MW00592942

The Legal and Regulatory Environment of e-Business

Law for the Converging Economy

John W. Bagby
Pennsylvania State University

F. William McCarty
Western Michigan University

Australia · Canada · Mexico · Singapore · Spain · United Kingdom · United States

The Legal & Regulatory Environment of e-Business: Law for the Converging World
John W. Bagby & F. William McCarty

Editor-in-Chief
Jack W. Calhoun

Vice President, Team Director
Michael Roche

Sr. Acquisitions Editor
Rob Dewey

Developmental Editor
Susanna C. Smart

Marketing Manager
Steven Silverstein, Esq.

Production Editor
Starratt E. Alexander

Manufacturing Coordinator
Rhonda Utley

Design Project Manager
Michelle Kunkler

Internal Designer
Craig Ramsdell/Ramsdell Design
Cincinnati, OH

Cover Designer
Ann Small/a small design studio
Cincinnati, OH

Cover Images
©Digital Vision and
©Greg Pease/Stone

Photography Manager
John Hill

Photo Researcher
Susan Van Etten

Production House & Compositor
Trejo Production

Printer
Quebecor World Taunton

Printed in the United States of America
1 2 3 4 5 04 03 02 01

For more information contact
West Legal Studies in Business,
5191 Natorp Boulevard,
Mason, Ohio 45040.
Or you can visit our Internet site at:
http://www.westbuslaw.com

Library of Congress Cataloging-in-Publication Data
Bagby, John W.
The legal and regulatory environment of e-business: law for the converging economy / John W. Bagby, F. William McCarty
Includes bibliographical references and index.
ISBN: 0-324-11079-0
1. Electronic commerce—Law and legislation—United States.
I. McCarty, F. William, 1941–
II. Title.
KF889.3 .B324 2003
343.7309'044—dc21
2002022525

Brief Contents

Contents

Part V Regulation

Chapter 19: Antitrust 653

Chapter 20: Labor and Employment 697

Table of Cases

Preface

A NEW KIND OF LEGAL ENVIRONMENT TEXTBOOK

This text was written to fulfill the needs of a traditional legal environment course, but it takes a nontraditional approach. Reflecting a new world that combines traditional commerce and emerging e-commerce, this book is the first to fully integrate both perspectives for the legal environment course. Traditional commerce and electronic commerce are merging today, as evidenced by the number of business-to-business transactions accomplished with significant e-commerce components in payments, electronic data interchange, or electronic processing of documents. Transactions between businesses and consumers are following a similar pattern, evolving to include significant elements of electronic assent, transaction processing, and performances. For example, most new car purchases involve some Internet activity, businesses advertise through the Internet, and consumers use retailing, travel, and other services available on the Internet. In addition, sectors such as government utilize the Internet through interactive processes with citizens (taxes, licensing, information), as well as the procurement of goods and services from vendors. Electronic marketplaces are also changing the face of consumer-to-consumer transactions as electronic auction markets make secondhand resale markets more liquid. As the legal environment of business is no longer based only on the traditional economy, this book captures the evolution toward regulations applicable to both traditional and e-commerce methods of business.

ADAPTING LAW AND REGULATION TO THE CONVERGING ECONOMY

The dot.com revolution of the late 1990s abruptly ended in a sobering realization that many aspects of traditional business models are still valid. The dot.com bubble economy misled venture capitalists, the securities markets, and a whole generation of entrepreneurs into believing that traditional measures of profitability and return on investment were inapplicable to Internet enterprises. Sole reliance on electronic commerce methods seems appropriate for only narrow sectors of the economy. Yet, smokestack industries that resisted the cyberspace revolution in the 1990s are increasingly involved in e-commerce. For example, traditional industries are progressively more involved in on-line business-to-business marketplaces. They are migrating their customer service networks to e-mail, electronic data interchange, and on-line customer information, including website catalogues, specification listings, and electronic contracting. Tremendous efficiencies are derived through the widespread use of electronic bill presentment and electronic payments, electronic commercial document processing, and enterprise software using computerized networks to connect multiple locations and with customers and suppliers.

Since the burst of the dot.com bubble, it has become evident that neither the traditional sector of the economy nor the e-commerce sector should be viewed in isolation. A few years ago, some commentators heralded the "new" economy, dubbing it "clicks" and predicting its superiority over the "old economy," the "bricks." There was widespread speculation of a long, steady decline in the traditional economy. Others rejoiced at the burst of the dot.com bubble, claiming that e-commerce lacked any real substance. This position overlooks the rather substantial influence and ongoing growth of computerized telecommunications and information technology on existing and emerging businesses. Increasingly, there is a recognition that most businesses in the future will converge on a hybrid of methods that must first retain the rigors of the traditional economy, including financial control, profitability requirements, disciplined management, and attention to supply chain efficiencies. At the same time, successful future businesses must implement effective information and communications technologies that were once considered the sole province of e-commerce companies: electronic communications, electronic data mining, electronic contract negotiation and formation, electronic transaction processing, electronic payments, and electronic performances.

The modernization of business techniques offered by e-commerce business models offers tangible productivity improvements, speeds the effectiveness of commercial interactions, and is replacing many traditional paper-based and hand-operated business processes of the traditional economy. All this suggests that a convergence of traditional business models with information technology methods requires major redesign of business models and business processes in order to sustain competitive advantage. The laws facilitating this transition must be understood and respected for the timeless aspects of traditional public policies. Recognizing which laws must be updated—sometimes even replaced with new laws—reflects the changing reach and functionality of new technology. Business managers need an understanding of traditional legal problem areas such as an employer's liability for workplace sexual harassment or service and product liability standards, as well as for emerging problem areas such as privacy laws or intellectual property protection.

The Legal and Regulatory Environment of e-Business: Law for the Converging Economy provides a comprehensive perspective on both traditional legal problems and new laws tailored for e-business. Traditional areas of administrative regulations, formation of business organizations, contract law, tort liability, and labor and equal opportunity laws continue to be important parts of the modern legal environment. This text combines a focus on those strategic areas with a focus on converging industries by providing unique insights into the blend of traditional and emerging principles that will equip managers to better understand and deal with their legal environment.

HOW THIS TEXT CONTRIBUTES TO SKILLS NEEDED FOR CONVERGENCE

The study of the legal and regulatory environment of business will have enduring relevance applicable today and in the future. It is intended to provide understanding of the evolution and the integration of traditional and new legal principles to the evolving marketplace. The evolution to e-commerce is forcing all business disciplines to reevaluate their basic principles, develop new models and analytical tools, and then integrate them into traditional disciplines. Managers must remain aware of the law underlying their existing business disciplines and how changes will require them to modify their decision making.

It is widely predicted that e-commerce practices will radically change traditional business methods as innovative methods are ever more frequently introduced. During such turbulence, a firm grounding in basic legal concepts is needed to understand potential legal pitfalls and to anticipate and forestall problems.

There are several reasons why business decision makers need both an understanding of basic legal principles that have been applied to traditional business methods and an understanding of e-commerce cyber law. First, the enforceability of contracts is essential to encourage use of, reliance upon, and investment in e-commerce. The risks of nonenforceability and even the risks of higher transaction costs are currently a significant barrier to faster growth in e-commerce. Second, many participants in cyberspace and many business decision makers have been proceeding into e-commerce without the benefit of careful strategic review by legal counsel competent in cyber law. Considerable risk of loss is already well documented for such underinformed ventures. Third, many businesspeople are more experienced with traditional commercial practice than with the unique property rights problems of intellectual property. Continued unfamiliarity with copyright and trademark ownership, licensing, and infringement are already leading to extensive and costly litigation. This book will enable business decision makers to better understand the law's effect on both traditional and e-commerce-related practices.

PHILOSOPHY OF THIS TEXT

Several major themes running throughout this text build student skills for careers in converging businesses. First, this text focuses on how existing laws are accommodating the transition and on what issues new perspectives are needed from legislation, regulation, judicial interpretation, private contracting, industry self-regulation, and public policy. Second, students are thoroughly exposed to electronic commercial practices and technology transfer. A firm grasp of the historical, social, political, and economic context of legal issues permits business decision makers to understand how traditional law is adapting to the new context. Third, substantive topics of the law of technology and cyber law are assembled into several major areas, including constitutional law, commercial law and practice, intellectual property, privacy, and regulation.

ORGANIZATION OF THIS TEXT

The Legal and Regulatory Environment of e-Business: Law for the Converging Economy is organized into five parts, each containing three to six chapters of related material. Part I, The Legal System, introduces law study, legal process, constitutional law, international law, and the administrative process of regulatory agencies. In Part II, Private Law is explored, including criminal and tort law, product and service liability, and business organization law. Part III has extensive coverage of e-commerce, including contract formation, performance, payments, writings and records, remedies, creditors' rights, technology transfer, employment and service contracts, and privacy. In Part IV, Intellectual Property, there is in-depth coverage of copyrights, database protections, trade secrets, patents, and trademarks. Finally, Part V, Regulation, covers a wide range of business regulations affecting both traditional and e-commerce business activities, including antitrust, labor and employment law, equal employment opportunities, securities regulations, environmental law, and Internet regulation. The breadth and depth of coverage is unprecedented in a legal environment text.

PEDAGOGY

The text and supporting instructional materials acquaint students in business and the information sciences with the laws of business and e-commerce. It identifies the key legal, regulatory, and public policy issues arising in the migration of society to cyberspace and in business's implementation of e-commerce methods. Students will learn about the legal and business issues of e-commerce with a view to gaining perspective on the transformation of traditional contracting behaviors and processes as they move into cyberspace.

Courses in e-commerce based on *The Legal and Regulatory Environment of e-Business: Law for the Converging Economy* may utilize traditional as well as emerging pedagogies: texts, outside readings, lecture, class discussion, guest lectures, videos, case law, Socratic dialog, and student-centered learning techniques such as team projects and presentations. The subject matter is particularly suitable for instructional support through technology-driven pedagogies such as multimedia presentations, Internet-based instruction, on-line exploration, and research in computer-equipped classrooms or outside the classroom via computer laboratories and students' personal computers. The subject matter permits students to conduct Internet search and research projects. These participative and active learning techniques are well suited for familiarizing students with the methods and architecture of cyberspace and the controversies of e-commerce.

KEY FEATURES

International and ethical aspects are integrated throughout the book, and the critical thinking approach is supported in the text and enhanced by the student study guide.

- **Cases:** Each chapter has two to four traditional excerpted cases relevant to traditional legal environment issues as well as to contemporary e-commerce concerns. Some examples are *Specht v. Netscape* on the enforceability of click-wrap assent to on-line contracts, *Universal City Studios, Inc. v. Corley* on the legality of decryption under the DMCA's anticircumvention rules, *RIAA v. Diamond Multimedia* on the copying of on-line music, *A&M Records, Inc. v. Napster* on the P2P sharing of music among strangers, *State St. Bank v. Signature Financial Group* on the patentability of business methods, *Shields v. Zuccarini* on cybersquatting, *PepsiCo, Inc. v. Redmond* on the inevitable disclosure doctrine, *U.S. v. Microsoft*

Corp. on antitrust and network effects of software standards, and *In re GeoCities* on privacy of on-line profiling.
- **Commentary** features highlight controversial or unsettled areas of law, including Automated Bargaining over License Terms, UCITA, Trademarks Meet the Internet, and Employee Privacy versus Employer Liability.
- **International Commentary** features draw in the international aspects of the issues being discussed in the chapter, such as "Trademark Protection for Generic Identifications of Origin" and "Discovery or Disclosure?"
- **Ethical Issues** cover ethical concerns in the business setting, including "Licensing Terms" and "Litigation Threat Chills Freedom of Speech."
- **Internet Margin Notes** send students to research tasks or additional information.
- **Internet Screens** highlight important Internet locations to help integrate technology issues with text narrative.
- The text is rich with **Examples** of real situations and companies.
- **Chapter Problems** provide review and case problems for each chapter.
- **Figures and Tables** enhance and clarify the chapter coverage, serving as graphic and visual aids.

OTHER COURSE SUPPORT MATERIALS

Extensive additional electronic courseware and instructional support specific to the text are also available.

For the Instructor

An *Instructor's Manual*, prepared by Ernest W. King of the University of Southern Mississippi, and John W. Bagby contains chapter outlines, solutions to case questions, and answers to the end-of-the-chapter questions.

The *Test Bank*, also prepared by Ernest W. King, contains more than 1,300 questions in multiple-choice, true-false, and essay formats, with answers.

PowerPoint® Lecture Slides, prepared by Jimidene Murphy of South Plains College, provide chapter highlights for lecturing.

The West Legal Studies in Business video library is available to qualified adopters of this text. You may be eligible to use selections from the library of West videos, a vast selection covering most business law and legal environment issues. There are some restrictions, and if you have questions, please contact your local Thomson Learning/West Legal Studies sales representative or visit http://www.westbuslaw.com/ video_library.html.

For the Student

A *Study Guide*, by Ronald L. Taylor, Metropolitan State College of Denver, provides students with review and study materials. It contains chapter outlines and objectives, as well as review questions in matching, completion, true-false, multiple-choice, short essay, and case problem formats.

For Both Students and Instructors

The text website provides on-line support at http://bagby.westbuslaw.com. This website provides links to all URLs in the text, online quizzes with immediate feedback for students, PowerPoint lecture slides that are useful for lectures and for study review, and more.

The West Legal Studies in Business website at http://www.westbuslaw.com directs students to the Student Resource Center for case updates.

Web Tutor™ on Web CT or Blackboard is an interactive, Web-based, student supplement that harnesses the power of the Internet to deliver innovative learning aids that actively engage students. The instructor can incorporate Web Tutor as an integral part of the course, or students can use it on their own as a study guide. Benefits to students include automatic and immediate feedback from quizzes and exams; interactive, multimedia, rich explanation of concepts; on-line exercises that reinforce what they've learned; flashcards that include audio support; and greater interaction and involvement through on-line discussion forums.

Infotrac® College Edition is an on-line library containing hundreds of scholarly and popular periodicals, including *American Business Law Journal*, Journal of International Business Studies, *Environmental Law*, and *Ethics*. It offers a database updated daily, full-length articles, and keyword searches that quickly and efficiently scan the entire database. Contact your local Thomson Learning/West Legal Studies sales representative to learn more.

Ten free hours of Westlaw, West's computerized legal research, are available for qualified adopters of this text.

ACKNOWLEDGMENTS

We wish to thank Dean Judy Olian of the Smeal College of Business Administration for inspiration about converging economies. We thank Ernest King for creating the *Instructor's Manual* and the *Test Bank*, Ron Taylor for the *Study Guide*, Jimidene Murphy for the *PowerPoint Lecture Slides* package, and Margaret McCamy for her work on the on-line quizzes. And we also thank our colleagues and reviewers for their input and help during the development of this book, especially the following:

Ernest W. King
University of Southern Mississippi
Robert L. Mitchum
Arkansas State University–Beebe
Paul Fiorelli
Xavier University
Lori K. Harris-Ransom
Caldwell College
T. Noble Foster
Seattle University
John M. Garic
University of Central Oklahoma
John C. Lautsch
California State University, Fullerton
Elizabeth A. Cameron
Alma College
Gary P. Sibeck
Loyola Marymount University
Marisa Anne Pagnattaro
University of Georgia
Jeanne Calderon
New York University
Susan J. Mitchell
Des Moines Area Community College
Susan D. Looney
Mohave Community College
Ann Morales Olazábal
University of Miami
Linnea McCord
Pepperdine University

We also would like to thank Rob Dewey, our acquisitions editor at West Legal Studies in Business, who believed in the vision of our text; Susan Smart, our developmental editor, whose constant and gentle reminders kept us on track throughout the considerable work to accomplish this innovative project; Starratt Alexander, our production editor, who pulled together the pieces to make this final product; and Nicole Moore, the marketing manager whose input and market savvy helped to get the word out.

AFTERWORD

The authors have considerable accumulated experience in instruction at various colleges and universities and in creating useful instructional materials. This experience is now adapted in a unique hybrid way to comfortably permit evolution from traditional business law and legal environment instructional approaches to the legal and regulatory environment for the converging economies. The thorough integration of technology law and cyber law into the traditional framework of law accomplished here will equip students with the skills needed for success in the twenty-first century.

John W. Bagby
F. William McCarty

The Legal System

PART I

This book's 24 chapters form five parts: the legal system, private law, e-commerce, intellectual property, and regulation. Each part focuses on a part of the law and the legal environment that is important to modern, competitive business firms.

Part I's six chapters provide the framework for a study of the more specific legal topics in the subsequent parts of the book. Chapter 1 notes the importance of the rules of law and legal institutions for both traditional and e-commerce business transactions. What is law and why is it important for business? As business has changed over years, what changes have taken place in the laws and legal institutions affecting business? How has the advent of e-commerce changed the business environment?

Both legal rules and ethical guidelines attempt to direct behavior in society. The ways legal rules are made and the legal institutions that make them vary significantly among the nations of the world. Most legal systems perform similar societal tasks, and each can be classified as part of a common law, civil law, or Islamic law legal system. Even nations that have similar legal systems may have different characteristics. Two important features of the U.S. legal system, which is a common law legal system, are the principles of federalism and separation of powers.

In addition to being guided by legal rules, corporations today often provide codes of conduct for employees and others who are affected by the corporation's activities. Chapter 2 discusses the interplay between legal rules and ethical guidelines that has become an important feature of the legal environment in the United States. It is clear that business corporations have a powerful role in many societies, often being able to shape the rules that seek to regulate their behavior. The public becomes outraged when businesses appear to try to buy political influence, act for self-interest rather than for the stakeholders they serve, or engage in transactions that serve the interests of a few insiders rather than the shareholders or the public at large. Public demands for privacy and security in commercial transactions are among the legal issues that affect e-commerce businesses.

Litigation as a means of resolving disputes is more common in the United States than in many other nations. As business firms continue to be involved in litigation, both as plaintiffs and as defendants, managers need to know the main features of the civil litigation process. As the title to Chapter 3 suggests, despite the critical role litigation occupies in the U.S. legal system, alternative dispute resolution methods such as arbitration and mediation are growing in importance throughout the world. The Internet provides access to websites to users throughout the world, but disputes between firms and their global e-commerce customers simply cannot use one nation's litigation processes to resolve business disputes. Knowing how to compare and when to utilize the various forms of alternative dispute resolution methods is becoming important for managers who will have responsibilities for both direct and e-commerce business transactions.

One of the ways to divide law into different categories is to consider the parties involved in and affected by different legal concerns. For example, public law deals with the laws involving business firms or individuals on the one hand and the government or society on the other hand. In contrast, private law deals with the laws that affect transactions between or among business firms and individuals but do not directly involve the society. Each of the last three chapters of Part I notes how an important area of public law affects business activities. The primary source of law in the United States is Constitutional law, and several parts of the Constitution are of particular concern to businesspeople. The applicability of commerce clause and the contract clause is quite evident, but several of the rights in the first ten amendments to the Constitution also affect business firms. These topics, as well as several important Constitutional principles, are reviewed in Chapter 4.

As Chapter 5 depicts, many firms today do business in more than one nation. Through trade and investments, they engage in numerous business activities with customers and other firms in nations with different legal environments. Some of those nations are also part of regional organizations such as the European Union that seek to more deeply integrate the economies of member countries. Several of these regional organizations, as well as a number of international organizations, have institutions with lawmaking powers. Many are attempting to harmonize different national laws while also providing processes for resolving international legal disputes. Although the Internet has made it easier for firms to engage in global business, the laws affecting international e-commerce activities are still developing.

The sixth and final chapter in Part I concerns administrative law. Administrative agencies have significant lawmaking responsibilities in most legal systems. In the United States, these agencies, which have been in existence for more than a century, make rules and regulations, adjudicate disputes that relate to the laws and rules they administer, and perform numerous ministerial duties that governments need to do. Administrative law is the law that regulates the administrative agencies and determines their powers and how they can act in carrying them out. These "rules for the rule makers" are important for businesses to understand because the rules of the agencies and the limits on their investigative and enforcement powers may affect regulatory actions the agencies impose on organizations. The actions of administrative agencies affect businesses in numerous ways, and businesses need to understand how those agencies perform their functions and how businesses can interact with them.

Law in Business

INTRODUCTION

This book describes and analyzes the legal environment of business in general and e-commerce in particular. The importance of law to business is not new. Hundreds and even thousands of years ago, some societies were codifying local customs and practices so that people would know what they were expected to do and not do. Today, these codes constitute the most important source of law in countries that have a civil law legal system.

In other societies, the customs and practices evolved into legal standards as courts resolved disputes by referring to those practices. Common law legal systems developed through the use of precedent court decisions that were grounded in the common law. In many societies, religion has played an important role in developing legal rules as well as ethical standards. Today, the Islamic legal system, based on the Qur'an, predominates in many countries.

This first chapter looks at how law affects business and at the importance of globalization and technology changes. After examining the role of law in society and its importance as a topic of study, particularly for business students, this chapter reviews important classifications of law. Law affects e-commerce in many ways, some quite different from the way law affects traditional methods of business. Particular problems for e-commerce are intellectual property concerns, from song copyright issues to business patents, and the global jurisdictional issues arising from the ubiquitous nature of Internet transactions.

Questions appear at the end of this and subsequent chapters to review the chapter's important concepts. Law is usually studied by applying legal analysis to specific cases. Although only one case is included in this first chapter, an appendix introduces case analysis at the chapter's end. That analysis includes a sample case to read and review and a method to use in reviewing the court cases found throughout the text, as well as those available through other sources.

HOW LAW AFFECTS BUSINESS

Whether their business transactions occur at a bricks-and-mortar site or in cyberspace, entrepreneurs and business managers need to understand the function of law and the characteristics of the legal environment in which businesses operate. Of course, the business legal environment has changed dramatically over the last century.

At the beginning of the twentieth century, antitrust laws were just emerging, and business employers and managers were not concerned with workplace safety regulations, equal opportunity requirements, or consumer protection warranties. Most business was conducted in person, and sellers and buyers knew each other or at least lived and worked in the same legal environment.

At the beginning of the twenty-first century, antitrust laws in Europe and the United States can block proposed corporate mergers or impose breakup requirements on firms whose practices restrict competition. Contract, property, and tort laws directly influence business agreements, the development and transfer of technology, and liability concerns. Laws regulate employee hiring, safety standards for the production of computer hardware, and the warranties that accompany the sale of products. The growing use of e-commerce means that many buyers and sellers never meet.

THE IMPORTANCE OF GLOBALIZATION AND TECHNOLOGY CHANGES

International, national, and even local news stories focus on legal matters every day. Decisions made in India about foreign investment regulations draw the attention of business managers in Tokyo, Detroit, and Barcelona. When the U.S. Congress places a moratorium on taxing the Internet, both on-line and bricks-and-mortar retailers are affected. Laws affect where business offices, plants, and employees locate. Local zoning restrictions, regulations affecting hiring practices, protection for intellectual property, and tax incentive packages can dissuade or attract businesses to particular countries or regions.

Increasing global competition and technological changes have brought the Internet to users around the world. According to 2001 Nielsen//NetRatings, 459 million people around the globe have home-based Internet access. The United States and Canada together account for 40% of the world's on-line population, but the greatest growth is occurring in Hong Kong, Germany, and Korea. Users in Singapore spend the most time on line at 24 minutes per session. According to the U.S. Census Bureau, in August 2000, more than half of U.S. households had one or more computers, and more than 80% of those households had at least one Internet user. That same survey of 50,000 U.S. households found that 95 million people used the Internet, a dramatic increase from the 57 million U.S. users in 1998.

NetValue has examined the users who seem most interested in purchasing goods and services over the Internet. Its study found that residents of Korea, Britain, Singapore, and Hong Kong had the highest percentage of visitors of secure sites with the capability to transmit credit card information for online processing.

As e-commerce continues to attract both businesses and consumers, both business-to-business (B2B) and business-to-consumer (B2C) transactions are increasing. Since the 2001 economic slowdown burst the bubble for most independent B2B exchange sites, B2B transactions have been dominated by the large global firms. IBM reported more than $43 million in electronic procurement in 2000, and Boeing processes more than 20,000 transaction daily via its website. Despite the economic slowdown, Boston Consulting estimates that worldwide B2B e-commerce will reach $4.8 trillion by

2004. Although North America now accounts for more than 70% of on-line trade, e-commerce in Europe and Asia is expected to rapidly catch up.

Although B2B Internet usage has not been as extensive as earlier predictions suggested, B2B transactions are having a major effect on business costs and profits. Some businesses claim to be saving up to 20% of their spending on services and materials by putting their supply chain on the Internet. Steve Butler, an analyst at eMarketer, says that "the majority of large enterprises continue to see e-business as a long-term strategy and they are moving into the next-generation of their e-business implementations."[1]

THE LEGAL ENVIRONMENT FOR BUSINESS

The term **legal environment of business** suggests something more than the simple memorization of the rules of law. The legal environment of business includes the laws, legal institutions, and processes that affect business. Law provides a set of rules and guidelines for business conduct. Headlines about the piracy of intellectual property, antitrust concerns with Microsoft's trade practices, and electronic signatures on contracts show but a few of the ways that the legal environment is important for business.

To explain how the legal environment affects both traditional and e-commerce-based business activities, we first focus on several key concepts. What is law? What are the components of the legal environment that affect business?

WHAT IS LAW?

What do business students gain from studying law? How can they analyze legal rules, decisions, and problems and apply them to business activities? The term **law** has several meanings, each of which captures a different sense of the source of law, its legitimacy, and its use as a process. According to *Black's Law Dictionary*, law is that which is laid down, ordained, or established. It is a rule or method according to which phenomena or actions coexist or follow one another. According to *Webster's Third New International Dictionary*, law is a binding custom or practice of a community. It is defined as a rule or mode of conduct or action that is prescribed or formally recognized as binding by a supreme controlling authority or is made obligatory by a sanction that is made, recognized, or enforced by the controlling authority.

In *Black's Law Dictionary*, the focus is on the "legal" behavior that results from the establishment, creation, or recognition of the law; it is law that guides people in a society to behave in certain ways. On the other hand, *Webster's* definition suggests that law is more concerned with its origins. Law is not generated by an outside source or higher authority but flows from the customs and practices followed by the people in a society. This definition also emphasizes that sanctions are what makes law effective. Therefore, not all customs or practices are laws; only those recognized as binding and enforced by authorities can be called laws. By combining these two definitions, we can conclude that the word *law* refers to established standards or guidelines for action or behavior in a society, whether the standards originate from a higher authority or from the practices and customs of people. To be law, however, the standards must be "binding"; they must be made obligatory by the authorities in a society.

1. The quotes and data in this section were found at the Cyber Atlas website: http://cyberatlas.internet.com.

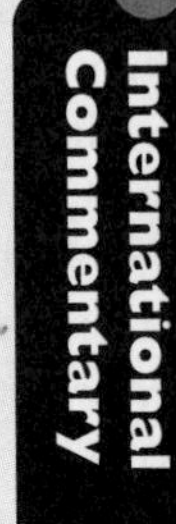

Some have suggested that the rule of law and strong legal institutions are critical to the economic development of a society. Although societies differ in the use of legal institutions, important components of a strong legal system include:

- requiring governmental actions to follow legal procedures
- providing private parties with meaningful access to courts and other independent institutions
- ensuring that property rights are protected

Research the legal institutions in several developing countries in Asia, Africa, the Middle East, and South America to determine if they have strong legal systems. Do you think there is a correlation between the existence of a strong legal system and economic development?

WHY STUDY LAW?

Law reaches pervasively into our personal and professional lives. From arbitration agreements to constitutional guarantees, from contractual requirements to securities or accounting regulations, the law and the legal environment affect almost all types of business activities. The rule of law is one of the most important attributes of a business environment, and where law is unstable or subject to governmental interference, businesses hesitate to venture. Although significant parts of the law affecting e-commerce are still developing, many of the existing legal principles are being adapted to this new environment.

One of the primary reasons that business students study law is to recognize how law is changing so that, as managers or entrepreneurs, they can better plan activities that hinge on what the law allows or requires. The legal environment in this new millennium is changing significantly to accommodate and adapt to e-commerce. Therefore, the study of the legal environment of e-commerce provides students with a vision of how the law may shape opportunities for business ventures in the coming years.

The use of e-commerce, of course, spreads the presence of businesses throughout the world. A business with a website can be accessed anywhere that the Internet is available. Clearly, some Web-based businesses hope to attract customers from the entire globe. As a business expands internationally, its managers must have a general knowledge of the governing legal system and the most important laws affecting business activities. A society's laws embody and reflect its customs and values.

The legal environment of business is dynamic; a society's laws, like its customs and values, change and evolve. Business managers must be aware of those changes and the forces that cause them. Businesspeople who are aware of important legal rules and emerging legal developments can perform more efficiently and effectively than those who lack such knowledge.

CLASSIFICATION OF LAW

Law can be classified in a variety of ways: substantive or procedural law, criminal or civil law, common or statutory law, and public or private law. Laws often fit into more than one classification. For example, contract laws are generally private, substantive, civil laws.

SUBSTANTIVE LAW AND PROCEDURAL LAW

Substantive laws define rights and impose on members of society the duty to respect those rights. Laws that detail the means by which those rights or duties will be enforced are **procedural laws.** For example, substantive law defines the elements necessary to create an enforceable contract. By examining these elements, we can determine if a person must be a certain age to make a valid contract. On the other hand, procedural law determines how substantive law will be enforced. Is the person who seeks to enforce another person's contractual commitment entitled to a trial? Should a jury be used at the trial? These questions can be answered by examining procedural laws.

CRIMINAL LAW AND CIVIL LAW

Another method of categorizing laws focuses on the rights that the law seeks to protect. If the purpose of a law is to protect society as a whole, not just a single member, the law is a **criminal law**. If a law concerns the rights of individuals (often including a corporation as a "person") or the duties owed to people in the society, the law is a **civil law**. Essentially, civil law focuses on rights and duties among the members of society, whereas criminal law focuses on possible wrongs committed against society as a whole.

Who Initiates the Case?

In a criminal case, society initiates the legal action because the society, rather than the individual victim, is the primary victim of the wrong. The commission of a crime makes all people, not just the victim of the crime, feel less safe and secure. As the society has more resources than any of its individual members, a person charged with a serious crime has a right to legal assistance paid for by society if that person is financially unable to afford to hire an attorney.

In a civil case, the lawsuit is brought by an individual person who claims that his or her rights have been infringed, and the individual selects and pays for legal representation. The society is not a party to lawsuits between two or more of its members.

Frequently, the title of a case tells whether it involves a criminal or civil action. A criminal case, brought by society, is titled *People v. Smith*, *United States v. Smith*, or *Michigan v. Smith*. Although most of the cases in which society is the accuser are criminal cases, sometimes they are not. A civil case, on the other hand, is titled *Jones v. Smith* or *ABC Corporation v. Smith* because individuals or organizations are parties on both sides.

Purpose

The purpose of a criminal case is to determine if the accused committed a criminal act and if the court must therefore impose some punishment. A person convicted of a crime might face a fine or temporary removal from society in jail or prison. The example of the criminal's punishment is also intended to deter would-be criminals from committing similar acts. The punishment may even rehabilitate the criminal so that he or she is less likely to commit future wrongs against the society.

In contrast, the purpose of a civil lawsuit is to determine if a wrong has been committed and, if so, to require the wrongdoer to compensate the injured party. The emphasis is on compensating the injured party, not on punishing the wrongdoer. If Laura breaks a contractual agreement that she made with David, he may bring a civil lawsuit against her. Generally, David would seek an award of damages as a remedy. He would want the court to order Laura to pay him a sum equal to the money he lost when she did not fulfill her part of the agreement.

Differences in Substantive Laws

Substantively, the law specifying what acts constitute robbery differs from the law specifying what acts constitute an enforceable contractual agreement. In criminal cases, most crimes are defined by federal or state statutory laws, administrative regulations, or municipal ordinances. In civil actions, a person's rights or duties toward others can be based either on statutory laws or on the common law of court decisions.

Differences in Procedural Laws

The procedures followed in criminal and civil lawsuits also differ. Legal standards, known as the **burden of proof**, indicate which party has the obligation to submit proof to the court and the quantity and quality of the evidence that is needed to prevail. The person bringing a lawsuit is the **plaintiff**, and the person being sued is the **defendant**. The person who represents society as the plaintiff in a criminal case is the **prosecutor** or district attorney. In a criminal lawsuit, the accused person is presumed innocent until proven guilty and will prevail unless the society can prove *beyond a reasonable doubt* that the accused committed the criminal act. In a civil lawsuit, the burden of proof is not the same. The plaintiff, or accuser, has to prove the case against the defendant, the accused, only *by the preponderance of the evidence*—that is, by more evidence against than in favor of the defendant.

For example, suppose that in a given civil case both the amount and the quality of the evidence are a little more in the plaintiff's favor than in the defendant's favor. Because a preponderance of the evidence is in the plaintiff's favor, the plaintiff would win the case. However, the same amount and quality of evidence in the plaintiff's favor in a criminal case would not be sufficient to convince a jury or a judge of the defendant's guilt beyond a reasonable doubt. Thus, the defendant, not the plaintiff, would win the criminal case. The amount and the quality of evidence required of the plaintiff to win a criminal case exceed what is required to win a civil case.

COMMON LAW AND STATUTORY LAW

In the United States, the term **common law** refers to law found in court decisions, and **statutory law** refers to legislative acts. Much of the law in the United States comes from court decisions. When a court has no statutory law to refer to in deciding a case, it turns to prior court cases—the common law—to make a decision. The court decisions that form the common law are based on the customs and practices in the society.

Statutory laws come from the U.S. Congress, state legislatures, and local city councils or commissions. The administrative rules and regulations of governmental agencies are also generally classified as statutory laws. Similarly, the laws and regulations of municipal bodies, referred to as **ordinances**, are also a type of statutory law.

PUBLIC AND PRIVATE LAW

Public law concerns the relationships between, on one side, people and, on the other, their government. Thus, criminal law is classified as public law because it involves a wrong against society. Constitutional law is also public law as it concerns the power of government to perform certain activities. **Private law** concerns the relationships between individuals and firms within the society. Parts II through V of this book deal with various private law topics that are important in the legal environment of e-commerce.

LAW AND E-COMMERCE

The changes that e-commerce has brought to the business world require adaptations in the legal rules affecting transactions. Intellectual property issues, in which the law seeks to balance the rights of the inventor of a business patent or the creator of copyrighted material with the almost immediate and global reach of material on the Web, present particularly difficult problems for e-commerce.

THE CHANGING ENVIRONMENT

The speed and scale of Internet legal problems pose immense challenges for the rule of law. Ira Magaziner, the architect of the Clinton White House Internet strategy, noted: "We're having problems of pornography distribution to minors, violations of intellectual property rights, potential violations of privacy and new types of crimes."[2] While international organizations are working on the basic tenets of Internet law, they continue to get hung up on liability and jurisdictional concerns. The passive, active, and interactive Internet business presence as a basis for jurisdiction is discussed later in this chapter.

Managers, business owners, and new entrepreneurs now must be aware of the legal concerns that affect both the traditional and e-commerce sides of their businesses. The recent passage of an e-commerce law in India is aimed at changing the way India does business and at advancing the country's position as an emerging power in the global high-tech industry. The law gives legal sanctity to digital signatures and Internet transactions, allows people to file their taxes electronically, and imposes prison terms and fines for hackers and other cyber criminals. India is just one of a growing number of countries that have adopted an e-commerce law.

Some legal concerns are more noticeable for e-commerce than for traditional methods of transacting business. According to an AT&T study, 87% of Internet users are concerned about on-line threats to their right to privacy. Similarly, according to a *Business Week*/Louis Harris poll, two-thirds of those who could, but choose not to use the Internet, say they would be more likely to use the Internet if the privacy of their personal information and communications would be protected. The lack of privacy is a global concern and the number one reason individuals are choosing to stay off the Internet.

In the European Union, a comprehensive data protection directive seeks to protect the right of natural persons to privacy in the processing of their personal data. Although there is no comparable federal law in the United States, the Federal Trade Commission (FTC) argues that federal mandatory on-line privacy standards are needed to make sure all providers are playing by the same rules. Currently, the FTC enforces the Children's On-line Privacy Protection Act (COPPA), which bars websites from collecting personal information from children under the age of 13 without parental consent. For adults, only voluntary industry guidelines and selective state privacy laws address complaints about access to personal data through the Internet.

ONLINE

Read the COPPA at **http://www.ftc.gov/ogc/coppa1.html**

2. "Taming the Wild, Wild Web," *Business Week*, October 4, 1999, p. 155.

INTELLECTUAL PROPERTY ISSUES

Many firms today have significant business assets based in their intellectual property—patents, copyrights, and trademarks. In 1995, the Patent and Trademark Office issued only one patent for what it called "Internet-related business methods"; in 1999, the total grew to 301, and the number of applications is doubling each year.[3] Amazon.com is seeking to prevent Barnes&Noble.Com from using Amazon's patented one-click checkout system. That system allows a shopper to place an order with a single tap of the mouse rather than reentering billing information. Although the trial court granted Amazon's request to stop Barnes & Noble from using a similar system, a federal court of appeals lifted the injunction and sent the case back to the district court for trial.[4]

Musicians and movie producers brought suit and stopped Napster—a file-sharing service—and similar sites from allowing their users to download copyrighted songs and movies without obtaining a license. Napster was reported to have had 20 million users downloading 500 million songs by the middle of the year 2000. Most downloaded songs were copyrighted, and all were downloaded for free.[5]

Numerous trademark owners lose significant revenue because products bearing their trademark or trade name are sold by unlicensed websites. Protecting valuable property from unlicensed access has become a major problem for many businesses, a problem that is exacerbated when portions of the property are immediately available to millions of people through the Internet.

OTHER REGULATORY CONCERNS

Since the September 11, 2001, attacks on the New York World Trade Center and the Pentagon, regulation of activities in a number of areas has been increasing. International terrorism has become a global concern since the attacks and the subsequent distribution of anthrax through the mail. Consequently, regulation of airplane traffic and airport security has dramatically increased. Governmental offices and facilities are less open, and banking and financial records are subject to greater governmental scrutiny.

In addition to the increased regulation brought about by the dramatic change in the U.S. environment after September 11, 2001, the regulation of business activities is also increasing in several traditional legal areas. As the number and size of mergers and acquisitions continue to increase, both within and across national boundaries, antitrust laws aimed at protecting consumers and competing firms have become more important. Growing awareness of environmental problems such as global warming and concerns with the safety of genetically modified food products raise problems that need to be addressed. The recycling of computer hardware and the disposal of a host of hazardous materials no doubt will lead to increased regulation in certain industries. As many countries have a more diverse workforce than previously, laws prohibiting discrimination are becoming more important for both employers and employees.

---

3. Scott Thurm, "The Ultimate Weapon," *Wall Street Journal,* April 17, 2000, p. A18.

4. The Court of Appeals decision in *Amazon.com, Inc. v. Barnes&Noble.Com, Inc.* is found at 239 F.3d 1343 (Fed. Cir., 2001).

5. Adam Cohen, "Taps for Napster," *Time,* July 31, 2000, p. 34.

GLOBAL, REGIONAL, AND NATIONAL LEGAL ISSUES

With globalization continuing to affect most industries, firms moving into new markets face a number of legal concerns. What is the nature of the legal system in the new market area? Which countries in the new market protect intellectual property? How does a specific country or region treat e-commerce contractual transactions? Is the country a member of the World Trade Organization, where trade disputes can be decided? Are countries in the region associated with others in a free trade area so that goods and services can be marketed more easily throughout the region?

What do a country's corporation and securities laws indicate is the best way for business activities in the new region to be organized and financed? How will the tort laws that establish the basis for liability to customers and other product users affect production and marketing operations? Are environmental regulations strictly enforced? These and many other questions will affect e-commerce for some time to come.

WHAT IS THE LEGAL ENVIRONMENT OF E-COMMERCE?

This book's focus on the legal environment of e-commerce is concerned with those traditional and new sources of law that affect electronic business transactions. These sources include the legal system, private law, intellectual property, regulatory law, and e-commerce contracting.

THE LEGAL SYSTEM

The study of the legal environment of e-commerce must begin with an overview of the legal system. A **legal system** includes the national legal, regulatory, and political institutions and legal processes affecting business activities. Other laws that are important to e-commerce are the international, supranational, and various national laws that affect global business and seek to harmonize the treatment of legal issues affecting the Internet.

PRIVATE LAW

Private law fields regulate and affect business and individual activities but do not directly involve governmental agencies. Although criminal law is not a part of private law, we include some aspects of computer crime in our review of this area. The private laws affecting e-commerce include product and service liability concerns based in tort and contract laws, as well as some aspects of business organization principles.

REGULATORY CONCERNS

Although certain industries and business activities are subject to significant focused regulation, other general regulatory laws affect almost all businesses. For example, labor and employment laws govern relations between employers and employees, and antitrust laws try to ensure that competition is not overwhelmed by monopolistic and trade restraint practices. Securities laws seek to protect investors, including those who invest on line. Environmental laws have become more important to manufacturers of computer products. In the United States, federal and some state regulations affect the disposal of plastic and petroleum-based products. In Germany, regulations require manufacturers who use boxes and shrink-wrap materials or who sell electronic equipment to take their products and packages back for recycling or disposal when consumers finish with them.

INTELLECTUAL PROPERTY

Because the protection of a firm's *intellectual property*, such as patents, copyrights, trade secrets, and trademarks, is so vital to many companies active in e-commerce, knowledge of these property interests and how they can be protected must be a part of the legal environment of e-commerce. The 1999 Anti-cybersquatting Consumer Protection Act is the major law used to combat cybersquatting that hijacks domain names. Both federal courts in the United States and international arbitral panels that are a part of the World Intellectual Property Organization (WIPO) have rendered hundreds of decisions involving domain name disputes. As technology has made it easier to access and copy information, the application of copyright and trademark law to cyberspace transactions is critical to many firms.

ONLINE

See the text of the 1999 Anti-cybersquatting Consumer Protection Act at **http://www.gigalaw.com/library/anti-cybersquattingact-1949-11-29.p1.html**

E-COMMERCE CONTRACTING CONCERNS

Finally, the e-commerce environment raises specific contracting concerns. How are e-commerce contracts formed? What payment and performance terms are a part of those contracts? What can be done to protect the transfer of technology through the Internet? What terms should be in consulting and technical services contracts dealing with computer usage? These topics constitute the heart of any review of the legal environment of e-commerce. In July 1999, the National Conference of Commissioners on Uniform State Laws promulgated the Uniform Computer Information Transactions Act (UCITA) as a commercial contract code for computer information transactions. It includes provisions for determining when and how an on-screen action establishes a contract, the enforceability of "shrink-wrap licenses," and remedies available for those contracting on line. UCITA's terms are discussed in greater detail in Part III, the e-commerce section of this book.

A recent case involving an e-commerce contract is *Specht v. Netscape*. The case deals with the enforceability of a clause in the click-wrap agreement that is at the heart of the way in which contracts are formed on the Internet. A person wanting to use a particular website is asked to read and review the terms the website host has drafted and that any user must agree to follow. If you don't agree to the terms of use, you cannot use the website. As is the case with most click-wrap agreements, one of the terms in the Netscape offer to contract is that the user, who accepts the offer by clicking his or her assent, agrees to settle any disputes with the website host through arbitration rather than litigation. Although this case, as well as Chapter 3, notes that arbitration agreements are usually enforced, in this case there is no consent to use arbitration. Is arbitration required for this dispute?

Before reading the *Specht* case, refer to the Appendix at the end of this chapter. It provides information on reading and analyzing a case and on preparing a sample brief of a case. This information will be useful for reading cases throughout this book and in other analytical reading you do.

Spececht v. Netscape

150 F.Supp.2d 585 (SDNY 2001)

Facts. Christopher Specht and several other plaintiffs sued Netscape and AOL for violating the Electronic Communications Privacy Act and the Computer Fraud and Abuse Act by using software that provided electronic surveillance of the plaintiffs' use of the Internet. The defendants each filed a motion to compel arbitration because they felt that by downloading the program the plaintiffs, like all other users of the defendants' software, had consented to its license agreement terms.

Netscape offered its "SmartDownload" software, a program that makes it easier for users to download software while still using the Internet for other activities, free of charge on its website. Most of the plaintiffs had selected and clicked on a box indicating they wanted to obtain the software and moved to a download page. The only reference on that page to the license agreement appeared in text that was visible only after scrolling down through the page to the next screen. There, a hypertext link took visitors to the license and support agreement, which included the following sentences: "For products available for download, you must read and agree to the license agreement terms BEFORE you install the software. If you do not agree to the terms, do not download, install or use the software." Another page included the license agreement, which provided that virtually all disputes be submitted to arbitration in Santa Clara County, California.

Legal Issue. If an Internet user is able to download and use a software package without first agreeing to its licensing agreement that includes a section requiring arbitration of any disputes, has the user consented to the use of arbitration by using the provider's software?

Opinion. Judge Hellerstein. The Federal Arbitration Act expresses a policy strongly favoring the enforcement of arbitration clauses in contracts.

A written provision in . . . a contract evidencing a transaction involving commerce to settle by arbitration a controversy thereafter arising out of such contract or transaction, . . . shall be valid, irrevocable, and enforceable, save upon grounds as exist in law or equity for the revocation of any contract.

On this basis, Defendants argue that this motion [to compel arbitration] is a generally accepted principle of contract law.

However, Defendants' approach eludes the distinction between two separate analytical steps. First, I must determine whether the parties entered into a binding contract. Only if I conclude that a contract exists do I proceed to a second stage of analysis: interpretation of the arbitration clause. . . . In determining which state law to apply, I look to the choice-of-law doctrine of the forum state, New York. . . . Although the record evidence on this point is spare at best, . . . I conclude that California has the most significant connection to the litigation, and I apply California law to the issue of contract formation.

Unless the Plaintiffs agreed to the License Agreement, they cannot be bound by the arbitration clause contained therein. . . . I must consider whether the website gave Plaintiffs sufficient notice of the existence and terms of the License Agreement, and whether the act of downloading the software sufficiently manifested Plaintiffs' assent to be bound by the License Agreement. In order for a contract to be binding, both parties must assent to be bound.

These principles enjoy continued vitality in the realm of software licensing. Software commonly is packaged in a container or wrapper that advises the purchaser that the use of the software is subject to the terms of a license agreement contained inside the package. The so-called "shrink-wrap licenses" have been the subject of considerable litigation. Not all courts to confront the issue have enforced shrink-wrap license agreements.

For most of the products it makes available over the Internet, but not SmartDownload, Netscape uses another common type of software license, one usually identified as "click-wrap" licensing. A click-wrap license presents the user with a message on his or her computer screen, requiring that the user manifest his or her assent to the terms of the license agreement by clicking on an icon. The product cannot be obtained or used unless and until the icon is clicked. The few courts that have had occasion to consider click-wrap contracts have held them to be valid and enforceable.

A third type of software license, "browse-wrap," was considered by a California federal court in *Pollstar v. Gigmania Ltd* (E.D. Cal, 2000). The court expressed concern about the enforceability of the browse-wrap license because many visitors to the site may not even be aware of the license agreement. The SmartDownload License Agreement in the case before me differs fundamentally from both click-wrap and shrink-wrap licensing, and resembles more the browse-wrap license of *Pollstar.*

Netscape's SmartDownload allows a user to download and use the software without taking any action that plainly manifests assent to the terms of the associated license or indicates an understanding that a contract is being formed. Netscape's failure to require users of SmartDownload to indicate assent to its license as a precondition to downloading and using its software is fatal to its argument that a contract has been formed.

Decision. The case law on software licensing has not eroded the importance of assent in contract formation. Because the user Plaintiffs did not assent to the license agreement, they are not subject to the arbitration clause contained therein. . . . Although the license agreement applicable to Netscape Communicator and Navigator is a conventional click-wrap contract that requires arbitration of "all disputes relating to this Agreement," the Communicator/Navigator license agreement is a separate contract governing a separate transaction. For the reasons stated, I deny Defendants' motion to compel arbitration.

Case Questions

1. What actions indicate that a user accepts the license agreement terms when using shrink-wrap or click-wrap products ? Are those actions present in this case? Why?
2. What action would you recommend Netscape take in revising access to its SmartDownload programs? What part of the judge's opinion makes you think that such a change would bring a different result than in this case?
3. Does this case determine the validity of plaintiffs' claims? Do you think this case now will be tried and decided in a court? Why?

Although this case refers to several relatively new statutes and to several cases dealing with e-commerce issues, as the opinion indicates, the law in this field is still developing. As of the beginning of 2002, more than a dozen countries had passed specific laws dealing with e-commerce. Typically, those laws address only a few of the many legal problems posed by the e-commerce environment.

QUESTIONS

1. Are all rules or standards that seek to guide personal or business conduct laws? Why? Give an example of a guideline or standard that seeks to regulate some of your conduct, and explain why it is not a law.
2. Classify each of the following as either a substantive law or a procedural law:
   a. A law that requires parties to a lawsuit to share information, documents, and data each has in its possession with the other litigant
   b. A law that requires contracts for the sale of goods valued at more than $500 to be evidenced by a writing
   c. A law that permits either party in a civil case in which damages for personal injuries are being sought to have the case tried before a jury
   d. A law that requires a person who negligently causes injury to another person to be liable for the damages the injured party suffers
3. What are three differences between civil and criminal lawsuits?
4. One of the most comprehensive sources of free legal information on the Internet is the Findlaw website at http://www.findlaw.com. Check that site and find an example of a *statutory law* passed by the legislature in your state and an example of a *common law* decision from a court in your state.
5. The text quotes Ira Magaziner, who was in the Clinton White House, as identifying three or four major Internet legal problems. Check some Web sources such as the Legal Information Institute at Cornell Law School, http://www.law.cornell.edu, as well as traditional sources like the *Wall Street Journal*, *Business Week*, and *Time*, and make your own list of the top five Internet legal problems affecting business today.
6. In 1998, Walker Asset Management Limited Partnership received U.S. Patent No. 5,794,207 (207) for the "name your own price" Internet reverse auction service. Walker Asset then started priceline.com. Later, Microsoft began to use a price-matching service at its Expedia.com site. Walker asserts that Microsoft's use of the process violates Walker's 207 patent. What defense would you expect Microsoft to

make to this suit? What could each party do to settle the case?

7. Is the case in problem 6 a civil or criminal case? Does it involve private or public law? The case will look at the Patent Act of 1952 to seek to resolve the dispute. What type of legal source is that?

8. A *legal system* includes the national legal, regulatory, and political institutions and legal processes affecting business activities. Assume your business sells specialized automobile parts to manufacturers who are located around the globe. If you are seeking to sell to firms located in Brazil, give an example of (1) a national law and (2) a regulatory requirement from a governmental agency in that country that can affect your business. How could knowlege of the legal processes and political institutions in places you hope to sell your products help your business?

9. The Taliban in Afghanistan imposed many restrictions on women. They could not go to school, work outside their homes, or travel with men. Using the definitions of *law* found in Webster's and Black's law dictionaries, explain if these restrictions are laws.

10. Find a recent law that affects e-commerce business and give examples of businesses that would be affected by the law. Check your state statutes or recent cases through the http://findlaw.com website, the virtual law library site at Indiana University at http://www.law.indiana.edu, the Lexis-Nexis database (see either http://www.lexisnexis.com or your university library's database), or this text's website at http:// bagby.westbuslaw.com. Recent newspaper or magazine articles may also be useful sources.

APPENDIX: USING LEGAL ANALYSIS

The study of law and the legal environment of e-commerce requires both a review of general principles and concepts and an analysis of how those principles are applied to specific case situations. Using **legal analysis** to study specific cases can lead to a better understanding of how legal concepts affect business activities. Through legal analysis we study court cases that solve specific disputes by applying general legal principles; extracts from court opinions are presented along with the text material. This mix permits our study to combine both inductive and deductive reasoning.

INDUCTIVE AND DEDUCTIVE REASONING

Inductive reasoning is the process of examining specific situations to determine if they have some common attributes. By studying related cases, we gain an understanding of how the application of legal principles in similar cases leads to the formation of general legal rules. Generalizations from specific decisions become the basis for solutions to similar problems.

Deductive reasoning is the process of examining general principles derived from induction or legislation and applying them to specific situations. By examining those general principles, we can deduce how to apply them to other specific problems. For example, consider the general principle that to be valid, all contracts for the sale of goods valued at $500 or more must be evidenced by a writing. This means that a specific contract for the sale of a $1,000 machine from the ABC firm to the XYZ firm must be evidenced by a writing. The same principle also should apply to a contract for a $600 television sold by the XYZ firm to John Jones. To fully understand a general legal concept, we need to examine its application to several different situations or cases. After reading and understanding a court's opinion in a specific case, generalizations can be made and used to resolve similar problems and cases.

Thus, to solve the questions and problems you see on examinations and in professional activities, you must go beyond memorizing important legal principles. Legal analysis requires you to understand how specific case decisions give rise to general principles and how general principles apply in specific case situations.

DEVELOPING CRITICAL THINKING SKILLS

Critical thinking skills enable students to become independent learners. Legal rules change frequently, so managers who understand the issues and policy-making processes underlying lawmaking, regulation, and litigation are able to make more informed and intelligent business decisions. Critical thinking approaches and inquiries are fundamental to legal analysis. Critical thinking requires an evaluation of the reasons, logic, and weight of evidence used in any argument. To perform the required analysis, we must understand the speaker or author's issue, conclusion, and reasons. These elements are also used in reading and briefing a judge's written court opinion. Only after the issue, conclusion, and reasons are identified can we evaluate the quality of the evidence and determine if the reasons support the conclusion.

IDENTIFYING ISSUE, HOLDING, AND REASONS

The *issue* is the primary subject for review. What is the problem or question being addressed by the author or by a judge's court opinion? The *holding* is the writer's judgment (in a court case, the judge's decision) about how that issue is to be resolved, based on the evidence reviewed. It answers the question(s) posed by the issue.

Next, identify the *reasons* given in support of the conclusion. Reasons explain why the conclusion should be accepted. Assume the facts show that A was driving his car too fast when he injured B as he crashed into B's car. Also assume the law says that negligent or careless drivers should compensate those who are injured by their actions. The conclusion, that A should compensate B, is supported by the reasoning that A's driving too fast was negligent and the cause of B's injuries.

READING CASE OPINIONS

The court opinions in this book are taken from the decisions of various state and federal courts. Some are recent cases dealing with problems affecting contemporary business managers. Others are classic cases that represent important developmental changes in the application of law to certain activities.

At first, cases can be difficult to read and understand. It helps to look for certain elements that facilitate the review of a case's important aspects. It is generally useful to write a short summary, known as a **brief**. A brief helps to clarify the opinion and helps you understand the issues addressed by the court. This Appendix contains a sample case, a discussion of items to include in a brief, and a sample brief.

READING A CASE AND WRITING A BRIEF

The following case gives you an opportunity to practice case analysis and brief writing. Carefully read the *Blue Note* case that follows; it is an important case dealing with jurisdiction questions related to e-commerce and the review questions that follow. Next, read the section on what items to include in a case brief. Prepare your own brief of the *Blue Note* case based on the format suggested. Finally, compare your brief with the sample brief. Although your brief should be similar to the sample, it need not be identical.

If you take the time to brief a number of the cases in this text, both your understanding of the cases and your writing of briefs will improve. Writing a brief also helps to improve your analytical skills. Writing a good case brief is almost impossible without first thinking about the important facts, determining how the legal principle is applied, and analyzing the court's reasoning and holding.

Items to Include in a Case Brief

Case Title and Citation In reading cases, look at the first several lines preceding the court's opinion. The first line states the title of the case and identifies the parties to the suit. Most cases in this book are appellate cases, not trial court cases, so generally the first party named is the **appellant**, the one who is bringing the appeal. The second party, known as the **appellee**, is the party who is satisfied with the trial court's decision. Some courts do not put the name of the appellant first; instead, they continue to place the names in the sequence used by the trial court.

In a trial court, the name of the party bringing the case to trial, the plaintiff, appears first, whereas the name of the party against whom the suit was brought, the defendant, appears last. These two sets of litigation designations (appellant-appellee and plaintiff-defendant) indicate different characteristics about the parties. Sometimes the terms are used together. A plaintiff-appellant, such as Bensusan in this case, is the party who originally brought the case to trial and who was not satisfied with the trial court's decision. King, doing business as the Blue Note, as the defendant-appellee, is the party who was sued and was satisfied with the trial court's decision because he won at that level.

The second line contains the **citation**, which tells the reader and legal researcher where the case may be found. Court opinions are collected and bound together in books known as *reporters*. The numbers and abbreviations in the citation indicate in which book and on what page to find a case. This case is found in volume 126 of the third series of the federal reporter. That reporter is used primarily for decisions of federal courts that review trial court decisions. The 1997 date indicates when the case was finally decided by that court. Sometimes several years pass between the original trial and the decision by the reviewing court.

The third line gives the name of the court that wrote the opinion. Here, it is a court of appeals located in New York City.

Facts Only those facts that provide information needed to resolve the problem confronting the court should be stated in a brief. You should read the entire case before beginning the brief so you can distinguish between those facts that are important to deciding the issue from those that are unimportant. Notice in the sample brief that only the more important facts are stated. Most of the cases in this text begin with a statement of the case facts. Some, but usually not all, of these facts should be in your brief.

Issue Court opinions frequently resolve several issues. Cases in this book are generally edited to present only the most important issue related to the book's topics. The issue identifies the legal problem that must be answered to determine which of the disputing parties wins the case. Generally, the issue should be posed in the form of a question permitting a yes-or-no answer in the holding. The cases in this text identify the legal issues.

Holding The holding contains the court's answer to the question posed by the issue. It states how the court answered the issue(s). A holding also usually notes which party won the lawsuit. The holding is the opinion of the majority of the judges of the court. It may not be the holding of all of the judges, and you may disagree with it. Look to both the Legal Issue and Decision to find a case's holding.

Reasoning The court's reasoning explains the decision it reached. Do not simply restate the decision as the rationale. To extract general rules from the court's decision, you must understand the court's reasoning. Ask yourself, "If the facts in this case were changed slightly, would the case be decided the same way? Why? Which facts or policies would lead a court in a slightly different case to reach the same opinion?" You should extract the reasons from the court's Opinion.

Dissent Some cases contain both majority and dissenting opinions so as to note legal controversies. A good brief should include a few sentences to summarize the views of the dissenting judges. Your comments should address the reasoning used to reach the dissenting opinion.

Comment and Rule of Law Include in your brief a section expressing your thoughts about the case. In this section, comment on the court's reasoning and on the consequences of the decision or the holding when it is later used as precedent. You also may want to summarize the rule of law from the case. The rule of law is generally limited to a one- or two-sentence statement that could be used as precedent in similar cases. Writing such a rule at the end of every case highlights the importance of that particular case to the development of law, as well as to the litigating parties.

SAMPLE CASE[6]

Bensusan Restaurant Corporation v. Richard King, (Individually and doing business as The Blue Note)

126 F.3rd 25 (2d Cir., 1997)
United States Court of Appeals

Circuit Judge Van Graafeiland. Plaintiff, Bensusan Restaurant Corporation, located in New York City, is the creator of an enormously successful jazz club, called the Blue Note. That name was registered as a federal trademark for cabaret services in 1985. Defendant King, a Missouri resident, has operated a small cabaret club featuring live entertainment in Columbia, Missouri, since 1980.

In 1993, a Bensusan representative wrote King, demanding he cease calling his club the Blue Note because Bensusan had registered the name as a federal trademark for cabaret services. King's attorney informed the writer that Bensusan had no right to make that demand of King.

In 1996, King authorized a company to create a website on the Internet for King's cabaret; the work was done in Missouri. Bensusan then filed this case in the Southern District of New York, alleging violation of the federal trademark law. He sought damages from King and an injunction to stop King's use of the mark "The Blue Note" or anything similar to it. He said that as King's website was accessible in New York, King could be brought to trial there.

King's website described his location and included a calendar of events at the club, as well as King's telephone number. It also had this text:

The Blue Note's Cyberspot should not be confused with one of the world's finest jazz clubs, Blue Note, located in the heart of New York's Greenwich Village. If you should ever find yourself in the Big Apple, give them a visit.

The text was followed with a hyperlink to a website maintained by Bensusan. When Bensusan objected to the text and hyperlink, King substituted this note:

The Blue Note, Columbia, Missouri, should not be confused in any way, shape, or form with the Blue Note Records or the jazz club, Blue Note, located in New York. The CyberSpot is created to provide information for Columbia, Missouri, area individuals only.

The district court dismissed the plaintiff's claim and the defendant appealed. In diversity or federal question cases, the court must look first to the long-arm statute of the forum state [where the court is located], in this instance New York. If the exercise of jurisdiction is appropriate under that statute, the court then must decide whether such exercise comports with the requisites of due process.

Because we believe that the exercise of personal jurisdiction in this case is proscribed by the law of New York, we

6. The authors have made minor changes in the court's language.

do not address the issue of due process. The New York law dealing with personal jurisdiction based upon tortious acts of a non-domiciliary [non-primary resident] who does not transact business in New York . . . provides that a New York court may exercise personal jurisdiction over a non-domiciliary who "in person or through an agent" commits a tortious act in this state. In *Feathers v. McLucas*, the New York Court of Appeals adopted the view that the statute reaches only tortious acts performed by a defendant who was physically present in New York when he performed the wrongful act. As construed by the Feathers decision, jurisdiction cannot be asserted over a nonresident under this provision unless the nonresident commits an act in this state. The failure to perform a duty in New York is not a tortious act in this state, unless the defendant or his agent enters the state.

Applying these principles, we conclude that Bensusan has failed to allege that King or his agents committed a tortious act in New York as required for the exercise of personal jurisdiction. The acts giving rise to Bensusan's lawsuit were performed by persons physically present in Missouri and not in New York. Even if Bensusan suffered injury in New York, that does not establish a tortious act in the state of New York within the meaning of the statute.

The Legislature in 1966 enacted a paragraph that said that New York courts may exercise jurisdiction over a non-domiciliary who commits a tortious act without the state, causing injury to person or property within the state. However, the Legislature limited the exercise of such jurisdiction to "persons who expect or should reasonably expect the tortious act to have consequences in the state and in addition derive substantial revenue from interstate commerce." Bensusan argues that King's hiring of bands of national stature and receiving revenue from people outside of Missouri, students of the University of Missouri, satisfies the interstate commerce requirement. We find that King's Blue Note café was unquestionably a local operation and the alleged facts were not sufficient to show he derived substantial revenues from interstate commerce.

We affirm the judgment of the district court.

SAMPLE CASE BRIEF

Facts

Bensusan owned a famous jazz club, the Blue Note, in New York City. In 1985, he registered the name "Blue Note" as a trademark for cabaret services. In Columbia, Missouri, defendant King owned a cabaret club that operated under the name Blue Note since 1980.

In 1993, Bensusan wrote to King, asking him to stop using the Blue Note name, but King did not do so. In 1996, King authorized people in Missouri to establish a website for him, using the name Blue Note in that site. Bensusan then sued King in a New York federal district court, alleging a violation of trademark law and seeking damages. He claimed that King's website, accessible in New York, made King subject to the New York court's jurisdiction.

New York law says there must be a tortious act in New York for New York to have jurisdiction. King claimed that New York courts did not have jurisdiction over him. The trial court agreed with King, and Bensusan appealed.

Legal Issue

If a trademark owner complains that an out-of-state resident violates his trademark on a website as well as at the place of business in the other state, does the fact that the website is accessible in the trademark owner's state subject the non-resident to a court's jurisdiction there?

Decision

No, for King. New York does not have jurisdiction over King.

Reason

The court looks to the New York laws dealing with personal jurisdiction. Those laws require that to have jurisdiction over a nonresident, that person must commit a tortious (wrongful) act in New York. Here, the website of King was developed in Missouri.

The court also reasoned that although the New York rules allowed its courts to exercise jurisdiction where that person derives substantial revenues from interstate commerce, here King's club was more local in nature.

Comment

The court did not decide if Bensusan's trademark was infringed by King. All it decided is that the case could not be decided in New York. There must be some connection between the defendant and the place where the case is brought, and here there was not a sufficient connection. The case raises questions as to whether accessing a website in another state, or perhaps another country, would give that state or country jurisdiction over the website owner.

CHAPTER 2

Ethics and the Legal System

Because of the close relationship between legal rules and ethical standards, this chapter first looks at business ethics and the growing concerns about the societal responsibilities of business. Although law seeks to guide people's conduct, many corporations and other organizations have promulgated codes of conduct for their employees to follow at work.

This chapter then examines the tasks performed by legal systems throughout the world and reviews their characteristics. The chapter concludes with a survey of the significant characteristics of the U.S. legal system, its state and federal judicial system, and the meaning and importance of the concept of jurisdiction. As noted at the end of this chapter, jurisdictional questions arise when an e-commerce user is located in one country, using a website in a second country, and sending or receiving information to people in yet other countries.

RELATIONSHIP BETWEEN LAW AND ETHICS

Both law and ethics prescribe guidelines for behavior. Some people believe that by obeying the law they are also behaving ethically. Others believe that laws establish minimum standards, whereas a system of ethics imposes stricter obligations. Despite the close relationship between law and ethics, some actions that are illegal can be ethical, and some legal actions may be unethical.

Some people argue that consideration of ethical standards may at times require people to violate the law. For example, the principle of civil disobedience, as practiced by Mahatma Gandhi and Martin Luther King Jr., is based on the belief that people should actively oppose unethical laws. This principle thus encourages doing what is illegal when the action is ethical. Similarly, if a driver races to extinguish a blazing fire at her home or hurries to the hospital with his pregnant wife, speeding, though illegal, is clearly ethical.

When a person distributes copyrighted music on the Internet in an MP3 format of CD quality, clearly this act violates copyright law and is therefore illegal. Is it unethical? Probably it is, because people know it is wrong. Thus, such actions are both illegal and unethical. Of course, many users suggest that, given the high cost of CDs and the low impact they perceive of MP3s on the profit of record companies, such actions are morally justified and ethical. What do you think?

When a businessperson sells a legal product at a reasonable price while making a profit, that action is both legal and ethical. There's nothing illegal or wrong with making a profit on what you sell. What if a doctor sells nonprescription drugs from his office? The American Medical Association (AMA) discourages doctors from selling vitamins and other health-related nonprescription drugs from their offices for profit. Although such practices are legal, the AMA thinks they can be unethical. Such practices pose conflict-of-interest problems while eroding the trust that normally exists in the patient-doctor relationship.

Although law and ethics are closely related because both reflect moral judgments, they are fundamentally different. Legal rules require all people to follow certain clearly defined standards or face explicit consequences. If we violate criminal rules, we could be imprisoned. If we do not adhere to contract formation requirements, our agreements may be unenforceable. Ethical standards, by contrast, are subjectively determined on an individual and institutional basis. Unethical behavior often goes unpunished by society. In some groups, unethical behavior is tolerated or accepted; in others, it is clearly discouraged.

ETHICAL ANALYSIS

Ethics is a field of philosophy that examines motives and actions from the perspective of moral principles. **Morality** refers to human behavior that is good and just. **Moral reasoning** is the process of moving from premises to conclusions in determining the right course of action. The moral principles that form the basis for evaluating behavior are generally drawn from several sources.

Ethical theories come from principles espoused by philosophers or from religious principles, such as the Golden Rule, the Ten Commandments, or similar precepts from the Buddhist, Hindu, or Muslim religions. The early Greek philosophers Socrates, Plato, and Aristotle focused on good and doing right. All major religions emphasize doing good for others, being fair, and treating people with respect. In countries with a religion-based legal system, legal and moral standards are not separate.

Like legal analysis, ethical analysis involves studying concepts and theories and applying them to particular situations. Using ethical theories requires asking questions, examining alternatives, and seeking solutions that coincide with ethical goals. Two important ethical theories influence the formation of our moral concepts today. They are the consequence-oriented utilitarian theory and the duty-based universal theory.

Utilitarian Theory

The **utilitarian theory** examines the consequences of a given action and defines an action as morally right and ethical if it produces the greatest amount of good for the greatest number of people. The utilitarian does not focus on the inherent correctness of a given action but instead examines its consequences. Maximizing the good from a given action or course of conduct requires measuring the costs and benefits from possible alternative activities. Thus, the utilitarian ethical analysis requires the performance of a societal cost-benefit analysis. The utilitarian theory is the dominant ethical theory used in business today. According to this theory, "good" is determined by maximizing the good consequences and minimizing the bad consequences of any action.

Universal Theory

The second major ethical theory is referred to as the universal theory. Immanuel Kant, commonly considered the founder of this theory, did not look at the consequences of actions to determine if they were ethical. Instead, he argued that a commitment to universal principles (the categorical imperative) should guide people. Kant believed that actions are moral only if they can be undertaken by everyone in good conscience. Thus, the **universal theory** suggests that your actions should be based on determining if your conduct could serve as the standard for universal conduct.

The Golden Rule exemplifies this duty-based standard: You should act as you expect others to act toward you. According to this duty-based theory, conduct should be guided not by looking at its resulting consequences but by whether it coincides with preexisting duties. Consider a business situation. What is ethical behavior for a person who sells at an on-line auction a product he believes is defective? The Ethical Issues box depicts how Kant might examine the seller's need to disclose to a potential buyer what he knows about the product by asking universal-based questions.

BUSINESS ETHICS AND CORPORATE SOCIAL RESPONSIBILITY

BUSINESS ETHICS

Business ethics can be viewed as an application of traditional ethical analysis to business decisions. However, although decisions made by individuals in a business organization obviously affect that organization's actions, a business organization often has its own history, tradition, rules, and ethical standards. The actions of a business firm may be influenced by values, interests, and principles that differ from those of its individual managers. Ethical analysis, therefore, can sometimes be difficult to implement in a business context. Problems arise in:

1. identifying common values within a firm or industry
2. deciding how much emphasis to place on collective benefits
3. projecting side effects
4. defining the extent of a firm's responsibilities to outside groups

Numerous business decisions require managers not only to know the law but to make ethical decisions as well.

Ethical Issue

Using Universal Ethical Analysis in Business Situations

We can apply Kant's universal theory to business problems by asking questions like the following:

1. Would I want everyone, regardless of the product being sold, to be able to refrain from disclosing what they know about a defect in the product?
2. Would I want the principle of nondisclosure applied if I were the buyer instead of the seller?
3. Am I treating the other people involved (the buyer) as an end, according them respect, and not just as a means (to achieve a sale and profit for me)?

Can you think of an ethical dilemma in business where each of these questions could be asked to help determine what is the ethical thing to do?

CORPORATE SOCIAL RESPONSIBILITY

The social responsibility of the business firm has developed in stages. Before the twentieth century, the corporate form was seldom used, and business owners were personally liable for business decisions. As the limited liability concept—in which the corporation became a legal entity and was held responsible for its activities—became more widespread during the late 1800s, the ownership and control of business were separated. Managers then had new ethical dilemmas in their shareholder relations because the managers were insulated from many of the consequences of their decisions. Today, the corporation is generally viewed as having responsibilities not only to its shareholders, but also to numerous groups affected by its actions.

Corporate Stakeholders

In their strategic planning, businesses should be aware of the diverse expectations of numerous groups. A business can actively identify its stakeholders and attempt to understand their reactions to and influences on corporate actions. **Corporate stakeholders** are groups or entities affected by the firm's activities. In addition to shareholders, customers, suppliers, and employees are the predominant stakeholders because they contract with the corporation. Employees, who by law must be loyal to the corporation, expect it to look out for their interests in return. Participants in the supply chain, from wholesalers on the one end to customers on the other, expect the corporation to act responsibly in satisfying their concerns as well.

The financial community is another important segment that demands the attention of the corporation. It consists of the shareholders, creditors, investment advisers, and potential investors. Firms must provide sufficient and accurate information about their financial status and about actions that may affect the value of its stock. The contributors of capital may use the legal system's proxy system to oust a firm's managers or change its policies to remedy perceived irresponsible behavior.

In addition, the local community near the firm's facilities is a stakeholder that can pressure the firm to consider its needs by denying zoning changes or operating permits or by publicizing actions that ignore its interests.

Stakeholders' Expectations and Influence

Business is expected to refrain from having a negative impact on various stakeholders. Some stakeholders expect the business to generate favorable benefits. For example, many expect corporate philanthropy, economic growth, freedom from pollution or industrial accidents, and beneficial research and development from businesses. If some stakeholders have sufficient political or economic power to pressure a firm to act in a "responsible" manner, then the firm should consider their influence in its decision making. To avert costly regulation, business must understand the complex power structure of government and the relationships among those in government that affect the legal environment.

Campaign Finance Laws and Political Action Committees

Business can exert political influence by advocacy during political campaigns or referenda. Today, elections usually are won by the candidate who spends the most. Political consultants and pollsters, television advertisements, and electioneering visits to voters are very costly. Many businesses are able to make such large contributions that some observers argue the political process makes politicians beholden to business.

In 1971, Congress enacted the Federal Election Campaign Act (FECA) that established the Federal Election Commission (FEC) to administer campaign finance laws. The FEC requires disclosure of political contributions, receipts, and expenditures by both contributors and candidates. The FECA permits the formation of political action committees to solicit campaign contributions from particular groups.

Political action committees (PACs) are groups formed by individuals, labor unions, corporations, trade associations, and other special interest groups to receive political contributions from more than 50 people and to spend the donations to elect candidates favorable to their interests. The regulations on PACs are not stringent. For example, direct PAC contributions to a presidential candidate are prohibited after the candidate receives federal matching funds for an election campaign. However, PACs may spend "independent" or "soft" money in favor of particular candidates or causes as long as the expenditures are made without the candidate's cooperation or knowledge. There have been numerous legislative proposals seeking to limit PACs' soft money expenditures and some legislation has been passed. It remains to be seen how successful it will be.

Corporate Philanthropy

Many firms seek to act responsibly by giving educational or research grants or by engaging in other philanthropic efforts. In a famous early court decision, a judge decided that philanthropy was an improper corporate goal. Henry Ford had a controlling interest in the Ford Motor Company. As the company expanded and its automobile became immensely popular, the company began paying a special dividend in addition to its regular quarterly dividend. Then, in 1915 Henry Ford declared he would discontinue the special dividend, announcing that he wanted to "employ still more men, to spread the benefits of this industrial system to the greatest possible number, to help them build up their lives and their homes."[1]

Subsequently, Ford profits were retained in the business. The Dodge brothers, who together owned 10% of all Ford Motor Company stock, sued the company, complaining that it should instead pay more of its profits to shareholders through dividends. The Michigan Supreme Court found for the Dodges in a decision that established "maximizing shareholder wealth as the goal of the firm."

The judicial attitude toward corporate philanthropy has evolved since the early twentieth century. Today, firms' charitable contributions often are viewed favorably. After the September 11 attack, corporations throughout the world pledged millions of dollars each to aid victims of the tragedy. Shareholders and firms recognize that corporations have responsibilities to the community at large. They see that firms that act philanthropically are viewed as acting responsibly and thus are likely to enhance their reputations.

CODES OF RESPONSIBILITY AND ETHICS

Laws regulating activities are often initiated when self-regulation is perceived as insufficient or nonexistent. The same could be said for codes of conduct. Rather than continuing to address behavior on a case-by-case basis, professional, industrial, and corporate codes of conduct lay out standards of behavior that can and are intended to be applied to a variety of situations.

Professional and Industrial Codes

Professional malpractice liability often depends on professional standards. For example, if an auditor does not follow "generally accepted auditing practices," a real

1. *Dodge v. Ford Motor Co.*, 170 N.W. 668 (Mich. 1919).

estate agent violates the realtors' code of ethics, or a lawyer violates the attorneys' code of conduct, that conduct is often considered to be evidence of malpractice.

Some industry groups have also adopted codes of responsibility. For example, many advertisers, broadcasters, trade association directors, and purchasing managers voluntarily abide by codes of conduct. Typically, these codes require professionals to be loyal to their clients' interests and to avoid conflicts of interest. Professionals must also exercise their best efforts for every client and maintain confidentiality.

Corporate Codes of Conduct

In recent years, numerous corporations have instituted codes of ethics for their employees. These codes are usually enforced with disciplinary sanctions and with termination for serious violations. Most codes, like the one from Boeing excerpted here, prohibit employees from offering or accepting bribes, trading on inside information, or otherwise violating legal standards. Some codes also focus on misappropriating corporate information, falsifying records, or working for other firms.

ONLINE

To access Boeing's code, see **http://www.boeing.com/companyoffices/aboutus/ethics/index.htm**

The Boeing Company has a policy that "sets standards of ethical business conduct at The Boeing Company." The company has an Ethics and Business Conduct Office, headed by a vice president of Ethics and Business Conduct. That office reviews ethical procedures and practices, compares them with the best practices of comparable companies, details policies and procedures, and publishes guidelines for company employees. Boeing's Statement of Values includes its commitment to leadership, integrity, quality, customer satisfaction, diversity, good corporate citizenship, and enhancing shareholder value.

In addition, Boeing's *Ethics and Business Conduct* Committee is responsible for oversight of the ethics program. The purpose of the Ethics and Business Conduct program is to communicate Boeing's values and standards of ethical business conduct to employees, inform them of policies and procedures regarding such conduct, establish companywide processes to assist employees regarding compliance with the standards of ethical conduct and the Boeing values, and to establish company-wide criteria for ethics education and awareness programs.

Among the 11 topics covered in Boeing's ethics policies and procedures guidelines are proper relationships with suppliers, offering and accepting business courtesies, conflicts of interest, and proper use of company, customer, and supplier resources. The Boeing policy regarding its communication systems—telephone, facsimile machines, voice mail, e-mail, and the Internet—permits personal use as long as the use:

1. is of reasonable duration and frequency
2. adds no cost to Boeing
3. is not related to an illegal activity or an outside business activity
4. would not cause embarrassment
5. does not support any religious, political, or outside organizational activity not endorsed by Boeing
6. does not adversely affect the performance of the employee, other employees, or the employee's organization

Two factors improve compliance with corporate codes of conduct. First, it must be clear that upper management endorses the code and appears to comply with its requirements. The "tone from the top" must signal a policy of commitment to ethical conduct in general and specifically to the firm's own code. Second, the system for investigating and punishing violations must be perceived as providing fair due process. It must routinely punish violations; if many exceptions are made,

International Commentary

International Standards

In 1996, the Executive Board of the International Chamber of Commerce based in Paris adopted "Rules of Conduct to Combat Extortion and Bribery." It also encourages companies to develop and implement mechanisms to enforce their own codes of conduct. The rules of conduct are intended as a method of self-regulation by international businesses. The basic principle of the rules is that all enterprises should conform to the relevant laws and regulations of the countries in which they are established and in which they operate and that they should observe the letter and the spirit of these rules. The rules deal with:

- Extortion: no demand or acceptance of a bribe
- Bribery and kickbacks: no indirect or direct offers of bribes; demands for bribes must be rejected; no kickbacks
- Agents: pay appropriate remuneration; keep records that are available to auditors and government
- Financial records and auditing: proper recording; no off-book accounts; use appropriate auditing system
- Responsibility of enterprises: use system of control; review compliance; take action against those who violate rules
- Political contributions: comply with law; disclose; inform senior management
- Company codes: develop clear policies, guidelines, training programs, and enforcement policies

Which of these do you think is of greater importance? Do you think other rules should be added?

employees will lose respect for the code. Does it appear that these two factors were present at the Enron corporation? If not, might the existence of a corporate code have changed the ethical environment in that firm?

ONLINE

Read the International Chamber of Commerce Extortion and Bribery guidelines at **http://www.iccwbo.org/home/menu_extortion_bribery.asp**

Legal Effect of Corporate Codes of Conduct

The proliferation of codes poses questions about their legal effect on the criminal, tort, and regulatory liability of both employees and their employers. In criminal prosecutions brought against corporate employees, the clear breach of a corporation's code of conduct provides evidence of, but does not prove, the breaking of a criminal law. The respondeat superior doctrine of tort law holds the master (employer) vicariously liable for the torts of an employee that are committed within the scope of employment. If employees or corporate managers break a corporate rule, government regulators may use the respondeat superior concept to punish a firm for the crimes or wrongs of its employees. If a firm strictly enforces its code of conduct and cooperates with law enforcement authorities in investigating wrongdoing, however, the punishment against the corporation may be less severe.

In the insider trading context, a corporate code that prohibits insider trading makes it clear that the employee is misappropriating information that belongs to the company. When investment banking firms enforce such codes, the code may help the firm avoid some vicarious liability for their employees' insider trading. For example, if a firm has "Chinese wall" procedures to prevent the leakage of information from the firm's underwriting division to its brokerage division, the liability of the firm for insider trading may be dramatically reduced. Where firms have effective compliance programs and they act in good faith and without knowledge of the illegal activities of the person(s) they control (employees), prosecutors, judges, and juries tend to be more lenient in punishing the firm for the acts of its employees.

Corporate Codes and E-Mail and Internet Usage

Companies of all sizes are wrestling with how to protect employee privacy while also minimizing the company's liability for employees' on-line activities. Employees

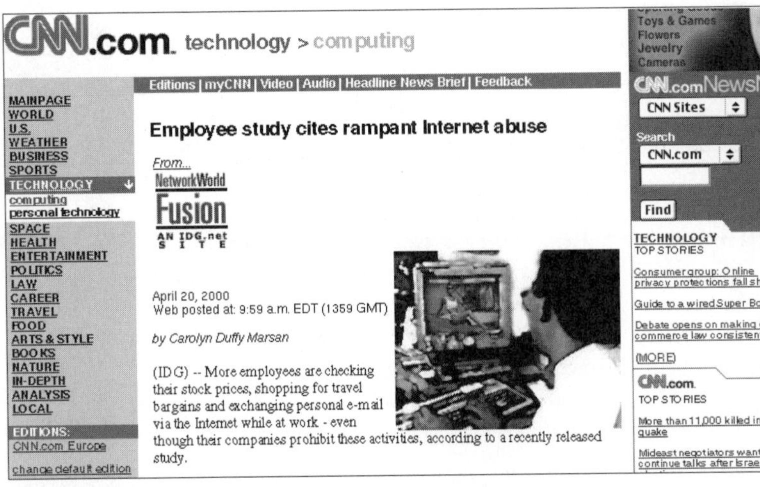

CNN.com technology > computing

Editions | myCNN | Video | Audio | Headline News Brief | Feedback

MAINPAGE
WORLD
U.S.
WEATHER
BUSINESS
SPORTS
TECHNOLOGY
computing
personal technology
SPACE
HEALTH
ENTERTAINMENT
POLITICS
LAW
CAREER
TRAVEL
FOOD
ARTS & STYLE
BOOKS
NATURE
IN-DEPTH
ANALYSIS
LOCAL
EDITIONS:
CNN.com Europe
change default edition

Employee study cites rampant Internet abuse

From...
NetworkWorld
Fusion
AN IDG.net SITE

April 20, 2000
Web posted at: 9:59 a.m. EDT (1359 GMT)

by Carolyn Duffy Marsan

(IDG) -- More employees are checking their stock prices, shopping for travel bargains and exchanging personal e-mail via the Internet while at work - even though their companies prohibit these activities, according to a recently released study.

Toys & Games
Flowers
Jewelry
Cameras

CNN.comNewsN
CNN Sites
Search
CNN.com
Find

TECHNOLOGY
TOP STORIES
Consumer group: Online privacy protections fall short
Guide to a wired Super Bowl
Debate opens on making e-commerce law consistent
(MORE)

CNN.com
TOP STORIES
More than 11,000 killed in Ind quake
Mideast negotiators want to continue talks after Israeli

at several large U.S.-based companies have been disciplined or fined for violating company policy regarding inappropriate e-mail and Internet usage. Xerox fired 40 employees for inappropriate use of the Internet at work, and the New York Times fired 23 workers who sent potentially offensive e-mail from their company computers. Merck instituted a company-wide standards and values program in early 2000. In February of that year, it announced it was terminating an unspecified number of employees for violating those policies. The firm would not say what specific events led to the terminations or how many employees had been fired.

http://

www.cnn.com/2000/TECH/computing/04/20/work.surf.idg/index.html

Dow Chemical had to deal with two successive cases involving its e-mail policies. In July 2000, it fired about 50 employees at its Midland, Michigan, facility, and in August an additional 40 employees at its Freeport, Texas, location were fired. In both cases, employees sent pornographic or sexually explicit e-mail to colleagues. Those who actively brought in, saved, and disseminated the material, those who had material that was extremely graphic or violent in nature, and those with histories of violating Dow policies were singled out for termination.

Employers worldwide are seeking to deal with cyberslacking by their employees. The dilemma for employers is that because the Internet is being integrated into daily operations, a large number of employees need to be given access. And while employers need to provide their employees with Internet access, they also need to avoid legal problems related to privacy and sexual harassment.

According to Stephen Whitlaw, chief executive of ACTIS Technology, a Glasgow, Scotland software firm, 79% of UK companies have found that their workers abuse their Internet access. In 2000, the British parliament passed a Regulatory Investigative Powers Act that gives companies the right to monitor employees' Internet and e-mail activities. New software from ACTIS enables companies to "fingerprint"

Ethical Issue

Employee Privacy Versus Employer Liability

At present, the law is unsettled regarding an employer's right to random computer monitoring unless the employer provides sufficient notification. From the employee's view, privacy protection should not end at the company door; there should be some right to privacy, even at work. Some states, including California, recognize an employee's right to a reasonable expectation of privacy, even in the workplace. On the other hand, the Electronic Communications Privacy Act of 1986 permits employers to monitor an employee's cellular, wire, or electronic communications where the monitoring is necessary for the protection of the rights or property of the employer.

How would you resolve the computer monitoring versus privacy issue? Would you decide differently if you were a company's manager instead of one of it employees?

every action carried out on their computer systems by employees.[2] Paul Grover of Value Added Distributors, the New Zealand distributor of JSB Software Technologies' surfCONTROL filtering software, says cyber-slacking has become a key security concern in New Zealand. He notes that "many IT managers are too afraid to provide Internet access to all their employees for security reasons and to avoid other risks. Yet, employees often benefit from having access to the Internet for research, training, and other genuine work-related tasks. Many businesses are also providing e-commerce solutions to their customers allowing them to do online ordering, for example, but have to somehow control access to the rest of the Internet."[3]

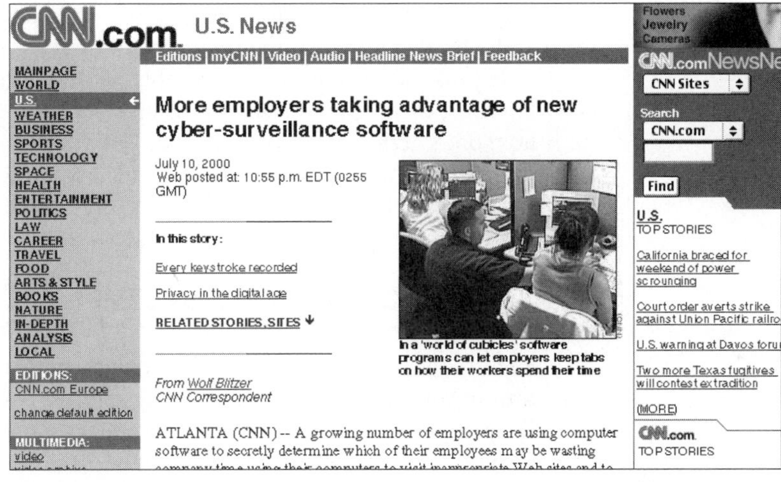

http://
www.cnn.com/2000/US/07/10/workplace.eprivacy/

Even where an employer assures employees that their e-mail communications would not be intercepted by management, employees who voluntarily use the company e-mail system have almost no protected privacy interest. The company's interest in preventing inappropriate and unprofessional comments—or even illegal activity—over its e-mail system usually outweighs any privacy interest an employee has in protecting those comments.[4]

ONLINE

See NASA Office of Inspector General, News Release 2002-027, December 2001, accessible at **http://www.hq.nasa.gov/office/oig/hq/press/pr2002-027.html**

If the employee uses a company's e-mail system—which is private property—to commit a tort or a crime, the employee can be held responsible (see Chapter 7). A former Intel employee who sent thousands of derogatory e-mails to Intel employees was held liable in tort for "spamming," which constitutes trespass. (*Intel Corp. v. Hamidi,* 98ASO5067 Cal. App. Dep't. S.Ct. 1999). A former subcontractor employee at the Jet Propulsion Laboratory in Pasadena was sentenced for receiving child pornography while using a NASA computer.

Legal Standards as Ethical Norms

Several well-established legal standards form a major basis for ethical analysis. First, the fiduciary duty imposed on agents who act on behalf of business organizations (discussed in Chapter 9) is the most fundamental legal and ethical principle. Agents owe their principals a duty of loyalty; this duty prohibits conflicts of interest and requires confidentiality. Second, laws such as the Uniform Commercial Code require business parties dealing at arm's length to act in good faith.

A third legal and ethical principle prohibits misappropriation of others' assets. Of course, the standard applies in criminal law for theft or embezzlement, but it also applies to intangibles. Because information is property, the laws of insider trading, unfair competition, and intellectual property infringement make it illegal to take

2. Stuart Macdonald, "ACTIS Software to Put Big Brother Right in the Office," *The Glasgow Herald,* April 20, 2001, p. 27.
3. Laurie Hilsgen, "The cost of slacking" *New Zealand Infotech Weekly* (Wellington), May 1, 2000, p. 13.
4. *Smyth v. Pillsbury,* 914 F.Supp. 97 (ED Pa. 1996).

corporate information for personal use or to provide it to an outsider. A fourth legal and ethical standard is the requirement to act with due care. The tort of negligence is based on the duty to act reasonably with regard to actions that may affect others. Finally, others' rights must be respected. This norm also requires an evaluation of how one's action affects others and requires that steps be taken to avoid infringing on the rights of others. Thus, cyber squatters who register a domain name that belongs to someone else are violating both ethical norms and legal trademark standards.

TASKS OF A LEGAL SYSTEM

Each society organizes its legal system to perform several different tasks. The institutions and functions of the legal system vary greatly from one society to the next. Despite the differences among these legal systems, all seek to maintain order and provide a forum for resolving disputes. Other common functions, such as protecting expectations and maintaining political authority while accommodating change, are also tasks of most legal systems.

TO MAINTAIN ORDER

The most important function of a legal system is maintaining order within the society. In a society without order, people cannot function efficiently because they must spend more time and energy protecting themselves and their property than in productive pursuits. Thus, the purpose of legal rules is to promote conforming conduct and to discourage nonconforming conduct. In a liberal society, customary rules rather than legal rules are used to maintain order. For example, littering on public property is generally nonconforming conduct in most societies; societies such as Japan rely more on custom to discourage such conduct, whereas other societies, such as Singapore, use legal rules to deter nonconforming conduct. The most important rules in a liberal society are those against rules—the rules that restrict the government's power.

TO PROVIDE A FORUM FOR THE RESOLUTION OF DISPUTES

A society's legal system usually provides methods and places for individuals and organizations to resolve disputes. The methods by which disputes are resolved do, of course, differ. In the Chinese legal system, private disputes are usually not settled in public courts. The emphasis on the duty to maintain peace and order (and thus amicably settle any dispute) outweighs any emphasis on the rights of the complaining party to have a public forum determine a resolution of the dispute.

In other societies, the greater emphasis on the rights of individuals and on achieving a settlement that meets established rules, applied by a neutral decision maker, generally leads to an important role for the legal system in resolving disputes. Of course, courts are not the only forums for settling disputes. Numerous alternatives exist, and many of them are increasing in popularity, as noted in Chapter 3.

OTHER TASKS

In addition to maintaining order and providing a forum for disputes, a legal system seeks to protect expectations while both maintaining the political authority and promoting social change. The legal system protects expectations by providing a framework of rules on which people in the society can rely. When a consumer buys a ladder, the legal system reinforces the expectation that the buyer will not suffer injury from a defective ladder. The legal system cannot guarantee that the consumer will not be injured. Instead, it requires the maker of a defective ladder to compensate the consumer who has been injured as a result of the defect.

The legal system thus encourages manufacturers to use reasonable care while assuring consumers that their expectations for the use of a nondefective ladder are protected. The legal system also sets minimum design or performance standards for some products that are to be sold in the society. If you want to sell an automobile, it must be equipped to meet established safety standards (seat belt, airbag, bumpers, shatterproof windshield) and anti-pollution requirements (use of lead-free gasoline and non-ozone-depleting refrigerants).

In almost all societies, one function of a legal system is to maintain a dominant political authority. That authority generally punishes or expels people who turn over secret governmental documents to its opponents. It may even permanently imprison or execute its opponents.

On the other hand, decisions of a legal institution such as a court, state agency, or legislative body may bring about social change because people generally support such decisions. Not everyone in society agrees with each new law, but once a decision is made, most people generally conform their behavior to its requirements. For example, the Occupational Safety and Health Administration (OSHA) has imposed new safety standards on many factories and firms. Generally, court cases requiring the use of safer equipment are adhered to, even when some of the rules and interpretations do not seem to make sense in certain situations.

LEGAL SYSTEMS

Each nation has its own legal institutions and legal environment, but all national laws can be classified as belonging to three or four major legal systems. Of course, the legal environment of some nations is based on more than one of these systems. The major legal systems are the common law, civil law, Islamic law, and socialistic law systems. Because many countries that once used the socialistic legal system are now using the civil law legal system, the civil law legal system is the most prevalent, and the socialistic legal system is no longer very popular.

COMMON LAW LEGAL SYSTEM

The legal system of the United States is a common law legal system. More than two dozen countries, including the United States, Australia, New Zealand, India, and most of Canada, use this legal system. In common law systems, the courts are recognized not only as interpreters of the law but also as creators of law.

Stare Decisis

As court decisions became recognized as a primary source of law, the doctrine of **stare decisis** developed. According to this concept, a judge's decision in a case not only interprets and applies the law to the controversy between the litigating parties but also sets a precedent for future cases involving similar facts. Stare decisis brings predictability to the law. Prior cases based on essentially the same facts predict the decision for later cases.

Stare decisis is applicable only where the courts are part of the same legal structure. Thus, a decision by the Michigan Supreme Court has to be followed by lower courts in Michigan but not by lower courts in Pennsylvania. Only the lower courts in the same jurisdiction are bound by the precedents set by a given higher court. A further limiting aspect of stare decisis is that in some cases the circumstances surrounding the decision made in the earlier case may have drastically changed. Thus, the same court, when faced with a similar case years later, could decide it differently. In such a case, the court generally expressly notes that it is overruling the prior decision, and it explains why.

The Adversarial Process

The common law legal system conducts trials by an adversarial process. The parties and their attorneys decide the evidence they will present in the case. The judge's only role in determining the evidence to be presented is to decide the validity of legal objections that are based on rules prohibiting consideration of certain types of evidence.

The jury is also used in some civil trials in most common law legal systems. The jury determines the facts, based on the evidence it hears; after hearing the judge's instructions on what law applies to the case, it renders its verdict.

CIVIL LAW LEGAL SYSTEM

A **civil law legal system** is based on a code of laws that organizes and codifies the legal rules of a society into one source or code. Civil law legal systems can trace their origin back to about 1750 B.C., when Hammurabi codified the laws of Babylon. A code also represents a reformation of the legal system. After the code becomes effective, past societal practices are no longer used as a basis for the law.

Code Law

Most of the civil law legal systems in the world today are based on Roman law. By the eighteenth century, the codified Roman law had become the basis of the legal system in more than 60 countries in Europe, Asia, South America, and Africa. Codes are large, comprehensive statutes, frequently covering every aspect of the legal system, including civil contracts, torts, commercial rules, criminal laws, and procedural requirements. The German and French codes have been models for codes in many other countries. The French code emphasizes certain principles such as the security of private property, freedom to contract, and family values, whereas the German code is more detailed and technical.

The Inquisitorial System

Trials in a civil law country use an inquisitorial system instead of the adversarial process of the common law legal system. Judges in a civil law legal system have a more hands-on role in the trial than do judges in a common law legal system. They direct the evidence that the parties are to provide for the court's review. Further, there are generally no juries in trials in a civil law legal system. The judge determines both the factual and legal questions. Exhibit 2.1 summarizes the differences between these two legal systems.

ISLAMIC LAW LEGAL SYSTEM

A third type of legal system, the **Islamic law legal system**, is found in more than 25 countries in the world today. Islamic rules of law are interpreted in harmony with the Shari'a (God's rules) found in the Qur'an (also referred to as the Koran) and the Sunna. Islamic law is not based on the will of the people acting through legislative

EXHIBIT 2.1 Comparison of Common Law and Civil Law Legal Systems

Common Law Legal System

1. The development of law by courts using a system of judicial precedent (stare decisis) in which prior court cases are a source of law
2. The use of an adversarial trial process
3. The use of a jury to decide issues of fact in many court cases

Civil Law Legal System

1. The development of law through applying general principles found in a code of law; administrative or governmental interpretations of the code are very important
2. The use of an inquisitorial trial process headed by the judge
3. The use of a judge to decide both facts and law in most court cases

bodies to establish legal rules. Instead, Muslims submit to the will of God, who they believe revealed to Muhammad the path (the Shari'a) for believers to follow. Scholars in the tenth century determined that the divine law had been sufficiently interpreted and that there was no further need for independent reasoning, meaning theoretically there is no need for new laws.

The Qur'an

The Qur'an is not a code of law but an expression of moral and ethical standards. It is a holy book that contains God's rules, as revealed to Muhammad during the period 610–622 A.D. Muslims believe it contains the very word of God. Only a few of its statements deal with what non-Muslims would see as legal issues. For example, it contains general statements that one should honor agreements and observe good faith in commercial dealings.

The Sunna

The Sunna are the traditions—the speeches or deeds of Muhammad or the practices that he is said to have approved. These are essentially past practices or traditions that constitute law because of their widespread acceptance over many centuries.

Differences in Interpretation

Among the many countries that adhere to the teachings of Islam, there are some clear differences, particularly between the Sunni and Shi'ite factions. For example, Iran's legal system is not the same as Saudi Arabia's. Saudi Arabia has no legislature, as only God can make rules for the people to follow. Its regulation of business activity must be in accordance with the Shari'a. A few countries, like Egypt, have a civil law legal system that is interpreted according to Islamic principles. Despite its being an Islamic country, the interpretations and legal system that were imposed in Afghanistan by the Taliban rulers would not be accepted in most other Islamic countries.

SIGNIFICANT CHARACTERISTICS OF THE U.S. LEGAL SYSTEM

The U.S. Constitution provides the framework for the organization of the U.S. legal system. Two significant characteristics, federalism and the separation of powers,

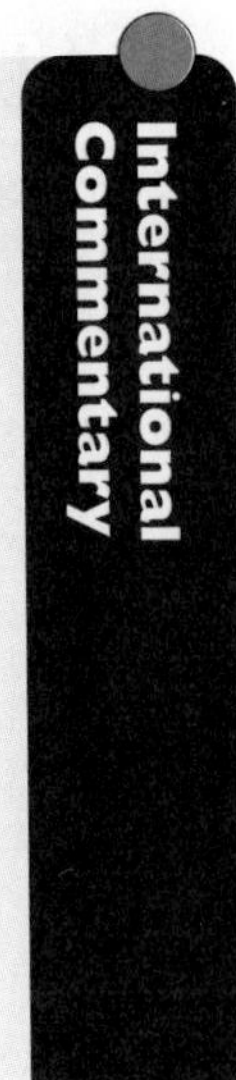

The Demise of the Socialistic Legal System

The most significant event affecting the world's legal systems in recent years has been the disintegration of the socialistic legal system. In the former Czechoslovakia (now the Czech Republic and Slovakia), Bulgaria, Romania, Poland, the former East Germany, Latvia, Lithuania, and other republics once part of the Soviet Union, the socialistic legal system has been abandoned. Monumental economic and political changes have reshaped many of these countries, and both the new and old countries are installing different legal systems.

Although each country is establishing its own system, most of the former socialistic-based legal systems are likely to be replaced with civil law legal systems. In some instances, the Islamic law legal system is being adopted. American judges and lawyers have provided significant assistance to a variety of countries looking to develop new legal systems, but most are patterning their legal systems after those in European countries. Several eastern and central European countries such as Poland and Hungary are currently seeking admission to the European Union (EU). The Baltic countries of Latvia, Estonia, and Lithuania are also working toward eventual admission to the EU. As all current EU members except Britain and Ireland have civil law legal systems, the former socialistic countries that have changed to a civil law system should have little difficulty integrating their societies with those of present EU members.

determine which governmental authority has law-making powers in a given situation. **Federalism** is the division of powers among federal, state, and local governments. The **separation of powers** is the splitting of law-making authority among the three branches of government: legislative, judicial, and executive.

FEDERALISM

The U.S. Constitution determines whether the state or federal legal system has the law-making powers to handle particular problems. The supremacy clause of the U.S. Constitution, which prohibits state law from contradicting federal law, provides:

This Constitution, and the Laws of the United States, which shall be made in Pursuance thereof; and all Treaties made, or which shall be made, under the Authority of the United States, shall be the supreme Law of the Land.

Some business representatives favor greater federal regulation so that they will face uniform federal rules rather than differing state laws. Peter Hutt, a Washington, D.C., lawyer who represents trade groups in the medical device and food industries, says, "One national rule is better than 50 inconsistent rules of any kind. Furthermore, as so many products and services are sold nationally, uniform laws may better suit our more homogeneous population."[5]

Despite the problems that result from the existence of two major legal systems, federalism has substantial benefits. Because state lawmakers are closer to a problem and can often act more quickly than Congress, state legal systems can deal with

5. The *Wall Street Journal*, May 10, 1993, p. 133.

many problems within the states more effectively than can a distant federal government. Moreover, the division of power between the state and federal legal systems means that special interest groups are less likely to dominate at all levels of the legal systems. Finally, the states do not all face similar problems. Some states are densely populated, and others are not. Coastal states have different concerns than many of the inland farming states. Federalism allows states to use diverse solutions for their own problems. Exhibit 2.2 illustrates the sharing of lawmaking powers between the federal and state legal systems.

SEPARATION OF POWERS

The government's powers, at both the federal and state levels, are separated into the executive, legislative, and judicial branches. Each branch is authorized to exercise only the powers it possesses. Generally, the legislative branch makes the law, the judicial branch interprets the law, and the executive branch executes and enforces the law. The separation of powers, depicted in Exhibit 2.3, provides checks and balances among the three branches of government. The framers of the Constitution included this principle because there was little accountability by the English crown to the American colonies. Although checks and balances are cumbersome and inefficient at times, they prevent any one branch of government from becoming too powerful.

EXHIBIT 2.2 Sharing of Federal and State Lawmaking Powers

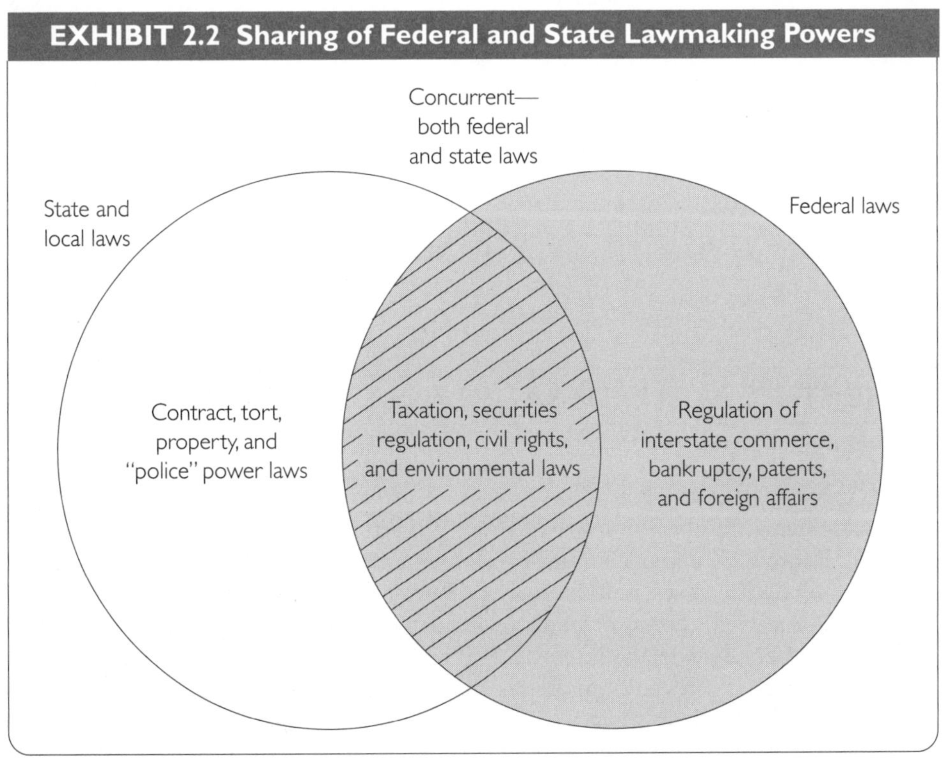

EXHIBIT 2.3 Separation of Powers in the Federal Legal System

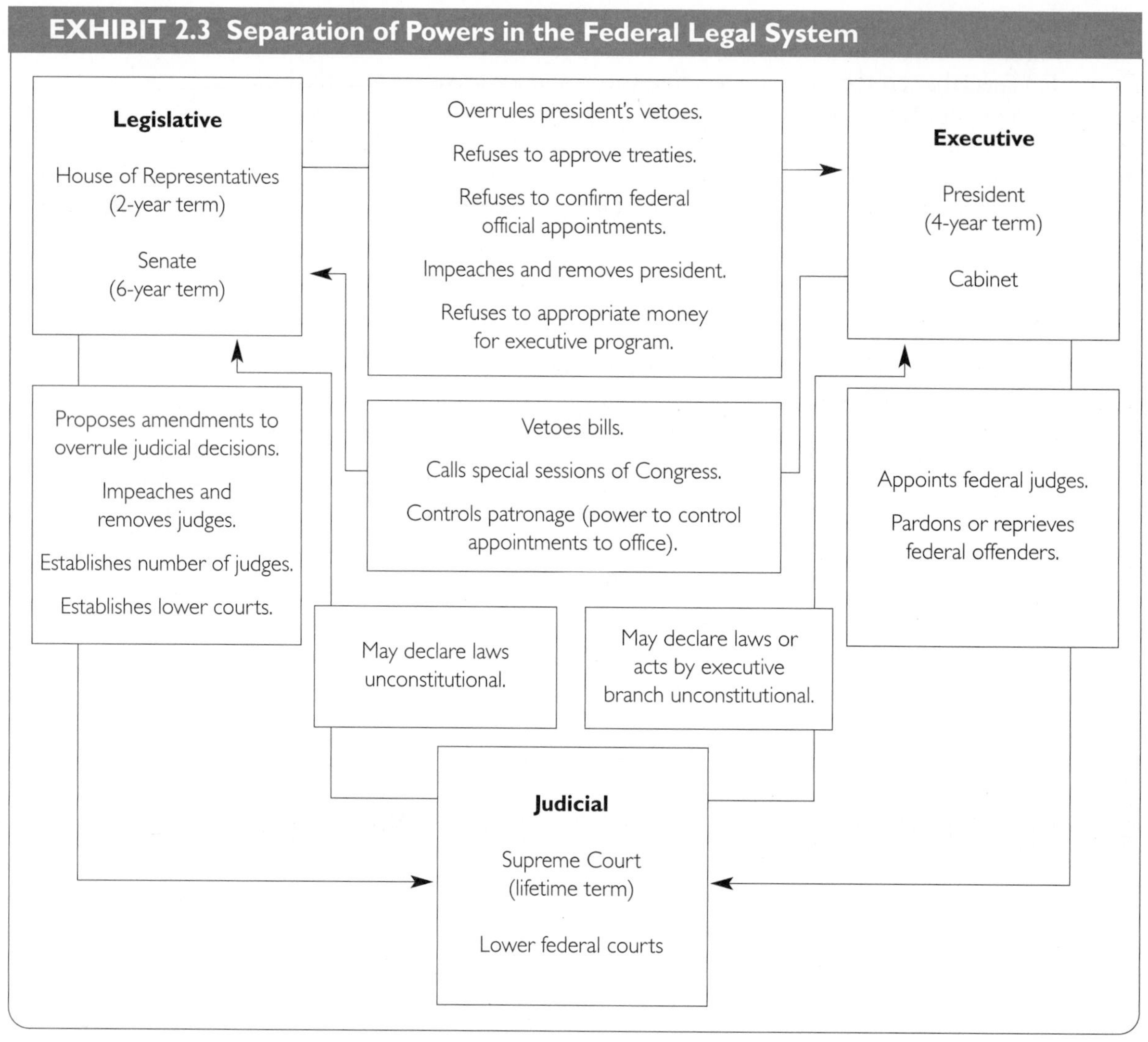

THE STATE AND FEDERAL JUDICIAL SYSTEMS

STATE COURTS

Each state has a number of courts; those at different levels have different tasks to perform. Exhibit 2.4 depicts a multilevel state court system. The power of any court to hear and decide cases is known as a court's **jurisdiction**. Courts at level 1 in Exhibit 2.4 are trial courts, or courts with original jurisdiction. Courts at levels 2 and 3 do not conduct trials; instead, they review the decisions of the trial courts. Because these courts review only cases that originated in other courts or agencies and are appealed to them, they have what is known as appellate jurisdiction. Some states have fewer than three levels of courts; the names of courts at each level differ among the states.

EXHIBIT 2.4 A Multilevel State Court System

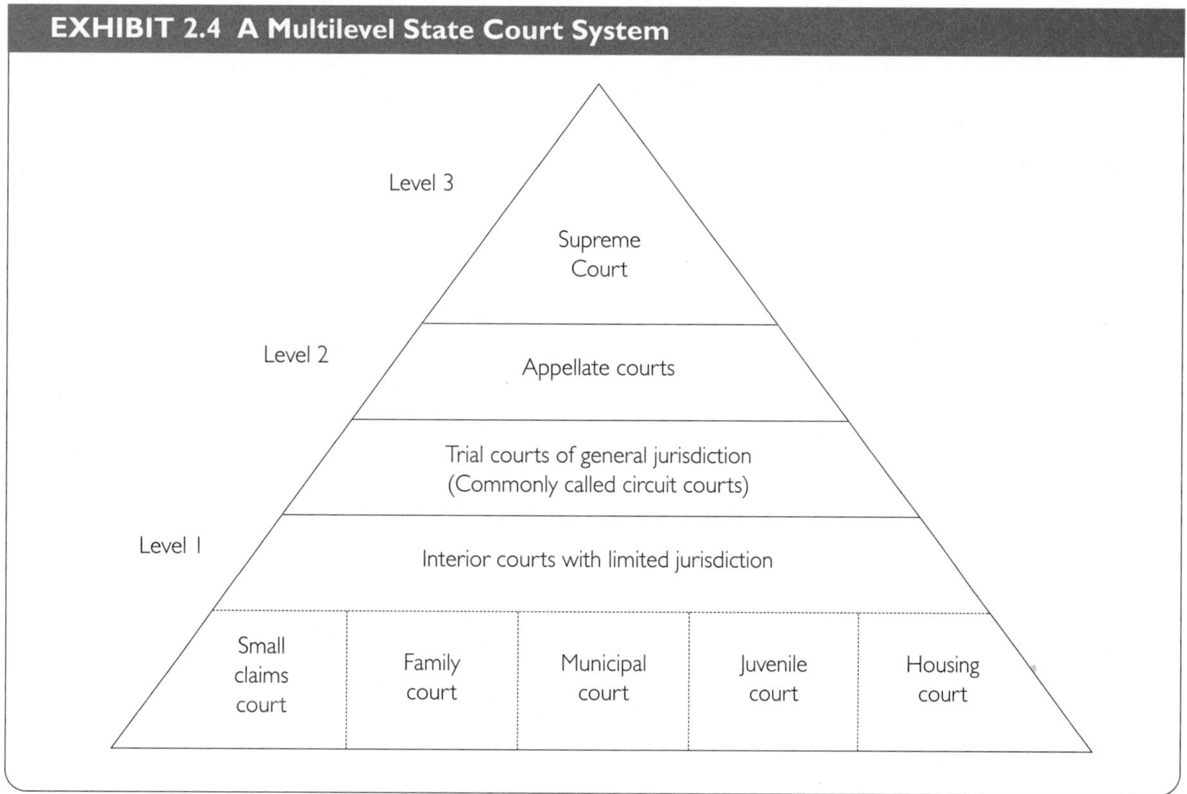

FEDERAL COURTS

As Exhibit 2.5 depicts, the basic three-tier system is used by the federal judiciary, with trial courts at the bottom, appellate courts in the middle, and the U.S. Supreme Court at the top. In addition to the regular three-tier courts, the federal judicial system includes several special courts, including the Court of Claims (determines monetary claims against the United States), the Tax Court, Bankruptcy Courts, and the Court of International Trade. Because these courts hear only certain types of cases, their jurisdiction is called limited subject matter jurisdiction.

The Supreme Court of the United States is expressly referred to in Article III of the U.S. Constitution. It hears appeals from the federal appellate courts and from the highest state courts. The Constitution also provides that a few cases, such as disputes between two states, may originate in the Supreme Court.

Federal appellate courts, known as the Circuit Courts of Appeal, are organized into 13 circuits, or groups of states, spread geographically across the nation. One circuit is the District of Columbia, one is for appeals from the Court of International Trade and the Court of Claims, and the remainder hear appeals from federal trial courts within each of 11 circuits across the country.

At the trial level of the federal judicial system are the federal district courts. There is at least one district court, often with numerous judges, in each state, and many states have several district courts. Although state courts at the trial level can generally hear any type of dispute, the jurisdiction of a federal trial court is limited to two basic types of cases: cases involving federal questions and cases involving diversity of citizenship.

EXHIBIT 2.5 The Federal Judicial System

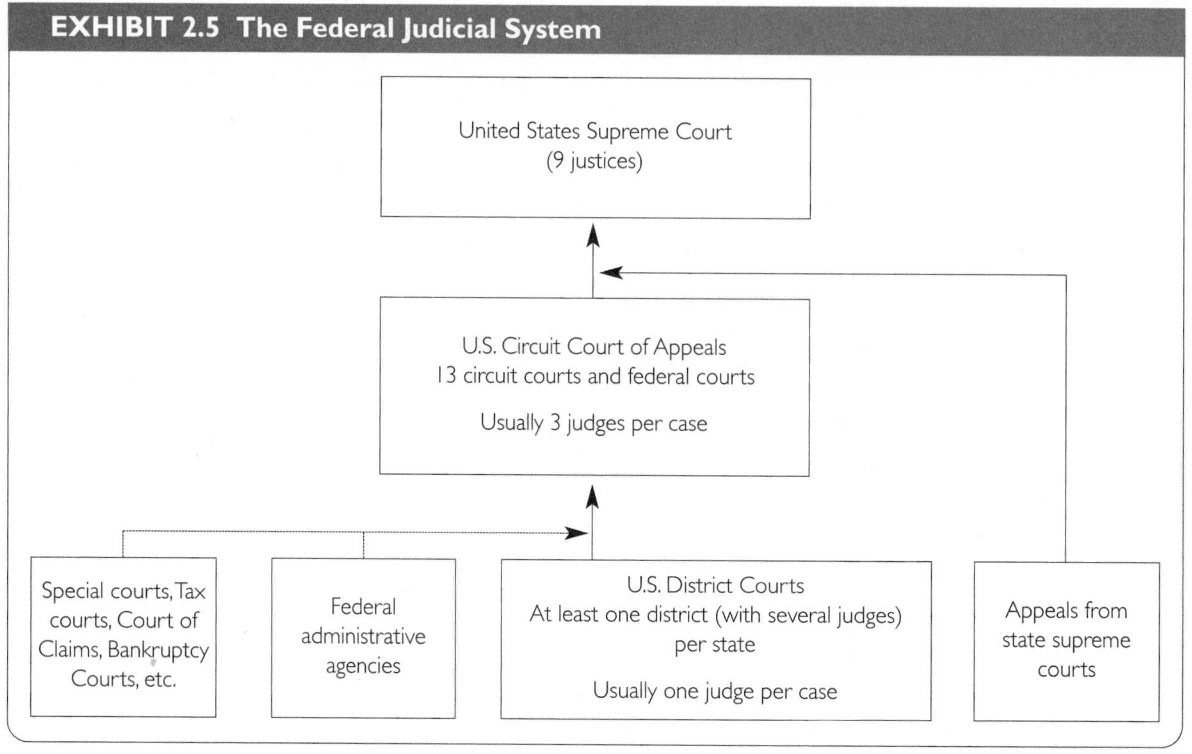

Federal question cases focus on the source of law that governs the case. Such cases are resolved by reference to federal statutes, the U.S. Constitution, a U.S. treaty, a federal administrative regulation, or an executive order of the president. On the other hand, diversity of citizenship cases focus on the parties' citizenship, regardless of the nature of their problem. Such cases require all plaintiffs to have state or national citizenship that is diverse or different from those of all defendants. Diversity of citizenship cases also require that the damages sought exceed $75,000.

The federal district court's diversity of citizenship jurisdiction is not exclusive; it is concurrent, or shared with that of the state courts. A plaintiff who wishes to sue defendants from other states may do so in either a state court that has jurisdiction or in a federal district court. If the suit is started in the state's judicial system, the defendants may be able to remove the case to a federal district court for trial. In most cases, however, the plaintiff selects the court system used.

For a case that is brought to a federal district court solely because of diversity of citizenship, the federal court must apply substantive state law (such as the contract law of Georgia), not federal law, to resolve the parties' dispute. However, the district court will apply federal, not state, procedural rules.

Finally, some cases must be filed in either the federal or state court system. For example, bankruptcy or patent cases must be heard in special courts in the federal court system because only federal laws apply to these subjects. Conversely, a contract dispute between two California residents with no federal questions must be heard in the California state courts. In such a dispute, there would be no subject matter jurisdiction for a federal court and probably no personal jurisdiction for the courts of other states.

Thus, it is important to distinguish between concerns focused on bringing a case in the federal or state legal system and concerns regarding the rules that determine the proper substantive law. Just as the federal courts apply state laws in most diversity of citizenship cases, the state courts sometimes apply federal law in resolving disputes brought to them. Determining where a case is heard and decided is not the same as determining which substantive laws apply. The latter determination is governed by conflict of law rules. They establish criteria to aid the judge in applying the most appropriate law.

JURISDICTION

We have already noted that a court's power to hear and decide cases is referred to as its jurisdiction. The term *jurisdiction* also refers to the political entity (the nation or state) that exercises the power to hear cases. Jurisdiction can also relate to a court's function.

THE MEANING OF JURISDICTION

The terms *original* (trial) and *appellate* (review) jurisdiction are used to describe the type of work performed by a court. Another aspect of jurisdiction concerns the relationship between the court and the case being considered. To make a valid decision regarding a case, a trial court must be legally authorized to hear the type of case involving the particular parties with a dispute. Thus, a trial court needs to have jurisdiction over the problem that a case concerns, referred to as *subject matter jurisdiction*, and jurisdiction over the participants in the suit, referred to as *personal jurisdiction*.

Because a general trial court has the power to hear almost any type of dispute, it normally has subject matter jurisdiction over almost all types of cases, except minor or special disputes heard by specialized courts. Personal jurisdiction, on the other hand, requires that the parties to the dispute be properly before the court—somehow connected to the place where the court is located. In that e-commerce frequently involves transactions between people from different states of the United States or different nations of the world, it can be difficult to determine the location of courts that are likely to have personal jurisdiction over parties to a dispute.

The person bringing a case to a court obviously consents to that court having jurisdiction to hear the dispute, but what about the defendant? When a potential defendant is outside the state where the court is located, a long-arm statute frequently is used. A *long-arm statute* is a law that makes people or entities located outside a territory (such as a state or nation) subject to court proceedings within the court's territory. For example, if a citizen of California is involved in an accident in Oregon that injures an Oregon citizen, the Oregon long-arm statute grants personal jurisdiction over the California defendant to an Oregon court because there is some minimum contact (traveling in Oregon) between the defendant and the state (Oregon) with the long-arm statute. In the United States, courts have held that without some minimum contact between the defendant and the court seeking to exercise personal jurisdiction, requiring an out-of-state defendant to appear in a court selected by the plaintiff would offend the U.S. constitutional requirement of due process, as well as traditional notions of fairness and justice.

JURISDICTION AND E-COMMERCE

Now, think about this concept as it applies to an e-commerce transaction between people or businesses from different countries. The American Bar Association has been studying cyberspace jurisdictional issues for several years. Its report recognizes that every Internet party should be subject to personal and prescriptive jurisdiction somewhere and that, as now occurs in physical transactions, sometimes more than one state may be able to assert jurisdiction over disputing parties.

The U.S. courts addressing this problem have looked at the different uses to which businesses put their websites and have found a continuum of contacts with the locations where their sites are accessible. The courts use a "sliding scale" approach that divides Internet activities into three categories for the purpose of jurisdictional analysis.

According to the court that originally developed the scale in *Zippo Manufacturing Co. v. Zippo Dot Com, Inc.*, 957 F.Supp.1119 (W.D.Pa. 1997): "The likelihood that personal jurisdiction can be constitutionally exercised is directly proportionate to the nature and quality of commercial activity that an entity conducts over the Internet." The sliding scale has become the standard by which courts determine if a business has minimum contacts or "does or transacts business within the state" where the court is located.

Look at the depiction of the scale in Exhibit 2.6 and then review the CoolSavings case.

EXHIBIT 2.6 Internet Transactions and Jurisdictional Concerns

1. **Active Internet Business:** Where there are repeated and purposeful actions such as initiating and continuing contracting, marketing, and distribution activities over the Internet with a business based in a particular state, the combination of such contacts satisfies the "transacting business" requirement. Thus, a firm that advertises and sells products, uses e-mail communication for sales orders, and provides an on-line news service into a state subjects the e-commerce business to jurisdiction there. See *CompuServe, Inc. v. Patterson*, 89 F.3d 1257 (6th Cir. 1996).
2. **Interactive Internet Business:** If a firm provides for only an exchange of information with residents of a state, who are without the ability to contract, and the firm has no other contact with the state in question, then that state does not have the necessary minimum contacts to support jurisdiction. In one case, an English defendant who had a beaniebabiesuk .com website, accessible in the state of Illinois, provided information about orders for Beanie Babies he owned that were created by the plaintiff. However, the defendant did not take orders or enter into contracts over the website. When he was sued by the plaintiff, an Illinois-based firm, the court held the defendant could not be forced to respond to a trademark infringement suit in Illinois because that court lacked personal jurisdiction over the defendant. See *Ty, Inc. v. Clark*, 2000 U.S. Dist. LEXIS 383 (ND.Ill. 2000). On the other hand, if a firm sets up an interactive website directed at the entire country, sends some representatives into the state, hires people there to help promote its technology, and obtains customers from that state, the state does have jurisdiction. See *CoolSavings.Com, Inc. v. IQ. Commerce Corp.*, 53 F.Supp.2d 1000 (N.D. Ill. 1999).
3. **Passive Internet Business:** If a firm's only presence in the state is a passive website, one that allows only viewing of the site's contents, the site cannot be subjected to jurisdiction merely because the site can be accessed within the state. See *GTE New Media Services, Inc. v. Bellsouth Corp.*, 199 F.3rd 1343 (D.C.Cir. 2000).

CoolSavings.Com, Inc. v. IQ Commerce Corp.

53 F.Supp.2d 1000, U.S. District Court (N.D.Ill. 1999)

Facts. Cool Savings, a Michigan corporation with its headquarters and principal place of business in Chicago, sued defendant IQ Commerce (IQ) for patent infringement. IQ is located in California and has no offices or physical presence in Illinois. CoolSavings's patent is for a data processing system that allows it to issue electronic certificates (advertisements and coupons) over interactive on-line networks.

IQ's "iSave" couponing program is intended to make various savings programs and promotional offerings by merchants available to consumers over the Internet. IQ's electronic discount coupon program was accessible in Illinois as well as in other states. People interested in IQ's program submit personal information, including their e-mail addresses, through IQ's website. In addition, IQ's website had "pop-up" windows that allowed customers to clip a coupon and save it in their computers for later use. It is this system that CoolSavings believes infringes its patent.

IQ claimed the Illinois courts did not have personal jurisdiction over it. At the time of the suit, IQ had 299 merchant members signed up for its "iSave" program, 11 of whom were from Illinois. IQ also made a concerted effort to market its capabilities by hiring a Chicago-based advertising and marketing firm to help it find interested merchants. IQ also had e-mail correspondence with the Chicago marketing firm, and it had sent representatives there to meet with the marketers.

Legal Issue. By setting up an interactive website directed at the whole country, including Illinois, and by contracting with a Chicago firm to promote its technology, does IQ establish minimum contacts with Illinois so it has jurisdiction?

Opinion. Chief Judge Marvin E. Aspen. In order to subject a non-resident defendant to personal jurisdiction, "due process requires that he have certain minimum contacts with the forum state such that the maintenance of the suit does not offend traditional notions of fair play and substantial justice." *International Shoe Co. v. Washington*, 326 U.S. 310 (1945). The Supreme Court has made it clear that the required minimum contacts must be purposeful, so that non-residents may anticipate being subject to litigation in the forum as a result of their activities.

The question before us, then, is whether IQ purposefully directed its activities at residents of Illinois and whether CoolSavings' claims arise out of or relate to those activities. Then, even if we decided that IQ did purposefully establish minimum contacts with Illinois, we must consider those contacts in light of other factors to determine whether asserting personal jurisdiction would be reasonable and fair.

We hold that by setting up an interactive website directed at the entire country, knowing and hoping that residents of all states would use it, and by using a Chicago-based marketing firm to promote its capabilities using the disputed technology, IQ purposefully established minimum contacts with Illinois.

It is undisputed that IQ intended its program to be accessible by residents of all states and that a number of Illinois residents did become iSave members. IQ's argument that its contacts with Illinois residents was negligible because Illinois residents' activity on its site amounted to only one-half of one percent of the total site activity is unpersuasive. We are dealing with specific personal jurisdiction and IQ's forum-related conduct—making its technology available for use by Illinois residents—forms the basis of the alleged infringement. Whether IQ's contacts are substantial and continuous is irrelevant. It is enough that IQ's couponing program, targeted at residents of all states, was accessed by people in Illinois. It may seem unfair to subject IQ to personal jurisdiction anywhere in the country, but it seems even more unfair to allow IQ to introduce its program to the entire country, while remaining subject to personal jurisdiction only in its home state, and thus requiring patentees from all over the country to go to California to litigate their infringement claims.

We need not rest our findings of specific jurisdiction on that ground alone however, because IQ also regularly dealt with a Chicago-based advertising and marketing firm—in person, on the phone, and by e-mail—with whom it worked to stimulate interest in the iSave product at issue here. It worked with that firm to help promote its coupon technology to corporate clients. These are purposeful contacts, not the unilateral activity of another party or third person that the Supreme Court warned us against attributing to a defendant for jurisdiction purposes.

We conclude that IQ's website activity in Illinois, coupled with its contacts with Frankel [the Chicago marketing firm], suffice to confer special personal jurisdiction over IQ in Illinois for this patent infringement case. IQ's contacts were purposeful, and they involved the technology that is the subject of this suit. . . . We must now consider these contacts in light of other factors to determine whether the assertion of personal jurisdiction would comport with fair play and substantial justice. Illinois has a strong interest in adjudicating injuries that occur within the state, and this interest extends to patent infringement actions. Even though the burden on IQ defending a lawsuit in Illinois may be significant, it is recognized that progress in communications and transportation has made the defense of a lawsuit in a foreign tribunal less burdensome. And the fact that it is advantageous to CoolSavings to litigate in its chosen forum does not militate against its right to have access to that court. IQ has not made a compelling case that asserting personal jurisdiction over it would be constitutionally unreasonable.

Decision. By setting up an interactive website directed at the entire country, knowing and hoping that residents of all states would use it, and by using a Chicago-based marketing firm to promote its capabilities in using the disputed technology, IQ purposefully established minimum contacts with Illinois. Illinois has an interest in hearing cases causing injury in that state, so it is fair for it to exercise personal jurisdiction over this defendant.

Case Questions

1. How would you categorize these activities? Do they fit as active, passive, or interactive Internet business activities? Why?
2. Which of the contacts that IQ had with Illinois seems to be more important in subjecting it to the jurisdiction of the Illinois courts? If there had been no contact with the Chicago marketing company, would this court reach the same decision? Why?
3. Is a patent infringement case one where a court is likely to exercise psersonal jurisdiction over an out-of-state defendant?

QUESTIONS

1. Who are a corporation's stakeholders? Which of those stakeholders are more important to most corporations?
2. Find a corporation with an Internet website that posts its code of conduct and compare it to Boeing's. What differences in emphasis do you see, and why do you think the codes are different?
3. What is one of the most distinctive features of an Islamic legal system?
4. Compare and contrast the civil and common law legal systems. In the United States, a court's decision can affect people who are not parties in the case, but the same is not true in Germany. Why?
5. Discuss the relationship between law and ethics. Give examples of acts that may be both legal and unethical and acts that may be both illegal and ethical.
6. Mrs. Vitullo and her husband purchased a boat from Modern Marine, a boat dealer in Michigan; the boat was manufactured by Velocity Powers, a Florida company. Velocity's only contact with Illinois was that it purchased parts from an Illinois manufacturer and that it had shown its boats in a boat show in Illinois. Velocity did have a website that was somewhat interactive and that could be accessed in Illinois. It did not allow any business to be conducted on line. Mrs. Vitullo was injured and her husband killed in a boating accident on Lake Michigan in Chicago. She brought suit in Illinois against Velocity for her injuries and her husband's wrongful death. Does Illinois have jurisdiction over Velocity Powers? Why? See *Vitullo v. Velocity Powerboats, Inc.*, 1998 U.S.Dist. LEXIS 7120 (N.D. Ill. 1998).
7. Mary, a 16-year-old high school student, had an opportunity to sing with a small band. To enhance her singing abilities, she entered into a contract with Mrs. Thompson for a course of vocal music lessons. The lessons were scheduled to occur for 15 weeks, and Mary agreed to pay Mrs. Thompson $1,500. She paid $500 at the beginning and was to pay the remaining $1,000 when the lessons were finished. Mary quit after completing 12 lessons and notified Mrs. Thompson that she was canceling the contract. She asked for the $500 she had paid to be returned, but Mrs. Thompson refused. Mary then sued Mrs. Thompson for the return of the $500. Assume that the law entitled Mary to have the $500 returned. Was it ethical for her to seek it? Do you think Mary had any ethical duty to pay Mrs. Thompson for the lessons she did have? Why?
8. You are the vice president for international sales of A-One Air Seat Corporation, which manufactures seats used in airplanes. Recently you have been discussing your product with an airline representative from Chinan Express, the government-subsidized airplane manufacturer in a heavily populated country in Asia. To sell products to this firm, you need a license from the government. In your discussion with the representative from Chinan Express, you learn that if you pay a certain individual $100,000 and have him apply for the license on behalf of your firm, it is very likely that the license will be granted within two months. On the other hand, if you apply directly, it may take up to two years for your firm to obtain the license. You hope to sell seats worth more than $5

million to Chinan Express. The president of your company asks what you think would be the right thing for the company to do. What would be your recommendation to the president regarding this transaction? Consider both the universal and utilitarian ethical theories in formulating your answer.

9. David Mink, a Texas resident, developed a computer program that could track information on sales made and opportunities missed on sales not made. He submitted a copyright and patent application for the software and hardware he developed. Later, at a trade show, he demonstrated the program to Richard Stark, a Colorado resident. Stark allegedly shared all of Mink's information with David Middlebrook, a Vermont resident, and two companies, one of which was AAAA Development. Mink brought suit in Texas against Middlebrook and AAAA. AAAA makes no sales in Texas and has no agents or representatives there. However, AAAA does have a website, accessible from Texas. The website provides an e-mail address by which website visitors can seek further information. Does the Texas court have personal jurisdiction over AAAA? See *Mink v. AAAA Development*, 190 F3d 333 (5th Cir., 1999).

10. Direct Access is a Florida-based company, with a satellite office in New York, that provides travel agents access to its database in Florida to book airline, automobile, and hotel reservations. Pres-Kap is a travel agency in New York. The parties negotiated a lease agreement in New York and then forwarded it to Florida, where it was signed by Direct Access. Payments due from Pres-Kap to Direct Access were sent to Direct Access in Florida. A dispute arose concerning the malfunction of the airline reservation system. After Pres-Kap stopped payment, Direct Access sued in Florida, claiming that the existence of the database in Florida and the fact that payments were sent there gives Florida the right to hear the dispute. Pres-Kap claims Florida has no jurisdiction over it. Who is correct? Why? See *Pres-Kap, Inc. v. System One, Direct Access, Inc.*, 636 So. 2d 1351 (Fla Dist.Ct. App. 1994).

CHAPTER 3

Litigation and Alternative Dispute Resolution

LITIGATION

Litigation is a dispute resolution process involving presentation of evidence by parties through their attorneys, to a jury and judge. Through court determinations of disputes, laws are interpreted, applied, and created. Although other methods are used to settle disputes, the most visible and formal method is the litigation process. Most court cases that are filed are not concluded in the courts; instead they are settled through negotiations. In other cases, mediation, arbitration, and other alternative dispute resolution (ADR) methods are often used.

Litigation is important not only for the parties to a controversy but also to the development of law. In the United States, almost all court decisions beyond the trial level generally must be explained in written opinions that become public information. It is through such opinions, exemplified by the cases in this book, that laws are applied to specific facts and legal principles are established.

THE USE OF LITIGATION

Although more publicity is given to criminal litigation than to civil litigation, civil litigation is of greater concern to both the average citizen and the business manager. Sometimes business managers use litigation as part of their management strategy. In the United States, there is little stigma to litigation and perhaps greater willingness than in some other countries to use it to solve problems that are not satisfactorily resolved through negotiation. For example, in Japan, the confrontation between parties that is part of litigation is not encouraged. Consensus practices aimed at harmonizing conflicting goals are such a part of the Japanese business environment that litigation between business firms is viewed as disruptive to long-term trust building.

THE AMOUNT OF LITIGATION

In almost all fields of business litigation, from advertising and bankruptcy to contract and tort law, the number of cases litigated has increased dramatically over the

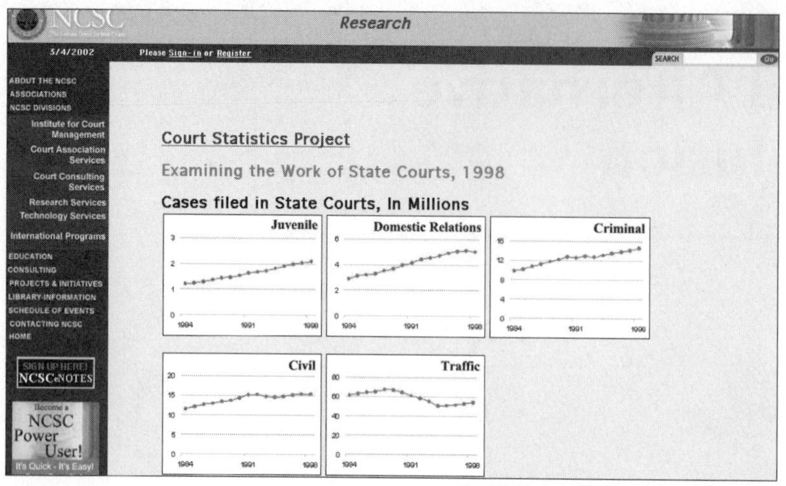

Court Statistics Project, The National Center for State Courts.

http://

www.ncsc.dni.us/divisions/research/csp/csp-stat02.html

past several decades. Both individuals and firms are more likely than they were in the past to bring disputes to the courts. In addition, recent changes in the environment, civil rights, and product liability fields have increased the potential for litigation. An increased familiarity with the legal system may also be making it easier for people to resort to litigation.

The United States is a litigious society—that is, a society in which people often prefer to sue than to settle disputes by other methods. More than 260,000 civil suits were filed in federal courts in 1999. However, fewer than 5% of these suits reached trial. By comparison, in 1990, 211,626 civil cases were filed in those U.S. district courts. In addition, well over a million (1.35 million in 1999) bankruptcy cases are filed annually in the federal court system. Those numbers have grown dramatically in the last several decades. In 1980, 331,000 cases were filed, and in 1990, the number was almost 783,000.

Because most civil cases involve questions of state law, such as contract, real estate, and personal injury law, they are generally litigated in state courts rather than federal courts. As the screen above depicts, in 1998, approximately 15 million civil cases were filed in state courts. Although the total number of civil filings in state courts has remained stable during the last decade, the charts show a continual rise in juvenile, domestic relations, and criminal cases from 1984.

Many cases and controversies litigated today involve problems that were practically unknown until recent times, such as biogenetic products, class-action suits regarding asbestos exposure, the role of cigarette smoking in causing cancer, the ownership and protection of computer programs, sexual harassment cases, the infringement of e-commerce business patents, and cyber squatting. The Internet has changed how some of the key concepts related to litigation are applied.

LITIGATION AND INTERNET ISSUES

VIOLATION OF EXISTING LAWS

Courts are already inundated with lawsuits involving the Internet. In his book *Code and Other Laws of Cyberspace*, Harvard law professor Larry Lessig argues that courts and legislatures must stop companies and governments from violating privacy, free speech, and open markets on the Internet. In 1999, the Federal Trade Commission filed 61 suits in response to consumer complaints about cyber get-rich schemes and auction items that were never sent, and it is seeking additional funding to increase its fight against cyber fraud. Patents that have been granted for Internet-related business methods are spawning dozens of lawsuits and counterclaims. Those who infringe patents could be forced to pay millions of dollars in damages, and companies that could lose patents will face unexpected competition. The biggest names in e-commerce have been involved in such disputes, including Amazon versus Barnes & Noble, Priceline versus Microsoft's Expedia, DoubleClick versus I.90, and dotNow's suit against AOL.

LITIGATION AND E-COMMERCE JURISDICTION

Chapter 2 notes that before accessing courts to decide legal disputes, a business has to know which courts have the power and authority to decide a case. Courts have the legal authority to hear and decide cases based on their jurisdiction over the parties to the case and the legal issues being disputed. Traditionally, courts have held that a court has jurisdiction if a company operates in or does business in the state or country where the court is located. But how does this apply to cyberspace, such as when someone posts something on an Internet site?

An overriding issue facing e-commerce business concerns jurisdiction. The jurisdictional problem—which court(s) can hear and decide specific cases—was briefly discussed in Chapter 2. Although courts in the United States and across the globe are beginning to develop criteria for answering jurisdictional questions, there is still a great deal of uncertainty about this important threshold litigation problem.

The U.S. courts divide cases involving website and Internet activities into three categories. In the first, significant activities such as accepting orders through the site from users in a country subject the website owner to that country's jurisdiction. Firms that use interactive e-commerce websites generally are subject to the jurisdiction of courts located wherever that site can be accessed. In the second category, with some degree of interaction between users in one country and the website owner based in another country, a number of factors need to be analyzed to determine if courts in the user's country have jurisdiction over the website owner. In the third category, when the site is not interactive and there are no other contacts between the website owner or developer and users in a specific country, courts in the users' countries do not have jurisdiction merely because the site can be seen in that country.

Businesses that develop websites that can be accessed throughout the world are very concerned with being the target of litigation in countries where their materials can be accessed. There is no question that Internet activities have increased jurisdictional exposure of most companies that have a cyber presence. An e-commerce website is a virtual storefront with worldwide exposure, and the Internet now connects more than 159 countries. How do courts determine (1) whether they have the authority to hear and decide cases involving websites created outside their country and (2) which country's laws will be used in deciding disputes? In some cases, the answer is clear. A European Community directive requires that in consumer contracts, the choice of law involving an e-commerce sale to a European consumer is always the law of the domicile of the consumer. The German Bundestag (parliament) has enacted a law that provides that German law applies to disputes related to use of a website that is accessible from Germany.

Being on the Internet exposes a firm to many different types of litigation. The World Intellectual Property Organization has decided hundreds of disputes over which firm has rights to a particular domain name. Trademark piracy can occur when cyber squatters register names similar to those used by established businesses or via meta-tagging practices that use competitors' names to attract searches to different sites. Posting protected material on a website or using legally protected business practices can lead to copyright, patent, and trade secret litigation. A company may be liable for employees' breach of confidentiality if employees transmit information to external websites or chat room discussions. Litigation over invasion of privacy issues related to use of personal data frequently involves cross-border disputes.

The broad discovery rules for civil litigation discussed later in this chapter have meant that the electronic data stored on servers, personal computers, disks, or personal digital assistants can be accessed by an opposing litigant. Corporate policies now must incorporate periodic reviews of all electronically stored data. As soon as there is notice of possible litigation, a firm has a legal duty to take steps to preserve possible electronic evidence.

Managers are employing a number of strategies to deal with the multiplicity of laws that could be applied to a website. In the terms and conditions that are expressed as a condition for using the site, firms are requiring that arbitration, one of the alternatives to litigation discussed in this chapter, be employed for any disputes between the firm and users.

Another strategy involves the use of a forum selection clause. A **forum selection clause** designates a specific forum (such as a specific court in a certain state) as the only place where any litigation claims are to be heard. The clause usually is included in click-wrap and terms of use agreements. Similar conditions may impose the law of the country selected by the website owner. Although courts in all countries do not always follow such terms, they do provide firms with greater control over where and how to resolve claims that can arise from around the world.

These clauses provide *some* protection against litigation being brought in any country selected by a user. Some website owners indicate that they do not make contracts through their website. Disclaimers specifically state that the website owner does not conduct sales, accept orders, or receive payments. Further language usually notes that the receipt of a file via Internet file transfer protocol (FTP) or e-mail does not constitute an order. The website may also specify the exclusive market that is served by its e-commerce business. Some courts have held that a website owner can limit its exposure by including a disclaimer that it will not sell products outside a certain geographic territory. The click-wrap agreement then defines the specific place where disputes are to be heard.

Many multinational firms set up different websites for different countries. If e-customers use a website outside their domicile, the website directs purchasers to use their "home" site. Developing this type of infrastructure is expensive, and the efficiencies associated with e-commerce are more difficult to extract. As the following case shows, it also may not be effective. In a controversial case that may establish legal precedent for countries seeking to impose their own restrictions on the use of the Internet, a French court ordered Yahoo! to block access for French users to a section of its U.S. site.

Union of Jewish Students v. Yahoo!

Tribunal de Grande Instance
Paris, France
November 20, 2000

Facts. The Union of Jewish Students and the International Anti-Racism and Anti-Semitism League assert that Yahoo! violates French law by making Nazi-related content available to web users in France. The law in France prohibits the exhibition or sale of Nazi-related objects. The items found on Yahoo.com's auction site include Nazi flags, war songs, daggers, and swastika-emblazoned gas valves.

Yahoo! has a separate website, yahoo.fr, that it has

designed for French users, and that site has none of the Nazi-related items. Nevertheless, the Yahoo.com website, though not designed for French users, is accessible in France. Although the display and sale of such items is legal in many jurisdictions where Yahoo! operates, including the United States, where it is based, the exhibition or sale of such goods is illegal in France under racial discrimination laws.

Legal Issue. If the contents of a website, accessible in France, violates French law, can a French court require the U.S.-website owner to use filters to block French users from accessing the prohibited web contents?

Opinion. Judge Jean-Jacques Gomez. The plaintiffs argue that Internet companies like Yahoo! are circumventing national legislation passed in France and other countries after World War II to prevent the spread of racist materials. Yahoo! insists it has taken steps to shield French users from the material by posting the exhibits on its U.S. site and not on its French site (Yahoo.fr). It also asserts that U.S. law, not French law, should govern what it posts on its Yahoo.com site located in the United States.

Yahoo! also argues that technical filtering solutions to block users is not feasible and that it would be too difficult to identify users originating from France. However, a panel of experts testified that a high percentage of French users could be blocked and that technology would allow Yahoo! to locate a user's origin with approximately 90% accuracy.

Decision. This court reaffirms its May 22 decision requiring Yahoo to prevent French users from accessing that portion of the auction site where the offending material is located. Yahoo! must adhere to the court's decision within 90 days or face daily fines of 15,000 euros per day [about $13,500]. Yahoo! is required to implement a three-part filtering system, based on blocking Internet protocol (IP) addresses that roughly correspond to the location of Internet service providers in France; blocking ten keywords as search terms; and requiring users to identify their geographic location.

Note. As a reaction to the decision, Yahoo! decided to ban all Nazi paraphernalia and other hate-related material from its on-line auctions effective January 10, 2001. A month later, e-Bay followed suit. Yet, Yahoo! said it would not comply with the French court's order. Instead, it filed suit in its home U.S. federal district court in California, seeking to have that court determine if a foreign court can determine what Yahoo! sells on its auction site. Despite French objections, in June 2001, Judge Jeremy Fogel granted Yahoo!'s motion for a determination that the French court's ruling was unconstitutional. Thus the case of *Yahoo! Inc. v. LaLigue Contre le Racisme et l'Antsemitisme (LICRA)* 145 F. Supp 2d 1168 and 169 F. Supp 2d 1181 (N. D. Cal. 2001) may help to determine the extent to which one country can impose its law on a website based in another country.

Case Questions

1. Shouldn't the laws of the place where material is accessible govern its use of a website?
2. What do you think would be the position of the Chinese government regarding the decision in this case? Why?
3. Some U.S. laws, such as most equal employment opportunity laws, do not apply to small businesses. Should the law make some exception for websites owned by small firms and exempt them from complying with the laws of dozens of different countries? Do you think most countries in the world would agree to such a provision? Why?

SEEKING ALTERNATIVES TO LITIGATION

In almost all fields of business litigation, the number of disputes brought to the courts has increased dramatically over the past several decades. Not only are there new e-commerce controversies that must be resolved but also even in traditional areas there are more people, more products, and more business and consumer transactions than ever before. Another reason for this increase may be advertising by law firms, televised court proceedings, and increasing education exposure that make people more familiar with and less afraid to access the legal system to resolve their disputes. As a result of the increased caseload, the legal system has become overburdened.

Both state and federal courts generally face a backlog of cases. Civil cases throughout the country face delayed resolution as criminal cases take priority on court dockets, because of the requirement that defendants accused of crimes be given a prompt trial. The increasing costs and delays associated with litigation have

International Commentary

Cyberlaw Debate

Under what circumstances should a firm with a website in one country need to comply with the laws of other countries where that site is accessible? Would it be prohibitive for small Web publishers to comply with laws in China, Brazil, Honduras, and New Zealand? Doesn't it make sense for Italian law to determine what is accessible in Italy?

Greg Wrenn, counsel for Yahoo!, refused to recognize the French court's jurisdiction. He argued that U.S. laws protect Nazi-related speech under the First Amendment. Yahoo! succeeded in getting the controversy before U.S. courts. Alan Davidson, an attorney for the Center for Democracy and Technology, worries that if every Internet publisher is liable under the laws of hundreds of countries, smaller Web publishers and individuals will be deterred from going global. He says complying with numerous local laws would place a prohibitive burden on the development of e-commerce.

On the other hand, companies doing business in foreign countries must always be aware of the laws where they do business. Some suggest that there's no reason why U.S. law should apply to a U.S. firm whose website is accessible in France. They argue that U.S. companies wishing to exploit the global markets need to tailor their content to local conditions and comply with orders of foreign courts.

Thomas Vartanian, who chaired an American Bar Association Internet project, notes "Courts want to protect their citizens." But, conducting business on the Internet on a country-by-country basis is not feasible. Jodi Kieley, a partner in Jenner and Block, who submitted an amicus brief supporting Yahoo! on behalf of the U.S. Chamber of Commerce, says, "You would have to survey the laws of every country in the world. As a practical matter, it's virtually impossible." Vartanian predicts that "courts are likely to continue to handle these issues on a nationwide basis. The only consensus we seem to be getting is that the rule of my country rules."[1]

led many firms to use alternative methods of resolving disputes and to find new ways to better manage their legal costs. The major alternative dispute resolution methods are discussed near the end of this chapter.

THE CIVIL LITIGATION PROCESS

Civil and criminal litigation differ significantly in their use of juries and in their parties, purpose, and processes. Whereas civil cases are initiated by individuals and organizations, criminal cases are brought by a public official representing society at large. These important differences should be noted in comparisons of civil and criminal litigation. Because many civil cases that are filed never reach trial, it is also necessary to look at the entire civil litigation process, not just the trial itself, to understand the nature of civil litigation.

USE OF AN ADVERSARIAL PROCESS

As noted in Chapter 2, in the U.S. legal system all litigation uses an **adversarial process** that entrusts the parties with responsibility for the development and proof of their claims. In the adversarial process, the parties, not the judge, decide what evidence to present, which witnesses to call, and when to object to something that

1. Tamara Loomis, "Yahoo Decision Affords Internet Companies a Temporary Respite from Worry," *The Internet Newsletter,* 6 (8), November 2001, p. 5.

the opposing party seeks to do. Because most people are not familiar with the complexities of litigation, the parties to a suit generally hire attorneys to represent them and to present the case.

Many other nations do not employ the adversarial principle in conducting litigation. Instead, they use the **inquisitorial process**, which requires all parties to assist the judge in investigating the facts of the controversy before the court. In the inquisitorial process, the judge, acting somewhat like an orchestra conductor, takes an active part in determining the facts. By contrast, the judge in a trial using the adversarial process is more like a referee at a sporting event, essentially reacting to objections posed by the attorneys.

The rationale for the use of the adversarial process is that truth and justice are more likely to emerge if each litigant is responsible for preparing, presenting, and defending his or her case. A neutral judge brings impartiality to the process, and the biased parties are expected to bring greater concern and dedication than would parties who are assisting in an investigation.

Critics of the adversarial system argue that winning or losing a case too often depends on the skill of the attorneys rather than the merits of the case. They also argue that the adversarial process leads parties to hide or distort facts to strengthen their positions. Accordingly, legal reforms adopted in recent decades have sought to lessen the impact of the adversarial principle in litigation. In addition, the utilization of the adversarial process has decreased as a result of increased use of administrative tribunals and the alternative methods of dispute resolutions noted later in this chapter.

STAGES OF CIVIL LITIGATION

The civil litigation process can be divided into five stages, beginning before a case has been filed and ending after a trial has been decided. These stages are prelitigation concerns, the pleading stage, pretrial activities, the trial process, and the post-trial and appellate stage.

Prelitigation Concerns

Before any lawsuit begins, there are matters the disputing parties should consider. Several important questions relate to the attorney's role. Should the party consult an attorney as soon as there is the possibility of litigation? Can the disputing parties investigate the facts and settle the dispute without seeking the assistance of attorneys? Would turning the dispute over to attorneys at an early stage take too much control away from the parties themselves? If the parties try to work things out themselves, will their discussions, notes, and documents hurt their cases if the dispute later results in civil litigation? Answering such questions helps determine when an attorney should be consulted.

Even after a decision has been made to consult and retain an attorney, the who, what, when, and where of the dispute must be addressed before any lawsuit begins (see Exhibit 3.1).

Pleadings Stage

A civil lawsuit is begun by filing a complaint with a court that has jurisdiction to hear and decide the dispute. Typically, the plaintiff's attorney files the complaint with the court and has a copy of the complaint and a summons delivered to the defendant(s). The complaint is a document that gives the plaintiff's version of the **historical facts**—allegations about the circumstances that led to the claimed wrongful acts by the defendant. It also generally includes **jurisdictional facts**—statements showing why the

EXHIBIT 3.1 Questions to Ask before Litigation

***Who* are the parties that could be sued?**
Because there can be multiple defendants, the plaintiff has to decide whether to sue some or all of the parties that might be liable. Although adding more parties generally increases costs, sometimes adding more parties increases the plaintiff's chance of winning and collecting damages.
***What* is the basis of the suit?**
A party who may be able to sue on the basis of a contract, breach of warranty, or tort may need to determine the advantages to pursuing one theory rather than another. Frequently, a suit initially alleges multiple theories so that evidence related to any of them can be discovered and potentially used in litigation.
***When* will the litigation begin?**
Should the party seek to file suit as soon as possible, or should the onset of litigation be delayed in the hope of achieving a settlement?
***Where* could the litigation take place?**
If a party has a choice of several courts, the place of suit may affect the applicable law, the procedures, and even who can be sued. Businesses with websites may be subject to litigation in numerous countries.

case is being brought before this particular court. Finally, the complaint concludes with a **prayer or request for relief,** which specifies the remedy that the plaintiff wants the court to impose. If the plaintiff is seeking to be compensated for loss, the prayer for relief requests damages.[2] A copy of a complaint appears in Exhibit 3.2.

The **summons** is a court order that gives the defendant notice of the lawsuit and requires the defendant to respond within a prescribed period of time (frequently 20 or 30 days). If no response is filed within that time period, a **default judgment** is entered. This judgment, in plaintiff's favor, is a result of the defendant's nonappearance.

The response to the plaintiff's complaint is generally found in the defendant's answer. The **answer** is a document that responds point by point to the allegations and statements of the plaintiff's complaint. If the defendant agrees with a statement, the defendant admits that the statement is true. If the defendant disagrees with an allegation, in the answer the defendant denies it. In this way, the defendant addresses each essential segment of the plaintiff's claim.

The answer may also include an affirmative defense. An **affirmative defense** provides a legal justification for the defendant's conduct. It states a legal reason why the defendant would be found not liable even if the plaintiff's claims were found to be true. A **counterclaim,** which is essentially a related or unrelated suit by the defendant against the plaintiff, may also be part of the defendant's answer.

If the defendant's answer raises facts not addressed in the plaintiff's complaint, in some, but not all, jurisdictions, the plaintiff may file a reply document. A **reply** either admits or denies the new facts raised by the defendant's answer.

In addition to the answer, which responds to the plaintiff's complaint, the defendant may also make a variety of other responses by motions. A **motion** is a request to the court for some type of court order. Motions may be made throughout the

2. A number of courts have already started to accept, or in some cases require, the electronic filing of court documents. The http://www.courts.net/efilings.htm summarizes the status of the electronic filing of court documents.

EXHIBIT 3.2 Complaint

State of Michigan
Kalamazoo County Circuit Court

Ace Electronics Plaintiff(s)	Judge Joyce Sanchez (Assigned Judge)
v.	
Jane Smith Defendant(s)	Civil Action No. 02-987654-MI (Year-File-Code)
Jones & Robinson (23232) Attorney(s) for the Plaintiff	
3825 N. Crosstown Parkway, Allegan, MI Address	
616-123-4567 Phone Number	

There is no civil action between these parties arising out of the same transaction of occurrence as alleged in this complaint pending in this court, nor has any such action been assigned to a judge.

COMPLAINT

Plaintiff. Ace Electronics, by its attorneys, Jones & Robinson states:

1. Between the dates of July 1, 2001 and October 10, 2001 Plaintiff sold and delivered certain goods, wares, and merchandise to the Defendant, upon open account, upon the promise of Defendant to pay for these goods.
2. There is now unpaid upon this account the sum of $12,250.00.
3. The account has become stated between the parties.
4. As a consequence, Defendant is justly indebted to Plaintiff in the amount of $12,250.00 plus interest from and after October 10, 2001 plus cost of suit.
5. A copy of the account and an affidavit verifying the account are attached as Plaintiff's Exhibits A and B.

PLAINTIFF REQUESTS judgment in its favor and against Defendant in the amount of $12,250.00 plus interest, cost, and attorney's fees.

Jones & Robinson
(Firm Name)

By Robert Robinson
(Typed Name of Attorney)

3825 N. Crosstown Parkway, Allegan, MI
(Address)

616-123-4567
(Phone Number)

pleading, pretrial, trial, and posttrial stages of litigation. During the pleadings stage, most motions are made in writing. Before the court acts on a motion, notice is provided to the opposing party, and oral arguments on the motion are presented to the judge. The judge either grants or overrules motions before litigation continues.

Once all of the pleadings have been filed, the framework or outline of the litigation emerges. Matters that the defendant admits in the answer are not at issue and need not be proved at trial. The disputed facts and allegations form the basis for further investigation during the pretrial stage and at the trial.

Pretrial Activities

After the pleadings have been filed but before the trial begins, each party, or litigant, seeks to discover as many important facts as possible about the dispute. The U.S. legal system has a very open approach to litigation in general and to discovery procedures in particular. Because both parties to a lawsuit have access to the same information, documents, and potential witnesses, any surprise at the time of trial is usually eliminated. The parties also keep the judge informed about their discovery and trial preparation through periodic **pretrial conferences** (discussed later).

Discovery Procedures. **Discovery procedures** are the methods each party in a lawsuit uses to uncover facts, documents, or other things that are in the exclusive knowledge or possession of the opposing party or that party's witnesses, and that may be used as evidence. Discovery is less significant in criminal litigation than in civil cases because in criminal litigation some of the defendant's information does not have to be made available to the prosecution. Discovery procedures used in civil suits include depositions, examinations, inspections, and interrogatories.

A **deposition** is transcribed testimony that a witness gives under oath but outside court. The witness is examined by the attorney for one party and then cross-examined by the attorney for the other party; all of the questions and answers are recorded by a court reporter. Depositions enable the parties to find out prior to a trial, when the witness's recall is fresh, what that person might say when called on to testify at the trial. If a witness is unable to appear at the trial, his or her deposition may be used and the testimony preserved.

Because both deposition and trial testimony are given under oath, conflicts between a deposition statement and trial testimony can be used to discredit a trial witness. Clearly, before testifying at a trial, well-prepared witnesses carefully review their deposition statements.

An **examination** may be a physical or mental examination of a litigant or an examination of personal or real property. Thus, a doctor hired by the opposing party may conduct physical examinations of a party to determine the extent of a claimed injury. A psychiatrist may conduct mental examinations to assist in determining a party's mental state. Examinations of buildings by contractors, engineers, and architects may reveal hidden defects in design or construction.

A unique feature of the U.S. legal system is that the records and documents of each litigant relating to the matters in dispute must be made accessible to the other litigant. The requirement for the **production and inspection of records and documents** means that bookkeeping records, correspondence, notes, medical files, electronic communications, data files, and financial documents in the possession of either party may be requested and must be made available for inspection and review by the opposing party. Only privileged or totally irrelevant information is exempt from such a request.

The discovery process has been profoundly affected by the proliferation of computers and the digitalization of data. As early as 1970, the Federal Rules of Civil

Procedure added language to expressly include data compilations from which information can be obtained. The rules governing the production of computer information are interpreted liberally. Thus, a litigant almost always includes *electronic evidence* in the discovery process.

Courts usually require that digitalized data be produced if relevant and useful to the case. If the data are not readable without codes or assistance from the producing party, courts generally require that such assistance be provided. Where the data are at issue, discovery rules may require that the underlying computer program be provided.

In a 1987 case involving the DuPont corporation (*Williams v. DuPont*, 119 F.R.D. 648), the court held that because DuPont was seeking to understand the statistical analysis of the plaintiff, it was entitled to discover copies of plaintiff's computerized database, codebooks, user's manual and all of the documents used in encoding the database," despite the fact that the information was based on documents that had already been provided in the form of paper records.

The importance of computerized data to the discovery process in modern litigation cannot be overstated. The screen of the Evidence.Finder.Com website illustrates the importance of computerized data in today's litigation. Consider, too, the following quote from an article *Electronic Evidence: Discovery in the Computer Age* by Susan J. Silvernail:

If a litigator does not pursue electronically stored data, he or she cannot be confident of complete discovery. Key evidence may await discovery on disks, hard drives, magnetic tapes and/or optical disks. Electronic mail, in particular, is an attractive source of discovery. . . . People communicate by e-mail what they would not commit to paper or even say out loud. . . . Electronically stored data is more permanent than paper. Paper can be shredded or thrown away, but electronically stored data is much harder to destroy. Long after memories have faded or an employee has been fired, electronically stored data, in part or in whole, remains stored on mainframes, personal computers, file servers, backup tapes and optical disks, and can be retrieved by the resourceful attorney who frames a request for the discovery of electronically stored data.[3]

Interrogatories. **Interrogatories** are written questions submitted to the opposing party that must be answered under oath. Although the opposing party need not provide answers that go beyond the questions asked, this discovery device sometimes reveals information that is known only to the opposing party. A plaintiff's interrogatory might ask, for example, if the defendant has or knows of any correspondence of any kind relating to defects in products sold to the plaintiff.

http://
www.finder.com/dockery/

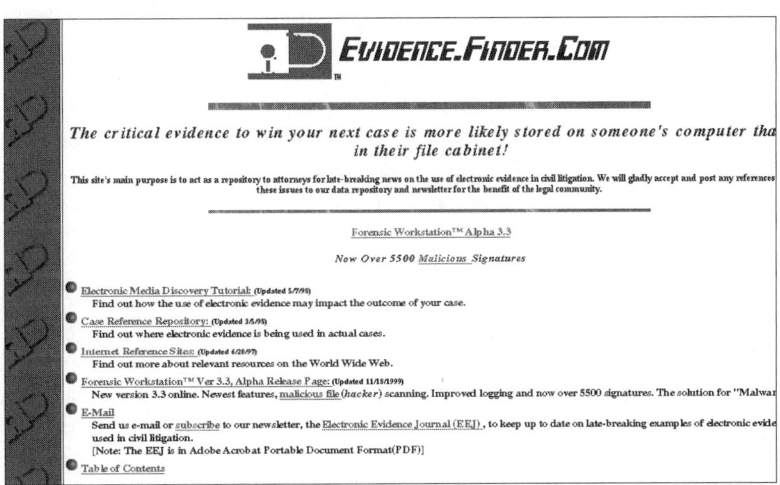

Well before a lawsuit begins, the parties often argue over how much discovery can be used and whether some requests are proper. In a case brought against Domino's Pizza

3. See 58 *Alabama Law Review* 176, at 182 (May 1997).

and its owner (now former owner) and CEO, Thomas Monoghan, the plaintiffs sought to take his deposition. After Monoghan refused to comply with the request for his deposition, the court had to determine if taking the deposition of the company's owner and CEO was proper.

Wauchop v. Domino's Pizza, Inc.

U.S. District Court, N.D. Indiana
143 F.R.D. 199 (1992)

Facts. Mrs. Wauchop was killed in an automobile accident involving a delivery vehicle owned by a Domino's Pizza franchisee. Her family filed a wrongful death suit against Domino's Pizza; Thomas Monoghan, the president of Domino's; the franchise owner; and the delivery vehicle driver. The plaintiffs said Domino's was negligent because its "30-minute delivery guarantee" caused the delivery personnel to drive negligently. According to the guarantee, if the pizza was not delivered in 30 minutes, it was free. At the time of the lawsuit, the news media had attributed 20 deaths to driving practices brought about by Domino's guarantee.

Monoghan claimed he had no responsibility for the injuries in the case and that he had no information that was not also available from others involved in the case.

Legal Issue. If a lawsuit related to a corporation's policy is filed against a corporation's president as well as against the corporation, can the plaintiff require the president to give testimony in a deposition even if the president claims he cannot be held personally liable for the policy decisions of the corporation?

Opinion. Judge Miller. In earlier proceedings, this court ordered the parties to complete all outstanding written discovery and all previously noted depositions by February 28. Mr. Monoghan's deposition previously had been noticed. During the status [pretrial] conference, counsel for Domino's and Mr. Monoghan stated that she would have a problem producing Mr. Monoghan for deposition.

Mr. Monoghan had moved for summary judgment on August 5th of the previous year contending he should not be held personally liable for the accident that forms the basis of this action. His motion was supported by his written statement that he was not personally involved in the operation of the franchise, that he never had any dealings with the driver, and that his only conduct in relation to the 30-minute guarantee was in his capacity as a corporate director or officer. Mr. Monoghan stated that the 30-minute guarantee policy went through corporate channels and was implemented after discussions with franchisees.

The plaintiff planned to test the assertions in Mr. Monoghan's written statement by deposing Mr. Monoghan and other employees of Domino's. Mr. Monoghan's refusal to make himself available for the deposition is based on several reasons. He claims he is not personally liable to the plaintiff because the only allegations against him relate to his implementation of the 30-minute policy in his capacity as a director, shareholder, and chief executive officer of Domino's. He further reiterates that he was never directly involved with the driver or with the operation of the franchise.

Mr. Monoghan also claims, surprisingly, that the 30-minute policy is not an issue in this case. He states ... that no reasonable trier of fact could find that the driver was trying to comply with the 30-minute policy when the accident occurred, because at the time of the accident he was returning to the store from a pizza delivery. Further, Mr. Monoghan claims that the 30-minute policy could be an issue only if the driver was speeding at the time of the accident and that the only evidence that he was speeding is a passenger's speculation during his deposition.

The plaintiffs are entitled to take Mr. Monoghan's deposition to inquire into his role in the development of the 30-minute policy, a topic central to the plaintiff's theory of Mr. Monoghan's liability and central to Mr. Monoghan's written statement. The plaintiffs point to discovery material that lends support to their contention that Mr. Monoghan was directly involved in the implementation of Domino's policy.

Under the discovery rules as they exist, Mr. Monoghan has no viable impediment to the taking of his deposition. The court cannot avoid the conclusion that Mr. Monoghan is willing to delay and frustrate discovery indefinitely, not withstanding the previous order regarding the discovery of the relationship between the 30-minute policy and the accident in this case.

Decision. The court ordered Mr. Monoghan to appear in Chicago for his deposition and to pay for the plaintiff's fees.

Case Questions

1. Why did Mr. Monoghan seek to avoid giving his deposition? Would it be appropriate to depose him in all cases that involved accidents of Domino's delivery people?
2. When should a court determine that it is not proper to involve the CEO or another executive in a company's deposition?
3. What would be the basis for holding Mr. Monoghan and Domino's liable for the injuries caused in the accident instead of only the franchisee and delivery person?

Pretrial Conference. A pretrial conference is a meeting of attorneys and the judge held before the trial to enhance the interchange of opinions and eliminate differences or disputes. Pretrial conferences seek to narrow the issues in dispute and to move the controversy toward either trial or settlement. Some conferences are quite formal: The judge, attorneys, and perhaps the parties meet in court and review unsettled issues. Other pretrial conferences are informal: The attorneys and judge discuss the case in the judge's office, and no formal record of their conversation is kept.

A judge may ask the parties to submit briefs showing the sources of law that back up their claims. If a trial is to be conducted, the use of expert witnesses may be discussed and the possible date and length of the trial determined. Similarly, if an injured

International Commentary

Discovery or Disclosure?

Different systems exist in the United States and in most European countries for obtaining information needed for trial. In the United States, a civil suit may be filed even though the plaintiff has very little information regarding potential witnesses and what their testimony may indicate about the issues in the trial. In the U.S. system, the filing of the case generally occurs first, and then the litigants seek to *discover* information that will enhance their case. The discovery process uses interrogatories to the opposing party, numerous depositions of the parties and their witnesses, and frequent requests for the production and inspection of documents and electronic files that have any possible bearing on the case. The objective of the discovery process is laudable—it seeks to produce all relevant evidence—but it often becomes too extensive, repetitive, and expensive.

In most European countries (including England, a common law country), a case is investigated before it is filed. The potential litigants *disclose* documents and possible witness information to each other before the case is filed. Once suit is filed, preliminary pleadings are filed to see if the case has legal merit. If it does, a trial date is set, and the parties exchange their witness lists and a short statement of what the witnesses will say. Exhibits to be used are exchanged, and the trial proceeds. As in the United States, depositions may not be used at trials unless a witness is outside the court's jurisdiction.

In contrast to the U.S. and the European systems, discovery procedures in Japan are very limited. For example, a consumer who brings a product liability case against the manufacturer of a product that has caused injury to him cannot either discover information or require the manufacturer to disclose reports regarding problems encountered in the manufacturing process. The manufacturer does not have to state whether it received complaints from other consumers of similar products.

As a consequence, plaintiffs in Japan, who usually have little knowledge about the manufacturing process or the safety record of a manufacturer's product, generally find it very difficult to prove the defendant's negligence or the product's defective nature. Thus, potential plaintiffs in Japan do not perceive that there is much to gain from litigation. Civil cases in Japan often take very long to resolve, the likelihood of success is low, and the society encourages settlement through negotiation or mediation rather than litigation. As a result, legal costs associated with product liability obviously differ significantly for Japanese, U.S., or European manufacturers.

party is seeking compensation, the parties may stipulate or agree to certain facts. For example, they may agree that plaintiff's medical expenses incurred since the injury amount to $100,000. The defendant may not admit liability, and the plaintiff may seek additional compensation, but the question of what medical expenses have been incurred will not need to be proved at the trial. Settlement options that could resolve the controversy without a trial are also reviewed at these conferences.

Trial Process

Most civil cases are not resolved through a trial. Instead, they are settled by the parties outside the courtroom. Typically, only 5% of the civil cases filed in federal courts are tried. Usually, when a trial does occur, it is because the parties are unable to agree about what actually happened. When opposing witnesses and parties hold contradictory views of what has happened, the resolution of their dispute comes down to determining whose view is more credible. In the American legal system, such questions of fact are usually determined by a jury.

Although most civil case trials do use juries, in some cases the parties do not have a right to a jury trial. The Seventh Amendment to the U.S. Constitution provides: "In suits *at common law*, where the value in controversy shall exceed twenty dollars, the right to trial by jury shall be preserved. . . ." Thus, suits that were tried in the chancery or equity courts (without benefit of a jury) instead of *at common law* are not covered by the Seventh Amendment's jury trial guarantee. In these *equity* cases, the plaintiff generally asks the court to grant an unusual remedy, such as an injunction or an order of specific performance. As those equitable remedies historically were not available in common law suits, such cases today are not tried before a jury.

In other cases, the parties waive their rights to a jury trial. In nonjury trials, the judge not only determines the legal questions but also decides the facts. When juries are used, the number of jurors varies with the type of case. Approximately three-fourths of the states have civil case juries consisting of six to eight people. In many states, the jury's decision or verdict need not be reached by unanimous vote. In Michigan, for example, all civil case juries consist of six people, and a decision on which five of the six agree constitutes the jury's verdict. A *hung jury* occurs if fewer than the minimum number of jurors required to make a valid decision agree.

Prospective jurors are chosen from various sources to obtain a cross-section of the community. Of course, some people who are called to serve may not be impartial with regard to the issues in specific cases. If it can be shown that a person's biases might influence his or her decision in a particular case, the judge will grant a challenge (known as a **challenge for cause**) to exclude that person from serving as a juror on that case. In addition to challenges for cause, each litigant has a certain number of discretionary challenges that do not have to be based on cause. These **peremptory challenges**, which cannot be exercised in a discriminatory way, provide each party with a role in selecting the jury that will hear and decide factual issues in the case.

Presentation of Evidence. Once the jury is selected, the presentation of evidence begins. First, each party is given a chance to make an **opening statement**, an overview of the case to be presented. This statement indicates to the judge and jury what testimony, documents, and exhibits the party intends to present as evidence. Opening statements are not considered evidence.

The plaintiff, who begins the presentation, has the burden of proving the complaint's allegations by the preponderance of evidence. Most of the evidence presented is the oral testimony of witnesses who are questioned by the attorneys. Documents, charts, other exhibits, and physical evidence may also be submitted.

After a witness has answered the questions of the plaintiff's attorney on direct examination, the defendant's attorney questions that witness through cross-examination. **Direct examination** is the questioning of a witness by the party on whose behalf the witness has been called; **cross-examination** is the questioning of a witness called by the opposing party. The questioning of a witness can continue through redirect and re-cross-examination if new issues are brought out in the witness's answers.

Once the plaintiff has called all of the witnesses who are to testify and has introduced the exhibits to be considered by the jury, the plaintiff's primary case is complete. If the testimony presented is not sufficient to allow a jury to decide for the plaintiff, the defendant can present a motion to the judge to direct the verdict and dismiss the case. If the judge agrees with the request, the judge grants the motion to **direct the verdict** in favor of the defendant. In this case, the jury has nothing more to do; the case is over and has been decided in the defendant's favor. If, as is usually the case, the judge does not grant the motion, the trial continues, and the defendant presents evidence.

Oral testimony of witnesses called by the defendant and cross-examined by the plaintiff is then presented to the jury and the judge. If either litigant believes that the rules of evidence prohibit the introduction of certain evidence, that party may object to the evidence. The judge then makes a legal decision to allow the evidence to be heard (overruling the objection) or to prohibit its use (sustaining the objection). An appellate court can later review the decisions the judge makes about the admissibility of evidence.

Rules of Evidence. The **rules of evidence** assure that information presented during a trial is relevant, unbiased, and reliable. Testimony that has been determined to be unreliable or irrelevant cannot be presented. For example, the fact that a witness committed several traffic offenses in the past five years would be irrelevant in a civil trial involving a contract dispute. If one of the parties seeks to ask the witness a question concerning those offenses, the other party can object to such evidence as irrelevant to the trial. The judge would then rule on the objection and should exclude the evidence by sustaining the objection. On the other hand, such evidence would be admissible in an auto accident case involving negligence.

Similarly, information contrary to a rule of evidence may be offered at a trial. One such rule concerns *hearsay* testimony. This rule of evidence, which has many exceptions, excludes as unreliable any testimony based on what a person has heard other people say. Testimony is restricted to statements based on the witness's knowledge and observation. For example, if LaMar witnesses a fight between Dave and Hernando, LaMar may testify as to what he saw. However, if LaMar tells Aretha about that fight, Aretha may not testify as to what she heard LaMar say. Hearsay testimony is excluded because the opposing party cannot probe LaMar's perceptions if only Aretha is available to report the hearsay.

Concluding the Trial. After both plaintiff and defendant have finished presenting evidence, each is usually given a chance to offer rebuttal evidence contradicting the evidence that was presented by the opposing party. The parties are then usually allowed to make **closing statements**, or summations that organize the evidence to assist the jury in arriving at that party's desired conclusion. Like the opening statements, these statements are not evidence, and the jury cannot consider them to be facts in reaching its decision.

After the closing statements have been presented, the judge gives the jury **instructions**—statements about the law that the jury should apply to resolve the dispute by evaluating the evidence presented by the parties. The judge's instructions summarize the law. Then, the jury reviews the evidence and deliberates as to the credibility of the testimony they have heard. Through these deliberations, the jury determines the facts. The **verdict** is the jury's determination based on the application of the law, as provided in instructions from the judge, to the facts, as determined by the jury from the evidence.

Although people often think of the jury's verdict as the end of a trial, the trial judge may legally set aside or change a verdict. Most judges are hesitant to alter a jury's verdict, but if a judge believes that a jury's verdict is not based on the evidence presented or does not follow the instructions of law, the judge may reverse the verdict by granting a **judgment notwithstanding the verdict** (JNOV). However, a judge's reversal of a verdict may be appealed.

Posttrial and Appellate Process

Posttrial Measures. It is the court's **judgment** or decision that ends the trial court proceedings. If either party considers the judgment wrong, that party can appeal the judge's decision by citing legal errors. Such errors may arise if the judge admits or denies the use of certain testimony or exhibits as evidence or makes mistakes in instructing the jury as to the law. A judgment that is not appealed within a specified period becomes final.

A plaintiff may obtain a judgment against a defendant for $100,000 yet fail to receive that amount. The judgment is a legal determination of the amount of money owed. If the defendant does not pay the determined amount voluntarily, the plaintiff may use legal means to enforce the judgment.

One method used to enforce a judgment is garnishment. **Garnishments** of wages or bank accounts are court orders to others, such as the defendant's employer or bank, to pay the plaintiff some of the defendant's money. Another method is to attach assets of the defendant, such as a car or other personal property. An **attachment** is an order allowing one person, such as the plaintiff, to sell the defendant's personal property—equipment, inventory, or furnishings—so that the proceeds may be used to pay off a judgment. The judgment also gives the plaintiff a **lien**, an interest in real estate owned by the defendant. If the real estate is sold, the sale proceeds are used to pay the plaintiff's judgment.

The judgment of a court usually remains in effect for several years and may be renewed. At any time during that period, property acquired by the defendant can be garnished, attached, or subjected to a lien so that it can be used to satisfy the judgment. The defendant's legal obligation to the plaintiff terminates only after the judgment has been fully paid or satisfied.

The Appellate Process. An appellate court reviews the legal ruling that one or both parties think were incorrectly made by the trial court judge. Note that it is the trial court, usually the jury, that decides factual discrepancies between the parties. In an appeal, there is no determination of facts because the factual issues were decided prior to or at the trial. Because appellate courts perform different functions than do trial courts, the appellate process varies substantially from the trial process.

Appellate court judges make decisions based on the trial court record, oral arguments, written briefs of the parties, and research and discussion conducted by the appellate court itself. The **trial court record** is the transcript of the testimony of all the witnesses, the exhibits used as evidence, the judge's rulings on all objections to the introduction of evidence, the judge's instructions to the jury, the jury's verdict, and the trial court's judgment.

On appeal, input of the parties generally is oral arguments, supported by written presentations called briefs. An **appellate brief** highlights the parts of the trial court record that support that party's position as to the correctness of the judge's decisions. It usually provides references to other cases that support those claims.

An appellate court generally is three judges who act by a majority vote. If the appellate court agrees with the trial court's judgment, it **affirms** that court's determination. If the appellate court determines that the trial court's judgment was incorrect, it **reverses** the judgment. The appellate court can either modify the legal remedy provided by the trial court or **remand** (return) the case to the trial court for some redetermination.

Suppose an appeal is made because the plaintiff who lost wanted to present certain testimony at the trial that the judge excluded. If the appellate court determines that the judge's interpretation was wrong and that the plaintiff's testimony should have been allowed as evidence, the appellate court usually returns the case to the trial court. If the excluded testimony was critical to the plaintiff's case, the jury's verdict against the plaintiff might have been different. Thus, the case is sent back to the trial court, which now must allow the plaintiff to use the excluded testimony so that the jury can consider it.

ALTERNATIVE DISPUTE RESOLUTION METHODS

Alternatives to court litigation have been studied and supported since early in the twentieth century. Congress passed the Federal Arbitration Act in 1925, and the American Arbitration Association was founded a year later. In that same year, Congress established a National Mediation Board, and in 1947 it created the Federal Mediation and Conciliation Service to assist in solving labor disputes. Today, the term *alternative dispute resolution* (ADR) covers a broad range of options to the adversarial system of litigating disputes. These options generally include arbitration, mediation, the minitrial, summary jury trial, and the private court or rent-a-judge methods. Each of these options is defined and briefly discussed in this chapter.

The term *alternative* not only contrasts these methods with litigation but also conveys a sense of choice and selection for the disputing parties. In some cases, this sense of choice is no longer true on account of statutes or court rules that require ADR to be used for certain problems. The Administrative Disputes Act specifically authorizes and encourages federal agencies to use alternative means of dispute resolution, including arbitration, conciliation, and mediation, in lieu of litigation. In many states, civil cases of less than a specified dollar amount and all divorce matters must be submitted to mediation before being litigated.

When contract clauses require arbitration, the contracting parties usually have no choice as to how to resolve disputes. Contracts requiring the use of arbitration, commonly used in e-commerce and in international business transactions, are also becoming common for health care providers, landlords, and securities brokers. Most e-commerce sites include mandatory use of arbitration in the event of disputes.

E-COMMERCE ADR AGREEMENTS

Arbitration in E-Commerce

In on-line agreements, the use of arbitration is contained in the click-wrap agreements, which a customer must click "accept" to proceed with a specific transaction or relationship. Here are two of the conditions of use found on Amazon.com's website in December 2000.

Applicable Law
By visiting Amazon.com, you agree that the laws of the state of Washington, without regard to principles of conflict of laws, will govern these Conditions of Use and any dispute of any sort that might arise between you and Amazon.com or its affiliates.

Disputes
Any dispute relating in any way to your visit to Amazon.com or to products you purchase through Amazon.com shall be submitted to confidential arbitration in Seattle, Washington, except that, to the extent you have in any manner threatened to violate Amazon.com's intellectual property rights, Amazon.com may seek injunctive or other relief in any state or federal court in the state of Washington, and you consent to exclusive jurisdiction and venue in such courts. Arbitration under this agreement shall be conducted under the rules then prevailing of the American Arbitration Association. The arbitrator's award shall be binding and may be enforced as a judgment in any court of competent jurisdiction. To the fullest extent permitted by law, no arbitration under this Agreement shall be joined to an arbitration involving any other party subject to this Agreement, whether through class arbitration proceedings or otherwise.

Other E-Commerce ADR Agreements

In May 2000, the European Extra-Judicial Network (EEJ-net) was launched to settle cross-border consumer disputes involving e-commerce. When consumers have problems with their e-commerce purchases, traditional litigation is neither practical nor cost-effective to resolve their disputes. The EEJ-net is designed to reduce costs, formalities, time, and language problems in cross-border disputes involving consumer complaints about goods and services. European countries are in the process of establishing common procedures and national clearinghouses to help dissatisfied consumers make claims in the out-of-court dispute resolution system in the country where the business supplying the service or product is located. Typically, the procedures combine mediation with arbitration to reach a binding resolution of such disputes.

Alternative dispute resolution is also important in business-to-business (B2B) transactions. The recommendations of the CPR Institute for Dispute Resolution (formerly the Center for Public Resources) address only B2B transactions. Companies that participate in the CPR's Global E-Commerce Commitment agree that disputes arising from electronic contracts subject to the commitment will be negotiated and, if necessary, mediated within a brief time period. The participants agree to postpone litigation for as long as the negotiation or mediation procedures continue, if doing so does not prejudice their legal rights. According to the institute's recommendations, "The global environment of e-commerce makes litigating business disputes particularly inappropriate. Jurisdictional and legal uncertainties also dictate that disputes be resolved in a non-adjudicative way, if at all possible. While court judgments and non-appealable arbitration awards have the virtue of finality, they are expensive to procure and highly uncertain as to outcome."

ONLINE

For more information on ADR in business-to-business e-commerce transactions, see **http://www.cpradr.org**

Problems with Internet-Based ADR Solutions

Although ADR methods are growing in popularity, some people feel that privatizing dispute resolution creates problems. In a recent law review article, Professor Thornburg of Southern Methodist University Law School notes that the Internet has accelerated the use of private rather than public methods of resolving disputes and cites four problems: (1) privatizing justice, (2) providing procedural advantages to powerful players, (3) lack of some due process components, and (4) decreasing role of government in shaping and enforcing substantive law.[4]

THE GROWING USE OF ARBITRATION AND MEDIATION

The use of ADR methods has been growing rapidly, both as part of the civil litigation process and as an alternative to it. **Arbitration** is a form of binding dispute resolution in which an arbitrator (or panel of arbitrators) hears evidence presented by the parties and then makes a decision resolving the dispute. As the most recognized form of ADR, arbitration is commonly used in international contracts, labor disputes, and many commercial transactions. Parties select arbitration by inserting clauses in a contract to govern future disputes or by agreeing to use arbitration after a dispute arises. Courts generally recognize and enforce both the disputing parties' choice of arbitration and the arbitrator's decision.

The American Arbitration Association (AAA) estimates that more than 500 employers—with workforces ranging from 800 to 300,000 workers—use some form of ADR to resolve many of their employment disputes. Almost 5 million workers are employed in these companies. Court and administrative backlogs are sizable. It often takes three to four years to resolve an employment law case at the district court level and up to eight years for the EEOC to resolve a case. The litigation and federal agencies are too slow and expensive. Accordingly, companies like Haliburton, TRW, Toys R Us, and Honda of America are using mediation, internal arbitration panels, and a variety of other ADR techniques to resolve employment disputes. Both arbitration and mediation provide an external decision maker. Some companies use a peer review system in which people from within the company engage in fact-finding as well as decision making for certain types of employment grievances.

ONLINE

See the AAA website at **http://www.adr.org/law/index.html**

Mediation is a process of dispute resolution whereby a third party, usually professionally trained, seeks to persuade the disputing parties to settle their differences. Unlike the arbitrator, the mediator usually has no ultimate authority to resolve disputes. Mediation is used in international conflicts, labor-management disagreements, and numerous contract disputes. The Federal Mediation and Conciliation Service (FMCS) is an independent agency created to promote sound and stable labor-management relations. Its mediators have experience in numerous labor-management disputes.

ONLINE

For more information about FCMS, visit **http://www.fmcs.gov**

One case in which FCMS mediators were involved concerned the health care industry. In 1998, changes in health care services in one of the nation's largest health care provider organizations led to long and turbulent negotiations between Kaiser Foundation Hospitals, operating 54 hospitals, clinics, labs, and administrative offices in northern California, and the California Nurses Association, representing approximately 8,000 nurses at Kaiser facilities. The negotiations, which took place in a politically charged atmosphere, focused on innovative approaches to quality care issues and changing strategies for cost containment. Two FMCS mediators were involved in negotiations for 15 months, beginning in January 1997. The FMCS deputy director teamed with the mediators to bring the parties together to lay out a framework for agreement in October 1997. Full negotiations resumed the next day and continued for several months until, following several around-the-clock sessions, a tentative agreement was reached in March 1998.

4. Elizabeth Thornbury, "Going Private: Technology, Due Process, and Internet Dispute Resolution 34, *University of California Davis Law Review* 151 (2000).

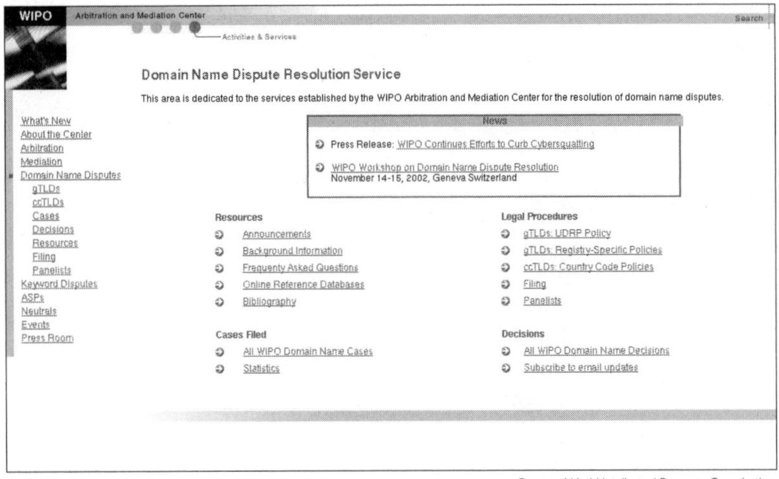

Courtesy, World Intellectual Property Organization.

http://

www.arbiter.wipo.int/domains/index.html

Other countries also show a trend toward using arbitration and mediation in employment disputes. A September 2001 report from the Advisory, Conciliation and Arbitration Services (ACAS) in the United Kingdom reveals that individual complaints to employment tribunals about discrimination in the workplace rose more than 20% in the last year. ACAS's Chief Executive John Taylor said: "While the number of complaints to tribunals for many types of cases has leveled off recently, there is still a significant rise in discrimination cases passed to ACAS. This is a worrying trend in today's increasingly diverse labour market. Many of the problems stem from simple lack of knowledge on the part of employers. . . ."

ONLINE

To see the text of this report, go to **http://www.acas.org.uk/news/news_14.html**

The Arbitration and Mediation Center of the World Intellectual Property Organization (WIPO) tries to settle domain name disputes arising in generic top-level domains such as .com, .net, or .org. The WIPO is also working with the Application Service Provider Industry Consortium (ASPIC) to establish a dispute settlement mechanism specifically tailored to meet the needs of service providers.

ARBITRATION

Arbitration is commonly used in international commercial transactions, health care provider-patient contracts, contracts between professional athletes and their team owners, and contracts between securities brokers and their clients. A sample arbitration offer from a patient information booklet given to health care patients is shown in Exhibit 3.3.

EXHIBIT 3.3 Arbitration Offer Found in Patient Information Booklet

Michigan Medical Arbitration Program Standard Offer

Arbitration is a method of deciding disputes without going to court. The offer of this agreement is authorized under Michigan law to provide the patient with a choice between arbitration or going to court to resolve any health care complaint which may arise.

In arbitration, a 3-person panel made up of a doctor or other health care professional, a lawyer, and a member of the public will hear and decide your case. In most cases a decision made by the arbitration panel is final and cannot be appealed to court.

Please take a moment to review the agreement. Signing the agreement is your choice. You will receive the same quality of health care whether or not you sign. If you do sign, you have 60 days after you are discharged to change your mind.

The patient information booklet you receive should answer any questions you may have. Questions can also be answered by calling the American Arbitration's toll-free number in the booklet.

*This provision appears in a booklet approved by the Michigan Commissioner of Insurance. It was written by the Michigan Arbitration Advisory Committee, a group of consumers, doctors, hospital administrators, nurses, and lawyers.

The procedural rules followed in arbitration are generally less complicated than those followed in court. The arbitrator is usually a specialist familiar with the type of problem underlying the dispute. Because the arbitrator handles fewer cases than a judge does, the dispute can be resolved more quickly than if it went through the courts. Further, arbitrators are often familiar with the nature of the dispute and the commercial practices of firms in the same or similar industries. By contrast, judges who are randomly assigned to the controversy may not have the specialized expertise to render appropriate decisions.

Voluntary Agreements to Arbitrate

The most important first step in initiating arbitration is the agreement to arbitrate. That agreement may be one of two kinds: (1) a future dispute arbitration clause in a contract or (2) when the parties did not agree to arbitrate in advance, a submission of an existing dispute to arbitration. If the parties agreed in advance to arbitrate a dispute, the party initiating the action serves a **demand for arbitration** on the other party and also files it with an arbitration association, such as the American Arbitration Association (AAA). The AAA rules of arbitration generally require the other party to be given a certain time period to respond to the claim before any documents are submitted or a hearing occurs.

Parties who have not agreed by contract beforehand to arbitrate may nevertheless use arbitration. They both sign a **submission to arbitration** agreement, a contractual obligation of the parties that will be enforced by the courts as long as it is not contrary to public policy or illegal. A future dispute arbitration clause and a submission agreement, both of which need to be signed by both parties, are shown here.

> **For the Arbitration of Future Disputes**
>
> Any controversy or claim arising out of or relating to this contract, or the breach thereof, shall be settled by arbitration in accordance with the Commercial Arbitration Rules of the American Arbitration Association, and judgment upon the award rendered by the arbitrator(s) may be entered in any court having jurisdiction thereof.

> **For the Submission of Existing Disputes**
>
> We, the undersigned parties, hereby agree to submit to arbitration under the Commercial Arbitration Rules of the American Arbitration Association the following controversy: (cite briefly). We further agree that the above controversy be submitted to (one) (three) arbitrator(s) selected from the panels of arbitrators of the American Arbitration Association. We further agree that we will faithfully observe this agreement and the rules, and that we will abide by and perform any award rendered by the arbitrator(s) and that a judgment of the court having jurisdiction may be entered upon the award.

One of the most significant recent cases to be decided by arbitration is the split-up of the Arthur Andersen accounting and auditing firm from Andersen Consulting (now known as Accenture). Internal disputes led to the consulting group's request to split from the accounting and auditing group. The accounting and auditing group then sought damages from the consultants. That case, noted in the Andersen Consulting screen depicted on page 69, was decided by an arbitrator appointed by the International Court of Arbitration of the International Chamber of Commerce.[5]

5. The Arthur Andersen accounting firm has been questioned about its auditing and consulting practices at several client firms, particularly the now bankrupt Enron corporation. While the case shows the split of Arthur Andersen into two firms, the conflict between them arose mainly because *both* firms continued to compete for consulting contracts.

Andersen Consulting Business Unit Member Firms v. Arthur Andersen Business Unit Member Firms and Andersen Worldwide Societe Cooperative

Case 9797/CKAER/ACS
Secretariat of the International Court of Arbitration
International Chamber of Commerce
Paris, France, July 28, 2000

Facts. Arthur Andersen & Co., which started as a public accounting firm, formalized its consulting activities into the Management Information Consulting Division (MIDC) in 1980. Some business consulting services were also being performed in the firm's Accounting and Auditing Division. In 1987, it created a new structure, known as the Andersen Worldwide Organization (AWO) to deliver its services in a uniform manner to clients across the world.

The Arthur Andersen & Co. Worldwide Societe Cooperative (AWSC), a Swiss firm, is the umbrella entity for the worldwide organization. It is responsible for developing policies, practices, and procedures to assure a consistent and uniformly high quality of professional services by all member firms (more than 100 worldwide).

As Andersen's business developed through the years, various difficulties began to strain the relationship between the partners practicing in the Accounting and Audit and Tax Divisions on one side and those practicing in the MIDC on the other. Over time, the MIDC unit evolved into the Andersen Consulting Business Unit (ACBU). The respective parties signed a member firms interfirm agreement (MFIFA) to settle any and all disputes by arbitration conducted by a single arbitrator pursuant to the Rules of Conciliation and Arbitration of the International Chamber of Commerce. The parties' agreement also said that the arbitration was to be in English and that the arbitrator "shall not be bound to apply the substantive law of any jurisdiction but shall be guided by the policies and considerations in the MFIFA provisions."

In December 1997, member firms of the ACBU filed a claim for arbitration of a dispute it had with the member firms of the Arthur Andersen Business Unit (AABU) and Andersen Worldwide Societe Cooperative (AWSC). It claimed both parties had breached their fiduciary and contractual duties to cooperate with them under the MFIFA. A counterclaim was later filed by AABU, claiming a breach of the obligations imposed on ACBU by the MFIFA. The claims were filed with the International Chamber of Commerce (ICC). The ICC then appointed Dr. Guillermo Gamba Posada of Colombia as the sole arbitrator.

Legal Issue. Where a worldwide corporation, formed to coordinate services performed by its member firms, fails to coordinate consulting services offered by different groups of member firms, did the worldwide organization breach its obligation to member firms in one of those units?

Opinion. Guillermo Gamba Posada, Arbitrator. Although the respondents initially objected to the tribunal's jurisdiction, the arbitrator earlier determined that the agreement of the parties gave the ICC jurisdiction over the parties and their controversy. As to the applicable law, based on the agreement of the parties, I apply the provisions found in the contract and the rule of law deemed most appropriate, generally by referring to the UNIDROIT Principles of International Commercial Contracts. Those provisions have enjoyed universal acceptance and, moreover, are at the heart of those most fundamental notions which have consistently been applied in arbitral practice.

The claimants accuse AWSC of disregarding its core function of acting as the coordinator of all Member Firms and the implementor of guidelines and policies to ensure compatibility among and the harmonious operation of all Member Firms. While the AWSC argues that it was under no such obligation, the MFIFA provisions demonstrate that AWSC's essential obligation is to coordinate the AWO member firms' diverse professional practices. Indeed, since its inception in 1977, AWSC's purpose has been the coordination of its member firms on an international basis. Those duties include the specific function, among others, of developing compatible policies and professional standards for the member firms, developing annual operating plans to ensure the effective coordination of the member firms' practice and determining the appropriate scope of practice for member firms.

Decision. I find that the AWSC materially breached its obligations to the claimants under the agreement by failing to coordinate the practices of the ACBU with those of the AABU and by failing to address the scope of the service conflict between the AABU and the ACBU. Due to the material breach by the AWSC of its obligation, ACBU is excused from any further obligations it would have under the Member Firm Interfirm Agreement to either AABU or to AWSC. The claimants are not obligated to pay any damages to AABU, but they also have no right to recover any damages from either respondent. ACBU is ordered to cease using the name Andersen or any other similar name as a part of its business as of the end of 2000.

Case Questions

1. Why do you think the parties selected arbitration as the method for resolving any disputes they might have?
2. Why did their agreement instruct the arbitrator to not follow the law of any particular jurisdiction? What sources did the arbitrator use as a guide in interpreting the agreements?
3. Do you think arbitration was a good choice for this dispute? Why?

Enforcement of Arbitration Agreements

Arbitration agreements are becoming more common in many areas. One recent concern is whether parties can be forced to arbitrate because of a rule imposed by a third party. Can a dispute between a securities broker-dealer and its customer be forced to be submitted to arbitration because the New York Stock Exchange (NYSE) requires most disputes between its members and nonmembers to be arbitrated? An NYSE rule provides that all members "must arbitrate all disputes with nonmembers that involve violations of the NYSE rules by members." In a 1984 case *Paine, Webber, Jackson & Curtis, Inc. v. Chase Manhattan Bank*, a court of appeals held that nonmember Chase Manhattan could not compel arbitration against Paine, Webber because their relationship and dispute were not "exchange-related." A little over a decade later (1996), the court of appeals for the same second circuit held in *Spear, Leeds & Kellogg v. Central Life Assurance Co.* that the nonmember (Central Life) could compel the member (Spear, Leeds) to arbitrate if the NYSE was investigating the conduct of its member.

In a recent case, excerpted next, a court of appeals in California said that, despite the trends toward requiring arbitration clauses to be enforced, if an employee is required as a condition of employment to submit all disputes with his or her employer to arbitration, then an arbitration clause cannot be used to force the employee to litigate discrimination claims.

Duffield v. Robertson Stephens & Co.

U.S. Court of Appeals
144 F.3d 1182 (9th Cir., 1998)

Facts. Tonyja Duffield was a securities broker-dealer who took a job with Robertson Stephens. In order to work there, she signed a form that registered her with various securities exchanges, including the New York Stock Exchange (NYSE) and the National Association of Securities Dealers (NASD). The form incorporated a mandatory arbitration provision by which Duffield agreed to arbitrate all employment-related disputes in accordance with the NASD's Code of Arbitration Procedures. In January 1995, she filed a claim for sex discrimination and harassment in violation of Title VII of the Civil Rights Act and a claim for breach of contract and intentional and negligent infliction of emotional distress. Robertson Stephens replied that her claim had to be submitted to arbitration. The trial court found for Robertson Stephens and Duffield appealed.

Opinion. Judge Reinhardt. The security industry's Form U-4 requires employees to submit to a system that is most fittingly described as "compulsory arbitration," the system under which employers compel their prospective employees as a condition of employment to waive their rights to litigate future employment-related disputes in a judicial forum (although the term applies as well to employees subjected to such a requirement for the first time during the course of their employment). Under Form U-4, as in many other form or standard agreements, future employment-related disputes include, among others, all claims of discrimination that may arise under civil rights or other statutes.

By compulsory arbitration, we do not, however, include systems under which employees agree, or otherwise elect, after disputes have arisen to submit them to arbitration. Nor do we include agreements in which at the time of hiring employers give prospective employees the choice to opt in advance for arbitration of all future employment-related disputes or for retention of their statutory right to litigate such disputes. In short, we refer to an arbitration agreement as "compulsory" when individuals must sign an agreement waiving their rights to litigate future claims in a judicial forum in order to obtain employment with, or continue to work for, the employer.

In this case, Duffield argues that she may not be compelled to arbitrate her statutory claims of sexual discrimination and sexual harassment under the waiver mandated by Form U-4. The Supreme Court has long recognized that in enacting Title VII Congress envisioned that decisions and remedies from the federal courts would play a unique and indispensable role in advancing the social policy of deterring workplace discrimination on the basis of race, sex, and national origin. [After review of the legislative history and several prior cases, the court notes as follows:] We conclude that in the passage of Title VII it was the congressional intent that arbitration is unable to pay sufficient attention to the transcendent public interest in the enforcement of Title VII.

In 1991, however, the Supreme Court held in *Gilmer v. Interstate/Johnson Lane Corp.*, 500 U.S. 20 (1991), that employees could be required under Form U-4 and NYSE Rule 347 to arbitrate age discrimination claims brought under the Age Discrimination in Employment Act of 1967 (ADEA). Without discussing the similarities or differences between the ADEA and Title VII, the Court distinguished Gardner-Denver [the ADEA] on the ground that it involved a collective bargaining agreement rather than an individual agreement to arbitrate.

The Court reasoned that "[a]lthough all statutory claims may not be appropriate for arbitration," individual agreements to arbitrate such claims should be placed on the same footing as other individual arbitration agreements "unless Congress itself has evinced an intention to preclude a waiver of judicial remedies for the statutory rights at issue." Finding no such congressional intention evidenced by any inherent conflict between the ADEA's underlying purposes and arbitration, the Court upheld the enforceability of Form U-4 in that circumstance. The Court's decision in Gilmer made it plain that its previous decisions finding arbitration generally inconsistent with the purposes of Title VII are now insufficient to "show that Congress in enacting Title VII intended to preclude arbitration of claims under the Act."

Duffield also argues that she cannot be required to arbitrate her claims because the arbitration agreement imposes an unconstitutional condition of employment. This argument, unlike the one we have just considered, is applicable to her state of tort and contract claims as well as to her claims that her civil rights have been violated. The argument is, in essence, that Form U-4 requires Duffield to forfeit her Fifth Amendment right to due process, her Seventh Amendment right to a jury trial, and her right to an Article III judicial forum. While this argument was not raised or addressed by the Court in Gilmer, it would, if meritorious, render Form U-4 unenforceable as applied to all of Duffield's underlying claims for relief.

Decision. The district court found it unmeritorious, holding that the essential prerequisite of state action was lacking. We agree. Duffield has met her burden of showing that Congress intended in enacting the Civil Rights Act of 1991 to preclude the compulsory arbitration of Title VII disputes. Form U-4 is, therefore, unenforceable with respect to her Title VII and FEHA [a California state statute] claims. Because no state action was involved in Duffield's mandatory waiver, however, there is no constitutional bar to enforcing Form U-4 with respect to her state tort and contract claims. Accordingly, the district court's order compelling arbitration is AFFIRMED IN PART and REVERSED IN PART.

Case Questions

1. What is the main reason the court concludes that employees who have claims against their employer under Title VII of the Civil Rights Act cannot be forced to arbitrate them?
2. Could the employer and employee voluntarily agree to arbitrate such a claim?
3. Give an example of an arbitration clause that the court would define as *not* being compulsory.
4. Do you think this case alters the policy of courts to favor arbitration?

International Arbitration

Arbitration is common in international business situations for several reasons. Each party fears bringing its dispute to hostile foreign courts with unfamiliar and perhaps bewildering procedures. Each party believes the judges or jurors in a foreign court will be partial toward the party from that country. Finally, each party generally perceives that prior disputes resolved through arbitration were handled more favorably than those resolved through litigation.

Arbitration is also desirable because, unlike many litigation decisions, arbitration decisions are usually recognized and enforced even if the arbitration does not occur in the country where it is being enforced. The United Nations Convention on the Recognition and Enforcement of Foreign Arbitral Awards has been ratified by more than a hundred countries. It is a multilateral treaty that provides for the recognition of arbitral awards and prevents courts from litigating disputes the parties agreed to arbitrate.

ONLINE

The text of the convention can be found at **http://www.jus.uio.no/lm/arbitration/arbitration.html**

In a 1985 case, *Mitsubishi Motors Corp. v. Soler Chrysler-Plymouth, Inc.* (473 U.S. 614), the U.S. Supreme Court forced a U.S. car dealer to arbitrate a contract dispute in Japan, saying:

There is no reason to assume at the outset of the dispute that international arbitration will not provide an adequate mechanism. To be sure, the international arbitral tribunal owes no prior allegiance to the legal norms of particular states; hence, it has no direct obligation to vindicate their statutory dictates. The tribunal, however, is bound to effectuate the intentions of the parties. Where the parties have agreed that the arbitral body is to decide a defined set of claims that includes, as in these cases, those arising from the application of American antitrust law, the tribunal therefore should be bound to decide that dispute in accord with the national law giving rise to the claim.

As international trade has expanded in recent decades, so too has the use of international arbitration to resolve disputes arising in the course of that trade. The controversies that international arbitral institutions are called upon to resolve have increased in diversity as well as in complexity. There is widespread recognition for arbitration.

MEDIATION

Characteristics of Mediation

Mediation, like arbitration, is used to resolve disputes, but there are important differences. In mediation, a third person, the mediator, attempts to reconcile a dispute between two parties by persuading them to adjust or settle their differences. The mediator usually acts as a go-between who encourages the parties to modify their positions. He or she usually has no authority to resolve the dispute.

The mediator's role is not to judge but to persuade and seek compromise and reconciliation. Whereas the arbitrator renders a decision and thus acts as a substitute for the judge, the mediator merely emphasizes the reasonableness of the parties' demands. Generally, if the contract or agreement between the parties provides for arbitration, the arbitrator's decision is final. By contrast, the mediator's recommendations are not binding and usually do not have to be accepted by the disputing parties. In most cases, those recommendations are not directly enforceable through the legal system.

Mediators have been used to settle international boundary disputes, baseball strikes, and numerous contract disputes. The Federal Mediation and Conciliation Service has experienced mediators who serve in labor-management disputes. In addition to settling disputes in the health care field, as has been noted, they assist in disputes between local school boards and teachers' unions, as well as between airlines and their mechanics' or pilots' unions. The Magnuson-Moss Product Warranty Act authorizes mediation in disputes regarding malfunctioning consumer products. Many companies, such as the Kellogg Company and DuPont, have agreed to mediate any business disputes they have with other businesses who also commit to use mediation.

Mediators are used for a variety of reasons. A mediator can diffuse emotions between parties who may be angry or upset with each other. Mediators may suggest

EXHIBIT 3.4 Neighborhood Dispute Resolution Centers

1. **Who are the mediators?** Mediators are community volunteers who receive at least 25 hours of specialized training in conflict resolution techniques and communication skills. They are laborers, counselors, attorneys, senior citizens, and employees of various community organizations.
2. **What kinds of matters are appropriate for mediation?** Each center has guidelines that generally include neighborhood disputes (fences and driveways), consumer merchant disputes, business and contract disputes, landlord-tenant problems, family disputes, and small claims. Disputes involving controlled substances and serious violence are not appropriate for mediation.
3. **Why do people use mediation?** Mediation is quick, usually within 10 days after both parties have agreed to mediate. The mediation usually lasts less than two hours. It is inexpensive because the centers provide free mediation to indigent people and low costs to others. It is successful because the goal is to have all parties satisfied. Mediation aims at a win-win situation. It offers privacy, in that all discussions related to the subject of mediation remain confidential and cannot be used in a lawsuit. Its effectiveness rates high, with approximately 80% of all mediations ending in agreement.

alternative strategies to the parties and encourage the use of unforeseen compromise positions. Mediators may point out weaknesses to each party in their respective positions, thereby encouraging more realistic settlement discussions.

Mediation in the Neighborhood

In the last decade, a network of diverse dispute resolution programs has evolved to mediate, arbitrate, and facilitate conflicts into agreement with a minimum of stress on the disputing parties and the courts. Today, these programs may be found in state, city, or county agencies. Trade associations have consumer action panels. University systems often use student volunteers and employ ombudsmen to serve as mediators. Some cities have independent organizations that provide mediation service for the community as a whole.

In Michigan, for example, the community Dispute Resolution Program was established by the legislature in 1988 and funded by an increase of filing fees at the circuit court trial level. At present, more than a dozen dispute resolution centers in the state provide mediation or other forms of voluntary dispute resolution to people as an alternative to litigation. Exhibit 3.4 answers several common questions about neighborhood dispute resolution centers.

OTHER FORMS OF ADR

In addition to arbitration and mediation, the minitrial, summary jury trial, and private court are sometimes used to resolve disputes.

The Minitrial

Some corporations use the minitrial, an informal presentation of a dispute by the parties and their attorneys to senior executives of each party or to independent outsiders. A neutral party is often present as a moderator or adviser. In some situations, the adviser is asked for an opinion; in others, the senior executives of the disputing firms meet to discuss settlement as soon as the presentation has been completed.

Once the senior executives have heard both sides of the dispute and become aware of the relative strengths and weaknesses of their companies' positions, settlement may be more likely.

The minitrial requires all parties to agree to its use. In a minitrial, the parties can resolve questions of law and fact in complex disputes through an abbreviated discovery process. The abbreviated discovery procedure, requiring exchange of key documents and names of witnesses, gives the parties fuller knowledge of the facts involved in the dispute and makes them more ready to reach a settlement. After the discovery stage, the adviser meets with the parties and seeks to resolve procedural issues. The actual trial generally lasts only a day or two and occurs months, not years, after the case begins.

The adviser at the hearing does not take the role of judge but instead derives his or her authority from the parties. In some cases, the minitrial is presented to the respective parties and the adviser merely conducts the hearing. In other cases, the adviser may be given authority to render an advisory opinion as to the outcome of the case if, in fact, it went to trial. Minitrials have been used in patent disputes, product liability cases, unfair competition, and antitrust claims. Some of the advantages are noted in Exhibit 3.5.

Summary Jury Trial

Sometimes parties want to put their case before a real jury to see how a jury reacts to their evidence. In a summary jury trial, each party presents to a jury some of the evidence that would be used in a full trial. The jury then deliberates and renders a nonbinding decision. After the jury verdict, the parties have the opportunity to talk to the jury to find out how and why they reached their decision.

By presenting their case to a jury in a trial type of setting and learning how and why the jury reached its verdict, each party can learn more about what an actual jury might do. Based on such evidence, the parties are more likely to settle the case, as the expectations of the parties usually move closer together.

Private Trials or Rent-a-Judge

Some businesses have sought to resolve disputes by using the paid services of retired judges or lawyers who assume the role of judge. The parties to such cases are able to select the judge who will hear the case and to have their case heard whenever they are ready to present it. In this dispute resolution method, referred to as the

EXHIBIT 3.5 Advantages of a Minitrial

1. The parties can design the processes and rules to be used.
2. The process allows mediation and creative problem solving.
3. The use of some discovery methods allows each party to learn the facts and pertinent issues about its opponent, thus promoting an informed settlement.
4. The adviser can be selected for his or her expertise and can be granted varying degrees of authority.
5. Both the preparation for the trial and the trial itself are relatively brief.
6. The case is generally presented to the executives of the parties—the people with authority to settle the dispute.
7. The hearings are confidential; the parties and the adviser agree not to disclose information regarding the proceedings to others.

rent-a-judge or private trial method, society does not vest the judge with the legal authority to impose a binding decision on the disputing parties. However, the parties frequently agree to accept the judge's determination, similar to voluntary arbitration.

A California statute, originating in the early 1990s, permits the parties to bypass the formal court system and use paid judges or referees. This statute allows the decision of the rent-a-judge to have the finality of trial court judgments. Nevertheless, in most cases the results of a private trial are not binding unless agreed to by the parties. Although private trials are quicker and use judges who usually are familiar with the type of dispute being submitted to them, some people believe private trials also pose problems of equal access. Why should some people be able to bypass the delays found in the public courts or be able to select the judge rather than be assigned to a judge via a random selection process?

LITIGATION AND ADR

Although litigation may be pursued as part of a business strategy in some cases, in many situations ADR techniques offer a less expensive and more effective means of resolving disputes. Business managers need to recognize the existence of these alternatives to litigation so that they can select the most appropriate method for any given dispute.

COMPARISONS

Both litigation and ADR constitute important segments of the U.S. legal system. The courts are established in the Constitution as a forum for resolving disputes. The courts are open to all people (although difficult for poor people to access), and they involve citizens in dispute resolution through juries. Although litigation is costly and somewhat inefficient, the courts play an important role as a check on the other branches of our government. Through the application of the Bill of Rights and due process guarantees (discussed in the next chapter), the courts enforce the rights of the minority. Most people support a strong and independent court system because it forces the government and other people in society to act according to rule of law.

The ADR techniques are generally fairly quick, not too expensive, and private. None of those attributes are shared with litigation. ADR involves the parties in a nonadversarial environment, encouraging each party to participate in seeking a solution that both parties can live with, both short and long term. Business managers need to be cognizant of different ADR techniques to select an optimal method for any dispute the business confronts. Effective dispute resolution management is too important to be ignored, either by individuals or by firm managers.

A comparison of the different methods of dispute resolution should consider a number of factors, including:

1. Is the decision reached through each method binding? Can the decision be reviewed?
2. How is the decision maker selected? Does that person generally have expertise in the particular industry involved?
3. Is the decision written? Are reasons given? Do the parties have to agree with and abide by the decision for it to be enforceable?
4. Is the process public or private?

DIFFERENCES

Several basic differences exist between the adversarial method of dispute resolution followed in civil litigation and the ADR processes. First, in the adversarial process, the neutral party (judge) makes a decision after hearing from the disputing parties, whereas in ADR the hearing officer may help formulate the result during the process. Second, in adversarial litigation, one party wins and the other loses. By contrast, ADR methods allow each party to benefit from the resolution. Third, whereas ADR requires communication and trust between the parties, the adversarial system nurtures distrust and animosity. Finally, the parties in litigation expect their case will be governed by a general legal principle found in a statute, administrative regulation, or court decision. In an ADR matter, the outcome of the dispute need not be based on general legal principles. Although legal rules are followed in most arbitration hearings, some ADR methods do not require the decision or result to be based on recognized legal rules. Exhibit 3.6 compares litigation's adversarial nature with ADR's emphasis on creative problem solving.

EXHIBIT 3.6 Comparison of Dispute Resolution Methods

Method of Dispute Resolution	Binding/ Reviewable	Selection of Decision Maker	Nature of Decision	Public/ Private
Civil trial	Yes—can appeal	Judge not selected by parties	Written decision with reasons	Public
Arbitration	Yes—limited review	Selected by parties; generally has expertise on subject in dispute	Sometimes a written decision with reasons	Private except when court reviews
Mediation	No, but can be enforced if in contract	Selected by parties	Based on agreement by parties; written decision is sometimes required	Private
Minitrial	No, but can be enforced if in contract	Selected by parties; sometimes has expertise on subject in dispute	Based on agreement by parties	Private
Private trial/ rent-a-judge	Sometimes—then subject to appeal	Selected by parties	Written decision sometimes with reasons	Private unless enforcement needed

ADR: PROS AND CONS

The use of ADR processes has grown because each of the methods possesses some advantage over litigation. The lower cost and quicker resolution of the dispute are significant advantages usually attributed to the ADR methods. Litigation sometimes is selected, however, because the cost or delay associated with it may be an advantage to one of the parties. Thus, if you might be held responsible for damage suffered by the other party, you might prefer to pay those damages later, after going through litigation, rather than soon.

Similarly, the cost of litigation may be a deterrent. A large firm may prefer to litigate with a small firm, hoping that the small firm's lack of financial resources will encourage it to settle. Litigation is generally more appropriate when a new legal policy is at stake because only the courts can establish the policy as precedent for future decisions. See Exhibit 3.7 for a summary of the pros and cons of ADR and litigation.

ETHICAL DILEMMAS IN LITIGATION AND ADR

Ethical considerations can play a part in selecting either litigation or ADR. Because litigation is so expensive and time-consuming, it can impose a hardship on some

EXHIBIT 3.7 Pros and Cons of ADR

Pros: Advantages of ADR over litigation

1. Less time from beginning of controversy to resolution of dispute.
2. Less cost because of lower attorneys' fees, less time away from work by corporate employees, and lower "court" costs for the prevailing party.
3. Parties can select a more experienced decision maker or facilitator rather than being randomly assigned to a judge.
4. Parties are able to select where the dispute will be heard; they are not bound to use the court system where each party does business.
5. The nonadversarial nature of ADR makes it easier to do business in the future with an opponent. The parties are actively involved in solving a problem and are not passive participants.
6. The informality of ADR methods is less formidable than are the evidentiary rules governing court procedures.

Cons: Disadvantages of ADR as compared to litigation

1. The longer time frame for litigation may be advantageous to one of the parties if it will have to make a payment to the other party once the dispute is resolved. Passage of time naturally decreases both the cost to the defendant and the value of the plaintiff's recovery.
2. The use of discovery in litigation allows each party to obtain valuable information from the other party.
3. The rule of law generally governs the dispute; if the law is on one party's side, the case is more likely to be decided in that party's favor.
4. Only the courts can establish precedent. If a party has a concern about future cases as well as the present controversy, litigation may establish the needed precedent.
5. Litigation is generally preferred if the case involved new or complex legal theories.
6. Litigation is more public and thus may be used to let other parties know that disputes will not be settled for their nuisance value.

defendants. On the other hand, most e-commerce contracts include mandatory arbitration clauses even where those in some way harmed by use of the site may prefer to use litigation—and its juries—to resolve disputes.

Ethical Dilemmas in Litigation

Although the use of ADR methods sometimes offers meaningful cost and time savings over litigation, parties often still choose to pursue litigation. Is it ethical for a party to seek to litigate a questionable case or to harass the opponent into settlement by threatening or conducting costly pretrial procedures? If a large firm has significant resources and easy access to legal counsel, is it ethical for that firm to pursue litigation if it suspects its small opponent will be unable to bear the time and cost such litigation will require?

Similarly, if the cost of litigation for a defendant is significantly more than the cost of settlement of a minor claim, is it ethical for the plaintiff to file a nuisance claim against the party? Before bringing suit, both the client and the attorney should have a reasonable belief that wrongful conduct has occurred, that damages have resulted, and that genuine legal issues exist. Litigation can be an ethical method of settling disputes, but unfounded or vindictive litigation wastes scarce societal resources and brings about disrespect of the law. The law does, however, provide some remedies for victims of unfounded litigation.

Ethical Dilemmas in ADR

Most websites include "terms and conditions" of use that require the user to approve the website provider's choice of law and choice of forum clauses prior to entering into any transaction out of which a dispute may later arise. Similarly, securities brokers and medical service providers often include arbitration provisions in all contracts in which they agree to provide services.

On the other hand, some countries require that in e-commerce transactions the consumer must have the right to bring the dispute before the courts or a special tribunal (depending on the legislation) in the country where the consumer resides. Is legislation needed to guarantee consumers a familiar dispute resolution process and substantive law, or should governments leave the parties to determine for themselves such contract terms?

Is it ethical for the provider of services to impose the terms of use on anyone who desires to use that firm's services? Most ADR processes are confidential, and decisions are not open to pubic scrutiny. Do people who accept click-and-wrap agreements or hospital arbitration agreements realize they are waiving any right to litigate disputes in court? If litigation is too expensive and time-consuming for use by the average person, should the law encourage use of the alternative dispute resolution procedures?

The goal of dispute resolution is to achieve a fair result. Whether they choose a civil trial, arbitration, mediation, minitrial, summary jury trial, or rent-a-judge, most people want what is rightfully theirs. The cost of alternative dispute resolution methods varies from one type to the next. Mediation through community dispute resolution centers generally is the least expensive method. Arbitrators are a bit more expensive, and rent-a-judges are generally the most expensive. If you pay for a more expensive method of dispute resolution, are you going to receive a better result? If the job of deciding cases is taken out of the hands of judges, what standards will be imposed on the parties who instead perform that task? What types of checks and balances will guarantee that they are doing a good job? Will poorer people get an inferior quality of justice merely because they cannot afford to use certain methods of dispute resolution?

QUESTIONS

1. What are the four most common methods of alternative dispute resolution?
2. Explain how the term *alternative* in ADR has more than one meaning.
3. Describe three situations in which a manager might prefer to use litigation rather than an ADR method to solve a dispute.
4. Compare and contrast the role of the parties toward each other, the role of the parties in determining the process and rules to be used, and the role of the decision maker in litigation with the comparable roles in most ADR methods.
5. Construct a scenario in which it would be best to use each of the various methods of alternative dispute resolution.
6. The OracleExchange.com website provides that anyone seeking to use the site for B2B purchases, sales, or exchanges must press its accept button, thereby accepting the website's terms for use. One of those terms is:

   You agree that OracleExchange.com marketplace is based in the U.S.A. and that all legal actions between You and Oracle that are related to these Terms and Conditions of Use shall be governed by the laws of the state of California, U.S.A., and shall be instituted in a state or federal court in San Francisco or San Mateo County, California.

   If a purchaser who used Oracle believes an automotive part purchased from a seller is not genuine but an imitation and that Oracle, as well as the seller, might be held responsible for providing a refund to the purchaser, would the seller have to bring its suit against Oracle and the seller in a court in San Francisco or San Mateo County, California? Could the purchase sue the seller, but not Oracle, in some other court?
7. The firm where you work is a large firm that is involved in a multimillion-dollar antitrust and breach of contract suit with another large firm. The two firms are competitors in the same industry, but each also has license agreements and a joint venture with the other. Each firm expects to spend several hundred thousand dollars in attorneys' fees and other costs to prepare for the suit. The case is scheduled to come before the court in about a year. The executives of your firm are upset with the slow pace of litigation and the long time required to get the case into and out of court. If there is an appeal, several years could come and go before the case is resolved. You are invited to a brainstorming session called by one of the executives who is in charge of managing the litigation. He has asked a group of people to suggest how this dispute could be solved without going to court. Which of the alternative resolution techniques would you recommend and why?
8. AMF and Brunswick both manufacture automatic scoring devices for use in bowling. Brunswick advertised that its automatic scoring device was more reliable than any others in use, and AMF brought suit, claiming the advertisement was false and deceptive. AMF sued Brunswick, and the litigation was resolved by an agreement whereby each party would submit any future disputes regarding advertising claims to an arbitration panel for nonbinding arbitration. Later, Brunswick ran several advertisements that claimed its laminated lanes were more durable than the wood lanes manufactured by AMF. AMF sued to have Brunswick submit its information to the arbitration panel, but Brunswick refused. Should the court force Brunswick to provide the arbitration panel with information on its laminated lanes?
9. Rodriguez de Quijas signed a standard arbitration agreement with Shearson/American Express brokerage house when he opened an account with that firm. The contract obligates the parties to settle any controversies through binding arbitration. De Quijas brought suit against Shearson, alleging that the broker made false and fraudulent transactions in his account, and he claims the broker violated the 1933 Securities Act. The Securities Act authorizes a person who is injured by a breach of that act to sue for damages, and de Quijas asserts that language allows him to bypass the arbitration. Do you agree?
10. Careful Construction Company entered into a contract with All-Right Electric Company whereby All-Right agreed to do electrical work on several commercial office buildings Careful had contracted to build. Their contract provided that any dispute between the parties was to be submitted to a private court. A dispute arose as to whether All-Right's work conformed to the standards it had agreed to in the contract. All-Right wanted to bring the dispute to trial, but it made a token appearance before a private judge. It presented no evidence, called no witnesses, but simply read statements indicating that its work did conform to the contract. The private judge decided in favor of Careful Construction Company, but All-Right refuses to abide by that judge's decision. Would a court enforce the private judge's decision and decline to hear a case if All-Right sues?

Constitutional Law

The U.S. Constitution establishes the basic framework for government, including the sphere of influence of various levels of government and the rights reserved to the people. It has always had a major impact on commerce. In early days it implemented the colonists' desire for free markets and self-determination. As the nation grew, the interpretation of several key constitutional provisions—the Commerce Clause, the Bill of Rights, and federalism—guided industrial development. More recently, as e-commerce evolves, the Constitution is again playing a major role. Governments and citizens are grappling with their evolving rights and duties that have been made much more complex by the Internet's borderless reach and the greater dependence on trade in intellectual property.

Nearly every major provision of the U.S. Constitution reflects a reaction to the tyrannical rule that the English crown exercised over the American colonies. To restrict the potential misuse of governmental powers by the central government, which the colonies experienced, the federal system spreads governmental powers among separate branches at each level of government and separates powers between the federal and local governments. The colonies first organized into a confederation to confine the central government's powers, but the **confederation** form of government did not coordinate the states' activities. The resulting protectionism and conflicting policies were finally seen as harmful to the whole country's strength. The Constitution became a compromise between the **Federalists**, who desired a strong central government, and the **Anti-Federalists**, who supported stronger states' rights. It forms the basis for all American law and represents the foundation for power at all levels of government. As the supreme law of the land, the Constitution establishes the basic structure of the federal government, provides for the states' self-government, and limits government encroachment on business and personal activities. The structure of the U.S. Constitution is so well balanced that it has been widely imitated.

The courts have reinforced the federal government's pervasive power to regulate business and interstate commerce. Nevertheless, there are still disputes over the relative roles of the states in our federal system. Many cases hold that the federal powers to regulate business activities are so pervasive that they preempt any state interference with interstate commerce. By contrast, other cases have carved out pockets of states' rights to regulate local business activity. However, state laws that interfere excessively with the federal government's enumerated lawmaking powers are held unconstitutional under the supremacy clause. The **supremacy clause** of the U.S. Constitution makes federal law supreme and permits the Supreme Court to declare unconstitutional any conflicting state law. This is a major component of federalism, a theme throughout this chapter.

The successful growth of e-commerce depends on the U.S. Constitution to encourage free markets, balance libertarian incentives and privacy with security, protect intangible property rights, and maintain open access to the infrastructure of e-commerce. Indeed, because electronic communication is the very essence of e-commerce, the U.S. Constitution's protection of free speech is the key legal infrastructure supporting the Internet. This chapter examines this and other basic constitutional issues triggered by activities in both the traditional economy and cyberspace.

The constitutional bases for some of the emerging e-commerce issues—states rights, obscenity, and intellectual property rights—are covered here in depth. Other issues—due process and jurisdiction, defamation, taxation of e-commerce, and privacy—are detailed in other chapters. Many of the most complex challenges in accommodating the convergence of the traditional and Internet economies trigger constitutional questions. Therefore, a basic understanding of the U.S. Constitution is essential to any participation in the public policy debate over Internet regulation.

ONLINE

Further reading on constitutional law can be found at **http://www.law.cornell.edu/constitution/constitution.overview.html**

THE BASIS FOR CONSTITUTIONAL POWERS

The Constitution has two major parts and several subparts. The first part contains the Preamble and seven substantive articles that establish and empower Congress, the executive branch, and the judiciary and then regulate relations among the states and authorize constitutional amendments. The second part contains amendments that were enacted after the founders' initial drafting. The first 10 amendments, the Bill of Rights, were ratified in 1791 to protect fundamental freedoms and liberties. Since then, thousands of amendments have been proposed, but only 18 have passed. They deal with liquor prohibition, taxation, the abolition of slavery and its effects, congressional pay, and election matters. Although 28 amendments have been passed, only 27 amendments are currently effective. In 1933, the Twenty-First Amendment repealed prohibition, the grand experiment, which was originally imposed by the Eighteenth Amendment in 1919.

Amendment proposals in recent years have sought to require equal rights for women, balance the federal government budget, outlaw desecration of the American flag, and establish the right to life for the unborn. The discussion in this chapter reorganizes this structure by first examining the historical context, next reviewing the basic powers of government, and then discussing the basic constitutional constraints on traditional and e-commerce activity.

THE HISTORICAL PERSPECTIVE

Conflict over the separation of powers has dominated the history of U.S. constitutional law since the Revolutionary War. Our government represents a compromise between opposing views of where are the most legitimate, efficient, and responsible places for governmental power to be. The country has continually struggled between two political forces in the search for the best model for government. The Federalists advocated the unitary form of central or national government. The Anti-Federalists represented regional interests that advocated stronger local governments. A general theory of government, known as federalism, sometimes called **dual federalism**, recognizes that power can reside at both the central level and at various local levels. Much of American history and the contemporary legal issues affecting business turn on federalism and the separation of powers between and within both state and federal levels of governments.

Constitutional Development during the Revolutionary War

England's pervasive and tyrannical rule over the American colonies led to the Revolutionary War. The English crown was dictatorial and abused the colonists, showing little respect for their opinions. Therefore, the constitutional framers included provisions to restrict any similar misuse of power by separating the power of the central government into three distinct branches. This separation of powers into many subunits of government may not seem efficient, but it is a proven deterrent to tyranny.

The original 13 colonies derived their political powers from colonial charters granted by the English crown. These documents eventually developed into separate state constitutions and were ultimately revised to parallel the U.S. Constitution so that the states have similar separations of powers. The colonies had divergent social and economic interests and considered themselves separate, distinct, and sovereign political entities. Although the colonies united during the Revolutionary War to oppose tyranny, they mainly sought to oppose their common enemy and provide for a collective defense, not to unify under a single model of government.

The Articles of Confederation

The colonies' first attempt to unify was an overreaction to the strong English central government. Soon after independence, the states used a confederation form of government that was no more than a loose aggregation of the states, similar to other experiments by the Swiss, Germans, and the Papal states. A confederation is a loose alliance of independent entities that seek to retain separate autonomy and self-determination. Confederating states join together for limited common goals, such as defense. They reject stronger forms of central government. The **Articles of Confederation** created the first American confederation. It provided a benchmark for the strongest form of states' rights in American federalism. Ever since these Articles of Confederation were ratified between 1777 and 1781, the trend has been generally toward increased central government powers and away from strong state powers. The Civil War was a notable example of conflict over states' rights.

The Articles of Confederation gave the new Congress very limited power to conduct foreign affairs, raise armed forces, and levy taxes. It created no branches of government with executive or judicial power. The early Congress had no power to raise money and could only request that the states contribute money for their collective efforts. The states had different currencies that created havoc in interstate commerce and eventually runaway inflation. The central government had great difficulty in maintaining domestic peace and preventing violence. In response, the states attempted to revise the Articles of Confederation; instead, they wrote an entirely new document, the U.S. Constitution.

Development of the U.S. Constitution

The U.S. Constitution is a compromise between the two dominant political groups of that time. The Federalist party initially succeeded in securing a strong national government in international affairs, interstate commerce, and taxation. The Federalist position was exemplified by well-to-do Northeastern merchants who stood to gain the most from unlimited interstate commerce. The Anti-Federalist position represented the states' rights advocates and the populist, agrarian interests of the South. They distrusted both the Federalists and central governments in general. This power struggle resulted in a compromise reserving the police power to the states and providing regional strength through each state's representation in the U.S. Congress.

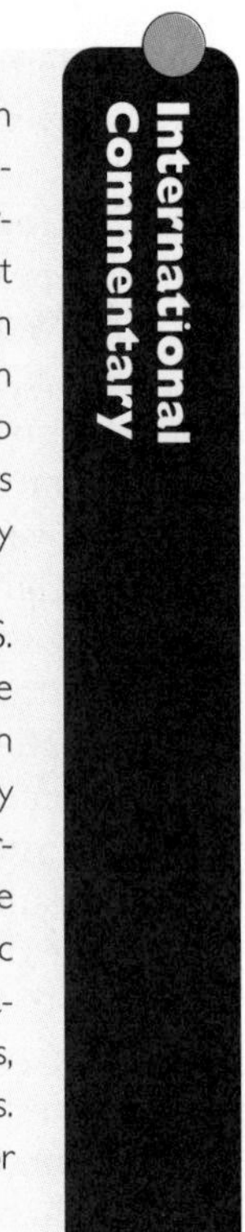

Other Nations' Constitutions

The U.S. Constitution is a unique document in world history. No other existing constitution has survived longer. This success is probably due to the Constitution's promise of freedom, the vastness of U.S. natural resources, the rugged individualism and motivation of immigrants from all over the world, and their rejection of the rigid feudal, class systems or autocratic rule evident throughout history. The U.S. Constitution provides a blueprint for minimum government intervention while permitting fundamental democratic principles. It balances efficiency with freedom and rewards individual achievement while protecting individual rights. It accommodates the powers of numerous competing economic, social, and political interests, unlike the ethnically dominated governments in many other nations at most other times in history.

The U.S. Constitution was influenced by other nations. The model for a republic was taken from the ancient Greeks. Principles of democracy were drawn from the early Romans. The common law tradition and the rule of precedent was drawn from England. The Magna Carta, reluctantly issued by England's King John in 1215, provided a model for due process by guaranteeing fundamental personal liberties such as the enjoyment of life, liberty, and property except after judgment by one's peers. However, the lack of a written English constitution inspired the American founders to rely on more than customs and conventions. The French also exerted considerable influence: Montesquieu's writings on the shortcomings of monarchy and its tendency toward despotism also inspired the new U.S. republic.

Today, Europeans stand to benefit from the U.S. experience under the Constitution. The nations of the European Union are moving through a confederation stage by lowering their mutual borders. They face many of the collective problems of balancing central governance with their culturally diverse sovereignties. The EU is following in many of the U.S. footsteps: economic harmonization, a common currency, encouraging intra-EU commerce, integrating varying laws and traditions, and seeking a unified interaction with outside nations. The U.S. Constitution provides a workable pattern for encouraging economic activity throughout the world.

THE POWERS OF GOVERNMENT

Most governmental powers are provided in the U.S. Constitution. **Enumerated powers** are expressly delegated to the federal government by the states. Implicit powers permit Congress to legislate where it is **necessary and proper** to implement particular enumerated powers. The **reserved powers** of the states include the police power to look after the general health, safety, welfare, and morals of their people.

Not all powers are allocated exclusively to either the federal government or the state governments. Both levels of government share or have **concurrent powers** to make laws in several areas (e.g., taxation). Certain potential powers are **prohibited** to both the state and federal governments. For example, neither level of government may make laws that establish a religion. The supremacy clause denies to the states the power to legislate in areas where the federal government power is exclusive.

Enumerated, Delegated, or Exclusively Federal Powers

The federal government has several **exclusive powers**. The most important to business is the power to regulate interstate commerce. The states are prohibited from making laws that would unduly burden interstate commerce. (The commerce clause is discussed in a later section.) Other exclusive powers give to only the federal government the power to act in matters of foreign affairs. For example, the states have no power to make war, sign treaties, naturalize citizens, or regulate aliens. The federal government has power over the post office, now the quasi-governmental U.S. Postal Service. The power to build post roads has given rise to federal interstate highways.

Reserved and Concurrent Powers

The Tenth Amendment reserves to the states any powers not specifically delegated to the federal government.

> **The Tenth Amendment**
> The powers not delegated to the United States by the Constitution, nor prohibited by it to the States, are reserved to the States respectively, or to the people.

Despite this reservation by the Tenth Amendment to the states of all remaining governmental powers, the states share many powers with the federal government. Examples include the power to tax and the powers of eminent domain.

The **police power** permits each state to protect its citizens' "health, safety, welfare, and morals." It enables the states to legislate in the areas of criminal law, tort law, contract law, commercial law, divorce law, regulatory law, and property rights. However, the state police power is not unlimited, so legislation is often invalidated when it imposes an undue burden on interstate commerce or constitutes an uncompensated taking of private property.

Takings

States have the power of **eminent domain**, permitting the **taking** of private property for public purposes, such as condemning homes to build a highway, a city lot to construct a government building, or farmland that will flood and become a lakebed when a dam is built. The power of eminent domain has also been important to create the **rights of way** for utilities and communications companies that are fundamental to Internet operations. Networks of wires are either strung overhead or put in pipes under public streets, but frequently they cross private land. The Fifth Amendment requires the government, or a private utility acting with eminent domain power, to pay "just compensation" for the value of property taken. This clause was included in the Constitution because of England's practice of confiscating colonists' property for use by the English crown. What constitutes a taking and what rights does a property owner have if the government or a utility wants to use the power of eminent domain to take that owner's property? Several recent takings cases illustrate balancing individual property rights with society's various interests.

Dolan v. City of Tigard

114 S.Ct. 2309 (1994)

Facts. Dolan applied for a permit to expand her plumbing supply store and pave the parking lot. The City Planning Commission of Tigard, Oregon, conditioned approval of the permit upon her dedication of land (1) for a public greenway along the adjoining Fanno Creek to minimize flooding and (2) for a pedestrian/bicycle pathway to relieve traffic congestion in the central business district. Dolan appealed the commission's denial of variances from these standards, alleging that the land dedication requirements were unrelated to her development proposal and therefore constituted an uncompensated taking of her property under the Fifth Amendment. The appeals board, the state court of appeals, and the state supreme court all affirmed, and Dolan appealed to the U.S. Supreme Court.

Legal Issue. Is the zoning commission's exaction for green space an uncompensated partial taking under the Fifth Amendment?

Opinion. Chief Justice Rehnquist. [In response to Oregon law] Tigard, a community of some 30,000 residents on the southwest edge of Portland, developed a comprehensive [land use management] plan [that] requires property owners in the area zoned Central Business District to comply with a 15% open space and landscaping requirement, which limits total site coverage, including all structures and paved parking, to 85% of the parcel. New developments [must] facilitate this plan by dedicating land for pedestrian pathways where provided for in the pedestrian/bicycle pathway plan. The city also adopted a Master Drainage Plan. Flooding occurred in several areas along Fanno Creek, including areas near petitioner's property. Increase in impervious surfaces associated with continued urbanization would exacerbate these flooding problems. Other recommendations included ensuring that the floodplain remains free of structures and that it be preserved as greenways. Cost of these improvements should be shared based on both direct and indirect benefits, with property owners along the waterways paying more due to the direct benefit that they would receive. Variances are granted only where it can be shown that, owing to special circumstances related to a specific piece of the land, the literal interpretation of the applicable zoning provisions would cause "an undue or unnecessary hardship."

One of the principal purposes of the Takings Clause is "to bar Government from forcing some people alone to bear public burdens which, in all fairness and justice, should be borne by the public as a whole." The authority of state and local governments to engage in land use planning has been sustained against constitutional challenge. "Government hardly could go on if to some extent values incident to property could not be diminished without paying for every such change in the general law." A land use regulation does not effect a taking if it "substantially advance[s] legitimate state interests" and does not "den[y] an owner economically viable use of his land." Undoubtedly, the prevention of flooding along Fanno Creek and the reduction of traffic congestion in the Central Business District qualify as the type of legitimate public purposes we have upheld. A nexus exists between preventing flooding along Fanno Creek and limiting development within the creek's 100-year floodplain.

We think a term such as "rough proportionality" best encapsulates what we hold to be the requirement of the Fifth Amendment. No precise mathematical calculation is required, but the city must make some sort of individualized determination that the required dedication is related both in nature and extent to the impact of the proposed development. It is axiomatic that increasing the amount of impervious surface will increase the quantity and rate of stormwater flow from petitioner's property. Therefore, keeping the floodplain open and free from development would likely confine the pressures on Fanno Creek created by petitioner's development. The Community Development Code already required that petitioner leave 15% of it as open space and the undeveloped floodplain would have nearly satisfied that requirement. But the city demanded more—it also wanted petitioner's property along Fanno Creek for its Greenway system. The city has never said why a public greenway, as opposed to a private one, was required in the interest of flood control.

The difference to petitioner, of course, is the loss of her ability to exclude others. As we have noted, this right to exclude others is "one of the most essential sticks in the bundle of rights that are commonly characterized as property." It is difficult to see why recreational visitors trampling along petitioner's floodplain easement are sufficiently related to the city's legitimate interest in reducing flooding problems along Fanno Creek, and the city has not attempted to make any individualized determination to support this part of its request. Petitioner would lose all rights to regulate the time in which the public entered onto the Greenway, her right to exclude would not be regulated, it would be eviscerated. We conclude that the findings upon which the city relies do not show the required reasonable relationship between the floodplain easement and the petitioner's proposed new building.

Dedications for streets, sidewalks, and other public ways are generally reasonable exactions to avoid excessive congestion from a proposed property use. But on the record before us, the city has not met its burden of demonstrating that the additional number of vehicle and bicycle trips generated by the petitioner's development reasonably relate to the city's requirement for a dedication of the pedestrian/bicycle pathway easement. The city simply found that the creation of the pathway "could offset some of the traffic demand . . . and lessen the increase in traffic congestion." No precise mathematical calculation is required, but the city must make some effort to quantify its findings in support of the dedication for the pedestrian/bicycle pathway beyond the conclusory statement that it could offset some of the traffic demand generated.

Cities have long engaged in the commendable task of land use planning, made necessary by increasing urbanization particularly in metropolitan areas such as Portland. The city's goals of reducing flooding hazards and traffic congestion, and providing for public greenways, are laudable, but there are outer limits to how this may be done. "A strong public desire to improve the public condition [will not] warrant achieving the desire by a shorter cut than the constitutional way of paying for the change."

Decision. The Fifth Amendment protects owners of real property from takings when zoning regulations require substantial open space and landscaping exactions.

Case Questions

1. What is a taking? For what reasons does the Constitution prohibit the "taking" of private property? What reasons might justify a governmental taking of private property?
2. Give examples of government takings of private real property.
3. How could public facilities or infrastructure be built without the power of eminent domain?

The *Dolan* case illustrates how a partial taking is of particular interest to business. When the taking is complete, the government or utility must pay the reasonable value of the property, essentially a measure of fair market value. However, when the taking deprives the owner of substantial rights, but does not take it all, there is a **partial taking**. This may arise where (1) a landowner is prevented from exploiting the property's greatest economic value, (2) a landowner must let others use the property, or (3) a landowner does not receive just compensation for the taking. Government regulations that limit land use, such as a zoning regulation, generally involve no compensable taking because the property is simply restricted from *some* uses. To do otherwise would severely restrict government's ability to regulate. Nevertheless, the Supreme Court considers some partial takings as compensable. For example, partial compensation was required when a government body took an easement for public beach access[1] and when the use of property in a flood plain was temporarily restricted.[2] A more expansive taking occurred when a regulatory agency sought to prevent coastal beach erosion by denying a building permit to a residential beach lot.[3] The Supreme Court balances the economic impact of a regulation against its anticipated public benefits in determining the extent of compensation for such regulatory takings.

Takings are also at issue in construction and maintenance of infrastructure for public services such as utilities and communications. For much of the twentieth century, state and federal statutes have authorized public utilities to condemn land through eminent domain so long as the land is taken for a public purpose, typically utility services.[4] This power permitted utilities to build and maintain their distribution networks that crisscross the nation: wires for electricity, telephone, and cable TV and pipes for water, natural gas, and sewers. Today, the public's hunger for high-speed Internet access will probably not decrease the need to build physical networks with at least some nonwireless elements, or **landlines**, which are needed for at least part of their networks. Most state statutes provide for structured condemnation proceedings in which the utility seeks to route its wires or pipes through private land or buildings. For example, there were such condemnation disputes when some apartment owners tried to prevent installation of lines as cable TV spread in the 1970s and 1980s. Eminent domain issues will continue as the nation becomes more connected.

Although wireless telephony would seem to alleviate some of the pressures and expenses of acquiring rights of way, it is not clear that wireless services will end the need for physical rights of way over land anytime soon. First, wireless is making only slow penetration into Internet access, and most Internet subscribers still use landlines through modems over traditional phone lines, DSL, or cable systems. Second, cell towers are needed for most wireless service. Many cell towers are sited on private property and are connected and/or powered by using landlines. Finally,

1. *First English Evangelical Lutheran Church of Glendale v. Los Angeles County*, 482 U.S. 304 (1987).
2. *Nollan v. California Coastal Commission*, 483 U.S. 825 (1987).
3. *Lucas v. South Carolina Coastal Council*, 505 U.S. 1003 (1992).
4. *Berman v. Parker*, 348 U.S. 26 (1954).

many wire-based utilities share pole space that strings the network wiring throughout each service area. For example, the power company's poles are often used by the phone and cable TV companies under a federal law that requires access but assures compensation. This law seeks to avoid excessive duplication of pole capacity, but it is argued that the law gives pole users a tremendous cost advantage over pole owners. Some other aspects of the regulation of public utilities and the electronic media are discussed in Chapter 24.

JUDICIAL REVIEW

The common law legal heritage in English-speaking nations like the United States has evolved into a hybrid of the common law and civil law legal systems. Both types of law periodically require interpretation, a function historically provided by the courts. Many constitutional provisions are precise enough to so that interpretation is unnecessary. For example, most of the numerical limitations seem clear enough. The minimum age is 35 years for the president, 30 for senators, and 25 for house members. Similarly, the simple majority vote required to pass legislation, the two-thirds needed to override presidential vetoes, and the three-fourths of state legislatures needed to amend the Constitution all seem quite precise. However, much of the remainder of the Constitution and many statutes contain vague terms. The founders and some legislatures deliberately use vague terms to permit flexibility as society's needs change. They realized they could not find precise and timeless language that would effectively anticipate the whole range of potential human behaviors. The courts' flexibility and discretion in interpretation helps to encourage compliance with the "spirit" and not just the "letter" of the law.

Judicial Restraint

The Supreme Court's power to interpret the Constitution is important because the formal constitutional amendment process is so cumbersome. Only 27 constitutional amendments are currently effective (Prohibition was repealed). By contrast, the Supreme Court constantly interprets the Constitution, thereby effectively changing it. Nevertheless, the courts' power to make laws is limited in several important ways. First, most courts may adjudicate and interpret only after a real **case or controversy** arises. Advisory opinions are not generally permitted except in a few states. Second, most judges exercise judicial restraint by trying not to make sweeping changes in the law. Judicial decisions are generally made in conformance with established precedents. The common law rule of precedent ensures consistency, provides some notice, and restricts judges from constantly imposing their personal economic or social beliefs. **Strict constructionism** is a view contrary to judicial activism in that it presumes the legislature is better suited to solve societal or economic problems because this is precisely the legislature's purpose and because it is more immediately responsible to voters.

Although courts have significant lawmaking powers, they are generally powerless to enforce their decisions. The legislature must appropriate funds for enforcement by the executive branch. Legal precedents are also subject to later legislation. In 1944, for example, the Supreme Court held insurance was within interstate commerce, which would have exposed the insurance industry to federal antitrust law.[5] However, Congress quickly passed the McCarran-Ferguson Act to reverse the decision and provide antitrust exemption to the insurance industry.

5. *United States v. South-Eastern Underwriters Association*, 322 U.S. 533 (1944).

Supreme Court Review of Legislation

Before 1803, judicial review of legislation was generally unknown. Today, any conflicts between the Constitution and a statute subject the legislation to **judicial review**. The power of judicial review flows naturally from both the common law of precedent and from the supremacy clause. Although no specific constitutional provision empowers the Supreme Court to hold legislation unconstitutional, the Supreme Court conferred this power on itself in the landmark 1803 case, *Marbury v. Madison*.[6]

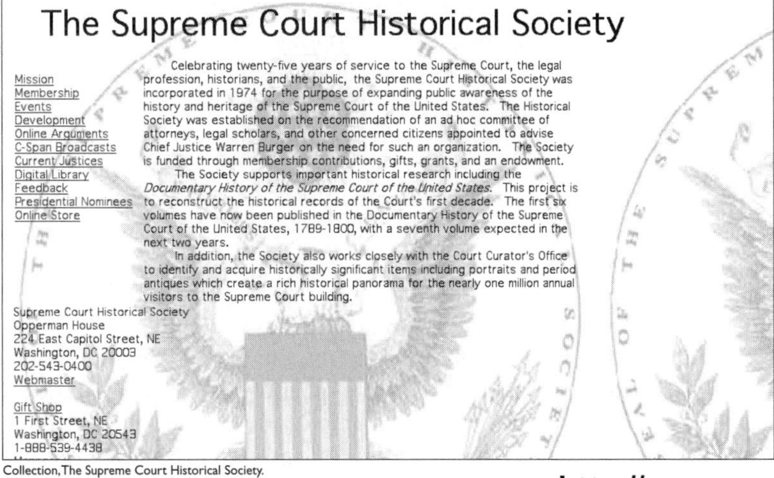

The Supreme Court Historical Society
Mission
Membership
Events
Development
Online Arguments
C-Span Broadcasts
Current Justices
Digital Library
Feedback
Presidential Nominees
Online Store
Celebrating twenty-five years of service to the Supreme Court, the legal profession, historians, and the public, the Supreme Court Historical Society was incorporated in 1974 for the purpose of expanding public awareness of the history and heritage of the Supreme Court of the United States. The Historical Society was established on the recommendation of an ad hoc committee of attorneys, legal scholars, and other concerned citizens appointed to advise Chief Justice Warren Burger on the need for such an organization. The Society is funded through membership contributions, gifts, grants, and an endowment.
The Society supports important historical research including the Documentary History of the Supreme Court of the United States. This project is to reconstruct the historical records of the Court's first decade. The first six volumes have now been published in the Documentary History of the Supreme Court of the United States, 1789-1800, with a seventh volume expected in the next two years.
In addition, the Society also works closely with the Court Curator's Office to identify and acquire historically significant items including portraits and period antiques which create a rich historical panorama for the nearly one million annual visitors to the Supreme Court building.
Supreme Court Historical Society
Opperman House
224 East Capitol Street, NE
Washington, DC 20003
202-543-0400
Webmaster
Gift Shop
1 First Street, NE
Washington, DC 20543
1-888-539-4438

Collection, The Supreme Court Historical Society.

http://

www.
supremecourthistory.org

In the last few days of his administration, President John Adams made several special appointments to federal office before the inauguration of the new president, Thomas Jefferson. After Senate confirmation, President Jefferson directed James Madison, the new secretary of state, to withhold the paperwork needed to legitimize several of Adams's appointments, including Marbury's commission as justice of the peace for the District of Columbia. Marbury sought a **writ of mandamus** in the Supreme Court, an order to force Madison to deliver Marbury's commission. Chief Justice John Marshall declined to grant Marbury's request because no statute gave jurisdiction to the Supreme Court to sit as a trial court in mandamus cases. In this ruling, Marshall effectively made it a judge's duty to interpret statutes in light of constitutional provisions.

Commentary

The Supreme Court: Ideology and Politics

From time to time, throughout American constitutional history, the Supreme Court's political independence has been questioned. Supreme Court judges are appointed by the president with the "advice and consent" of the U.S. Senate. This provides a check on the power of the executive branch, balancing the executive's and judiciary's powers. However, critics often charge that the nomination process is too political, thereby assuring the appointment of political ideologues. When the president and a Senate majority are from the same political party, the president can appoint and the Senate will probably confirm justices clearly sympathetic to their own party's ideology. For example, Democratic President Franklin D. Roosevelt (FDR) used the politically sympathetic Senate majority of Democrats to appoint liberal Supreme Court justices supportive of FDR's New Deal and more aggressive government regulations.

Supreme Court justices' political and ideological leanings become important in close questions. A single swing vote on constitutional questions is decisive, possibly changing established interpretations. For example, *Roe v. Wade*[7] inferred the abortion rights rule from a constitutional right to privacy. When the presidency is held by a member of one party and the Senate is controlled by the other party, new justices may reflect ideological balance; Senate hearings usually reveal a nominee's extremist views, forcing the president to nominate more moderate candidates who are acceptable to the Senate.

6. 1 Cranch 137 (1803).
7. 410 U.S. 113 (1973).

When a controversy involves the constitutionality of legislation, Marshall's decision empowered the courts to invalidate legislation in conflict with the Constitution.

The advice and consent process was designed to permit open debate of a nominee's ideology and qualifications. The president should be given some free rein to select ideologically compatible individuals for the cabinet. These people must regularly work with the president's team and harmonize with the administration's objectives. However, judges and other independent government officials, like Securities and Exchange Commission or Federal Trade Commission commissioners or the Federal Reserve chairman, are separate from the presidential administration. Their experience and job qualifications are more important than ideological conformity. The nomination and confirmation process has permitted a shift of emphasis from ideological compatibility to qualifications that suit the position. The president and Senate might do well to return to the true spirit of the U.S. Constitution's "advice" provision, which appears to require the president to first seek counsel from the whole Senate. Doing so could help avoid the divisiveness of nominating an ideologically unacceptable candidate.

SPECIFIC POWERS OF GOVERNMENT

THE COMMERCE CLAUSE

The power over commerce is an enumerated power of the federal government. The commerce clause forms the primary basis for economic regulation and is probably the most important constitutional provision with impact on business.

> **The Commerce Clause**
>
> The Congress shall have the Power . . . To regulate Commerce with foreign Nations, and among the several States, and with the Indian Tribes.

Two major aspects of the commerce clause affect business. First, it gives Congress power to regulate interstate commerce. Second, by implication it denies the states power to regulate or impede interstate commerce. It seems to leave the states with somewhat freer control over **intrastate commerce**—that is, the local incidents of commerce. States may validly use their police power to protect the health, safety, welfare, and morals of their citizens. In practice, both federal and state laws may regulate certain aspects of commerce, providing the state law's purposes are proper.

Regulation of Foreign Commerce

Under the Articles of Confederation, the states made inconsistent compacts with foreign nations. The Constitution makes the regulation of trade with foreign nations an exclusively federal power. This provision presumes that decisions to make treaties, conduct foreign relations, and regulate foreign commerce are best made by a single, unified entity representing the will and needs of the whole nation.

The definition of foreign commerce is unclear because foreign commerce with the United States necessarily begins or ends within a state. In practice, the states have been prohibited from regulating certain aspects of foreign commerce. For example, state regulation of imports from or exports to foreign nations is invalid if it restricts trade or requires any special treatment of foreign goods. The states may exercise limited regulation over foreign goods once these goods are in the hands of a retailer and the bulk of a wholesale lot has been broken down into smaller commercial units, for example, when a large shipping container has been broken down into pallets or boxes. State regulation is invalid if it discriminates between domestic and foreign commerce, even if the regulation is arguably based on public welfare concerns. Some nations permit their political subdivisions to affect foreign commerce. For example, the Canadian provinces regulate Canada's securities markets. Provincial regulators can make international agreements with other nations' regulators and have done so on enforcement matters with the U.S. Securities and Exchange Commission (SEC).

Federal Regulation of Commerce

The constitutional framers intended the commerce clause to grant Congress sufficient power to govern in all areas of economic activity. In 1824, however, the Supreme Court, in *Gibbons v. Ogden*,[8] restricted Congress from regulating *intrastate* (matters wholly within only one state) by narrowly interpreting the word *interstate*.

> **Interstate Commerce**
>
> Commerce, undoubtedly, is traffic, but it is something more: it is . . . commercial intercourse between nations, and parts of nations, in all its branches, and is regulated by prescribing rules for carrying on that intercourse.[9]

By the early twentieth century, the Supreme Court restricted Congress's interstate commerce powers to include only those matters involving actual transportation of goods across state lines. This left almost all manufacturing as intrastate and therefore not subject to federal regulation.

Commerce Power and the New Deal

New Deal political economy influenced the Supreme Court's interpretation of the commerce clause. During the Great Depression, public pressure mounted for federal solutions to the economic devastation. The legislative efforts of FDR and Congress pitted them against the Supreme Court's laissez-faire predisposition. After FDR's 1937 power struggle with the Supreme Court, the Court validated nearly all of Congress's remedial legislation regulating commerce, including such major laws as the National Labor Relations Act, the securities laws, and the Fair Labor Standards Act. Since 1937, the commerce clause has become the most significant source of congressional power to regulate business. Today, federal legislation is upheld even when it develops a federal police power to preserve health, safety, and welfare. The **affectation doctrine** invalidates regulation over interstate commerce unless some reasonable link exists between that activity and an aspect of interstate commerce. The determination by Congress that such a link exists is usually sufficient to satisfy the courts, even though the link may be tenuous.

Necessary and Proper Clause

The broad commerce power to regulate business can be further implemented through the necessary and proper clause, a catchall phrase in Article I, Section 8, following the list of delegated powers. It permits regulation even beyond an enumerated power. Legislation covering such additional matters is valid when it makes regulation of an enumerated power more effective. For example, a limit on tort remedies against nuclear power generators was based on the necessary and proper clause as a way to encourage development of the nuclear power industry.

8. 6 L.Ed. 23 (1824).
9. Ibid.

The Necessary and Proper Clause
The Congress shall have Power . . . To make all Laws which shall be necessary and proper for carrying into Execution the foregoing Powers.

State Regulation of Commerce

Although the Constitution does not specifically deny the states power to regulate interstate commerce, case law has limited state power. The dual federalism concept permits the states to regulate intrastate activities so long as they impose only minor burdens on interstate commerce under a "balancing test." First, the state regulation must bear a rational relationship to a valid state goal. Second, the effect of the state regulation on interstate commerce must be slight. Third, the extent to which the state regulation discriminates against interstate commerce must be small. Fourth, the necessity for the state regulation must be great. These four factors balance the state's interests in regulating against the need for federal uniformity. If a state law regulating commerce is reasonably related to a strong and necessary state goal and the burdens and discrimination that it places on interstate commerce are small, the law should be valid. A long line of cases on the states' powers to regulate interstate commerce fall into three basic groups: (1) state regulation of interstate transportation, (2) state regulation of production and trade, and (3) state taxation of multistate and multinational businesses.

In the 1925 case of *Buck v. Kuykendall*,[10] a Washington State statute for licensing common carriers was an invalid burden on interstate commerce. Buck was refused permission to use the Washington State highways to operate an "auto stage line" because the territory was "already being adequately served." The Supreme Court found that the state was attempting to unconstitutionally regulate interstate commerce, not simply the safety of its highways. In the 1938 case of *South Carolina State Highway Dept. v. Barnwell Bros.*,[11] the state's restriction on truck width and weight was upheld as a legitimate safety concern, despite the incidental burden that the restrictions placed on interstate commerce. Long trucks presented similar safety concerns to Iowa, which validly restricted double trailers over 60 feet long.[12]

State safety concerns must be actual and not conjectural, a problem addressed by the arbitrary train-length restrictions in the 1945 case of *Southern Pac. Co. v. Arizona*.[13] Arizona attempted to collect penalties from Southern Pacific Railway for violating the 14-car passenger-train maximum limit and the 70-car freight-train limit. This case introduced the "balancing test," and the Supreme Court then used it to invalidate the Arizona statute as arbitrary. *Bibb v. Navajo Freight Lines, Inc.*[14] presented a similar problem in 1959. Illinois attempted to require all trucks to use a particular type of curved mudguard for their wheels. The statute was found unconstitutional because the mudguards, manufactured by an Illinois company, were expensive and offered little additional protection compared with the equipment already in use by most trucking companies. This ruling illustrates that there must be a compelling local interest before local regulations imposing burdens on interstate commerce are upheld as constitutional.

Most state restrictions on out-of-state products are discriminatory and therefore impose an undue burden on interstate commerce. However, there is an exception for state quarantine restrictions. For example, laws prohibiting transportation of diseased

10. 267 U.S. 307 (1925).
11. 303 U.S. 177 (1938).
12. *Kassel v. Consolidated Freightways Corp. of Delaware*, 450 U.S. 662 (1981).
13. 325 U.S. 761 (1945).
14. 359 U.S. 520 (1959).

cattle into Iowa and New York were upheld. To protect their fruit trees from disease, Arizona and California can legitimately restrict the import of fruit. However, local efforts to prevent local disposal of imported solid wastes are generally unsuccessful.[15] Although state regulations may ostensibly try to prevent the spread of disease, unwholesome foods, or undesirable materials, their economic effect is to favor in-state producers. There is seldom a justification to burden interstate commerce when a state or local law gives preference to locally produced products, conserves local resources, maintains favorable local prices, or otherwise restricts exports outside the state.

The celebrated **milk import cases** have been particularly troublesome. Although states may use the police power to assure food safety, several milk regulations have been invalidated. States have attempted to control the price, place of production, or distance that milk travels to market on the pretext of maintaining the milk's wholesomeness. The New York State Milk Control Act of 1933 established minimum prices for milk to ensure sanitary conditions. The city of Madison, Wisconsin, restricted milk sales in the city to milk produced within 25 miles of the city.[16] A Mississippi regulation allowed the sale of milk produced out of state only if the state of origin permitted the import of Mississippi's milk. All these state laws were found to be excessive regulation for their limited objective because other means existed to control milk purity.

States may tax interstate commerce if the out-of-state business has some connection, local operations, or nexus with the taxing state. Several types of tax are valid, although each must apply fairly to both in-state and out-of-state businesses: property taxes on real estate or personal property residing within the state on "tax day," income taxes on the portion derived from within the taxing state, and use taxes on an out-of-state mail, phone, Internet, or other direct marketing method. These state taxation methods are so important to the future of e-commerce that this subject is covered in detail in Chapter 24.

CONTRACT CLAUSE

The **contract clause** prohibits the states from impairing private contracts. This limitation restricts the states, but not the federal government, from passing statutes or administrative regulations that modify the duties owed under *existing* contracts. Nineteenth-century Supreme Court decisions interpreted the contract clause so pervasively that states were effectively prohibited from imposing economic regulations.

> **The Contract Clause**
> No State shall . . . pass any . . . Law impairing the Obligation of Contracts.

The framers included the contract clause in response to the economic chaos that existed under the Articles of Confederation and to prevent the passage of **debtor relief laws** by political pressure. Because more people were debtors than creditors, the framers feared that the debtors might elect legislators who promised to pass laws modifying debt contracts.

Some early interpretations of the contract clause restricted public grants by the states to individuals and institutions (colleges). Modern interpretations of the contract clause permit the states to modify existing contracts only in emergency situations, for example, when necessary to protect the public's health, safety, welfare, or morals.

15. *Fort Gratiot Sanitary Landfill, Inc. v. Michigan Dept. of Natural Resources*, 504 U.S. 353 (1992).
16. *Dean Milk Co. v. Madison*, 340 U.S. 349 (1951).

FULL FAITH AND CREDIT CLAUSE

An important element of federalism is that each state must recognize the laws and legal processes of the other states. Without this recognition, some of the states could become a refuge for those evading their legal obligations elsewhere. To prevent such misuse of the states' borders, the constitutional framers formulated the **full faith and credit clause.**

> **Full Faith and Credit Clause**
> Full Faith and Credit shall be given in each State to the public Acts, Records, and judicial Proceedings of every other State.

Full faith and credit is distinguished from stare decisis, the rule of precedent. Precedents are previous cases that establish rules of law applicable to different but similar disputes arising later in that jurisdiction. Full faith and credit does not require states to adopt other states' precedents, only to enforce other states' laws or judgments between particular disputing parties when suit is brought in another state. The full faith and credit clause requires application of the doctrines of **res judicata** and **collateral estoppel.** These doctrines require that when a competent court with jurisdiction over the subject matter renders a final decision, there can be no further litigation, except for appeals. These two doctrines are similar to the criminal law doctrine of **double jeopardy,** which prohibits the prosecution of an individual twice for the same crime. All of these doctrines require a halt to litigation so that a defendant cannot be subjected to repeated suits on the same issues. The courts of other states must recognize and enforce the final decisions of all other states. For example, if a creditor wins a judgment against a debtor in one state and the debtor flees to another state, the creditor may enforce the decree in the second state, even if the second state does not have the same law as the state rendering the decree. Thus, Indiana need not require the payment of alimony in divorce actions between its citizens. However, it must enforce the alimony awards decreed in other states. Otherwise, Indiana could become a haven for alimony defaulters from other states.

Another important effect of the full faith and credit clause is that the courts of each state must apply the law of the state having the closest relationship to the events at issue in a suit. For example, parties may form a contract in one state, but one of the parties might bring suit for breach of the contract in another state. The **forum state** in which the suit is brought must apply the law of that state with the closest connection to the contract. The Supreme Court has approved several definitions of this "closeness." A complex **conflicts of law** analysis may be required to predict the proper choice of law if the forum state's substantive law differs from that of the other states involved. Similar problems exist in tort, domestic relations, and corporation law. For example, the law of the state of incorporation applies to questions of corporate governance. Conflicts of law rules often make it difficult to **forum shop**—that is, look around for a court in a state with a more favorable law. Similar difficulties about international law are discussed in other chapters.

PRIVILEGES AND IMMUNITIES

The **privileges and immunities clause** is another aspect of federalism that prohibits the states from erecting barriers at their borders.

> **Privileges and Immunities Clause**
> The Citizens of each State shall be entitled to all Privileges and Immunities of Citizens in the several States.

No state may discriminate against the citizens of other states by prohibiting travel or denying access to its courts. Corporations do not have all the same rights as natural persons under the privileges and immunities clause. Thus, out-of-state corporations may be charged higher taxes than domestic corporations as long as the taxes are not unfair or confiscatory. Foreign corporations, those chartered in another state, must register when doing business in other states to have the privileges and immunities of domestic corporations chartered in that state. Because state taxes support state educational institutions financially, nonresident students may be required to pay higher college tuition at state universities than do resident students. The commerce, full faith and credit, and privileges and immunities clauses work together to unify the nation while preserving states' rights.

TAXING AND SPENDING POWER

The federal government has the power to tax to raise revenue or even to discourage particular activities. Even if Congress does not have a specific power to directly regulate a particular activity, its taxing and spending power may be used for that purpose. Earlier cases invalidated taxes intended only as indirect regulation rather than for revenue raising. However, the Supreme Court today focuses less on Congress's motives to levy the tax and more on whether the tax is valid as a regulatory measure. For example, taxes have been validated to discourage sales of marijuana, firearms, and gambling. These taxes are, in reality, indirect regulation of these activities.

Congress also has the constitutional power to spend tax receipts on matters both connected to an enumerated power and on matters not directly related to an enumerated power. Funds raised by taxes may be spent on nearly any policy Congress chooses, so long as it does not violate another constitutional provision. Both the taxing and spending powers of the federal government are used to expand its powers to regulate in many areas not originally enumerated in the U.S. Constitution. Today, political constraints are more influential than are constitutional constraints on Congress's taxing and spending habits.

INTELLECTUAL PROPERTY CLAUSE

Many areas of government regulation are derived, but only indirectly, from some broad grant of power. For example, most of the federal regulations of antitrust, the securities and investment markets, labor and employment relationships, consumer protection, and environmental quality are based on the commerce clause. Congress infers its power after experience with problems in these substantive areas and after political pressure is triggered to regulate. There is direct legislative power in the Constitution in only a few areas. The power of taxation is one well-known example of a regulatory power directly enumerated as a federal power. However, e-commerce and cyberspace are also intimately affected by another directly enumerated federal power, the grant to enact and administer intellectual property (IP) laws (e.g., patent, copyright).

Intellectual Property Clause of the U.S. Constitution (Article I, Section 8, Clause 8)

[Congress shall have the power] To promote the Progress of Science and useful Arts, by securing for Limited Times to Authors and Inventors the exclusive Right to their respective Writings and Discoveries.

The IP clause is unusual; few other regulatory areas have such comprehensive enablement. The IP clause not only directly *grants* the specific regulatory power but also states the framer's *purpose* to promote science and useful arts, as well as the *method* Congress should use to achieve this purpose in the grant of exclusive rights for limited times. Congress has had IP laws since 1790. The commerce clause has also been an important source of IP law, providing the constitutional authority for antitrust, trademark,[17] and unfair competition law. More recent **sui generis** IP rights, such as plant patents and chip designs, are based on both the IP clause and the commerce clause.

The IP clause does not answer many nuances of IP law. However, legislation and/or regulators have defined many of these details, and the courts sometimes limit or confirm these details. For example, the Supreme Court has confirmed Congress's power to establish standards for patentability (novelty, obviousness) and copyrightability (originality). The courts also must balance federalism. In the IP realm, this means there are still state police powers about some IP matters, such as trade secrets, trademarks, and trade dress, as well as the property rights, criminal, tort, and contract law aspects of technology transfer. Many of these issues are addressed throughout this book.

CONSTITUTIONAL RIGHTS OF BUSINESSES AND INDIVIDUALS

The adoption of several fundamental rights known as the **Bill of Rights** amended the Constitution shortly after the initial ratification. Those amendments with the greatest impact on business are discussed here. The **First Amendment** contains several rights, most notably freedom of speech, freedom of the press, freedom of assembly, and freedom of religion. The **Fourth Amendment** ensures the right to be secure from searches and seizures except on the issuance of a warrant. The **Fifth Amendment** includes several provisions ensuring fair judicial process, such as protection against self-incrimination, the right to a grand jury indictment, protection against double jeopardy, and the right to due process. The **Sixth Amendment** guarantees a speedy trial, an impartial jury, the right to confront witnesses, subpoena powers, process to obtain witness testimony, and the right to legal counsel. The **Seventh Amendment** preserves the right to a trial by jury in actions at common law. The **Eighth Amendment** prohibits excessive fines. The Ninth, Tenth and Eleventh Amendments limit federal powers and preserve states' rights.

These constitutional rights are not absolute; they have been interpreted and refined over two centuries. Courts balance the need for constitutional protection against other important policies. The Bill of Rights protections specifically apply to natural persons, but they frequently extend to other entities, such as corporations, because they are considered artificial persons. Corporations have the protection of many constitutional rights, particularly during criminal investigations and proceedings. Constitutional rights affect nearly every field of law, as reflected in recurring references and further discussion in other chapters throughout this book.

THE FIRST AMENDMENT

The First Amendment has been one of the most important collections of fundamental rights: freedom of speech, press, assembly, and religion. People are specifically

17. *The Trademark Cases*, 100 U.S. 82 (1879) (holding that the commerce clause, not the IP clause, is the source of legislative power to enact trademark laws because trademarks are neither writings nor discoveries).

protected from action by the federal government under this amendment. There are also protections from a state's action under the absorption doctrine: the Fourteenth Amendment applies the Bill of Rights and other constitutional protections to governmental action at all levels and branches of government.

Freedom of religion was a major reason that many colonists left for the New World. Religious freedom was so important that it was made an integral part of the First Amendment. The First Amendment's freedom of religion has two parts. First, government may not "establish" any religion. Contemporary establishment issues are raised by school voucher proposals for use at schools sponsored by religious groups. Second, government may not enact laws that interfere with the "free exercise" of religion. Many of the constitutional issues concerning the freedom of religion are beyond the scope of this book. Nevertheless, religious freedom can have a significant impact on business, particularly because the First Amendment requires that employers must provide reasonable accommodation for observance of the Sabbath and varying religious holidays and for other religious customs. Employees' religious rights are discussed further in the Chapter 21 coverage of the equal employment laws.

The First Amendment

Congress shall make no law respecting an establishment of religion, or prohibiting the free exercise thereof; or abridging the freedom of speech, or of the press; or the right of the people peaceably to assemble, and to petition the Government for a redress of grievances.

The freedom of speech guaranteed by the First Amendment provides society with open access to the general marketplace of ideas. It protects speakers by affording expressive access to the public and improves the quality and quantity of available ideas. It protects the ability of recipients of this expression to listen, read, and learn. Speech includes written, verbal, and nonverbal methods of expression. For example, the courts uphold union picketing for lawful purposes as nonverbal speech. However, the First Amendment's right of free speech is *not absolute*. Laws may regulate some incidents of speech to preserve safety and public order. For example, in a labor strike, local law may limit the number of pickets and the manner of picketing.

Not all types of speech are protected because society's need for some types of expression does not outweigh the social costs of allowing them. For example, obscenity, defamation, incitement to riot, fraudulent statements, and subversive speeches receive little protection under the First Amendment. **Prior restraint** laws that prohibit certain classes of speech are suspected to violate the First Amendment. Prior restraint arises, for example, if a city denies a permit to assemble, a court prohibits a public meeting even though the potential for violence is quite low, or a magazine is banned because it might have some obscene content. It is impermissible prior restraint when government restricts speech opposing politicians in power. There are three rough classifications of speech for First Amendment analysis: (1) commercial speech, (2) political speech, and (3) unprotected speech.

The First Amendment has a broad impact on various business issues, many of which are introduced in this chapter and discussed in detail. However, some aspects of the First Amendment's impact on particular business problems are discussed in other chapters where specific areas of law are covered. For example, the impact of the First Amendment on defamation and trade libel is discussed more fully in Chapter 7, the First Amendment's impact on privacy is covered in Chapter 14, the interaction between the First Amendment and intellectual property is discussed in Chapters 15 and 18, and commercial free speech in the advertising context is detailed in Chapter 24.

Commercial Speech

Initially, the courts were not sympathetic to the protection of commercial speech. Legislation regulating advertising was approved under the presumption that advertising and other forms of commercial speech are less justifiable than political speech. The underlying reasoning was that commercial speech primarily results only in personal gain for the advertiser and therefore that advertising was not presumed to have the lofty social legitimacy of political speech. However, more recent cases recognize that commercial speech disseminates important information. By making adequate information available to all market participants, commercial speech contributes to the efficient operation of markets.[18]

Despite the increasing recognition of the social value of commercial speech, it may be regulated as to time, place, and manner, but only if society's need for such restrictions outweighs the speaker's interest. The criteria for regulation of commercial speech are listed in Exhibit 4.1. Consider how these criteria apply to restrictions on advertising tobacco, pornography, and alcohol.

During the energy crisis, some states believed that the need to conserve energy clearly outweighed an electric utility's right to advertise. The New York Public Service Commission issued an order that prohibited electric utilities in New York from advertising to promote electricity use. The order permitted only informational advertising to encourage consumption shifts from peak to off-peak times. The U.S. Supreme Court invalidated the order under the First Amendment as a

"highly paternalistic" view that government has complete power to suppress or regulate commercial speech. [P]eople will perceive their own best interests if only they are well enough informed, and . . . the best means to that end is to open the channels of communication, rather than to close them. Even when advertising communicates only an incomplete version of the relevant facts, the First Amendment presumes that some accurate information is better than no information at all. . . . [This] governmental interest could be served as well by a more limited restriction on commercial speech, [so] the excessive restrictions cannot survive.[19]

The analysis in the *Central Hudson* case is important in Chapter 24, where there is a more detailed discussion of the regulation of advertising generally and of the regulation of Internet advertising in particular.

The commercial speech doctrine may also be important for **encryption** software that converts recognizable expression (e.g., text/data file, e-mail message, digital music, video) into a coded, unrecognizable format sometimes called "ciphertext."

EXHIBIT 4.1 Criteria to Regulate Commercial Speech

1. The commercial speech must concern lawful activity and not be misleading.
2. The degree of restriction must directly relate to the degree of governmental interest.
3. The restriction must reach no further than necessary to protect the governmental interest, and no other practical method may exist to protect this interest.
4. The time, place, and manner of the speech may be regulated, provided that no change is made in the substance of the speech.

18. *Virginia Pharmacy Board v. Virginia Citizens Consumer Council*, 425 U.S. 746 (1976).
19. *Central Hudson Gas & Electric Corp. v. Public Service Commission*, 447 U.S. 557 (1980).

Using various means (e.g., symmetric encryption, public/private key encryption), an encrypted file is made difficult or nearly impossible to read or use without a decryption "key." Strong encryption is fundamental to reliable e-commerce, the security of electronic payment systems, and the confidentiality of electronic messages (e.g., digital signatures, PGP). However, encryption is also important to maintain military secrecy. Law enforcement agencies have difficulty monitoring criminal and terrorist activities unless encryption is weakened, either with "back door" access for law enforcement or by limiting available encryption technologies to weaker forms.

ONLINE

For a discussion on cryptology, visit the Center for Democracy and Technology website **http://www.cdt.org**

The U.S. State Department once limited exports of strong encryption by classifying them as "munitions" subject to strict export controls. There have been recent changes in export regulations covering encryption software and encryption devices, as well as the electronic dispatch of messages or files protected by strong encryption. Exports have been banned only to certain listed nations (e.g., Cuba, Iran, Iraq, Syria, Sudan, Libya, North Korea). Nevertheless, exporters may be required to obtain an export license granted only after review by the U.S. Commerce Department's Bureau of Export Administration (BXA). By contrast, free speech advocates support the general availability of strong encryption. Contradictory encryption case law is confusing. Is encryption protected free speech under the First Amendment? Are export controls or law enforcement access to encrypted messages impermissible prior restraint on free speech? Is encryption given less protection under the First Amendment because it is "merely" commercial speech? The following case addresses some of these points.

Junger v. Daily

209 F3d 481 (6th Cir., 2000)

Facts. Peter Junger, a professor of law at Case Western Reserve University, sought to post parts of his textbook *Computers and the Law*, and software source code listings to his websites. Posting these programs to a website is considered an export under BXA regulations because they can be accessed from nearly anywhere in the world. The BXA determined that an electronic version of several chapters of Junger's book that listed the source code for encryption software programs would constitute restricted exports under the Export Administration Regulations of the BXA. This ruling effectively required Junger to acquire a license before exporting encryption software by posting his programs and chapters. Junger challenged the BXA regulations, seeking declaratory and injunctive relief to permit him to engage in the unrestricted distribution of encryption software through his website.

Legal Issue. Is encryption source code protected speech under the First Amendment? Are the BXA regulations permissible content-neutral regulations so they are not subject to facial challenge on prior restraint grounds? Remanded.

Opinion. Chief Judge Martin. The issue of whether or not the First Amendment protects encryption source code is a difficult one because source code has both an expressive feature and a functional feature. The district court concluded that the functional characteristics of source code overshadow its simultaneously expressive nature. The fact that a medium of expression has a functional capacity should not preclude constitutional protection. Rather, the appropriate consideration of the medium's functional capacity is in the analysis of permitted government regulation. The Supreme Court has explained that "all ideas having even the slightest redeeming social importance," including those concerning "the advancement of truth, science, morality, and arts" have the full protection of the First Amendment. This protection is not reserved for purely expressive communication. The Supreme Court has recognized First Amendment protection for symbolic conduct, such as draft-card burning, that has both functional and expressive features.

Though unquestionably expressive, [many forms of expression] are not traditional speech. Particularly, a musical score cannot be read by the majority of the public but can be used as a means of communication among musicians. Likewise, computer source code, though unintelligible to many, is the preferred method of communication among computer programmers. Because computer source code is an expressive means for the exchange of information and ideas about computer programming, we hold that it is protected by the First Amendment. The functional capabilities of source code, and particularly those of encryption source code, should be considered when analyzing the governmental interest in regulating the exchange of this form of speech. Under intermediate scrutiny, the regulation of speech is valid, in part, if "it furthers an important or substantial governmental interest." The government "must demonstrate that the recited harms are real, not merely conjectural, and that the regulation will in fact alleviate these harms in a direct and material way."

We recognize that national security interests can outweigh the interests of protected speech and require the regulation of speech. In the present case, the record does not resolve whether the exercise of presidential power in furtherance of national security interests should overrule the interests in allowing the free exchange of encryption source code. Before any level of judicial scrutiny can be applied to the Regulations, Junger must be in a position to bring a facial challenge to these regulations. In light of the recent amendments to the Export Administration Regulations, the district court should examine the new regulations to determine if Junger can bring a facial challenge. [Therefore,] we REVERSE the district court and REMAND the case to the district court for consideration of Junger's constitutional challenge to the amended regulations.

Decision. The First Amendment's protection of free speech extends to software and computer code despite the fact that software is a mixture of functional and expressive features.

Case Questions

1. Compare and contrast encryption software with other forms of digital content: e-mail message, spreadsheet program, MP3 music file, video on DVD.
2. Try to reconcile the First Amendment's general policy of encouraging broad dissemination of political speech with the primary purpose of encryption, to prevent comprehension of the contents of communications.

Political Speech

First Amendment protection also extends to political speech by individuals as well as commercial entities. Corporations may validly disseminate ideas and influence political thought. However, the subject of the political speech should be more general. Political speech may not receive full protection if it identifies specific political parties or candidates, or violate the campaign finance laws.

In *First National Bank of Boston v. Bellotti*,[20] a Massachusetts statute prohibited a corporation from making expenditures or contributions for the purpose of influencing the vote on questions submitted to voters unless the questions materially affected the corporation. The statute also prohibited corporate advocacy on legislation involving taxation. Corporate violators could be fined up to $50,000, and the corporate officer who authorized the expenditures could be fined and imprisoned for up to one year. First National Bank of Boston and others desired to publicize their views that a ballot question on a graduated individual income tax was unconstitutional. The court held:

[The First] Amendment protects the free discussion of governmental affairs. . . . The inherent worth of the speech in terms of its capacity for informing the public does not depend upon the identity of its source, whether corporation, association, union, or individual. . . . The press does not have a monopoly on either the First Amendment or the ability to enlighten. . . . The First Amendment goes beyond protection of the press and the self-expression of individuals to prohibit government from limiting the stock of information from which members of the public may draw.

20. 435 U.S. 765 (1978).

Ethical Issue

Litigation Threat Chills Freedom of Speech

The Bill of Rights includes constitutional freedoms most Americans consider sacred, fundamental rights. These rights are the product of political struggles over the several millennia that track the evolution of civilization. However, the First Amendment freedom of speech may appear to conflict with other civil rights and property rights. This problem has arisen in recent years with public participation by individuals and interest groups. They may write editorials, give speeches, organize boycotts, complain to regulators, testify before public bodies, or post derogatory materials to websites. For example, some interest groups have made public attacks on real estate developers, alleging environmental or aesthetic destruction. In other cases, citizens have complained to regulators about a manufacturer's allegedly unsafe products. Dot.sucks websites using URLs that may be confusingly similar to the targeted businesses' URLs are discussed further in Chapter 18.

As a result of these attacks, the targeted business can suffer declining sales, a loss of reputation, or toughened new regulations. Some of these targeted businesses have responded by suing for damages, injunctions against the speech, or blocked access to websites critical of the business. Some of these responses are termed ***SLAPP suits***, an acronym that stands for strategic litigation against public participation. Such suits by either side may sometimes involve an ethical dilemma of constitutional proportions. Either unfair pressure is brought on the targeted business or costly litigation is brought by affluent firms, chilling individuals' the free speech or government participation and thereby frustrating these fundamental constitutional rights.

Some targeted businesses bring SLAPP suits alleging the public participants of one or more torts: defamation (libel, slander), trade disparagement, trademark infringement, misrepresentation or fraud, tortious interference with contract relations, interference with prospective advantage, and/or privacy violations. In many cases, merely bringing the suit intimidates the public participant, effectively silencing them. Some public participants challenge SLAPP suits and can be successful in blunting the SLAPP to vindicate their participation rights. Indeed, in some "SLAPP-back suits," the public participants have won damages for abuse of process or malicious prosecution against the originally targeted business. A few states have passed anti-SLAPP statutes.

Targeted businesses should never be denied judicial access to redress malicious damage by a public participant acting in bad faith. However, public participants should not be intimidated from exercising legitimate First Amendment rights of free speech and petitioning the government for redress of grievances. Vindicating constitutional rights and abusing the political and legal systems pose ethical problems for all involved.

If a legislature may direct business corporations to "stick to business," it may also limit other corporations—religious, charitable, or civic—to their respective "business" when addressing the public. Such power in government to channel the expression of views is unacceptable under the First Amendment. The First Amendment is plainly offended when a statute suppresses speech and thereby gives one side an advantage in any debate. The proliferation of content on corporate websites is another example of political speech that should receive First Amendment protection.

Obscenity

The third classification of communications not protected under the First Amendment is **unprotected speech**. This includes incitement, sedition (advocating violent overthrow of the U.S. government), fraud, defamation, fighting words, words posing a clear and present danger (shouting fire in a crowded place), and obscenity, which is discussed here. Regulation of some of these forms of speech, such as fraud and defamation, are discussed elsewhere in this book.

Many forms of written and visual expression are subject to assessment as pornographic or obscene. Indeed, novels, magazines, movies, and interpretive dance have all been tested under local ordinances or state laws that ban obscenity. The states retain

http://
www.aclu.org/

police powers to protect the health, safety, welfare, and morals of their citizens from the harmful effects of obscenity. Indeed, there is strong sentiment to protect children from pornography. However, there are two major difficulties. First, it is difficult to distinguish genuinely obscene materials from materials that are not obscene. The First Amendment prohibits censorship, a form of prior restraint, unless the materials are obscene. Local laws might not provide law enforcement with sufficient guidance, and the public's definition of obscenity differs, based on many demographics (e.g., religious belief, gender, age, location). Second, society is generally more protective of children and therefore more willing to limit minors' access to pornography.

The Internet upsets the traditional balance between freer adult access to pornography and the controls that society has fairly effectively exercised over children's access to pornography in its traditional forms—restrictions on selling print pornography to minors, movie ratings, and pay-per-view TV controls. These traditional controls are generally ineffective to block children's access to obscene materials on the Internet. Of course, technological solutions are filling some of this gap. For example, the V-chip on TVs, Internet service provider (ISP) filtering for known pornographic sites, and Internet security software (firewalls, virus protection, block lists for known pornography sites) may all enhance parental control capability. Federal telecommunications regulations are validly used to prohibit broadcast of indecent material when children are most likely to be watching (daytime, prime time).[21] Nevertheless, the Internet has reawakened controversy over the definition of obscenity and the effectiveness of controlling children's access to it.

What *is* obscene? A long line of cases, many in the U.S. Supreme Court, have resulted in a localized test that balances the offensiveness of the suspect expression with its social value. Under the formulation of obscenity announced in *Miller v. California*,[22] the trier of fact in a criminal prosecution may determine whether the expression is obscene using the three factors in Exhibit 4.2.

EXHIBIT 4.2 *Miller* Test of Obscenity

Basic Obscenity Guidelines for the Trier of Fact

1. The average person applying *contemporary community standards* would find that the work, taken as a whole, *appeals to prurient interest*.
2. The work depicts or describes, in a *patently offensive* way, sexual conduct specifically defined under state law,
3. The work, taken as a whole, *lacks serious literary, artistic, political, or scientific value*.

21. *Sable Communications of California v. FCC*, 492 U.S. 115 (1989).
22. 413 U.S. 14 (1973).

The definition of the terms in this three-part test is the subject of additional court interpretation. **Prurient interest** requires a "tendency to excite lustful thoughts" and can be expanded to include "a shameful or morbid interest in nudity, sex, or excretion." *Patently offensive* probably defines "hard core" pornography that exhibits ultimate sexual acts, normal or perverted, actual or simulated, including masturbation, excretory functions, and lewd exhibition of the genitals. The suspect expression must also **lack serious literary, artistic, political, or scientific value.** This objective test requires the use of the mythical reasonable person and not the impression of a single juror. Testimony of experts and local community members may be relevant on this point. The local standards of the *Miller* test can be met once a community's contemporary definitions of *patently offensive* and *prurient interest* are understood. For example, Larry Flint's *Hustler* magazine is still banned from Hamilton County, Ohio (Cincinnati). Local TV affiliates sometimes refuse to carry broadcasts believed to be obscene under local standards. However, such local standards seem impossible to apply when the suspect expression is available nearly anywhere from the Internet.

The U.S. Congress responded to mounting political pressure to control Internet pornography with the Communications Decency Act (CDA), passed as part of the Telecommunications Act of 1996. The CDA made it a federal crime to knowingly transport obscene material for sale or distribution through an interactive computer

Ethical Issue

Jurisdiction: Obscenity Defined under Local Community Standards

Physical distribution resulting in the sale of magazines, books, tapes, or posters is different than electronic delivery over the Internet. Local merchants can know local obscenity law and can then make an informed estimate as to whether the particular expression they might want to stock and sell is obscene under local community standards. It is possible to manage the risks of an obscenity conviction when the seller of a suspect expression resides in that community. By contrast, the Internet is available everywhere, and sellers of expression or providers of free content cannot easily estimate whether a particular suspect expression would be obscene under all the different local community standards that vary according to the local demographics and culture. Internet sites risk obscenity liability by simply posting an expression that may be illegal under stricter interpretations of obscenity in some communities.

Consider the example in a famous Internet jurisdiction case.[23] Robert and Carleen Thomas operated a bulletin board, e-mail, and chat sites from their home in Orange County, California. Sexually explicit magazine photographs were scanned and posted as .gif files capable of being downloaded and displayed anywhere in the world. A U.S. postal inspector in Tennessee downloaded materials from the Thomas site and then placed an order for videotapes that were likely to be considered obscene under local community standards in Tennessee. The Thomases were tried and convicted of criminal obscenity under federal law, using Tennessee's local community standards. In upholding the Thomases' conviction, the Court of Appeals recognized that the jurisdictional reach of another state's local community standards "may result in prosecutions of persons in a community to which they have sent materials which are obscene under that community's standards though the community from which it is sent would tolerate the same material." This decision permitting jurisdiction in a faraway place with potentially different local community standards forces website operators to censor their content, refuse passwords to persons from certain other places, and/or find technological solutions to block access from other communities, states, or nations with laws forbidding the availability of such content. There have been similar difficulties for Internet service providers (ISPs) like AOL and Yahoo!, as some foreign nations exert other forms of content regulation. For example, there are laws prohibiting the display or sale of Nazi memorabilia in France and Germany. These nations have pressured some ISPs into either deleting material or filtering requests so that such content is not downloaded into those nations.

23. *U.S. v. Thomas*, 74 F.3d 701 (6th Cir.) *cert. denied* 117 S.Ct. 74 (1996).

service, with fines up to $100,000 and imprisonment up to five years for the first offense and ten years for subsequent offenses. The CDA covers expressive "matter" including magazines, books, pictures, paper, film, video and audio recordings. The CDA also prohibits on-line communications, involving comments, requests, suggestions, proposals, images, or other communications, that are obscene, lewd, lascivious, filthy, or indecent if intended to annoy, abuse, threaten, or harass another person. It is a separate crime to transmit such material to a minor under 18 years old. The CDA has created major comfort for ISPs, with various defenses against secondary, contributory, or republisher liability for merely carrying the communication containing prohibited obscenities. Key terms in the CDA are not well defined, particularly the term **indecent**. Although the prohibitions against transmitting obscene materials to minors is still valid, the following case invalidated some CDA provisions.

Reno v. ACLU

521 U.S. 844 (1997)

Facts. The Communications Decency Act (CDA) makes it criminal to transmit or display indecent, patently offensive, or obscene material through computerized communications if the recipient is a known minor. After passage of the CDA, the American Civil Liberties Union (ACLU) and many others immediately challenged §§223(a) & (d) as invalid under the First Amendment as a prior restraint on protected speech because the terms *indecent* and *patently offensive* were vague. Congress anticipated the challenge, so the CDA included "severability" provisions that attempt to allow other provisions of the act to survive the challenge if some provisions were invalidated.

Legal Issue. Are §§223(a) & (d) of the CDA so vague that they violate the First Amendment, casting a chilling prior restraint on Internet communication?

Opinion. Justice Stevens. The many ambiguities concerning the scope of [the CDA's] coverage render it problematic for purposes of the First Amendment. For instance, each of the two parts of the CDA uses a different linguistic form. The first uses the word "indecent," while the second speaks of material that "in context, depicts or describes, in terms patently offensive as measured by contemporary community standards, sexual or excretory activities or organs," §223(d). Given the absence of a definition of either term, this difference in language will provoke uncertainty among speakers about how the two standards relate to each other and just what they mean. Could a speaker confidently assume that a serious discussion about birth control practices, homosexuality, or the consequences of prison rape would not violate the CDA? This uncertainty undermines the likelihood that the CDA has been carefully tailored to the congressional goal of protecting minors from potentially harmful materials.

The vagueness of the CDA is a matter of special concern for two reasons. First, the CDA is a content-based regulation of speech. The vagueness of such a regulation raises special First Amendment concerns because of its obvious chilling effect on free speech. Second, the CDA is a criminal statute. In addition to the opprobrium and stigma of a criminal conviction, the CDA threatens violators with penalties including up to two years in prison for each act of violation. The severity of criminal sanctions may well cause speakers to remain silent rather than communicate even arguably unlawful words, ideas, and images.

The second prong of the *Miller* test contains a critical requirement that is omitted from the CDA: that the proscribed material be "specifically defined by the applicable state law." This requirement reduces the vagueness inherent in the open-ended term "patently offensive" as used in the CDA. Moreover, the *Miller* definition is limited to "sexual conduct," whereas the CDA extends also to include (1) "excretory activities" as well as (2) "organs" of both a sexual and excretory nature.

We are persuaded that the CDA lacks the precision that the First Amendment requires when a statute regulates the content of speech. In order to deny minors access to potentially harmful speech, the CDA effectively suppresses a large amount of speech that adults have a constitutional right to receive and to address to one another. That burden on adult speech is unacceptable if less restrictive alternatives would be at least as effective in achieving the legitimate purpose that the statute was enacted to serve. In evaluating the free speech rights of adults, we have made it perfectly clear that "[s]exual expression which is indecent but not obscene is protected by the First Amendment." It is true that we have repeatedly recognized the governmental interest in protecting children from harmful materials. But that interest does not justify an unnecessarily broad suppression of speech addressed to adults. As we have explained, the Government may not "reduc[e] the adult population . . . to . . . only what is fit for children." "[R]egardless of the strength of the government's interest" in protecting children, "[t]he level of discourse reaching a mailbox simply cannot be limited to that which would be suitable for a sandbox."

The District Court found that at the time of trial existing technology did not include any effective method for a sender to prevent minors from obtaining access to its communications on the Internet without also denying access to adults. The Court found no effective way to determine the age of a user who is accessing material through e-mail, mail exploders, newsgroups, or chat rooms. As a practical matter, the Court also found that it would be prohibitively expensive for noncommercial—as well as some commercial—speakers who have Web sites to verify that their users are adults. These limitations must inevitably curtail a significant amount of adult communication on the Internet. By contrast, the District Court found that "[d]espite its limitations, currently available user-based software suggests that a reasonably effective method by which parents can prevent their children from accessing sexually explicit and other material which parents may believe is inappropriate for their children will soon be widely available."

We agree with the District Court's conclusion that the CDA places an unacceptably heavy burden on protected speech, and that the defenses do not constitute the sort of "narrow tailoring" that will save an otherwise patently invalid unconstitutional provision. In *Sable*, we remarked that the speech restriction at issue there amounted to "'burn[ing] the house to roast the pig.'" The CDA, casting a far darker shadow over free speech, threatens to torch a large segment of the Internet community.

Decision. Prohibition against "indecent" content on websites found in the Communications Decency Act is unconstitutionally vague.

Case Questions

1. How could Congress have made the CDA less susceptible to invalidation under the First Amendment?
2. Describe the chilling effect on permissible speech that the CDA provisions in question would have had.

THE FOURTH AMENDMENT

Of all the constitutional provisions discussed, the Fourth Amendment provides business with the greatest protection from unfair governmental investigations. Typically, the Fourth Amendment protection arises before a criminal defendant is indicted or before a civil administrative case is filed. The Fourth Amendment protects both natural persons and corporations from unreasonable searches and seizures.

Fourth Amendment: Unreasonable Searches and Seizures

The right of the people to be secure in their persons, papers, and effects, against unreasonable searches and seizures, shall not be violated, and no Warrants shall issue, but on probable cause, supported by Oath or affirmation, and particularly describing the place to be searched and the persons or things to be seized.

The Fourth Amendment is a major constitutional source of privacy. The constitutional basis for privacy is detailed in Chapter 14.

THE FIFTH AND FOURTEENTH AMENDMENTS

The Fifth and Fourteenth Amendments contain two major provisions to maintain fundamental fairness: the due process and equal protection clauses. The Fifth Amendment applies these protections to actions taken by the federal government.

Fifth Amendment: Due Process Clause

No person shall be . . . deprived of life, liberty, or property, without due process of law.

The Fourteenth Amendment applies the Fifth Amendment to the states under the **absorption** or **incorporation** doctrine. This doctrine assures that the fundamental protections of most constitutional rights also apply to the actions of state government.

> **Fourteenth Amendment: Due Process and Equal Protection Clauses**
> . . . nor shall any State deprive any person of life, liberty, or property, without due process of law; nor deny to any person within its jurisdiction the equal protection of the laws.

The Fifth Amendment also includes the well-known right against self-incrimination. This is a fundamental constitutional right to privacy that is discussed more completely in Chapter 14.

Equal Protection of the Laws

The need for equality under the law after the abolition of slavery demanded a definitive constitutional statement. The equal protection clause of the Fourteenth Amendment was originally intended to provide blacks with protection from arbitrary legislative distinctions. Today, that clause applies to all types of arbitrary and unreasonable classifications in legislation and to all ethnic and demographic groups. By its very nature, legislation necessarily selects which persons or entities are subject to the law, based on such classifications as conduct, size of business, or level of income. However, establishing fair classifications of this kind is difficult, requiring careful statutory design. For example, only murderers should receive punishment under criminal statutes prohibiting murder. Similarly, the Uniform Commercial Code imposes special obligations on merchants; it requires a higher level of conduct in commercial transactions from merchants than from nonmerchants. These classifications are fair only when they adequately discriminate.

Legislative classifications with no reasonable purpose are unconstitutional under the equal protection clause. There are three tests of equal protection, and each is progressively stricter in its standards for valid legislation. Under the least restrictive approach, the rational basis test, laws should have general applicability unless there is sufficient reason to discriminate against certain people. This test applies in many situations, but it seldom invalidates legislation. Another test, the strict scrutiny test, applies in situations involving discrimination against protected classes of persons or discrimination in matters of fundamental rights. When strict scrutiny applies, many statutes are held unconstitutional. Quasi-strict scrutiny is an intermediate test that is important in some business contexts.

Equal protection issues arise most often in cases of racial segregation. Equal protection has required reapportionment of state legislatures under the principle of "one person, one vote," as when two nearby congressional districts in a state have grossly unequal numbers of citizens. The courts have ruled military regulations as unconstitutional that afford spouses of servicewomen lesser benefits than the spouses of servicemen. The denial of voting rights in school district elections to nonparents or nonowners of property was found unconstitutional under strict scrutiny.

Rational Basis. The equal protection clause does not disturb the constitutionality of a statute if there is a rational connection between the statute's classification scheme and a permissible governmental purpose. Under this **rational basis** test, the statute is first presumed constitutional. Government may regulate in areas that are normally and legitimately the role of government. For example, Congress may pass laws pursuant to an enumerated power, such as the regulation of interstate commerce. State legislatures may pass criminal laws implementing the police power. Any classifications used in statutes enacted for such purposes must have a reasonable basis and not be arbitrary.

In *Minnesota v. Clover Leaf Creamery Co.*,[24] the Supreme Court found that a Minnesota statute provided adequate equal protection even though it prohibited only plastic disposable packaging for milk. The statute sought to diminish the solid waste problem and save energy by banning nonreturnable plastic milk containers, yet it permitted the use of nonreturnable plastic containers for other products. The rational basis test, which was used here, invalidates only the most outrageously arbitrary classification schemes. This case permits states to implement a regulatory program in steps, eliminating evils only partially at first and deferring complete elimination to future regulations.

Strict Scrutiny. In more recent years, courts have used the **strict scrutiny** test to invalidate legislation that violates certain fundamental rights or discriminates against suspect classes. When the rigorous criteria of the strict scrutiny test are applied, legislation is seldom acceptable if any conceivable alternative could achieve the same legitimate regulatory end. Under strict scrutiny, the suspect legislation must be necessary and the only means to achieve a compelling governmental interest. To survive a strict scrutiny attack, a statute must relate to the governmental interest more closely than is required under the rational basis test, and the governmental purpose must be more important. There must be clear legislative intent to reach the legitimate governmental goal.

Strict scrutiny applies only to fundamental rights and to discrimination against suspect or protected classes. **Fundamental rights** include voting rights, interstate travel, immunity from mandatory sterility, and criminal procedural protections. **Suspect classes** are demographic classifications of people who deserve greater protection because they have been subjected to intentional discrimination. Suspect classes include classifications based on race, national origin, and alien status. Employment discrimination is more directly governed by the antidiscrimination laws discussed in Chapter 21.

Quasi-Strict Scrutiny. A third classification, **quasi-strict scrutiny**, has arisen in recent years. It falls between the rational basis and the strict scrutiny tests. This standard applies where the rights involved are clearly important but are not quite considered fundamental rights, or where the classifications in the statute are only partially suspect. For example, classifications based on gender or legitimacy must be substantially related to an important government objective under this middle-ground test. The quasi-strict scrutiny test validates some classifications while invalidating others. Clearly, every equal protection inquiry is quite fact-specific.

Due Process of Law

The due process clause is intended to prevent unfair and predetermined outcomes at criminal trials like those in colonial times held before English judges. Due process requires that governments observe at least a minimum level of fairness in trial pro-

24. 449 U.S. 456 (1981).

cedures. This fairness doctrine prohibits arbitrary, biased, and unreasonable outcomes in trials and administrative hearings. The due process clause applies to a wide variety of criminal, civil, and administrative hearings. Certain private determinations by nongovernmental entities are also subject to some form of due process. However, due process rights are not identical in all cases. Criminal defendants usually receive more specific and extensive protections than do the parties in civil trials or administrative hearings.

Due process prohibits government from depriving any person of **life, liberty, or property** without due process of law. A person in this context is broadly construed to include both natural persons and artificial persons, such as corporations or unincorporated associations. A **deprivation of life** usually denotes capital punishment and also arises in right to die or euthanasia cases. A **deprivation of liberty** occurs when one is denied the ability to move freely in public areas—that is, while not trespassing on private property. A **deprivation of property** occurs when a person must pay a fine or money damages or when property is taken by government. Be aware that due process actually *permits* government to deprive one of life, liberty, or property, *but only if* due process is followed.

Due process has developed into two separate limits on unreasonable governmental action. **Procedural due process** incorporates the traditional issues regarding the processes of investigation, arrest, detainment, trial, and appeal. **Substantive due process** involves issues concerning the fairness of legislation in the way it defines rights and duties. These due process issues arise whenever government attempts to vindicate rights, whether those attempts are prosecuted by government attorneys, initiated in court or administrative agencies, or conducted by private entities affected with a public character (e.g., private universities). To successfully claim a due process right, some form of **state action** or governmental process must be involved because constitutional rights provide protection only from oppressive governmental actions, not oppressive private acts. There is no constitutional protection from an individual's actions unless the individual is acting under the color of government. For example, a basketball coach suffered no due process violation when the National Collegiate Athletic Association (NCAA) required the university to punish its coach for alleged NCAA rule violations. The NCAA is a private organization, so there was no state action involved, even though the state university implemented the NCAA's order.[25]

Procedural Due Process. Two basic rights in litigation involve due process protections. The first right is intended to assure defendants a fair opportunity to offer a defense and the use of fair trial procedures. In some cases, a notice of suit, a **service of summons**, must be personally delivered to the defendant. **Substituted service** of process is a valid alternative if it is impossible to deliver the notice directly.

The second stage where basic due process rights exist is in litigation and the conduct of trials. The precise fair trial procedures vary according to the rights adjudicated, the type of trial, and the severity of the penalties. The trial procedures should afford the utmost protection to a criminal defendant charged with a capital crime. At the other extreme, a college disciplinary proceeding can provide sufficient due process even without many of the procedural technicalities of a criminal trial. The Fifth, Sixth, and Seventh Amendments also require several fair trial procedures. These procedural rights are detailed in Chapters 7 and 14, where criminal procedure

25. *National Collegiate Athletic Ass'n v. Tarkanian*, 488 U.S. 179 (1988).

and privacy are discussed. Of particular note is a discussion of the **USA Patriot Act.** This antiterrorist law passed following the September 11, 2001, terrorist attacks. The new law may significantly diminish the rights of suspected terrorists.

Is a full trial by jury necessary to review a university's dismissal of a student for poor scholarship? Informal administrative processes need not include the full spectrum of evidentiary rules to provide minimum due process. In *Board of Curators of the University of Missouri v. Horowitz,*[26] Horowitz was dismissed from the university's medical school for failure to meet academic standards. She had been fully informed of the faculty's dissatisfaction with her progress and the adverse impact on her timely graduation. The ultimate dismissal decision was deliberate and careful. Horowitz sued the university, claiming a lack of due process in the dismissal process. The Supreme Court compared academic dismissal to disciplinary proceedings, reserving the broader due process procedural steps like notice and opportunity to present evidence for only disciplinary proceedings. Justice Rehnquist said that:

The decision to dismiss respondent rested on the academic judgment of school officials that she did not have the necessary clinical ability to perform adequately as a medical doctor and was making insufficient progress toward that goal. Such a judgment is by its nature more subjective and evaluative than the typical factual questions presented in the average disciplinary decision. Like the decision of an individual professor as to the proper grade for a student in his course, the determination whether to dismiss a student for academic reasons requires an expert evaluation of cumulative information and is not readily adapted to the procedural tools of judicial or administrative decision making.

The tort and product liability system has evolved to permit significant awards of damages beyond those needed solely to compensate the plaintiff. In the more egregious product liability, malpractice, and negligence cases, the jury (or sometimes the judge) has ordered a further component of damages, called punitive damages, amounts in addition to the compensatory portion of the damage amount. Unlike compensatory damages, which simply reimburse the victim, punitive damages are a form of punishment, justified as a heightened incentive that deters harmful behavior or carelessness. However, many critics argue that recent history in product liability cases shows punitive damages may be unfair and violate both due process and the Eighth Amendment prohibition against excessive fines. Several states have specified limitations on punitive damages, and some recent cases now require controls on juries ordering punitive damages. This topic is discussed in more detail as a form of tort reform in Chapters 7 and 8.

Substantive Due Process. The substantive due process doctrine allows a court to declare a statute unconstitutional if the statute fails to provide due process. In the late nineteenth and early twentieth centuries, the **economic due process** doctrine was applied to invalidate early regulatory statutes that required minimum wages or maximum working hours or that allowed union membership. Many such statutes were unconstitutional because they unjustifiably restricted the freedom of business to contract or they deprived business of its property without due process. Today, this economic substantive due process is inapplicable.

In the area of personal liberty and rights, the substantive due process doctrine retains some validity. It requires that legislation meet two tests. The first test is an

26. 435 U.S. 78 (1978).

ends-means test similar to that in equal protection cases. This test requires that legislation be directed toward a legitimate governmental purpose and that the means used be closely connected to that purpose. Second, the test prohibits vague legislation. A statute is unconstitutional if it does not provide ascertainable criteria for the identification of unlawful conduct. For example, a law enforcement officer cannot arrest someone based on the officer's interpretation of what constitutes wrongdoing. Laws permitting this level of discretion are vague. In *Coates v. City of Cincinnati*,[27] the city passed a criminal ordinance prohibiting "three or more persons to assemble . . . on any of the sidewalks . . . and there conduct themselves in a manner *annoying* to persons passing by . . ." (emphasis added). On the basis of this ordinance, the Cincinnati authorities prosecuted Coates for participating in a student demonstration. The ordinance violated due process because it subjected Coates's constitutional right of assembly to an imprecise standard, the term "annoying conduct." Conduct that some people find "annoying" does not annoy others, so people of common intelligence must necessarily guess at the word's meaning. Substantive due process also protects business from prosecution under vague laws.

THE ELEVENTH AMENDMENT

Much in the original U.S. Constitution concerns federalism—the proper balance between power given to the central government versus powers distributed to state and local governments. Federalism is also the issue at the heart of several amendments. For example, the Second Amendment authorizes state or local militias. The Ninth Amendment reserves rights to the people even if such rights are not enumerated in the Constitution. The Tenth Amendment reserves powers not delegated to the federal government to the people or to the states. The Twelfth, Fifteenth, Seventeenth, Nineteenth, Twenty-Fourth, and Twenty-Sixth Amendments prohibit states from restricting election matters. The Thirteenth, Fourteenth, and Fifteenth amendments prohibit states from tolerating slavery.

Since the 1980s, the U.S. Supreme Court has shifted firmly to support states' rights. Among the tools used in this shift is the Eleventh Amendment, a relatively inactive provision that has been reawakened with significant impact on e-commerce and a particular impact on IP. The Eleventh Amendment prohibits jurisdiction in the federal courts for many types of suits against the states.

The Eleventh Amendment

The Judicial power of the United States shall not be construed to extend to any suit in law or equity, commenced or prosecuted against one of the United States by Citizens or another State, or by Citizens or Subjects of any Foreign State.

The Eleventh Amendment stands alongside common law precedents as the strongest sources of sovereign immunity for the states. **Sovereign immunity** is a government's immunity from suit, based on the outmoded old English notion that the "king can do no wrong." Since the 1940s, many states, as well as the federal government, have relaxed or partially waived their sovereign immunity, thereby subjecting themselves to civil liability on some matters. For example, most states have opened themselves to civil tort liability for various types of physical injury,

27. 402 U.S. 611 (1971).

such as those resulting from defective conditions on state owned and operated roads.

The **abrogation of state sovereign immunity** may also be accomplished by Congress. However, under recent Supreme Court decisions, this is not easily done, so one of three avenues is open to enforce federally created rights against the states. First, suits may be brought against state officers who violate federal law,[28] such as a state university employee who reproduces copyrighted expression either without permission or outside an exemption such as fair use. These suits are against the officer and not against the state itself. However, the copyright owner can be awarded only prospective relief, such as an injunction against future infringement. There could be no damage suit for past infringement under this theory. Second, states may validly waive their Eleventh Amendment sovereign immunity. Some IP strategists suggest that Congress should amend the IP laws to withhold from states the right to enforce the states' own IP rights in copyrights or patents unless each state specifically waives its sovereign immunity for IP infringement suits brought against the state. The third method is for Congress to abrogate the states' Eleventh Amendment sovereign immunity. Under this method, Congress would enact legislation that subjects the states to jurisdiction for infringement in the federal courts. Although Congress did this several times prior to 1996, a recent series of IP abrogation cases has thrown this third method into question, as illustrated in the following case.

College Sav. Bank v. Florida Prepaid Postsecondary Educ. Expense Bd.

119 S.Ct. 2219 (1999)

Facts. The College Savings Bank sold deposit contracts (CDs) for funding college education. The bank brought suit against a Florida state agency that used a similar tuition repayment program, alleging unfair competition under the federal trademark law, the Lanham Act, based on the board's alleged false advertising. An individual may sue a state if Congress has authorized such a suit in the exercise of its power to enforce the Fourteenth Amendment or if a state has waived its sovereign immunity by consenting to suit. The Trademark Remedy Clarification Act (TRCA) sought to subject states to suits brought under the Lanham Act for false and misleading advertising.

Legal Issue. Can states be made subject to federal trademark liability under TRCA, despite the sovereign immunity granted in the Eleventh Amendment?

Opinion. Justice Scalia. Though its precise terms bar only federal jurisdiction over suits brought against one State by citizens of another State or foreign state, we have long recognized that the Eleventh Amendment accomplished much more: It repudiated the [assumption that] the jurisdictional heads of Article III [of the Constitution] superseded the sovereign immunity that the States possessed before entering the Union. This has been our understanding of the Amendment since the landmark case of *Hans v. Louisiana*. While this immunity from suit is not absolute, we have recognized only two circumstances in which an individual may sue a State. First, Congress may authorize such a suit in the exercise of its power to enforce the Fourteenth Amendment—an Amendment enacted after the Eleventh Amendment and specifically designed to alter the federal-state balance. Second, a State may waive its sovereign immunity by consenting to suit.

This case turns on whether either of these two circumstances is present. Our decision three Terms ago in *Seminole Tribe*, held that the power "to regulate Commerce" con-

28. See *Ex Parte Young*, 209 U.S. 123 (1908).

ferred by Article I of the Constitution gives Congress no authority to abrogate state sovereign immunity. As authority for the abrogation in the present case, petitioner relies upon §5 of the Fourteenth Amendment, which we held in *Fitzpatrick v. Bitzer*, and reaffirmed in *Seminole Tribe*, could be used for that purpose. Section 1 of the Fourteenth Amendment provides that no State shall "deprive any person of . . . property . . . without due process of law." Section 5 provides that "[t]he Congress shall have power to enforce, by appropriate legislation, the provisions of this article." We made clear in *City of Boerne v. Flores*, that the term "enforce" is to be taken seriously—that the object of valid §5 legislation must be the carefully delimited remediation or prevention of constitutional violations. Petitioner claims that, with respect to §43(a) of the Lanham Act, Congress enacted the TRCA to remedy and prevent state deprivations without due process of two species of "property" rights: (1) a right to be free from a business competitor's false advertising about its own product, and (2) a more generalized right to be secure in one's business interests. Neither of these qualifies as a property right protected by the Due Process Clause.

We have long recognized that a State's sovereign immunity is "a personal privilege which it may waive at pleasure." The decision to waive that immunity, however, "is altogether voluntary on the part of the sovereignty." Accordingly, our "test for determining whether a State has waived its immunity from federal-court jurisdiction is a stringent one." Generally, we will find a waiver either if the State voluntarily invokes our jurisdiction, or else if the State makes a "clear declaration" that it intends to submit itself to our jurisdiction. Thus, a State does not consent to suit in federal court merely by consenting to suit in the courts of its own creation. Nor does it consent to suit in federal court merely by stating its intention to "sue and be sued," or even by authorizing suits against it " 'in any court of competent jurisdiction.' "

Concluding, for the foregoing reasons, that the sovereign immunity of the State of Florida was neither validly abrogated by the Trademark Remedy Clarification Act, nor voluntarily waived by the State's activities in interstate commerce, we hold that the federal courts are without jurisdiction to entertain this suit against an arm of the State of Florida.

Decision. The states are immune from suit by private parties based on the infringement of federally created intellectual property rights.

Case Questions

1. If the abrogation difficulties described in this case apply to all forms of federal IP rights, what could this case mean for copyright and patent owners?
2. Does the Supreme Court indicate how Congress might impose the obligation on states to avoid infringing IP rights?

QUESTIONS

1. What is meant by judicial review? Does it give the Supreme Court the final word on what the law and the Constitution mean?
2. Is there any limit to the ability of Congress to regulate intrastate activity under the commerce clause? Consider the case of an Ohio farmer, Filburn, who was fined $117.11 for exceeding his 1941 acreage allotment for wheat under the Agricultural Adjustment Act of 1938. Filburn was allotted 11.1 acres for this purpose, but he sowed and harvested 23 acres. He sold some of his wheat but used most of it as food for his family and as feed for his cattle. Filburn sued for an injunction against the enforcement of the fine. He argued that his activity had been completely intrastate and that Congress could not regulate it under the commerce clause. How should the Supreme Court decide the case? Why? *Wickard v. Filburn*, 317 U.S. 111 (1942).
3. An Arkansas statute requires that all rental cars picked up within the state be equipped with cell phones and a global positioning system (GPS) so that rental car companies can track their fleet's whereabouts. A federal statute requires that all automobiles sold in interstate commerce be equipped with a new mechanism that detects and warns drivers of dangerously low tire inflation. Both statutes have been passed for the purpose of safety. Are both statutes enforceable? Why or why not?
4. Harry Homeowner resides within the city of Lake City, which the state recently granted a huge sum to erect a civic center. To build this civic center as

planned, Lake City condemned the property and residence owned by Harry Homeowner, mailed Harry a check for an amount equal to 25% of the appraised value, and ordered Harry and his family to leave the premises with all of their belongings within two weeks. Lake City conducted no hearing concerning this matter. What constitutional issues are raised?

5. The city of Atlanta passes an ordinance banning the sale of all toys with toxic paint and sharp edges. The effect of this ordinance is to ban the sale of foreign toys, which amount to 70% of the toys sold in the Atlanta area. The Atlanta ordinance is much stricter than the federal statutes governing toy safety. Answer the following questions:
   a. Where does the city of Atlanta get the power to ban hazardous toys?
   b. Is a problem presented by the fact that the Atlanta ordinance is more stringent than the federal statutes?
   c. Does the city of Atlanta have the power to regulate the sale of foreign toys?
6. New Hampshire enacted a commuters' income tax that taxed the New Hampshire–derived income of nonresidents. New Hampshire did not tax the income of New Hampshire residents. Residents living in adjoining parts of Maine and from New Hampshire challenged the validity of the tax. The case was transferred directly to the New Hampshire Supreme Court, which upheld the statute. The case was then heard by the U.S. Supreme Court on appeal. What was the result and why?
7. Under an Alabama state divorce law, a wife may recover alimony from her husband if cause is shown. When Mr. and Mrs. Orr filed for a divorce, Mr. Orr claimed alimony from his wife and was denied it under the state statute. He appealed, claiming that the statute denying alimony to husbands was unconstitutional. On what grounds is his claim based? What was the result, and why? See *Orr v. Orr*, 440 U.S. 268 (1980).
8. The plaintiffs, consumers of prescription drugs, claimed that they would benefit from the advertising of prescription drugs. They brought a suit against the Virginia State Board of Pharmacy to challenge the constitutionality of a Virginia statute declaring it unprofessional conduct for a licensed pharmacist to advertise the price of prescription drugs. The board had the power to revoke a license or to impose a fine for violation of the statute. As a result of the statute, all advertising of the price of prescription drugs was effectively forbidden. The Citizens Consumer Council sued the Virginia State Board of Pharmacy. On what grounds would its lawsuit be brought, with what result, and why? See *Virginia State Board of Pharmacy v. Virginia Citizens Consumer Council*, 425 U.S. 748 (1976).
9. What role has the conflict over centralized or local government played in the development of American constitutional law? How can the U.S. Constitution remain relevant to technological, social, and economic developments of the Internet?

CHAPTER 5

International Business Law

CONDUCTING INTERNATIONAL BUSINESS

Every day, the number of international business activities increases. WIPO—the World Intellectual Property Organization—is responsible for wiping out hundreds of domain name disputes for Web users across the globe. Two U.S.-based firms, General Electric and Honeywell, find their proposed merger is vetoed—not by U.S. antitrust authorities, but by the European Union. New investment and tax laws make Ireland and India attractive locations for foreign investments by technology-based firms. Global firms doing business in Europe carefully review their privacy protection policies to see if they comply with the personal data protection directive from the European Union.

INTRODUCTION

Although international trade has existed for thousands of years, the accelerating globalization of business activities and the worldwide accessibility of the Internet are creating greater interest in international business law. As firms trade and make investments in countries and regions far from their origins, they need more knowledge about the laws and legal environment in other parts of the world. Although national laws continue to be at the heart of the regulation of business, today a combination of national, regional, and international laws affect global business.

Significant legal changes, many of which deal with e-commerce concerns, are occurring at the national level. In addition, as global business has become so important to nations and businesses, national laws and regulations are increasingly being harmonized with those of other countries. Regional organizations such as the European Union (EU), the Association of South East Asian Nations (ASEAN), and the Southern Common Market (MERCOSUR) are emerging as important sources of law. In addition to the protection of personal data, recent directives from the European Commission (the executive arm of the EU) concern electronic copyrights, e-commerce contracts and liability issues, and Internet jurisdictional standards for civil and commercial matters. International organizations such as the World Trade

Organization (WTO) and the International Chamber of Commerce (ICC) play important roles in promoting reforms in international business law.

Although this chapter focuses on "international" business, it is also concerned with the legal environment for "global" business. This book and many others use the terms *international* and *global* interchangeably, but sometimes the two terms have distinct meanings. For example, an international investment fund differs from a global investment fund because the international investment fund makes investments only outside the country where the fund is listed, whereas a global fund invests both inside and outside its home country. From a legal perspective, international law concerns the law among nations (inter-national), and the global legal environment involves the laws, institutions, and legal processes that affect private firms doing business globally.

This text uses the term **international business law** to examine the international, regional, and national laws affecting international business transactions. The two major methods of conducting international business are international trade and international investment. **International trade** occurs when goods or services produced in one country are purchased by firms or individuals located outside the country of origin. **International investment** occurs when individuals or firms purchase a significant interest in foreign firms or start business operations there.

INTERNATIONAL TRADE

International trade, which involves exports and imports, is the most common and least complex method of conducting international business. **Exports** are goods sold outside the country where they are produced. When foreign goods or services enter into the commerce of a country, they are regarded as **imports**. Thus, when a Chinese firm (the exporter) sells toys to a U.S. firm (the importer), the toys are a Chinese export and a U.S. import.

Although the developed countries account for the majority of world trade, the rate of growth of world trade for developing countries is increasing. Developing countries now account for almost 28% of world exports. The United States is the world's largest trading country. Its total trade in goods and services, which reached the $500 billion level at the beginning of the 1990s, doubled to $1 trillion by the year 2000.

The U.S. balance of trade, which compares total exports to total imports, continues to be a deficit (greater imports than exports). Although the United States maintains a trade surplus in the services it exports and imports, the large volume of goods it imports has raised the overall trade balance to a $260 billion deficit. The United States and Canada are the world's largest trading partners. Approximately $400 billion was traded between these two countries in 2000. Other important U.S. trading partners are Mexico, Japan, China, and Germany.

INTERNATIONAL INVESTMENT

Although international trade is generally more visible, international investment has reached significant levels in many countries. If an investment by a foreign firm gives that firm at least a 10% ownership of a local firm, the investment is known as a **foreign direct investment**. An investment that results in the purchaser's owning less than 10% of the local firm is known as a **foreign portfolio investment**.

Firms doing international business are most concerned with the legal environment for foreign direct investment. As such investments generally bring human and physical as well as financial resources, many countries have designed their laws to attract foreign direct investments. In Ireland, the tax laws are very attractive, and there is a well-educated work force; the many young people with engineering skills and the more open environment for foreign firms in India are making it a more desirable investment location.

SOURCES OF INTERNATIONAL LAW

International law comes from at least four major sources. Most scholars consider **international law** as coming from national laws, treaties, generally accepted practices, and regional and international organizations. **National laws**, such as those on foreign direct investment, are the most important source. **Treaties** are agreements among different countries. They may be bilateral, such as between two countries that seek to minimize conflicts in their income tax laws, or global, such as the Law of the Sea Convention that many countries have signed. **Generally accepted practices** are those customs and practices that over time have been accepted by most nations of the world. Such practices have been recognized by courts and other legal institutions in many different countries. Some of the customs regarding the determination of a country's borders are based in generally accepted practices. **Regional organizations**, such as the European Union, and **international organizations**, such as the World Trade Organization, are playing an increasing role in shaping the international environment for business activities.

Firms doing business internationally face several challenges in adapting to their legal environment. In addition to dealing with laws from many different sources, such firms find that national laws are often based on social, political, and economic values that differ from those prevalent in their home countries.

In the Middle East and in other countries such as Pakistan and Indonesia, businesses must be cognizant of the influences of Islam on the legal system. Moreover, the role of law and even the type of legal system in other countries often are not the same as those found in the domestic legal environment. For example, foreign firms may have difficulty competing in Japan because some regulations either are not in writing or are written in general terms with interpretations known only to local firms.

NATIONAL LAWS AND LEGAL SYSTEMS

The national law of the country in which a firm is doing business usually has a greater impact on the firm's activities than does any other source of law. As noted in Chapter 2, most national laws can be classified as belonging to one of the major legal systems—the civil law, common law, or Islamic law (see Exhibit 5.1).

Although Chapter 2 details the significant differences among the world's major legal systems, they are also briefly noted here. Approximately half of the countries in

EXHIBIT 5.1 Major National Legal Systems

1. Civil law or code law system, as in France
2. Common law legal system, as in the United States
3. Islamic legal system, as in Pakistan

the world, including most European and South American countries, use a **civil law legal system**. The primary source of law in a civil law legal system is a legislative code. The comprehensive code systematically details the important legal principles that govern commercial and individual activity within the territory where it is controlling.

Approximately a fourth of countries use a **common law legal system**. This system, which is the basis of U.S. law, is found mainly in countries that were influenced by British law. In countries with a common law legal system, there is no systemized code. Instead, both court decisions and legislative acts are important sources of law. Common law courts not only interpret legislative laws but also rely on the precedent of prior court cases, through the concept of stare decisis.

In an Islamic legal system, the source of the law is the Qur'an and the Shari'a. The Shari'a describes the Islamic legal system and the Qur'an is based on the Sunna, sayings or decisions of the prophet Muhammad. Islamic law is found in approximately a fourth of the world's countries, such as those located in the Middle East and in several Asian countries. Because of the different interpretations of Islam, national legal systems in countries like Iran and Saudi Arabia vary significantly.

Comparison of National Legal Systems

Despite the different legal systems in the world, the recognized legal sources within most countries are customs, judicial practices, and legislation. Significant differences, however, lie in how each legal system uses these sources of law. For example, judicial decisions are recognized as a primary source of law in a nation with a common law legal system. In some of those countries, courts may interpret legislative acts and declare them void if they conflict with the nation's constitution. By contrast, civil law or code law legal systems give a more limited role to courts. For example, because in France only laws derived directly from the *Code Civil* are considered primary sources of law, French court decisions have a lower status as a source of law than do the code provisions. Conversely, the administrative interpretation of the code has greater importance than in a common law legal system.

Important differences also exist in the application of substantive laws. For example, even though contract laws occupy an important role for individuals and business firms in almost all countries, the details of a particular contract may differ significantly. In the United States, the approach of businesspeople and their lawyers is to use the contract as the written expression of everything the parties have agreed to do. If the parties did not include something in the contract, the law assumes they intentionally omitted possible terms.

By contrast, in Germany contracts do not need to include all the terms on which the parties agree. If there are standard practices and ways of conducting business in a certain industry, the parties are expected to know and abide by those practices; reference to them is not included in a contract. In Japan, the parties undertaking the same type of business activity might not even make a written contract. If a contract is prepared, it will be less extensive than its counterpart in either the United States or Germany. In Japan, if conditions assumed by the contract do change, the parties will expect to renegotiate the contract, regardless of what the contract provides. The contract terms are regarded as less important than the relationship between the parties. Consequently, each party expects that the other will accommodate changes needed to allow the other party to profit from and continue the relationship.

Legal institutions also have varying degrees of independence and authority in different countries. Even where the letter of the law seems to be similar, its interpretations, application, and enforceability can differ greatly. For example, although Japan's legal system is modeled on Germany's civil law legal system, cultural factors in each country influence the legal processes. In Japan, there is greater dependence on extralegal and informal means of enforcing social control and less emphasis on legal institutions and officials than is true in Germany.

Conflicting National Laws

Treaties between countries are usually aimed at resolving conflicts in how national laws treat particular transactions. Absent treaty provisions to resolve conflicts between national laws, a business should assume that a transaction could be subject to the law of more than one nation because the laws of a nation sometimes can regulate activities or transactions outside its geographic boundaries (referred to as extraterritorial laws). In such situations, a business has to comply with the laws of both the nation where the activities occur and the nation where the firm originates.

REGIONAL LAWS AND ORGANIZATIONS

Different Objectives

The regional coordination of laws and policies by different nations significantly affects the conduct of international business. In several cases, such as the European Union (EU) and the Andean Common Market (ANCOM), regional economic integration has led to legal institutions that provide a larger framework for the regulation of business activities than the individual nation. On the other hand, some regional organizations cooperate for rather limited and specific purposes.

For example, the member nations of the Organization of Petroleum Exporting Countries (OPEC) cooperate in seeking to stabilize the price at which oil is sold. The countries in the Association of South East Asian Nations (ASEAN) seek to promote regional growth and development. Instead of establishing legal institutions, the members of this regional association have agreed to create a free trade area to promote trade among their countries. The ASEAN countries intend to eliminate most tariffs by 2003.

Stages of Regional Economic and Legal Integration

There are four stages of regional economic integration, summarized in Exhibit 5.2. A **free trade area** is formed when two or more countries agree to eliminate or phase out tariffs and other trade barriers among member countries. The North American Free Trade Agreement (NAFTA) aims at removing all tariffs among the countries of Canada, Mexico, and the United States. It also includes important legal guarantees for investment in the area by the region's firms. NAFTA also establishes a variety of dispute resolution panels for financial services, labor, and environmental problems.

EXHIBIT 5.2 Stages of Regional Integration

Free Trade Area	No tariffs among members	NAFTA
Customs Union	Free trade area plus common external tariffs	goal of MERCOSUR
Common Market	Customs union plus free movement of goods, services, people, and capital	European Community
Economic Union	Common market plus integrated economic policy and common currency	EU members that are in EMU

A **customs union** goes further than a free trade area. In addition to eliminating tariffs among members, all members agree to have a common external tariff. Thus in a customs union, unlike a free trade area, the tariff rates assessed by any member for goods coming from outside the area will be the same. Argentina, Brazil, Paraguay, and Uruguay, which have formed the Southern Common Market (MERCOSUR) are pushing their integration toward a customs union.

A **common market** or economic community goes further than a customs union by trying to make uniform standards and laws among the member countries. The goal of a common market is to have free movement of people, goods, services, and capital. This goal is sometimes referred to as achievement of the four freedoms. A court with jurisdiction to enforce its rulings is critical to a common market. The current European Union, once known as the European Community, was the first regional organization to attain this goal. Both the ANCOM and MERCOSUR countries in South America have a common market as an eventual goal.

Finally an **economic union** requires member countries to adopt a common currency and to integrate their economic policies. The Maastricht Treaty agreement among the European Union (EU) countries created an economic monetary union (EMU). Economic policies of member countries are coordinated by the European Central Bank, and one currency, the euro, has replaced 11 different national currencies. Not all members of the European Union are members of the economic monetary union.

INTERNATIONAL ORGANIZATIONS

The nations of the world have given lawmaking powers to several international organizations. The United Nations (UN) is the best known international organization. The rules and actions of such organizations as the World Trade Organization (WTO), the World Intellectual Property Organization (WIPO), the International Monetary Fund (IMF), and the World Bank (WB) frequently have significant effects on the international legal environment. The following sections of this chapter provide examples of laws originating in international organizations. WIPO is one of the international organizations most concerned with the legal environment affecting e-commerce. The TRIPS Agreement of the WTO and the United Nation's Convention on the International Sale of Goods (UNCISG) exemplify the role of international treaties and agreements.

http://
www.wipo.org/about-wipo.en/

Headquartered in Geneva, Switzerland, WIPO's Arbitration and Mediation Center is best known for its decisions on domain name disputes. A business or individual who has registered a domain name or has a trademark permitting the use of that name in e-commerce as well as in other business ventures can submit to WIPO a dispute with another firm seeking to use the same or a similar name. The WIPO arbitration panel's consideration and review of evidence is similar to that in civil court cases. Consider the *Madonna* case discussed next. The format for this case varies from others in this book because it was established by WIPO.

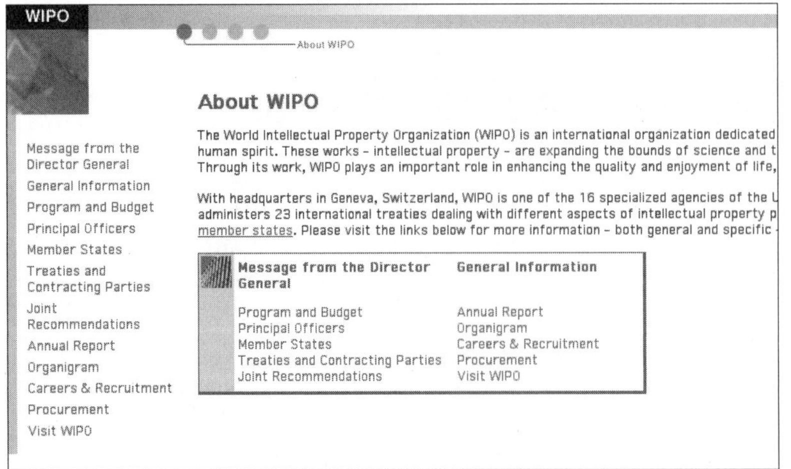

Courtesy, World Intellectual Property Organization.

Madonna Ciccone, p/k/a Madonna v. Dan Parisi and "Madonna.com"

WIPO Arbitration and Mediation Center
Administrative Panel Decision
Case No. D2000-0847

Facts

1. The Parties
The Complainant is Madonna Ciccone, an individual professionally known as Madonna.
The Respondent is "Madonna.com," the registrant for the disputed domain name, located in New York, New York, U.S.A. or Dan Parisi, the listed contact for the domain name.
2. The Domain Name(s) and Registrar(s)
The disputed domain name is madonna.com.
The registrar is Network Solutions, Inc., 505 Huntmar Park Drive, Herndon, Virginia 20170, U.S.A.
3. Procedural History
This action was brought in accordance with the ICANN Uniform Domain Name Dispute Resolution Policy and the ICANN Rules for Uniform Domain Name Dispute Resolution Policy. Respondent elected to have the case decided by a three-member panel.
4. Factual Background
Complainant is the well-known entertainer Madonna. She is the owner of U.S. Trademark Registrations for the mark MADONNA for entertainment services and related goods. She has used her name and mark MADONNA professionally for entertainment services since 1979. Complainant's music and other entertainment endeavors have often been controversial for featuring explicit sexual content. In addition, nude photographs of Madonna have appeared in Penthouse magazine, and Complainant has published a coffee-table book entitled "Sex" featuring sexually explicit photographs and text.

Respondent is in the business of developing websites. On or about May 29, 1998, Respondent, through its business Whitehouse.com, Inc., purchased the registration for the disputed domain name from Pro Domains for $20,000. On June 4, 1998, Respondent registered MADONNA as a trademark in Tunisia. On or about June 8, 1998, Respondent began operating an "adult entertainment portal website." The website featured sexually explicit photographs and text, and contained a notice stating "Madonna.com is not affiliated or endorsed by the Catholic Church, Madonna College, Madonna Hospital or Madonna the singer." By March 4, 1999, it appears that Respondent removed the explicit sexual content from the website.

On June 9, 1999, Complainant, through her attorneys, objected to Respondent's use of the Madonna.com domain name. On June 14, 1999, Respondent through its counsel stated: "As I assume you also know, Mr. Parisi's website was effectively shut down before you sent your letter, and is now shut down altogether. He is in the process of donating his registration for the domain name."

The word "Madonna," which has the current dictionary definition as the Virgin Mary or an artistic depiction of the Virgin Mary, is used by others as a trademark, trade name and personal name. By his own admission, Respondent has registered a number of other domain names, including names that matched the trademarks of others. Other domain names registered by Respondent include wallstreetjournal.com and edgaronline.com.
5. Parties' Contentions
Complaint contends that the disputed domain name is identical to the registered and common law trademark MADONNA in which she owns rights. She further contends that Respondent has no legitimate interest in the domain name.

Respondent claims that Complainant cannot show he lacks a legitimate interest in the domain name because Respondent (a) made demonstrable preparation to use the domain name for a bona fide business purpose; (b) holds a bona fide trademark in the word MADONNA; and (c) has attempted to make bona fide noncommercial use of the name by donating it to the Madonna Rehabilitation Hospital.
6. Discussion and Findings
A. The Evidentiary Standard For Decision
Paragraph 4(a) of the Policy directs that the complainant must prove each of the following:
   (i) that the domain name registered by the respondent is identical or confusingly similar to a trademark or service mark in which the complainant has rights; and,
   (ii) that the respondent has no legitimate interests in respect of the domain name; and,
   (iii) that the domain name has been registered and used in bad faith.

Since these proceedings are civil, rather than criminal in nature, we believe the appropriate standard for fact finding is the civil standard of a preponderance of the evidence (and not the higher standard of "clear and convincing evidence" or "evidence beyond a reasonable doubt"). Under the "preponderance of the evidence" standard a fact is proved for the purpose of reaching a decision when it appears more likely than not to be true based on the evidence. We recognize that other standards may be employed in other jurisdictions. However, the standard of proof employed in the United States seems appropriate for these proceedings generally, and in particular for this proceeding which involves citizens of the United States, actions occurring in the United States and a domain name registered in the United States.

B. Similarity of the Disputed Domain Name and Complainant's Mark

As Respondent does not dispute that its domain name is identical or confusingly similar to a trademark in which the Complainant has rights, we find that Complainant has satisfied the requirements of Paragraph 4(c)(i) of the Policy.

C. Lack of Legitimate Interests in Domain Name

Complainant has presented evidence tending to show that Respondent lacks any rights or legitimate interest in the domain name. Respondent's claim of rights or legitimate interests is not persuasive.

Respondent has failed to provide a reasonable explanation for the selection of Madonna as a domain name. Although the word "Madonna" has an ordinary dictionary meaning not associated with Complainant, nothing in the record supports a conclusion that Respondent adopted and used the term "Madonna" in good faith based on its ordinary dictionary meaning. We find instead that name was selected and used by Respondent with the intent to attract for commercial gain Internet users to Respondent's website by trading on the fame of Complainant's mark.

Second, Respondent contends that it has rights in the domain name because it registered MADONNA as a trademark in Tunisia prior to notice of this dispute. Certainly, it is possible for a Respondent to rely on a valid trademark registration to show prior rights under the Policy. However, it would be a mistake to conclude that mere registration of a trademark creates a legitimate interest under the Policy. If an American-based Respondent could establish "rights" vis à vis an American Complainant through the expedient of securing a trademark registration in Tunisia, then the ICANN procedure would be rendered virtually useless. To establish cognizable rights, the overall circumstances should demonstrate that the registration was obtained in good faith for the purpose of making bona fide use of the mark in the jurisdiction where the mark is registered, and not obtained merely to circumvent the application of the Policy.

Here, Respondent admits that the Tunisia registration was obtained merely to protect his interests in the domain name. Respondent is not located in Tunisia and the registration was not obtained for the purpose of making bona fide use of the mark in commerce in Tunisia. A Tunisian trademark registration is issued upon application without any substantive examination. We find at a minimum that the registration does not evidence a legitimate interest in the disputed name under the circumstances of this case.

We find that Complainant has satisfied the requirements of Paragraph 4(a)(ii) of the Policy.

D. Bad Faith Registration and Use

Under Paragraph 4(b)(iv) of the Policy, evidence of bad faith registration and use of a domain name includes:

(iv) by using the domain name, you have intentionally attempted to attract, for commercial gain, Internet users to your website or other online location, by creating a likelihood of confusion with the complainant's mark as to the source, sponsorship, affiliation, or endorsement of your website or location or of a product or service on your website or location.

The pleadings in this case are consistent with Respondent's having adopted madonna.com for the specific purpose of trading off the name and reputation of the Complainant, and Respondent has offered no alternative explanation for his adoption of the name despite his otherwise detailed and complete submissions.

Respondent's use of a disclaimer on its website is insufficient to avoid a finding of bad faith. First, the disclaimer may be ignored or misunderstood by Internet users. Second, a disclaimer does nothing to dispel initial interest confusion that is inevitable from Respondent's actions. Such confusion is a basis for finding a violation of Complainant's rights. We conclude that bad faith acquisition satisfies the requirement of bad faith registration under the Policy.

Respondent's reliance on a previous ICANN decision involving the domain name sting.com is misplaced. See *Gordon Sumner p/k/a/ Sting v. Michael Urvan*, Case No. 2000-0596 (WIPO July 24, 2000). In the Sting decision there was evidence that the Respondent had made bona fide use of the name Sting prior to obtaining the domain name registration. . . . Here, there is no similar evidence of prior use by Respondent and the evidence demonstrates a deliberate intent to trade on the good will of complainant.

Because the evidence shows a deliberate attempt by Respondent to trade on Complainant's fame for commercial purposes, we find that Complainant has satisfied the requirements of Paragraph 4(a)(iii) of the Policy.

7. Decision

Under Paragraph 4(i) of the Policy, we find in favor of the Complainant. The disputed domain name is identical or confusingly similar to a trademark in which Complainant has rights; Respondent lacks rights or legitimate interests in the domain name; and the domain name has been registered and used in bad faith. Therefore, we decide that the disputed domain name madonna.com should be transferred to the Complainant.

Mark V. B. Partridge, Presiding Panelist
James W. Dabney, Panelist
David E. Sorkin, Panelist
October 12, 2000

Case Questions

1. What are the three requirements of the ICANN Uniform Domain Name Dispute Resolution Policy that the complainant must prove? What is the basis for showing that the respondent registered and used the mark in bad faith?
2. The panel determines that its role is to make findings of fact based on the evidence presented. What standard should it use in making those findings? How does that standard compare with the standard normally used in criminal or civil cases? Why is that standard used here?
3. What is the basis for showing that the respondent registered and used the mark in bad faith?

The Madonna case is only one of more than a thousand domain name cases decided by the WIPO Arbitration and Mediation Center during a year. The following chart depicts the total number of generic top level domain name cases that the center decided in 2000.

TREATIES

The laws of different countries often have conflicting aims. As countries frequently regulate overlapping aspects of business transactions, often they seek to resolve conflicting rules by entering into treaties with other countries. Generally such treaties have both national and international effects. Treaties involving a large number of countries are sometimes referred to as conventions. The Convention on Contracts for the International Sale of Goods is discussed later in this chapter. Most treaties, though, are bilateral—entered into by two countries. Bilateral treaties govern the conditions under which firms from other countries are permitted to do business in the host country and the taxation of income earned in one country and sent to an affiliate firm in the other country. These and other relevant treaties are an important source of law that should be consulted before transacting international business.

Two of the most important treaties and conventions affecting the international legal

www.arbiter.wipo.int/domains/statistics/2001/filings.html

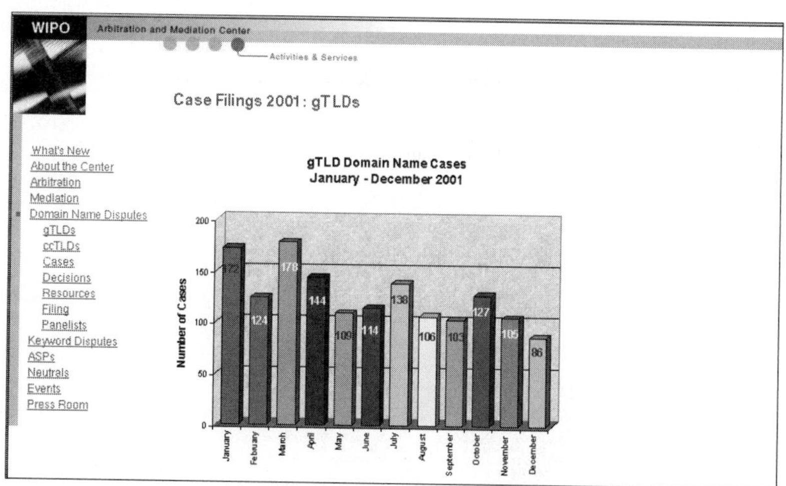

Courtesy, World Intellectual Property Organization.

environment are the WTO Trade Related Intellectual Property rights agreement, known as TRIPS, and the UN Convention on Contracts for the International Sale of Goods (CISG). The TRIPS Agreement establishes standards for the protection of intellectual property; the Convention on CISG establishes contractual interpretations when parties from different countries enter into sales agreements for goods.

The TRIPS Agreement and Intellectual Property

The members of the WTO make a number of commitments to each other. They commit to periodically negotiate to lower tariffs and other trade barriers and to use the organization's dispute settlement body for their trade disputes. They also agree to accord other members most-favored nation treatment and national treatment.

The **most-favored nation** (MFN) requirement, now generally known as **normal trade relations** (NTR), provides that there can be no discrimination among WTO members. Thus, tariffs and other barriers to products from all WTO members must be the same. The treatment a country accords to goods from another country must be as favorable as it gives to goods from any other WTO member country. The **national treatment standard** forbids discrimination between a member's own nationals and the nationals of other members. Taken together, these two standards provide treatment for nationals of all other members that is the same as for nationals of a member.

With the advent of e-commerce, it became increasingly important to seek international agreement on the treatment accorded to intellectual property. Thus, the trade-related intellectual property rights agreement, known as **TRIPS**, became effective in 1995. It was negotiated by the parties to the WTO and is administered by that organization. It covers a broad range of intellectual property, including (1) copyright and related rights, (2) trademarks, (3) geographical indications including appellations of origin, (4) industrial design and patents, (5) layout-design of integrated circuits, and (6) trade secrets.

ONLINE

The webpage for the TRIPS agreement is found at the WTO site **http://www.wto.org**

The three main features of the TRIPS agreement are establishing minimum standards, providing for enforcement of intellectual property rights, and subjecting disputes to the WTO's dispute settlement provisions. The minimum standards of protection are specified in the main treaties and conventions that protect intellectual property. Thus, the Paris Convention for the Protection of Industrial Property, known as the Paris Convention, establishes the standards for protecting patents, and the Berne Convention for the Protection of Literary and Artistic Works (the Berne Convention) establishes the standards for copyright protection. Other treaties that establish the standards that the TRIPS members must meet include the International Convention for the Protection of Performers, Producers of Phonograms, and Broadcasting Organizations (Rome Convention), and the Treaty on Intellectual Property in Respect of Integrated Circuits (IPIC Treaty). The TRIPS agreement also adds some obligations that are not included in these basic treaties.

http://

www.wto.org/english/tratop_e/trips_e/intel2_e.htm

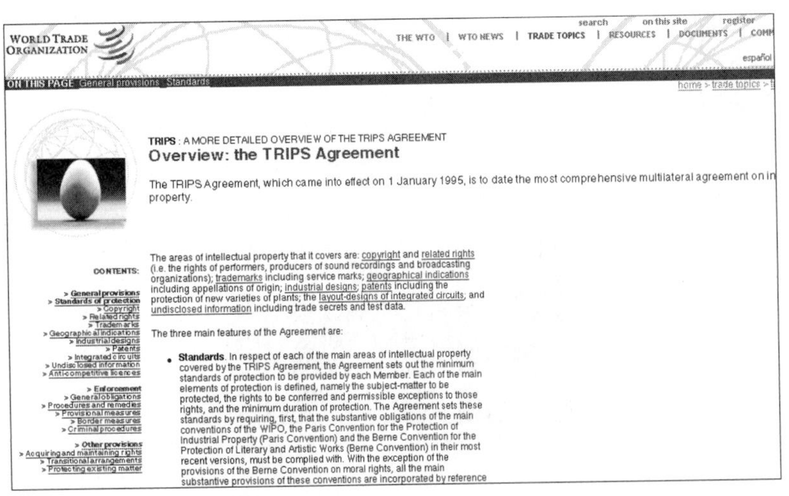

The second set of provisions in the TRIPS agreement deals with the enforcement of intellectual property rights. These sections include significant detail on civil and administrative procedures, criminal procedures and special requirements related to border measures. For example, the agreement requires that in all countries civil judicial procedures must be available for any activity infringing intellectual property rights covered by the agreement. Parties must be allowed to be represented by counsel, and to present evidence. Courts must be empowered to order parties to produce relevant evidence, as well as to grant damages or order infringing goods to be disposed of or, in appropriate cases, destroyed. Criminal provisions must be made for willful trademark counterfeiting or copyright piracy on a commercial scale. Sanctions must include imprisonment and/or monetary fines consistent with the penalties applied in crimes of a corresponding gravity.

The third set of provisions makes disputes between WTO members subject to the WTO's dispute resolution procedures. These procedures include consultation, with possible mediation by the WTO, followed by arbitration before a three-person panel. The panel decisions can be appealed to the appellate body of the WTO. Enforcement provisions list several unilateral remedies to the winning party in the event the other party does not comply with the arbitration decision.

The CISG Convention

All commerce and trade requires a stable legal environment. Special laws and customs known as the **law merchant** govern the sale and movement of goods. These laws, which spread through England and other countries centuries ago, remain in effect today. In recent years, the international community has agreed on a common body of international sales law, the **United Nations Convention on the Contracts for the International Sale of Goods** (**CISG**).

The CISG applies to contracts for the commercial sale of goods between parties whose places of business are in different nations that have agreed to the terms of the convention. Note that this law concerns only the sale of goods; the sale of services is not covered by this law. The CISG, which is discussed in Chapter 10's treatment of commercial law, was drafted by representatives from countries with common law, civil law, and socialist legal systems. It embodies principles from each. The CISG has been adopted by more than 50 countries, including France and Germany. Two of the CISG articles relating to nonconforming goods are discussed in the following case from France's Supreme Court.

ONLINE

A database on the CISG and International Commercial Law can be found at **http://cisgw3.law.pace.edu**

KARL SCHREIBER GmbH v. Thermo Dynamique Service et al.

Cour de Cassation Premiere Chambre Civil
26 mai 1999
[Supreme Court—First Civil Part, 26 May 1999]

Facts. Thermo Dynamique Service, the buyer, is a French company with its main office in Marseille, France. Karl Schreiber GmbH, the seller, is a German company, with its principal office in Postrach, Germany. On August 5, 1992, the buyer ordered 196 rolled metal sheets from the seller. The first part of the order was delivered on October 28, 1992. Then the buyer conducted some tests on the materials on November 9 and 11. The buyer sent some faxes seeking further information on November 16 and 19. On December 1 of that year, the buyer notified the seller of its intent to cancel the contract, principally on grounds that the products did not conform with the order as regards both quantity and quality. On December 16, buyer brought suit seeking to have the contract declared void. The seller claims the buyer did not notify it of a defect of conformity within a reasonable time period, as required under the CISG.

Legal Issue. Does a buyer who notifies a seller of a defect of conformity within 3 weeks after its inspection, but 5 weeks after delivery, comply with the CISG requirement to notify the seller within a reasonable time period?

Opinion. Chief Justice M. Lemontey. This case was brought before the Toulon Tribunal of Commerce. That court's 1994 decision dismissed the buyer's complaint and ordered it to pay the seller the sum of F 353,535 plus interest. The buyer then appealed to the Court of Appeals of Aix-en Provence. The Appeals Court noted that Article 38 of the CISG requires the buyer to inspect delivered goods within as short a period of times as is practicable. Article 39 adds that a buyer cannot rely on defects of conformity if it does not notify the seller of the nature of the defect within a reasonable time, beginning at the moment it was noticed or should have been noticed.

The Court of Appeals said the trial revealed that the seller knew the use envisioned for the ordered goods and that the dimensions of some of the plates were outside the contractually established limits and not suitable for the use. The Court of Appeals held that, bearing in mind the heavy handling the plates called for and some incompressible periods of time needed for the inspections, the buyer did warn the seller of unacceptable nonconformities with a reasonable period of time. The seller then appealed to the Supreme Court.

Decision. We reject any further appeal and uphold the decision of the Court of Appeals. The Court of Appeal was solely exercising its sovereign discretion when, after considering the chronology of events, it concluded that the buyer had arranged for the goods to be inspected within what was a short and normal period and had given the seller notice of the lack of conformity within a reasonable time, within the meaning of article 39 CISG.

Case Questions

1. Based on the text information just prior to the case, why is the law of this case based on the CISG?
2. If some of the goods were delivered on October 28, what are the factors that led the Court to conclude that the buyer's notice of cancellation more than a month later is timely?
3. Why do you think the CISG requires notice of cancellation within a "reasonable period" instead of setting a certain number of days? Would there be situations where a notice of cancellation would have to come within a week or two?

LAWS AFFECTING INTERNATIONAL TRADE

Laws affecting international trade may be imposed on either the exporting or the importing of goods and services. Usually, legal restrictions affect imports more than exports.

LAWS AFFECTING EXPORTS

Because exports bring money to exporters and create jobs, most national laws encourage it. But most nations have some laws that discourage or regulate exports.

Laws Regulating Exports

Laws may discourage the export of products that are scarce in the exporting country. For example, U.S. export quotas have been imposed on wheat and soybeans during crop shortages. Laws may also discourage exports out of concern over their possible misuse by the importer. The United States restricts the export of some technologically advanced computer hardware that may have adverse military uses.

Businesses should investigate the laws of their home country to be certain that the goods in question may be freely exported. Laws may require prior approval before particular goods are allowed to leave the country. Such laws may impose a general restriction that prohibits any export of the goods or a more targeted ban that imposes export controls on goods destined for specific countries. For example, U.S. computer parts may be freely exportable to many countries, but not to Iraq.

Laws Encouraging Exports

Despite the use of some export controls, laws usually encourage exports because the penetration of foreign markets by domestic producers helps a country's balance of trade. Governmental assistance and tax benefits are among the most common methods used to encourage exports. Governmental programs assist exporters by providing valuable information. Through publications and programs, the U.S. Department of Commerce assists potential exporters in identifying countries and firms that seek certain products. It also sponsors exhibits and trade shows throughout the world so that exporters can meet and contact foreign representatives.

Governments also make financial assistance available to exporters. The Export-Import Bank (EX-IM) of the United States offers medium- and long-term loans and credit guarantees. Loans are made directly to exporters, as well as to commercial banks that then lend to exporters. Special programs often give tax assistance to exporters.

Countries can provide tax assistance for their exports in several ways. For example, the turnover or value-added tax (VAT) levied in many European countries is often refunded to the seller if the goods are sold for export. Thus, the cost of goods purchased in these countries will be less for the foreign buyer than for the local buyer (as long as the rebate of the tax is passed along to the purchaser). In the United States, the Foreign Sales Corporation Act of 1984 exempts from U.S. tax approximately 5% of the income of corporations organized as foreign sales corporations. (Tax laws require such corporations to be mainly engaged in exporting.) However, if other countries think the tax assistance one country provides to its exporters violates agreed-upon WTO rules, the dispute can be brought to the WTO. The following case summarizes actions the WTO took concerning a complaint that the U.S. law violates WTO rules. Subsequent to the decision, the United States adopted new legislation to provide some of the same benefits to exporters in a way that, according to the United States, does not violate the WTO rules. But the legality of the U.S. law was still in question in mid-2002.

European Community v. United States

Dispute Settlement Body of the World Trade Organization (1997–2000)

Facts. This request, dated 18 November 1997, is in respect of Sections 921–927 of the U.S. Internal Revenue Code and related measures, establishing special tax treatment for "Foreign Sales Corporations" (FSC). The EC contends that these provisions are inconsistent with U.S. obligations under Articles III:4 and XVI of the GATT 1994, Articles 3.1(a) and (b) of the Subsidies Agreement, and Articles 3 and 8 of the Agreement on Agriculture. On 1 July 1998, the EC requested the establishment of a panel. At its meeting on 22 September 1998, the Dispute Settlement Body (DSB) established a panel. The panel found that, through the FSC scheme, the United States has acted inconsistently with its obligations under the Subsidies Agreement as well as with its obligations under the Agreement on Agriculture. The report of the panel was circulated to members on 8 October 1999.

On 26 November 1999, the U.S. notified its intention to appeal certain issues of law and legal interpretations developed by the panel to the WTO's Appellate Body.

Legal Issue. If the United States provides tax benefits to its companies using a "foreign sales corporation," does that constitute a subsidy contrary to the agreements it entered into with other members of the World Trade Organization?

Opinion. Chairman Crawford Falconi. The report of the Appellate Body was circulated to members on 24 February 2000. The Appellate Body upheld the panel's finding that the FSC measure constituted a prohibited subsidy under Article 3.1(a) of the Subsidies Agreement. However, the Appellate Body reversed the panel's findings that the

U.S. had acted inconsistently with its obligations under Article 3.3 of the Agriculture Agreement.

The Appellate Body further found that the U.S. had acted inconsistently with its obligations under the Agriculture Agreement by applying export subsidies, through the FSC measure, in a manner which results in, or threatens to lead to, circumvention of its export subsidy commitments with respect to agricultural products. The Appellate Body also emphasized that it was not ruling that a member must choose one kind of tax system over another so as to be consistent with that member's WTO obligations.

Decision. The Dispute Settlement Body (DSB) adopted the Appellate Body report and the panel report, as modified by the Appellate Body report, at its meeting on 20 March 2000.

Case Questions

1. What does this summary indicate is the relationship between national laws affecting exports (such as the U.S. tax code) and the trade rules found in the agreements of the World Trade Organization?
2. This case begins with a 1997 request by the EC to the WTO's Dispute Settlement Body (DSB) and ends with the DSB adopting the report of the Appellate Body. Summarize the other steps used to resolve disputes between members at the WTO.
3. Why do you think the EC brought this dispute to the WTO? How would the EC or companies located there be affected by the U.S. tax provisions?

LAWS AFFECTING IMPORTS

All countries impose some restrictions on imports. Import controls are levied for a number of reasons. Foremost usually is the desire to protect domestic products from competition with foreign products. In other cases, importing countries may want to ensure that scarce capital resources are used to meet other needs. Occasionally, a country places an embargo on another country. The **embargo** is meant to halt or significantly restrict all trade, whether exports or imports.

Legal restrictions against imports range from prohibitions, which declare that certain products cannot be imported, to quotas, which limit the number of products imported, to tariffs, which impose taxes on imported products, to various types of discrimination against foreign goods or in favor of domestic goods. Although each nation may adopt its own import policy, as with export subsidies, a nation's commitment to honor its international trade agreements, such as those made through the World Trade Organization (WTO), limits the restrictions that it may impose.

Prohibitions on Imports

A **prohibition** totally restricts the import of a product. For example, in the United States, the Trading with the Enemy Act grants the president the power to restrict all imports from countries considered enemies of the United States. Thus, there may be a prohibition on all or some products from Libya or Cuba into the United States. Brazil prohibits the import of small computers and light passenger airplanes, and Taiwan keeps out chemicals used in making drugs if those chemicals can be produced domestically.

Quotas on Imports

A **quota** limits the quantity of a product that may be imported. It is less restrictive than an outright prohibition but more restrictive than merely taxing the product. Although the rules of the WTO prohibit certain quotas, there are significant exceptions to the ban. Quotas, which are widely regarded as an effective form of restricting imports, are frequently disguised as "voluntary" agreements between trading partners. The EU has pressured Japan to limit its shipments of quartz watches, stereo equipment, and computer-controlled machine tools. The United States has obtained similar promises from European and South American countries to limit some of their steel exports.

Tariffs

A **tariff** is a tax on an imported product. Tariffs are invariably discriminatory because domestic products are not subject to the same taxes. Usually, tariffs are levied to protect infant industries from the better-developed industries of foreign countries. Two types of tariffs are the ad valorem and flat rate tariffs. An **ad valorem tariff** is levied on a value basis (the tariff represents a percentage of the value or price of the item imported); a **flat rate tariff** is levied on each unit imported (such as a barrel of oil, a meter of pipe, or a pound of nails).

Other Duties

In addition to tariffs, two other duties may be imposed on imports that are regarded as unfairly traded goods. **Antidumping duties** are used when goods are *dumped*, or sold in the importing country at a price lower than the price in their home market. Rules of the WTO permit an importing nation to impose an antidumping duty that is equal to the difference between the sales price of the imported product and the price of a comparable product in the home market.

Countervailing duties are assessed to counteract foreign subsidies of imported products that materially injure competing domestic products. The foreign subsidy may be in the form of tax rebates, favorable financing terms, or other special governmental assistance. Under international agreement, if a subsidy can be proved to cause or threaten to cause material injury to a domestic industry, countervailing duties may be levied, as long as they do not exceed the amount of the subsidy.

Nontariff Barriers

Any governmental regulation that discriminates against imports or in favor of exports is a **nontariff barrier**. The long list of the major types of nontariff barriers includes prohibitions, quotas, import licensing controls, foreign exchange controls, import fees, financial deposit requirements for imported producers, and duplicative or unnecessary product testing and certification requirements. Some nontariff barriers effectively prevent goods from entering a country; others are effective only after the goods are already in the country.

For example, an import license may be needed before goods are admitted into a country. The license may require payment of a fee, completion of extensive documentation regarding the products and the manufacturer, or approval by regulatory agencies. In some Central American countries, officials are given complete discretion to approve or deny such licenses. Nontariff barriers that are effective subsequent to entry include governmental procurement policies, internal tax policies, subsidy programs, and other practices giving domestic industries an advantage.

INTERNATIONAL LICENSING

In addition to exporting and importing, another method of conducting international business is through licensing. A **license** is a certificate or document from the licensor that gives the licensee permission to produce or distribute the licensor's product under the licensor's name.

Use of License

Licensing is becoming more common as a method of conducting international business, as it generally offers greater rewards than exporting with fewer risks than direct investing. Intellectual property in computer software programs, music recordings, and production processes are often licensed to foreign manufacturers or distributors for use in designated countries or regions. For example, a German firm with a patent on a particular production process may authorize a licensee to make or use the patented process for a limited time in Hungary. Although some governmental regulations affect licensing agreements, generally the agreement of the parties establishes the terms of use.

Terms of a Licensing Agreement

A license agreement generally contains the grant of a license from the licensor, details the conditions of its use, establishes other assistance that the licensor may provide to the licensee, fixes the compensation payable to the licensor, determines the governing law, and establishes methods for resolving disputes.

The agreement usually states the nature of the license being granted and the terms for its use. Confidentiality requirements are usually imposed on the licensee, particularly if trade secrets, rather than patents, are being licensed. In addition, both parties will be concerned about new technologies that are developed under the agreement. The licensor will seek the right to use any new related know-how that the licensee develops. Likewise, the licensee will want any updated information and improvements developed by the licensor so that the licensee can maintain its competitive position.

Manufacturing and marketing limitations may also be imposed on a licensee. For example, a licensee may be allowed to manufacture or sell products only in certain locations. Permitted use limitations may restrict the applications for which the licensed technology may be used. For example, licensed plastics manufacturing technology might be allowed to be used for cups, boxes, and other containers but not for automotive products.

In addition to granting the license, the licensor may also agree to provide training assistance, marketing programs such as advertising prepared by the licensor or a financial contribution to advertising prepared or purchased by the licensee, or manufacturing guidance in laying out the manufacturing or assembly processes to use.

As compensation for the use of the license, the licensee generally pays a royalty to the licensor. The royalty must be at a rate that allows both the licensee and the licensor to make a fair return on their investment in developing and using the licensed technology. The parties must determine the frequency of the royalty period, decide whether royalties are determined on net or gross income, and designate the currency of payment. Some countries restrict the methods used to determine royalties. For example, in India the government, which must approve all licensing agreements, will not allow the licensor to require a minimum guaranteed royalty to be paid. Instead, royalties must be tied to income earned: if no income is earned, no royalty can be due.

The designation of governing law for the licensing agreement may be difficult. In some situations, the country where the licensee is located will not approve contracts if the law of the licensor's country is selected. In most countries, however, the parties are free to select the governing law, and the courts of each nation will enforce the law selected by the parties. Although each party often prefers its own country's law, the critical question is whether the governing law effectively recognizes and protects intellectual property. Some countries fail to adequately protect all forms of intellectual property, and others take no steps to discourage piracy of transferred technology.

Taxation of Licenses

The tax treatment of licensing agreements concerns both the licensor and the licensee. Both the licensor's country and the country in which the licensee manufacturers, uses, or sells the licensed product will probably seek to tax a share of the royalties. In the absence of tax treaties, royalties are usually subject to income tax in the licensee's country, the *host country*, for the activity that creates royalties. The host country's tax authorities generally withhold the tax due from royalty payments that the licensee makes to the licensor. However, royalty income received by the licensor is also taxed, for what is now the second time, in the licensor's country, the *home country*. To avoid double taxation, tax treaties usually provide that if the licensor has a permanent establishment (place of business) in the host country, the home country will not tax the licensor's royalty income.

Franchising

Franchising is a well-known form of licensing by which the owner (franchisor) of trademarks and copyrights grants a license to another person or firm (the franchisee) to use the trademarks and copyrights in selling the goods or services under certain specified conditions. The franchisee pays a percentage of the gross or net sales of those goods to the licensor in the form of a royalty. Holiday Inn, Avis, McDonald's, and The Gap are examples of well-known international franchises.

LAWS AFFECTING INTERNATIONAL INVESTMENTS

WHY USE DIRECT INVESTMENTS?

Legal constraints on exporting and licensing often make international investment a more desirable method of engaging in international business. If significant barriers to international trade exist, investment may be the only means of selling products in a foreign market. Local laws may discriminate against imports so that only the establishment of plants in those countries can overcome the barriers. For example, many Japanese firms have made investments in European countries to bypass the tariff barriers on imports imposed by the EU.

Crucial business factors may also make investment preferable to exporting or licensing. The on-site locations obtained through investment enable foreign firms to market goods and to provide after-sales service on them more effectively. For large items, the transportation expenses incurred in exporting often make trade arrangements so costly that foreign direct investment may be the only profitable means of selling internationally. Major sites for foreign direct investment in recent years have been in China, India, Ireland, and Mexico.

NATIONAL POLICIES AND DIRECT INVESTMENTS

Nations have different policies and laws regarding the conduct of business by foreign-based firms. Even within any one country, some laws may promote foreign investment, while other laws restrict its influence. As early as the 1950s, some governments began to realize that their national goals could conflict with the goals of multinational firms. Consequently, some nations impose a variety of laws, administrative rules, and investment codes to regulate foreign direct investments.

By contrast, other nations welcomed foreign investors because those investments provide many people with jobs and help to improve the country's economic conditions. These nations modified their tax laws, currency exchange regulations, and administrative policies to attract global business enterprises.

TYPES OF FOREIGN DIRECT INVESTMENTS

Direct investing usually occurs when a new operation is begun or an existing business is bought. Typically, a new firm or enterprise is established for the business. When that investment is totally (or mostly) owned and controlled by a foreign investor, the new firm is referred to as a **wholly owned foreign enterprise** (WOFE). If the foreign firm partners with another firm located in the country where the investment is being made, the new firm is referred to as a joint venture (JV). An international joint venture always has two or more active participants and usually involves the establishment of a separate corporation. Frequently that new corporation, owned partially by a foreign firm and partially by a local firm, is organized in the host country. In a joint venture, each party shares in contributions and ownership. For example, a foreign firm may contribute capital and management experience, and a local firm may contribute raw material resources and local marketing expertise.

The laws of the countries in which the operations are conducted must be closely examined to determine the benefits of international investment. However, international investment is also affected by certain rules of international law, extraterritorial aspects of the laws of the home country, treaty obligations between the host country and the home country, and relevant rules of international institutions. Of course, there are also ethical concerns when investments are made in other countries.

JOINT VENTURES

Joint ventures have recently replaced wholly owned foreign enterprises as the most prevalent method for establishing foreign manufacturing facilities. In some countries,

Ethical Issue

Many ethical questions arise when a firm does business internationally. These questions occur most frequently with direct investments.

Should a product that is banned in one country be sold in other countries? This question poses ethical dilemmas when manufacturers are faced with substantial inventories of products that the legal institutions, regulators, or consumers in one country have determined are too dangerous to sell. Such ethical dilemmas arise for food products, pharmaceuticals, and pesticides that do not meet governmental standards in one country. Should those products then be sold instead to other countries that have less stringent regulations?

What special obligation do firms owe to people in less developed countries who may lack information and awareness of the possible hazards associated with products? When products designed for use by parents of infants or by elderly people require careful preparation or mixing of ingredients, will the producers ensure that consumers in countries wherever the products are sold are properly advised about how to prepare those products? What about the possible consequences of the improper or proper use of pesticides?

Environmental concerns also affect the disposal of waste. *Is it ethical to contract with governments in poor countries to dispose of trash or toxic waste that was generated in more developed countries?* What if the disposing firm has reason to believe that money paid to foreign officials will not be used to protect people from the hazards associated with the product?

Another area that poses ethical dilemmas for firms doing international business concerns the payment of money to foreign officials. Although most countries have laws against bribery, sometimes significant differences exist regarding customary and acceptable practices for payments made to officials. *What standards should a firm doing business in different countries follow?* Although recent commitments to several treaties now make foreign bribery illegal in more than 50 countries, the enforcement of these laws sometimes varies significantly from one country to the next.

investment codes prohibit many types of wholly owned foreign investments. These codes may also require that a specific percentage of a joint venture be owned by local individuals, firms, or government units. Thus, the joint venture is frequently the only means of making a foreign investment.

Absent legal restraints requiring joint ventures, this method of international direct investment may nevertheless be preferable. Political and business risks may be so great that sharing them may be best. There may be critical ingredients of business success, such as access to local capital, political contacts, personnel, and local suppliers, that only a local partner can provide. Review the following case that briefly describes one recent international joint venture.

- What is the business reason for forming this joint venture?
- What is each party contributing to the venture—money, talent, intellectual property, marketing know-how, plant facilities?
- As these are both large companies, why would it be important for them to create a new firm for their joint venture?
- How has the e-commerce environment influenced these firms?

The number of mergers between firms that originated in different countries is increasing. If a proposed merger is likely to affect the competitive environment in different locations, the antitrust or competition authorities in each of those locations must approve the merger. The Commission of the European Union is the controlling authority for mergers or joint ventures affecting competition in the Common Market. (The case format for this case varies from others in this book, because the format for this case is set by the commission.)

Bertelsmann/Mondadori/BOL Italia

Case CompJV.51, Commission of the European Communities, September 1, 2000

In August 2000 the Commission received notification of a new joint venture between Bertelsmann, a global German-based media firm, and Mondadori, an Italian-based publisher.

The Parties

Bertelsmann heads a German-based media group that operates internationally. Bertelsmann will hold the BOL Italia shares through its wholly-owned German Subsidiary Bertelsmann Multimedia GmbH.

Mondadori heads the Mondadori group of companies. Its main business includes the publishing of books, magazines, graphics and printing. Mondadori is a part of the Fininvest group.

BOL Italia is a corporation under Italian law. Its business activity is the online sale of books in the Italian language and for music cassettes, CDs, CD-ROMs, VHS and DVDs to consumers worldwide.

The Operation

The transaction creates a full-function joint venture between Bertelsmann and Mondadori under joint control of both parties. The parties will establish the joint venture by Mondadori acquiring 50% of the shares in the currently wholly owned Bertelsmann subsidiary BOL Italia. The parties will concentrate in BOL Italia their online sales activities in Italy of Italian books, CDs, CD-ROMs, VHS and DVDs.

Concentration

The decision-making structure consists of a board comprised of 4 members. Each parent company appoints two of the board members and each member has one vote. Board decisions must be passed by an absolute majority of the board members. In case of a deadlock, the situation will be resolved through negotiations rather than providing either party with a decisive, tie-breaking vote. Consequently, the parents' companies have the joint control of BOL Italia as specified within the Regulation.

BOL Italia is a full-function joint venture that has been agreed on for an unlimited term. The joint venture will be able to perform all the functions of an autonomous economic entity in the book-publishing and book-retailing sectors on a lasting basis. Therefore the joint venture will be a lasting basis as specified by the Regulation.

Community Dimension

The undertakings concerned have a combined world-wide turnover (sales) of more than EU 5 billion. The Community-wide turnover of both companies is in excess of EU 250 million, but they do not achieve more than two-thirds of that within one Member state. The operation therefore has a Community dimension.

Competitive Assessment

For purposes of the present assessment, the precise scope of the relevant product market and the relevant geographic market can be left open, since on the basis of all plausible market definitions considered, the operation will not lead to the creation or strengthening of a dominant position. Mondadori is very active in the Italian book publishing market, but Bertelsmann has virtually no publishing activities in the Italian market. The joint venture will not lead to the creation or strengthening of a dominant position in the market for the sale of music cassettes and CDs, CD-ROMs and other multimedia products. The operation will not lead to any coordination of the parents' competitive behavior in any upstream market and in the market of the joint venture.

Decision. For the above reasons, the Commission has decided not to oppose the notified operation and to declare it compatible with the Common Market and the EEA Agreement.

Case Questions

1. How did these parties form the joint venture company? Was it already in existence or was it created for this venture?
2. Why do you think the commission is interested in who is on the board of directors of the joint venture? What does the composition of the board of directors suggest about the control of the joint venture firm?
3. Will both parent companies be in existence after the joint venture? Are they likely to continue their own business activities?
4. How does the e-commerce environment affect this venture?

LEGAL ASPECTS OF DIRECT INVESTMENTS

Firms engaging in international business realize that direct investments, whether through wholly owned or joint venture enterprises, generally involve not only the greatest reward but also the greatest risk. A number of well-known firms that once made direct investments in China are no longer there. Numerous legal questions must be answered about such proposed investments (see Exhibit 5.3).

Investment Laws and Policies

The impact of foreign investment laws is probably the first area that should be investigated. Many countries attempt to attract foreign investors by creating a

EXHIBIT 5.3 Legal Questions Affecting Foreign Direct Investments

1. What are the country's investment laws or policies?
2. Which form of business organization is most appropriate for an investment?
3. Are there exchange controls that affect movement of money into or out of the country?
4. What is the taxation policy of the source country?
5. Do labor laws require worker representation on a company's board of directors or the hiring of a certain percentage of the labor force from the source country?
6. Is expropriation or nationalization a possibility?
7. What are the antitrust policies and how have they been developing?
8. Is intellectual property (patents, trademarks, and copyrights) protected?

favorable legal environment. They use incentives like tax holidays, increased depreciation, or other benefits aimed at making the country's tax rate favorable for foreign investors. Ireland and Scotland have attracted numerous manufacturing operations through tax incentives.

Because a number of countries try to stimulate some foreign investments while restricting and controlling others, an analysis of both the country's investment code and its more specialized policies is required to determine whether its encouragement of foreign investments is counteracted by other legal regulations.

Forms of Business Organization

The choice of a particular form of business organization for international investment often has critical tax consequences. Several options are usually available to a firm seeking to do business in another country. The first option is to organize a corporation in the country where business is to occur or in a country with favorable corporation and taxation laws. Typically, an affiliate known as a **foreign subsidiary** firm (foreign to the firm organizing the new entity) is incorporated under the laws of the country where its business activity is to take place, thereby increasing the likelihood that it will be treated by that country as a local company. Generally, such firms are separate legal entities and are not usually considered part of the parent corporation. In the Bertelsmann case, Bertelsmann Multimedia GmbH is a German subsidiary of Bertelsmann, and BOL, the new joint venture, was an Italian subsidiary of Bertelsmann.

Another choice is a special corporation. The Internal Revenue Code permits U.S. corporations with international sales to establish a **foreign sales corporation** (FSC). This firm is incorporated under one of several specified foreign laws, but not the law of the place where the firm does business. It is referred to as a foreign sales corporation because its sales and income must come from outside the United States. The U.S. parent firm that establishes an FSC subsidiary owns all the shares of the subsidiary's stock. As noted earlier, because of objections by the European Communities before the WTO, the United States has recently changed the details of this law.

Another option is to establish a foreign branch of a firm's existing corporation. **Branches** of any corporation are not independent entities but a part of the parent corporation. Thus, legally, for a U.S. firm with its headquarters in New York and branches in Chicago, Frankfurt, and Mexico City, each branch is regarded as a part of the firm in the United States.

Exhibit 5.4 on the next page illustrates the differences between the foreign subsidiary, the U.S. foreign sales corporation, and the branch form of business organizations.

Exchange Controls

Foreign direct investment decisions may be affected by currency exchange controls designed to limit the investing firm's right to withdraw profits, interest, dividends, or portions of the invested capital. Some protection against the most severe restrictions is available to U.S. corporations pursuant to treaty provisions. Firms may also secure insurance protection against the risk of inability to convert investment receipts from the local currency into dollars.

Tax Considerations

Foreign direct investors must examine both direct and indirect taxes. Many countries derive most of their income from indirect taxes, such as sales taxes, turnover taxes, or excise taxes. Indirect taxes are easier to collect than direct taxes and are less dependent on a high level of taxpayer income. For example, almost 50% of

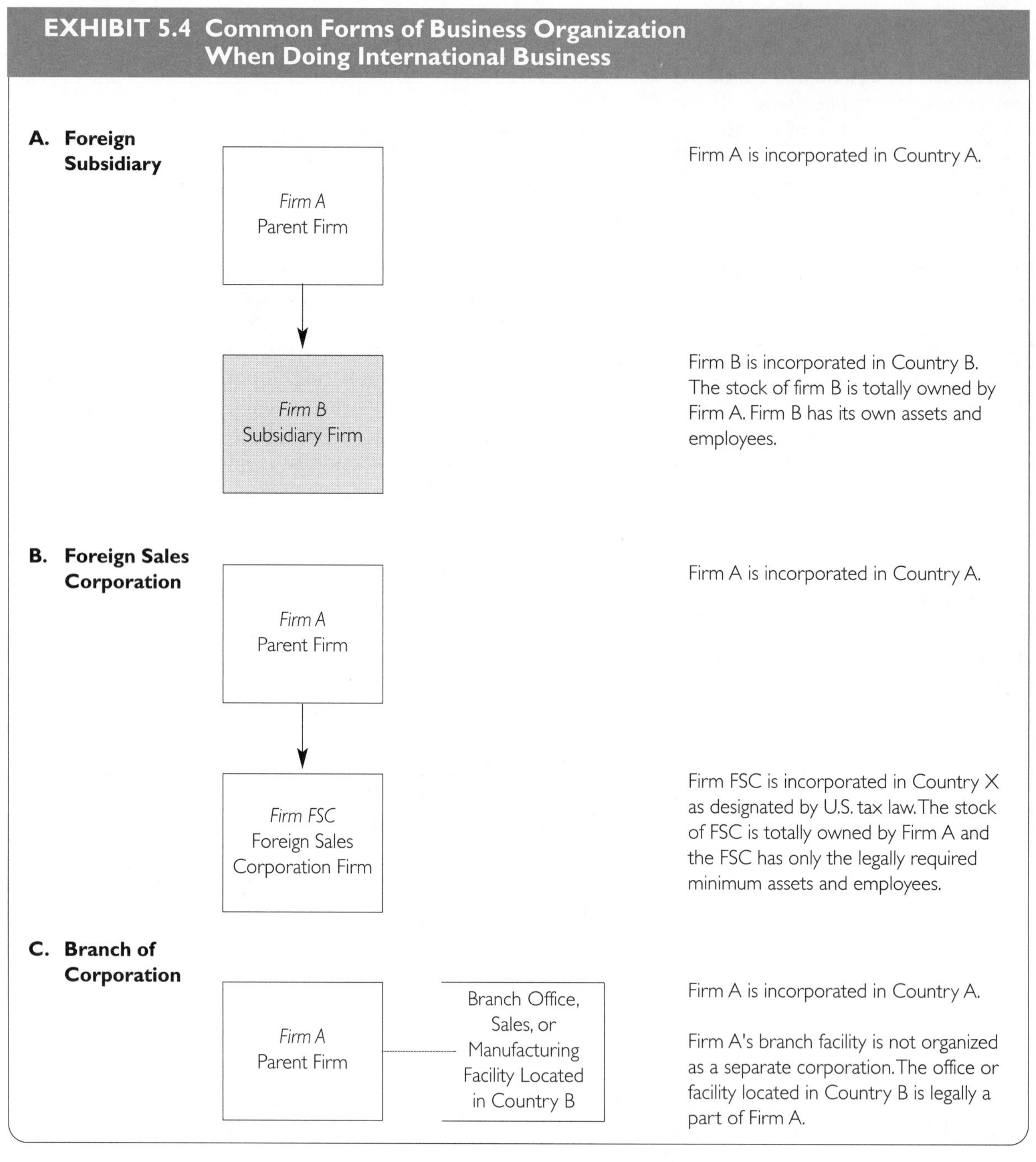
EXHIBIT 5.4 Common Forms of Business Organization When Doing International Business
A. Foreign Subsidiary
Firm A
Parent Firm
Firm A is incorporated in Country A.
Firm B
Subsidiary Firm
Firm B is incorporated in Country B. The stock of firm B is totally owned by Firm A. Firm B has its own assets and employees.
B. Foreign Sales Corporation
Firm A
Parent Firm
Firm A is incorporated in Country A.
Firm FSC
Foreign Sales Corporation Firm
Firm FSC is incorporated in Country X as designated by U.S. tax law. The stock of FSC is totally owned by Firm A and the FSC has only the legally required minimum assets and employees.
C. Branch of Corporation
Firm A
Parent Firm
Branch Office, Sales, or Manufacturing Facility Located in Country B
Firm A is incorporated in Country A.
Firm A's branch facility is not organized as a separate corporation. The office or facility located in Country B is legally a part of Firm A.

France's taxes are indirect taxes. Municipal or state taxes, as well as national taxes, must be reviewed to determine the total tax burden. In Switzerland, for example, the municipal or canton taxes on corporate income are far more significant than the Swiss federal tax.

Tax treaties play an important role in determining the tax burden of some transactions. They can alleviate the double taxation imposed by conflicting or overlapping tax laws of the country of source and the country of origin.

Labor Laws

International investments are affected not only by minimum or prevailing wage laws but also by legal provisions regarding hours of work, workers' compensation, retirement benefits, and vacation bonuses. In most European countries, for example, bonuses of one month's pay generally are required by legislation or practice for salaried and hourly workers. In Japan, bonuses of at least one month's pay are awarded to many workers in July and December; in good years, each semiannual bonus may be as high as four months' pay. Severance payments equal to at least six months' salary must accompany any notice of termination for many workers in numerous countries.

In some countries, workers have a vested right to their jobs; Mexican and Colombian laws restrict an employer's right to discharge workers except under specifically prescribed conditions. Local laws often require foreign workers to obtain work permits, such as work visas or green cards in the United States. Further, laws may require that local nationals comprise a minimum percentage of the labor force in a firm owned by a foreign enterprise. For example, all foreigners working in Saudi Arabia must obtain work permits, and all companies in Saudi Arabia that employ foreigners must employ 75% Saudi nationals and pay at least 51% of their total payroll to Saudi nationals.

Safety of Investment

Expropriation or nationalization occurs when a government takes over the ownership and management of private firms. Although the terms are often used interchangeably, they are different. The government pays compensation to the former owner when **nationalization** takes place, but no compensation is paid when **expropriation** occurs. In 1982, France nationalized many of the banks operating in France, both foreign and domestically owned. In the 1960s and 1970s, Cuba expropriated many of its foreign banks.

If sizable investments are contemplated, legal protection against the risk of expropriation should be considered. Firms should analyze the risk of expropriation or nationalization before investing in politically unstable foreign countries.

Antitrust Laws

Firms operating in the United States, whether of domestic or foreign origin, have long been aware of the possible effects of the antitrust laws on their operations. The U.S. antitrust laws, discussed in Chapter 19, are intended to preserve a relatively free system of competition by controlling anticompetitive practices and by regulating the growth and use of economic power.

Antitrust laws were enacted in most of the major European countries after World War II. Those national laws were subsequently supplemented and to some extent replaced by Article 85-90 of the Treaty of Rome, which created the European Communities. Article 85-90 of that treaty prohibits practices and agreements that restrict or distort competition within the EU or among its member states. Furthermore, the EU Commission has clearly indicated that Article 85-90 also applies to extraterritorial activities that affect trade or commerce in the member states, even if one of the parties to such activities is not a member of the European Communities or the European Economic Area (EEA).

In a 1999 case, *DuPont/Sabanci Case No. COMP/M.1538*, the Commission of the European Communities reviewed a joint venture between two companies, both of which were based outside the EEA. The joint venture was between DuPont, a global, diversified U.S.-based corporation, and Sabanci, a conglomerate holding company based in Turkey. The two firms formed a joint venture to develop, manufacture, and sell various polyester products. Because the two firms had sales of more than EUR 100 million in France, Germany, and Italy in 1998, their joint venture had to be approved by the commission. Although the parties accounted for approximately 25% of the Western European market for the three polyester end-use segments of the market, the commission declared their joint venture compatible with the common market and the EEA agreement.

Intellectual Property Protection

Intimately connected with antitrust law is the legal protection afforded intellectual property—trademarks, copyrights, and patents. Whereas antitrust law is antimonopolistic, patent law gives a limited monopoly to certain processes, products, or designs, and copyright and trademark law gives a limited monopoly to words or symbols.

A patent confers rights that are protected only within the boundaries of the country in which the patent is issued. As firms often need global protection for their patents, they must register and otherwise meet the requirements in each country or region (such as the EU) where they seek protection. Thus, a U.S. patent and a Canadian patent, even when granted for the same invention, create separate and distinct rights; those rights may differ in scope and effect in each issuing country.

International treaties such as the Paris Convention for patents and trademarks and the Berne and Universal Copyright Conventions for copyrights create some uniformity among national laws by allowing applications from one country to be protected in other countries if specified registration requirements are met. The Trade-Related Intellectual Property (TRIPs) provisions of the World Trade Organization also promote uniformity in the protection of intellectual property by requiring WTO members to agree to conform their patent, trademark, and copyright laws to certain standards.

INTERNATIONAL DISPUTE RESOLUTION

Despite the best planning and intentions, disputes between a licensor and licensee, between joint venture partners. or between the seller and purchaser of internationally traded goods do occur. When such disputes arise, there are a variety of ways to seek resolution. In addition to direct negotiation by the parties, litigation, mediation, and arbitration are frequently used.

As noted in Chapter 3, firms that frequently engage in international business transactions often select arbitration when they enter into contracts because it is quicker and less complicated than litigation and because the decisions are binding on the parties involved. There is significant international consensus regarding the enforceability of both the agreement to arbitrate and the arbitrator's award. More then a hundred countries have signed the United Nations Convention on the Recognition and Enforcement of Foreign Arbitral Awards.

ONLINE

The UN Convention can be found at **http://www.jus.uio.no/lm/arbitration/arbitration.html**

Bodies that determine the rules and processes for international arbitration include the American Arbitration Association, the International Chamber of Commerce in Paris, the Euro-Arab Chamber of Commerce, and the United Nations Commission for International Trade Law (UNICTRAL).

QUESTIONS

1. Assume that a firm is doing business in three countries: one with a common law legal system, one with a civil law legal system, and one with Islamic law. Which particular aspects of the laws affecting the firm are likely to vary significantly among these countries?
2. Why do governments regulate imports more than exports?
3. Assume that you read that of all firms investing in country X last year, 75% formed joint ventures and only 25% invested through wholly owned firms. The article's author then concludes that "joint ventures are obviously the preferred method of doing business in country X." Explain why that conclusion might *not* be correct.
4. A U.S. firm is planning to open a new manufacturing facility in Poland. Before it makes a direct investment there, it seeks your advice on the type of laws it should review before making the investment. Assume that Poland welcomes foreign investments like those planned by this firm. What advice would you give?
5. The United Kingdom imposes quality standards on domestic producers of milk and dairy products. It has also passed a regulation prohibiting the import of pasteurized milk and unfrozen dairy products as a measure to protect its people from milk that may not meet its standards. Other European Union member countries protest that the regulation does not provide a method whereby their milk and dairy products can pass the U.K. health and safety standards imposed on its producers. Does the U.K. regulation violate the "free movement of goods" provisions governing the EU countries or the directives of its commission prohibiting national laws that interfere with that free movement?
6. Assume that the United States, France, and Germany have signed the UNCISG Treaty, but Portugal and Mexico have not done so. Baachus Wines, a U.S. importer of wine and beer, contracts with a French winery to buy French wines. A dispute arises regarding the quality of the wines sent to Baachus. Does the UNCISG apply? What if the contract is for German beer? What if Portuguese wine is being purchased? Would your answers be different if Baachus wants the products delivered to its Mexican office?
7. What are the four types of economic integration? There has been some discussion between NAFTA members and some South American countries about either extending the geographical scope of the free trade area or perhaps formating a customs union. How does a customs union differ from a free trade area? What problems do you foresee in extending the geographic scope of NAFTA?
8. Give an example of laws originating from each of the following sources—a treaty, national laws in another country, regional laws, laws from international organizations—that could affect a U.S. firm that does business in Asia and South America.
9. The European Union's directive on the protection of personal data, including data on employees, requires that data subjects have access to data about themselves, that they be allowed to challenge and correct wrong information, and that sensitive data—relating to race and age—be subjected to special rules. It also requires that employees have a right of action to obtain relief in an administrative agency or court. How are U.S.-based firms with subsidiaries in Europe affected by this law?
10. A pornographic website in Italy is accessible by foreign residents. Users at the website can download pictoral images and store them on their computers. If such access is illegal in the user's country, does the Web owner have to comply with that country's law?

CHAPTER 6

Administrative Law

INTRODUCTION

CREATION OF ADMINISTRATIVE AGENCIES

An **administrative agency** is a governmental body that is not included in the Constitution as part of the legislative, executive, or judicial branches. There are two types of administrative agencies: executive agencies and independent regulatory agencies. **Administrative law** concerns the organization and operation of what is known as the fourth branch of government—the administrative agencies. Much of administrative law is concerned with the **administrative procedures** these agencies use to perform three different types of activities: rule-making, adjudication, and ministerial duties. Federal and state statutes establish the procedures governing most of these agencies.

This chapter examines the creation of administrative agencies and the legislative delegation of their powers. It then reviews the processes these agencies use as they make rules, adjudicate cases, and perform numerous informal actions. The role that courts play in reviewing agency functions is also noted. We discuss, too, some ways in which the administrative regulation of e-commerce is still evolving.

Congress established the first executive branch administrative agencies, the State Department and the Treasury Department, in 1789 to deal with foreign imports and to provide pensions to disabled soldiers. The Office of the Attorney General and the Department of War were created that same year. The Department of Defense emerged from the Department of War, and the Department of Justice is the successor to the Office of the Attorney General.

In the late nineteenth century, Congress wanted to institute a system for establishing railroad rates. However, it lacked the expertise that it felt was needed. Should the rates throughout the country be equal on a per mile basis? Should the rates differ with the amount of freight or passenger traffic or with the distance traveled? How could Congress draft one law that would apply to many different situations? Similarly, if general railroad rates were established, the courts would later have to determine how the rates should apply to specific situations.

But both the courts and the existing agencies in the executive branch were very busy and ill equipped to handle the problems that needed to be resolved. Thus, in 1889 Congress created an independent regulatory agency, the Interstate Commerce Commission (ICC). The ICC was granted the power to determine general rates, a rulemaking or legislative type of power, as well as the power to resolve disputes regarding the application of those rates, an adjudicative type of power.

TYPES OF ADMINISTRATIVE AGENCIES

Executive Agencies

Those that assist the president in carrying out the functions of the executive branch are **executive agencies**. Of course, the heads of these agencies serve at the pleasure of the president. Many agencies, known as **subagencies**, are in fact part of executive agencies. The Occupational Safety and Health Administration is a subagency in the Department of Labor, and the Internal Revenue Service is part of the Treasury Department.

Independent Regulatory Agencies

The Interstate Commerce Commission and the Federal Trade Commission are agencies with executives who serve for fixed terms and cannot be removed from office without just cause. As the years passed, Congress created other administrative agencies to deal with specialized problems. In 1914, the Federal Trade Commission (FTC) was created to curb monopolistic practices that the Sherman Antitrust Act, passed in 1890, had failed to address. As radio transmission became common, the need to allocate the available bandwidths led to the creation of the Federal Communications Commission (FCC). The airplane brought us the Federal Aviation Administration (FAA), and the Food and Drug Administration (FDA) was established to deal with impure foods and quack medicines. The stock market crash of 1929 led to the creation of the Securities and Exchange Commission (SEC), and the development of atomic energy brought about the Atomic Energy Commission (AEC) and subsequently its conversion to the Nuclear Regulatory Commission (NRC).

Additional independent agencies arose as new problems emerged that appeared too complicated for Congress to address and monitor, and included the Environmental Protection Agency (EPA), the Occupational Safety and Health Administration (OSHA), and the Consumer Product Safety Commission (CPSC), among others. The development of additional executive department agencies somewhat parallels the growth of independent agencies. Exhibit 6.1 depicts the functions performed by some well-known independent federal agencies, and Exhibit 6.2 lists the activities undertaken by some executive branch agencies.

ADMINISTRATIVE LAW AND E-COMMERCE

Initially, the Internet and e-commerce were perceived to be like the wild, wild West, where few rules were in place and the government's role was barely noticeable. The "Wild Wild Web" has disappeared. Today, administrative agencies, which make and apply governmental regulations, are hard at work revising existing regulations and formulating new rules to deal with a host of e-commerce concerns.

EXHIBIT 6.1 Selected Federal Independent Regulatory Agencies

Agency	Activities
Interstate Commerce Commission http://www.icc.gov	Regulates interstate surface transportation
Federal Trade Commission http://www.ftc.gov	Protects the public from anticompetitive behavior and unfair and deceptive business practices
Equal Employment Opportunity Commission http://www.eeoc.gov	Enforces civil rights and equal opportunity laws regarding discrimination in employment
National Labor Relations Board http://www.nlrb.gov	Conducts union certification elections and attempts to prevent unfair labor practices by employers and unions
Environmental Protection Agency http://www.epa.gov	Administers laws related to air and water pollution, solid waste, and other environmental concerns
Securities and Exchange Commission http://www.sec.gov	Enforces federal securities laws regulating the sale of securities to the investing public

- Commerce Department regulations ease export restrictions on encryption products to EU members.
- Internet sweepstakes are subject to U.S. federal and state laws, as well as to laws in each country where they are accessible.

EXHIBIT 6.2 Selected Federal Executive Department Agencies*

Department	Activities and Subagencies
State http://www. state.gov	Conducts foreign affairs through embassies and consular offices; includes passport, foreign service, and consular affairs
Treasury http://www.treas.gov	Raises money for governmental needs; includes IRS, Customs Service, and the Bureau of Alcohol, Tobacco, and Firearms
Justice http://www.usdoj.gov	Represents the U.S. in litigation; includes the FBI, Drug Enforcement Agency, and Immigration and Naturalization Service
Commerce http://www.home.doc.gov	Represents commercial interests of U.S.; includes Bureau of Census, Patent and Trademark Office, and Bureau of Economic Analysis
Education http://www.ed.gov	Promotes and regulates educational services; includes Office of Special Education and Rehabilitation Services, Office of Elementary and Secondary Education, Office of Postsecondary Education
Labor http://www.dol.gov	Issues labor safety standards; includes OSHA, Bureau of Labor Statistics, Office of Labor-Management Standards

* Other U.S. federal government websites can be accessed through the Federal Web Locater at http://www.nfoctr.edu/fw/.

- Oklahoma says that the Oklahoma Board of Dentistry has authority to regulate out-of-state individuals who practice dentistry in Oklahoma over the Internet.
- The Federal Trade Commission asserts that it has a vital role to play in electronic commerce markets. It views competitive concerns in e-commerce as similar to those found in more traditional markets, tempered by a number of special characteristics.
- Significant antitrust issues arise in the electronic marketplace, where pricing information is easily exchanged among competitors.
- Lobbyists representing software developers and marketers are seeking (yes—seeking, not opposing) new federal rules regarding consumer rights in computer software and other information products from the Federal Trade Commission. (They want one uniform standard.)

ADMINISTRATIVE PROCEDURES

Both executive agencies and the independent regulatory agencies follow the same procedures for carrying out their duties. Although the activities of these many different agencies vary a great deal, all agencies follow similar procedures. Congress enacted the Administrative Procedures Act, which details the procedures to be used by agencies involved in any of three main types of activities: rule-making, adjudication, and informal ministerial activities.

Rule-making actions affect a large number of people and do not depend on facts about people's individual circumstances. The Administrative Procedures Act defines a **rule** as an "agency statement of general or particular applicability and future effect designed to implement, interpret or prescribe law or policy." Rule-making procedures must follow three steps—notice, comment, and publication—to be effective.

In contrast, when an administrative agency determines existing facts, applies rules or laws to those facts, and reaches a conclusion or decision by some type of hearing process, it is involved in **adjudication**. Most agency adjudications or hearings usually follow trial types of procedures.

The majority of administrative agency activities are **informal actions**, such as granting permits, determining eligibility for governmental benefits, or collecting information. The procedures used in informal activities vary. In most cases, there is no judicial review of these activities.

ADMINISTRATIVE AGENCIES

ROLE OF ADMINISTRATIVE LAW

Administrative agencies, which were created to deal with specific societal problems, clearly illustrate the connection between law and the changing society. However, administrative law is not concerned with the substance of regulatory laws or with the specific regulations promulgated by these agencies. The substantive rules of the agencies are dealt with in Part V of this book. Chapters 19–23 deal with specific regulatory concerns such as antitrust law, labor law, equal employment, securities regulations, and environmental laws. The last chapter in Part V addresses Internet regulation.

Administrative law is concerned with the procedures agencies use to perform the tasks legislative bodies delegate to them. The Administrative Procedures Act is the primary authority that governs the procedures to be used by administrative agencies in performing most of their work.

DELEGATION OF AUTHORITY TO ADMINISTRATIVE AGENCIES

Because administrative agencies are not mentioned in the U.S. Constitution, their powers must originate from one of the three branches of government expressly granted powers by the Constitution. Administrative agency powers originate with legislation known as **enabling acts**. As noted in Chapter 5, the Constitution grants legislative powers to Congress and other powers to the executive and judicial branches. These powers are intentionally separated to prevent their concentration and abuse. However, because administrative agencies may have all three types of governmental powers, several constitutional questions were raised when Congress first created them.

If an agency had the power to make rules and regulations, was Congress giving away its legislative power? Could legislative power, granted to Congress by the Constitution, be exercised by other governmental organizations? Was the separation of powers violated if agencies possessed legislative, judicial, and investigative authority? Although a few early cases found that the delegation of authority from Congress to administrative agencies violated the separation of powers, since early in the twentieth century the courts have generally upheld the legislature's delegation of authority to administrative agencies.

Delegation is the transfer of power by one governmental body (such as the legislature) to another (such as an administrative agency). Although it is unconstitutional for the legislature to transfer *all* of its legislative powers to an administrative agency, the legislature can delegate to an agency *part* of its authority to make rules and regulations. The laws that grant some lawmaking authority to an agency and specifies the activities that the agency may perform are known as **enabling legislation**.

The Federal Trade Commission Act, for example, created the Federal Trade Commission and gave it the authority to protect the public from noncompetitive behavior and unfair and deceptive acts or practices. Similarly, the Securities and Exchange Act of 1934 granted the Securities and Exchange Commission authority to regulate the securities markets. The activities that specify the concerns to be addressed by an agency are commonly referred to as **standards**. If the legislature does not adequately define the standards by which agency actions are guided, the courts may find that the grant of authority to the agency is unconstitutional. When Congress does define the standards, the agency must follow them. In the *Iowa Utilities* case, the U.S. Supreme Court said that although Congress established standards for the FCC to follow in making rules for the telecommunications industry, the FCC did not follow those standards.

AT&T Corp. v. Iowa Utilities Board

525 U.S. 366 (1999)
Supreme Court of the United States

Facts. By enacting the 1996 Telecommunications Act, Congress ended the exclusive franchise in local markets for local exchange carriers (LECs), which owned the equipment that constituted a local network. The act required the LECs to share their network equipment with competitors to facilitate their entry into the market. After the Federal Communications Commission issued rules implementing the act's local competition provisions, numerous challenges were filed in a number of courts. Those cases were consolidated in the Court of Appeals for the Eighth Circuit. The Court of Appeals found that the FCC lacked jurisdiction to issue some of the rules but held that other rules were valid as reasonable interpretations of the act. The Supreme Court's opinion that follows deals with one part of its review of that decision.

Legal Issue. Is the FCC's rule that the Telecommunications Act requires local exchange carriers to open all of its network elements to any competitor seeking entry into its market a reasonable interpretation of the Act?

Opinion. Justice Scalia. The LECs challenged the FCC's requirement of unbundled access. The FCC's rules set forth a minimum number of network elements that must be made available to requesting carriers. The LECs said the FCC virtually ignored the 1966 Telecommunications Act's requirement that it consider whether access to proprietary elements was "necessary" and whether lack of access to nonproprietary elements would "impair" an entrant's ability to provide local service. Because the FCC declined to impose a requirement of facility ownership on carriers who sought to lease network elements, the LECs argued that the competitors could lease "all elements" from the LECs without developing their own facilities.

We are of the view that the FCC did not adequately consider the "necessary and impair" standard when it gave blanket access to these network elements. The rule requires an incumbent to provide a minimum of seven network elements and allows the state commission to determine whether to grant a requesting carrier access to additional elements on a case-by-case basis. Section 251 (d)(2) of the Act provides: In determining what other network elements should be made available.... the Commission shall consider, at a minimum, whether

(A) *access to such network elements as are proprietary in nature is necessary, and*
(B) *the failure to provide access to such network elements would impair the ability of the telecommunications carrier seeking access to provide the service that it seeks to offer.*

The incumbents argue that section 251 (d)(2) codifies something akin to the "essential facilities" doctrine of antitrust law, opening up those "bottleneck" elements unavailable elsewhere in the market. We ... agree with the incumbents that the Act requires the FCC to apply *some* limiting standard, rationally related to the goals of the Act, which it has simply failed to do.

In the general statement of its methodology, the Commission announced that it would regard the "necessary" standard as having been met regardless of whether "requesting carriers can obtain the requested proprietary element from a source other than the incumbent" since "requiring new entrants to duplicate unnecessarily even a part of the incumbent's network could generate delay and higher cost for new entrants, and thereby impede entry by competing local providers and delay competition, contrary to the goals of the 1996 Act."

And it announced it would regard the "impairment" standards as having been met if "the failure of an incumbent to provide access to a network element would decrease the quality, or increase the financial or administrative cost of the service a requesting carrier seeks to offer, compared with providing that service *over other unbundled elements in the incumbent LEC's network.* This means that comparison with self-provision, or with purchasing from another provider is excluded. Since any entrant will request the most efficient network element, it is hard to imagine when the incumbent's failure to give access to the element would not constitute an "impairment" under this standard.

That judgment allows entrants, rather than the Commission, to determine whether access to proprietary elements is necessary, and whether the failure to obtain nonproprietary elements would impair the ability to provide services. The Commission cannot, consistent with the statute, blind itself to elements outside the incumbent's network. That failing alone would require the Commission's rule to be set aside. . . . [I]f Congress had wanted to give blanket access to incumbents' networks on a basis as unrestricted as the scheme the Commission has come up with, it would not have included section 251(d)(2) in the statute. It would simply have said that whatever requested element can be provided must be provided.

Decision. As the FCC did not adequately consider the "necessary and impair" standard when it gave blanket access to these network elements, we find its rules to be contrary to the standard established by Congress and therefore invalid.

Case Questions

1. What was the standard that Congress told the FCC to use in determining the network elements a local exchange had to provide to new entrants?
2. The Court says the FCC did not follow the congressional requirement to consider both the "necessary" and "impairment" issues when determining the parts of a local exchange network that must be made available to new entrants. What standard did the FCC use?
3. Why is there a constitutional problem if the FCC determines that potential entrants to the local exchange market should determine the elements the existing local carrier needed to provide to them?
4. Suppose Congress does not provide any standard for the FCC to use when making rules that affect an industry like the telecommunications industry. What constitutional problem would be raised?

CONTROLS OVER ADMINISTRATIVE AGENCIES

Administrative agencies are not directly accountable to the people. Administrators, unlike legislators, many judges, and the president, are not elected. Thus, controls on administrative agencies are needed to ensure that the agencies are responsive to the country's needs. Each of the three branches of government maintains some control over administrative agencies. The *Iowa Utilities* case illustrates the control a court has in reviewing the actions of administrative agencies. The legislature that delegates power to an administrative agency and appropriates money for it also has significant control over an agency's activities. Similarly, the executive who appoints a person to head an agency and the courts that review its activities also exercise some control. Finally, some control is exercised by the public, through its access to agency information.

Legislative Controls

In the enabling legislation, Congress generally specifies which activities an agency may perform. If the legislature does not authorize an agency to regulate certain products or activities, the agency lacks the power to do so. In a high-profile case, the U.S. Supreme Court recently examined whether Congress had authorized the Food and Drug Administration to regulate cigarettes and smokeless tobacco when it passed the Food, Drug and Cosmetics Act granting the FDA jurisdiction over "drugs" and "devices."

Food and Drug Administration v. Brown & Willamson Tobacco Corp.

529 U.S. 120 (2000)
United States Supreme Court

Facts. Under the Food, Drug, and Cosmetic Act (FDCA), Congress granted to the Food and Drug Administration (FDA) the authority to regulate, among other items, "drugs" and "devices." In August 1996, the FDA asserted jurisdiction to regulate tobacco products in the United States after concluding that nicotine was a "drug" and that cigarettes and smokeless tobacco were "devices" that delivered nicotine to the body. Pursuant to its asserted authority, the FDA promulgated regulations governing tobacco products' advertising, promotion, labeling, and accessibility to children and adolescents. A group of tobacco manufacturers, retailers, and advertisers filed suit in the United States District Court for the Middle District of North Carolina challenging the FDA's regulations. The trial court found some of the FDA rules to be constitutional and others unconstitutional. Upon appeal, the Court of Appeals determined that Congress had granted no authority for the FDA to regulate tobacco. The FDA then appealed to the U.S. Supreme Court.

Legal Issue. When Congress passed the Food, Drug, and Cosmetics Act granting the FDA jurisdiction over "drugs" and "devices," did it thereby give the FDA the authority to regulate cigarettes and smokeless tobacco?

Opinion. Justice O'Connor. Because this case involves an agency's construction of a statute it administers, the Court's analysis is governed by *Chevron U.S.A. Inc. v. Natural Resources Defense Council, Inc.* under which a reviewing court must first ask whether Congress has directly spoken to the precise question at issue. If so, the court must give effect to Congress' unambiguously expressed intention. If not, the Court must defer to the agency's construction of a statute so long as it is permissible. In determining whether Congress has specifically addressed the question at issue, the court should . . . place the provision in context, interpreting the statute to create a symmetrical and coherent regulatory scheme. In addition, the meaning of the statute may be affected by other Acts. Finally, the court must be guided to a degree by common sense as to the manner in which Congress is likely to delegate a policy decision of such economic and political magnitude to an administrative agency.

Considering the FDCA as a whole, it is clear that Congress intended to exclude tobacco products from the FDA's jurisdiction. A fundamental precept of the FDCA is that any product regulated by the FDA that remains on the market must be safe and effective for its intended use. That is, the potential for inflicting death or physical injury must be offset by the possibility of therapeutic benefit. In its rulemaking proceeding, the FDA quite exhaustively documented that tobacco products are unsafe, dangerous, and cause great pain and suffering from illness. These findings logically imply that, if tobacco products were "devices" under the FDCA, the FDA would be required to remove them from the market under the FDCA's misbranding and device classification.

Congress, however, has foreclosed a ban of such products, choosing instead to create a distinct regulatory scheme focusing on the labeling and advertising of cigarettes and smokeless tobacco. Its express policy is to protect commerce and the national economy while informing consumers about any adverse health effects. Thus, an FDA ban would plainly contradict congressional intent. Various provisions in the Act require the agency to determine that, at least for some consumers the product's therapeutic benefits outweigh the risk of illness or serious injury. This the FDA cannot do, because tobacco products are unsafe for obtaining any therapeutic benefit. The inescapable conclusion is that there is no room for tobacco products within the FDCA's regulatory scheme. If they cannot be used safely for therapeutic purpose, and yet they cannot be banned, they simply do not fit.

The history of tobacco-specific legislation also demonstrates that Congress has spoken directly to FDA's authority to regulate tobacco products. Since 1965, Congress has enacted six separate statutes addressing the problem of tobacco use and human health. This tobacco-specific legislation has created a specific regulatory scheme for addressing the problem of tobacco and health. And it was adopted against the backdrop of the FDA consistently and resolutely stating that it was without authority under the FDCA to regulate tobacco products as customarily marketed. In fact, Congress several times considered and rejected bills that would have given the FDA such authority. Indeed, Congress' actions in this area have evidenced a clear intent to preclude a meaningful policymaking role for any administrative agency.

Finally, the Court's inquiry is shaped, at least in some measure, by the nature of the question presented. In extraordinary cases, there may be reason to hesitate before concluding that Congress has intended an implicit delegation to the agency. This is hardly an ordinary case. Contrary to the agency's position from its inception until 1995, the FDA now asserts jurisdiction to regulate an industry constituting a significant part of the American economy.

Decision. Given tobacco's unique political history . . . the Court is obliged to defer not to the agency's expansive construction of the statute, but to Congress' consistent judgment to deny the FDA this power. We affirm the Court of Appeals determination that Congress did not grant the FDA the authority to regulate tobacco.

Dissent by Breyer joined by 3 other justices. The FDA has the authority to regulate "articles (other than food) intended to affect the structure or any function of the body. I believe that tobacco products fit within this statutory language. In its own interpretations, the majority nowhere denies two salient points. First, tobacco products fall within the scope of this statutory definition, read literally. Cigarettes are "intended to affect" the body's "structure" and "function" in the literal sense of these words.

Second, the statute's basic purpose—the protection of public health—supports the inclusion of cigarettes within its scope. In short, I believe that the most important indicia of statutory meaning—language and purpose—along with the FDCA's legislative history, are sufficient to establish that the FDA has authority to regulate tobacco.

Case Questions

1. According to the majority opinion, which two reasons indicate that Congress did not want the FDA to regulate tobacco products?
2. What has been the position of the FDA with regard to its regulation of tobacco until 1995? What effect does this have on the Court's decision?
3. What two sources does the dissent consult before determining that the FDA should be allowed to regulate tobacco?

Congress also establishes the procedures an agency must follow in making rules and adjudicating cases. The **Administrative Procedures Act** (APA) specifies these procedures for most federal agencies. Several important provisions of this act are reviewed later in this chapter. Most states have similar acts.

In many states, an automatic periodic review of agencies is provided by **sunset laws.** Under such laws, the legislature reexamines an agency's records and determines whether to continue its authority. Another method of legislative oversight over agencies is through the legislature's control of agency funding. When agencies request funding, special legislative committees carefully scrutinize their activities.

The legislature also has significant power through its control of the budget. The budget for an agency whose mission or recent action is not popular with the legislature may be cut back. At both the federal and state levels, legislatures are willing to exercise their "power of the purse" to signal their concerns to administrative agencies. This fiscal power is shared with the executive branch because the president proposes the annual budget. Finally, the legislature may revoke rules of administrative agencies. Such control is rarely exercised, but the legislature retains this power through its delegation of rule-making powers to administrative agencies.

Executive Controls

The executive branch has the clearest line of authority over administrative agencies. Most agency heads are appointed to their positions by the president, who retains the authority to hire and fire them. Subject to the civil service system and Senate approval, the president can control the policies of many agency administrators. The administrators of independent agencies do have some independence from the executive, however. They have fixed terms of office, and they can generally be removed only *for cause*. The Securities and Exchange Commission, Federal Trade Commission, and Federal Reserve Board are among these independent agencies. Agencies may also be reorganized by the president with the consent of Congress. Thus, functions and powers of one agency can be transferred to other agencies.

Judicial Controls

As the *Iowa Utilities* case illustrates, the courts have the authority to review the rules, informal actions, and adjudications of administrative agencies. Review of agency actions by the judicial branch is discussed in a subsequent section of this chapter. These controls are often important in ensuring that administrative agencies do not act in an arbitrary manner.

ONLINE

The website at the Florida State University Law School provides a summary of the many agencies that are using the Internet to help them perform their various tasks.
http://www.law.fsu.edu/library/admin/admin2.html

http://
www.law.fsu.edu/library/admin

Public Internet Access and Public Control

The Internet allows the government to get closer to the people, and many federal agencies are using it to make the government less distant. From providing rule-making notices to on-line sources for needed documents such as renewed vehicle registration, or forms and information needed to obtain public assistance, governmental agencies are now providing the public with access to a great deal of their information through the Internet.

As to public control, concern over secret agency activities and agencies' misuse of information led to passage of the Freedom of Information Act (FOIA) in 1966. Congress sought to increase agencies' accountability to the public by mandating that agency files be open to public interest groups, scholars, journalists, and other interested parties. Businesses sometimes use the FOIA to review agency information about competing firms. Cases have sought to limit this use of agency files, but the

FSU COLLEGE OF LAW

ABA ADMINISTRATIVE PROCEDURE DATABASE

On Site Digital Text
Search
Federal Resources
State Resources
Organizations
Journals
Discussion Lists
Other Resources
Email Us

Welcome to the ABA Administrative Procedure Database, developed and maintained with the cooperation and support of the American Bar Association's Section of Administrative Law and Regulatory Practice and the Florida State University College of Law.

This site is designed to facilitate the exchange of information about federal and state administrative law among legislators, lawyers, hearing officers, judges, and citizens. This site contains links to federal and state Administrative Procedure Acts (APA), reform proposals, and organizational and other resources.

courts have held that the FOIA requires all agencies, departments, and independent commissions to make all agency documents publicly available *unless* the documents qualify for one of the statute's nine exemptions (see Exhibit 6.3).

In 1996, the president signed the Electronic Freedom of Information Act Amendment (EFOIA), clarifying the view that the FOIA include information to include information in electronic format. The act aso requires agencies to search for records in electronic format and to electronically publish frequently requested records. By way of comparison, the green paper (proposal) noting the need in EU countries for governments to provide information to the public was released in early 1999. It noted that public information should be made more accessible in electronic format. Public information is also seen as a key resource, one that can improve the competitiveness of European firms.

Almost all agencies provide Internet access to freedom of information requests for those seeking public or nonexempt information. Take a look at the Department of Labor site, http://www.dol.gopv/public/agencies/agency.htm, and click on its FOIA/Privacy link to see an example of one agency's way of handling such requests electronically.

FUNCTIONS OF ADMINISTRATIVE AGENCIES

ONLINE

The United States Department of Justice has a list of the FOIA websites for many federal agencies. **http://www.usdoj.gov/04foia/other_age.htm**

Administrative agencies usually perform several different functions. Of the more than 100 agencies at the federal level, the two that affect the most people are the Internal Revenue Service and the Social Security Administration. The Internal Revenue Service interprets the tax statutes, collects taxes, and makes rules and regulations that specify how taxpayers are to compute the taxes they owe to the federal government. The Social Security Administration provides information on the current status of individual accounts, determines eligibility for social security benefits, and issues millions of checks to eligible recipients.

Most administrative agency activities can be classified into three general functions. The first of these functions is rule-making. Many administrative agencies are authorized to make rules and regulations that have the effect of law. The second general function of administrative agencies is adjudication. Many agencies conduct **adjudicatory hearings** to determine whether a particular individual or business has violated a legislative statute or an administrative regulation. In a hearing, an agency finds facts and applies either laws or rules to those facts. Generally, the procedures

EXHIBIT 6.3 Freedom of Information Act Exemptions

1. Documents classified by the president in the national interest
2. Documents related to agency internal personnel practices
3. Documents whose disclosure is prohibited by other statutes
4. Documents containing trade secrets or financial data
5. Documents reflecting the deliberative process of agency policy formulation or containing advisory opinions
6. Personnel, medical, and similar files whose disclosure would be an unwarranted invasion of privacy
7. Selected law enforcement records
8. Documents regarding the operation of financial institutions
9. Geological and geophysical maps and data

at administrative hearings are similar to, but less formal than, those used in the courts. The federal courts process several hundred thousand cases each year, whereas several million claims are processed annually by federal agencies, and even more are processed by state and local agencies.

The third general function of administrative agencies is the performance of ministerial or informal actions. Agencies administer grants and assistance programs, undertake investigations, gather and analyze data, and issue reports. Some agencies grant patents, and others regulate immigration, classify grain, or review waste disposal plans.

ADMINISTRATIVE RULE-MAKING

Rule-making can be distinguished both from adjudication and from informal acts such as providing interpretations. Although both rule-making and adjudication use hearings, an agency action that affects a large number of people and does not depend on facts about individual circumstances is considered to be rule-making rather than adjudication. In contrast, adjudications usually concern only a few parties and are based on specific facts presented at a hearing.

On the other hand, it is the procedures that are used that distinguish interpretations from rules. Through the APA, Congress has directed agencies that want to issue rules that can have the effect of laws to use established rule-making procedures. Agency interpretations of laws or rules do not use those rule-making procedures. Consequently, an agency's interpretations do not have the same legal effect as its rules. Nevertheless, those interpretations are given significant weight when a court reviews agency actions. In *Thomas Jefferson Univ. v. Shalala* (512 U.S. 504, 514), the U.S. Supreme Court noted: "An agency's interpretation of its own regulation must be given controlling weight unless it is plainly erroneous or inconsistent with the regulation."

RULE-MAKING POWER

The power to make rules originates with the legislature, which then delegates some of its rule-making power to an administrative agency. Of course, the legislature also can later limit or revoke the agency's rule-making power. In the early 1980s, for example, the Federal Trade Commission (FTC) ruled that used car dealers had to disclose certain information about the defects of the cars they sold. After the dealers lobbied Congress, it specifically revoked the FTC's authority to make such rules. In the *Willamson Tobacco* case, we've seen that the FDA cannot make rules to regulate tobacco use or advertising.

According to the General Accounting Office, during fiscal year 2000 federal agencies issued 4,528 nonmajor rules and 65 major final rules. Among these rules were:

- 265 rules from the Internal Revenue Service
- 701 rules from the Environmental Protection Agency
- 263 rules from the Federal Communications Commission, including those establishing licensing requirements for wireless telecommunications and satellite service broadcasts
- 91 rules from the Agricultural Marketing Service, including ones regulating the quantity of Irish potatoes grown in Colorado and dried prunes in California
- 280 rules from the National Oceanic and Atmospheric Administration, such as those regulating the fishing for Pacific cod, Atlantic tuna, and Maine quahogs.

IMPOSING PROCEDURAL REQUIREMENTS

The legislature specifies the process agencies must use to make legislative types of rules or regulations. Sometimes the legislature tailors those procedures to a specific agency in the enabling legislation. More frequently, the legislature refers to another statute that governs rule-making and other administrative activities. Both Congress and state legislatures have passed special laws detailing the procedural requirements that agencies must follow in making rules and in performing adjudicative functions. The Administrative Procedures Act (APA) establishes such procedures for federal agencies.

Providing Notice

An agency engaged in rule-making must provide public notice that it will hold a hearing to receive comments about a particular problem or a specific rule proposal. Such notice must generally be provided at least 30 days before the hearing date.

Holding a Hearing to Receive Comments

Unlike a court trial or an administrative adjudicatory hearing, at a rule-making hearing there is usually no trial or adversarial proceeding. Instead, people affected by the proposed rule offer oral or written comments on the proposals, and the agency is represented by people who listen to those comments.

Preparing the Final Rule

After the hearing, the administrative agency reviews the comments offered by interested parties and affected businesses. It is required to provide a general and concise summary of the comments. It may revise or withdraw the proposed rule to reflect those comments, but it has no legal obligation to do so. If only a few people with a similar view offered comments, the hearing alone would not provide enough diversity of views. The agency is free to prepare its final rule in the most appropriate form, and it must then publish the rule. All federal rules appear in the *Federal Register* and are later compiled into the *Code of Federal Regulations* (CFR). Rules adopted by state administrative agencies may sometimes be found in sources such as the *Michigan Register*.

According to the General Accounting Office, for the 1998 year, the *Federal Register*—the daily governmental publication in which all proposed and final regulations are announced—was 68,571 pages long. The *Code of Federal Regulations* (a compilation of federal rules over a number of years) filled 114 volumes in 1970; by 1998, it filled 201 volumes and of those, fewer than 100 were classified as major rules, ones that would have an annual effect on the economy of at least $100 million.

http://

www.regulation.org/keyfacts.html

Key Regulatory Facts & Figures

THE FACTS

Although President Ronald Reagan succeeded in reversing the growing federal regulatory burden for a time, regulatory growth accelerated under President George Bush and exploded during President Bill Clinton's first term. Initially, the Republican-led 104th Congress made the reduction of spending by federal regulatory agencies a priority, and this focus led to a slower rate of growth in new regulations. Unfortunately, those efforts were short-lived.

THE NUMBER OF FEDERAL REGULATIONS [1]

FACT: Since 1997, the size, scope, and cost of the federal regulatory system has returned to pre-1994 levels and once again is increasing at record rates.

According to the U.S. General Accounting Office (GAO), between April 1, 1996, and March 13, 2001, federal regulatory agencies issued 21,653 final rules and sent them to Congress for review. Of this startling number, 335 were defined as "major" rules--rules that will have an annual effect on the economy of more than $100 million. [2]

- By the end of 1998, the *Federal Register*, the daily government publication in which all proposed and final regulations are announced, was 68,571 pages long, and 4,000 pages longer than in 1997. [3]
- The massive Code of Federal Regulations (CFR), an annual listing of executive agency regulations published in the *Federal Register*, includes all regulations now in effect. In 1998, the CFR filled 201 volumes with a total of 134,723 pages; it occupies 19 feet of shelf

Courtesy, The Heritage Foundation.

In the following case, the agency did not follow the APA's rule-making procedures. Secretary of Health and Human Services Heckler established a policy that imposed new duties on hospitals. The court discussed the agency's duty to consider "relevant factors to prevent arbitrary and capricious decision making and to assure rational consideration of the impact of the contemplated regulatory action." What concerned the court most regarding the establishment of this agency policy?

American Academy of Pediatrics v. Heckler

561 F.Supp. 395 (D.C.D.C. 1983)
United States District Court for the District of Columbia

Facts. This case involved the validity of an administrative rule published without benefit of public comment by Secretary of Health and Human Services (HHS) Heckler. The rule concerned the care and treatment of newborn infants in hospitals receiving federal funds. The rule was sparked by a case involving an infant born with Down syndrome and a surgically correctable blockage of his digestive tract that precluded normal feeding. The infant's parents refused to consent to surgery, and the hospital turned to the state for guidance. Despite the appointment of a special guardian, no judicial intervention occurred. Because the infant needed immediate surgery, he died within six days of birth.

Soon after that incident, the HHS published a rule in the *Code of Federal Regulations*. On behalf of HHS, Heckler asserted that because of the need to put a new policy into effect quickly, it would not seek public comment about its proposal. The rule published by the HHS required hospitals and other medical institutions receiving federal aid to post a sign warning that failure to feed and care for handicapped infants violated federal law. It authorized an immediate investigation by a squad from the HHS office to protect the health of such an infant, and it required institutions receiving federal aid to give 24-hour access to hospital records and facilities during the investigation.

Heckler asserted that as the new policy was an agency interpretation, not a proposal rule, she did not need to follow the rule-making process specified by the Administrative Procedures Act (APA). The American Academy of Pediatrics disagreed and sued Heckler. Heckler submitted a record to the court of the factors she considered before interpreting the policy.

Legal Issue. Was Heckler's implementation of the new policy, without following the APA's rulemaking procedures, arbitrary and capricious?

Opinion. Judge Gesell. The Administrative Procedures Act was designed to curb bureaucratic actions taken without consultation and notice to persons affected. Broad delegations of rulemaking authority from the Congress were intended to be tempered by assuring a degree of due process for those to be governed by the rule. The greater the impact of the regulation upon established practices or the greater the number of people directly affected, the more the courts have insisted that the right of comment by those affected be preserved.

Thus the Act has been generally construed to curtail rulemaking without comment. Moreover, the Act requires that all regulations shall issue only after the rulemaker has considered relevant factors to prevent arbitrary and capricious decision making and to assure rational consideration of the impact of the contemplated regulatory action. The instant regulation offends these established precepts to a remarkable extent.

The Court is well aware that the agency rulemaking must be considered deferentially and that this Court is prohibited from substituting its own judgment for that of the agency's decision. Nevertheless, this Court may not, on the other hand, "rubber-stamp" challenged agency decisions and must inquire whether the agency's action was based on a consideration of the relevant factors. Lacking such consideration, the regulation fails to satisfy the test of rationality and cannot be sustained because it is arbitrary and capricious.

The record tendered in support of the Secretary's action here clearly establishes that many highly relevant factors central to any application of section 504 to medical care of newborn infants were not considered prior to promulgation of the challenged rule. All matters considered by the Secretary are documented in Court Exhibit A. However, that record reflects no consideration whatsoever of the disruptive effects of a 24-hour, toll-free "hotline" upon ongoing treatment of newborns. As indicated, any anonymous tipster, for whatever personal motive, can trigger an investigation involving immediate inspection of hospital records and facilities and interviewing of involved families and medical personnel. In a desperate situation where medical decisions must be made on short notice by physicians, hospital personnel and often distraught parents, the sudden descent of "Baby Doe" squads on the scene, monopolizing physician and nurse time and making hospital charts and records unavailable during treatment, can hardly be presumed to produce higher quality care for the infant.

It is clear that a primary purpose of the regulation is to require physicians treating newborns to take into account only wholly medical risk-benefit considerations to prevent parents from having any influence upon decisions as to whether further medical treatment is desirable. The Secretary did not appear to give the slightest consideration to the advantages and disadvantages of relying on the wishes of the parents who, knowing the setting in which the child may be raised, in many ways are in the best position to evaluate the infant's best interests.

None of these sensitive considerations touching so intimately on the quality of the infant's expected life were even tentatively noted. No attempt was made to address the issue of whether termination of painful, intrusive medical treatment might be appropriate where an infant's clear prognosis is death within days or months or to specify the level of appropriate care in futile cases.

. . . Even if the regulation could withstand the requirements of [the APA], it must be declared invalid due to the Secretary's failure to follow procedural requirements in its promulgation. It is undisputed that the rule was not issued in accordance with either the public notice or 30-day delay-of-effective-date requirements of the APA. The Secretary argues that the rule is either a "procedural" or "interpretative" rule not subject to the requirements of these provisions, or that waiver of these requirements is appropriate given the need "to protect life from imminent harm." Neither of these arguments has merit.

This regulation cannot be sustained. It is arbitrary and capricious. . . . At the minimum, wide public comment prior to rulemaking is essential. Only by preserving this democratic process can good intentions be tempered by wisdom and experience.

Case Questions

1. What two requirements does the Administrative Procedure Act impose on agencies contemplating rule-making actions?
2. What are some of the appropriate factors that the agency did not consider in this case?
3. If the agency had considered the appropriate factors, would the regulation have been legal?
4. After the September 11, 2001 terrorist attack, several governmental agencies proposed new rules that included restricting access to governmental buildings and requiring airports to enhance their security. Should these rules be invalid if they did not follow the APA rule-making requirements?

Commentary

The APA and Internet Domain Names

Professor Michael Froomkin at the University of Miami School of Law has written a provocative article in the *Duke Law Journal* that suggests that the regulation of domain names by the Internet Corporation for Assigned Names and Numbers (ICANN) probably violates the Administrative Procedures Act for notice and comment in its rule-making activities. In "Wrong Turn in Cyberspace: Using ICANN to Route around the APA and the Constitution," he argues that ICANN has been making domain name policy for several years under contract with the Department of Commerce, which gave ICANN regulatory authority to control the domain name system.

According to Professor Froomkin, either the Department of Commerce is violating the APA by having ICANN make rules that violates the procedural requirements the Administrative Procedures Act places on the Department of Commerce, or it is unconstitutionally delegating its powers over domain names to ICANN. ICANN is a private, nonprofit California corporation that was created by an international group after a U.S. interagency task force called for the creation of such an organization instead of having the Department of Commerce issue substantive rules. Such substantive rules would be subject to the APA requirements and to judicial review of the agency's action.

The U.S. government came to control the domain name system because it came into the hands of people whose work on it was funded by government grants. The movement of the regulation of the domain name system from government to a private nonprofit corporate entity raises, according to Froomkin, a number of problems:

1. It reduces public participation in decision making over public issues.
2. It vests key decision-making power in an essentially unaccountable private body that is capable of abusing its authority.
3. It nearly eliminates the possibility for judicial review of critical decisions regarding the domain name system.

ADMINISTRATIVE ADJUDICATION

An administrative adjudication usually concerns only a few people and uses trial types of procedures at a hearing. Many administrative agencies perform adjudication functions. They determine facts, apply rules or laws to those facts, and reach a decision. In performing adjudicative functions, both federal and state agencies generally follow court types of procedures. The most important differences between agency adjudicative procedures and those used in traditional court trials are that an administrative hearing does not use a jury and most hearings do not follow all of the traditional rules of evidence. Most of the procedures governing administrative adjudications are specified in the APA or similar laws.

ADJUDICATION PROCESS

Most administrative adjudications follow the traditional sequence of (1) investigation, (2) complaint and answer, (3) hearing, and (4) decision or order. Of course, many of the matters that are investigated never reach the complaint stage. Even after a complaint has been filed, most controversies are settled without a full hearing. At the end of a hearing, the administrative law judge issues an order based on the application of relevant law to the facts presented at the hearing. Frequently, that order may be appealed first to some other person or the governing board of the agency and then into a court of appeals.

NEED FOR A TRIAL TYPE OF HEARING

Although agencies engaged in adjudication generally do follow the trial-like procedures noted in the previous section, some hearings that are adjudicatory in nature do not require that type of process. Administrative agencies and the businesses they regulate frequently have different views regarding what procedures the agencies should follow in carrying out their activities. If an agency plans to revoke a license held by a business, does it first have to hold a trial type of hearing? This issue is addressed in the following case.

Gallagher & Ascher v. Simon

678 F.2d 1007 (1982)
Seventh Circuit Court of Appeals

Facts. The Customs Service, a division of the Department of the Treasury, determined that Gallagher, an importing business, should lose its license as a customs broker because it had violated a "timely entry" Treasury Department regulation. Gallagher argued that, before suspending its license, the Treasury Department should have held an adjudicatory hearing and granted it all the rights and procedures generally available in a trial. Because the Customs Service was a division of the Department of the Treasury, Gallagher sued Simon, the secretary of the Treasury. After the federal district court decided in Simon's favor, Gallagher appealed to the Court of Appeals.

Legal Issue. If an agency is going to suspend a customs broker's license, does it first have to hold an adjudicating hearing?

Opinion. Circuit Judge Cudahy. At the time this case began, Gallagher was a licensed customs broker in Chicago. It had been issued a special permit by the Treasury Department which allowed it to secure the immediate release of imported goods by submitting invoices to customs inspectors for examination at the point of entry. Gallagher was allowed to complete the entry documents and pay the duty at a later time, referred to as making a "timely entry."

Regulations defined timely entry as being within 10 days after the day on which the imported merchandise was first released under a special permit.

If a broker fails to make timely entry, the District Director of the Customs Service initiates a claim for liquidated damages. Generally, warning letters are then sent to offending brokers. Notice of the suspension of the special permit follows if brokers continue not to make timely entries.

On July 23, 1976, District Director Hertz issued a warning letter to Gallagher, accusing it of making 9 late entries in the preceding month. The warning letter stated the number of violations was unacceptably large and advised that if Gallagher's performance did not improve, its special term permit would be suspended in September. Gallagher took no action. . . . When Gallagher made 21 untimely entries in August, District Director Hertz, in a September 12 letter, issued an order suspending Gallagher's special term permit for a period of 30 days commencing . . . September 17, 1976. . . . Gallagher then filed suit in district court.

The APA provides that the formal adjudication procedures described in sections 556 and 557 must be followed "in every case of adjudication required by statute to be determined on the record after opportunity for an agency hearing. . . ." The APA, as many courts have recognized, does not itself mandate that a trial-type hearing be held where none is required under the administrative agency's own governing statute; the APA simply dictates the procedures to be followed when another statute provides for a hearing. Thus, if the governing statute does not require that a hearing be conducted in connection with a particular agency action, [the adjudication provisions] "do not come into play." In the instant case, the regulation authorizing the District Director to suspend a broker's special term permit does not provide an opportunity for an agency hearing. Consequently, . . . the APA does not require that a permit suspension comply with the procedures to be used in an adjudicatory hearing.

The plaintiffs argue that all license suspension and revocation cases [include] an independent right to an adjudicatory hearing. Section 558(c) of the APA provides in pertinent part:

When application is made for a license required by law, the agency . . . shall set and complete proceedings required to be conducted in accordance with sections 556 and 557 of this title or other proceedings required by law and shall make its decision. Except in cases of willfulness or those in which public health, interest, or safety requires otherwise, the withdrawal, suspension, revocation, or annulment of a license is lawful only if, before the institution of agency proceedings therefore, the licensee has been given—(1) notice by the agency in writing of the facts or conduct which may warrant the action; and (2) opportunity to demonstrate or achieve compliance with all lawful requirements.

The instant case involves an agency decision to suspend a license and thus is governed by the second sentence in section 558(c). Read literally, all that this sentence requires of an agency proposing the suspension of a license is that the licensee receive prior written notice of the facts warranting the suspension and an "opportunity to demonstrate or achieve compliance" with all legal requirements. It does not mandate any sort of hearing, let alone a trial-type hearing described in sections 556 and 557.

The legislative history . . . indicates that the special treatment accorded licensees was not intended to trigger a right to an adjudicatory hearing. The district court concluded that the District Director had met his obligations under this section, and we agree. The notice requirement was satisfied in the instant case by the warning letters sent by the District Director to Gallagher.

The second requirement—an opportunity to demonstrate or achieve compliance—was also met in the instant case. An opportunity to achieve compliance was, indeed, the very purpose of the warning letters, which threatened suspension of the term special permits only if the broker's conduct did not improve. Such a notice of violations and a request to comply in the future meet the requirements of section 558(c).

Decision. We conclude that the impact of the two suspensions, relatively short in duration and affecting only a portion of the customs broker's business, was not so great as to require more formal procedures than were afforded. We conclude that these government interests outweigh the factors supporting additional procedural safeguards, the costs of which would be unduly great. Affirmed.

Case Questions

1. Under what circumstances should an administrative agency consult the Administrative Procedures Act to determine whether a trial type of hearing is required?
2. What provision of the APA controlled the need for a trial type of hearing in this case?
3. What procedures does the APA require an administrative agency to follow in suspending or revoking a license? How were those procedures followed here?

Administrators involved in rule-making, adjudication, or even in informal actions must be aware of the important role they play in our legal system. People interacting with administrators have a right to expect fairness and impartiality. Political considerations or personal preferences regarding the outcome of adjudications or the wording of proposed regulations should not influence their judgment.

INFORMAL ADMINISTRATIVE ACTIVITIES

GENERAL ACTIVITIES

Most agency actions are informal rather than adjudicative or legislative. Administrative agencies engage in a wide variety of informal actions, many of which are not subject to court review. In some instances, however, such decisions are reviewed informally within the agency. Frequently, the action taken by the initial decision maker can be reviewed by an immediate supervisor and again by a person at the agency's highest level. Critics suggest that such reviews are merely perfunctory and perhaps not impartial. It is important, however, that all of the expert agency personnel consider and review decisions affecting regulated business to assure consistency within the agency in matters affecting similar firms.

INFORMATION-GATHERING ACTIVITIES

Administrative agencies gather information through three types of activities. First, many agencies gather and analyze information as they engage in rule-making or adjudication. Many legislative statutes and administrative regulations require regulated companies to submit reports, financial records, and other documents. Because such records are usually considered public documents, the U.S. Constitution's Fifth Amendment privilege against self-incrimination does not protect them from disclosure. Further, an agency may share documents in the public record with other agencies. Because various agencies require many different reports, the cost of complying with agency requests for information can be a significant burden for businesses, particularly small firms. This expense has led to the Paperwork Reduction Act and to the regulatory cost-benefit analysis discussed later in this chapter.

Ethical Issue

Regulators, administrative law judges, and caseworkers in administrative agencies hold powerful positions because of their role in making, interpreting, and enforcing the law. An administrator engaged in rule-making may assign greater importance to the public comments made by parties in favor of a proposed rule than to those made by parties opposed to the ruling. Administrators may decide to proceed to a hearing in some cases while declining to initiate cases based on individual complaints in other situations. Administrative law judges may consider individual circumstances in one situation where a rule or statute is not followed but refuse to overlook violations in other cases. In seeking to perform informal activities, some caseworkers may apply one administrative policy in certain cases and another in different cases, even though the facts of the problems appear to be similar.

When impartiality or fairness is lacking or policies are not applied evenly, the actions of administrators are unethical.

Second, administrative agencies hold informal hearings to gather information. Many agencies use subpoena power to compel the testimony of witnesses or the production of needed documents at such hearings. For instance, in the *Pediatrics* case, the HHS secretary could have held informal hearings with hospital administrators, doctors, and parents to determine whether the department should respond to the situation with a rule.

Third, agencies often have the power to inspect the books and records or the premises of regulated businesses. The Securities and Exchange Commission (SEC) investigates complaints against securities brokers. If some basis for such a complaint exists, the SEC may want to inspect a broker's books and records. During the late 1980s, the SEC conducted numerous investigations about possible violations of insider trading laws and stock manipulations. The investigations led to both criminal and civil charges against individuals and securities firms.

Occupational Safety and Health Administration inspectors visit factories and plants to determine if conditions are unsafe and whether OSHA's safety rules are being violated. Because regulatory inspections serve the public interest, sme have argued that courts give special interpretations to the Fourth Amendment with regard to administrative inspections. Perhaps the probable cause requirement usually followed in criminal cases should be relaxed in dealing with administrative warrant procedures. The extract from the following case shows that inspections conducted by administrative agencies are in fact subjected to a less onerous standard than inspections conducted by criminal investigators.

Marshall v. Barlow's, Inc.

436 U.S. 307 (1978)
United States Supreme Court

Facts. An OSHA inspector sought to inspect and search Barlow's plumbing business in Idaho. The inspector said that OSHA was simply conducting a routine inspection of the premises. Barlow's refused to permit the inspection, claiming the Fourth Amendment protected it against unreasonable searches, and required OSHA to obtain a warrant before conducting an inspection. The trial court granted Barlow's an injunction to prevent OSHA from conducting a warrantless search. Marshall, the Secretary of Labor who oversees OSHA, appealed to the Supreme Court.

Legal Issue. Does OSHA have to obtain a search warrant before it conducts a routine inspection of the safety conditions at a business firm? If a warrant is required, must the agency prove probable cause of a crime to obtain the warrant?

Opinion. Justice White. The Occupational Safety and Health Act of 1970 (OSHA) empowers agents of the Secretary of Labor (Secretary) to search the work area of any employment facility within the Act's jurisdiction. The purpose of the search is to inspect for safety hazards and violations of OSHA regulations. No search warrant or other process is expressly required under the Act.

The Secretary urges that warrantless inspections to enforce OSHA are reasonable within the meaning of the Fourth Amendment. . . . The Warrant Clause of the Fourth Amendment protects commercial buildings as well as private homes. To hold otherwise would belie the origin of that Amendment, and the American colonial experience. The Fourth Amendment's commands grew in large measure out of the colonists' experience with the writs of assistance [that] granted sweeping power to customs officials and other agents of the King to search for smuggled goods. Against this background, it is untenable that the ban on warrantless searches was not intended to shield places of business as well as of residence. This Court has already held that warrantless searches are generally unreasonable, and that this rule applies to commercial premises as well as to homes.

As we explained in *Camara*, a search of private houses is presumptively unreasonable if conducted without a warrant. The businessman, like the occupant of a residence, has a constitutional right to go about his business free from unreasonable official entries upon his private commercial property. The businessman, too, has that right placed in jeopardy if the decision to enter and inspect for violation of regulatory laws can be made and enforced by the inspector in the field without official authority evidenced by a warrant.

The Secretary submits that warrantless inspections are essential to the proper enforcement of OSHA because they afford the opportunity to inspect without prior notice and hence to preserve the advantages of surprise. . . . The risk is that during the interval between an inspector's initial request to search a plant and his procuring a warrant following the owner's refusal of permission, violations of this latter type could be corrected and thus escape the inspector's notice.

We are unconvinced, however, that requiring warrants to inspect will impose serious burdens on the inspection system or the courts, will prevent inspections necessary to enforce the statute, or will make them less effective. In the first place, the great majority of businessmen can be expected in normal course to consent to inspection without warrant; the Secretary has not brought to this Court's attention any widespread pattern of refusal.

Whether the Secretary proceeds to secure a warrant or other process, with or without prior notice, his entitlement to inspect will not depend on his demonstrating probable cause to believe that conditions in violation of OSHA exist on the premises. Probable cause in the criminal law sense is not required. For purposes of an administrative search such as this, probable cause justifying the issuance of a warrant may be based not only on specific evidence of an existing violation but also on showing that "reasonable legislative or administrative standards for conducting an . . . inspection are satisfied with respect to a particular [establishment]."

A warrant could be based on a showing that a specific business has been chosen for an OSHA search on the basis of a general administrative plan for the enforcement of the Act derived from neutral sources such as, for example, the dispersion of employees in various types of industries across a given area, and the desired frequency of searches in any of the lesser divisions of the area, would protect an employer's Fourth Amendment rights. We doubt that the consumption of enforcement energies in the obtaining of such warrants will exceed manageable proportions.

Decision. We hold that Barlow's was entitled to a declaratory judgment that the Act is unconstitutional insofar as it purports to authorize inspections without warrant or its equivalent and to an injunction enjoining the Act's enforcement to that extent. The judgment of the District Court is therefore affirmed.

Case Questions

1. What will OSHA have to do if it still wants to search Barlow's premises?
2. How does the need for a warrant protect the businessperson if a government official determines that a search is necessary?
3. Does the requirement of an administrative search warrant make it more difficult and expensive for OSHA to conduct inspections?

JUDICIAL REVIEW AND ADMINISTRATIVE AGENCIES

The scope of judicial review of administrative decisions is limited because administrative agencies are considered experts in the activities assigned to them. Because courts, unlike agencies, hear a wide diversity of cases, they seldom have the specialized knowledge possessed by agencies.

DETERMINING WHETHER AN AGENCY ACTIVITY IS REVIEWABLE

As some agency actions are not subject to judicial review and the standards of review differ depending on the type of activity being reviewed, a court contemplating a review of some agency action must first answer three questions about its possible review.

1. Is the agency activity subject to judicial review?
2. If so, are there reasons not to review this particular problem or decision?
3. What standards or criteria should be used to determine the legality or propriety of the agency's activity?

Agency Activities That Are Not Reviewable

Sometimes Congress dictates that certain agency actions are final—not to be reviewed by courts. If the legislature clearly specifies that the agency has the final authority over a matter, the courts will follow the **statutory preclusion** of judicial review. For example, the administrator of Veterans Affairs has the final authority to determine the benefits due to veterans:

[T]he decisions of the administrator on any question of law or fact under any law administered by the Veterans Administration providing benefits for any veterans and their dependents or survivors shall be final and no other official or any court of the United States shall have the power or jurisdiction to review any decision.

In other cases, the decision not to review certain agency actions is made by the agency itself, with the approval of the courts. For example, the Food and Drug Administration was asked to investigate a state's use of drugs in administering capital punishment. The agency declined to do so, and the court refused to review this agency action. Thus, an agency's decision not to act, not to investigate, or not to file a complaint against a firm is often considered an unreviewable decision. This stance is justified because the agency has discretion to make decisions on the use of its resources to carry out the policies set by the legislature. Thus, **discretionary activities** of agencies generally are not reviewable by the courts.

Reasons Not to Review

The second judicial review question focuses on whether there are reasons that a court should not review an administrative agency action, even though it could do so. Answering these questions depends on (1) the person seeking review (a matter of *standing*), (2) the finality of the agency's decision (a matter of *ripeness*), (3) the extent to which the agency has reviewed the activities (a matter of *exhaustion of administrative remedies*), and (4) whether the agency should review before a court does so (a matter of *primary jurisdiction*). These questions are summarized in Exhibit 6.4.

STANDARDS FOR JUDICIAL REVIEW

Finally, a court must determine the standards it will use to judge or measure the administrative agency's activity. Over time, the courts have provided answers to

EXHIBIT 6.4 Reasons Why a Court May Not Review Agency Actions

Topic	Concern of Courts	Reasons for a Court Not to Review
Standing	*Who* seeks review?	If the person is not injured in some way, there may not be a disputed case.
Ripeness	*When* will the problem be ready for review?	If the agency activity is not final, the court should not act.
Exhaustion	*When* is the party seeking review?	If the affected person has remedies available in the agency, the court should not review at this time.
Primary Jurisdiction	*Where* is review to take place?	If a review can be obtained from the agency and the court, perhaps the court should defer to the agency.

disputes involving each of the three types of administrative activities: the legislative activity of rule-making, the judicial activity of adjudication, and the review of informal agency actions. In general, courts examine whether an agency has clearly explained why and how it reached a decision. However, courts do not second-guess agency decisions.

REVIEW OF AGENCY LEGISLATIVE AND RULE-MAKING ACTIVITIES

When an agency performs a legislative function such as rule-making, the reviewing court seeks to answer several specific questions.

1. Is the delegation of legislative authority to the agency sufficiently limited?
2. Did the agency's action fall within the powers granted to the agency by the legislature?
3. Did the agency's action violate any constitutional or statutory requirements imposed on the agency?
4. Did the agency follow proper procedures (usually specified by statute)?
5. Is the action of the agency "arbitrary or capricious"?

Courts uphold an agency legislative action if these five questions are answered satisfactorily. In the *Vermont Yankee* case, the lower court found the agency's rule-making procedures improper. The U.S. Supreme Court's review clearly indicates that judicial review has a limited role with regard to the rule-making of administrative agencies.

Vermont Yankee Nuclear Power Corporation v. Natural Resources Defense Council, Inc.

435 U.S. 519 (1978)
United States Supreme Court

Facts. This case involved granting a construction permit and later an operating permit for the Vermont Yankee nuclear power plant. The Atomic Energy Commission was authorized to make decisions regarding applications for such a permit. The commission's decision-making process required a three-member Atomic Safety and Licensing Board to conduct a public adjudicatory hearing. At that hearing, the Natural Resources Defense Council (NRDC) unsuccessfully sought to require the board to consider the environmental effects of plant operations concerned with reprocessed nuclear fuel. The commission did, however, begin rule-making proceedings to examine the concern raised by the NRDC.

During those rule-making proceedings, the commission indicated that it would not allow cross-examination of the participants' testimony but that any person giving oral testimony would be subject to questioning by the commission. After the rule-making hearing, the commission adopted a rule dealing with the impact of fuel reprocessing in licensing procedures. The NRDC objected to the rule-making process and appealed the commission decision to the Court of Appeals, which found the rulemaking procedure inadequate.

Legal Issue. If an agency complies with the APA's rule-making requirements, can a court require it to use additional procedural safeguards?

Opinion. Justice Rehnquist. In 1946, Congress enacted the Administrative Procedures Act, which was not only a "new, basic and comprehensive regulation of procedures in many agencies," but was also a legislative enactment which settled "long-continued and hard-fought contentions, and enacts a formula upon which social and political forces have come to rest."

Section 4 of the Act, dealing with rulemaking, requires in subsection (b) that "notice of proposed rulemaking shall be published in the Federal Register . . . ," describes the contents of that notice, and goes on to require in subsection (c) that after notice, the agency "shall give interested persons an opportunity to participate in the rulemaking through submission of written data, views, or arguments with or without opportunity for oral presentation. After consideration of the relevant matter presented, the agency shall incorporate in the rules adopted a concise general statement of their basis and purpose."

In interpreting this provision of the Act, we [have] held that generally speaking this section of the Act establishes the maximum procedural requirements which Congress was willing to have the courts impose on agencies in conducting rulemaking procedures. Agencies are free to grant additional procedural rights in the exercise of their discretion, but reviewing courts are generally not free to impose them if the agencies have not granted them....

Much of the controversy in this case revolves around the procedures used in the rulemaking hearing which commenced in February 1973. The Commission indicated that while discovery or cross-examination would not be utilized, the Environmental Survey would be available to the public before the hearing along with the extensive background documents cited therein.

The Licensing Board identified as the principal procedural question the propriety of declining to use full formal adjudicative procedures.... In some circumstances additional procedures may be required in order to afford the aggrieved individuals due process. But, this much is absolutely clear. Absent constitutional constraints or extremely compelling circumstances the "administrative agencies should be free to fashion their own rules of procedure and to pursue methods of inquiry capable of permitting them to discharge their multitudinous duties."

NRDC argues that section 4 of the Administrative Procedures Act, merely establishes lower procedural bounds and that a court may routinely require more than the minimum when an agency's proposed rule addresses complex or technical factual issues. We think the legislative history does not bear out its contention. The Senate Report explains what eventually became section 4 thus:

"The bill is an outline of minimum essential rights and procedures.... It affords private parties a means of knowing what their rights are and how they may protect them. And the Attorney General's Manual on the Administrative Procedures Act ... further confirms that view. In short, all of this leaves little doubt that Congress intended that the discretion of the agencies and not that of the courts be exercised in determining when extra procedural devices should be employed."

There are compelling reasons for construing section 4 in this manner. In the first place, if courts continually review agency proceedings to determine whether the agency employed procedures which were, in the court's opinion, perfectly tailored to reach what the court perceives to be the "best" or "correct" result, judicial review would be totally unpredictable. And the agencies, operating under this vague injunction to employ the "best" procedures and facing the threat of reversal if they did not, would undoubtedly adopt full adjudicatory procedures in every instance. Not only would this totally disrupt the statutory scheme through which Congress enacted "a formula upon which opposing social and political forces have come to rest," but all the inherent advantages of informal rulemaking would be totally lost.

Secondly, it is obvious that the court in these cases reviewed the agency's choice of procedures on the basis of the record actually produced at the hearing, and not on the basis of the information available to the agency when it made the decision to structure the proceedings in a certain way. This sort of Monday morning quarterbacking not only encourages but almost compels the agency to conduct all rulemaking proceedings with the full panoply of procedural devices normally associated only with adjudicatory hearings.

Finally, and perhaps most importantly, this sort of review fundamentally misconceives the nature of the standard for judicial review of an agency rule. Thus, the adequacy of the "record" in this type of proceeding is not correlated directly to the type of procedural devices employed but rather turns on whether the agency has followed the statutory mandate of the Administrative Procedures Act or other relevant statutes.

Decision. We find that the Commission did follow the APA requirements. This sort of unwarranted judicial examination of perceived procedural shortcomings of a rulemaking proceeding can do nothing but seriously interfere with that process prescribed by Congress. We reverse the Court of Appeals judgment and remand the decision to the District Court.

Case Questions

1. What element of the rule-making procedures was questioned by the Court of Appeals?
2. What are the sources of law that might be consulted to determine the rule-making procedures that an agency should use?
3. What source does the Supreme Court indicate should generally determine the appropriate agency rule-making procedures?

REVIEW OF AGENCY ADJUDICATORY ACTIVITIES

When a court performs a review of an agency's adjudication function, its review process is different from its review of rule-making, because adjudication leaves a formal record of the hearing that can be examined. The following questions are generally examined when a court reviews an agency adjudicatory action.

1. Did the agency violate any constitutional or statutory provisions imposed on it?
2. Does the agency have proper jurisdiction to decide the case?
3. Did the agency follow proper procedures (usually established by statute)?
4. Is the agency's decision supported by "substantial evidence" in its record?

REVIEW OF AGENCY INFORMAL ACTIVITIES

Although agency informal actions are often discretionary and not subject to court review, courts do sometimes review an agency's informal activities. In the *Overton Park* case that follows, the court first examines the question of reviewability. Once a court determines that an agency's action is subject to review, what other factors influence that review? (See Exhibit 6.5.) Read the case and see how the court determines the answers to other questions affecting the judicial review of informal agency activities.

EXHIBIT 6.5 Questions Affecting Review of Agency Informal Actions

1. Is the action in question subject to judicial review?
2. Did the agency act within the scope of its authority?
3. Did the agency follow the procedural requirements?
4. Was the agency's action "arbitrary and capricious"?

Citizens to Preserve Overton Park v. Volpe

401 U.S. 402 (1981)
United States Supreme Court

Facts. Secretary of Transportation Volpe determined that a federal highway (Interstate 40) could be built through a park in Memphis, Tennessee. Several federal laws prohibited the agency from authorizing the use of park property to construct a highway if feasible and prudent alternative locations were available. Citizens to Preserve Overton Park sued in federal district court, claiming that the agency's decision was invalid because it did not make formal findings of fact in support of the decision. This group also claimed that the agency's decision should be reviewed by the courts. Both the district court and the appellate court rejected the group's claim because they found the secretary's decision to be unreviewable by the courts. The group then appealed to the Supreme Court.

Legal Issue. Can a group of citizens seek court review of an agency's determination that a federal highway can be built through a park?

Opinion. Justice Marshall. A threshold question—whether petitioners are entitled to any judicial review—is easily answered. . . . The Administrative Procedures Act provides that the action of "each authority of the Government of the United States," which includes the Department of Transportation, is subject to judicial review except where there is a statutory prohibition on review or where "agency action is committed to agency discretion by law." In this case, there is no indication that Congress sought to prohibit judicial review and there is most certainly no "clear and convincing evidence of a legislative intent" to restrict access to judicial review.

Similarly, the Secretary's decision here does not fall within the exception for action "committed to agency discretion." This is a very narrow exception. The very existence of the statutes indicates that protection of parkland was to be given paramount importance. The few green havens that are public parks were not to be lost unless there were truly unusual factors present in a particular case or the cost or community disruption resulting from alternative routes reached extraordinary magnitudes. If the statutes are to have any meaning, the Secretary cannot approve the destruction of parkland unless he finds that alternative routes present unique problems.

Plainly, there is "law to apply" and thus the exemption for action "committed to agency discretion" is inapplicable. But the existence of judicial review is only the start: the standard for review must also be determined. For that we must look [again] to . . . the Administrative Procedures Act, which provides that a "reviewing court shall hold unlawful and set aside agency action, findings, and conclusions found" not to meet six separate standards. In all cases agency action must be set aside if the action was "arbitrary, capricious, an abuse of discretion, or otherwise not in accordance with law" or if the action failed to meet statutory, procedural, or constitutional requirements.

The generally applicable standards . . . require the reviewing court to engage in a substantial inquiry. Certainly, the Secretary's decision is entitled to a presumption of regularity. But that presumption is not to shield his action from a thorough, probing, in-depth review.

The court is first required to decide whether the Secretary acted within the scope of his authority. . . . The reviewing court must consider whether the Secretary properly construed his authority to approve the use of parkland as limited to situations where there are not feasible alternative routes. . . . And the reviewing court must be able to find that the Secretary could have reasonably believed that in this case there are no feasible alternatives or that alternatives do involve unique problems.

Scrutiny of the facts does not end, however, with the determination that the Secretary has acted within the scope of his statutory authority. [The APA also] requires a finding that the actual choice made was not "arbitrary, capricious, an abuse of discretion, or otherwise not in accordance with law." . . . To make this finding the court must consider whether the decision was based on consideration of the relevant factors and whether there has been a clear error of judgment.

Although this inquiry into the facts is to be searching and careful, the ultimate standard of review is a narrow one. The court is not empowered to substitute its judgment for that of the agency.

The final inquiry is whether the Secretary's action followed the necessary procedural requirements. Here the only procedural error alleged is the failure of the Secretary to make formal findings and state his reason for allowing the highway to be built through the park. Here, there is an administrative record that allows the full, prompt review of the Secretary's action that is sought without additional delay which would result from having a remand to the Secretary. That administrative record is not, however, before us.

Decision. It is necessary to remand this case to the District Court for review of the Secretary's decision. That review is to be based on the full administrative record that was before the Secretary at the time he made his decision.

Case Questions

1. What was the court's answer to the allegation that the administrative action was not subject to judicial review?
2. How did the court determine whether the agency's actions were arbitrary and capricious?
3. Why did the court send this case back to the district court for further review?

BUSINESS INTERACTION WITH AN ADMINISTRATIVE AGENCY

INFORMATION AND INFLUENCE THROUGH TRADE ASSOCIATIONS

Because administrative agencies perform a variety of functions, businesses interact with them in different ways. Almost all businesses try to keep informed about relevant agency rulings and regulations. Small businesses frequently rely on trade associations to alert them to agency proposals. Trade associations also offer conventions, training courses, and programs that keep members abreast of current political developments. Today, more than 2,500 trade associations are based in Washington, D.C., and hundreds more are found in each of the state capitals and in major cities. Trade associations generally seek the adoption of administrative rules and legislation favorable to their members.

COST-BENEFIT ANALYSIS

Every business must comply with administrative requirements, orders, and regulations, whether or not it can stay informed about them and comment on their development. What is the cost of such compliance? Several executive orders issued in the 1980s require executive agencies to make a cost-benefit analysis of all new rules. In addition, some of the independent agencies perform cost-benefit analyses.

There are several ways to determine the cost of regulations. According to estimates given in 1999 by the Office of Management and Budget, the total direct cost of regulations is in the range of $200 billion to $300 billion. Other estimates by business groups suggest the overall direct costs to be more than $500 billion.

Although the direct cost of compliance with agency regulations can be estimated, the benefit gained from administrative agency activities is more difficult to assess. What effects do EPA regulations mandating cleanup of air, water, and land pollution have on the health of individuals? If the FDA prevents drugs with significant side effects from being marketed, how many deformities, injuries, and even deaths are prevented? If the FAA requires increased maintenance on commercial airplanes, how many crashes are prevented? What is the value to society of less pollution, fewer dangerous drugs, safer air travel, and fewer injuries and deaths?

ONLINE

Information about some of the agencies of the European Union can be found at **http://www.europa.eu.int/agencies/carte_en.htm**

International Commentary

Administrative Law and European Administrative Space

From the time of Napoleon, administrative law has had a major role in the legal environment of Europe. Governmental regulation and the administrative "state" have met with greater acceptance there than in the New World. Of course, the sources of administrative regulation in Europe have changed dramatically in recent years. Although each country maintains its own administrative structure, more major administrative decisions are now being made at the regional or community level than at the national level.

In the European Union, the ***Commission***, which now has 20 members, acts as the executive branch. Each commissioner supervises a directorate encompassing a functional area such as transportation, energy, or agriculture. The Commission proposes regulations and directives to the ***Council***, the legislative body, and seeks to ensure that European Community laws are followed. Regulations proposed by the Commission and approved by the Council are directly applicable in EC countries, whereas directives leave to the member country the method of achieving the aims noted in the directive.

The administrators and bureaucrats employed in the executive agencies of the European Commission are known as *Eurocrats*. Like their counterparts in Washington, D.C., the 15,000 Eurocrats in Brussels draft rules, bring enforcement actions, and recommend changes in the legislation of member countries. Rule-writers are divided into 22 administrative directorates-general. They, and the staff of the commissioners, are at the center of the Brussels bureaucracy. A number of recent directives from the European Commission directly affect the legal environment of e-commerce, including:

1. Personal data privacy protection in the electronic communications sector
2. Internet jurisdiction in civil and commercial matters
3. E-commerce in the internal market
4. Copyright and related rights in the information age and digital signatures
5. Value-added taxes on e-services

Moreover, the costs and benefits of specific regulations do not accrue to the same people, further complicating the measurement of their relative values. Finally, it is impossible to assign objective values to the social benefits and sometimes even to the costs. Thus, cost-benefit analyses cannot accurately assess either the efficiency or value of government regulation.

QUESTIONS

1. Define and give examples of the rule-making and adjudicatory functions of an administrative agency in your local or state government.
2. Compare and contrast the procedures used to make administrative rules and administrative orders.
3. Describe the various sources of controls on administrative agency action. Which of these do you think is the strongest? Why?
4. The federal Mine, Safety, and Health Act of 1977 requires federal mine inspectors to inspect underground mines at least twice a year. The inspection is intended to ensure compliance with health and safety standards. The act also grants inspectors the right to enter any mine without advance notice of an inspection. If a mine operator refuses to allow a warrantless inspection, the secretary of the Labor Department is authorized to bring a civil action for an injunction. When a federal mine inspector attempted a follow-up inspection of one company's stone quarries, an officer of the company refused to allow the inspection. The company relied on the *Marshall v. Barlow's* case as authority for denying the inspector admission to the quarries without a search warrant. Was the company's action legal?
5. What is the main difference between an agency adjudicatory proceeding and a court trial?
6. A Florida administrative rule permits a warrantless search of child day-care facilities, including private homes used as day-care centers, at any time of day. The Florida legislature's concern is to protect the health and safety of children at these centers by eliminating such hazards as inadequate capacity, access to poisonous materials, open pools, and sexual abuse. Is the Florida warrantless search scheme constitutional as applied to private homes?
7. The state of Georgia has regulations granting compensation to employees for work-related injuries. The Workers' Compensation Board awards compensation after conducting hearings. The findings of the Workers' Compensation Board are subject to judicial review and reversal only if the board acts outside its powers or if the award is not supported by substantial evidence on the record taken as a whole. Does the Workers' Compensation Board exercise legislative or adjudicatory powers in making awards? Explain your answer.
8. The Interstate Commerce Commission (ICC) published a general notice in the *Federal Register* outlining proposed legislation to be submitted to Congress. The notice asked for comments from the general public. Following a period allowed for written comments, instead of submitting legislation to Congress, the ICC issued final rules that affected tour brokers. These regulations put new, expensive "surety bond" requirements on tour brokers. The National Tour Brokers' Association sued the ICC, claiming the notice provided was inadequate under the APA. Did the ICC comply with the procedural requirements under the Administrative Procedures Act? See *National Tour Brokers' Association v. United States*, 591 F. 2d 896, 1978.
9. The Clean Air Act requires the EPA to set and periodically revise national ambient air quality standards (NAAQS) for each air pollutant identified by the agency as meeting certain statutory criteria.

   In 1997, the EPA issued final rules revising the primary and secondary NAAQS for particulate matter and ozone. The EPA set two concentration levels (e.g., 0.08 parts per million level of ozone), one to protect the public health with an adequate margin of safety and a less stringent level, necessary to protect the public welfare. The EPA indicated the factors it used in determining the permissible concentration levels, but it did not indicate any criterion for why those particular levels were selected. There was no indication of why the level was not 0.06 or 0.13. Although the EPA relied on the recommendation of the Clean Air Scientific Advisory Committee in setting the standard (it should not be less than 0.08), that body gave no specific reasons for its recommendation. The American Trucking Association said that when the EPA establishes health standards without adequately explaining the reasons for doing so, it and Congress are violating the delegation of authority doctrine that requires clear and explainable standards for agency rules. Do you agree? See *American Trucking v. U.S. E.P.A.*, 175 F.3d 1027 (D.C. Cir., 1999).

10. The government obtains people with expert knowledge for its regulatory agencies from the very industries that they are supposed to regulate. Conflicts of interest often arise, and this revolving door problem is a concern of almost every government agency. The best place to get experts for the Food and Drug Administration is from the food industry or the pharmaceutical industry. If an executive from ABC Drug Company is appointed director of the Food and Drug Administration, how should he or she treat a product that ABC is trying to convince the FDA to approve? The reverse of that situation is equally perplexing. If a top-ranking official of the Food and Drug Administration quits and is hired by ABC Drug Company, how should that person's prior affiliation with the FDA influence its approval of ABC's drugs? How could government regulations limit the potential conflicts of interest from the revolving door?

Private Law

PART II

Of the many areas of law, among the best known are those that concern the law's punishment of those who commit wrongs against society or against private parties. The two distinct, but related, branches of law that address these concerns are criminal law and tort law. Criminal laws set standards for duties that all persons, including business firms and their managers, owe to society. Criminal prosecutions, brought by a representative of society, seek criminal punishments to protect the society and deter future wrongdoers. By contrast, tort law cases are brought by individuals or firms, who usually seek compensation for a wrongdoer's breach of a duty, a duty that is based in a societal obligation, not in a voluntary contractual commitment.

Just as a burglar who breaks into someone's home and makes away with valuable property while causing damage to the premises violates both criminal and tort law, so, too, does the hacker who intrudes into computer networks to steal valuable data, implant a virus, or cause a hard drive to crash. Chapter 7, the first chapter in this unit, outlines the main characteristics of both criminal and tort law. Although violent crimes such as murder, rape, and robbery and property crimes such as theft, larceny, and arson are well known, others, such as white-collar crimes and computer crimes, are more directly related to business firms and to the e-commerce environment. Because computers are an integral part of nearly every business endeavor, computer crimes, such as cyber crime that is committed over telecommunications networks, are a major concern to most business organizations.

Although tort law, as a type of civil law, differs from criminal law in many respects, intentional torts are closely aligned to criminal laws. Tort law is a pressing legal concern for business because it is the most common basis for holding a firm liable for the wrongful acts of its employees and agents. All torts require some proof of a causal connection between the tortious or wrongful act and the legal injury that occurs. Each of the three major categories of tort law—intentional, negligent, and strict liability torts—is reviewed in Chapter 7. The subsequent chapter, Chapter 8, focuses on the various theories of product and service liability, including several tort-based theories, that are used to hold business organizations liable for problems caused by their products or services.

The origins of product and service liability laws in the United States can be traced to cases brought in the early twentieth century. A classic case, involving a car with damaged spokes in wooden wheels, depicts not only how far automobile manufacturing has evolved but also how different are today's legal standards for manufacturers and other organizations in the supply chain. Although most of the theories of liability are based on tort law principles, the warranty theory of liability emerges from contract law concepts. In addition to any express warranties, sellers who are merchants have warranties imposed on them by law, known as implied warranties, whenever they sell goods. The breach or nonperformance of a warranty is an important basis for product and service liability.

The tort-based negligence and strict liability principles are also important standards that can be applied to hold liable the business firm providing faulty or defective products and services. The service provider may be a computer software firm, network installer, or computer usage consultant. The tort of misrepresentation applies when a firm's brochure or advertisement represents that a product or service will perform to specified standards and it does not do so. Some misrepresentations are intentional and deceitful; others are unintentional. Both can have legal consequences if someone who relies on the representations thereby suffers a legal injury.

The tortious acts of a person acting as an agent for a business can make the business, as well as the agent, liable for any damages those actions cause. Chapter 9 discusses the agency relationship between a firm and its employees or agents. The basis for holding the firm liable for the agent's wrongful actions is the concept of respondeat superior. In exchange for allowing a business to use agents as representatives of the firm, the law imposes liability on the firm when those agents, while acting for the firm, cause injury to others.

Liability concerns constitute one of the major factors firms consider in determining how to organize a business. Today, firms have a number of different forms of business organization they can use to operate a business. Because of its ease in creation and the control it provides to the firm's owner, the sole proprietorship is the most common form of business organization.

The partnership form of business organization has been the form of choice for many professional accounting, engineering, and legal services firms. However, as newer forms of business organizations, such as the limited liability company and the limited liability partnership, offer business owners limited liability that is not available in traditional partnerships, the use of the traditional partnership is in decline. Instead of using a partnership, the organizers and owners can choose to organize as a limited liability company, a subchapter S corporation, or even a limited partnership. Each of these forms combines some of the taxation and management benefits found in traditional partnerships with the limited liability that has been a major reason for organizing as a corporation.

The corporation form of business organization, used by almost all major business entities throughout the world, is unique in that it splits the ownership and management of the firm between the shareholders on the one hand and the directors and officers on the other. The corporation is an attractive form because its shareholder-owners, who may number in the millions, can select directors to oversee a firm's operations, and they, in turn, can hire professional managers to carry out the business of the firm. Determining which form of business organization to use depends on the features that are most important and the type of activities that will be performed. Agency and business organization laws are central to the organizational and operational concerns of all businesses.

CHAPTER 7

Crimes and Torts

Among the best known areas of traditional law is the punishment or vindication of wrongs. These wrongs may have been committed against society generally or more specifically against individual private parties. They may be committed intentionally or result from unintentional, negligent acts. Two distinct but related branches of law that address these wrongs are covered in this chapter: criminal law and tort law. Imagine that a hacker invades a computer network, intercepts orders for goods, captures credit card account numbers, and then uses them to make fraudulent purchases. Many of these acts would be illegal under criminal law, exposing the hacker to criminal prosecution and penalties (fines, imprisonment). The very same acts could also expose the hacker to civil liability to those directly injured: the credit card issuer, card holders, and the Internet service provider (ISP).

CRIMINAL LAW VS. CIVIL LAW

The purpose of criminal law is to punish wrongdoers and isolate them from society. Criminal law sets standards for duties that all persons and businesses owe to society. Criminal prosecutions are brought by the government, most typically by a local or state prosecutor or district attorney. There are also federal crimes prosecuted by the Justice Department. Prosecutors seek criminal punishment remedies, including fines and imprisonment, and even the death penalty in capital punishment cases, to protect society and deter future wrongdoing. Criminal prosecutors must generally prove the defendant's guilt **beyond a reasonable doubt**, that is, the trier of fact (jury or, if there is no jury, judge) must be thoroughly convinced of criminal guilt.

By contrast, civil law enforces duties owed primarily to individuals or business entities. The civil law of torts imposes duties on persons to act carefully or refrain from intentional aggression. The civil law of contracts enforces duties that are voluntarily assumed by the contracting parties. A civil plaintiff must generally prove the defendant's liability by a **preponderance of the evidence** (more likely than not); this standard of proof is lower than for criminal guilt.

Government units are sometimes the victims of crimes or torts, and governments are sometimes the wrongdoers held responsible in tort suits. Governments can also make, enforce, and be held responsible on contracts, although government contracting and government procurement are specialized fields with rather esoteric rules, not covered in this book. In some tort cases, the judge or jury sometimes assesses punitive damages. Deterrence is a secondary objective of tort law in the most egregious cases.

THE CHALLENGES OF CYBERSPACE FOR LAW ENFORCEMENT

Cyberspace poses many new problems in deterring crime, punishing it, and compensating victims for injuries that wrongdoers commit against society and individuals. Consider these difficulties in the following comparison. First, think of the malicious injury resulting from a burglar's physical intrusion into someone's home or a place of business. Once inside the premises, the wrongdoer might steal property or money, perhaps by cracking open a wall safe. While inside, the burglar might discover valuable secrets by examining confidential files, maybe without leaving fingerprints or a trace of DNA evidence. The burglar might also damage physical property, such as breaking the door and lock while entering, or a burglar might destroy information or records. Now compare this example with the intrusions a computer hacker makes by using networked telecommunications to access others' computers. Hackers can perpetrate similar injuries: After breaking codes to enter a computer or network, the hacker might steal software or data, otherwise wreak havoc with a virus, orchestrate a denial-of-service attack, or crash a hard disk.

The differences between traditional unlawful physical intrusions and cyberspace intrusions are key to the evolution of law to make cyberspace a safer place for individuals and electronic business activity. First, computer intrusions can be committed from far away, sometimes without leaving any of the electronic or physical evidence that is usually recovered from crime scenes by forensic investigators. This distance impedes investigations by hiding evidence, and it complicates jurisdiction over remote defendants, witnesses, and ISPs. Second, many observers believe that computer security measures, such as passwords or encryption, can never be as effective as well-established physical controls. Physical controls include fences, locked doors, security guards, serial numbers, video monitoring, and the difficulty of concealing the mass and distinctiveness of physical assets. Third, hackers sometimes "anonymize" their communications and cover up evidence that could identify them or reveal their whereabouts and accomplices. Some experts believe that many more computer intrusions than physical intrusions go undetected. Fourth, computer attacks, fraudulent schemes, and other harmful communications can too often be carried out on a much broader scale than was possible with traditional technologies. For example, securities fraud, virus attacks, and obscenity or defamatory remarks can be more widely and cheaply disseminated than with traditional means such as face-to-face contacts, the telephone, or postal mail.

FACTORS DISTINGUISHING CRIMINAL LAW FROM CIVIL LAW

This chapter addresses criminal law and tort law, both as they are applied in the traditional physical world and as these bodies of law are adapting to the tough challenges of cyberspace. Some crimes, such as assault and battery, trespass, and false imprisonment, are also unlawful under civil law as intentional torts. For such crimes, the act that may be prosecuted as a criminal offense may also be the complaint in a civil tort suit, and the defendant may be exposed to criminal prosecution as well as civil liability to the individuals, firms, or even governments that are injured.

Criminal Law vs. Tort Law

A wrongful act that results in personal injury may also be a criminal act. Although criminal law was originally derived from common law precedents, it is now based primarily on statutory laws passed by the federal and state legislatures. Similarly, tort law principles emerge primarily from common law precedents, although an increasing number of statutes affect tort law liability. Most crimes and torts are made unlawful by state law.

How can a person be tried twice for the same offense, first under criminal law and then under tort law? Would that not constitute unconstitutional double jeopardy under the Fifth Amendment, as introduced previously in Chapter 4? The answer is generally no. Criminal law punishes wrongdoers, and civil law compensates victims. The law's purposes would be frustrated if prosecutors and injured victims were required to race against each other to the courthouse or if one type of suit preempted the other. Therefore, there is no competition between criminal and civil suits over the same wrongful conduct. In fact, the two paths are often complementary, as when a conviction precedes a civil suit and makes the civil plaintiff's case easier to prove.

Double jeopardy is interpreted so that it is not violated by parallel proceedings. Recall the multiple cases triggered by the O. J. Simpson events. He was successfully sued for the civil ort of wrongful death by the relatives of Nicole Brown Simpson despite his previous acquittal by a jury on criminal charges of murder. Therefore, there is no double jeopardy if a person is sued in a civil tort action and tried for the same criminal act under the same facts. Double jeopardy occurs only when a person is tried twice for the same "crime." The substantive law, trial procedures, and burdens of proof are different for tort cases than for criminal cases. Thus, although a tortious action could be a crime, it need not be. A tort is a wrong for which the injured party can be compensated.

Tort Law vs. Contract Law

Tort law and contract law are both branches of civil (noncriminal) law. If a business or an individual breaches a contractual obligation while also committing a tort, the injured party may bring both a breach of contract case and a tort case. Because both cases are civil actions arising from the same events and involving the same parties, the two actions can be brought together in one legal proceeding. For example, suppose an on-line consumer purchases a software program over the Internet. After downloading and installing the program, the consumer discovers the program has destroyed important data stored in the consumer's hard drive memory. Contract law requires that the software be fit for its ordinary purpose. In that the software did not meet that standard, the seller breached the contract, as discussed further in Chapters 8 and 13 on contract warranties and licensing. However, the purchaser could also sue the seller or manufacturer of the software in tort because the manufacturer breached its responsibility for being reasonably careful in the design, manufacture, or shipment of its software. Both the manufacturer and the seller could be sued in one suit, alleging a negligent tort against the manufacturer and a breach of contract by the seller. Money damages could be recovered if the plaintiff could prove breach of contract, the commission of a tortious act by the defendant, or both. Punitive damages are generally not available in the breach of contract portion of the suit. Distinctions between criminal and civil law are so important to this chapter that these matters are summarized in Exhibit 7.1.

EXHIBIT 7.1 Criminal Law vs. Civil Law

Comparative Factor	Criminal Law	Civil Law
Plaintiff/complaintant	State or federal prosecutor or district attorney	Injured party: individual, business entity, or government
Objective of law	Protect society, punish wrongdoers, deter wrongdoing	Compensate particular injured parties; only in egregious cases, punishment as deterrence
Nature of wrongful act	Duty owed to society Violation of criminal statute prohibiting certain conduct and intended to protect society	Wrongful act violates private tort duty imposed by law or violates contractual duty voluntarily assumed
Burden of proof	Beyond a reasonable doubt	Preponderance of the evidence
Remedies/penalties	Fines and/or imprisonment; capital punishment in only the most severe cases	Money damages, declaratory judgment, and/or equitable remedies of specific performance or injunction

CLASSIFYING CRIMINAL LAW

Crimes are classified in a number of ways. Most common and street crimes are made illegal under state law, and some crimes are illegal under federal law. The traditional classification scheme for crimes focuses on the severity or seriousness. First, **misdemeanors** are less serious crimes traditionally punishable by smaller fines or incarceration in jail or imprisonment for a year or less. Examples include trespass and theft of low-value property. Petty offenses are usually considered misdemeanors and can include building code violations or drunk driving (DUI/DWI). Civil or summary offenses, which are even less serious, can include minor traffic or parking violations for which no criminal record is kept. As with most other crimes, the precise name of the crime, its classification, the precise definition, and the range of applicable penalties vary considerably from state to state.

Second, **felonies** are crimes more serious than misdemeanors, and there are a full range of constitutional protections because the penalties are more serious, such as larger fines and/or longer prison terms. Felonies include homicide, robbery, and arson. The **model penal code**, not one of the uniform laws, further divides felonies into four categories reflecting society's assessment of seriousness, use of deadly weapons or force, the perpetrator's intent, and the suffering inflicted by the criminal act: (1) **capital offenses** possibly punishable by death, (2) **first-degree felonies** punishable by up to life imprisonment, (3) **second-degree felonies** punishable by up to 10 years imprisonment, and (4) **third-degree felonies** punishable by up to five years imprisonment.

CONTEMPORARY CLASSIFICATION OF CRIME

Crimes are also now popularly classified according to other factors, such as the general nature of the damage caused, the means used to commit the crime, or even generalizations about the perpetrators. Although the hundreds of different particular crimes could be classified in many other ways, the following taxonomy is useful to describe crimes. First, **violent crimes** are usually directed against human individuals (such as the familiar urban *street crimes*); they can include homicide (murder, manslaughter), assault and battery, rape, robbery (taking property from another by using force or fear), kidnapping, and "aggravated" forms of various crimes such as assault or robbery, when a deadly weapon is used. Second, **property crimes** cause destruction or deprive owners of their property. They include theft, burglary, extortion, larceny, receiving stolen goods, forgery, fraud, false pretenses, theft of services, infringement, arson, trespass, and vandalism. Third, **public order crimes** generally encompass acts that violate society's mores or threaten order, responsibility, or government, for example, intoxication; use, possession, or sale of controlled substances or items (illegal drugs, weapons, explosives, bioterrorism agents); prostitution; gambling; pornography; hate crimes; stalking or harassment; bribery; treason, sedition, or espionage; incitement to riot; counterfeiting; and various forms of terrorism.

A fourth category includes **white-collar crime**, which is illegal, nonviolent behavior by employees of business firms, and **corporate crime**, illegal behavior intended to benefit business firms. These two categories obviously overlap and often are financial crimes and property crimes that are made to appear part of a legitimate, ongoing business activity. For example, fraud, mail and wire fraud, embezzlement, theft of intellectual property (including trade secrets), industrial espionage, bribery, insider trading, and criminal forms of regulatory offenses such as antitrust law, securities regulations, transportation system regulations, and banking regulations fall in this category. A fifth category, **computer crime**, includes these crimes when the activities at least partially involve computers. Computer crime also includes theft of hardware, software, or computer time, as well as the destruction or deprivation from use of others' computers. **Cyber crime** is a fairly new subclass that describes computer crime committed over telecommunications networks. Cyber crime may cause much broader injuries than other computer crimes. For example, the intentional spread of a computer virus or the launch and orchestration of a denial of service attack against a website or ISP affects hundreds, even thousands of others. Other contemporary examples of cyber crime include stalking, pornography, gambling, hacking, electronic terrorism, and theft.

The final broad category of crimes is **organized crime**. Organized crime is often the result of racketeering activities by criminal gangs or syndicates, many of the most infamous of which have been operated by crime families and ethnic clans. Organized crime is operated by a centrally controlled, formal structure and most often the participants satisfy the public's demand for illegal activities such as liquor, drugs, gambling, weapons, prostitution, pornography, and loansharking. Organized crime frequently uses terroristlike tactics of selective violence and intimidation to discipline their members and the public, protect their turf, and insulate their illegal markets. Money laundering is often needed to funnel illegal profits into legitimate investments. Laundering, discussed further later, helps to reinforce the organization's strength and can permit its members to withdraw and use illegal criminal profits. In recent years, organized crime has expanded into financial crime, including credit card and securities fraud.

Clearly, the traditional and more contemporary classifications of crimes are neither exclusive nor exhaustive. Some crimes belong in two or more categories. More detailed discussion of some particular crimes and the applicable law enforcement tools are discussed throughout this chapter. Several other particular crimes involving intellectual property, trade secret theft, securities fraud, insider trading, antitrust

Ethical Issue

Business Ethics vs. Criminal Law

For many centuries, both religious principles and laws have been a primary source of ethical guidance. Religious precepts and ethical standards outline ideal behavior, and they are often called ***normative principles*** because they suggest ideal goals for conduct. Laws, by contrast, are ***prescriptive*** because they do more than suggest normative or "ought to" standards; they require, or prescribe, minimal levels of conduct. However, criminal law is usually ***proscriptive*** because it forbids certain actions that society views as unacceptable. Society constantly makes choices between flexible ethical standards, industry self-regulation, regulation by expert administrative agencies, and the less flexible criminal laws. This dilemma poses both threats to free choice and opportunities for responsive businesses. Nearly every business decision can be analyzed for ethical impact, a moral reasoning process that was introduced in Chapter 2.

Several other well-established legal standards outside the criminal law context form the major bases for ethical analysis. First, the ***fiduciary duty*** standard discussed further in Chapters 9 and 12 is a fundamental legal and ethical principle. Agents owe their principals a duty of loyalty that requires confidentiality and prohibits conflicts of interest. Second, there are several laws, most notably the UCC discussed throughout Chapters 10, 11, and 12, that require commercial parties dealing at arm's length to act in ***good faith***. This means they must act honestly in fact in the transaction in question. Dishonesty and bad faith are often specifically penalized in commercial litigation.

A third ethical principal with strong parallels in law prohibits ***misappropriation*** of others' assets. Although this legal and ethical standard seems to be stated clearly enough in the criminal law of theft, larceny, or embezzlement, it also applies to intangibles. For example, information is property that should not be misappropriated by another. The laws of insider trading, unfair competition, trade secrets, and intellectual property infringement discussed throughout this book make it illegal to misappropriate information for personal use or for communication to an outsider.

A fourth legal and ethical standard is the requirement that everyone and every entity act with ***due care***. The tort of negligence requires that all activities be undertaken with reasonable consideration of the possible external impact on others. Physically dangerous or financially damaging activities must be performed with due diligence. Finally, ***respect for others' rights*** should be observed. This legal and ethical norm also requires evaluating how one's acts affect others and taking steps to avoid infringing the rights of others. Many ethical dilemmas can be resolved by reference to one or more of these five norms.

violations, tax evasion, environmental pollution, and violations of regulations in food and drug safety, consumer product safety, and health care privacy are discussed in other chapters.

CRIMINAL PROCEDURE

The criminal procedure followed by state and federal law enforcement officials and the criminal courts varies somewhat according to which governmental units have jurisdiction and on the seriousness of the alleged crime. Criminal prosecutions differ from civil cases because the plaintiff is a local prosecutor, staff attorney in the office of the state's attorney general, or a U.S. attorney working for the U.S. Department of Justice (DOJ). Prosecutors are bound to protect the public, which is a different perspective than that followed by a private party vindicating personal rights. Of course, private citizens are often involved in initiating criminal actions when they report suspicious activity to prosecutors, bring charges, or supply key evidence. Criminal procedure begins with investigations and proceeds through arrest, booking, indictment, arraignment, and plea bargaining. If the charges are not dropped or settled in the plea bargain, the matter goes to trial, and criminal procedure governs the trial process, sentencing, and appeal or punishment.

CRIMINAL INVESTIGATIONS

http://
www.usdoj.gov/

Detection of a criminal act initially prompts an investigation, including the questioning of suspects, possible accomplices, and witnesses. This may lead to an arrest by law enforcement officials. Thereafter, the investigation may continue with interviews of the accused and witnesses and perhaps seizure of hard evidence such as documents, weapons, articles with fingerprints, DNA samples, other identifying evidence, and increasingly computer memories and other records. Criminal charges may be initiated if the district attorney's office believes the defendant can be convicted, given the weight of the evidence and their limited prosecutorial resources. The prosecutor files charges in an affidavit, complaint, accusation, or an information brought against the person or persons implicated in the crime.

Constitutional Protections for the Accused

The U.S. Constitution constrains the tactics used by investigators and requires fairness in trial procedures. The Sixth Amendment requires notice of criminal charges, a speedy and public trial, trial by an impartial jury, representation by legal counsel, confrontation of accusers, cross-examination of witnesses, and the right to call witnesses. Recall the discussion in Chapter 4 of the Fourth, Fifth, and Fourteenth Amendments. The Fourth Amendment prohibits unreasonable searches and seizures, a topic further detailed in Chapter 14. Various testimonial privileges promise secrecy for confidential communications between attorney and client, between spouses, and with some others, also discussed in Chapter 14. Chapter 4 also introduced the due process requirements of the Fifth and Fourteenth Amendments, which provide other general criminal procedure safeguards and set fairness standards for the conduct of all trials.

The Fifth Amendment also requires an indictment and provides the double jeopardy right and the self-incrimination privilege. Since the landmark 1966 case *Miranda v. Arizona*,[1] law enforcement officials must give **Miranda warnings** to all suspects who may be subjected to custodial interrogation. More recent Supreme Court cases have limited this right by creating exceptions to the Miranda rights. For example, there is a limited public safety exception, convictions will not be overturned if there is sufficient evidence for conviction outside the confession, and the suspect must clearly assert the right to counsel during questioning.

Miranda Warning

You have the right to remain silent. Anything you say can and will be used against you in a court of law. You have the right to consult with an attorney and to have one present with you during interrogation. If you cannot afford an attorney, one will be appointed for you.

1. 384 U.S. 436 (1966).

The use of evidence acquired through search or seizure for proof of criminal guilt is subject to the Fourth Amendment's protections. They are interpreted to require that law enforcement officials must generally have a search warrant issued by a judge, magistrate, or other public officer before conducting the search. Warrants may be issued only if based on **probable cause**, a legal standard discussed further in the Chapter 14. Generally, search warrants are granted only when law enforcement officials can convince the judge that evidence of a crime is likely to reside in the area to be searched and that if the evidence were found it would be relevant to their investigation. The warrant must describe both the evidence sought and the location to be searched. With some exceptions, only the evidence described may be used to prove criminal guilt. Warrants for arrest must also be based on probable cause that the suspect committed the crime described in the warrant.

When these constitutional rights are violated, the evidence obtained is generally inadmissible to prove guilt under the **exclusionary rule**. Further, if investigators acquire leads from illegally acquired evidence, that further evidence is tainted, which means it will be excluded from use at trial as **fruit of the poisonous tree**. For example, assume e-mail records are seized in an illegal search for obscene materials on a suspect's hard drive. If investigators find evidence of illegal gambling on that hard drive, or if the original sender of the e-mail messages is contacted and then provides additional incriminating evidence, then all this additional evidence would be excluded as tainted fruit of the poisonous tree.

In cyberspace, law enforcement needs to access information quickly, given that evidence of wrongdoing is often fleeting and temporary; that is, computer records are easily erased and may exist only for moments as electronic impulses. This impermanence may be counterbalanced by the often large number of intermediate electronic copies made. As discussed in Chapter 14, it is becoming difficult to erase e-mail messages or their file attachments. Many people mistakenly believe there are no copies of their e-mail, clickstream, or on-line activities, but most messages can be intercepted, and they are not easily disavowed. In litigation, the prosecutor can subpoena most print and electronic records from the accused or from others. Many still fail to recognize that their frank, hostile, or incriminating e-mail and other electronic records are preserved on many hard drives, that copies often are saved on their employer's server and at their ISP, and that printouts and electronic copies are made by recipients or are forwarded widely to others. Crime statistics can be found at the FBI's website.

ONLINE

FBI website
http://www.fbi.gov/ucr/ucr.htm

USA Patriot Act

In the wake of the September 11, 2001, terrorist attacks on the Pentagon and World Trade Center, Congress strengthened federal law enforcement's investigatory powers by passing antiterrorism legislation, the Uniting and Strengthening America Act (USA Patriot Act). This law permits the U.S. Attorney General to detain aliens suspected of terrorist activity, the U.S. State Department to designate **terrorist organizations** to prevent their fund-raising, and the FBI to use **roving wiretaps** on any phone line used by suspected terrorists (e.g., business line, home phone, cell phone, etc.) in a single warrant. Widespread public support quickly developed to lift investigatory obstacles and thereby protect U.S. citizens, property, and free markets from terrorist attacks. Indeed, a major shift in public opinion resulted in huge new majorities favoring the use of facial recognition technologies, TV monitors in public places, and broader government monitoring of various communications. It remains uncertain whether this represents a temporary or permanent shift in public opinion to trade off privacy for security. In most past situations, citizens tolerated increased intrusions only until the threats subsided, but some law enforcement officials argue that the threat of terrorism requires a permanent reduction in privacy.

To ease the difficult task of coordinating antiterrorism activities by various government agencies, as well as the responsibilities of the new director of homeland security, the USA Patriot Act permits greater sharing of investigatory files among various federal agencies. It authorizes secret searches of certain information without notifying the investigation's target. Some aspects of bank secrecy are now relaxed; investigators can obtain payment information such as credit card and bank account numbers of suspected terrorists. The provisions to detect money laundering are discussed later in this chapter. The act also substantially increases funding for U.S. border control. Several of the USA Act's provisions are subject to automatic expiration under a sunset provision.

The USA Patriot Act also enhances law enforcement surveillance powers over on-line activities. For example, the federal government now has authority to subpoena ISPs for e-mail addresses, URLs visited, e-mail recipients, and sender information. Federal law enforcement officials need not have probable cause but need only show that the information sought is relevant to an ongoing investigation. Federal investigators will now routinely have access to information similar to the on-line profiling data collected by the private data industry. Profiling is discussed further in Chapter 14. Many state law enforcement personnel are now seeking similar powers under revised state laws.

PRETRIAL PROCEDURES

A valid arrest initiates pretrial criminal procedure. Arrests are generally made in two ways. First, law enforcement officials may directly observe a suspect in suspicious or criminally related activity, which provides sufficient probable cause to make the arrest. Alternatively, after criminal activity is reported, law enforcement may learn sufficient information to seek an arrest warrant from a judge. Under the Sixth Amendment, warrants are issued only if evidence is presented to show probable cause—a sufficient likelihood that the suspect has committed or is about to commit a crime. Formal arrest includes statements indicating the nature of the activity, and law enforcement usually takes the suspect into custody, a form of temporary detention.

After charges are filed by the arresting officer, there are screening processes to prevent law enforcement officials from abusing the criminal process or bringing false accusations against the innocent. In a **preliminary hearing**, the prosecutor must demonstrate the existence of probable cause that the evidence connecting the defendant to a crime is sufficient to "hold the defendant over" for prosecution. These proceedings are held before a magistrate, who possesses judicial power to permit a prosecution to proceed. When there is sufficient evidence of wrongdoing, the magistrate issues an **information**, which represents the formal criminal charges. Alternatively, in cases alleging more serious crimes, a grand jury may be used. The **grand jury**, consisting of numerous local citizens, performs a similar function by reviewing the evidence against the accused for probable cause. When grand juries recommend prosecution, they issue an **indictment** showing that there is sufficient evidence against the defendant. Grand juries operate in secrecy to encourage reluctant witnesses to volunteer forthright testimony because the secrecy deters retaliation by the accused.

Following these formal charges, the accused defendant makes an appearance before a judge or other magistrate at an **arraignment**. The defendant may then file a **plea**—that is, the accused's answer to the prosecution's allegations. The most common pleas are not guilty, guilty, or **nolo contendere** (no contest, no admission of guilt but submitting to the court's resolution). A defendant who does not plead not guilty may be immediately sentenced. Indigent defendants may be assigned a free public defender attorney under the constitutional right to counsel. **Bail** may be set to ensure that the defendant will appear at the trial. Bail is often provided by a bail bondsman or, in some cases, may be waived if the judge believes the defendant will not flee, thereby releasing the defendant on his or her own recognizance. The defendant may waive the right to a preliminary hearing or review by the grand jury.

Many accused suspects negotiate the type of crime they plead guilty to, often submitting to the prosecution's preferred sentence. This process is known as **plea bargaining**, and it is memorialized in a **plea bargain agreement**. For example, the prosecutor might initially argue that the defendant's conduct amounted to a serious crime, such as murder. However, during plea bargaining, the defendant may show remorse or agree to provide evidence or testify against other criminals. The plea bargain might obligate the defendant to plead guilty to a lesser offense, such as manslaughter rather than murder, or to fewer from among several charges. This process conserves public resources when the defendant understands that the prosecution could probably win a conviction on some of the charges. By some accounts, plea bargaining is highly successful in resolving criminal cases, probably accounting for nearly 90% of all criminal complaints.

Before trial, both parties may conduct additional investigation, the prosecution to strengthen its case and the defense to prove innocence, find the real perpetrator, gather evidence for cross-examination of opposing witnesses, or show improper evidence gathering by law enforcement. Often each side must provide its information, witness lists, and other sources to the opposition. Hard evidence includes weapons, documents, computer information, and objects with fingerprints or other identifying information. As in civil discovery, the process is intended to elicit the truth.

CONDUCT OF THE CRIMINAL TRIAL

Criminal trials follow a sequence similar to civil trials: (1) a jury is impaneled, (2) both sides make opening remarks, (3) the prosecution presents its case-in-chief by examining and cross-examining witnesses and showing tangible evidence, (4) the defense similarly presents its case-in-chief, (5) both sides make closing remarks, (6) the judge instructs the jury with the applicable law, (7) the jury deliberates, and (8) the jury renders its verdict. Criminal verdicts must usually be unanimous; otherwise, a "hung jury" results, necessitating either another trial or the defendant's release. When defendants are found guilty, they are sentenced, an official judgment as to the punishment, sometimes by the judge but meted out by the jury in many serious crimes.

Juries are impaneled in a process known as **voir dire**. Prospective jurors are questioned to determine whether they have severe biases that would invalidate the accused's due process. For example, the judge should dismiss a prospective juror **for cause** if the prospective juror is related to the parties, has already formed an opinion about guilt from news coverage, or does not believe in the illegality of the particular crime charged or the potential form of punishment (opponent of capital punishment). In addition, sociological and demographic factors about particular prospective jurors might make their participation inappropriate. Each side in criminal trials and in many civil trials has a limited number of **peremptory challenges** to remove such jurors when their attorneys or their trial consultants believe that the prospective juror might not treat the accused or litigating party objectively.

Criminal prosecutors must usually prove two elements of an alleged crime to gain a conviction. First, a criminal act, also known as ***actus reus***, as defined by the criminal code, must have been committed by the defendant. Second, the defendant must have had the **criminal intent** to commit the criminal act, which is known as **mens rea.** These elements must be proved beyond a reasonable doubt, a much higher burden of proof than the preponderance of the evidence standard used in civil cases.

SENTENCING

Sentencing is a process in which the judge and/or jury metes out the punishment to the defendant. Many criminal statutes create a range of potential penalties between a minimum and maximum fine and/or imprisonment of those convicted. The defendant may be sentenced immediately if the law requires a mandatory sentence. Sentencing may be postponed in capital crimes or if sentencing guidelines give the judge discretion. In some serious cases, a later hearing is held to consider additional evidence—a **bifurcated trial.** In such a sentencing hearing, the judge or jury may consider the defendant's background and likelihood of **recidivism** (return to crime).

Federal Sentencing Guidelines

Congress established the U.S. Sentencing Commission in the Sentencing Reform Act of 1984. The commission issued the U.S. Sentencing Guidelines to standardize sentencing in the federal courts and respond to evidence that any two defendants convicted of the same crime could receive vastly different punishments. Generally, federal judges must consider a specified range of sentences for particular crimes by considering factors such as the defendant's prior criminal record, the seriousness of the offense just convicted, and any other factors specified in the guidelines.

Many states have also enacted sentencing guidelines to standardize sentencing. For example, a few states have adopted "**three strikes you're out**" laws. These effectively mete out life sentences after three felony convictions. Such sentencing guidelines force judges to sentence repeat offenders with this maximum penalty.

In 1991, the commission promulgated sentencing reforms for federal white-collar and business crimes. Firms with a strictly enforced compliance program or corporate code of conduct may receive leniency.[2] The **U.S. Sentencing Guidelines** promulgate a formula judges must use to calculate a **culpability multiplier** that can supply credits that reduce a defendant firm's criminal sentence. For example, a corporation's criminal sentence could be reduced to as low as 15% of the potential maximum penalty for violations committed by their employees. To qualify, the corporation must have a compliance program that is reasonably designed, implemented, and enforced to be generally effective in preventing and detecting criminal conduct. This "mitigation" of the corporate penalty depends on whether the firm (1) reported the violation voluntarily, (2) instituted an effective compliance program (such as a code of conduct and effective enforcement mechanism) before and after the violation, (3) had no high-level policy-setting official with knowledge of the violation, (4) cooperated fully with the government's investigation, and (5) accepted responsibility and took prompt, reasonable steps to remedy the harm. Other mechanisms include the use of an ombudsman and executive training programs to reinforce the importance of compliance programs. Sentencing reforms like the U.S. Sentencing Guidelines add force to the trend to adopt effective **compliance programs** that enforce corporate codes of conduct.[3]

2. *United States v. Beusch*, 596 F.2d 871 (9th Cir., 1979).
3. *In re Caremark Int'l, Inc.*, 698 A.2d 959 (Del.Ch., 1996).

CRIMINAL APPEALS

Generally, the defendant may appeal a conviction. However, criminal appeals generally address only defects in the criminal process, often constitutional issues from the Bill of Rights. In some states such as California, appeal is automatic in capital punishment cases. The appeals court may permanently dismiss the charges or order a new trial. Absent a trial court error, the double jeopardy provision prohibits another prosecution on the same charges.

SECONDARY LIABILITY

Many criminal prosecutions are complicated by the difficulty of assessing individual responsibility. Consider crimes committed by groups or by a business. Businesses are large organizations that perform complex acts in which many people have a part, which can make the legal determination of criminal intent problematic. It is difficult to assign direct responsibility for the overall effect of such complex behavior. However, there are several legal doctrines that assign criminal liability for major and minor participants in complex or group crimes. For example, parent corporations can sometimes be held liable for crimes committed by subsidiaries under the civil theory of piercing the corporate veil. When the parent so controls the subsidiary's decision making, it would be inequitable to shield the parent from responsibility for the deeds of a related corporation within the larger unified enterprise.[4]

An **accessory** is someone who aids the perpetrator of a crime but is not present at its commission. An **accessory before the fact** provides assistance before the commission of the illegal acts, and an **accessory after the fact** provides assistance after the commission. A **conspiracy** is an agreement among two or more persons who plan the commission of a crime. A criminal **attempt** includes all the activities of the perpetrator(s) to plan and carry out a criminal act, such that, if successful, would result in the criminal act. All these are separate crimes for which additional convictions and penalties can be assessed if adequately proven. Should corporate officers be held responsible for crimes committed by the corporation? The following case illustrates the heightened responsibilities of corporate officials under some, but not all criminal laws.

United States v. Park

421 U.S. 720 (1975)

Facts. Park was the chief executive officer of Acme Markets, Inc., a national retail grocery chain headquartered in Philadelphia. Acme employed approximately 36,000 employees at 874 retail outlets and 12 warehouses. Acme pleaded guilty to numerous charges of violating the FDA Act by failing to maintain sanitary conditions at some food warehouses. During 1971, for example, a food safety inspector found rodent infestation in the Baltimore warehouse. After Acme received FDA citations, the FDA inspector commented that "there was still evidence of rodent activity in the building and in the warehouses and we found some rodent-contaminated lots of food items." Park testified that although all Acme employees were theoretically under his control, the company had an "organizational structure for responsibilities for certain functions" and assignments "to individuals who, in turn, have staff and departments under them." When Park received notice of the FDA inspections, he conferred with the Acme department responsible for

4. See *U.S. v. NYNEX*, 788 F.Supp. 16 (D.D.C., 1992).

sanitation, which was investigating and attempting to correct the unsanitary conditions. Although Park believed that there was nothing more he could have done to remedy the problem, he conceded that sanitation was ultimately his responsibility, despite delegation of that responsibility to other managers. Park was convicted of violating of the FDA Act.

Legal Issue. Can a CEO be held liable under a criminal statute requiring particular public health conditions at corporate facilities?

Opinion. Chief Justice Burger. The rule that corporate employees who have "a responsible share in the furtherance of the transaction, which the statute outlaws" are subject to the criminal provisions of the Act was not formulated in a vacuum. Cases under the Federal Food and Drugs Act of 1906 reflected the view both that knowledge or intent was not required to be provided in prosecutions under its criminal provisions, and that responsible corporate agents could be subjected to the liability thereby imposed. Moreover, the principle had been recognized that a corporate agent, through whose act, default, or omission the corporation committed a crime, was himself guilty individually of that crime. The principle had been applied whether or not the crime required "consciousness of wrongdoing," and it had been applied not only to those corporate agents who themselves committed the criminal act, but also to those who by virtue of their managerial positions or other similar relation to the actor could be deemed responsible for its commission. It was enough in such cases that, by virtue of the relationship he bore to the corporation, the agent had the power to prevent the act.

Courts of Appeals have recognized that those corporate agents vested with the responsibility, and power commensurate with the responsibility, to devise whatever measures are necessary to ensure compliance with the Act bear a "responsible relationship" to, or have a "responsible share" in, violations. This is by no means necessarily confined to a single corporate agent or employee—the Act imposes not only a positive duty to seek out and remedy violations when they occur but also, and primarily, a duty to implement measures that will insure that violations will not occur. The Act, in its criminal aspect, does not require that which is objectively impossible. The theory upon which responsible corporate agents are held criminally accountable for "causing" violations of the Act permits a claim that the defendant was "powerless" to prevent or correct the violation to "be raised defensively at a trial on the merits."

Congress has seen fit to enforce the accountability of responsible corporate agents dealing with products, which may affect the health of consumers by penal sanctions cast in rigorous terms, and the obligation of the courts is to give them effect so long as they do not violate the Constitution. The Government established a prima facie case when it introduced evidence sufficient to warrant a finding by the trier of the facts that the defendant had, by reason of his position in the corporation, responsibility and authority either to prevent in the first instance, or promptly to correct, the violation complained of, and that he failed to do so. The failure thus to fulfill the duty imposed by the interaction of the corporate agent's authority and the statute furnishes a sufficient causal link. We conclude that the charge was not misleading and contained an adequate statement of the law to guide the jury's determination.

Decision. Corporate officers may be convicted under some criminal statutes when the corporation commits the criminal offense.

Case Questions

1. Is criminal intent required in corporate crime prosecutions?
2. For what reason should managers be held responsible for criminal violations?
3. Does this decision unfairly expose all employees to potential criminal liability?

BUSINESS CRIMES

Society increasingly believes it is wrong for business to generate undesirable side effects. Unique temptations and opportunities encourage some business crimes, and criminal acts are often blended with legitimate transactions to avoid detection. Enforcement is frustrated because existing laws do not address all aspects of corporate crime. Many laws target individual conduct or organized crime groups while ignoring the unique attributes of criminality within the business firm. Increasingly, however, new laws specifically address white-collar crime and corporate crime.

Many corporate crimes involve fraud or violations of various regulatory schemes (e.g., labor, environmental, manufacturing) that are not immediately obvious. Unlike the more common street crimes involving violence, property damage, or disturbance of public order, corporate crimes often go undetected because their effects do not surface immediately. The traditional law enforcement emphasis on immediate and personal crimes also tends to shield corporate crime from attention.

Law may not be a sufficiently effective control over much of this aberrant corporate behavior.[5] Some structural and procedural aspects of law reduce its effectiveness as a motivator of corporate responsibility. For example, business crimes tend to affect much larger financial interests than do personal crimes. In addition, judges tend to be more lenient with corporate wrongdoers than with "common" criminals. Why this special leniency? Corporate officers are usually seen as upstanding community members with reputations for responsibility who can usually afford to hire the best defense lawyers. Defendants charged with corporate crime often claim that their actions were motivated not by personal greed or hatred but by the goal of business survival. In communities where the business has many employees and suppliers, these people may be sympathetic to the corporate defendant, and they are the ones who elect the local prosecutor or district attorney.

EMBEZZLEMENT

Embezzlement is the wrongful appropriation of property entrusted to an individual. Embezzlement differs from larceny or theft in that the embezzler is initially given rightful possession of the misappropriated property. A thief has no rightful possession of stolen property. Therefore, embezzlement is committed by those who are entrusted with another's property, typically agents, brokers, consultants, accountants, attorneys, or corporate officials. Consider, for example, cashiers, who receive currency from customers as payment for goods or services. A cashier can rightfully possess the cash during working hours, even though it really belongs to the employer. However, handling the money becomes embezzlement when the cashier takes money from the cash register while on the job. By contrast, it is larceny for a cashier to steal cash out of the employer's unguarded safe because the cashier has no rightful custody of that money. The act of embezzlement may also trigger civil tort liability for conversion, as discussed later in the torts section.

MAIL AND WIRE FRAUD

Federal statutes make it a criminal offense to perpetrate fraud by communicating misrepresentations in the mail or by telephone, telegraph, radio, television, or most other electronic telecommunication means. These laws prohibit the use of the mail or wire to conduct an intentional scheme or artifice to defraud in order to obtain money or property. Most businesses communicate to potential clients or customers by mail, over the phone, and increasingly by some electronic means (e.g., electronic data interchange, computer modem, satellite, e-mail, Internet, cell phone, pager). When even an incidental part of perpetrating the fraud includes such communication, the businessperson may be liable for mail and wire fraud. These crimes carry stiff penalties of fines up to $1,000 and imprisonment for up to five years per count.

5. See Christopher D. Stone, *Where the Law Ends: The Social Control of Corporate Behavior* (New York: Harper Colophon, 1975).

Elaborate fraudulent schemes may constitute numerous separately punishable crimes, and this pattern is also illegal under racketeering laws.

Mail and wire fraud is often combined with prosecution of other regulatory crimes such as copyright infringement over the Internet, hacking as a form of computer fraud and abuse, electronic publication of pornography, and theft of trade secrets by electronic means. For example, the mail and wire fraud statutes were used in the infamous insider trading case involving the *Wall Street Journal*'s "Heard on the Street" columnist. The reporter used the phone to tip his friends about a forthcoming article in which he discussed particular stocks. The friends then traded in the stocks before stock prices were affected by the publication of the stories. The Supreme Court decisively outlawed the participants' insider trading under the misappropriation theory when the case was prosecuted under the mail and wire fraud statutes.[6] Insider trading is illegal as mail or wire fraud if confidential information is misappropriated and securities are traded by mail or coconspirators are tipped by phone or wire. These activities are separately illegal under Rule 10b-5 of the Securities Exchange Act of 1934, discussed further in Chapter 22.

Online fraudulent schemes plagued the early days of e-commerce. The mail and wire fraud statutes apply to communications and computer crimes.[7] For example, fraudulent stock fraud, devices promising antiterrorism protection, and various get-rich-quick schemes have been perpetrated via e-mail and websites. These activities are a form of wire fraud, even though some links in these communications do not use traditional phone calls or they use wireless devices. There may be a mail and wire fraud violation if nearly any part of the fraudulent transaction uses the mails or wire (wireless, computer networks), including the knowing use of an electronic payment.[8]

COMPUTER CRIME

Today, computers are an integral part of nearly every business. This ubiquity significantly raises the potential for computer crime. Computer crimes include criminal activities at least partially involving computers and increasingly cyber crime, computer crime committed over telecommunications networks. Computers and networks provide many new opportunities for creative forms of crime. Computer crime includes more than the following list of examples: embezzlement by unauthorized computerized funds transfer; industrial espionage or misappropriation of confidential computer files; theft of hardware, software, or valuable computer-use time; sabotage through tampering with computer files or destroying data, programs, or hardware (e.g., virus infections, denial of service attacks); fraud in making misrepresentations in computer-collected data; destruction or deprivation of computer use by others; and criminal infringement. A new federal agency, the National Infrastructure Protection Center, acts as a clearing house to coordinate the response to cyber crime, hacking, and other unlawful Internet attacks.

ONLINE
National Infrastructure Protection Center
http://www.nipc.gov

Computer crimes are difficult to detect because the more artful hackers carefully cover their tracks to conceal any audit trail. Firms must be vigilant in using effective computer security controls (e.g., encryption, restricting access to computer hardware, firewalls, passwords, ID codes). Until recently, the enforcement of computer crime has simply required the extension of existing law. Today, most states, the federal

6. *Carpenter v. United States*, 484 U.S. 19 (1987).
7. *U.S. v. Riggs*, 739 F.Supp. 414 (N.D.Ill., 1990).
8. *U.S. v. Bentz*, 21 F.3d 37 (3d Cir., 1994).

government, and many other nations are now customizing computer laws to accommodate these unique problems. Some of these laws, such as the Economic Espionage Act, are discussed further in Chapter 16, and the Computer Fraud and Abuse Act is discussed in Chapter 14. The next case illustrates the difficulties of adapting existing law to computer crimes in particular and to white-collar crimes in general.

State v. McGraw

480 N.E.2d 552 (Ind., 1985)

Facts. The City of Indianapolis leased computer services at a flat-rate fee, which was irrespective of the actual on-line processing time used. McGraw, a city employee, was authorized to access the system from his desktop terminal. City employees were forbidden to make unauthorized use of city property. McGraw began moonlighting by selling the direct-marketed product NaturSlim to his coworkers. He used the city's computer system to keep the associated business records: correspondence, client lists, inventory records. McGraw was reprimanded for making sales during office hours and was eventually terminated for poor job performance. After his discharge, McGraw requested a former coworker to make a printout of his personal business records and to delete all associated computer files from the city's system. The former coworker provided the printout to McGraw's supervisor, thereby triggering an investigation into McGraw's criminal theft of computer time. The state appealed the trial court's dismissal of his conviction for the theft.

Legal Issue. Does the unauthorized use of unmetered computer capacity by an employee constitute criminal theft?

Opinion. Judge Prentice. It is fundamental that penal statutes must be construed strictly against the State. They may not be enlarged by implication or intendment beyond the fair meaning of the language used and may not be held to include offenses other than those which are clearly described, notwithstanding that the court may think the legislature should have made them more comprehensive. The Act provides: "A person who knowingly or intentionally exerts unauthorized control over property of another person with intent to deprive the other of any part of its value or use commits theft, a felony."

It is immediately apparent that the harm sought to be prevented is a deprivation to one of his property or its use—not a benefit to one which, although a windfall to him, harmed nobody. The Court of Appeals focused upon Defendant's unauthorized use of the computer for monetary gain and upon the definition of "property" as used in the statute. We think that it would be more accurate to say that the information derived by use of a computer is property. Having determined that Defendant's use was property, was unauthorized and was for his monetary benefit, it concluded that he committed a theft. Our question is, "Who was deprived of what?"

There is no evidence that the City was ever deprived of any part of the value or the use of the computer by reason of Defendant's conduct. Defendant's unauthorized use cost the City nothing and did not interfere with its use by others. He extracted from the system only such information as he had previously put into it. He did not, for his own benefit, withdraw City data intended for its exclusive use or for sale. Thus, Defendant did not deprive the City of the "use of computers and computer services" as alleged. We find no distinction between Defendant's use of the City's computer and the use, by a mechanic, of the employer's hammer or a stenographer's use of the employer's typewriter, for other than the employer's purposes. Under traditional concepts, the transgression is in the nature of a trespass, a civil matter—and a de minimis one, at that. Defendant has likened his conduct to the use of an employer's vacant bookshelf, for the temporary storage of one's personal items, and to the use of an employer's telephone facilities for toll-free calls. The analogies appear to us to be appropriate.

Intent is a mental function and, absent an admission, it must be determined by courts and juries from a consideration of the conduct and natural and usual consequences of such conduct. There was no evidence presented from which the intent to deprive, an essential element of the crime, could be inferred. A companion statute to the theft statute, proscribing conversion, [states] as follows: "A person who knowingly or intentionally exerts unauthorized control over property of another person commits criminal conversion, a class A misdemeanor."

The only difference between the statutory definitions of theft and criminal conversion is that the definition for conversion omits the words "with intent to deprive the other of any part of its value or use." At most, the evidence in this case warranted a conviction for criminal conversion. The decision and opinion of the Court of Appeals are ordered vacated, and the judgment of the trial court is affirmed.

Pivarnik, Judge (dissenting). I must dissent from the majority opinion. In the first place, intent is clearly shown in that Defendant used the City computer system for his personal business, well knowing that he was doing so and well knowing that it was unauthorized. I think the Court of Appeals properly focused upon Defendant's unauthorized use of the computer for monetary gain and upon the definition of property as used in the statute. Time and use are at the very core of the value of a computer system. To say that only the information stored in the computer, plus the tapes and discs and perhaps the machinery involved, are the only elements that can be measured as the value or property feature of that system is incorrect.

It is irrelevant that the computer service was leased to the City at a fixed charge and that the tapes or discs upon which the imparted data was stored were erasable and reusable. The fact is the City owned the computer system of all the stations including the defendant's. The time and use of that equipment at that station belonged to the City. Thus, when the defendant used the computer system, putting on data from his private business and taking it out on printouts, he was taking that which was property of the City and converting it to his own use, thereby depriving the City of its use and value. I therefore would allow the Court of Appeals opinion to stand.

Decision. Where there is no deprivation of assets, a criminal charge of theft should be dismissed.

Case Questions

1. Does information constitute property? Why?
2. How could a new statute be written to specifically eliminate the ambiguities inherent in applying traditional criminal law to computer crime?

Stalking

Stalking is another traditional crime that has moved to the Internet. **Stalking** is a fairly recently defined crime involving the pursuit of another by tracking them, in a stealthy manner, often anonymously. It usually involves repeated acts of harassment perceived as threatening to the victim. The harm is in fear and apprehension about a credible threat of potential physical assault to the victim or the victim's family or damage to the victim's property. The federal government and most states outlaw stalking when it results in harassment, annoyance, or alarm. Stalking may involve tortious activity such as the infliction of emotional distress, as discussed in the torts section later.

Cyber stalking may involve the use of hacker methods to intercept the target's e-mail and Web activity or to pose as a friendly correspondent in chat rooms or other communications. Arguably, cyber-stalking is less threatening because of the anonymity and distance between the stalker and the victim. However, experience shows that the potential for fear or electronic theft is realistic. Therefore, several states are amending their stalking laws to include acts of stalking that use telecommunications devices. Children are vulnerable to cyber stalking by predatory adults when trusting children are lured to unprotected places where they may suffer physical, emotional, or financial harm.

ONLINE

DOJ cyber stalking website
http://www.usdoj.gov:80/criminal/cybercrime/cyberstalking.htm

Identity Theft

There has long been a crime of impersonation, a form of identity fraud. Today, the Internet makes it easier to acquire an individual's personal information (e.g., name, address, social security number, bank or credit card account numbers) and then misuse that information to convincingly pose as the person, either on or off line. In cyberspace, it is often too easy to evade traditional physical safeguards: examining IDs, observing an impersonator's demeanor, or authenticating signatures. Identity thieves can ruin an individual's reputation, credit history, or insurability or even create a false criminal record. Congress enacted the Identity Theft and Assumption and Deterrence Act in 1998. Most states have identity theft protections for victims, as well as penalties for the thieves.

The Fair Credit Reporting Act (FCRA) is a financial privacy law detailed in Chapter 14. The FCRA is increasingly used to vindicate identity thefts. Victims are suing credit reporting bureaus when they wrongfully provide the victim's credit history to impersonators. In one form of this crime, the identity thief uses credit history information to pose as the victim and thereby obtain credit cards, or utility accounts, borrow money, or obtain fake IDs. Credit bureaus are liable to the victim if they release such information to the wrong person.

In *TRW v. Andrews*,[9] the U.S. Supreme Court limited credit bureau liability by starting the FCRA's two-year statute of limitations when the credit reports were wrongfully supplied rather than later, when the victim discovered her or his identity was stolen by the impersonator. A receptionist in a Los Angeles doctor's office used a patient's personal information to obtain a credit report from TRW (now Experian). Thereafter, the receptionist posed as the patient to obtain a credit card and a utility account. The patient did not discover the damage to her credit rating until a year later and sued TRW on some of the claims more than two years after the receptionist obtained the patient's credit history. This important decision puts much more responsibility on the shoulders of the victims of identity theft; they must discover and resolve such problems quickly. Many states help the victims of identity theft with the often daunting task of discovering and correcting errors in their credit histories caused by identity thieves.

Many antiterrorism tools are readily adaptable to reduce identity theft and can also inspire confidence in the safety of e-commerce. For example, identity technologies useful in both areas may include **biometrics** (fingerprinting, retinal scanning, facial recognition, DNA analysis) or **national ID cards** containing digitized records of biometric, password, photographs, signature specimens, and account numbers. These techniques are controversial among privacy advocates.

www.consumer.gov/idtheft/

Gambling

Gambling has had a long and varied past. Ancient people believed that gambling outcomes were an expression of supernatural powers. This idea survives today because many gamblers believe in luck. Eventually, gambling became a widespread pastime. However, by the nineteenth century, pressures to regulate gambling mounted as it became associated with many negative consequences. For example, gambling restrictions were rationalized after experience with "Old West" saloons, where gambling was linked with alcohol abuse, prostitution, and violence. Many naive gamblers and their families suffered financial ruin. In the twentieth

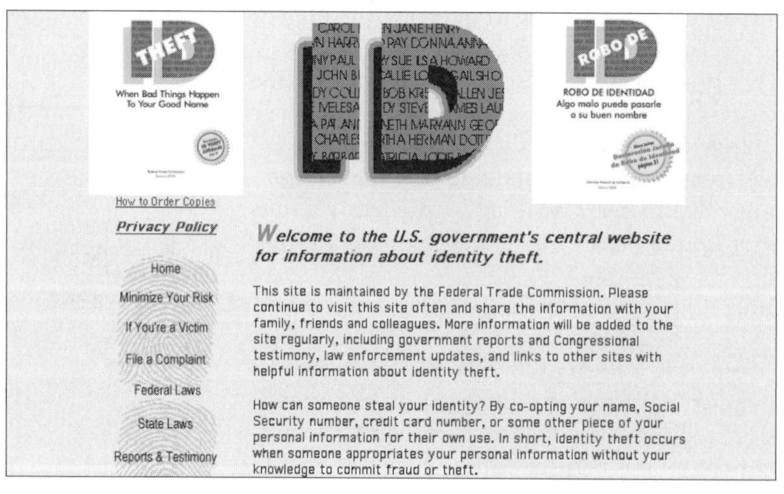

9. 122 S.Ct. 441 (2001).

century, gambling became connected with organized crime and with manipulation of sporting events. By the late twentieth century, government regulation relaxed somewhat, as revenues rose from gambling taxes and from state-run lotteries. At least some forms of gambling are illegal in all 50 states and in most foreign nations. However, enforcement of illegal gambling varies considerably. As discussed in Chapter 12, contracts to pay illegal gambling debts are unenforceable.

Gambling is the creation of a risk with no prior existence primarily for the purpose of shifting the risk to expose the parties to gain or loss. These risks are usually based on uncertain events that solely rely on chance (simple card games, dice, roulette), rely entirely on external factors (sports outcomes), or are based on a combination of chance and the gambler's skill (complex card games). Gambling proliferates on the Internet for several reasons. First, local law enforcement officials have great difficulty detecting illegal on-line gambling. Gamblers usually operate from the privacy of their homes, and electronic settlement of gambling debts uses credit cards or peer-to-peer payment systems that are difficult to police. Illegal gambling can involve money laundering, as discussed in a later section. Second, on-line gambling sites operate most successfully from states or foreign nations where on-line gambling is legal. States or nations that generally outlaw gambling or specifically prohibit on-line gambling face very difficult enforcement problems. The jurisdiction problems of the Internet are particularly daunting in cyberspace. Opponents of new restrictions on on-line gambling argue that the costs of enforcement outweigh any benefits, that legalizing gambling would weaken organized crime, and that the negative social context of gambling has changed.

RACKETEER INFLUENCED AND CORRUPT ORGANIZATIONS

A portion of the Organized Crime Control Act of 1970 is known as **RICO**, an acronym for that law's provisions on racketeer influenced and corrupt organizations. RICO has criminal and civil provisions. Civil RICO permits private plaintiffs to sue for civil treble (triple) damages against persons found guilty of racketeering activities. RICO outlaws a pattern of illegal activities that include the **predicate offenses** of securities fraud, murder, arson, extortion, drug dealing, mail and wire fraud, bribery, loan sharking, and other enumerated state and other federal crimes. Many of these crimes can be committed by using telecommunications and computer networks, such as the Internet.

RICO requires a private plaintiff to prove the following essential elements to win triple damages: (1) the defendant committed at least two prohibited acts (2) that constituted a pattern (3) of racketeering activity (4) by which the defendant (5) invested in, maintained an interest in, or participated in (6) an enterprise (7) that affected interstate or foreign commerce. Critics claim RICO has been expanded to cover many activities that were not traditionally considered part of organized crime.

RICO makes it unlawful to invest proceeds derived from racketeering activities, a practice used by organized crime to launder its illegal profits. In one case, the proceeds from the sale of a firm tainted by securities fraud were invested in another firm. In another case, a fraud was perpetrated by general partners who sold their brokerage business. The pattern of racketeering activity outlawed by RICO may be proved, for example, by the artificial inflation of a company's market price. RICO's special powers and penalties promise treble damages and attorney's fees to civil plaintiffs. Criminal conviction can carry fines of up to $25,000 and/or imprisonment for up to 20 years per violation. RICO authorizes judges to order the defendant to forfeit any property acquired with the illegal racketeering profits, which permits prosecutors to request a pretrial freeze or seizure of the defendant's assets. This powerful settlement inducement was allegedly used to bring down the "junk bond king" Michael Milken and his employer, the investment banking firm of Drexel Burnham Lambert.

Nearly half of the states have passed RICO-type statutes. The state laws combined with the expansive federal RICO provision make significant liabilities possible in business litigation. In addition, the RICO criminal procedures provide stiff penalties and permit prosecutors to freeze the defendant's assets during a criminal RICO trial. This tactic has allegedly been used to bully investment banking firms accused of stock manipulation and securities fraud into settling RICO charges.

Dissatisfaction with civil plaintiffs' and federal prosecutors' alleged misuse of RICO has led to reform. For example, the Supreme Court in *H.J. Inc. v. Northwestern Bell Telephone Co.*[10] required better proof of a relationship between the predicate offenses, such as the same or similar purpose, results, participants, victims, or methods of commissions. Prosecutors cannot easily prove the required "pattern" from only two isolated events unless they clearly pose a threat of continuity. *Reeves v. Ernst & Young*[11] held that most auditors, investment bankers, and legal counsel are relieved from RICO liability for such crimes as securities fraud committed by their clients. RICO requires that the defendant must actively "participate" in committing the predicate offense to be held liable. The RICO threat on auditors of fraudulent financial statements is eliminated unless they knowingly participate in the management or operations of the client. This point was further reinforced with passage of the Private Securities Litigation Reform Act (PSLRA), discussed further in Chapter 22. Under PSLRA, securities fraud and securities fraud applications of the mail and wire fraud statutes are no longer predicate offenses for civil RICO. However, they still remain part of criminal RICO.

BRIBERY AND THE FOREIGN CORRUPT PRACTICES ACT

Scandals in the 1970s focused public inquiry on the misuse of corporate funds for unethical and illegal purposes. The SEC investigated questionable payments made by domestic firms, including bribery of domestic and foreign officials, illegal campaign contributions, and kickbacks. This prompted Congress to pass the **Foreign Corrupt Practices Act (FCPA)** in 1977. The FCPA was amended twice, first with the Foreign Corrupt Practices Act Amendments of 1988 and again with the International Anti-Bribery and Fair Competition Act of 1998. The FCPA outlaws foreign bribery and establishes accounting standards to prevent bribery. The accounting standards provisions require publicly traded companies to keep books and records that accurately and fairly reflect the transactions of the corporation and to devise and maintain an adequate system of internal accounting controls. These standards are designed to prevent the accumulation and use of bribery funds. The SEC is discussed further in Chapter 22. Bribery is also a criminal offense under other state and federal laws.

After 20 years' experience with the "high ground" represented by the FCPA, the United States convinced the governments of more than 30 other nations to agree to adopt similar antibribery legislation. This was accomplished with the implementation of a treaty negotiated through the Organization for Economic Cooperation and

10. 492 U.S. 229 (1989).
11. 507 U.S. 170 (1993).

Ethical Issue

Ethical Dilemmas in Foreign Trade

Nearly all nations outlaw bribery. However, bribery receives varying degrees of acceptance in other nations. Some firms doing business abroad may be induced to bribe foreign officials to gain business in nations where bribery is tolerated by the culture or encouraged by corrupt officials. It may be difficult to do business without bribes in some nations. These foreign officials act unethically when other nations' firms must bribe them to gain business. Bribery contradicts the basic assumptions underlying the perfect competition model by diverting transactions from freely negotiated market outcomes into suboptimal transactions based on factors other than price, service, and quality. The officials who personally profit by taking bribes do so at the expense of their own citizens and nations. Bribery becomes possible only where there are primitive control systems, lax accountability and ineffectual enforcement, or outright concealment. The FCPA establishes a higher standard in law and in accounting practice by requiring internal corporate accountability over funds that might be used as bribes.

Development (OECD), the Convention on Combating Bribery of Foreign Officials in International Business Transactions. Congress implemented the convention with passage of the 1998 amendments to the FCPA.

Prohibited Bribery

The FCPA criminalizes foreign bribery intended to "secure improper advantage" when made by all persons, including publicly traded corporations, companies of various legal structures (e.g., **domestic concerns**), various unincorporated organizations, persons within the United States, and persons outside the United States who are working for a U.S. company. The FCPA antibribery provisions outlaw any corrupt payments, offers to pay, and offers to give **anything of value** to foreign officials to influence decisions to grant business. **Foreign officials** include government officials, officials of foreign political parties, candidates for foreign public office, and officials of international organizations.

Grease payments (facilitating payments) are not considered bribes under the FCPA. **Grease** payments are made to lower-echelon foreign government agents when they make **routine governmental actions.** In some countries, for example, customs officials routinely expect a "gratuity" to expedite the clearance of incoming goods. An exporter might feel pressured to make a grease payment to get a shipment of perishable goods quickly cleared through foreign customs. In this situation, the payment would not be an illegal bribe so long as it is permissible in the foreign country. Bona fide promotional expenditures and contract performance expenses, including lodging for foreign officials, are not illegal bribes.

Foreign Corruption Practices Act Enforcement

The FCPA gives enforcement powers to both the SEC and the U.S. Justice Department (DOJ). The DOJ conducts criminal investigations, prosecutes criminal bribery, and may seek civil penalties and injunctions. The SEC has civil enforcement powers over publicly traded firms and enforces the accounting standards provisions of the FCPA. Violators of the FCPA bribery provisions are subject to fines of up to $2 million, and individual violators are subject to possible imprisonment for up to five years. The SEC may assess civil penalties of up to $10,000 for individuals, whether or not they are U.S. nationals. An employer may not pay an individual violator's fine.

The 1988 amendments give the U.S. attorney general power to issue guidelines and to assist compliance by providing opinions on the legality of specific proposed conduct by U.S. companies, persons, or their foreign agents in the DOJ's FCPA

Opinion Procedure Releases. The new antiterrorism law, the USA Patriot Act, includes foreign bribery as a form of illegal money laundering, discussed later in this chapter.

TERRORISM

Increasingly, the criminal law is directed at **terrorism**, a threatened use of violence reinforced by actual violent, criminal acts, usually for political or religious purposes. Terrorism is often performed by small, zealous groups who intend to coerce and intimidate. They rely on fear from widespread publicity of their illegal acts. Terrorism targets particular victims who are usually linked together by a demographic factor such as their religion, race, ethnicity, or national origin. The impact of terrorism is often much broader, going beyond national borders. Terrorist acts include the development and use of weapons of mass destruction, erratic murders and bombings, hijackings, kidnappings, and creating fear of credible threats of various criminal acts.

Several waves of terrorism in modern times have encouraged public support for new criminal laws and enforcement procedures. For example, infamous waves of terrorism accompanied Nazi expansionism, the Irish Republican Army, the Palestinian crisis, and associated Arab-Israeli conflicts in the Middle East. Except for the Ku Klux Klan's long-standing terrorism against blacks, terrorism was largely unknown in the United States until the Oklahoma City bombing in 1995 and then the attacks on the World Trade Center and Pentagon on September 11, 2001. Increasingly, terrorists use modern tools and technologies that increase the impact of their acts, such as high-powered explosives, hijacking of transportation systems, computers, and telecommunications networks. Terrorists often use these means for spying, malicious destruction or disturbance, and transactions to finance and organize their terrorist networks.

Cyber Terrorism

Cyber terrorism involves activities by **hackers**, people skilled in computer programming. *Hacker* is now generally perceived as a derogatory term. Malicious hackers pride themselves in overcoming the security features of computer networks, and many gain unlawful entry into others' computer systems to steal information or money or do damage. Malicious hacking involves illegal acts that use computer networks for spying, financial fraud, malicious destruction (denial of service, virus attacks, falsifying data), or exerting unauthorized control over dams, power systems, air traffic, transportation systems, utilities, or other systems with broad impact.

Counterterrorism

The United States took steps to combat terrorism and cyber terrorism following several incidents in the 1990s, and particularly after the terrorist attacks of September 11, 2001. First, the United States has negotiated international agreements with other nations and through international organizations such as the United Nations. These agreements require signatory nations to cooperate in antiterrorist activities. For example, many nations are cooperating in apprehending, prosecuting, and terminating terrorist organizations and their networks by using various law enforcement tools. Second, the United States now designates various groups as suspected terrorist organizations, which expands law enforcement monitoring and triggers greater financial scrutiny for money laundering. The FBI's Internet monitoring software program, **Carnivore**, selectively searches for e-mail containing language believed to suggest terrorism and other criminal activity. Third, the United States offers rewards for assistance in apprehending known terrorists. Fourth, antiterrorism preparedness, or **counterterrorism**, has been enhanced by the creation of coordinating agencies such as the U.S. Office of Homeland Security and the State Department's Office of the Coordinator for Counterterrorism. Fifth, the United States and other cooperating nations have increased the effectiveness of their border controls and travel documents (visas). These nations are also monitoring and restricting terrorist fund-raising and improving their information exchange and antiterrorism law enforcement.

ONLINE

U.S. Counterterrorism website
http://www.state.gov/s/ct/

MONEY LAUNDERING

Criminal law increasingly focuses enforcement efforts on **money laundering**, a varied set of practices that create an illusion of transactions to disguise the origin and movement of criminal proceeds. The critical element is to mimic legitimate transactions so that criminals can provide plausible explanations for their cash flow and cash reserves. This practice has led to a reliable enforcement method to find the criminal leaders and their accomplices: "Follow the money." Law enforcement often examines a suspect's finances for suspicious expenditures beyond the suspect's reported earnings and financial means.

The term *money laundering* literally means to "clean" or legitimize the appearance of money made "dirty" as the proceeds of crimes. The term may have originated from the 1920s and 1930s gangster era, when legal slot machine gambling proliferated. The cash flow of coins from this gambling and from coin-operated laundries provided plausible and practically untraceable excuses for handling huge amounts of currency and coins from criminal activities. Today, a major argument against gambling is that it facilitates money laundering and organized crime. However, money laundering has probably been done for more than 4,000 years. It was originally used to hide legitimate earnings from taxation or from unfair confiscation by oppressive governments.

The tools of money launderers are well known but are still in use because detection is difficult and enforcement is costly. Launderers use transaction methods that minimize records. Cash payments of $10,000 and more must be reported by businesses and banks, creating an audit trail. Using cash rather than checks, wire transfers, or credit cards reduces the record keeping and thereby hides transactions. Conversion of criminal proceeds into gold, diamonds, or other valuable hard assets can also conceal the flow of value. The use of "fronts" is another component of successful money laundering. These apparently respectable businesses are used as a cover for illegal activities.

In recent years, government has tried harder to restrict money laundering, which is an indispensable component of many illegal schemes that society seeks to eliminate: the illegal drug trade, terrorism, organized crime, and smuggling. The purposes of laws against money laundering are to (1) identify criminals and their accomplices for prosecution, (2) reveal the criminals' accessories and coconspirators, who may provide incriminating evidence that brings down criminal organizations, (3) seize the money or freeze accounts holding laundered money, and (4) deter crimes generally because the incentive is reduced if it becomes risky to spend the criminal proceeds. Civil penalties for each money laundering violation can include fines of either twice the amount involved or $1 million, whichever is greater. Several of the key U.S. statutes used to stop money laundering are listed in Exhibit 7.2.

ONLINE

Money laundering guidance for financial institutions
http://www.moneylaundering.com

EXHIBIT 7.2 U.S. Laws Against Money Laundering

Federal Statute	Purposes and Methods
Bank Secrecy Act of 1970 (BSA)	Currency transaction report ("paper trail" for transactions over $10,000); civil and criminal penalties
Money Laundering Control Act of 1986	Creates three new federal money laundering crimes: (1) assistance in laundering, (2) engaging in $10,000 transactions involving property from criminal activity, and (3) structuring transactions to avoid BSA disclosures of currency transaction reports
Anti–Drug Abuse Act of 1988	Increased civil and criminal sanctions. Forfeiture of property involved in violating BSA or other anti-laundering statute. Requires record keeping of large cash purchases of monetary instruments (bank drafts)
Crime Control Act of 1990, §2532	Federal banking regulators authorized to negotiate with foreign banking regulators for help in certain criminal investigations
Federal Deposit Insurance Corporation Improvement Act of 1991, §206	Federal banking regulators given discretion to disclose information to foreign banking regulators to enforce anti–money laundering laws
Housing and Community Development Act of 1992, Title XV (Annunzio-Wylie Anti-Money Laundering Act)	Authorizes seizure, closing, and/or revocation of charter of financial institutions guilty of money laundering or BSA offenses; specifies mitigation factors
USA Patriot Act of 2001	Broadens definition of financial institutions regulated under money laundering laws, requires anti–money laundering programs and training, regulates private and correspondent banking; FCPA now defines money laundering as a form of bribery; stiffens civil and criminal penalties for money laundering

DEFENSES TO CRIMES

Defendants guilty of some crimes may offer an excuse or justification for the criminal act. As in other areas of law, a **defense** either partially or completely relieves the defendant from liability. These defenses are in addition to the basis for acquittal if the accused's constitutional rights are violated during criminal processing or the defendant creates reasonable doubt about guilt or can disprove the prosecution's allegations.

Some defenses directly undermine the prosecution's proof of *mens rea* or criminal intent. **Infancy** is a defense for defendants under the legal age of majority, usually 18. Most states have a separate **juvenile court system** for children, although some older minors may be "tried as an adult" in the regular system for particularly serious crimes. **Intoxication** and **insanity** are also defenses that may show the defendant could not have had the criminal intent needed to be found guilty. Courts are generally more willing to accept intoxication as a defense if it is involuntary—the defendant was forced or tricked into ingesting the intoxicating drugs or alcohol. There are several different tests of criminal insanity: (1) the **M'Naghten rule**, still used in several states, shows the defendant to be incapable of distinguishing right from wrong, (2) the **irresistible impulse** test is used in a few states, and (3) the Model Penal Code's test, used in most states and federal courts, shows the defendant is lacking substantial capacity to appreciate wrongfulness because of mental disease or defect. **Mistake** of fact may be a defense if the defendant has a genuine mistaken belief in the objective of the act, such as someone who mistakenly takes another person's coat from a checkroom because it looked like the defendant's coat. Ignorance of the law is almost never a defense.

Other defenses examine the circumstances that might justify the criminal act. A victim might grant **consent**, as football players do for assault and battery during practice or games. **Duress** involves a credible threat of serious bodily harm to the defendant, and the defendant commits the crime to avoid the threatened harm. **Self-defense** is similar to duress—the justifiable use of force to repel a physical attack or in defense of one's home or family. The defendant can use only as much force as is needed to repel the attack. Deadly force is justified only when the defendant is threatened with death or serious bodily harm. **Necessity** is another derivation of self-defense. **Entrapment** prevents law enforcement from promoting a crime by staging the circumstances and suggesting that the defendant do the criminal act. There is no entrapment if the defendant was predisposed to the crime. Law enforcement may set up traps so long as they do not push the defendant into the criminal act. The **statute of limitations** prevents prosecution after the statutory period has run out. Finally, some defendants may be granted **immunity**, barring prosecution in exchange for the defendant's cooperation and information leading to successful prosecutions against other criminals.

TORTS

Unlike most of criminal law, which seeks to punish and deter unlawful wrongs committed against all of society, tort law seeks to award compensation to remedy wrongs committed against individuals or identifiable groups. Many intentional torts closely parallel the similar crimes. For example, assault, battery, and trespass entitle the victim to compensation under tort law but are also are criminal acts. The growth in tort law mirrors somewhat the evolution of society. Tort law has become concerned with protecting the individual's reputation, right to privacy, freedom from interference with property rights, and freedom from externally caused mental distress. In recent years, tort liability has expanded to cover interference with personal rights (sexual harassment), interference with economic relations, and injuries from defective products and malpractice.

There are four types of torts: intentional torts, quasi-intentional torts, negligence, and strict liability. Although each type has distinctly different proof requirements, all four require both proof of a causal connection to the tortious act and proof that an injury occurred that the law would compensate. Tort law is much broader and more pervasive than the coverage it is given in this chapter alone. Indeed, tort law is the source of many other forms of liability discussed throughout this book. For example, tort law is the direct foundation for product and service liability, privacy liability, civil securities law liability, and environmental cleanup liability, which are discussed in Chapters 8, 14, 22, and 23. Tort law is closely related to intellectual property infringement (discussed in Chapters 15, 16, 17, and 18) and to agency and employment liability (discussed in Chapters 9, 13, 20 and 21). Finally, civil remedies in other regulatory programs closely resemble tort law, such as antitrust and Internet regulation (discussed in Chapters 19 and 24). Clearly, this introductory discussion of tort fundamentals is a necessary prerequisite to most other discussions of civil remedies. Exhibit 7.3 compares the four major types of torts.

EXHIBIT 7.3 Comparison of the Four Types of Torts

Type of Tort	Requirements	Examples
Intentional torts	Intent to commit tortious act Causation Injury	***Battery:*** hit another person ***Trespass:*** unconsented touching of land or personal property of another person
Quasi-intentional tort: defamation	Defamatory (false) statement about the plaintiff Publication by the defendant Damage to plaintiff's reputation	***Libel:*** false written statements made in newspaper ***Slander:*** false spoken statement made on TV
Negligence	Duty to act as reasonable person Breach of duty Proximate and actual causation Injury	Careless driving Unskilled professional malpractice in person or remotely (over the Internet)
Strict liability	Ultrahazardous activity or inherently defective product that is unreasonably dangerous Defect existed while under defendant's control Defendant in business as seller Causation and injury	Use of dynamite that destroys structures on adjoining property Product liability injuries

BUSINESS AND VICARIOUS LIABILITY

Tort law is a pressing legal concern for business because there may be liability for the actions of employees. Most businesses act through other people: officers, employees, and independent agents. Corporations, partnerships, and many sole proprietorships employ people and other firms to implement their activities. The law holds a business responsible for acts of employees if the business has the right to control the employee.

The Agent and the Independent Contractor

If an agent commits torts while working on behalf of a business, the injured person can sue the business, the agent or employee, or both. This type of risk exposure is **vicarious liability**. In this analysis, the business is a **master** or principal, and its agents or employees are **servants** or agents. Vicarious liability arises when an agent causes injury to a third party—to an individual or to another business—while acting on behalf of the principal.

A business is not held vicariously liable for the act of an agent if the business has no right to control that agent's means or methods of conducting the act. For example, if a person is employed by a business solely to do a particular job without the business having any control over how the job is to be done, only the agent is responsible for his or her acts. The business is not generally liable for the torts of such a person, referred to as an **independent contractor**. The vicarious liability of businesses for the acts of agents or contractors is also discussed in Chapter 9 and is a major basis for determining ownership of copyrights under the work made for hire doctrine discussed in Chapter 15.

Vicarious Liability and Individual Direct Liability

Although a business is held vicariously liable for an employee's torts, this fact does not alter the **direct liability** of the employee. All persons are directly liable for their own tortious acts. The vicarious liability imposed on a business for the torts of servants is an alternative source for compensation. For example, if ABC Trucking employs Jeff to drive a delivery truck and Jeff's negligent driving causes injury to pedestrians, Jeff is directly liable *and* ABC is vicariously liable to the pedestrians for their injuries. However, such victims are permitted only one recovery. Vicarious liability provides some greater assurance that the victim will be fairly compensated, not overcompensated.

There are several reasons why the vicarious liability of a business is generally more significant than the direct liability of an employee. First, because both the business and the employee may be held liable, the injured party usually sues both of them. The injured person may be unsure whether the employee is solely responsible as an independent contractor or whether the business is also liable because the employee is a servant acting within the scope of employment. By suing both, the injured plaintiff forces the business and the employee to determine through litigation the extent of the control that the business can exercise over the employee. Second, the business usually has greater financial resources than the employee. This basis for suing the business is known as the **deep pocket theory**. Most businesses are well advised to insure these risks. Too often, the employee's wages or assets are

Commentary

Jurisdiction in Tort Cases: Where to Hear a Tort Case and What Law to Apply

The general legal principle governing a tortious act is that the law of the place where the tort occurs is usually applied. Of course, it is not always easy to determine where a tort action occurs. In the Union Carbide[12] case, a U.S. court was asked to hear a tort case against Union Carbide Ltd. (an Indian corporation) and Union Carbide, Inc. (a U.S. corporation), which owned a majority of stock in the Indian corporation. The plaintiffs alleged that the lack of supervision by the U.S. firm made it responsible for the deaths and damage caused by an explosion at an Indian facility that manufactured methyl-isocynanate, a dangerous and deadly gas. Plaintiffs asked the U.S. court to hear the case and to apply U.S. tort law in determining liability.

The U.S. court refused to hear the case because the parties, witnesses, and documentary evidence were primarily in India. The court applied the concept of ***forum non conveniens***, determining that the U.S. court was not a convenient forum in which to hear and decide the case. Likewise, the court looked at the conflict of law rules and determined that the substantive law to apply in determining liability for the explosion should be the law of the place where the wrong occurred: India. This decision dramatically affected the financial liability of Union Carbide because the computation of damages under U.S. law can result in very large damage amounts.

Similar jurisdictional problems exist today as torts are committed on the Internet. For example, when a website publishes false, defamatory statements damaging to the reputation of an individual in another state or nation, which law should apply, and which place should hold the trial? The state or nation where the victim is located may successfully assert jurisdiction if the ***tortfeasor***, who committed the tortious act, directed the wrongful activity through the Internet and into the plaintiff's state or nation. Jurisdiction is a recurring theme throughout this book. Because it remains unsettled, it is a subject to which managers must be constantly attentive.

12. *In re Union Carbide Corp. Gas Plant Disaster*, 809 F.2d 195 (2d Cir., 1987).

insufficient to satisfy large damage awards. Given this disparity in resources, the business, with its deep pockets, is often the injured person's primary target. The deep pocket theory is justified because the master should screen and monitor its servants to assure safe operations.

INTENTIONAL TORTS

An intentional tort is an intentional, wrongful act performed by the person committing the tort, the tortfeasor. The plaintiff must prove that the defendant intended to do the act that caused the injury. Tortious actions that interfere with personal rights can cause physical or mental injury, interference with private property (trespass), or interference in economic relations. Intentional torts require the plaintiff to prove only that the defendant intended to do the act that caused the injury; it is not necessary to prove that the defendant intended to cause the resulting injury. If, however, the plaintiff can prove evil motive or desire to harm, then punitive damages may be appropriate in addition to compensatory damages. **Compensatory damages** are payments to reimburse damages such as medical expenses, lost income, and pain and suffering. The standard is that compensatory damages are awarded only to compensate the injured person for the losses actually suffered. By contrast, punitive damages are additional amounts intended to punish the wrongdoer for the wrongfulness and to deter similar wrongful acts. Punitive damages are discussed in the last section of this chapter.

The clearest cases of intentional torts generally occur when one person causes physical injury to another. For example, a punch in the nose can be a battery if it causes injury. The law requires that people refrain from intentional actions that injure others. It allows recovery of damages for an injury caused by someone's intentional interference with the right not to be injured. Some types of intentional acts interfere with personal rights, and some result from physical or mental injury, interference with property rights, or interference with economic relations.

INTENTIONAL TORTS THAT INTERFERE WITH PERSONAL RIGHTS

Assault

Assault is a crime and intentional tort resulting from an intentional act of putting another person in apprehension of immediate offensive harmful touching. The victim may be afraid but need not be; **apprehension** here means expectation. Words alone do not typically constitute an assault because they are not sufficient to make an ordinarily reasonable person apprehensive of immediate harm. Words coupled with a menacing gesture, however, can constitute an assault. The relevant intent in assault is that of the actor. The apprehension is based on the victim's state of mind, judged by a reasonable person standard. Note that actual physical contact need not take place for an assault to occur. A person who points a gun or a knife at another person in a threatening manner commits an assault, even though the victim is not actually touched. Given that words alone are insufficient for an assault, it may be difficult to commit assault using e-mail, in chat rooms, or otherwise over the Internet.

Battery

Battery is the intentional offensive touching of another person without justification or consent. Battery also includes the unprivileged touching of another with some instrumentality put in motion by the aggressor. For example, shooting a bullet that hits someone constitutes a battery. Like self-defense and use of force in criminal law, a **reasonable justification** is usually the key to determining whether a battery is wrongful under tort law. A person imminently threatened or battered by another may respond in self-defense with similar force without incurring liability. However, if another person is the victim or the victim's property is threatened, many courts would not excuse a "defensive battery" as self-defense. Minimal, social, or unavoidable touching, as on a crowded bus or at a sporting event, is usually not considered battery because it is expected, justified, and not offensive to a reasonable person. However, "crowd surfing" at a concert might result in unconsented contacts that are more invasive than would be reasonable to expect in most crowded public situations.

False Imprisonment

False imprisonment is the intentional confinement of a nonconsenting individual within a bounded area for an appreciable time. False imprisonment may be charged against a business that attempts to deal with suspected shoplifters or with employees suspected of dishonest behavior. Under common law, a storekeeper could be held liable for detaining a suspected shoplifter if that person was later found to be innocent.

Most states have statutes that limit the false imprisonment liability of storekeepers to unreasonable actions or bad faith detentions. If storekeepers have probable cause or act in good faith in detaining a suspected shoplifter, they are not liable. The privilege is a qualified one; if it is abused, the storekeeper could be held liable for detention without reasonable cause. It is unlikely that false imprisonment could be committed over the Internet. However, where security controls like gates or doors are controlled electronically or with computer networks, there might be liability for false imprisonment.

Intentional Infliction of Emotional Distress

The courts are beginning to recognize that the **intentional infliction of emotional distress** is a separate tort. Liability is usually limited to outrageous acts that cause detectable emotional injury. Although courts frequently hold that there has to be some physical injury to allow recovery for mental distress, some courts allow recovery even in the absence of physical injury.

Invasion of Privacy

The right of privacy provides tort remedies that are intended to protect a person from unwarranted interference with the right to be left alone. The Internet and the reawakening of antiterrorism law enforcement have thrust privacy rights forward as a major public policy issue for the foreseeable future. Privacy has become multifaceted; that is, privacy is not simply a tort but also subject to constitutional rights, property rights, regulatory requirements, and contractual agreements. Given the increasing importance of balancing individual privacy rights with societal rights, all of Chapter 14 is devoted to the various aspects of privacy.

INTENTIONAL TORTS THAT INTERFERE WITH PROPERTY RIGHTS

Interference with property rights concerns one person's unauthorized use or appropriation of another's property. The person owning or possessing the property may be injured even if the property is not damaged. Trespass and conversion are torts that interfere with property rights. The right to exclusive possession and use of real property is violated by trespass. Similarly, rights in personal property are also violated by interference or by a conversion that takes or destroys the personal property. Trespass is often a separate crime.

Trespass to Land

A person who enters someone else's real property without consent is committing a trespass. The intentional act of entering the possessor's property causes the injury. Even if the property is not damaged, the possessor is harmed by the unpermitted entry. A person who owns land or is a tenant on real property has the right to have that property remain free from interference. This right protects the owner's exclusive possession and use of land, the growing crops attached to it, the minerals underground, and/or the buildings and structures built thereon, Of course, if the trespass causes damage to the property, such as pollution, greater compensation is needed. Airplane overflights are not actionable as trespass as long as sufficient minimum altitude is maintained under aviation regulations. By contrast, subsurface trespass is wrongful, such as when a mineshaft or oil well drilling crosses property lines under the surface.

Trespass to Chattels

Trespass to chattels is an intentional and wrongful interference with the possession or use of personal property. The rightful owner, possessor, or tenant (lessee) may sue for an injunction. When the trespass is so severe that there is considerable damage, the owner may prefer to sue for conversion. Trespass to chattels is experiencing resurgence as malicious hackers carry out destruction on others' networks or computer systems. For example, denial of service and virus attacks may constitute trespass or even conversion if the damages are severe. Is it a trespass to gather data from "free" websites if their terms and conditions of service prohibit access except in furtherance of the website owner's business? This question was answered in favor of the website owner in *eBay v. Bidder's Edge*,[13] disfavoring the operation of shopping bots, a topic discussed in greater detail in Chapter 16.

Conversion

Conversion occurs when one person appropriates personal property that is rightfully in another person's possession. The theft of goods from someone's house represents not only a crime but also the tort of conversion. Thus, the defendant may be held responsible both for the criminal act of larceny and for compensatory damages. Conversion also occurs when a person fails to return borrowed property or property placed in a bailment for a specific purpose. For example, if Joe lends Sue his computer for one month but she keeps it for three months, Sue commits conversion. Sue has wrongfully denied Joe the use and enjoyment of his computer for two months. Generally, a successful conversion suit requires proof of the owner's demand for the return of property, followed by the tortfeasor's intentional refusal to return it.

The victim of conversion may sue for damages measured by the rental value of the converted property. Thus, in the example, Joe could sue for damages based on two months' rental value of a similar computer. If the defendant destroys or permanently deprives the owner of property, the damages would equal the market value of the property. A related tort is misappropriation, which is appropriate for intangibles such as intellectual property rights. For example, the infringement

13. 100 F.Supp.2d 1058 (N.D.Cal. 2000).

of trade secrets is often vindicated in a civil tort suit for misappropriation, as discussed further in Chapter 16.

INTENTIONAL TORTS THAT INTERFERE WITH ECONOMIC RELATIONS

Both individuals and businesses are protected from unreasonable interference with their economic relations. The intentional torts of disparagement, interference with contract rights, and interference with prospective business relations all pertain to economic relations. The economic interference aspects of privacy rights, such as appropriation, are discussed in Chapter 14. Fraud is another intentional tort covered as a defense to contract liability and as securities fraud and in Chapters 12 and 22.

Disparagement

The tort of **disparagement** protects against the tortfeasor who makes disparaging statements about the business activities of a person or a business. This tort arises if the plaintiff can prove that specific business losses occurred as a result of the statements. For example, if one company's advertising falsely claims that a competitor's products are inferior, that the competitor stocks stolen goods, or that the competitor does not pay its bills, the disparaged business could sue in tort.

Disparagement is sometimes referred to as **trade libel**. Unlike traditional defamation, disparagement protects only an individual's business or trade; it does not protect an individual's personal activities. Further, the plaintiff in a disparagement suit must prove that the disparagement is false. By contrast, the defendant in a defamation suit must prove that the statements were true to have a defense. Trademark law may also be implicated when the disparaging statements are directed at registered trademarks of a firm or at its trademarked products. The problem of using trademark law to block criticism targeting firms is discussed in Chapter 18. Many of the problems that the Internet has thrust into modern defamation law, discussed later, may also apply in disparagement cases.

Interference with Contract Rights or Prospective Business Relations

The tort of **interference with contract relations** involves intentional tampering with the contract of a person or a business. This tort covers existing contracts between an employer and an employee, between a business and a supplier, or between a business and a customer. Intentionally causing the breach of a valid contract constitutes wrongful interference with contractual relations. The tort occurs if the defendant, knowing of a contract between the plaintiff and another party, intentionally induces that other party to breach the contract, and if the breach injures the plaintiff.

The tort of interference with the prospective economic advantage of an individual or a business is similar to the tort of interference with contract relations. Individuals and firms have a legal duty not to tamper with the business relations of others, whether those business relations involve currently enforceable contracts or merely the expectancy of contracts. A famous case involved Pennzoil's fight with Texaco to takeover Getty Oil Company. Pennzoil sued Texaco for its wrongful interference with an agreement between Pennzoil and Getty Oil. Texaco claimed that it did not knowingly interfere with their agreement. Texaco's takeover was successful, but Pennzoil initially won the largest punitive damage award in history in the case.[14]

---

14. *Texaco, Inc. v. Pennzoil Co.*, 729 S.W.2d 768 (Tex.Ct.Ap. 1987), *cert.denied* 108 S.Ct. 1305 (1988).

QUASI-INTENTIONAL TORTS: DEFAMATION

Defamation is the publication of an untrue statement about another person that injures the person's reputation or character. **Slander** is oral defamation; **libel** is written defamation. Libel was traditionally considered the more serious offense for two reasons. First, the spoken word is ephemeral; it lasts only as long as the words are spoken. Second, published writings, particularly newspapers and books, are more permanent and influential, so the damage is potentially more widespread. Today, however, technology may draw into question the distinction between libel and slander. For example, radio, TV, and now the Internet are very widely influential. Although radio and TV broadcasts are ephemeral, lasting only the duration of the statements, they can be recorded and replayed. Many broadcasts are heard or seen by millions of people. Internet communications are increasingly considered published writings, so the rules of libel may be more appropriate. Most of this discussion focuses on defamation, a general tort that includes both.

The reason for the publication requirement is that a person's good name exists only when perceived and evaluated by others. If the audience does not consider the statement derogatory or if no one hears or reads the statement, there is no injury. The interest protected is the subject individual's reputation, so money damages are computed as the victim's lost reputation and lost economic advantages resulting from the extent of publication of the untrue and damaging statements.

DEFENSES TO DEFAMATION

In the United States, the First Amendment is a major component of defamation law. Freedom of speech requires that **truth is a complete defense.** True statements are justified under the U.S. Constitution's protection for the open marketplace of ideas. Certain statements are **defamatory per se**; that is, liability is established automatically and without further proof of the injury to reputation. For example, accusing a person of murder or alleging that a person has a venereal disease could be defamatory per se. Another defense to defamation exists if the person who makes the statement has a qualified or absolute privilege to do so. During litigation, judges, attorneys, and witnesses have an **absolute privilege.** A **qualified privilege** exists for private matters if the statement is made by someone who has a duty to make statements and if the statement is communicated only to those with an immediate interest in the information. For example, in many states, if a prospective employer asks a former employer about a former employee's character, the former employer's statement is probably privileged. Thus, if the former employer acts in good faith and not in malice, there is usually no defamation, even if the statement is untrue.

There is another defense when the defamation is about public figures. No defamation of a person who is a public figure exists unless the statement is both untrue and made with malice. **Malice** is often difficult to prove. However, if, for example, a reporter writes an untrue story about a public figure, the defamation may be regarded as malicious if the reporter did not take reasonable steps to substantiate the sources. Malice is a particularly important problem for the news media—print, broadcast, or on-line.

Liability of ISPs

Internet defamation may occur in several contexts. Defamatory statements could be posted to a bulletin board or website, they may be uttered in chatrooms, the statements may be included in e-mail messages, the statements may be **webcast** as streaming audio or video from websites, or the statements may be made over Internet telephony (the use of the Internet to carry phone calls). Computer telecommunications networks such as the Internet might eventually be used for new forms of communications still unforeseen today.

Should ISPs whose services transmit defamatory statements be held liable for publishing defamatory statements as **republishers**? The question forces the application of laws developed for older technologies to the Internet. Generally, the courts have not held phone companies liable for spoken defamation because they are common carriers that distribute communications and have no control over the sender's content. Similarly, bookstores are not held liable as republishers of defamation if they have no knowledge of the defamatory contents.[15] This status contrasts with the potential republication liability (1) by publishing companies for statements made in books, (2) by broadcast networks for defamatory broadcasts, and (3) by newspaper publishers for defamation contained in editorials, articles, or ads.

The groundbreaking case of *Cubby v. CompuServe* recognized that ISPs are more like common carriers and should not be liable as republishers when they do not monitor or mediate the communications on their facilities. CompuServe Information Service (CIS) was a component product of CompuServe's ISP service that supplied many special interest bulletin boards, interactive chat rooms, and databases of related information. Derogatory statements about Cubby were initially published by an independent daily newsletter, *Rumorville, USA*. These statements were distributed on one of the CIS services, the *Journalism Forum*, which focuses on the media industry. In shielding CompuServe from republication liability, the court stated:

"CompuServe has no more editorial control than does a public library, bookstore or newsstand, and it would be no more feasible for CompuServe to examine every publication it carries for potentially defamatory statements than it would for any other distributor. Technology is rapidly transforming the information industry. A computerized database is the functional equivalent of a more traditional news vendor."[16]

A key concept in *Cubby v. Compuserve* is whether it would be practical for an ISP to monitor all communications. To the extent an e-mail list, chatroom, bulletin board, or website is monitored by the ISP or sponsor, there may be republication liability under defamation law or even liability for publishing criminal obscenity. The following case illustrates the risks of mediating such on-line facilities.

Stratton Oakmont v. PRODIGY

1995 WL 323710 (N.Y.Sup.Ct., 1995)

Facts. PRODIGY is an ISP that claims family-oriented content on many of its chat rooms, bulletin boards, and other electronic databases. PRODIGY's statement of policy guidelines reserve it the right to exercise editorial control and remove materials it finds objectionable. In one posting, PRODIGY claimed, "We make no apology for pursuing a value system that reflects the culture of millions of American families we aspire to serve." Allegedly defamatory statements were posted to PRODIGY's *Money Talks* financial bulletin board about Stratton Oakmont. They included allegations of criminal and fraudulent acts by Stratton Oakmont and by its president, as well as calling Stratton Oakmont's brokers a "cult" of liars.

15. *Smith v. California*, 361 U.S. 147 (1959).
16. 776 F.Supp. 135, 140 (S.D.N.Y. 1991).

Legal Issue. Is PRODIGY a republisher?

Opinion. A finding that PRODIGY is a publisher is the first hurdle for Plaintiffs to overcome in pursuit of their defamation claims, because one who repeats or otherwise republishes a libel is subject to liability as if he had originally published it. In contrast, distributors such as book stores and libraries may be liable for defamatory statements of others only if they knew or had reason to know of the defamatory statement at issue. A distributor, or deliverer of defamatory material is considered a passive conduit and will not be found liable in the absence of fault. However, a newspaper, for example, is more than a passive receptacle or conduit for news, comment and advertising. The choice of material to go into a newspaper and the decisions made as to the content of the paper constitute the exercise of editorial control and judgment, and with this editorial control comes increased liability. In short, the critical issue to be determined by this Court is whether the foregoing evidence establishes a *prima facie* case that PRODIGY exercised sufficient editorial control over its computer bulletin boards to render it a publisher with the same responsibilities as a newspaper.

The key distinction between CompuServe [in the *Cubby* case] and PRODIGY is two fold. First, PRODIGY held itself out to the public and its members as controlling the content of its computer bulletin boards. Second, PRODIGY implemented this control through its automatic software screening program, and the Guidelines that Board Leaders are required to enforce. By actively utilizing technology and manpower to delete notes from its computer bulletin boards on the basis of offensiveness and "bad taste", for example, PRODIGY is clearly making decisions as to content, and such decisions constitute editorial control. That such control is not complete and is enforced both as early as the notes arrive and as late as a complaint is made, does not minimize or eviscerate the simple fact that PRODIGY has uniquely arrogated to itself the role of determining what is proper for its members to post and read on its bulletin boards. Based on the foregoing, this Court is compelled to conclude that for the purposes of Plaintiffs' claims in this action, PRODIGY is a publisher rather than a distributor.

PRODIGY has virtually created an editorial staff of Board Leaders who have the ability to continually monitor incoming transmissions and in fact do spend time censoring notes. Indeed, it could be said that PRODIGY's current system of automatic scanning, Guidelines and Board Leaders may have a chilling effect on freedom of communication in Cyberspace, and it appears that this chilling effect is exactly what PRODIGY wants, but for the legal liability that attaches to such censorship.

Computer bulletin boards should generally be regarded in the same context as bookstores, libraries and network affiliates. It is PRODIGY's own policies, technology and staffing decisions which have altered the scenario and mandated the finding that it is a publisher. PRODIGY's decision to regulate the content of its bulletin boards was in part influenced by its desire to attract a market it perceived to exist consisting of users seeking a "family-oriented" computer service. This decision simply required that to the extent computer networks provide such services, they must also accept the concomitant legal consequences.

Decision. Continuous monitoring of content by an ISP subjects it to duty not to republish defamatory postings.

Case Questions

1. What is the practical difference between the rigor of review presumed in republisher liability and that promised by PRODIGY?
2. Will ISPs undertake any monitoring under the threat of republication liability if this case becomes widely cited as precedent?

As the *Stratton-Oakmont* case was winding through the New York courts, Congress was passing the Communications Decency Act (CDA). As noted previously in Chapter 4, ISPs have the benefit of a safe harbor from republisher liability for defamation, obscenity, or infringing materials. However, Congress still sought to encourage ISPs and other technology companies to continue developing methods and software to block and filter offensive or unlawful content. Therefore, §230 of the CDA eliminates ISP liability as a republisher if the ISP makes good-faith action to restrict access or availability of obscene, harassing, or otherwise objectionable content posted by others. The effect of *Cubby* and the CDA are to make the Internet into an effective new outlet for nonmediated speech. Before the Internet, only the traditional print and broadcast media could effectively reach large segments of the population. The CDA's safe harbor nearly assures that some uncensored outlets will persist.

NEGLIGENCE

Under the law of negligence, all persons and businesses must act responsibly in all their activities. Nearly anyone can be held liable for breach of the duty of care if others are injured as a result. Negligent torts differ from intentional torts because the tortfeasor may be liable for unintentional, careless acts. Negligence is based on fault, not intent. When the carelessness injures others, tort law holds the individual or business liable for the injury.

GENERAL REQUIREMENTS

Four requirements must be proved by a plaintiff in a negligence case. First, the defendant must be shown to owe a duty of care to the plaintiff. Second, it must be proved the defendant breached or did not perform that duty. Third, the plaintiff must link the defendant's breach to the plaintiff's injury as the actual and proximate cause. Fourth, the plaintiff must prove that an injury was suffered and that money damages can be determined as compensation.

Duty of Care

All individuals and businesses must act carefully when others could be affected—that is, when it is foreseeable that a lack of reasonable care could cause injury. Many actions involve a predictable danger of injury. It is not necessary to foresee the precise harm that could occur if the defendant was negligent, only that the failure to exercise reasonable care poses an unreasonable risk of some harm. By contrast, if no risk of harm is foreseen, there is no **duty to use reasonable care.** In such situations, causing an injury to someone would not be negligence. For example, it is reasonable to foresee that driving a car too fast risks harm to other drivers and pedestrians. The duty to use reasonable care requires the driver to guard against such harm. A driver who fails to perform the duty of driving carefully may be committing a negligent tort. Some states apply no-fault laws to motor vehicle accidents, and the injured party need not prove the driver's negligence to be entitled to compensation.

Breach of Duty

The plaintiff must prove that the defendant did not perform the duty of care or is responsible for the nonperformance of that duty. For example, if you have a party in your home or apartment, the law imposes a duty to use reasonable care in maintaining the property and in conducting the party so guests are protected from foreseeable risks. Does a room have loose rugs on which a guest could slip and fall, or loose ceiling tiles that could fall on someone? If the homeowner or apartment tenant does not take precautions with regard to such items of foreseeable danger, the duty of care is not performed; that is, the duty is breached. Thus, nonperformance of the duty of care occurs if a person acts in a careless, reckless, or unreasonable manner. For example, in a case filed against the Los Angeles International Airport,[17] the airport was not liable for the death of a person killed by a bomb left in a public coin-operated locker. The airport was not in a dangerous condition, and the city had taken reasonable steps to guard against terrorism.

The law does not require that a person or a business be an insurer or a guarantor of the absolute safety of others. Negligence is based on a comparison of a

17. *Moncur v. City of Los Angeles Dept. of Air*, 137 Cal. Rptr. 239 (1977).

person's actions with the standard for the actions expected from the mythical **ordinary, reasonable person.** Sometimes a person or a business acts reasonably yet still causes injury to others. For example, a company that manufactures room heaters uses a process to ensure that they do not overheat and cause fire. If the company has acted reasonably, as compared with the standard expected of manufacturers of similar products, there would be no negligence even if the heater became defective and caused injury to its user. In such a case, the company could not be held liable for negligence, although it might be held liable on some other basis, such as an implied warranty or strict liability.

Proximate Cause

Once the plaintiff has shown that the defendant breached the duty of care, the defendant's act must also be shown to be the proximate cause of the plaintiff's injury. **Proximate cause** is the standard used in negligence cases to establish the reasonability of a causal relationship between the defendant's nonperformance or breach of duty and the plaintiff's injury. Only injuries with a close (proximate) causal connection to the defendant's actions are negligent. These injuries are caused by actions whose consequences are reasonably foreseeable. There is no liability for actions with only a weak or remote link to an injury. For example, it is reasonably foreseeable to expect pedestrian bystanders to be harmed by reckless driving. By contrast, it is probably unforeseeable that the injured pedestrian's best friend would suffer emotional distress from that injury.

Injury

To win a case, plaintiffs must prove they sustained some **injury** that can be compensated for by an award of money damages. Injuries include physical injury, property damage, lost profits, pain and suffering, and many other components that are the consequence of the defendant's negligent act. Expert witnesses are often used to prove and disprove damages. For example, economists testify as to lost profits, orthopedic surgeons as to the diminished capacity of the victim's arms, legs, and hands, and appraisers as to the repair costs of damaged property. The jury considers this testimony in its assessment of a compensatory damage amount.

Negligence Per Se and *Res Ipsa Loquitur*

In two circumstances—negligence per se and *res ipsa loquitur*—the burden of proof on the plaintiff is lessened. **Negligence per se** enables the plaintiff to use the defendant's violation of a criminal statute to prove the defendant was negligent. For example, if a statute imposes criminal penalties if a moving firm does not have certain safety equipment on its trucks, the statute creates a conclusive presumption that the defendant was negligent. Some states allow the presumption to be rebutted by other evidence. This is another important relationship between criminal law and tort law.

Res ipsa loquitur means "the thing speaks for itself." In some situations, circumstantial evidence is used to establish a prima facie case of negligence. Unless the defendant counters this evidence, the doctrine of *res ipsa loquitur* is sufficient to prove negligence. This doctrine is used when the plaintiff cannot know the exact cause of negligence, as in cases involving product liability or negligent building construction. A building will not usually crumble or collapse unless there was some negligence in its design or construction; thus, even though the exact cause of the failure is not known, circumstantial evidence suggests that there was negligence.

DEFENSES TO NEGLIGENCE

There are three basic defenses to negligence claims: contributory negligence, comparative negligence, and assumption of risk.

Contributory Negligence

The defendant may raise **contributory negligence** as a defense when the plaintiff was also somewhat negligent. Even though the defendant may have been negligent, the law prohibits any recovery for the plaintiff. This defense is commonly known as the **all-or-nothing rule** because the plaintiff wins all if contributory negligence is not proved and nothing if contributory negligence is proved. The harshness of this rule prompted an innovation of comparative fault, the comparative negligence defense.

Comparative Negligence

Most states use comparative negligence rather than contributory negligence as the most common defense in negligence cases. **Comparative negligence** weighs the relative negligence of the plaintiff against the negligence of the defendant. In some states, it does not matter how much negligence is attributable to the plaintiff. Even if the plaintiff can prove that the defendant is only 15% negligent in causing the plaintiff's injuries, the plaintiff (who would be 85% negligent) can still recover damages equal to 15% of the money needed to totally compensate for those injuries.

Consider the following examples. Suppose that a two-car accident occurs in a state using this type of comparative negligence defense. Assume that the plaintiff driving Car 1 is found to be 85% at fault for his own injuries. If $100,000 were needed to totally compensate the plaintiff for his injuries, the plaintiff would be able to recover $15,000 from the defendant driving Car 2, who was 15% at fault. Other states permit the plaintiff to recover damages from the defendant only if the defendant is responsible for at least 50% of the plaintiff's injuries. In these states, the plaintiff in this example above would recover nothing.

Assumption of Risk

The assumption of risk defense is also based on comparative fault. If the plaintiff knew, or should have known, of the risk inherent in a particular situation and voluntarily assumed that risk, the defendant is not responsible for the plaintiff's injuries, even though the defendant was also negligent. A classic example of this defense occurs when a plaintiff is injured while riding in a car with an intoxicated driver. Although the defendant driver is negligent in driving while intoxicated, the plaintiff, who knows the risk of riding with an intoxicated driver, nevertheless voluntarily does so. In such cases, the plaintiff may be denied recovery because of the assumption of that known risk.

Some states using the comparative negligence defense do not use assumption of risk. Under this view, the plaintiff's assumption of risk is a form of negligence that is compared with the defendant's negligence, which effectively merges assumption of risk and comparative negligence into one defense. **Assumption of risk** occurs when a person who knows of a risk nevertheless proceeds in the face of that risk. Contributory or comparative negligence compares the action of the one person with the action of the reasonable person (to determine whether there is any negligence) and of the defendant (to determine the relative negligence of the parties). A person's actions can contribute to causing an injury even if he or she does not know of the risk involved.

Tort Law and the European Community

Tort law in the European Union (EU) is governed by Article 215 of the Treaty of Rome. It provides that the noncontractual liability of the EU is governed by the "general principles common to the laws of the member states." Much of the work of the European Court of Justice is now handled by the European Court of First Instance. This court was authorized by the 1987 Single European Act, and its jurisdiction is limited to actions or proceedings by individuals or legal persons (firms).

When damages are sought in litigation involving EU law, the European Court of Justice and the Court of First Instance must determine what principles of noncontractual liability (tort law) are common to the laws of member states. This determination is not easy, as there are now 12 member nations. Two members are common law jurisdictions, whereas the others are civil or code law countries. The European Community tort liability principles are not based on those national laws, which impose the highest duty. Instead, it is common law national principles, such as fault being required for a finding of negligence, that create EU liability principles.

STRICT LIABILITY

Strict liability is held against a person who engages in inherently dangerous or **ultrahazardous activity**. There is liability to any injured party, regardless of the actor's intent or fault. Therefore, strict liability is different from intentional torts and negligence because strict liability requires proof of neither intentional wrongdoing nor fault.

GENERAL REQUIREMENTS

The plaintiff's recovery under the strict liability theory is somewhat easier than under the proofs required for either negligence or intentional torts. A strict liability tort occurs if one person does something dangerous and the act injures another person who is within the scope of risk. The determination of whether an activity is ultrahazardous is the most important question in strict liability cases. The precedents can be summarized, although not exhaustively, in the following list: the dusting of crops, the keeping of wild and vicious animals, and the use of explosives and dangerous chemicals. On the other hand, such activities as mining coal, driving automobiles, and keeping gasoline in service station tanks are not ultrahazardous.

Strict liability is also generally applicable to product liability cases. This application of strict liability is detailed in Chapter 8. A product is defective if the product is unreasonably dangerous and the danger is not readily apparent to the buyer. Typical strict liability cases involve such products as foods and drinks, playground equipment, consumer appliances, and automobiles.

DEFENSES TO STRICT LIABILITY

Because proof of negligence is not required in strict liability cases, the defenses of contributory or comparative negligence are not available. However, most states recognize the assumption of risk and misuse defenses. **Misuse** is a form of assumption of risk based on improper product use. For example, a misuse might exist if the injured plaintiff used inside a house an insecticide labeled for only outdoor use. Similarly, if a cigarette package warns users of a specific risk such as lung cancer, the manufacturer is generally not liable for those injuries.

POLICY UNDERLYING STRICT LIABILITY

Society tolerates some ultrahazardous activities that have sufficient social value. Compensation for a victim is more likely in strict liability cases than in negligence cases. Strict liability allows the defendant to spread the costs of the injury among many users, enabling society to receive the benefits of the ultrahazardous activity while sharing the cost of compensating the injured party. For example, society benefits when the mining and road-building industries use explosives. Strict liability balances the danger with society's needs as long as the costs of compensation are shared by society.

TORT REFORM

Because there are so many product liability cases and the ever-increasing jury awards are widely publicized, strong pressures have built to reform tort and product liability laws. Even the U.S. Congress has repeatedly considered imposing national tort reform, preempting this area of traditional states' rights. Existing federal reforms extend to securities litigation, accountants' malpractice liability, civil aviation, and airline disaster litigation. State reforms have passed in many states for strict product liability and other torts such as negligence, warranty, and misrepresentation. The 1980s were a period of dramatic growth in litigation. Tort law expanded as the courts recognized more extensive duties. Juries became more sympathetic to victims of accidents, product failures, and unsafe conditions, applying the deep pocket theory to hold accountable corporate defendants that were perceived to have extensive financial resources. Eventually, insurers claimed they were unable to accurately predict the outcome of tort litigation, and insurance premiums skyrocketed. Some types of insurance became unavailable. Insurers and potential corporate defendants called for tort reform in the media, through various legislatures, and in the courts.

COMPONENTS OF TORT REFORM

Proponents of tort reform claim that reforms create a fair, predictable, and equitable fault system while reducing the costs of litigation. They assert that a tort crisis has increased the cost of goods and services, stifled innovation in new products, delayed the introduction of new drugs, and postponed the sharing of benefits in many research breakthroughs. Tort reforms enacted in some states include changes in the allocation of liability among several defendants, limits on certain types of damages, restriction of double recoveries by plaintiffs, reduction of the contingency fee incentives of plaintiff attorneys, sanctions against frivolous suits, and structured settlements made in periodic damage payments over several years. Astute managers must closely monitor reform legislation and judicial decisions.

Joint and Several Liability

Joint and several liability requires the complete satisfaction (full payment) of a plaintiff's damage award from any or all of the responsible defendants, regardless of the degree of fault of any single defendant. In some cases, a particular defendant may be required to pay more than its share of the damage award. For example, a deep pocket insurer of a local retailer might have to pay the whole judgment if the manufacturer is **judgment-proof**—that is, uninsured or insolvent.

Joint and several liability provides an incentive for plaintiffs to include deep pocket entities as named defendants. Even when they are only slightly at fault, the whole compensatory and punitive amount must be paid by any defendant with sufficient financial resources. For example, drivers injured in traffic accidents often sue the state as well as the other driver because the state is responsible for the safety of road conditions. If the other driver is at fault but has insufficient insurance to satisfy the plaintiff's damages, the state's deep pocket may be held liable for the remainder. Most proposals to reform joint and several liability would impose **proportionate liability** among defendants. This system is similar to comparative negligence because it would require the jury (judge, if no jury is used) to assign percentage proportions of fault between defendants and limit their financial exposure to their proportionate amount.

Damage Caps

Tort reform efforts usually attempt to significantly limit or eliminate such **noneconomic damages** as (1) pain and suffering, (2) loss of consortium with a spouse, (3) emotional distress, (4) embarrassment, and (5) punitive damages. For example, some states have imposed specific dollar-amount ceilings for noneconomic damages in all negligence cases. Other states have such ceilings for only specific types of suit, most notably medical malpractice, product liability cases, or cases in which the state is a defendant (hazardous road conditions). Still other states require "clear and convincing evidence" before allowing noneconomic damages to exceed the ceilings.

Punitive Damages

There is a widespread perception that juries are awarding increasingly larger punitive damage awards. **Punitive damages** are an additional component of damages above and beyond compensatory damages. Compensatory damages reimburse the plaintiff for losses actually suffered. Advocates of retaining punitive damages argue they deter the adverse side effects of business activities. Their argument is that without the threat of severe penalties, business managers have little incentive to avoid endangering the public with harmful products, manufacturing processes, or business practices. Additionally, managers are personally too well insulated from lawsuit pressures; that is, they seldom directly bear the wealth effects of their decisions because the firm pays. Finally, they argue that highly visible punitive awards send signals to managers that convince them to act more carefully and consider the impact of their decisions on others.

Opponents of punitive damages argue that they adversely affect companies. Punitives damages can be unpredictable and counterproductive for the economy. For example, a multimillion-dollar punitive award could wipe out a company's profitability for several years, force it to drop useful products, slow its innovation, force the closing of facilities, require layoffs, or even drive the company into bankruptcy.

Several comprehensive empirical studies of damage awards contest the exaggerated claims of some tort reformers. Critics of the tort reform movement charge that stories about punitive damages are distorted to advocate abrupt legislative changes. Researchers find that most large damage awards (1) were made in asbestos cases, (2) have declined since 1986, (3) are made in state courts, (4) predominate in the South, (5) are usually based on the failure to warn consumers of known defects, and (6) have plaintiffs who are victims of catastrophic injuries.[18] Other studies

18. Michael Rustad, *Demystifying Punitive Damages in Product Liability Cases: A Survey of a Quarter Century of Trial Verdicts* (Washington, D.C., Roscoe Pound Foundation, 1991).

confirm that few of the huge damage awards publicized are ever paid out in full. Although most large punitive awards receive widespread news coverage, they are eventually reduced after settlement or on appeal through the legal device of **remittitur**. Many newsworthy awards are never paid out, and many tort reformers fail to acknowledge these facts.

Recent challenges to punitive damages allege that they violate two fundamental constitutional rights: (1) Punitives allegedly constitute excessive fines prohibited by the Eighth Amendment, and (2) unrestrained jury discretion to assess punitives violates the defendant's Fourteenth Amendment due process rights. In *Browning-Ferris Indus. v. Kelco Disposal,*[19] the Supreme Court rejected the Eighth Amendment argument. A regional BFI executive instructed the local BFI office to cut prices and drive Kelco, a competing waste collector, out of business. The Supreme Court reaffirmed the jury's award to Kelco of $51,146 in compensatory damages and $6 million in punitive damages in Kelco's monopolization suit. The Eighth Amendment was intended to protect convicted defendants from excessive punishment by government, not from civil actions between private parties.

In *Pacific Mutual Life Ins. Co. v. Halsip,*[20] an insurance company was held liable for its agent's misappropriation of health and life insurance premiums. The coverage lapsed when the agent failed to remit premiums deducted from the insured's paychecks. The agent concealed cancellation notices sent out by the insurance companies. A jury verdict held the insurer vicariously liable under *respondeat superior.* Halsip was awarded $1,040,000, of which nearly $840,000 was punitive damages. In upholding the Alabama punitive damage computation procedure, the U.S. Supreme Court held that the common law method for assessing punitive damages is not so inherently unfair as to deny due process and be per se unconstitutional. The Alabama procedure to review punitive damages considered the following factors: (1) the relationship between the punitive damages award, the harm likely to result from the defendant's conduct, and the harm that actually occurred; (2) the degree of responsibility of the defendant's conduct, the duration of that conduct, the defendant's awareness, any concealment, and the existence and frequency of similar past conduct; (3) the profitability of the wrongful conduct and the desirability having the defendant sustain a loss; (4) the "financial position" of the defendant; (5) all the costs of litigation; and (6) mitigation from the imposition of criminal sanctions or other civil awards against the defendant for the same conduct.

Courts after *Halsip* are in conflict. Many are narrowing punitives, some invalidate limits on damage awards, and others continue awarding punitives without any arbitrary dollar limitation. In the much publicized decision of *BMW of North America v. Gore,*[21] a punitive award of $2 million was reversed when weighed against the $4,000 representing compensatory damages for the decreased value of a new BMW automobile. The BMW distributor had repaired a paint scratch that occurred during shipment for a cost of about $600. In 2001, the punitive award of $5 billion was reduced in the infamous case about the *Exxon Valdez* oil tanker spill off the Alaska coast. The appeals court held that the punitives were excessive in relation to the $287 million in compensatory damages. The trial court was ordered to lower the amount of punitives.[22]

19. 492 U.S. 257 (1989).
20. 499 U.S. 1 (1991).
21. 517 U.S. 559 (1996).
22. *In re Exxon Valdez,* No. 99-35898 (9th Cir., 2001).

Punitives are also available in several state and federal regulatory programs, such as treble damages in antitrust and securities litigation and in employment discrimination cases, as discussed elsewhere in this book. In 2001, a federal appeals court held that there is no prerequisite for compensatory damages for the award of punitives in hostile work environment discrimination cases under the federal civil rights law.[23]

QUESTIONS

1. Discuss why the law has not proven to be the most effective control over aberrant behavior. What aspects of criminal law, tort law, and business ethical analysis are interrelated in answering this question?
2. McClean and Uriarte were employees of International Harvester Company. International Harvester supplied equipment and acted as a subcontractor to Crawford Enterprises, which had contracted to build a plant for the National Petroleum Company of Mexico. McClean and Uriarte were indicted for violating provisions of the Foreign Corrupt Practices Act and for bribing officials of the National Petroleum Company. They filed motions to dismiss the charges against them on the grounds that the failure to convict their employer was a bar to their prosecution. Does the Foreign Corrupt Practices Act permit the prosecution of an employee if the employer has not been, and cannot be, convicted of similarly violating the act?
3. Big Smokes Tobacco Corporation used questionable marketing practices to sell chewing tobacco in developing countries. Some users in these countries heated the tobacco to make it taste stronger. As a result, mouth and throat cancers proliferated among smokeless tobacco users. Certain groups urged a consumer boycott of Big Smokes Tobacco in the United States, claiming that it contributed to causing cancer and even death of smokeless tobacco users in developing countries. As Big Smokes Tobacco vice president for marketing, how would you respond to this accusation?
4. Susan left work after dark one evening. She was assaulted and battered in the parking lot. The security guard detained the assailant. Both Susan and the local district attorney brought separate cases against the defendant. Did their cases cause double jeopardy for the defendant? Compare and contrast the differing procedural aspects for the causes of action Susan brought on the basis of tort assault and battery with the causes of action the district attorney brought on the basis of criminal assault and battery.
5. Identify, define, and give an example of the four requirements that a plaintiff must prove to recover damages in a suit based on negligence.
6. Mrs. Davis was in debt to a finance company. She informed the company that she was no longer employed, that she was on public aid, and that she was unable to make payments on her loan. Over an eight-month period, in attempting to collect the debt, employees of the finance company called her several times a week, sometimes more than once a day, and used obscene and threatening language. Employees of the finance company visited her home weekly to demand payments on the debt. Daily threatening e-mails were sent to her mailbox, and threatening voicemail messages were left on her telephone. On one occasion, an agent from the finance company even telephoned her at a hospital where she was visiting her sick daughter. Mrs. Davis sued the finance company for damages, alleging emotional distress. Explain how the finance company's conduct was tortious.
7. John, a novice skier, brought a negligence action against Big Bear Ski Resort for injuries that allegedly occurred when he became entangled in underbrush concealed by loose snow. John was skiing on the resort's novice trail designed for inexperienced beginners. No warning signs regarding the underbrush were posted. What would be the basis for holding Big Bear Ski Resort liable?
8. The plaintiff was injured in an automobile accident caused entirely by the defendant driver. The plaintiff

23. *Cush-Crawford v. Adchem Corp.*, 271 F.2d 352 (No. 00-7617, 2001).

was not wearing his seat belt. He was thrown from the car and sustained a head injury when he landed on the pavement. The defendant offered evidence that had the plaintiff been wearing his seat belt, he would not have been thrown from the car. If the doctrine of comparative negligence is followed, will this reduce the damages to which the plaintiff is entitled? Explain.

9. Mr. Black sued a retail store for injuries. He slipped on rainwater as he stepped on a mat just inside the door to the store. Prior to the fall, a store employee placed a "Caution: Wet Floor" sign approximately five feet in front of the door. In accordance with store procedure, the employee mopped the entrance area periodically on rainy days. What defense will the retail store assert? Is this defense different from contributory negligence?

10. Explain the concept of joint and several liability, how it is applied, the grounds on which it is criticized, and the workings of the tort reforms that most directly address joint and several liability.

Product and Service Liability

INTRODUCTION

Product and service liability laws in the United States concern manufacturers and service providers across the globe. We all know of lawsuits against McDonald's for serving its coffee too hot to handle and of public disputes between Firestone and Ford as to what causes accidents on Ford SUVs equipped with Firestone tires. Product liability cases make the headlines because they can affect so many people and they frequently result in multimillion-dollar verdicts.

The liability of firms for the asbestos in their products has forced dozens of firms into bankruptcy. Although U.S. service and product liability laws offer compensation to consumers who use defective or unsafe products and services, the laws of many countries seem to offer more protection to the producer than to the consumer. What happens when a U.S. consumer purchases toys manufactured in China? Even if the Chinese manufacturer could be held liable, from whom can the U.S. consumer recover?

A century earlier, a buyer was generally responsible for investigating products before making a purchase. Known as **caveat emptor** or buyer beware, the law placed legal duties on the buyer. A seller could defeat any claims by showing that the buyer did not sufficiently examine products. Today, the law has moved in the opposite direction. The U.S. product liability laws now impose liability on the manufacturer and seller of products that cause injury, even where there is no fault in the manufacturing or selling of the products to consumers. And it is not just manufacturers and retailers who are affected by these laws. Accounting, consulting, financial, and legal service providers may also be liable if they intentionally or unintentionally cause injury while providing their services.

TYPES OF PRODUCT LIABILITY

There are four primary theories of product liability: breach of warranty, negligence, strict liability, and misrepresentation. **Warranties** may be either *express*—based on the seller's written or oral expressions—or *implied*, derived from the law, not from the expressions of the seller. *Express warranties* arise when the seller makes affirmations of fact or provides a description, sample, or model of the goods. *Implied warranties* are imposed by the law, the Uniform Commercial Code (UCC) or the Convention for the International Sale of Goods (CISG), on merchants and on sellers who select goods for the buyer.

Negligence in product liability is usually based on the seller's failure to properly design, inspect, or package the goods or warn users of known dangers. Negligence requires proof of four elements: (1) There must be a *legal duty*, such as the duty to warn or the duty to use reasonable care; (2) that duty must be *breached* or not performed; that is, there was no warning, or there was a lack of reasonable care; (3) the nonperformance of the duty must be the *proximate cause* of (4) some *legal injury*. Thus, reasonable care by the manufacturer or seller or lack of proximate cause can defeat a claim of negligence.

Under strict liability, the burden of proof on the purchaser or user is not as difficult. It is usually easier to prove that a product's defects render it unreasonably dangerous or defective, as is required under strict liability, than to meet the requirements of negligence or breach of warranty. There is no need to prove lack of reasonable care, as with negligence, or to prove that there is a warranty that the buyer relied on, as in the breach of warranty case.

The fourth theory is **misrepresentation**. Misrepresentation requires a false representation of a material fact (a fact that the seller knows or should know that the buyer is relying on) and reliance by the buyer on the representation, with the reliance leading to injury. Fraud is a type of misrepresentation because the seller intentionally makes a statement of fact that the buyer relies on in making a purchase. Even if the misrepresentation is innocent—that is, the seller did not know the statement was false but believed, although wrongly, that it was true—the buyer has a legal remedy. The buyer would be able to cancel the contract and have any purchase money returned. However, damages are generally not recoverable for an innocent misrepresentation.

Product liability laws also impose liability on any seller in the distribution chain. However, the retailer and/or distributor often have recourse against the manufacturer if either of them is held accountable to a consumer because of a manufacturing defect. Sellers do usually have several defenses in product liability cases, including contributory or comparative negligence, assumption of risk, and product misuse.

This chapter discusses the theories, remedies, and regulatory environment of product liability laws. Today, most product liability concepts are also applicable to service providers such as accountants, bankers, computer software consultants, and graphic or Web designers. The first section briefly notes the historical development of suits against sellers of products. Next, the chapter explores the four theories used in product liability cases: breach of warranty, negligence, strict tort liability, and misrepresentation. The defenses to each of these theories are also identified. The risk for a business is directly related to several procedural concerns: who may sue, what parties may be liable, what facts need to be proven, and what the available defenses are. The last section discusses product safety regulation by government agencies. Preventive regulatory programs seek to avert product liability harms by enforcing minimum standards for goods and services, consistent with the adage that "an ounce of prevention is worth a pound of cure."

THE ORIGINS OF PRODUCT LIABILITY

The most famous product liability case occurred nearly 90 years ago, shortly after automobiles were mass produced and sold to ordinary consumers. Although the automobile was not considered inherently dangerous, there were obvious dangers to its users if some of its parts were not properly manufactured. Would an auto manufacturer be held liable to the consumer, even though the part in question—a wheel—was made by another manufacturer and even though a dealer, not the manufacturer, sold the car to the consumer?

MacPherson v. Buick Motor Co.

217 N.Y. 382, 111 N.E. 1050 (1916)
New York Court of Appeals

Facts. MacPherson bought a new Buick from a retail dealer who had originally purchased the car from the manufacturer, Buick Motor Company. The spokes of the car's wooden wheels crumbled, causing the car to collapse and injure MacPherson. The wheel was purchased from a component part manufacturer. A reasonable inspection would have disclosed the defect.

Legal Issue. Can the purchaser of a car, whose contact is with a dealer, bring suit against the manufacturer if the product is defective, even if there is no contact between the purchaser and manufacturer? If the defect was caused by the manufacturer of a component part, rather than the automobile manufacturer, can the latter still be liable?

Opinion. Judge Cardozo. For a neglect of ordinary care or skill whereby injury happens, the appropriate remedy is an action for negligence. The right to enforce this liability is not limited to the immediate buyer. The right extends to the persons or class of persons for whose use the thing is supplied. It is enough that the goods "would in all probability be used at once . . . before a reasonable opportunity for discovering any defect which might exist," and that the thing supplied is of such a nature "that a neglect of ordinary care or skill as to its condition or the manner of supplying it would probably cause danger to the person or property of the person for whose use it was supplied, and who was about to use it."

We hold that the principle of *Thomas v. Winchester* [the principle of strict liability] is not limited to poisons, explosives, and things of like nature, to things which in their normal operation are implements of destruction. If the nature of a thing is such that it is reasonably certain to place life and limb in peril when negligently made, it is then a thing of danger. Its nature gives warning of the consequences to be expected. If to the element of danger, there is added knowledge that the thing will be used by persons other than the purchaser, and used without new tests, then, irrespective of contract, the manufacturer of this thing of danger is under a duty to make it carefully.

We have put aside the notion that the duty to safeguard life and limb, when the consequences of negligence may be foreseen, grows out of contract and nothing else. We have put the source of the obligation where it ought to be. We have put its source in the law.

From this survey of the decisions, there thus emerges a definition of the duty of a manufacturer which enables us to measure this defendant's liability. Beyond all question, the nature of an automobile gives warning of probable danger if its construction is defective. This automobile was designed to go 50 miles an hour. Unless its wheels were sound and strong, injury was almost certain. It was as much a thing of danger as a defective engine for a railroad. The defendant knew the danger. It knew also that the car would be used by persons other than the buyer. This was apparent from its size; there were seats for three persons. It was apparent also from the fact that the buyer was a dealer in cars, who bought to resell. The maker of this car supplied it for the use of purchasers from the dealer.

The dealer was indeed the one person of whom it might be said with some approach to certainty that by him the car would not be used. Yet, the defendant would have us say that he was the one person whom it was under a legal duty to protect. The law does not lead us to so inconsequent a conclusion. Precedents drawn from the days of travel by stagecoach do not set the conditions of travel today. The principle that the danger must be imminent does not change, but the things subject to the principle do change. They are whatever the needs of life in a developing civilization require them to be.

In this view of the defendant's liability there is nothing inconsistent with the theory of liability on which the case was tried. There is nothing anomalous in a rule which imposes upon A., who has contracted with B., a duty to C. and D. and others according as he knows or does not know that the subject matter of the contract is intended for their use.

Decision. We think the defendant was not absolved from a duty of inspection because it bought the wheels from a reputable manufacturer. It was not merely a dealer of automobiles. It was a manufacturer of automobiles. It was responsible for the finished product. It was not at liberty to put the finished product on the market without subjecting the component parts to ordinary and simple tests. The lower court's finding that the Buick Motor Company is liable for the injuries sustained by the plaintiff is affirmed.

Case Questions

1. The court says that the source of Buick's duty to the purchasers of its car is not in contract but "in the law." What does this mean for the manufacturers of products or for service providers?
2. What is the nature of the duty imposed on Buick with regard to parts, such as wheels, it uses in its automobiles? What does this case suggest about the liability of a manufacturer who incorporates component parts made by other manufacturers into products that the manufacturer sells?
3. To whom does the automobile manufacturer owe a duty?
4. Compare this case to the case of a purchaser of a Ford SUV with Firestone tires that become defective. Could the purchaser sue Ford? Could Ford hold Firestone liable?

HOW LONG DOES PRODUCT LIABILITY LAST?

Once courts began to hold manufacturers strictly liable for defects in their products, the potential for liability seemed limitless. Manufacturers became especially concerned with the possibility that they would be liable for defects in products long after the items were manufactured. Today, two problems cause the greatest concern. One issue deals with the delayed manifestation of injuries. What if the victim of a defective product is unable to detect an injury for several years after he or she begins using the product? The statute of limitations laws generally require any suit to be brought within a few years after an injury occurs, but how would those laws be interpreted if the injury was not noticeable until later? Does the statute of limitations run out so that the victim's suit is then prohibited?

A related problem is that sometimes the delayed manifestation of injuries, such as possible harmful side effects caused by using a new medication, may make it difficult to later identify which firm was the manufacturer of the specific product used by the injured party. Can anyone be held liable if the injured party cannot identify with certainty the firm that manufactured the product alleged to have caused the injury? Recent decisions have addressed both of these concerns.

Delayed Manifestation

In a new type of information-age injury case, most courts rule that the statute of limitations for repetitive stress injury (RSI) claims begins to run at either the onset of symptoms or at the date of last use of a keyboard made by a particular manufacturer, whichever date is earlier.

In *Blanco v. American Telephone and Telegraph* 692 N.E. 2d 133 (Ct. App. NY, 1997), the court reached a middle ground as to when the statute of limitations begins. It rejected suggestions that the "first-use" rule would apply. Under that standard, the first time an operator begins to use a keyboard starts the statute of limitations period. Usually, this standard would mean that several years after that date, any claims related to injuries caused by the use of the keyboard would be barred. Obviously, most keyboard workers who suffer from repetitive stress injuries like carpal tunnel syndrome would have no reason to complain when they first begin using the keyboards. By the time the operators would suffer any symptoms of RSI and before they could allege any damages, the statute of limitations (normally about three years) would expire.

On the other hand, the manufacturers did not want a standard that would have the claim arise only when the injury is discovered. Applying this standard would mean starting the statute of limitations period only after an injury in fact is or should be noticeable. Although that standard is used for some toxic torts, it could lead to cases brought perhaps a decade or more after keyboards are used if the RSI symptoms do not develop until then.

With RSI cases, there is really no discernible first date of injury; instead, the injury occurs gradually and sometimes without the victim's knowledge. The adoption of a **delayed manifestation** statute of limitations that begins either with the onset of symptoms or with the last use of the manufacturer's keyboard, whichever is *earlier*, provides some protection to plaintiffs who cannot be faulted for failing to exercise their legal rights before the symptoms begin. However, manufacturers now can better assess their risk of liability, as this approach effectively bars claims against remote manufacturers whose products were made years ago. If the product was last used more than three years ago, the statute prevents the injured party from recovering against the keyboard manufacturer.

Market Share Liability

Some drug cases, such as *Sindell v. Abbott Laboratories*, 607 Pd 924 (Cal. S.Cst., 1980) have introduced new theories to address the difficulty of identifying the manufacturer of the particular product causing the victim's damage. To prevent miscarriage, Sindell's mother took a prescription drug, DES, while pregnant with Sindell. Many years later, Sindell developed cervical cancer due to her mother's use of DES. Sindell could not identify which one of the several manufacturers that made the drug actually produced the prescription her mother used.

The court developed the concept of **market share liability** to permit victims to bring suit against any or all producers of DES. This concept makes it unnecessary to precisely identify the brand of drug in the actual prescription used. Instead, the extent of a manufacturer's liability may be based on the defendant's actual market share of the drug sales at the time the drug was used. Recent cases prohibit third-generation plaintiffs (granddaughters) from recovery.

WARRANTY LIABILITY

As manufacturers and sellers of goods can be held liable for defective products in several ways, managers need to be aware of the range of legal theories, and they should understand the limitations and special features of each theory. The first of these, the contract-based theories of express and implied warranty, usually applies any time that goods are sold. In contrast, the negligence and strict liability theories expose sellers to the greatest potential liability. Those tort-based theories can be used by anyone who is injured as a result of using a product that becomes defective. The misrepresentation theory can be used when advertisements or brochures specify that products will meet certain performance standards. As each of the theories is based in state laws, different states may apply their own interpretation as to what substantive and procedural requirements must be met to establish liability.

A **warranty** is an affirmation of fact or a promise of performance made in any product sale governed by the Uniform Commercial Code (UCC). In either warranty or strict liability cases, it is unnecessary to determine who is "at fault." Many states apply warranty liability to any business in the chain of distribution. However, some contractual relationship requirements for warranty actions still exist in about one-third of the states.

Warranty provisions are most often contract terms that impose additional duties on the seller. There are three types of product quality warranties: (1) express warranties, (2) implied warranties of merchantability, and (3) implied warranties of fitness for a particular purpose. The UCC also implies a warranty of title, requiring sellers to have the right to pass full ownership to buyers unless the possibility of adverse claims is evident to the buyer.

EXPRESS WARRANTIES

Express warranties are contractual promises about the future performance of goods. Goods are defective if they fail to meet the express warranty standards. Warranty liability arises if the seller agrees to provide a remedy to the purchaser. The buyer need not prove any seller misrepresentation or fault. An express warranty arises under UCC 2-313 if the seller's promise forms a *basis of the bargain*; that is, the parties must consider that the warranty is part of the description of the goods. No particular reliance needs to be proved for the warranty to become enforceable. The promises that form the terms of the express warranty may come from (1) an affirmation of fact or any promise relating to the goods, (2) a description of the goods, (3) a sample, (4) technical specifications, or (5) a model used by the seller in making representations to the buyer.

Express warranties are formed by either the seller's promises or conduct. For example, if the seller presents technical specifications or a blueprint to the buyer, that conduct constitutes an express warranty. An express warranty may also be inferred from past conduct; for example, a seller's prior deliveries of goods of a certain type or standard leads the buyer to assume that future deliveries will involve similar goods. A sample of the goods, such as grain or chemicals drawn from a larger bulk, may represent the expected average quality. A model may be used when the actual goods to be delivered are not available. The making of an express warranty is illustrated in Exhibit 8.1.

Generalized statements of value are usually too vague to be warranty promises; instead, such expressions are considered a seller's **puffing**. For example, when an auto dealer claims that an automobile is "great" or "a bargain," no warranty arises. On the other hand, warranty statements need not be in any special format or labeled as a warranty or guarantee. Similarly, the seller need not intend to create warranty obligations. Express warranties are enforceable to the extent that the seller promises satisfaction. The precise timing of the seller's promise or the seller's display of a sample is not important; even promises made after the sale can create or modify the warranty. What is important is that the statement becomes part of the basis of the bargain and is seen as part of the contract.

An express warranty may be written or oral as long as the parol evidence rule does not require that it is written. The **parol evidence rule** applies when a written contract of sale is intended to be the complete contract between buyer and seller. If the written contract is considered an integration—it contains all of the terms the parties agreed on—and the written agreement contains no written warranty, then no oral evidence of an express warranty is admissible. Thus, if a car dealer promises a warranty but an integrated written agreement clearly states there are no warranties, the parol evidence rule prevents the oral statement of the dealer from being considered. However, if there is no written agreement and a car dealer makes a promise, that promise can create an express warranty.

THE IMPLIED WARRANTY OF MERCHANTABILITY

A warranty of merchantability is implied under UCC 2-314 whenever goods are sold by a merchant. A **merchant** is a seller or buyer who deals in goods of the kind involved in the contract or who professes to be an expert in the particular trade.

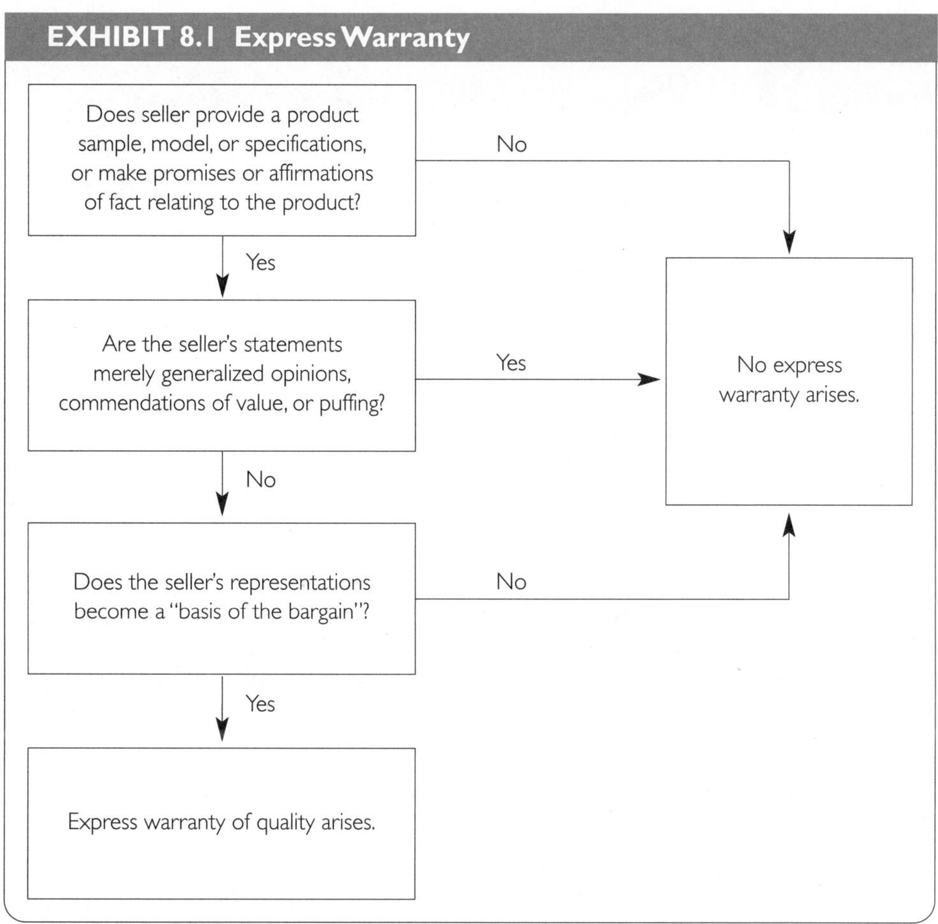
EXHIBIT 8.1 Express Warranty
Does seller provide a product sample, model, or specifications, or make promises or affirmations of fact relating to the product?
No
Yes
Are the seller's statements merely generalized opinions, commendations of value, or puffing?
Yes
No express warranty arises.
No
Does the seller's representations become a "basis of the bargain"?
No
Yes
Express warranty of quality arises.

Sellers are considered merchants when they employ agents who are merchants. Even secondhand goods must conform to the merchantability standard when sold by a merchant. As Exhibit 8.2 illustrates, a sale of goods by a "merchant" carries with it an implied warranty that the goods are merchantable. In isolated sales occurring out of the ordinary course of business, no merchantability warranty applies. For example, if one sells a personal car to a neighbor, there is no implied warranty of merchantability.

An implied warranty may be inferred from trade customs. A usage of trade is a common practice among most of the firms in a particular business. A **course of dealing** refers to a common practice followed by contracting partners in their previous dealings. For example, an obligation to provide pedigree papers to substantiate the lineage of a show dog may arise from a usage of trade. Merchantable goods must at least conform to the six UCC characteristics of merchantability:

1. Pass without objection in the trade under the contract description
2. Are of fair average quality if *fungible* (i.e., all units equivalent or interchangeable, as with grains or chemicals, and lose their identity when mixed together)
3. Are fit for the ordinary purposes for which they are used
4. Are of even kind, quality, and quantity within the variations permitted
5. Are adequately contained, packaged, and labeled as required by the agreement
6. Conform to the label or container description

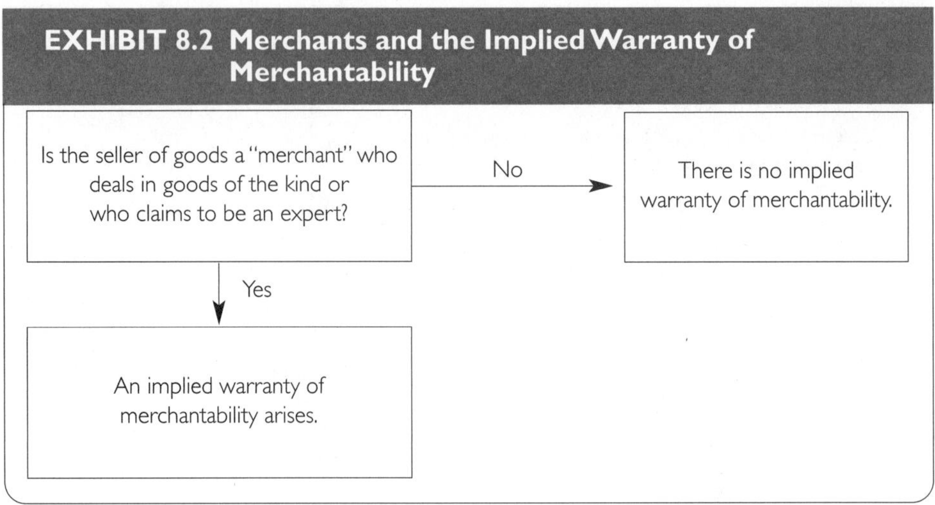
EXHIBIT 8.2 Merchants and the Implied Warranty of Merchantability
Is the seller of goods a "merchant" who deals in goods of the kind or who claims to be an expert?
No
There is no implied warranty of merchantability.
Yes
An implied warranty of merchantability arises.

These definitions for merchantable goods also provide guidance for the interpretation of an unclear express warranty. The *Northern Plumbing Supply* case, noted in the next section, illustrates how the implied warranty of merchantability establishes minimum consumer expectations for a product's performance.

THE IMPLIED WARRANTY OF FITNESS FOR A PARTICULAR PURPOSE

The **implied warranty of fitness for a particular purpose** arises under UCC 2-315 whenever the buyer relies on the seller's expertise to select goods to suit the buyer's intended use. It may be made by any seller, whether or not the seller is a merchant. This "fitness warranty" occurs, for example, if a paint dealer is asked to select non-toxic paint for use in a child's room. When the dealer presents paint to the buyer, this act implies a warranty that the paint contains no lead. Even if the buyer does not directly communicate the need for a no-lead paint to the seller, the fitness warranty arises if the seller has reason to know the purpose. The buyer must actually rely on the seller's expertise and selection decision before there is a fitness warranty.

Unlike the ordinary purpose that is the basis for the merchantability warranty, a particular purpose is specific and relates to uses peculiar to the buyer's household or business. Ordinary purposes, on the other hand, are the uses customarily made by most buyers. For example, shoes must be fit for the ordinary purpose of walking on normal ground, but a buyer may instead want shoes that will fit a particular purpose, such as those that would be fit for mountain climbing. A buyer who relies on the seller's selection of a particular pair for this purpose has the benefit of a fitness warranty. However, no fitness warranty arises if the buyer ignores the seller's suggestions and insists on a particular brand or model of goods, because in that case the buyer does not rely on the seller's expertise.

What circumstances might surround a seller's understanding of the buyer's business, permitting an inference that the buyer is relying on the seller's selection expertise? In *Northern Plumbing Supply, Inc. v. Gates*,[1] Gates sought to purchase pipe

1. 196 N.W.2d 70 (N.Dak. 1972).

from Northern Plumbing Supply to make a farm implement. Northern's president, Luxem, knew of Gates's purpose because he had visited Gates's farm. Gates showed Luxem a section of pipe with a wall thickness of 0.133 inch as a model for the pipe he desired, but he simply requested "standard" pipe. Northern then supplied Gates with "standard" pipe with a thinner wall thickness of 0.116 inch, which was too weak for the farm implement attachments that Gates made.

Even though Luxem conceded the thinner-walled pipe would not hold up to the stress of Gates's use, he insisted it was not his responsibility to second-guess Gates's request for "standard" pipe. The court held Gates was a farmer with no way of knowing that "standard" pipe had an insufficient wall thickness for his purposes. He was, instead, relying on Luxem's expertise to buy pipe that fitted his particular purpose. As a seller, Luxem knew all about pipes and also about Gates's intended use. All the elements of an implied warranty of fitness were present in this case.

WARRANTY EXCLUSIONS

Although sellers frequently offer an express warranty to distinguish their products from those of competitors, some sellers want to exclude all warranties whenever possible. All exclusions of *implied* warranties must be conspicuous in the sale contract. They must be written in common language that draws the buyer's attention to the exclusion. The exclusion of the implied warranty of merchantability must mention the word **merchantability** or otherwise clearly exclude the warranty. The wordings **as is** and **with all faults** are examples of language that in common understanding attract the buyer's attention, so they are effective to exclude all warranties.

A Typical Warranty Exclusion

The seller hereby disclaims all other warranties, either express or implied, including any implied warranty of merchantability or fitness for a particular purpose.

Buyer's Inspection of Goods

A warranty is automatically excluded to the extent that the seller gives the buyer a reasonable opportunity to inspect the goods prior to contracting if the inspection would reveal the defect. The seller can demand that the buyer make an inspection. For example, if a salesclerk requests the buyer of a cellular telephone to test the clarity of its reception but the buyer does not do so, no warranty as to the clarity of transmissions will arise. The scope of the examination necessary is based on the buyer's opportunity to inspect and on the buyer's expertise in discovering a particular type of defect. A usage of trade, a course of dealing, or a course of performance may also exclude a warranty.

Inconsistent Warranties and Exclusions

If the terms of an express warranty are inconsistent with an exclusion or a disclaimer, the inconsistency is resolved in favor of the buyer. For example, a two-year express warranty in bold typeface is inconsistent with a fine print exclusion of an express warranty. In that case, the buyer has the benefit of the express warranty. However, it is completely consistent to provide a warranty on some aspect of the goods while disclaiming warranty on other aspects. Automobile manufacturers often provide warranties limited to the car's drivetrain (engine and transmission) and expressly exclude any warranty on the tires and battery. The excluded parts are usually covered by warranties from separate manufacturers, against which the buyer must make warranty claims. Goods sold "as is" carry no warranty; thus, using that term effectively excludes both implied and express warranties.

THE MAGNUSON-MOSS WARRANTY ACT

Some sellers make outlandish claims about the performance or characteristics of goods. They may promote warranties as a major inducement to purchase, calling them "full" warranties when they are not. Thus, in 1975, Congress passed the Magnuson-Moss Warranty Act to increase consumer information, prevent deception, and improve consumer product competition. The Federal Trade Commission (FTC) is responsible for implementing the act.

The regulations apply to all consumer product sales of $15 or more. Although the FTC does not require any express warranty, it requires that any warranty given must be: (1) conspicuous, (2) found in a single document, and (3) written in readily understood language. A warranty must also identify the parties it covers and clearly describe the parts or characteristics excluded from coverage. If a warranty claim is made, the warrantor must state precisely the services provided. The dates of the warranty's commencement and cessation, along with step-by-step procedures for submitting warranty claims, must be stated. If arbitration is used, the arbitration procedures must be described. Usually, the consumer must attempt to resolve the claim through these procedures before taking further action. If the seller provides an express warranty, limitations on implied warranties are invalid, with the exception that implied warranties can be limited to the duration of the express warranty.

If consumer merchandise costing more than $10 is sold and a warranty is given, the warranty must be conspicuously classified as "full" or "limited." A **full warranty** must provide the consumer with reasonable replacement or repair rights without other charges or conditions. Return of the warranty registration card is not a condition to honor the warranty. **Consequential damages**, those that replace lost profits or earnings if the user is injured by a defective product, may be limited with conspicuous language. If the consumer makes repeated unsuccessful attempts to remedy defects, a refund or free replacement option must be available. This practice avoids the seller's attempt to wear down the buyer and sets minimum standards for "lemons."

As a matter of practice, full warranties are so costly that few sellers provide them. Consequently, most warranties are either limited or provided as extracost options. Several states have enacted *lemon laws* that require the dealer to refund or replace certain consumer goods that it is unable to fix after repeated attempts.

Ethical Issue

Consumer Confusion about Warranties

The UCC warranty exclusion/disclaimer provisions are an important example of legislated ethics in the warranty area. The UCC requires all parties to exercise good faith and observe fair dealings to meet consumers' reasonable expectations. Sellers have strong incentives to win sales by promising extensive warranties. However, the rising cost of defective product claims gives sellers a conflicting incentive to limit warranties.

In the past, some unethical sellers promised warranties in sales literature, in the salesperson's representations, and sometimes even in the sale contract. However, those sellers also included fine print warranty disclaimers in the contract to prevent the seller from being held liable for the warranty. This problem is reinforced by the parol evidence rule, which, when there is an integrative contract representing all of the agreed-upon terms, effectively prevents consumers from proving that a warranty promise was made.

Sellers can avoid this ethical dilemma by (1) complying with the UCC warranty exclusion provisions, (2) prohibiting sales personnel from making outlandish claims that appear to be warranties, and (3) providing an effective repair and replacement process.

NEGLIGENCE LIABILITY

Negligence was the first tort theory used in product liability cases. The plaintiff must prove the damage sustained was the "fault" of the defendant's negligent conduct. The four requirements of negligence, discussed in depth in Chapter 7, are briefly reviewed here.

ELEMENTS OF NEGLIGENCE

First, the plaintiff must prove the defendant had a *duty to exercise due care*. The duty is based on the ability to foresee that an unreasonable risk of harm could result from using the goods or services sold. The seller must minimize risks of injury by adequately designing, building, or inspecting the goods. Primary responsibility to minimize product defects rests with the product's manufacturer or assembler. In some situations, wholesalers and retailers should inspect, assemble, or prepare the goods before delivery. For example, auto dealers have the duty to inspect new cars sold to consumers. Manufacturers must warn consumers and give instructions for safe use. *Failure to warn* is now the most prevalent type of negligence in product liability cases.

A *breach or non-performance of these duties* may result in liability to any person who might reasonably be expected to use or be affected by a defective product. For example, it is negligent not to inspect empty beverage bottles before filling them because it is reasonable to expect that foreign substances may injure a consumer.

A causal relationship must exist between the injury suffered and the breach or nonperformance of the duty. The term *proximate cause*, which requires both a cause in fact and a reasonably close connection between the breach of duty and the injury, is required in negligence cases.

Finally, the injury that is required is not necessarily a physical injury but instead is a *legal injury*. Thus, interference with a person's rights may constitute an injury.

A wide range of injured victims may sue under negligence, including the purchaser, members of the purchaser's family, the purchaser's guests, and even bystanders if they fall within the zone of foreseeability. Foreseeable bystanders are those reasonably expected to be affected by defective products. For example, it is foreseeable that a defective automobile could injure a pedestrian.

DEFENSES TO NEGLIGENCE

Defenses ordinarily available to a negligence defendant may also be asserted in product liability suits. If the plaintiff contributed to the negligence by not using reasonable care to guard against dangers, the defendant may be partially or completely relieved of liability through application of the *comparative or contributory negligence* defense. Similarly, if the plaintiff misused the product or voluntarily **assumed a known risk** in using the product, the defendant is relieved of negligence liability. The statute of limitations for negligent torts, often a two-year period, is usually applied in negligence product liability actions.

STRICT LIABILITY

The most common theory of product liability used today is based neither on fault nor on warranty provisions in the sales contract. Under the strict liability in tort theory, a manufacturer, wholesaler, or retailer in the business of selling products may be liable for injuries resulting from defects that render those products unreasonably dangerous.

The strict liability theory places the burden for defective products on the manufacturer—primarily because that party, rather than the injured party, can best bear the cost of compensating for any injury caused by the products. The classic case establishing modern strict liability law is the *Yuba Power* case.

Greenman v. Yuba Power Products, Inc.

377 P.2d 897 (1962)
Supreme Court of California

Facts. Greenman wanted a Shopsmith power tool that could be used as a saw, drill, and wood lathe after he saw one demonstrated by a retailer and studied a brochure for it that had been prepared by the manufacturer. Greenman's wife bought a Shopsmith and gave it to Greenman for Christmas.

More than a year later, a piece of wood flew out of the lathe while Greenman was using the Shopsmith tool, causing him serious injury. Greenman then sued in a California state court against both the retailer and the manufacturer for breach of warranty and negligence. The trial court found for the plaintiff and the defendant appealed. Ultimately, the case was heard by the California Supreme Court.

Legal Issue. Can a person injured as a result of a defect in a product he or she uses receive on the basis of a strict liability even if the manufacturer did not breach a warranty or commit negligence?

Opinion. Justice Traynor. To impose strict liability on the manufacturer under the circumstances of this case, it was not necessary for plaintiff to establish an express warranty as defined in section 1732 of the Civil Code. A manufacturer is strictly liable in tort when an article he places on the market, knowing that it is to be used without inspection for defects, causes injury to a human being. Recognized first in the case of unwholesome food products, such liability has now been extended to a variety of other products that create as great or greater hazards if defective.

Although in these cases strict liability has usually been based on the theory of an express or implied warranty running from the manufacturer to the plaintiff, the abandonment of the requirement of a contract between them, the recognition that the liability is not assumed by agreement but imposed by law, and the refusal to permit the manufacturer to define the scope of its own responsibility for defective products make clear that the liability is not one governed by the law of contract warranties but by the law of strict liability in tort. Accordingly, rules defining and governing warranties that were developed to meet the needs of commercial transactions cannot properly be invoked to govern the manufacturer's liability to those injured by their defective products unless those rules also serve the purposes for which such liability is imposed.

We need not recanvass the reasons for imposing strict liability on the manufacturer. . . . The purpose of such liability is to insure that the costs of injuries resulting from defective products are borne by the manufacturers that put such products on the market rather than by the injured persons who are powerless to protect themselves. . . .

The remedies of injured consumers ought not be made to depend upon the intricacies of the law of sales. In the present case, for example, plaintiff was able to plead and prove an express warranty only because he read and relied on the representations of the Shopsmith's ruggedness contained in the manufacturer's brochure. Implicit in the machine's presence on the market, however, was a representation that it would safely do the jobs for which it was built. Under these circumstances, it should not be controlling whether plaintiff selected the machine because of the statements in the brochure. . . .

Decision. To establish the manufacturer's liability, it was sufficient that plaintiff proved that he was injured while using the Shopsmith in a way it was intended to be used [and that it was] as a result of a defect in design and manufacture, of which plaintiff was not aware, that made the Shopsmith unsafe for its intended use. The judgment is affirmed.

Case Questions

1. Could Greenman recover on his breach of warranty case? Why?
2. What does a plaintiff like Greenman have to prove to find Yuba Power liable under the strict liability theory? How does this differ from proving negligence?
3. What is the public policy behind holding a manufacturer strictly liable for injuries caused by defective products?

Many states have adopted the strict liability standard based on Section 402A of the *Restatement of Torts Second.*

Standard for Strict Liability in Restatement of Torts Second, Section 402A

1. One who sells a product in a defective condition unreasonably dangerous to the user or consumer or to his property is subject to liability for physical harm thereby caused to the ultimate user or consumer, or to his property, if
   (a) the seller is engaged in the business of selling such a product, and
   (b) it is expected to and does reach the user or consumer without substantial change in the condition in which it is sold.
2. The rule stated in Subsection (1) applies although
   (a) the seller has exercised all possible care in the preparation and sale of his product, and
   (b) the user or consumer has not bought the product from or entered into any contractual relation with the seller.

UNREASONABLY DANGEROUS OR DEFECTIVE

The strict liability claimant must prove the product is either (1) defective or (2) in unreasonably dangerous condition. These standards are purposely vague to cover a wide variety of products and situations.

Defectiveness generally depends on the customer's expectations for product performance. Products with weak parts or mechanical limitations are defective. The merchantability standards provide some guidance for defectiveness. Products with inadequate safety warnings, that are unfit for ordinary purposes, with inadequate packaging or labeling, or that would not pass without objection in the trade are probably defective for strict liability purposes.

Unreasonable danger is also closely tied to customer expectations. A product dangerous beyond what an ordinary consumer would expect is unreasonably dangerous. Consider alcohol, caffeine, and tobacco, common substances with dangerous side effects when used improperly or excessively. Most consumers know the risks, so the products are not unreasonably dangerous unless adulterated with foreign substances.

DEFENSES TO STRICT LIABILITY

The strict liability theory exposes business to the broadest potential liability of all product liability theories because of its lesser burden of proof. There is no contractual (privity) relationship requirement, and the defenses of contributory and comparative negligence are inapplicable. Most states do recognize defenses such as assumption of risk, product misuse, or failure by the plaintiff to discover a defect or danger that the plaintiff should have discovered.

The **assumption of risk** defense requires knowledge of the risk by a plaintiff and a voluntary assumption of that risk. In most of the cases brought against tobacco companies for injuries caused to addictive smokers, the plaintiffs argued they did not know that they would be unable to quit smoking, so they did not assume that risk. The tobacco companies, who argue that the dangers of smoking are well known and are expressed on each pack of cigarettes, have been quite successful in using this defense against possible liability. The assumption of risk defense is also discussed in Chapter 7.

The **product misuse** defense is similar to the assumption of risk defense, but it focuses on the plaintiff's use of a product in a manner for which the product was not designed. As courts have held that sellers must design and warn users about foreseeable uses, even ones that are not the use for which the product is designed, this defense is not usually effective. Similarly, the plaintiff's failure to discover an obvious danger or defect can sometimes be at least a partial defense to liability. Plaintiffs are supposed to know that knives and power saws are sharp and dangerous, and a defendant does not have to warn potential users about such dangers. Although this defense is more common in negligence cases, many courts now consider the conduct of the plaintiff, as well as that of the defendant, in determining liability and assessing damages in strict liability cases.

Commonly, plaintiffs in product liability cases allege breach of warranty, negligence, and strict liability theories against all sellers in the chain of distribution. In some cases, a fourth theory of liability, misrepresentation is also asserted.

MISREPRESENTATION

The final theory of product liability, **misrepresentation**, is based on a false representation of material facts. Merchants and others engaged in the business of selling goods to the public may be liable for misrepresentations of the quality or characteristics of products. Unlawful misrepresentations may result from either negligence or from conscious and knowing misstatements. The *Restatement of Torts Second* notes that misrepresentation is a common basis for product liability.

Standard for Misrepresentation in the Restatement of Torts Second, Section 402B

One engaged in the business of selling chattels who, by advertising, labels, or otherwise, makes to the public a misrepresentation of a material fact concerning the character or quality of a chattel sold by him is subject to liability for physical harm to a consumer of the chattel caused by justifiable reliance upon the misrepresentation, even though

(a) it is not made fraudulently or negligently, and

(b) the consumer has not bought the chattel from or entered into any contractual relation with the seller.

CHARACTERISTICS OF MISREPRESENTATION

Although the misrepresentation theory is similar to a breach of express warranty, the two differ in several important respects. Misrepresentation is a tort; it is not based on the UCC or other contract principles. The tort statute of limitations applies, and contractual limitations of remedy, exclusions of warranty, or exclusions of consequential damages are ordinarily not applicable. Because there is no need for a contractual relationship, the manufacturer, wholesaler, retailer, or other distributor may be potentially liable. Consumers entitled to sue are broadly defined to include employees who use the goods on the job and family members with permission to use the goods. The misrepresentation must be material and concern the characteristics of the goods or services.

FRAUD AND MISREPRESENTATION ON THE INTERNET

Unfortunately, fraud and misrepresentation remain a common problem for investors seeking information or actually investing on the Internet. Although the SEC monitors websites, chat rooms, and message boards for fraudulent practices and misrepresentations, when one type of scheme is attacked and disappears, others arise.

In a complaint filed in January 2000, the SEC alleged that a self-proclaimed Internet stock-picking guru, Yun Soo Oh Park, who was known as Tokyo Joe, operated a website where members who paid a monthly fee to his company would have access to his stock picks. However, Tokyo Joe had already purchased shares of the stock he recommended, and when his members sought to buy on his recommendations, he sold the stock—committing an illegal practice known as scalping. The complaint against Tokyo Joe also charged that the past performance results posted on his website were materially false and misleading. A consent order settled the case after Park was ordered to disgorge profits he had made and pay several penalties. He was also required to post a hyperlink to a copy of the final order on the home page of his website for 30 days.

The WallStreet Prophet's website claimed an 85% success rate on his stock recommendations. However, the SEC found that those statements were fraudulent misrepresentations and that Ricky Gaspard, the owner and operator of the WallStreet Prophet, was a former roofing contractor who in fact had never been licensed or had any experience in the field. Gaspard agreed to refrain from future SEC violations and to provide a copy of the SEC's order against him to all current and future subscribers for a year.

Soon after the September 11, 2001, attacks and the subsequent finding of anthrax in a number of mailed letters, the SEC also took action to stop several firms from representing that they had technologies capable of killing anthrax in mail packages. The actions against Disease Sciences, Inc., and Classics Group, Inc. were noted in the SEC's news website at http://www.sec.gov/news/press/2001-136.txt. While the SEC is chasing after violators, it seems that when one scheme is stopped, another "scheme du jour" begins.

ONLINE

To review the status of current cases, check the litigation link at **http://www.sec.gov/litigation/litreleases/shtml**

MARKETING AND MISREPRESENTATION

Misrepresentations may be inferred from the way goods are merchandised, even if the marketing efforts are directed toward only a segment of the population. A policeman purchased a riot helmet from his department, relying on a package illustration showing a motorcyclist wearing the helmet, and wore the helmet while riding his motorcycle. The helmet was designed to release quickly on impact and came off his head in a motorcycle accident. The manufacturer was held liable based on the misrepresentation because the helmet was not suitable for motorcycling. Misrepresentation and the other theories of product liability are depicted in Exhibit 8.3.

THE PARTIES IN PRODUCT LIABILITY CASES

THE PLAINTIFFS

Selection of the proper parties as plaintiffs and defendants is an important part of product liability cases. Substantive and procedural laws applicable in the state where the wrong occurred and in the forum state—where the suit is brought—may restrict or expand the number of parties that are potential plaintiffs and defendants. The clear trend is to expand the classes of persons who can be compensated for injuries caused by defective products.

Of course, the purchaser and user of the product are potential plaintiffs. A second group that can sue is the employees of a commercial consumer who use or may be

EXHIBIT 8.3 Product Liability Theories

Theory	Eligible Defendants	Eligible Plaintiffs	Damages Recoverable	Elements Required	Defenses
Negligence	Manufacturers are primarily liable; some jurisdictions hold retailers to a duty to discover and disclose defects that are discoverable upon an inspection Service and product providers can be liable for negligent design	Any person within the traditional negligence risk perimeter as determined by the concepts of duty and proximate cause, i.e., those within the zone of forseeability	General and special damages that result directly from the breach Punitive if negligence is willful; trend to limit Trend to limit noneconomic damages (pain and suffering)	Duty Breach of Duty Actual cause Proximate cause Damages *Res ipsa loquitur* may establish duty and breach	Contributory or Comparative negligence Assumption of risk Misuse of product Statute of limitation State of the art
Strict liability *(Restatement [Second] of Torts,* §402A)	Sellers, manufacturers, retailers, suppliers, or lessors if in the business Franchisors if they retain control over defective manufacture or misrepresentations in advertising	Users and consumers; bystanders are increasingly included	General and special damages for personal injury, physical harm, or property destruction No punitives Trend to limit noneconomic damages (pain and suffering)	Defect Unreasonably dangerous Consumer expectations Causation Damages	Assumption of risk Misuse of product Statute of limitations Unavoidably unsafe
Breach of warranty (UCC)	Merchants as to implied warranties of merchantability Any seller as to implied warranty of fitness or express warranties	All natural persons who might reasonably be expected to use, consume, or be affected by defective product In most states only the family, guests, or those in household can sue on a warranty; some states have wider coverage	Trend to limit to purely commercial economic losses, but some states impose no such limits No punitive damages	Contract of sale Warranty Breach of warranty Warranty was not excluded Damages	Most contract defenses Failure to notify of breach Lack of contractual privity Misrepresentation Fraud Duress Undue influence Statute of limitations
Misrepresentation *(Restatement [Second] of Torts,* §402B)	Sellers, manufacturers, retailers, suppliers, or lessors if in the business	Users, consumer, or bystander if relying on misrepresentation	General and special damages for physical harm	Merchant seller Misrepresentation to public Justifiable reliance Causation Damages	Misrepresentation not made publicly Dealer was only puffing No reliance Statute of limitations

International Commentary

Product Liability in Japan

In the September 25, 2000, issue of *Time* magazine's Asian edition, the following story served to depict the recent state of product liability protection in Japan.

On an autumn afternoon 10 years ago, Masumi Iijima was at home giving piano lessons when she heard a loud bang. She looked out the window and saw white smoke spewing from the house. When she ran to the living room, she saw a melted black object in the spot where the family's wide-screen Mitsubishi TV usually sat. The fire quickly spread, destroying a valuable collection of Edo-period paintings and killing Masumi's beloved Shetland sheepdog. Pieces of the TV set were later found scattered around the scarred remains of the house.

A slam-dunk legal case? That's what Masumi's husband, Eiwa, thought when he took Mitsubishi Electric to court. But, the company put up a simple and surprisingly effective legal defense. "It's physically impossible for a TV to explode," its lawyers claimed in court. After a five-year legal battle, the Tokyo Regional Court ruled against the family.

The article notes that later, after learning that some other owners with the same model had also had their TVs explode, design defects were discovered and a successful appeal was filed with a higher court. Subsequently, Mitsubishi admitted that over the years it had kept secret 66 claims of TV sets overheating, including seven that caught fire. Even though the law required Mitsubishi to report the information to government authorities, the company did not do so. Apparently, that wasn't all that unusual. In August 2000, Mitsubishi Motors, another major member of the Mitsubishi group, revealed that it had failed to report safety problems with some of its cars for a period of 23 years.

Although Japan has passed a new product liability law and other laws intended to aid consumers, structural problems still make it very difficult for consumers to prevail. Japan lacks the discovery laws that in the United States allow injured parties access to company records in litigation. Lawyers can't even access governmental records, and the new Freedom of Information Act (which became effective in 2001) exempts consumer complaint records. Since the end of World War II, there have been 129 verdicts in product liability cases in Japan. By contrast, more than 200,000 such cases are filed every year in the United States. There's also still significant social pressure for consumers to stay silent rather than litigate against any highly regarded business. The *wa*, or harmony, would be greatly disturbed. Clearly, the legal environment for the Japanese consumer who may be injured by defective products is far different than it is for his or her U.S. counterpart.

affected by the product. A third, more remote group is bystanders who may be affected by the product if it fails. In addition to these groups, class action laws now allow a plaintiff to sue on behalf of all others who may have been injured by using a defective product. Such class action suits clearly expose businesses to increasing risks.

THE DEFENDANTS

Product liability law has significantly expanded the number of defendants potentially liable for defective products. Most entities in the chain of distribution, illustrated in Exhibit 8.4, are potential defendants, including component part manufacturers, assemblers, wholesalers, and retailers. Most products begin with the refinement of raw materials or the manufacture of component parts. The manufacturer or assembler combines components into finished products. A wholesaler may then purchase the products for resale to retailers, who purchase in order to resell to ultimate consumers.

Component Manufacturers

Component part manufacturers and assemblers of finished products can be held liable under all product liability theories. Component part manufacturers may be

EXHIBIT 8.4 Possible Defendants and Plaintiffs in Product Liability Cases

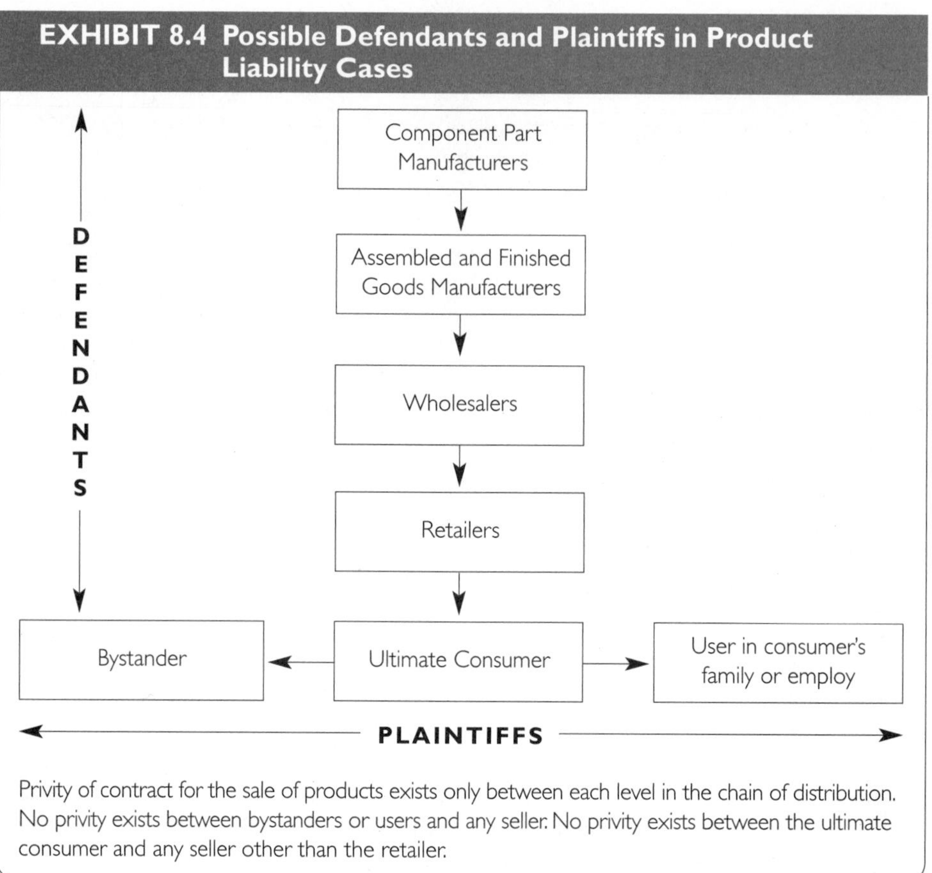

Privity of contract for the sale of products exists only between each level in the chain of distribution. No privity exists between bystanders or users and any seller. No privity exists between the ultimate consumer and any seller other than the retailer.

shielded from liability if (1) the finished product assembler converted the component to an unexpected use or (2) the component reached the consumer after the assembler, dealer, or buyer made substantial changes to it. In one example, a punch press manufacturer sold a machine without safety devices, expecting the industrial customer to add the safety devices best suited to the specific work application. Because the machine was altered by the customer, who attached a safety device to fit its needs, the punch press manufacturer was not liable when the failed safety device caused injury to a customer's employees.

Wholesalers or Distributors

Although wholesalers and distributors are not usually named as defendants in product liability actions, they may be held liable under any of the product liability theories. Typical suits against wholesalers are those brought against the domestic distributors of foreign-made goods. If a Chinese toy manufacturer does not have a presence in the United States, those who are injured by defective toys may instead sue the U.S. distributor of those products.

Retailers

Retailers are the most likely to be sued because they make contractual commitments to the buyer. Retailers can be held liable under all product liability theories. However, one possible defense is the **sealed container doctrine**. Under this theory, the retailer has no duty to discover concealed or latent defects. For example, some states relieve retail food stores from liability if a sealed container (e.g., bottled liquids or soft drinks) explodes or leaks, causing injury or slippery conditions. Certainly, it would be impractical for a retailer to conduct scientific tests or to regularly dismantle all goods for inspection. The retailer's duty arises only when the sealed container is opened, when the retailer suspects poor quality, or when the retailer provides some assembly or installation service, a dealer-introduced defect.

If the manufacturer leaves some of the final steps of production, assembly, or investigation to the retailer, both the manufacturer and the retailer could be liable for defects occurring at the retail or dealer stage. Such delegation of duties is a common practice in the automobile industry.

Franchisors

Increasingly, patented product designs are licensed by franchise owners to franchisees for manufacturing. Because the franchisee actually manufactures the product, the franchisor may be shielded from warranty or strict liability suits. However, if the design is defective, the franchisor may be liable for negligent design. Additionally, many franchise agreements reserve to the franchisor control over the franchisee's quality control, approval of product modifications or adaptations, and oversight of product advertising. Such control over the franchisee manufacturer usually exposes the franchisor to greater liability.

ALLOCATING PRODUCT LIABILITY AMONG SELLERS

Because most parties in the distribution chain may be liable for defective products, there is concern as to how to allocate the liability among those parties. In addition to joint and several liability, which was noted in Chapter 7, and the market share liability discussed earlier in this chapter, several other doctrines affect how liability is allocated among various parties. They include the principles of subrogation, indemnification, and successor liability.

Employees who are injured while using industrial machinery for their employers' operations may have a product liability claim against the machinery manufacturer and a workers' compensation claim against their employer. Employers or their workers' compensation insurers who pay these claims are given the right of **subrogation** to sue the defective equipment manufacturer. For example, if the injured employee's claim is paid by workers' compensation, the insurer is substituted as the claimant in the product liability suit against the defective equipment manufacturer. Thus, subrogation is a form of reimbursement from the equipment manufacturer for the workers' compensation claim paid by the insurer.

Any party ordered to pay a product liability judgment may have the right of **indemnification** from the party that is ultimately liable. For example, if a wholesaler was held liable for a defectively manufactured product, it could seek indemnification from the manufacturer who was ultimately responsible for a defect in design, manufacture, handling, or warnings.

The ongoing restructuring of businesses has led to mergers, acquisitions, and corporate breakups involving the sale of various product lines. These organizational changes raise the question of **successor liability**: Are the purchasers of these businesses liable for defective products that were manufactured or designed by the selling corporation? Generally, the answer is no. Business purchasers generally are liable only for debts they consciously assume, and because common acquisition practices often exclude such claims, they remain the selling corporation's liability. Of course, if the corporation being purchased is totally absorbed or merged into the successor company, that company does have the liability for defects in products sold prior to the merger. On the other hand, if a corporation files for bankruptcy or the seller of a product line is liquidated, product liability claimants could be left with nothing. Some states require purchasing corporations to assume the product liability risks of the seller. However, such laws apply only where the transaction is designed as a sham to avoid liability.

LIABILITY OF SERVICE PROVIDERS

BREACH OF WARRANTY

The service provider could be liable for failing to meet a contractual warranty of satisfaction or success. For example, few doctors would promise total success in a medical operation, and few lawyers would promise such success in litigation. Such promises would obligate them to provide that success and therefore give the patient or client an enforceable contract right.

NEGLIGENCE

Providers of services can be liable if injuries result from their activities. Because the service provider is held to a duty of due care, most service liability cases are based on negligence. To avoid liability for negligence or other unreasonable or poor practices (**malpractice**), professionals such as doctors, lawyers, accountants, and engineers must perform services that are equal to the reasonably prudent professional standard. Suits alleging medical malpractice, audit failures, and attorney malpractice have increased significantly in recent years.

Courts have wrestled with the liability of accountants for more than 80 years. In 1919, the *Landell v. Lybrand* decision held that an accountant could not be held liable in negligence by a party who was not in contractual privity with the accountant. In the 1931 *Ultramares v. Touche* case, third parties who could be identified as primary beneficiaries when an audit was performed were allowed to bring negligence suits. By 1983, *Ultramares* had been significantly weakened. The standard of foreseeability was applied to accountants; they could be held liable for any foreseeable consequences of their actions. The pendulum swung the opposite way several years later when subsequent cases sought to limit the accountant's liability in the absence of a contractual relationship. Today, the law again seems to hold accountants liable for negligence, even to third parties who are not in contractual relationships with them.

Negligence liability also affects the financial community. In a case in which damages could exceed $150 billion, Unilever in late 2001 sued Merrill Lynch over alleged mismanagement of its huge pension fund. The case relates to the 1997 and 1998 period, when Merrill Lynch underperformed the benchmark by more than 10% over five consecutive quarters. The case made headlines in London, where the trial was held, and, according to Denis Bastin, a European consultant, "It's a very important case for the industry. It's a litmus test. Everybody's retirement money and how it is being managed is being questioned."[2] The case was settled when Merrill

2. Sara Calian, "As the Portfolio Turns: Merrill-Unilever Saga Grips London," *Wall Street Journal*, December 3, 2001, p. C1.

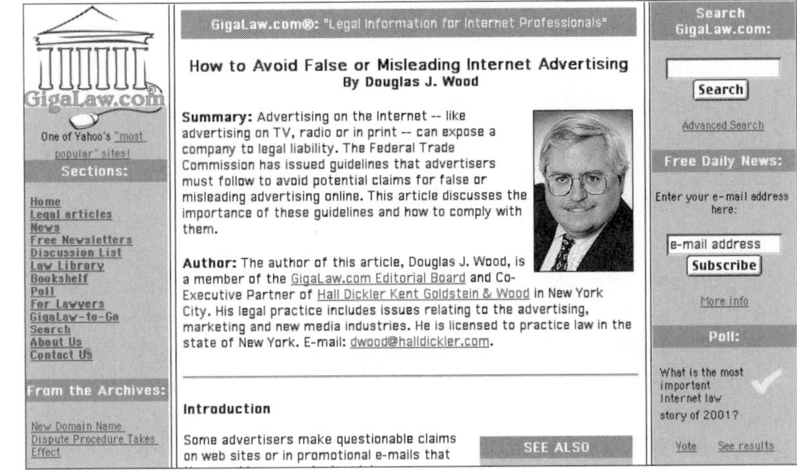

Lynch agreed to pay Unilever $105 million without any admission of liability.

http://
www.gigalaw.com/articles/2001/wood-2001-12.html

STRICT LIABILITY

An important distinction between service providers and the manufacturers or sellers of goods is that strict liability is usually not applied for the sales of services unless the services are very closely tied to sales of goods. For example, strict service liability generally could occur when a restaurant serves adulterated food or a hairdresser misuses hair chemicals that physically injure a client.

The Digital Millennium Copyright Act expressly exempts Internet service providers (ISPs) for copyright violations that might occur on websites accessed through an ISP's network.

MISREPRESENTATION

As for misrepresentation, service providers and consultants increasingly advertise their services. If statements in advertisements on a website or in brochures constitute untrue representations, service providers can be held accountable for injuries the representations cause. The FTC seeks to apply all consumer protection laws and regulations to on-line marketing.

ONLINE

The Gigalaw website at provides a summary of the applicable laws affecting online advertising.
www.gigalaw.com/articles/2001/wood-2001-12.html

INTERNET SERVICE PROVIDERS

Internet service providers (ISPs) are often sued for defamatory postings that appear on their websites. Generally, the cases argue that the ISPs were negligent in not warning people about what may appear on their website or that, as they allowed others to cause injury, they, too, should be held liable. The following case, brought against America Online, Inc., notes that the liability of the ISPs has been definitively determined by the federal Communications Decency Act.

Doe v. America Online, Inc.

783 So.2d 1010
Supreme Court of Florida (March 2001)

Facts. Doe filed a complaint in 1997 against Richard Lee Russell and America Online (AOL), ISP, to recover for emotional damages suffered by her son, John Doe. Doe claimed that in 1994, Russell lured her son and two other minor males to engage in sexual activities with each other and with Russell. She asserted that Russell photographed and videotaped these acts and used AOL chat rooms to market them. Her complaint said AOL violated several Florida criminal statues. She also asserted that AOL was negligent in not taking action against Russell when it should have known that he and others like him would use AOL services to market and distribute child pornography. Doe also alleged that AOL should terminate Russell's services because it had received complaints about his transmission of obscene photographs.

AOL moved to dismiss the claim, alleging they were barred by section 230 of the Communication Decency Act. That act provides, among other things, that "No provider or user of an interactive computer service shall be treated as the publisher or speaker of any information provided by another information content provider." The trial court and court of appeals agreed with AOL and dismissed Doe's case, and she appealed to the state supreme court.

Legal Issue. Several legal issues are raised by this case.

(1) Does section 230 of the Communication Decency Act (CDA) apply to complaints filed after its effective date where the cause of action is based upon acts occurring prior to its effective date?

(2) If the answer to question 1 is in the affirmative, does section 230 of the CDA preempts Florida law?

(3) Is a computer service provider without notice of a defamatory third part posting entitled to immunity under section 230 of the Communication Decency Act?

Opinion. Chief Justice Wells. The certified questions in this case focus upon the application of 47 U.S.C. sec. 230 [the CDA] to Florida tort actions based upon alleged "distributor" liability of ISPs. We first address the second and third certified questions. We find that section 230 does preempt Florida law as to such a cause of action based upon alleged negligence. We find persuasive the reasoning of the United States District Court in *Zeran v. America Online, Inc.* 958 F.Supp. 1124 and the Fourth Circuit in *Zerani, 129 F.3d at 331-32.*

The importance of this certified question is obvious in light of the current explosive growth in worldwide use of the Internet. The fundamental issue here is whether companies that provide access to the Internet are subject to common-law civil tort causes of actions based upon the laws of each of the fifty states or whether Congress has acted to make ISPs immune from such common-law civil actions. In reaching our conclusion, we find instructive the analysis of the congressional adoption of section 230 that was provided in the *Zeran* decisions and in commentaries concerning the *Zeran* decisions. These sources indicate that two reported judicial decisions from courts in the State of New York were significant in congressional passage of the CDA. According to one commentator, those decisions created a paradox in that those ISPs who tried to control what was placed in the Internet would be subject to defamation lawsuits and liability on account of their efforts, while ISPs who made no efforts to control content would be free of liability.

In 1996, Congress enacted 47 U.S.C. Sec. 230, which was adopted as Title V of the Telecommunications Act of 1996. The Congressional Conference Report on section 230 specifically states:

One of the specific purposes of section 230 is to overrule Stratton-Oakmont v. Prodigy *and any other similar decisions which have treated such providers and users as Publishers or speakers of content that is not their own because they have restricted access to objectionable material.*

In Zeran, the Court describes this history of section 230: Fearing that the specter of liability would deter service providers from blocking and screening offensive materials, Congress enacted 230's broad immunity to remove disincentives for the development and utilization of blocking and filtering technologies. . . . In line with this purpose, 230 forbids the imposition of publisher liability on a service provider for the exercise of its editorial and self-regulatory functions.

In *Zeran*, the court said that "the preemption issue reduces to the question of whether imposing common law distributor liability on AOL amounts to treating it as a publisher or a speaker. If so, the state claim is preempted." The key to answering this question is that distributor liability, or more precisely, liability for knowingly or negligently distributing defamatory material, is merely a species or type of liability for publishing defamatory material.

Congress' clear objective in passing sec. 230 of the CDA was to encourage the development of technologies, procedures and techniques by which objectionable material could be blocked or deleted by the interactive computer service provider itself or by the families and schools receiving information via the Internet. If this objection is frustrated by the imposition of distributor liability on Internet providers, preemption is warranted. Closely examined, distributor liability has just this effect. . . . AOL falls squarely within this traditional definition of a publisher and, therefore, is clearly protected by sec. 230's immunity.

We next turn to the first certified question, which is whether section 230 applies to complaints filed after its effective date where the complaint alleges a cause of action based upon acts occurring prior to its effective date. Section 230 clearly reflects Congress' intent to apply the CDA to all suits filed after its enactment, notwithstanding when the operative facts arose. In section 230 (d)(3) the CDA provides:

No cause of action may be brought and no liability may be imposed under any State or local law that is inconsistent with this section.

Decision. We specifically concur that section 230 expressly bars "any action" and we are compelled to give the language of this preemptive law its plain meaning. We concur . . . that Doe's cause of action against AOL is barred.

Case Questions

1. Based on the product liability theories discussed in this book, why do you think the New York cases referred to by this court held that ISPs who took action to provide filters could be liable while those who took no action to filter content could not be held liable?
2. If Congress had not passed the CDA, and if you worked for an ISP, what action would you suggest your firm take in imposing restrictions on the materials that can be provided through sites using your services? Why?
3. Does it make sense for Congress to preempt state laws that would regulate ISPs? Why?

DEFECTIVENESS—A NEW APPROACH TO STRICT LIABILITY?

The central requirement in a product liability suit is proof of the product's defectiveness. *The Restatement (Third) of Torts: Products Liability*, released in 1997 by the American Law Institute, segments product defects into three categories: design defects, manufacturing defects, and warnings defects. The new Restatement sets out a single test for each type of defect, regardless of the nature of the legal claim. If courts adopt this approach, the distinction between cases brought on negligence, strict liability, or breach of warranty theories will be less important.

DEFECTIVE DESIGNS

Products must be designed to eliminate defects that could lead to injury. A manufacturer is liable only if the plaintiff can show that there is a more reasonable alternative design. Some states have looked closely at the expectations of the consumer to determine the features that should be included in a product's design. However, the consumer's expectation is not the only factor that should be considered. If the manufacturer can show that the design it used—considering the cost of the product, the design's effect on the appeal of the product, its anticipated life, and its required maintenance—appeared reasonable at the time of design, it may escape liability.

Restatement (Third) of Torts: Defective Design

A product is defective in design when the foreseeable risks of the harm posed by the product could have been reduced or avoided by the adoption of a reasonable alternative design by the seller or other distributor, or a predecessor in the commercial chain of distribution, and the omission of the alternative design renders the product not reasonably safe.

However, reasonable design activities are still subject to absolute liability for unreasonably dangerous products. The manufacturers must design obviously dangerous products with safety devices or warnings where practical. For example, chain saws are inherently dangerous because of a tendency to "kick back," so chain saw manufacturers must issue warnings and install chain-stop safety devices to limit their liability. The following case involving silicone breast implants was based in part on negligent or defective design. The court's decision revises its warranty law, but those changes do not affect this case. Note, too, the other theories of liability that are reviewed in the case and the court's reference to the design-based theories of liability.

Vassallo v. Baxter Healthcare

696 N.E.2d 909 (1998)
Supreme Court of Massachusetts

Facts. Plaintiff Florence Vassallo claimed that Baxter Healthcare Corporation was liable because silicone breast implants, manufactured by a predecessor company, that had been implanted in her were negligently designed, lacked adequate product warnings, and breached the implied warranty of merchantability. A jury at the trial level found for the plaintiff, and the defendant appealed.

Legal Issue. Can defendants be held liable for negligence or breach of warranty for not giving adequate warning of defects they knew about or should have discovered through testing?

Opinion. Justice Greaney. At the age of forty-eight, Mrs. Vassallo underwent breast implant surgery. The silicone gel breast implants were manufactured by Heyer-Schulte Corporation and through a series of corporate transactions, the defendants assumed liability for breast implants that firm manufactured. In 1992, Mrs. Vassallo underwent a mammogram that revealed that her breast implants might have ruptured. The implants were removed surgically in 1993 and the surgeon noted severe, permanent scarring of Mrs. Vassallo's pectoral muscles.

Several doctors testified that Mrs. Vassallo was suffering from atypical autoimmune disease related to her exposure to silicone gel. There was also extensive testimony as to the knowledge, attributable to the defendants, of the risks of silicone gel breast implants up to the time of Mrs. Vassallo's implant surgery in 1977. Heyer-Schulte was aware that some of their implants were rupturing, having received 129 complaints of ruptured gel implants in 1976. As a result, Heyer-Schulte knew that its implants were "not consistent as far as durability or destructibility is concerned." Despite this knowledge, Heyer-Schulte conducted few animal and no clinical studies to document the safety and efficacy of its silicone gel implants. Heyer-Schulte did furnish warnings to physicians concerning their silicone gel implants in 1976, but that warning did not address the issue of gel bleed, the fact that a rupture could result from normal stress and could persist undetected for some time.

The judge's decision that the plaintiff's general evidence of causation was scientifically valid despite the absence of supporting epidemiological data is consistent with decisions by other courts. The defendants correctly point out that evidence of failure adequately to test a product is relevant *to claims of design, manufacturing or warning defects*, but does not furnish a separate, independent basis for liability. The judge's instruction that the jury could consider product testing in evaluating the design defect claim was not error. The evidence warrants the jury's finding on the negligence claims. Because the plaintiff's recovery can be upheld on the jury's finding of negligence, we need not address the defendant's claim of error concerning the breach of warranty count.

Our current law regarding the duty to warn under the implied warranty of merchantability presumes that a manufacturer was fully informed of all risks associated with the product at issue, regardless of the state of the art at the time of the sale, and amounts to strict liability for failure to warn of these risks. The majority of states follow the principle that the seller is required to give warning against a danger if he has knowledge, or by the application of reasonable, developed human skill and foresight, should have knowledge of the danger. An overwhelming majority of the jurisdictions support the proposition that a manufacturer has a duty to warn only of risks that were known or should have been known to a reasonable person. The rationale behind the principle is explained by stating that unforeseeable risks arising from unforeseeable product use . . . by definition cannot specifically be warned against. However, a seller is charged with knowledge of what reasonable testing would reveal.

Decision. A defendant can be held liable under an implied warranty of merchantability for failure to warn or provide instructions about risks that were reasonably foreseeable at the time of sale or that could have been discovered by way of reasonable testing prior to marketing the product.

Case Questions

1. What reasonable actions should the defendant have taken with regard to its breast implants to try to ensure that they were not negligently designed?
2. The discovery of what the defendant knew about its implants and when it knew it was critical. What obligations did that knowledge impose on the defendant?
3. Would a Japanese consumer be likely to have access to such information? Why or why not?

MANUFACTURING DEFECTS

The manufacturer is liable for manufacturing defects without regard to whether it used due or reasonable care. The strict liability for manufacturing defects is a no-fault standard; the use of reasonable care is not a defense.

> **Restatement (Third) of Torts: Manufacturing Defects**
> A product contains a manufacturing defect when it departs from its intended design even though all possible care was exercised in the preparation and marketing of the product.

WARNING DEFECTS

The law places an obligation on the manufacturer to provide a consumer with a warning if the manufacturer should foresee a risk of harm. The duty to warn is not imposed, however, if the risk of harm is obvious or commonly known. The defense that the risk of use is commonly known arises in cases like the coffee spill situation mentioned in this chapter's Introduction. In one such case, a judge dismissed the need for a warning that might require the manufacturer to deliver a "medical education" with every cup of coffee sold. The judge concluded that a detailed warning of the type needed would only obscure the principal point—that precaution should be taken to avoid spills.[3]

On the other hand, the duty is imposed even if there is a foreseeable risk of harm from misusing a product. The key question is whether the risk is one that is foreseeable.

> **Restatement (Third) of Torts: Warning Defects**
> A product is defective because of inadequate instructions or warnings when the foreseeable risks of harm posed by the product could have been reduced or avoided by the provision of reasonable instructions or warnings by the seller or other distributor, or a predecessor in the commercial chain of distribution, and the omission of the instructions or warnings renders the product not reasonably safe.

Sellers are shielded from liability when adequate directions and warnings of known dangers are provided. However, warnings alone do not replace the manufacturer's duty to provide obvious safeguards. For example, a conspicuous warning about the dangers of a punch press would be insufficient if a simple guard device would protect the operator from serious injury.

To be effective, warnings must be understandable and conspicuous. Sellers are reluctant to place too many warnings on products because the warnings might alarm purchasers. Such a concern does not constitute an adequate justification for a failure to warn of known dangers. If serious danger would arise when directions are disregarded, then the warning must be made more conspicuous. A warning must be calculated to reach the likely users of the product. In one case, employees used machinery purchased by their employer, and separate warnings for the employer and the employees were required. In the case of a machine tool used in a factory, the warnings must be conspicuously noted on the machine tool and be understandable by the average worker. Warnings placed in a bulky user's manual may be insufficient if users are unlikely to ever see or consult the manual.

Hazardous processing machinery is often covered with many warnings. Manufacturers should foresee and warn against dangers related to all uses and even to service procedures. In *Nelson v. Hydraulic Press Mfg. Co.*,[4] a maintenance worker

3. *McMahon v. Burn-O-Matic Corp.*, 150 F.3d 651 (7th Cir., 1998).
4. 404 N.E. 2d 1013 (Ill. App., 1980)

was injured while attempting to repair an injection molding machine. Melted plastic was placed into a feed tube and forced into molds to manufacture various plastic parts. Nelson climbed a ladder to observe a hardened plastic plug when molten plastic suddenly erupted, causing him severe injury. No warnings appeared on the machine. The court said:

The jury, as reasonable persons, could have concluded that the defendant manufacturer knew or should have known of the danger to maintenance men from exposure to hot plastic material erupting through the feed hole during maintenance operations to purge the machine of hardened plastic, As a result of the failure to warn or instruct concerning said danger, the machine in question was unreasonably dangerous and in a defective condition when it left the control of the defendant. That defective condition was a proximate cause of plaintiff's injuries and damages.

ESTABLISHING DEFECTIVENESS

Proof of a product's defects may come from several sources. Conflicting expert testimony about the product's performance and design characteristics is often heard from engineers, scientists, designers, and production experts. The many documents from the seller's files that must be produced during discovery may show whether a particular design or warning was considered and rejected as too costly by the manufacturer's designers or production managers.

The legal doctrine *res ipsa loquitur*, which stands for "the facts speak for themselves," permits an injured plaintiff to prove that the defects caused the injury even if there is no proof of causation. An injured plaintiff may sometimes prove a defect even if the product failure destroys the product. In *Escola v. Coca-Cola Bottling Co.*, 150 P. 2d 436 (Cal S.Ct. 1944) a waitress was injured when a bottle of Coca-Cola exploded in her hand because of carbonation pressure and/or the weakness of the bottle. The injured plaintiff's burden of proof under *res ipsa loquitur* was established for product liability actions:

Defendant is not charged with the duty of showing affirmatively that something happened to the bottle after it left its control or management; . . . to get to the jury the plaintiff must show that there was due care during that period. Plaintiff must also prove that she handled the bottle carefully. The reason for this prerequisite is . . . to eliminate the possibility that it was the plaintiff who was responsible. . . . It is not necessary, of course, that plaintiff eliminate every remote possibility of injury to the bottle after defendant lost control, and the requirement is satisfied if there is evidence permitting a reasonable inference that it was not accessible to extraneous harmful forces and that it was carefully handled by plaintiff or any third person who may have moved or touched it. Upon an examination of the record, the evidence appears sufficient to support a reasonable inference that the bottle here involved was not damaged by any extraneous force after delivery to the restaurant by defendant. It follows, therefore, that the bottle was in some manner defective at the time defendant relinquished control.

It thus appears that there is available to the industry a commonly used method of testing bottles for defects not apparent to the eye, which is almost infallible. Since Coca-Cola bottles are subjected to these tests by the manufacturer, it is not likely that they contain defects when delivered to the bottler which are not discoverable by visual inspection.

AFFIRMATIVE DEFENSES

Sellers may assert several defenses to prevent or lessen their liability. Disclaimers of warranties and lack of contractual relationship (privity) are defenses to a breach of warranty suit. Situations in which plaintiffs place themselves in danger are the most widely recognized defenses. These defenses include contributory and comparative negligence, assumption of risk, and misuse of the product. If the plaintiff failed to exercise due care in using the product, contributory or comparative negligence may completely or partially bar recovery in a negligence or warranty case.

COMPARATIVE AND CONTRIBUTORY NEGLIGENCE

Because strict liability and breach of warranty are *not* based on fault, the courts are hesitant to apply the negligence doctrines of contributory or comparative fault to these two theories. However, some courts consider the plaintiff's actions, as well as those of the defendant, in assessing liability and calculating damages.

ASSUMPTION OF RISK

Both assumption of risk and product misuse are recognized defenses to strict liability and warranty actions. In many cases involving latent (hidden) defects or the delayed manifestation of injuries, the plaintiff may have trouble proving causation. Successful defendants challenge the plaintiff's weak evidence that the defect led directly to the injury, particularly if scientific research is inconclusive to link the use of a drug or substance to an injury like the plaintiff's.

Should sellers of products be held liable for injuries sustained by people who have knowingly exposed themselves to danger? The following case illustrates the assumption of risk doctrine in a warranty case.

Hensley v. Sherman Car Wash Equipment Co.

520 P.2d 146 (Colo. 1974)
Colorado Supreme Court

Facts. The plaintiff, an employee at a car wash, was injured when she fell into a hole in the floor used for a hookless conveyor. The conveyor moved the cars through the wash area. Although a pivoting safety hood swung down over the hole to permit the cars' tires to pass over it, it reopened after a car passed.

Plaintiff relied on an information sheet provided to her by the defendant that said:

"SAFE WORKING CONDITIONS. Car wash personnel are assured safe working conditions on all areas of the vehicle by the pivoted safety hood at exit end, over drive box which swings down as tire rides over, and then swings back up to cover the opening after tire has passed over; eliminates all possibility of persons stepping into an open pit."

She brought suit, alleging breach of express warranty. Defendant contends that plaintiff's inattentiveness amounted to contributory negligence and barred recovery, and that plaintiff "assumed the risk" as she was aware that the safety hood had not been operating properly since the installation of the equipment approximately one month earlier.

Legal Issue. Is plaintiff's alleged contributory negligence or assumption of risk a defense that prevents her recovery in a breach of warranty suit?

Opinion. Judge Pierce. Plaintiff testified that on the morning of the accident, a representative of Sherman had worked on the equipment and, specifically, had adjusted the safety hood, assuring her and the manager of the car wash that the device was working properly. Furthermore, she testified that she had observed the hood through the morning; it had operated properly each time a car came through the process and therefore she assumed that it had been properly repaired. Other jurisdictions have held that the concept of contributory negligence, as it is known in negligence case law and as distinct from the doctrine of assumption of risk, has no place in actions premised on breach of warranty. In the absence of established Colorado law, we adopt that view.

This case presents a clear example of the distinctions between warranty and negligence theories. While the conduct of plaintiff in looking backwards as she stepped into the opening at the end of the conveyor might well constitute negligence on her part, this part was within the scope of the risk warranted against by defendant. It is uncontested that the purpose of the safety hood was to prevent a person from stepping into the opening at the end of the conveyor unit. As the language relied on by the plaintiff makes clear, the safety hood was designed to assure safe working conditions for employees and to "eliminate all possibility" of persons stepping into the opening. The very risk which defendant warranted not to exist was encountered by plaintiff, and her negligence or lack of due care is irrelevant. Contributory negligence is not a defense where plaintiff's conduct only puts the warranty to the test.

The most common accepted affirmative defense to a warranty claim is unreasonable use of the product by the plaintiff with knowledge of the defective condition and the risk it creates. Defendant was entitled to an instruction to the effect that plaintiff could not recover if she unreasonably exposed herself to a known defective condition. Such activity on her part would be disregard of a known danger, and she would not be proceeding in reliance upon defendant's warranty.

It is uncontested that plaintiff was aware of the fact that the safety hood had not been operating properly at all times. However, if her testimony is to believed, the fact of her knowledge is attenuated by her apparent reliance on the assurances from the defendant's representative that the safety hood had been repaired and her own observation of the hood just prior to the accident.

Decision. The issue is her awareness of a defect in the mechanism *at the time of the accident*. Whether or not her reliance on the statements of the repairman and her own observations was justifiable is a question for the jury. We remand the case to the trial court.

Case Questions

1. What representations created the warranty in question?
2. Why is the plaintiff's negligence not a valid defense to the breach of warranty case?
3. Do you think the facts show that the plaintiff exposed herself to a "known defective condition"?

PRODUCT MISUSE

Abnormal use or misuse of the product by the plaintiff is similar to the assumption of risk defense. A *misuse* is an unreasonable use of the product in a manner that was not intended by the seller or designer. A misuse is sometimes foreseeable by the seller, so warnings or design changes may be necessary. The courts have not been consistent in their application of the misuse defense. Some courts have recognized this defense in strict liability cases, whereas others have refused to apply it.

In one case, the manufacturer of a chair claimed that it was misuse for the buyer to stand on the chair and use it as a stepladder. The court found this use to be foreseeable and required that the chair be designed to remain stable even under the pressures of a person standing on it.

PRODUCT SAFETY REGULATIONS

The product liability laws intended to promote safe products are supplemented by product safety regulations that require certain products to maintain minimal safety levels. Food products, drugs, consumer products, and motor vehicles must meet established safety specifications. Taken together, the law provides both protective and curative remedies. The product liability system seeks to cure product safety

Ethical Issue

Consumer Responsibility for Product Safety
Consumers face ethical dilemmas when they misuse products. Sellers are increasingly considered principally responsible for safety, and knowing the seller is liable may lead some consumers into complacency. They may disregard their obligation to use products responsibly. Safety is a concern for all parties: the manufacturer, dealer, and user. Consumers have commonsense duties to avoid exposing themselves, their families, and bystanders to potential dangers.

Some states apply the concept of comparative fault to auto accidents so that an injured party's compensation is reduced if that party's injuries were partly due to not wearing seat belts. Do you think comparative fault should play a part in strict liability cases?

problems by compensating victims after an injury, whereas the regulatory system attempts to prevent injuries caused by unsafe products.

There are numerous interactions between the state product liability compensation systems and the federal and state administrative regulatory systems. Evidence from product liability trials that show defects in product design, manufacture, or warnings often triggers action by a product safety administrative agency. Whenever a recovery suit creates adverse publicity about unsafe products, public opinion may force regulators to consider further action.

FOOD AND DRUG SAFETY AND PURITY

One of the first areas of product safety was consumable foods and drinks. Early state statutes concerned the wholesomeness of milk. Today, state and local governments exercise police power to regulate the impact of food and drugs on the health, safety, and welfare of citizens. Regulated foods include bread, milk, milk products, imitation milk products, soft drinks, intoxicating liquors, fruit, fruit products, grain, grain products, and eggs. Regulatory oversight often covers the production, manufacturing, processing, sale, marketing, and transportation of food, sometimes through licensing. The outbreak of foot and mouth disease among animals in Great Britain and then in Europe led many countries to prohibit the transport of dairy and food products into their borders. Even though this disease does not cause injuries to humans, such strict regulations seek to ensure a safe food supply in the countries where animals are not yet affected by the disease.

The Food and Drug Administration

The Food and Drug Administration (FDA) and the U.S. Department of Agriculture (USDA) also regulate the purity of foods and drinks. Federal statutes dating back almost 100 years enable these agencies to regulate milk, meat, poultry, bottled drinking water, vitamins, infant formulas, eggs, food additives, and tea. The federal agencies control adulterated and misbranded foods, food-level tolerances for poisonous ingredients, and the use of pesticides and additives in foods or raw agricultural commodities. Labeling standards require disclosure of the contents of food products and nutritional profiles.

Drug Safety

The Federal Food, Drug, and Cosmetic Act of 1938 authorizes the FDA to regulate drugs and devices: any article or component intended to diagnose, cure, mitigate, treat, or prevent disease or to affect the bodily structure of humans or animals.

http://
www.cpsc.gov/

Devices include most medical instruments and apparatuses such as an intrauterine device (IUD) or prosthesis.

In early 2001, the FDA imposed some of the stiffest fines in its history, suspended manufacturing operations, and issued pointed warnings to a number of pharmaceutical manufacturers that ignored demands to correct substandard manufacturing procedures. The FDA said its action reflects its concern that the manufacturing violations may pose a risk to the safety and effectiveness of the products marketed to the consumer.

States also regulate drugs, including drugs sold over the counter and prescription drugs sold by state-licensed pharmacists. Municipal boards of health often have regulatory power over drugs. Misbranding and adulteration are common classifications of defects. In one case, a manufacturer was held to have overpromoted an antibiotic drug that effectively concealed its warning, leading to liability. State regulatory schemes usually provide remedies to consumers and local boards of health, including the power to ban, seize, condemn offending articles and substances.

Consumer Product Safety

The most comprehensive federal statute affecting defective consumer products is the Consumer Product Safety Act of 1972 (CPSA). The CPSA created the Consumer Product Safety Commission (CPSC) to administer the act. The Injury Information Clearinghouse compiles product failure statistics, collects research on defects, and funds research to discover defects. The CPSC has the power to establish minimum product standards and to enforce regulations for noncomplying products. It also administers the Federal Hazardous Substances Act and the Poison Prevention Packaging Act, which cover the labeling and misbranding of poisons and hazardous substances, and the Flammable Fabrics Act, which sets minimum standards for the fire-retardant qualities of fabrics.

ONLINE

Information on recent recalls and other enforcement activities of the CPSC is available at **http://www.cpsc.gov/**

MOTOR VEHICLE SAFETY

The federalization of automobile safety regulations began with the National Traffic and Motor Vehicle Safety Act of 1966. Congress sought to reduce traffic accidents, deaths, and injuries by establishing vehicle safety standards, supporting related research, and providing mechanisms to remedy defective vehicles. Two major systems were designed to prevent injuries. The first system empowers the Department of Transportation (DOT) to promulgate practical safety standards for motor vehicles. All newly manufactured domestic and foreign vehicles sold in the United States must be certified as complying with these standards. Extensive civil fines may be imposed for noncompliance. The second system requires remedies for defects arising after sale, such as nonfunctioning or malfunctioning auto parts. These defects may be discovered by customers, testing agencies, manufacturers, or the DOT. The

International Commentary

Maintaining U.S. Competitiveness

Critics charge that U.S. manufacturers are becoming less competitive in world markets because the product liability system imposes excessive costs on U.S. industry. Many nations with a civil law legal system have more extensive statutory liability provisions, similar to implied warranties, than do common law nations like the United States.

The liability systems in most other countries are not as financially favorable to injured plaintiffs as the U.S. system. For example, New Zealand prohibits common law tort actions against the sellers of goods. Instead, New Zealand has a state-run no-fault compensation system for most types of defective product injuries. In 1985, the European Union adopted a product liability directive that holds manufacturers or producers strictly liable for injuries caused by defects in their products. That directive fundamentally changed laws in member countries that had required proof of either privity of contract or negligence to recover for defective products. Liability for services is not covered by the directive.

The burden of product liability laws arguably falls evenly on foreign and U.S. manufacturers when they sell in the United States. However, differences in safety and testing standards can impose greater costs in selling abroad. Foreign nations may impose more stringent standards on imported goods than on those domestically produced. Some nations protect their domestic producers by imposing stringent safety, packaging, labeling, and warranty regulations on imported products. For example, the U.S. automobile industry has long argued that U.S.-built vehicles are priced 40% higher in Japan than in the United States because of discriminatory technical, safety, and inspection requirements for imported automobiles.

Ethical issues arise in product liability when a domestic manufacturer withdraws a defective product from the home market and turns to foreign markets to dispose of existing inventories. For example, critics charge that after U.S. manufacturers were prohibited from selling the IUD birth control device in the United States, they cut their losses by unloading excess inventories in the lesser developed countries. As information spreads about businesses' global social responsibility, the impact of defective products is becoming both an international and ethical dilemma for manufacturers from all nations.

manufacturer may be required to (1) recall and repair defective vehicles, (2) replace defective vehicles, or (3) refund the purchase price.

Other state and federal statutes and agencies regulate the safety of particular products. The Federal Aviation Administration (FAA) sets private and commercial aircraft safety standards. The Occupational Safety and Health Administration, discussed in Chapter 20, indirectly regulates tool and workplace defects by setting minimum safety standards for tools.

THE ADMINISTRATIVE REMEDIES

Safety regulations establish standards and minimum specifications for the structural integrity and performance of products. Sample products are tested to evaluate their "breaking point," which can facilitate the redesign. A product's resistance to typical operating stresses and patterns must hold within a range reasonably expected under normal use. A hammer, for example, might be required to withstand a minimum pounding pressure before fracturing. Its claw might be required to withstand a normal prying pressure.

ONLINE

Further information on the new regulations against tobacco products can be found at **http://www.usatoday.com/news/smoke/smoke01.htm.**

Agencies are often empowered to "rule in" as legal all safe products and thereby to "rule out" unsafe products. Drugs and food additives may not be sold or used unless they appear on the "legal list." The FDA has established several lists of approved food additives. For example, the Generally Recognized as Safe (GRAS) list includes foods and food additives that were considered safe for consumption when the list was first published in 1958. The artificial sweetener NutraSweet was separately approved for use in certain goods. The FDA also lists drugs acceptable for prescription and over-the-counter sales. Experimental drugs, such as several AIDS drugs, may not be prescribed or sold until placed on the list after extensive testing.

Certain products and food additives are excluded from distribution. The FDA, USDA, CPSC, and Congress have each banned the sale of certain new items. A product ban may be implemented simply through the issuance of a new rule creating the ban or through withdrawal of the authority from manufacturers to produce and sell an existing product. For example, the use of cyclamates as artificial sweeteners was banned in 1969 after evidence mounted about their health hazards.

Warning Labels and Advertising

Nearly all safety regulators require that products be branded and that they include instructions for use. Warnings may be necessary to prevent product misuse consistent with the duty to warn. Foods, drugs, cosmetics, and toys are typical of products required to carry conspicuous warnings of known dangers and directions for safe use. Warning labels may help prevent misuse. Mandatory warning labels may also help manufacturers establish misuse by consumers who disregard a conspicuous and known warning. The *Cipollone* case later in this chapter illustrates this point.

Several advertising issues arise under product safety regulations. Electronic media advertising of cigarettes is banned, relegating tobacco ads to only the print and billboard media. The Surgeon General has required that a warning about the dangers of cigarettes be placed on cigarette packages.

The legislation greatly strengthens both the federal and state governments' regulatory arsenal and furnishes them with additional resources to address the public health problems related to tobacco use. Among other things, the regulations:

- Confirm FDA's authority to regulate tobacco products under the Food, Drug, and Cosmetic Act, making FDA the preeminent regulatory agency with respect to the manufacture, marketing, and distribution of tobacco
- Ban all outdoor tobacco advertising and eliminate cartoon characters and human figures, such as Joe Camel and the Marlboro Man, as advertising appealing to the nation's youth
- Impose and provide funding for an aggressive federal enforcement program, including a state-administered retail licensing system, to stop minors from obtaining tobacco products
- Empower the federal government to set national standards controlling the manufacture of tobacco products and the ingredients used in such products.

Searches, Seizures, Forfeitures, and Condemnations

Speedy action is often critical in food and drug cases. To avert widespread disaster, the various food and drug regulators have immediate powers to search for adulterated foods and drugs. The spread of foot and mouth disease in some animals exemplifies situations when immediate and summary action is justified. The administrative remedies of seizure, forfeiture, condemnation, and impoundment are used when speedy action is necessary.

Repair, Refund, or Replacement

Both the Consumer Product Safety Act and the National Traffic and Motor Vehicle Safety Act require manufacturers and sellers to remedy common defects with a repair following public announcement of recall. Although recalls are intended to cure defects, the repairs also prevent injuries. Recalls often follow consumer complaints or failure reports. Because recalls enable manufacturers to repair defective products, they probably decrease product liability suits based on product failure.

Regulatory Noncompliance and Damage Suits

Plaintiffs in traditional product liability recovery actions can lessen their burden of proof by simply proving that the product fails to meet regulatory standards. In a case involving a poisonous chemical, for example, the manufacturer's failure to include the skull and crossbones or other warning symbol required by regulations triggered liability, even though a textual warning was provided. The package failed to adequately warn two migrant workers who could not read English. Several state and federal statutes provide for private damage suits. For example, the CPSA has a right of action independent of common law product liability theories.

Regulatory Compliance as Due Care

Although defendants in product liability cases often show their compliance with safety regulations as evidence of their reasonable care, many courts have held that government regulations create only minimum standards. Even if firms meet those standards, they can still be held liable for negligence, breach of warranty, or unreasonably dangerous defects. Nevertheless, compliance with regulations generally provides some evidence of reasonable care. Some product liability reform laws limit damages recoverable against drug manufacturers if they comply with government regulations.

The *Cipollone* case illustrates the impact that federal cigarette warning requirements have on various state product liability theories. Similar concerns may apply to other products requiring federal or state warnings, including alcoholic beverages, automobiles, pharmaceuticals, medical devices, and pesticides. The court's discussion also provides a review of the various theories of product liability.

Cipollone v. Liggett Group, Inc.

505 U.S. 504 (1992)
United States Supreme Court

Facts. Rose Cipollone smoked cigarettes from 1942 until she died shortly after removal of a cancerous lung in 1984. Thereafter, Antonio Cipollone, her husband, continued her product liability suit against three cigarette manufacturers. Cipollone presented extensive evidence that she was addicted to smoking and that the cigarette manufacturers made misleading advertisements assuring smokers of safety and favorably depicting smokers. The cigarette manufacturers alleged that the Federal Cigarette Labeling and Advertising Act of 1965, as amended by the Public Health Cigarette Smoking Act of 1969, preempted state law, thus displacing the product liability laws on which Rose Cipollone's claims were based. A jury awarded Antonio $400,000 for breach of warranty for advertising before the 1965 warning label requirement but found that Rose was 80% comparatively negligent, denying her any damages. After Antonio Cipollone's death, the couple's son Thomas appealed the decision of a U.S. Circuit Court of Appeals that reversed the jury's damage award.

Legal Issue. Are all state-based product liability laws that could apply to cigarette manufacturers preempted by the 1965 federal law, as amended?

Opinion. Justice Stevens. "WARNING: THE SURGEON GENERAL HAS DETERMINED THAT CIGARETTE SMOKING IS DANGEROUS TO YOUR HEALTH." A federal statute enacted in 1969 requires that warning (or a variation) to appear in a conspicuous place on every package of cigarettes sold in the United States.

Article VI of the Constitution provides that the laws of the United States "shall be the supreme Law of the Land ...

any Thing in the Constitution or Laws of any state to the Contrary notwithstanding." State law that conflicts with federal law is "without effect." Consideration "start[s] with the assumption that the historic police powers of the States [are] not to be superseded by ... Federal Act unless that [is] the clear and manifest purpose of Congress."

In the 1965 preemption provision regarding advertising, Congress spoke precisely and narrowly: "No statement relating to smoking and health shall be required in the advertising of [properly labeled] cigarettes." A warning requirement promulgated by the FTC and other requirements under consideration by the States were the catalyst for passage of this act, which reflected Congress' efforts to prevent "multiplicity of State and local regulations pertaining to labeling of cigarette packages."

The plain language of the preemption provision in the 1969 Act is much broader than that of its predecessor. First, the later act bars not simply "statements," but rather "requirement[s] or prohibition[s] . . . imposed under State law." Second, the 1969 act reaches beyond statements "in the advertising" to obligations "with respect to the advertising or promotion" of cigarettes. The 1969 Act worked substantial changes in the law: rewriting the label warning, banning broadcast advertising, and allowing the FTC to regulate print advertising. The phrase "[n]o requirement or prohibition" sweeps broadly and suggests no distinction between positive enactments and common law. We must look to each of petitioner's common law claims to determine whether it is in fact preempted. The central inquiry in each case is straightforward: We ask whether the legal duty that is the predicate of the common law damages action constitutes a "requirement or prohibition based on smoking and health ... imposed under State law with respect to ... advertising or promotion."

Failure to Warn

Petitioner offered two closely related theories: first, that respondents "were negligent in the manner [that] they tested, researched, sold, promoted, and advertised" their cigarettes; and second, that respondents failed to provide "adequate warnings of the health consequences of cigarette smoking." Petitioner's claims are preempted to the extent that they rely on a state law "requirement or prohibition ... with respect to ... advertising or promotion." [Petitioner's] claims that respondents' post-1969 advertising or promotions should have included additional, or more clearly stated, warnings are preempted. The Act does not, however, preempt petitioner's claims that rely solely on respondents' testing or research practices or other actions unrelated to advertising or promotion.

Breach of Express Warranty

A manufacturer's liability for breach of an express warranty derives from, and is measured by, the terms of that warranty. The "requirements" imposed by an express warranty claim are not "imposed under State law," but rather imposed by the warrantor. While the general duty not to breach warranties arises under state law, the particular "requirement ... based on smoking and health ... with respect to the advertising or promotion [of] cigarettes" in an express warranty claim arises from the manufacturer's statements in its advertisements. In short, a common law remedy for a contractual commitment voluntarily undertaken should not be regarded as a "requirement . . . imposed under State law." To the extent that petitioner has a viable claim for breach of express warranties made by respondents, that claim is not preempted by the 1969 Act.

Fraudulent Misrepresentation

Petitioner alleges two theories of fraudulent misrepresentation. First, respondents, through their advertising, neutralized the effect of federally mandated warning labels based on a state law prohibition of advertising that tends to minimize health hazards of smoking. Such a prohibition, however, is merely the converse of a state law requirement that warnings be included in advertising and promotional materials. Section 5(b) of the 1969 Act preempts both requirements and prohibitions; it therefore supersedes petitioner's first fraudulent misrepresentation theory.

Petitioner's second theory alleges intentional fraud and misrepresentation both by "false representation of a material fact [and by] concealment of a material fact." Petitioner's claims that respondents concealed material facts are not preempted insofar as those claims rely on a state law duty to disclose such facts through channels of communication other than advertising or promotion. Petitioner's fraudulent misrepresentation claims that arise with respect to advertising and promotions are not preempted. Such claims are not predicated on a duty "based on smoking and health" but rather on a more general obligation—"the duty not to deceive." Congress offered no sign that it wished to insulate cigarette manufacturers from longstanding rules governing fraud. To the contrary, both Acts explicitly reserved the FTC's authority to identify and punish deceptive advertising practices—an authority that the FTC had long exercised and continues to exercise. This indicates that Congress intended the phrase "relating to smoking and health" to be construed narrowly, so as not to proscribe the regulation of deceptive advertising.

State law prohibitions on false statements of material fact do not create "diverse, non-uniform and confusing" standards. Unlike state law obligations concerning the warning necessary to render a product "reasonably safe," state law proscriptions on intentional fraud rely only on a single, uniform standard: falsity. The phrase "based on smoking and health" fairly, but narrowly, construed does not encompass the more general duty not to make fraudulent statements. Petitioner's claims based on allegedly fraudulent statements made in respondents' advertisements are not preempted by the Act.

Conspiracy to Misrepresent or Conceal Material Facts

Petitioner's final claim alleges a conspiracy among respondents to misrepresent or conceal material facts concerning the health hazards of smoking. This duty is not preempted for it is not a prohibition "based on smoking and health."

Decision. The judgment of the Court of Appeals is accordingly reversed in part and affirmed in part, and the case remanded. It is so ordered.

Case Questions

1. What product liability theories are preempted by the federal warning requirement?
2. Why are warranty claims not preempted?
3. Why is one of the fraudulent misrepresentation claims preempted while the other is not?
4. Discuss the immunity a manufacturer receives for compliance with all regulations.

QUESTIONS

1. A Texas statute requires manufacturers of defective products to indemnify the seller for any loss arising out of a product liability action unless the seller caused the loss. A truck driver who was injured while opening the hood of his truck claimed the truck's design, which required him to stand on the front bumper while opening the hood, caused him injury. He later added a claim that the Ruan Leasing Company, the lessor of his truck, was negligent in maintaining the truck's hood. Although the truck driver settled with the manufacturer and agreed to dismiss the claim against the lessor, the lessor, Ruan, sued to recover from the manufacturer for the costs associated with its defense of the negligence claim the truck driver brought against it. The manufacturer said it did not have to indemnify Ruan for the expenses incurred in defending itself against negligence, because those expenses did not arise out of the product liability action brought by the truck driver. Do you agree? See *Menitor v. Ruan Leasing*, 6 S.W.3d 729 (Supreme Court of Texas 2000).
2. Rand McNally and Company published a chemistry textbook in which the author provided instructions for a chemistry experiment. The instructions provided no clear warning of dangers associated with the experiment. When several students who were injured by an explosion that resulted after they followed the textbook instructions, they sued the publisher, claiming it, as well as the author, should be held liable. Do you agree?
3. Define *strict liability*. How does this theory differ from liability based on a contractual promise or warranty liability? How does it differ from liability based on negligence or fault?
4. Identify the basis for possible liability for participating in one of the following schemes listed by the FTC In its dirty dozen scams most likely to appear by e-mail:
   a. A bulk e-mail solicitation offers to sell you lists of millions of e-mail addresses to which you can send your own bulk e-mail solicitation.
   b. You're asked to send a small amount of money ($5 to $20) to each of five names on a list, replacing one name with your own, and then forwarding the message by bulk e-mail. A product, such as a recipe or a report, is transferred to each of the recipients.
   c. A credit repair service offers to erase negative information from your credit files so you can quickly qualify for a credit card, auto loan, or job.
5. What type of warranty is involved in the following fact situation? A customer asked for a pair of hiking boots that would be suitable for mountain climbing above the timberline of the Rockies. The customer said that she would be carrying packs with a weight of more than 75 pounds. The salesperson recommended a pair of traditional hiking boots with waffle soles and no extra support. As a result of wearing the boots (which lacked adequate support), the customer became disabled while on the climb and was heli-

coptered out of the wilderness. What is the best ground on which to sue?

6. Several recent laws have been aimed at restricting information on people gathered for one purpose to be transferred to others who could use that information without the prior consent of the subject person. What specific firms and organizations are most affected by these restrictions found in the Driver's Privacy Protection Act, the Health Insurance Portability and Accountability Act, and the Financial Services Modernization Act?
7. Harry Handyman, an accountant, prides himself on doing all the work on his home himself. When the floor in his kitchen needed replacing, he went to the local hardware store and purchased a roll of linoleum and, after a lengthy discussion with the owner, a can of Super-Bind Linoleum Glue. Harry followed all of the warnings and instructions on the can. He left all the windows in the kitchen open, and he positioned a fan to blow the toxic fumes out of the room. Nevertheless, while he was spreading the glue, an explosion ripped through the kitchen, severely burning him and damaging his home. Later investigation revealed that the cause of the fire was the ignition of the fumes from the glue by the pilot light of a hot-water heater in the utility room outside the kitchen. What cause of action does Harry have, and against whom? Explain.
8. Jones purchased a steel-belted radial tire. The tire had a design defect that caused it to separate, but she was not warned of this defect, even though the manufacturer had received several complaints. The tire blew out when she was driving the car on rough terrain. Is Jones entitled to recover for injuries from the manufacturer?
9. Two golfers playing golf met up with another pair of golfers on the tenth hole and agreed to play the rest of the course as a foursome. On the sixteenth hole, an errant ball hit off the tee by the defendant struck the plaintiff in the right eye, causing personal injuries. The defendant claimed he motioned the defendant to move aside prior to his striking the ball. The plaintiff said the defendant hit a second shot, a "mulligan" from the tee, which he, the plaintiff, did not expect. The plaintiff argued that the defendant was negligent and thus liable. The defendant argued that in golf, as in other sports, participants are held liable only if their conduct is reckless or intentional and not for ordinary negligence. Which standard of care, ordinary negligence or reckless conduct, should apply in this case? Why? Could a jury interpret the plaintiff's conduct as being reckless?
10. Describe the relationship between government regulation of product liability and the traditional common law theories of recovery for product liability. Give two examples of how governmental regulation could affect specific cases or how the outcome of cases could affect governmental regulation.

CHAPTER 9

Agency and Business Organizations

INTRODUCTION

Most businesses in the United States are small businesses—started by entrepreneurs. An **entrepreneur** is someone who organizes, manages, and assumes financial responsibility for a business or other enterprise. In determining how to organize a business, an entrepreneur considers many options—from a sole proprietorship to a corporation. The business organization portion of this chapter reviews the options for organizing a business and notes the advantages and disadvantages of each different form.

As no one person can perform all the activities required to operate a business, businesses use agents to represent the organization in dealing with customers, suppliers, and other parties. An **agent** acts on behalf of or represents another person or firm. The business firm or person who is represented by the agent is the **principal.** Today's students will be the agents and principals of tomorrow's business firms. Although employees are agents, a person does not have to be an employee to be an agent. Firms often hire independent contractors to act on their behalf in performing specified tasks. Such contractors are agents who work on a firm's behalf, but they are not subject to control by the firm, and they are not regarded as employees.

Determining whether the relationship between a firm and one of its agents is an employment relationship can be critical. As noted in Chapters 20 and 21, the employment relationship is subject to significant regulation. Most of those regulations do not apply if the agent is not also an employee of the firm. On the other hand, although businesses by necessity must enter into principal-agency relationships, the law generally does impose liability on the business for actions performed by its agents. The nature of the relationship between a business firm and its agents determines the tort and contract liability of the business for the acts of its representatives.

AGENCY RELATIONSHIPS

An agency relationship is based on the consent of both parties; neither can force the other to accept the relationship. The essence of an agency relationship is the agent's agreement to act on behalf of the principal. Essentially, an agent acts on behalf of and in the principal's place in negotiating contracts, selling goods, and accepting payments from third parties. The term **fiduciary** is at the heart of the agency relationship. As a fiduciary, or a person with a fiduciary duty, an agent has the obligation to be faithful to the principal who places trust and confidence in the agent.

TYPES OF AGENCY RELATIONSHIPS

The basic agency relationships are the principal-agent relationship and the employer–independent contractor relationship. The essence of the **principal-agent relationship** is that the principal (firm) authorizes another (the agent) to carry out a broad range of activities on the principal's behalf. The principal-agency relationship is not always based on an employment relationship. If you authorize a friend to take care of your home and to pay some bills for you while you are out of the country for an extended period, you have entered into an agency relationship but not an employment relationship.

In such a case, you usually give the friend a **power of attorney**, a document that shows others that you have authorized the friend to act for you and that the friend has consented to an agency relationship. The friend is known as an attorney because he or she acts on your behalf; the person need *not* be an attorney at law, who acts in legal matters on behalf of someone else.

Principal-Agent

A corporate officer, a store manager, and a sales representative are all agents, people who have agreed to act on behalf of a firm. If the store manager decides to refund money to a customer or the sales representative agrees to reduce the listed price of goods for a potential purchaser, their actions are regarded as those of the principal. Most principal-agent relationships are between employers and employees. Although the employment contract controls many of the duties each party has toward the other, agency law also imposes certain obligations on each party as a result of their agency relationship.

The principal (firm) authorizes the agent to act for it and gives the agent broad powers to represent it. Of course, the principal retains the right to control the agent's activities. A firm generally establishes policies that its agents must follow, such as setting working hours, determining the place of employment, and limiting the authorized work of the agent to certain activities.

Employer–Independent Contractor

The employer–independent contractor relationship differs from the principal-agent relationship because the employer lacks the right to control the physical activities of the agent. The essence of the **employer–independent contractor relationship** is that the person or firm hiring the contractor to perform specific tasks does *not* have the right to control the method of performance of the contractor. A truck driver who owns his own equipment and hires himself out on a job basis is an independent contractor; his employer does not have a right to control his activities. On the other hand, a truck driver who drives a company truck, under rules established by the firm that she drives for, is an agent and an employee. Building contractors, plumbers, and air conditioning service people are usually independent contractors. The firm or employer who hires them has no right to control their physical conduct in the performance of their job.

An accountant or an attorney could be either an independent contractor or an agent, depending on whether the firm for which they perform work has the right to control their performance. Some attorneys are employees and agents of General Motors, subject to the rules and policies of that firm. On the other hand, an attorney who is a member of an independent firm may contract to perform specific jobs for companies like General Motors.

If an attorney is doing work that is not subject to control by the client firm, the attorney is an independent contractor, not an employee-agent. An accountant who works independently or as a part of an accounting firm, but who independently or as a part of another firm contracts to provide services to various corporations, is also an independent contractor. However, if an independent contractor is hired to assist a firm in consulting with other parties, that contractor is also the firm's agent for the specific purpose for which the contractor was hired. Thus, an independent contractor can also be an agent of a firm.

Determining the Nature of the Relationship

An Internal Revenue Service (IRS) website, http://www.irs.gov/prod/forms_pubs/pubs/p15a04.htm, provides a good summary of the factors that determine whether, for the IRS tax purposes, an individual is an employee or an independent contractor. Under IRS rules, while employers do have to withhold and pay a number of taxes on behalf of its employees, an employer generally does not have a similar obligation on payments made to independent contractors. According to the IRS, all evidence related to the degree of control by the employer and the independence of the employee-contractor needs to be considered. Three categories are examined: behavioral control, financial control, and the type of relationship of the parties. The IRS site also contains several case examples, many of which lead to a finding of an employer-employee relationship rather than that of employer and independent contractor.

ONLINE

Type in "topic 762" or "independent contractor vs. employee" to view the factors listed by the IRS.
http://www.irs.gov

Recently, a case involving workers at Microsoft made it clear that persons originally considered by an employer to be independent contractors who are later found to be employees are entitled to specified employee benefits, even if they had agreed that they would not be eligible for such benefits.

Vizcaino v. Microsoft[1]

120 F.3d 1006 (1997)
U.S. Court of Appeals, 9th Circuit

Facts. In 1989 and 1990, the Internal Revenue Service examined Microsoft's records and determined that it should have been withholding and paying taxes for some workers the IRS decided were employees. Microsoft agreed and made the corrections for the employees. Some of the people in that category were tendered offers to become acknowledged employees, but others, like Vizcaino, were not. She did have the opportunity to work for a temporary employment agency, but she refused to do so. The workers then asserted they should have had the opportunity to take part in Microsoft's stock purchase plan and its employee stock purchase plan. Microsoft disagreed and Vizcaino brought suit. The district court found for Microsoft. Vizcaino appealed to the Court of Appeals, where a three-judge panel reversed and held for her and the other workers. The Court of Appeals then decided to rehear the matter en banc (with all judges).

1. A subsequent opinion from the Court of Appeals is found at 173 F.3d 713 (1999). It does not materially change this case. The U.S. Supreme Court declined to review the case.

Legal Issue. Where temporary employees originally treated as independent contractors are later determined to be employees, are the "employees" entitled to participate in company stock purchase plans in the same manner as other employees?

Opinion. Circuit Judge Fernandez. It is important to recognize that there is no longer any question that the workers were employees of Microsoft and not independent contractors. The IRS clearly determined that they were. Microsoft admits that they were employees. However, Microsoft entered into agreements with the workers that stated that each worker was "an Independent Contractor" and that the worker "agreed to be responsible for all of his federal and state taxes . . ." and that "you are not either an employee of Microsoft, or a temporary employee of Microsoft." We now know that most of this was not, in fact, true because the workers actually were employees rather than independent contractors. What are we to make of that?

Viewed in the proper light, it can be seen that the workers were indeed hired by Microsoft to perform services for it. We know that their services were rendered in their capacities as employees. Therefore, the workers were employees, who did not give up or waive their rights to be treated like all other employees under the plans. The workers performed services for Microsoft under conditions which made them employees. [The court then noted that the SPP (stock purchase plan) was an ERISA plan and that the plan administrators, not the courts, determine who are employees. Their decision could, however, be reviewed by the courts. The courts did review these issues.]

The ESPP (employee stock purchase plan) was an offer to employees to become shareholders of Microsoft by purchasing its stock. Most employee benefits are for services rendered or for the purpose of inducing the further rendering of services. They help to guarantee a competent and happy work force. The mistake Microsoft made brought difficulties with the IRS, but it has resolved those difficulties by making certain payments and taking other actions.

Decision. We now determine that the plan administrators' reasons for rejecting the workers' participation in the SPP and the ESPP [that they were not employees] were invalid. Any remaining issues regarding the right of any or all of the workers to participate in the SPP must be decided by the plan administrator upon remand.

Case Questions

1. Review the IRS website regarding the factors that are to be considered in determining the status of a worker as an independent contractor or employee. Which of those factors do you think are most important in the Microsoft case?
2. What is the legal effect of the agreement between Microsoft and the workers in question that stated that they were independent contractors? Why do you think it was used?
3. What are the consequences for the Vizcaino and the other plaintiffs of being eligible to participate in the employee plans? What would the present value of her stock be if she had been able to purchase or receive Microsoft stock in 1990?

CREATION OF AGENCY RELATIONSHIPS

Although many agency relationships are based on contracts, agency relationships can also be created without contracts so that one person (an agent) can be authorized to act for another (the principal). The three methods of creating authority are by actual authority, apparent authority, and ratification.

Actual Authority

When supplier S contracts with UPS to deliver parts from S to its customers, such as manufacturer M, S and UPS are entering into an agency and contractual relationship. UPS's authority to act for S is based on the contractual agreement between them. Similarly, if I expressly state to a stockbroker, "Please sell 100 shares of my IBM stock at today's market price," I am expressly authorizing the broker as my agent to act on my behalf.

On the other hand, if a firm hires a person to manage one of its stores, that manager would have the implied authority to make necessary purchases for the store and to hire needed help unless the firm as principal made clear statements to the contrary. Here, the manager's actual authority is implied from being hired as the store manager. Thus, **actual authority** is authority granted to an agent by a principal either based on express statements or implied from those statements or from actions of the principal.

Apparent Authority

Apparent authority is created when the principal does something that leads a third party to believe the agent is authorized to act for the principal. The principal must be the source of the agent's authority. The third party, who relies on the apparent authority of the agent, cannot look to the agent to create the authority. It must instead look to expression or conduct from the principal.

If S tells manufacturer M that "UPS will pick up the part you are returning," S (the principal) is indicating to M that UPS (its agent) is authorized to act on its behalf in its dealings with M (the third party). Here, the principal S is by its conduct and expressions to M indicating that UPS has the apparent authority to act on its behalf. Although M does not know whether UPS actually is authorized for this work by S, S's conduct provides apparent authority to M to accept UPS as being authorized to pick up S's part.

If you go to a store and offer to pay by check and the clerk accepts your check as payment for goods being purchased, you can reasonably assume that the clerk has authority to accept checks as payment. If there are no notices to the contrary in the store, even if the clerk was not actually authorized to accept a check, the absence of any notice that checks are not acceptable would lead you to believe that a check is an acceptable method of payment.

Sometimes firms place in written contracts statements related to warranties such as "The warranty for this product is as noted in this written agreement. Agents are not authorized to alter the terms of the contract's warranty provisions." This provision indicates to prospective purchasers that salespeople lack the authority to extend or alter the warranty. The contract provision effectively limits the apparent authority of the salesperson.

Ratification

The act of accepting and giving legal effect to an unauthorized act constitutes **ratification.** In the *Schoenberger* case, Schoenberger argues that the CTA ratified a manager's promise to pay him a higher salary. But the court found that once the supervisor discovered that the unauthorized promise to pay more had been made, he immediately indicated the promise would not be honored. If, instead, the supervisor had said, "That should not have been done, but we will honor the promise this one time," then ratification would have occurred. For ratification, there must be an act that is originally unauthorized that the principal later accepts, by word or by action.

The case that follows, *Schoenberger v. CTA,* deals with the hiring of an employee and a promise a representative of the CTA made to him regarding his salary. Many students of the legal environment will soon be seeking permanent employment. When you are interviewing for a job, whose statements and promises can be relied on? The case reviews whether the CTA representative had actual authority or apparent authority or whether his actions were ratified later and thus authorized by the CTA.

Schoenberger v. Chicago Transit Authority

405 N.E.2d 1076 (1980)
Appellate Court of Illinois

Facts. Schoenberger sued the Chicago Transit Authority (CTA) to recover contract damages. At issue was whether the CTA was liable under agency principles for a promise, allegedly made by its employee ZuChristian when Schoenberger was hired, that he would receive an automatic $500 increase in salary a year after beginning work. Schoenberger stated that he did not question ZuChristian's authority to discuss salary with him, but he believed that ZuChristian's authority overrode the authority of the placement department, which he thought had only a "perfunctory" role in hiring.

ZuChristian testified that his supervisor had told him to make informal offers to prospective employees. However, ZuChristian also stated that when he told Schoenberger of his desire to hire him, he intended for Schoenberger to regard this as an offer. He also stated that he lied to Schoenberger when he told him that the $19,300 salary offer was merely a clerical offer, which would automatically be raised to $19,800. This story, he said, was agreed upon by his supervisor, John Hogan. Both ZuChristian and Hogan thought their story would lead to Schoenberger's acceptance of the lower salary that had been approved by the human relations department. When the increase in salary was not given at the promised time, Schoenberger resigned and filed suit. The trial court ruled in favor of the CTA, and Schoenberger appealed.

Legal Issue. Is ZuChristian's promise to Schoenberger that the CTA would automatically be raised by $500 a year after Schoenberger's employment began binding on the CTA because ZuChristian was the CTA's agent?

Opinion. Justice Campbell. The authority of an agent may only come from the principal and it is therefore necessary to trace the source of the agent's authority to some word or act of the alleged principal. Authority may be actual or apparent, actual being express or implied. The authority to bind a principal will not be presumed, but rather the person alleging authority must prove its source unless the act of the agent has been ratified.

Both Hogan and Bonner, ZuChristian's superiors, testified that ZuChristian had no actual authority to either make an offer of a specific salary to Schoenberger or to make any promise of additional compensation. Furthermore, ZuChristian's testimony corroborated the testimony that he lacked the authority to make formal offers. From this evidence, it is clear that ZuChristian lacked the actual authority to bind the CTA for the additional $500 in compensation to Schoenberger.

Nor can it be said that the CTA clothed ZuChristian with the apparent authority to make Schoenberger a promise of compensation over and above that formally offered by the placement (human relations) department. Here, Schoenberger's initial contact with the CTA was with the Placement Department where he filled out an application and had his first interview. There is no evidence that the CTA did anything to permit ZuChristian to assume authority to hire and set salaries. He was not at a management level in the CTA nor did his job title, Principal Communications Analyst, suggest otherwise. The mere fact that he was allowed to interview prospective employees does not establish that the CTA held him out as possessing the authority to hire employees or set salaries. Moreover, ZuChristian did inform Schoenberger that the formal offer of employment would be made by the Placement Department.

Our final inquiry concerns plaintiff's contention that irrespective of ZuChristian's actual or apparent authority, the CTA is bound by ZuChristian's promise because it ratified his acts. Ratification may be expressed or inferred and occurs when the principal, with knowledge of the unauthorized transaction, takes a position inconsistent with non-affirmation of the transaction. Ratification is the equivalent of an original authorization and confirms that which was originally unauthorized. Ratification occurs when a principal attempts to seek or retain the benefits of the transaction.

Upon review of the evidence, we are not convinced that the CTA acted to ratify ZuChristian's promise. According to Bonner's testimony, when he took over the supervision of Zuchristian's group in the fall of 1976 and was told of the promise, he immediately informed ZuChristian that the promise was unauthorized and would not be honored. He subsequently also informed Schoenberger of this same fact. Mere delay in telling Schoenberger does not, as plaintiff contends, establish the CTA's intent to ratify.

Decision. For the reasons we have indicated, the judgment in favor of the defendant CTA is affirmed.

Case Questions

1. What did Schoenberger have to prove to show that ZuChristian was acting as the CTA's agent when he discussed the automatic $500 increase in Schoenberger's salary?
2. What should lead Schoenberger to question whether ZuChristian had the authority to act on behalf of the CTA?
3. Who had the authority to commit the CTA to a definite salary for a prospective employee such as Schoenberger? Who would normally have such authority for most corporations or organizations similar in size to the CTA?

TERMINATION OF AGENCY RELATIONSHIPS

The principal-agent relationship may be terminated either by operation of law or by the parties. In addition to sometimes terminating an agency relationship, the law also restricts the ability of the parties to terminate their relationship.

Termination by Law

The law terminates a relationship when either of the parties dies or when the subject matter of the relationship is destroyed. As the agent's authority is based on the agreement of the principal, if the principal dies, the agent is no longer authorized to transact business for the principal. If I hire an agent to sell my summer cottage and the cottage is later destroyed by fire, the law terminates the relationship I had with the agent.

Similarly, if the law changes, the authority of an agent is automatically terminated. If a sales agent is initially authorized to sell certain nonprescription drugs and the law changes so that a purchaser now needs a prescription to buy those drugs, the agent's authority to sell the drugs without a prescription is revoked by law.

Termination by the Parties

In an agency relationship, generally the parties may terminate an agreement at the end of a term or whenever the parties so desire. For example, they may provide in their agreement that "this agreement terminates one year from today." As Chapter 20 indicates, most employment relationships can be terminated at will—that is, when either party determines they want to end the relationship. That chapter also notes, however, several exceptions to the "at will" termination of the employment relationship.

In addition to the exceptions noted in Chapter 20, the law provides that an agency relationship, which includes most employment relationships, cannot be terminated without the agent's consent *if* the agent has a property interest in the relationship. An agent in this relationship has an **agency coupled with an interest** and is protected from unilateral terminations by the principal. For example, professional athletes or movie stars often have agreements with agents whose compensation is based solely on the earnings of their principal. The agent has a property interest in the earnings of the principal; therefore, if the principal wants to terminate the relationship, the agent must either consent to termination of the agency or receive some severance pay from the principal.

Today, many businesses often use agents and distributors to represent them in selling their products throughout the global marketplace A **distributor** usually is a person or firm that purchases products from a seller and that assumes the economic and legal risk involved with reselling them. Unlike the distributor, the agent acts on behalf of the firm that sells the product. Thus, the agent has fiduciary duties to the principal firm that the distributor, who deals on a contractual basis, does not have. The agent also has less risk, as it is not purchasing the product from the selling firm; instead, it is paid a commission or a commission and salary for using its efforts to sell the seller's products. A firm's right to terminate a relationship with an agent or with a distributor is subject to significant regulation in many countries.

DUTIES OF PRINCIPAL AND AGENT

Once an agency relationship exists, each party owes certain duties to the other. As has been noted, the agent has fiduciary duties to the principal. These duties, based on the relationship of the parties and not on their contractual agreements, arise in every

The law of most countries clearly distinguishes between agents and distributors. The Hieros Gamos network maintains a number of websites where lawyers in other countries provide outlines and brief commentaries about the laws of other countries. Known as *lex mundi*, Latin for laws of the world, these sites usually include information about doing business in the country under discussion.

For example, the site for Denmark includes "A Lawyer's Guide to Doing Business in Denmark," prepared by Michael Budtz. Found at http://hg.org/guide-denmark.html, the guide includes the following language:

Under Danish law, no special form is required for concluding an **agency** *agreement. The agent is not an employee of the principal and, unless otherwise agreed to, the agent does not acquire any additional rights as an employee. In the case of termination the agent is entitled to compensation for the loss of goodwill. . . . Furthermore, the compensation shall be considered "reasonable." . . .*

According to the law, a reasonable period of notice is 1 month during the first year of the agency agreement increasing by 1 month per year to a maximum of 6 months. The parties may not agree on shorter periods of notice.

A distributor concludes contracts in his own name and for his own account. This constitutes the main distinction between the agent and the distributor. It is customary in the distributorship agreement to include provisions concerning the termination of the agreement. Depending on how long time the agreement has been in force and on other relevant circumstances, the required notice to terminate a distributorship usually should be 3 to 6 months . . . and in extraordinary cases even up to 1 year.

transaction the agent undertakes. The agent's role as a fiduciary is the basis for many ethical and legal problems in business today. A significant portion of the litigation against businesses and their officers, employees, and agents relates to the fiduciary obligation of agents. The agent generally owes the principal five duties, depicted in Exhibit 9.1, based on the fiduciary relationship. The principal's duties to the agent are more general and are not based on the fiduciary relationship (see Exhibit 9.2).

Agent's Duty of Loyalty

The duty of loyalty is the most important of the agent's fiduciary duties. Agents have to act for their principals and cannot act for anyone else, even themselves. The duty of loyalty means that an agent cannot have a conflict of interest—representing both the principal and someone whose interest is different than that of the principal. If there is a conflict of interest between the agent's interest (or those of another party) and that of the principal, the agent must disclose the interest to the principal. Investment bankers are often underwriters for companies' new stock issues. An underwriter is paid by the seller for its role in underwriting. Thus, if the investment

EXHIBIT 9.1 Agent's Fiduciary Duties to Principal

- Duty of loyalty
- Duty to use reasonable care and skill in its performance
- Duty to communicate information
- Duty of obedience
- Duty to account

banker is to serve potential purchasers or recommend to them that they consider purchasing the securities, the investment banking firm must disclose to the possible purchasers that it is also representing and being compensated by the firm that will be selling the stock.

Consulting firms, advertising firms, and law firms often have to carefully monitor whom they represent so that they perform their fiduciary duty and disclose potential conflicts of interest if some clients have interests that are opposite to those held by other clients. Most health-related firms will not hire lobbyists who represent the interests of tobacco companies. These firms, as principals, believe their agents cannot adequately represent both interests.

The law does allow a broker or middleman to bring different parties together. Some firms seek to place venture capitalists with new firms in need of capital. If neither party is relying on the broker for advice and assistance, the firm can perform the **finder or middleman** role.

Agent's Duty to Use Reasonable Care and Skill in Its Performance

The degree of care and skill required from the agent is that expected of a reasonable person under similar circumstances. A person with special skills, such as an attorney or an engineer, is held to the standard expected from those with such special skills. An agent must use reasonable care and skill in looking after the principal's property. If you use a company car, you must use reasonable care in operating and maintaining it. If you receive money on the principal's behalf, you must keep it reasonably safe. However, the agent is not liable for any and all losses. He or she needs to use only reasonable care; the agent is not an insurer or a guarantor of the principal's property.

Agent's Duty to Communicate Information

A principal depends on an agent to provide information received from third parties. Insurance agents must pass on to the insurance companies they represent any information about policy changes that insured customers want to have made in their insurance policies. A failure to perform this duty can result in the agent's being held personally liable to the principal for any loss caused to the principal. Consider the following case: A savings and loan association had lent money to someone planning to purchase a home. The savings and loan association hired a firm to check for termites in the home. The inspection report, given to the savings and loan association, was not passed along to the purchaser. Although the savings and loan association argued that the termite inspection was to protect its interest in the home, not that of the purchaser, the Supreme Court of Ohio found that the association violated its duty to disclose the inspection information to the purchasing homeowner.[2]

One who acts as agent for another becomes a fiduciary with respect to matters within the scope of the agency relation. . . . An agent owes his principal a duty to disclose all information which the agent learns concerning the subject matter of the agency relation and about which the principal is not apprised. Furthermore, where a principal suffers loss through his agent's failure to function in accordance with his duty, the agent becomes liable to the principal for the resulting damage.

Agent's Duty of Obedience

The principal has the right to direct the agent to perform certain activities, and the agent must obey all reasonable instructions regarding the agency. Of course, the

2. *Miles v. Perpetual Savings & Loan*, 30 N.E.2d 1364 (1979).

agent does not have to follow illegal instructions from the principal. The agent is not free to use his or her own judgment regarding what to do if the principal has provided clear and reasonable guidelines. Many firms have ethical policies about accepting gifts, lunches, dinners, or gratuities from those with whom their employees do business. Agents are obligated to follow such policies, regardless of their own views on whether such gifts might create ethical problems. Only during emergency situations, when the principal cannot be consulted, can the agent deviate from instructions without violating her or his duty.

Agent's Duty to Account

The agent has a duty to keep and make available to the principal a record of all property and money received and paid out on behalf of the principal. Note that this obligation affects agents who are either receiving money for the principal or spending money that belongs to the principal. Thus, gifts agents receive from suppliers or others doing business with the principal do not belong to the agent who receives them. They are the property of the principal and must be accounted for unless there is a clear policy that allows the agent to keep gifts of little value. Even the president of the United States is unable to keep all gifts given to him; instead, those of significant value belong to the people he represents. If an agent is paying out money received from the principal, or for which the agent-employee expects to be reimbursed, the agent must provide an accounting. Expense account policies often provide details or the level of accounting expected from employees who are spending the principal's funds.

Principal's General Duties

The principal's duties to the agent are based both on the contractual agreement and on agency law. While the agent has the duty to act for the principal and to be loyal to the principal, the principal has the duty to cooperate with the agent. In addition, the principal has the duty to reimburse the expenses of the agent, to indemnify the agent from loss, and to provide the agent with a safe working environment (see Exhibit 9.2).

Principal's Duty to Cooperate The principal who hires an agent as a salesperson cannot compete with the agent. For example, a person wanting to sell a home often hires a real estate agent to represent the seller. Generally, the contract provides that during the term of the agency agreement, the agent has an exclusive right to sell the home. The homeowner agrees not to compete in trying to sell the home or to otherwise interfere with the agent's work.

EXHIBIT 9.2 Principal's Duties to the Agent

- Duty to cooperate
- Duty to reimburse expenses
- Duty to indemnify against loss
- Duty to provide a safe working environment

Principal's Duty to Reimburse Expenses and to Provide Indemnification. Whenever an agent spends her or his own money to pay for necessary expenses in the reasonable performance of agency duties, the principal has the duty to reimburse the agent for those expenses. When an agent is delivering goods for a principal, the cost of highway tolls, reasonable food and accommodation expenses, and normal supplies paid for by the agent have to be reimbursed within a reasonable time by the principal. If an agent has to pay money to third parties for the principal, those funds have to be reimbursed.

Usually, the principal also has to **indemnify** the agent—that is, make good any losses the agent suffers on account of doing the principal's business. If a third party claims a pizza delivery driver caused injury to the third party, the third party could bring suit against both the driver and the pizza firm. The firm must compensate the driver not only for any funds he or she is required to pay to the third party but also for costs incurred in defending the lawsuit. Usually, if the agent commits an intentional tort or is acting outside the scope of her or his authority (such as if the accident occurred while the driver was doing personal business), the principal need not provide indemnification to the agent.

Principal's Duty to Provide a Safe Working Environment. The law requires the employer-principal to provide the agent with a safe working environment. The common law based on court decisions imposes on the employer an obligation to inspect the premises and warn the employee of any hazardous areas. Federal and state statutes add other requirements, such as the Occupational Safety and Health Act requirements discussed in Chapter 20.

PRINCIPAL'S LIABILITY IN CONTRACT AND TORT FOR AGENT'S ACTIONS

CONTRACTUAL LIABILITY OF PRINCIPAL FOR CONTRACTS FORMED BY AN AGENT

The principal's liability for contracts that an agent negotiates and signs with third parties depends on the knowledge that the third party has regarding the principal. *The Restatement of the Law Second, Agency* classifies principals as being disclosed, partially disclosed, or undisclosed.

Disclosure

If a third party knows the identity of the principal when it is contracting with the principal's agent, the principal is **disclosed.** If you purchase office supplies for XYZ Company and indicate to the seller that you are an agent for XYZ, the office supply store, as the third party, is dealing with a disclosed principal. It knows it is not dealing with you personally as a contracting party.

On the other hand, if a third party contracts with a party who in fact is an agent, but who keeps the existence and identity of his/her principal hidden from the third party, the principal is **undisclosed**. Frequently, real estate developers hire people to purchase property in an area where they plan some future development. They want the people who are making the purchase to keep the agency relationship and the developer's (principal's) identity secret so that the current landowners will not seek higher prices for land they contract to sell. The sellers who contract with the purchaser have no knowledge of either the existence of the principal-agency relationship or the identity of the principal. The Disney Company purchased much of the land around what later became Disney World by using other people as agents without disclosing that the purchasers were acting for Disney.

In between these alternatives is a partially disclosed principal. The principal is **partially disclosed** if the third party the agent deals with knows that there is a principal-agent relationship but does not know the identity of the principal. When a business is planning to move a large facility into a new location, it often hires agents to purchase land and make contracts with local governments and other organizations. Generally, the business requires its agents and local officials to keep its identity hidden until the proposed transactions are finalized. Because the landowners (third parties) with whom the agents deal know that the agents represent someone, they know of the existence of the principal-agency relationship. However, because they do not know the identity of the principal, the principal is only partially disclosed to them.

Liability

If a third party deals with a disclosed principal, the principal is liable to the third party on the contract made by the agent. The contract is the principal's contract and not the agent's, so the principal can be held liable and the agent cannot be held liable. If the principal is undisclosed, however, the third party can hold the agent liable because the third party, who was unaware of the agency relationship at the time of the contract, contracted with the person who is the agent. If the third party finds out about the principal, the third party can instead hold the principal liable. However, the third party cannot hold both the agent and the principal liable on the same contract; it must elect to hold one of them to be the responsible contracting party.

Suppose that at the time of the contract, not knowing the principal's identity, the third party contracts with the agent. If the contract obligates the agent to pay money to the third party over a number of years, the third party can seek performance from the agent. However, a third party who discovers the identity of the principal could instead hold the principal liable for the future performance. The principal is liable because the agent was acting within the scope of his or her authority in contracting with the third party. Similarly, the principal can seek to enforce the contract against the third party because, in reality, the contract was made on behalf of the principal.

If you as an agent do not want to be held liable for a contract you are negotiating on behalf of a principal, you need to disclose the existence and identity of your principal to the party you deal with. If you sign a contract as Ashley Tate, no one knows that you are in fact representing someone else. The other party to the contract will seek to hold you liable on the contract you signed. Similarly, if you sign the contract as Ashley Tate, Agent for Fourth Bank, it is not clear whether you or the bank is liable on the contract. To make it obvious that you should not be held liable, you should sign the contract as Fourth Bank, by its agent, Ashley Tate. This signature makes it clear that the bank, not Ashley Tate as its agent, is the party to be held liable on the contract.

TORT LIABILITY OF PRINCIPAL FOR AGENT'S TORTS

Respondeat Superior

The principal's liability for the torts of its agents depends on the nature of the relationship between the principal and its representative and on how the action in question relates to the principal's work. Generally, because liability follows the right to control, if the principal has the right to control the actions of its agent, the principal will be held liable if the agent commits a tort that injures a third party. Note that the principal's liability is vicarious liability; it is based on the actions of someone else—the agent. As long as the acts of the agent are within his or her scope of authority, the principal can be held liable.

The rule of ***respondeat superior***, "let the superior respond," holds the principal liable even though the principal is not at fault. The principal's liability is not based on its committing a wrong; instead, it is based on the wrong committed by the agent if the agent was at the time acting in the scope of her or his authority to further the principal's business. The agent is also liable for committing the tort, as indicated in Chapter 7. Although the third party can hold both the agent and the principal liable for the agent's tort, it can collect only once—either totally from one party or partially from each party. If the principal has agreed to indemnify the agent, the agent can recover from the principal for any loss he or she suffers.

Liability is imposed on the principal because the principal directed or authorized the agent to act in its place. Essentially, in exchange for allowing the principal to do business through its agents, the law imposes liability on the principal when those agents, acting within the "scope of their authority," commit torts. As the "scope of the authority" of the agent limits the principal's liability, it is often important to determine whether an agent's actions are considered to be outside the agent's authority. When the agent acts on her or his own, not in furtherance of the principal's business, the principal is not held liable for the agent's torts. The acts of an agent that are outside or beyond the scope of the agent's authority are the agent's actions, not done in furtherance of the principal's business. Review the following case and how its decision could be applied to a business firm.

Tall v. Board of School Commissioners of Baltimore

706 A.2d 652 (1998)
Court of Special Appeals of Maryland

Facts. William (Roy) Tall Jr. was a nine-year-old boy who had Down's syndrome. He participated in a special education program at Harbor View Elementary, a school sponsored by the Board of School Commissioners (Board) in Baltimore. While at school in July 1995, Roy urinated in his pants. His teacher, Mr. Manning, responded by disciplining Roy by beating him on his arms and legs with a ruler. When Roy arrived home, his mother discovered raised welts and bruises on her son's arms and legs and took him to the hospital emergency room, where he was treated for his injuries.

Roy's parents reported the injuries to the police, who, after an investigation, filed criminal child abuse and assault and battery charges against Manning. Manning pleaded guilty to assault and received a suspended sentence and five years of supervised probation. William Tall, Roy's father, then sued the Board, seeking damages for his son.

The trial court found that because both the Board and state law had a clear policy against corporal punishment, Manning's actions were outside the scope of his employment and not in furtherance of the Board's business of educating students. Its decision for the Board noted that Manning had been specifically instructed not to use corporal punishment. Tall then appealed to the Court of Appeals.

Legal Issue. Is a teacher, who while teaching beat a student with a ruler, despite a clear school policy against any kind of corporal punishment, an agent acting within the scope of his employment?

Opinion. Justice Hollander. Appellant's claims against the Board are all premised on the doctrine of *respondeat superior.* Under this doctrine, the Board, as employer, cannot be liable for Manning's actions unless his conduct was within the scope of employment. Appellant asserts that Manning's conduct was incidental to conduct authorized by the Board for educating special needs children, it was foreseeable, and it is in furtherance of appellee's objective of educating these children. According to appellant, Manning's physical contact with Roy was foreseeable because, as a result of Roy's disability, Manning was required to give him special attention, which included clothing, touching, and cleaning Roy.

As we see it, Manning did not act within the scope of employment in beating Roy. We explain. It is well settled that an employer may be held vicariously liable under the doctrine of *respondeat superior* for tortious acts committed by an employee, so long as those acts are within the scope of employment. An employee's tortious conduct is considered within the scope of employment when the conduct is in furtherance of the business of the employer and is authorized by the employer. Even if the employee's acts were willful or reckless, an employer may be held liable for the wrongful acts of an employee, so long as the employee's acts were within the scope of employment and in furtherance of the employer's business.

In order to be deemed within the scope of employment, an employee's tortious conduct need not be expressly authorized by an employer. An employee's unauthorized conduct might fall within the scope of employment if it was of the same general nature as conduct that was authorized or incidental to that conduct. In analyzing the scope of employment in the educational context, *Hunter v. Board of Education of Montgomery County* is instructive. There, the Court observed that a school board "can only be held liable for the intentional torts of its employees committed while acting within the scope of their employment." In the case under review, we do not see how a nine-year-old child with Down's syndrome would view a physical assault by his special needs teacher, after that child had urinated in his pants, as being within the scope of the teacher's apparent authority.

Other jurisdictions have refused to hold employers liable under the doctrine of *respondeat superior* for sexual assaults perpetrated by school employees. Manning's conduct constituted a drastic departure from the Board's policy, as reflected in the local rules and the Supplement. Moreover, as a result of his conduct, Manning was convicted of assault. The criminal conviction surely establishes the egregiousness of Manning's misconduct, and lends support to the Board's claim that his action was outside the scope of his employment. We recognize that there are legitimate occasions when a teacher may have to touch a student. We fail to see how the act of physically striking a disabled child could be considered in furtherance of the Board's objective of educating disabled children, particularly when, as here, both State and local law forbid the use of corporal punishment for discipline purposes.

Decision. We conclude that Manning's conduct was neither expected, foreseeable, nor sanctioned. Rather, it was so extreme in nature, and so far beyond the bounds of appropriate behavior, that it cannot possibly be considered to have been in furtherance of appellee's objectives. Judgment Affirmed.

Case Questions

1. Under what circumstances might it be within the scope of a teacher's employment to touch a student?
2. What is the effect of the criminal case on this case?
3. What does this case indicate about the conduct of employees in business firms that is contrary to the clear policies of those firms? What does it suggest to you that firms and other organizations should do regarding employee behavior?

LIABILITY OF THE EMPLOYER FOR TORTS OF THE INDEPENDENT CONTRACTOR

Frequently, businesses contract with other firms to provide special services for them. Despite an employment relationship, because the hiring firm has no right to control the actions of the representative of the contracted firm, usually the lack of control also means that the employer is not liable for any torts the agents of the contracting firm commit. In such an employer–independent contractor relationship, the employer generally is *not* liable for the torts committed by the independent contractor.

However, there are exceptions to the rule of not holding the employer liable. As the *Massey v. Tube Art* case notes, if the employer has a legal duty that the law does not allow the employer to delegate or transfer to another party, the employer can be held liable for actions performed in its place by an independent contractor.

Massey v. Tube Art Display, Inc.

551 P.2d 1387 (1976)
Court of Appeals of Washington

Facts. Tube Art contracted to move a sign for its client, McPherson Realty, to a new location. It hired Redford, a backhoe operator, to dig a hole at a spot it marked. While digging the hole, Redford struck a gas pipeline. He examined the pipeline but, finding no leak, left the site. The next morning, an explosion in the building served by the pipeline killed several people and injured others. Massey, a tenant in the building whose property was damaged by the explosion, sued Tube Art. He claimed Tube Art was liable for Redford's negligence because Redford was Tube Art's employee and agent. Tube Art argued that its relationship with Redford was that of employer–independent contractor and that, as such, it could not be held liable for Redford's negligence. The trial court found for Massey, and Tube Art appealed.

Legal Issue. Is a person who digs holes for a sign company, pursuant to specific directions from the company, an "employee" of that company rather than an independent contractor?

Opinion. Judge Swanson. Traditionally servants and non-servant agents have been looked on as persons employed to perform services in the affairs of others under an express or implied agreement, and who, with respect to physical conduct in the performance of those services, is subject to the other's control or right of control. An independent contractor, on the other hand, is generally defined as one who contracts to perform services for another, but who is not controlled by the other nor subject to the other's right to control with respect to his physical conduct in performing the services.

In determining whether one acting for another is a servant or an independent contractor, several factors must be taken into consideration as listed in the Restatement (Second) of Agency:

a. the extent of control which, by the agreement, the master may exercise over the work details;
b. whether or not the one employed is engaged in a distinct occupation or business;
c. the kind of occupation, with reference to whether, in the locality, the work is usually done under the direction of the employer or by a specialist without supervision;
d. the skill required in the particular occupation;
e. whether the employer or the workman supplies the instrumentalities, tools, and the place of work for the person doing the work;
f. the length of time for which the person is employed;
g. the method of payment, whether by the time or by the job;
h. whether or not the work is a part of the regular business of the employer;
i. whether or not the parties believed they are creating the relation of master and servant (now referred to as principal and agent);
j. whether the principal is or is not in business.

All of these factors are of varying importance in determining the type of relationship involved and, with the exception of the element of control, not all need be present. It is the right to control another's physical conduct that is the essential and oftentimes decisive factor in establishing vicarious liability whether the person is a servant or a non-servant agent.

Our review of the evidence supports the trial court's evaluation of both the right and exercise of control even though Redford had been essentially self-employed for about 5 years at the time of the trial, was free to work for other contractors, selected the time of day to perform the work assigned, paid his own income and business taxes and did not participate in any of Tube Art's employee programs. The testimony advanced at trial, which we find determinative, established that during the previous three years Redford worked exclusively for sign companies and 90 percent of his time for Tube Art. He had no employees, was not registered as a contractor or subcontractor, was not bonded, did not himself obtain permits or licenses for his jobs and dug the holes at locations and in dimensions in exact accordance with the instructions of his employer. In fact, Redford was left no discretion with regard to the placement of the excavations that he dug. We therefore find no disputed evidence of the essential factor—the right to control—nor is there any dispute that control was exercised over the most significant decisions—the size and location of the hole.

Assuming for the sake of argument that Redford acted as an independent contractor, this court does not accept Tube Art's argument that its liability is, therefore, negated. In the present case, Tube Art exercised control over where the hole was to be dug, the day it was to be dug and how deep the hole was to be. Moreover, it was not unreasonable to expect Tube Art to know that gas pipes might very well be lurking in the vicinity of the proposed excavation. In such case, it was incumbent on Tube Art to ascertain where service pipes might be located. Failing this, Tube Art cannot now disclaim liability.

Decision. Rather, where the danger to others is great, a duty is imposed upon an employer to make such provisions against negligence as may be commensurate with the obvious danger. It is a duty which cannot be delegated to another so as to avoid liability for its neglect. The decision of the trial court is affirmed.

Case Questions

1. Evaluate each of the factors listed by the *Restatement, Second, Agency* and determine if in this case the facts indicate a principal agent or an independent-contractor relationship.
2. Why does the court conclude that Tube Art is liable even if Redford is regarded as an independent contractor?
3. Could Tube Art be held liable for Redford's negligence? Why? Could Tube Art be held liable because it (Tube Art) was negligent?

BUSINESS ORGANIZATIONS

Entrepreneurs who are establishing a business can select from different forms of business organization. The proprietorship, partnership, and corporation are the traditional forms of business organizations. Several alternative forms are also now available to entrepreneurs.

FORMS OF BUSINESS ORGANIZATION

ONLINE

For a comparison of the traditional forms of business organizations, see **http://www.lectlaw.com/files/buo06.htm**. It provides excerpts from a U.S. Small Business Administration publication.

Among the traditional forms of business organizations, the sole **proprietorship** is the easiest to form and the most commonly used. There are few legal formalities to comply with, and the owner is assured of maintaining control. However, other forms, such as a partnership or corporation, may be more attractive for many businesses, especially as they grow and hire more agents and employees. A partnership brings two or more people together to collaborate in operating a business and making a profit. The corporation is the form selected by most businesses that reach a certain size. Its limited liability for owners and separation of management from ownership make it especially attractive for larger businesses.

In addition to the three traditional forms of business organizations, several newer forms—the limited liability company, the limited liability partnership, and the subchapter S corporation—combine some of the favorable attributes in each of the more traditional forms. These forms are discussed in detail in the next section of this chapter. Franchise businesses also play a unique role in the organization of business activities, and special laws govern certain aspects of franchise operations.

An entrepreneur or student looking at the forms of business organization should note the benefits and disadvantages of each form so that the most appropriate form for each individual situation can be selected. How easy or difficult is it to create the organization? How is the income taxed? Are owners personally liable for the debts of the firm? Who controls the firm's management? Can the owners easily transfer their interests to others? Is it easy to change the management of the firm? Will the firm dissolve if an owner leaves? Is significant record keeping required after the firm is organized? Exhibit 9.3 and the text that follows answer these questions and compare the important characteristics of each major form of business organization.

THE PROPRIETORSHIP, PARTNERSHIP, AND CORPORATION

THE SOLE PROPRIETORSHIP

A person who is the only owner of a business is called a **sole proprietor**. Of course, the proprietor often hires employees and agents to perform the work of the firm and to conduct transactions with other businesses.

Creation of a Proprietorship

A sole proprietorship is the easiest type of business organization to form. Generally, if a special name is used for the business, a certificate for doing business under an assumed name is filed in the county where the business operates. If Chris wants to form a business, to be known as "Custom Climate," to provide heating and air conditioning services, he would file a certificate to register that name in the county where the business is located. The registration of trade names is discussed in Chapter 18.

Local, state, and federal laws require the owner of any business to comply with certain governmental regulations. A restaurant needs to obtain a permit from the local health department, provide a specified number of parking spaces, and comply with applicable zoning restrictions. State law imposes insurance requirements for unemployment compensation and workers' compensation for employees. Federal and state laws control pollution permits and the disposal of waste products. Both federal and state taxes must be withheld from the wages of employees. Despite all these requirements, which are also imposed on other forms of business organizations, the sole proprietorship is subject to less governmental regulation than any other form.

Characteristics of a Proprietorship

A sole proprietorship is not considered to be an entity separate from its owner. If someone sues the business, the suit is filed against the owner. For example, a suit against Custom Climate would be filed against Chris, doing business as Custom Climate, and all of Chris's assets, whether they are in his personal bank account or in the business account, are exposed to liability for any legal judgment against the business. Thus, a major problem with the sole proprietorship is the risk the owner takes. Chris has unlimited liability; his personal assets are not legally distinct from his business assets. Another problem with the sole proprietorship is that when Chris dies, the business is automatically dissolved. Although other family members can take over the operation of the business, they do so as a new business organization. Finally, sole proprietorships often have difficulty in attracting capital. Few investors want to put their funds in someone else's control without having a voice in the management of the organization.

Of course, a major benefit of the sole proprietorship is that all profits go to one person—the owner. The owner does not file two income tax returns, a business return and a personal one. Instead, business income is listed on the personal tax return (usually on Schedule C for the federal income tax return). Another major benefit is the ease of starting a sole proprietorship. The sole proprietorship form of business is popular because it is so easy to organize and to operate. Approximately 80% of U.S. businesses are organized as sole proprietorships.

EXHIBIT 9.3 Comparison of the Forms of Business Organization

	Sole Proprietorship	**General Partnership**	**Limited Partnership**	**Limited Liability Partnership**	**Limited Liability Company**	**Corporation**
Creation	No formalities or expenses are required other than those specific to the business to be operated.	No formalities or expenses are required other than those specific to the business to be operated. A written agreement among the partners is advisable.	Must file a formal certificate. Written agreement is normal as roles of limited partner must be distinguished from general partner(s).	It is designed for professionals doing business as partners. Formation expenses are comparable to that of a corporation	Must file articles of incorporation. Formation expenses comparable to that of corporation.	Expense and time required to comply with statutory formality. Must receive charter from state. Usually required to register and pay fees to operate in states other than the state of incorporation.
Taxation	Profits are taxed as ordinary income to the proprietor; losses are deducted by the proprietor.	A federal income return is filed by the partnership for informational purposes. Profits are taxed to each partner as ordinary income; losses are deducted by each partner. Profits and losses are shared equally unless the partnership agreement provides otherwise.	No tax on entity; tax liability flows through to partners. Partner cannot offset regular income with passive tax loss.	It is usually taxed as a partnership—taxes are passed through to the partners.	If it does not possess all the attributes of a corporation, it is taxed like a partnership.	Profits taxed first as income to the corporation and a second time as dividends are distributed to owners. Losses are deductible only by the corporation.
Liability of Owner	Sole proprietor has unlimited personal liability.	Each partner has unlimited personal liability for partnership debts.	General partner has unlimited liability; limited partners' liability is limited to capital contribution.	Each partner has liability limited to his/her interest in the firm.	Liability of shareholders is limited to loss of capital contribution unless an extraordinary event requires piercing the corporate veil.	Liability of shareholders is limited to loss of capital contribution unless an extraordinary event requires piercing the corporate veil.

EXHIBIT 9.3 Comparison of the Forms of Business Organization (continued)

	Sole Proprietorship	General Partnership	Limited Partnership	Limited Liability Partnership	Limited Liability Company	Corporation
Control of Management	Sole proprietor has total control.	Each partner is entitled to equal control unless the partners provide otherwise in the partnership agreement.	General partner exercises all management powers. Written consent from all partners usually required for new general or limited partners.	(same as general partnership).	All members can participate in management; can have numerous shareholders.	Separation of ownership and control. Owner generally has no control over daily management decisions.
Transferability of Ownership Interest	Transferable with sale of assets and business.	Nontransferable unless the partners unanimously agree.	Interest of partners are assignable, but new partners cannot be admitted without consent unless in partnership agreement.	Nontransferrable unless agreement provides otherwise.	Members can limit transferability of shares.	Freely transferable unless shareholder agreements provide otherwise.
Duration	Limited to life of the proprietor.	Limited to life of the partners.	Limited partners can be added or dropped; change in general partner can cause dissolution, but agreement usually provides otherwise.	A change in partnership can cause dissolution, but agreement usually provides otherwise.	If one member drops out, all others must agree to continue; similar to general partnership.	Unlimited.
Recordkeeping Requirements	Minimal.	Depends on agreement—usually moderate.	Moderate—some state requirements imposed.	Significant.	Significant.	Extensive annual reports, bylaws, shareholder meetings, board of director meetings.

The Partnership

A **partnership** arises from any agreement between two or more people to carry on a business for profit. A partnership involves a sharing of rights and responsibilities. Usually, partners sign a partnership agreement that details their respective rights and duties. Until recently, most law firms and accounting firms were organized as partnerships. Although some partnerships involve only a few partners, others involve numerous parties performing complex business transactions.

Creation of a Partnership

Any agreement, whether implied or express, written or oral, is sufficient for the creation of a partnership, but most partnerships start with a written partnership agreement. The parties detail their responsibilities and rights and how the work of the partnership is to be performed. A procedure for admitting new partners or removing existing partners is also generally specified in the agreement.

Characteristics of the Partnership

Partners have duties and rights toward other partners. A partner in a partnership acts both as an agent, in acting for other partners, and as a principal, when other partners act on her or his behalf for partnership purposes. The partnership is regarded as the principal, and each of the partners, as a member of the partnership, has the obligations that a principal has toward agents such as other partners. A violation of a duty owed by a partner acting as agent can result in a suit by the partnership. A partner's relationship with third parties (people with whom the partner and the agent do business) is also based on agency law. The partner's authority to represent the partnership is based on actual and apparent authority given to that partner by the partnership.

One of the advantages of the partnership form of business organization is that it allows the parties to contribute their different talents and resources to a common business and to share them in any lawful manner they choose. Neither the contributions nor the shares of the partners need be equal. Frequently, some partners contribute greater financial resources while others bring managerial skills, important contacts, or knowledge-based resources to the firm.

A partnership, like a sole proprietorship, is subject to only one level of tax on its income. Although a partnership must file an informational return with state and federal officials, the partnership as such does not pay a tax. Instead, the income of the partnership is passed through to the partners, who report it on their individual tax returns. The partner's share of the partnership income, even if not distributed to the partner by the partnership, is subject to tax.

A disadvantage of the partnership form of organization is that its members, like the sole proprietor, are subject to unlimited liability for the debts and obligations of the partnership. If the partnership does not have sufficient assets to satisfy a judgment against it, the judgment creditor may seek satisfaction of the judgment from the assets of the individual partners. Another disadvantage of the partnership is that it terminates on the death or withdrawal of a partner. However, as the partnership agreement usually allows the remaining partners to carry on the business in the form of a new partnership, this disadvantage can be overcome. Similarly, the revised uniform partnership that has been adopted in a number of states as a replacement for the uniform partnership, which had been adopted by all states except Louisiana, specifically provides that the withdrawal of a partner need not lead to dissolution of the partnership.

Partnership, Joint Venture, or Corporate Merger

A **joint venture** is an agreement between two or more parties to cooperate together for a specified time and in specified and limited activities. A joint venture is *not* a separate form of business organization, but it is a way in which individuals or business organizations cooperate. However, because joint ventures are used extensively in business, particularly among parties from different countries, they are discussed here.

A joint venture shares some characteristics of a partnership in that it involves two or more parties who join together in some business project. A partnership, however, is organized to carry on a business for an indefinite period, whereas a joint venture is limited to a specific time period (which can be extended by the parties). Further, the joint venture does not envision the parties cooperating together in all of their business activities. In fact, business competitors often continue to act independently in some actions while cooperating with other firms in selected activities.

For example, IBM and Apple Computer have agreed to work together on some chip design projects while competing in many other areas. Most of the major automotive companies have joint ventures to learn certain things from their partners or to reduce development and manufacturing costs. The joint ventures of GM and Toyota, Ford and Mazda, and DaimlerChrysler and Mitsubishi have benefited each of the participants in various ways.

The British-based Saatchi & Saatchi Agency in 1998 formed a joint venture with French-based Publicis Communications. The French firm provided technical and logistical services and media strategy while the British firm provided creative input and account management services. As often occurs with joint venture partners, a few years later (2000) one of the partners (Publicis), bought out its partner (Saatchi & Saatchi). To participate in a joint venture, two corporations frequently create and jointly own a third corporation. The two original corporations continue to exist and to operate independently, but they cooperate in the activities the third corporation performs.

A merger has the effect of eliminating one or two of the existing business organizations. For example, some U.S. firms that began to do business in China in the early 1990s entered into joint ventures with a Chinese company. Originally, then, three firms—the Chinese firm, the U.S. firm, and the Chinese-based joint venture—existed.

In some cases, the U.S. firm either bought all of the interest in the joint venture owned by the Chinese company (as Publicis did with Saatchi & Saatchi) or sold all of its interest to the Chinese firm. In that case, the joint venture firm no longer existed, but the U.S. firm and the Chinese firm continued. Thus, there were two separate firms, probably both cooperating and competing, but there was no longer a joint venture firm.

In yet other cases, the U.S. firm bought the Chinese firm's interest in the joint venture and also purchased all other assets of the Chinese firm. In this case, the Chinese firm went out of business and the joint venture's business became part of the U.S. firm's business. Thus, the three firms had become one through a merger. The DaimlerChrysler firm is the result of a merger between Daimler and Chrysler. It is not a joint venture between two firms; the Chrysler firm no longer exists, and the Daimler firm (formerly DaimlerBenz), with the assets of Chrysler added to it, is now DaimlerChrysler.

THE CORPORATION

The third traditional form of business organization is the corporation. Unlike the other forms, a **corporation** is an organization that is created by state law, and it is regarded as an entity that is distinct from its owners. Although fewer than 20% of the business organizations in the United States are corporations, they account for

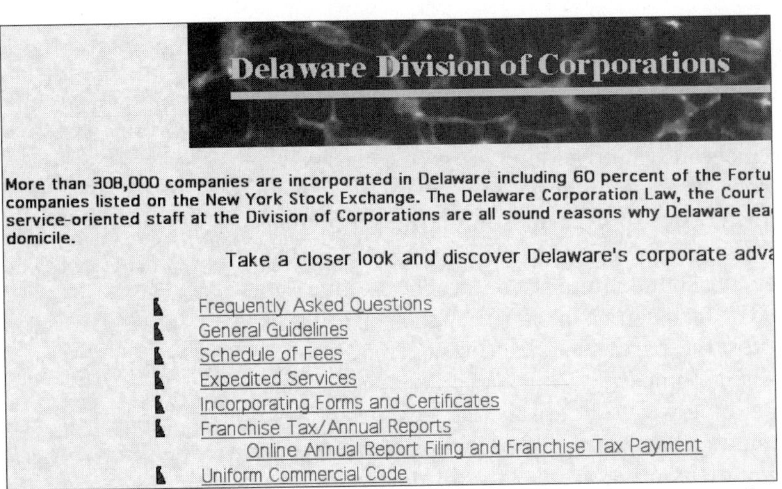

Used with permission from the Delaware Secretary of State.

http://

www.state.de.us/corp/

90% of total sales and annual revenue for all business firms. In recent years, the banking, telecommunications, pharmaceuticals, and airline industries have become more concentrated as larger corporations have acquired or merged with smaller ones. Many businesses are incorporated each year by entrepreneurs and by people who are new to the business world.

Creation of a Corporation

A corporation is created by state law. State corporation laws specify the requirements that must be met to organize a business as a corporation. State laws often specify a minimum capitalization, require a minimum number of people on the board of directors, and mandate certain methods for shareholder voting. A corporation can elect to incorporate in any state; it need not be incorporated in the state where it does most of its business. Some states have laws that are favorable to the management of a corporation. For example, Delaware is known for its statutory and court decisions that allow officers and directors significant control over the actions of the corporation. The home page of Delaware's corporate division indicates that 50% of the companies listed on the New York Stock Exchange are incorporated in Delaware. (See http://www.state.de.us/corp/.) Other states, such as California, have laws that offer greater protection to the corporation's shareholders.

A document known as the **articles of incorporation** must be submitted to the secretary of state's office, or to another designated state agency, by incorporators who intend to form a corporation. Generally, corporations are authorized to engage in any business that is lawful in that state. The **bylaws** state the rules by which the corporation is to be governed: the number of people on the board of directors, their powers, and how they are to be elected.

Once the initial directors are in office, the incorporators' role is completed. In small corporations, the same people frequently serve as incorporators, shareholders, members of the board of directors, and officers and employees of the company.

Characteristics of a Corporation

A corporation provides for separation of the ownership and management of the organization. Three groups are involved in owning and operating a corporation. The **shareholders** are the owners, and they elect a **board of directors** to provide management oversight and establish policies for operating the corporation's business. The board of directors, in turn, hire **officers**, who oversee the day-to-day operations of the business. Of course, the officers can also hire employees and agents to perform the work of the business.

One of the most important advantages of the corporate form of business organization is the limited liability of its owners, the shareholders. Their liability is limited to their investments; they are not personally liable for the debts of the corporation. In a few circumstances, individual shareholders can be held liable for a corporation's debt. In these instances, regarded as "piercing the corporate veil," the shareholders usually have not kept the corporate business separate from their own personal business.

Another important advantage is that a corporation can more easily raise capital than can the other forms of business organizations. The transferability of a shareholder's interest and the corporation's ability to sell shares, which are often publicly traded, make it easy for investors to place their capital in the corporation. Those investors' limited liability of course adds to the attractiveness of a corporation as a form of investment. Another advantage of the corporation is that it generally has perpetual existence. It does not dissolve with the death or withdrawal of owners or managers.

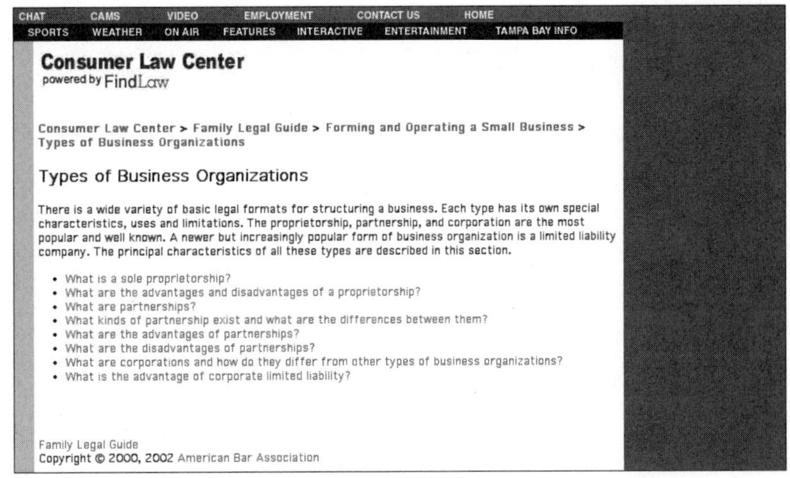

CHAT CAMS VIDEO EMPLOYMENT CONTACT US HOME
SPORTS WEATHER ON AIR FEATURES INTERACTIVE ENTERTAINMENT TAMPA BAY INFO

Consumer Law Center
powered by FindLaw

Consumer Law Center > Family Legal Guide > Forming and Operating a Small Business > Types of Business Organizations

Types of Business Organizations

There is a wide variety of basic legal formats for structuring a business. Each type has its own special characteristics, uses and limitations. The proprietorship, partnership, and corporation are the most popular and well known. A newer but increasingly popular form of business organization is a limited liability company. The principal characteristics of all these types are described in this section.

- What is a sole proprietorship?
- What are the advantages and disadvantages of a proprietorship?
- What are partnerships?
- What kinds of partnership exist and what are the differences between them?
- What are the advantages of partnerships?
- What are the disadvantages of partnerships?
- What are corporations and how do they differ from other types of business organizations?
- What is the advantage of corporate limited liability?

Family Legal Guide
Copyright © 2000, 2002 American Bar Association

Courtesy, FindLaw.

http://
www.tampabaylive.findlaw.com/newcontent/flg/ch12/st2/t1.html

One of the major disadvantages of the corporate form of business organization is that the corporation's profits are taxed twice. The corporation, as a separate entity, pays tax on the income it earns. Then, some of the income remaining after taxation is distributed to shareholder-owners. These individuals are then taxed via their personal tax returns on the money they receive as dividend income, even though that money has already been taxed as part of the corporation's income. The corporate form of business also requires greater record keeping than does the partnership. Minutes of the board of directors, annual meetings by the shareholders, and annual reports to the state of incorporation have to be prepared.

ONLINE

A brief summary of the essential characteristics of the corporate form of business organization appears at the website **http://tampabaylive.findlaw.com/newcontent/flg**

ALTERNATIVE FORMS OF BUSINESS ORGANIZATIONS

Although the proprietorship, partnership, and corporation continue to be the major forms of business organization used in the United States, several other forms are also common, such as the limited liability company, the subchapter S corporation, and the limited partnership. These forms of business organization are attractive because they combine some of the favorable features of each of the more traditional forms. The limited liability company and the subchapter S corporation provide similar features. The limited partnership combines some of the features of a partnership with features of a corporation.

ONLINE

The Lnet website provides information about limited liability companies and partnerships in the 50 states. **http://c2.com/w2/bridges/LnetStatePages**

THE SUBCHAPTER S CORPORATION

A **subchapter S corporation** is organized according to the regulations of subchapter S of the Internal Revenue Code. Unlike the traditional corporation, subchapter S corporations are not taxed on their income; instead, that income is passed through to the individual shareholders, who pay tax on their share of the corporation's income. Thus, there is no double taxation, as there is with a traditional corporation, yet the shareholders continue to have the limited liability that general corporation law provides. The requirements that must be met to qualify for a subchapter S corporation are noted in Exhibit 9.4.

The problems of the subchapter S corporation are found in its requirements. In days when corporations are doing business throughout the world, the requirement

EXHIBIT 9.4 Subchapter S Corporation Requirements

- No more than 75 shareholders, each of whom must be a U.S. citizen or resident alien or a certain type of other organization.
- Corporation must have only one class of stock.
- Corporation cannot own 80% or more of another corporation.
- Corporation must file a timely election to be treated as an S corporation.

that all shareholders must be U.S. citizens or resident aliens limits a firm's ability to have a European, Mexican, or Chinese individual as a shareholder. Similarly, as a firm grows, it will probably want to attract investments from more than 75 shareholders. The limitations on owning other corporations and on having other corporations as shareholders are also quite restrictive.

THE LIMITED LIABILITY COMPANY

Like the subchapter S corporation, a **limited liability company** combines the pass-through, one-level taxation treatment that benefits partnerships with the limited liability advantage of a corporation. In 1997, the Internal Revenue Service issued regulations that clarified the tax status of limited liability companies (LLCs). The LLC has become a very popular form of business organization because it is treated as a corporate entity for liability purposes, is taxed like a partnership, and lacks the limitations imposed on the subchapter S corporation or even on the limited partnership (discussed later).

State laws generally require the use of the term "Limited Liability Company" or the initials LLC in the name of a firm organized in this way. Under the current federal tax laws, the Internal Revenue Service automatically taxes an LLC as a partnership unless it elects to be taxed as a corporation. The lack of double taxation leads most such firms to decide to be taxed as partnerships rather than as corporations. However, if LLC members wish to reinvest the profits of the business in the firm rather than distribute it to the members, they might prefer to be taxed as a corporation if the corporate tax rates are no higher than the personal tax rates.

Another advantage of the LLC is that the members can enter into an **operating agreement** that details the firm's methods of making decisions, allocating profits, and dealing with the transfer of membership in the organization. The firm's operating agreement is similar to partnership agreements. The existence of the LLC provides U.S. businesses with two corporate forms of business organization: the LLC and the general corporation.

THE LIMITED PARTNERSHIP

In a **limited partnership**, some of the partners are allowed to limit their liability to the amount of their original investment; each limited partnership must have at least one general partner, who has unlimited liability, and one limited partner with limited liability. The general partners act the same as partners in a general partnership. They can act on behalf of the partnership in dealings with third parties, and they can be held personally liable for partnership obligations. In contrast, the limited partner

International Commentary

Although the limited liability company is new to the United States, it has been a standard feature of corporation law in many other countries for years. In Germany, for example, the two corporate forms are the GmbH *(Gesellschaft mit beeschrankter Haftung)* and the AG *(Aktiengesellschaft)*. In the United Kingdom, the two forms are the PLC (public limited company) and the Ltd (private limited company), and in Brazil they are the SA *(sociedade anonima)* and the *limitada*. The GmbH, Ltd, and *limitada* are comparable to the U.S. LLC. Each has stock that cannot be traded on a stock exchange, and they are usually used for smaller companies. The other corporate form in each country is for publicly traded companies, such as those that would use the general corporation in the United States. This distinction between publicly traded corporations and more closely held or privately owned companies is common in most countries' corporation laws.

One relatively effective way to check how the laws of other countries compare with federal and state laws in the United States is through the Hieros Gamos network. Its *lex mundi* (Latin for laws of the world) sites usually include information about how to incorporate a business in the country being discussed. For example, see: http://www.hg.org/guide-india.html or http://www.hg.org/guide-austria.html for comparable limited liability company law provisions in India and Austria.

cannot participate in the management of the partnership. Unlike a general partner's interest, a limited partnership interest can be transferred to other parties. The partners can, however, impose restrictions on such transfers. Generally, the resale market for a limited partnership interest is small and informal.

Limited partnerships are frequently used to raise capital for the development of special projects. Thus, a wealthy limited partner could invest significant funds in such a project without risking his or her other assets to creditors of the project. Oil well drillings, Broadway shows, shopping centers, movies, and other rather risky ventures are often organized as limited partnerships. A limited partnership cannot use a limited partner's name in the business, and it must use either the words *limited partnership* or the abbreviation LP so that third parties will realize that the organization includes some limited partners.

THE LIMITED LIABILITY PARTNERSHIP

In a **limited liability partnership**, each partner has limited liability for his or her own actions and for the some or all actions of other partners. The first statute authorizing the use of a limited liability partnership (LLP) was enacted in Texas in 1991. Currently, all states have some similar form of business organization. The limited liability partnership is designed primarily for professionals who do business as partners. Its major advantage is that it combines the pass-through, one-level taxation common to partnerships, but it limits the liability of the partners, as is the case with the LLC and the general corporation. Accounting and law firms that were organized as partnerships easily converted to the LLP form of business organization because the organizational structure is still that used by partnerships.

A major advantage of the LLP form of business is that one partner can avoid liability for the malpractice of other partners. Although an LLP partner would be liable for his or her own malpractice, and for the malpractice of those persons he or she supervises, the law limits the partner's liability for negligence or other wrongful acts of other partners. Statutes do vary from state to state, but all limit a partner's liability for some actions of the other partners.

COMPARISON OF FORMS OF BUSINESS ORGANIZATION

Each of the forms of business organization offers advantages and disadvantages. Factors that should be compared include the ease of creation, taxation, the liability of the owners, the transferability of an owner's interest, the duration of the organization in the event ownership changes, the need for record keeping, and the control of management. Each of these factors was noted in Exhibit 9.1.

FRANCHISES AND BUSINESS ORGANIZATIONS

A **franchise** is a privilege granted or sold, such as the privilege of using a name or process to sell products or services. A franchise may be considered a form of business organization in that it defines how a firm's assets are financed, controlled, and distributed. A **franchisor** develops a product or service that is generally protected by a trademark or trade name. Usually, the franchisor consists of several corporations, each commonly owned. It then licenses the product or service to **franchisees** as a uniform method of doing business. The franchisees—who pay royalties, usually based on a percentage of gross sales, to the franchisor in exchange for the license to use the franchised products and services—invest in their own business operations and usually organize their own corporations. Frequently, one franchisee operates a number of different stores or outlets as part of its license with the franchisor.

Characteristics of a Franchise

The most distinctive aspect of a franchise is the franchisor's exercise of substantial control over a business owned by the franchisee. In exchange for being able to use the franchisor's unique name, trademarks, and special products and techniques, the franchisee permits the franchisor to establish the products that may be sold, the hours of operation, and the types of supplies and equipment to be used. Although fast food restaurants like McDonald's, Little Caesar's Pizza, and Burger King are highly visible franchises, franchises are common in many service businesses. The hotel industry (Hilton, Sheraton, Marriott), the tax preparation business (H & R Block), the muffler and brake business (Tuffy, Midas), and even the legal business (Hyatt Legal Services) all have significant franchise operations.

The franchise agreement usually provides that the franchisor will provide managerial assistance to the franchise, aid in selecting the site for operating the franchise, and regulate the purchasing, advertising, and record keeping of the franchise. The franchisee agrees to provide monetary investment in the business, comply with the regulations established by the agreement, and compensate the franchisor through royalty payments.

Franchise Laws

Most states have enacted legislation aimed at protecting the franchisee. One set of laws requires the franchisor to disclose specific information to prospective franchisees before any sale. Most states use the uniform franchise offering circular, which requires balance sheet and income statements from the franchisor, along with the material terms of the franchise agreement. It also requires the franchisor to provide a description of any territorial restrictions imposed on franchisees and the circumstances under which the franchisor can unilaterally terminate the franchise agreement.

At the federal level, the Federal Trade Commission franchise rules establish guidelines as to the information to be provided to franchisees. Specific information on the number of new franchisees, the average revenue per franchise, the required supplies that must be purchased from the franchisor, and certain historical data must be provided 10 days prior to any agreement. Federal antitrust law also affects the franchise relationship. The application of antitrust laws to vertical restraints imposed by a franchisor is briefly discussed in Chapter 19. A checklist of some of the terms used in franchise agreements is found at the CCH website: http://toolkit.cch.com/tools.franch_m.asp.

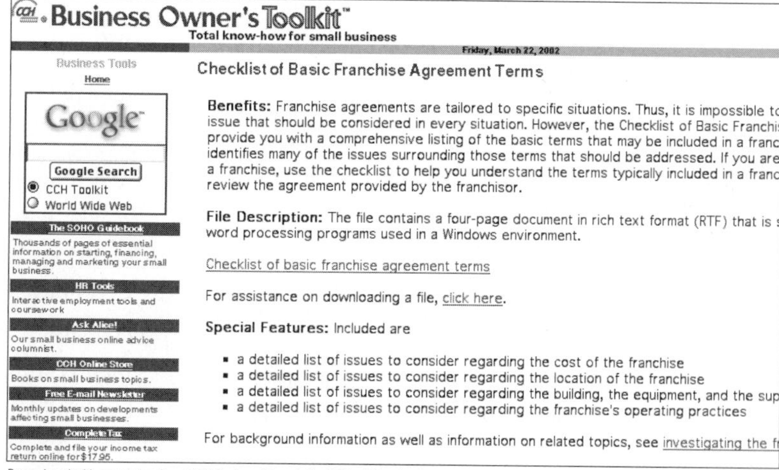

http://
www.toolkit.cch.com/tools/franch_m.asp

QUESTIONS

1. Dave, a general contractor, contracts to build a house for Jim and Cari. Dave subcontracts the carpentry work on the house to Chris. Chris is building the stairwell from the ground level to the basement level but does not enclose it while he is working on it. Laura has a contract to install windows in the house, and she goes on the property to finish her measurements and begin the installation. While in the house, she falls through the open stairwell and suffers injuries. Would Dave, Jim and Cari, or Chris be liable to compensate Laura for her injuries? Why?
2. Sean Rogers worked for Pacesetter Corporation, a home improvement firm. Although Rogers worked mostly at Pacesetter's offices, he also regularly worked at home. He normally worked on performance reviews at home on Monday evenings to be ready to discuss them with the employees he supervised on Tuesday morning. On the evening in question, at the invitation of his supervisor, Sean met the supervisor at a bar to discuss a promotion. He then drove home to work on his performance evaluations. On the way home, he was injured in an accident. Sean claims that as an employee he is eligible for workers' compensation. Pacesetter Corporation said his injuries occurred while he was on personal business and his injuries did not arise out of and in the course of his employment. Who is correct? Why? See *Rogers v. Pacesetter Corporation*, 972 S.W.2d 540 (1998).
3. Stokely–Van Camp, Inc., hires Lennen & Newell as its advertising agency. Lennen & Newell contracts with CBS to purchase advertising time on behalf of Stokely–Van Camp. The contract between CBS and Lennen-Newell is not signed by Stokely–Van Camp. If CBS is not paid for the advertising time that was used for Stokely–Van Camp, can it hold Stokely–Van Camp liable? See *CBS v. Stokely–VanCamp, Inc.*, 456 F.Supp. 539 (1977).
4. Darden, an agent for Nationwide Mutual Insurance Co., had numerous payments credited to his retirement account by Nationwide based on his business performance. The plan provided that if he sold policies for a competitor within 25 miles of his home after retirement or termination, he forfeited his right to any unpaid benefits. Darden was terminated by Nationwide and then began to sell for competitors out of his same insurance office. Nationwide informed Darden that his prospective benefits would be forfeited. He claimed they were vested under the ERISA law for employees and that he was an employee. Nationwide claimed that he was an independent contractor. What factors should the courts examine to determine if he should be regarded as an employee with vested retirement benefits? What decision should the court make? See *Darden v. Nationwide*, 503 U.S. 318 (1992).
5. Why does the agent have fiduciary duties to the principal even though the principal does not have fiduciary duties to the agent? Which of the principal's duties to the agent are more likely to be the source of litigation between agent and principal? Why?

6. What is the major advantage of the corporation form of business organization over the partnership? What is the advantage of the partnership over the corporation?
7. Why did the alternative forms of business organizations arise?
8. Jones, a limited partner in a tax preparation business, invests $100,000 in the business.
   a. What are the requirements for creating a limited partnership?
   b. Can Jones transfer his membership to his wife on his death?
   c. Will he as a limited partner be responsible for partnership debts that are not covered by the partnership assets?
9. Tom and Susan are wealthy businesspeople in a high income tax bracket. They wish to enter into a business venture, but it has a high risk of potential product liability suits. They expect a loss for the first three years of the business, owing to significant capital expenses and the difficulty of entering into a market. Which forms of business organization are best suited to their proposed venture? Why?
10. Define the following terms:

    Corporation

    Franchise

    Joint venture

    Limited liability company

    Limited liability partnership

    Limited partnership

e-Commerce

PART III

Commercial contracts are enforced so that trade proceeds in an orderly fashion and property rights are protected. If businesses could not expect reliable performance on contracts, commerce would become unstable and diminish. In such an uncertain world, only face-to-face agreements could be made with reasonable certainty, and many agreements would be breached. However, with reliable commercial law, businesses can plan for future purchases, production, and sales, thereby spreading the benefits of prosperity throughout the economy. With enforceability of contracts made remotely—by mail, phone, or on-line—new efficiencies have become possible as never known in the history of commerce.

Contracts are the most basic of all business relationships. All sales of personal property, goods, real estate, services, intangibles, and employment result from enforceable agreements. The interactions of businesses with suppliers, customers, and employees are all based on various forms of contracts for sales of land, sales of goods and services, and licensing of intellectual property (IP). Commercial practices, commercial documents, and electronic records are forms of contract needed to facilitate trade. Traditionally, many contracts are made in written documents. However, there is no tangible "contract," only the intangible but legally enforceable rights resulting from the parties' agreement, whether made orally, in writing, or electronically. When the parties successfully finish negotiations, they conclude the contractual agreement and thereby have binding obligations. A **contract** is an enforceable set of mutual obligations for which the law recognizes a duty and provides for enforcement of remedies.

Contract-like devices were recognized as early as ancient Egypt. In the United States, traditional contract law evolved from common law court decisions. Also influential were the common practices of medieval merchants that were consolidated into the law merchant. Modern commercial statutes such as the Uniform Commercial Code (UCC) are based on the law merchant. As transaction volume increases and the geographical distance between parties grows, commercial law is needed to bring certainty. Modern contract law facilitated the industrial revolution, and it supports modern capitalism.

The U.S. Constitution's libertarian ideals emphasize individual free will, limit the intrusion of government, and restrict states from interfering with existing contracts. The U.S. vision of laissez-faire, or **freedom of contract**, is created when these Constitutional ideals are implemented through legal structures and ultimately applied to commercial activity. Of course, parties are not completely free to contract for just anything; for example, illegal objectives are impermissible. Nevertheless, freedom of contract provides incentives that encourage free enterprise, permitting better planning and better satisfaction of expectations. Freedom of contract is a basic assumption of commercial law because it facilitates rather than regulates: The parties are generally free to adapt legal principles to their transaction, thus encouraging innovation. Just as commercial law evolved to accommodate past technological changes in transportation and communications, the law discussed throughout Part III is evolving to accommodate new methods of making contracts, performing contractual duties, making payments and deliveries, and otherwise facilitating e-commerce.

The five chapters in Part III cover the major areas of contracting and related commercial practice for both traditional commerce and e-commerce. Chapter 10, Introduction to Contracts and Their Formation, details the differences among the various commercial laws, depending on the subject matter (employment, goods, licensing). It analyzes e-commerce by using traditional contracting models and discusses the formation of contracts. Chapter 11, Payments and Performances, examines the operations of commercial obligations. The various regimens of payments, deliveries, and third-party rights in both traditional commerce and e-commerce are discussed. Chapter 12, Writings and Records, Defenses, Remedies, and Creditors' Rights, further explores contract practices such as requirements for signed, written contract documents or authenticated records, the authority of agents to make contracts, and key obligations such as warranties, remedies, and creditors' rights. Chapter 13, Technology Transfer: Employment, Service, and Distribution Contracts, explores the methods for economic exploitation of technology, with particular emphasis on transferring IP rights by license and assignment. It covers IP infringement and remedies and explores employment contractual and fiduciary duties, with particular emphasis on technology. Finally, Chapter 14, Privacy, discusses an increasingly important area for traditional businesses such as financial services and health care, as well as an essential aspect of e-commerce. Taken together, these five chapters cover the major legal aspects of transaction practice for both traditional and e-commerce businesses, in addition to the convergence of transaction modes.

Introduction to Contracts and Their Formation

In just a few years, the formation of contracts on line has evolved from an esoteric process designed by lawyers and data processing experts into something most college students and businesspeople do regularly. Nearly every time computer users click "OK" or "I agree" to install software on line or use databases, a contract is formed. How can we integrate our understanding of traditional written contracts resulting from face-to-face negotiations into this emerging world of electronic contracting? This is a pressing question confronting most businesses today as their bricks-and-mortar storefronts converge with their growing on-line presence. Contract law must adapt to new and future forms of communication and automated negotiation.

This chapter discusses the law applicable to contracts and the early-stage aspects of most forms of traditional and e-commerce transactions: their formation and enforceability. The laissez-faire principle is alive and well in the U.S. law of contracts. Therefore, with very few exceptions, contract law does not set the terms of any contract; instead, most terms are negotiated. Contract law sets the ground rules for formation, interpretation, and performance of commercial relations. The following discussion focuses on contracting for most types of business involved in the sale of goods, services, intellectual property licensing, and real estate.

SOURCES OF COMMERCIAL LAW

The many sources of commercial law complicate planning for the wide variety of potential transactions and potential parties from different states or nations. Traditionally, such difficulties concerned only large firms engaged in interstate or international commerce and their expert consultants advising on collateral matters such as transportation, financing, law, or import-export regulations. However, the Internet now permits individuals and small businesses to directly participate in many aspects of global commerce, and many people unaccustomed to these matters need a broader understanding of commercial law. The onset of e-commerce also suggests the need for greater uniformity and harmonization in commercial laws between states and nations.

The starting point for analysis of commercial contracting is with the common law of contracts. The common law comes from case law precedents and was the original basis for U.S. contract law. Today, the common law of contracts applies to sales of interests in land; to employment, services, and consulting contracts; and to many transactions in intellectual property rights. The common law has been collected and rephrased by legal scholars into a compilation, the ***Restatement of the Law Second, Contracts***. Although the *Restatement* is not the definitive law, many courts nevertheless have made it authoritative by citing it as if it were legislation to resolve disputes. In the United States, contract law is a combination of common law precedents, the *Restatement,* and statutory contract law.

The most important statutory law of contracts is found in uniform laws passed by the states. The **Uniform Commercial Code (UCC)** is a product of the National Conference of Commissioners on Uniform State Laws (NCCUSL). The UCC is based on the common law and on the law merchant. The UCC governs the sale of goods and some other types of contracts. The UCC now applies throughout the United States and is summarized in Exhibit 10.1. It is divided into several parts called articles that govern most aspects of commercial transactions: sales of goods, various payment mechanisms and their intermediaries, investment securities, title documents and collateralization.

NCCUSL's website
http://www.nccusl.org

EXHIBIT 10.1 Articles of the Uniform Commercial Code (UCC)

No.	Title of Article	Coverage
Article 1	General provisions	Concepts and definitions common to all UCC Articles
Article 2	Sales	Formation, enforcement, performance, and remedies for sales of goods
Article 2a	Leases	Formation, enforcement, performance, and remedies for leases of goods
[UCITA, formerly Article 2b]	[Uniform Computer Information Transactions Act, only in Va. & Md.]	[Formation, enforcement, performance, and remedies for licensing software, data, and computer-delivered information]
Article 3	Commercial paper	Issue, negotiation, and transfer of payment by checks, notes, drafts, and certificates of deposit
Article 4	Bank deposits and collections	Defines relations among banks and their depositors; governs payment and collection process
Article 5	Letters of credit	Defines rights and duties of parties financing or paying in international trade by using letters of credit
Article 6	Bulk transfers	Notice requirement to protect creditors from merchant debtor disposing of all inventory to abscond with proceeds
Article 7	Warehouse receipts, bills of lading, documents of title	Negotiation and transfer process for documentary titles covering goods in transit or in storage
Article 8	Investment securities	Negotiation and transfer of investment securities (e.g., corporate stocks, bonds)
Article 9	Secured transactions	Creation and enforcement of liens on goods; priorities among creditors established

Certainty in international transactions is complicated because different nations have varying approaches to contracting that reflect their cultural, political, and historical differences, their different legal systems, and their differing views on the role of government intervention in commerce. The common law system, based on the rule of precedent, is applicable in the United States, Canada, and most other nations of the former British Empire. The civil law system, based on comprehensive codes or statutes, generally applies in nations with a continental European heritage. There are further differences with Islamic law, socialist law, and the law in some developing nations. Despite some uniformity, each system's unique differences can have an impact on contract duties, formation, performance, and expectations. Civil law nations fill in contract gaps with statutory terms common to all contracts. This policy is adopted by the UCC. Indeed, the most successful commercial law is suppletory, as found in most industrialized nations. **Suppletory law** furnishes common terms to agreements the parties have left incomplete in some way(s). Economists believe it is efficient for commercial laws to allow freedom of contract yet provide standard-form, gap-filling terms if these automatic terms are similar to the ones that would have been negotiated by parties dealing at arm's length.

ONLINE

Find the complete UCC on the Internet **http://www.law.cornell.edu/ucc/ucc.table.html**

Trade between developing countries and industrialized nations reflects an imbalance in bargaining power and in the development of their legal systems. The United Nations Vienna Convention on Contracts for the International Sale of Goods (CISG) governs international sales of goods unless the parties choose by contract to apply some other law.

Dealings between firms in developing and developed nations raise ethical concerns because contracts are negotiated with foreign government officials. Officials in some nations have been known to expect special favors before granting business to foreigners. Concern over such practices led the United States to enact the Foreign Corrupt Practices Act (FCPA), discussed in Chapter 7, to prohibit bribery by U.S. firms or corrupt payments to gain business. The CISG reflects concerns over these problems.

ONLINE

CISG **http://www.uncitral.org/en-index.htm**

Privately adopted rules for commercial practice, the original basis for the law merchant, still have significance in both domestic and international trade. The International Trade Commission (ITC) promulgates commercial rules, called INCOTERMS, which parties may choose to implement in their contracts. Affiliated trading groups like North American Free Trade Association (NAFTA) and the European Union (EU) also regulate some aspects of international trade. In the e-commerce area, the EU has become proactive in promulgating new laws that cover several aspects of e-commerce. Many of these new laws, called EU directives, are discussed throughout this book.

Specific e-commerce laws are also passing in many U.S. states. Two of these new laws are discussed in depth in Part III of this book. The Uniform Electronic Transactions Act (UETA) legitimizes the use of electronic documents, electronic signatures, and electronic agents. UETA has become law in nearly 30 states and is likely to pass soon in the other states. It could eventually become applicable to

http://

www.uncitral.org/

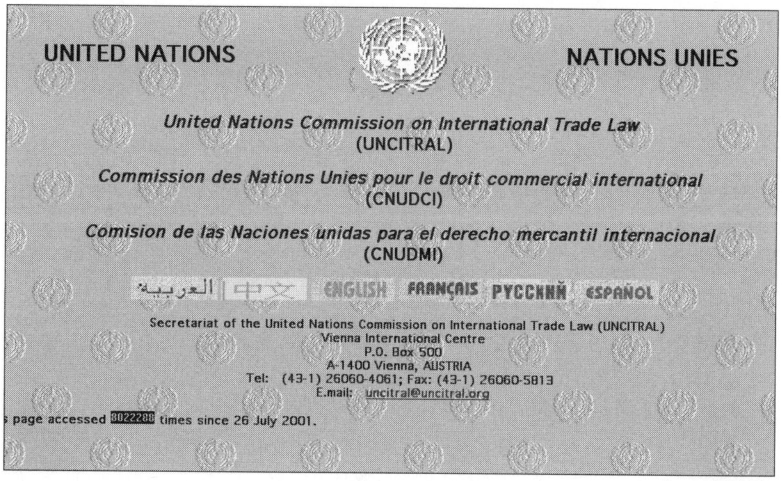

UNITED NATIONS NATIONS UNIES

United Nations Commission on International Trade Law
(UNCITRAL)

Commission des Nations Unies pour le droit commercial international
(CNUDCI)

Comision de las Naciones unidas para el derecho mercantil internacional
(CNUDMI)

العربية | 中文 | ENGLISH FRANÇAIS PYCCKИЙ ESPAÑOL

Secretariat of the United Nations Commission on International Trade Law (UNCITRAL)
Vienna International Centre
P.O. Box 500
A-1400 Vienna, AUSTRIA
Tel: (43-1) 26060-4061; Fax: (43-1) 26060-5813
E.mail: uncitral@uncitral.org

s page accessed 8022288 times since 26 July 2001.

Courtesy, UNCITRAL.

most types of contracts and other legal documents. The Uniform Computer Information Transactions Act (UCITA) was formerly intended to become UCC Article 2B but now stands outside the UCC. UCITA applies to the formation, enforcement, performance, and remedies in contracts for the licensing of software, data, and computer-delivered information. However, it has passed in only two states, Virginia and Maryland, and its prospects for further passage are uncertain. If UCITA is not held to apply to a particular licensing transaction, the common law and the UCC would probably apply.

TYPES OF COMMERCIAL CONTRACTS

Contracts are classified in several ways. **Express contracts** arise from the parties' outward expressions of mutual assent, such as their oral or written statements, gestures, or on-line communications. **Implied in fact contracts** are inferred from the parties' actions. For example, a written employment agreement is an express contract. By contrast, a taxi passenger's contract is often implied in fact. **Bilateral contracts** require two promises, one from each party. In a **unilateral contract**, one of the parties does not expect a return promise but instead asks the other party to actually perform. For example, an offer of reward seeks a unilateral contract: The

Commentary

Jurisdiction: Choice of Law and Forum

When contract interpretation is needed during litigation or settlement negotiations, the law of the jurisdiction *where the contract was made* is usually applied. Some courts would instead apply the law of the jurisdiction *where the major part of contract performance occurs*. This difference in interpretation creates uncertainty that many commercial parties find risky. They seek greater certainty and an opportunity to avoid unfavorable results from the application of law hostile to their position. Experienced commercial contracting parties commonly insert specific contractual terms that select the law of a particular jurisdiction to govern any interpretation of their contract. Such ***choice of law*** provisions are generally enforceable in most industrialized nations. Choice of law is generally optimal when the chosen law is well developed and equitably balances the rights of both sides. For example, Delaware's law of corporations is recognized as fairly well balanced.

Choice of law clauses sometimes favor one party, so they are imposed by the stronger and better informed party on the weaker or less sophisticated party. The stronger party is usually a corporate seller in a business-to-consumer (B2C) transaction or the party with greater market power in a business-to-business (B2B) transaction. Selection of a forum, the jurisdiction where the trial or hearing is conducted, is also commonly made with ***forum selection*** clauses. In many commercial contracts, the parties try to avoid the uncertainties or disadvantages of litigation by choosing alternative dispute resolution (ADR) methods. For example, international B2B supply contracts regularly choose ***arbitration*** of contract disputes rather than risk litigation in the courts of some foreign and potentially hostile court system.

Most contract disputes are governed by the state or national law with the strongest relationship to the contract's formation or performance. However, e-commerce involves a significant component of intellectual property (IP) rights that are generally established by national laws. Many of the IP rights discussed later in Part IV are created under U.S. federal law or under the national laws of other nations. Therefore, although state law generally governs the commercial aspects of e-commerce relations, sometimes the federal law of patents, copyrights, or trademarks must also apply. Consequently, the federal courts usually will hear disputes involving federal IP questions. When an e-commerce dispute involving IP is heard in a federal court, that court usually also decides the accompanying state contract disputes.

offeror makes an express promise to pay the reward if some other party does an act—provides the information sought. The performing party does not accept the reward contract by *promising* to provide the needed information but instead accepts the reward offer by *performance* in actually providing the information. Both bilateral and unilateral contracts are possible under common law, the UCC, and UCITA. Most contracts are bilateral in nature.

A **valid contract** is completely enforceable by either party if it meets all of the necessary legal requirements. A **void contract** is invalid and unenforceable because the contract has an illegal objective or one party is adjudged to have been insane or incompetent during negotiations. A **voidable contract** allows one or both of the parties to rescind or cancel if there is a problem with incapacity, fraud, misrepresentation, duress, undue influence, or mistake. When all the duties have been fully performed by both parties, this contract is an **executed contract.** An **executory contract** has at least some duties by either or both parties that are not yet fully performed. An **unenforceable contract** is one for which a written document was required by the statute of frauds, but none was signed. These contract problems are discussed further in Chapter 12.

ANALYSIS OF E-COMMERCE, USING TRADITIONAL CONTRACTING MODELS

It is useful to analyze emerging e-commerce methods by reference to traditional commercial practice. Electronic contracting is based on existing contract rules and commercial practices. Although some new cyber laws and commercial practices will probably develop to supplement current practice, existing law remains the backbone for e-commerce. Traditional contracting is based on a sequence of conventional activities and resulting conditions that create legally binding mutual obligations between the parties. Contracting between parties has four major components: (1) exchange of information, (2) reaching an agreement with mutual assent, (3) consideration, and (4) performance and payment. Enforceable contracts in both the traditional and on-line environments must have all these elements present.

INFORMATION EXCHANGE MODEL

Under the informational model, prospective buyers and sellers become interested in contracting as they identify each other, begin communicating their interest in contracting, and advertise and describe their products and services. Outside cyberspace, the parties often request and provide information by using various advertising media, trade shows, sales representatives, catalogues, brochures, specifications, and price lists. When third parties are needed to complete the transaction, the parties hire them (e.g., brokers, lenders, carriers). Before the contract is finalized, counterparties often make inquiries regarding terms, revise their product specifications, and modify proposed terms.

Although similar methods are now used in cyberspace, electronic contracting will eventually benefit from the faster speed of communications and the greater access to on-line resources. For example, there will be real-time updates of price and of product availability, and all parties will be able to access larger computer databases of product information. The advantages of cyberspace will permit efficiencies heretofore unavailable in most markets, making it possible to collect and distribute private data about counterparties (e.g., interests, preferences, tastes, creditworthiness, performance quality, reliability). Unless constrained by privacy laws, website operators will collect private information about customer demographics and preferences to target their marketing or assemble into dossiers for sale or barter to other firms. Commercial parties will participate in B2B exchanges, where buyers can post specifications, sellers will help design customized products, specific terms will be negotiated, and final agreements concluded. Internet information exchange also permits the use of business models based on website exposure, measured as "hits" or "eyeballs," and thereby receive compensation for directing visitors to other sites (hyperlinked referrals) or for banner advertisements. All this customer exposure helps build a brand image that enhances the value of trademarks and goodwill and permits heightened use of customer relationship management techniques.

MUTUAL ASSENT MODEL

A wide variety of contract negotiation and conclusion techniques are used both inside and outside cyberspace. Even though the common law traditions were modified by the UCC to conform to modern commercial practice, the basic framework of common law mutual assent dictates the legal expectations for contracts formed in and out of cyberspace. Contracts are formed when an offer is communicated. An offer confers a power of contracting on the offeree, thereby creating a contract when the power is exercised in an acceptance. Contract negotiations via the Internet will mirror these and other common law behaviors, including revocations, rejections, modifications, and repudiations. Contemporary commercial practices prevailing under the UCC will also be adopted in e-commerce. For example, parties will use electronic versions of purchase orders, confirmations, and invoices—each with different terms. This creates a **battle of the forms** problem. Standard terms will be included to improve the predictability and reliability of contracting, particularly in contracts between consumers and merchants. Standard form contracts between merchants will develop from trading partner agreements for electronic data interchange (EDI).

It seems unlikely that written contracts will be abandoned. Documentary evidence of the parties' agreement and contract terms will still be required and is nearly always advisable. The requirement of the statute of frauds for a signed memorandum and the dependability and completeness of writings under the parol evidence rule should play as significant a role in e-commerce as it plays under traditional practice. Indeed, UETA legitimizes the use of computer communications as electronic records that are legally equivalent to written documents. UETA sanctions the use of digital signatures to satisfy the need for authorized signatures on written contracts. The authentication evidencing that the parties actually signed a record may be performed by cybernotaries. Similar assurance may be provided by various encryption techniques. As in the traditional world, contracts may be implied from the parties' on-line conduct. Parties will be bound to only those agreements negotiated and concluded by agents with proper authority, although UETA legitimizes the use of electronic agents. UETA and the redundant federal e-sign law are discussed in Chapter 12.

CONSIDERATION MODEL

The consideration requirement has always posed conceptual challenges for students of contracting. Traditional contracts are enforceable only when each party's promised performance is supported by consideration, a legally binding obligation arising from the parties' mutual assent. The consideration requirement is used to test the seriousness of the bargained-for exchange. A party's promise is unenforceable unless made in exchange for a legally sufficient counterpromise by the other party; that is, each party must make a new and irrevocable commitment to the other. The significance of the consideration requirement has diminished. For example, consideration is not required in some sales of goods under the UCC, or it may be presumed. In B2B contracts, careful contract drafting by experienced lawyers nearly eliminates consideration risks.

However, e-commerce business models purporting to give users "free access" are again raising consideration questions. The mere accessing of a site may obligate users to the website's license restrictions and require them to provide private information or accept privacy-tracking "cookies" that the website or its affiliates may access later. It is still useful to analyze e-commerce by using the consideration model because it can resolve legal rights when the profit-making expectations of website operators must accommodate the Internet culture's expectations for "free-surfing."

PERFORMANCE MODEL

The performance of contracts via computer communications poses some of the greatest challenges for e-commerce. Currently, only intangible personal property can be transmitted electronically via communications networks like the Internet. Today, it is physically possible to download documents, data, artistic expression or literary works, music, consulting reports, professional advice, software, images, audio or video files, orders, notices, and documentary transfers. For the foreseeable future, the performance of contract duties involving the delivery of tangible property will not be made via the Internet. Physical delivery of tangibles must be made personally or through agents such as a delivery service.

Money, document, and title transfers are contract obligations that can be made electronically. The electronic transfer of payments (e-payments) and electronic recording, custody, transmittal, presentment, and endorsement of formal contracts such as commercial documents (e.g., documents of title, warehouse receipts) can be made via the Internet. Wire transfer of funds began soon after the first transatlantic telegraph cable was laid in the 1800s. Today, electronic funds transfers (EFT) are a majority of all funds transferred.

The law and commercial practice developed under these four traditional contract components are useful in analyzing e-commerce because they are the paradigm for the evolution of commerce into cyberspace. Although a few cyber laws may radically change this traditional practice, many if not most traditional contracting elements will probably survive the evolution to e-commerce. It is now useful to analyze the needs for new cyber laws by reference to the emerging types of on-line contracts already in use.

TYPES OF ON-LINE CONTRACTS

Several types of e-commerce commercial contracting are in current use. Further innovation in communications, computers, and business methods are likely to encourage additional advances. An accepted method of classifying e-commerce is through traditional supply chain concepts, which generates three distinct on-line markets, each with its separate architecture and differing legal requirements. First, the B2B market involves procurement transactions among suppliers of raw materials or component parts to assemblers, as well as from wholesale suppliers to retailers. There have been extensive e-commerce developments in the B2B markets, including the widespread development of EDI. The ABA's Electronic Messaging Services Task Force defines EDI as "the transmission, in standard syntax, of unambiguous information between computers of two or more independent organizations."

In practice, EDI refers to a system of interconnected computers, using dedicated and secure telephone lines and/or satellite connections to link merchant buyers, sellers, their banks, carriers, warehouses, customs officials, and trade brokers. EDI systems envision repeated transactions between regular suppliers and customers that use electronic ordering, confirmation, invoicing, record keeping, payment or financing, and transmittal or negotiation of trade documents. The terms of EDI contracts are generally stated in an umbrella contract, which the ABA refers to as a trading partner agreement. This contract permits the sale of varying quantities and types of goods at various delivery dates and at changing prices. However, most other terms are held constant. EDI systems may permit some human intervention. Some EDI systems may automatically make daily merchandise restocking orders, much like Wal-Mart's pioneering EDI system. At this writing, there are in development several hundred B2B exchanges (online electronic marketplaces) that envision using the Internet rather than dedicated, secure communications. Many of these markets would permit participation by many competing buyers and sellers.

The second major type of e-commerce market is consumer retail or business to consumer (B2C). Such markets sell goods generally through website shopping transactions, such as Amazon.com, or dispense computer services and information through fee-based subscription services, such as America Online (AOL). Website B2C shopping usually involves customers browsing on-line catalogues, specifications, and price lists before communicating a purchase order directly online, through other electronic means (e.g., fax, phone), or via the mail. Consumer payments may be effected on line or via other means (e.g., phone credit card, check). Deliveries of tangible goods are usually made off line by delivery service, although customers can sometimes pick up the goods physically at a distribution center. The B2C subscription services include on-line service providers (OSPs), also known as Internet service providers (ISPs), which charge subscribers a periodic fee for access, a pay-per-view fee charged by the amount of time used, or at various rates depending on the different costs of the particular content accessed. The standard subscription agreement often has aspects of a license. Most ISPs have abandoned charging fees in favor of business models deriving revenue from banner ads or the collection and resale of private data. LexisNexis and Westlaw are fee-based subscription computer information and research services that charge variable pay-per-view rates; they are commonly used in legal and financial research.

The third type of e-commerce market is consumer to consumer (C2C). They most resemble electronic want ads, flea markets, or auctions but use Internet facilities such as electronic bulletin boards, chat sites, or e-mail communications. At this writing, e-Bay is the best known example of this e-commerce model. The contractual terms of trade range quite broadly. Some are open, permitting the parties to negotiate and arrange for payment and delivery, such as those often found on an electronic bulletin board. Other systems impose rules of trade that are set by system software and security features, such as those found in many of the more successful on-line auction sites.

TRANSACTIONS' SUBJECT MATTER DETERMINES WHAT LAW APPLIES

The essential threshold inquiry in analyzing transactions is the classification of the transaction's subject matter; that is, the main consideration exchanged must be identified. Transactions primarily for the purchase of land, professional service engagements, or regular employment are generally governed by the common law of contracts as supplemented by various regulatory regimens. The UCC Article 2 governs contracts for the sale of goods. **Goods** are tangible personal property (not real estate), which the UCC defines in §2-105(1) as "all that are movable at the time of contracting." While the UCC is based in the common law, it also conforms to commercial practice. Therefore, UCC provisions often supplement and occasionally change the common law rules. International sales of goods are covered by the CISG, although many international B2B supply arrangements may choose to apply other laws or private commercial rules. Auctions of goods are covered by the UCC, supplemented by each auction's own rules. Auctions of services were so infrequent historically that the applicable law is uncertain. However, the service auctions beginning to appear in cyberspace will probably follow the common law but be modified somewhat by practices used in goods auctions and with each auction's own unique rules.

E-commerce transactions often involve the licensing (temporary right to use) or assignment (outright sale) of intellectual property (IP) or other data and information. The common law governs licensing and assignments but is supplemented by federal IP law. However, a new licensing law, the Uniform Computer Information Transactions Act (UCITA), may apply to IP licensing. UCITA is discussed throughout the chapters in Part III and is applicable in those states that have adopted it, thus far only Virginia and Maryland. Additionally, UCITA may also apply to contracts where local law permits the contract to invoke the licensing law from another state that has adopted UCITA. UCITA exempts transactions in electronic information in several industries with stable contracting environments: TV, movies, recorded music, and print publishing. The mere use of e-mail or other electronic communications to reach an agreement for land, goods, or services does not make UCITA applicable. At this writing, there is an effort to apply the UCC Article 2 to transactions in software, perhaps preempting the application of UCITA.

Despite the apparent complexity of e-commerce transactions, the discussion in this book usually begins with the common law rules and then considers when other laws may be applicable. Exhibit 10.2 summarizes the application of major laws that affect the formation, interpretation, performance, and terms of e-commerce transactions.

Most commercial contracts have multiple subject matters. For example, most buyers believe that the predominant subject matter in the contract are the goods, the land, or the services purchased. By contrast, the seller is much more concerned with the buyer's payment. The UCC has several other articles (3, 4, 5, 7, and 9) governing performance of the payment, credit, and transfer or custody obligations. In addition, many transactions have subject matter mixed between goods, services, and information. One classic example is the warranty accompanying a sale of goods; another example is a restaurant's sale of food (goods) accompanied by the service of preparing and serving the food. In such transactions, the UCC applies if goods predominate in the transaction, such as the sale of a new car sold with a warranty for service and repair. The common law applies if land or services predominate and the goods sale is only incidental, such as a restaurant's service of food. Despite this latter general rule, the UCC's warranties discussed in Chapter 12 cover restaurant food services.

UCITA is intended to cover transactions to create, modify, transfer, or license computer information or information rights (e.g., software, data) when in electronic form either obtained from or through a computer or if licensed for computer processing (UCITA §103(a)). UCITA applies only to the information aspects of a transaction, leaving other appropriate laws to apply to the noninformation subject matter. For example, the UCC applies to the goods aspects of a transaction unless

EXHIBIT 10.2 Application of Various Laws to E-Commerce Contracts

Subject Matter of Contract	Law Applicable to Contract Formation, Interpretation, and Performances	Other Laws Potentially Relevant to E-Commerce Transactions
Interest in land	Common Law	Agency; real estate conveyancing; mortgages; environmental regulations; UCC Articles 3, 4, 5, 7, and/or 9, E-SIGN or UETA if enacted
Professional Services	Common Law, UCITA where enacted for independent contractors in information service contracts	Agency; professional ethical regulations; UCC Articles 3, 4, 5, 7, and/or 9, E-SIGN or UETA if enacted
Employment	Common Law	Agency; labor law; regulation of equal employment and compensation; UCC Articles 3, 4, 5, 7, and/or 9, E-SIGN or UETA if enacted
Goods [software]	UCC Article 2	Agency; UCC Articles 3, 4, 5, 7, and/or 9, E-SIGN or UETA if enacted
Leases of goods	UCC Article 2A	Agency; UCC Articles 3, 4, 5, 7, and/or 9, E-SIGN or UETA if enacted
Information, software, IP, data: contracts to license, create, modify, or transfer	Common Law or UCITA where enacted [Va. & Md.]	Agency; federal or international IP laws
Securities	UCC Article 8	Agency; state corporation laws; federal securities regulations; UCC Articles 3, 4, 5, 7, and/or 9
Performances: payments, credit, and Goods Transfer or Custody	UCC Articles 3, 4, 5, 7, and/or 9	Agency, E-SIGN or UETA if enacted

computer information is the "primary subject matter" and the goods aspects are merely an incidental portion. The UCC applies when computer information is embedded in goods, such as the diagnostics in a car engine's control computer. Contracting parties may either "opt in" to the application of UCITA or "opt out" of UCITA, as long as the safeguards of UCITA §103(e) are satisfied.

UETA enables business and government to agree to use electronic forms of records, signatures, acknowledgments, and notarization. UCITA permits the use of either electronic or paper documents, calling them **records,** to effect the communications for contracting or to satisfy any need for written contract documents. Both UCITA §102(54) and UETA §2(13) define **record** as "information that is inscribed on a tangible medium or that is stored in an electronic or other medium and is retrievable in perceivable form." UETA defines **electronic record** as a "record created, generated, sent, communicated, received, or stored by electronic means." UETA is more procedural than substantive, a perspective dramatized by this caricature: "The medium shall not be the message." UETA requires no standard or particular form of electronic transaction. Instead, UETA validates the use of electronic means where traditional paper documents and signatures were previously required. It permits but does not require electronic contracting; that is, parties must agree to use electronic records and electronic signatures rather than their written counterparts. When parties agree to transact electronically, their records, signatures, and contracts must be enforced if made in electronic form. Therefore, electronic records and electronic signatures will satisfy the requirements of other laws that require signatures and writings. UETA must be applied to facilitate electronic transactions, and it must be construed to be consistent with reasonable commercial practice and to promote uniformity among the states. It applies only prospectively—that is, to transactions using electronic records or electronic signatures that are created, generated, sent, communicated, received, or stored after the adopting legislation becomes effective. For states that do not adopt UETA, these matters are governed by the federal **E-SIGN** law officially known as the Electronic Signatures in Global and National Commerce Act. UETA and the federal E-SIGN law are discussed in Chapter 12.

CONCLUDING AN AGREEMENT

The formation of a contract is generally known as mutual assent. In international parlance, these are the activities that **conclude an agreement.** Before a bilateral contract arises, the parties must agree to the contract's terms, a step known as **mutual assent.** In traditional and "big ticket" contracting, the parties begin preliminary negotiations by communicating expectations about what they consider to be favorable terms. For example, an advertisement, salesperson's pitch, or website information may start the negotiations. By contrast, contracts with smaller "stakes" have smaller profit margins and generally lesser consequences for both buyer and seller, which usually make it uneconomical for most sellers and many buyers to engage in extensive negotiating formalities that impose high transactions costs. Indeed, **form contracting** is a twentieth-century efficiency innovation that has nearly eliminated the transaction costs of negotiating, particularly in B2C transactions. In most retail contracts, large sellers set "take-it-or-leave-it" terms, sometimes called **boilerplate.** Consumers have little power to change these standardized terms. In a few instances, some sellers find a competitive advantage in varying a few contract terms, particularly the price on big-ticket items. Still, consumers seldom negotiate much, and many prefer the low stress and simplicity of not haggling at all.

Populist pressures for consumer protection legislation illustrate the major exception to laissez faire. Consumer protection laws usually are not passed until after long experience with entire industries that uniformly adopt nearly identical terms that favor sellers. It appears that e-commerce B2C transactions could follow this model. Despite the potential for lower transaction costs with the use of electronic negotiations, most B2C on-line transactions are largely "take-it-or-leave-it," based on arcane boilerplate terms that largely benefit the seller. Buyers often ignore this "legalese," choosing to quickly click through and thereby accept them, often ignorant of the rights they surrender and the duties they accept. The discussion of UETA and UCITA in Part III examines a few such consumer protection provisions in both laws.

The stated terms of a contract must usually identify the parties, adequately describe the subject matter, state the price (i.e., the cash, property, or services), indicate the quantity of the product or services, fix the time for each party's performance, and include any other key terms (e.g., credit, warranties). The parties' early communications may be merely informational or can be cast in the form of offers and counteroffers. A fine line distinguishes mere informational communications from the five operative contracting communications: offer, acceptance, revocation, rejection, and counteroffer. This distinction is based on the objective theory of contracts.

OBJECTIVE THEORY OF CONTRACTS

All expressions of the contracting parties are judged objectively by a reasonable person's interpretation. The objective theory of contracts applies to all communications between parties to distinguish mere (1) preliminary negotiations and (2) inquiries regarding terms from more serious communications such as (3) offers, (4) counteroffers, (5) acceptances, (6) revocations, and (7) rejections. The first two of these are informational communications that do not create, exercise, or terminate the power of contracting. By contrast, the latter five do affect the power of contracting. An offeror's statement is a legal offer if a reasonable person would conclude that the offeror clearly intended to confer a power of acceptance on the offeree and that the offeree need only accept to create a contract. The offeror's hidden intent or secret hesitation is irrelevant. For example, a casual person might make a proposal, but only in jest. Such a proposal might be an offer irrespective of the emotional person's intent if a reasonable person believes it was intended as an offer. Many behavioral observers of cyberspace communications believe that e-mail messages are all too often flippant or emotionally inspired. Therefore, care must be taken in making electronic communications or interpreting them as operative contracting communications. Offers and acceptances are particularly critical because society believes that frivolous statements should not lead to binding contract obligations.

THE OFFER

An **offer** is a proposal to contract that contains all of the necessary contract terms. The proposal must be intended by the offeror to confer a power of acceptance on the offeree. An offer becomes effective only after it is communicated—that is, when received by the offeree. The offer is usually oral or written, but occasionally it can be communicated by gestures, such as the way bids are made at some auctions. Written offers may be made in electronic communications, such as by telephone, fax, e-mail, website response or submission, chat room communication, or bulletin board posting. As additional electronic communications become commonplace, they will probably satisfy the requirement for effective communication among contracting parties. Consider the digital order entry using the telephone keypad in the following case.

The Formation of Contracts

Dealings between companies residing in the Pacific Rim contrast with U.S. contracting practices. For example, the Japanese respect long-term B2B supplier-customer relations that are nurtured slowly to form a reasonable basis for trust, long-term commitment, and sustained performance. There is generally no rush into contracts with foreign firms. Instead, Japanese firms rely on a drawn-out negotiation of relationships, not contracts. They prefer to focus on the prospects for harmony and the evolution of their relationship. They focus less on the immediate favorability of particular contract terms. In Japan extensive socializing probes the intentions of another firm's representatives before deals are finalized. Negotiators in Mexico follow a similar model. Although this practice may appear extremely time-consuming and inefficient to impatient Americans, it is fundamental to making sound relationships of trust in the view of Asians and Latin Americans.

Since the 1990s, an increasing number of U.S. B2B customers and suppliers have established ongoing relationships using EDI. These relationships generally use an umbrella agreement, called a ***trading partner agreement***, to govern all future orders. EDI is discussed later in this chapter. The Japanese contracting model has high transaction costs, so it is efficient only for enduring B2B supply relationships. By contrast, the fast pace of e-commerce dealings suggests there will be a growth in on-line negotiations and continued use of boilerplate to reduce the transaction costs of prolonged negotiations.

Corinthian Pharmaceutical Systems v. Lederle Laboratories

724 F.Supp. 605 (S.D.Ind. 1989)

Facts. Corinthian is a drug wholesaler and customer of Lederle, a pharmaceutical manufacturer. Lederle implemented a telephone-actuated computer order entry system, called Telgo, to facilitate customer orders. The customer enters order data by using the telephone keypad. When Corinthian learned of an impending future price increase for DPT vaccine to $171 per vial, Corinthian placed an order via Telgo for 1,000 vials of DPT at an old price list amount of $51 per vial. Corinthian was automatically provided a confirmation by Telgo with an order-tracking number indicating a price of $64.32 per vial. Lederle shipped only 50 vials at the $64.32 price with a accompanying letter stating the remaining 950 vials would be priced at $171, that the 50 vials were an accommodation, and that Corinthian could cancel the orders. Corinthian sued for breach of contract when Lederle refused to perform at the $64.32 price.

Legal Issue. Does an electronic order constitute an acceptance of an offer at the prevailing posted price?

Opinion. A sale of goods is covered by the Uniform Commercial Code, and both parties are merchants under the Code. The starting point in this analysis is where did the first offer originate. An offer is "the manifestation of willingness to enter into a bargain, so made as to justify another person in understanding that his assent to that bargain is invited and will conclude it." The only possible conclusion in this case is that Corinthian's "order" for 1,000 vials at $64.32 was the first offer. Nothing that the seller had done prior to this point can be interpreted as an offer. First, the price lists distributed by Lederle to its customers did not constitute offers. It is well settled that quotations are mere invitations to make an offer, particularly where, as here, the price lists specifically stated that prices were subject to change without notice and that all orders were subject to acceptance by Lederle.

The letter, just like the price lists, was a mere quotation (i.e., an invitation to submit an offer) sent to all customers. As such, it did not bestow on Corinthian nor other customers the power to form a binding contract for the sale of one thousand, or, for that matter, one million vials of vaccine. Thus, as a matter of law, the first offer was made by Corinthian when it phoned in and subsequently confirmed its order for 1,000 vials at the lower price. The next question, then, is whether Lederle ever accepted that offer.

Under the Code, an acceptance need not be the mirror-image of the offer. However, the offeree must still do some act that manifests the intention to accept the offer and make a contract. Under §2-206, an offer to make a contract shall be construed as inviting acceptance in any manner and by any medium reasonable in the circumstances. The record is clear that Lederle did not communicate or do any act prior to shipping the 50 vials that could support the finding of an acceptance. When Corinthian placed its order, it merely received a tracking number from the Telgo computer. Such an automated, ministerial act cannot constitute an acceptance.

Under the Code a seller accepts the offer by shipping goods, whether they are conforming or not, but if the seller ships non-conforming goods and seasonably notifies the buyer that the shipment is a mere accommodation, then the seller has not, in fact, accepted the buyer's offer. An accommodation is an arrangement or engagement made as a favor to another. The term implies no consideration. In this case, then, even taking all inferences favorably for the buyer, the only possible conclusion is that Lederle Labs' shipment of 50 vials was offered merely as an accommodation; that is to say, Lederle had no obligation to make the partial shipment, and did so only as a favor to the buyer. The accommodation letter, which Corinthian is sure it received, clearly stated that the 50 vials were being sent at the lower price as an exception to Lederle's general policy, and that the balance of the offer would be invoiced at the higher price. The letter further indicated that Lederle's proposal to ship the balance of the order at the higher price could be rejected by the buyer.

Thus, the end result of this analysis is that Lederle Lab's price quotations were mere invitations to make an offer, that by placing its order Corinthian made an offer to buy 1,000 vials at the low price, that by shipping 50 vials at the low price Lederle's response was non-conforming, but the non-conforming response was a mere accommodation and thus constituted a counteroffer.

Decision. Phone order using keypad to communicate data is an offer, not acceptance of catalog and price list advertisement.

Case Questions

1. Why was Lederle's electronic response with an order-tracking number to Corinthian not considered an acceptance of Corinthian's order?
2. Why should a supplier have the opportunity to consider an order for standard goods at a posted price before a binding contract is formed?

Problems may occur in interpreting whether business communications are really offers. Generally, advertisements for goods or services are merely intended as invitations to deal; they are seldom actual offers. The objective reasonable person would presume that advertisements, solicitation letters, catalogues, and price lists are intended merely to arouse the interest of a potential buyer who would negotiate after receiving such information. If advertisements were routinely considered offers, then a contract could be too easily created. For example, not many sellers would be prepared with sufficient inventory if too many of these "offerees" responded to a particular advertisement. Because it is reasonable to assume that advertisers do not want this out-of-stock problem, their advertisements are not offers, only preliminary negotiations. This is not to say that an advertisement could not be worded to clearly indicate an offer. An advertiser could invite immediate acceptance. For example, language such as "while they last" in an advertisement could create an offer. Offer and acceptance are illustrated in Exhibit 10.3.

TERMINATION OF OFFERS

As long as an offer remains open, the offeree is free to create a contract by accepting the offer. However, the offeree's ability to exercise the contracting power can be terminated. Offers are terminated by the passage of time (lapse), revocation, rejection, acceptance, the death of either party, or the destruction of the contract's subject matter.

Lapse of Time

Offers do not confer a permanent power of acceptance. Offers are terminated by the passage of a reasonable time, a period that varies, depending on the circumstances. Offers terminate quickly in volatile markets (e.g., stock, currency, or commodities exchanges) and when parties leave a face-to-face encounter. By contrast, in more stable markets, such as real estate, an offer can have a longer life, perhaps days, weeks, or even months. These rules should apply to e-commerce negotiations. For example, assent to on-line investments in the financial markets is usually instantaneous or subject to publicized rules permitting market-induced delays in executing trades. An offer may expire in virtual negotiations if the parties cease communicating for even a few minutes. An offeror who wants the offer to terminate at a specific time may limit its duration by specifying that the offer lapses under its own terms after the time passes. For example, prospective home buyers often specify that their offers

EXHIBIT 10.3 Offer and Acceptance

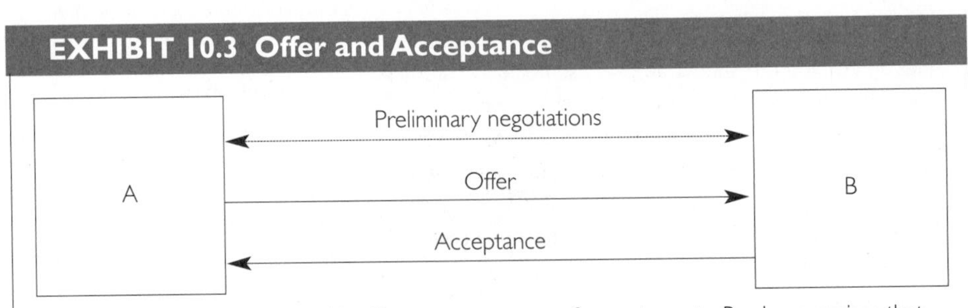

After preliminary negotiations, A's offer passes a power of acceptance to B, who exercises that power and a contract results when B dispatches an acceptance to A. For example, if A offers to purchase B's house and B mails an acceptance to A, an enforceable contract exists.

lapse in a few hours or days. This tactic creates an imminence to induce a reluctant seller to accept a particular price.

Revocations

Usually, the offeror may withdraw an offer by the act of **revocation** at any time before acceptance. A revocation is effective when expressed directly by the offeror to the offeree. A revocation may be implied, such as when the offeree receives reliable knowledge that the offered property was sold to another person. Revocation is illustrated in Exhibit 10.4.

In some instances, an offeror can make a binding promise *not to revoke* an offer. **Irrevocable offers** are useful, for example, when the offeree must spend time and money to survey or research the subject matter before agreeing. If the offer is held open, the offeree has more time to study it without fear of losing the deal. There are two ways to make an offer irrevocable: option contracts and firm offers. An **option contract** is formed when the offeree pays a price (consideration) for irrevocability. The option becomes a separate contractual commitment in which the offeror gives up the right to revoke in return for the consideration. Options are valid in sales of goods, but they are used extensively to tie up real estate while buyers consider other alternatives. Options to purchase securities, called puts and calls, are common forms of speculative investment.

Options to purchase *goods* under the UCC can be made without any consideration paid by the buyer. A **firm offer** can be made by a merchant in a signed writing, which creates an irrevocable offer even without payment of consideration. A firm offer is irrevocable for a reasonable time, as stated in the offer, but no longer than three months. An offeror who revokes a firm offer or sells optioned property to another person breaches the option contract and would be liable for damages. For example, assume that in a signed writing a merchant makes an offer to sell a buyer 500 widgets at $30 each. If the merchant promises to keep the offer open for two weeks but then withdraws it the next day, the buyer may enforce the contract. In some civil law nations, offers must stay open for a minimum period, such as three days. The CISG makes firm offers enforceable even if they are not made in writing.

Rejection

An offeree may refuse an offer by communicating a **rejection**, which terminates the offeree's power of acceptance. However, care is necessary because not every response

EXHIBIT 10.4 Revocation

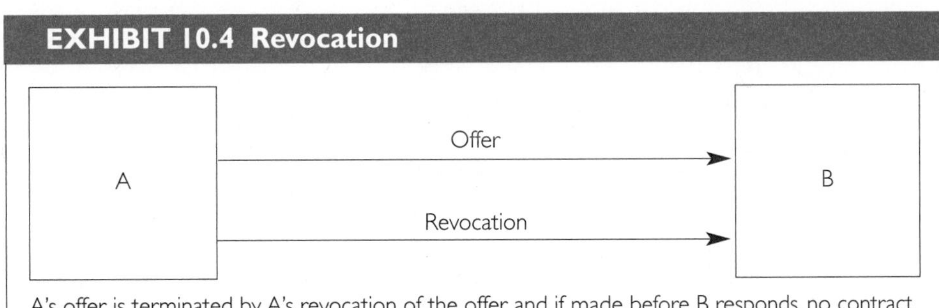

A's offer is terminated by A's revocation of the offer, and if made before B responds, no contract results. For example, if A offers to purchase B's house but has a change of heart before B responds, A may withdraw the offer by revocation and no contract results.

by an offeree constitutes an unequivocal rejection. For example, it is not a rejection for an offeree to merely request additional information or to ask the offeror to consider changing the terms. This is an **inquiry regarding terms**, which is compared with rejection in Exhibit 10.5.

Counteroffer

By contrast, an offeree might appear to accept an offer but also attach additional or different conditions to the apparent acceptance. This type of response is often called a **conditional acceptance.** When an offeree revises the offered terms in this or any other way, it is still considered a counteroffer. Both conditional acceptances and counteroffers reject and terminate the offer because they lack exact agreement with the offered terms. When negotiating with counteroffers, the parties exchange several offers, none of which is accepted. If the offered terms and the accepted terms deviate, no contract results because the parties have failed to agree; that is, the offer and the offeree's response are not a mirror image of each other, so there is no meeting of their minds. Instead, each response to the previous offer is a counteroffer. Eventually, a contract may result when the last counteroffer is *un*conditionally accepted by the last offeree. Counteroffers are often the negotiating method used in residential real estate sales. *Counter* is a slang term for making a counteroffer.

Both the UCC and UCITA treat conditional acceptances as counteroffers, and contracts are enforceable only when any new conditions are accepted. No contract arises until the original offeror accepts the different terms that the offeree imposes in the conditional acceptance or counteroffer. If the parties use standard forms that include a conditional acceptance, they must wait for acceptance of the conditional terms before performing. Otherwise, a contract exists, but the conditional or additional terms are not accepted. Counteroffer is illustrated in Exhibit 10.6.

ACCEPTANCE

For a contract to be formed, the offeree must accept the offer (recall the illustration in Exhibit 10.3). A contract comes into existence when the offeree accepts all the terms, exactly as proposed. This results in an express agreement, a clear **meeting of the minds**. In one form of negotiating, informal communications between the parties take place before either actually makes an offer. Later, a formal offer, containing all of the terms already acceptable to both parties, is made by one party and formally accepted by the other. Businesses often use this form in more complex contracting,

EXHIBIT 10.5 Rejection

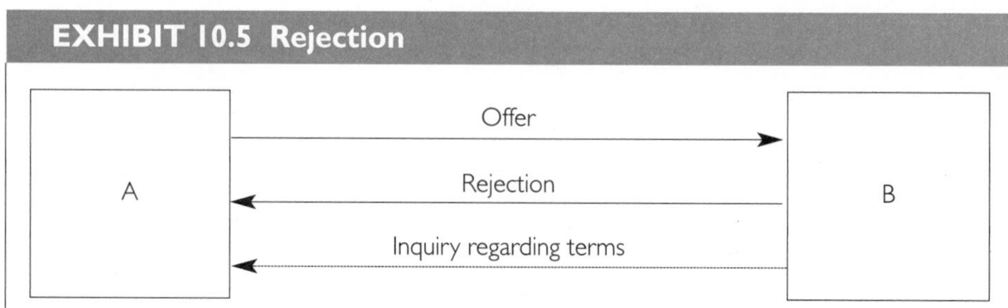

A's offer is terminated by B's rejection of the offer so no contract results. For example, if A offers to purchase B's house and B immediately rejects the offer, no contract results. However, a mere inquiry regarding terms does not terminate the offer.

EXHIBIT 10.6 Counteroffer

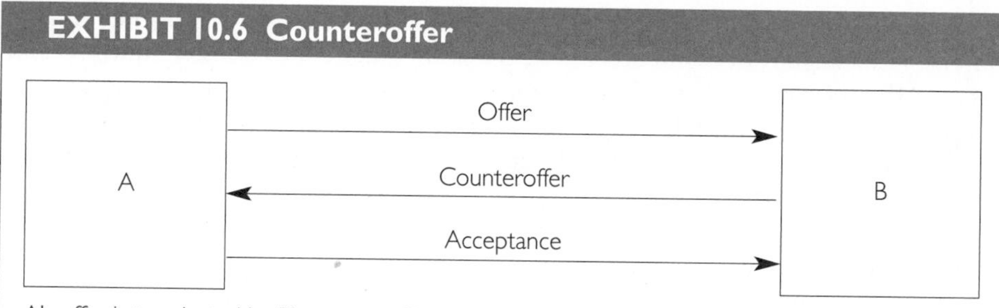

A's offer is terminated by B's counteroffer or conditional acceptance, but B extends a new offer to A. The contract results when A dispatches an acceptance in response to B's counteroffer. For example, if A offers to purchase B's house but B counteroffers at a higher price, then no contract exists unless A accepts B's counteroffer.

such as with a supplier or commercial customer. Another form of contracting involves negotiating by changing the offered terms, with each party making a counteroffer to the prior offer. In a third variation, the offeree neither inquires nor objects but accepts on the offered terms. Much of the on-line e-commerce in B2C markets uses this third form, a "take-it-or-leave-it" approach using standard terms and form contracts. UCITA has some special rules for **form contracts.**

> Form contracts under UCITA §102(60): "records containing terms prepared for repeated use in transactions [when used if] there was no negotiated change of terms by individuals except to set the price, quantity, method of payment, selection among standard options, or time or method of delivery."

An acceptance need not be communicated to be effective. An acceptance can be implied from the offeree's conduct. For example, a Web user who continues accessing a free website, after learning of particular terms in the access license, could be bound to those terms. Consider the many websites that restrict access to users who agree to the website's use license. Many websites collect information about users' Web surfing and access history (clickstream) for advertising, target marketing, and resale. Use of the website under these conditions could obligate users not to defeat the website's collection of private data if the user has impliedly accepted the license's privacy policy.

TIMING AND EFFECT OF CONTRACTING COMMUNICATIONS

For a contracting communication to confer, exercise, or terminate the power of acceptance, the sending party must intend the communication to affect the power of contracting. Most communications between parties are effective only when actually received. Generally, offers, revocations, rejections, and counteroffers are effective when and if received. However, one major exception, the **mailbox rule**, makes certain acceptances effective when dispatched. A dispatch occurs when the offeree has done everything that can be done to send off the acceptance. For example, a contract immediately comes into existence the moment a diligent offeree drops a properly addressed, stamped letter of acceptance into a U.S. Postal Service mailbox. Acceptances are also effective upon dispatch if any other reasonable method is used that has been invited by the offeror. The acceptance is effective even if a rejection or revocation arrives before the acceptance ultimately arrives or is lost.

The relevance of the mailbox rule has diminished. First, if the offeree uses an unreasonable means of communication, the acceptance is not effective until receipt. Second, the offer may specify that no contract becomes binding until the acceptance is actually received. Third, UCC §2-206 is more lenient. An acceptance is effective if it is communicated by any reasonable method under the circumstances in common use, and if it is as fast as or faster than the means used by the offeror. For example, a faxed acceptance would be effective to create a contract based on a mailed letter of offer. Fourth, acceptances communicated by instantaneous communications, such as telephone or telex, are effective upon receipt. However, e-mail is not always instantaneous, so analysis under some special rules of UCITA and UETA may be necessary. Fifth, UCITA §203(4)(a) makes electronic acceptance or performance effective on receipt. Sixth, under international law, the CISG makes acceptances effective upon receipt, and a similar rule applies under the civil law of many nations.

There is a rebuttable presumption that the U.S. mail reliably delivers mail. A return receipt or electronic acknowledgment helps prove delivery. These factors should also apply to private mail services, as should a signature tracing saved to a delivery driver's electronic tablet. As nearly instantaneous electronic messaging becomes more widespread in contract negotiation, all electronic messages are likely to be considered delivered and effective when they arrive in retrievable format on the recipient's system. UCITA encourages the use of electronic acknowledgments; essentially, these are automatic, semiautomatic, or manual electronic replies indicating a message was received by the intended recipient. However, under UCITA §215(b), "Receipt . . . by itself does not establish that the content sent corresponds to the content received." As regular users of e-mail will recognize, replies and forwards often include the text of the prior message(s), but it can be difficult to determine if the earlier text remains unaltered.

UETA does not attempt to change substantive commercial laws; it seeks only to validate use of electronic communications. In UETA §15, electronic records are considered sent when (1) properly addressed to a system designated by the recipient, (2) in a form capable of processing by the recipient's system, and (3) the information enters a system outside the sender's (or sender's agent's) system. Receipt under UETA occurs when the record reaches the recipient's designated system and is capable of processing by that system. Therefore, under UETA, sending and receipt are nearly simultaneous for many contracting partners, almost eliminating the risk of competing revocation and acceptance timing. UETA does not require that the individual recipient must receive personal notice for the receipt to be valid.

CONTRACT FORMATION UNDER THE UCC

The UCC generally requires the same elements of a valid contract as the common law: mutual assent, consideration, no defenses to formation, and legality. The UCC adopts most common law offer and acceptance doctrines but simplifies the formation of sales contracts as is done in commercial practice. UCC §2-206 permits both bilateral and unilateral contracts. The UCC rejects the rigid common law acceptance rules by permitting acceptance in any commercially reasonable manner. An acceptance of an order (offer) is possible with either a prompt promise to ship or with an actual, prompt shipment of goods that conform to the order's specifications. The shipment of nonconforming goods is the simultaneous acceptance of the order, and it also breaches the contract unless the seller indicates the shipment is made as an accommodation.

Auctions

The century-old auction device is changing; many successful auctions today are conducted on line. In the traditional "open outcry" form of auction, the owner of goods or land hires an auctioneer to advertise the public sale event to attract bidders. At the appointed time, interested purchasers physically attend the event or communicate bids remotely by telephone or other electronic means. Bidding generally starts low, although some sellers set a minimum bid. Bidders then make successively higher competing bids until only one winning bidder remains—the one who made the last and highest offer. Under free market economic theory, the auction mechanism is the primary method of transaction exchange.

Auction sales present a problem of identifying which party is the offeror and which is the offeree. Under the common law of auction sales, the identities of the offeror and offeree are defined by the apparent intent of the parties. Sellers at many auctions want to retain the right to withdraw goods from the auction block if they decide the bids are too low. To accomplish this, the bids must be designated offers. This means the auctioneer's final act of knocking down the goods to the highest bidder would work as an acceptance. Most auctions concern goods, so UCC rules often apply. Under UCC §2-328, an auction of this kind is called an **auction with reserve** because the seller is considered to reserve the right to withdraw goods from the auction block before final sale.

Of course, the offeror-offeree designations can be switched in an auction, so that each bid is an acceptance of the auctioneer's offer in placing the goods on the block. A fiction is created to accomplish sales under this system. Each next higher bid is considered to replace the previous bid and cancel the contract created by the previous bid. The final acceptance occurs when the bidding stops, and the enforceable contract is formed when the goods are finally knocked down to the last and highest bidder. An auction of this kind is called an **auction without reserve** because the auctioneer does not reserve the right to withdraw the goods after bidding starts. Most auctions choose to operate with reserve unless the auction notice explicitly indicates otherwise. Auctions without reserve may be necessary when sellers are desperate because auctions without reserve tend to draw bargain hunters.

On-Line Auctions

In practice, few markets still use the traditional auction method. Indeed, there are many auction variations. For example, there are **sealed bids** in which the identity of competing bidders and/or their bids is kept confidential. The time open for receiving bids can be extended for hours, days, or even weeks. Electronic facilities can match orders for sale and purchase much like stocks trade on the New York Stock Exchange's computer, the NYSE DOT. Electronic auctions hold promise for C2C, B2C and B2B markets.

ONLINE

eBay's transaction security measures description
http://www.ebay.com

On-line auctions in the future will probably enforce terms of auction trade that increase their reliability. Auctions failing to provide such assurance are unlikely to succeed in the long run. Auctions involving B2B commerce are also developing, and some may radically change the supply chain because of **disintermediation**—the elimination of middle men, wholesalers, and resellers who add no real value for buyers.

E-B2B Exchanges

The Internet has spawned interest in the auctioning of goods and services. Auctions for services were historically limited to charity events. However, B2B and B2C

Commentary

E-Commerce Controversy: eBay's Transaction Security Measures

The popular eBay Internet C2C and B2C auction market may form a model for on-line auctions in the future. An analysis of the eBay user agreement reveals many of the auction rules needed to build user confidence in the reliability of this exchange method. Membership and contractual capacity are required for bidders and sellers. Registration permits the auction house to facilitate binding transactions and deny access to abusers. Sellers pay agency fees to eBay for the privilege of selling, and eBay asserts it is only a venue—that is, a place for others to conduct transactions. It does not close transactions; instead, the parties must process payments, assure deliveries, and take the risk that the goods are described accurately and that the buyer is creditworthy. Moreover, eBay has facilities to reduce transaction risks: (1) an escrow service to withhold payment until the buyer inspects, (2) a reputation bulletin board about regular buyers and sellers where previous counterparties can comment on a participant's reliability, (3) a dispute resolution method between buyers and sellers and an arbitration requirement for disputes with eBay, and (4) insurance coverage for undelivered or wrongly described items.

auctions of professional services are emerging. For example, outside independent attorneys can bid on corporate work. The rules for these markets are uncertain, but they may resemble competitive, sealed-bid procurement, processed at Internet communication speed with potential transactions visible to many more parties. Corporate clients will probably post detailed descriptions of packages of related work to the electronic market, essentially a secure bulletin board, and make a request for quotes (RFQ). Law firms could register to gain access to the electronic market, view the RFQs on line, forecast the work effort needed, formulate a bid, and finally communicate it via e-mail to the potential client. The client might then select the best price from among firms considered reasonably competent and then award a binding contract, either via return e-mail, phone, mail, or other means. The involvement of corporate counsel in posting RFQs and law firms in bidding probably assures that reasonable auction rules will be adopted and carefully constructed. As the on-line auctions become reliable, other professionals' services (e.g., accountants, consultants), and financing for corporate or consumer loans is moving on line.

http://
www.ftc.gov/ftc/consumer.htm

By early in 2000, nearly 1,000 B2B exchanges had been announced, largely to be implemented on the Internet. The Federal Trade Commission (FTC) calls them **B2B electronic marketplaces.** The FTC provisionally defines them as "software systems that enable buyers and sellers of similar goods to carry out procurement activities using common, industry-wide computer systems." At the time of this writing, only a few are functioning. Nevertheless, they hold promise for substantial efficiencies in procurement and probably involve four major areas of law: membership rights, commercial law, IP, and antitrust. In the first area of legal concern, B2B exchanges

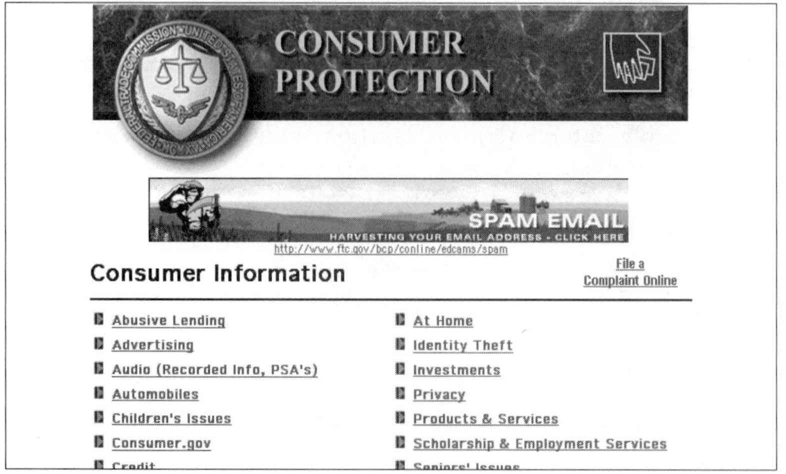

will probably enforce membership rules, impose terms and conditions for use, and allocate risks among participants by using warranties, indemnification, and dispute resolution methods.

The second major area involves the processing of transactions and the terms of sale. Most goods sales must conform to UCC Article 2. Electronic means of mutual assent will be used, so many of the UETA and UCITA mechanics of contract formation and performance are implicated. Four major transaction methods are envisioned. First, participants may solicit and identify each other on line and then move off line to negotiate and conclude a binding contract by using the RFQ format. Second, there are direct auctions in which many parties can bid on specified goods during a finite open time period. *Prices rise* as more bids are made, and the goods are typically sold to the highest bidder.

Another major method is the **reverse auction**, essentially an electronic posting of a buyer's needs. Bidding typically *drives prices down* during a fixed time period, and the lowest bidder wins the contract. Of course, these price movement dynamics may differ if bids are sealed or the bidders' identities are kept confidential. A fourth possible method may emulate the financial markets, which are sometimes called **dual auctions** because they involve the posting of bid and ask prices. Prices for standardized goods, such as in the markets for currencies, commodities, or securities, are bid up to prices asked by sellers or down to prices bid by buyers.

The third major area of legal concern is the unique intellectual property that will emerge. Two types are likely: (1) transaction information and (2) transaction processing methods. First, data are largely protected under trade secret law, and participants may be unwilling to permit other exchange participants or outsiders to benefit from such confidential information. Contractual confidentiality restrictions and various computer security methods are likely. Second, some transaction processing methods will be novel and nonobvious enough to be protected under a business method patent. For example, an Internet-based reverse auction method, as described in Priceline.com's patent, may become the common method for purchaser-initiated B2B systems. IP law is detailed in Part IV.

The fourth area of B2B legal concern involves any potentially collusive activity among competitors. There are always antitrust concerns about price fixing, particularly in vertical procurement markets, if they largely involve a single industry. These potential anticompetitive aspects of B2B exchanges are discussed further in Chapter 19. There are precedents to aid in developing these markets: travel reservation systems, agricultural auctions, and the securities and commodities markets.

E-CONTRACTING DEPARTURES FROM TRADITIONAL PRACTICE

Emerging e-commerce methods depart from traditional contracting practices. Two related practices that are coming into widespread use are likely to shape much of the future for B2C and C2C commercial practice on line. First, shrink-wrap and click-wrap may operate both as a manifestation of assent and as conclusive proof of the agreement's terms. Second, in B2B commercial practice, many parties already engage in EDI, an electronic form of ordering based on agreed and standardized terms of trade.

Shrink-Wrap Agreements

The software industry has long sought to impose standardized license terms on mass market purchasers by enclosing a printed copy of the license that is viewable from within a clear plastic wrap that is sealed around the software package. This **shrink-wrap agreement** resembles a unilateral contract in which purchasers' assent to the terms is inferred when they open and use the software product. A shrink-wrap typically provides that the act of opening the package constitutes an acceptance of the license on the stated terms. These terms are not negotiated but are imposed on individual licensees, and they generally favor the seller. By contrast, license terms negotiated as part of a **site license** to large purchasers, such as corporations or universities, may differ significantly from shrink-wrap licenses. When shrink-wrap agreements are enforceable, they automatically obligate the licensee to the stated terms. Shrink-wraps are probably enforceable if drafted carefully and clearly, displayed conspicuously to permit review, and do not deviate substantially from industry norms. However, some courts refuse to enforce shrink-wraps or find that particular terms are unconscionable (unfair). Some have been invalidated as a postnegotiation attempt to unilaterally impose additional but unfavorable terms on the buyer.[1]

Shrink-wraps are becoming ubiquitous; arguably, they are so common they constitute a usage of trade that sets a precedent for interpreting similar licenses. Another basis for enforcement is that shrink-wraps simply modify any preexisting contract terms. For example, many software purchases are clustered into periodic shipments: First, the terms for some trial copies are negotiated; then, later shipments include shrink-wraps with modified terms. Some courts refuse to enforce these shrink-wrap terms if unconscionable. The following watershed case enforced a shrink-wrap license limitation on using data contained in a CD-ROM telephone directory.

ProCD, Inc. v. Zeidenberg

86 F.3d 1447 (7th Cir., 1997)

Facts. Zeidenberg sold data stored on his website, including data found with his search engine. This on-line database included telephone directory listings Zeidenberg extracted from a licensed copy of SelectPhone, a national directory of 3,000 telephone directories produced by ProCD. Zeidenberg had purchased the ProCD product on CD-ROM. The ProCD package had a shrink-wrap license that referred to terms contained in an accompanying user manual that prohibited the commercial use of the telephone listings like that done by Zeidenberg.

Legal Issue. Are shrink-wrap license limitations enforceable against purchasers who have ample opportunity to see or object to the terms and therefore are not automatically unconscionable or in violation of contract law or public policy?

Opinion. Circuit Judge Easterbrook. Must buyers of computer software obey the terms of shrinkwrap licenses? Shrinkwrap licenses are enforceable unless their terms are objectionable on grounds applicable to contracts in general (for example, if they violate a rule of positive law, or if they are unconscionable). The "shrinkwrap license" gets its name from the fact that retail software packages are covered in plastic or cellophane "shrinkwrap," and some vendors, though not ProCD, have written licenses that become effective as soon as the customer tears the wrapping from the package. The district court held the licenses ineffectual because their terms do not appear on the outside of the packages. The court added that a purchaser does not agree to—and cannot be bound by—terms that were secret at the time of purchase. [W]e treat the licenses as ordinary

1. *Step-Saver Data Systems, Inc. v. Wyse Technology*, 939 F.2d 91 (3d Cir., 1991).

contracts accompanying the sale of products, and therefore as governed by the common law of contracts and the Uniform Commercial Code.

Vendors can put the entire terms of a contract on the outside of a box only by using microscopic type, removing other information that buyers might find more useful (such as what the software does, and on which computers it works), or both. The "Read Me" file included with most software, describing system requirements and potential incompatibilities, may be equivalent to ten pages of type; warranties and license restrictions take still more space. Notice on the outside, terms on the inside, and a right to return the software for a refund if the terms are unacceptable (a right that the license expressly extends) may be a means of doing business valuable to buyers and sellers alike.

Transactions in which the exchange of money precedes the communication of detailed terms are common. Consider the purchase of insurance. The buyer goes to an agent, who explains the essentials (amount of coverage, number of years) and remits the premium to the home office, which sends back a policy. On the district judge's understanding, the terms of the policy are irrelevant because the insured paid before receiving them. Yet the device of payment, often with a "binder" (so that the insurance takes effect immediately even though the home office reserves the right to withdraw coverage later), in advance of the policy, serves buyers' interests by accelerating effectiveness and reducing transactions costs. Or consider the purchase of an airline ticket. The traveler calls the carrier or an agent, is quoted a price, reserves a seat, pays, and gets a ticket, in that order. The ticket contains elaborate terms, which the traveler can reject by canceling the reservation. To use the ticket is to accept the terms, even terms that in retrospect are disadvantageous. Just so with a ticket to a concert. The back of the ticket states that the patron promises not to record the concert; to attend is to agree. A theater that detects a violation will confiscate the tape and escort the violator to the exit. One could arrange things so that every concertgoer signs this promise before forking over the money, but that cumbersome way of doing things not only would lengthen queues and raise prices but also would scotch the sale of tickets by phone or electronic data service.

Consumer goods work the same way. Someone who wants to buy a radio set visits a store, pays, and walks out with a box. Inside the box is a leaflet containing some terms, the most important of which usually is the warranty, read for the first time in the comfort of home. Drugs come with a list of ingredients on the outside and an elaborate package insert on the inside. The package insert describes drug interactions, contraindications, and other vital information. Next consider the software industry itself. Only a minority of sales take place over the counter, where there are boxes to peruse. A customer may place an order by phone in response to a line item in a catalog or a review in a magazine. Much software is ordered over the Internet by purchasers who have never seen a box. Increasingly software arrives by wire. There is no box; there is only a stream of electrons, a collection of information that includes data, an application program, instructions, many limitations.

What then does the current version of the UCC have to say? We think that the place to start is §2-204(1): "A contract for sale of goods may be made in any manner sufficient to show agreement, including conduct by both parties which recognizes the existence of such a contract." A vendor, as master of the offer, may invite acceptance by conduct, and may propose limitations on the kind of conduct that constitutes acceptance. A buyer may accept by performing the acts the vendor proposes to treat as acceptance. And that is what happened. ProCD proposed a contract that a buyer would accept by using the software after having an opportunity to read the license at leisure. This Zeidenberg did. He had no choice, because the software splashed the license on the screen and would not let him proceed without indicating acceptance.

Competition among vendors, not judicial revision of a package's contents, is how consumers are protected in a market economy. ProCD has rivals, which may elect to compete by offering superior software, monthly updates, improved terms of use, lower price, or a better compromise among these elements. As we stressed above, adjusting terms in buyers' favor might help Matthew Zeidenberg today (he already has the software) but would lead to a response, such as a higher price, that might make consumers as a whole worse off.

Decision. Shrink-wrap licenses are enforceable where the seller imposes terms and conditions which the buyer accepts by opening the shrink wrapping from the software.

Case Questions

1. Should the rationale in *ProCD* permitting the enforceability of shrink-wraps be limited to sales of packaged software or packaged database information to consumers, or should it be more broadly applied to corporate purchases of customized software or data?
2. How could electronic commerce achieve its potential to significantly reduce transactions costs if standardized shrink-wrap licenses were not enforceable?

Shrink-wraps often limit the customer's rights of use as well as the customer's rights against the seller. For example, many licenses limit warranties or the damages recoverable if the software or information is defective, they deny the right to sue by requiring arbitration, and they often apply laws favorable to the vendor. Customers unwilling to assent to the shrink-wrap terms are usually permitted to return the package under a term that gives a choice: to **accept or return**—that is, accept all the standard license terms or return the goods to the seller. Some cases refuse to enforce such take-it-or-leave-it contracts, calling them **adhesion contracts** if customers are unlikely to read or understand terms that are unconscionable or violate public policy. Nevertheless, a few state statutes have attempted to validate shrink-wrap licenses, and UCITA would validate them, as discussed in the following sections. License terms are discussed further in Chapter 13.

Click-Wrap Agreements

Shrink-wraps have evolved into the **click-wrap agreement** encountered while operating a computer. Use of the software or access to a website is often prevented unless the user clicks affirmatively "I Agree" during software installation or before accessing website content. Packaged software using a click-wrap license can record the assent on the user's computer, although it is more reliable to transmit the assent back to the seller during online registration through the user's modem or Internet connection. Websites requiring click-wrap assent may cause an immediate transmission of the agreement back to the website operator. The click-wrap is similar to the shrink-wrap because both impose standardized licensing terms to which users agree by conduct. Click-wraps are likely to be enforceable under the same standards applicable to shrink-wraps. However, both may be vulnerable to invalidation as unconscionable or an adhesion contract. Recall the case discussed in chapter 1, *Specht v. Netscape*,[2] which refused to enforce a click-wrap unless the user had scrolled down through all the terms, indicating the opportunity to read them all. They differ mainly in that assent is demonstrated by clicking through rather than by opening the transparent plastic wrapper. Also, click-wraps are more likely than shrink-wraps to govern all future transactions.

ONLINE

FTC's click-wrap enforceability advisory
http://www.ftc.gov/bcp/conline/pubs/buspubs/dotcom/

Contract Formation under UCITA

The Uniform Computer Information Transactions Act (UCITA) was originally proposed to be part of the UCC, as Article 2B, and to validate shrink-wrap mutual assent. Since then, UCITA's scope grew initially but is now limited to traditional and electronic transactions in software, multimedia, data, and on-line information. As of this writing, UCITA has been enacted only in Virginia and Maryland. Iowa law prohibits vendors from imposing UCITA on Iowa consumers. Controversy surrounds UCITA, and many observers believe it will not be as successful as the UCC. Despite this controversy, UCITA settles on electronic contracting rules that may eventually become some of the norms for other forms of on-line contracting. UCITA parallels UETA in legitimizing the parties' use of electronic records, electronic signatures, authentication, and electronic agents. UCITA's broad terms are discussed throughout the electronic commerce chapters of Part III. This section discusses the impact that UCITA may have on the formation and conclusion of a contract.

2. 150 F.Supp.2d 585 (D.N.Y. 2001).

UCITA's contract formation rules parallel existing sales law because many UCITA rules were derived from the *Restatement of Contracts* and from UCC Article 2. The new law speaks in terms of "manifesting assent," so much of the focus in UCITA mutual assent is on what a reasonable person would infer from the contracting parties' conduct. UCITA §202 permits contract formation in any manner, including traditional offer and acceptance, and by the parties' conduct. Contracts formed using electronic agents are also authorized. UCITA §203 provides that offers can be accepted in any reasonable manner including by shipment or promise to ship a copy of the subject computer information. UCITA §203(4)(a) rejects the mailbox rule when electronic communications are used: Acceptances are effective upon receipt of an electronic message or upon the receipt of an electronic performance.

UCITA §211 establishes an important rule in facilitating mutual assent in Internet types of transactions. UCITA makes it unfavorable for information vendors to prevent customers from exercising the opportunity to review, print, or store the license terms before performance. Of course, customers may choose not to read the terms, so a contract under UCITA is enforceable so long as customers had an opportunity to review. UCITA creates special rules for **mass market transactions.** Generally, these are licenses sold at retail to consumers containing standardized terms, UCITA §102(43). There are special remedies for consumers of mass market licenses.

ONLINE

UCITA adoptions and controversy
http://www.ucitaonline.com

Electronic Data Interchange

In the 1990s, commercial customers began to use electronic methods for customizing B2B contracts, orders, and documents for recurrent purchase transactions with regular customers from their long-standing suppliers. **Electronic data interchange (EDI)** transactions usually anticipate a course of dealing with continuing orders, invoices, payments, and shipments based on standard terms in an umbrella contract, the **trading partner agreement.** The International Chamber of Commerce (ICC) first developed EDI practices with Uniform Rules of Conduct for Interchange of Trade Data by Teletransmission (UNCID).

EDI is a flexible contracting method permitting various models. For example, in an EDI model perfected by Wal-Mart, a large purchaser may provide incentives so that its many suppliers will implement EDI with particular computer and communications hardware and EDI software based on standard trade terms and conditions.

International Commentary

European Union's Distance Selling Directive

The EU adopted a Directive on the Protection of Consumers in Respect of Distance Contracts in 1997. This EU directive requires EU members to enact national laws that protect consumers, largely with disclosure requirements similar to those in UCITA. This EU directive applies to ***distance contracts*** concerning goods or services that are accomplished by means of technology. For the foreseeable future, this directive will cover direct marketing contracts using Internet communications. Consumers must be provided with certain information that is durable and accessible before a distance contract may be concluded, including (1) identity and address of supplier, (2) description of the goods or services, (3) price including taxes, and (4) terms for performance, payment, and delivery, among other terms. The EU directive goes beyond UCITA in that it directs EU member nations to grant consumers a cooling off period of at least seven working days to cancel the transaction. This EU directive exempts certain financial transactions, periodicals, and audio or video recordings if the consumer has opened the sealed package.

In another model, the start-up costs and complexity of all this EDI "infrastructure" is best provided by a third-party EDI firm that specializes in electronic transaction processing. EDI trading partners often expect their counterparty to implement adequate EDI systems and then regularly keep accurate records and log all transactions and transmissions. The amount of human intervention varies in different implementations of EDI systems.

The Electronic Messaging Services Task Force of the American Bar Association (ABA) developed the **Model EDI Trading Partner Agreement**[3] that provides some standard or benchmark EDI terms that balance the burdens and risks among EDI parties. Terms of the Model EDI Trading Partner Agreement may be adjusted to suit the special needs of particular parties. The ABA model agreement envisions that the parties will use a secure, closed, and dedicated communications system to reduce both errors and unauthorized interference by hackers. Confirmation messages are encouraged to provide "functional acknowledgment" that each counterparty's electronic message was received. EDI messages are typically made effective upon receipt, eliminating the mailbox rule. The parties may agree to use communication methods that clearly indicate the formation of their contract.

ONLINE

Accredited Standards Committee's EDI standards
http://www.x12.org

TERMS OF THE AGREEMENT

Parties often use a written agreement, even if contract law does not require one, because long experience shows that it is prudent to "get it in writing." For example, circumstances can change after the agreement is concluded and before all performances are rendered. These changed circumstances often make it less advantageous for one party to perform the duties as they originally agreed. Of course, the primary purpose of enforceable contracts is to permit parties to allocate the risk of changed circumstances and thereby gain certainty so they can plan for the future. For example, a seller might agree to supply a commodity at a particular price, but the price rises by the time shipment is made. Alternatively, a retailer might agree to buy popular goods from a manufacturer but be unhappy about receiving the shipment several weeks later when an item's popularity has declined.

Written contracts make it difficult for the party disadvantaged by economic or other circumstances to deny terms plainly stated or to add terms not originally stated in the written contract. Experienced business parties prepare written contracts that anticipate many changes in circumstances. Typically, the more sophisticated party, both in business decision-making and legal drafting abilities, takes the initiative to author the written agreement. The author, called the **scrivener**, often takes advantage of the situation by including terms more favorable to the author's side. However, when both parties are relatively sophisticated, the contract is drafted in successive versions that eventually reach some middle ground that reflects the parties' relative bargaining power and the market conditions for the underlying goods or services. Despite the certainty provided by written contracts, it is often necessary for contract law to assist in interpreting the parties' contract by determining what terms should be in a vaguely worded contract, filling in gaps the parties overlooked, defining contract duties by interpreting contract language, and implementing later modifications. This section discusses interpretation of terms.

---

3. *The Commercial Use of Electronic Data Interchange: A Report and Model Trading Partner Agreement*, 45 Bus.Law 1645 (1990).

MIRROR-IMAGE RULE

The common law **mirror-image rule**, applicable to land sales, services, or employment, requires that the acceptance mirror the offered terms. This rule requires that the accepted terms agree in every detail to the offered terms with no variations. The UCC, applicable to sales of goods, is more liberal, permitting some deviations between the offered and accepted terms. Commercial organizations often fail to adhere strictly to the common law mirror-image rule. Goods sales often involve a "battle of the forms" in which buyers and sellers, with the aid of their attorneys, construct invoices, order forms, and confirmation notices containing terms very favorable to themselves. Inevitably, there are differences between terms found in the offer and acceptance forms. Minor differences usually go unnoticed unless a dispute arises. UCC §2-207 provides a complex solution to this problem.

Additional Terms in Acceptance or Confirmation (UCC §2-207)

1. A definite and seasonable expression of acceptance or a written confirmation which is sent within a reasonable time operates as an acceptance even though it states terms additional to or different from those offered or agreed upon, unless acceptance is expressly made conditional on assent to the additional or different terms.
2. The additional terms are to be construed as proposals for addition to the contract. Between merchants such terms become part of the contract unless:
   (a) the offer expressly limits acceptance to the terms of the offer;
   (b) they materially alter it; or
   (c) notification of objection to them has already been given or is given within a reasonable time after notice of them is received.
3. Conduct by both parties which recognizes the existence of a contract is sufficient to establish a contract for sale although the writings of the parties do not otherwise establish a contract. In such case the terms of the particular contract consist of those terms on which the writings of the parties agree, together with any supplementary terms incorporated under any other provisions of this Act.

UCC §2-207 applies to forming a contract when there are only minor deviations between the parties' written documents in sales of goods. Unlike under the common law mirror image rule, slight differences between the offer and the acceptance do not always cause mutual assent to fail. A contract is formed if there are no material differences on key terms in the parties' communications. However, either party may reimpose the mirror-image rule. Counteroffers are possible only if highly material terms are in dispute between the writings. **Highly material terms** include essential terms like the parties' identity, the price, and significant differences in the quantity or subject matter. For example, differences in the size, color, or grade of apples would be highly material, and a return communication that contains these differences would be a counteroffer.

If the additions, deletions, or changes in the acceptance or confirmation form are not highly material, perhaps they are just material, and this does not prevent mutual assent. In this case, the parties still have an enforceable agreement. If different terms appear in the second communication, they are considered mere proposals to modify, but the contract still exists on the terms as originally offered. Such proposals to modify may be accepted or rejected by the offeror. **Material terms** are those that would cause surprise to either party, such as changes in standard warranty protection or customary credit terms.

When both of the parties are merchants, immaterial differences in the second communication may actually become part of the contract without further negotiation, providing the offeror does not object to the offeree's immaterial new terms. If the parties conduct themselves as if they have a contract despite different terms in their forms, their conduct implies that they acknowledge a contract exists and that it is enforceable. In that case, the contract's terms are those on which the writings agree, together with other terms automatically supplied by the UCC. For example, if the buyer pays for the goods or the seller delivers them, then a contract exists even if the parties' forms do not agree. The CISG rejects UCC §2-207 and follows the mirror-image rule.

The UCITA approach to the battle of the forms is found in §204. It retains much of the UCC §2-207 regimen. A contract is not created if the acceptance materially alters the offered terms, unless the material term is accepted or the parties conduct themselves as if a contract exists. If the additional terms are not material, a contract exists on the offered terms. If the additional terms are immaterial, they are not part of the contract except between merchants, where they can become part of the contract unless the other party objects. In UCITA licensing contracts, the scope, geographical region, field of use, and duration of a license are likely to be material terms in most situations.

OPEN TERMS

Most reasonable and careful parties express all or nearly all the terms they foresee as essential when they make an offer or otherwise negotiate. However, such foresight is not always necessary: The parties may presume that reasonable or customary terms are in use even if some terms are not expressed. UCC §2-204 provides for terms of a contract to be left as **open terms** for future determination or to be inferred later from the circumstances. In such situations, the contract will be enforced as long as a "reasonably certain basis" exists "for giving an appropriate remedy."

The UCC provides **gap-filling terms** to supplement vague sales contracts. For example, the price of goods may be determined later if the parties leave the price term open, if they say nothing about price, or if they intend to use the market price prevailing at the time of delivery. UCC §2-304 infers a reasonable price determined at the time for delivery. An open delivery term is interpreted as requiring delivery at the seller's place of business and at a reasonable time after contracting. A payment term left open obligates the buyer to pay when the goods are received. Even the quantity term can be left vague until determined by the sellers' actual **outputs** or the buyers' actual **requirements.** Terms can also be supplied by trade custom, as discussed in the next section. The CISG does not clearly encourage the use of open terms, except in setting the price according to some outside force, such as by market prices, a market index, formula, or third party. The CISG imposes no good faith duty on the parties, but the UCC and UCITA both do impose a **duty of good faith** on all parties.

UCITA permits open terms and provides several default rules, essentially gap-filling terms, to supply terms when the parties fail to be specific. Not all terms must be conspicuous, negotiated, or expressly assented or agreed to, unless UCITA expressly requires such formality. Under UCITA §305, "An agreement that is otherwise sufficiently definite to be a contract is not invalid because it leaves particulars of performance to be specified by one of the parties." Any such particulars of performance may be specified by a party but only in good faith and only in a commercially reasonable manner. There may be several excuses for breach if the other party fails to specify a term "seasonably" (within the time agreed or within a reasonable time) and this failure materially affects the other party. For example, if the purchaser of data delays in setting specifications for the data needed, the supplier is excused for any resulting delay in its performance and may perform, suspend performance, or treat the failure to specify as a breach of contract. UCITA §306 requires that performances under open terms be "reasonable in light of the commercial circumstances existing at the time of agreement." UCITA special licensing terms are discussed in Chapter 13.

INTERPRETATION

Disagreements over the meaning of contract terms are all too frequent and are resolved under the objective rule of contracts. Terms are interpreted by how an objective, reasonable person would understand the words used in the particular context. Common words are given their general meaning unless the particular line of business applies a unique usage to the words in question. For example, consider the word *gross*. In common parlance, gross means overall, total, flagrant, disgusting, or bizarre. However, among wholesalers and retailers, gross is a measure of unit quantity, precisely 12 dozen, or 144.

Three levels of trade custom or commercial precedent are useful in interpreting contracts. The first level applies precedents set in a whole industry, and the two other levels progressively provide guidance developed from narrower experiences among fewer parties. The broadest source of industry precedent comes from **usages of trade**, which are methods or expectations in the commercial dealings common to a whole trade or business, derived from its customs and practices. It may take some time before the Internet community establishes solid usages that most participants regularly observe. A narrower source of trade customs comes from a recognized course of dealing. These are practices derived from previous dealings directly between the contracting parties.

The narrowest of the three is a **course of performance**, which looks to a single contract between the parties in which there were several or repeat performances, such as installment payments or deliveries. For example, a buyer who fails to object to consistently late deliveries establishes a precedent that causes the seller to reasonably expect that tardy future deliveries are acceptable. Once this course of performance is set, the buyer would be unable to claim breach of contract for another late delivery before first notifying the seller that future late deliveries would not be tolerated. Both the UCC and UCITA permit these trade usages to help interpret vague contracts or to define terms. The UCC's provision is similar to UCITA §302, which provides that when there are inconsistencies, the parties' agreement and conduct are given precedence over trade usages. For example, the express terms of a contract override all inconsistent trade usages; course of performance prevails over course of dealing and usage of trade, and course of dealing prevails over usage of trade. Trade usages are proven as facts.

MODIFICATIONS

Laissez faire dictates that contract law should not inhibit the parties from modifying an existing agreement. Circumstances change, and parties are often willing to accommodate each other to preserve their ongoing relationship. However, experience has shown that a powerful party may pressure the weaker party into a modification more favorable to the stronger party. As a result, the common law requires that any contract modification be regarded as another contract that should be properly formed and supported by consideration. This rule usually means that both parties' obligations must be changed by the modification. The UCC and UCITA were drafted to ease these requirements. Modifications of goods sales and computer information licenses are enforceable even without consideration and even if only one party's obligation changes.

Many contracts anticipate such changing circumstances and require that particular processes be followed for modifications. Generally, oral contracts may be modified orally. However, many written contracts require that modifications are enforceable only if made in writing and sometimes only if approved by particular parties. Under UCITA §303, an authenticated record may validly require that later modifications be effected only by use of another authenticated record. In a B2C transaction, using the merchant's standard form, the consumer must separately manifest assent to the clause requiring an authenticated record for a modification. On-line subscription contracts have frequent periodic changes in terms. Generally, the subscriber must be given an opportunity to "terminate the contract as to future performance if the change alters a material term and the party in good faith determines that the modification is unacceptable." UCITA requires that whenever opposing parties are asked to accept a modification, they must be given an opportunity to review the proposed modification before it becomes binding.

Consideration

As introduced earlier as the consideration model of e-commerce, the law does not enforce all agreements. For two reasons, mutual promises must go beyond a certain minimum threshold to create a contract: First, many promises are made idly or lightly, with no intention of creating binding obligations. For example, promises to make a gift, do a favor for another, or participate in a social arrangement are considered less serious than are business promises. Second, only sufficiently important cases should burden the judicial system. Although it might be socially desirable to rely on all promises, there must be some limit on the enforceability of promises, a limit corresponding to the seriousness and motivation of the promisor and the reasonableness of the promisee's expectations. These reasons justify the **consideration** requirement. Consideration distinguishes serious, enforceable promises from less serious and unenforceable promises. The rule of consideration requires that the parties mutually give value or make obligations. This is the principal measure of the importance of promises, but its significance is declining. The mutual promises necessary for adequate consideration are illustrated in Exhibit 10.7.

EXHIBIT 10.7 Consideration

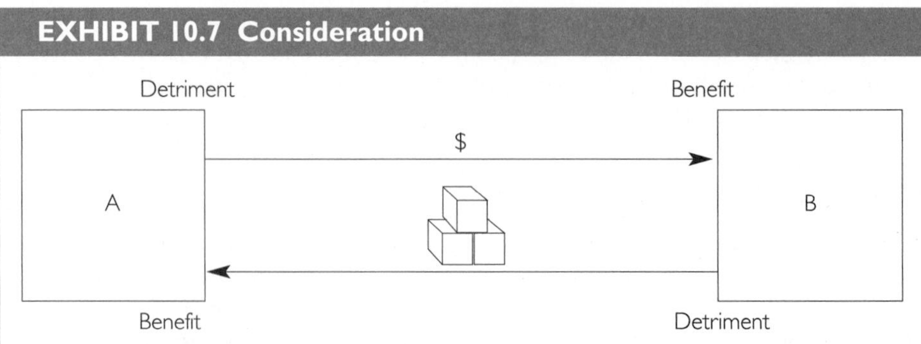

Consideration exists for a contract when the two parties exchange new promises. A promises to pay money to B because B promises to deliver goods to A, and B promises to deliver goods to A because A promises to pay money to B. A's promise to pay B for the goods that B delivers is a benefit to B and a detriment to A. B's promise to deliver goods to A is a benefit to A and a detriment to B.

TESTS FOR THE PRESENCE OF CONSIDERATION

There are several tests of consideration. They vary conceptually and are stated in terms of value, benefits, detriments, mutuality of obligation, and the exchange of promises. A common misconception about consideration is that value must pass physically between the parties. Another misconception is that there must be a real detriment to the promisor and a real benefit to the promisee. Although the consideration requirement is usually satisfied if property or labor is exchanged, it can be satisfied with less, simply by the parties' new promises. Only **legal detriments** or **legal benefits** need be present in the new promises, such as when the parties make promises that obligate themselves in the future. A promise to do something new, something the promisor was not previously obligated to do, is sufficient consideration to support a counterpromise. A promise is quite different from an actual transfer of property or services pledged in a promise. All that is necessary is that the promise creates a legally binding obligation. Promises alone have sufficient legal value to show seriousness. Actual performance satisfies the consideration requirement but is not necessary.

A **forbearance** is *promising not to do* something or to actually refrain from doing it. A forbearance can also constitute sufficient consideration. In the settlement of a dispute over an automobile accident, for example, the party at fault usually promises to pay money in exchange for the victim's promise to refrain from suing for damages. This explains why contracts to release a negligent driver are enforceable to prevent suit after the victim accepts an insurance company settlement. The proper test of consideration is whether the parties make mutually binding new promises. Enforceable promises may be either promises to do something new or promises to refrain from doing something previously permissible. To satisfy the consideration test, the promises made by both parties must change their legal obligations.

MUTUALITY OF OBLIGATION

The exchange element of consideration is an important concept. Parties that exchange promises are more likely to intend to be legally bound because each party's promise is made "on the condition" that the other party is making an acceptable return promise. With few exceptions, the mutual or bilateral nature of the promises clearly indicates their seriousness and the parties' intent to be bound. Each party makes a promise "in consideration" of the other party's promise, so the promises are mutually given in exchange. Each party is induced or motivated to promise something new because the other party has made a new promise in return. Stated another way, each party's promise must be supported by the consideration found in the other party's counterpromise.

The classic formulation of consideration holds that there must be a legal detriment to the promisee or a legal benefit to the promisor when the promises of the parties are analyzed (illustrated in Exhibits 10.8 and 10.9). These tests are efficient because each demonstrates that two new promises are made. Either of these tests also shows that each party gives and receives legal value. Another formulation holds that each party must consciously give legal value in an outgoing promise in return for the incoming promise. Still another formulation holds that consideration exists whenever the offer and acceptance result in two new promises made in exchange. Each of these consideration formulations includes elements of legal value given for and legal value received from the conscious mutual exchange of interdependent promises. Although the theoretical nature of consideration too often seems obtuse, it need not pose interpretation problems because situations in the following sections more clearly indicate when consideration is lacking.

EXHIBIT 10.8 Detriments to the Promisee

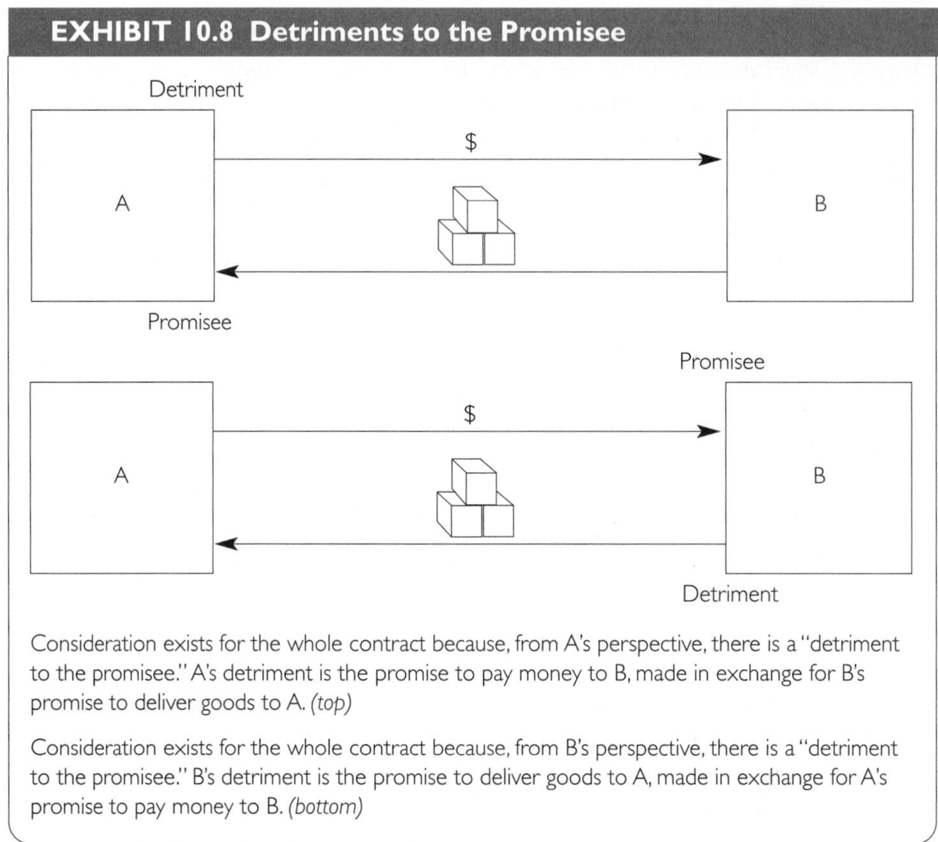

Consideration exists for the whole contract because, from A's perspective, there is a "detriment to the promisee." A's detriment is the promise to pay money to B, made in exchange for B's promise to deliver goods to A. *(top)*

Consideration exists for the whole contract because, from B's perspective, there is a "detriment to the promisee." B's detriment is the promise to deliver goods to A, made in exchange for A's promise to pay money to B. *(bottom)*

UNENFORCEABLE PROMISES: CONSIDERATION IS LACKING

In several common situations, consideration is found to be lacking, which makes the agreement unenforceable. If either party's promise is subject to that party's wish, will, or desire, then the promise is **illusory**. For example, an unlimited right to cancel the contract gives the promisor a way to back out at any time. A promise that is never binding is an illusion, so a contract supported by such a promise lacks consideration. However, if the cancellation right is limited, such as with 30 days' notice, then the promise is not illusory and provides good consideration.

When one party is already legally bound to perform an obligation and later simply repromises it, that second promise is a mere stale repetition. Nothing new is given in the newly repeated old promise when it is in exchange for the promisee's return new promise. When there is a **preexisting legal duty,** the promisor is already legally obligated to do or refrain from doing some activity and then attempts to use the repromise as consideration for a new contract. However, there is no new consideration, and the second contract based on a restated promise is unenforceable. Consider a jockey who is already under contract to ride a horse in the Kentucky Derby. If that jockey pressures the horse's owner for higher pay as the odds of winning become more favorable, the owner may feel pressure to promise to pay more. However, this owner's promise is not supported by any new consideration. The jockey has a preexisting legal duty to ride in that race under the terms of the original contract.

EXHIBIT 10.9 Benefits to the Promisor

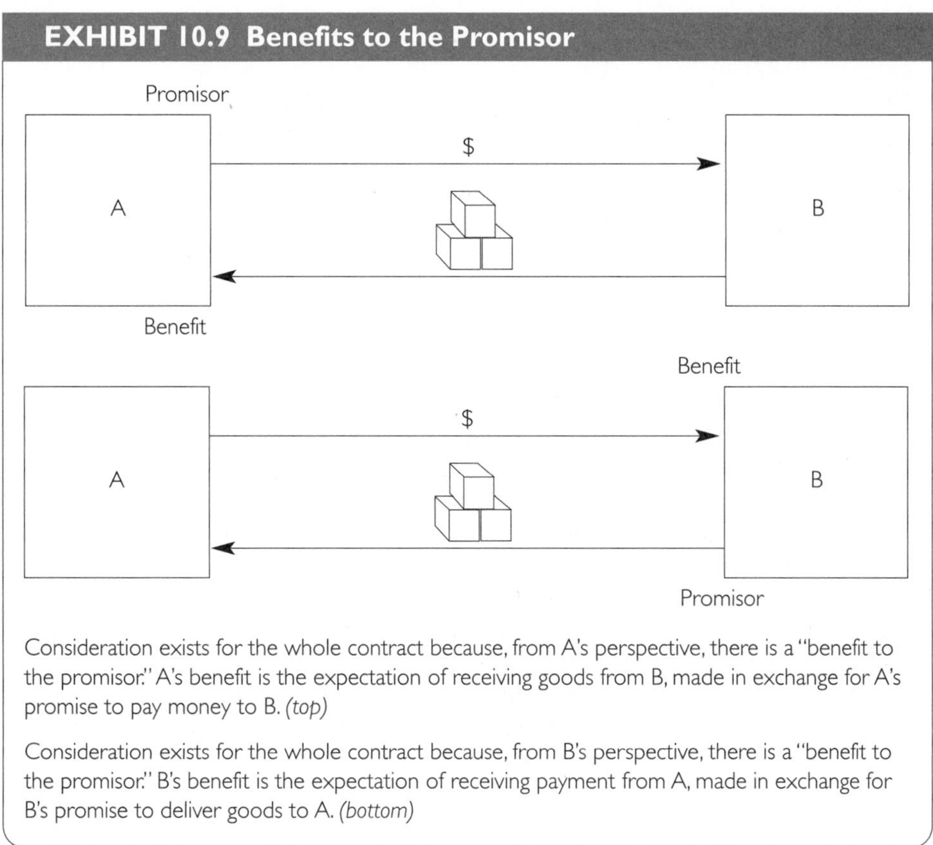

Consideration exists for the whole contract because, from A's perspective, there is a "benefit to the promisor." A's benefit is the expectation of receiving goods from B, made in exchange for A's promise to pay money to B. *(top)*

Consideration exists for the whole contract because, from B's perspective, there is a "benefit to the promisor." B's benefit is the expectation of receiving payment from A, made in exchange for B's promise to deliver goods to A. *(bottom)*

There is sufficient consideration in an **accord and satisfaction** when a debtor agrees to settle a disputed or **unliquidated debt**. For example, a client may not have agreed to a consultant's fee before the services are rendered. When the bill arrives, the client may dispute the amount or particular itemized entries. When the consultant and client settle their dispute over the bill, the disputed claim becomes liquidated. Each has given up rights by settling, and the settlement amounts to an accord and satisfaction that is supported by consideration. By contrast, agreements to settle undisputed or liquidated debts by which the debtor promises to pay less are usually not supported by consideration because the debt amount is the debtor's preexisting legal duty. However, if the debtor promises to pay the amount sooner or in a different medium, then the creditor receives something different than was originally promised, and consideration is again present to validate the contract.

PROMISES ENFORCEABLE WITHOUT CONSIDERATION

Enforceable obligations do not always require consideration. In a few unusual cases, a single, one-way, or gratuitous promise, though unsupported by consideration, becomes enforceable to preserve fairness and equity. The doctrines of **promissory estoppel** and **charitable subscriptions** permit enforcement by balancing the unfairness when the promisee suffers damage by relying on a promisor's promise (see Exhibit 10.10).

EXHIBIT 10.10 Elements of Promissory Estoppel

1. Under the circumstances, should the promisor reasonably expect that the promisee will rely on the promise and then act in some definite and substantial way? This is a ***detrimental reliance.***
2. Has the promisee ***in fact relied*** on the promise to his or her own detriment?
3. In ***balancing the equities*** of enforcing or not enforcing the promise, would substantial unfairness be avoided if the promise is enforced?

The doctrine of charitable subscriptions is similar to promissory estoppel. It applies when a charity relies on a donor's promise to contribute. Typically, the promisor pledges to donate something, and the charity relies on that pledge to its detriment by changing its position. For example, if a church member's promise to make a big contribution induces the church to remodel its building, the one-way charitable subscription becomes enforceable as soon as the church contracts with a builder, even though the charity has not given consideration.

The consideration requirement is waived in several other limited situations. For example, a debt barred by either the statute of limitations or the debtor's discharge in bankruptcy may be revived if the debtor reaffirms the original promise to pay the debt or makes partial payment without new consideration. The repayment of debts barred by bankruptcy must be approved by the bankruptcy court judge. **Composition** agreements entered into by several creditors and a debtor are enforceable without new consideration because the parties have a mutual interreliance similar to actual consideration. Although common law modifications require consideration, UCITA and the UCC permit contract modifications without consideration, and the UCC requires no consideration for written merchants' firm offers and for modifications of existing sales contracts. Consideration is generally unnecessary under UCITA for waivers or releases, which are one party's surrender of rights under a contract.

UCC §2-302 permits the court hearing a contract dispute to modify an adhesion contract—that is, a contract with unfair provisions—under the **unconscionability** doctrine. The parties may present evidence of the purpose and commercial setting of any clause brought into question. A consumer contract may be designated unconscionable if it is one-sided and oppressive, causes unfair surprise, and unfairly allocates risks because one side clearly has superior bargaining power. Courts have applied unconscionability as a form of consumer protection beyond the UCC context to achieve fairness. Unconscionability seldom applies to commercial parties. It is generally reserved for the uniquely vulnerable position of consumers. Commercial parties are presumed to be more experienced and better informed, to have better access to legal counsel, to possess stronger bargaining power, and to negotiate contracts more carefully than most consumers.

Internet transactions may reawaken the quiet area of contract consideration. The law increasingly recognizes that visitations by Web users to websites, downloads, and website interactivity often involve a license between the website and user. Licenses are contracts that must be supported by consideration. Many Web users have accepted license terms at some websites, essentially manifesting their assent by clicking "I agree." As the website license theory takes hold, users may be limited in the defensive acts taken to preserve their privacy. For example, many websites are expressly accessible only on the condition the user truthfully and completely supplies private information and accepts cookies to track the user's clickstream. User access to the website would constitute consideration from the website in exchange for the user's private information. If the user were to provide incorrect or incomplete data in a website registration license application or thwart use of cookies, this act could constitute a failure of consideration or even a breach of the license agreement. Of course, website operators who insist on enforcing this contract consideration theory to compel the surrender of private data from privacy-sensitive and savvy users may forfeit advantageous visits from a considerable part of the market. The pressures for privacy laws as a form of consumer protection are discussed further in Chapter 14.

QUESTIONS

1. Compare the formalities of traditional mutual assent with manifesting assent under electronic commerce. What are the similarities? What are the differences? How does evolving electronic commerce law accommodate the differences?
2. Explain the major differences between the common law of contracts and the statutory law for sales of goods under the UCC. What is the difference between the subject matter covered by both? For what reasons has the UCC changed the specific rules?
3. How are the rules of physical and electronic auctions determined? How is assent manifested in a physical auction? How is assent manifested in an electronic auction?
4. A customer purchased software from a local retailer. During the installation, a dialog box appeared, stating license terms that limited the manufacturer's liability for defects in the software. The customer clicked through, accepting these limitations. When software defects damaged the customer's business, the manufacturer claimed only the retailer was liable because the click-through agreement released the manufacturer. Should the retailer and not the manufacturer be responsible for defects in the product? See *Step-Saver Data Systems, Inc. v. Wyse Technology*, 939 F.2d 91 (3d Cir., 1991).
5. A commercial customer of an electronic mail service acquired the e-mail addresses of hundreds of other e-mail customers. The commercial customer used these e-mail addresses to send out notices of its business—that is, spam. The e-mail service provider sought to prevent further use of these customer lists. Can an e-mail service enforce its click-wrap term forbidding customers from using mailing lists acquired through the e-mail service provider for commercial purpose? See *Hotmail Corp. v. Van Money Pie Inc.*, 47 USPQ 2d (BNA) 1020 (N.D.Cal. 1998).
6. A pricing mistake was wrongly introduced when an electronic communication of contract negotiations was mistakenly modified. Is the electronic communications provider liable for the damages? See *Germain Fruit Co. v. Western Union Telegraph Co.*, 70 P. 658 (Cal. 1902).
7. For what reason has the concept of consideration remained in the law of contracts? When is consideration required? How might the consideration requirement be applied to a seller's collection of consumer private data? Explain how the consideration requirement might apply when the seller gives a discount in return for an individual's private data. What would be the ethical and legal impact if a consumer provides false private data while involved in on-line activity?
8. How does the objective theory of contracts clarify ambiguities in the communications of contracting parties during negotiations? Does this analysis change as Internet users click through various notices and agreement boxes?
9. The plaintiff, a website developer, requested that the defendant telecommunications company extend broadband lines to a new industrial park. No contract promising to pay for the installation was ever signed. After the telecommunications company completed the installation of the new lines, the plaintiff sought a declaratory judgment that it was not liable for the cost of extending the lines. Under what theory and analysis would the website developer be liable?
10. Larry and Amy were playing a friendly on-line game of "Medieval Pillager," each remotely from their own separate home computers. As Larry was about to drive his sword into Amy's white knight, Amy typed

into the chat box back to Larry: "If you kill my white knight in one thrust, I'll give you $500." Larry killed Amy's white knight; must Amy pay?

11. Nancy had a contract to work for Ace dot.com for two years when financial difficulties developed at the company. In oral conversation with the owner of Ace, Nancy offered to resign. Although, the owner did not accept Nancy's oral offer at that time, he later wrote Nancy a letter accepting her oral offer to resign. Has the offer lapsed?

12. The plaintiff purchased an option to buy the defendant's server computer. The written option agreement stated that the option to purchase was to expire on May 1. On April 15, the plaintiff sent a notice to the seller refusing to exercise the option. However, on April 29, the plaintiff had a change of heart and attempted to exercise the option by sending a notice to the seller. If an offeree (here the plaintiff) sends a notice refusing to exercise an option but then subsequently decides to exercise it, does the first refusal extinguish the offer? Does it make a difference if the offeror (the defendant-seller in this case) has not yet sold the server computer to someone else?

Performances and Payments

Commerce was at great risk before the law became a reliable incentive to perform contracts as promised. At one time, there were many perils and much intrigue in commercial transactions. Deliveries made over long distances could be lost at sea, damaged by weather, or stolen by pirates. Even as commercial law developed more fully, some parties too often failed to fulfill their obligations: Checks bounced, some goods were defective, and the quantities delivered were late or short. Parties generally trust repeated transactions with reliable counterparties or face-to-face exchanges where the consideration can be inspected before completing the transaction. The development and enforcement of safe commercial law and practices have very substantially reduced transaction risks. Today, commercial law provides highly reliable recourse when contract performance is inadequate or fails completely. This consistency may be among the most important factors supporting trade and prosperity.

Unprotected commerce over the Internet has caused a reversion to the commercial risks of the past. Anonymous interactions and transactions with unknown and untrusted counterparties are again raising many of the same risks that existed before commercial law improved dependability. Goods, data, and software from unknown vendors are too frequently defective or misdescribed. Electronic payments are at risk of interception by hackers or cancellation. Counterparties are often in remote jurisdictions where legal process is expensive, often greater than the value of the transaction at stake. The progress of e-commerce will be inhibited unless commercial law can adapt to reduce these risks. Adaptations of commercial law and practice that made early commerce safe may be the solution to transaction safety in e-commerce.

The primary objective of contracting is to make and receive a performance: the actual transfer of valuable goods, services, information, and payment. In this chapter, the performance of contracts is reviewed, including how contract terms and other standards may condition or assess the accomplishments of each party. This chapter also reviews the participation of outside third parties who may assist in processing or assuring performance. In some instances, a third party is entitled to receive a performance. Payment systems are discussed because, except for barter transactions, payments are the most common form of performance. Parties that satisfactorily fulfill their obligations are entitled to discharge, which recognizes that adequate performance releases them from their duty to perform. Throughout this discussion, it is important to remember that the contract's primary subject matter determines what law applies: common law, Uniform Commercial Code (UCC), Uniform Computer Information Transactions Act (UCITA) and/or Uniform Electronic Transactions Act (UETA).

PERFORMANCES

Most parties hope to discharge their contractual duties quickly and effectively. Contract law measures their performance by examining several basic performance questions: *When* should performance have been made and were these duties performed in a timely manner, *what* was performed, *who* performed it and to whom was the performance made, and *where* was performance made? Adequate and **full performance** by both parties fulfills their duties, and the contract is effectively discharged. These questions are examined in this chapter. With the convergence of e-commerce and the traditional economy, this chapter focuses on traditional physical performances and also integrates an understanding of how traditional performance rules extend into e-commerce through electronic payments, the processing of electronic documents, and electronic deliveries.

CONDITIONS

Conditions address the timing of performance. Certain events or **conditions** are often necessary before a party's rights become enforceable. The parties can expressly agree that some event is the triggering condition, often by using phrases such as "provided that," "contingent on," or "on the condition that." Conditions may also be implied with express conditions or with the circumstances. Some contracts contain **conditions precedent**, uncertain future events that must happen *before* a duty is owed. For example, in a software development contract, the contract terms might not require the purchaser to pay until the software is proved to satisfactorily perform according to prescribed standards. In e-commerce, an on-line seller might require the buyer's payment as a condition precedent before the seller will deliver. A website development contract might condition the client's payment duty on the client's personal satisfaction with the website's appearance and functionality. **Concurrent conditions** arise when each party's performance is conditioned on the other party's nearly simultaneous tender of counterperformance. For example, in most face-to-face retail store sales, the buyer's payment is concurrently conditioned on the seller's delivery. Similarly, the seller's delivery is concurrently conditioned on the buyer's payment. Occasionally, there is a **condition subsequent**. This is an event that occurs *after* a duty is being performed that relieves one party of any further duty to perform. For example, a customer's failure to pay the monthly bill for Internet service might be interpreted to relieve the ISP from a duty to provide future service.

TITLE AND RISK OF LOSS

Before the UCC, under the common law, the concept of **title** or ownership of property was very important for many reasons. Title gave the owner a right to insure the property, and title gave the owner legal remedies against the seller or a wrongdoer. An owner is liable for taxes. An owner risks financial loss if the property is damaged or destroyed. The UCC has changed some of this by separating the incidents of ownership that title implied from two other concerns: insurable interest and risk of loss. Today, title to goods affects mainly ownership, creditors' rights, and taxation. As discussed further in Chapter 13, ownership of information and intellectual property is distinguished from the more limited licensee rights that most purchasers obtain when acquiring these intangibles.

Title

Title does not pass from the seller to the buyer until *after* the goods are identified to the contract. Goods are **identified** when particular goods are designated as being for the buyer, which can occur in several ways. The contract may explicitly designate particular goods by, for example, listing serial numbers. Identification also occurs when particular goods are shipped or the seller otherwise labels them as intended for the buyer. Generally, the contract of sale dictates when title passes. However, if the timing of title transfer is not mentioned, then title passes when the seller completes delivery. Delivery can happen: (1) when they are delivered to the carrier in a contract requiring the seller to "ship," (2) when they are delivered to the buyer in a contract requiring the seller to "deliver," (3) at the time of contracting if delivery is not mentioned or will occur without moving the goods, such as when the goods are held in an independent warehouse, or (4) when negotiable documents of title are delivered. If the buyer rejects the goods, title immediately reverts to the seller. Most title transfers in international trade are determined by separate, formal documents of title.

Documents of Title

Many domestic and international commercial transactions use formal written documents that accompany the goods in transit for various purposes. For example, commercial documents make or guarantee payment, prove the contents of shipment to various officials (customs, public safety, law enforcement, carrier, bankers, buyer), and prove or actually transfer ownership. These are formal documents, and they are intangible interests in personal property. They are traditionally written on paper; many are still printed on official-looking certificates.

Since the 1960s, many commercial documents have been replaced by **uncertificated** rights, which are generally mere book entries or electronic records held by another party, for example, insurance policies, ATM transactions, savings accounts, and corporate securities (stocks or bonds). This change has been made possible by innovations in technology, such as computerized electronic communication, encryption, and biometrics. Also, UETA now permits many such formal documents to be officially archived as electronic records on computers as well as transferred and negotiated by electronic endorsement. Security measures to minimize errors and irregularities in this electronic world must eventually become as reliable—perhaps even more reliable—than the security measures traditionally used with paper documents.

Traditionally, an intimate understanding of these commercial documents was largely of interest to logisticians, carriers, warehouses, auditors, lawyers, financial service firms (securities, insurance, banking), government officials, and, of course, delivery drivers, loading dock foremen, and mail room clerks. Today, with the migration of commercial practice to e-commerce, such details are becoming important to entrepreneurs, information technologists, marketing and finance people, and professionals in nearly all other business functions because their design of new systems for the converging economy *must* use them effectively.

Many important commercial documents transfer legal rights when negotiated by endorsement. This exchange of commercial documents works to reduce risk, particularly in transactions conducted at a distance. These risks include wrongful payment or delivery, malicious tampering, fraud, and theft. Payment by check is the most familiar form of transferable or **negotiable instruments. Commercial paper**, a subset

> **Ethical Issue**
>
> ### Ethical Controversy over Forgery
>
> Probably the biggest challenge for commercial practice has been in building and maintaining trust and confidence. Transaction anxiety has plagued commercial parties for thousands of years. The 16th Century mercantilists invented documentary transfers of title and payments. This has been one of the most significant developments to encourage reliance on standard commercial practices and therefore, contributes greatly to increasing safe commercial activity. Nevertheless, fraud still raises transactions costs. Consider the unethical practice of forgery—to fashion or reproduce for fraudulent purposes. Forgeries of endorsements on checks, notes and other commercial documents immediately results in the victim mistakenly giving property rights, goods or money to the forger. Obtaining property under false pretenses has long been a crime and tort but is also wrongful under commercial laws like the UCC. As more commerce moves to electronic documents, the forgery problem only increases, from imposters forging signatures to the illegal interception and decryption of encrypted electronic messages and other hacking methods. Forgery has moved high tech with counterfeiting of cash, checks and other commercial documents using color copiers and laser printers. Such activities are illegal and unethical. General trust and reliance on e-commerce will improve only as these security concerns are adequately addressed by law and technology.

of negotiable instruments, is governed by UCC Article 3. It includes familiar forms of payment obligations, including checks, notes, drafts, certificates of deposit, and bankers' acceptances.

The usefulness of negotiating documents by endorsement is best seen with the classical example of buyers' and sellers' "transaction anxiety." Sellers are often unwilling to transfer title or physical custody of goods to an unknown or uncreditworthy buyer without some kind of assurance. Similarly, buyers are often unwilling to make payment to unknown or untrustworthy sellers, without some assurance. These expectations can be fulfilled when the system uses **trusted and reliable third-party intermediaries**, including the seller's and buyer's banks, the carrier or other freight forwarder, or the warehouse. These trusted intermediaries perform nearly concurrent conditions in transferring the payment to the seller and transferring title to the buyer. In other words, after inspections and government clearances are verified, intermediaries condition their endorsement of payment on the endorsement of the title transfer, and vice versa.

UCC Article 7 governs the use of **documents of title**, which include bills of lading, dock receipts, dock warrants, and warehouse receipts. Documents of title are written instruments entitling the holder to possess, receive, or dispose of specified goods usually then held by a bailee, carrier, or warehouse. **Bailees** are temporary custodians of goods who usually act for the true owner's benefit. Carriers and warehouses are common bailees. A **bill of lading** is a document of title used by carriers and freight forwarders. A bill of lading can also serve as the contract of carriage Exhibit 11.1). A **warehouse receipt** is a title document issued by a warehouse and it can also serve as the storage contract (Exhibit 11.2).

Documents of title may be nonnegotiable. However, when they are negotiable and physically accompany the flow of documents handled by trusted intermediaries, certainty rises significantly. An endorsement is required to transfer rights from the transferor to the transferee of a negotiable document of title. There is a special status for bona fide purchasers of negotiable documents of title, similar to the holder in due course status for commercial paper discussed later. During shipment, carriers must take reasonable care of the goods in their possession. Carriers must deliver them to the recipient, called a **consignee**, which is designated in the document of title. Similarly,

EXHIBIT 11.1 Bill of Lading

BILL OF LADING

Shipper	
Consignee: (Complete name and address)	Forwarding agent
	Point and country of origin / Place of receipt
Notify party	Domestic routing instructions
Pier	Place of delivery
Ocean vessel / Port of landing	
Point of discharge	

CARRIER'S RECEIPT — PARTICULARS FURNISHED BY SHIPPER

Marks and numbers	Number of packages	Description of goods	Gross weight	Measurement

- Received in apparent good order and condition except as otherwise noted hereon the goods, containers, or other packages for transportation from the place of receipt or port of loading subject to exceptions, limitations, and conditions and to be delivered to the consignee or assigns.

(TERMS OF THIS BILL LADING CONTINUED ON REVERSE.)

TOTAL FREIGHTS $ ____________________

DATE ______________________________ BY ______________________
(Agent)

EXHIBIT 11.2 Warehouse Receipt

WAREHOUSE RECEIPT—NOT NEGOTIABLE

Receipt and lot number ________________ Vault no. ____ ____ ____ ____ ____
____ ____ ____ ____ ____

Date of issue ______________ 20 ____

Received for the account of and deliverable to ______________________________
of (address) ____
the goods enumerated on attached schedule and stored in Company warehouse, located at ______________________________. These goods are accepted upon the following conditions.

That the value of all goods stored is not over $ ________________ per pound unless a higher value is noted on the schedule, for which an additional monthly storage charge of $ ________________ on each $ ________________ will be made.

Ownership. The Customer, Shipper, Depositor, or Agent represents and warrants that he is lawfully possessed of goods to be stored and/or has the authority to store or ship said goods. (If the goods are mortgaged, notify the Company of the name and address of the mortgagee.)
Payment of Charges. Storage bills are payable monthly in advance for each month's storage or fraction thereof. The Depositor will pay reasonable attorney's fee incurred by the Company in collecting delinquent accounts.
Liability of Company. The Company shall be liable for any loss or injury to the goods caused by its failure to exercise such care as a reasonably careful person would exercise under like circumstances. The Company will not be liable for loss or damage to fragile articles not packed, or articles packed or unpacked by other than employees of this Company.
Change of Address. Notice of change of address must be given the Company in writing, and acknowledged in writing by the Company.
Transfer or Withdrawal of Goods. The warehouse receipt is not negotiable and shall be produced and all charges must be paid before delivery to the Depositor, or transfer of goods to another person; however, a written direction to the Company to transfer the goods to another person or deliver the goods may be accepted by the Company at its option without requiring tender of the warehouse receipt.
Access to Storage, Partial Withdrawal. A signed order from the person whose name the receipt is issued is required to enable others to remove or have access to goods. A charge is made for stacking and unstacking, and for access to stored goods.
Building-Fire-Watchmen. The Company does not represent or warrant that its building cannot be destroyed by fire. The Company shall not be required to maintain a watchman or sprinkler system and its failure to do so shall not constitute negligence.
Claims or Errors. All claims for non delivery of any article or articles and for any damage, breakage, etc., must be made in writing within ninety (90) days from delivery of goods stored or they are waived. Failure to return the warehouse receipt for correction within ________ ( ) days after receipt thereof by the depositor will be conclusive that it is correct and delivery will be made only in accordance therewith.
Warehouseman's Lien. The Company reserves the right to sell the goods stored, in accordance with the provisions of the Uniform Commercial Code (Business and Commerce Code if stored in Texas), for all lawful charges in areas.
Termination of Storage. The Company reserves the right to terminate the storage of the goods at any time by giving to the Depositor thirty (30) days' written notice of its intention to do so, and, unless the Depositor removes such goods within that period, the Company is hereby empowered to have the same removed at the cost and expense of the Depositor, or the Company may sell them at auction in accordance with state law.

THIS DOCUMENT CONTAINS THE WHOLE CONTRACT BETWEEN THE PARTIES AND THERE ARE NO OTHER TERMS, WARRANTIES, REPRESENTATIONS, OR AGREEMENTS OF EITHER DEPOSITOR OR COMPANY NOT HEREIN CONTAINED.

Storage per month or fraction thereof	$ ________	Wrapping and preparing for storage	$ ________
Warehouse labor	$ ________	Charges advanced	$ ________
Cartage	$ ________	$ ________	$ ________
Packing at residence	$ ________	$ ________	$ ________

By ______________________________

warehouse operators must take reasonable care of goods in their possession, deliver them to the designated consignee, and accurately prepare the warehouse receipt. Risks that the goods may be lost, damaged, or stolen in transit are discussed later.

Electronic Commercial Documents

Negotiable documents can be processed electronically. Currently, this is largely done within secure Electronic Data Interchange (EDI) systems operating among regular trading partners who previously agreed to use electronic commercial documents. However, as UETA is proven reliable, electronic commercial documents will migrate from EDI into more general practice. Theoretically, documents need not physically accompany the goods in transit. Indeed, printed documents cannot physically accompany electronic deliveries of information or software. Instead, various electronic methods may cause electronic documents to arrive right before or soon after the goods arrive. They could directly accompany electronic delivery of information or software. For example, documents showing endorsements can be transferred by fax machine, scanned for attachment to e-mail messages, downloaded from a secure website, or sent via EDI.

An original document is first prepared, perhaps by word processor in ASCII characters or by a webpage development tool using the HTML Web markup language. Perhaps a more suitable and emerging new language is **XML**, extensible markup language. XML is broader than HTML, it permits the use of graphics for diagrams, and designers can construct forms for easy and accurate data storage and retrieval. Alternatively, the document can be printed for faxing, or an electronic version can be transmitted via computerized facsimile, sent as an e-mail attachment, or uploaded or downloaded through a secure website. As the electronic document is transmitted electronically, all necessary intermediaries can apply their endorsements. Endorsements can be written signatures made either on the original or on a copy printed from the electronic version or made by using some other acceptable electronic signature technology (e.g., encryption). Further endorsement and transfer can be made physically or by another electronic conversion that uses the same or a different technique, such as fax, e-mail, scanning, Web access, or some future developed electronic or digital communication method. As UETA and the federal E-SIGN law are expanded to cover more types of commercial documents, endorsements may alternatively be made with electronic signatures on electronic records.

As of this writing, neither UETA nor the federal E-SIGN law applies to checks, notes, drafts, or letters of credit. The banking industry has reliable systems and may want to await the proven security of newer systems. However, experience with EDI and the electronic negotiation of real estate promissory notes should eventually demonstrate a workable model for electronic negotiable instruments of all types. As the banking system becomes able to reliably process electronic checks, simple changes in the UETA and E-SIGN exceptions for electronic transferable documents may expand their use. Chapter 10 introduced UETA's approach to electronic commercial documents.

Under UETA §16 and the federal E-SIGN law, electronic **transferable records** can be used as negotiable documents if the parties expressly agree to use them. However, for now, UETA permits the use of electronic transferable records for only real estate promissory notes and documents of title. The mortgage industry appears ready to reduce the paperwork expenses of negotiable documents. The federal E-SIGN law is even more restrictive, in that it permits electronic transferable records for only real estate promissory notes. By permitting electronic promissory notes for real estate loans, UETA and E-SIGN facilitate cost savings for the secondary mortgage industry. All the federal E-SIGN exceptions will be reviewed by 2003, and some exceptions may then be removed by Congress or by federal regulators. The states might also expand coverage to other types of commercial paper.

Like their paper counterparts, transferable records must be created, transferred, and stored under secure conditions that permit only one party at a time to control or possess them. Absent forgery in the paper world, when a negotiable instrument is transferred, it is no longer held by the transferor, only by the transferee. Significant technological difficulties must be overcome before many computer systems could be sufficiently reliable and secure to assure such exclusive control over transferable records. For example, after an electronic transfer, the sending system must be prevented from having any control over the record, and the recipient must have exclusive control. Some possible combination of security methods is needed, including encryption, physical access controls, and/or third parties that record every transfer. Endorsement could be approved or made by humans who review each transaction by computer. Alternatively, the electronic agent provisions of UETA and E-SIGN are intended to permit cost savings with computerized transaction processing and endorsement via electronic agents.

Like many citizens, some courts are suspicious of the validity of electronic documents. Electronic commercial documents must have enough security to build confidence that the system is not prone to alteration, forgery, or other fraud. The judge's language in the following case rather bluntly illustrates that proof of key commercial concepts, such as title, require reliable evidence, and the Internet may have a long way to go before it builds confidence that it is accurate.

St. Clair v. Johnny's Oyster & Shrimp, Inc.

76 F.Supp.2d 773 (S.D.Tx. 1999)

Facts. Teddy St. Clair was injured while working as a seaman for Johnny's Oyster & Shrimp, Inc., aboard the vessel *Capt. Le'Brado*. Teddy St. Clair sued Johnny's Oyster & Shrimp, Inc., for personal injury compensation, and his employer filed a motion to dismiss the claim, arguing it was not responsible for the injuries because it did not own the vessel *Capt. Le'Brado*. Teddy St. Clair offered proof of ownership retrieved from the Internet.

Legal Issue. Is information obtained off the Internet sufficient to prove title to a vessel?

Opinion. District Judge Kent. A motion to dismiss should be granted only when it appears without a doubt that the plaintiff can prove no set of facts in support of her claims that would entitle her to relief. Defendant alleges that it does not now, and did not at the time of the alleged incident, own or operate the vessel CAPT. LE'BRADO. Defendant notes that on July 1, 1999 ownership was transferred to Oysters R Us, Inc. and on August 1, 1999, Oysters R Us, Inc. transferred ownership of the vessel to Shrimps R Us, Inc. Plaintiff responds that he has discovered "evidence"—taken off the Worldwide Web on December 1, 1999—revealing that Defendant does "in fact" own CAPT. LE'BRADO.

Plaintiff's electronic "evidence" is totally insufficient to withstand Defendant's Motion to Dismiss. While some look to the Internet as an innovative vehicle for communication, the Court continues to warily and wearily view it largely as one large catalyst for rumor, innuendo, and misinformation. So as not to mince words, the court reiterates that this so-called Web provides no way of verifying the authenticity of the alleged contentions that Plaintiff wishes to rely. There is no way that Plaintiff can overcome the presumption that the information he discovered on the Internet is inherently untrustworthy. Anyone can put anything on the Internet. No web-site is monitored for accuracy and nothing contained therein is under oath or even subject to independent verification absent underlying documentation. Moreover, the Court holds no illusions that hackers can adulterate the content on any web-site from any location at any time. For these reasons, any evidence procured off the Internet is adequate for almost nothing.

Instead of relying on the voodoo information taken from the Internet, Plaintiff must hunt for hard copy back-up documentation in admissible form from the United States Coast Guard or discover alternative information verifying what Plaintiff alleges.

Decision. Information obtained off the Internet is not sufficiently reliable to prove ownership of a vessel.

Case Questions

1. If websites were regularly archived by third parties, could they be used to prove the timing and accuracy of website content? How might that change this judge's rationale about the accuracy of Web content?

2. Many disputes about information posted on the Internet may not require proof of the truth stated in the posted material; in this case, that would be accuracy of ownership of the boat in this case. Instead, in many other situations, it is useful simply to prove the material was posted. In what situations might evidence of mere posting satisfy courtroom evidentiary requirements and prove key facts?

Warranty of Title

The UCC implies in every contract for sale that the seller has the right to sell the goods, there are no outstanding liens on the goods, and the seller can pass good title to the buyer. This is known as the **warranty of title**. It differs from express warranties and implied warranties of fitness or merchantability, which address product quality, not ownership. For example, the warranty of title would make the seller liable if the true owner of stolen goods were to reclaim them from the buyer after the sale. The warranty of title can be specifically disclaimed. It does not arise if the circumstances suggest the goods are of questionable origin, such as in a sheriff's sale. However, a general statement disclaiming "all warranties" does not eliminate the warranty of title. UCITA's noninterference and noninfringement warranty would serve a function similar to the warranty of title.

Risk of Loss

Risk of loss is still important because goods can be damaged, lost, or stolen during shipment. Loss may result from an intentional act, negligence, or a natural catastrophe. Importantly, before risk of loss passes to the buyer, the seller is liable for breach of contract if a loss occurs. By contrast, after risk of loss passes to the buyer, the purchase price must be paid even if the goods are damaged or lost. Therefore, the parties have conflicting incentives for the timing when they shift the risk of loss. One sensible risk management technique is for both parties to insure the goods during transit. The buyer has the right to insure, called an **insurable interest**, as soon as the goods are identified, and the seller retains an insurable interest for as long as the seller has either title or a security interest (lien) in the goods.

Passage of risk of loss is made according to numerous technical rules. First, the parties may specify in their contract when risk passes. Second, if they do not include such a term and no carrier is used to transport the goods, then risk passes when a nonmerchant seller tenders delivery to the buyer or a merchant seller makes actual delivery to the buyer. Third, when a carrier is used, risk generally passes at either the point of the shipment's origin or at the point of arrival at the destination according to the **mercantile terms** used: FOB, FAS, CIF, C&F, or Ex-Ship. Mercantile terms are established by the UCC and are called **INCOTERMS** by the International Chamber of Commerce. See Exhibit 11.3 for common mercantile terms.

ONLINE

International Chamber of Commerce
http://www.iccwbo.com

Consider the example of goods shipped from a Pittsburgh manufacturer to a Detroit wholesaler. In an "FOB Pittsburgh" contract, risk and title pass when the seller tenders the goods to the carrier in Pittsburgh. In an "FOB Detroit" contract, risk and title pass when the carrier makes actual delivery of the goods to the buyer in Detroit. The risk remains on the seller in a **sale on approval** until the buyer confirms the purchase after testing or other trial period. Risk remains with the buyer in

EXHIBIT 11.3 Mercantile Terms

Mercantile Abbreviation	Mercantile Term	Mercantile Term Meaning
FOB	Free on board	Requires payment of freight charges: (1) by buyer if FOB (named place of seller's shipment), (2) by seller if FOB (named place of buyer's destination), (3) by seller if FOB (named carrier vessel, car, or vehicle). Title and risk of loss pass from seller to buyer at the named place.
FAS	Free alongside	Requires seller to deliver goods alongside vessel designated by buyer. Title and risk of loss pass from seller to buyer alongside the vessel.
CIF (CF)	Cost, insurance, freight	Seller's price includes cost of goods, loading, transit, insurance, and freight charges for transport to the named destination. Seller must contract for the transportation. Title and risk of loss pass from seller to buyer when the goods are delivered to the carrier.
C&F	Cost and freight	Seller's price includes cost of goods, loading, and freight charges for transport to the named destination. Seller must contract for the transportation. Title and risk of loss pass from seller to buyer when the goods are delivered to the carrier.
Ex-Ship	Ex-Ship	Requires unloading of goods from ship at named port; title and risk of loss pass from seller to buyer when unloaded.

a **sale or return** until the goods are returned to the seller. If the goods are rightfully rejected or there is a rightful revocation of acceptance by the buyer, risk reverts to the seller. These latter two remedies are discussed later in this chapter.

THIRD-PARTY RIGHTS

One might think that only the contracting parties may seek enforcement of their contracts. However, in four distinct situations, outsiders have legally enforceable rights or responsibilities in the contracts of other persons or firms. The first two situations involve contracts that specifically identify and intend an outside third party to receive contractual benefits. Such third parties are either creditor beneficiaries or donee beneficiaries. The third and fourth situations arise when a contracting party transfers to an outsider either contractual rights or contractual duties under an existing contract. In such situations, the outsider may enforce the contract or could be required to perform a contractual duty.

Third-Party Beneficiaries

An outsider intentionally identified as a beneficiary to receive the performance is an **obligee** in the original contract and is known as a **third-party beneficiary**, illustrated in Exhibit 11.4. The party who must make the performance is the **obligor**. A third-party beneficiary may enforce the contract against the original obligor. If the person who is promised a performance intends that the contract should confer a gift on the third party, then the third party has no right to sue this promisee. For example, assume someone purchases flowers from a florist, intending them to be a gift for the purchaser's spouse. The spouse, known as a **donee third-party beneficiary**, could enforce the contract against the florist as obligor, but obviously not against the spouse who purchased the flowers. The spouse conferring the gift simply used the florist's services to make the gift. The donee of a gift cannot generally sue the donor for the performance.

Contrast the restrictions on donee third-party beneficiaries with the greater rights of third parties who were previously owed a duty by the promisee. If the promisee uses the obligor to discharge a *duty already owed* to the third-party beneficiary, this is a **creditor third-party beneficiary** situation. Creditor beneficiaries may enforce the obligation against *either* of the contracting parties. The promisee was already previously liable to the third party because that duty preexisted, independent of the third-party beneficiary contract. For example, a home sale contract might identify the seller's lender as a creditor third-party beneficiary. If the buyer assumes the seller's mortgage and promises to repay the original mortgage loan, the lender can generally sue either the seller or the buyer. The seller is liable as the original borrower, and the buyer voluntarily assumed the duty to pay. Unless the bank releases the seller from making the

EXHIBIT 11.4 Third Party Beneficiary

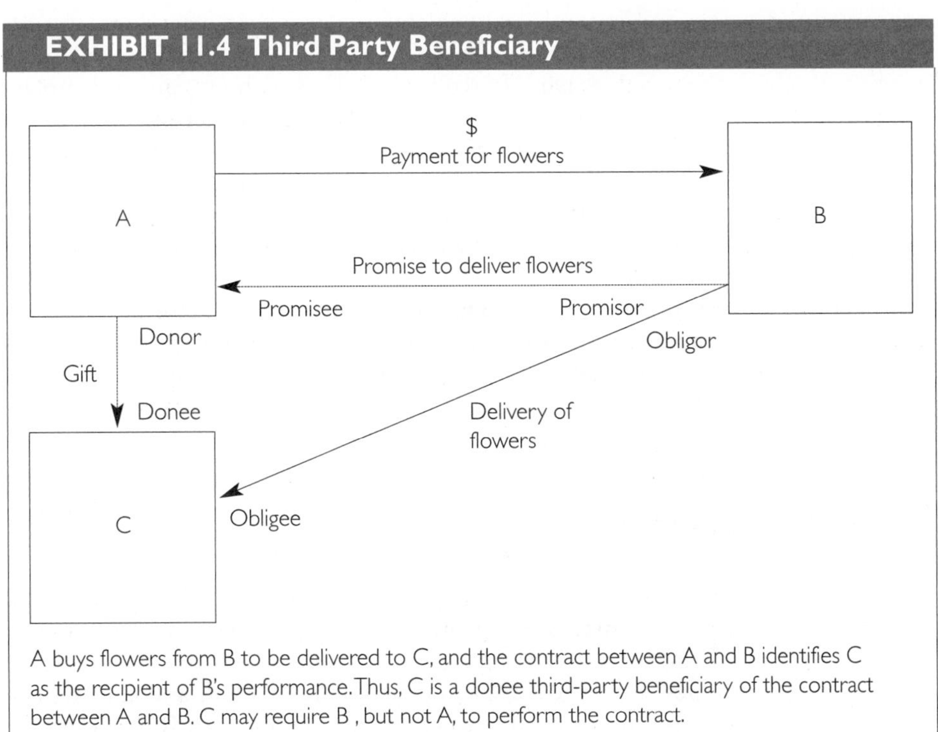

A buys flowers from B to be delivered to C, and the contract between A and B identifies C as the recipient of B's performance. Thus, C is a donee third-party beneficiary of the contract between A and B. C may require B , but not A, to perform the contract.

payments in a **novation** contract, the bank may sue either the seller or the buyer for loan default, because the seller originally borrowed the money and the buyer promised to perform to the lender on the original loan.

Some outsiders are mere **incidental beneficiaries.** Incidental beneficiaries receive benefit only by coincidence from the side effects produced by others' contracts. These side effects are called **externalities**, or benefits enjoyed by outsiders who are not contracting parties. Incidental beneficiaries have no rights to enforce the contract because they are neither identified in the contract nor intended to benefit from it. For example, contracts for the construction of a new factory often generate significant economic benefits for the surrounding community. However, community members cannot enforce the construction contracts because they are merely unintended and incidental beneficiaries.

Assignment and Delegation

Contract rights and/or duties are sometimes transferred to an outsider in a separate contract. Such **transfer contracts** are often made after the original contract. The law distinguishes between the **assignment of rights** to enforce the original contract, (Exhibit 11.5) and the **delegation of duties** to perform under the original contract (Exhibit 11.6). Consider the sale of a business. The seller assigns rights to enforce contract duties owed to the business *from* others (e.g., accounts receivable) and usually delegates duties previously owed *to* outsiders (e.g., accounts payable). The purchaser of the business receives both rights and duties so it may collect previously outstanding accounts receivable and must perform contract duties the seller formerly owed to other customers.

The transfer of rights or duties can sometimes be accomplished without getting permission from the other party to the original contract. Such unconsented transfers are effective only when they do not materially change the obligations or rights of the nonconsenting party. For example, a wholesaler may assign past-due accounts receivable to a collection agency or factor. A seller of goods may assign the buyer's payment by check to the seller's bank for collection. These debtors cannot complain as long as they are notified. Notice permits the debtor to redirect payment to the new payee, the assignee. Rights and duties are freely transferable if they involve obligations to pay money or are standard repair and construction contracts. The test for transferability focuses on the nonconsenting contracting party. A transfer is unenforceable if the nonconsenting party would suffer a **material change** in duty or right. Personal service contracts are typical examples of unassignable or nondelegable contracts. Nevertheless, it is possible for the original contractor to grant permission for the assignment or delegation, consenting to substitute the new party as assignee or delegate. The original contract can validly limit delegation. Assignment is a commonplace technique, particularly in the endorsement and transfer by negotiation of payments and other commercial documents, as discussed next.

PAYMENT SYSTEMS

By the Industrial Revolution, commerce had evolved beyond the limits of payment by barter or cash. Fundamental to the growth in trade has been the development of alternatives to concurrent payment and delivery of goods. Performances by barter or money (e.g., currency) for large transactions in goods, services, and land are seldom made simultaneously by both sides. Key to this evolutionary advance were the banking practices of medieval European **mercantilists**, who developed important

EXHIBIT 11.5 Assignment of Rights

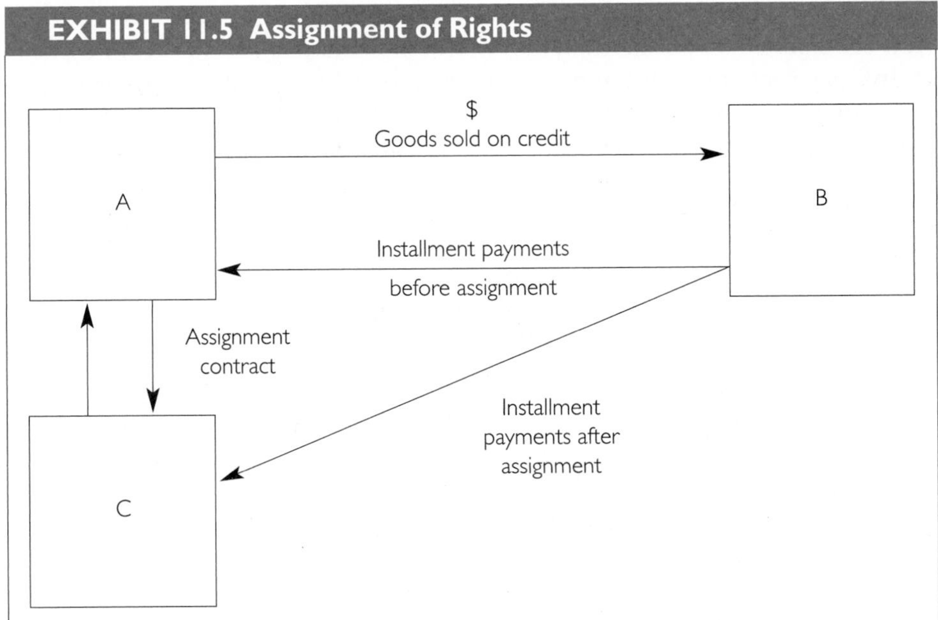

A's account receivable is factored to C, an assignment of rights. C is the factor that obtains the right to receive the installment payments that B originally promised to A. B's consent is necessary only for the assignment of personal services, not this payment duty.

EXHIBIT 11.6 Delegation of Duties

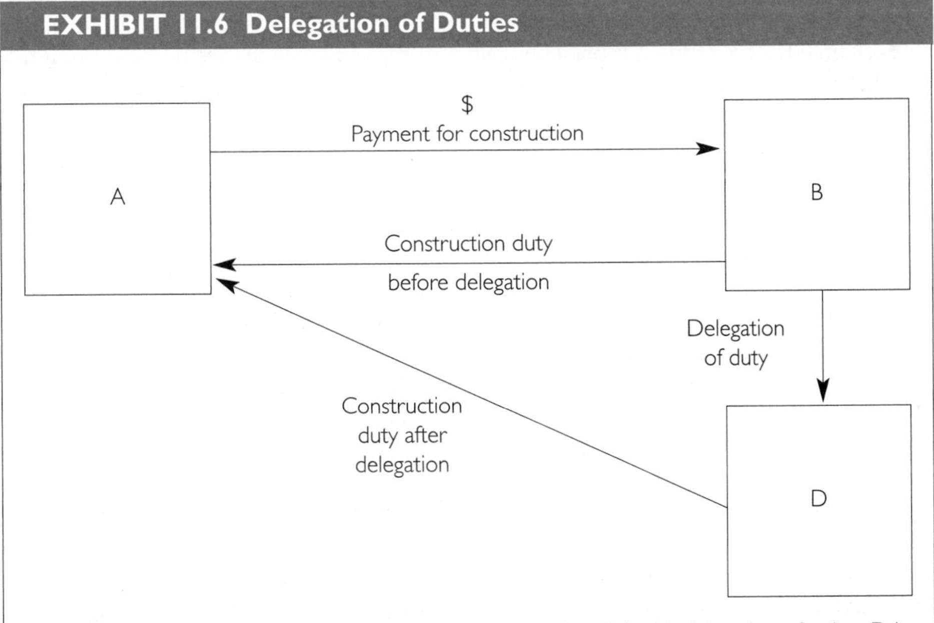

B's obligation to perform construction services is delegated to D. In this delegation of a duty, D is the delegate that becomes obligated to perform the construction services to A. A's consent is necessary to delegate personal services and also to release B's original duty to perform.

payment mechanisms. Generally, today's documentary and electronic payment systems are modeled on the mercantilists' system of permitting the transfer of **rights to receive payment** given by buyers and borrowers, who used these payment documents to pay for goods and services. The mercantilists' customs and practices eventually became the law merchant. Documentary payments facilitated trade, and they eventually permitted negotiable instruments to become reliable substitutes for currency. These are very successful payment mechanisms. The Federal Reserve processes more than 50 billion negotiable instrument payments annually, mostly the familiar personal and corporate checks.

Contemporary law encourages payment with paper instruments and increasingly with electronic alternatives. This transactional infrastructure was made possible as lawmakers recognized that uniformity among the states and between nations is needed to facilitate commerce. The payments section of this chapter discusses the traditional paper-based payment schemes governed by UCC Article 3, "Commercial Paper," and Article 4, "Bank Deposits." Also, electronic payment schemes are discussed, including Article 4A covering electronic funds transfers, Federal Reserve System rules on debit, point of sale, and credit card transactions, and innovations in electronic payments.

Recall that negotiable documents of title, discussed previously, are processed by third parties, including carriers, warehouses, and banks. Similarly, negotiable payments are processed by the seller, the seller's bank, the buyer's bank, and other intermediaries. When the buyer pays using commercial paper, the seller accepts the buyer's check or note as the buyer's performance. Typically, the seller then negotiates the paper, transferring it through the banking system by endorsement for eventual payment by the buyer or the buyer's bank. This concept of **negotiability** is essential to making commercial paper an adequate substitute for money. Negotiable instruments are formal contracts that must meet strict requirements for contents and location. They are transferred by the negotiation process. The law gives a special status to intermediaries, which stand between the payor and payee, to encourage intermediaries to willingly accept the paper in exchange for the value it represents. Most of these intermediaries become **bona fide purchasers for value** or **holders in due course**, who are given greater rights than are assignees of a simple, informal contract as just discussed.

DEFINITIONS

UCC Article 3 covers two types of commercial paper: notes and drafts. A **note** (promissory note, installment note, collateral note, mortgage note) is a *two-party* instrument in which the **maker** promises to pay the **payee** a specified amount in the future. A bank's **certificate of deposit** (CD) is a type of note in which the bank acknowledges the receipt (deposit) of customer funds and promises to repay them at a future time with interest. A **draft** is a *three-party* instrument in which a **drawer** issues a draft that orders a **drawee**, usually the drawer's bank, to pay money to the third-party payee. **Checks** are the most common form of draft. When a drawer writes the check, it directs their drawee bank to pay the specified amount of money to the payee or to someone else to whom the payee endorsed the check. Other forms of draft are widely used in commerce. For example, the **time draft** is payable on a specified date in the future, possibly days, months, or even years away. A **sight draft** is payable on sight—that is, immediately when presented and after a demand is made for payment. A **trade acceptance** is a commercial draft used to pay for goods (also known as a **sales draft**). It can be drawn by the seller of goods on the buyer's bank and sent for the buyer's approval.

NEGOTIABILITY

Negotiable instruments must meet strict rules of form to facilitate accurate and efficient verification of the terms and validity. This regularity encourages participants in the banking system to willingly take the paper by assignment in exchange for value, usually by paying money for the paper or crediting a customer's bank account. Can you imagine the commercial difficulty if sellers and their banks would not accept documentary payments?

Commercial paper must meet the negotiability requirements of UCC §3-104 by being strictly (1) in writing and (2) signed by the maker or drawer, (3) containing unconditional promise or order to pay, (4) indicating a fixed amount of money (sum certain), (6) being payable on demand or at a definite time and (7) payable to order or to bearer, and (8) containing no other undertaking. These requirements create certainty, reducing the risk of forgeries or fraud by imposters. The migration to electronic payments over many years has been slow but steady to permit management of these risks and thereby retain stability in the banking and financial systems.

The writing requirement permits the use of handwritten, typed, preprinted, or mixed inscriptions in a tangible form. Although the use of paper is traditional, it is unnecessary. Computer and telecommunication transfers are covered by UCC Article 4A on electronic funds transfers. The **signature** may be handwritten in cursive or printing; supplied by stamp, computer, or check-cutting device; or provided by some other mechanized form or symbol intended to authenticate a writing. UETA does not yet require use of electronic signatures on notes or drafts. However, if favorable experience accumulates, the states or the Federal Reserve may expand UETA's coverage to electronic payments. Importantly, forgeries do not obligate the maker or drawer who is wrongly named on a forged instrument.

Notes and drafts must include an **unconditional promise or order to pay**, thereby setting the terms of payment. A **promise** makes a commitment to pay. By contrast, a simple IOU is not a promise to pay because it is merely an acknowledgment of a debt. Alternatively, an **order** directs some agent to make the payment. Typically, an order directs the customer's bank or lender to make the payment. The payment cannot be made conditional on some event or on another agreement; otherwise, no one would freely accept such paper in commerce. For example, a promissory note would be nonnegotiable if it was written by a buyer who included an express condition that the payment promise was not binding until the payee (e.g., seller) delivered specified goods. Similarly, paper is nonnegotiable if made expressly subject to or governed by some other writing or contract like a warranty. Why? Banks and other intermediaries would have no easy way to confirm whether the goods were delivered, and they could not easily verify the contents of some other writing. Banks would probably be reluctant to accept such conditional paper if extra work was needed to verify other documents.

Many people write notations on their checks. It is permissible for commercial paper to merely mention another obligation or writing without destroying negotiability. For example, check writers often use a memo line in the lower left-hand corner to reference a particular payment, invoice number, transaction, or the underlying contract. It is also permissible to state that a note is secured with a lien on specified collateral. A payment can be limited to be taken from a particular fund, such as when a customer's check is drawn against only one of several accounts held in a particular bank.

Instruments are negotiable only if the extent of the obligation can be easily ascertained by looking *only* at the paper. Importantly, a **fixed sum of money** (sum certain) must be stated. Nevertheless, some adjustments are permissible. For example, interest may be stated at a specified rate. A formula can state the applicable interest if it is clearly stated on the paper or can be determined by an index that is generally available as a published rate (e.g., "three points over prime rate"). Variable-rate paper is now negotiable under the 1990 revision to UCC Article 3. Paper remains negotiable even if the fixed amount can be adjusted by a stated discount for early payment or a premium charged for late payments. There can also be adjustments for additional costs of collection, such as attorney's fees. Payment must be promised or ordered only **in money**—that is, domestic or foreign currency sanctioned by a government. Payment promised in foreign currency can also be paid in domestic currency; the exchange rate is determined at the spot market rate quoted by banks as prevailing on the date of payment. However, payment cannot be promised or ordered in goods, services, or other intangible, nonmoney credits. A check to pay in gold leaf, cigarettes, bus tokens, frequent flyer miles, or some Internet currency is nonnegotiable even if such "currency" becomes acceptable as a medium of exchange in some communities. This is the most important requirement restraining the use of traditional payment mechanisms in electronic form by using nonmoney credits, as discussed later.

Negotiable paper must make it clear *when* payment is promised or authorized. There is a "time value of money." Intermediaries are willing to handle commercial paper only if their obligations and rights can be determined easily. A **demand instrument** is payable "on demand," when presented, or "at sight" if no time is stated, like most personal checks. Many notes and time drafts are often made payable at a definite future time on a specified date. Sellers and lenders take these instruments as a form of credit, effectively giving the buyer some time to settle up. The **definite time** that payment will be made must be readily ascertainable when the instrument is originally made. Negotiable time instruments include those made payable a fixed period after a stated date (30 days after June 1, 2002), on or before a particular date (payable October 30, 2003), on stated alternate dates, or payable on some other readily ascertainable date. However, paper is nonnegotiable if made payable only after some uncertain event. For example, a note made payable "after I sell my house" is nonnegotiable because when or whether the house might be sold is uncertain. Notes remain negotiable even if they contain an **acceleration clause**, giving the holder a right to demand early payment for some stated reason. For example, it is common in real estate purchases for the buyer to borrow much of the purchase price. The real estate loan is evidenced by a note that may include an acceleration clause requiring full and early repayment if the owner sells the house before the loan is completely repaid. Borrowers are also often given the right to prepay their loan early without destroying their note's negotiability. A note remains negotiable even if the holder is given the right to extend payment to some later date as stated on the note. However, it is nonnegotiable if the maker alone can extend payment.

Commercial paper must contain the **magic words of negotiability**, "payable to order or bearer," which tells intermediaries that they should willingly take the paper because it will flow freely to others and ultimately the maker or drawee will honor the payment. **Bearer paper** is negotiable by anyone who rightfully possesses it. For example, "pay to bearer," "pay to Joan Doe or bearer," and "pay to cash" all contain sufficient magic words of negotiability. **Order paper** is somewhat more restrictive than bearer paper because only a stated person can rightfully demand payment. Order paper requires negotiation; usually an endorsement must be supplied by the person named in the order or by someone else who is the rightful transferee. For example, order paper is negotiable if there are magic words such as "pay to the order of Joan Doe" or "payable to the assigns of John Doe." However, paper is nonnegotiable if it says only "pay to Joan Doe" because this does not encourage intermediaries to handle the paper. The person must be clearly identified, by name, account number, or office. Some preprinted forms use both order and bearer language such as "pay to the order of ___named person___ or bearer," and a specific name will be written into the blank when issued. Paper with both order and bearer language is treated as bearer paper. By a special UCC exception, checks commonly indicate "pay to the order of ___named person___" but remain negotiable even if the maker crosses out the wording "~~to the order~~" or if the preprinted form says simply "pay to ______."

A negotiable instrument may be antedated, postdated, or undated without affecting its validity. Written words are given preference over contradictory numeric writing, so the written amount on a personal check must be honored even if the numerals do not match. Handwritten terms are given preference over typed or preprinted terms, and typewritten terms are given preference over preprinted terms. An incomplete instrument may be completed by some authorized person. Consider a blank check that the maker authorizes someone else to fill in with the correct purchase price. It is enforceable. However, a blank check completed for a higher amount contains a **material alteration**. The negotiability of instruments must be readily determinable by looking only at the instrument itself for the elements discussed here. These elements must all appear on the face of the paper, with the few exceptions noted. Exhibit 11.7 illustrates the formal negotiable instrument requirements appearing directly on a check.

NEGOTIATION AND TRANSFER

The transfer of commercial paper is much like an assignment of contract rights covering the right to receive the stated payment. However, in commercial practice, intermediaries generally want better rights than would exist for an assignee under a

EXHIBIT 11.7 Negotiability Determined on Face of Draft

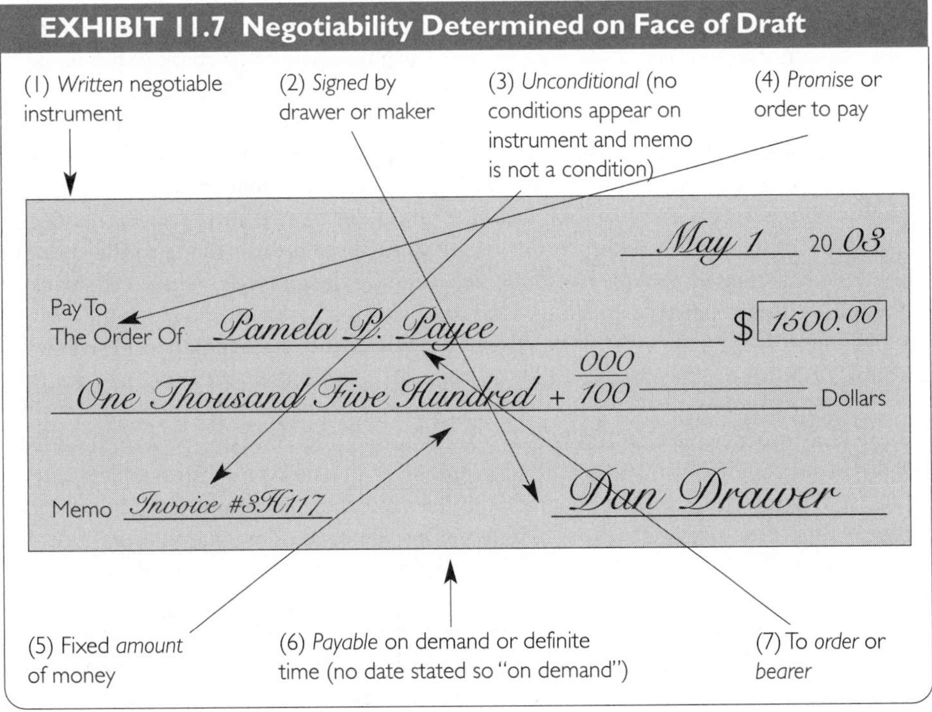

simple contract. An assignee of a simple contract receives only the rights held by the assignor, nothing more. However, to encourage their participation, commercial paper law adds a special status for intermediaries that transfer the paper. To achieve this special status, it is not enough that the instrument be in the formal negotiable form just discussed. The instrument must be transferred and assigned by due negotiation. Intermediaries thus have a special status, called a holder in due course, generally assuring that payment will be free from many defenses the original maker might assert against a normal contract assignee. Obviously, some clarification and context for the concept of the holder in due course is now needed.

When a maker or drawer initially drafts the instrument and makes the first delivery to another person, this is known as **issue**. Most paper is subsequently delivered many times in later **transfers** from **transferors** to **transferees**. Consider an individual who issues a personal check. First, the check may be issued by the drawer to a merchant in exchange—that is, as payment—for goods or services. The merchant is a transferee who further transfers the check to the merchant's own bank in exchange for crediting the merchant's account by the check amount. The check is likely to be negotiated further—that is, transferred through other correspondent banks—and is ultimately presented for payment to the drawee, which is the buyer's bank. **Negotiation** is a special type of transfer to a **holder** who rightfully possesses (has actual physical control) and has good title (ownership) to the instrument. Anyone in rightful possession of bearer paper has good title. Clearly, it is less risky to make paper to order, to endorse with restrictions, and to safeguard negotiable instruments as if they were cash. Order paper is negotiated when the previous holder physically transfers it after making an endorsement. Endorsement shows the transferor knowingly grants the transferee rights in the paper. If paper is made payable to multiple transferees in the conjunctive (e.g., "to Jack *and* Julia") then both must indorse. If the paper is made payable in the disjunctive (e.g., "to Jack *or* Julia") then either of their endorsements alone will suffice.

Endorsements

An **endorsement** is the signature of a payee, usually made on the back of the instrument. An endorsement is not invalid if it corrects a misspelling or changes the name to that of the holder. If the payee's name is misspelled, it is preferable to endorse by spelling the name both ways. An endorsement can broaden or limit further negotiation. In a **blank endorsement**, the payee simply supplies her or his signature converting the paper from order to bearer paper. In a **special endorsement** the payee supplies a signature but restricts further negotiation to a person named in the special endorsement. This implies that it retains order paper status because it is made to the order of only the newly named person. For example, compare the endorsements on the back of two checks made payable to John Doe in Exhibits 11.8 and 11.9. John's blank endorsement in Exhibit 11.8 makes the order paper into bearer paper. However, in Exhibit 11.9 John alternatively made a special endorsement over to "pay to Joan Roe." This endorsement serves as a security measure because it preserves the check's character as order paper that can be lawfully negotiated by only one person, Joan Roe. Bearer paper can be given a special endorsement, which converts it into order paper.

A **restrictive endorsement** that adds some condition generally does not destroy negotiability. Some restrictive endorsements are ignored. For example, assume the payee John Doe adds the restriction to "pay only if the maker performs the contract." This is a restrictive endorsement, but the added words would not be given any effect. By contrast, further negotiation can be somewhat restricted, such as transfer only through the banking system. "Pay any bank" and "for deposit only" are common and enforceable restrictive endorsements that do not destroy negotiability. For example,

EXHIBIT 11.8 Blank Endorsement

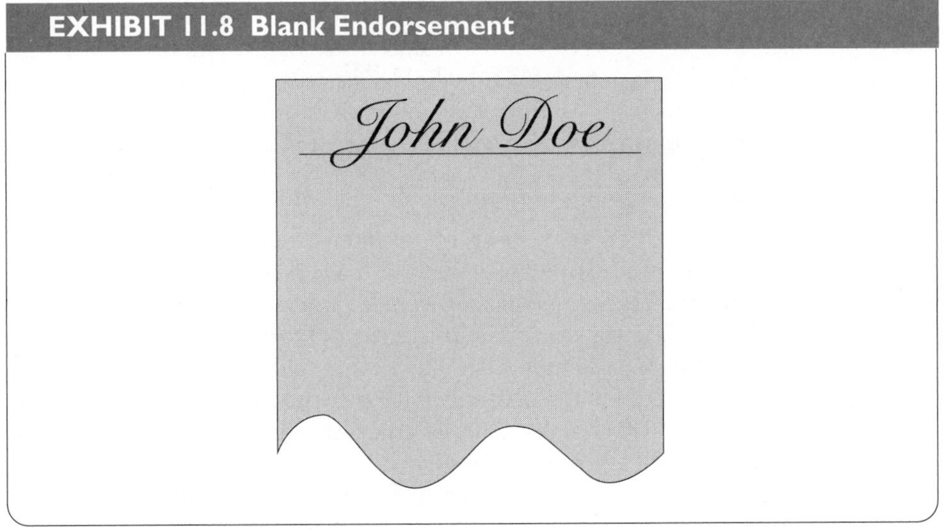

EXHIBIT 11.9 Special Endorsement

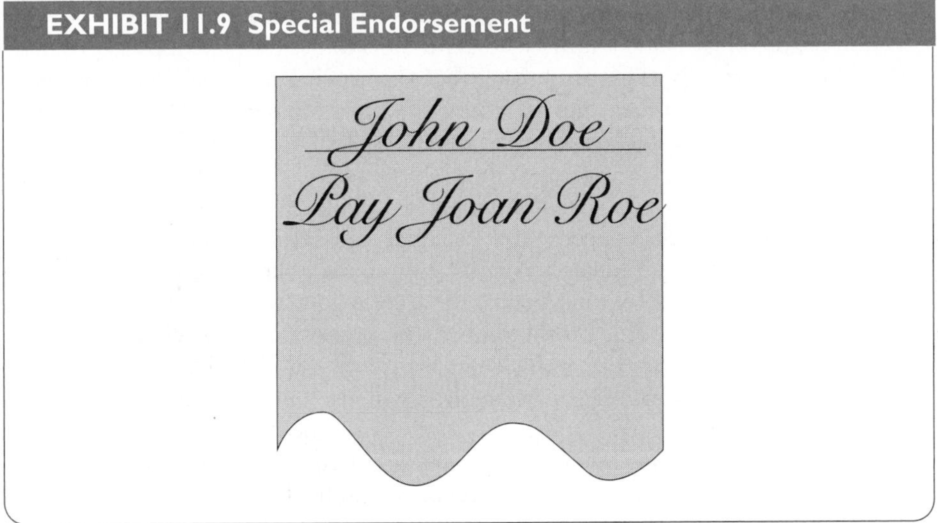

anyone giving cash for a stolen check with the restrictive endorsement "for deposit only" may be required to pay a second time to the check's rightful owner.

All endorsers are presumed to make **unqualified endorsements;** that is, they imply that they promise to pay on any instrument they endorse if it is not paid when due. Therefore, all intermediaries usually must deal with a bounced check if the drawee bank dishonors the check for insufficient funds or other reasons. Any endorser may limit this risk by making a **qualified endorsement** by endorsing and writing "without recourse" on the back. Of course, qualified endorsements reduce the willingness of further intermediaries to accept or give value for the paper.

Forged endorsements on bearer paper are irrelevant because the forged endorsement is unnecessary to negotiate. Recall that the bearer need only tender delivery, not supply an endorsement. However, forgeries might be unlawfully used to negotiate order paper. A forgery is ineffective to pass title. Therefore, understanding the **chain of title** on the paper becomes important if forgery is suspected. This often requires identifying each transferor and each successive transferee, noting dates where possible. Although a forged drawer or maker's signature will not obligate the true drawer or maker, it does not affect the holder's status with respect to others in the chain of title. Therefore, the ultimate dishonor gives holders the right to collect from their immediate transferors. This complex concept is discussed next.

Holders in Due Course

Intermediaries in the banking system are encouraged to participate in transferring payment rights so long as they need not worry that they have much risk if the commercial paper is dishonored. Holders can obtain an even more special status as a holder in due course (HDC) if they take a transfer of an instrument (1) for **value**, (2) in **good faith**, and (3) **without notice** of any defenses or another's claim to the paper. The HDC's special status is much better than that of a contract assignee or even another holder. Ordinary assignees take commercial paper or other contract rights subject to *any* defense the maker or drawer could assert in the original and underlying contract. The HDC takes commercial paper free of such **personal defenses**, which encourages intermediaries to participate in handling commercial paper. For example, assume a retailer purchases goods from a wholesaler and pays with a nonnegotiable promissory note. Because it is nonnegotiable, the wholesaler then assigns (factors) the note to a finance company, which immediately pays the wholesaler a discounted amount in cash. What effect on negotiability is there if the wholesaler fails to deliver the goods as promised or if the goods actually delivered breach the warranty? The finance company is an assignee of a simple contract right to receive the buyer's payment. The finance company could not force the buyer to pay because the seller has breached the contract.

Commercial practice has developed the HDC as a special status to encourage intermediaries such as banks and finance companies to willingly handle notes and drafts. The HDC takes commercial paper free of personal defenses to the underlying contract; that is, the HDC will not be denied payment even if the maker or drawer has the personal defense of breach of contract against the seller who was the original payee.

The HDC must give value for the instrument; otherwise, there would be no out-of-pocket losses to protect. Generally, value is given if the HDC pays money for the transfer of the paper. However, the value given will also be sufficient when the HDC acquires the paper as collateral, takes the paper as payment for a separate, previous debt (antecedent claim), gives another negotiable instrument in exchange (e.g., pays for a note with a check), or makes an irrevocable obligation to a third party (e.g., issues a letter of credit). Banks usually give value when they pay out cash in return for a check or when a customer's account is given unrestricted credit for the amount of a deposited check. HDC status is given only to a holder who takes the paper in **good faith**—that is, honesty in fact—a subjective standard that inquires whether the person actually knew of any wrongdoing.

The UCC imposes an objective standard of sincerity by prohibiting HDC status to a holder with any *notice* (actually knew) of several specified problems: The paper is overdue, is unpaid after demand, or was accelerated; the paper was obviously altered or forged; the paper was dishonored; or anyone has defenses or claims to payment on the underlying transaction. Checks are presumed overdue 90 days after the issue date, so intermediaries after that date are not HDCs. Nevertheless, the drawee bank may still pay such a check if sufficient funds are available.

Later transferees from an HDC inherit the HDC's special status under the **shelter rule.** Unless a transferee from an HDC was a party to the fraud, the transferee also shares the HDC's special rights to ignore personal defenses in the underlying transaction. For example, assume the buyer of goods issued a note to a seller who, in turn, negotiated the note to an HDC. If the HDC made a gift of the note to his spouse, the spouse would have HDC protections, even though the spouse gave no value to the HDC in return.

The HDC takes free of personal defenses; that is, the HDC can demand payment even if the original maker or drawer can assert a defense against the original payee. Personal defenses include the usual contract law defenses, such as breach of contract, fraud in the inducement (intentional misrepresentation), misrepresentation, mistake, failure of consideration, failure of a condition precedent, and impossibility. However, the HDC will take a negotiable instrument subject to real defenses. This means that in such cases the special HDC status is inapplicable and the HDC may be prevented from receiving payment. The following are **real defenses:** incapacity (incompetence, infancy), fraud in the execution (tricked into signing the wrong instrument, such as a note rather than an autograph as pretended), instrument discharged in bankruptcy, forgery, material alteration, and illegality.

The Federal Trade Commission (FTC) has promulgated a rule that supersedes the HDC rule when the note's maker is a consumer purchasing goods or services. Consumers who purchase on credit can still assert personal defenses like breach of contract for the sale of the goods. The FTC rule constrains the transfer of consumer financing notes, which puts pressure on sellers of goods. If sellers breach the underlying sale contract, they risk holding all consumer financing contracts as their own receivables rather than easily factoring them for immediate cash to third-party finance companies.

LIABILITIES OF THE PARTIES

Holders, HDCs, and other intermediaries in the commercial banking system willingly participate because their rights and liabilities are predictable when a negotiable instrument is dishonored. UCC Article III provides for both contract liability and warranty liability. On these bases, most transferees are assured of recourse against either an immediate or remote transferor when a check bounces or a note is not paid. Many of these parties are not natural persons—for example, corporations—so their negotiable instruments are signed by their authorized agents. Only an authorized agent can obligate an entity to liability on an instrument. The agent is not personally liable on the instrument if the principal is identified and the agent clearly signs in a representative capacity.

Different forms of liability are implied by contract for nearly everyone signing a negotiable instrument. There is nearly absolute and unconditional **primary liability** for makers, drawers, and drawees after an instrument is accepted. Endorsers generally have only **secondary liability**; their liability is typically conditioned on certain events or rights. A maker is primarily liable to pay a note according to its terms. The drawer on a check or draft also has primary liability, but it does not arise unless the drawee dishonors the draft. A drawee is not primarily liable until acceptance of the draft by the drawee, which usually occurs after the drawee, usually a bank, verifies the drawer's signature and concludes that a sufficient balance is available to make the payment. However, if a check presented is not dishonored by midnight on the next business day, then it is accepted. Acceptance makes the drawee into an acceptor.

An endorser becomes secondarily liable after payment is refused. This happens after the holder made **presentment** of the instrument demanding payment from the drawee or maker; there was **dishonor** by inaction or refusing payment, and a notice of dishonor was given to the endorser, either orally, in writing, or electronically. A **protest** is a notarized certificate of dishonor sometimes used in international banking. As stated earlier, an endorser can avoid liability by endorsing "without recourse." If presentment of a check is not made within 30 days from the date of endorsement, the endorser no longer has endorser liability.

Endorsers are also liable to all subsequent transferees under five **implied warranties:** (1) the transferor had *good title* to the instrument, (2) *all signatures are authentic*, (3) the instrument has *no material alterations*, (4) there are *no claims or defenses* against the transferor, and (5) the endorser has *no knowledge of insolvency* by the maker, drawer, or acceptor. If one of the warranties is breached, an endorser may be liable to any subsequent transferee who gave value for the instrument. A subsequent transferee is someone later in the chain of title. Warranty liability is a further inducement, in addition to the protections provided by primary and secondary liability, to encourage holders to participate in handling paper. Both warranty and endorser liability can be disclaimed.

BANK RELATIONS WITH CUSTOMERS

UCC Article 4 governs bank relationships with its customers. The drawee bank is a debtor holding its customer funds, and the bank's customers are creditors, depositors, and drawers. A bank's basic obligation runs only to its customers, not to third-party holders who present checks for payment. The bank must honor drafts or other items by making payment upon presentment. Wrongful dishonor makes the bank liable to the bank's customer for compensatory damages that may arise if, for example, the drawer is arrested for bouncing the check. But, of course, banks need not pay an item if there are insufficient funds available on deposit.

Forgeries

The bank may charge the customer's account with properly paid items. However, in certain situations, the bank may not charge a customer's account or, if the bank makes a mistaken payment, the account must be recredited for items with the following problems: (1) forged signatures of the drawer or an endorser, (2) altered items, (3) payments made before the date stated on the draft, or (4) payments made in violation of a valid stop-payment order.

Bank customers must use reasonable care by promptly examining each periodic bank statement for forgeries or bookkeeping errors. A customer who delays may lose the right to contest forgeries or material alterations. Banks can recover from anyone forging a necessary endorsement. The bank, not the customer, is liable for payment on an item with a forged drawer's signature. However, if the bank dishonors a check with a forged signature of a drawer or endorser or because the item has a material alteration (e.g., zeros added to raise dollar value), the first transferee who took the check from the forger bears the loss.

INTERNATIONAL SALES TRANSACTIONS

Domestic and international commercial law evolved from international practice and the law merchant. International sales transactions are generally far less certain than domestic transactions. The physical distance between parties grows, language and cultural barriers arise, currency fluctuations too quickly eliminate profitability, and the cross-border enforceability of contracts is uncertain in many legal systems. Indeed, some systems are outright hostile to foreigners. Commerce could be significantly reduced if the legal machinery was generally believed to be unreliable. To raise expectations, much of international law is designed to improve the reliability of commercial performances.

International Documentary Sales

The bill of lading is often transferred between the seller's bank and the buyer's bank. This practice permits payment to be conditioned on title transfer using negotiable document of

International Commentary

International Trade: Documentary Transactions Reduce Transaction Anxiety

Absent long-standing and trusted relations between international buyers and sellers, both buyer and seller risk nonperformance by the other party, the classic "transaction anxiety." The buyer is uncertain whether the goods will arrive as described and when promised. The seller is uncertain whether payment will be made on a timely basis, if made at all. Both parties risk that the goods or payment might be lost in transit. International commercial practice uses several documents to reduce these risks. A document of title is used to condition delivery and title transfer on the buyer's payment. The buyer can condition payment on documentary proof of inspection, physical delivery, and title transfer. These documents are commonly processed as concurrent performances when the documents are verified and exchanged simultaneously. The parties rely on each carrier, warehouse, dock operator, and other intermediary along the route to check and assure the authenticity of these important commercial documents. Long-standing successful experience with international documentary transfers has significantly reduced losses and transaction anxiety.

title. Similarly, the simultaneously delivery and title transfer is conditioned on payment by draft or letter of credit. There are four major methods by which the international buyer makes payment. First, many buyers and sellers have long-standing and trusted relations, so the seller has well-founded confidence that a particular buyer, who has made reliable payment of prior bills, will again be "good for this payment." In such situations, sellers may ship based on the buyer's **open account** and expect timely payment in the near future or as agreed. Second, some sellers insist on prepayment from an unfamiliar buyer or from a buyer with uncertain credit risks. Of course, the risk shifts to buyers who prepay: The seller might default by not making delivery. Third, payment can be made by draft (e.g., bill of exchange, check, sight draft) payable out of the buyer's bank account or credit line. A seller authorized in the contract of sale may actually prepare the draft and send it to the buyer's bank for payment, along with the bill of lading. Such a sight draft is due immediately upon arrival at the buyer's bank. A time draft is not payable until some future date; essentially, the seller provides credit. The fourth method uses a letter of credit.

Letters of Credit

The buyer's method of payment in much of international commerce is a **letter of credit (L/C)**, a bank's documentary assurance to the seller that the buyer will pay. The L/C is based on the buyer's bank's creditworthiness and on its international reputation. To facilitate processing through the international banking system, L/Cs are often made negotiable. The L/C often accompanies the transaction documents. They can also be made nonnegotiable. **Standby L/Cs** are used for nonpayment purposes, such as performance bonds, guarantees, or other collateral.

In the United States, L/Cs are governed by UCC Article 5. However, most international L/C transactions specifically incorporate the **Uniform Customs and Practices for Documentary Credits (UCP)** issued by the International Chamber of Commerce (ICC). The newest revision of the UCP is **UCP 500**. The UCP governs when the L/C specifies the UPC. When there is any conflict between the UCP and the UCC, the UCC governs only if there is no UCP provision. Exhibit 11.10 shows a sample L/C form.

The typical international sales transaction using the L/C as payment involves four parties: (1) The buyer is the account party, who applies to (2) its bank, the **issuing bank**, to establish a line of credit and issue the L/C in favor of (3) the seller, the **L/C beneficiary**, and documents are forwarded and payments transmitted through (4) the seller's bank, known as either a **confirming bank** or **advising bank**. The whole process involves two other primary documents: the underlying contract for

EXHIBIT 11.10 Letter of Credit

ORIGINAL

Date: April 6, 1992

Call 828-8327 concerning inquiries on Documents submitted under this letter of Credit.

DOCUMENTARY CREDIT—IRREVOCABLE	CREDIT NUMBER Of Issuing Bank 0/00/000 Our No. 0000000
FOR ACCOUNT OF Taiwan Steel Products Co., Ltd. Taipei Taiwan	CORRESPONDENT First Bank Taipei Taiwan
BENEFICIARY John Doe Exporters, Inc. Chicago, Illinois U.S.A.	AMOUNT Six Thousand and 00/100 U.S. Dollars U.S. $6,000.00 EXPIRY June 15, 2003

IN ALL COMMUNICATIONS WITH US, PLEASE MENTION OUR REFERENCE NUMBER

Gentlemen:
We have received from the above named bank a **cable** dated **April 5, 2003** requesting us to inform you that they have opened in your favor their irrevocable Credit particulars of which are as follows:
Available by your drafts at **sight ON US.**
Accompanied by the following documents (full sets required unless otherwise specified):

Signed commercial invoice in triplicate, describing the merchandise as mentioned below, stating that goods shipped conform with purchase order No. 0/00/0 dated March 5, 2003.

Packing list in triplicate.

Insurance policy or certificate in duplicate covering all risks including war risks.

Full set of clean on board ocean bills of lading issued to shippers' order and blank endorsed, marked "Freight Prepaid" and notify International Forwarders, Keelung.

Evidencing shipment from U.S. Port to Keelung, Taiwan not later than May 25, 2003 of the following merchandise: 200 sets of cookware at the price of $30.00 per one set CIF Keelung, Taiwan.

Partial shipments permitted.

Transshipments prohibited.

Drawings under this letter of credit must be presented for negotiation not later than ten days after the date of issuance of the bills of lading.

☐ This credit is not confirmed by us and therefore carries no engagement on our part, but is simply for your guidance in preparing and presenting drafts and documents.

☒ This credit is confirmed by us and we undertake that all drafts drawn and presented in accordance with the terms of the credit will be honored by us.

The above mentioned correspondent engages with you that all drafts under and in compliance with the terms of the Credit will be duly honored on delivery of documents as specified.
If the Credit has been opened by cable, this advice is subject to correction upon receipt of the mail confirmation.
Drafts must be marked "Drawn under **First Bank, Taipei, Taiwan, Letter of Credit No. 0/00/0** " and presented at our office on or before the above indicated expiry date.
The credit is subject to the Uniform Customs and Practice for Documentary Credits [1974 revision the International Chamber of Commerce Publication No. 290]
Should the terms of the above mentioned Credit be unsatisfactory to you, please communicate with your customers and request that they have the issuing bank send us amended instructions. Original credit must be returned with documents for negotiations.

J. Smith — FOR CASHIER

G. Black — FOR CASHIER

sale of goods and the bill of lading. Many international sales transactions also include one or more of the following supplementary documents and relationships: contract(s) of carriage with one or more common carriers, storage contracts with dock and warehouse facilities, customs clearances, inspection documents, the buyer's application for credit, insurance polic(ies), export licenses, certificates of origin, packing slips, and the relationship of trust built up between the two banks. The 1994 UCP revision creates greater flexibility for L/C parties to use new and electronic documents in international sales transactions. Carefully review the order and flow of documents in the typical L/C process as depicted in Exhibit 11.11.

The seller often prepares the primary documents after negotiating the sales contract with the buyer. All matters called for in the sale contract must be included exactly as they are stated in *all* the other documents. This is a strict form of the mirror image or perfect tender rule from contract law. It prohibits the issuing bank from paying on the L/C if there are *any* discrepancies—that is, major or even minor differences among the documents in the terms stated. For example, discrepancies include any variance among the documents in the goods description (e.g., size, quantity, quality, color, specifications), misspellings, missing documents like an inspection certificate, late delivery, different named shipping vessel or carrier, expired L/C, and most other errors.

This **strict compliance rule** is so exacting because time and cost pressures make banks generally unsuitable and unable to investigate or resolve discrepancies. Banks must examine L/C documents quickly, or they are presumed to accept them and then become obligated to pay on the L/C. UCC Article 5 gives domestic banks just three banking days to do their document examination. The UCP requires banks to use a "reasonable time," which cannot be more than seven banking days. The general rule is that banks need not "look behind the documents" to determine negotiability and performance of an international sales transaction. Therefore, the parties must draft the documents very carefully and provide for others to verify matters, such as inspecting the shipment to assure exact compliance with the sales contract description. The 1994 UCP revision directs banks to ignore any L/C conditions not contained in the documents.

Should an issuing bank pay on an L/C if it knows the seller committed fraud? The next case illustrates the fraud exception to the strict compliance rule. The UCP has no fraud exception, so this subject is left to national law.

Sztejn v. J. Henry Schroder Banking Co.

31 N.Y.S.2d 631 (N.Y.App.Div. 1941)

Facts. Sztejn negotiated a purchase of hog bristles from Transea Traders, Ltd., an Indian corporation. The price was paid with an irrevocable L/C issued by J. Henry Schroder to Transea. The actual shipment from Transea included 50 cases of cowhair and other refuse under a bill of lading erroneously mirroring the L/C description showing hog bristles. Sztejn sought to enjoin Schroder from honoring a draft sent by Transea's advising bank, the Chartered Bank of India. Sztejn claimed payment should be withheld because of the fraud in the transaction.

Legal Issue. Is the strict compliance rule applicable if the seller commits fraud?

Opinion. Justice Shientag. It is well established that a letter of credit is independent of the primary contract of sale between the buyer and the seller. The issuing bank agrees to pay upon presentation of documents, not goods. This rule is necessary to preserve the efficiency of the letter of credit as an instrument for the financing of trade. One of the chief purposes of the letter of credit is to furnish the seller with a ready means of obtaining prompt payment for his merchandise. It would be a most unfortunate interference with business transactions if a bank before honoring drafts drawn upon it was obliged or even allowed to go behind the documents, at the request of the buyer and enter into controversies between the buyer and the seller regarding the quality of the merchandise shipped. If the buyer and the seller intended the bank to do this they could have so provided in the letter of credit itself, and in the absence of such a provision, the court will not demand or even permit the bank to delay paying drafts which are proper in form. Of course, the application of this doctrine presupposes that the documents accompanying the draft are genuine and conform in terms to the requirements of the letter of credit.

This is not a controversy between the buyer and seller concerning a mere breach of warranty regarding the quality of the merchandise. It must be assumed that the seller has intentionally failed to ship any goods ordered by the buyer. In such a situation, where the seller's fraud has been called to the bank's attention before the drafts and documents have been presented for payment, the principle of the independence of the bank's obligation under the letter of credit should not be extended to protect the unscrupulous seller. It is true that even though the documents are forged or fraudulent, if the issuing bank has already paid the draft before receiving notice of the seller's fraud, it will be protected if it exercised reasonable diligence before making such payment. However, in the instant action Schroder has received notice of Transea's active fraud before it accepted or paid the draft.

Although our courts have used broad language to the effect that a letter of credit is independent of the primary contract between the buyer and seller, that language was used in cases concerning alleged breaches of warranty; no case has been brought to my attention on this point involving an intentional fraud on the part of the seller which was brought to the bank's notice with the request that it withhold payment of the draft on this account. The distinction between a breach of warranty and active fraud on the part of the seller is supported by authority and reason. As one court has stated: "Obviously, when the issuer of a letter of credit knows that a document, although correct in form, is, in point of fact, false or illegal, he cannot be called upon to recognize such a document as complying with the terms of a letter of credit."

While the primary factor in the issuance of the letter of credit is the credit standing of the buyer, the security afforded by the merchandise is also taken into account. In fact, the letter of credit requires a bill of lading made out to the order of the bank and not the buyer. Although the bank is not interested in the exact detailed performance of the sales contract, it is vitally interested in assuring itself that there are some goods represented by the documents. Accordingly, the defendant's motion to dismiss the supplemental complaint is denied.

Decision. While strict compliance under letter of credit practice prevents the issuing bank from "going behind the documents" to verify the seller's performance, the strict compliance rule is inapplicable if the seller commits fraud.

Case Questions

1. What is the primary issue in cases like this that seek to invalidate an L/C?
2. Why do courts attempt to enforce L/Cs whenever possible? How could the buyer have better protected itself in this type of situation?
3. What forms of electronic communication might cure this type of problem?

The bank issuing the L/C has a duty to "pay against the documents" by first checking for discrepancies, endorsing documents as necessary to process the transaction, and then either notifying the seller of discrepancies causing dishonor of payment or honoring the payment by paying the seller or crediting the seller's bank. The UCP presumes L/Cs are irrevocable, although the buyer's bank can make them revocable, but this substantially reduces their usefulness. The L/C is often confirmed, obligating the seller's bank (confirming bank) to credit the seller's account as soon as the issuing bank honors payment. If the L/C is unconfirmed, the seller's bank provides only advising functions as a correspondent of the issuing bank by processing paperwork but does not credit the seller's account. In most cases, the seller's bank assists in preparing the documents and reviewing them for discrepancies. It forwards the documents to the issuing bank and may need to redraft any noncomplying documents returned by the issuing bank if there is still time remaining.

A standby L/C is not used for payment but instead as a performance guarantee or collateral. Payment is due if the account party breaches some duty. For example, Manufacturers Bank was required to pay on a standby L/C that guaranteed the performance of AT&T's contract to install a telephone system in Iran. AT&T stopped performance after the Shah was ousted and the Islamic regime did not pay its AT&T bills. Despite

EXHIBIT 11.11 Letter of Credit Process

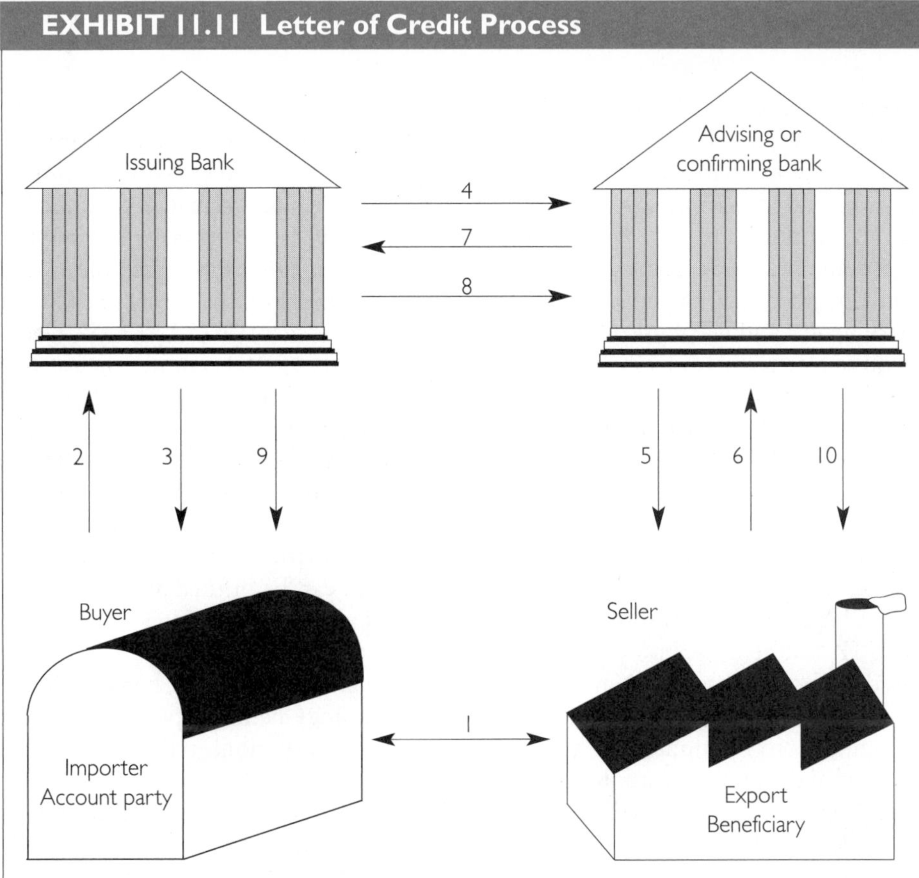

Typical Order of Events:

1. Contract for the international sale of goods.
2. Buyer (account party) applies to the issuing bank for an L/C designating the seller as beneficiary.
3. Issuing bank makes commitment to buyer to issue L/C specifying buyer's terms of full performance.
4. L/C is forwarded from issuing bank to the seller's advising or confirming bank.
5. Advising or confirming bank forwards buyer's L/C to seller for seller's preparation of documents in conformance with L/C.
6. Seller forwards completed documents (e.g., bill of lading, inspection certificates, export license, customs clearance) to advising or confirming bank.
7. Advising or confirming bank carefully checks for discrepancies, advises seller to make any necessary revisions, and forwards documents to issuing bank.
8. Issuing bank carefully checks for discrepancies and either (a) honors L/C by paying seller or confirming bank; or (b) bank dishonors L/C if there are discrepancies or bank revokes a revocable L/C.
9. Issuing bank forwards bill of lading and any other documents to buyer as necessary to claim goods from carrier.
10. Advising bank pays seller, credits seller's account, or pays transferee if beneficiary negotiated L/C.

Iran's breach of the installation contract, the bank was still required to pay the standby L/C because AT&T's performance bond was not conditioned on Iran's payments.[1]

Electronic Letters of Credit

Letters of credit need not be transferred physically by mail or trusted courier. For many years, international practice has recognized and employed electronic L/Cs that are transmitted among participating banks through secure electronic communication networks such as SWIFT, the Society for Worldwide Interbank Financial Telecommunications. Article 11(a)i of UCP 500 specifically authorizes the use of "authenticated teletransmissions." They are regarded as "the operative Credit instrument," and no physical mail confirmation is necessary. UCC Article 5's recognition of electronic L/Cs is somewhat less definite; UCC §5-104 requires the use of a "record" authenticated by signature or other authentication method acceptable under standard practice by financial institutions or a method otherwise specifically permitted in the L/C. Electronic L/Cs are clearly envisioned by the UCC §5-102(14) definition of the term **record**, which permits "information inscribed on a tangible medium, or that is stored in an electronic or other medium and is retrievable in perceivable form." The comments to UCC Article 5 authorize current use of electronic L/Cs if the transmission and its data are durable and can be printed as a paper document for controlling and recording payments and assignments.

UCP "authentication" predates UETA, so no traditional signature or symbol-based method is required. Nevertheless, the UCP makes the advising bank responsible to assure that the L/C is authentic. This technology-neutral approach permits authentication by numerous methods, including encryption, password, return acknowledgment, verification by telephone, or a traditional signature or symbol. Authentication under the UCC is also flexible and technology-neutral, encouraging the evolution of practices by the banking industry. Authentication is necessary only for the identity of the L/C issuer, confirmer, or adviser. If there are incomplete or garbled teletransmissions, the electronic L/C is not effective. In such cases, the advising bank should request that the issuing bank resend clear and complete information, which the issuing bank should promptly provide.

Alternatives to Traditional Documentary Sales

International commercial contracting retains some ancient contracting methods while it also evolves with technology. Alternatives to the traditional documentary sales process previously described are widely used today. **Countertrade** is a complex reciprocal barterlike exchange in which international brokers match buyers and sellers who trade goods and services without transferring cash. Many developing countries and former Soviet bloc nations have negative trade balances, their currencies do not convert well into hard currency, they have large debt burdens, or their government restricts currency outflows. These problems restrict the very foreign trade so badly needed to invigorate their economies. There are several types of countertrade. **Barter** is the direct exchange of different types of goods or services between the two parties. In a **swap**, two sellers of the same goods exchange delivery obligations to reduce transportation costs. The most common form of countertrade is counterpurchase: A seller from an industrial nation exchanges goods or services for other goods from the buyer, often through an intermediary such as the government or a firm in the developing nation. In a buyback, industrial machinery acquired from the seller is paid for with goods eventually produced with those machines.

---

1. *American Bell International v. Islamic Republic of Iran,* 474 F.Supp. 420 (S.D.N.Y. 1979).

Countertrade raises many legal, electronic commerce, ethical, trade policy, and economic policy questions. Legal questions include product safety compliance, complex contracting, and the antitrust laws. Electronic commerce questions involve computerized matching and communications among counter trading parties. Ethical issues include foreign bribery and allegations that rich industrial nations take unfair advantage of developing nations. Trade policy issues include trade restrictions and the dumping laws. Economic problems include circumventing foreign currency translation and the rather significant inefficiency of countertrade. Consider the role that the Internet could play in barter and the more fine-tuned adjustments that could be made among all the parties.

ELECTRONIC PAYMENT SYSTEMS

Money, the primary subject of payment obligations, has a long history, an understanding of which informs the design of reliable electronic payment systems. Dating from hundreds of years B.C., the successful forms of money traditionally have two major functions: (1) **storehouse of value** and (2) medium of exchange. Money was once considered a storehouse of value because gold or silver coins had intrinsic value from their precious metal content. Today, few circulating coins are struck from precious metal, and few paper currencies are backed by government promises to redeem them for gold or silver. Therefore, today money serves as a storehouse of value only while the public has confidence in it. Public confidence is also essential to money's function as a medium of exchange. Money must be widely available so that most people can use it. Money must also be widely acceptable: most people must be willing to take it in payment for services, intangibles, goods, or land.

The experience with various competing currencies in early U.S. history was negative. During colonial and post-Revolutionary times, paper notes were issued by governments (England, colonies, states, U.S. federal), by private banks, and even by other private parties. Some were backed by agricultural products, such as tobacco, meaning the currency could be redeemed (exchanged) for something of tangible value. However, the proliferation of these currencies caused inflation; many were not universally accepted for payment. The Constitution framers reacted to a proliferation of currencies before the Revolution and during the time of the Articles of Confederation. They envisioned a single predominant currency, so Congress was granted the power to coin and regulate money, and that power was prohibited to the states. The states have since had the power to charter (license) banks. Currency was issued by both federally chartered banks and by state-chartered banks until the taxes levied on nonfederal notes diminished their use. Public confidence in money is enhanced when control is concentrated in a trusted government entity like the Federal Reserve.

Background: Contemporary Use of Electronic Payment Systems

Electronic payments are hardly new. The first international wire transfer of funds occurred soon after the transatlantic telegraph cable was laid in the 1880s, linking the United States with the United Kingdom. The lives of few people today remain untouched by electronic payments. The most frequent experiences are cash withdrawals from bank accounts or credit card accounts via automated teller machines (ATMs). Most credit card charges use electronic account verification and transaction processing. Indeed, the physical handling of credit card carbon impressions is nearly an extinct practice, although it resurfaces occasionally when electronic networks become temporarily inoperative. Most retail merchants offer point-of-sale (POS) transaction processing for debit and ATM cards via electronic networks similar to credit card networks.

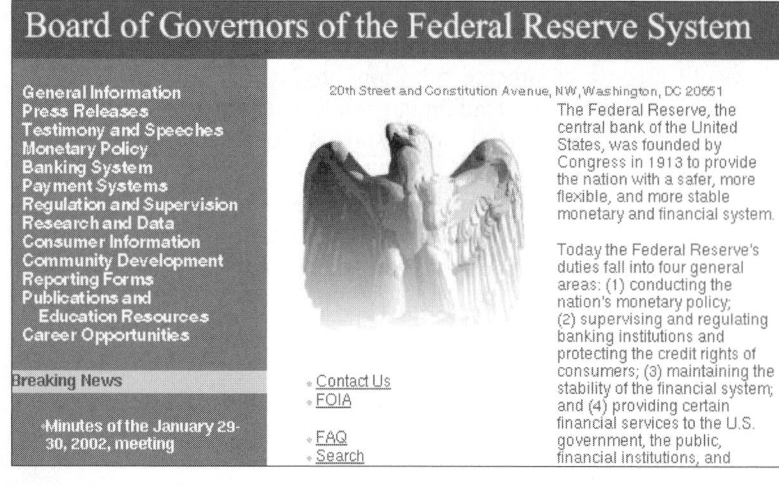

http://
www.federalreserve.gov/

Electronic payments systems are less visible, but no less important, in other areas. Consider the growing use of electronic payment systems in transportation: toll tag use at turnpikes, bridges, and tunnels and gasoline purchases charged with electronic token-readers at the pump. Even people who do not use "plastic" are affected by electronic processing of payments at the wholesale level. Nearly all interbank transactions between the buyer's bank and the seller's bank are processed electronically, including the total fund transfers clearing all paper checks, direct deposits, and clearance of credit card or debit transactions by ATM or POS. Electronic payment systems can be viewed broadly to include preconditions to payment such as metering, bill calculating, and invoicing.

The electronic metering and recording of customer transactions facilitates billing of regular and long-distance telephone use, wireless airtime, pay-per-view deliveries, and on-line subscription services (ISP, LexisNexis, Westlaw). **Electronic bill payment and presentment (EBPP)** to customers or to their automated payment services may also trigger electronic payments. Many transactions use analog or digital electronic means to transmit billing and payment information, such as use of the telephone (voice), fax (documents), or e-mail (electronic records) to communicate credit card account numbers and expiration dates to authorize payments, to identify the payor, or to transfer bank draft payment using **automated clearing house (ACH)** facilities. Electronic bill presentment is the first step to performance of payment obligations. It may occur through e-mail, Web banking, or some third-party electronic bill payment service.

The following section discusses the existing legal framework for electronic payment mechanisms, as well as the technical and legal challenges to successful development of alternative electronic payment mechanisms. First is an introduction to the retail electronic transfer of payments involving both credit and debit transactions under federal law. Next, wholesale electronic funds transfer under Federal Reserve regulations, the federal Electronic Funds Transfer Act, and UCC Article 4A are examined. Finally, emerging electronic payment systems are reviewed in light of the key enduring legal and practical characteristics of successful payment systems. These principles are projected onto proposed systems to predict the obstacles and opportunities for reliable electronic payment innovations.

Retail Electronic Funds Transfer: Credit Cards

When consumers directly use electronic funds transfer (EFT), these are retail transactions that can occur in two modes. First, credit card transfers are debt transactions, essentially advances made from a line of credit established between the consumer and the credit card issuer. Credit EFT transactions are based on push technology because a series of payment orders directs banks to make payments through the system to the ultimate payee. Second, debit transfers are deducted directly from assets held by a financial institution or from an existing deposit account with a bank. Like traditional paper-based checks and drafts, debit EFT are based on pull technology because they order or request payment through the system from the payor bank.

Commentary

Controversy over New Money: Network Effects and Payment Systems

The obstacles to innovations in electronic payments are similar to the challenges of introducing a new currency. The first barrier is switching costs. Before a payment innovation can succeed, people must believe the new system will be as convenient to use as their existing money and certainly no more costly. A new currency may not be as stable as the old one. The Euro sustained considerable losses after its initial introduction. Some Europeans are reluctant to use stored-value cards because they find their traditional currency works just fine. They find no compelling reasons to switch because fees are charged to use stored-value cards. Of course, some consumers may pay for convenience. As bank tellers become less convenient, consumers may learn to tolerate ATM fees charged both by their own banks and by the ATM owners.

The second barrier is network economics. ***Network effects*** are economies of scale derived from standardization and universal acceptance. Payment innovations are unlikely to succeed until critical mass is achieved. Consider the ubiquitous fax machine. It was nearly worthless until all fax machines used the same communications protocol, and only then did most offices install them. As the fax network expanded, the value of the fax technology expanded. The same holds true for money and payment systems. As more consumers and merchants learn to trust particular currencies ($) or forms of payment (checks, credit cards), they become the standard forms for payment.

The implication of network economics for innovative payment systems is that critical mass must be achieved. Enough customer subscribers, participating merchants, and infrastructure must come on line to facilitate frequent and reliable use. ***Critical mass*** is the essence of network effects. Many systems must achieve very wide acceptance before they will be financially successful. Of course, not all markets are controlled by network effects to the same extent as are communications, payments, and computer compatibility. Indeed, the measure of success for many tangible products is the achievement of small but profitable market shares. Network economics is discussed further as it affects the antitrust laws in Chapter 19.

Credit cards were first developed in the 1950s. They proliferated in the 1960s as many banks issued cards indiscriminately and without careful screening for the creditworthiness of prospective cardholders. After many issuing banks sustained significant losses, Congress passed the Consumer Credit Protection Act in 1970, as part of the Truth in Lending Act. The Federal Reserve is authorized to implement the act and has done so with the strong consumer disclosure protections of Regulation Z.

Credit card transactions are also regulated by three major types of contracts: (1) There are contracts between merchants and their banks to process credit cards accepted as payment, (2) there are contracts between consumers and their banks that issue credit cards, and (3) all participants are bound by the transaction clearing rules of the sponsoring credit card association (e.g., Visa, MasterCard, Discover, American Express). They are closed systems in several respects. The parties' rights and duties are defined by system rules regulating acceptance of payments, processing of transactions, and the honor or dishonor of the ultimate transfer of funds. Also the transmission of transaction information is often sent via secure networks. However, consumers become vulnerable as they transmit credit card account information via the Internet. Security concerns will require the use of encryption or other protective means. For example, the SSL (secure socket layer) communications technology is in wide use, essentially an encryption of account information during transmission.

The revenue that supports the credit card system is derived from various fees. First, a percentage of gross credit card sales, the "discount," is charged-back against the merchant who accepts credit cards. Effectively, this is a percentage-of-gross-sales fee (1%–5%) the merchant must pay on the amount received in payment for the consumers' use of credit. Second, consumers pay interest on unpaid balances, typically between 10% and 24%. Third, some cardholders pay an initiation fee or annual fees.

Credit card issuers profit from these fees, which allows them to give consumers another big incentive to use credit cards: the rather considerable advantage of float. Those consumers who can time their credit card transactions and payments optimally actually borrow the amount of the purchase, interest free, for up to 50 or 60 days if they have no outstanding unpaid balances. Float has been a double-edge sword for many years, affecting both the credit and debit sectors of the banking industry. The float causes many banks to lose profitable opportunities, yet some banks find ways to take financial advantage of float. Float is the result of slow and inefficient transmittal of instruments and documents, as well as less than fully automated record keeping. Today, the elimination of float is a primary incentive driving advances in electronic payment systems.

Regulation Z imposes considerable consumer protection obligations on card issuers. In turn, card association rules shift many of these risks to merchants. Cards may be sent to consumers only upon consumer requests or as a renewal. A cardholder becomes liable for charges only after the issued card is accepted, either by signature, by use, or by authorizing another person's use. Increasingly, acceptance is accomplished when consumers call to activate new cards they receive. Periodic statements of account and notices of the card issuer's error resolution process must be sent to cardholders. Cardholders must attempt to settle disputes that arise over a transaction (e.g., warranty breach) directly with the merchant. Regulation Z gives the consumer a bargaining advantage in this: Payments to the merchant can be suspended until the dispute is resolved. Regulation Z limits this right to contest only those charges over $50, and only those made within the cardholder's state or within 100 miles of the cardholder's home. Some credit card issuers currently waive these restrictions. Without this extension of consumer protection, consumers charging purchases in distant transactions via the Internet, phone, or mail order would not have this dispute-bargaining advantage.

Cardholder liability is limited to $50 for any unauthorized charges made before the issuer is notified that the card was lost or stolen. Merchants who do not inspect the card they accept may not contest the cardholder's claim that a particular charge is unauthorized. Card association rules shift most of this risk to merchants, who must verify the identity of the cardholder. The most common verification methods include a comparison of signatures, although other methods are available, such as a comparison of the cardholder's photograph on the card or other ID, verification using a PIN (personal identifying number), or perhaps some biometric method (fingerprint, retinal scan). Merchants accepting cards via mail, telephone, or the Internet seem particularly vulnerable to credit card fraud. Increasingly, credit card issuers insure these risks in an effort to make Internet credit card use more secure and safe for consumers. Clearly, the relatively high credit card interest rates payable on unpaid balances also defray the expenses of credit card fraud and subsidize losses on delinquent accounts of uncreditworthy cardholders. These consumer protections are unequaled for any other payment method, electronic or otherwise. For this reason, Regulation Z probably accounts for the overwhelming dominance of credit card payments in retail transactions consummated by phone, by mail, or over the Internet. In other words, in the Internet space, "credit card is king" of electronic payments by dollar volume.

Retail Electronic Funds Transfer: Debit Cards

The other predominant mode for consumer electronic funds transfer is the debit EFT transaction. Since the 1970s, financial institutions have offered electronic access to retail customer deposit accounts or other assets through customer use of debit cards at ATMs or POS devices. Debit EFT also includes computer or telephone transfers, regular direct deposits such as paychecks or social security benefits, and direct withdrawals such as periodic bill payments, and, more recently, Internet bill payment services. Congress passed the Electronic Funds Transfer Act (EFTA) in 1978, authorizing the Federal Reserve to implement the act, which it has done with Regulation E. Regulation E requires financial institutions to issue an **access device** when EFT debit services are used. Various security methods serve as components of an access device. Redundant controls are usually best. Consider the security involved in using a debit card to withdraw cash from an ATM. The actual card must be used, a secret PIN must be entered, photographs are taken, and the amount of the withdrawal is often limited so an account cannot be quickly depleted. Now consider the authentication process for bill payment by using a home computer. This process might include a written preauthorization for such transactions, an on-screen notice detailing each transaction, identification using a PIN, and a paper receipt for reconciliation of records. The EFTA and Regulation E cover only the bank-to-consumer portion of these transactions. The wholesale, interbank transfer of consumer transactions is discussed later.

Regulation E is less consumer-protective than Regulation Z because it places greater responsibility on consumers. For example, consumers who completely fail to notify the bank of a lost or stolen debit card could conceivably suffer unlimited losses. The $50 limit applies only if notice is given within 2 days after the consumer learns of the loss. The limit rises to $500 if notice is given after 2 days but by 60 days. Increasingly, debit cards are branded as credit cards to broaden their acceptance beyond ATMs and POS devices to include certain merchants. As of this writing, some credit card companies are not enforcing the higher loss limits for these cards. Such lenient policies could change as consumers become reliant on them. Debit cards may not be issued or activated unless requested by the consumer, and some employers now refuse to offer paper paychecks, pressuring employees to authorize direct deposits.

Regulation E has no provision similar to the right under Regulation Z to withhold payments during the consumer's dispute with the merchant for breach of contract. Debit transactions offer more disciplined spending management to financially responsible consumers because consumers have difficulty spending more than is available as deposited assets. Nevertheless, users of credit EFT methods have stronger regulatory protections under Federal Reserve Regulation Z than do users of debit EFT methods under Regulation E.

Regulation E gives consumers a right to stop payment similar to the right under commercial paper law. For example, a preauthorized EFT may be prevented, before it is actually executed, such as the regular payment of a utility bill. Regulation Z requires that banks investigate and document errors, and consumers must be given documentation of all EFT transactions actually completed. Disclosures of consumer rights under the EFTA are also required. In June 2000, the Federal Reserve proposed revisions to Regulation E to expand disclosures required for ATM fees and to allow recurring EFT from a consumer account when authorized in a signed writing or "similarly authenticated." If the proposal is promulgated, it could permit use of some electronic or biometric means of authenticating regular EFT transactions.

Wholesale Funds Transfers

Before the 1989 introduction of UCC Article 4A, the only guidance for wire transfer of commercial payments among business parties was industry practice. Since then, the widespread adoption of UCC Article 4A has codified many of these practices to achieve a balance of the risks. A typical wholesale business-to-business payment occurs when a commercial customer pays its suppliers. This wholesale transfer of funds totals several trillion dollars each business day. These EFTs are typically made in large amounts, at high speed, and at low cost, using reliable electronic technologies. UCC Article 4A is technology-neutral; it governs wholesale funds transfers whether transmitted by electronic means or by traditional means such as U.S. mail.

Much of the money transferred to or from banks by consumers or other customers is eventually transferred between banks. Federal Reserve Regulation J applies essentially similar rules to the EFT between financial institutions routed through Fedwire, using their regional Federal Reserve branches as conduits. Although the consumer-initiated credit or debit EFTs previously discussed are excluded from UCC Article 4A, this law was prescient because its objectives and methods anticipated the problems with electronic payments arising in contemporary e-commerce. A more detailed example of a wholesale EFT transaction helps identify the parties and provides a better understanding of their major functions and the steps typically involved.

Wholesale EFT Transaction Illustration

Assume that East Corp. owes $45,350 for a truckload of widgets it purchased from InterWidgCo. East Corp. typically pays its bills from an account with All-National Bank. InterWidgCo. has an account with First State Bank. An EFT commences when an authorized person in East Corp.'s accounts payable office uses a computer to issue a ***payment order*** directing All-National Bank to transmit a second payment order to First State Bank. The All-National Bank payment order specifies that $45,350 currently held in East Corp.'s account will be transferred to First State Bank and the amount should immediately credited to InterWidgCo.'s account. When First State Bank accepts the second payment order, it notifies InterWidgCo. that the $45,350 has become available. Settlement of these payment orders usually occurs later, when accounting entries are made netting all the transactions between the two banks, perhaps by the close of that business day.

In this example and under UCC Article 4A, both East Corp. and All-National Bank are senders of payment orders. Each order, in turn, is triggered by its predecessor. East Corp. is the originator. First State Bank is the receiving bank, and InterWidgCo. is the **beneficiary** of the payment orders. If these two banks have not had regular, frequent transfer activity between them, one or more **intermediary banks** may be needed to act as conduits to process these payment orders.

Today, most EFT payment orders are transmitted electronically through communications systems called value-added networks (VAN). Significant VANs include the regional automated clearing houses (ACH), the New York Clearinghouse Interbank Payments System (CHIPS), and, in international commerce, the Society for Worldwide Interbank Financial Telecommunications (SWIFT). Payment orders can also be transmitted by EDI, fax, e-mail, phone, and even on paper. When an EFT transaction is processed through intermediary banks, several VANs may be involved. VANs are closed and secure information-processing systems transmitting EFTs only among members or as intermediaries for other banks or other parties.

UCC Article 4A requires that security procedures be established to authenticate transactions, verify the parties' identities, and detect errors. These concerns are similar to the problems addressed by electronic signatures, discussed in Chapter 12. UCC Article 4A encourages banks to develop, regularly use, and impose security procedures on customers, so long as they are commercially reasonable. Security procedures can be expected to evolve and improve over time. Examples include the use of algorithms or other codes, identifying words or numbers, encryption, callback procedures, or similar security devices.

The overriding incentive of EFT is to reduce the cost of individual verification of payment orders, making EFT more efficient. When commercially reasonable security procedures are in place but an unauthorized payment order is processed, the loss allocation rules of Article 4A and the parties' contract usually shift this risk to the customer. UCC Article 4A helps settle disputes concerning potentially costly errors, such as mistaken beneficiaries or amounts, improper notices, fraudulent payment orders, and even bank failures. EFTs are typically large dollar amounts, and their transaction costs are low. UCC Article 4A helps the transmitting and receiving banks to carefully design EFT procedures for themselves and their commercial customers with a view to minimizing the risk of costly errors and the opportunity for fraud.

Future Prospects for Electronic Payment Systems

Many experimental consumer electronic payment systems have been announced. The accompanying promotional fanfare has attracted dot.com venture capital and investor attention. However, most of these systems have eventually failed, and none has yet achieved widespread success. Nevertheless, electronic payment systems may experience the greatest near- to medium-term growth in peer-to-peer (P2P) payments systems like PayPal, smart card use, electronic customer loyalty point systems, escrow services, electronic bill presentment, and electronic access and manipulation of account records at banks and vendors. All these systems rely on computerized, electronic telecommunications to do one or more of the following: authorize or order payments, verify customer identity and availability of account status, documentation, and record keeping.

ONLINE
PayPal P2P system
http://www.paypal.com

Some day, secure electronic packets of value may actually transfer electronic currency without the assistance of trusted third-party intermediaries (e.g., banks). However, third parties will remain involved with all forms of payment until electronic payment innovations are much more reliable and resistant to tampering, legal, and commonplace. E-commerce will probably rely on credit cards for at least part of most consumer transactions in the near to medium term. An estimated 95% of Internet commerce payments in 2000 involved credit cards, and many electronic payment innovations depend on credit cards.[2]

As with most other cyber law concerns, returning to the basic principles underlying our existing law and financial institutions may be necessary. With a clearer understanding of the function of these institutions, we can then project how such legal protections should be configured in e-commerce and determine whether existing law can adapt. If not, society can consider new legislation that is technology-neutral, will accommodate existing payment methods, and then will foster the development of new payment methods.

The barriers to widespread use of electronic payment innovations are considerable. Uncertainties about the safety and security of payment innovations may slow acceptance by the public and businesses. The Federal Reserve is reluctant to surrender its control over the money supply, and banks are not eager to relinquish their control over payments. However, the economic incentives to reduce the transaction costs of payment performances are substantial. Compare the estimated cost (in 2000) of an in-person bank transaction with a human teller at $1.07, an ATM transaction at 27¢, and a smart card transaction (discussed later) less than 1¢.[3] The

2. See e.g., Julia Angwin, "E-Money: And How Will You Be Paying for That?," *Wall Street Journal*, October 23, 2000, p. R37.
3. Thomas P. Vartanian, "The Future of Electronic Payments: Roadblocks and Emerging Practices," testimony before the Subcommittee on Domestic and International Monetary Policy of the Committee on Banking and Financial Services, U.S. House of Representatives (September 19, 2000) citing Kevin P. Sheehan, *Electronic Cash*, Banking Rev. (FDIC) 1.

combined costs of billing consumers and their payments by check are estimated at 85¢ per transaction. As discussed in Chapter 17, there are significant incentives to innovate in electronic payment systems, now that business methods are clearly patentable. Indeed, as of 2000, the U.S. Patent and Trademark Office (PTO) had issued nearly 100 patents covering electronic payment systems. As payment laws are modernized in the future to facilitate innovation, many more patent applications for electronic payment systems can be expected.

Adapting Payment Law and Business Practices to E-Commerce

The law of electronic payments is developing slowly. Before the Internet's full potential can be unleashed, the constraints of law and business practice must be accommodated. A central constraint is that compliance is required with banking and payment laws.[4] First, state laws require licensing banks. Banks have a near oligopoly control over the deposit and payment order business. Electronic payment products have been proposed by nonbanks. Nonbanks that accept customer deposits or link their payment products to a bank account may violate state banking laws. Nonbanks may engage in the business of transmitting money (e.g., Western Union, GE Credit, money orders), including the movement, distribution, and clearing of payments. However, such nonbanks must also be licensed under most states' money transmitter laws. Second, Regulation E may apply to electronic payments, such as the stored value systems discussed later, which would trigger the Regulation E consumer protections previously discussed. Third, the Stamp Payments Act of 1862 makes it a criminal felony to circulate coins, tokens, or obligations under $1 if they are intended to circulate as money. Unless repealed, this old law could severely constrain the development of micropayments, point systems, and the electronic coin purses. Fourth, the deposit insurance system is designed to protect depositors from bank failures. Some firms can be expected to try to remain outside the extensive regulations of the FDIC. However, customers of some other firms may still seek the safety of deposit insurance.

Innovation in the design of electronic payment schemes must also account for business practices and economic incentives. The lessons learned from the major characteristics of money and from the evolving payment schemes should be addressed. As innovations in electronic payments are analyzed, consider the following factors:

- Confidence in money is gained when its value is linked or it can be converted into something of value, such as an acceptable denomination of a respected currency ($, £, ¥, €) or another liquid asset with reliable value (gold).
- Electronic payment forms should be as convenient as cash—that is, readily transferable, capable of convenient exchange in scalable denominations, and easily stored and transmitted to or received from various locations.
- There must be security and accuracy in transactions.
- There must be reliable means to authenticate electronic money as genuine, not counterfeit or forged.
- Anonymity for the purchaser is a contentious issue. Some users may seek an audit trail of all prior transactions, including the identity of payors, payees, and intermediaries. This capability is now possible with checks, wire transfers, POS, or credit card transactions. Law enforcement prefers traceable payments for evidence of criminal activity, such as the money laundering discussed in Chapter 7.

4. Ibid.

Paper currency has serial numbers and can be marked, and contemporary coins have too low a value to be practical for large transactions. By contrast, many other users prefer to maintain transaction anonymity. Some privacy advocates suspect that comprehensive transaction records weaken personal freedoms and can become a tool for a repressive government.

- Few payment schemes are practical without the participation of trusted and reliable third-party intermediaries. Third parties, like banks, provide useful services such as experience, transmission of orders, account information or documents, useful relations with correspondents; they provide security and safekeeping; and they can connect the payment scheme to reliable sources of value.
- New forms of money created outside the traditional framework of regulatory oversight may weaken control over the economy. Alternative forms of money and payment schemes processed outside the banking system threaten the power of the Federal Reserve and other financial regulators to control the money supply, maintain the solvency of financial institutions, and maintain the integrity of deposit insurance (FDIC).

The involvement of third parties seems indispensable to the success of electronic payment innovations. These third parties would usually include banks, financial institutions, credit card issuers, and VANs. The emerging electronic payment innovators might also find additional third parties useful, including lenders, Federal Reserve, FDIC, clearing houses, and escrow agents. Aside from the network effect problems of scale economies, the success of electronic payment innovations must find the right mix of third party involvement and hit the market at the right time. Consider the potential range of involvement of such third parties: (1) investment, ownership, and operation of the electronic payment system; (2) research, development, standards setting, and system design; (3) issuance of electronic value to consumers and financial liability for the electronic value; (4) resale agent for other issuers of electronic value; (5) recruitment of participating merchants; (6) recruitment of consumers; (7) operation of computer data and storage; (8) operation of telecommunications network infrastructure; and (9) escrow services.

Electronically Stored Value and Smart Cards

Persistent efforts to use electronic memory devices to store value for ultimate use in payments probably will continue. Value stored on computers could be used in Internet transactions. Value stored on plastic cards or other portable storage devices could be used to shop in person through computer communications terminals physically held at a merchant's premises or mounted as a PC peripheral. Stored value is really an electronic wallet, purse, or piggy bank. Most such systems envision that value is added into storage by a third party who accepts traditional payment by cash, check, or credit and/or debit card transfer and converts this to the storable electronic value. When purchases are made, precise deductions of the appropriate value are made from the storage device. Optional features of the transaction include remote authentication and authorization, documentation, transmittal of notices, private consumer behavior information accumulated, creation of permanent records, and even anonymity maintained. The precise combination of these factors, as well as identity of the third party, the computer and communications infrastructure used, and other architectural aspects, help to distinguish the stored value experiments thus far attempted.

In the United States, most smart card experiments have failed (e.g., 1996 Atlanta Olympics, 1998 Manhattan Upper West Side). Stored-value cards offer consumers less protection than do credit or even debit cards under Federal Reserve Regulations

Commentary

Stored Value in Closed Communities: The Case of a College Campus

An analysis of the college environment illustrates how barriers to stored value might be overcome. Most important, the economies of scale from network effects can occur promptly in a closed community like a college or university. The enlistment of thousands of student consumers could be accomplished by a single administrative decision. For example, university administrators can order mandatory use of smart card technologies on student ID cards (chips, magnetic strips), force standardization of communication and security protocols, and select a single third party to administer the tasks of a financial institution (bank, credit union). Remaining student reluctance can be overcome if smart cards store other data, such as customer loyalty points that entitle cardholders to discounts or free merchandise. At large campuses, a single decision also immediately enlists some key merchants that conveniently reside on campus: vending machines, photocopiers, computer labs, food services, fees, event tickets, refreshments, and bookstores. Local, independent, off-campus merchants may have little choice but to adopt the technology or risk losing significant student business. The lesson for electronic payment innovations is that critical mass must be achieved quickly because of the difficulties in overcoming consumer satisfaction with existing technologies and merchant reluctance to invest in expensive new technologies with unknown reliability.

Z and E (limitation on theft losses, unauthorized use). The Mondex and CyberCoin projects are repeatedly mentioned. However, American consumers seem satisfied with existing payment technologies. By contrast, smart cards are becoming popular in Europe, Japan, and U.S. college campuses, where the finality of cashlike transactions is appreciated and there are no realistic expectations to benefit from the float.

Federal Reserve Proposal for Electronic Check Presentment

In 2000, the Federal Reserve proposed a system to reduce the costs of physically moving checks between banks and Federal Reserve branches and around the country. This system involves automated clearinghouse debits or **electronic check presentment (ECP)**. Under this proposal, the bank that "cashes" the payee's check would retain the paper check rather than return it for payment as done currently under UCC Articles 3 and 4. Instead, the depository bank would make and transmit an image of the check to collect from the drawee bank. If the drawer who issued the check ever requested a copy, the depository bank would electronically produce and mail an **image replacement document (IRD)** to the drawer. Federal Reserve regulations would make this IRD an equivalent of the original check for all legal and evidentiary purposes. Although a few rights and duties must be revised under Federal Reserve regulations and the UCC, the ECP proposal described here appears to be a substantial efficiency innovation for the back office handling of traditional paper checks and may be a step toward broader acceptance of electronic checks.

Micropayments

Considerable Internet content is not particularly valuable and will probably not be sold for high prices, which is not to say that healthy markets cannot develop in low-priced content such as clips of sound, music, or video, images, data, information, and analysis. Rather, the availability of such content is restrained until efficient and effective payment schemes are devised. As of this writing, most "low-value content" is available only under one of three models: (1) free, supposedly as part of building elusive "brand image," (2) ostensibly free sites that generate revenue from banner advertisements, referrals, or secondary use and resale of users' private information profiles, or (3) subscription and metered pay-per-view services. Until content providers can be paid fairly for their low-value content, the willingness to supply more content will be restrained. Website practices may not respect visitor privacy. Content providers will remain unwilling or unable to have their content effectively bundled with other subscription services. An obvious solution to this problem is the development of effective **micropayment** technologies—small, electronic payments made automatically and at low transaction costs.

Most existing payment schemes pose transaction costs that may consume too large a percentage of low-value transactions. Consider the difficulties with credit card use. The transaction fees force many merchants to require minimum purchases of $10 to $20 per charge. Some credit card issuers charge merchants up to 5% of the total sale in fees for processing the payment. These economics make it difficult to profitably use credit cards for sales of low-value content. It is generally uneconomical to make micropayments to access Web content on a pay-per-view basis. Potentially lucrative new business models would be possible if Web users could make small electronic payments, perhaps as low as a few pennies, to receive low-value website content. For example, reliable micropayment capabilities might replace some of the free access to Internet sites under current usage. Micropayments could stimulate accessibility to more creative and useful webpage information, video and audio content, images, and networked data if website operators had greater incentive from more direct profits. Of course, many in the Internet community are unreceptive to this pay-per-view model because Web content has long been freely available. However, their fears may be an overraction. There is a compelling analogy: Video content proliferated as television viewing migrated from free advertiser-supported broadcast transmission to subscription cable television, premium channels, video rentals, and pay-per-view.

The lack of universal micropayment capabilities relegates Web commerce to either (1) larger transactions for goods, software, or subscription services or (2) speculative and uncertain business models. Although this dilemma probably constrains very few B2B transactions, it forces business-to-consumer and consumer-to-consumer transactions into a few controversial business models, such as (1) banner advertising and referrals, (2) the collection and resale of private user data, and (3) brand image building. The introduction of reliable and efficient micropayment technologies arguably would release a flood of content, reducing reliance on models that are contingent on revenues from advertising or private data profiling. At this writing, the most promising models permitting micropayments are subscription services, e-malls, and e-wallets. Although some form of digital coin might be more effective, failures of the Millicent, flooz.com, and CyberCoin experiments because of insufficient critical mass probably reflected a user population that was not ready to pay for content they still believed should remain free.

Electronic Payment Epilogue

As of this writing, at least four broad types of experimental electronic payment systems were underway. First, digital cash requires the involvement of an intermediary (InternetCash Corp., DigiCash Inc.). The intermediary takes in money from registered consumers who establish a credit balance with initial payment by cash, check, or credit card. Payments are then dispensed for Internet purchases made from registered vendors. Second are digital wallets, which also require consumers and vendors to register with an intermediary (Yahoo!, AOL's Quick Checkout, Microsoft's Passport). The intermediary's software holds the consumer's credit card numbers and shipping address, facilitating quicker on-line transaction processing. In a variation of this type of system, the vendor assigns a different credit card number for each new transaction so that the vendor never learns the consumer's actual credit card number, which enhances security. Third, systems that more closely resemble frequent flyer points, bonus coupons, or green stamps are typically issued by point-granting intermediaries (Beenz.com, E-Centives, MyPoints.com). Both consumers and vendors must register and points are earned for providing personal information or viewing ads. Fourth, escrow agents are trusted third parties who hold the consumer's payment for the vendor's benefit until the consumer notifies the escrow agent that the goods actually arrived and conform to the vendor's description. Escrow payments must be released to the vendor when the escrow terms are satisfied. Escrow has long been used to protect both parties in various types of transactions, notably sales of real estate.

Despite all the publicity surrounding electronic payment experiments, the most successful systems are largely extensions of existing systems, illustrating two important points. First, consumers' and commercial parties' acceptance of new payment systems will depend on the proven security and reliability of those systems. Second, payment system performance depends on trusted third parties—commercial banks and other financial intermediaries—which will probably control the handling of most payment processes. E-commerce must rely on credit cards, checks and drafts, and EFT until there is widespread acceptance of reliable electronic currency. Indeed, Federal Reserve Chairman Alan Greenspan has predicted, "Electronic money is likely to spread only gradually and play a much smaller role in our economy than private currency did historically."

QUESTIONS

1. Commercial transactions have historically depended more on customs and practices than on enforcement under national laws. For what reasons have the UCC and UCP developed the mechanisms that encourage parties to accept, endorse, and give value for instruments like checks, notes, drafts, letters of credit, and documents of title?
2. Fekkos purchased a tractor from Lykins Oil Co. that was later found to have numerous defects. Lykins agreed to pick up the tractor, and Fekkos could leave the tractor in his front yard. When the tractor was stolen, Lykins sued to recover the price. On whom was risk of loss and why? See *Lykins Oil Co. v. Fekkos*, 507 N.E.2d 795 (Oh.Ct.Cmn.Pleas, 1986).
3. Compare and contrast the function of title and risk of loss in the past and how it operates today under UCC Article 2 in sales transactions.
4. Explain the distinction between an assignment of rights and a delegation of duties. How can these two mechanisms be present in the same transaction? How can a transaction include one but not the other? Provide an example.
5. Discuss how a third-party beneficiary contract is distinguished from a transfer of rights or duties. How could an assignment of rights or delegation of duties create rights in a third-party beneficiary?
6. A commercial buyer pays for goods with a signed note to the order of the seller, promising to pay the agreed sale price in 30 days. Consider the alternative decisions of the buyer to either (a) make a notation on the bottom of the note showing the invoice number of the goods sale or (b) write the invoice number followed by this statement: "payment on this note is conditioned on the goods delivered meeting the description in the invoice." What is the issue raised by these notations? What is the impact of these two alternative notations? How would notations be accomplished with electronic records or documents?
7. The buyer of goods from a foreign seller applies to its bank for an L/C to finance the purchase. The buyer's

bank issues the L/C containing the language that the L/C "will remain in force for a period of 6 months." What issue will arise if the bank seeks to revoke the L/C in three months? What interpretation should be given the L/C language and why? See *Conoco, Inc. v. Norwest Bank Mason City*, 767 F.2d 470 (8th Cir., 1985).

8. ePmt.com plans a new system for micropayments over the Internet. This system promises to enable payment of small but reasonable amounts for Internet access to content at websites of ePmt.com's clients. What are the obstacles confronting the development of new payment systems such as ePmt.com proposes? What are the characteristics of any reliable and successful payment scheme?

9. The law of commercial paper and other negotiable instruments has many highly technical and rigid requirements for form. They have been justified as needed routine that makes the payment and performance systems work quickly and reliably. Try to envision how similar requirements for electronic promises or orders to pay might be accomplished, including parallel reasons for each requirement. Justify any reasons to abandon particular formality requirements as electronic payment forms are devised.

10. Explain the network effects of money. What are the key factors in building general acceptance of a form of payment? What are the major obstacles to electronic payment schemes that are not sponsored by a reliable and trusted government entity?

Writings and Records, Defenses, Remedies, and Creditors' Rights

Individuals and businesses make on-line agreements daily, from complex loan applications and brokerage account applications to simple website access agreements. These contracts are made and performed as discussed in the previous two chapters. Should signed writings be necessary to enforce these contracts? How is an electronic contract proved if there is no traditional written contract? Can either party get out of their duty by pleading some defense or coercion to enter the contract? What good are legal rights without some reasonable remedy? These matters were critically important in the traditional economy and are of equal importance to e-commerce. This chapter addresses various remaining commercial law and regulation issues. First, the requirement for written contracts and its evolution into electronic records are explored. Next, defenses to contract formation are examined, followed by a discussion of the authority of agents to make and perform contracts, including both human and electronic agents. Then the failure to complete obligations and remedies for such breach of contract are covered. The chapter concludes with a discussion of special remedies for creditors when the debtor fails to make timely payments or otherwise defaults on a financial obligation.

WRITINGS AND SIGNATURES, RECORDS AND AUTHENTICATION

Contrary to a popular misconception, most oral contracts are fully enforceable and legally binding. Generally, contracts need *not* be in writing. Indeed, retail purchases are contracts, and there are usually no written contracts used, other than the ubiquitous receipt. Of course, if a dispute over any contract's interpretation arises, proving the precise terms may be difficult without consulting a reliable written document. There are several purposes for signed writings. It may be difficult to authenticate who really accepts an offer if the acceptance is done remotely and without witnesses. A signed writing helps prevent **forgery**. Signing a contract also serves a cautionary purpose: The ceremonial execution of a written contract more clearly demonstrates each party's approval of the particular terms memorialized in the writing, and it reminds them of the seriousness of their new duties.

To reduce the possibility of inaccurate fact findings in court, the law does require that some contracts be evidenced by a writing that includes all essential terms. For contracts that fall into one of several special classes, the **statute of frauds** requires a written contract *signed by the party to be charged*. The party to be charged is the one who denies the existence of a contract and who may be sued for breach. Written contracts need be signed only by the party against whom the plaintiff seeks enforcement. As discussed in Chapter 10, writings or records are often used to communicate the offer and the acceptance. Even when no writing is required by the statute of frauds, most parties consider writings and records to be very important to contract enforceability.

MEMORANDUM

To be effective in satisfying the statutes of frauds, a written contract must appear in a certain form, known as a **memorandum.** A memorandum may be an informal document or even a collection of several documents if they refer to the same transaction. A memorandum may be pieced together from separate documents, receipts, telegrams, mailgrams, letters, order forms, confirmations, addressed envelopes, and the like.

There is now no good reason to exclude electronic documents or records from satisfying the writing requirements. In the same way the courts have validated telegraph, telephone, and Telex communications, various communications tools (e.g., fax, e-mail, Web-interactive communications) are likely to be adequate substitutes for writings. How have the courts responded to changes in communications to validate the use of new technologies as legally effective documents? The following case illustrates an early authentication problem with electronic communications.

Howley v. Whipple

48 N.H. 487 (1848)

Facts. Two adjoining landowners, Ira Gould and Charles Bellows, were in dispute over the boundary between their parcels of land. Ira Gould left the area before a survey was completed, so the parties agreed to abide by the surveyor's determination of the boundary. After the survey was completed, Ira's son Joseph Gould sent a telegram to Ira, using the local telegraph agent. The only evidence authenticating that Ira was the sender of the telegram was the responding telegrapher's records.

Legal Issue. Could a telegraph message be a sufficient writing to satisfy the statute of frauds requirement that contracts be evidenced by a signed writing? Is a telegrapher's electronic transmission of the replying party's name inadmissible as evidence to prove the identity of the sender?

Opinion J. Sargent. Telegraphic messages are instruments of evidence for various purposes and are governed by the same general rules which are applied to other writings. If there be any difference, it results from the fact that messages are first written by the sender, and are again written by the operator at the other end of the line, thus causing the inquiry as to which is the original. The original message must be produced, it being the best evidence. If there was a copy of the message existing it should be produced, if not then the contents of the message should be shown by testimony. So when a contract is made by telegraph, which must be in writing by the statute of frauds, if the parties authorize their agents to make a proposition on one side and the other party accepts it through the telegraph, that constitutes a contract in writing under the statute of frauds; because each party authorizes [the telegrapher] to write for him; and it makes no difference whether that operator writes the offer or the acceptance in the presence of his principal and by his express direction, with a steel pen an inch long attached to an ordinary penholder, or whether his pen be a copper wire a thousand miles long. In either case the thought is communicated to the paper by the use of the finger resting upon the pen; nor does it make any difference that in one case common record ink is used, while in the other case a more subtle fluid, known as electricity, performs the same office.

The only way to prove such a message in a court of law would be to summon both the intermediate agents or bearers of the message, and in that way to trace the message from the lips of the one party until it was received in the ear of the other party. Anything short of that would be to rely upon hearsay evidence of the loosest character.

We know that by the admirable system regulating the telegraphic companies, the original dispatch is preserved and may be at all times procured for the proper purposes. The paper filed at the office from which the message is sent is of course the original, and that which is received by the person to whom it was sent purports to be a copy. If the dispatch is sought to be used in evidence the original must be produced and its execution proved precisely as any other instrument, or its absence accounted for in the same mode, before the copy can be received. Whilst we know that the operators employed by the company are unusually accurate and reliable in the mode of doing business, still they do not act under the sanction of an oath, and even if they did, a copy coming from the office where delivered must be proved to be a true and compared copy, before it can be admitted in a proper case.

Decision. Electronic communication such as telegraph, is sufficient to satisfy the statute of fraud's writing requirement if the agents are authorized and can authenticate the message.

Case Questions

1. Using the reasoning in this precedent, what argument could prevent the validation of fax, e-mail, or other electronic communications in negotiating a contract or satisfying the memorandum requirement of the statute of frauds?
2. What role do the telegraphers play as transcribers or intermediaries that might be analogous to modern forms of electronic communications of contract terms and assent?

SIGNATURES

The signature required for a memorandum may be satisfied by any tangible sign that is used to authenticate a writing. Of course, a cursive signature of the party is the traditional method. However, parties may also use a stamp, corporate seal, initials, the signatory's name as printed or typed, or even a fingerprint or the letter X. The key factor is that the party making the sign must intend that it be used for authentication at the time the sign is affixed to the writing or record. **Authentication** under UCITA means either (1) to sign or (2) with the intent to sign a record, otherwise to execute or adopt an electronic symbol, sound, message, or process referring to, attached to, included in, or logically associated or linked with, that record.

Electronic forms of authentication are becoming satisfactory as signatures. A few courts have held that audiotape or videotape recordings of the parties executing the agreement could be sufficient authentication. Facsimile signature devices, which are essentially signature machines, can make valid signatures if there is reliable proof that the machine was operated by someone with authority. Authority to negotiate and authenticate contracts is discussed at the end of this chapter. Electronic signature pads record signatures needed for credit card payments at many retailers and are used increasingly in commercial transaction documents, such as by UPS. These machines record, archive, and transmit a digital copy of the actual cursive signature as proof of the transaction or delivery.

Digital signatures are encrypted data bits used to authenticate electronic records. They are attached to a communication to attest to one or more of the following: a particular person created the record, access to view or modify the record is limited to designated persons or recipients, and/or verification of the source of the communication. In the future, other digital signature technologies may develop, including biological certification (e.g., biometrics such as retinal scan, fingerprint, voiceprint) and third-party certification authorities, effectively **cyber notaries** that perform a function for electronic commerce similar to that performed by notaries public on paper documents. Electronic signature enforceability is addressed further as part of the discussion of UETA later.

STATUTE OF FRAUDS CATEGORIES

Written contracts in the form of a memorandum are necessary in several major business-related activities, including (1) sales of land, (2) guarantees to pay the debts of others, (3) contracts incapable of performance within one year of their making, and (4) sales of goods worth $500 or more under the UCC. UCITA adds another category in computer information contracts: A record must be authenticated (the cyberspace equivalent of a signed writing) if the agreement requires the payment of a contract fee of $5,000 or more. Many other signed writing requirements are found in variations of the statute of frauds spread over various commercial laws. For example, the UCC requires signatures and endorsements for negotiable instruments (checks, notes), documents of title, warehouse receipts, bills of lading, and sales of investment securities.

Sales of Land

A contract that calls for the transfer of any **interest in land** must be evidenced by a memorandum to be enforceable. This requirement applies to contracts that transfer a variety of real estate interests, including full ownership (called a fee simple), an easement, covenant, mortgage, condominium ownership, mineral rights, growing vegetation, and leases lasting more than one year in most states (three years in a few states, such as Pennsylvania).

The **part performance** exception to the statute of frauds permits enforcement of an oral land sale contract if the buyer has (1) paid part or all of the purchase price and (2) either taken possession of the property with the seller's knowledge or made valuable improvements on the land. Enforcement of an oral land sale is justified because it would be unfair to let the seller use the technicalities of the statute of frauds to back out of an oral deal later turned unattractive after the buyer takes possession. In such instances, most courts grant a specific performance, ordering the seller to formally deed the property over to the buyer. It is expected that the passage of UETA will encourage expanded use of electronic records in place of the many current paper-based documents for real-estate transactions (e.g., contracts of sale, inspection certificates, deeds), land use processes (e.g., zoning applications, subdivision plats), and real estate financing (e.g., loan applications, mortgages, recording).

Guarantee Contracts

If an outside third party promises a creditor that the outsider will pay the original debtor's debt, the promise must be in writing. These promises are known as collateral contracts of **guarantee**. Although the original debtor's contract of debt need not be in writing, the guarantor's promise to pay if the debtor defaults *must* be evidenced by a memorandum. A true collateral contract of guarantee is enforceable only after the debtor defaults. For example, assume that C, a creditor, is willing to extend credit to D, the debtor, only if G, the outside guarantor, provides additional assurance that the debt will be repaid. G's promise to pay D's debt if D defaults is a collateral contract of guarantee that must be evidenced by a memorandum.

An exception to this requirement exists when the guarantor's **main purpose** or **leading object** is merely to protect the guarantor's own interests. An oral guarantee is enforceable in this situation because fraud is less likely. For example, a corporation in financial difficulty may be able to borrow money only if its president agrees to guarantee the loan. Because the president's main purpose in guaranteeing the loan is to protect the company and his position as president, the guarantee need not be in writing. Guarantee contracts should also be distinguished from some forms of collateral and security arrangements that need no writing to be enforceable. Because loan cosigners or comakers are both primarily liable on the debt, their promises are not collateral guarantees that must be evidenced by a memorandum.

Contracts Incapable of Performance within One Year

Long-term and complex contracts are more susceptible to problems of proof as time passes. If a breach of contract suit is brought long after contracting, witnesses may forget the facts or the circumstances may have changed. Therefore, a contract that is incapable of being performed within one year after the contract was made must be evidenced by a memorandum. The statute of frauds does not require writings for all long-term contracts. In many instances, the parties choose to take longer than a year to perform contracts that were capable of full performance within a year. The fact that a contract *might* take longer than a year to perform is not the important factor. No writing is required if the contract could reasonably be completed within one year.

Generally, only those contracts that require more than one year from the date the contract was made and the last day on which a performance is required must be memorialized with a memorandum. The one-year time begins to run when the contract is made and ends with the last required performance. Contracts that require several years for full performance must be evidenced by a memorandum. For example, a two-year employment contract or a professional engagement requiring performance at a time more than a year after the contract is made must be in writing under this provision.

UCC's Sales of Goods over $500

The common law statute of frauds has been amended by the UCC for contracts involving the sale of goods for $500 or more. The UCC statute of frauds is less restrictive than the common law. The memorandum required by the UCC need not state all the terms of the contract, but it will be enforced only up to the quantity stated in the writing. The UCC has "gap fillers," automatic terms that are implied in a goods sale contract if there are missing terms. For example, testimony may supply terms of price, delivery, quality, or industry customs. There are four major exceptions to the UCC statute of frauds in which oral contracts are enforceable.

First, if both parties to an oral contract are merchants and one party sends a written confirmation of an oral agreement to the other party, then no writing is necessary if the recipient fails to object within 10 days. This is the **receiver bound** exception. It provides an incentive for merchants to carefully read and quickly respond to their mail. A second UCC exception exists for **specially manufactured goods**, defined as goods unsuitable for sale in the seller's ordinary course of business. Consider an oral telephone order for $1,000 of unique manufactured goods. Even without a writing, the oral contract becomes enforceable as soon as the seller makes a substantial beginning in procuring or making the goods. Goods requiring special printing, embossing, unusual colors, trademarks, or emblems are typical examples of specially manufactured goods.

A third UCC exception permits enforcement of an oral contract if the party seeking to deny the contract nevertheless confirms the agreement by making a judicial **admission**. The admission may appear in testimony, in pleadings, or otherwise in a court proceeding. The statute of frauds will not aid a party to renege on a contract actually entered into orally. The fourth UCC exception permits enforcement of oral contracts if there has been either a **part payment** for goods by the buyer or an acceptance of a **partial delivery** by the seller. Contracts are enforced under this part performance doctrine only for the quantity paid for or accepted.

Statute of Frauds for Licenses under UCITA

UCITA's statute of frauds is based on the UCC. Most important, and consistent with UETA, the focus turns away from a primary reliance on cursive signatures written on paper documents by pen. UETA and UCITA now permit the use of physical or electronic records. A record is sufficient even if it omits or incorrectly states a term. No contract is enforceable beyond the number of copies or subject matter as shown in the record. Terminology under UCITA changes; instead of a signed writing, UCITA requires an **authenticated record**. Recall that a **record** includes both information inscribed on a tangible medium (writing) or stored in a retrievable format (electronic record), and authentication is either a signature or the execution of an electronic symbol linked with that record. UCITA validates current digital signature technologies and many other technologies that may develop in the future.

The main UCITA rule is that contracts requiring payment of a contract fee (price) of $5,000 or more must be supported by an authenticated record showing that a contract was formed. The party against whom enforcement is sought must authenticate the record, and the record must reasonably identify the subject matter. However, a party can agree that any future UCITA license between the parties need not be stated in authenticated records if the party against which enforcement is sought agrees to this in the first authenticated record.

UCITA's exceptions to the statute of frauds expand on exceptions found in both the common law and in the UCC. First, no authenticated record is needed if the license terms call for an agreed duration of one year or less. Also, no authenticated record is needed if the license may be terminated at will by the party against whom the contract is asserted. Second, there is a part performance exception: No authenticated record is needed when a tendered performance is accepted or the information licensed is accessed by the licensee. For example, no writing is required when the buyer takes and accepts the goods or downloads the information. Third, there is no authenticated record requirement when a party admits in court, by pleading or by testimony or otherwise under oath, that a contract was made. An admission is not enforceable beyond the number of copies admitted or the subject matter admitted. Fourth, there is a merchant's receiver bound exception. No authenticated record is required between merchants if, within a reasonable time, a record confirming the contract and sufficient against the sender is received and the party receiving it has reason to know its contents. Like the UCC, this exception is inapplicable if a notice of objection to the contents of a merchant's confirming record is given by way of a record within 10 days after the confirming record is received. UCITA's statute of frauds would govern only licenses of information.

UNIFORM ELECTRONIC TRANSACTIONS ACT

The Uniform Electronic Transactions Act (UETA) may be the most significant cyber law for electronic commerce. UETA validates electronic contracts, electronic signatures, and the use of electronic agents for electronic contracting. UETA's passage by all the states seems likely, following passage in Congress of the Electronic Signatures in Global and National Commerce Act (federal E-SIGN) in June 2000. This federal law effectively encourages states to adopt the more favorable provisions of UETA.

Impact of UETA

A working understanding of UETA is important to businesses that create, process, and accept paper-based contracts but seek to convert to electronic forms of these documents. Many states' regulatory agencies will implement UETA in government documents. Most state agencies must promote consistency and interoperability between their agencies and with other states and the federal government.

Electronic forms of various traditionally paper-based negotiable instruments are now valid, including notes, bills of lading, warehouse receipts and other documents of title. However, UETA does not yet apply to several key classes of documents, such as wills, codicils (revisions of a will), and testamentary trusts, or to the most common negotiable documents, such as checks, drafts, letters of credit, and investment securities. Nevertheless, the experience of UETA should influence how all negotiable instruments eventually migrate to electronic form. UETA does not alter many states' consumer protections, such as requirements for written or mailed notices. UETA should be distinguished from UCITA; the latter applies only to transactions in computer information. UETA applies to transactions in several but not all underlying subject matters, including land, services, and goods, with the exceptions noted previously. UETA does not apply to computer information transactions covered by UCITA; however, these two laws have many similar provisions.

ONLINE

Online Information about UETA

http://www.uetaonline.com

Overview of UETA's Provisions

UETA establishes several new terms of commercial practice and thereby expands traditional contracting concepts to work in the digital age. As in UCITA, a UETA record is information inscribed in a tangible medium or stored and retrievable in perceivable form. An **electronic record** is a record that is created, generated, sent, communicated, or received by electronic means. Information means data, text, images, sounds, codes, computer programs, software, databases, and the like. An **electronic signature** is an electronic sound, symbol, or process attached to or logically associated with a record, used with the intent to sign the record. It is the equivalent of an authentication under UCITA. UETA permits the use of electronic agents to effect automated transactions, as discussed later in this chapter.

Electronic Records and Electronic Signatures

The centerpiece of UETA is found in §7, which validates the use of electronic records and signatures. Electronic records satisfy legal requirements for writings so that the enforceability of a record or signature cannot be denied simply because it is in electronic form. Electronic records must still satisfy any other formal requirements, such as notices, disclosures, and completeness of terms. For example, if the parties' e-mail messages show an agreement on the sale of widgets, these electronic records would still need a quantity term to create a valid contract for the sale of goods under the UCC. Electronic records and signatures simply satisfy requirements under existing law, such as the statute of frauds, when they require documents to be signed writings.

Legal requirements to provide information in a memorandum are satisfied with an electronic record if it is capable of retention (printing and storing) by the recipient when received. UETA makes electronic records the equivalent of writings but does not alter other substantive requirements of contract law. Many other laws have specific requirements for the posting, display, communication, and transmittal of records; usually a physical, printed form is required. Although UETA validates electronic records, it does not override these existing legal requirements under other laws mandating particular methods of posting, sending, or formatting records. For example, eviction notices generally must be posted where the tenant is most likely to see it, right on the front door of the dwelling. Even if the landlord and tenant agree to electronic transactions, UETA cannot override property law requirements for physical posting of paper eviction notices.

Electronic transactions pose different security problems than traditional practices that use printed documents or voice telephone conversations. Electronic information is vulnerable to corruption by electronic interference or intentional forgery by hackers. UETA authorizes the use and innovation of security procedures (e.g., encryption) to verify the identity of the sender. UETA makes an electronic record or electronic signature attributable to a particular sender if it was the act of that person, which can be shown in any manner from the context and surrounding circumstances, such as an effective security procedure.

UETA's recognition of electronic signatures differs somewhat from existing digital signature law and practice; the latter focuses on security and encryption. By contrast, UETA simply permits the substitution of an electronic sound, symbol, or process when the law requires a physical signature if it is attached to or logically associated with a record and used with the intent to sign the record. Electronic signatures may take many forms, including a PIN number, password, server identification, biometrics, clickwrap using the "I Agree" button or some form of encryption.

Changes and Errors in Electronic Transmissions

Electronic transmissions can be prone to errors caused by individual users, and sometimes they are prone to changes caused by electronic computers or during communication. UETA encourages the use of security procedures to detect and correct changes or errors. In §10, UETA provides that if one party fails to use a security procedure that both parties had previously agreed to use, the conforming party may avoid the change or error if the security procedure would have discovered it and permitted its correction. Additionally, UETA strongly encourages simple error-checking mechanisms in business-to-consumer transactions, such as confirmation screens that help detect errors. These and other types of changes or errors are resolved under the doctrine of mistake discussed later.

Retention of Electronic Records

Many laws require certain documents to be saved as evidence for future use. UETA §12 permits the retention or presentation of electronic records to satisfy these retention requirements if the information accurately reflects the original and remains accessible for future reference. Accessibility of electronic records becomes problematic over time. Obsolete computer systems may become incompatible or accessible only by data-recovery experts. Floppy disks are not stable over time, and conversion between systems is time-consuming and expensive. Nevertheless, electronic records must remain accessible if they are to satisfy legal requirements for retention. For example, if a law requires retention of a check, that requirement is satisfied by electronic retention of all information on the front and back of the check. Unless there is a requirement to the contrary, written documents can be discarded once transferred to electronic form. Care should be taken until electronic archives are proven reliable.

Sending and Receipt of Electronic Records

The law often requires inquiry into the time or place that a document is sent or received. For example, recall that a contract is created under the mailbox rule when the acceptance is dispatched. Similarly, the UCC requires that some notices must be delivered to a party's place of business. UETA §15 does not address proof of time of receipt. In the situation of multiple e-mail addresses, the recipient can designate the particular e-mail address to be used. When the precise location is an issue—for example, in a conflict of laws, or tax issues—the location is that of the sender or recipient, not the location of the information system. General broadcast messages that are sent to systems rather than individuals are not considered a sending. The key element is whether the sender or recipient has control.

Transferable Records

UETA facilitates electronic negotiable instruments but only in the limited areas of the electronic equivalent of paper promissory notes and paper documents of title, and then only if the issuer agrees that the electronic record should also be an **electronic transferable record.** UETA does not apply to checks, drafts, investment securities, or letters of credit. Rules parallel to UETA may be developed in the future, but the banking system is not yet ready for these documents to "go electronic" under UETA.

UETA creates the concept of "control" over an electronic record, which should be the equivalent of the concept of "possession" as traditionally used in a paper context. Systems must be in place to ensure that the record is transferred in such a manner that there is only one "holder" of the record. The transferable record must remain unique, identifiable, and unalterable. UETA's provisions are summarized in Exhibit 12.1.

Additional Laws Covering Electronic Signatures

The original impetus for UETA in 1996 was the international effort by UNCITRAL, which drafted the Model Law on Electronic Commerce. UETA was intended to displace the proliferating number of electronic and digital signature laws passed by the states in recent years. UETA is technology-neutral and intended to avoid state laws that favor particular technologies. For example, a few state statutes, such as Utah's, validated electronic signatures only if dual-key encryption was combined with third-party certification of the encryption keys. Such technology-specific laws could lock in particular technologies and dampen the incentive to innovate.

Now UETA has spawned imitation. A federal electronic signature law was passed in June 2000, formally known as the **Electronic Signatures in Global and National Commerce Act** (E-SIGN). The E-SIGN law preempts—that is, it overrides—all state electronic signature laws, with an important exception. UETA's electronic contracts and signatures provisions, §§1–16, will apply in states where UETA is enacted without substantial change from the official version discussed previously. Although Pennsylvania's UETA is nearly identical to the official version, California's initial passage of UETA contained more than 50 amendments. E-SIGN may preempt California's UETA if the courts interpret it as not being uniform. Therefore, the applicability of UETA or E-SIGN law may depend on the outcome of future court challenges.

There are some key differences between UETA and E-SIGN. UETA covers more types of transactions than does E-SIGN. For example, as discussed before, UETA covers attribution, defines when records are sent or received, covers mistakes or errors, requires the admission of electronic records in legal proceedings, permits the use of transferable records in transactions beyond real property, and better defines the use of electronic agents in automated transactions. E-SIGN does not cover these subjects precisely. By contrast, E-SIGN provides more consumer protection by requiring notices and protection from unannounced electronic communication system changes. Where UETA merely requires the retention of electronic records for later reference, E-SIGN requires more: that records be accessible to all who are entitled under

EXHIBIT 12.1 Summary of UETA Provisions

Section	Subject	Summary of Provisions
§1	Short title	Cite as Uniform Electronic Transactions Act (UETA)
§2	Definitions	Definitions for 16 key UETA terms
§3	Scope	Applicable to electronic records and electronic signatures in contracts, notes, documents of title, and certain government documents; not applicable to wills, codicils, testamentary trusts, checks, UCITA transactions, and others prescribed by law
§4	Prospective application	Applies to validate electronic transactions only after the effective date chosen in the adopting state statute
§5	Use of electronic records and electronic signatures; variation by agreement	Use of electronic means is not required; applicable only if parties agree to conduct transactions by electronic means, determined by context and circumstances; any party may refuse to conduct future transactions electronically, and this right cannot be waived; other UETA provisions may be varied by agreement
§6	Construction and application	Construed and applied to facilitate electronic transactions, be consistent with reasonable commercial practice, and facilitate uniformity
§7	Legal recognition of electronic records, signatures, and contracts	Records, signatures, and contracts may not be denied enforceability solely due to their electronic form; electronic records and electronic signatures satisfy legal requirements for signatures and writings
§8	Provision of information in writing; presentation of records	Legal requirement to provide information in writing is satisfied with electronic record if capable of retention (printing and storing) by recipient when received. Validity of electronic records under UETA does not override legal requirements of other laws requiring paper document posting, sending, or formatting
§9	Attribution and effect of electronic record and signature	An electronic record and electronic signature are attributed to a particular sender if they were the act of that person; shown in any manner from the context and surrounding circumstances, such as an effective security procedure (e.g., encryption)
§10	Effect of change or error	Use of security procedures encouraged to verify changes and correct errors; penalizes party using electronic agent in automated transaction with an individual unless an opportunity is provided to verify communication and check errors
§11	Notarization and acknowledgment	Notarization requirements satisfied by electronic signatures made by the authorized person if all required information is attached or logically associated with the electronic signature or electronic record
§12	Retention of electronic records; originals	Electronic record satisfies laws requiring document retention if the information accurately reflects the original and remains accessible for future reference; check retention requirements satisfied by electronic retention of all information from front and back of check; written documents may be discarded after transfer to electronic form; laws passed later may specifically require retention of nonelectronic records
§13	Admissibility in evidence	Evidence of a record or signature cannot be excluded from a legal proceeding solely because it is in electronic form
§14	Automated transaction	Machines acting as electronic agents can form contracts; the lack of human intent does not negate the transaction, inferred from computer programming and use; contract may be formed between electronic agent and individual, e.g., click-through; no legal relationship created with unidentified site access if user is not identified; validates user's click-through license agreement, constitutes a sufficient signature
§15	Time and place of sending and receipt	Parties may agree as to effective timing of electronic messages; otherwise, electronic record is sent when properly addressed or directed to an information processing system designated by the recipient, in a form capable of processing, and it enters a system outside the sender's; receipt occurs when the record reaches the recipient's designated system in a form capable of processing, not when recipient becomes aware of it; return receipt of acknowledgment verifies the record's receipt but not its contents

EXHIBIT 12.1 Summary of UETA Provisions (continued)

Section	Subject	Summary of Provisions
§16	Transferable records	Framework for negotiation of electronic promissory notes and documents of title but not for other commercial paper (checks, drafts), letters of credit, or investment securities; issuer must agree to use electronic transferable records; "control" over an electronic record depends on the reliability of the system to identify the person as rightful transferee; copies must be identifiable as not the authoritative original; systems must assure there is only a single authoritative copy and only one "holder" of the record; the transferable record must remain unique, identifiable, and unalterable

law. E-SIGN specifically excludes the use of several documents in electronic form—in family law matters (divorce or custody settlements, antenuptial agreements) and for various cancellation notices (utility shutoffs, insurance benefits)—and it prohibits giving notice only by electronic means concerning a primary residence (eviction, mortgage default, repossession, foreclosure). E-SIGN requires assessment of its exceptions and the effectiveness of electronic consumer notices. On balance, the states have an incentive to avoid federal preemption by E-SIGN, so most are likely to pass UETA in its original form. Nearly 30 states have passed UETA as of this writing.

PAROL EVIDENCE

Before a contract is finalized, the parties frequently negotiate or dicker about its terms. The negotiation process often involves proposals and counterproposals of alternative terms that replace previously offered but withdrawn terms. As the negotiators change their proposed terms, they grant advantages to the other party and may take on new performance burdens. The final agreement is usually a compromise in which both parties give up some of their original demands and find agreement in a middle ground. This process of give-and-take through negotiation has led to the parol evidence rule.

The **parol evidence rule** prohibits either party from proving any different terms than those stated in the written document. If the parties litigate over breach of contract, the parol evidence rule prevents the jury from considering any oral or written evidence that would alter or vary the terms in the written contract. Neither party may seek the jury's sympathy by introducing evidence of a contract term that might have been proposed during preliminary negotiations but was later omitted when the parties reached a complete and final agreement. It also prevents fraud because false evidence of terms allegedly adopted is excluded.

The statute of frauds is further distinguished from the parol evidence rule because the latter is "triggered" when the court finds the writing is an **integration.** This means that the parol evidence rule excludes evidence of terms not in the writing when the court finds that the writing was intended by the parties to be so complete that it should not be supplemented. The parties can make this outcome even more certain by including a **merger clause** that clearly states that the writing is intended as an integration. As a practical matter, the rule requires the party that did not prepare the writing to read it carefully before signing. This extra care assures that all of the finally agreed-upon terms actually appear in the written contract. The parol evidence rule does not exclude evidence needed to clarify ambiguities or to show fraud, duress, mistake, illegality, incapacity, or later modifications.

UCITA §301 adapts the traditional parol evidence rule to protect the integrity of records felt to provide the exclusive source of terms, called **confirmatory records.** UCITA permits the explanation or supplement of confirmatory records by using evidence of usage of trade, course of dealing, or course of performance, even if the confirmatory record is not deemed ambiguous or does not amount to an integration. However, under some circumstances, the court may find that the proposed additional terms would not have been omitted from the confirmatory record, so the evidence will be excluded. It is also useful to consider UETA's transferable record rules as an alternate form for safeguarding the terms in a record. Transferable records must be secured by technical means, such as by system architecture or encryption, to prevent alterations.

CONTRACT DEFENSES

Canceling an agreement is difficult. The law generally favors stability and thereby satisfaction of the reasonable expectations of the parties. However, in some cases public policy finds that the circumstances of the parties' mutual assent favor releasing one party from a bad bargain because of actual or potential coercion during negotiations. A contract defense may exist if the parties' mutual assent is not genuine, such as when either party is coerced. An agreement can be canceled if the misunderstanding or coercion is so great that enforcement would be unfair. Such situations typically arise in dealing with incompetents, when one party misrepresents material facts to the other, when certain mistakes are made, or when there is coercion. Neither UETA nor UCITA displaces contract defenses. Indeed, UCITA §114 specifically embraces the contract defenses discussed next with this provision: "principles of law and equity, including the law merchant and the common law of this State relative to capacity to contract, principal and agent, estoppel, fraud, misrepresentation, duress, coercion, mistake, and other validating or invalidating cause, supplement [UCITA]."

CAPACITY

Not all persons are legally capable of entering into contracts. Some persons lack the mature judgment, experience, cognitive development, or ability needed to understand the effects of their promises. Minors as well as drunken, drugged, and insane persons lack contractual capacity, so they are protected from the harsh dealings of another party. However, the mental and negotiating capabilities of incapacitated persons are not usually evaluated in every case. Rather than invalidating outright all the contracts of incompetents, the law gives each incompetent the right to avoid unfair contracts at their choice. An incompetent may usually withdraw or **disaffirm** a contract. This protection lasts until the minor reaches the age of majority, usually 18, or the drunken, drugged, or mentally impaired person becomes lucid. Adults cannot disaffirm contracts made with incompetents.

In most states, both deserving and shrewd minors are protected by the right to disaffirm a contract. For example, a minor can disaffirm a reasonable contract even if the adult party is damaged by the disaffirmance. Adults can protect themselves by assuring they deal only with adults or by insisting an adult parent or guardian join in, cosign, or guarantee the contract. Much of the contemporary regulation of Internet activity involves interaction with minors, with particular emphasis on regulating the collection and use of private information and regulating minors' access to "adult content." Regulation of on-line activity with children is covered in greater depth in Chapter 14.

Although identifying minors is a well-understood problem in face-to-face transactions, it is more problematic when transactions are remotely concluded via phone, fax, or mail. Electronic commerce transactions pose even more difficulty because many use automated transaction processing or electronic agents that are not sufficiently sophisticated to reliably identify the customer's incapacity. Two major methods appear in current use: (1) customer affirmation that they are adults, usually to access adult material, and (2) requiring the use of credit cards to access website material, based on the assumption that few customers under age 18 legitimately possess credit cards.

Voidability of an Incompetent's Contracts

Before majority, minors may disaffirm their contracts at any time but must generally return the contractual benefits still in the minor's possession. It is usually irrelevant that some of these benefits are missing or depreciated. Many states now limit this absolute right of disaffirmance if the minors misrepresented their age. In such situations, the minor may disaffirm but is held liable for the adult's losses. After a minor attains majority or after a mental incompetent becomes lucid, there is a short window of opportunity for disaffirmance, which must be done within a reasonable time. During this grace period, the incompetent is enabled to assess the fairness of contracts made during minority and decide to either disaffirm or ratify them. Once a minor reaches majority and accepts the contract by **ratification**, the right to disaffirm is lost.

The contracts of minors and other incompetents are not automatically considered void. Instead, they are voidable contracts, and only the minor's intentional act of disaffirmance releases the minor from liability. A voidable contract may be ratified only after the incapacity is removed. A minor cannot make a legally binding contract during minority, and it follows that it is impossible to ratify a contract during minority. Ratification can occur only after the minor reaches majority or after an impaired person becomes lucid. The law may imply ratification if the incompetent either has not disaffirmed within the reasonable time or acts in a manner inconsistent with disaffirmance. For example, if after reaching 18, the person continues to use property bought during minority, the courts will imply a ratification from that conduct.

Necessaries

In some instances, an incompetent's right to disaffirm is further limited by making them responsible to pay for **necessaries,** the necessities of life: food, clothing, and shelter. Necessaries may also include contracts for services and property that aid in sustaining life, such as tools of the trade, employment placement services, vocational education, and medical services or supplies. This determination is subjective. Of course, the possibility of an unfair bargain still exists, for example, overpriced or defective necessaries. Balancing these considerations, the law implies quasi-contractual duties on the incompetent to pay the reasonable value of the necessary items, which may be less than the price originally agreed to. Items are not necessary if the incompetent's parent or guardian could have provided them.

MISREPRESENTATION AND FRAUD

It is unjust for either party to provide incorrect information to the other about the contract's subject matter. From an economic perspective, the allocation of resources is not optimal if contracting parties have inaccurate or incomplete information. The law prohibits a wrongful party from enforcing a contract based on such misrepresentation.

The innocent victim may rescind a contract tainted by misrepresentation if it involves material facts on which the victim has justifiably relied and has suffered damages. The UCC imposes good faith requirements of "honesty in fact in the conduct or transaction concerned," and UCITA further requires the "observance of reasonable commercial standards of fair dealing" in every contract or duty.

The initial focus in a misrepresentation case is on the misstatements themselves and also on the person making the misstatements. Not all statements are facts that can be misrepresented. Facts are matters susceptible to exact knowledge and verification, such as past events or current conditions. Usually, predictions of future events are not facts but merely opinions, so they cannot be misrepresented as facts. However, if the opinion is made by a recognized expert or appraiser, then their statements of opinion or prediction could actionable as misrepresentation if they are untrue. For example, a salesperson's use of generalized statements concerning the value or quality of goods is known as **puffing**. Most reasonable buyers understand that puffing statements are usually too vague to be misrepresented as facts. However, if the person making representations of facts knows, or should know, that their statements are false, then this behavior is more serious and the act of misrepresentation becomes fraudulent. **Fraud** is not only a reason to cancel a contract but also the basis for monetary damages based on the tort of deceit. Fraud is a criminal act and a regulatory violation under state and federal law.

The next focus in a misrepresentation case is on the victim. In negotiating a contract, the victim's reliance on the other party's representations must be reasonable. Sometimes the victim should not believe a particular representation. If the victim has superior experience with the contract subject matter, then the victim should make an independent investigation. If there is no actual reliance by the victim, then there is no causal link between the misrepresentation and the victim's alleged damage. A lack of reliance releases the misrepresenter from liability, because contract law aids only victims damaged as a direct result of another's wrongdoing. However, if the victim of fraud honestly and reasonably believed the misrepresenter's statements, the contract may be canceled. For example, if a landowner promises that no toxins were ever dumped on the land, the buyer may rescind if later there is proof the landowner knowingly contaminated the land.

MISTAKE

In most instances, the law refuses to aid those who blunder in contract negotiations by making mistakes of judgment either in assessing the contract's value or in estimating their own capability to perform. However, some mistakes concern such key terms as the identity, existence, or character of the contract's subject matter. When both parties are mistaken about the subject matter, a **bilateral** or **mutual mistake** occurs, permitting either party to rescind or cancel. If only one party is mistaken, then there is a **unilateral mistake**. The contract is voidable for a unilateral mistake only if the nonmistaken party knows of or should have known of the victim's mistake and takes advantage of the victim.

UETA and UCITA both recognize recurrent areas for error with provisions to prevent mistakes in computer transactions. A mistake may occur in the execution by completing or authenticating the wrong document or misentering keyboard information. A mistake may be the result of computer interface frustration, such as madly clicking through. UETA §10 was introduced previously; it addresses this problem when automated transactions are made with an individual. The party using an electronic agent must give the individual an opportunity to prevent or correct the error. For example, consider an individual who strikes the numeric key "1" to order a single copy of a book from an on-line bookseller but the "1" key sticks or delays in displaying the "1," causing "111" to be sent, or the "1" is mistakenly rekeyed. In such a situation, the electronic agent facility of the on-line bookseller must send a confirmation screen that permits the individual to review the quantity ordered. This confirmation might be as simple as a box saying, "You ordered 111 books; click yes if this is correct." UETA §10 provides that without using some such security procedure, the individual may avoid the mistaken contract for the quantity of 111 books. Electronic agents are discussed further at the end of this chapter.

Restitution is usually required to unwind a mistaken transaction. If UETA gives one party a right to rescind a mistaken transaction, any consideration already received must be either returned or destroyed or instructions from the other party followed. However, a party may be prohibited from rescinding if the consideration was already received and used. For example, it may be impossible not to have used information after it is revealed, because the information *is* the consideration. Once information is received and understood, it may be impossible to avoid using it or receiving its value, and this situation limits the right to avoid the error or change.

UCITA §206 empowers the courts to grant appropriate relief if the use of electronic agents results in an automated contract involving fraud, electronic mistake, or the like. UCITA §214 gives consumers a defense to avoid contracts resulting from electronic errors. An **electronic error** occurs in an electronic message if the information processing system provides no reasonable method to detect and correct or avoid errors. In an automated transaction, a consumer is not bound by an electronic message that the consumer did not intend and that was caused by an electronic error, if the consumer promptly notifies the other party, returns the computer information or destroys all copies, and has not already used the benefits of the information or redistributed it to a third party.

DURESS

The terms of most contracts are dictated by market forces or by one party's business needs. Laissez-faire freedom of contract prevents the law from changing the terms of freely negotiated contracts. However, if one party unduly pressures the other party, the resulting contract may be voidable. The threat or actual use of force is an obvious type of coercion that might make a person to agree to unfavorable terms. This constitutes **duress**, and the victim may rescind the contract. The threat of criminal prosecution is duress, but the threat of civil suit is not duress unless the claim is unfounded and malicious. The threat of force may seem nearly impossible in electronic transactions because of the anonymity and separation of the parties. However, hackers have done considerable damage from their remote locations. Some parties identify themselves, or their locations may become known by various means. Some contracting partners can access the other party's assets, perhaps even taking control over another party's computer, information system, or critical website. Therefore, duress may become a problem even in the seemingly isolated Internet environment.

Economic duress arises if one party threatens to breach an existing contract unless the victim agrees to another, usually unfavorable, contract. However, economic duress is not a justifiable basis for cancellation if the economic circumstances are imposed by the market or if the victim makes mistakes of judgment. Tying is another form of economic duress discussed further in Chapter 19 on antitrust law. Unfair commercial contracts may be modified under the UCC concept of **unconscionability**, discussed in Chapter 10.

In a more subtle form of coercion, **undue influence** is exerted by someone owing a fiduciary or close relationship to the victim. Victims of undue influence may rescind a contract if a position of trust was used to divert property from its normal course. For example, a young boy's grandmother became his guardian after his parents died, leaving him as the heir to their corporate stock. However, the grandmother induced the boy to sign over the stock to her. Her undue influence deprived him of the stock, so he later disaffirmed the stock transfer to his grandmother and the corporation was required to replace his shares after he became an adult.

ILLEGALITY

The common law doctrine of illegality holds that the law should not aid lawbreakers; therefore, the courts usually do not assist either party to an illegal contract. Illegality arises if the principal contract objective calls for the commission of a criminal or tortious act. Illegal contracts are void and unenforceable. However, the illegality doctrine is not so straightforward if the contract calls for acts that may not appear illegal but an illegal performance is likely. When the most likely method of performing the contract's legal objective is through illegal means, the contract itself may be illegal. By contrast, an otherwise legal contract is not made illegal simply because one party may do an illegal act during performance. Courts must determine the legality of the subject matter and assess how the principal duties are likely to be performed.

Because the courts refuse to enforce the duties of either party to an illegal contract, it is often said that the parties will be left as the court finds them. For example, if one party has already paid for an future illegal act, the other party will not be required to perform that act or ordered to repay for the unperformed illegal act. Despite the apparent unfairness, illegal contracts cannot be rescinded or enforced when both parties are ***in pari delicto***, that is, they both know of the illegality.

Types of Illegality

There are four common areas in which illegality seems to exist but the rule prohibiting enforcement is relaxed: (1) licensing, (2) gambling, (3) public policy, and (4) restraints of trade. Restraints of trade are covenants not to compete (discussed in Chapter 13) or antitrust offenses (Chapter 19).

Licensing Statutes. Many states and municipalities require certain professionals and most businesses to obtain licenses before doing the licensed activity. A court may refuse enforcement of certain contracts made with unlicensed persons, but first the type of license must be determined. Some licensing statutes, such as municipal business licenses, have only a **revenue-raising** objective. These laws do not usually require a test of the licensee's expertise or qualifications, so contracts made by unlicensed persons or businesses are generally enforceable, even if they have neglected to obtain the required license. However, penalties may apply.

On the other hand, all states and most nations require the licensing of many professionals. The primary objective of professional licensing is to protect the public from unscrupulous and unskilled practitioners. **Regulatory licensing statutes** require satisfaction of certain minimum qualifications before professional practice. For example, lawyers, doctors, engineers, teachers, real estate brokers, and barbers must be licensed before practicing by demonstrating their good character and professional skills. An unlicensed professional's contracts to provide regulated services are illegal and unenforceable. Therefore, a customer or client is usually permitted to rescind such a contract for professional services and regain any funds they paid because they are the type of person protected from unskilled and unscrupulous practitioners by the statute.

Gambling. In all states, the unrestricted free exercise of gambling is illegal. Legal gambling generally occurs in licensed casinos, at licensed pari-mutuel racetracks, at licensed off-track betting parlors, at sales locations for state lotteries, or at limited charitable functions (e.g., bingo games). Contracts to pay illegal gambling debts are unenforceable. The proliferation of Internet gambling sites has challenged law enforcement because gambling sites are often located outside the state or in international havens, generally beyond the practical reach of local law enforcement. Problems of illegal Internet gambling were discussed in Chapter 7.

One of the most perplexing problems with gambling is determining what activities are really illegal gambling. **Gambling** occurs when the parties enter a gaming transaction that creates a risk from an uncertain event. That risk had no prior existence and is created primarily to shift that risk and expose the parties to gain or loss. For example, neither party has a risk of losing the bet before they start the game. However, as a result of playing, they both risk loss. If two parties bet on the price level that a particular stock will reach on a particular day, they create an unenforceable gambling contract. A similar economic event seems to occur if one party sells a stock and another party buys it. However, there is a fundamental difference between betting and a legitimate securities transaction. Stock ownership carries the risk of uncertain price movements, a previously existing risk. By contrast, betting on stock prices creates a brand-new risk that is not associated with stock ownership but is created only in the gambling contract.

Insurance contracts are also susceptible to characterization as gambling. An insurance contract is legal and not gambling if the beneficiary or loss payee (the person selected to receive the policy proceeds) has a close connection with the insured person or property. The beneficiary's risk existed before the insurance was purchased. This close connection or nexus is called an **insurable interest.** An insurance policy is not illegal gambling when there is an insurable interest. An insurable interest in a person's life exists if there is a close family relationship (e.g., spouse, child, parent) or the insured is a key employee of a business. An insurable interest in property exists if the beneficiary owns, leases, or holds a lien on the property (collateral) or arises for the buyer after the seller identifies specific goods as destined for shipment to a particular buyer under the UCC. If the purchaser of insurance has no insurable interest, the insurance contract is illegal gambling. In the case of a loss, no benefits are paid, but the premiums are returned to the insured party.

Public Policy. As a matter of public policy, the courts usually do not enforce agreements that violate society's ethical and moral norms as found in statutes and court decisions. Public policy prohibits contracts that seek to bribe or unduly influence public officials, fiduciaries, agents, or law enforcement officials in the performance of their duties. Such contracts are illegal and unenforceable. For example, public policy prohibits certain terms in the contracts of parking lot operators, pawn shops, or checkrooms. These parties are **bailees** because they hold custody of other people's property. Bailees often try to enforce **exculpatory clauses** in an attempt to escape liability if the owner's property is damaged or lost while the bailee has custody. However, such clauses are generally unenforceable if the bailee tries to avoid liability for willful misconduct. Exculpatory clauses are valid only to relieve the bailee of liability for negligence and only if the terms are effectively communicated to the property owner.

AUTHORITY TO NEGOTIATE AND CONCLUDE CONTRACTS

Few contemporary businesses can expect to manage significant growth without hiring employees to do production, administration, procurement, and sales activities. Although the Internet may seem to permit sole entrepreneurs to go it alone, eventually in the expansion of most successful start-ups, they must use other people or firms as agents to perform the increasing workload. This section discusses the parts of agency law needed for others to negotiate, conclude, and perform contracts. The discussion includes the agent's duties, the agent's authority, and the principal's duties resulting from contracts made by agents or from automated transactions that use electronic agents. Agency law is largely taken from case law precedents and summarized in the *Restatement of the Law Second, Agency*, produced by the American Law Institute.

ONLINE
American Law Institute
http://www.ali.org

NATURE OF PRINCIPAL AND AGENT RELATIONS

An **agency** is initially a two-party relationship between the **principal**, who hires or otherwise consents to accept the services of a second party, the **agent**. An agency is a fiduciary relationship in which the principal consents to have the agent only act for the principal. All corporations are artificial persons under the law that can act only through agents. All corporate contracts, including purchasing, hiring, and selling, are performed by corporate agents. Corporate agents may be persons—usually managers and employees or other firms such as independent contractors. The law of agency becomes important when the principal's legal relationships with outside third parties are affected by the agent's actions. These acts regularly include negotiation, conclusion or performance of contracts, receipt of information, processing of payments, and various forms of decision making. Agencies are most often created formally in a written or oral contract for employment or retainer. However, agencies may also arise by implication from the circumstances, even if there is no formal employment relationship.

Agents are fiduciaries that generally owe duties to perform carefully and with loyalty to the principal. Agents must avoid conflicts of interest; they cannot simultaneously represent the counterparty in a contract. Agents may not favor their own personal interests over their principal's interests. It is unethical and unlawful for an agent to take a profit in a transaction made for the principal without the principal's fully informed consent. An agent must also keep the principal's trade secrets confidential. Agents must obey all the principal's reasonable and lawful orders in connection with the subject of the agency. Agents must use reasonable skill and care by giving the principal's business reasonable diligence and attention. These and other topics related to the rights and duties owed by agents and their principals are detailed further in Chapter 13. The agency relationship is depicted in Exhibit 12.2.

AGENT'S AUTHORITY

The most important point about agency in the contracting context is that the agent's contracting activities bind the principal only if the agent is authorized. This point is significant both for contracting by traditional means and in most electronic commerce activities. Principals may assent to a contract by using their authorized agents. An authorized agent's actions bind the principal to the third party in the contract. Much of this chapter has been devoted to the creation of binding contracts via

EXHIBIT 12.2 Authority of Agents

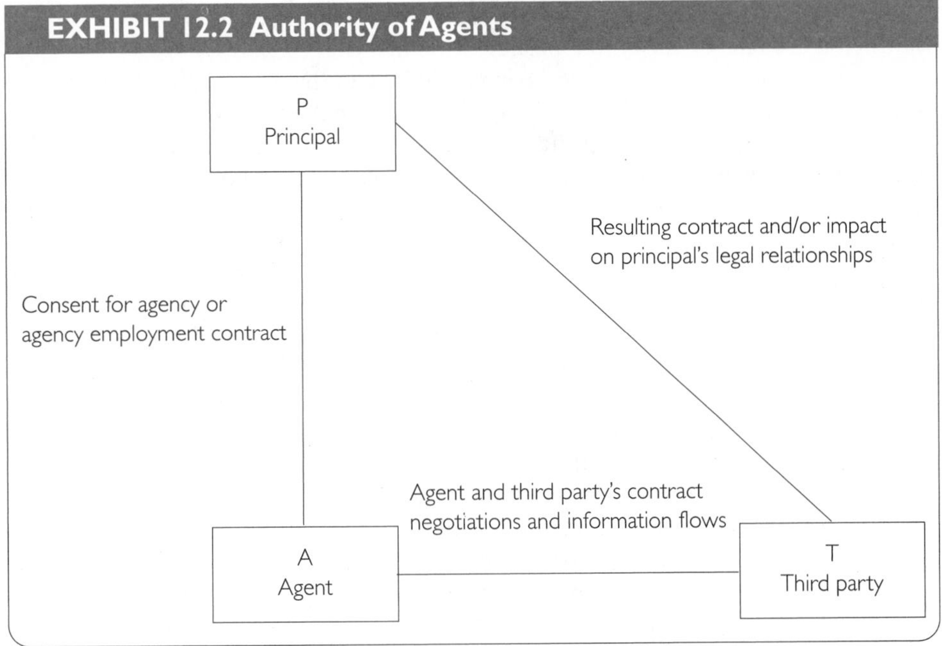

traditional offer and acceptance or with substitute technological methods. Principals may use agents to negotiate and conclude agreements, and when they do, the resulting agreements are binding, but only if the agents are authorized.

Authorizing agents in a clear manner is critically important to commerce and to understanding the principal's contractual duties. Of the four major methods to authorize agents, the first two forms are actual authority: (1) express authority and (2) implied authority. The second two forms are **circumstantial authority**: (3) apparent (ostensible) authority and after-the-fact authorization by (4) ratification. The clearest and most effective method for authorizing an agent is by **express authority**. As illustrated in the section on written contracts, express authority is best given in a written contract. Express authority can also be granted orally but must be in writing in a few instances. The **equal dignities rule** requires a written authorization if the agent negotiates a contract for the principal that the statute of frauds requires must be in writing: land sale, guarantee, performance for more than one year, sales of goods worth more than $500, and computer information or securities worth more than $5,000.

The principal has the power to control the amount, scope, and timing of the agent's authority. However, if an agent has been granted at least some express authority, the law may permit these powers to expand as an **implied authority** when needed to implement the express grant. For example, assume that a web-based retailer has authorized its purchasing agent to negotiate and conclude contracts with suppliers at prevailing market prices for up to 5,000 units in any month. One supplier with excess inventory offers a steep discount, but only if the Web retailer's agent will commit to purchase 7,000 units. In some instances, courts may imply the agent has authority to purchase the additional 2,000, even though this quantity exceeds the agent's express authority, because the discount is so favorable. Of course, given sufficient time and an immediately accessible principal, the agent should request express authority. Implied authority is intended to permit the agent to push the limits in an urgent or emergency situation. Implied authority also supplements an express grant of authority when it is vague or silent on a particular point.

An agent's authority may also be expanded when the principal's acts suggest to third parties that the agent is authorized. The principal gives the agent apparent or ostensible authority when the principal's words or actions hold out or intimate that the purported agent has some authority. Even volunteers, who are not authorized agents, may be given apparent authority in some instances. For example, imagine that the trademarked logo of a retail company appears on a manufacturing company's website. Additionally, text on the manufacturer's site strongly suggests that the retailer can negotiate prices in sales made directly to the consumer from the manufacturer. In this example, even if the retailer has no actual authority, the manufacturer has held consumers to believe that the retailer is an authorized agent and can make binding contracts.

Authority is best when clearly expressed before the agent negotiates a contract. However, a fourth type of authorization is conferred *afterwards* by ratification. **Ratification** may arise either when agents exceed their actual authority or when nonagents volunteer to represent the principal. The contract becomes binding on both the principal and the third party when the principal learns of the unauthorized agent's act and retroactively approves the entire transaction. Ratification may also be implied if the principal remains silent while retaining the benefits of an unauthorized contract with the third party. For example, an unauthorized friend might buy insurance for you. You are not liable to pay the premiums, but if you do, the payment is a ratification of your friend's unauthorized act.

CONTRACT LIABILITY OF PRINCIPAL AND AGENT

Under the **conduit theory**, the contract made by an authorized agent binds only the principal and the third party. Agents usually take on only a representative role and seldom expect to have personal liability if the principal breaches the contract. For example, a corporate purchasing agent would not expect to be held liable if the corporation failed to pay a supplier for goods the agent ordered. The purchasing agent is a mere conduit through whom the principal and third party negotiate. When two corporations are contracting, they each use agents as conduits for their negotiations. However, if the agent is unauthorized, the conduit theory does not apply, and the agent can be held liable for the unauthorized commitment. For example, many corporate employees are not authorized to assent to a click-wrap software license or to bind their employer to a website agreement. Some employees may be unaware that the employer may not be responsible on these agreements and that the employee may have personal liability on these electronic commerce agreements.

An agent is also personally liable when pretending to represent a nonexistent principal. An agent may be legally responsible in two additional instances, even if the principal authorizes the negotiations. First, an agent can voluntarily assume the liability of a principal when the agent cosigns or comakes the contract. Second, an agent may be personally liable if the principal's existence or identity is withheld from the third party. Agents are generally not liable when the third party knows that a principal exists; that is, the agent is known to be only a representative, and the principal's identity is also known to the third party. However, some agents withhold the principal's identity to preserve the principal's confidentiality. For example, a principal's negotiating experience may be so well known that third parties might hope to seek better terms when dealing with that principal. To avoid this, the principal might use an agent to negotiate contracts and hide the principal's identity. In such situations, the agent may be specifically instructed to conceal the principal's existence and/or identity and thereby preserve the principal's confidentiality. This is not illegal; it is an undisclosed principal situation.

When the third party knows the agent represents someone else but does not know who the principal is, the principal is **partially disclosed.** Few third parties are willing to accept uncertain responsibility from some unknown principal, so they insist the agent assume responsibility on the contract. When the third party does not even know that there is a principal, the authorized agent appears to actually be the principal in the contract. This is an **undisclosed principal** situation. The third party may elect to hold either the agent or the principal liable on the contract, but not both. This election cannot be made until the third party learns the principal's identity and verifies authority. Undisclosed principals are frequently used in land sales to conceal the identity of a purchaser such as a big company or a wealthy individual.

ELECTRONIC AGENTS UNDER UCITA AND UETA

UCITA and UETA both accept the law of agency. They further envision the use of automated, mechanical, or computerized communications as substitutes for human agents to negotiate or conclude contracts. UCITA §107(d) authorizes electronic agents to authenticate, perform, or manifest assent to create a contract. UCITA §102(27) defines an **electronic agent** as a computer program (or electronic or other automated means) used by a person to initiate an action (take a step in an electronic transaction) or to respond to electronic messages or performances on the person's behalf without review or action by an individual. The UETA definition is similar. The principal is bound by the operations of the electronic agent, even if no individual is aware or reviews the electronic agent's actions. The acts of an electronic agent may be attributable to that person or company.

Electronic agents may conclude **automated transactions**, contracts formed without human intervention by one or both parties. Automated transactions may also be formed with interaction between a human and an electronic agent. Electronic agents may manifest assent to a record or term after an opportunity for review. The assent may occur after the electronic agent has an opportunity to authenticate the record or term. Alternatively, assent may occur after the electronic agent starts to perform by delivering the licensed information or by making a payment due. For an electronic agent to have sufficient opportunity to review a record or term, it must be in a form that a reasonably configured electronic agent could be technically capable of using. Eventually, electronic agents may develop artificial intelligence, enabling totally autonomous negotations.

DISCHARGE OF OBLIGATIONS, BREACH OF CONTRACT, AND REMEDIES

The vast majority of contracts are performed satisfactorily; goods are delivered and accepted, services are adequately rendered, land ownership is transferred and possession taken, and payments are accurately made and credited. Small disputes may arise concerning the quantity, quality, form, or timeliness of both parties' performance, but most are quickly settled amicably. Of course, there are two major incentives to avoid contract disputes. First, most parties genuinely seek repeat business and need to build and maintain their good reputations by performing satisfactorily.

Breach of contract is generally believed to harm commercial reputations. Second, the threat of legal process looms over contract performances. The law provides aggrieved parties with a remedy.

Early experience with e-commerce shows that performance and payments pose a challenge to the effectiveness of traditional economic and legal incentives. These traditional methods of resolving contractual disputes are under stress in the e-commerce world. For example, many on-line retailers in the B2C world have failed to provide adequate customer support, failed to accurately deliver customer orders in a timely manner, or failed to process payments fairly. As a result, some e-commerce businesses have collapsed. Many e-commerce firms are developing new policies and procedures, including the use of trusted third parties to oversee or assist in performance. Two key observations should be made. First, initial designs of e-commerce transaction processing, particularly by dot.com entrepreneurs inexperienced in traditional commerce, may not satisfy customers. This undermines confidence in e-commerce generally and may delay its growth. Second, political and economic pressures will mount to prevent recurrence of e-commerce service failures. If the public comes to believe that remedial efforts are failing, additional consumer protection regulations seem likely.

In this section, the traditional methods of determining satisfactory performance are explored, including the discharge of contractual duties, measures of adequate performance, breach of contract, and legally enforceable remedies. Measures of performance and remedies are standardized under contract law. Nevertheless, laissez-faire allows the parties considerable flexibility to customize such terms to best suit their needs. This section also discusses the difficulties in fashioning new laws that balance the need to encourage e-commerce growth and the need to adequately protect both sides in e-commerce transactions. The primary focus is on the common law as modified for goods sales by the UCC and for licenses under UCITA where it is the law. Many of UCITA's provisions define licensing, and they are detailed in Chapter 13. Warranties trigger remedies that were discussed as part of product and service liability in Chapter 8.

DISCHARGE BY PERFORMANCE

Each party's performance is judged by the degree of perfection that a reasonable person can objectively expect to receive. To adequately discharge their contract duties, both parties must perform exactly as promised; otherwise, they will have committed a **material breach.** This is the **perfect tender rule**: The buyer must pay fully and on time, and the seller must deliver on time exactly the quality and quantity. If either party materially breaches its obligation, the innocent party may postpone counter-performance and sue for a remedy. In many instances, contract law relaxes this strict rule. Strict and exact performance of many complex contracts is not always realistic. In some situations, the law or the parties may permit something less than perfect and full performance.

Consider two compelling examples that support relaxing the perfect tender rule when the seller produces a product customized for the buyer's particular needs. The first is a classic example, a building construction contract. The contractor, acting in good faith, is permitted by law to deviate slightly from the plans and specifications if the deviations are only minor and unintentional and they scarcely cause the buyer any real harm. For example, the building materials called for in the contract may become unavailable, permitting the contractor to make substitutions. The law requires that the contractor should still be paid. The second example is similar:

the design and production of complex software or websites. Technology and consumer tastes change quickly during performance. Sometimes the customer may call for changes after construction starts; perhaps the vendor takes advantage of new tools or technological capabilities. When the performance made is not exactly as stated in the contract, it may be best to adjust the purchase price to reflect the slightly lesser but still reasonably acceptable quality because it still amounts to a **substantial performance.**

The distinction between the perfect tender rule and the substantial performance doctrine is illustrated by the difference between mass production and individually customized production. The industrial revolution made much higher efficiency and more consistent quality possible. Innovations included routine tasks and repetitive production with standardized and interchangeable parts. Mass production permits more consistent quality, which justifies the perfect tender rule for standardized goods. By contrast, the difficulties of achieving perfection in specially manufactured products is complicated by uncertainties in production and materials availability, justifying a relaxation of perfection.

How these two rules of performance quality will adapt to the "mass customization" plans of some e-commerce companies is uncertain. **Mass customization** promises the quality control and efficiency advantages of mass production with the made-to-order customization that customers increasingly demand. Mass customization promises to reduce inventory costs and shorten production delays. The closest contemporary example of this manufacturing-to-order concept is the on-line ordering and configuration of personal computers. It may take some time before mass customization of hardware or software products can achieve its promise of cost savings with consistent reliability. Until manufacturers can adequately test the performance of all combinations of options, the unknown interactions among them can conceal reliability problems.

The lateness of deliveries, payments, or performance of services is also judged. If the delay in performance is too serious, it may constitute a material breach. If there is a material breach, the innocent party is relieved from performance and may sue for a remedy. Slight delays must be tolerated, though, perhaps with small price adjustments made. However, at the time of contracting either party may insist the contract include a provision making **time of the essence.** This provision requires perfect tender and timely performance. For example, a real estate sale contract might require the buyer to search diligently for financing and require that time is of the essence so that if the financing cannot be found the seller can quickly find another buyer or the buyer another property.

Anticipatory Breach

Either party may notify the other party of an inability or unwillingness to perform in the future. This is an **anticipatory breach** under the common law and an anticipatory repudiation under the UCC or UCITA. Such a preannounced breach gives the innocent party a choice if breach is threatened before the time set for performance: either await performance or immediately sue. In either case, the aggrieved party may suspend its performance after receiving this anticipatory notice. Anticipatory repudiation permits the innocent party to sue for damages, cancel the contract, or ignore the repudiation and await performance. The breaching party may withdraw the repudiation if the aggrieved party has not yet acted on it, such as by contracting with someone else or by bringing suit. At any time, either party may demand adequate assurances of performance from the other party. For example, if a seller is uncertain about the buyer's solvency or if a buyer is disturbed about recent erratic deliveries, either party could lose trust. If the other party fails to give assurances after a request, the innocent party may pursue remedies for breach even though the time for performance has not yet arrived.

IMPOSSIBILITY OF PERFORMANCE

The doctrines of delegation and **impossibility of performance** are interrelated. Sometimes an obligor becomes ill and cannot perform services or cannot deliver goods that were destroyed or unobtainable if a supplier halted production. A strike or a boxcar shortage might also prevent performance. In such situations, the contract becomes *subjectively impossible* to perform. That is, the obligor (the subject) cannot personally perform as promised, but perhaps another could be substituted to perform as a delegate.

Consider the differences between a contract for the services of a famous portrait painter and those of a house painter. If the artist becomes ill, there is simply no direct substitute for the quality of the expected performance. Because no one else can paint like the artist, performance is either justifiably delayed or excused altogether by impossibility. By contrast, if the house painter suffers a strike, there is no objective legal impossibility of performance because house painting is not generally considered so unique. Why? Because another house painter could be appointed to paint the building. In such cases, the obligor *must* delegate the duty or risk breaching the contract. The doctrine of impossibility excuses performance only when unique services are justifiably excused or unique subject matter is destroyed before performance. Other variations of this defense are the **frustration of purpose** and **commercial impracticality** doctrines. Some courts release an obligor if, after the contract has been made, events occur that render the other party's performance worthless or too costly.

Force Majeure Clauses

The parties may agree to define the particular events or conditions that trigger impossibility of performance. **Force majeure** clauses are often used when one or both parties could be exposed to uncertain and debilitating events. Force majeure clauses are enforceable as privately bargained-for impossibilities. They are customized to the parties' particular needs or their industries. For example, oil and gas supply contracts typically contain force majeure clauses that excuse performance if oilfield difficulties are experienced. Force majeure clauses are generally enforceable if, through no fault of either party, performance becomes impossible because of listed events. Typical subjects of force majeure are labor troubles (strikes), war, transportation failures, acts of God, and any other event the parties mutually agree to include in the clause.

DAMAGES

Contract law is intended to satisfy the parties' reasonable expectations of performance. In most cases, money damages are an efficient and satisfactory remedy. **Compensatory damages** are the most typical damage awards because they represent the losses actually suffered in obtaining a replacement, realizing the promisee's original expectations, or obtaining a substitute performance. For example, the party breaching a contract must usually pay any of the innocent party's out-of-pocket expenses. Of course, the nonbreaching party has a **duty to mitigate damages** by avoiding and minimizing their damages when possible. Punitive damages are rarely awarded in breach of contract cases unless the promisor is also guilty of tortious and willful misconduct.

Damages for breach can sometimes be made more certain if the parties agree to a **liquidated damage** provision in which the parties specify the amount of damages if one party breaches. Liquidated damage clauses are enforceable only if they are legitimate estimates of uncertain future damages. An attempt to use liquidated damages to penalize and discourage breach is generally unenforceable. For example, if a wholesaler presold a quantity of goods to be acquired from a manufacturer, it would be unreasonable to charge the manufacturer liquidated damages that were considerably more than the wholesaler might expect to profit on the transaction. A large liquidated damage provision in such a supply contract would be unenforceable as a penalty because the wholesaler's potential loss is limited to the difference between wholesale and resale price, plus expenses or diminished goodwill and reputation. However, if the wholesaler had not presold the goods and the market for the goods was uncertain, a liquidated damage provision approximating the wholesaler's markup could be a reasonable amount.

SPECIFIC PERFORMANCE

Although damages are the most typical remedy, a specific performance of the contract may be ordered in cases involving unique property such as land, collectibles, or goods previously designated for purchase. **Specific performance** is a court order requiring the parties to perform exactly as originally promised. When money damages are inadequate to satisfy the promisee's expectations, the extraordinary remedy of specific performance may be ordered. No specific performance will be ordered for personal services. Both the UCC and UCITA provide for specific performance in appropriate circumstances.

ARBITRATION CLAUSES

Arbitration is a traditional dispute-settlement mechanism in international commerce. It is used increasingly in domestic commercial disputes for the reasons discussed in Chapter 3—namely, efficiency, privacy, and avoidance of litigation difficulties. However, an arbitration clause may not always result from balanced bargaining. Indeed, critics charge that the stronger party usually *imposes* arbitration on the weaker party, who may have little choice but to accept. How are these arguments affected by the following influential "terms in the box" case?

Hill v. Gateway 2000, Inc.

105 F.3d 1147 (7th Cir.) *cert.denied* 522 U.S. 808 (1997)

Facts. The Hills purchased a Gateway 2000 PC that included an arbitration clause among the considerable documentation included inside the computer's shipping box. The Hills waited longer than the 30 days offered in Gateway's return policy to object to the inclusion of an arbitration clause for the settlement of warranty and other breach of contract disputes. Gateway moved to dismiss the Hills' fraud and racketeering claims by arguing that the Hills' failure to return the PC within the 30 days constituted acceptance of the arbitration clause, thereby barring the Hills from litigating claims against Gateway in court.

Legal Issue. Is an arbitration clause enforceable against a consumer if it is contained in a shrink-wrap agreement enclosed among considerable documentation inside the new computer's box?

Opinion. J. Easterbrook. An agreement to arbitrate must be enforced "save upon such grounds as exist at law or in equity for the revocation of any contract." A contract need not be read to be effective; people who accept take the risk that the unread terms may in retrospect prove unwelcome. Gateway shipped computers with the same sort of accept-or-return offer ProCD made to users of its software [in the case *ProCD v. Zeidenberg*]. ProCD is about the law of contract, not the law of software. Payment preceding the revelation of full terms is common for air transportation, insurance, and many other endeavors. Practical considerations support allowing vendors to enclose the full legal terms with their products. Cashiers cannot be expected to read legal documents to customers before ringing up sales. If the staff at the other end of the phone for direct-sales operations such as Gateway's had to read the four-page statement of terms before taking the buyer's credit card number, the droning voice would anesthetize rather than enlighten many potential buyers. Others would hang up in a rage over the waste of their time. And oral recitation would not avoid customers' assertions (whether true or feigned) that the clerk did not read term X to them, or that they did not remember or understand it. Writing provides benefits for both sides of commercial transactions. Customers as a group are better off when vendors skip costly and ineffectual steps such as telephonic recitation, and use instead a simple approve-or-return device. Competent adults are bound by such documents, read or unread.

Shoppers have three principal ways to discover these things. First, they can ask the vendor to send a copy before deciding whether to buy. The Magnuson-Moss Warranty Act requires firms to distribute their warranty terms on request; the Hills do not contend that Gateway would have refused to enclose the remaining terms too. Concealment would be bad for business, scaring some customers away and leading to excess returns from others. Second, shoppers can consult public sources (computer magazines, the Web sites of vendors) that may contain this information. Third, they may inspect the documents after the product's delivery. Like Zeidenberg, the Hills took the third option. By keeping the computer beyond 30 days, the Hills accepted Gateway's offer, including the arbitration clause.

The Hills' remaining arguments, including a contention that the arbitration clause is unenforceable as part of a scheme to defraud, do not require more than a citation to *Prima Paint Corp. v. Flood & Conklin Mfg. Co.*, 388 U.S. 395 (1967). Whatever may be said pro and con about the cost and efficacy of arbitration (which the Hills disparage) is for Congress and the contracting parties to consider. Claims based on RICO are no less arbitrable than those founded on the contract or the law of torts.

The decision of the district court is vacated, and this case is remanded with instructions to compel the Hills to submit their dispute to arbitration.

Decision. "Terms in the box" included on documentation sealed inside the shipping containers may be enforceable against the buyer if they can be inspected after delivery and the buyer has the option to reject the goods on these terms.

Case Questions

1. What are the consumer's realistic options, given the "terms in the box" dilemma discussed in this case?
2. How do the courts reconcile the expectations of consumers as created by the vendor's advertising with the limitation of remedies inherent in "hidden" arbitration clauses?
3. Under this judge's reasoning, which is the more appropriate forum, the courts or the legislature, to create consumer protections against unfair surprise in contract terms or the alleged unfairness of arbitration?

UCC REMEDIES

The UCC remedies are intended to put the innocent party in the same position as if the breach had not occurred. An innocent but aggrieved party may seek a court order, the recovery of money damages, or other rights designed to give the innocent party benefits equivalent to what full performance would have given. The UCC imposes a general duty of good faith on all parties. The remedies for breach of contract track the steps in each party's performance so that the impact of a breach can be corrected precisely and quickly. Both parties must stand ready to perform until the other party fails to **tender** performance as required; that is, they must indicate a willingness and an immediate ability to perform ("here, take the money!").

The UCC generally permits either buyer or seller to recover **consequential damages**, those additional damages that flow naturally from the breach, including lost income or profits. However, the UCC requires any aggrieved party to mitigate damages by trying to minimize them whenever practical. Either party can cancel the contract if the other party is in breach of contact. The UCC imposes a four-year **statute of limitations** period, which requires suit for breach of contract within four years after the contract was performed. However, much of the focus of the UCC is providing reasonable self-help mechanisms to avoid confrontation or litigation. The UCC releases parties from performing if an unforeseen event makes the obligor's performance highly impractical. For example, if a seller's cost of goods increases by 10 times or more, then the contract might be discharged for commercial impracticality.

Seller's Obligations and Buyer's Remedies

In addition to rights under the extensive UCC express and implied warranties of quality discussed in Chapter 8, the buyer has several more remedies. The most fundamental buyer remedy is the right to receive **conforming goods** that exactly meet the contract description. The seller must tender delivery at a reasonable time and place, give the buyer notice, and hold the goods for a reasonable time to give the buyer the opportunity to take delivery. The buyer has the right of **inspection** before accepting goods to assure they conform to the description, unless the delivery is COD or a "shipment against documents" (e.g., document of title, draft, letter of credit). However, the inspection right imposes a duty on the buyer that may limit warranty protection. For example, to the extent the buyer fails to discover a defect while making a reasonable inspection, the buyer's warranty is excluded, and there is no remedy.

If the seller delivers **nonconforming goods** that do not meet the contract specifications, then the buyer has three choices: (1) accept the nonconforming goods, (2) reject nonconforming goods and sue for damages, or (3) accept whatever commercial units (e.g., case, crate, pallet) that are reasonable under the circumstances and sue for damages. An **acceptance** of goods occurs when the buyer indicates willingness to keep them, fails to reject within a reasonable time, or treats the goods as belonging to the buyer (e.g., uses or resells them). Even after an acceptance, the buyer has a limited right of revocation of acceptance; the buyer may withdraw or cancel the acceptance if there are defects that were difficult to discover in a normal inspection (latent defects) or the buyer reasonably believed the seller would cure but the seller never did. After the buyer rejects or revokes acceptance, the buyer must reship the goods back to the seller or hold them for the seller to pick up.

The buyer's rights after rejecting nonconforming goods are limited by the seller's right to cure. **Cure** is the seller's right to correct the breach by notifying the buyer that substitute conforming goods will be provided. Then the buyer must receive the conforming goods before the time originally set for performance. If the seller fails to deliver conforming goods by the time set for performance, the buyer may **cover** (purchase substitute goods from another seller). Alternatively, the buyer may sue for specific performance to force the seller to give up unique goods or for **replevin** of goods already identified in the contract. The buyer has the right to collect compensatory damages when the seller fails to perform. Damages are computed as the difference between the contract price and the higher market price on the day of the breach. An alternate measure is the increased price paid for cover, including incidental and consequential damages.

Consider how these remedies would affect a retailer who was promised a shipment of desktop personal computers on Thursday just before the retailer's well-advertised Saturday sales event. If the wrong goods arrive (laptop computers) on

Tuesday, the supplier still has until Thursday to cure this by delivering conforming goods—desktop PCs. However, if nothing shows up by Thursday, the buyer may cover by purchasing desktop PCs from another supplier on Friday. The buyer is not required to cover, so if no goods arrive for the Saturday sales event, the buyer can still sue the supplier for consequential damages, probably lost profits from the desktop PCs that would have been sold on Saturday.

Buyer's Obligations and Seller's Remedies

The seller's most basic right is to receive payment of the contract price on or before the time set for performance of the payment obligation. The seller has four basic monetary remedies if the buyer refuses to accept delivery of conforming goods: (1) collect damages equal to the difference between the contract price and a lower market price prevailing at the time of breach, (2) collect damages on the difference between the contract price and a lower resale price to some other buyer, (3) recover lost profits if the buyer's breach causes the sale of fewer units by the seller, or (4) sue for the total sale price if the goods are unsuitable for sale to anyone else (highly customized).

When the buyer's solvency is in question, the seller has some additional remedies: (1) stop the shipment of goods already in transit with a common carrier, (2) refrain from delivering goods the seller still holds, or (3) demand return of goods anytime during the 20 days following delivery if the buyer is insolvent. However, the seller must deliver as promised if an insolvent buyer tenders cash. The CISG closely mirrors the UCC remedies for both buyer and seller.

REMEDIES UNDER UCITA

In those states where UCITA is effective, the remedies parallel the UCC's remedies in many ways. UCITA's laissez-faire perspective permits the parties considerable freedom to design their own remedies by contract. This makes the UCITA remedies controversial because licensing is unique and many of the balances the UCC draws between vendor and buyer rights in goods sales may not work well for the licensing of software or information. Indeed, many observers predict that transactions governed by UCITA will show systematic bias favoring sellers in consumer transactions and bias favoring large corporate buyers in B2B transactions. Generally, UCITA includes a cancellation right after notice to either party if the other party breaches. The parties may agree to a liquidated damage provision. UCITA has a complex statute of limitations of ostensibly four years. However, the statute of limitations may be changed in nonconsumer contracts, but not to less than one year. Limited forms of money damages are a primary focus of UCITA remedies, but they are much more regulated than under the common law or the UCC. As in other areas of the law, the parties must mitigate damages whenever it is reasonable to do so.

Limitations on Electronic Self-Help

UCITA has a controversial contractual remedy that some software producers and information providers apparently are hoping to use widely: **electronic self-help**. The licensor can disable some software with several possible technologies. One clear example of electronic self-help termination occurs when the licensor shuts off the licensee's access to programs or databases at the licensor's server. This electronic self-help remedy may be legitimate if the licensee has missed payments and is nearly insolvent. The licensor should not be required to continue supplying when the licensee is in breach of contract.

It is typical for software or data to reside on the licensee's system. However, even when the licensee physically controls the information, it can still be remotely shut off by electronic means. Examples of these electronic self-help methods include

- Periodic electronic reauthorization
- A time-activated shut-off device (electronic time bomb)
- Periodic entry of changing authorization codes
- Web-based probes from the vendor that disable the system, or the system may require periodic retrieval of reauthorization from the licensor over the Web, by telephone, or by mail

Self-help has long been acceptable in leasing and in secured lending (discussed later). Repossession of automobiles is a prime example. However, there is strong public opinion that electronic self-help is an intrusive violation of privacy. Public policy tolerates self-help only if it does not cause great surprise, does not breach the peace or damage third parties, and does not permit economic abuse of a vulnerable customer. For example, if electronic self-help were used to shut down key accounting software or disable an essential data system, there could be potentially huge consequential damages for the licensee. Therefore, electronic self-help may be deemed to be *illegitimate* if the licensee is not really in breach, the licensor pressures the licensee to pay more or buy other products, or there are risks to public safety, potential harms to third parties, or the risk of personal injuries, property damage, or information destruction. Without these safeguards, electronic self-help could actually serve to hold the licensee's business for ransom.

UCITA prohibits electronic self-help in mass market licenses. In other licenses, the licensee must specifically consent to the self-help provision, but this could be a "take-it-or-leave-it" proposition. The licensor must give the licensee 15 days notice before invoking electronic self-help. UCITA remedies are derived from licensing practices; other details are discussed in Chapter 13.

ONLINE

Controversy over UCITA's Self-Help Provisions
http://www.ucitaonline.com

CREDITORS' RIGHTS AND DEBTOR PROTECTIONS

A critical underpinning to the commercial law system is the protection given parties when contracts are breached. Much of commerce depends on seller-financed transactions or on transactions financed by third-party financial institutions. Long experience with abuses by both debtors and creditors shows a need for legal and contractual safeguards that balance their interests. When a debtor's insolvency leads to default on a loan, two major sources of law are implicated: (1) state commercial law including secured transactions and (2) federal bankruptcy law. Insolvency protections include the orderly and fair administration of the insolvent debtor's remaining assets, which can minimize creditor losses if the debtor tries to disappear with the assets or if the debtor favors some creditors over others. It also addresses the creditor's harsh treatment of the debtor. This section examines the planning and practice of "definancing," first, as provided by contract and state law on creditors' rights and then under federal bankruptcy law. Federal bankruptcy law is divided into components generally called chapters, which are frequently referred to in this discussion: Chapters 7, 11, and 13.

ONLINE

Insolvency information and data
http://www.bankruptcydata.com

SECURED FINANCING

The creditor's willingness to extend credit depends on the probability of default and on how adequately the debtor can assure repayment. The debtor's promissory note provides the basic legal right to debt repayment. **Insolvency**—the unwillingness or inability to make debt payments—too often makes it impractical for creditors to collect. This reality has led to the development of other repayment assurances. For example, a creditor should investigate the debtor's creditworthiness before making the loan. Credit insurance, surety, and guarantee contracts are sometimes used, making third parties accountable if there is a default. Frequently, creditors insist that the debtor grant a lien in collateral—that is, **pledge** property actually held by the creditor or grant a right to foreclose on property the debtor uses.

A **lien** permits the creditor to take steps to repossess and foreclose on the collateral if the debtor defaults. **Foreclosure** is a regulated process of selling the collateral to produce proceeds, usually money paid by the buyer at the foreclosure sale. Foreclosure proceeds are used largely to pay down the outstanding debt. Common examples of **security interests** include mortgages on land, new car liens, and a corporate bondholder's lien on factory machines.

UCC Article 9 provides the legal machinery for securing loans by creating lien rights in personal property but not in real estate. A major revision of Article 9 became effective in July 2001 and is being adopted by most states, effective when designated in the state's adoption statutes. During the transition from old Article 9 to Revised Article 9, it is still useful to understand both versions, even if all 50 states adopt the revision. Although Revised Article 9 continues the use of paper documents, it now recognizes electronic records; it permits the use of traditional signatures while also recognizing electronic authentication. These advances should enhance efficiency and accuracy in credit transactions, such as electronic loan applications, electronic communications between debtors and creditors, and electronic creation of liens using public filing and retrieval. Revised Article 9 also makes new distinctions between consumer debtors and commercial borrowers.

The only party who can grant a lien and create a security interest is the owner or rightful possessor of property. Often, the **secured party** (lender) will not make a loan unless the owner grants a lien. A security interest gives the secured party special rights to keep or sell the collateral if the debtor defaults. **Default** is not defined in Article 9, which gives the parties freedom of contract to define default in the loan documentation. Default is most often triggered by missed periodic loan payments. Default can also be triggered by other financial conditions or behaviors that lenders find typical of an imminent breach.

Commonly, the borrowed money is used to purchase the collateral. This creates a **purchase money security interest (PMSI)**. Many UCC Article 9 rules depend on the type of property: intangibles, accounts, inventory, consumer goods, farm products, or equipment. Revised Article 9 adds several new classes of property important to the information economy, including software, payment intangibles, investment property, health care insurance receivables, and commercial tort claims.

Security interests must generally be created in two basic steps. The first step is attachment, the grant of a security interest. The second step is **perfection**, determination of the secured party's priority. Priorities are important if a debtor grants several liens in the same collateral to different secured parties. Article 9 priority rules settle these conflicting claims when the proceeds of a foreclosure sale are insufficient.

Attachment

The creditor is responsible for making the security interest become effective. Attachment using a **security agreement** is the most common method. The security agreement is a written document or electronic record, signed or authenticated by the debtor, describing the collateral and granting the lien. Attachment makes the lien effective between the debtor and the creditor. Attachment is accomplished when three things occur. First, the borrower must sign a security agreement or authenticate such an electronic record. Alternatively, the creditor could take possession of the collateral to make attachment possible. Second, the secured party must give **value**, a form of consideration. Usually a lender advances the loan principal to be used for the purchase of either the collateral or some other property. Third, the borrower must have some rights in the collateral, although full ownership is not necessary. After the security interest attaches, the secured party should be careful to assure that no other secured party acquires superior rights in the collateral. Assurance of this priority is the second major step: the perfection process.

Perfection by Public Filing

Debtors are usually free to grant numerous security interests in the same collateral to several lenders or secured parties. This practice may be appropriate if the asset is so valuable that it could cover several loans or be useful in a later round of financing. For example, homeowners commonly borrow money by taking out a second mortgage on their home. However, disputes inevitably arise among several secured parties who all have security interests in the same collateral. For example, if the collateral is worth less than the total of all outstanding debts, some lien holder(s) may not be fully paid. To be assured of their precedence, secured parties must take the additional step of perfection. This puts other potential lenders on notice that the secured party has priority. Perfection usually occurs when the secured party files a **financing statement**, known as Form UCC 1. This document or electronic record is separate from the security agreement. A financing statement describes the collateral and the security interest and must be filed at the local government office (county courthouse) or state government office (secretary of state) as required by law.

The public filing of liens on both real estate and personal property serves a very important function: It facilitates efficient financing. The availability of these public databases permits potential lenders to make a loan conditional on a reliable foreclosure value of particular collateral. The lender can search for other security interests on the property that the borrower is offering as collateral. Lenders can avoid making loans if liens are already outstanding on the property. Public policy disfavors secret liens because they pose excessive risk to later lenders and thereby restrict the availability of credit. The current local and state filing system for secured transactions is archaic and fragmented, frustrating efficiency. A comprehensive, national, searchable electronic database of secured transaction filings could greatly enhance the protection of lenders.

The revision of Article 9 should help advance the filing system from today's numerous local and state paper-based databases into a national electronic system. Electronic databases may be inherently more efficient, rigorous, and potentially exhaustive in retrieving relevant data. Today, a few private vendors are integrating access to many states' electronic filing systems. Further, there are national secured transaction filings for a few types of collateral—IP and mobile equipment like railroad cars and commercial aircraft. However, a single, federally operated, secured transaction database for most types of property would be difficult to achieve politically. The efficiency and fairness of secured financing may not reach its potential until search costs and accuracy are improved. Revised Article 9 holds great promise but may not eliminate secured transaction costs so long as the information trail is easily broken by debtors moving the collateral to other states, changing their individual or business names, or becoming acquired by other companies.

Perfection: Alternatives to Filing

UCC Article 9 allows alternative methods of perfecting a secured transaction. First, the secured party may perfect by taking possession of the collateral. If other potential lenders act carefully, another lender's possession is a clear signal that a security interest exists. Second, most vehicles have title certificates that are needed to transfer ownership. Notice of a security interest is typically written directly on a vehicle's certificate of title, and this clearly notifies buyers or lenders considering a transaction that a lien exists. Third, perfection of a PMSI is automatic for consumer goods, instruments, and health care insurance receivables. Fourth, floating liens are particularly useful for rolling inventories through the use of **after-acquired property clauses**. For example, inventory collateral can be generally or vaguely described, so that liens on goods sold to consumers from the inventory are released upon sale. However, the secured party's lien can then be automatically extended, via the after-acquired property clause, to any replacement goods that replenish the inventory. Fifth, the lien on property the debtor sells can extend to the proceeds received in that sale; that is, the security interest covers the money received by the seller or any goods the seller receives in trade for the secured property that was sold.

Financing Transactions in IP and Telecommunications Intangibles

Intangibles such as IP pose conceptual and practical financial problems. Of course, all assets, tangible or intangible, are most reliably valued *ex post*, using the hindsight of completed transactions and cash flows. Tangible assets seem much easier than intangibles to value with reliability and precision *ex ante*, particularly if there are liquid markets that can value similar assets. Traditional accounting principles do not adequately standardize the valuation techniques for IP and many other intangibles. Most IP assets are valued at acquisition cost. It is inherently misleading to simply capitalize research and development (R&D) expenses. R&D is frequently irrelevant to the IP asset's potential for cash flow. Research is inherently risky, and the commercialization of innovation is uncertain. IP is often a mere component of other products or services, raising additional uncertainty. Even modern techniques of financial forecasting (e.g., discounted cash flow, options pricing) are more speculative when applied to intangible assets.

Goodwill is a convincing example of the difficulties in valuing IP. Goodwill cannot be recorded as an asset unless it is acquired in a transaction involving tangible assets. Goodwill may be valued for financial accounting purposes only to the extent the purchase price for an acquired company or a business unit exceeds the fair market value (FMV) of its tangible assets. This surplus is simply presumed to be goodwill if the tangible assets purchased are available in a liquid market at FMV. Goodwill is often represented by trademark(s) so the trademark's value may be inferred from the value of goodwill.

Secured transaction law also poses risk in the financing of intangibles. Given the higher inherent risk that intangibles will be profitable, creditors need even more effective techniques to reduce the risk of debtor default. The legal process for securing loans on IP and other intangibles is fragmented and uncertain. The acquisition of effective liens on trademarks, patents, *unregistered* copyrights, and FCC broadcast licenses is governed by UCC Article 9. These assets are classified as **general intangibles** under both the old and the revised versions of UCC Article 9. Case law legitimizes the traditional UCC attachment process using a security agreement and the UCC perfection process through filing in the applicable state or local office. Although the IP laws generally require federal filings for outright assignment (a complete sale of the IP asset), cases hold that the federal IP laws allow UCC filings for secured transactions because they are not outright assignments. The trademark and patent laws have no secured transaction provisions. Therefore, the only method to create enforceable liens in trademarks, patents, *unregistered* copyrights, and broadcast licenses is by using state UCC law and processes. Although domain names are closely related to trademarks, how liens on domain names will be resolved is uncertain. It is also unclear whether domain names are assets available to satisfy creditors' claims. UCC security interests can also be extended to cover the proceeds of IP, which essentially are the royalties and other fee income from licensing the IP.

All this stands in stark contrast to the process required for *registered* copyrights. The *only* method to create enforceable liens in registered copyrights is to follow the federal secured transaction filing process at the federal Copyright Office. Copyright law opens the Copyright Office's filing system only to registered copyrights. Therefore, *unregistered* copyrights generally cannot use the Copyright Office services, so they must rely on the UCC secured transaction process. Federal law will likely trump state law in the growing area of telecom licenses. The FCC appears to have the legal right to recapture licenses to use portions of the airwave spectrum that had been auctioned to a wireless firm that went bankrupt. A license to use a portion of the airwave spectrum is a very valuable intangible asset, essential to wireless service providers. Although this federal right of recapture is not really a contractual form of lien, it nevertheless works to preempt other creditors' claims on the license.

Priorities

Disputes are inevitable among secured parties competing for the proceeds of a foreclosure sale. Generally, the secured party that perfected first will have its debt completely satisfied out of the foreclosure sale proceeds before other creditors with lower priority receive anything. If the dispute is among unperfected parties, the party whose security interest attached first will win. UCC Article 9 provides for many complex additional priority rules based on a number of factors: the types of secured parties, the types of collateral, whether the loan created a PMSI, whether the debtor is in bankruptcy, and whether the collateral was purchased by a good faith purchaser for value.

Default

After priority problems are resolved, the secured party may choose between remedies: selling the collateral in a public or private sale or simply keeping the collateral to satisfy part or all of the debt. If the sale brings more money than is needed to pay off the secured party's debt, the surplus first pays the expenses of the repossession and sale. Next it repays all other secured debts, and then any remainder is returned to the debtor. The debtor is responsible for any deficiency if sale proceeds are insufficient to pay all debts.

BANKRUPTCY

The Constitution empowers Congress to pass uniform bankruptcy laws. The Bankruptcy Act of 1898, which governs bankruptcy in the United States, has been revised several times. Substantial amendments were made in the Bankruptcy Reform Acts of 1978, 1984, 1986, and 1994. Another revision effort that is likely to favor creditors began in 2000 and was still unresolved by 2002. After a bankruptcy filing, the debtor may lose control and ownership of many assets. These assets are liquidated (sold), and the proceeds are eventually distributed to creditors. Usually, most of the unpaid portion of the bankrupt's debts are **discharged**—that is, eliminated

ONLINE

American Bankruptcy Institute
http://www.abiworld.org

altogether—resulting in the debtor receiving a "clean slate." Thus, bankruptcy law provides the overextended debtor with a fresh start and assures fair and equal treatment of all creditors within each of several creditor classes. There are several different forms of bankruptcy that may be used by individuals, businesses, and certain government units.

Straight Bankruptcy

The best known form of bankruptcy is Chapter 7 of the bankruptcy code. Known as **straight bankruptcy**, it provides for a complete liquidation of the debtor's assets and partial satisfaction of most debts. The bankruptcy courts oversee the process of (1) collecting and selling the debtor's assets, (2) verifying creditor claims, (3) distributing the proceeds, and (4) granting the debtor a discharge of most remaining debts. Insolvent individuals, partnerships, and corporations may be liquidated in straight bankruptcy. A debtor may choose to file a **voluntary petition** with the bankruptcy court, or creditors may "throw" a debtor into bankruptcy by filing an **involuntary petition.** The fact of **insolvency** is determined on either the cash flow basis or the balance sheet basis. A debtor unable to pay debts as they come due is insolvent on the cash flow basis. A debtor with liabilities in excess of assets is insolvent on the balance sheet basis. Either debtor may take advantage of bankruptcy laws. From the time that the bankruptcy petition is filed until the final disposition of the case by the bankruptcy court, a stay or suspension order is in effect. The **bankruptcy stay** prevents creditors from collecting debts or foreclosing on collateral.

To qualify for a discharge from debts, the debtor must perform several duties and cooperate in good faith during bankruptcy proceedings. The debtor must file documents with the bankruptcy court, including (1) a list of creditors, (2) a schedule or list of assets and liabilities, and (3) other financial statements. The debtor must give up all nonexempt property to the bankruptcy trustee, who becomes the legal owner until liquidation. Most tangible and intangible property, such as goods, real estate, intellectual property rights, and accounts receivable are surrendered.

The bankruptcy trustee is elected by majority vote of creditors to manage the proceeding by carefully collecting and disposing of the property and thereby accumulating a fund used to pay off creditor claims. The trustee determines whether each creditor's claim is genuine and may challenge any fraudulent claims against the debtor. The trustee must collect property and debts owed to the debtor and may choose to reject executory contracts, excusing the bankrupt debtor from performing in the future. The trustee must keep adequate accounting records and file a detailed accounting with the bankruptcy court. Professionals such as accountants, appraisers, attorneys, and auctioneers are hired as necessary to assist the trustee. The

Ethical Issue

Ethical Considerations in Credit and Insolvency

The framers of the Constitution intended the bankruptcy laws to eliminate the English practice of imprisoning defaulting debtors. Although such imprisonment was a strong disincentive to avoid default, it prevented debtors from earning money to repay their debts. Society believes that fairness demands that debtors who have borrowed more than they can repay should be given another chance through bankruptcy. The cost of credit is raised both by debtors who misuse credit and the bankruptcy process, as well as by creditors who offer easy credit to the noncreditworthy. Both abuses probably limit the availability of credit to all individuals and businesses. Creditors as well as debtors face ethical dilemmas in credit and bankruptcy.

trustee uses the proceeds from liquidating the bankrupt's property, called the bankrupt's estate, to pay these and other costs of bankruptcy before proceeds are distributed to creditors.

There are three basic types of creditors in bankruptcy proceedings. First, **secured creditors** have security interests, such as mortgages or liens on specific property. Security interests give these creditors a preference on the sale proceeds after the secured items are sold in liquidation, but only up to their contractual security or up to the liquidation value of the collateral, whichever is less. To the dollar extent that the collateral sale is insufficient to satisfy a secured creditor's claim, the secured creditor becomes equivalent to an unsecured creditor. Second, **unsecured** or **general creditors** have no security interests. They must take their shares of the distribution proceeds equally as a group on a pro rata basis after secured creditors are paid from the proceeds of their collateral. For example, trade creditors that supply inventory or equipment without retaining a lien are unsecured. Credit card issuers are unsecured on most of their customer accounts. Third, priority creditors generally have priority over unsecured creditors. Each class of priority creditors may have its claims totally paid before the next class receives payment. Priority creditors include bankruptcy administration expenses, certain wages and benefits of the bankrupt's employees, taxes, certain consumer claims, and alimony and child support. If there are insufficient funds to pay all the claims of a particular class of priority creditors, they share the remainder of the fund pro rata and all lower priority creditors receive nothing.

After liquidation, a discharge in bankruptcy is usually ordered, giving the bankrupt a clean slate for preexisting debts. However, a discharge can be denied if the bankrupt conceals assets, makes fraudulent transfers, destroys books or records, disobeys a bankruptcy court order, fails to explain the loss of assets, or makes fraudulent statements in the bankruptcy proceeding. If no discharge is granted, the bankrupt will lose its assets in the liquidation yet still owe the unpaid portion of all debts. Some debts, such as alimony, child support, federal taxes, and federally insured student loans, cannot be discharged in bankruptcy, so they are still owed after discharge of other debts.

ONLINE

Bankruptcy forms online
http://www.uscourts.gov/bankform/

Alternatives to Liquidation

All debtors in financial difficulty need not be completely liquidated. A debtor with only moderate financial difficulties may be able to work out suitable arrangements with creditors under alternative procedures. Under a Chapter 13 debt adjustment, an individual person with regular income from salary, wages, or commissions as an employee may have debts adjusted but not discharged. Usually a very strict subsistence budget is imposed on the debtor until solvency is reached via various work-out techniques. The debtor's employer or the debtor pays a certain sum periodically (usually monthly) to the bankruptcy trustee. The trustee apportions that sum among the creditors according to the adjustment plan. **Composition** arrangements with creditors may allow the debtor to pay lower principal and/or interest rates. Extension terms permit the debtor to make smaller payments and extend the maturity date and/or the number of debt payments. If the debtor complies with the plan, there is a discharge, even if some creditors receive less than the original amount of their debts plus interest and penalties.

For corporations, Chapter 11 provides a **reorganization** process somewhat similar to the Chapter 13 arrangement just discussed. Chapter 11 permits businesses with going-concern value to continue operating during financial difficulties. The purpose is to minimize the negative impact of business failures on the economy, creditors, customers, suppliers, employees, and the community. In a Chapter 11 proceeding, a debtor corporation is reorganized pursuant to a voluntary or involuntary petition. Texaco may be the largest firm to have successfully emerged from Chapter 11. At this writing, Enron continues to operate under the "protection from creditors" provided by Chapter 11.

The reorganization process is usually more complex and time-consuming than a Chapter 13 proceeding. Each class or group of similar creditors and shareholders forms a separate committee to propose, negotiate, modify, and approve a master reorganization plan. The plan may include elements of composition, extension, and/or reduction, which means that the debtor corporation's shareholders, bondholders, and creditors are likely to receive less than their full claims. For example, some creditors may be converted into shareholders, preferred shareholders may be converted into common shareholders, and common shareholders, as residual claimants, may lose most of their stock.

If the bankruptcy court finds that a particular plan is fair and equitable to all the classes of creditors, then the whole plan may be approved, even if some committees have not approved it. The final court approval of the plan discharges the corporation from its former debts and equity interests and substitutes the new claims as defined in the plan. In some Chapter 11 proceedings, referred to as "prepacks," the various claimants negotiate the plan before filing the bankruptcy petition. This practice permits the plan to be worked out amicably and reduces the bankruptcy court's involvement to approval of a plan that the parties already feel is fair. A prepack can be more efficient and avoids goodwill losses because the proceeding occurs quickly and without much fanfare. A corporate reorganization can be converted into a Chapter 7 liquidation proceeding when it is in the best interest of all involved.

Insolvency and the Dot.coms

By the year 2000, much to the disappointment of "new economy" supporters, dot.com start-up companies finally became subject to traditional financial expectations. The mere promise of revolutionary new e-commerce business models could not overcome the need for conventional cash flow and enduring wealth creation. Many overvalued stock prices fell to levels more consistent with customary models of revenue production. Without solid cash flows, many new ventures could not long maintain their high cash "burn rates" (underfunded expenditures). Firms in the information economy pose commercial and financial challenges because many rely heavily on intangible and intellectual property assets that are difficult to evaluate and can be risky collateral. Investors and venture capitalists can be expected to withdraw or discontinue financing when dot.coms appear headed for financial trouble.

Unlike firms in the bricks-and-mortar economy, many dot.com start-ups have few tangible assets to secure loans. Many also are equity financed, making it less appropriate to seek the debt relief of bankruptcy. Bankruptcy administration expenses may quickly overwhelm a troubled dot.com's tangible assets. Financial difficulties in e-commerce are widespread; they destabilize intellectual property asset values and therefore are harmful to creditors and investors. At least three insolvency problems can plague financially troubled dot.coms. The first and most fundamental is that the primary intellectual assets of most dot.coms are their employees. Many dot.com employees hold stock options. However, employees can too easily lose their incentive to remain employed when the company's financial troubles depress their options' value.

Licensing of IP both *to* a dot.com and *from* a dot.com raises two more important areas of insolvency issues. If the IP is "licensed-in" to a financially troubled company from a financially healthy outside third party, the license may not survive in the licensee's bankruptcy to be available as an asset of the bankruptcy estate. Recall the discussion of contract assignments earlier in this chapter. Contracts are not assignable without the permission of the obligor if the contract's subject matter is unique. The IP licensed-in to a financially troubled dot.com from a licensor may not be freely assignable by the trustee to raise cash. Royalty payments fundamentally depend on the licensee's unique products, so the licensor's permission to assign is probably needed. Such licensors may often be better off abandoning the bankrupt, in which case new licenses can be negotiated with other licensees without interference from the trustee.

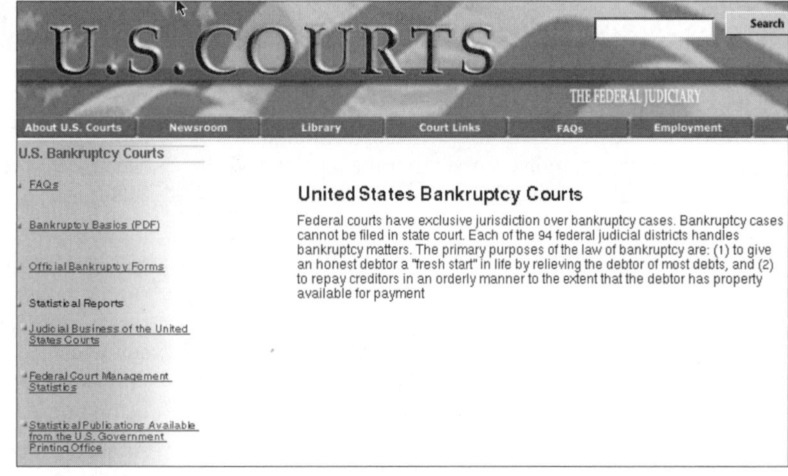

http://

www.uscourts.gov/bankruptcycourts.html

A third problem area arises when the IP is "licensed-out" from a financially troubled company. Generally, bankruptcy law permits the trustee to use reasonable business judgment to either accept or reject any of the bankrupt's executory contracts in order to maximize the bankrupt's estate. The outside licensee can be left in limbo until such a choice is made. Under bankruptcy law, ongoing IP licenses are considered **executory contracts** because both parties continue to owe some future duty to perform. For example, the licensee must make future royalty payments, and the licensor must continue to grant permission to use the licensed technology. Until 1988, bankruptcy law permitted the trustee to reject ongoing licenses, thereby canceling the bankrupt debtor's permission, and the licensee was often left in limbo until the rejection decision was made. However, the Intellectual Property Bankruptcy Act now requires the trustee to respect ongoing licenses by giving the licensee an option to terminate or continue the license.

Intangible information is a primary asset for many financially troubled dot.coms. As discussed in Chapter 14 of this book, private data can be valuable both to the individuals profiled in the information and as a marketing tool in commerce. ToySmart, an Internet toy retailer, collected considerable private information about children who visited the ToySmart site. ToySmart's announced privacy policies prohibited resale of this information without each individual's permission. However, when ToySmart filed for Chapter 11 bankruptcy protection in June 2000, it proposed to sell the database of names, addresses, and other information to raise cash and help it survive as a going concern. The FTC intervened to block the data sale. Nevertheless, the value of private data might still be realized in this or similar situations if, rather than selling the data outright, the financially troubled dot.com were acquired by another company and survived as a subsidiary. Such a survival technique would probably leave the dot.com free to use its intangible assets as originally permitted by its privacy policy. Restrictions on a dot.com's ownership are not generally part of privacy policies.

QUESTIONS

1. How does the parol evidence rule resolve ambiguities in a written integration contract that the parties envision to be the whole and compete embodiment of their agreement? Do the assumptions underlying the parol evidence rule hold in on-line contracting on the Internet?

2. SupplyCo's sales representative, Jack Jenkins, has made numerous sales calls on ABC Manufacturing, usually negotiating with Henry Smith, ABC's purchasing manager. SupplyCo sells industrial solvents that could be used in ABC's circuit board manufacturing processes. ABC's solvent needs currently amount to several hundred thousand dollars annually and are fulfilled by IndusSolvCo under a long-term supply contract. Henry suggested to Jack that if SupplyCo would permit Henry's family to use the SupplyCo corporate beach house for Henry's family vacation, he would terminate the IndusSolvCo contract prematurely to make future purchases from SupplyCo. None of this is put in writing, and Henry's family used the beach house for their two-week summer vacation. Thereafter, Henry did not terminate the IndusSolvCo supply contract and never made any orders from SupplyCo, although he was apologetic when Jack again visited ABC. What ethical issues are apparent for both men and their companies? Comment on the role of the statute of frauds in controlling the unethical behavior of these parties.

3. Jane purchased a life-cycle exercise machine at Body Workers. The written installment sales contract disclaimed any warranty obligations to the buyer. Jane experienced several problems with the exercise machine that Body Workers refused to repair. Jane sued the Body Workers on its oral promise that, if problems arose, it would "take care of them." Is this oral promise admissible in court? Explain.

4. Jones had an oral agreement to purchase 1.3 acres of land in a 10-acre tract. The seller refused to close on the contract. If the buyer sues for specific performance, will the statute of frauds be a valid defense?

5. MMI contracted to supply software to Gregory and be compensated at an hourly rate. When the software failed to perform to Gregory's satisfaction, he denied payment and refused to permit MMI to cure the defects. MMI sued for the price, and Gregory counterclaimed breach of warranty of fitness under the UCC. Does the UCC or common law apply to this contract? Explain your reasoning. See *Micro-Managers, Inc. v. Gregory*, 434 N.W.2d 91 (Wisc. 1988).

6. It can be argued that the creditors' rights system of collateral, foreclosure, debtors hiding behind bankruptcy protection, and balanced treatment of creditors is more costly than if debtors and creditors were simply left to their own devices. Criticize this laissez-faire statement from the perspective of the intent behind our creditors' rights laws and practices.

7. Assume a supplier sells a shipment of goods to a retailer with the sale of goods contract calling for the buyer to make three installment payments each month for the next three months. The seller wants to assure repayment by using the secured transaction method available under UCC Article 9. Describe the type of transaction, and indicate what two basic steps are important to the supplier's objectives.

8. What are the challenges facing creditors and bankruptcy administrators when the bankrupt firm has "burned" though considerable financing and most of its assets are intangibles such as data, customer lists, software, and IP?

9. Software that the Mortenson Co. licensed from Timberline Software was designed to assist construction contractors in assembling complex bids on projects. A bid Mortenson made using the software was computed at $2 million less than was accurate. The Timberline license included a disclaimer against consequential damages resulting from defects in the software. In a breach of contract suit against Timberline, will the disclaimer eliminate Timberline's liability for the $2 million? See *M. A. Mortenson v. Timberline Software Corp.*, 970 F.2d 803 (Wash.App. 1999).

10. Wisconsin law requires physician signatures on all prescriptions before a pharmacist is permitted to fill the prescription. Walgreen's Pharmacy was censured by the Wisconsin Pharmacy Examining Board for filling prescriptions contained in an e-mail message. On appeal, how should the court decide before UETA and after UETA? Does it matter that signatures were not needed for telephone prescriptions? See *Walgreen Co. v. Wisconsin Pharmacy Examining Board*, 577 N.W.2d 387 (Wis.Ct.App. 1998).

Technology Transfer: Employment, Service, and Distribution Contracts

How does a firm protect its intellectual assets? This problem is becoming more acute as job tenure practices change. Increasingly, employees change jobs several times during their careers, broadening their skills and experience, and lifetime employment with a single firm is becoming rare. Imagine a typical modern scenario: Employees work on projects developing new products and services. They become attractive to competitors and to other firms for two main reasons: (1) These employees know secrets about the particular products or processes of their current employer, and (2) employees have valuable general experience in developing products, giving them strong potential on related projects. Successful employees are often lured away to other firms with offers of higher salaries, stock options, and challenging new assignments. The departure of one influential employee can stimulate other employees to change employers. The exodus of their cumulative knowledge effectively transfers significant intangible assets about technologies to the new firm.

Can the original firm protect its knowledge base with contractual and other legal restrictions? If they can, how do employees retain the flexibility to advance their careers? The law balances these parties' rights. Employees need to maintain freedom of job mobility, they have the right to seek rewarding work, and they need financial support. Society is best served when workers are most productive by working up to their greatest potential in their chosen fields of expertise.

Increasingly, the value of firms depends less on the fair market value or cash flow potential of tangible assets (real estate, product, plant, and equipment) and more on ideas, as created and implemented by employees. In the knowledge economy, value is derived increasingly from information and expertise supplied by employees. Firms have legitimate interests in protecting any intellectual property (IP) resulting from investment in R&D or from employee training. IP is valuable whether held as registered patents, copyrights, and trademarks or held as proprietary information and trade secrets secured in filing systems and known only by key employees. These two realities, job-hopping and the ascendance of intangible assets, raise risks for both employers and employees. The law creates technology transfer mechanisms that balance these often conflicting interests.

EXHAUSTIBILITY OF TANGIBLE VERSUS INTANGIBLE PROPERTY

The risk of losing proprietary information from employee movement is one example of the main problem in technology transfer: the exploitation of intangible property. Information and other intangible property are seemingly inexhaustible, making them uniquely different from tangible property. Tangibles are totally **exhaustible**; when tangibles are transferred or wrongfully misappropriated, the rightful owner loses *all* value in the property, and the ownership advantages are completely exhausted. For example, when an automobile is sold or stolen, the owner is suddenly aware of the obvious fact that the property is gone. The owner cannot economically exploit the tangible asset because no one would buy it without tangible proof that it exists.

By contrast, intangible property is only partially exhaustible. The original persists even when copied. Intangible property can be possessed simultaneously by many people. Often, the value of intangibles to the original owner is not immediately or completely eliminated when only a few copies are sold, licensed, or even stolen. For example, when patented processes, computer software, sound and video recordings, or information are licensed, sold, or misappropriated, only a "copy" is taken. The owner still has the "original," which can be exploited financially when the original owner sells additional licenses to others. Indeed, the original owner could make a nearly infinite number of copies, which makes the intangible seem to be inexhaustible. However, eventually the market would become saturated, eliminating all paying customers. Therefore, intangibles are only **partially inexhaustible**, or partially exhaustible. If too many licenses are sold or too many illegal copies are made, eventually the marketability becomes exhausted. For example, if numerous illegal copies of a rock group's latest album are pirated, eventually royalties from legitimate sales diminish. This is the result predicted by the artists and record companies in the case that shut down Napster,[1] as discussed in Chapter 15. The same holds true for illegal copies of books, software programs, games, data, videotapes, or nearly any digital media. Similarly, if a competitor's spy obtains a company's newly developed secret production process, the innovation loses much of its value to the original inventor.

Most people understand the partial exhaustibility of intangibles. For example, most people understand that use of unauthorized copies often goes undetected. As long as the original remains intact, the owner of intellectual property may never even know about the unauthorized copies. Some people believe that no harm is done if the owner is unaware of the misappropriation. However, the owner receives decreasing profits when there is uncontrolled and unauthorized distribution of intangible IP. Society gives incentives to inventors and creators by establishing IP rights and enforcing the technology transfer contracts needed to exploit IP. Licensing permits the owner to control distribution. Without a method to identify what IP legitimately belongs to a particular owner, people could ignore the license and misappropriate the IP. The federal laws concerning patents, copyrights, and trademarks and the state common law protecting trade secrets, trademarks, and technology transfer contracts are essential to an owner's exclusive claim to IP.

This chapter discusses the methods used to exploit intangibles and distribute them through the supply chain. IP laws prohibit most unauthorized uses, as discussed

1. *A&M Records, Inc. v. Napster*, 239 F.3d 1004 (9th Cir., 2001).

in the intellectual property chapters, 15 through 18. IP law endows the owner, inventor, or creator with a bundle of rights to exploit their IP largely through technology transfer. Employment contracts are examined first in this chapter. They specify the employer's and employee's rights in IP, inventions, and job experiences, often through assignments of innovations. Next, licensing is discussed because it is the primary method to distribute technology. Leases and franchising are then discussed at the end of this chapter.

LAWS APPLICABLE TO TECHNOLOGY TRANSFER AND DISTRIBUTION

Technology transfer creates business relationships that are formed by contract. These relationships manage and structure the financing, allocate property rights, arrange production, establish control, provide funds, anticipate expansion, and/or create uniform controls for a business that is often composed of numerous related yet independent parts. Managers negotiating employment or distribution contracts hire employees and independent contractors. These relationships create the design of the supply chain. Under American law, laissez-faire freedom of contract is given great weight. The parties may design their contract terms to achieve nearly any desired result unless public policy is offended. Most subjects of bargaining are open to negotiation, resulting in a mix of terms that reflect the parties' needs and relative bargaining power. Of course, the stronger party can often extract concessions at the other party's expense.

Agency law supplements these employment and distribution contracts by clarifying the various parties' duties, automatically providing for allocation of certain business risks, and implying fiduciary duties of care and loyalty. Regulation addresses some problems in employment and distribution contracts, although no single and coherently integrated body of law has developed. During the twentieth century, the laws of contracts and agency have been supplemented by various employment regulations. Employment law is a general umbrella term for various state and federal regulatory programs such as the antidiscrimination laws administered by the Equal Employment Opportunity Commission (EEOC), workplace safety rules from the Occupational Safety and Health Administration (OSHA), workers' compensation, regulation of wages and working conditions, collection of employment taxes, and laws concerning lie detector use, drug testing, immigration, garnishment, plant closing duties, and termination of employment. Labor law governs unionization and collective bargaining between employers and employees. These topics are covered in Chapters 20 and 21. The antitrust laws discussed in Chapter 19 constrain supply chain relations with distributors, franchisees, and in licensing IP.

EMPLOYMENT CONTRACTS

An employer generally has the incentive to specify contract terms that enhance the employer's flexibility, business opportunities, and profitability. Employers usually desire to minimize expenses, protect assets, and retain flexibility to deploy their employees as needed. On the other hand, employees desire stability in their compensation and work environment, job security, fair treatment, and generally increasing compensation and benefits. Some employees seek stable work tasks, but many others expect ever-changing challenges in their work assignments that permit them to grow professionally. Employees also want freedom to resign at will, go work elsewhere, or even start their own businesses, using all their accumulated skills and experience. Sometimes these goals come into conflict, presenting a zero-sum struggle, much of which is resolved during negotiation of the employment contract. Sometimes public policy intervenes to equitably balance the parties' reasonable expectations or protect outsiders affected by the employment relationship.

The parties to employment and distribution contracts understandably seek to control performances in the contract. For example, manufacturers and wholesale distributors often require retail outlets to carry large inventories, hire knowledgeable sales staffs, use only trained repair technicians, and diligently promote their product lines. Employers may impose work rules to assure product quality and employee loyalty while maintaining a congenial workplace. The flow of benefits and funds between the parties is also an essential contract term. Both sides must be concerned with termination provisions as changes occur in the parties' needs or performance quality. This section discusses several contract terms that can protect these interests. Many are applicable to both employment and distribution contracts.

EMPLOYER'S RIGHT TO AN EMPLOYEE'S INNOVATIONS

There is a shift in innovation today; less is developed by independent individuals than by institutions. The complexity and technical sophistication of most processes and new products require considerable expenditures for research. Many important discoveries could not be developed except with the use of extensive scientific equipment in expensive laboratory settings. Today, teams of researchers employed in corporate R&D departments, government labs, or research universities predominate. The institutional sponsorship of R&D raises critical questions of ownership and the permissible use of these innovations.

An employer may lay claim to ownership of innovations developed by employees, based on agency law, the employment contract, and/or IP law. Most fundamentally, the fiduciary duty generally prohibits an agent from competing with the principal. If an employee develops and sells something that is close to the employer's line of business, the employee's acts could violate the duty of loyalty. An employer's claim to ownership becomes stronger when it is based on contract. An employee may be specifically hired to do research, create expression, or develop a particular technology. The employment contract may shift ownership and control of copyrights, patent rights, or trade secrets to the employer, often in an assignment.

An employer may not own the innovations produced by an employee if the employee's duties do not specifically include conducting research or fostering innovations. If the employee can prove that personal investment of time, money, and effort was made to develop an invention, innovation, or trade secret, then the employee may own it. This claim is even stronger if the innovation was developed entirely on the employee's own time. Employee ownership gives the employee exclusive rights to use it personally or license it to others. Contrast this innovation with an invention that was developed on the employer's time and using the employer's resources and facilities. Most savvy employers specifically include **assignment** provisions in employment contracts that transfer ownership of such innovations to the employer. Assignments were introduced in Chapter 11.

Even without an assignment, the employer may still have a limited shop right to use the invention. Under the **shop right doctrine**, the employer has a *nonexclusive right to use* the innovation without paying royalties to the employee. This right persists after the employment terminates and can also apply to an inventor who is an independent contractor. During the negotiation of an employment contract, some employers clearly inform each new hire that they are **hired to invent** particular innovations or in specific technologies. This statement generally vests ownership in the employer. The following case illustrates why savvy employers now routinely require assignment of inventions or specify a "hired to invent" relationship so that the invention is among the new employee's primary duties.

Aetna-Standard Engineering Co. v. Rowland

493 A.2d 1375 (Pa. 1985)

Facts. Rowland's resume touted his engineering design expertise. He was hired by Aetna-Standard without any explicit understanding that he would design new equipment. There was no written employment contract or any oral agreement to assign inventions designed during employment; he was not specifically informed that his duties included devising new inventions. Rowland received no pay increase when appointed to Aetna- Standard's IHI project, but he was later instructed that his new job included the development of a "plug mill receiving table." After the table design was completed, Rowland signed a disclosure document as a joint inventor with his project supervisor, Remmer. Thereafter, Rowland met with Aetna's patent attorney to explain the drawings of the table and signed the patent application naming himself and Remmer as joint inventors. After Rowland was laid off, Rowland refused to assign his interest in the patent when requested by Aetna. Remmer had assigned his interest but no longer worked for Aetna. Aetna made no claim to the patent until after Rowland was terminated.

Legal Issue. Will the law imply an assignment of Rowland's interest in the invention by virtue of the employment relationship? Does Aetna-Standard have a shop right to use the invention?

Opinion. Judge Cirillio. The major body of law on an employer's and employee's respective rights in the inventive or creative work of the employee evolved in the nineteenth and early twentieth centuries during our nation's industrial revolution. The United States Supreme Court has announced several rules for defining these rights. In the leading case of *United States v. Dubilier Condenser Corp.*, the Court stated that the mere existence of an employer-employee relationship does not of itself entitle the employer to an assignment of any inventions, which the employee devises during the employment.

At the same time, however, the absence from the employment contract of an express agreement to assign will not preclude the employer as a matter of law from asserting a claim to the employee's invention. Instead, a court must closely scrutinize the employment contract, so that, absent an express contrary agreement, an employee must assign his invention to his employer if he was hired for the purpose of using his inventive ability to solve a specific problem or to design a certain procedure or device for the employer; in such a case, the invention is the precise subject of the employment contract.

Although an employer might not be entitled to an assignment of the employee's invention, that is, of his patent, the employer will likely have a license or "shop right" to use the invention without paying the employee any additional compensation as royalties; the shop-right rule thus creates an exception from the employee's patent right to exclude others from making or using his invention. As in the law on assignment of invention, the employment relationship, standing alone, does not give the employer a shop right; the employer might have to show an express agreement for the right. A shop right will arise, however, where the employee devises the invention on the employer's time and at the latter's expense, using his materials and facilities, and allows him to use the invention without special compensation. Under this rule, an employee may not recover on an implied contract for payment for the shop right.

Quaker State Oil Refining Co. v. Talbot presented a factual situation seemingly similar to that in the case now before us. In Quaker State, the defendant employee was hired by an oral contract to design a specific oil-dispensing drumhead for the plaintiff to manufacture. He designed the drumhead, but incorporated into it several devices, which he had invented before his employment with the plaintiff. The plaintiff sought to compel the defendant to assign to it legal title to, any patent application or patents. The Court noted:

Where an employee by contract is hired to make a particular invention or solve a specific problem for the employer the property in the inventions of the employee belongs to the employer; the employee has sold in advance the fruit of his talent, skill and knowledge, to his employer, who is equitably entitled to it; in making such inventions or solving such problems the employee is merely doing what he was hired to do.

The Quaker State Court also commented that, independent of the employer's right to the completed drumhead, it has no rights in any of the individual component devices which the employee had patented before commencing work for it, unless it paid him appropriate compensation.

Deciding an employer's and employee's rights in an invention patented by the employee thus requires close examination of the employment contract, of any assignment provisions in that contract, of the nature of the employment, and of the circumstances surrounding the invention in dispute. Proof of an employer-employee relationship does not alone give the employer rights in the invention, particularly where the contract was for general employment. On the other hand, the existence of a patent in the employee's name does not itself bar the employer's claim. During our examination, we keep in mind that a court must hesitate to imply agreements to assign, although it may readily grant the employer a shop right to use the invention. The table was designed at appellant's place of business and with its resources. While appellant has no right to appellee's patent interest, it is entitled to the royalty-free, non-exclusive use of the table.

Decision. Employers do not own inventions employees create on the job when there is no assignment to the employer, however the employer retains a shop right to use such inventions.

Case Questions

1. If Rowland or Remmer refuses to provide assistance in patenting the plug mill receiving table, does the invention move into the public domain? What could Aetna-Standard have done to prevent this outcome?
2. What justifies an employer having a shop right in innovations developed with the employer's resources? What could justify the employer in claiming innovations developed on the employee's own time?

An invention may be developed by a single individual or by several members of a design team. Patent applications must by made or authorized only by the inventor(s) unless excused, such as when an inventor cannot be found or refuses to participate. The inventor is the person who conceives of the essential "kernel" of features or elements that makes the invention novel—an advance over known prior art. Two or more persons may be co-inventors if each collaborates to contribute, even if their work is done separately or at different times.

Employee's Assignment of Innovations

To avoid the uncertainties in the *Aetna-Standard* case, employers often insist that a term appear in the employment contract requiring the employee to assign to the employer all patents, inventions, innovations, or trade secrets. Because patents are typically issued to individual inventor(s), employers need employees' cooperation to own them. Patent-assignment clauses usually say that: (1) inventions developed during employment are transferred to the employer, (2) the employee will assist in securing the patent but usually at the employer's expense, and (3) any patent issued is assigned to the employer.

Before R&D starts, it is difficult to know which employees will be successful innovators. To confidently capture control over all new technologies, many employers simply require all employees to assign their rights, usually when first hired, even if few employees actually invent anything useful. Some very valuable employees may have the bargaining power to refuse assigning all their patent rights. Many progressive research universities split patent royalties with the faculty researchers responsible for the development. These policies are argued not only to be more equitable but also to enhance faculty motivation by retaining and attracting high-quality researchers. Employment, salary, and bonuses are valid consideration for an employee's assignment of patent rights.

The courts may choose not to enforce an unreasonably broad assignment clause. For example, an assignment would probably not be enforceable for an invention made entirely off the employer's premises, financed wholly with the employee's funds, and developed on the employee's time. A few states have statutes that reinforce the employee's ownership of personal developments. However, this can be a gray area, particularly for inventors actually employed to do R&D and who are exposed to component technologies developed for the employer that could arguably contribute to the employee's invention. Clear guidance is particularly problematic for inventions made during an employee's off-work time but in the same general area of expertise used in employment.

Work Made for Hire

Copyrighted works generally belong to the author or coauthors of the work. Joint authors create a work when they intend that their contributions be merged into inseparable or interdependent parts of a single whole work. For example, joint authors include the composer and lyricist of a song or the coauthors of a textbook. Authors are generally the human individuals who actually create the work. However, a corporate or business firm may be the author holding all the bundle of rights in copyright if it hires employee(s) or independent contractors to create part or all of a work under a **work made for hire**, including (1) works created by employees **within the scope of their employment** or (2) specially commissioned works created by independent contractors. **Specially commissioned works** can be used only as part of a (1) collective work, (2) motion picture or other audiovisual work, (3) translation, (4) compilation, (5) supplementary work, (6) instructional text, (7) test, (8) answer key, or (9) atlas. Additionally, the written contract must be signed by both parties and must be executed before the work starts to expressly designate it as a "work made for hire." The employee–independent contractor distinction was created in the 1976 revision to the copyright law. Works created by employees or commissioned before 1976 generally belong to the employer. The Supreme Court reinforced the individual author's rights in interpreting control over a commissioned statue in *Community for Creative Nonviolence v. Reid.*[2]

Consider how these ownership problems can complicate contracts for writing software or for website creation and maintenance. For example, a computer programming company might develop software or Web pages under a supply contract for a client. The customer is generally best served if they get an assignment of all copyrights developed during the course of the contract's performance. However, if the contract does not include an assignment of the program's copyright or fails to include wording that the agreement is a "work for hire," the programmer will own the program. Software and web pages may not qualify under one of the nine categories of works made for hire. Under the federal copyright law, the programming company would own the source code and could sell a second copy to the client's competitor. Such copyright ownership issues can extend to written text, computer programming, sound recordings, website pages, browser applets or plug-ins, and film or television video sequences. These issues are discussed in the final section in this chapter.

Master-Servant and Scope of Employment

The two forms of work made for hire use the two major criteria for vicarious tort liability under *respondeat superior* introduced in Chapter 7: the master-servant relationship and activities within the scope of employment. Courts evaluate several factors in distinguishing servants from independent contractors. First, the parties' intent may provide some insight, although this form of relationship may be chosen to achieve tax benefits. Second, the level of supervision commonly required for the type of work is important. Where employers usually supervise closely the type of

2. 490 U.S. 730 (1989).

work in question, the master's right to control the servant is implicated. However, if the employee is generally left to work independently with only cursory monitoring, the employee is more likely an independent contractor. Third, an independent contractor usually has a higher level of skill than a servant. Servants typically possess more generic skills possessed by many people. An independent contractor usually has extensive experience, training, and education, particularly if it leads to a recognized profession or occupation. The supervision factor is also related to the skills factor. An employer's supervision is more likely when the employee's skills are lower and the employer's skills are higher.

A fourth factor concerns the employee's service arrangements. Servants generally work exclusively, regularly, and continuously for the same employer. By contrast, independent contractors tend to work for numerous employers on specific tasks and only when needed. An independent contractor may reject an employer's instructions and may refuse engagements for various reasons. Fifth, the manner of payment is often indicative: Servants are paid a recurring salary based on pay periods. Independent contractors are usually paid by the job. Sixth, if the employer owns the facilities and tools required for the work, the employee is probably a servant. Independent contractors typically have many of their own tools and often work at their own premises. Finally, the local customs for the type of work involved may also be relevant.

These criteria are helpful to decide close cases. For example, consider the two primary methods for hiring an attorney. When an attorney in private practice is retained by a client, the parties probably enter a contract for services that may contain a clause preserving the attorney's independence. Second, the attorney probably supervises his or her own work. Third, in most situations, the attorney is hired specifically to render professional expertise. Therefore, the client's direct and close supervision would be improper. Fourth, many attorneys in private practice work for several different clients on an irregular basis. Fifth, the attorney is paid for the particular job. Sixth, the attorney typically works at the courthouse, the attorney's law office, and at various other locations. These factors strongly suggest that the attorney in private practice is an independent contractor. However, an attorney working for a corporation is viewed quite differently. A corporate staff attorney is typically subject to the employer's supervision, works exclusively at the employer's site on a regular and continuous basis, and is paid a salary. These examples emphasize that it is difficult to reliably designate an employee except by using a preponderance of these factors. In some states, it is difficult to regularly retain personnel and designate them as independent contractors if that would reduce their rights.

The second element, **scope of employment**, is also ambiguous and unpredictable in close cases. There is an enormous amount of case law interpreting the phrase "scope of employment." Two main inquiries have developed. First, was the servant pursuing the master's business objectives? Second, was the servant's act foreseeable by the master? Both of these tests are ambiguous and could lead to conflicting results. Acts that are most clearly outside the scope of employment are done solely for the servant's benefit. The *Restatement of the Law Second, Agency* in §228 attempts to clarify this confusion:

Section 228 of the *Restatement of the Law, Second, Agency*

(1) Conduct of a servant is within the scope of employment if, but only if:
   (a) it is of the kind he is employed to perform;
   (b) it occurs substantially within the authorized time and space limits;
   (c) it is actuated, at least in part, by a purpose to serve the master; and
   (d) if force is intentionally used by the servant against another, the use of force is not unexpected by the master.

The general law of agency is the method used to analyze work made for hire issues under federal copyright law. This ignores any special exceptions under a particular state's law. This analysis should not give sole reliance to the control issue—that is, whether the employer had the right to control or took actual control over the author's activities.

ONLINE

American Law Institute's Restatement of the Law
http://www.ali.org

RESTRICTIONS ON COMPETITION

An employer risks several potential losses when an employee disassociates from the firm. First, it may be difficult to replace the employees whose services are unique or who know the business thoroughly. New employees must be trained for complex tasks and must become familiar with the employer's business. This problem has led to the use of fixed-term employment contracts that require notice before termination.

A second problem is the information an employee learns or develops while on the job. The employer could suffer irreparable harm if an employee quit and immediately joined a competitor or started a competing firm and used confidential information. For example, sales personnel are given lists of existing customers and develop lists of new customers. They learn about new products before their release and may learn innovative sales tactics. Top management, designers, engineers, and production personnel learn trade secrets about new products and secret production processes before they are disclosed outside the firm. This information and other competitive strategies and marketing plans could be immensely useful to a competitor.

The employer confronts a dilemma: Can employees be effective without learning such information, or will the employer's success be compromised if employees quit and take or disclose valuable confidential information? To analyze this question, an understanding is needed of how freedom of employment contracting is affected by the balancing of interests between employers and their employees.

Covenants Not to Compete

An employee's rights after termination may be limited by a **covenant not to compete**; a contract term prohibiting the employee from competing with the employer after termination of their employment. These provisions are also known as **restrictive covenants**, **noncompetition clauses**, or simply **noncompetes** for short. They restrict an employee's freedom to work, usually irrespective of whether the employee is fired or quits. Noncompetes supplement the general fiduciary duty of loyalty (discussed later), which requires confidentiality and prohibits competition during employment. Today, most savvy employers require new hires to sign noncompetes as one of many hiring documents. However, many smaller firms or employers without knowledge or experience with competition by former employees may seek to impose noncompetes in midstream on existing employees. These employees may argue that their employer gives them no new consideration in return for the noncompete restriction. Such a lack of new consideration could bar enforcement of the noncompete if the employee is already working under a fixed-term employment contract. However, many employees work under an employment-at-will contract, so the employer's consideration for imposing a noncompete in midstream could simply be the promise of continued employment, making the noncompete enforceable. Employment-at-will is discussed later in this chapter.

Reasonable Restriction

Some employers attempt to make excessive restrictions on their former employees' activities. The law generally disfavors such overrestrictive covenants because they restrain trade. Noncompetes may deprive former employees of a livelihood or restrict their use of professional talents and skills used at a former job. Indeed, as a matter of public policy in California, noncompetes are generally unreasonable and invalid. In other states, a noncompete must be reasonable to be enforceable. Some courts and a few state statutes limit the use of noncompetes to executive, managerial, or professional employees, those who are more likely to have access to valuable confidences. For example, noncompetes are most likely to be enforceable on agents who deal with clients, like brokers of real estate, securities, and commodities. A few states outright refuse enforcement to unreasonable noncompetes, leaving the employer totally unprotected. Employers seeking reliable protection from restrictive covenants generally must draft them narrowly, precisely limiting their effect as to time, space, and field of use. Some states use the **blue pencil test**, which permits the judge to limit the unreasonable aspects of a noncompete to more reasonable dimensions.

The restriction may be only as broad as necessary to prevent misappropriation of the former employer's trade secrets and confidences or unique relationships with customers (goodwill). For example, assume an employee is required to sign a restrictive covenant when first hired. The covenant will be considered unreasonable and unenforceable if it restricts competitive employment for an excessive period of time, say 10 years. Six months to two years is usually considered the useful life of the former employee's confidential knowledge. Thereafter, confidential information becomes obsolete, or competitors obtain it by other means. Clearly, the reasonable time varies by industry, permitting the employer and employee to present evidence on labor markets in their industry, as well as the useful life of confidential information. For example, a two-year restriction might be reasonable in traditional manufacturing industry but an "eternity" (unreasonably long) in the website design industry. In the sale of a business or professional practice, the time restriction may be much longer, even permanent. No reasonable person would purchase a business at a price including a premium for goodwill unless the seller is restricted by a noncompete for a long time. In such situations, the seller is usually prohibited from competing against the purchaser because competition would dilute the value of the purchased business.

Restrictions are also unenforceable if they extend to geographic regions where the former employer is not doing business. Geographic restrictions may be larger if the employer is engaged in interstate or international commerce. Restrictions are generally unenforceable outside the field of use made during the former employment. For example, it would probably be unreasonable to restrict a computer programmer from working for a bank unless their former duties included writing financial software. Employers are at increasing risk when they impose, rather than negotiate, unreasonable or vaguely defined restrictions without evidence that the former employee was exposed to real and valuable trade secrets. Increasingly, the terms of contracts with suppliers and customers are considered proprietary. Along with unique business methods potentially patentable as methods of doing business, the trade secrets protected by noncompetes and confidentiality agreements may include such business transaction information.

Ancillary to an Agreement

The restrictive covenant must be **ancillary**; that is, it must be necessary to protect interests transferred in a contract. A noncompete is ancillary when it is necessary to protect trade secrets divulged during an employment contract or to protect goodwill purchased in a business. Restrictive covenants unconnected with employment, franchise, or the sale of a business are generally unenforceable. It is never legitimate to use noncompetes to simply prevent competition. Although stating a separate consideration paid for the noncompete may not be necessary, it can be useful to do so. For example, a noncompete could be written to protect the sale of business, stating a lower value for the business's tangible assets and a premium separately stated for the intangible goodwill. In such a situation, it is easier to conclude that a separate consideration was paid for the restrictive covenant to protect the goodwill. In many states, an employer's agreement to hire is sufficient consideration for a noncompete if the employment probably involves sharing trade secrets or confidences with the employee.

Inevitable Disclosure Doctrine

Some observers argue that noncompetes are draconian—that is, more stringent and severe than needed, like killing a fly with a hammer. Former employers have legitimate interests in restricting only the *use* of confidential information; they have no legitimate interest in preventing former employees from vigorously competing against the former employer. However, noncompetes do both these things and sometimes provide the former employer with a wider margin of protection than is deserved. It would be much fairer to former employees to use more precise methods to limit the *misuse* of particular confidential information, such as the confidentiality duties that are discussed in the next section. However, employers may be justified in arguing that they are at greatest risk when former employees move into very similar jobs at direct competitors. It may be impossible for these former employees not to divulge confidences. Indeed, many observers argue that firms routinely hire employees away from their competitors more to gain confidences than to gain employees generally experienced in the field. If this is true, then it may be that disclosure of the former employer's confidences is inevitable when employees change jobs.

For some years now, a few courts have enjoined former employees from working for a direct competitor in a job with nearly identical duties under the **inevitable disclosure doctrine**. It applies to employees not bound by a noncompete but who have such intimate knowledge of the former employer's trade secrets that the employee could not possibly work for a competitor without using or disclosing the confidences. For the inevitable disclosure doctrine to apply, the trade secrets allegedly involved must be precisely and validly defined and highly valuable to both employers.[3] What should be the remedy? Courts use an **inevitability injunction** that prevents the employee from taking the new job immediately. It might extend for only short periods (e.g., six months) as was ordered in the following case.

PepsiCo, Inc. v. Redmond

54 F.3d 1262 (7th Cir., 1995)

Facts. William Redmond, PepsiCo's general manager for the California market division, accepted an offer from Donald Uzzi, a former PepsiCo employee, to join Quaker Oats's fledgling "new age" beverage unit (Snapple) and "sports drink" unit (Gatorade) as vice-president of field operations. PepsiCo's confidentiality agreement prohibited Redmond from disclosing:

at any time, to anyone other than officers or employees of [PepsiCo], or make[ing] use of, confidential information relating to the business of [PepsiCo] ... obtained while in the employ of [PepsiCo], which shall not be generally known or available to the public or recognized as standard practices.

3. *EarthWeb, Inc. v. Schlack*, 71 F.Supp.2d 299 (S.D.N.Y. 1999).

PepsiCo sought an inevitability injunction to prohibit Redmond from divulging PepsiCo trade secrets and confidential information at Quaker and from assuming any duties relating to beverage pricing, marketing, and distribution. PepsiCo argued that Redmond had trade secrets information about (1) PepsiCo's highly confidential emerging strategy to dramatically expand its "All Sport," Lipton, and Ocean Spray beverages, (2) PepsiCo's operating plan (financial goals, marketing plans, promotional event calendars, growth expectations, operational changes), (3) PepsiCo's proposed "pricing architecture," (4) PepsiCo's "attack plans," and (5) PepsiCo's selling and delivery systems to retailers.

Legal Issue. Was there sufficient evidence that PepsiCo would suffer irreparable harm without an injunction prohibiting Redmond's disclosure of PepsiCo's trade secrets and barring him from assuming the new job for 6 months?

Opinion. Circuit Judge Flaum. The Illinois Trade Secrets Act ("ITSA"), which governs the trade secret issues in this case, provides that a court may enjoin the "actual or threatened misappropriation" of a trade secret. A party seeking an injunction must therefore prove both the existence of a trade secret and the misappropriation. The ITSA, [the *Teradyne* and *AMP* cases] lead to the same conclusion: a plaintiff may prove a claim of trade secret misappropriation by demonstrating that defendant's new employment will inevitably lead him to rely on the plaintiff's trade secrets. The district court concluded on the basis of that presentation that unless Redmond possessed an uncanny ability to compartmentalize information, he would necessarily be making decisions about Gatorade and Snapple by relying on his knowledge of [Pepsi Cola North America] PCNA trade secrets.

It is not the "general skills and knowledge acquired during his tenure with" PepsiCo that PepsiCo seeks to keep from falling into Quaker's hands, but rather "the particularized plans or processes developed by [PCNA] and disclosed to him while the employer-employee relationship existed, which are unknown to others in the industry and which give the employer an advantage over his competitors." PepsiCo has not contended that Quaker has stolen [traditional trade secrets like] the All Sport formula or its list of distributors. Rather PepsiCo has asserted that Redmond cannot help but rely on PCNA trade secrets as he helps plot Gatorade and Snapple's new course, and that these secrets will enable Quaker to achieve a substantial advantage by knowing exactly how PCNA will price, distribute, and market its sports drinks and new age drinks and being able to respond strategically. This type of trade secret problem may arise less often, but it nevertheless falls within the realm of trade secret protection under the present circumstances. PepsiCo believes that Quaker, unfairly armed with knowledge of PCNA's plans, will be able to anticipate its distribution, packaging, pricing, and marketing moves. Redmond and Quaker even concede that Redmond might be faced with a decision that could be influenced by certain confidential information that he obtained while at PepsiCo. In other words, PepsiCo finds itself in the position of a coach, one of whose players has left, playbook in hand, to join the opposing team before the big game.

Thus, when we couple the demonstrated inevitability that Redmond would rely on PCNA trade secrets in his new job at Quaker with the district court's reluctance to believe that Redmond would refrain from disclosing these secrets in his new position (or that Quaker's [prohibition against disclosing confidences from a former employer] would ensure Redmond did not disclose them), we conclude that the district court correctly decided that PepsiCo demonstrated a likelihood of success on its statutory claim of trade secret misappropriation. For the foregoing reasons, we affirm the district court's order enjoining Redmond from assuming his responsibilities at Quaker through May, 1995 [six months] and preventing him forever from disclosing PCNA trade secrets and confidential information.

Decision. Under appropriate circumstances, an employer may be entitled to an inevitability injunction that prohibits a former employee from working for a competitor for limited times if the former employer would likely suffer irreparable harm from the former employee's disclosure of the trade secrets.

Case Questions

1. What does this case suggest about the useful life of confidential marketing plans?
2. What are an employee's job options after terminating from the former employer and before joining a new employer? Does it make any difference if the new employer is a direct competitor of the former employer?

FIDUCIARY DUTY OF LOYALTY

The most fundamental duty that agents or employees owe to their principals and employers is the **fiduciary duty of loyalty**. It is a duty of trust and confidence requiring the agent to act with the utmost good faith in relation to the principal's business affairs. The agent must also render service with reasonable care and skill, which requires the agent to perform the contract duties promised and give due attention to the principal's business. Additionally, the agent must communicate information about the principal's business, account for money and property received for the principal, and act with obedience to the principal's reasonable directives.

The agent must conduct the principal's affairs with the highest integrity. The principal's business and financial interests must be put first and all other interests subordinated. While authorized, the agent must act solely for the principal's benefit in all business matters concerning the subject matter of the agency. This duty prohibits the agent from acting in the interests of others or in the agent's own personal interests if it conflicts with the principal's interests. Some aspects of the fiduciary duty may continue even after the agency is terminated. The fiduciary duty is necessarily stated imprecisely in the abstract but becomes more specific in certain recurring situations: (1) potential conflicts of interest, (2) the agent's comminglement of the principal's property, (3) the agent's competition with the principal, and (4) the maintenance or misappropriation of the principal's confidential information.

Conflicts of Interest

From biblical times, there has been a fundamental principle that no one can serve two masters. Any action that would favor one principal necessarily causes harm to the other. This zero-sum assessment assumes that benefits flowing to one principal must necessarily come at the expense of the other. It is best illustrated where the two principals are contracting together or are competing for the same limited stakes. An agent who represents both principals is a dual or double agent. An agent representing both sides in the same transaction is incapable of satisfying fiduciary duties to both principals simultaneously. Gains by one side are translated into losses by the other.

For example, a real estate agent representing both the seller and the buyer is incapable of fully satisfying the seller's need for a high price and the buyer's need for a low price. The dual agent provides professional judgments to each and learns confidential knowledge about the seller's willingness to reduce the price and pressures to sell quickly and about the buyer's ability to pay more than initially offered. In all probability, one of the principals will receive more information or better advice than the other. Even if the agent scrupulously attempts to "split the difference" by negotiating "fair terms," both principals receive a lesser caliber of service than if each had an independent and loyal agent. Today, several states specifically permit buyer's agents who owe their loyalty only to the buyer. Fidelity and trust given to one principal is incompatible with the trust owed the other.

Agents violate the fiduciary duty of loyalty by receiving secret gifts, gratuities, commissions, kickbacks, or bribes from the other party in a transaction. Such payments are believed to influence the agent's judgment, and this harms the principal. Both the agent and the third party are liable for the principal's losses when the two collude to breach the agent's fiduciary duty. For example, a corporate purchasing agent might be treated to extensive entertainment or provided gifts by a supplier to influence the agent's decision to make corporate purchases. Receipt or solicitation of such inducements amounts to kickbacks, even bribes made as compensation that violates the agent's fiduciary duty.

Despite this prohibition against an agent's adverse interests, in some instances an agent may lawfully represent two parties to a transaction. An agent must generally disclose to the principal all matters that have an impact on the agency, including the existence of another principal. There is no fiduciary violation where both principals are fully informed that the other principal exists and then give consent to the dual agency. An agent may also act as a finder to bring together two potential contracting partners without informing either of the dual agency if neither principal expects advice or help with negotiations. A **nonexclusive agent** may represent numerous principals and the agent's own interests even if the multiple representation competes with any one principal. Consent for such competition must appear in the employment contract or be inferred from the parties' past dealings or other circumstances. For example, theatrical agents typically represent many different performers. The agent's reputation for representing numerous performers is probably sufficient to communicate any potential adverse interests. High-quality theatrical agents must have flexibility to decide whether a particular performer is suitable for a particular role. These agents can then provide a reliable clearinghouse to fulfill the varying needs of third parties for different characters or styles of music.

Self-Dealing

Another form of conflict occurs when the agent's own financial interests directly conflict with the principal's interests. Any personal interest the agent has in a transaction that is adverse to the principal's interests breaches the fiduciary duty. For example, without the principal's fully informed consent, an agent cannot secretly purchase the principal's property. Even if the price was allegedly "fair" or was determined by an appraiser or closed at the market price, this practice is self-dealing. Similarly, the agent may not advance the interests of close friends or relatives if doing so conflicts with the principal's interests.

During the agency, an agent may not compete with the principal in matters that fall within the scope of the agent's employment without the principal's fully informed consent. An exclusive agency prohibits the agent from competing with the principal on either the principal's time or even on the agent's own time. For example, most corporate employees are required to apply themselves full-time and only for the corporation's business interests. This rule probably does not prohibit the agent's moonlighting on the agent's own time in a line of business distinct from the principal's business.

Duty to Account

Agents often hold property and funds belonging to the principal. Any such property received by the agent during the course of operating the principal's business must be safeguarded for the principal's benefit. Any payments the agent receives must be forwarded directly to the principal unless the agent is permitted to retain amounts as reimbursement for expenses, compensation, or commissions. For example, it is customary for waiters to retain tips given by restaurant patrons.

The duty to account has two additional aspects: the duty to keep accurate records and the duty not to commingle the agent's property with the principal's property. Accurate records are essential if the agent executes numerous transactions for the principal and the principal's profits come into question. When the principal requests to see these records, the agent must produce them. Additionally, the agent must not commingle the principal's property with the agent's property. This generally requires an agent to open a separate bank account before depositing the principal's funds. For example, the agent may not use the principal's funds as a short-term loan or for the agent's personal investment purposes, even if the funds are eventually returned. The agent must keep accurate records. Any doubts about the true ownership of commingled funds are resolved in favor of the principal.

Confidentiality Duty

Another aspect of loyalty is the agent's duty to maintain confidentiality. Principals commonly expose their agents to numerous confidential matters to facilitate the effective operation of the business. Confidences are facts that are not known widely or that could harm the principal if they became widely known, including the principal's trade secrets, formulas, manufacturing processes, business plans, financial condition, customer lists, sales tactics, and new product information. Such information is often communicated to agents but is intended solely for the principal's benefit. The agent is prohibited from using such information for personal purposes and may not communicate it to a competitor. Information is the principal's property, and the agent is prohibited from misusing it, irrespective of whether the information was originally produced by the agent, the principal, or another agent.

After termination, an agent may always use any generalized knowledge and skills acquired during the agency. The employer has no right to demand confidentiality for matters that are generally known or for information the employee has a privilege to use personally. A distinction is drawn between "generalized knowledge" of a profession or trade, which a former employee may use or reveal, and "confidences," which may not be used or revealed because they belong to the employer.

A general framework for distinguishing generalized professional information from proprietary information requires analysis of several factors. First, consider the employer's restriction on the employee's ability to compete and the reasonableness of any restriction. Second, the employee's participation in developing the confidential information may be relevant. Third, the employee's knowledge of the employer's claim of exclusive rights to the information is important. Fourth is the extent of the employer's investment in developing the information and how the disclosure would affect future incentives to invest. Under the various testimonial privileges, such as the attorney-client privilege, a client may require confidentiality for communications made to receive legal advice. The privilege may also require confidentiality by secretaries, accountants, and other technical experts.

Nondisclosure Agreements

Of increasing importance are **confidentiality agreements**, also widely known as **nondisclosure agreements (NDA)**. They are often signed between suppliers, customers, and all their employees involved in a transaction. For example, consider the scenario where one party is presenting a proposal or other innovative ideas to attract the other party into a business relationship. During preliminary negotiations, the parties evaluate the proposed contract by making presentations and submitting data, specifications, or strategic plans. The NDA requires confidentiality and thereby prohibits disclosure of any secrets revealed in such presentations.

Increasingly, contracting parties insist on confidentiality for secret information for assessing contract feasibility or during contract performance. An NDA can be required before permitting outsiders' access to confidential information. The NDA may limit the purposes for the communication, itemize the particular information covered, indicate how it is transferred, and require its use only for the contract in question. Each document can be identified separately by number, such as customer lists, drawings, reports, specifications, and confidential exhibits. Anyone agreeing to receive confidential information should attempt to limit his or her duty to maintain secrecy to a particular time frame. Information that will be revealed when a patent is granted can be made confidential for a few years. However, trade secret information should be kept confidential indefinitely or until the secrets become known publicly.

Such NDAs may create a level of trust that can encourage other revelations of proprietary information. For example, information can be discovered during plant tours or disclosed in separate discussions explaining the itemized documents. Therefore, it is often prudent to extend the coverage of the NDA to all confidential information exchanged or discovered during the parties' relationship. However, the NDA should not cover information that is already known by someone else in the firm or information that is already in the public domain.

The NDA should prohibit copying the information, transferring it to outsiders, or divulging it to consultants. All documents should be returned when demanded by the disclosing firm. All individuals exposed to confidential information covered by the NDA should also sign. Often both parties sign the NDA, particularly if both parties disclose and both parties are to receive information. Recipients of confidential information should attempt to limit their duty to maintain secrecy to a particular time frame. NDAs are an essential safety net for employers if an employee's noncompete might ever become unenforceable.

TERMINATION OF EMPLOYMENT

The employer's and the employee's interests may conflict when the employee is terminated. The injury suffered by the parties can depend on the circumstances. The employee must find new work if laid off by the employer. By contrast, the employer must find a replacement employee if the employee quits. The employer's IP and trade secrets can be protected by noncompetes and NDAs, as discussed previously. However, there is a continuing fiduciary duty owed by the employee after termination. This section discusses how the law further constrains the employee's activities after the employee's departure from the employer. Constraints on the employer's freedom to terminate employees are discussed in Chapter 20.

Preparatory Steps

A former employee's conduct just before leaving the firm is often closely examined after termination for evidence of conflicts of interest. A former employee may legitimately take preparatory steps to start or join a new business before quitting the former employer. For example, contracts with suppliers and leases may be negotiated, a new corporation may be formed, and customers not then serviced or sought by the former employer may be solicited. However, these acts can appear sinister, or even conflicts of interest. The former employer's documents should not be taken. Many firms today try to avoid such thefts by escorting a terminated employee from the building. Additionally, customers or coworkers should not be solicited. An employer may validly prohibit the hiring of coworkers with a separate contractual covenant. Solicitation of employees serving under fixed-term contracts exposes the departing employee who solicited them to liability for tortious interference with contractual relations.

SETTLING WORK RULE DISPUTES

The increasing complexity of employment, service, and distribution contracts raises the likelihood of disputes among the parties. Increasingly, employers impose work rules, often embodied in employee manuals that supplement the employment contract. These terms may include additional employee duties. Many employment contracts **incorporate by reference** employee manuals that thereby become express terms of the employment contract with binding legal effect on the legal obligations of both the employer and employees. The same effect may be given to other company documents that carry various titles: company handbook, management handbook, corporate code of conduct, and corporate policy manuals. For example, such handbooks may be introduced as evidence to clarify an ambiguous employment contract. Publicity of the code projects a public image of ethical and socially responsible behavior. Codes of conduct may be required by law or by a self-regulatory body. Some become part of a consent decree made with a government agency that was investigating the company. For example, the U.S. Department of Defense has insisted that several defense contractors institute codes of conduct to prevent defense-procurement fraud or overcharging the government.

Corporate codes of conduct often prohibit employees from engaging in a wide range of illegal or unethical activities, including bribery, sexual harassment, destruction of documents, insider trading, environmental violations, software piracy, misappropriation, fraud, and copyright infringement. Additional policies address the employee's duties during government investigations, antitrust compliance, international boycotts, and relations with suppliers and customers.

Arbitration

Arbitration was initially introduced in Chapter 3. Increasingly, employment and distribution contracts require the parties to arbitrate disputes, a form of alternative dispute resolution (ADR), rather than litigate. Nearly 1 in 12 U.S. workers are covered by agreements to settle employment disputes through arbitration. Many labor union contracts require arbitration of workplace disputes between union members and the employer. **Arbitration** is a binding ADR method by which the parties' dispute is submitted to a nonjudicial third party who renders a legally enforceable decision. The arbitrator's decision is an award of damages or other relief (reinstatement, restored seniority). The recent Supreme Court case *Adams v. Circuit City*,[4] reaffirmed that the Federal Arbitration Act (FAA) applies to employment disputes and that employers can require the settlement of employment disputes with arbitration. The Supreme Court remanded the case back to the Ninth Circuit Court of Appeals to reconsider whether the Circuit City arbitration clause was valid. The Ninth Circuit held that even though the FAA validates employment arbitration, if the employer drafts the arbitration clause to be too favorable to the employer, it can be invalidated under state contract law.[5] Therefore, litigation, rather than arbitration, for workplace disputes can occur in three ways; first, when arbitration clauses are not used; second, when arbitration clauses like the one used in the Circuit City case are held invalid; and third, when Congress specifically exempts employment disputes from the Federal Arbitration Act, such as it has done for transportation workers.

LICENSING

License is a very broad yet vague term because it refers both to governmental privileges and private contracts. The **governmental privilege** aspect is familiar to anyone who licenses vehicles or businesses and to those who become qualified to drive a vehicle or practice their profession. Usually a governmental entity seeks to raise revenue and/or control the persons conducting the licensed activity. For example, businesses must obtain a municipal business license to conduct their activities. Professionals such as doctors, lawyers, engineers, and more than 100 other trades and callings must have government licenses to assure professional character and

4. 532 U.S. 105 (2001).
5. *Circuit City v. Adams*, 279 F.3d 889 (9th Cir., 2002).

competence and protect society. Although governmental licenses are important in technology transfer, the following discussion concerns private licenses.

A **private license** is a special privilege that is defined and conferred by contract on some firm or person, called the **licensee** by the owner of property or producer of a service, the **licensor**. A license usually confers lesser rights that would be transferred in an outright sale or assignment. The licensor usually retains rights in the property. Many licenses permit the licensor to revoke the license if the licensee breaches limitations on use as stated in the license. Licenses are often standardized form contracts with nonnegotiable terms to reduce transaction costs. However, under the laissez-faire, freedom-of-contract principle, licenses may be individually negotiated, so they can have an almost infinite variety of forms. Like all contracts, licenses are created with valid mutual assent and must be supported by consideration. Some licenses must be in writing and are subject to limitations, such as defenses to formation. As discussed in Chapter 10, the mutual assent that concludes many contemporary licensing contracts in the consumer mass market is accomplished with click-wrap or shrink-wrap. Licenses are a common part of contracts for employment, distribution, franchising, and software purchases and are becoming increasingly important in Internet use and information sales.

Licensing is a common method to distribute property directly to consumers. Licensing is also essential in organizing franchise businesses because independent outsiders distribute the franchise system's products. Limited property rights are created, narrowing the licensee's use of intangible property. Usually, licensing is only a limited sale of intangible property, unlike transactions in tangible property such as the temporary lease or permanent outright transfer of land or goods. Tangible property has material substance that can be possessed physically and exclusively. Leasing is the primary method to create and transfer limited property rights in tangible real estate (e.g., office, building) or personal property (e.g., vehicles, computers, telecommunications equipment). By contrast, intangible property rights are not directly related to physical property but are recognized as rights between persons. This point is sometimes confusing because intangible IP can be represented in physical objects, such as a copyrighted book, a patented process using machines, a patented component in a product, or the trademarked logo on a sign or product packaging. Licensing most often involves a transfer of the right to use intangible property: ideas, information, discoveries, knowledge, expressions, designs, writings, words, program steps, symbols, logos, trade names, slogans, endorsements, or software. Some transactions are a hybrid of leasing and IP licensing. For example, the tickets to watch a movie or sporting event, attend a concert, or view a theatrical performance are usually called licenses despite the incidental real estate interest in occupying a seat for a short time.

The licensor's primary incentive is to exploit its IP to maximize revenue. The licensor, in **licensing out** the IP, usually tries to impose restrictive license terms and retain maximum rights so they can be relicensed to others. The licensee has somewhat rival interests when **licensing in** IP rights, attempting to minimize license restrictions and lower the compensation paid while maximizing its opportunities for exploitation.

Licenses almost always grant lesser rights than transfer in a sale or assignment. An **assignment** is generally an outright transfer that forever conveys all or a substantial part of the seller's rights to the buyer. When the seller assigns IP, the seller cannot generally assign that same IP to anyone else. Therefore, assignment is inappropriate if the seller's business model depends on multiple resales of the same IP. An assignment of IP is most appropriate if the buyer purchases a customized IP product that will not be sold to another customer.

GENERAL LICENSING TERMS

Many standardized licenses are similar to other types of form contracts: Consistency in terms and conditions reduces transactions costs. Lower licensing costs can be passed on to consumers, and eventually more content should become available to the public. Consider how appropriate it is to use standard, mass-market licensing for Internet content. Much Web content is of such low value—worth just pennies per page—that individually negotiating each license for user access would be prohibitively expensive. In high-volume, consumer transactions, many licensors carefully craft a single, uniform contract. This "take-it-or-leave-it" approach uses a single statement of terms and conditions. For example, the conditions for website use become a license to access the website's material. Sometimes an incentive emerges to modify these set terms, such as when the market resists by demanding a better deal. A contemporary example is that many websites are increasing privacy protections under pressure from consumers and the threat of regulation.

In the future, automated electronic agents could negotiate some terms, particularly where the trade-offs between factors are susceptible to deterministic substitution. For example, a user's browser could initially specify the user's privacy expectations. Next, the website could either change its privacy policy to conform to the user's demand or it could counterpropose somewhat less privacy protection in exchange for giving the user free access to normally pay-per-view data. If the user's electronic agent were programmed to accept this counteroffer, the transaction costs of negotiating a low-value license could be accomplished automatically. Automated bargaining by electronic agents raises some interesting new complications.

Many of the licenses that cover high-value content or become the major foundation for ongoing business relationships are custom tailored to the specific situation with deliberate and thoughtful human oversight. Few terms in such contracts are standard because the stakes are high enough for the parties to commit human resource investments to customize their relationship, balancing the relative risks and rewards in the package of terms. An important feature of licensing is evident in the adage that "there are many ways to slice the [IP] salami." This means that laissez-faire freedom of contract is alive and well in the law of licensing. Parties negotiating

Commentary

Future Controversy: Automated Bargaining over License Terms

Someday, negotiations may be automated without human intervention, perhaps using electronic agents. For this scenario to be successful, standards must emerge to define the range and increments of these automatically negotiated terms. Automated bargaining may raise trespass questions. Consider how shopping bots today automatically probe auction sites to determine prices. Many auction sites' terms and conditions prohibit such automated price collection, and some have implemented technical blocking methods. Now consider electronic agents that could feign negotiating a license by expressing phony seriousness to negotiate a deal while having no real intention or human authority to actually conclude the deal. The electronic agent might simply be interested in probing the other party's site for valuable confidential negotiating postures. But negotiating flexibility is a trade secret, quite valuable if learned by counterparties. For example, knowing another party's fallback or deal-breaker positions would give the counterparty a bargaining advantage. Only time will tell whether automated bargaining will develop into a reliable method. The prospect of secret bargaining positions revealed on the false pretext of serious negotiations could become a serious deterrent to the development of electronic agents.

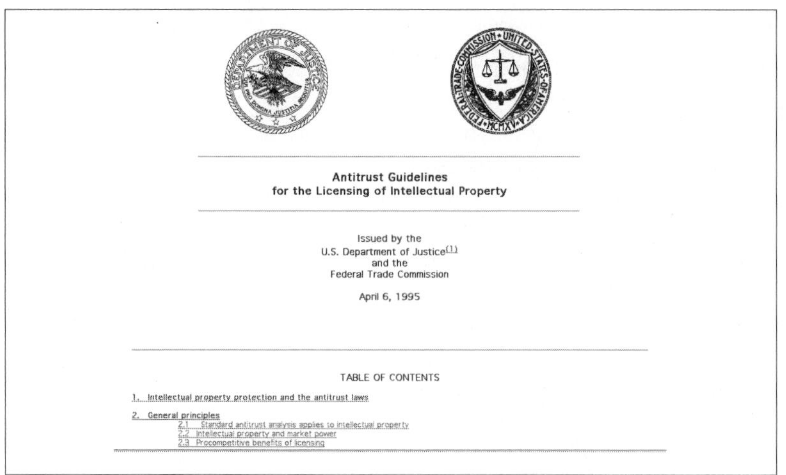
Antitrust Guidelines
for the Licensing of Intellectual Property

Issued by the
U.S. Department of Justice[1]
and the
Federal Trade Commission

April 6, 1995

TABLE OF CONTENTS

http://

www.usdoj.gov/atr/public/guidelines/ipguide.htm

licenses can make conscious trade-offs by varying any or all contractual terms and thereby define the rights created and conveyed in the license.

Many license terms are actually limitations on the licensee's right to use or exploit the IP. The following terms are typically used to limit the license granted: field of use, duration, territory, noncompetition, transferability, termination, and liability for consequential damages. Other typical terms define the form of compensation, make warranties, may require confidentiality, and provide for dispute settlement. Some of the principal licensing terms are discussed in the following text. Licenses restrain trade to some extent, so they are scrutinized under antitrust law as discussed in Chapter 19. The Federal Trade Commission and the Justice Department have issued antitrust guidelines for IP licensing.

Scope of Grant

The heart of any license is the **grant**, the clause(s) that describes the IP involved, creates the right, and then transfers it to the licensee. The grant defines the content. For example, data sets are described, official titles are used for registered copyrighted work(s) or a description of the invention(s), and patent number(s) and/or registered trademarks are separately listed. Commonly, the rights are **nonexclusive,** which permits the licensor to use the IP as well as license it to others. In an **exclusive** license, only the licensee may use the IP, thereby prohibiting use by either the licensor and/or other licensees. **Sublicensing** is the licensee's right to further license the IP to others. It is often prohibited. However, when sublicensing is permitted, the licensor may require the licensee to use particular licensing terms or a specified form for all sublicenses. The licensor may specify particular rights retained, thus expressly permitting the licensor to use certain aspects of the IP rights.

A problem concerning the technological scope of grants in both assignments and licenses reemerged in the mid-1990s. When a license is first negotiated, the terms usually address uses and technologies known at that time, raising the question of whether old grants should be interpreted to include each new technology as new markets are built. Consider how negotiations for an author's rights to a novel written in the 1950s could not have foreseen the development of consumer electronics or digital technologies. The publisher may have had standard form contract language that effectively captured the rights to adapt the novel into known technologies such as a script for a Broadway play, a Hollywood movie, or a TV drama. However, few publishers would have thought to include grant language to capture unknown fields of use such as videotape sales or rentals. These technologies did not exist in the 1950s when the contracts were drafted. Similarly, few publishers in the early 1990s were farsighted enough to capture an author's rights to many current electronic formats such as DVDs or Web downloads of streaming video. This gap creates uncertainty about whether a license or assignment will cover uses involving future technologies. The law implies that many book authors retain electronic distribution rights to their books unless the grant specifically included all technologies presently known or developed in the future.

A recent controversy illustrates the problem of publishing in new technologies not specifically described in the original grant. Freelance writers are independent contractors who supply stories to newspapers, magazines, and the trade press. The publisher evaluates each story, and the parties enter into a new contract each time a story is published. The grant is often made according to the publisher's standard form contract that traditionally granted rights for publication only on paper and not in electronic formats. As publishers have moved their content onto the Internet, they have electronically republished stories originally granted only for print uses.

One recent Supreme Court case caps a developing line of similar lower court cases to illustrate part of this problem. In *Tasini v. New York Times Co.*,[6] the U.S. Supreme Court held that grants in one medium do not extend to grant uses in other media. Tasini was a freelancer who wrote stories for various media outlets. This practice permits the newspapers to have smaller in-house staffs while encouraging a thriving group of writers who cherish their status as independent contractors. Tasini's assignment to the *Times* granted print rights but did not mention electronic rights. Tasini sued for infringement when the *Times* posted his article to its electronic archive of stories. Many large media companies like the *New York Times*, *Wall Street Journal*, *Washington Post*, *Business Week*, and *Time* have found value in archiving all their previously published articles to provide access free or to fee-paying customers via the Internet. Some authors have demanded additional royalties or sought to block use of their articles in electronic databases of published articles.

Tasini's victory for freelance writers may come at a price—a loss for the public. Many publishers refuse to negotiate new royalty agreements for electronic rights, choosing instead to remove these writers' content from their electronic databases. This creates a "gap in history." Cases like *Tasini* have led publishers to change their standard form contracts for both licensing and assignments. Many publishers now specifically acquire rights to future but currently unknown technologies, as illustrated in the following sample language. Of course, famous authors and talented inventors have stronger bargaining power. These authors may be able to insist on retaining rights to some future technologies or negotiate more favorable royalties for themselves.

Grant for Use in Future Technologies

The author grants all rights to the Work, including reproductions, whether in media now existing or hereafter developed, including, but not limited to, print, electronic communication or storage by magnetic or optical means, including all video, movie, audio rights and the public performance or display of the Work or any derivative works using electronic means now existing or which may come into existence.

IP Audit

Licensors must assure they have solid rights to the IP they license out. An **intellectual property audit** is advisable to marshal all of the firm's IP assets and determine the enforceability of rights. Audits help the firm precisely monitor assets and avoid licensing out IP when the licensor does not have full rights. Licensees frequently insist that licensors must make a warranty of title, possibly called warranty of noninfringement, assuring that they have the right to license and that the licensee's allowable use

6. 533 U.S. 483 (2001).

under the license will be rightful. Audits may also be advisable for licensees and during mergers and infringement litigation, and they are a prerequisite to cross-licensing.

Duration and Termination

An important business issue is the duration, length of time, or term of the license, the starting date and the ending date outside of which the licensee has no rights. Licensees naturally seek longer terms to permit full development of the licensed IP, particularly if it is successful. By contrast, some licensors may prefer retaining control, perhaps to substitute potentially more successful licensees or to renegotiate more favorable terms when it becomes clear the IP is becoming successful. The duration may be defined by precise calendar dates or could be indefinite, such as when terminated by specified events: "for as long as the licensee sells the licensed product."

Sometimes the licensor may have the right to terminate the license earlier if certain conditions are not met. For example, grounds for termination may include the licensee's failure to make required payments, failure to reach milestones (production quantities, quality), or the licensee's breach of key license terms. After termination, a licensor may find it desirable to obligate the licensee to a continuing confidentiality duty and to complete unfinished performances after termination.

The **first sale doctrine** prohibits the licensor from exercising control after the product embodying the IP is sold the first time. Buyers of patented goods or copyrighted expression are not bound by the licensor's restrictions. For example, a patent holder cannot prevent the consumer from reselling an automobile containing patented technologies. Similarly, the copyright holder cannot prevent a consumer from reselling a music CD, video, or used textbook. By contrast, licensors hope to restrict further use or transfer of digital copies of licensed software or information, precisely the issue holding back Web music.

Territorial Limitations to a Geographical Region

Many licenses limit the particular geographic regions in which the licensee may do business using the IP. For example, in the entertainment industry and in franchise businesses, the licensee is commonly granted marketing rights solely within a specified metropolitan area, in a particular state or states, within the continental United States, or in particular nations. This practice permits the licensor to license out to different firms in other regions that have local expertise or a successful track record. Sometimes differences in cultural aspects or language, as well as local regulatory restrictions, make it necessary to license differently in various locations, particularly in international transactions.

The Internet makes enforcing traditional geographic limitations more difficult. Markets are becoming global, advertising extends beyond borders, and the Internet's architecture works against restricting marketing activities to particular regions. Nevertheless, licensees can be prohibited from directing their selling efforts to particular regions, states, or nations.

Another method of limiting marketing rights is to restrict the field of use by prohibiting the licensee from selling in particular supply chains, outside particular industries, or to particular customers or markets (wholesale, retail). Such supply chain restrictions have antitrust implications, discussed in Chapter 19.

Compensation

Payment is usually the most important licensing term. Compensation structure can vary widely. The license typically requires payment of some consideration for the privilege granted in the license. Consideration may come from a number of sources:

money, the cancellation of past debts the licensor owed to the licensee, the settlement of a infringement claims between the parties, or cross-licensing of the licensee's other IP back to the licensor. The licensee frequently pays a monetary licensing fee or royalty. Licensees typically must keep accurate records so that royalties can be precisely paid, the licensee's success determined, and audits facilitated.

Royalty traditionally refers to consideration paid for mineral interests under lease or for the licensed use of a registered patent, copyright, or trademark. Running royalties are computed at a percentage rate that is applied to a **royalty base**, which depends on the volume of the licensee's unit production, dollar sales activity during the license duration, or other quantity measure of production or sales. Royalties for Internet content can be metered in other ways, such as website "hits," the number of viewers or downloads, and time of viewing (eyeballs). **Residuals** are royalties paid in the entertainment industry. **Running royalties** are set annual fees and generally not variable by units or dollar volume. A **license fee** generally refers to an initial or fixed payment made to purchase the license right or to acquire a franchise that includes license rights. Such fees are generally fixed and are not paid periodically or in variable payments. Compensation schemes under many licenses combine fixed fees with variable fees.

How much should the licensor charge? The licensee can be successful only when the fees are reasonable, considering the contribution made by the licensed IP to the value of the whole product. For example, the royalties charged for a patented automobile component could not exceed the cost of a reasonable substitute component. Similarly, the consumer cost of basic cable TV service would probably not support fees for premium movie channels. Therefore, pricing a royalty requires analysis of economic factors such as the existence of substitute components, price elasticity for substitute components, the added utility that the IP contributes to the product, and the competitive environment for the finished products. Adjustments are often needed to better balance the burdens of production expenses, taxes, shipping, returns, and discounts. Finally, licensors are often obligated to indemnify licensees if the IP licensed infringes a third party's IP rights.

Ethical Issue

Ethical Dilemma in Licensing Terms

Long, long experience illustrates that some one-sided tactics are all too frequently used in IP licenses and assignments. The stronger party often controls the drafting of license terms and takes advantage of this opportunity to cast the terms more favorably than necessary. Licensees are often required to give up reasonable rights and assume liability for consequences beyond their control. This problem is aggravated because many licensees fail to read the fine print, and even fewer take the time to understand the consequences of the legalese used in complex license terms and conditions. The licensee's ignorance permits the licensor to insert terms favorable to the licensor.

The history of content contracting in the entertainment industry is similar—the main difference is that the stronger parties are assigned, rather than licensed, works written by songwriters, screenwriters, and playwrights. For example, many of the great blues musicians of the twentieth century had their songs acquired for a pittance. These songs became the foundation of the most lucrative properties the music industry ever acquired: soul, rock, and jazz. With such treatment, it is no wonder that much of Hollywood's labor force became unionized and instituted inflexible work rules. So long as license terms are drafted by the stronger party, they will be complex, ambiguous, and one-sided. Cynicism will continue prompting pressures to regulate licensing. Licenses actually negotiated between parties with more equal bargaining power are much more likely to occupy a reasonable middle ground.

PATENT LICENSING

Patent license grants a privilege to practice the patent—that is, permits the licensee to engage in conduct that the patent owner could otherwise attack as patent infringement, such as manufacturing the patented product or using the patented process. Licenses are made for existing patented technologies and can be made for technologies covered by patent applications even before they are issued. The U.S. patent law requires that licenses be in writing. Licensees are often in the best position to observe the performance of a patented invention and design improvements. However, the licensor's consent may be necessary to experiment with or modify the patented process or goods and then to regularly practice the improvement developed by this R&D. The licensor of the original technology cannot practice the improvement without a license from the licensee who developed the improvement. These patents block each other unless the parties enter into cross-licensing.

Cross-Licensing

This problem underscores the importance of having a portfolio of patents and the benefits of cross-licensing. Under **cross-licensing**, each party owns IP and exchanges licenses in one or more of their technologies with an opposing party. Cross-licensing is an efficient process. Often no money changes hands, and only licensing rights are exchanged. Cross-licensing can be used whenever mutually beneficial, such as in settlement of IP disputes between the parties. The promise of cross-licensing has led to strategic behavior by many technology firms: They build up IP portfolios, particularly patents, so they can use the threat of patent infringement litigation to negotiate settlements based on cross-licensing. Therefore, some licensing does not produce much royalty revenue but instead provides a shield against the threat of infringement damage liability. Royalties cannot be collected after a patent expires.

TRADE SECRET LICENSING

A common misconception is that trade secrets are used only by the firms that develop them. The very nature of secrecy makes it difficult to conceal such information if it were to become widely known. However, many trade secrets cannot be effectively exploited by their discoverer, and perhaps full exploitation can be accomplished only by sale or license to others. Two key secrecy conundrums create challenges in the licensing of trade secrets. First, the buyer must be convinced of the value in a technology, but, if it is revealed, the information might no longer be secret. Second, the licensee must agree to maintain confidentiality. Trade secrets are often described in documents, but they may also be discovered by reverse engineering, such as in dissecting a product or decompiling software, as discussed in Chapter 16.

The owner of a trade secret faces a potentially daunting dilemma in licensing the technology. Potential licensees are often unwilling to license a technology without knowing many of the key secret factors that make it valuable. However, the owner could lose its value when the secret is divulged. To engage serious interest by a potential licensee, one or both of the following conditions must exist: (1) The secret product has a well-known reputation for value and quality, or (2) the licensor must divulge enough to stimulate the recipient's serious interest. When the trade secret is too new to have developed a reputation, the licensors must hope to persuade the recipient that the idea has value. To do so, the recipient must enter a confidential relationship to allow a review of the secrets by using the strategies discussed next.

Submission of Unsolicited Ideas

Many inventors are unable, by themselves, to effectively exploit their innovations. Some are simply not interested in undertaking all the trouble and risk of starting up a new business. They often seek the interest of a successful firm already in the field or in a related trade. Established firms have acknowledged goodwill and may be better able to develop and market the innovation. It's a big strategic challenge for an inventor to find the right firm and then provoke interest without running the risk that the firm will simply use the idea without paying. Unless patented, ideas are "as free as the air,"[7] so the law does not generally protect an innovator who blurts out an innovative idea without first making a contract for compensation. Sometimes the law provides protection under an express or implied contract for compensation or if the innovator had a confidential relationship with the recipient firm. However, without such confidentiality, the recipient is generally free to use the idea after disclosure.

What types of ideas might be submitted? Submissions can concern trade secrets, possibly patentable inventions, business strategies, marketing plans, new products, new designs, business methods, and other forms of inspiration. Some ideas are **know-how**, the expertise to make innovations work or work better. Copyright law largely protects only the form of expression and not the underlying ideas. Therefore, it is not easy to protect an abstract concept or story line for a movie, television show, or theatrical work; a slogan and skit underlying an advertising campaign; or the abstract concepts underlying a sculpture, artwork, or website. A submitter would nearly always have a stronger position if the idea could first be patented. However, patenting is often prohibitively expensive for independent inventors. Submission to another firm may seem attractive if the recipient has special expertise that is needed to analyze the idea's profitability, if the idea may not be patentable, or if it could be better protected as a trade secret.

The submitter may be entitled to compensation from a recipient under any one of four theories from state law. Many states recognize rights in novel, original, and concrete ideas once they are well developed and nearly ready for implementation. Industry customs are also relevant to show the practice in compensating for idea submissions. First, there is a property rights theory in ideas presented orally, in writing, or in a mock-up. To be protected as property, such ideas cannot be already in common use or well known. The recipient may be liable for misappropriation by having access to the idea and then producing a product substantially similar to the one submitted without the inventor's permission. Second, recipients are bound to express contracts to compensate the submitter, but there must be contractual consideration. Waivers that release the recipient from liability must clearly state their terms, and some states require them to be reasonable.

The last two theories are implied contracts. The third theory examines the parties' conduct. A contract may be implied-in-fact by considering four factors: (1) whether the recipient solicited the idea, (2) whether the recipient could prevent disclosure, (3) whether the disclosure was confidential, and (4) the nature of the parties' interactions. The submitter's case is strengthened when the idea submission was intentionally solicited by the recipient; the recipient could have prevented the disclosure and knew the submitter expected compensation. By contrast, an implied contract is less likely if the submission was received involuntarily and there was no

7. *Desny v. Wilder*, 299 P.2d 257 (1965).

expectation of confidentiality. The fourth theory is quasi-contract, a form of equitable relief that is implied-in-law. A remedy could be required if the disclosure was confidential, the recipient would be unjustly enriched by using the disclosed idea, and the parties intended to agree on compensation later. Remedies under these four theories could include actual value or the reasonable value of the recipient's benefits. Alternatively, the industry's going rate for reasonable royalties might be used as a benchmark.

Recipients also have risks when unsolicited ideas are submitted. Many large firms are inundated with submissions of unsolicited ideas. Some firms may already have similar R&D efforts underway somewhere in their various divisions or at some other location. No recipient should ever agree to pay for ideas that it already knows, are in the scientific literature, or are in the public domain. However, screening submitted ideas for utility and profitability can be costly. Submitters can sue, claiming misappropriation. Many large technology firms use routine procedures to handle and review submissions. For example, submissions can be handled by separate offices within the firm or even by an independent third party. These procedures create a **Chinese wall** to isolate the actual recipient from the firm's operating divisions that might use the idea.

Many firms require the submitter to sign a **waiver** before the recipient will evaluate the idea. Waivers are essentially contracts that release the recipient from liability for misappropriating the idea or breaching confidentiality. They frequently allow copies to be made and can permit disclosure onward to others. Unless the submitter has a patent, many of these waivers could allow the recipient to keep or use the idea. Filing for a patent before submission may protect the submitter. However, if a patent is unaffordable or impossible, the submitter must devise a strategy to entice the recipient into confidentiality. One method is to gradually reveal just enough information to convince the recipient of the idea's value, and then the recipient may agree to maintain confidentiality while the idea is further evaluated.

Database Licensing

Until databases are given **sui generis** status as a separate and unique type of statutory IP right, their protection must rely primarily on trade secret law. Therefore, databases are most effectively licensed when kept secret or when technical features deter misappropriation or enhance the database's utility. For example, data stored on a website could be effectively licensed if users consent to confidentiality and they have difficulty copying substantial portions of the data. Data that must be constantly revised or updated has an inherent licensing advantage if the original owner has preferred access to the updated data stream, such as a stock exchange has to daily trading information. In sum, the best current methods to protect databases include limited licensee access, a valuable brand image, a unique user interface, and contractual confidentiality.

COPYRIGHT LICENSING

Licensing of copyrighted IP is probably the most common form of licensing. Most Web content is protected by copyright, although Web licensing may also involve trademarks, trade secrets, patents, and endorsements. Copyright licensing is somewhat more complex than licensing of these other forms of IP because copyright is a bundle of rights with separate licensable interests in reproduction, derivative works, and distribution, as well as performance and display. Distinctions are made between exclusive and nonexclusive licenses. Over the years, the licensing of copyrighted works has become less complicated, as the owners of works recognize new business models and forms for the use of their works. The most influential factors are standardized license contracts, reasonable fees, recognition of profit potential in customized content, technological solutions that permit selective unbundling of content, and a greater willingness to explore new marketing channels.

Consider the example of **custom anthologies** created by college faculty for their students' readings. For many years, professors collected articles from newspapers and trade magazines, scholarly research, and book chapters to produce an optimal readings package. In many subjects, this practice is necessary because textbooks lag behind the understanding of emerging and fast-changing fields. However, many such anthologies were made without the permission of the publishers or authors. Before the 1980s, the permissions process was cumbersome, and many publishers resisted any attempt to parcel out portions of their works in independent compilations, occasionally preferring to assemble their own custom anthologies. However, after the famous Kinko's case,[8] most publishers, copy shops, and university printing services have started to work together more effectively to provide timely and efficient permissions clearance. Today, most such anthologists respect the copyrights of the owners by securing permissions more easily, and they pay royalties to the publishers. Still, many professors complain that the high costs of permissions are passed on to students, which forces much higher prices, and many professors have deleted important materials as too costly. Nevertheless, the Internet holds great promise for efficient permissions licensing by connecting licensors with licensees.

Licensing Music

There are many practical differences in copyright licensing depending on the type of expression involved: literary; musical; dramatic; choreographic; pictorial, graphic, and sculpture; audiovisual; sound recordings; and architectural works. Digital fixation and storage and Internet transfer add further complexity. In the United States, practices have developed to facilitate the licensing of copyrighted expression, such as the compulsory licensing of music and broadcasts and the private management of the permissions process by performing rights organizations. Chapter 15 illustrates several separate copyrightable interests in music. Foremost are the typically inseparable interests in the **composition** for which the tune or melody is written by the composer-songwriter and the words are written by the lyricist. Most often, the composer and lyricist assign these interests to a music publisher, either a corporate affiliate of a recording company or an independent firm. Sheet music and "fake books" are often published. However, today the larger market involves a separate copyright interest in a **sound recording**, made by a particular group of musicians who join to record their rendition of the composition. There may be several individuals or firms with rights in the copyright of the sound recording, including the author of the **arrangement** (adaptation or modification to different voices, instruments, rhythms, verses, etc.), the musicians, vocalists and singers, and recording technicians who modify (morph) many aspects of the sound. In most instances, the rights of these parties are assigned to the record company in exchange for marketing, regular employee compensation, and/or royalties. Some of these persons may be employed under a work made for hire contract, obviating the assignment. The classic treatise explaining licensing music is *Kohn on Music Licensing*.

ONLINE

Kohn on Music Licensing
http://www.kohnmusic.com

8. *Basic Books, Inc. v. Kinkos Graphics Corp.*, 758 F.Supp. 1522 (S.D.N.Y. 1991).

The Europeans have a strong tradition in according **moral rights**—the artist or author's right to accurate attribution and to maintaining the integrity of the original work. Moral rights are generally weaker in the United States than in Europe. Consider the issue of compulsory licensing and cover. In the United States, very few IP rights are subject to **compulsory licensing**, by which the government mandates permission to use an owner's IP for a fee set by the government, not by market forces. Under a compulsory license, the owner may neither refuse to license nor negotiate license fees. Compulsory licensing was initiated in the 1909 Copyright Act to balance rights in the automated playing of player pianos.

The 1976 Copyright Act continues compulsory licensing for five types of content: (1) nondramatic phonograph records, called the **mechanical right;** (2) cable television retransmission of broadcast TV; (3) jukebox playing of phonograph records; (4) noncommercial, public broadcasting of certain copyrighted works; and (5) satellite retransmissions to the public. Compulsory licenses are administered by the Copyright Royalty Tribunal, but there has been significant litigation. The Recording Industry Association of America (RIAA), a trade association, is closely involved in music licensing and infringement enforcement.

ONLINE
Recording Industry Association of America
http://www.riaa.org

The **mechanical license** for phonograph records is among the most significant compulsory licenses. The mechanical license arises after a musical composition is recorded by one band or group of musicians and it is distributed to the public. Thereafter, another musical group may apply for and receive a mechanical license to make an independent recording of that composition, even if it will be recorded in a different style. That is, once a composition is **covered**, others may record and distribute to the public or publicly perform their version. It is also significant for Internet music because the Digital Millennium Copyright Act (DMCA) applies the mechanical license to **digital phonorecord deliveries**, essentially streaming or downloading music via the Internet. There are limitations on the mechanical license: It does not require licensing for dramatic musical works (operas, soundtracks), and the original song cannot be distorted; that is, the basic melody cannot be changed without infringing the composition owner's right to adapt the original into a derivative work.

Performing Rights Associations

Public performance licenses are needed when a sound recording from a phonorecord is broadcast via radio, TV, or the Internet. Licensing is also needed for a public performance of a musical composition, played by some other group of musicians. For example, a license is needed when a "cover band" plays others' compositions or the rendition is styled like the sound recording of a particular musical group. How could composers, musicians, and record companies monitor all the radio airplay or live band performances and negotiate reasonable royalties? The administration of such permissions, licensing, and collection and distribution of royalties could be prohibitively cumbersome without form contracting. To simplify this process, **performing rights associations** provide clearinghouse services by supplying **blanket licenses**, which are standardized licenses at standardized rates. They substantially increase the economies of scale by reducing transaction costs and probably increase the replay and cover of compositions and sound recordings. As discussed in Chapter 19, these societies are generally pro-competitive but are regulated under antitrust law to prevent price-fixing or bias favoring established composers or musicians.[9]

9. *Broadcast Music Inc. v. CBS*, 441 U.S. 1, 32 (1979) (J. Stevens dissent).

Performing rights associations include the American Society of Composers, Arrangers, and Performers (ASCAP), Broadcast Music Incorporated (BMI), and the Society of European Stage Authors and Composers (SESAC). Licensees may license through these organizations or can approach copyright owners, mostly the record companies, to negotiate licenses directly.

ONLINE

Performing rights licensing organizations
http://www.ascap.com
http://www.bmi.com
http://www.sesac.com

The mechanics of the music-licensing process usually comes after the selection of the best music to use in the licensee's particular application. This is itself an art and a challenging process because of the many styles and tastes involved in optimally selecting compositions and particular recordings or excerpting the most useful passages. As discussed later, the personnel involved in designing a complex collection of IP must understand IP law and how it is licensed. It is also possible to draw music from the public domain or from music libraries. Public domain music must still be arranged and performed by musicians the user hires. Sound recordings from music libraries may be the easiest method to acquire rightful use, but care must be taken to acquire *all* the rights the user may conceivably need as the product's success expands. Finally, the licensing of digital copies of software, information, music, images, and video is unsettled at this time. Chapter 15 discusses the peer-to-peer (P2P) exchange of copyrighted works through Internet music-trading facilities such as Napster, Morpheus, Gnutella, and MP3 that poses potentially irreconcilable conflicts between copyright holders and emerging consumer expectations. It is possible that the technical and legal issues will crystallize to enable Web delivery of such works, perhaps on a subscription or pay-per-view basis.

SOFTWARE LICENSING

Software licensing primarily involves creating and transferring copyrighted IP because software is expression written in symbolic language that defines process steps to control computer hardware. However, software licensing can sometimes be a hybrid of various forms of IP. Software can include methods and processes that are protectable as trade secrets, and some software programs may be sufficiently novel and nonobvious to be patentable. In addition, many successful software programs have brand images protected by trademarks that are used in various places to complement and reinforce the other IP protections. Increasingly, software licensing is accomplished through the shrink-wrap or click-wrap techniques discussed in Chapter 10.

Software licenses are perhaps unique largely because of the reproduction right under copyright that gives exclusive rights to the copyright owner to make and distribute copies. To use software effectively, it is necessary to make several types of software copies and then to use the copies in various ways. To be useful, software licenses must permit users to do at least some copying. Nearly all purchasers of software licenses receive a copy of the original program, whether distributed on disk, on CD, as written lines of code, or as a file when downloaded. Loading the software on a system's hard drive makes another copy, and most users seek the right to make backup copies to restore their systems after hardware failures. Each time the software loads up for use, substantial parts of the software must be copied into temporary storage (RAM). Some software licenses permit installation on a single user's desktop and another copy on their laptop computer, so long as both are not in use simultaneously. **Site licenses** give firms and other large institutions the right to make multiple copies for employees, members, or students. Therefore, at least some attention must focus on the extent of copying permitted under a software license. Many information licenses must accommodate intermediate, ephemeral or temporary copies as necessary to use information contained in a database.

To adequately protect the trade secrets contained in many software programs, licenses typically forbid reverse engineering. The user may not **decompile** or otherwise convert the machine-readable **object code** back into **source code**—the form in which programmers write software. Trade secrets could be discerned if the software was analyzed to determine how its components work. The prohibition against decompiling can create problems, particularly if the licensor is unwilling, unable, or unreasonable about providing later services for the software. Repairs to fix bugs or modifications to evolve the software's functionality usually require making changes to source code. Many software programs anticipate this need and build in some user flexibility. However, the prohibition against reverse engineering could severely inconvenience the licensee, particularly if the licensor went bankrupt. In special situations, a **source code escrow** may be an appropriate compromise. It employs the services of an independent third party to protect the trade secret confidentiality but gives the licensee a right to decompile and repair or customize when needed.

The furor during 1999 over the Y2K problem helps underscore the central role that software plays in successfully running government, business, safety-related aspects of the transportation system, flood control, and electric power generation and distribution. The importance of software licensors' quality warranties was highlighted. Considerable societal cost to update software systems had been delayed until the Y2K crisis. There is good news in all the Y2K difficulties in that millions of dollars were expended to upgrade software that will probably have lasting positive impact. Nevertheless, experience and litigation over these expenditures emphasize the importance of carefully analyzing software warranties and then developing strategies for substitutes that replace mission-critical software systems.

Multimedia Works

Multimedia works are combinations of various types of content, largely protected under copyright, that can include text, audio, graphics, and video expression. Multimedia products are generally embodied in software that is designed to be used in education and entertainment and will run largely on computers or networks. Multimedia products may also include other types of IP, such as trade secrets, patents, trademarks, and data.

A multimedia project poses three broad challenges in technology transfer. First, its development must be commissioned. Content experts, programmers, pedagogical experts, and media experts are generally all needed to create a high-quality product. Second, the developer must create or acquire rights to many small bits of content that are to be orchestrated into the multimedia collage or montage. Third, the product must be distributed, usually under license, using either fixed storage (CD-ROM) or network delivery (Web-streaming) via a potentially profitable business model. Multimedia products are very complex and require significant IP management of permissions. They have many of the same cyber law problems as any other e-commerce project, including general IP, copyright in particular, payments, e-contracting, privacy, and constitutional protection of First Amendment expression.

COMPUTER INFORMATION LICENSING UNDER UCITA

At the heart of UCITA is the different treatment given licensing of computer information (software, data) than the traditional commercial practice for sales or leases in goods, land, and services. UCITA's drafters made many aspects of licensing consistent with the familiar practices of UCC. UCITA attempts to strike a balance that preserves innovation incentives without inhibiting the growth of simple and efficient network distribution. Many of UCITA's contract law provisions were introduced in previous chapters. Formation and consideration rules were introduced in Chapter 10; recall that UCITA embraces the transaction costs savings in the developing law of shrink-wrap and click-wrap assent. Chapter 11 introduced UCITA's title warranties. Chapter 12 details UCITA's integration with UETA, as well as discussing how UCITA establishes a visionary framework for the evolution of contractual writings and remedies applicable to electronic contracting and performances. In this section, some of UCITA's unique licensing aspects are introduced.

Mass Market Licenses

Like most other uniform laws, UCITA creates a legal framework around recognized and common commercial practices. Current licensing practice generally falls into two broad categories: (1) large, wholesale, B2B transactions and (2) retail transactions that are both B2B and B2C. The large transactions require considerable customization. The law has generally presumed large transactions are negotiated at arm's length and that both parties are reasonably sophisticated and represented by legal counsel competent in licensing. These underlying assumptions and these contracts are explored later in this chapter.

Under UCITA, **mass market** licenses are small-dollar, routine transactions that include all consumer contracts. In addition, they include B2B transactions in which marketing efforts are directed to the general public, under substantially similar terms consistent with retail transactions, and are not for customized products, site licenses, or access contracts. For example, both consumers and employees use Web-browsing software and various plug-ins to display particular types of documents (pdf) or play audio and video clips. UCITA covers licensing in both markets because they are mass market transactions based on similar terms and they are neither customized products nor site licensed in the corporate market.

UCITA imposes special rules for mass market licenses, largely to recognize the needs for consumer protection while promoting economies of scale to achieve efficiency in standard form licenses. Consumer protections for mass market licenses include a requirement for mutual assent before or during initial access to the information, an opportunity to review and retain copies of the license terms, and restrictions on unconscionable terms. If the licensee's assent comes after payment, then there is a right to return the product, and certain consequential damages are recoverable. UCITA's efficiency provisions expressly condone the use of shrink-wrap and click-wrap as a legitimate manifestation of mutual assent to create licensing contracts.

Access Contracts

UCITA may bring some clarity to subscription service contracts with Internet access providers (ISPs). UCITA covers **access contracts**—contracts "to obtain by electronic means access to, or information from, an information processing system of another person."[10] This category includes ISP contracts with providers such as AOL, AT&T, and CompuServe, as well as remote data processing such as Reuters, LexisNexis, and Westlaw; e-mail systems such as Hotmail; and automatic database updating. UCITA §611 sets default rules for ISP service quality, including (1) keeping the system available in a manner consistent with contract terms and industry practice but permitting occasional access failures, (2) permitting periodic change to content unless specific content availability is guaranteed, and (3) clearly indicating use

10. UCITA §102(a)(1).

restrictions for the information accessed. In the future, UCITA could conceivably apply to wireless telematics (OnStar) and telecommunications (wireless Web services) and to permitting license termination without notice if the licensee is in breach of contract.

Other Licensing Terms in UCITA

UCITA provides default rules for most of the standard licensing terms discussed here. In most instances, laissez faire gives the licensor the freedom to negotiate a contract that specifies these terms, although some licensees may be able to negotiate more favorable provisions. Care must be taken when the license is prepared by one party because surprise and disappointment to the other party are likely. First, if the number of permitted users is not expressly limited, although it often is, UCITA limits it to a reasonable number of users in light of the information involved and the commercial circumstances. For example, if UCITA applied to recorded music, sharing one licensed sound recording with all students attending a particular university would be unreasonable. Second, there is no automatic right to receive error corrections, updates, improvements, or new versions of software or information. Third, UCITA favors licensors in matters involving ownership, transfer restrictions, and inspection rights.

Finally, UCITA licenses are not perpetual; they last for a term that is reasonable in light of the information involved and the commercial circumstances. Great care must be taken that the licensor's right to terminate does not permit the extortion of huge fees under threat of termination when the licensee has become highly dependent on the information. For example, a threat to terminate enterprise software just before the licensee's annual inventory needed for preparation of financial statements and its tax returns could amount to economic duress. UCITA provides no automatic protection from such extortion. To avoid such pressure, licensees must carefully examine license terms and negotiate fairer termination provisions.

ONLINE

UCITA report
http://www.wsba.org/businesslaw/lcc/report/2000/ucita.htm

TRADEMARK LICENSING

The licensing of trademarks is usually a B2B matter between two parties: (1) the licensor, who either manufactures a trademarked product or who owns a business service system, and (2) licensees, who independently do business selling the licensor's products or services. Trademark licensing benefits both the licensor and licensee because sales are enhanced with a strong brand image of the product or service. This image is created from the licensor's reputation for product quality, as enhanced by advertising and by the product's visibility at the licensee's retail level.

Consistency and coherence in the supply chain are key to maintaining the enforceability of trademark-licensing contracts. Early cases held that a licensor abandoned and lost rights in its trademark when it failed to control licensees' use of the trademark.[11] Today, the Lanham Act requires that the trademark owner must exercise control over the quality and nature of the products sold under the trademark. As discussed in Chapter 18, the basis of trademark rights is to assure that consumers are protected. Trademark is not premised on a pure private property rights theory that commercial symbols constitute a separate type of property. Instead, the validity of trademark licensing is tested by the fundamental principle

11. *Everett O. Fisk & Co. v. Fisk Teachers' Agency, Inc.*, 3 F.2d 7 (8th Cir., 1924).

Commentary

Controversy over UCITA

The public is still uncomfortable with the limitations imposed on the rights they acquire in licensing transactions. Most people are accustomed to having broad freedoms in using the products they buy: They can share them with friends and use them for personal or business purposes, most goods can be used anywhere in the world, buyers can resell goods, and the useful life of a purchase is determined by physical quality or durability. Everyone has the common experience that the limitations of tangible property are grounded in the physical limits of the property. This experience leads to a fundamental difference between sales and leases of tangible property on the one hand and the licensing of intangibles on the other. The attributes of owning rights in intangibles are not defined by their physical embodiment. In purchasing a license to use software or data, the disk is not the product. This point is not easily understood if the product purchased is encoded on a disk and packaged in a box. Instead, the *license is the product*, and the product is defined by the license terms. Licenses differ significantly.

Even with mounting experience on the Internet, the public is only slowly learning about the nonstandard and restrictive nature of license terms. Licenses create the property rights purchased. However, many people are not yet sufficiently experienced to ask questions about the license's duration, geographic limitations, fields of use restrictions, or transferability. Much of the controversy over UCITA is really founded in public ignorance of the long-standing licensing practices contained in UCITA. Furthermore, mass market licenses are generally nonnegotiable, which has clearly caused public confusion and indifference. Indeed, the public too often ignores the terms of shrink-wrap and click-wrap licenses inside computer packages or downloaded from online. The problem is aggravated because most licensors spend considerable resources to compose their mass market licenses. The resulting legalese is incomprehensible to the average person, and the mass market license terms are heavily biased in favor of the licensor.

Historically, the IP the public purchased was embodied in a physical object: Musical recordings are on tape or disk, literary works are printed in books, and information is printed in periodicals. Of course, licensees could make unauthorized copies by using technologies such as xerography or electronic recording, although people generally understand that most of these overt acts are prohibited as infringement. Anyway, there are natural limits on the proliferation of such imperfect copies. Such copies are unlikely to be mass-produced or to divert significant sales from the licensor. Content owners have relied on physical controls to prevent large-scale unauthorized copying and distribution. Today, because digital formats (MP3), digital storage (CD-R/W), and Internet distribution weaken these controls, content owners must turn to restrictive licensing.

The license defines computer information products; they are not defined by the public's common understanding of well-established commercial relationships. Although consumers blindly accept many licenses, they are much savvier about the terms and restrictions in other forms of limited use transaction, such as a lease on a car or an apartment. The most cogent criticism of UCITA is that it applies unfamiliar licensing conventions to mass market transactions. The public's inexperience with the diversity of licensing creates numerous opportunities for surprise and disappointment. Today, few consumers have the experience or expertise to understand most licenses. Given the lower stakes of Internet licensing transactions, few consumers ever take the time to do the analysis or obtain competent legal advice. UCITA may eventually raise public consciousness that the uniqueness of intangibles necessitates at least some restrictions on licensing. Eventually the public may acquire a better understand of licensing economics, and the public may embrace licensing restrictions.

UCITA is not without more legitimate concerns over its shortcomings. Critics charge that the introduction of UCITA provides content owners a rare opportunity to turn back some long-cherished IP user rights. Chapter 15 explains that IP users directly benefit from the first-sale doctrine and from the fair use exception to copyright infringement. UCITA and the Digital Millennium Copyright Act (DMCA) will make it difficult to do the reverse engineering that sparks incremental and evolutionary innovation. UCITA may facilitate pay-per-view pricing, effectively metering customer usage by charging for each use. Competition in licensing terms may come only slowly, limiting customer choice in negotiating more favorable mass market license terms at first. Licensors should exercise some restraint in drafting adhesion license contracts with unconscionable terms. If consumers perceive licenses are unfair, negative reaction seems inevitable, and the public will exert pressure for consumer protection legislation.

that commercial symbols function as a method to prevent consumer confusion. In modern business practice, trademark licensing is the fundamental organizing principle for a highly successful business method: the franchise.

FRANCHISES

Franchise, like *license*, is a somewhat imprecise term because it refers generally to the grant of a privilege. Franchise describes both governmental grants and private-contract relations. The early governmental grants of franchises were to public utilities (e.g., electric, gas, water, telephone). They were essentially legal monopolies to provide the service within a fixed geographic area. By contrast, the **private franchises** discussed here grant a privilege to conduct the business defined in the franchise agreement. Franchises are a form of business organization because they permit an owner to profit from the business's growth while retaining some control and limited liability.

Since the 1950s, franchises have grown tremendously and contribute significantly to retail sales of manufactured products and consumer services. Common franchise businesses include automobile dealerships, fast food and other types of restaurants, soft drink bottlers, and gas stations. There are also numerous service franchises such as hotels, motels, photocopying, vehicle rentals, tax preparation, cleaning or laundry, law, hair salons, and real estate brokerages.

What Is a Franchise?

There is no single definition of franchise. A **franchise** is generally recognized to be a contract that grants a license to conduct business under a registered trademark in which all participants share a community of interest in selling goods or services under specified conditions. A franchise system is a business-distribution organization composed of numerous independent retail units, the **franchisees**, which pay franchise fees and royalties to the **franchisor**, which supplies products, formulas, a trademark, and/or methods of operation. An FTC trade regulation rule defines a franchise as any continuing commercial relationship in which franchisees distribute goods or services identified by a trademark, service mark, trade name, or other commercial symbol. The franchisee is required or advised to meet the franchisor's quality standards, the franchisor secures a retail outlet or location for the franchisee, and the franchisee is obligated to make a payment or commits to make future payments to the franchisor or an affiliate.

The rights and duties of the franchisor and franchisee are largely defined by their franchise agreement. Although the parties may initially execute a vague commitment letter, the relationship is precisely defined in the franchise contract. The terms in franchise agreements vary among industries and even between brands within a product market. Most franchise agreements include trademark licenses as well as many of the distribution contract terms discussed throughout this chapter.

The FTC definition classifies several key franchise features into three general groups: control, assistance, and supply. The **control feature** is satisfied when the franchisor exerts significant controls over the franchisee's business operations: business organization, promotional activities, management, marketing plan, or business affairs. Control is an essential feature because the Lanham Act requires a trademark owner to enforce quality-control standards over all who use the trademark. This factor contributes to the success of fast-food franchises because consumers can rely on consistent quality at any restaurant in the system. The **assistance feature** exists when the franchisor provides significant assistance to the franchisee on managerial or operational matters. The **supply feature** is characterized by the franchisee's sale of goods or services supplied by the franchisor, its affiliate, or sourced from a third party designated by the franchisor. Most successful franchises include all these features.

Table of Contents

Rule Overview
Rule Requirements
Business Relationships Covered
Disclosure Options
Potential Liability for Violations
Legal Resources

I. Rule Overview

http://
www.ftc.gov/bcp/franchise/netrule.htm

The FTC further classifies franchises into package franchises, product franchises, and business-opportunity franchises. In a **package franchise**, the franchisee must use a uniform business format specified by the franchisor and identified by the trademark. The franchisee usually pays a periodic royalty determined by the level of sales. The franchisee in a **product franchise** distributes goods bearing the franchisor's trademark and produced by the franchisor or under the franchisor's control. Automobile dealers and soft drink bottlers are the best known examples of product franchises. They are usually required to pay an initial fee to purchase the franchise. The franchisor earns additional profits as part of the price of goods distributed through the franchisee (new cars, replacement parts, soft drink concentrate). The **business-opportunity franchise** is a catchall category that includes other franchises in which the franchisor supplies goods to the franchisee, the franchisor secures retail outlets for the franchisee, and a fee is paid.

Franchise Regulation

The regulatory approach to franchising has been decidedly laissez-faire. There is no single comprehensive regulatory scheme, and the parties have the freedom to negotiate varying terms in their franchise agreements. Some franchisors exercise strong controls over their franchisees, but others exercise only weak control. Therefore, as the states and federal governments have gained experience with franchises, they have passed narrow regulations to target specific aspects after abuses are discovered. Franchise regulation generally falls into three major areas: (1) protection of franchisees, (2) protection of customers, and (3) protection of competition and the markets.

Franchises are most successful when the franchisor designs a popular product and business method and then sustains the system's growth by recruiting numerous successful franchisees. For the large, well-known franchises, it is easy to recruit competent franchisees. However, newer, smaller, and unestablished franchises must aggressively market their franchise systems to be successful. Franchisors often use seminars and information packages that describe business prospects to potential franchisees in glowing terms. The failure of many franchises in the late 1960s and early 1970s led to federal disclosure requirements and to state regulations in nearly half the states. Franchisors or brokers dealing in franchises must disclose sufficient information for the prospective purchaser to make an informed decision. This disclosure often includes the name, address, and business experience of the franchisor and its affiliates; its litigation experience; recent financial statements; a copy of the franchise agreement; and a description of all the fees, royalties, or hidden costs necessary to operate the franchise. The antitrust aspects of franchises are discussed in Chapter 19.

ONLINE
State Franchise Laws
http://www.ftc.gov/bcp/franchise/netdiscl.htm

Franchise Termination

Franchise agreements typically provide for termination of the parties' obligations so that neither is required to continue if the relationship becomes unprofitable or unsuitable. The franchise relationship usually runs for a renewable fixed term but can be terminated "for cause" after notice is given. Most franchisees invest considerable time and money to start and maintain their businesses, but individual franchisees are relatively powerless to modify the termination provisions. Experience with arbitrary terminations by some franchisors has led to litigation and legislation to protect franchisee rights.

Automobile dealer franchisees are protected from bad-faith termination by a federal statute, the **Automobile Dealer Day in Court Act**. This law also prevents automobile manufacturers from threatening dealers with termination unless they accept more cars, parts, or other services from the manufacturer. The **Petroleum Marketing Products Act** gives gas station operators an opportunity to purchase the premises when the franchisor refuses to renew the lease. Several states have passed similar statutes to protect franchisees in other types of business. Absent such statutory protection, some franchisees have been successful convincing courts to limit the franchisor's right to terminate at will. These suits are often based on the UCC's good faith provision. Some courts award damages to the franchisee equal to the out-of-pocket expenses in purchasing the franchise. Other courts have expanded the allowable damages to include the loss of future profits expected in operating the franchise.

PUBLICITY, ENDORSEMENT, OR AFFILIATION

Marketing increasingly claims that relationships among firms and persons mutually enhance their individual brand images. For example, advertisers use the appeal of celebrity endorsement to enhance the desirability of their products. Websites post trademarked logos of independent firms to enhance each firm's goodwill with the other firm's brand image—cobranding. Independent firms join in strategic alliances to leverage their specific advantages into stronger products. The reputation of search engines and portals improves with more reliable links to useful sites. How do affiliations raise legal or regulatory questions?

Affiliation requires some compliance with consumer protections, privacy, IP, and licensing law. First, the descriptions and actual performance of such affiliations should be accurate to avoid liability for fraud or false advertising. Second, licenses may be needed before the parties begin their public activities and before they create or publicize their relationship. Generally, such licensing may cover interests such as an individual celebrity's right to privacy, copyrights in another firm's content, and trademarks of other firms used by each firm to demonstrate a relationship exists with other firms. Contracts between these participants are often needed to create the affiliation. Third, linking may involve moral rights because the linked site's reputation is at stake. Licenses may also be needed in two key areas: (1) celebrity endorsements and (2) Internet affiliations.

Licensing Celebrity Endorsement

Celebrities have the exclusive right to control the commercial exploitation of their endorsements or personae. This right is based on an inherent property interest derived from the state law of privacy rights, discussed in Chapter 14, called misappropriation or the right of publicity. The publicity right can also be based on two tort theories that an unauthorized endorsement (1) causes damage to the celebrity's reputation or (2) constitutes a misrepresentation. What are the elements of a celebrity's persona that can be protected? Endorsement law protects the celebrity from unauthorized use of various separate elements of the persona: name, likeness (photo, drawing, look-alike), and voice or style (the unique "sound" of Bette Midler's singing voice).[12]

Authorization is needed to use a celebrity's endorsement; New York law makes such an endorsement a crime without written authority. This permission should be granted in a written license by the celebrity or by the estate of a deceased celebrity (in 13 states). Licensing terms should include the duration, the elements authorized, geographic limitations, itemization of products endorsed, compensation, and the celebrity's approval over the particular use (creative control). A license to use a **stock photo** from a photographer does not assure that the photographed celebrity gave permission. A **morals clause** may create grounds for termination if the celebrity's image is tarnished by scandal or illegal activity. Perhaps the celebrity should have a similar right to terminate if the manufacturer or its product line falls into disrepute.

Internet Affiliations: Linking, Framing and Metatags

Affiliations on the Internet have grown rapidly. Websites link to unaffiliated sites or otherwise use their content. Most are not authorized by the site linked. Does this raise IP infringement or other legal issues? If so, would it be best to secure permission to link or frame, using an authorization by license? Downloading creates a copy of copyrighted expression to the user's RAM and screen and is often printed or saved. Those who post to websites know the whole World Wide Web can access their content, so it can be argued that posting material to a website by implication grants permission to view. Does any such permission extend to linking, framing, saving, printing, or sending such files to others?

Linking or hypertext links occur when one website, the **linking site**, provides a complete uniform resource locator (URL) to another website, the **linked site**, to access a document. The link may appear on the linking site's page in its raw form [http://www.thompson.com], or the raw form URL can be embedded within a highlighted word, phrase, title, button, or graphic. Browsers (Netscape Communicator, Microsoft Explorer), Web-authoring tools (FrontPage), viewers (Adobe Acrobat), word processors, and many other computer applications automatically convert URLs directly into clickable links when keyed into a document as it is created or modified. When these webpages are posted, downloaded, or otherwise distributed (e-mail attachment), they are used by other users to automatically launch the download of material contained at that linked site.

The culture of the Internet expects linking to flourish unhindered by property rights claims by the linked site's owner. Further, it is argued that site owners wishing to block access to unauthorized or unknown outsiders may simply use password protection, cookie technology, or some other authentication scheme to exclude unwanted downloads. Under copyright infringement law, linking is not a reproduction or public display of another's copyrighted expression. Linking simply points the way and saves the user from typing in sometimes long and tedious URLs. However, there is potential liability in linking. For example, if a website provides notice or has a user license requiring permission to link, then an unauthorized link might constitute a trespass. The use of a copyrighted graphic or trademarked logo as the link

12. *Midler v. Young & Rubicam*, 944 F.2d 909 (1991), *cert.denied* 503 U.S. 951 (1992).

without permission from the IP's owner could constitute infringement. Further, if users are led to believe that the linking site is affiliated or endorsed by the linked site, two other theories of liability may arise: palming off and tortious interference with business, discussed in Chapters 7 and 18.

Deep linking bypasses the home page of a linked site and directly accesses internal pages. Website owners often want users to pass through shallower pages for various reasons: Users are exposed to banner ads, information is collected, cookies set or retrieved, and the user might make different choices instead. Website owners might claim that deep linking alters the sequence of pages that users see, which constitutes an unauthorized derivative work infringing the linked site's copyright. As of this writing, no case has held that deep linking is infringement. However, in *Ticketmaster Corp. v. Tickets.com, Inc.*,[13] the trial court dismissed a trespass theory of deep linking but permitted three other claims to go to trial: infringement, palming off, and tortious interference with business. The case was later settled.

Until the legal risks of linking become better settled, both netiquette and careful risk management suggest getting permission to link whenever the linked site demands permission and for deep linking. Deep linking may deprive linked sites from collecting banner ad revenues from advertisers. Linking licenses may include many of the usual licensing terms: grant clause, termination, and duration. They may also include aesthetic and presentation requirements and some sharing of data or ad revenues when collected by the parties. Linking to illegal, terrorist, or pornographic materials may eventually become illegal. For example, both Germany and Japan prohibit some such links.

Framing displays parts of two websites simultaneously. Usually the linking site creates a perimeter frame or border, often displaying its logo and other links of its own choosing. Inside the frame is displayed content from the linked site. Some novice users may think there is an affiliation between the sites unless there is conspicuous notice to the contrary. The outer edges of the framed site, including its ads, may be partially blocked by the frame. Alternatively, the framed site may be shrunk to fit inside the frame. This may infringe on the framed site's right to make derivative works. Framing raises the linking site's value by free-riding on the linked site's value. However, experienced users know their browsers permit the framed site to be opened separately in an unframed page.

Metatags are hidden html codes in webpages that ostensibly describe the website's content to signal search engines. Metatags help users screen for sought-after content or screen out objectionable content (obscenity). Search engines give precedence to websites when the search term appears numerous times. Some unscrupulous website operators include famous trademarks belonging to others or use inaccurate descriptions in their metatags. This practice is arguably fraudulent because these intentionally misdescriptive search terms cause search engines to more prominently display these websites when users are looking for other sites, causing users to suffer initial confusion.[14] Website traffic counters credit such hits to the fraudulent website, and some users may stay at the websites even if they were searching for other content. Such misuse of metatags may cause consumer confusion or dilution that infringes a trademark owner's rights. The fraudulent inflation of website hits may also violate the banner advertising contract or constitute false advertising.

---

13. 54 U.S.P.Q.2d 1344 (C.D.Cal. 2000).

14. See *Brookfield Communications v. West Coast Entertainment Corp.*, 174 F.3d 1036 (9th Cir., 1999).

International Commentary

Challenges in International Licensing

Licensing in international markets poses some additional challenges and complexity. The usual difficulties of international commerce can plague licensing, such as risks of asset appropriation by foreign governments, litigation uncertainties in potentially hostile foreign courts, misunderstood cultural biases, and exchange rate risks when the compensation is denominated in a foreign currency. Care should be taken before directing selling efforts to foreign markets. Foreign nations may control the movement of information, encryption, and currency flows across their borders. Some content may be illegal in foreign nations (blasphemy, obscenity, nonnative language, differing accounts of historical events, unpopular political ideas). Domestic export restrictions can also be problematic; encryption software was once classified as munitions (military weaponry), severely restricting its export outside the United States.

Various nations have somewhat different IP law that may impose unexpected standards of infringement. For example, the Europeans believe in stronger moral rights. It may be necessary to hire local agents in foreign markets to administer licenses: distribution, collection, and remittance of licensing fees. Territorial limitations are particularly difficult to monitor and enforce in foreign markets. Some nations, particularly developing countries, fail to respect IP and prefer to capture ideas freely that could improve their standards of living. It is advisable to identify and insist on dispute resolution methods and forums that promise fair treatment to all parties.

LEASING

Many transactions are neither sales nor licenses but occupy a middle ground, leases. A **lease** is a contract granting possession and use of property in exchange for the payment of rent. The owner of the property who sells rights to use the property is the **lessor**. The party acquiring temporary possession and use under the lease is the **lessee**. Leases of real estate (land, buildings) have been a common form of contract for hundreds of years in markets for residences and for business uses such as agriculture, manufacturing or warehouse facilities, and office space. Real estate leases are governed by the common law of real property and various landlord-tenant statutes. Leases of goods are governed by the UCC Article 2A, which has been passed by 49 states (but not Louisiana). Goods leases became quite popular in the twentieth century as their tax and financing advantages became better understood and then were widely accepted. Long experience with unconscionable lease terms led to consumer protections in leasing.

Between the 1950s and the 1980s, many of the original technologies that serve as infrastructure for cyberspace were leased, not purchased. Telecommunications equipment, mainframe computers and their peripherals, and the software to run them all were leased by the manufacturers or their leasing subsidiaries to both commercial customers and to consumers. The proportion of computers and phone systems under lease dropped dramatically after the AT&T antitrust breakup and after PCs became more commonplace. Since then, most customers purchase their own equipment. Leasing was imposed on customers because it permitted greater control over the uses of these technologies and arguably legitimized the tying that lessors once commonly required.

Today, leasing of such equipment is not just an interesting phase of business history. Leasing is making a comeback, particularly of PCs to business clients. Web hosting agreements may include the lease of server and storage capacity. In the future, software leasing may reemerge because vendors are attempting to extract higher revenues for the use of their programs. However, a revision of UCC Article

ONLINE

NCCUSL website of uniform laws
http://www.nccusl.org

IIA that is underway by the National Conference of Commissioners on Uniform State Laws (NCCUSL) could exclude software from leasing in favor of licensing under UCITA.

The leasing of goods under UCC Article 2A essentially mirrors the structure of UCC Article 2 (Sales): both cover transactions in goods. Many contractual elements of sales and leases are similar, and Chapters 10, 11, and 12 have already covered the elements of contract law, such as mutual assent, consideration, defenses, writings, warranties, legality, and performance. Each lease is created in a **lease agreement** that defines the transfer of rights and possession. It includes the lessee's duties to pay rent and preserve the property leased. The statute of frauds requires a written lease if the total of payments is more than $1,000. A **sublease** provision may permit the lessee to further lease the property to another person, a sublessee, or it might prohibit such activity. **Consumer leases** made by merchant lessors have special protections if the total payments are less than $25,000 and the goods are leased primarily for personal, family, or household use. **Finance leases** are three-party transactions involving the lessee, a lessor who simply finances the lease, and the original supplier of the goods. The lessee's duty to make lease payments to the lessor is independent of the supplier's breach in supplying the goods. This arrangement substantially protects the lessor from loss if the goods are defective and the lessee tries to pressure the supplier by threatening to stop making payments to the lessor. The pending revision of UCC Article 2A would better enable electronic lease contracting, as in other revised articles.

COMPUTER SERVICES AND DEVELOPMENT

Major areas of concern are contracts with outside vendors to provide computer services: the development of software or websites, the hosting and delivery of software applications, the hosting of websites, and the development of multimedia. Only the largest and most technically savvy firms have the expertise to do all these functions in-house. Most firms developing Internet commerce strategies must manage the technology transfer issues raised by computer service contracts, including ownership and control of IP and information, limitations on their scope of use, and the duration of the relationship.

An important distinction was made in the discussion of mass market licenses under UCITA: Computer services are generally long-term B2B transactions that must be separately negotiated. They are rarely the standard form contracts used in most transactions. Standard forms are only a starting point for the parties to further customize their relationship and the products provided. Negotiations generally begin with the customer's first draft that defines the requirements. The draft is then often communicated in a **request for proposals** (RFP), and one or more candidate firms may respond with a concrete proposal.

Negotiations move smoothly if the client has done some planning beforehand, understands what is needed, and has researched comparable software or websites to specify functionality. Preparing proposals is costly and risky. If another bidder wins the contract or the customer withdraws the RFP, there may be no legal basis to bill the customer for the time and expense of developing the proposal. Although proposals are protected by copyright, the bidder's ideas or trade secrets are not protected without an NDA from the customer. Negotiations should result in a written engagement contract, specifically defining the compensation, system requirements, delivery, testing and acceptance of deliverables, ownership, rights to make updates, confidentiality, and warranties on IP, functionality, and scalability.

The creation of IP rights discussed in Chapters 15 through 18 and the licensing of IP rights discussed in this chapter are critical to developing useful terms in both software and web development contracts. When IP belonging to third parties is used, the burden of obtaining and paying for permission to license that content must be allocated between the developer and the client. The parties should also agree on the ownership of IP created during the development: software, websites, and website content. Developers want ownership in order to resell the software, information, or content in similar projects for other clients. Also, developers can raise their clients' switching costs by holding ownership, which tends to lock in clients to do most of their future business for maintenance, updates, and upgrades with that developer. By contrast, many clients seek ownership to reduce their switching costs. Clients legitimately hope to prevent the developer from supplying their competitors. If the developer retains ownership, the client usually needs to negotiate the right to update and modify as needed to change the software's functionality or update websites.

Software development contracts raise similar issues. Ownership, control, and licensing of the software are the key points of contention. Parties are most satisfied and suffer the least costly surprise when ownership and control are balanced to satisfy both sides' interests. For example, there is considerable development expense in creating an enterprise software package. Software developers must be able to repackage their work for other clients, or must charge higher fees. Generally, the software developer owns the major functional subroutines, tools, and templates, which can be adapted for other clients' use. Clients must be free to use, modify, and adapt the software efficiently as their business needs evolve. A client will seek to own any new code written to customize the software for that client's particular application. The parties arrive at this balanced split through several stages of negotiations, first creating a scope for the project in which the client's needs are defined, then iteratively adding details to the development work plan, and establishing specifications, milestones, deliverable dates, performance testing, and progress payments.

Web hosting relationships are bundles of services that provide Internet access for users to the client's content. Web hosts hold the key to the client's success in using the web for commercial purposes. The host may agree to obtain domain name registrations, operate sufficient and reliable Internet gateways and server capacity, post and update clients' website content, collect and maintain data (users' private information and transaction information), and administer the transaction processing needed for e-commerce sites. Another form of hosting involves application service providers (ASP). ASP relations involve a client's access to software and data, licensed from a second-party vendor but hosted by a third party, the ASP, using the ASP's servers and telecommunications facilities. ASP relationships are emerging as an important business model for e-commerce because the client need not install the software on its computers. The ASP model permits the vendor to use various forms of compensation, such as flat fees or metered according to usage.

QUESTIONS

1. XYZ Computer Corp. hired Mr. A as a staff electrical design engineer under an employment-at-will with no written contract. A and several other engineers were assigned to design a new scientific workstation computer terminal. Part way through the project, A quit to form his own computer workstation firm. Before

he left, he attracted several other engineers from the project to join him. Eventually A's new firm developed a competing workstation that used several new technologies originally developed at XYZ. What rights does XYZ have against A?

2. In question 1, what contract terms could XYZ insert into its employment contracts with engineers to avoid some aspects of the competition from A and the others?

3. What is the essential difference between leasing tangible property that is protectable by possession and licensing intangible intellectual property that must be registered or otherwise controlled for effective protection?

4. Ms. B was hired by the ABC Investment Management Corp. as an account broker. B's superior tipped her with some confidential inside information, ordered her to share it with numerous clients, and told her to actively encourage them to invest in the subject companies. B strongly believed this was illegal insider trading under the securities laws and could subject her and ABC to criminal prosecution. B was fired after refusing to tip the inside information to clients. Explain how the confidentiality duty could apply to this situation.

5. What are the various legal controls over franchise operations, and why did they arise?

6. Discuss the major terms in license agreements that control the scope and extent of the IP transferred. Relate these terms to the various "methods to slice the salami."

7. Licensing transactions are significantly different from other common limited use transactions, such as leasing. This leads to confusion, indifference, and surprise. Explain the controversy over consumer acceptance of information-licensing practices.

8. Microsoft hosted an entertainment information website, Seattle Sidewalk, with links to activities in Seattle. Links were provided to purchase tickets to various entertainment events that were deep links to TicketMaster.com. These links permitted users of the Microsoft site to bypass Ticketmaster's front pages. Explain the legal difficulties that could arise if a website operator made unauthorized use of other websites through the practices of linking, framing, or metatags. What IP theories are involved? What economic interests are allegedly violated? See *Ticketmaster Corp. v. Microsoft Corp.*, Civ.Action No. CV 97-3055 (C.D.Cal. 4/28/97).

9. Michigan Document Services provided services to instructors at the University of Michigan who created anthologies and "coursepacks." These are customized collections of articles, other published works and the instructors' own problems and graphics into a readings packet appropriate for the instructors' courses. Various publishers of the copyrighted works used in these anthologies sued Michigan Document Services for copyright infringement for failure to secure permission and remit royalties or permission fees. What logistical and legal difficulties are there for instructors to develop and rightfully create such anthologies? See *Princeton University Press v. Michigan Document Services, Inc.*, 99 F.3d 1381 (6th Cir., 1996).

CHAPTER 14

Privacy

Privacy assumed major prominence during the twentieth century. Technological advances have made it progressively easier and cheaper to discover, record, and use **personally identifiable information (PII)**. Society is so crowded that few people can withdraw into isolation, either in our communities or in cyberspace. Humans are social and industrious animals with strong emotional and practical needs to interact. Yet privacy remains an aspiration for most, during at least part of our lives. Accommodating privacy requires an understanding of abstract privacy concepts. Society must then balance each individual's interest in confidentiality and seclusion with some legitimate use of private information for society's protection.

Privacy will probably remain a *balance* between individual interests in secrecy or solitude and society's interests in order and efficiency. Privacy questions arise in many aspects of law enforcement, as well as in business relations. Data about individuals' past conduct, their interests, and future plans are needed to exercise discipline, maintain order, assess risks, and predict future performance, such as in contracts of employment, loans, and insurance. Individuals' privacy rights are limited for public health, national security, and the public's right to know. Such data may also become useful to more precisely market products to the most interested users. The effective use of PII may finally permit marketing efficiencies long promised by economic theory.

It seems natural and rational for individuals to resist revealing their PII. Long experience justifies the fear that exposure of private information makes individuals vulnerable. History reveals that several aspects of privacy interests have been fundamental to civil liberty and essential to individual freedom, autonomy, dignity, and good taste. Privacy issues can be expected to engender strong emotional, even visceral, reactions that can translate into draconian regulatory reactions to suppress what the public perceives as privacy abuses.

This chapter discusses the development of privacy law, its application in traditional transactions, and its adaptation to cyberspace and e-commerce. First, the baseline of existing privacy law and society's expectations are discussed. Second, the concept of privacy is explored because it forms the basis for privacy regulation both in the traditional economy and in cyberspace. Third, the basic architecture of data collection and data management is reviewed to pinpoint the workings of privacy law and policy. Fourth, the economic incentives of private data collection are examined to explain the evolution of current privacy law and predict what new privacy laws will emerge. Finally, existing privacy law is examined from constitutional sources, statutes, and regulations. A comparison is made of privacy laws in key sectors: on line, telecommunications, children, financial, workplace, and health care. Law affecting these key sectors is examined from various sources, including international, federal, state, and private self-regulation levels. Society will look to self-regulation and privacy law to resolve the challenges as technologies advance in the collection, archiving, analysis, and distribution of private information.

POLITICAL AND SOCIAL CONTEXT OF PRIVACY

With all the controversy emerging over privacy on line and even in traditional contexts, the lack of comprehensive U.S. privacy protection and policies is not surprising. Privacy laws are narrowly drawn to particular industry sectors—the **sectoral approach**. Privacy law is generally enacted only after considerable experience with activities the public views as abusive. This approach is consistent with both laissez-faire economics and the common law approach to lawmaking. As a result:

U.S. Privacy Law Protection is a hodge-podge, patch-work of sectoral protections, narrowly construed and derived from constitutional, statutory and regulatory provisions of international, federal and state law.

The U.S. sectoral approach to privacy is different from the European approach, discussed in a later section examining the European Union's (EU's) **omnibus** method. The essentially comprehensive and uniform EU approach to privacy covers most industries and governments with strong privacy rights. Privacy advocates urge the United States to follow this European approach, but many business and government interests oppose the EU's strong, omnibus privacy rights.

Most people in a free society realize that privacy is a fundamental right, a civil liberty interest essential to individual freedom, autonomy, and dignity. The current intensity of the public's interest in privacy probably arises because technological advances in data collection, storage, integration, and secondary use heighten people's concern about potential abuse of private information. Computerized telecommunications and the perceived value of private data result in the **commoditization of private information**, by transforming private information to a commodity easily shared, traded, sold, and presumably valued. In the words of Sun Microsystem's CEO Scott McNealy, "You have zero privacy anyway. Get over it!"

Private information is subject to **data creep**; that is, data collected for one purpose eventually finds its way to secondary and even tertiary uses. For example, Social Security numbers (**ssn**) were originally intended only for keeping records of payments made through the Federal Insurance Contributions Act (FICA) and retirement benefits paid out from the Social Security system. However, the ssn is now the primary individual information locator for both government and the private sector. Information collected for one limited purpose is inevitably used for other purposes, often without the knowledge or consent of the **subject individual**, the person described by the information. Often, the PII is used to the subject individual's disadvantage to deny a loan, insurance coverage, or a job.

Although the public may never know about *all* the methods and uses for their PII, there is a general unease developing about misuse. Many people are suspicious about requests for their PII when it seems irrelevant to transactions, and e-commerce and e-government may suffer without changes in substantive privacy rights. This impacts the public's perception of privacy practices by both governments and private firms. The American public's attitudes towards privacy are changing; most people are becoming savvier and more careful with their PII. According to Alan F. Westin, a privacy expert and director of the Center for Social and Legal Research, a privacy think tank, the public is segmented into three fairly distinct groups in their privacy attitudes and expectations.[1]

SEGMENTATION OF THE AMERICAN PUBLIC ON PRIVACY ISSUES

- **Privacy fundamentalists** value privacy highly, summarily reject business claims that PII needs are legitimate, advocate that individuals refuse to disclose PII, and seek strong regulation of privacy rights.
- **Privacy pragmatists** balance their personal privacy with societal needs for PII, examine privacy policies and practices, disclose PII when economically rational and appropriate, favor industry self-regulation of privacy (voluntary privacy standards and practices), and support privacy regulation only when self-regulation fails.
- **Privacy unconcerned** are typically indifferent about disclosing PII, trust in the benefits derived from disclosing PII, and are unlikely to support strong privacy rights or regulation.

Studies show that the number of privacy fundamentalists has remained steady throughout the 1990s at about 25% of the population. The number of privacy pragmatists has been growing, from 55% during the early 1990s to 63% by year 2000. The proportion of privacy unconcerned has fallen from 20% down to 12%. These data probably reflect the growing public awareness of data collection practices and the uses for their PII.

WHAT *IS* PRIVACY?

Privacy is an imprecise yet complex term. In its most general sense, **privacy** refers to several distinct interests, individual expectations, legal rights, and PII data practices. Some synonyms for *privacy* are helpful to gain perspective: seclusion, solitude, retreat from intrusion, intimacy, isolation, secrecy, concealment, and separateness. Consider the formal *Webster's* definition of privacy.

> ***Privacy:*** withdrawn from company or public view, secrecy, one's private life or personal affairs.

Privacy probably has only one absolute meaning: maintaining secrecy over PII. However, in the business context, privacy has no absolute meaning. Instead, it is a relative term determined by the societal balance between disclosure and secrecy as set forth in public policy by privacy laws and actual practice.

The variety of privacy interests may be better understood through the lens of societal motives. Privacy was one of the American colonists' main hopes in their

1. Alan F. Westin, Interpretive Essay, in *Public Records and the Responsible Use of Information*, (Hackensack, N.J.: Choicepoint, 2000), p. 5.

risky move to the New World. Many colonists sought to leave behind government oppression in their native lands. As detailed later, many U.S. Constitutional freedoms are actually forms of privacy: religious freedom, restrictions on search and seizure, prohibitions against the quartering of soldiers, freedom of speech, freedom of press and association, due process, and equal protection. Under this vision, privacy is a fundamental right necessary to achieve liberty, without interference from government or from powerful private interests. Privacy actually promotes competition, a point clearly made in Chapter 16. When individual or firm activities can be held secret, this private information is actually a form of property if the individual or firm exploits it for economic advantage. Privacy rights are critical to excluding the intrusion of others who might appropriate the property rights in private information. Privacy also seems essential to intimacy.

Privacy is a fundamental and enduring expectation of biblical origins. Consider the story of the Garden of Eden. When Adam and Eve ate of the forbidden fruit, they were condemned to suffer *shame* for their transgressions and feel *modesty* about their bodies. Shame throughout history demonstrates that imperfect human decision making and behavior are inevitable and that humans want to avoid embarrassment. When zones of privacy are plentiful, individuals risk less public contempt and retribution. Shame may be a sufficient consequence for many people to repent and voluntarily correct their own bad habits when motivated by the promise of redemption and the self-satisfaction of virtue. Similarly, modesty serves important societal purposes as another form of privacy. Shyness or prudent dress and appearance probably protect individuals from harmful intrusions by societal predators.

Acquiring, maintaining, and overcoming privacy are all costly pursuits. Privacy is argued to be a benefit earned, inherited, or acquired, either with specific effort or as the result of obscurity and public indifference. Consider the extensive efforts of the rich and famous to obtain seclusion. Many spend heavily on isolated residences, gated communities, private clubs, and security systems to keep the public out. Millionaire recluse Howard Hughes feared disease from physical exposure to common people, so he hid from the public and even from his old friends. However, privacy deteriorates as outsiders expend resources to breach the veil of privacy. Consider the **paparazzi**, freelance photographers who hound the famous for candid and revealing photographs. They overcame the privacy efforts of the late British Princess Diana when they concentrated their efforts to stalk, track and pursue her.

Maintaining privacy in cyberspace is similar. Technological advances in capturing, archiving, processing, and disseminating information can be frustrated with clever but often expensive counter-measures and with privacy regulations. Consider the famous words of Phyllis McGinley, a twentieth-century American poet and essayist:

Who could deny that privacy is a jewel? It has always been the mark of privilege, the distinguishing feature of a truly urbane culture. Out of the cave, the tribal tepee, the pueblo, the community fortress, man emerged to build himself a house of his own with a shelter in it for himself and his diversions. Every age has seen it so. The poor might have to huddle together in cities for need's sake, and the frontiersman cling to his neighbors for the sake of protection. But in each civilization, as it advanced, those who could afford it chose the luxury of a withdrawing-place.[2]

2. Phyllis McGinley, A Lost Privilege, in *The Province of the Heart*, New York: Viking (1959).

PUBLIC-SECTOR VERSUS PRIVATE-SECTOR

In exploring the boundaries of privacy, distinguishing between the public sector and the private sector is also helpful. This dichotomy is useful for two major reasons. First, public versus private often differentiates the ownership and control of institutions. In a democracy, **public sector** activities are owned and controlled politically—that is, by *all* the public equally, as implemented through various government entities. By contrast, **private sector** enterprises are owned and controlled largely by only *some* individuals or business firms. Private sector ownership is seldom in equal shares; instead, it is most often in varying proportions according to the size of the owner's investments. Second, many fundamental privacy laws, particularly those in the U.S. Constitution and many federal statutes, are aimed at preventing privacy abuses by governments acting in the public sector. Until recently, prohibitions against privacy intrusion by private individuals or private firms were much less pervasive. Concern over private sector intrusions has increased in importance, along with the growth of the Internet.

In part, the traditional notion of privacy underlies the public sector versus private sector distinction, at least in most democratic nations; that is, open records laws expose to public scrutiny much of the inner workings, transactions, and other decisions governments and their agencies make. The public accountability of public sector institutions means that many records are openly disclosed and government meetings are open to press coverage and public attendance. Most of the private sector can keep much more of its activity confidential because the right of privacy is a fundamental component of individual autonomy, liberty, and dignity.

PRIVATELY HELD VERSUS PUBLICLY TRADED

Another use of the public-private distinction relates to the extent that ownership of a business firm is closely held by a few shareholders and is not traded on a national securities exchange—that is, **privately held**. This is distinguished from large "for-profit" private-sector firms that have their securities traded on national exchanges. These are called **publicly traded**, or sometimes simply **public firms**. The securities laws limit the confidentiality of internal information from publicly traded firms. Public firms must generally disclose considerable strategic, financial, and operational information before they may access the public capital markets. This privacy balance favors the role corporate information plays in assuring fair capital markets over an individual firm's interests in concealing information from competitors, suppliers, customers, employees, shareholders, or law enforcement.

PRIVACY VERSUS CONFIDENTIALITY

The similarities and differences between confidentiality and privacy are important to understand. The laws, contracts, and practices used to protect confidential corporate information are somewhat different from those protecting PII. Both situations involve secret information that could be used to the advantage of outsiders and possibly to the disadvantage of the subject. The incentive for secrecy by individuals and firms is also similar: Both seek to avoid misuse of secrets that would disadvantage the subject individual or firm. However, corporate confidentiality and individual privacy are often treated differently (1) because individuals may not be as sophisticated as business firms and (2) because of transaction costs. Privacy law provides more automatic protection of PII because individuals may lack the sophistication and bargaining power to adequately protect themselves. Individual PII is collected in numerous, low-value transactions that are more efficiently regulated through default rules.

Business firms can fend for themselves, and they are expected to recognize the value of particular information. Firms should determine what pieces of information should be kept confidential and then limit information transfers with restrictions in their contracts of employment, supply, consulting, and sales. To minimize transaction costs, firms can develop and impose appropriate restrictions in **form contracts** that precisely define their relations with others. Confidentiality is a fundamental part of all agents' fiduciary duties. The legal methods and protections for corporate confidentiality are discussed in the trade secret section of Chapter 16 and also in the employment and distribution contracts sections of Chapter 13.

Shift in Privacy Focus: From Intrusions by Government to Include Intrusions by Private Parties

Privacy rights protect individuals from intrusion by government and from intrusion by private parties (other individuals, institutions, business firms). In America, privacy rights initially focused on protection for citizens from the government intrusions suffered during the colonial era. Indeed, much of the law of criminal process affords zones of privacy from oppressive and arbitrary government action. In those days, businesses were small, making it impractical, even futile, for businesses to collect or analyze PII data for large segments of the population.

The focus of privacy concerns shifted as the frontier was tamed and the population density increased, particularly in the cities. During the Industrial Revolution, the focus of privacy began to shift from concern over government intrusion to concern about privacy intrusions from private parties. Concern for the sanctity of private property rights reemerged in the late nineteenth century. In the mid-twentieth century, another wave of privacy concern followed, this time over PII, as consumer credit proliferated and the consumer use of insurance became common. This era resembles much of the current privacy debate. The question again is what PII business should use to make employment decisions, grant or deny credit, underwrite or set premiums for insurance, hone their marketing efforts, adjust pricing, or refuse to sell to particular individuals. High-tech investigatory tools are accessible to individuals and business firms that once were available only to government spies. Employers feel a greater need to monitor employee activities and performance because of the growth in individual autonomy and responsibility. Of course, concern over government privacy intrusion will persist as long as government is large and powerful enough to create a realistic threat of repression and tyranny.

REGULATION OF PRIVATE DATA MANAGEMENT

In the United States, privacy rights are imposed only *after* disputes show a need to settle competing forces. This is a clash over two important values: (1) individual autonomy and (2) personal experience. Privacy must be compared with ownership of data, the informational meaning given that data, and the intangible intellectual property right to use this knowledge or sell it as a service. The controversy over privacy regulation is essentially a struggle to resolve these often conflicting claims when society finds it appropriate to intervene by setting policies for the benefit of individuals and society. For example, this conflict is settled in favor of individual privacy interests when restrictions are placed on data collection or use, such as the financial and health care information privacy restrictions discussed later. By contrast, the balance can also favor the rights to use and own observations and perceptions; examples include broadening law enforcement investigatory powers and the protectability of corporate information and data as trade secrets.

BASIC MECHANICS OF MODERN PRIVATE DATA ACTIVITIES

The basic structure of data management activities shows how and where privacy regulations will be focused. The privacy balance is reconciled by restrictions placed at several major choke points along the sequence of events typical to the data management process. Most of these regulatory approaches are *preventive*; they seek to deter the intrusion. However, if prevention fails, damage suits are a *curative* solution for past, unprevented privacy violations. No privacy regulation could long be effective without a clear, technical understanding of data management practices. New techniques could be developed to circumvent weak restrictions. Privacy regulation can encourage or limit particular activities at each or any stage during data management.

There are three basic steps in the data management of PII: (1) collection, (2) analysis, and (3) use. These steps can be further broken down into additional discrete segments. Consider the flow and processing of PII in Exhibit 14.1.

Data Acquisition

The first step in PII data management is collection, or **data acquisition**, the observation of some activity, followed by collecting and coding into data storage. In cyberspace, much observed information is captured as it flows through telecommunications wires, along the airwaves, within networks, or at particular websites. Information **capture** generally refers to the interception and storage of data during its creation, entry, discovery, detection, or transmission by an interception device installed somewhere en route. For example, in traditional commerce, information is directly observed and captured as transactions are recorded. Vendors and delivery services must make reports of consumer purchases, loan payments or defaults must be recorded by lenders, an insured's careful or risky acts are highly relevant data routinely gathered by insurers for underwriting, and employers must record and analyze employee activities as they accomplish job-related goals or engage in misconduct. In the on-line world, websites are visited, hot links are clicked, queries are answered with PII data, cookie data is available to servers from user's PCs as electronic probes read data files, and numerous other types of activities become more readily observable. This on-line data is captured when electronic records are made.

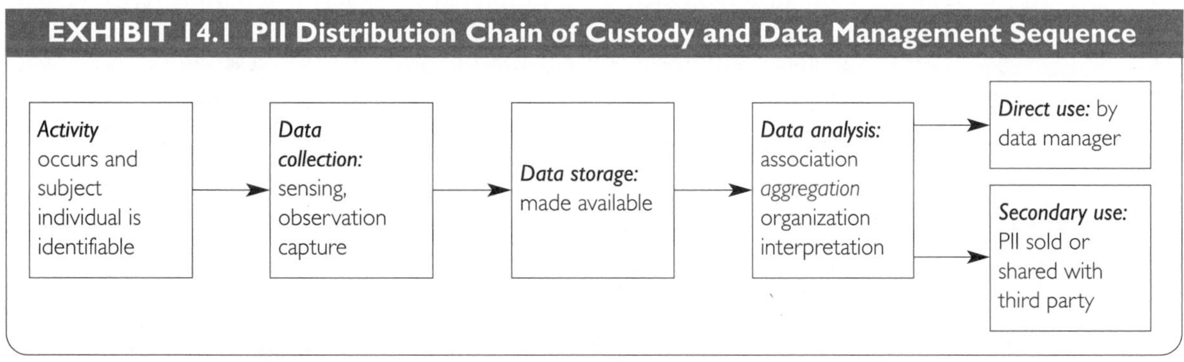

The **right to learn** from our direct experience generally permits us to observe, record, and remember these data. Although not expressly stated in the U.S. Constitution, the right to learn can be inferred from First Amendment speech and association. Learning is more than a right; it is a duty in some contexts, from the obligation to attend school to various regulatory duties to collect, analyze, disclose, and act upon business-related information. The right to learn is clearly critical to people's growth and development because learning underlies nearly all progress.

From this perspective, privacy regulation intercedes only as an exception to learning when the balance favors individual privacy or commercial confidentiality. Some privacy laws prohibit even the observation or recording of some data. For example, a common law privacy right restricts outsider intrusion upon the seclusion of others, criminal and tortious trespass laws forbid entry into the sanctity of another's property, it is generally illegal for voyeurs or Peeping Toms to use surreptitious means to visually observe others, and some forms of employer monitoring are restricted. With some law enforcement exceptions, wiretap laws prohibit listening to landline or wireless telephone transmissions, and it is generally illegal to intercept computerized telecommunications (e.g., e-mail, file attachments). In the future, further prohibitions on direct observation seem likely, such as restrictions on the monitoring of children's activities, unauthorized decryption, prohibitions on taking human tissue samples for genetic testing, and the unauthorized interception of financial transactions. In all these activities, public policy views the collection of these data as unduly intrusive because it violates intimacy, solitude, and modesty or gives the observer an unfair advantage over the subject individual.

Information Analysis

The second step in the sequence of data management is the organization and analysis of the data to create information useful for some purpose. Before computerized telecommunications and storage, most data was transcribed by hand into paper databases. For example, the primary function of double-entry accounting systems was to create a discipline for handwritten bookkeeping entries. The use of simultaneous debit and credit entries permitted systematic organization of accounting records that reduced errors, permitted correct classification of items, and allowed reconciliation—the subsequent inspection for quality control purposes. Similarly, analysis of PII must also follow systematic handling and pragmatic evaluation before valid conclusions can be drawn.

As data collection and organization have become mechanized, these activities are termed **data warehousing**. The impromptu analysis of this data in real time is often called **data mining**. Innovative methods of analysis of huge databases can reveal important and useful relationships, but not all firms are capable of effective information analysis. Often the PII captured is disclosed to third-party firms that specialize in gathering PII from several sources to provide analysis for clients. The verb **aggregate** (suffix pronounced *-gate*) is often used to describe the process of combining PII about one or more individuals from multiple sources. An **aggregator** is a database manager who usually combines partial bits of PII data about an identified individual from several sources. When collected and properly organized, these data form a profile or dossier about that subject individual that is useful in making marketing, insurance, credit, and employment decisions.

Contrast this activity with the adjective form of the same word: *aggregate* (suffix pronounced *-git*). When used to describe databases composed of PII about many individuals, the term *aggregate data* generally means that personal identifiers are not captured or are stripped away. Therefore, no PII can be linked to a subject individual from aggregate data. To illustrate the difference between aggregate (adjective) and aggregate (verb), consider the following example of traffic counts. Vehicle traffic can be counted using detector loops embedded in the pavement without identifying drivers or their license plates. This "aggregate data" of traffic volume is used to plan for new traffic signals or to maintain highways. By contrast, this highway planning could also be based on data from highway video cameras that can identify each car's license plate. An aggregator could combine this information with PII data from wireless calls and credit card purchases made en route to profile the continuing whereabouts of each subject individual caught traveling on that highway.

Data analysts often "drill down" into large accumulations of data to draw conclusions that are useful to their own decision making or useful when further disclosed to their clients. Key to these efforts are evolving methods of data organization, structuring, filtering, aggregation, association, and analysis. Nearly all conclusions are based on theories and conjecture or on generalizations from empirical testing. Of course, some forms of analysis are based on faulty assumptions, erroneous calculations, or premature generalizations (e.g., junk science). For example, law enforcement is generally prohibited from interpreting lie detector evidence to disprove an alibi. In the future, other restrictions may prohibit the use of some data analysis methods. For example, employers and health care providers may be prohibited from using genetic testing of human tissue samples to infer predisposition to disease. Health insurers and employers resist extending coverage to individuals if they or their families have the potential to require high-cost medical treatment. Employers might try to avoid hiring people or fire them if genetic propensity to disease or dishonesty is discovered. Privacy advocates believe that genetic testing should not be used in these ways until there is very strong and reliable scientific consensus connecting particular genetic markers with these undesirable predispositions.

Use of Knowledge

Data are collected and analyzed to give them value. This value is realized as knowledge is used. This is the third stage in the sequence of data management. Without the promise of some economic gain when resources are expended to produce knowledge, then only intellectual curiosity would motivate the collection and analysis of data. High-quality information is presumed in economic theory, but it is only common sense that valuable and accurate knowledge is too often a scarce commodity. Most people have personal experience with an underinformed transaction that confirms this point. Data are collected and information produced for **direct use** by the data manager or for **secondary use** when sold to clients, shared with partner firms, or bartered in return for other information.

This focus on the third stage of data management serves at least two important purposes. First, by prohibiting particular uses of information, use-restriction policies recognize that collection and analysis of PII can often be inevitable. The greatest injury to the subject individual comes with use of PII. The incentive to improve decision making with information is so strong that some firms inevitably learn PII, despite restrictions on collection and analysis. Use restrictions are nearly the last resort because they are intended to prevent the privacy intrusion from actually causing injury to the subject individual. A second reason to focus on use restrictions is that data management is similar to other industries. When information moves from acquisition, through analysis, to ultimate use, these activities are actually a *chain of distribution*. It illustrates that there is value in information; there is value added by intermediate services (e.g., compilation, selection, customization, interpretation), and there are markets for knowledge that is useful to consumers of information.

However, if the "handlers" of PII are regulated under privacy law, this focus shifts from a chain of distribution to a *chain of custody*. Custody recognizes that subject individuals have rights in their own information and that privacy regulation constrains the activities of these PII handlers during the three basic stages of collection, analysis, and use. It also implies that firms involved in data management have general custodial duties of reasonable care, safeguarding, and sometimes even more specific statutory duties. A chain of custody approach suggests that privacy regulation could restrict the transfer, transmission, communication, or receipt of PII. A focus on information handling recognizes the vulnerability of flowing data and reinforces the handler's responsibilities to the subject individual regarding security. It could also be used to more directly control intermediaries and purchasers.

Privacy rights cast as restrictions on use are also quite common. Consider some of the following examples: (1) In underwriting or setting premiums for automobile insurance, the insurer is often prohibited from considering moving violations after a few years pass; (2) potential creditors are forbidden from considering an individual's former bankruptcy in making credit decisions after several years pass; (3) financial and health care privacy rules require the subject individual's consent before the release or sale of private data; and (4) law enforcement is prohibited from using a confession to prove guilt unless Miranda warnings were given.

NATURE OF PRIVACY RIGHTS

Privacy is a fragmented, sectoral assortment of "rights" found in international law, constitutions, federal statutes and regulations, state statutes and regulations, common law, and private contracts. Why is privacy noted in so many sources? What is the impact of all this diversity? First, privacy should not be viewed as simple or monolithic because privacy law is a balance among several often competing complex interests. Second, privacy rights may occupy niches in almost all of the major fields of law: constitutional protections, criminal law, tort law, contract rights, and technical requirements from regulations. Some scholars even advocate a property rights vision for private information,[3] based on the opinion that privacy rights are classified as torts but really function more like a part of property law.[4] It is also possible to extend the law of trade secrets, insider trading, and database protections to recognize that "information is property,"[5] thus PII is also property.

When privacy rights are included within a major field of law, this classification has some significant impact: procedurally, substantively, and remedially. Generally, constitutional rights are so fundamental that they cannot be waived or eliminated by contract. Penalties under the criminal law are generally perceived as more severe than other prohibitions or remedies. Although individuals injured by privacy violations may press for criminal charges, criminal prosecutions are generally discretionary matters within the powers of government prosecutors, who must make resource allocation decisions on whether to seek indictments or prosecute privacy crimes. Violations of privacy regulations are generally enforced by regulators (e.g., FTC, SEC, HHS) and not by injured individuals or by local prosecutors. Regulatory enforcement is generally initiated when proposed or approved by the agency's leadership. Some agencies have independence from the executive administration of the governor at the state level or from the president at the federal level (e.g., FTC).

3. Lawrence Lessig, The Architecture of Privacy, *Vanderbilt Journal of Entertainment Law and Practice* 1 (1999) 56.
4. Richard A. Posner, *The Economics of Justice* (Cambridge, Mass.: Harvard University Press, 1981), chapters 9 and 10.
5. *Carpenter v. United States*, 108 S.Ct. 316, 321 (1987).

However, the enforcement policies of most other regulators are subject to political influence, such as the emphasis given particular types of crimes prosecuted by the U.S. attorney general or by cabinet-level departments. For example, enforcement priorities for violations of health care information privacy regulations under the Health Insurance Portability and Accountability Act (HIPPA) rules discussed later are within the discretion of the Department of Health and Human Services (HHS). HHS must conform its regulatory enforcement policies to the current president's priorities.[6]

The objective of U.S. civil law is generally not preventative but curative because it compensates victims. When private rights of action for money damages exist, these suits are initiated by the injured individuals and not by prosecutors or regulators. Criminal violations do not always carry an automatic private right of action for the victim to recover damages, although some do exist (e.g., assault, battery). A potential consequence of tort reform may be that privacy rights classified as torts are weakened. In a few instances, federal laws have been passed to enforce Constitutional rights that include tort remedies for damages, such as in the civil rights area.[7] Property rights in private information could conceivably be treated like torts: private rights of action initiated by the subject individual, damages recoverable including other remedies, and perhaps some special constitutional protections extended (e.g., no takings under Fifth Amendment). Privacy policies of websites and business firms may be treated as contract duties, giving website visitors certain rights to sue for breach of contract. Then privacy policies probably would be enforceable if the contract is properly formed, and such contracts would be subjected to the performance rules of contract law. It seems unlikely that punitive damages for breach of privacy would be recoverable under contract law.

Finally, the burden of proof in most civil private rights of action (e.g., tort, contract, property rights) is preponderance of the evidence, a relatively low threshold. The preponderance standard makes it easier for plaintiffs to prove a case than it is for a prosecutor to prove criminal guilt. Criminal law generally requires proof beyond a reasonable doubt. In some regulatory actions, the burden of proof is clear and convincing evidence, a standard somewhere between the civil and criminal extremes. Exhibit 14.2 illustrates some of the potential differences in privacy rights, depending on the field of law from which they originate.

EXHIBIT 14.2 Fields of Law That Include Privacy Rights

Field of Law	Enforced by	Remedies
Constitutional protection	Subject individual, prosecutor or attorney general, regulatory agency	Money damages, injunction
Tort rights	Subject individual	Money damages, injunction
Contract duties	Subject individual	Money damages, injunction, delete information
Regulatory requirements	Regulatory agency	Civil penalties, delete information
Criminal prohibitions	Prosecutor or attorney general	Fines, imprisonment, delete or deny use of information
Property rights	Subject individual	Money damages, injunction, delete information

6. Exec. Order No. 12,498.
7. Civil Rights Act of 1871, 42 U.S.C. §1983.

LAW AND ECONOMICS OF PRIVATE INFORMATION

Plotting the intersection between information economics and privacy law helps to predict the likely conduct of individuals and data managers. The economics of privacy is complex, as is the range of privacy interests. The incentives and behaviors of the players will change as society struggles to balance personal rights of privacy against society's needs for PII. Three basic principles are fundamental to the economic analysis of privacy: (1) Markets function best with complete information, (2) information is costly and often incomplete, and (3) information often defies exclusive control, making it difficult to maintain secrecy, control its use, or prevent misappropriation.

Under the perfect competition model, perfect information is presumed. Many economists assume that sufficient information is always freely available to inform all parties when they make contracts. With perfect information and rational action by contracting parties, economists predict that efficient markets will result: Market prices correctly assess asset values when well-informed parties bargain for their transactions. As transactions are completed, an information signal communicates the preferences of consumers. Thus, consumer demand attracts optimal investment to produce products and services, using the most promising technologies and businesses. By contrast, lack of demand diverts investment away from less promising alternatives. In sum, many economists presume that the information that parties need to bargain, including the transaction data about their completed contracts, is widely available to guide what Adam Smith called the "invisible hand" optimally for society.

Although neoclassical economics traditionally presumed that information is complete, increasingly some economists admit the existence of market anomalies, a form of market failure where information is imperfect and leads to market inefficiencies. The imperfection of information explains why so many resources are spent to collect and improve the quality of information. Imperfect information is often regulated where there has been a history of secrecy that society eventually discovers to be harmful (e.g., corporate financial reporting, toxic chemical disclosures, Megan's laws governing whereabouts of sex offenders).

Information is seemingly inexhaustible: The original copy usually persists even if numerous copies are made. However, inexhaustibility is only an illusion because it is difficult to make a profit from information without maintaining exclusive control over it. After information is published or otherwise becomes available to competitors or suppliers, its value to the owner steadily erodes until it is totally lost. When these two factors combine, this pithy observation is often made: Information wants to be free. That is, there are strong pressures to learn or share information, and information is vulnerable to unauthorized communication and even unlawful misappropriation.

After information is revealed, it cannot be withdrawn. Important information will become widely known. When analogized to intellectual property (IP), information almost defies exclusive possession. Information is not like tangible property: Tangibles can be possessed by only one person at a time. By contrast, unauthorized copies of information can proliferate even without the rightful owner knowing that copies were made, who has these copies, or for what purpose the copies are used. Consider how profit-making opportunities are siphoned off from the rightful owner of data, software, music, or video when illegal copies are obtained by serious potential buyers. The rightful owner is deprived of all the marginal revenue from those who would have paid for a copy. The effect is similar for private information. Others who use PII concerning a subject individual deprive the subject individual of the power to control whether their PII may be used or how it will be used. When other people trade in a subject individual's information, this activity siphons off the individual's opportunity to receive its value.

This analysis illustrates the basic economic conundrum of private information: Who should capture the value of a subject individual's information, the **intruder** or the subject individual? Advocates of database rights argue that experience belongs to each person and that the finder of information should become the owner. Without such incentives, highly valuable information will be lost, and the result will be less economic efficiency, a bad outcome for society. By contrast, privacy advocates seek limitations on database property rights because PII is a product of each subject individual's right of self-expression (thought, action, ingenuity). Society cannot accommodate both these extreme positions. A balance must be drawn; adjustments are needed to accommodate societal interests in efficient markets, justice, and social order while still indulging individual liberty and autonomy and incentivizing other forms of well-being derived from privacy.

Drawing the Privacy "Balance"

This chapter repeatedly describes privacy as a balance between each individual's rights and society's rights set within the context of our long cultural and legal history. However, there is not much practical guidance on how that balance is drawn because there is really no deterministic or formulaic balancing method. Instead, balancing is a compromise resulting from social, economic, and political pressures. Experience with repeated privacy intrusions from government or private entities leads society to evaluate two major factors: (1) the usefulness to society of the type of information acquired in the intrusion and (2) the repugnance of such intrusions. This balance has inspired various social pressures and legal responses. The extent of privacy protection depends on existing mores and society's legitimate needs for information to function properly. Society then chooses either to permit such intrusions, to regulate them, or to prohibit them.

Richard A. Posner, the noted professor of law and economics, Seventh Circuit federal appeals court judge, and influential writer, suggests this balancing can be conceptualized by using an adaptation of Judge Learned Hand's formula for tort liability.[8] Applied generally to privacy, Judge Learned Hand's model might help solve privacy problems by balancing three factors.[9] First, society must consider the probability (P) that particular types of intrusions will discover critically useful information. Second, society should consider the costs of the intrusion (B), both in collecting the data and in damage to the subject individual from the loss of privacy. Third, the model requires a determination of the losses (L) suffered by society (e.g., other individuals, other firms) if the information is *not* discovered. Hand's formula would support privacy protection when intrusion costs are greater than the likely losses ($B > P * L$). It would permit the intrusion when the likely losses are greater than the costs of intrusion ($B < P * L$). Of course, it is difficult to operationalize this model because it requires probability, cost, and loss valuations that are arbitrary, are difficult to estimate, or defy quantification. Nevertheless, the legislative process for privacy law probably makes rough approximations of these factors.

Arguments *against* Strong Privacy Rights

The most potent argument economists advance against strong privacy rights stems from the drive to achieve economic efficiency. Markets are less prone to failure when all parties are relatively well informed. Data are needed to evaluate the subject matter of transactions as well as the counterparty *before* contracts are negotiated.

8. Richard A. Posner, *Economic Analysis of Law*, 3d ed. (Boston: Little Brown, 1986), chapter 29.

9. *United States v. Carroll Towing Co.*, 159 F.2d 169, 173 (2d Cir., 1947).

Strong privacy rights restrict the potential availability of highly relevant information potentially leading to **adverse selection**; that is, when underinformed contracting parties are ignorant of critical information, they cannot effectively evaluate the transaction or the counterparty's ability to perform satisfactorily. This lack of information leads to bad decision making. For example, consider the underwriting of risks by an insurance company or a creditor's decision to make a loan. If prospective insureds can hide information about their health risks or their dangerous driving records, the insurer will suffer losses that could have been prevented if PII were used. Eventually, insurers must charge higher premiums to all customers to stay profitable. Similarly, the solvency of lenders is endangered and the cost of credit rises for all borrowers if loan applicants keep secret their previous loan defaults.

Richard Posner calls such "bad information" about someone's reputation **deservedly discrediting information.**[10] This approach creates an important distinction in PII between favorable information about an individual—"good information"—and disfavorable information about an individual—"bad information." Those opposing strong privacy rights argue that information showing the subject individual in a bad light should be made available because it helps society better assess the risk that these individuals might breach their contracts. Firms have obligations to their shareholders and to their employees to investigate new recruits and monitor employees. Of course, contract law encourages candor about many matters: The laws of fraud and misrepresentation, as well as disclosure regulations, protect innocent parties when the counterparty provides material misinformation and sometimes when key information is withheld.

Economists generally believe that efficiency is enhanced when an activity is provided by the party who has the lowest cost of performing. This is the concept of the **least cost provider**. It suggests that subject individuals should reveal all their relevant PII. Thereby, society would spend less in the aggregate on investigations, data collection, and analysis. Curiously, economists also believe that developing new markets whenever possible is usually a good thing. If subject individuals regularly and cheaply revealed discrediting information, they would slow the development of new markets in PII.

The mass customization of products and the advertising needed to attract such sales requires significant PII. Many economists now argue that consumers will find more precisely targeted marketing to be much more advantageous than traditional marketing. For example, strong privacy laws could stifle a reduction in inefficient junk mailings or the annoyance of irrelevant telemarketing calls. Weak privacy protections enable the construction of personal profiles, clickstream dossiers, and digital silhouettes that could reveal individual interests, purchasing habits, characteristics, and judgments that could enable sellers to predict future interests and buying habits. Therefore, to achieve this optimal marketing system, the public must not insist on strong privacy rights.

Some sellers apparently have another objective in assuring weak privacy protections: **perfect price discrimination**. Classical economics has never adequately solved a major problem: variable pricing of goods or services according to each individual customer's utility function. More precise customer ranking would permit sellers to charge more to rich individuals or those who take pride in owning superior technologies. Simultaneously, consumers of moderate means would pay lower prices, closer to what they could afford. Discriminatory pricing would permit sellers to

10. Richard A. Posner, *Economic Analysis of Law*, 2d ed. (Boston: Little Brown, 1986), p. 545.

maintain economies of scale by producing larger quantities while avoiding the lower profitability of conventional, single-tier pricing.[11] Some observers predict an opposite result from data warehousing of consumer PII.[12] They point to the mounting experience with banks and their credit card divisions that charge higher fees to unprofitable customers while giving special discounts to their "best," most profitable customers. PII can also lock in customers, a major objective of customer loyalty programs (e.g., frequent flyer, grocery bonus member programs). Of course, both discriminatory pricing systems could succeed if consumers accept these practices.

Most consumers are unlikely to willingly tolerate price discrimination, particularly if revealing their PII could cost them more for goods or services. Many people would condemn the favoritism of lower prices for some and the punitive exploitation of higher prices for others. Chapter 19 discusses the Robinson-Patman Act, an antitrust law that prohibits many forms of price discrimination. However, it applies to only the markets for goods. Nevertheless, consumers are forced to tolerate some price discrimination in a few areas. Price discrimination is not generally illegal in services. Price discrimination occurs frequently in goods that have new technology; the early adopters pay off the R&D costs, allowing later purchasers to pay less once economies of scale are achieved.

In the service sector, price discrimination regularly occurs. Consider travel services: lodging, airfares, and vehicle rentals that are often priced higher for customers seeking convenience, last-minute bookings, or first-class accommodations. Discounts are readily available for those consumers who can tolerate some uncertainty or inconvenience (e.g., Saturday night stayover, weekend rates, return vehicles to the same location). Some toll roads and public transit systems use **congestion pricing** by charging higher prices during rush hour because the market will bear it and it encourages carpooling and public transit.

PII profiles permit deep knowledge about consumers that may be particularly useful to sellers of luxury goods. Such sellers can choose not to sell to customers considered inappropriate to the maintenance of their luxury reputation. For example, a seller of luxury-class automobiles might try to maintain brand image by refusing to make sales to consumers that PII databases classify as not among the "executive class." Sales outside this "target demographic" group might depreciate the brand's desirability among their target group of loyal customers. Critics compare this practice with **redlining**, a discriminatory technique of refusing home mortgage lending in neighborhoods with particular demographic or criminal activity profiles.

Several organizations are likely to fight strong privacy protections. The U.S. Chamber of Commerce and many other trade associations can be expected to protect their members' access to PII as long as the data seems useful. The credit bureau industry—including Equifax, TransUnion, Experian, and TRW—has a substantial business that could be adversely affected if privacy rights were strengthened. Another segment of the PII data industry is ramping up: aggregators who facilitate the collection, archiving, and warehousing of PII, notably DoubleClick, Acxiom, Naviant Technologies, and HotData. These organizations and firms can be expected to engage in data warehousing activities both inside cyberspace and from sources in traditional commerce.

---

11. Soon-Yong Choi, Dale O. Stahl, & Andrew B. Whinston, *The Economics of Electronic Commerce* (Indianapolis: Macmillan Technical Publishing, 1997), chapter 8.
12. Marcia Stepanek, Weblining, *Business Week* (April 3, 2000), EB 26–34.

Law enforcement at all levels (local, state, federal, regulatory, self-regulation) is highly conscious of the useful insights possible from PII data warehousing. The law enforcement community was one of the original focal points for strong privacy rights. Indeed, the most powerful Constitutional rights to privacy were generally directed at the long history of intrusion by government agents. The law enforcement community may better understand the potential for negative political and public relations implications because they have long negative experience with too publicly advocating weak privacy.

Arguments *for* Strong Privacy Rights

Privacy advocates make economic arguments in favor of strong privacy protections that challenge the arguments just discussed. Proponents of strong privacy protections maintain there are market failures in PII data management practices. These generally relate to the incentives of the data management industry as well as the discipline exerted by the market and by law on that industry. First, the data manager "gains the full benefit of using the information in its own marketing or in the fee it receives when it sells information to third parties."[13] This is related to the observation made in the previous section that PII is useful because it so often informs better decision making.

The second economic reason supporting strong privacy rights is that while the subject individual may suffer injury when their PII is disclosed (e.g., bad information), the data manager disclosing the information does not suffer any injury. Indeed, PII helps the data manager or its clients reject contracting with subject individuals or change the terms of their contracts. Third, the data management industry generally does not fully reveal all PII dossier details to the subject individual. Similarly, subjects are generally unaware of the use of their data or the identity of the purchaser and even the identity of the collector. All this secrecy in collection and use of PII means the subject individuals cannot effectively monitor the use of their data. Subject individuals have difficulty in correcting erroneous data or explaining the context of accurate data. Of course, the customers purchasing erroneous data might eventually gain enough experience to discipline the data manager for poor product or service quality. However, the subject individual has the stronger and more immediate incentive to assure accuracy, which is precisely why subject individuals have "access rights" under the Fair Credit Reporting Act, discussed later, to view their credit histories and correct errors after an adverse credit decision is made.

Finally, there are many potential terms regarding the handling of each individual's PII and thus far little bargaining between data managers and subject individuals over them. Competition within the data management industry is only beginning, so there is little market discipline to even offer competitive terms or negotiate unique terms. Most data managers refuse to bargain over individual terms of privacy policies, partly because bargaining costs are high relative to the small value of most PII. In sum, the data management industry can capture most of the benefits of PII, yet it bears little responsibility for the data until required to do so by competitive market conditions or privacy regulations.

The property rights approach to PII recognizes that individuals have ownership and control rights over their PII. An individual's information is a form of currency belonging to the subject individual that can be useful in bargaining with business

13. Peter P. Swire and Robert E. Litan, *None of Your Business: World Data Flows, Electronic Commerce, and the European Privacy Directive* (Washington, D.C.: Brookings Institution Press, 1998).

firms. Subject individuals lose some of this advantage when their PII is first revealed. However, further sale and disclosure of the subject individual's PII decreases its value to the subject individual unless privacy policies or privacy rights restrict resale or secondary use. Individuals are unlikely to overcome the market power of the data management industry, particularly in that the industry has an incentive to hide its activities and generally most subjects remain ignorant of how their PII is used.

In the future, **digital rights management** systems, somewhat like the systems coming into use to deter and track on-line copyright infringement, could be adapted to PII collection, aggregation, use, and resale. Such systems attach hidden data along with the primary data (text, music, images, video, PII). For example, **metatags** and **digital watermarks** are hidden data of this type, used to identify and track sources and then enforce restrictions. A **digital privacy rights management** system could include a profile of the subject individual's privacy preferences. This information could accompany digital copies of their PII records to enforce restrictions on the collection and use of their PII. Electronic agents may also implement these privacy restrictions and keep records about secondary uses. Privacy advocacy organizations such as the Electronic Privacy Information Center (EPIC.org) can be expected to advocate stronger privacy rights for PII of subject individuals.

ONLINE

The Electronic Privacy Information Center (EPIC)
http://www.epic.org

The following excerpt is from an article in *ITS Quarterly* discussing legal issues in intelligent transportation systems (ITS). ITS generally includes smart cars and highways: the application of high-technology, computer, and telecommunications systems to improve transportation safety, reduce congestion and adverse environmental impacts, and provide better traveler information and logistics management. This excerpt addresses privacy problems arising when PII can pinpoint the time, location, and activities of travelers. This discussion implicates **location referencing** technologies such as electronic toll tags for bridges, tunnels, and turnpikes; wireless phones; global positioning systems (GPS); traffic video; global information systems (GIS); and many other emerging technologies creating the field of mobile commerce.

Ethical Issue

Litigation Risk Management for Intelligent Transportation Systems (Part II)
by John W. Bagby & Gary L. Gittings
***ITS Quarterly*, 8(3), 60–67, 1999**

The examination of litigation risk . . . should begin with a stakeholder analysis of the incentives regarding collection and use of data about private individuals. . . . Understanding these incentives helps predict the use of such data and the likely responses made through the political, legal and regulatory systems, at all government levels. . . .

The individual subjects of data collection have a group of incentives motivating the preservation of confidentiality. . . . All can be summarized as defensive. Many individual subjects can be expected to seek legal protection or even take defensive, self-help measures to protect their personal privacy or thwart the collection, archiving and use of such personal data. This conduct will most likely include efforts to eliminate publication or use of false data or defamatory content. Privacy advocates may also likely seek to eliminate and conceal truthful data they view as damaging to their reputations or solitude. Some privacy advocates seek simply to avoid the "fishbowl exposure" of public revelation of highly private facts. Privacy advocates also worry such data archives are insecure and entirely too vulnerable to misuse of financial and personal safety data by electronic hackers or societal predators (e.g., extortion, stalking). . . .

It is expected that privacy advocates will seek public policies to more narrowly define the legitimate uses of personal data. Privacy advocates will likely seek broad definitions for the illegitimate, misuse of private data and seek imposition of severe sanctions for data misuse. Further, they will likely seek legal protections for personal privacy by constitutional provision or interpretation, statute, regulation, and through provisions in pri-

Ethical Issue

vate contracts. . . . Privacy advocates may be expected to publicly expose the misuse of private information and seek public denunciation and censure of those seen to misuse private data. There can be expected continued growth in the general movement to thwart the collection, archiving and use of personal data.

In stark contrast to most individuals' privacy expectations, the users of data clearly have rival interests. Data users will likely seek to collect any data perceived to be helpful in their business decision-making or that has profit potential. . . .

Despite users' immediate incentives to broadly collect and utilize private individual data, some data users can be expected to eventually respond to market pressures by providing some individual privacy. Two major responses are emerging in the e-Commerce world and are easily transferable to ITS. First, many users will be pressured by privacy advocates to adopt privacy protection standards. These are most likely to be privately orchestrated efforts that would be advanced to preempt pressures for further government privacy regulations. Such preclusive efforts may be implemented in various forms: vendor/users' unilateral adoption of privacy procedures, industry sponsored self-regulatory codes of conduct, and/or third party privacy certification schemes. Second, vendor/users may bargain with individuals for the use of personal data. Users may either pay outright for some data or they may offer discounts or special services in exchange for particular data elements. In competitive markets, individuals might possibly have the choice to purchase products or services from vendors promising privacy or alternatively from other vendors expecting to collect and use data. Presumably, different contracts would emerge for different terms of service and/or prices depending on the level of privacy made available.

However, such consumer choice depends directly on the existence of competitive markets, that is, that several vendors will emerge in each service market to be available as alternative vendors for customers in each relevant geographic market. More realistically, during the early phases of this market development, it is less likely that there will be abundant competition among vendors of similar services or that several competitors would offer varying service packages, some with and some without privacy protections. Only after full competition eventually develops would the promise of competitively dictated privacy terms be achieved. . . .

Opponents of strict privacy protections can be expected to lobby for weakness in privacy laws, undertake perfunctory industry efforts to protect privacy, be slow to invest or innovate in privacy protections, and advocate broader definition of "business necessity" to justify their data collection and use. Data users which become convinced about the profitability of data warehousing can be expected to aggressively push new items for refining, collecting and archiving data, to develop new uses for personal data, and resell data whenever profitable. Data users and their trade associations can be expected to closely monitor the progress of privacy advocates. As individual aversion to data warehousing becomes better understood by data users, there will be further incentive to hide their practices of collection, warehousing and the sale and use of such data. Data users will tenaciously protect their future data use from any forms of privacy protection they view as obstructionist. For example, regulations requiring users to give notification to individual subjects every time data is used would likely be seen as arousing pressures from subjects to more closely regulate privacy. Therefore, data users have an incentive to obscure their collection, use and sale of private data. . . .

DEVELOPMENT OF FAIR INFORMATION PRACTICE PRINCIPLES

Underlying many contemporary privacy laws and privacy policies are five key **fair information practices** that had their origins in a 1973 advisory committee report to the U.S. Department of Health, Education and Welfare, *Records, Computers and the Rights of Citizens*. The advisory committee's recommendations have had a lasting impact, influencing the work of modern privacy task forces. They have been adopted in numerous privacy statutes, regulations, and privacy policies discussed here.

The first fair information practice principle is **notice**. Subject individuals should be given notice and have a clear awareness whenever an entity's PII capture practices might affect that individual. Before any information is collected, the subject individual must be given reasonably adequate, conspicuous, and comprehensible notification of the data capture practices. Notice is necessary before the subject individual can make an informed choice regarding the data capture. Notice enables individuals to take measures to protect their privacy. The notice should identify all details needed to permit informed choice. At a minimum, this information should include (1) who is collecting the data, (2) who will receive the data, (3) how the data will be used, (4) what data is collected, (5) what means, methods, or mechanisms will collect the data, (6) whether the data to be collected is required for access to a website or required for initiating a relationship with the collector, and (7) a description of the quality and security controls used. Other terms may also become important with further sophistication of PII capture methods and as subject individuals begin to see how their PII is used.

The second principle of fair information practice is **choice**. The subject individual must be given a choice as to whether and how their PII is collected. Choice must be made by the subject as a clear and intentional manifestation of consent. The consent should extend to primary uses of the information necessary for the immediate transaction or purpose. Additionally, consent must address any *secondary uses* of the PII, those uses beyond the immediate needs in the current transaction. Consent for secondary use should address the collector's expected future use, as well as any transfer of the PII for use by others. An **opt-out** consent requires the subject individual to take a clear and affirmative act to *prevent* collection and use of PII. By contrast, an **opt-in** form of consent requires the subject individual to take a clear and affirmative act to *permit* collection and use of PII Collector. Opt out versus opt in is detailed later. As parties become more sophisticated, the consent should become more complex than a simple, binary yes or no. As the terms of privacy become more complicated, the form of consent should also allow subject individuals to tailor the nature of their PII use.

The third principle of fair information practice is **access**. The subject individual must be given timely, accurate, and inexpensive access to review their file: the PII archived about themselves. Long experience with credit bureaus and with other databases shows that errors too often occur in such databases that are disadvantageous to the subject individual. Participation by the subject individual is essential to both the accuracy and the legitimacy of PII information in databases. The subject individual has the strongest incentive to review and assure accuracy of the data. When errors are discovered, there should be a simple and effective method to contest and correct inaccurate data.

The fourth principle of fair information practice is **security**. There are two major custodial duties for the owners and operators of PII databases: quality control and safeguarding. The PII collector must continually take reasonable steps to assure the accuracy of PII. Also, the PII database operator must take precautions, including careful maintenance of administrative and technical security measures to prevent unauthorized access, destruction, misuse, or unauthorized disclosure of PII.

The fifth principle of fair information practice is **enforcement**. The PII collection and database management process must have mechanisms to enforce the privacy practices, including self-regulation or legal protections such as private rights of action for redress and/or regulatory enforcement. The implementation of these fair information practices is evident in the following sections of this chapter and summarized in Exhibit 14.3.

EXHIBIT 14.3 Fair Information Practice Principles

Fair Information Practice Principle	Explanation of Fair Information Practice Principles
Notice/awareness	Subject individuals should be given notice of an entity's practices before any information is collected from them by identifying details about the data collection, security and uses.
Choice/consent	Subject individual has choice on whether and how PII is collected. Consent might be manifested with an *opt out* (an affirmative act *preventing* PII collection and/or use) or an *opt in* (an affirmative act *permitting* collection and/or use).
Access/participation	Subject individual can gain timely and inexpensive access to review PII about themselves. A simple and effective method should exist to contest and correct inaccurate data.
Integrity/security	Collector takes reasonable steps to assure accuracy of PII, as well as administrative and technical security measures to prevent unauthorized access or disclosure, destruction, or misuse of PII.
Enforcement/redress	Mechanisms exist to enforce privacy practices, including self-regulation, private rights of action, and criminal or regulatory enforcement.

EFFECTING CHOICE: OPT IN VERSUS OPT OUT

Consumer choice can be achieved in various ways. Both voluntary privacy policies and several new privacy laws require a form of choice. Some laws relate primarily to Internet activities, and other laws apply more broadly to data collection on line and off line. Notice and consent in traditional commerce can be made expressly in written contracts or inferred from conversations or conduct. However, for low-stakes transactions and in much activity on line (e.g., e-commerce) there may be only one practical method for consumer privacy notice and consent: on-line access to notice of privacy policies and click-through consent. As discussed previously, someday it may be possible for firms using electronic agents to implement a digital privacy rights management system. Electronic agents could conceivably negotiate and enforce restrictions on the collection and use of PII automatically. However, until these technologies become reliable and commonplace, most consumer privacy consent will be made through simple click-through choices. Most U.S. privacy consents in use today are opt-out systems. However, there is a trend to use the European-style opt-in system.

Generally, a privacy consent system is either opt-out or opt-in. Opt-out systems require the consumer to make an affirmative act that *denies* authorization for the collection and/or use of PII. They contrast with other systems using the opt-in approach, in which an affirmative act *grants* authorization to collect and/or use PII. Opt out is supported by many business firms and by data managers. Opt out is likely to provide an immediate increase in the value of PII databases. An opt-out default permits collection and use, unless and until consumers take the trouble to opt out, meaning that the group of consumers from whom data can be collected legally starts out very large, nearly the whole population. Thereafter, as individuals exercise their choice to withdraw by opting out, the number of subject individuals eventually declines. This decline will happen slowly if it is difficult to exercise the option, the option process is unclear, or individuals do not think their PII is used to their disadvantage. Of course, if the option is easily exercised or individuals quickly learn that their PII is being misused, then the rate of opting out would rise. Therefore, data managers have an incentive to make it more difficult to opt out, with confusing privacy notices or lengthy and complex opt-out procedures. In sum, an opt-out form of privacy consent is more desirable for data managers because initially the population participating is large and the decline in its size is slow, depending on several factors largely within the data manager's control. Exhibit 14.3 illustrates this point.

Contrast opt-out procedures with opt-in procedures. Opt in poses serious disadvantages to data managers: They cannot collect PII until and unless the subject individual consents. When opt in is used or required, data managers have an incentive to make it easy, quick, and simple for consumers to choose to participate. The default number of individuals participating necessarily starts at zero. All growth in participation depends on several factors: Consumers perceive that they benefit by sharing their PII, opting in is simple, or access to many Internet sites is blocked unless they share PII. Therefore, websites and other firms hoping to collect PII must work hard to lure participation. Additionally, the mere existence of opt-in rights strongly suggests that individuals have property rights in their PII. This concept makes database maintenance more problematic than under opt-out conditions because the collector's rights are subject to stronger consumer privacy protections. Exhibit 14.4 illustrates the contrast between opt out and opt in.

Currently, many U.S. privacy laws favor self-regulation and businesses' right to build and use PII databases under opt out. However, there is a shift underway from opt out to opt in. First, certain aspects of health care and children's on-line privacy in the United States may become opt in. Second, the EU's privacy data directive, an opt-in regime, is becoming influential. Third, opt in is being adopted by many progressive Internet sites and will probably be advocated persistently by privacy fundamentalists. Finally, some observers argue that websites or firms use opt in only when the subject individual is purchasing goods or services. If competing sellers can divert sales with greater privacy protections, businesses may find it necessary to use the more privacy-conscious opt-in procedure. These observers then argue that opt out should still be appropriate for websites offering free content. As discussed in Chapter 10, this view presumes the individual's PII is payment to gain access to content on the data collector's site. Therefore, for free website access, providing PII is price of website admission and the PII data constitute contractual consideration. Under this theory, opt-in regulations constitute a taking of private property, as suggested in the following case.

EXHIBIT 14.4 Proportion of Participants: Opt-in versus Opt-out Consents

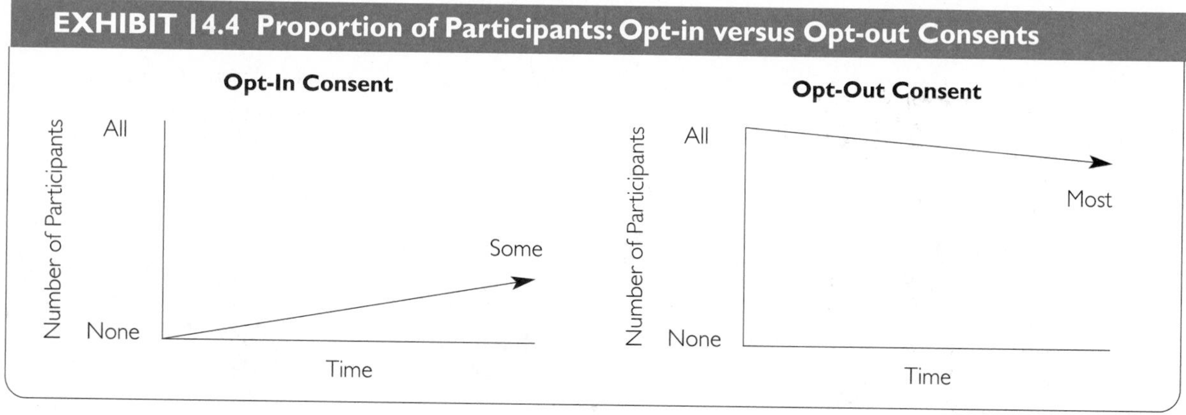

U.S. West v. FCC

182 F.3d 1224 (10th Cir., 1999) *cert.denied*
120 S.Ct. 2215 (6/5/00)

Facts. FCC regulations under the Telecommunications Act of 1996 required phone companies to guard the privacy of consumer proprietary network information (CPNI) to their parties. CPNI is "information that relates to the quantity, technical configuration, type, destination, ***location***, and amount of use of a telecommunications service subscribed to by any customer." The Act states "[e]very telecommunications carrier has a duty to protect the confidentiality of proprietary information of, and relating to . . . customers." The FCC regulations require phone companies to get opt-in permission from their customers before using or disclosing CPNI onward to third parties.

Legal Issue. Does the FCC privacy regulation violate the phone company's First Amendment rights of free speech to disclose CPNI to third parties? Does the FCC regulation constitute an impermissible taking under the Fifth Amendment of the phone company's private property rights in its customers' CPNI?

Opinion. Circuit Judge Tacha. The government argues that the FCC's CPNI regulations do not violate or even infringe upon petitioner's First Amendment rights because they only prohibit it from using CPNI to target customers and do not prevent petitioner from communicating with its customers or limit anything that it might say to them. This view is fundamentally flawed. Effective speech has two components: a speaker and an audience. A restriction on either of these components is a restriction on speech. Although speech that merely proposes a commercial transaction is at the "core" of commercial speech, it does not constitute the universe of commercial speech. When the sole purpose of speech based on CPNI is to facilitate the marketing of telecommunications services to individual customers, we find the speech integral to and inseparable from the ultimate commercial solicitation. Therefore, the speech is properly categorized as commercial speech.

[Under the commercial speech doctrine of the *Central Hudson* case] the government may restrict the speech only if it proves: (1) it has a substantial state interest in regulating the speech, (2) the regulation directly and materially advances that interest, and (3) the regulation is no more extensive than necessary to serve the interest. The breadth of the concept of privacy requires us to pay particular attention to attempts by the government to assert privacy as a substantial state interest. Although we may feel uncomfortable knowing that our personal information is circulating in the world, we live in an open society where information may usually pass freely. A general level of discomfort from knowing that people can readily access information about us does not necessarily rise to the level of a substantial state interest under *Central Hudson* for it is not based on an identified harm. The government presents no evidence showing the harm to either privacy or competition is real. Instead, the government relies on speculation that harm to privacy and competition for new services will result if carriers use CPNI.

While protecting against disclosure of sensitive and potentially embarrassing personal information may be important in the abstract, we have no indication of how it may occur in reality with respect to CPNI. The FCC's failure to adequately consider an obvious and substantially less restrictive alternative, an opt-out strategy, indicates that it did not narrowly tailor the CPNI regulations regarding customer approval. The FCC record does not adequately show that an opt-out strategy would not sufficiently protect customer privacy. The respondents merely speculate that there are a substantial number of individuals who feel strongly about their privacy, yet would not bother to opt-out if given notice and the opportunity to do so. Such speculation hardly reflects the careful calculation of costs and benefits that our commercial speech jurisprudence requires. We conclude that based on the record before us, the agency has failed to satisfy its burden of showing that the customer approval regulations restrict no more speech than necessary to serve the asserted state interests. Consequently, we find that the CPNI regulations interpreting the customer approval requirement violate the First Amendment.

Decision. Regulations that limit telephone companies' use of CPNI about telephone users violate the First Amendment rights of the telephone companies.

Dissent. Circuit Judge Briscoe. Congress made it abundantly clear it intended for telecommunications carriers to obtain customer "approval" prior to using, disclosing, or permitting access to individually identifiable CPNI. Although Congress did not specifically define the term "approval" in the statute, its ordinary and natural meaning clearly "implies knowledge and exercise of discretion after knowledge." In addressing U.S. West's takings argument, the threshold question is whether CPNI constitutes "property" for purposes of the Takings Clause. U.S. West gives short shrift to this issue, arguing that CPNI is protectable property for purposes of the Takings Clause. U.S. West has failed to take the requisite step of demonstrating that CPNI qualifies as trade secret property, or any other kind of protectable property interest, under state law.

Case Questions

1. The court essentially views phone company use or disclosure of CPNI as protected speech under the First Amendment. What would happen to privacy rights if this approach is used to prevent other privacy laws from prohibiting use or disclosure of PII?
2. What dangers might individuals risk if their cell phone carrier sold wireless CPNI, including the phone customer's real-time location information, to any third party?

JURISDICTION OVER PRIVACY PRACTICES

Jurisdiction is a key question in privacy, much as it has been in other areas where activities span state and national boarders. Increasingly, many jurisdictions are enacting privacy protection regulations. Many nations, notably member states of the EU, the United States, and Canada, have passed privacy legislation in recent years that affect both traditional commerce and Internet activities. During 2000, nearly 1,000 pieces of proposed legislation were introduced in the United States. Although few were enacted, many new privacy laws should be expected over the next few years.

Other institutions are competing to seize jurisdiction and regulate privacy. First, privacy-conscious individuals should take responsibility for their own privacy by carefully reviewing privacy policies, pursuing every opportunity to limit others' use of their PII, keeping up-to-date on privacy matters, and monitoring the use of their PII to control misuse. Many individuals can also participate in the formulation of privacy regulations. Second, many industries, trade associations, and their member firms now actively seek jurisdiction over privacy by promoting self-regulation. Third, states and local governments have traditionally regulated privacy and probably will continue to do so. State and local governments are generally closest to their citizens, making them more responsive when the public demands stronger privacy rights. Fourth, there is considerable activity in privacy regulation at the federal level and among the various federal regulators (e.g., FTC). Finally, some international organizations, such as the EU, that are effectively supernational councils of government are leaders in creating strong privacy rights.

With this much activity, there is a clear potential for inconsistent and incompatible requirements. In the United States, it is traditional for the states to exercise **police powers** to protect the health, safety, welfare, and morals of their citizens. Clearly, the creation and strengthening of privacy rights are within state police powers, particularly when privacy is conceived as protecting property rights in PII, avoiding intrusions from societal predators, or preventing contacts that endanger health, safety, or morals. Conflicts between the privacy regulations from various jurisdictions seem inevitable. Traditional jurisdictional conflicts arise when on-line or traditional commerce involves consumers in one jurisdiction and either the product or service vendor or the data manager in another jurisdiction. For example, does the law of the subject individual's residence apply when PII is collected by an Internet site owned by a firm from another state or nation? Generally, the principles of jurisdiction discussed in Chapter 3 apply.

Traditionally in the United States and to some extent in the EU, when such conflicts become intolerable, there are three possible resolutions. First, the Constitutional framers enumerated particular powers to be exercised only by the federal government (e.g., international relations, defense, foreign and interstate commerce). Second, the states have been quite successful in drafting and adopting uniform laws when inconsistent state laws would needlessly raise transactions costs (e.g., commercial law). Third, federal law can preempt state law if the potential for inconsistent state law very significantly deters progress.

EU PERSONAL DATA PROTECTION DIRECTIVE

In the past, many European people suffered at the hands of many tyrannical governments (e.g., feudal lords, Nazis, Fascists and Communists) that used PII to oppress and punish dissenters. It is not surprising that this experience led the EU to become a model for strong privacy rights. EU privacy rights span all industries and all EU nations. The flow of private data is severely restricted across borders. The **EU Personal Data Protection Directive** was enacted by the EU Parliament in 1995. EU directives like this one require all the **member states** (European nations) to enact national laws consistent with the directive. A majority of EU nations have now done so. The term used in the EU Directive for PII is **personal data**, which includes any information relating to an identifiable person. The directive regulates the **processing** of personal data, which includes operations performed on personal data either by automated or manual means and personal data that becomes part of a **filing system**. Data managers and their clients are called **data controllers**, which gives them various duties concerning processing of personal data.

Substantive articles (sections) of the EU Directive parallel the Fair Information Practice Principles, but the EU adds some other detailed privacy concepts. First, Articles 10 and 11 provide for notice and awareness, called **data controller identification**, which includes the collector's identity, the purposes for data processing, and other information needed to assure fair and lawful processing. Second, Article 7 requires **legitimacy of data processing**, a less restrictive concept than consent because it includes other circumstances that may justify data collection. Generally, personal information may be processed only if there is unambiguous consent, essentially an opt-in system. However, processing is also lawful without consent for other reasons, such as when processing is necessary: (i) to perform a contract or protect the interests of the data subject (subject individual), (ii) to comply with legal obligations of the subject or controller, (iii) for the controller to exercise its legitimate rights so long as the data subject's fundamental rights are not violated, and (iv) for the public interest. A unique opt-out provision exists for data subjects to avoid automated processing that evaluates personal aspects of the data subject or that would otherwise have a significant effect on the data subject. For example, the opt out would apply if a decision to extend credit would be made by computer or electronic agents using defined creditworthiness criteria (e.g., earnings, credit histories).

Articles 12 and 14 of the EU Directive give the data subject rights similar to the third principle, access. Subjects have the right to confirm that there is processing of data concerning them, including the purpose, categories of data, and recipients receiving the personal data. The data subject has **objection rights** to prevent use of data in direct marketing. When the data is incomplete or inaccurate, the data subject has the right to rectify or correct and to erase or block to data processing. The EU Directive has several provisions addressing data integrity and security. Article 6 requires the personal data to be accurate and current and to be retained as PII no longer than necessary. This provision appears to permit longer retention and use of aggregate data stripped of personal identifiers. Article 17 requires the data collector

Commentary

Why Should Congress Preempt State Privacy Laws?

Are the on-line capture of PII, its archiving, analysis, and use inherently borderless activities? If so, does their regulation require uniformity? Many industry advocates believe that the potential for inconsistent state regulations of privacy make it appropriate for Congress to impose uniformity through ***preemption*** of all states' privacy laws. They argue that different privacy requirements from the states and for different sectors increase the costs of data management. With such fragmented privacy laws, they argue that the only safe compliance strategy is to satisfy the privacy laws of the most restrictive state. They argue that an express preemption of all state privacy laws would foster e-commerce by limiting the costs of privacy compliance. This is similar to the EU's approach, an omnibus and multinational harmonization of privacy.

Privacy fundamentalists counter that federal preemption will not result in the same strong privacy rights consumers enjoy in Europe. Instead, federal preemption simply makes it easier and cheaper for these industries to focus lobbying efforts on one legislature, the U.S. Congress, which might too easily bow to pressure and enact weak privacy rights and permanently prevent more protective state laws. Preemption could also stall useful experimentation. Classic justification for federalism is that the states may try different approaches to a problem—here privacy—and some states may find the right balance. Other states can then learn from this experience. Congressional preemption of state privacy law does not respect states' rights.

to use technical and organizational security and integrity measures to avoid data loss, unlawful destruction, or unauthorized access, alternation, or disclosure. Articles 22, 23, and 24 provide that the national laws of the EU member nations are the primary source for enforcement and redress. However, a private right of damages for the data subject is specifically required in suits against the responsible data controller.

In addition to provisions paralleling the five Fair Information Practice Principles, there are some additional rights. Use restrictions under Article 6 require fair and lawful data processing and only for the use originally collected. Data collected must be adequate, relevant, and not excessive, considering the authorized purpose for processing. Article 8 creates a class of **highly sensitive data** that receive greater protection, including ethnic or racial demographics; opinions or beliefs based on political, religious, or philosophical views; health or sex life information; and membership in unions. For example, cross-border data flows cannot be permitted by member states unless adequately safeguarded in the destination nation.

EU Safe Harbor

Article 25 of the EU Personal Data Protection Directive prohibits member nations from permitting any transfer of personal data to some other nation that does not provide an *adequate level of protection* to privacy matters. Adequacy is assessed from all the circumstances, including (i) nature of the data, (ii) purpose and duration of the proposed processing, (iii) nation where data originates, (iv) nation of final destination, and (v) privacy laws, professional rules, and security measures in the final destination nation. EU member nations should evaluate these factors whenever data transfers to non-EU nations are contemplated by an EU data collector. The guidelines envision that the EU will keep **white lists** that publicize which non-EU nations have been evaluated and provide an adequate level of protection.

Transfer of data to nations not certified as providing adequate protection may still be possible. However, EU nations are expected to more carefully examine proposed data transfers to such nations. The relevant factors about the proposed transfer include whether the data transfer would involve highly sensitive data, the

http://

www.export.gov/safeharbor/

potential for financial loss (e.g., Internet credit card payment), personal safety risks (e.g., PII showing subject's location), data are intended for decision making significantly affecting a data subject, repetitive transfers of mass volumes of data, and covert or clandestine practices to collect data (e.g., Internet browser cookies). Permission to transfer PII satisfying one or more of these factors would be less likely to be granted.

The U.S. Department of Commerce negotiated a **safe harbor** with the European Commission to recognize when U.S. privacy protection meets the adequacy standard. The safe harbor specifies adequate PII data-handling methods and practices that, if carefully followed, will shield U.S. firms from EU legal action for privacy violations. The safe harbor may become very important for U.S. and multinational businesses doing business inside and outside EU nations. For example, any severe restriction on personal data flows from an EU nation to the United States could prove difficult for those firms with personnel information (e.g., skills databases, employment history, benefits) or client information in industries like insurance, consulting, banking, and auditing. Unfortunately, the EU Parliament voted to reject this safe harbor. Nevertheless, the EU Commission overrode the rejection and formally recognizes that U.S. firms complying with the safe harbor will be deemed as providing adequate protection.

Adequacy can be demonstrated with self-certification showing that a firm's privacy policies meet the safe harbor requirements. Additionally a U.S. regulator in that firm's industry must serve as a forum for appeals. Each U.S. firm must submit an annual letter to the U.S. Commerce Department self-certifying its compliance with the safe harbor either through participation in a self-regulatory privacy program or by using its own privacy policy. Updates are found on the U.S. Commerce Department website.

Uncertainties of EU Safe Harbor

A transfer of personal data out of an EU nation could be accomplished without using the safe harbor. For example, transfer is permissible if the data subject gives an unambiguous consent (generally opt in) or there is a contract that requires adequate privacy protection made between the European data controller and a U.S. data processor. What are the other major uncertainties under the safe harbor? First, many European critics complain that U.S. privacy law is not adequate. These parties may challenge the safe harbor in the European Court of Justice. Second, not all U.S. firms are in industries covered by the safe harbor; thus far, only firms subject to the FTC and United States Department of Transportation (DOT) are covered. However, firms in financial services, insurance, investment and commercial banking, and telecommunications should eventually be covered as their respective regulators agree to oversee their privacy policies. Finally, the safe harbor's application is uncertain when European individuals provide PII directly to U.S. firms over the Internet.

EXHIBIT 14.5 EU Safe Harbor Principles

Principle	Explanation of EU Safe Harbor Principle
Notice	Must notify individuals about the purposes for data collection and use, provide contact information for inquiries or complaints, list which third parties will receive the information, and explain the choices and means offered to limit use and disclosure.
Choice	Opt out if their PII will be disclosed or used outside the original purposes for collection. Opt in for highly sensitive information.
Onward transfer	Transfer of personal data to third-party agents must bind the third party to the safe harbor, assure that the third party is subject to the directive or have a contract with such third party requiring at least the same level of privacy protection as required by the relevant principles.
Access	Individuals must have access to PII held by an organization to permit correction, amendment, or deletion if inaccurate unless such access would be excessively burdensome or expensive compared with the risks to the individual's privacy.
Security	Must take reasonable precautions to protect PII from loss, misuse, and unauthorized access, disclosure, alteration, and destruction.
Data integrity	PII must be relevant for the purposes to be used. Must take reasonable steps to ensure that data are reliable for the intended use, accurate, complete, and current.
Enforcement	There must be readily available and affordable independent recourse mechanisms to investigate and resolve complaints and disputes, with damages awardable where provided by law; procedures verifying commitments to adhere to implementation of the safe harbor principles; and obligations to remedy failures to comply with the principles. Sanctions must be sufficiently rigorous to ensure compliance. Safe harbor benefits are no longer assured for failure to provide annual self-certification letters.

The self-regulatory regime must provide a dispute-resolution system to investigate and resolve individual complaints. It must also have procedures for verifying compliance and provide a remedy for problems arising out of a failure to comply. Examples include the seal programs discussed as self-regulation. Additionally, an appeal process must be available through a federal or state regulator that must have authority to remedy the U.S. firm's failure to comply with the firm's self-regulation by bringing action under a federal or state law that prohibits unfair and deceptive acts. A self-regulatory regime must assure compliance with seven personal data protection principles (listed in Exhibit 14.5). that closely resemble the Fair Information Practice Principles and the EU Directive.

CONSTITUTIONAL BASIS FOR PRIVACY RIGHTS

Several provisions of the U.S. Constitution create or affect privacy rights for individuals in their homes and in their other activities. Most are derived from the Bill of Rights and other Constitutional amendments. Some provisions explicitly protect privacy, and other protections are inferred from broader principles. However, a few provisions actually limit privacy rights. The U.S. Constitution is the supreme law so its privacy principles are very strong and cannot be overridden by federal, state, or local law. Exhibit 14.6 summarizes these Constitutional rights applicable to privacy rights.

The Fourth, Fifth, and Ninth Amendments have been most influential. The 1965 case of *Griswold v. Connecticut*[14] became the foundation for a **zone of privacy** for

14. 381 U.S. 479 (1965), holding unconstitutional a Connecticut statute outlawing use and advice on using birth control devices as an intrusion into zone of privacy.

EXHIBIT 14.6 Constitutional Provisions Affecting Privacy

Constitutional Provision	Rights Protected	Impact on Privacy
First Amendment	Freedoms of speech, religion, press, assembly, petitions	Privacy of literature, entertainment, ideas, absorbed political and religious beliefs, worship practices, group membership; but permits observation and learning.
Third Amendment	No quartering of soldiers	Protection from military's physical intrusion and surveillance into the home.
Fourth Amendment	No unlawful search and seizure; warrants, subpoenas, or court orders are required	Protection from unreasonable search of persons, homes, papers, or effects without warrant based on probable cause; secrecy of communications and correspondence.
Fifth Amendment	No double jeopardy; no self-incrimination; due process (federal); no uncompensated taking of private property	Protects from repeated legal process, forced revelation of information, enhances autonomy; but protects from federal action taking ownership of observation and knowledge acquired about others' private activities.
Sixth Amendment	Trials in the public record, confront witnesses	Prevents secrecy of trials; permits intrusion into witnesses' solitude to require testimony, and cross-examination opens up witnesses' past and conduct to scrutiny.
Ninth Amendment	Enumeration of rights in Constitution does not deny the people other rights	Basis to infer privacy rights, even though not expressly stated in Constitution.
Tenth Amendment	Reserves power of government to the states or to the people	Basis to infer state authority to enact privacy laws and to the people to protect their privacy.
Fourteenth Amendment	Due process (states); privileges and immunities; equal protection of the laws	Basis to withhold or limit access to information, freedom of personal choice; but protects from state action taking ownership of observation and knowledge acquired about others' private activities.

individuals.[15] Later cases reserve this zone whenever there is a **reasonable expectation of privacy:**

- Subject individual exhibits actual expectation of privacy.
- Society recognizes that the expectation of privacy is reasonable.

The Fourth Amendment restricts government from capturing information where there is a reasonable expectation of privacy. It forms the basis for prohibitions against wiretapping, electronic eavesdropping, disclosure of prescription drug records,[16] and the right to reproductive freedom. *Katz v. U.S.*[17] is an early electronic eavesdropping case illustrating how society's expectations expand the zone of privacy to a public place. This case found that individuals may have a reasonable expectation of privacy even when talking in a public phone booth. Law enforcement did not use direct wiretapping but installed a listening device mounted outside a phone booth. The lack of visual privacy in a glass-walled phone booth does not forfeit the aural privacy of the enclosed space. One possible implication for cyberspace may be that unencrypted communications, if too easily intercepted, may not exhibit a sufficient privacy expectation to be protected.

15. Samuel Warren and Louis Brandeis, The Right to Privacy, *Harvard Law Review* 4 (1890), 193.
16. *Whalen v. Roe*, 429 U.S. 589, 599 (1977).
17. 389 U.S. 347 (1967).

One of the most controversial Supreme Court cases of modern times is a privacy case. *Roe v. Wade* chronicles the development of the Constitutional basis for privacy as a **fundamental right**, creating the right to an abortion.

Constitutional protection is lost when the information is given to another person. After private information flows into commerce, there is an "assumption of risk" that Constitutional privacy protection is lost by the subject individual. For example, there is no Constitutional expectation of privacy in bank records, phone numbers dialed, trash container contents left at curbside, or activities subject to aerial observation from aircraft. Nevertheless, other state and federal privacy laws may protect some of these activities.

The Fifth Amendment self-incrimination privilege limits *how* government can capture incriminating information, such as in police interrogation or tax returns. However, this right does not protect the contents of papers of any kind because record keeping is not a compelled act of self-incrimination. This raises an important distinction: The Fifth Amendment protects mental thoughts but not physical manifestations. This may be the reason that courts increasingly find that physical examinations and samples are not protected by the Fifth Amendment. For example, individuals accused of criminal activity are not protected by the Fifth Amendment from requirements to submit samples of fingerprints, voiceprints, tissue for DNA testing, blood, urine, or hair follicles.

It will be interesting to see how these rules will adapt to electronic records and security methods in cyberspace. Consider a critical distinction made in *Doe v. United States*. The defendant was "forced to surrender a key to a strongbox containing incriminating documents, but not to reveal the combination to his wall safe" or to force him to actually use the combination he knew would open the safe.[18] In the electronic and cyberspace world, passwords or software keys are needed to access files on computer hard drives, retrieve files from network storage, access e-mail accounts, or restore encrypted files. Such protection may not be available for an employee who is hiding information on systems owned by her or his employer.

Commentary

Roe v. *Wade* and the Right to Privacy as a Fundamental Right

"The Constitution does not explicitly mention any right of privacy. In a line of decisions, however, going back perhaps [to 1891,] the Court has recognized that a right of personal privacy, or a guarantee of certain areas or zones of privacy, does exist under the Constitution. In varying contexts, the Court or individual Justices have, indeed, found at least the roots of that right in the First Amendment, in the Fourth and Fifth Amendments, in the penumbras of the Bill of Rights, in the Ninth Amendment, or in the concept of liberty guaranteed by the first section of the Fourteenth Amendment. These decisions make it clear that only personal rights that can be deemed "fundamental" or "implicit in the concept of ordered liberty," are included in this guarantee of personal privacy. They also make it clear that the right has some extension to activities relating to marriage, procreation, contraception, family relationships, and childrearing and education."[19]

18. *Doe v. United States*, 487 U.S. 201 (1988).
19. *Roe v. Wade*, 410 U.S. 113 (1973).

PRIVACY IN LITIGATION, REGULATION, AND LAW ENFORCEMENT

Recall the discussion of litigation and trial process in Chapter 3. The Fourth Amendment provides business with the greatest protection from unfair criminal or regulatory investigations. Fourth Amendment protection generally arises before a criminal defendant is indicted or before a civil administrative case is filed. Both natural persons and corporations are protected from unreasonable searches and seizures. In all types of cases, after suit has been filed, all parties, including defendants, prosecutors, private litigants, and administrative agencies, may use discovery to obtain information from the opposing side to help prove its case. **Discovery** devices include written **interrogatories** to question opposing parties and **depositions** to orally question witnesses. A **production of documents** request permits the examination of private files. Before suit is filed, investigators may get information from various sources: investigators, required reports, on-site inspections, and subpoenas. After assessing this information, the plaintiff, prosecutor, or agency enforcement division may decide whether there is sufficient evidence to sue or prosecute.

Many other nations prohibit such expansive discovery in noncriminal cases. In most civil law nations of Europe and Latin America, the criminal judges also serve as the prosecutor, which gives them very broad **inquisitorial** powers of discovery. However, civil plaintiffs do not share these rights to obtain documents from opposing parties. It can be very difficult to prove wrongdoing in such nations because of their strong secrecy norms.

Statutes require the keeping of many records for the public's benefit, so they are considered **public records** with no right to privacy. Administrative agencies may share with other agencies any nonprivileged evidence they gather. For example, federal agencies may generally refer investigative files to the Justice Department (DOJ) for criminal prosecution. The FTC may inform the DOJ about information it discovers about privacy violations, which could lead to DOJ criminal charges.

Administrative agencies are created by **enabling legislation** that empowers the agency to act and often authorizes the agency to subpoena witnesses and documents. Criminal prosecutors generally have similar powers once a criminal indictment is issued. **Subpoenas** require pretrial and trial testimony from witnesses. A ***subpoena duces tecum*** requires the production of documents. Regulatory agencies may not abuse the subpoena power for ulterior motives. For example, agencies may not harass businesses by issuing excessive subpoenas, and they may not publicly disclose trade secrets and other private matters examined under subpoena. Administrative subpoenas are not self-executing. This is a limitation to discourage agencies from exceeding their subpoena powers. The recipient of an administrative subpoena may validly refuse to testify or to produce the documents requested until ordered to do so by a court.

An agency must justify a subpoena before a court will order enforcement. Four fairness standards, established in *United States v. Powell*,[20] require the agency to prove that its investigation is legitimate and that the information it seeks is relevant. The subpoena recipient can be ordered to comply if the agency satisfies the *Powell* criteria.

---

20. *United States v. Powell*, 379 U.S. 48 (1964).

United States v. Powell Subpoena Enforcement Standards

1. Agency has a *legitimate purpose* to investigate.
2. Inquiry must be *relevant* to that legitimate purpose.
3. Agency may *not* already have the requested information *in its possession.*
4. Agency must *follow* its own *administrative procedures* in issuing the subpoena.

The protection of witnesses from compelled self-incrimination constitutes one of the best known aspects of the Fifth Amendment. By "pleading the Fifth," witnesses may refrain from giving evidence that might tend to show their own guilt. However, documents that are required to be kept for governmental purposes are not privileged. The Fifth Amendment constrains the investigatory activities of administrative agencies, prosecutors, police, and Congressional committees. It protects the most intimate and private thoughts of those accused of wrongdoing. An important limitation on the protection against self-incrimination has developed. That protection is a personal right, so it protects only a natural person from whom testimony is sought. Therefore, corporations and other business entities do not receive protection against incriminating evidence taken from an employee's testimony in matters involving the corporation. Employees may assert the privilege of protection against self-incrimination to protect only their personal privacy interests. The privilege does not protect the employer from incrimination.

In many instances, evidence that incriminates one party is in the hands of someone else. For example, an ISP may hold subscriber's e-mail and file attachments on its server. Accountants or attorneys often hold tax or litigation documents for their clients. When government officials seek this information, the clients may try to plead the Fifth to keep the information secret. This argument usually fails because the privilege is testimonial, so it protects only verbal and not documentary evidence. Several statutes remove the privilege if the person receives immunity from prosecution.

PRIVILEGED COMMUNICATIONS

Other types of evidentiary privileges can be used to keep information private. Most are based on state common law and not directly on Constitutional provisions. These privileges usually protect the accused from the release of confidential information known by close associates. Such associates include spouses, attorneys, priests or ministers, doctor-patient, and accountant-client (in about 20 states but not in federal cases). These privileges have developed around the relationships among these persons to encourage frank and open disclosure and to foster the relationships. The attorney-client privilege may be available to keep information secret if (1) information passes (2) from client to practicing attorney (3) in confidence, (4) not from some other source, and (5) for the purpose of receiving professional advice. Attorneys can generally communicate confidentially by using e-mail or intranet schemes if their clients consent after being informed of the risks of interception.

In the corporate context, there are additional requirements to gain the secrecy benefits of the attorney–corporate client privilege: (1) The employee must be ordered to communicate to the attorney (2) about information gained within the employee's duties (3) that is not immediately available to upper management. The Supreme Court has observed that the potential for expanding the attorney-client privilege to idle communications is too great. Unprivileged idle communications are those not made in confidence or not seeking legal advice. Additionally, the strict privilege requirements enumerated here are designed to prevent misuse of the privilege. Communications with corporate attorneys should not be made intentionally to shield information if the purpose is not primarily for the attorney's professional advice.

SEARCH AND SEIZURE

Some agencies have the authority to search private areas of personal or business premises without a warrant. These privacy intrusions may be illegal as unreasonable searches or seizures unless certain conditions are met. A few industries have a long history of close and pervasive regulation and cannot reasonably expect total privacy. For example, in the sales of firearms, liquor, food, and drugs, the public's interest in safety outweighs the individual businesses' right to privacy. Also, in emergency situations, where consent is given, or where the regulated activities are in open and plain view, agencies may conduct surprise inspections even without a search warrant. Law enforcement cannot open mail without the recipient's consent or a search warrant. However, transactional information on the outside of the envelope, called **mail covers**, is not private. Postcard correspondence also seems vulnerable.

In almost all other situations, regulators must obtain a warrant from a federal magistrate before searching employees, premises, and paper or computer files. The warrant should be issued only on the agency's showing of **administrative probable cause.** Three factors can form the basis for the grant of an **ex parte warrant** when the target is not present at the hearing: (1) "specific evidence of existing violations," (2), employee complaints, or (3) "reasonable legislative or administrative standards" (i.e., random, regular, and routine inspections, reinspections, or follow-up inspections). The surprise element may be necessary to avoid destruction of evidence, intimidation of witnesses, or correction of the violation.

PRIVACY UNDER FEDERAL FREEDOM OF INFORMATION AND STATE OPEN RECORDS LAWS

The investigatory powers of government permit the collection of considerable private information. The **Freedom of Information Act (FOIA)** and **state open records laws** were passed because regulatory agencies were widely believed to operate in a cloud of secrecy. To make government more responsive to the public will, these laws now require federal and state governments to disclose most information contained in government files. Government must disclose information whenever a specific request is made by nearly anyone: individuals, public interest groups, research scholars, journalists, and even foreigners. There is thus very little privacy for PII or corporate information held by regulators. However, every president since George Washington has claimed a constitutional right to an **executive privilege**, exempting sensitive information from public disclosure. Today, there can still be some privacy covering information in government hands under FOIA and most state open records laws, which provide a few specific statutory exemptions to disclosure (Exhibit 14.7).

All reasonably well-described requests for records from whatever internal agency source must be disclosed. Under amendments made in the **Electronic Freedom of Information Act (eFOIA)** of 1996, the same standards apply to both "hard-copy" and electronic files. Thus, e-mail, letters, and notes must be accessible, and the same FOIA exemptions apply to electronic records. The agency must publish an on-line index and provide on-line reading rooms where those documents likely to be requested frequently are made available. The agency may charge reasonable fees for document search and photocopying, although many agencies regularly decline to charge fees in

EXHIBIT 14.7 FOIA Exemptions

- National defense, national security, or foreign policy matters designated by presidential executive order
- Agency's internal personnel rules and practices
- Exemptions required by other statutes
- Trade secrets and commercial or financial information that is privileged or confidential concerning regulated entities, but only in the agencies' discretion
- Internal deliberative process in interagency or intra-agency memoranda or letters
- Agency personnel or medical files
- Investigatory files compiled for law enforcement purposes
- Bank secrecy condition reports of financial institutions
- Geological and geophysical information concerning oil and gas wells

the public interest. An appeal may be made to the agency's head when a lower echelon official withholds disclosure. These appeals must be processed within 20 working days. When agencies do not provide information, a complaint can be made to the U.S. District Court to seek an injunction. Courts may issue contempt citations against agency personnel for refusing to comply with court-ordered disclosure.

The selective release of information by agencies may represent an abuse of its discretion. If an agency publicly discloses or leaks information, a private entity's trade secrets may be lost, destroying a competitive advantage. An agency that threatens disclosure of confidential information to force settlement or compliance is clearly abusing its discretion. In such cases, the information supplier may sue for a **protective order** prohibiting disclosure. The Justice Department may prosecute disclosures that are illegal under the Trade Secrets Act. However, such issues are not ripe for adjudication until after the disclosure is made, and the damage may already be done. In the alternative, regulated entities may seek judicial review of an agency's decision to release information. Unfortunately, an agency might not notify the suppliers of information until after the secret is already disclosed. Initially, the **Privacy Act of 1974** appeared to block federal agencies from disclosing PII from their files without the consent of the subject individual. However, a 1984 amendment makes it clear that unless exempt under FOIA or another law (e.g., IRS records) PII must be disclosed in a FOIA request.

PRIVACY RIGHTS UNDER STATE LAW

A few states have constitutional provisions explicitly directed to protect privacy. Alabama, California, and Florida have broad privacy rights for individuals that prohibit government intrusion; a few are listed as inalienable rights. Some other states, including Pennsylvania, Colorado, and New Jersey, interpret their constitutional search and seizure provisions more broadly than the Fourth Amendment. For example, in some states, people can keep their banking records secret, and other states give people the right to keep secret the telephone numbers they dial. However, state constitutions are not the major source of privacy rights. State privacy law most often comes from state statutes and the common law. State privacy statutes are discussed later, in sections covering privacy in various specific contexts (e.g., on line, children, financial, health, employment, telecommunications).

This section reviews the four major common law privacy rights: (1) intrusion upon seclusion, (2) public disclosure of private facts, (3) false light, and (4) misappropriation. These rights were first organized into four distinct categories by the eminent tort law scholar, William L. Prosser.[21] Today, most exist in some form in all 50 states, largely by common law precedent and now enshrined in the *Restatement of the Law Second, Torts*. A few states have codified them into statutory provisions. Generally, these privacy torts offer remedies of money damages or an injunction to halt the privacy intrusion when a subject individual's privacy is violated.

INTRUSION UPON SECLUSION

Section 652B of the *Restatement of the Law Second, Torts* is the most common form of the **intrusion** tort that protects the sanctity of the "right to be let alone." It is defined by §652B as arising when another person:

intentionally intrudes, physically or otherwise, upon the solitude or seclusion of another or his private affairs or concerns . . . if the intrusion would be highly offensive to a reasonable person.

A subject individual must prove three elements to obtain a remedy based on the tort of intrusion: (1) The intruder intended to intrude, (2) there was a reasonable expectation of privacy under the circumstances, and (3) the intrusion is substantial and therefore highly offensive to a reasonable person.

First, like other intentional torts, the intrusion cannot be accidental or unknown by the intruder. Although there is no requirement that the subject individual knows of the intrusion when it happened, the intruder must have known of the acts taken that caused the intrusion. For example, it might not be wrongful to read an e-mail or file attachment mistakenly sent to your e-mail client (computer program) if you reasonably believed the message was intended for you. However, a hacker's knowing use of a "sniffer" program to read files from another person's computer or while files are in transit over the network would clearly show an intent to intrude.

The second element of intrusion considers the surrounding circumstances. In what contexts does society recognize that activities include a reasonable expectation of privacy? Most people expect that their activities at home hold a reasonable expectation for privacy. However, the expectation of privacy might be lost when an activity is done in clear and plain view by a passer-by. Typically, the inquiry focuses on whether the situation is open to view or closed to intrusion without the use of mechanical or electronic surveillance techniques. For example, activities visible on a public street, viewable in public areas of a private building, or easily monitored with standard radio receivers generally offer no expectation of privacy. These situations contrast with the intruder making an "informational breaking and entering" into spaces typically closed to casual view.

Although the tort of intrusion does not protect any particular "place," it does protect persons in particular types of places that society believes people should reasonably expect not to be under surveillance. An intrusion can occur when there is a physical trespass into private space, such as tapping telephones, opening mail, intercepting Internet communications, or using secret cameras or listening devices to surveil inside a home, personal vehicle, or office. However, an intrusion can be unreasonable even without a physical trespass. Trespass is a separate but related and

21. William L. Prosser, Privacy, *California Law Review* 48 (1960), 383.

sometimes overlapping tort. It is also a crime. Trespass involves an intentional, physical entry into another's real estate or the physical interference with another person's personal property. Trespass protects the exclusive right to use real property (e.g., land and buildings) or personal property (e.g., computer).

The third requirement is for the intrusion to be highly offensive to a reasonable person. This element assesses the seriousness of the intrusion, and some courts may require the intrusion to be outrageous. It is not a subjective test that simply asks whether the subject individual is offended, which should be presumed if a suit is brought. Instead, it is an objective test using the mythical person of ordinary sensibilities. It is probably often satisfied by the jury's collective sensibilities or by the judge's estimation of society's revulsion with the seriousness of the intrusion.

There is no requirement that an intrusion be published (disclosed to others); the wrongful activity is in the mere surveillance. All three of the other privacy torts and many other privacy rights prohibit particular uses of private data, such as publication or disclosure. The intrusion tort simply focuses on the earlier actions that intrude and not on the actual use of information discovered thereby. Although publication might be protected expression under the First Amendment if the story is newsworthy, "The First Amendment is not a license to trespass, to steal, or to intrude by electronic means into the precincts of another's home or office."[22] Subject individuals who give permission or consent to the intrusion cannot complain. Similarly, there is generally no wrongful intrusion claim for activities conducted in public view. However, the consent must be examined carefully, as an intruder gaining admittance under false pretenses would probably not have genuine consent. For example, it could be an intrusion or trespass for a website to access a user's hard drive to read cookies or other data without specific consent.

PUBLIC DISCLOSURE OF PRIVATE FACTS

Section 652D of the *Restatement of the Law Second, Torts* has been called an extension of the tort of defamation. It prohibits only highly offensive and broad-based disclosures of highly embarrassing and **private facts** that are not newsworthy, when someone:

gives publicity to a matter concerning the private life of another . . . [if it] (a) would be highly offensive to a reasonable person, and (b) is not of legitimate concern to the public.

The subject individual whose private facts are revealed is seldom successful. Courts must balance the media's First Amendment rights to exercise news judgment in determining the public's interest in the facts. Factors likely to excuse the publicity include (1) a long time passing between the events and the publicity, (2) the publicity is not simply tastelessly pandering, (3) society has a legitimate interest in the information, and (4) the impact is not shockingly harmful to the subject individual.

The publicity must be made to such a large group of the **public at large** that it would probably become public knowledge. Nevertheless, some cases find a violation if the main audience includes the subject individual's coworkers, family, neighbors, or members of her or his church or clubs. The facts must have been private before the wrongdoing, so publicity of information already in the public domain, information obtained legally, or information that was a matter of public record are

22. *Dietemann v. Time, Inc.*, 449 F.2d 245 (9th Cir., 1971).

not actionable. Community standards of what is "highly offensive to a reasonable person" are used to evaluate whether the publicity shocks the ordinary sense of decency or propriety. This privacy right has been most clearly applicable to the traditional news media (e.g., print, radio, TV), particularly to the tabloid, scandal, and gossip press. However, it may expand to include persons not a regular part of the press. For example, new forms of mass communication (e.g., website postings, chat rooms, bulletin boards) and databases of personal information (medical and credit histories) may become involved. These database matters are discussed later.

FALSE LIGHT

Section 652E of the *Restatement of the Law Second, Torts* provides for another privacy tort that closely resembles defamation. The **false light** tort prohibits making a false connection between a person and illegal, immoral, or embarrassing activity that causes injury to the subject individual. This tort is similar to private facts discussed previously. False light is triggered whenever someone gives:

publicity to a matter concerning another that places the other before the public in a false light . . . (a) . . . highly offensive to a reasonable person and (b) the actor had knowledge or acted in reckless disregard as to the falsity . . . and false light in which the other would be placed.

It would be a false light violation to attribute to a subject individual false statements, authorship, or political views. Fictional dramatizations of identifiable, often famous people can be actionable under the false light tort if they falsely depict relationships, dialogue, thoughts, or activities. The elements include intentionally or recklessly making a connection between the subject individual and the untrue description. For example, a preliminary finding of false light was made in a magazine's publication of nude beach photographs of Brad Pitt with a former girlfriend because it implied his consent to the publication.[23]

In recent years, activity resembling false light has been recognizable in cyberspace. For example, websites falsely connect individuals to activities, and e-mail attachments often circulate that falsely depict famous people in caricatures or photographs modified to be insulting or falsely showing the subject individual in untrue or compromising situations. Some states now refuse to recognize the false light tort. Nevertheless, it may emerge as an important constraint on unreasonable personal attacks in e-mail and on websites.

MISAPPROPRIATION

The fourth traditional state common law privacy right is found in the *Restatement of the Law Second, Torts* in §652C. This **right of publicity** subjects to liability anyone who:

appropriates to his own use or benefit the name or likeness of another . . . to advertise the defendant's business or product, or for some similar purpose.[24]

This privacy tort resembles a property right in one's own personality because it protects the subject individual's right to control the commercial exploitation of her

23. *Pitt v. Playgirl*, 178 BC 503 (Cal.Sup.Ct., 1977).

24. *Restatement of the Law Second, Torts* in §652C and comment b.

or his own personal endorsement. As a practical matter, only celebrities have much commercial potential in their endorsement and public reputation. The right is also known as the **appropriation right** because it resembles the misappropriation right in IP law. The tort's impact is illustrated in a case enjoining the publication of a frontal nude drawing of Muhammed Ali, the famous heavyweight prizefighter:

The distinctive aspect of this common law right of publicity is that it recognizes the commercial value of the picture or representation of a prominent person or performer and protects his proprietary interest in the profitability of his public reputation or persona.[25]

Although the media is a for-profit industry, it is not generally liable for misappropriation when pursuing its primary purpose of news gathering and reporting. Even parodies of famous public figures do not generally trigger misappropriation liability as long as the stories are newsworthy. This illustrates the **incidental use** doctrine, which uses the First Amendment to permit news reporting on a celebrity or even when the media touts its own accomplishments. Web posting of Howard Stern's nude buttocks was a protected incidental use because the website was devoted to his candidacy for the New York governorship.[26] However, the First Amendment defense has its limits when a media organization appropriates the celebrity's entire performance, act, or exhibition under the pretext of news reporting.

The potential for misappropriation liability in on-line activity seems considerable. The migration of news services as well as audio and video entertainment to the Internet suggest that precedents from the traditional media will apply to on-line activity. For example, celebrity **look-alike** and **sound-alike** advertising is vulnerable to liability. Jacqueline Kennedy Onassis and Woody Allen won judgments against advertisers that used look-alike models. Bette Midler won damages against an ad agency for using a convincing impersonation of her voice, sung by her former backup singer.[27]

The states differ on whether the misappropriation right survives the celebrity's death. For example, in some cases the celebrity's heirs can continue to enforce the property right for many years, up to 50 years in California. In other states, the right terminates at death, putting the celebrity's persona into the public domain for use by anyone. Finally, a few states permit suits by heirs only if the celebrity's persona was commercially exploited prior to death.

ELECTRONIC PRIVACY: COMPUTER, INTERNET, AND TELECOMMUNICATIONS

Much of the contemporary concern over privacy focuses on how greatly the Internet expands the amount of PII that can be captured, analyzed, and transferred onward. On-line privacy concerns may become the main focus for the privacy debate as more businesses use the Internet for record keeping and as they exploit the value of PII from on-line databases. The regulation of on-line privacy will probably involve applications of federal and state laws originally designed to regulate telephone privacy, computer security, and secrecy of entertainment preferences. This section

25. *Ali v. Playgirl, Inc.*, 447 F.Supp. 723 (S.D.N.Y., 1978).
26. *Stern v. Delphi Internet Services Corp.* 626 N.Y.S.2d 694 (N.Y.Sup.Ct., 1995).
27. *Midler v. Young & Rubicam*, 944 F.2d 909 (1991), *cert. denied* 503 U.S. 951 (1992).

discusses the convergence of various privacy laws in the online environment, including the special treatment of children's privacy. E-mail privacy is discussed later, in the employment privacy section.

PROFILING

Currently, the major objective in collecting clickstream and on-line behavior data is to permit the emerging network advertising industry to target banner advertisements to Web users. Targeting is intended to reduce marketing expenses and raise sales. Through the use of cookies, **Web bugs**,[28] and other emerging technologies, website operators and third-party firms can track Web users' browsing habits and product interests. This PII is organized into dossiers that provide profiling services to advertisers, websites, and data aggregators. Sometimes the data are non-PII; the user is not identified by name, but the targeting of ads is still possible. The FTC's *Online Profiling: A Report to Congress* describes **profiling:**

*[M]any of the banner ads displayed on Web pages are not selected and delivered by the Web site visited by a consumer, but by network advertising companies that manage and provide advertising for numerous unrelated Web sites. In general, these network advertising companies do not merely supply banner ads; they also gather data about the consumers who view their ads. Although the information gathered by network advertisers is often anonymous (*i.e., *the profiles are linked to the identification number of the advertising network's cookie on the consumer's computer rather than the name of a specific person), in some cases, the profiles derived from tracking consumers' activities on the Web are linked or merged with personally identifiable information. This consumer data can also be combined with data on the consumer's offline purchases, or information collected directly from consumers through surveys and registration forms.*[29]

Inferences are drawn from these profiles in an attempt to predict consumer purchasing habits and tastes. This practice permits automatic, split-second decisions to deliver particular ads targeted to each different consumer's specific interests.

Cookies are small files that websites cause to be saved on a Web user's hard drive. They contain **values**, alphanumeric expressions that are sometimes encrypted as well as coded. Few users know when cookies are in use or how to interpret them. Cookie files are generally less than 4 Kb in size, up to the equivalent of a full typed page of characters. They typically identify the website URL (content) once visited, include a set date and an expiration date, often many years in the future. Cookies are usually sent back to the originating website or to a third party, such as DoubleClick, which supplies website tracking services. Some cookies are temporary; session cookies are deleted when the browser program closes because they are useful only during that session. For example, a cookie can prove a user is registered with rightful access to a secure website after the initial logon. It is argued that cookies are harmless to users' computers and cannot spread viruses, but this may not remain true. Also, cookies raise questions of trespass; few users grant permission to set cookies. For example, German law requires users' consent because setting cookies is con-

ONLINE

Cookie demonstration
http://www.privacy.net/track/

28. Web bugs are tiny graphic image files embedded in a webpage, generally the same color as the background on which they are displayed, invisible to the naked eye, and detectable only by looking at the page's source code. The Web bug sends back considerable data to its home server: computer's IP address, the URL of the viewed page, the time of viewing, the type of browser used, and the identification number of any cookie previously placed by that server.
29. See http://www.ftc.gov/os/2000/07/onlineprofiling.htm.

sidered an invasion of another's computer.[30]

The FTC has taken the lead among all regulators in overseeing on-line privacy policies. The FTC has no general authority to prescribe privacy policies, require their posting, or assure compliance by websites or their partners. However, as discussed in later sections, the FTC has authority over privacy in both consumer finance and children's on-line activities. Nevertheless, the FTC Act gives the agency authority to prohibit unfair methods of competition and unfair or deceptive trade practices, such as the following landmark enforcement action for deceptive privacy practices.

FEDERAL TRADE COMMISSION

Privacy Initiatives

Advances in computer technology have made it possible for detailed information about people to be compiled and shared more easily and cheaply than ever. That's good for society as a whole and individual consumers. For example, it is easier for law enforcement to track down criminals, for banks to prevent fraud, and for consumers to learn about new products and services, allowing them to make better-informed purchasing decisions. At the same time, as personal information becomes more accessible, each of us - companies, associations, government agencies, and consumers - must take precautions to protect against the misuse of that information.

The Federal Trade Commission is educating consumers and businesses about the importance of personal information privacy. Read more about our efforts, what we've learned, and what you can do to protect the privacy of your personal information.

FTC Chairman Announces Aggressive, Pro-Consumer Privacy Agenda
October 4, 2001

http://
www.ftc.gov/privacy/

In re GeoCities

FTC Docket No. C-3849, 9823015 (1999)
http://www.ftc.gov/os/1998/9808/geo-ord.htm

Facts. The GeoCities website provided home pages for free and fee-based personal services, e-mail, contests, and children's clubs. The application form requests certain mandatory PII. GeoCities allegedly falsely represented the PII would be used only to provide members with target ads. However, the PII was allegedly sold or rented to third parties, who have used it for purposes beyond what GeoCities promised. GeoCities also allegedly falsely represented that GeoCities was the collector of PII from children at the official GeoCities GeoKidz Club, when, in fact, third parties actually collected and maintained the children's PII.

Legal Issue. Is it an unfair and deceptive trade practice for a website to violate its own announced privacy policy by transferring the PII onward to third parties?

Opinion. IT IS ORDERED that respondent [GeoCities], in connection with any online collection of personal identifying information from consumers, in or affecting commerce, . . . shall not make any misrepresentation, in any manner, expressly or by implication, about its collection or use of such information from or about consumers, including, but not limited to, what information will be disclosed to third parties and how the information will be used.

. . . shall not misrepresent, in any manner, expressly or by implication, the identity of the party collecting any such information or the sponsorship of any activity on its Web site.

. . . shall not collect personal identifying information from any child if respondent has actual knowledge that such child does not have his or her parent's permission to provide the information to respondent.

. . . shall provide clear and prominent notice to consumers, including the parents of children, with respect to respondent's practices with regard to its collection and use of personal identifying information. Such notice shall include, but is not limited to, disclosure of: A. what information is being collected (e.g., "name," "home address," "e-mail address," "age," "interests"); B. its intended use(s); C. the third parties to whom it will be disclosed (e.g., "advertisers of consumer products," mailing list companies," "the general public"); D. the consumer's ability to obtain access to or directly access such information and the means by which (s)he may do so; E. the consumer's ability to remove directly

30. Cookies are explained in detail at http://www.cookiecentral.com/.

or have the information removed from respondent's databases and the means by which (s)he may do so; and F. the procedures to delete personal identifying information from respondent's databases and any limitations related to such deletion.

. . . shall deliver a copy of this order to all current and future principals, officers, directors, and managers, and to all current and future employees, agents, and representatives having responsibilities with respect to the subject matter of this order.

. . . shall establish an "information practices training program" for any employee or GeoCities Community Leader engaged in the collection or disclosure to third parties of consumers' personal identifying information. The program shall include training about respondent's privacy policies, information security procedures, and disciplinary procedures for violations of its privacy policies.

Decision. It is an unfair and deceptive trade practice for websites to violate their own privacy rules.

Case Questions

1. What does this case mean for website PII practices of profiling and selling PII to third parties?
2. How can websites change their privacy policies to broaden their use of PII they collect?

UNSOLICITED COMMERCIAL E-MAIL: SPAM

Spam is an emerging area of privacy that resembles the intrusion tort because it arguably violates the right to be left alone. **Spam** is the e-mail version of mass distributions of direct marketing solicitations traditionally achieved by flyer, junk mail, or telemarketing calls. Spam may also be called **unsolicited commercial e-mail** (UCE). The rise in UCE volume and the controversy suggest that this marketing tool can be cost-effective. Indeed, there are low marginal costs to the sender of spam who expands an e-mail recipient list. However, consumers are responding negatively to these unwanted, annoying, and time-wasting solicitations. Spammers free-ride on the computer and communications capacity of ISPs,[31] which forces ISPs to add expensive Web servers, technicians, and bandwidth to accommodate the growing volume of spam. An ISP unable to handle spam could suffer a tarnished reputation when spam overloads crash their servers. Spam is triggering both litigation and legislation. Antispam laws that focus on fraud, trespass, hacking, or infringement are most likely valid. However, there may be Constitutional problems because the First Amendment freedom of speech and press and the commercial speech doctrine may protect some forms of spam. Also, the commerce clause may prohibit state antispam laws if they unduly burden interstate commerce.

Four federal laws can probably be adapted to prohibit some aspects of spam. First, the **Telephone Consumer Protection Act (TCPA)** regulates several phone telemarketing activities: (1) it prohibits automated dialing systems that charge the call to the receiving landline or wireless phone, (2) it prohibits fax flooding (unsolicited ads sent by fax), and (3) it gives consumers the right to be removed from telemarketing lists. The TCPA could be applied to e-mail spam, probably with recognition that phone, cable, and wireless networks are converging. Second, the **Computer Fraud and Abuse Act (CFAA)** provides for civil and criminal penalties for unauthorized access or molestation of protected computer systems. Spam is likely unlawful under CFAA provisions prohibiting intrusions into a protected computer system: (1) intentional access that causes damage; (2) sending commands, data, or software that causes damage; or (3) intentional fraudulent access to obtain something of value. At

31. *Report to the Federal Trade Commission of the Ad-Hoc Working Group on Unsolicited Commercial Email* (July 1998) at http://www.cdt.org/spam.

least two CFAA cases involved spam: *Hotmail v. Van$ Money Pie, Inc.*[32] (transmission of false e-mail addresses, resulting in a denial of service) and *AOL v. LCGM, Inc.*[33] (extraction of e-mail accounts to evade ISPs' spam-blocking software). The third federal law is **FTC Act** §5, prohibiting unfair and deceptive trade practices, which could apply to fraudulent, unsolicited e-mail spam. ReverseAuction.com settled FTC §5 charges that it violated an agreement with eBay by harvesting e-mail addresses and spamming e-mail recipients with the deceptive subject line "will EXPIRE soon."[34] Fourth, spam misrepresenting the sender's identity may violate the federal trademark law, the **Lanham Act,** for false designation of origin.

The states are cracking down on spam, although most state laws apply only to spam originating from within their state or destined into their states. One California law requires spam to include return addresses or toll-free numbers in the first message line so the recipient can opt out and get off the list. The subject line must include ADV to indicate the message is an ad. The Nevada law was the nation's first opt-out spam law. Another California law requires spammers to comply with ISPs' privacy policies and makes it criminal to falsify or impersonate the domain name of the spam sender, a form of **technical fraud.** The Washington and Virginia laws also prohibit this form of technical fraud. The law in Maryland criminalizes harassing or obscene e-mail.

Constitutional law and tort law are also important to the spam controversy. In *Cyber Promotions, Inc. v. AOL, Inc.,*[35] the ISP refused to deliver nearly 2 million UCE ads daily that Cyber Promotions attempted to send. In its refusal, AOL did not violate Cyber Promotions' First Amendment rights. Given that there are other communications channels available for ads, the AOL decision does not amount to state action blocking free speech. Spam may not always be advertising; sometimes it is political speech or just vindictive. Intel won an injunction against a former employee who sent 30,000 e-mails on six occasions to all Intel employees discussing the work environment. The spam constituted a trespass to chattels because the employee evaded Intel's e-mail controls. Consider the damage to Intel: If each employee spent an average of two minutes reading each of the six e-mails, the firm lost more than 1,000 hours of employee productivity.

TELECOMMUNICATIONS

Wiretapping, the interception and recording of telephone calls during transmission, is a major privacy intrusion. Under authority of the search and seizure provision of the Fourth Amendment, Congress passed the federal wiretap statute in 1968 as part of the **Omnibus Crime Control and Safe Streets Act.** Government, private parties, and employers are generally prohibited from wiretapping or recording oral communications. Exceptions permit wiretapping with either party's consent, employer monitoring "in the ordinary course of business" after notification of employees, national security and foreign intelligence matters, and for law enforcement under a court order. Unauthorized wiretapping carries criminal penalties. Evidence obtained from an unauthorized wiretap is *not* admissible at trial, and any further evidence discovered by leads obtained from an unauthorized wiretap is also inadmissible under the **fruit of the poisonous tree doctrine.**

32. 47 U.S.P.Q.2d (BNA) 1020 (N.D.Cal., 1998).
33. 46 F.Supp.2d 444 (E.D.Va., 1998).
34. *In re ReverseAuction.com* (Civ. Action No. 000032); see http://www.ftc.gov/opa/2000/01/reverse4.htm.
35. 948 F.Supp. 436 (E.D.Pa. 1996).

Wiretapping warrants can be issued only by a judge upon the showing of probable cause when law enforcement demonstrates a reasonable probability that the wiretap will capture conversations related to criminal activity. These proceedings are **ex parte**; that is, the subject of the wiretap is not present, and the court must supervise the wiretapping. Clearly, the subject individual should not even know of the wiretap; otherwise, any information useful to the investigation is unlikely to be spoken over that phone line. Other laws may prohibit placing listening devices in homes or offices to capture one side or all of phone conversations. For example, the FCC has a **phone rule** that prohibits the media from recording a phone call for broadcast without first notifying the caller of the recording.

The original federal wiretap law applied only to voice communications and not to the transmission or storage of computerized communications. As a result, Congress amended the wiretap law with the **Electronic Communications Privacy Act (ECPA)** in 1986 to expand the wiretapping provisions to wireless telephony (cellular) and e-mail communications. The ECPA has criminal penalties and civil remedies, including punitive damages. The ECPA prohibits unauthorized interception or disclosure of **electronic communications**, defined as:

any transfer of signs, signals, writing, images, sounds, data or intelligence of any nature transmitted in whole or part by wire, radio, electromagnetic, photoelectric or photooptical system.

Therefore, the ECPA covers communications via pager, cellular and wireless telephony, browser requests, Internet downloads, chat room traffic, voice mail, and e-mails (including attachments) when transmitted by common carriers in interstate commerce. ISPs are prohibited from disclosing these to outsiders. There are prohibitions against **unlawful access to stored communications**—that is, probing into computer storage, such as RAM or disk drives, for information in source or destination computers or during transit while the communication in temporary intermediary storage such as on a server.

Exceptions under the ECPA allow some interception or access. An **intranet** or in-house system is not covered, and the wiretap exceptions mentioned previously also apply under the ECPA. An ISP can monitor its subscribers' electronic communications as necessary to provide ISP services (quality control) or protect the ISP's rights or property. **Parties to a communication** may collect, analyze, and disclose electronic communications. This provision presumably would permit a website's profiling activities about its visitors. Prior consent by either the sender or the recipient is a defense. However, it is uncertain whether the mere posting of a monitoring policy would suffice, without a clear consent using something like a click-wrap. Law enforcement must obtain a warrant to intercept transmissions or access information in storage. However, an ISP may disclose evidence of criminal activity it discovers if the monitoring is permitted by an exception.

Wireless devices are proliferating: cell phones, wireless Web connections, personal data assistants (PDAs), and intelligent transportation systems (ITS, in-vehicle information and toll payment systems). Some systems come equipped with global positioning system (GPS) capability that can determine location by triangulating from satellite signals. Another technology is increasingly used: Cellular service providers can use signal strength, triangulation, and other technologies to pinpoint the user's location within only a few meters. The **Wireless Communications and Public Safety Act of 1999 (WCPSA)** requires wireless carriers (cell phone companies) to capture location data of 911 emergency calls (E911) made by cell phones.

This should help in the dispatch of emergency assistance (e.g., police, fire, ambulance, HazMat teams) more quickly and precisely than the haphazard experience of many emergency control centers. Although 911 calls are easily located by using caller ID systems on landlines, cellular E911 callers often cannot accurately describe their location, delaying the emergency response. For example, automated crash notification systems like GM's OnStar provide pinpoint location data.

Privacy fundamentalists are concerned that mobile location referencing could lead to constant monitoring of individuals' location and movements, with grave potential for privacy intrusions. As a result, the WCPSA added "location" to the list of **customer proprietary network information** (**CPNI**) that must be kept private by a telephone carrier. CPNI is now defined as:

information that relates to the quantity, technical configuration, type, destination, location, *and amount of use of a telecommunications service subscribed to by any customer.*

CNSI may be used for emergency and billing purposes, but the customer must opt in to any resale of CNSI to third parties for marketing purposes. For example, electronic coupons could appear on a cell phone or PDA whenever the customer passed by the particular retailer.

Two federal laws protect the privacy of video viewing habits. The **Cable Communications Policy Act of 1984** (**CCPA**) requires that subscribers to cable TV services consent before PII is captured through the cable system, such as pay-per-view purchases or regular viewing habits. The CCPA prohibits disclosure of such PII and requires annual disclosures to subscribers about PII policies and their capture practices. Subscribers must have access to inspect and correct such records. PII about video rental and purchase habits was restricted by the **Video Privacy Protection Act of 1988** (**VPPA**). The VPPA is also known as the Bork bill because PII about Supreme Court nominee Robert Bork's viewing habits influenced his Senate confirmation. The VPPA requires a customer's consent before disclosing PII about video purchase or rental habits. The CCPA and VPPA could be applied to video entertainment delivery over the Internet.

CHILDREN'S ON-LINE PRIVACY

Congress passed the **Children's Online Privacy Protection Act** (**COPPA**), encouraged by the FTC's 1998 report criticizing self-regulation as ineffective.[36] COPPA charged the FTC to issue implementing regulations resembling the Fair Information Practices, which became effective in April 2000. PII of children under age 13 generally cannot be collected, used, or disclosed onward unless notice and opt-in parental consent is given. Websites targeting children or websites that actually know they collect PII from children must comply. PII under COPPA includes first or last name, e-mail address, phone number, home address, ssn, product preferences, or personal interests when collected on line. Notice must indicate what PII is collected and how it will be used or disclosed. The notice must also recite the COPPA requirements and detail **parental refusal rights**, a form of continuing opt out.

Verifiable parental consent, an opt in, is COPPA's key feature. It is defined as:

36. *Privacy Online: A Report to Congress* (June, 1998); see http://www.ftc.gov/reports/privacy3/index.htm.

reasonable efforts to ensure that before personal information is collected from a child, a parent of the child receives notice of the operator's information practices and consents to those practices.[37]

Initially, the FTC used a *sliding scale* to judge the sufficiency of consent, depending on how the operator uses the child's personal information. A less rigorous method of consent was required for PII used for internal purposes, such as parental e-mail and follow-up. However, a more reliable method of consent is required if the PII was disclosed onward to others because this raises the danger to children (e.g., credit card, postal mail, digital signature). New consent is required if the website materially changes its PII practices.

COPPA rules require access: Parents must be able to verify what PII has been collected and may revoke their consent and require the website to delete all PII collected. After revocation, the website may terminate the child's future website privileges. Parental consent is not required in a few instances, such as acquisition of an e-mail address for the child's one-time inquiry or the parent's name or e-mail address for consent purposes. Websites are prohibited from refusing to permit participation to a child who does not provide additional PII that is unnecessary to participate (e.g., contest requirement to provide parent's credit card number). COPPA has substantive requirements for the content and format of children's privacy policies. At this writing, the FTC is certifying safe harbors: self-regulatory programs that will oversee industry guidelines to provide incentives and independently assess compliance.

FINANCIAL PRIVACY

Financial privacy has assumed major importance for many years. The United States probably has more experience with federal regulation of privacy in the reporting of credit histories than with privacy regulation in any other sector. Creditworthiness is judged by a **credit history**, data archived about a debtor's timely payments or payment defaults. This information is sold as consumer reports to lenders, insurers, prospective employers, and others to infer character and general reputation. Many people insist this information is relevant to decisions in employment, bonding, and insurance underwriting. Financial PII about most individuals is increasingly available from confidential credit records and from publicly available court filings, mortgage records, personal property liens, and other sources. Financial PII based on transaction history directly with a creditor is **experience information**, and information from all other sources is **nonexperience information**.

The principal piece of financial privacy legislation is the 1970 **Fair Credit Reporting Act (FCRA)**. It is intended to assure fairness in credit reports without unduly burdening the credit reporting system. More recently, financial privacy has taken on new urgency. Considerable financial PII has migrated onto computerized databases and may become accessible through telecommunications. The merger of financial institutions seems to promise the combination of each formerly separate firm's incomplete data into larger, comprehensive, and more valuable financial PII databases. New financial privacy concerns have led to the passage of various state

37. *How to Comply with the Children's Online Privacy Protection Rule: A Guide from the FTC, Direct Marketing Assn. and the Internet Alliance* (June 2000); see http://www.ftc.gov/bcp/conline/pubs/buspubs/coppa.htm.

financial privacy laws and the federal privacy provisions of **Gramm-Leach-Bliley Act (GLB)** in 1999. This section discusses how compliance with both laws is necessary under contemporary regulation.

FAIR CREDIT REPORTING ACT

A "good credit rating" is essential to get access to credit to finance a car, home, or business. The debtor has ultimate responsibility for good credit through personal discipline: by exercising restraint in borrowing, budgeting wisely, and making timely payments. Hundreds of small credit reporting agencies (credit bureaus) and a few huge financial information service firms (Equifax, TransUnion, Experian, TRW) sell creditworthiness reporting services to lenders, insurers, and prospective employers. These services include the investigation, archiving and reporting of financial and other PII concerning debtors. **Consumer reports**, also known as credit histories, are compiled from lender reports about the promptness and fullness of installment repayments on loans and credit cards. Credit reporting agencies also collect information about the reputation and character of debtors. The FCRA provides debtors with access to their credit histories on a limited basis, permitting them to correct mistakes in these reports. FCRA also requires the removal of obsolete information. For example, bankruptcies more than 14 years old and bad debt information more than 7 years old may not be included in a consumer report.

Any entity in interstate commerce that is regularly engaged in the collection or evaluation of consumer credit information provided to third parties must comply with the FCRA. Reports concerning transactions between the consumer and the reporter are not regulated. Credit reporting agencies must verify the accuracy of the information. If a consumer disputes information in an agency's files, whether or not that information has yet been reported, the agency must reinvestigate unless the consumer's dispute is frivolous. If the objectionable information is not deleted, consumers are entitled to include a brief statement of their version of the dispute. For example, if two consumers have the same name, but with different spellings (e.g., Johnson vs. Johns*e*n), an inaccurate report might be made. Either is permitted to include a statement in the files concerning this potential confusion. If adverse information on a consumer is not deleted from an agency's files, all reports on that consumer sent out from the agency must include the consumer's statement or an accurate abstract of it. The consumer may insist that the statement be given to anyone who received the adverse information within the prior two years for employment purposes or within the prior six months for other purposes.

The customers of credit reporting agencies are usually potential creditors, insurers, or employers. However, these users must have legitimate purposes to request a report. Reports may be legitimately supplied pursuant to a court order, on written request of the consumer, or to any entity reasonably expected to use the reports in making decisions on such matters as (1) the granting of consumer credit, (2) the issuance of insurance policies, (3) employment, (4) the granting of governmental licenses, or (5) other legitimate purposes. Many lenders request potential borrowers to give written authorization before credit histories are purchased.

There are strong principles of enforcement under FCRA and under some states' common law, as well as remedies for unconscionable conduct in credit investigations. The FTC may designate particular activities of violators as unfair and deceptive trade practices or issue cease and desist orders. Users who obtain information from credit reporting agencies under false pretenses may be criminally liable. For example, falsification of the prospective debtor's authorization for request of credit information is a federal crime. Credit reporting agencies that knowingly provide information for illegitimate purposes may also be held criminally liable, with fines of up to $5,000 and/or imprisonment for up to one year. Agencies that willfully or negligently violate the act may have civil liability for actual damages, reasonable attorney's fees, and court costs. Punitive damages may be assessed for willful violations.

Enforcement is also used to motivate financial PII security. Credit reporting agencies may be held liable for negligence if they do not install and maintain reasonable procedures to ensure the accuracy of reports and supply the reports only for legitimate purposes. A damaged consumer may also use the common law torts of defamation and invasion of privacy. Users, credit reporting agencies, and those who supply inaccurate information to credit reporting agencies may be held liable for damages if the information is false or violates the common law or other privacy rights. In the early 1990s, evidence surfaced that sloppy procedures at some credit reporting agencies showed individuals' records full of inaccuracies, causing damage to their prospects for credit, insurance, licenses, and employment. The FTC and 19 states' attorneys general settled charges with TRW based on allegations it sold sensitive data to junk mailers, permitted errors to recur, and inadequately investigated customer complaints. This settlement pressures other credit reporting agencies to adopt similar protections or risk further federal financial privacy regulation like the Gramm-Leach-Bliley Act.

GRAMM-LEACH-BLILEY ACT

The Gramm-Leach-Bliley Act (GLB, the Financial Modernization Act of 1999) was primarily intended to break down the separation between the three major sectors of financial services: commercial banking, investment banking, and insurance. GLB repealed a New Deal–era law—the Glass-Steagall Act—permitting a form of **universal banking** prevalent in most other industrialized nations. GLB signals an inevitable consolidation of financial service firms. It permits the merging firms to combine their separate financial PII into huge new databases containing customers' banking, brokerage, and insurance information. GLB required the major federal regulators of financial services to coordinate new privacy regulations to restrict the onward transfer of financial PII outside these affiliating firms. GLB requires security measures, notice, and opt-out consent.

Substantially identical GLB regulations have been issued by the FDIC, SEC, FTC, Federal Reserve Board, Office of Thrift Supervision, and Comptroller of the Currency. Each agency regulates a separate part of the financial services business. The precise definition of the **financial institutions** subject to the GLB financial privacy rules is unclear. Eventually, any firm regularly engaged in financial transactions could become subject to the GLB financial privacy rules. Initially, the financial service businesses regulated under GLB privacy rules include securities brokers, banks, thrifts, credit unions, check cashing services, retailers issuing credit cards, appraisers, vehicle lessors, check printers, tax preparers, investment advisers, mortgage brokers, trust services, and credit counselors. GLB authorizes the states to regulate privacy in the gap of federal regulation over the insurance industry, and states may enact stronger financial PII protections than does GLB.

GLB financial privacy applies whenever a customer inquires about or obtains a financial product for personal, family, or household purposes. GLB also applies to the resulting transaction data. Whether the financial PII is collected on line or by traditional means is irrelevant. The PII can be collected either directly from the subject individual or from third parties. Financial institutions must develop privacy policies and notify customers when accounts are opened and annually thereafter. An opt-out consent must be offered for the customer to prevent onward transfer of financial PII. The exercise of opt out must be reasonable: E-mail, website forms, checkoffs on paper forms, and toll-free numbers are probably reasonable but not requiring each customer to initiate the opt out by writing a letter. Before GLB, banks could sell their customers' "transactions and experience" financial PII data to third parties. Now, such sales are permissible only after adequate notice and as long as customers choose not to opt out. GLB further restricts third parties from redisclosing some of the financial PII they receive from a financial institution.

GLB does not require financial institutions to notify customers exactly how their financial PII will be used. Instead, GLB requires that the notice simply describe general categories of financial PII collected and disclosed and to whom it is disclosed. GLB does not require that customers have access to their financial PII. Financial PII may be shared freely and without any consent privilege among related affiliates of the financial services firm, such as a broker, bank, or insurer controlled by the same holding company. GLB critics expect that privacy bills will be introduced to close this loophole.

HEALTH CARE PRIVACY

Health care information may include a wide variety of diagnostic and treatment PII. These data often show the subject individual's former and present health condition (e.g., test results for blood pressure, HIV, biopsy). Such PII informs predictions about the physical condition and future health care costs of subject individuals and their families. Physicians cannot render effective diagnosis and treatment without much of the test data and prior record of treatments and responses. Health insurers must have truthful treatment information to accurately and efficiently make health care payments. These are immediate uses of health care information needed for the rendering of essential health care services, called **uses and disclosures for treatment, payment, and operations**.

Privacy fundamentalists warn that secondary uses of these data, called **uses and disclosures other than for treatment, payment, and operations**, are less valid. These secondary uses might include such things as a determination of those who should not be hired, insured, or treated. Most people would find public disclosure of such sensitive data repulsive. Imagine video replays of embarrassing surgery or public revelation of medical treatment history. Such exposure would be among the most basic attacks on human dignity. Indeed, the confidentiality of doctor-patient relations is among the most sacred of societal mores. The theory underlying confidential relationship privileges is that loss of this privacy through disclosure by PII databases will deter patients from seeking necessary medical treatment. Therefore, health care privacy is a fundamental human precept found in many state and federal laws. Of course, we all benefit from medical research that identifies cures or alleviates suffering. Secondary use of health care information is essential to the progress of medical science.

Congress passed the Health Insurance Portability and Accountability Act (HIPAA) in 1996 to permit freer movement of employees among the different health care insurance plans of different employers. HIPPA also restricts disclosure of health care PII by the medical profession, hospitals, health insurers, employers, and health care intermediaries. The health care PII issues were so contentious that it took nearly four years after HIPPA's passage for the Department of Health and Human Services (HHS) to finally issue the HIPPA privacy regulations in December 2000. These rules are extremely detailed and potentially costly to implement. HHS used estimates for implementation costs that ranged from $5 billion to $17 billion annually, with $9 billion to $21 billion in annual benefits. As with most potentially costly regulatory programs, industry estimates the costs will be higher and the benefits lower.

HIPPA defines health care–related PII as **protected health information (PHI)** and restricts the data management and disclosure activities of several **covered entities**, including health care providers, plans, clearinghouses, HMOs, Preferred Provider Organizations (PPOs), and their affiliates. Oral, written, and electronic PHI are all covered. The general rule is that patients must give prior written consent—opt in—before PHI can be used for treatment or can be disclosed for other uses. The forms of consent are different in various contexts and are subject to highly technical requirements. It appears that covered entities in the health care industry can decline to provide services or payments unless patients give consent, except for emergency medical services. Patients have notice, access, and correction rights and may demand an accounting of disclosures made (date, recipient, brief description of PHI). Exceptions were created for obvious purposes: emergency treatments, imminent threats to public health, and some law enforcement and judicial uses. Conflicting state laws are largely preempted. The HIPPA regulations are being phased in until full implementation in 2004. There are strong security and enforcement provisions. For example, violations are punishable by civil and *criminal* penalties. At this writing a rule proposal from HHS would eliminate the consent requirement.

EMPLOYMENT AND WORKPLACE PRIVACY

Employers increasingly use tests and gather other PII to predict the performance of new hires and monitor existing employees. References and PII from former employers seem relevant. Information about individuals' lifestyles, habits, use of substances, and past behaviors could conceivably have a bearing on their honesty and prospects. However, many people view tests and background checks as excessive intrusion. Some tests have questionable validity (e.g., polygraph) on account of scientifically fallacious theories or slipshod testing procedures. The employment privacy controversy illustrates a growing tension between employers' stated needs and rights advocated by employees.

Many employers require interviewees to take batteries of tests, including psychological, medical, drug, intelligence, and skills tests. Psychological testing may reveal an applicant's work ethic, criminal tendencies, ability to work with others, performance under stress, and aptitude for leadership. Intelligence and skills tests can reveal knowledge and ability to perform necessary job tasks. Medical tests may reveal that the predisposition of an applicant or immediate family to certain diseases could require expensive treatment. For example, mandatory HIV testing for the AIDS virus is a controversial procedure disapproved by some courts.[38] Some employers may try to administer genetic testing, hoping to predict an applicant's honesty, criminal tendencies, or future burden for health care expense. The administration, management, and use of PII based on intrusive tests raise contentious public policy, legal, and privacy issues.

38. *Glover v. Easter Nebraska Community Office of Retardation*, 686 F.Supp. 243 (D.Neb. 1988).

SUBSTANCE ABUSE

Employees' abuse of certain substances can adversely affect performance, productivity, health, and workplace safety. For example, tobacco use is strongly linked to lung cancer and emphysema. Whereas workplace smoking bans and hiring bans on smokers are probably legal, firing smokers may not be legitimate. Thousands of local ordinances and employer work rules regulate smoking. Similarly, alcohol and drug abuse can be directly related to jobsite accidents and public safety, as well as employees' diminished capacity and productivity. Many large firms have drug testing programs for prospective new hires, usually performed through urinalysis or the assay of hair samples.

Some firms monitor employee drug use. Drug testing poses numerous legal issues. Policies covering unionized employees must be negotiated with the union because testing is a term or condition of employment. Random drug testing of existing employees may not be permissible, with some exceptions for federal employees where there is "reasonable suspicion" or "probable cause" that drug abuse has impaired the employee's job performance. The justification for drug testing is clearest when the employee's job affects public safety, such as operators of dangerous equipment, transportation workers, pilots, train engineers, air traffic controllers, and bus drivers. The Drug-Free Workplace Act of 1988 requires private contractors supplying the federal government to establish and enforce drug-free policies, although the act requires neither drug testing nor rehabilitation services. The following case illustrates how some states balance drug prevention with privacy.

Twigg v. Hercules Corp.

406 S.E.2d 52 (W.Va., 1990)

Facts. Twigg performed his job satisfactorily as a materiel planner at Hercules's Allegany Ballistics Laboratory in Mineral County, West Virginia. Twigg protested but submitted to two random drug urinalyses in 1986. Both tests were negative. However, Twigg refused to submit to a third test in 1987 and was discharged. Twigg challenged his discharge in federal district court, which sought clarification of West Virginia privacy policy from the West Virginia Supreme Court of Appeals.

Legal Issue. Are employers restricted in their drug testing of employees?

Opinion. This court first dealt with the issue of employers being held liable where an employee's discharge contravenes a substantial public policy in *Harless v. First National Bank in Fairmont*. A bank employee was allegedly discharged after he attempted to bring to the attention of the bank's vice-presidents, and a member of the bank's board of directors, the fact that the bank "had intentionally and illegally overcharged customers on prepayment of their installment loans and intentionally did not make proper rebates,'" all in violation of state and federal consumer credit and protection laws. We recognized in the Harless case a new cause of action for at-will employees who are discharged when the employer's motives for such discharge contravene a substantial public policy.

Subsequently, in *Cordle v. General Hugh Mercer Corp.*, we dealt with whether the discharge of an employee for refusal to take a polygraph test as a condition of employment violated substantial public policy. In applying the holding of the *Cordle* case to the present case, it is unquestionable that since we do recognize a "legally protected interest in privacy" and have previously found that requiring employees to submit to polygraph examinations violates public policy based upon this privacy right, we likewise recognize that it is contrary to public policy in West Virginia for an employer to require an employee to submit to drug testing, since such testing portends an invasion of an individual's right to privacy.

We do, however, temper our holding with two exceptions to this rule. Drug testing will not be found to be violative of public policy grounded in the potential intrusion of a person's right to privacy where it is conducted by an employer based upon reasonable good faith objective suspicion of an employee's drug usage or where an employee's job responsibility involves public safety or the safety of others.

Where a business is engaged in an activity which involves either public safety or safety concerns for others, we find that there exists a legitimate reason for the implementation of a drug testing program since a drug-impaired employee would potentially increase the risk of harm to others. However, there must be a showing by the employer that the employees required to undergo such testing have responsibilities or duties which are connected to the safety concerns of others. Thus, in the present case, it is obvious that a company involved in manufacturing highly explosive and dangerous fuels does employ individuals who, if drug-impaired, could increase the risk of harm to others, whether they are members of the general public or other employees.

Generally, courts have held that "(t)he proscription against unauthorized searches and seizures embodied in ... the Fourth Amendment to the United States Constitution ... applies exclusively to government or state action. Therefore, generally a private employer can conduct drug testing without having to concern themselves with requirements of the Fourth Amendment. Thus we recognize that the imposition of an obligation upon the employer to meet the high standards of probable cause before conducting a drug test on an employee would place an intolerable burden upon the employer. That is why we choose to impose the lesser standard of reasonable suspicion upon the employer. [This recognizes] the employer's right to be free from potential liability brought on by an employee's drug usage which may ultimately result in harm to the others or in mismanagement, misfeasance or incompetence in the workplace. We refuse to allow an employer to intrude upon this right of his employee absent some showing of reasonable good faith objective suspicion, unless the employer can articulate either a public safety concern or concern for the safety of other employees. To hold otherwise would effectively render an employee's right to privacy meaningless.

Decision. Employers are restricted in their use of mandatory drug testing for employees unless there are legitimate public safety concerns or a reasonable suspicion of drug use.

Case Questions

1. For what reasons is it legitimate to override an employee's right to privacy with a drug or lie detector test?
2. What other reasons aside from safety and liability might an employer have to institute drug or other substance abuse testing?

FEDERAL LIE DETECTOR PROHIBITIONS

The **Employee Polygraph Protection Act** prohibits most employers' use of lie detectors without a reasonable suspicion of losses caused by employees. A lie detector test may be conducted if the employer provides a written statement showing a reasonable suspicion that the employee had access to damaged or missing material and was involved in the matter. The questions must relate only to the alleged misconduct and may not be the only basis for an employee's dismissal. Employers may not retaliate against employees who refuse to take a lie detector test. Violators are subject to liability for punitive damages, civil fines, and attorney's fees. Some exemptions exist for governments, government defense contractors, drug producers, and security protection companies. The unreliability of polygraph PII makes the results generally inadmissible to prove guilt in a criminal trial.

WORKPLACE SURVEILLANCE AND E-MAIL PRIVACY

Workplace surveillance is nothing new. Laziness, disloyalty, and mistrust long have inspired close supervision. However, technological advances enable new and creative forms of secret surveillance. Many employers are expanding their privacy intrusions, which severely limits each employee's expectations of zones of privacy in the workplace.[39] Indeed, the business necessity exceptions to prohibitions on workplace wiretapping and on-line surveillance provide employers with a fairly strong basis for surveillance. On-line surveillance is generally permissible if the employer owns the networks and computers. The use of cameras and listening devices is also increasing.

These realities must be balanced with the widespread encouragement employees receive to explore the Internet generally or e-commerce sites specifically and to use computerized communications to achieve the firm's efficiency and competitiveness goals. Only recently have many employees acquired broadband Internet and high-speed e-mail access at their homes. Workplace access has been the predominant medium for most employees' on-line activity. There is an ongoing tension between two major forces. On one hand, there are workplace rules prohibiting unauthorized use of employer facilities (phone, e-mail, Internet) and the employer's increasing legal risks for employees' unlawful activities. On the other hand, employees apparently will make inevitable use of the employer facilities for at least some personal purposes. Lax enforcement of these policies expose employers to considerable liability (copyright infringement, pornography, defamation, privacy violations, discrimination). Legislation may be proposed to specifically prohibit harassing, obscene, or abusive e-mail. Overly stringent policies risk both absenteeism and employees inevitably finding work-arounds, such as moving their on-line activities to personal wireless devices (pagers, cell phones, wireless Internet).

Employers generally lay claim to ownership of internal workplace computers, networks, and other communications facilities, which allows the employer to (1) maintain confidentiality of trade secrets and (2) prohibit personal uses of employer assets, often justifying closer surveillance. Any lingering doubts are eliminated with workplace rules. Employees must bind themselves to restrictions, often with a separate part of their employment contract, as introduced in Chapter 13. Privacy policies that are clearly communicated and rigorously followed reduce liability risks for the employer. It seems unlikely that wiretapping laws will protect the workplace privacy of employees. The ECPA's exceptions for workplace notice support the employer's surveillance of e-mail and Internet activity. However, smaller firms using public e-mail systems may risk liability under the ECPA for unlawful interception.

Yet, many people still mistakenly believe that e-mail and on-line activity are evanescent, remain unrecorded, are not intercepted, and can be easily disowned. Anonymous remailers can forward e-mail messages with the sender's identity stripped. However, as the world discovered in the Microsoft antitrust litigation, confidential and damaging e-mail from Bill Gates concerning competitive strategies is very difficult to erase. Both electronic and print copies too often proliferate. In litigation, it is now routine to subpoena print and electronic records during pretrial discovery. It may take some time for Internet newcomers and even seasoned e-mail users to recognize the permanence of their too often frank, hostile, or incriminating e-mails, as well as other records of their workplace Internet activities. Employer policies generally extend to prohibit unauthorized sharing of user IDs and passwords to access the firm's computers, either at the workplace or remotely by computer. By contrast, home e-mail and Internet activities are much more likely to maintain some protection under privacy law.

39. *Smyth v. Pillsbury Co.*, 914 F.Supp. 97 (E.D.Pa. 1996).

PRIVACY AND SELF-REGULATION

The United States will probably continue to try to supervise privacy policy with self-regulation rather than government regulation or private rights of action. The pioneers who developed the Internet generally despise legal regulation and often insist that the Internet can never be regulated. This position is becoming untenable and unrealistic. Nevertheless, many "netizens" are proponents of **netiquette**, an unofficial form of self-regulation that emphasizes courtesy, respect, and self-restraint. The success of netiquette should probably unclog bandwidth and avert overregulation. Self-regulation enhances trust that may also avert more stringent regulation. Many firms realize the costly stakes if privacy policies are not forthcoming. Increasingly, firms' privacy efforts are more serious, and **chief privacy officers** are taking responsibility for compliance and coordinating the diverse, sectoral privacy problems for employee PII, financial PII, health care PHI, and their on-line presence. Self-regulation may be essential for firms dealing with the EU.

Industry may be able to avert more stringent privacy regulation with more objective self-regulation that is supplemented by industry associations and third parties. Trade associations traditionally have served to mediate disputes with outsiders. When such programs build the trust of outsiders and prove to be objective, they can win the support of regulators and even the public.[40] For example, the Direct Marketing Association has created privacy guidelines and works closely with the FTC to assure compliance with the COPPA privacy regulations. Another approach is for independent third parties to establish guidelines and provide some verification that firms are compliant. For example, the Better Business Bureau has established BBBOnline, a code of on-line business practices and dispute resolution through arbitration. It is a form of **seal program** that is intended to raise the public's expectation of trust in the fairness of online privacy practices. The TRUSTe program is similar. The stakes are enormous: If self-regulation of privacy practices fails, more stringent legislation seems inevitable.

ONLINE

http://www.truste.org
http://www.bbbonline.org

Of course, effective self-regulation begins inside each firm. Privacy issues must be taken seriously and commitment made by the firm's leadership. Privacy policy making and enforcement should be an important organizational goal, perhaps managed by high-ranking form officer. Privacy policy making and implementation must be seen as important and revised as privacy developments unfold. Periodic privacy audits may be appropriate to assure that compliance and privacy practices are current. Most firms will have at least some employees who need privacy training to comply with privacy policies, privacy law, and society's evolving privacy expectations. Recall that the United States negotiated a safe harbor from the EU Data Directive that relies on self-regulatory programs.

40. *Self-Regulation and Privacy Online: A Report to Congress* (FTC, July 1999); see http://www.ftc.gov/os/1999/9907/pt071399.htm.

QUESTIONS

1. Explain how privacy is not an absolute. Consider the interests that subject individuals have in retaining their privacy and the interests that society has in overcoming privacy, particularly the compelling societal reasons to allow privacy intrusions.

2. Explain how Judge Hand's method of balancing privacy might work if it was possible to estimate the probability that particular types of intrusions might discover critically useful information, the costs of the intrusion, and the losses society suffers if the information is *not* discovered.

3. As part of a routine audit of the Amerada Hess Corp.'s 1972–1975 tax returns, the IRS sought tax accrual work papers held by Arthur Young & Co., the auditor. An administrative summons was issued to Arthur Young. The appeals court applied state law giving an accountant-client privilege. May an accountant's client assert the privilege to resist an IRS subpoena for potentially incriminating work papers held by the accountant? See *United States v. Arthur Young & Co.*, 104 S.Ct. 1495 (1984).

4. The Occupational Safety and Health Act (OSHA) authorizes personnel from the OSHA Administration to inspect work areas for worker safety violations. Although there were no employee complaints and no search warrant was obtained, the OSHA inspector attempted to enter Barlow's site. However, the business owner denied access to the non-public areas of the facility. Must an OSHA inspector secure a warrant to search regulated premises if administrative probable cause is absent? See *Marshall v. Barlow's*, 436 U.S. 307 (1978).

5. The victim was struck by a vehicle and received blood transfusions while hospitalized. Within a year, he was diagnosed with AIDS and died a year later. In a wrongful death suit against the driver, the victim's representative attempted to prove that AIDS was contracted in the transfusion by serving a subpoena on the blood bank for the names and addresses of blood donors. Should the blood bank be required to disclose this private information, or is public policy better served by respecting donor's privacy? See *Rasmussen v. South Florida Blood Service*, 500 So.2d 533 (Fl., 1987).

6. New York State maintained a central database of patients using some particular prescription drugs. There was evidence that some physicians and patients were reluctant to use the listed drugs because the security of the database was in question. Is there a constitutional right to maintain privacy of prescription drug records? See *Whalen v. Roe*, 429 U.S. 589 (1977).

7. A large quantity of political e-mail was sent to advocate the defeat of a proposal to raise school taxes. An Ohio state law prohibited the anonymous distribution of campaign literature. As applied to e-mail spam, is the prohibition against anonymous literature a violation of the sender's privacy and First Amendment rights of free speech? See *McIntyre v. Ohio Elections Commission*, 514 U.S. 334 (1995).

8. Explain what laws might be used by privacy fundamentalists to prohibit websites from tracking users' on-line activities. What laws might be used to prohibit either the aggregation of PII or the resale onward of these data to third parties?

9. How might businesses use the "business necessity" concept to justify surveillance of employees, customers, suppliers, and others? Consider the following situations.
    a. Using network computer logs to monitor employee e-mail.
    b. Using network computer logs to monitor employee surfing habits and clickstream on the Internet.
    c. Using hidden cameras to monitor employee activities in the workplace.
    d. Using hidden cameras to monitor customer activities in commercial areas.

Intellectual Property

PART IV

Before the twenty-first century, tangible property was the primary source of value. Enterprises exploiting products, plants, equipment, livestock, and land produced the most economic return. Growth was possible with expansion that gave access to more tangible raw materials, increased production of tangible products, and enhanced distribution methods to deliver physical commodities and finished goods. However, at the dawn of the twenty-first century, there is a marked shift to the significance of intangible assets. **Intangibles** are assets without physical substance, such as the value derived from ideas, knowledge, and relationships. Part IV introduces an important subset of intangible property, known as **intellectual property** rights (IP). IP is produced, protected, and exploited for economic gain in quite different ways than are tangible properties such as goods or land. A misunderstanding of these differences will be very costly for managers of converging businesses in the twenty-first century.

A major difference between tangible property and IP is exhaustibility. Tangibles are totally **exhaustible**, but IP is seemingly inexhaustible. Transfer, theft, or destruction of the physical embodiment of a tangible asset eliminates the benefits previously held by its owner or possessor. For example, the sale of land or theft of a computer (personal property) does away with (exhausts) the original owner's benefits. By contrast, copies can be made of IP without disturbing the owner's original. For example, the owner of a music CD, book, or movie may still have the original even after copies are made or distributed to others. If the copying is done secretly, the owner may not even know about the theft. Of course, the market becomes saturated when enough copies are floating around, making it difficult for the owner to sell legitimate copies. IP law protects the owner from such infringement. It is unfortunate that the technical ease of photocopying books, burning CDs, and distributing unauthorized copies is causing widespread disrespect for IP rights. People with limited knowledge of IP may come to wrongly believe that making unauthorized copies or distributing such copies to strangers is not theft. These activities are wrong and constitute civil and sometimes criminal infringement.

IP law attempts to balance two important things: the public domain and private property. The **public domain** is all the knowledge and expression accumulated during human experience since the beginning of time. Society, culture, and civilization would not have developed unless people could freely build upon the discoveries and ideas of all past generations. IP law defines the public domain by giving IP rights only to creators and inventors of new things. All other knowledge remains in the public domain for others' use. Much of the four chapters in Part IV is about how IP laws distinguish between the public domain and those truly new developments that deserve protection as IP. Therefore, IP rewards inventors and authors with limited monopolies to produce and sell IP so that society will eventually be enriched by their creativity.

Part IV explains the most important laws addressing IP. Chapter 15, Copyrights, introduces how expression is protected. Chapter 16, Trade Secrets and Database Protection, examines the protections for a wide variety of valuable secret information. This part concludes with Chapter 17, Trademarks, which considers the use and protection of commercial symbols and Internet domain names. Taken along with Chapter 13 in Part III, Technology Transfer, Employment, and Service Contracts, these chapters cover the major IP property rights and exploitation methods in wide use today and for the foreseeable future.

Throughout Part IV, watch for recurring themes that help to distinguish IP rights. Copyright covers only works of authorship—the form of expression that authors use in their writings, software, and visual arts. Trade secret law protects information with economic value but only if it is adequately kept secret. Databases are collections of information or works. Patents are inventions, and trademarks are commercial symbols. Throughout these chapters, be alert to these differences and to the different ways these intangible rights are created, protected, and vindicated through infringement litigation, as well as the regulatory agencies and processes involved. Also recognize that although IP is a very complex and esoteric area of professional practice, innovation would not happen without the creativity of scientists, artists, writers, technology experts, business strategists, applied economists, and many other professionals. Innovation is the engine for growth into the twenty-first century.

Copyrights

Business law in the twentieth century largely addressed tangible assets (e.g., product, plant, equipment, real estate) as the predominant form of property. However, in the twenty-first century, intangible property rights, like the expression protected by copyright law, are becoming the central theme. As noted in the discussion of Constitutional law in Chapter 4, expression is protected under the First Amendment because it is essential to democracy and to commerce. Expression describes the research results that specify inventions, which makes expression both the object and the medium of most creativity. Now consider the human need and passion for entertainment, news, and personal interaction. It is easy to see how expression contains information that lies at the heart of all communications and commerce.

Expression is the most pervasive of all forms of intellectual property (IP). Patents and trade secrets protect ideas but are described in text and drawings. Some creative designs can be protected as design patents, and others function as commercial symbols protectable as trademarks. Even with all these alternative forms of IP, none of them is possible without expression, making copyright as the most pervasive form of IP. This point is particularly important to e-commerce, given that nearly everything on the Internet is expression.

IP is intangible property that suffers greatly when compared with tangible property, a difficulty introduced in Chapter 13. Recall that owners must invest often large amounts to invent, create, or acquire IP assets, and IP is much more easily misappropriated than is tangible property. Therefore, it is good that government fosters creativity and innovation by establishing special forms of property rights for IP: copyrights, patents, trade secrets, and trademarks. Technologies such as encryption can also play important roles in preventing misappropriation. Copyrighted expression is particularly vulnerable, and several emerging technologies intensify these risks.

Digital copying and distribution has great potential to weaken traditional business models in the software, music, and video industries. In the 1990s, these industries successfully lobbied for new copyright protection laws. Given the public attention over the modern subject matter of copyright (digital entertainment, Internet communication, creative websites), copyright law is ascending to a central role in e-commerce and in cyberspace. This chapter discusses how copyright law protects traditional forms of expression and how expression is adapting to digital forms.

Commentary

Technical Vulnerability of Copyrighted Works

Four technological developments have exacerbated the vulnerability of artists, authors, and owners of IP. First, the digitization of expressive content makes it easy to duplicate. Copying digital content is cheaper, easier, and more reliable than was generally possible in analog formats because tape recorders and photocopiers make imperfect copies. Second, copies are stored more easily, cheaply, and secretly. Consider how modern computer storage practices use huge hard drives, optical "burning" technologies, transportable mass storage, or the accumulation of big files on remote servers. Many individuals can now build up large collections of content heretofore practical only for libraries. Third, computerized telecommunications technologies have fostered the development of networks like the Internet. Widespread networking makes it possible to distribute content precisely or very broadly and over long distances. Just a few years ago, such distribution was only available to broadcasters and media conglomerates. Fourth, digital technologies facilitate the modification or transformation of creative works, such as by digital morphing. Creative works can be changed to hide their original authorship or easily palmed off as the product of someone else. Moreover, digital works can be transformed into new, sometimes even better works. These capabilities raise ethical questions for equipment makers and consumers.

Consider how the digital revolution has destabilized the traditional business models used by the entertainment industry. Authors, artists, creators, and distributors of software, games, music, and video are now much more vulnerable to misappropriation. Each form of content is more easily, cheaply, and flawlessly copied, archived, shared, and altered than was possible just a decade ago. Recorded music is digitized into various formats, "ripped," and stored for playback on assorted devices. In many cases, this recorded music is just exchanged with close friends. However, peer-to-peer (P2P) technologies such as Napster encouraged global publication among countless strangers. In some instances, expression has been modified in sophisticated home studios. Similarly, since the 1980s, large quantities of unauthorized and infringing copies have been made of software and games. Going forward, other industries may also become at risk. For example, the technologies are finally developing that make digital infringement of video even more widespread than was possible with the analog VCR. Is it ethical to take copies of music without paying?

The music, motion picture, and software industries claim they have suffered huge financial losses from such unlawful infringement. However, many of these claims are based on estimates of lost profits from sales that "might" have occurred. Industry often projects losses as if every recipient of an illegal copy definitely would have purchased at full retail price. Clearly, this is a specious and deceptive assumption.[1] Indeed, the evidence of any media industry harm has only begun to surface, and other economic factors can explain some of the entertainment industry's lost profitability. Further, the evidence may only be beginning to emerge that P2P file sharing undercuts the incentive to invest in creation and marketing of sufficiently diverse content. Society faces a huge ethical dilemma in reconciling these opposing interests.

---

1. See *RIAA v. Diamond Multimedia*, 180 F.3d 1072, 1074 (9th Cir., 1999). Whether piracy causes such financial harm is a subject of dispute. Critics of the industry's piracy loss figures have noted that a willingness to download illicit files for free does not necessarily correlate to lost sales, for the simple reason that persons willing to accept an item for free often will not purchase the same item, even if it is no longer freely available. See Lewis Kurlantzick and Jacqueline E. Pennino, "The Audio Home Recording Act of 1992 and the Formation of Copyright Policy," *Journal of the Copyright Society U.S.A.* 45 (1998), 497, 506. Critics further note that the price of commercially available recordings already reflects the existence of copying and the benefits and harms such copying causes. Thus, they contend, the current price of recordings offsets, at least in part, the losses incurred by the industry from home taping and piracy.

OVERVIEW OF COPYRIGHTS

The law of **copyright** protects original **works of authorship** once they are fixed in a tangible medium. Initial copyright protection arises when an author or creator writes, saves, records, or otherwise forms expression in a physical process. The resulting product is called a **work**. For example, literature, music, or software is written on paper or input into a computer. Music, drama, or dance is also recorded in a medium. For example, images are created, drawn, formed, recorded, or captured as photographs, architectural plans, sculpture, maps, or other visual works. Authors and creators of copyrighted works must often transfer some or all of their rights to others who are more skilled, better connected, or better financed to effectively exploit the work.

Copyright law gives the creator or author several important exclusive rights. These rights are often called a "bundle of rights" because they represent different interests in the work. They include the right to **reproduce** (make copies), **distribute** (sell copies), make **derivative works** (adapt), perform or display (exhibit to the public), make **digital transmissions**, and transfer rights by license or assignment. It is an unlawful infringement when other people use the copyrighted work in these ways but are unauthorized to do so. **Infringement** entitles the owner to legal remedies (compensation). Purchasers of a physical embodiment of the copyrighted work, such as a book, CD, or video, may resell these. This very important right for purchasers is called the **first sale doctrine**. A few infringements are excused under the **fair use** exception. For example, it may be a fair use to use another's work for teaching, scholarship, or research or to parody, criticize, or comment, such as in news reporting. Fair use is one of the most contentious copyright issues today because digital technologies make copying easier.

Copyrights last for a very long time. The **copyright term** has been lengthened for works created after 1978 to more than 70 years in some instances and up to 120 years for some works. The owner's rights under copyright law become stronger when the work is registered and deposited with the Copyright Office of the Library of Congress, although doing so is not always necessary. Similarly, it is no longer mandatory to place a copyright notice on the work, although doing so is still advisable. These matters are detailed throughout this chapter.

THE EVOLVING HERITAGE OF COPYRIGHT

The U.S. Constitution gives Congress the power to make IP laws for copyrights and patents. Before passage of the 1976 Copyright Act, the state common law provided an alternate protection scheme. However, Congress has made the federal law of copyrights exclusive, so the states may no longer provide rights or remedies covering copyrightable subject matter. Much of the ongoing and probable future struggle over copyrights will explore how much the public may use expression protected by copyright. This conflict is really over the **public domain**. A majority of the copyright litigation and regulation concerns how soon, how much, and how others may use expressive works.

Contemporary copyright law had its beginnings in England with Parliament's passage of the **Statute of Anne** in 1710. By the late eighteenth century, the U.S. Constitution had recognized the unique role government plays in providing copyright as an incentive to creativity. Various copyright laws have been passed since that first U.S. statute in 1790. The 1909 and 1976 U.S. copyright laws are the most important.

Today, copyright law is again in transition. Most of the world's copyright laws still reflect traditional conceptions of the range of expression, turn-of-the-twentieth-century technologies, and the traditional business models used to exploit copyrighted works. These laws were designed mainly for literary, musical, and artistic expressions and not for functional or coded methods like software or encryption.

Radical changes in technology have pushed traditional copyright concepts to the limit, requiring Congress, regulators, and the courts to improvise as they adapt copyright law to new technologies. Some well-financed interests such as publishing and media conglomerates have been extraordinarily successful in getting legislation passed that favors their interests. Many critics argue these recent law revisions have unduly benefited copyright owners at the expense of consumers, users, and the public domain. They argue that the traditional concepts such as "ideas are not copyrightable, only the expression of ideas is protected under copyright," fair use, and the first sale doctrine are being whittled away. Other nations are also a source of pressure to change copyright law.

The impact of international treaties and domestic laws with an effect on international copyright is significant, as discussed throughout this chapter. A key copyright treaty, the **Berne Convention**, has become the focal point of the different conceptions of expression from various nations and cultures. Other important laws and treaties include the U.S. Tariff Act, the Universal Copyright Convention, the "TRIPS" provisions of the World Trade Organization (WTO), and the regional trade agreements covering the European Union and North America. The United States is often a bellwether in first identifying new copyright issues and has exerted leadership in providing compromise to accommodate the opposing factions of creators and owners versus users and consumers. Nevertheless, some observers charge that the United States fails to protect some rights adequately (e.g., moral rights) and overprotects others (e.g., copyright duration). Some of the more significant international copyright laws and treaties are summarized in Exhibit 15.1.

EXHIBIT 15.1 Major International Copyright Treaties and Laws

International Agreement, Treaty, or Law	Major Participants and Successes	Major Provisions
Tariff Act §337	U.S.	Authorizes International Trade Commission (ITC) hearings; ITC may issue *exclusion order* directing U.S. Customs Service to block imports of infringing products
Berne Convention	U.S. is among 79 nations; now the leading treaty	Requires national treatment; no formalities for acquisition of copyright rights; strong moral rights
Universal Copyright Convention	Initially favored by U.S. as preferred alternative to Berne	Requires national treatment; substantive provisions: notice, registration
WTO trade-related intellectual property (TRIPS)	Many nations; most successful of all international IP treaties	Requires compliance with Berne, except for moral rights, software, and data compilation protections; permits copyright owner to prohibit rental
EU Treaty of Rome	19 EU "member states"	Various EU directives requiring consistent and harmonized national laws
North America Free Trade Agreement	Canada, Mexico, and U.S.; some slow progress	Calls for harmonization and effective enforcement of national laws

COPYRIGHTABLE SUBJECT MATTER

The Copyright Act defines the types of expression that may be protected.

> **Copyrightable Subject Matter**
> original works of authorship fixed in any tangible medium of expression, now known or later developed, from which they can be perceived, reproduced, or otherwise communicated, either directly or with the aid of a machine or device.[2]

There are several elements to copyrightability. First, the work must be **original;** that is, it is not copied but created independently by the author. This standard is not as rigorous as the novelty standard required under patent law. Further, litigation is not a good forum to assess artistic merit.[3] Nevertheless, the work must have at least a minimum level of creativity or authorial ingenuity. Second, the expression must be **fixed in a tangible medium of expression**, which requires a stable, permanent, and physical rendering either in a copy or in a phonorecord. The term **phonorecord** is a catchall for recording media; it includes most recordings of sound, video, or software in various media: vinyl, tape, disk.

Copyright does not protect oral renditions or performances unless there is recording or documentation of the original. However, **ephemeral copies** of software or other works loaded into a computer's RAM are potentially infringing copies, even though they disappear when the computer is turned off or moves on to do another activity.[4] Live performances have been problematic but now may be fixed if they are simultaneously broadcast. Third, the work must be perceivable by humans either directly or indirectly. **Direct perception** occurs while a person reads a book or views a photo, painting, or sculpture. **Indirect perception** requires the aid of a machine or device, such as listening to an audio CD or watching a DVD movie played on a machine. Video games in software or on a cartridge are fixed, even though the user's progress through the game can change the images actually viewed from all those possible in the game's memory.

CLASSIFICATION OF WORKS OF AUTHORSHIP

What types of works are copyrightable? The Copyright Act lists eight types of works of authorship permitted copyright protection: (1) literary works, (2) musical works (including accompanying words), (3) dramatic works (including accompanying music), (4) pantomimes and choreography, (5) pictorial, graphic, and sculptural works, (6) motion pictures and other audiovisual (A/V) works, (7) sound recordings, and (8) architectural works. These categories can be complex because some works may not fit neatly in just one category. Categorization can be important because some of the special rights discussed in the next section are not available for all types of works. The classification of copyrightable works is summarized in Exhibit 15.2.

Literary works are the most basic and include expressions in words or numbers. Novels, nonfiction books, databases, and poetry are all literary works. There was significant litigation about the copyrightability of computer software until Congress

2. 17 U.S.C. §102(a) (2000).
3. *Bleistein v. Donaldson Lithographing Co.*, 188 U.S. 239 (1903).
4. *MAI Systems Corp. v. Peak Computer Inc.*, 991 F.2d 511 (9th Cir., 1993).

EXHIBIT 15.2 Types of Copyrightable Works

Works of Authorship	Definition	Examples
Literary	Expressions in words or numbers	Novels, nonfiction books, databases, poetry, software
Musical	Composition: tune, melody, parts, and words but not if in motion picture or other A/V soundtrack	Sheet music, arrangements
Dramatic	Directions guiding portrayal of story in performance using dialogue or acting; includes associated music	Script with accompanying sheet music
Pantomime, choreography	Dance movements and patterns (successive static and kinetic body movements) following rhythmic relationships	Video, film, dance notation
Pictorial, graphic, sculpture	Two- and three-dimensional works of fine, graphic, and applied art; must be physically or conceptually severable from functional aspects	Photographs, maps, paintings, 3D sculptures, pottery, textiles, macramé, jewelry, furniture, computer graphics, still cartoon and characters, prints, art reproductions, maps, globes, charts, technical drawings, diagrams, models, games
Motion picture, audiovisual	Series of related images shown by machine, accompanied by sounds	Disks or tapes shown by projector or TV
Sound recordings	Series of musical, spoken, or other sounds	Phonorecords (tape, disks)
Architectural	Building design, architectural plans, or drawings, including overall form, arrangement, and composition of spaces and design elements	Plans, blueprints, drawings, models, structures built after 1990

implemented the recommendations of the National Commission of New Technological Uses of Copyrighted Works (CONTU) with passage of the **Computer Software Copyright Act** in 1980. Software is now classified as literary work when composed of "a set of statements or instructions to be used directly or indirectly in a computer in order to bring about a certain result." It includes source code written by either programmers or another computer. Software also includes object code that runs on computers, as well as operating systems and applications programs.[5]

Musical works include the words and tune as fixed in sheet music, sound recordings, and arrangements but arbitrarily do not include the soundtrack to a motion picture or other types of A/V work. Sound recordings were not protected until after the passage of the **Sound Recording Act** in 1971. **Sound recordings** capture the performance of a music, literary, or dramatic work by fixing it as a series of musical, spoken, or other sounds regardless of the medium: disks, tapes, or phonorecords. There is an important distinction between the composition and the sound recording: The owner of the composition can prevent performances of the composition, but the sound recording owner cannot. This point was made in Chapter 13 when the compulsory license was discussed. No federal copyright provides protection for sound recordings made before 1972.

The Copyright Office defines **dramatic works** as directions guiding the portrayal of a story in a performance by use of dialogue or acting. **Pantomimes** and **choreographic**

5. *Apple Computer Inc. v. Franklin Computer Corp.*, 714 F.2d 1240 (3d Cir., 1983), *cert.denied* 464 U.S. 1033 (1984).

works are dance movements and patterns, including both successive static and kinetic body movements that follow rhythmic relationships. They are typically fixed in video or film but can be recorded in notation form. **A/V** and **motion picture** works are series of related images shown by machine (projector, TV) and are accompanied by sounds. The music accompanying A/V works is protectable as part of the A/V work and not separately as a sound recording.

Pictorial, graphic, and sculptural works include two- and three-dimensional works of fine, graphic, or applied art. This classification includes photographs, prints, art reproductions, paintings, maps, three-dimensional sculptures, pottery, jewelry, globes, furniture, textiles, charts, technical drawings, computer graphics, diagrams, models, still cartoons, characters, and other forms. Artistic items that have some physical function have always raised concerns about the public domain. There is continuing concern that copyright protection of a particular artistic design might preempt similar useful objects. When copyright protection is so extensive that it covers the functional aspects of a work, other artists could be prevented from designing artistically different but functionally similar objects. For example, outdoor lighting fixtures were held not copyrightable unless the artistic aspects deserving copyright protection (artistic lampshade) could be separated physically from the functional aspects (mounting bracket). The **severability rule** requires that functional aspects must remain in the public domain.[6]

Since passage of the **Architectural Works Protection Act** in 1990, copyright protection now extends to architectural plans, drawings, blueprints, and models. The 1990 act protects the design of a building, architectural plans, and drawings, including the overall form, arrangement, and composition of spaces and design elements. Protection does not cover standard features but does cover both habitable (e.g., houses, office buildings) and uninhabitable structures (e.g., bridges, walkways). The severability rule discussed previously applies to buildings already standing before the act's passage; that is, functional aspects are in the public domain. However, for buildings constructed after the act's 1990 passage, copyright protection extends to the whole design.

NONCOPYRIGHTABLE SUBJECT MATTER

Ideas are not copyrightable; only the expression of ideas is protected under copyright. This statement is so often quoted because it underlies much of the controversy about infringement, it defines the public domain, and it also separates fair use from infringement. The Copyright Act specifically excludes the following from copyrightability: ideas, procedures, processes, systems, methods of operation, concepts, principles, and discoveries. This rule makes the public domain richer, enabling other creators to build upon the public domain as new expression reveals new ideas. Creators can maintain control over ideas only if they qualify as patentable or remain concealed as trade secrets.

This rule is the **idea-expression dichotomy**. It was clarified in *Baker v. Selden*, the original case in which copyright protection was denied to a system of bookkeeping, essentially because bookkeeping is a functional process.[7] Often the essential inquiry in distinguishing ideas from expression is whether another person would be prevented from using the idea unless they also used some form of the expression. As discussed in

6. *Esquire, Inc. v. Ringer*, 591 F.2d 796 (D.C.Cir., 1978).
7. 101 U.S. 99 (1879).

Chapter 16, sweat of the brow is not protectable under copyright; that is, when facts, data, or their interpretations are produced by hard work (the "sweat"), the result is ideas, not expression. Ideas standing alone are not copyrightable subject matter.

Idea versus Expression Dichotomy
Ideas are not copyrightable; only the expression of ideas is protected under copyright.

Generally, documents produced by the U.S. government are not copyrightable. This rule increases the public domain, particularly for public affairs. Citizens as a group own government documents because they were produced at taxpayer expense and are intended to benefit the public. Most federal and many state government documents are immediately placed in the public domain. In the United States, no copyright is possible for the reports, opinions, guidance, or other works prepared by government employees performing their government duties. This rule makes it difficult for the U.S. government to protect software produced by government agencies. However, federal agencies may purchase, license, and own software produced by others. Although there is no explicit copyright exclusion for state government works, nevertheless, the laws, regulations, and court decisions contained in many state documents are generally in the public domain. Some nations, such as the United Kingdom, claim proprietary interest in many of their government documents.

THE BUNDLE OF EXCLUSIVE RIGHTS

Copyright law grants several different rights to the author, creator, or owner of the work. These rights essentially define what the copyright owner can do with the copyrighted work and what rights the owner can license or assign to others. These rights are actually a **bundle of exclusive rights**, called **statutory rights**. They include the right to reproduce, make derivative works, distribute, perform or display, license and/or assign, and the newest right of digital transmission. The importance of these rights varies considerably and depends on the type of work and on the business models used in the particular industry involved. The exclusive rights sometimes overlap and can be combined to fully exploit the copyright. Exploitation is often best done by others, such as publishers or studios. The media industry commonly requires authors to assign their interests in their work before they will market the work. Copyright ownership and the licensing or assignment of some or all of the exclusive rights in the bundle are complex matters introduced in Chapter 13 as forms of technology transfer contracting.

REPRODUCTION

The most basic right under copyright is to **reproduce**—that is, to fix the work in a tangible and fairly permanent medium. Copying can also be done without fixation, such as when performed or displayed. The owner typically makes copies by the most efficient production process available: high-speed printing presses for printed materials, high-speed presses for vinyl phonorecords, high-efficiency burning of optical media (CDs), and deliberate, authorized downloads. Unauthorized copying is the most typical form of infringement, whether for personal use or for further distribution or sale. It does not matter that the copier is unaware that the work is protected under copyright. Unauthorized copies are often made by low-efficiency, consumer-oriented copying technologies such as photocopies, tapes, scans, CD burners, and PCs. Of course, there have been cases of large-scale pirating of entertainment products and software in efficient, modern factories. Many such Asian operations have been the focus of international trade negotiations and the grant of "most favored nations" status with the United States as a trading partner.

Unauthorized copying is a persistent and emotion-driven problem. Purchasers of copyrighted works believe they should have the right to make copies and use the work in any way they please. By stark contrast, copyright owners repeatedly use complex technicalities of copyright law to inhibit owners from freely using their works in ways made possible by new technologies. This tension is not easily resolved and has repeatedly resulted in compromise legislation that preserves some aspects of copyright owners' existing business models but permits the emergence of new technologies for copying, performance, and distribution. Nearly perfect digital copying poses a huge threat to the entertainment industry if endless copies are made from legitimately acquired originals and legitimate sales of new copies are prevented that would have otherwise occurred.

The right of purchasers to make tapes from vinyl records, off-the-air broadcasts, or CDs for home use was an unsettled question until the 1992 passage of the **Audio Home Recording Act** (AHRA). Negotiations among the powerful record and electronics industries were triggered by the entertainment industry's fear that digital audio tape (DAT) would lead to widespread illegal copying. The Copyright Office now refers to DAT and other digital recording technologies as **digital audio recording technology (DART)**. The AHRA requires that **digital audio recording devices** be equipped with copy protection technologies, called **serial copy management systems (SCMS)**, that prevent making copies from copies. Copies from originals are not prevented by the law. It is ironic that the infringement threat of DAT never really materialized but was reborn in the late 1990s as MP3 and CD burner technologies proliferated.

A compulsory royalty must be paid from the sales proceeds of both digital audio recording devices and blank digital recording media. These proceeds are pooled for distribution to copyright owners and artists by the Register of Copyrights of the Library of Congress. Purchasers may not be sued for infringement if they make non-commercial home copies. There is a similar exception for software purchasers but not for licensees to make backup copies of their software. Some software vendors nevertheless authorize licensees to make limited backup copies.

Are computer-based music-recording devices exempt from restrictions on the use of digital sound recording devices? The following case weakened enforcement rights of digital music rights owners. It may also have contributed to the migration of consumer listening from a preference for traditional hi-fi quality audio equipment using phonorecords, CDs, and tapes to portable and computer-based listening methods.

ONLINE
Recording Industry of America (RIAA)
http://www.riaa.org

RIAA v. Diamond Multimedia

180 F.3d 1072 (9th Cir., 1999)

Facts. Before the 1980s, a person wishing to copy an original music recording was limited to using reel-to-reel or cassette tape of a vinyl record or compact disk using analog, rather than digital, recording technology. Each successive generation of copies suffers from an increasingly pronounced degradation in sound quality, hiss, and lack of clarity characteristic of older recordings. Digital recording introduces almost no degradation in sound quality, no matter how many generations of copies are made. Thousands of perfect or nearly perfect copies of copies can be made from a single original recording. Music "pirates" use digital recording technology to make and distribute nearly perfect but unlicensed copies of commercially prepared recordings. The Internet was not useful to distribute digital music because music computer files required hundreds of computer floppy disks to store, and downloading even a single song took hours. However, various compression algorithms make audio files "smaller" by limiting bandwidth. MPEG-1 Audio Layer 3, commonly known as "MP3," is a standard, nonproprietary compression algorithm freely available for use by anyone. MP3 has become a most popular digital audio compression algorithm by creating audio files smaller (approximately 1/12) without significantly reducing sound quality. MP3 technology has upset traditional business models used in the record industry to secure their sound-recording properties. Various pirate websites offer free downloads of copyrighted material, and a single pirate site may contain thousands of pirated audio computer files.

The Rio is a small device with headphones that allows a user to download MP3 audio files from a computer, store them on flash memory cards, and listen elsewhere. Before the Rio, MP3 users could listen to their downloaded digital audio files only from playback off their hard drives through their computers by using headphones or attached speakers. The Rio renders these files portable. The Recording Industry Association of America (RIAA), the record industry's primary trade association, sought to enjoin the manufacture and distribution of the Rio by Diamond Multimedia Systems ("Diamond").

Legal Issue. Is the Rio portable music player a digital audio recording device subject to the restrictions of the Audio Home Recording Act of 1992 (AHRA) that require a serial copyright management system ("SCMS") that sends, receives, and acts upon information about the generation and copyright status of the files that it plays?

Opinion. Circuit Judge O'Scannlain. The AHRA does not broadly prohibit digital serial copying of copyright protected audio recordings. Instead, the AHRA places restrictions only upon a specific type of recording device;

[n]o person shall import, manufacture, or distribute any digital audio recording device . . . *that does not conform to the Serial Copy Management System ["SCMS"] [or] a system that has the same functional characteristics.*

The AHRA defines a "digital audio recording device" as:

any machine or device of a type commonly distributed to individuals for use by individuals, whether or not included with or as part of some other machine or device, the digital recording function of which is designed or marketed for the primary purpose of, and that is capable of, making a digital audio copied recording *for private use. . . .*

A "digital audio copied recording" is defined as:

a reproduction in a digital recording format of a digital musical recording, *whether that reproduction is made directly from another digital musical recording or indirectly from a transmission.*

A "digital musical recording" is defined as:

a material object—

(i) in which are fixed, in a digital recording format, only sounds, and material, statements, or instructions incidental to those fixed sounds, *if any, and*

(ii) from which the sounds and material can be perceived, reproduced, or otherwise communicated, either directly or with the aid of a machine or device.

In sum, to be a digital audio recording device, the Rio must be able to reproduce, either "directly" or "from a transmission," a "digital music recording."

Hard drives ordinarily contain much more than "only sounds, and material, statements, or instructions incidental to those fixed sounds." Indeed, almost all hard drives contain numerous programs (e.g., for word processing, scheduling appointments, etc.) and databases that are not incidental to any sound files that may be stored on the hard drive. The Rio appears not to make copies from digital music recordings, and thus would not be a digital audio recording device under the AHRA's basic definition.

The AHRA expressly provides that the term "digital musical recording" does not include:

a material object—

(i) in which the fixed sounds consist entirely of spoken word recordings, or

(ii) in which one or more computer programs are fixed,

Thus, a hard drive is excluded from the definition of digital music recordings. This provides confirmation that the Rio does not record "directly" from "digital music recordings," and therefore could not be a digital audio recording device. There are simply no grounds in either the plain language of the definition or in the legislative history for interpreting the term "digital musical recording" to include songs fixed on computer hard drives. The district court concluded that the exemption of hard drives from the definition of digital music recording, and the exemption of computers generally from the AHRA's ambit, "would effectively eviscerate the [AHRA]" because "[a]ny recording device could evade regulation simply by passing the music through a computer and ensuring that the MP3 file resided momentarily on the hard drive." While this may be true, the AHRA seems to have been expressly designed to create this loophole.

Under the plain meaning of the AHRA's definition of digital audio recording devices, computers (and their hard drives) are not digital audio recording devices because their "primary purpose" is not to make digital audio copied recordings. Unlike digital audio tape machines, for example, whose primary purpose is to make digital audio copied recordings, the primary purpose of a computer is to run various programs and to record the data necessary to run those programs and perform various tasks.

Diamond asserted at oral argument that the exclusion of computers from the AHRA's scope was part of a carefully negotiated compromise between the various industries with interests at stake, and without which, the computer industry would have vigorously opposed passage of the AHRA. In turn, because computers are not digital audio recording devices, they are not required to comply with the SCMS requirement and thus need not send, receive, or act upon information regarding copyright and generation status. The Rio's operation is entirely consistent with the AHRA's main purpose—the facilitation of personal use. As the Senate Report explains, "[t]he purpose of [the AHRA] is to ensure the right of consumers to make analog or digital audio recordings of copyrighted music for their *private, noncommercial use*."

For the foregoing reasons, the Rio is not a digital audio recording device subject to the restrictions of the Audio Home Recording Act of 1992. The district court properly denied the motion for a preliminary injunction against the Rio's manufacture and distribution.

Decision. General purpose PCs are not digital audio recording devices subject to the copy protection requirements of the AHRA. The Diamond Multimedia Rio player using MP3 conversion and compression technologies is legitimate under the AHRA's assurance of consumer rights to make private, noncommercial analog or digital audio recordings of copyrighted music.

Case Questions

1. What impact would this decision's reasoning have on sales of CD burners for PCs? What impact might it have on stereo hi-fi components that record CDs?
2. What other technological means might the music industry use to prevent serial copying on PCs using MP3 or CD burner technologies?

DERIVATIVE WORKS

A copyright owner has the exclusive right to base further works on the original by adapting or changing the original work into an abridgment, newer version or translation that caters to another market or is fixed in another medium. Derivative works are more than copying; they arise when editorial changes are made to a preexisting work, annotations or elaborations are added, or detail is removed to condense the original. For example, a book might be abridged, transformed into a screenplay for a motion picture, or rewritten into a stage play. Musical compositions may be arranged differently or interpreted differently by other musicians during a performance. A dramatization might change a literary work.

Derivative works usually add enough original, new expression to be considered an authorial work in and of themselves. The right to make a derivative work belongs to the copyright owner, although this right can be licensed or assigned to others. The digital practice of **morphing** usually results in a derivative work. For example, web designers who base their website on another's website by adding, subtracting, or modifying the original could be guilty of infringing on the original owner's exclusive right to make derivative works.

DISTRIBUTION

Many of the exclusive rights of copyright owners would be nearly worthless unless copies or phonorecords could be sold, rented, leased, or otherwise transferred to paying customers. Publication was required under prior law before the author or owner could have rights under federal copyright law. **Distribution** is a form of publication. For example, it would infringe the distribution right if pirated copies of musical recordings were sold by street vendors. The unauthorized posting, downloading, uploading to bulletin boards, and forwarding of e-mail or its attachments are infringements on the distribution right. Ignorance is no excuse for this type of infringement.

First Sale Doctrine

The distribution right is limited by the first sale doctrine. This rule allows the buyer to resell, give, lend, or even destroy the work after the first sale. Without this limitation, copyright owners could prevent a used market from developing in copyrighted products. The record and software industries were successful in lobbying Congress to prohibit commercial rentals of music in 1984 and software in 1990. This first wave of potential widespread piracy triggered industry fears of lost profits. A resale royalty exists in Europe that requires payment of a royalty from the proceeds of resales after the first sale. Imagine if such a right were to become politically and practically feasible in the United States. Software companies and the entertainment media might be willing to relax their insistence on copy protection or soften their resistance to P2P file-sharing techniques such as Napster if there were a reliable method to collect royalties on used sales.

PERFORMANCE AND DISPLAY

Performance and display are similar in that the copyrighted work is viewed by the public, whether for an admission fee or for free. **Performance** is the more active method used to recite, render, play, dance, or act the work directly or with a device or process such as a projector or public address system. For example, an orchestra performs when the live rendition is broadcast, and another performance occurs if a videotape of the live broadcast is rebroadcast. Among the several limitations on this right is that it applies only to public performances. Individuals may sing in the shower or play their CDs and DVDs in private. Of course, this is precisely what many consumers expect to do when entertainment products are purchased.

Public performance occurs in public places, where there are a substantial number of persons outside a normal circle of friends and family. There is no precise guidance on what constitutes a substantial number of outsiders, although it would approach substantiality as the audience becomes larger and the number of outsiders increases. Probably routine meetings of business associates is not substantial. The owner can also control transmission, such as by radio, TV, or webcast, when this results in a public performance. Other details of music licensing are discussed in Chapter 13.

The right to display was traditionally a right to more passive activity. **Display** of a work entitles the copyright owner to show a copy directly or by mechanical means such as projection of film or slides or on TV. An exception permits the purchaser of a copy of the work to exhibit or project up to one image at a time if the viewers are physically present where the copy is located. The display right does not apply to sound recordings or architectural works.

DIGITAL TRANSMISSION RIGHT

The **Digital Performance Right in Sound Recordings Act** was passed in 1995 to manage rights and uses when digital sound recordings are transmitted. It prohibits unlicensed digital transmissions and creates a compulsory license similar to the mechanical license discussed in Chapter 13. This act requires copyright owners to license digital transmissions of their works when these are made in interactive, on-demand specific requests to order particular types of music or particular titles. For example, XM Satellite Radio is a subscription automobile music service with a hundred different channels, mostly of various music styles or talk programming. Such services may someday have the capacity to broadcast precisely the consumer's

Commentary

The Expanding Concept of Performance Rights

There are a plethora of performance rights. They are really a hodgepodge, a patchwork of narrow uses added by legislation from time to time. These new performance rights balance traditional rights essential to existing business models with the greater functionality promised by emerging technologies. New technologies often make distribution more efficient or broaden the spectrum of offerings. Revisions to the copyright laws have also helped to manage the transition from monopolistic markets, such as a local TV broadcast, to new methods of transmission, aggregation, and performance. For example, cable or satellite TV services would not have flourished without regulation by the Federal Communications Commission (FCC) and statutory exceptions to the performance right.

Through a very complex set of revised laws, Congress and the FCC have addressed performance and transmission of audio and video entertainment works. For example, businesses, restaurants, and bars may use background music and video but only by complying with complex rules found in another legislative compromise, the ***Fairness in Music Licensing Act*** of 1998. That law actually specifies the maximum size of a business and the number of speakers and TV screens used to obtain advantageous licensing terms. Similar legislative compromises have made exceptions to the performance right to help foster the ***secondary transmissions*** of cable television and satellite companies.

particular selection on demand. Other visions of such services could "webcast" music to a customer's PC on demand. Digital transmissions are a hybrid of distribution and performance. Traditional analog radio broadcasts and existing music subscription services like Muzak are not affected.

Consider how digital transmission technologies could change the record companies' current business model. If they can devise effective security technologies to prevent customers from repetitiously replaying these sound recordings, there would be little need to distribute physical copies of music through record stores. Further, record companies could charge fees every time the music is played. The lack of physical copies of new music would give record companies complete control over listening and user fees. If consumers accept this "pay-per-use" model, similar revenue models could then spread to computer software and become even more prevalent than pay-per-view video is currently. License fees for digital sound transmissions such as these are negotiated.

Disputes about many forms of licensing are settled through arbitration held by **Copyright Arbitration Royalty Panels (CARP)**. These panels are essentially royalty rate-making tribunals for several licensing schemes, including cable TV, digital audio recording technologies (DAT), digital phonorecord deliveries, and satellite broadcasts. Loopholes in the law were addressed by the Digital Millennium Copyright Act. For example, interactive services that supply consumers with durable copies, rather than simply supplying one-time broadcasts, must negotiate royalties directly with copyright owners or perhaps through performing rights societies discussed in Chapter 13. The bundle of exclusive rights under copyright are summarized in Exhibit 15.3.

ONLINE

Copyright Arbitration Royalty Panels (CARP)
http://www.loc.gov/copyright/carp/

DIGITAL MILLENNIUM COPYRIGHT ACT (DMCA)

In 1997, the United States signed two international copyright treaties negotiated in the **World Intellectual Property Organization (WIPO)**. The two WIPO treaties

EXHIBIT 15.3 Comparison of Rights in the Copyright Bundle

Statutory Right	**Definition**	**Examples**
Reproduction	Fix the work in a tangible and fairly permanent medium	Make copies using tapes, photocopiers, computer disks
Derivative work	Adapt or change original work for another market or medium, using editorial changes, adding annotations or elaborations, and/or removing detail	Screenplay made from book, new musical arrangement, abridgment or translation of literary work, morphing digital work
Distribution	Initial public transfer of copyright work through sale, rental, lease, or other transfer; limited by first sale doctrine	Retail sale, rental, or lease of copies or phonorecords (not wholesale); copy shelved at public library; downloading
Performance and display	Performance: public viewing or other sensory reception (touch, see, hear) directly or using device or process; public includes substantial number of persons outside a normal circle of friends and family Display: show copy directly or by mechanical means	Recite, render, play, dance, or act the work; live orchestral performance; videotape rebroadcast; projection of film or slides or on TV
Digital transmission	Digital broadcast of sound recordings, on demand	Satellite or webcast of listener's selections
License or assignment (discussed in Chapter 13)	License: temporary, revocable transfer of right to use work Assignment: permanent and irrevocable transfer of element(s) of bundle	Most agreements for use of software Author's transfer of a work to publisher in exchange for publication, marketing, and royalties

obligate all signatory nations to pass legislation implementing provisions of two treaties.[8] One result is the **Digital Millennium Copyright Act (DMCA)**, which creates civil and criminal prohibitions against tampering with copy protection schemes or tampering with the billing data that may accompany a digital copy of the work. The DMCA does not add a new exclusive right to the bundle held by copyright owners. Indeed, the DMCA is not well integrated into existing copyright law because it prohibits *access* to a work rather than *use* of a work. Use is the traditional focus taken by infringement law. As a result, some commentators argue the DMCA may eventually make it unlawful to make a fair use of copyrighted material, as discussed in a later section.[9] At this writing, bills may be introduced in Congress to change this difficulty.

The DMCA applies to a variety of digital works, including sound recordings, A/V works, software, and literary works. Four of the DMCA's major provisions are discussed here: (1) anticircumvention rules, (2) anticircumvention exceptions, (3) copyright management information, and (4) the safe harbor for ISPs. Discussion of the DMCA's civil and criminal penalties and on its impact on fair use follows.

8. The two treaties are the WIPO Copyright Treaty and the WIPO Performances and Phonograms Treaty. They were originally adopted by WIPO in 1996, signed by the United States in 1997, and implemented by the DMCA in 1998.
9. See, e.g., Julie E. Cohen, *Lochner* in Cyberspace: The New Economic Orthodoxy of Rights Management, *Michigan Law Review* 97 (1998), 462.

ANTICIRCUMVENTION

Owners of copyrighted works have always relied on standard technologies to inhibit infringement of their rights. Over the years, control over choke points in the creation, production, distribution, or performance of works has been reasonably effective to prevent pervasive misappropriation—at least until the digital age. For example, media and entertainment companies have controlled the capacity of printing presses, vinyl and CD mass production, and broadcast of TV and radio. However, new technologies have opened up substantial leaks in these physical controls. Copyright owners have reacted by plugging them with contract restrictions or by seeking new protective legislation. For example, software has stronger protection when copy-protected, reverse engineering is prohibited, and software is licensed or leased rather than sold. The DMCA attempts to plug a widening hole in the copyright owner's technical or legal protections by making it illegal to evade technologies that impede access or copying. The DMCA anticircumvention rules prohibit unauthorized access to a work protected by **standard technical protection measures** intended to restrict access. Separately, the DMCA has **antitrafficking provisions** that prohibit the manufacture or sale of software or devices that circumvent access controls. The following case involves the constitutionality of the DMCA. This case is similar to *Junger v. Daily* in Chapter 4.

Universal City Studios, Inc. v. Corley

273 F.3d 429 (2d Cir., 2001)

Facts. In September 1999, Jon Johansen, a Norwegian teenager, collaborating with two unidentified individuals, reverse-engineered a licensed DVD player, and culled from it the "player keys"—information necessary to decrypt the Content Scramble System (CSS). Johansen was trying to develop a DVD player operable on Linux, an alternative operating system that did not support any licensed DVD players at that time. Johansen wrote a decryption program called DeCSS. Corley publishes a print magazine and maintains an affiliated website geared toward "hackers." In November 1999, Corley posted a copy of DeCSS on his website 2600.com. The trial court enjoined further posting of DeCSS and enjoined hyperlinking to postings of DeCSS.

Legal Issue. Does the decryption program DeCSS violate the anticircumvention and antitrafficking provisions of the DMCA?

Opinion. When the Framers prohibited Congress from making any law "abridging the freedom of speech," they were not thinking about computers, computer programs, or the Internet. But neither were they thinking about radio, television, or movies. Just as the inventions at the beginning and middle of the 20th century presented new First Amendment issues, so does the cyber revolution at the end of that century. Congress sought to combat copyright piracy in its earlier stages, before the work was even copied. The DMCA backed with legal sanctions the efforts of copyright owners to protect their works from piracy behind digital walls such as encryption codes or password protections.

The movie studios were reluctant to release movies in digital form until [there were] adequate safeguards against piracy of their copyrighted movies. First, they settled on the DVD as the standard digital medium. They enlisted the help of members of the consumer electronics and computer industries, who in mid-1996 developed the Content Scramble System ("CSS"). CSS is an encryption scheme that employs an algorithm configured by a set of "keys" to encrypt a DVD's contents. The algorithm is a type of mathematical formula for transforming the contents of the movie file into gibberish; the "keys" are in actuality strings of 0's and 1's that serve as values for the mathematical formula. Decryption in the case of CSS requires a set of "player keys" contained in compliant DVD players. Without the player keys and the algorithm, a DVD player cannot access the contents of a DVD.

Computer code conveying information is "speech" within the meaning of the First Amendment. Content-based restrictions are permissible only if they serve compelling state interests and do so by the least restrictive means available. A content-neutral restriction is permissible if it serves a substantial governmental interest, the interest is unrelated to the suppression of free expression, and the regulation is narrowly tailored, which "in this context requires . . . that the means chosen do not 'burden substantially more speech than is necessary to further the government's legitimate interests.' " "[G]overnment regulation of expressive activity is 'content neutral' if it is justified without reference to the content of regulated speech." "The government's purpose is the controlling consideration. A regulation that serves purposes unrelated to the content of expression is deemed neutral, even if it has an incidental effect on some speakers or messages but not others." The Supreme Court's approach to determining content-neutrality appears to be applicable whether what is regulated is expression, conduct, or any "activity" that can be said to combine speech and non-speech elements.

In considering the scope of First Amendment protection for a decryption program like DeCSS, we must recognize that the essential purpose of encryption code is to prevent unauthorized access. Owners of all property rights are entitled to prohibit access to their property by unauthorized persons. Homeowners can install locks on the doors of their houses. Custodians of valuables can place them in safes. Stores can attach to products security devices that will activate alarms if the products are taken away without purchase. These and similar security devices can be circumvented. Burglars can use skeleton keys to open door locks. Thieves can obtain the combinations to safes. Product security devices can be neutralized. CSS is like a lock on a homeowner's door, a combination of a safe, or a security device attached to a store's products. DeCSS is computer code that can decrypt CSS. The initial use of DeCSS to gain access to a DVD movie creates no loss to movie producers because the initial user must purchase the DVD. However, once the DVD is purchased, DeCSS enables the initial user to copy the movie in digital form and transmit it instantly in virtually limitless quantity, thereby depriving the movie producer of sales. The advent of the Internet creates the potential for instantaneous worldwide distribution of the copied material. As a communication, the DeCSS code has a claim to being "speech," and as "speech," it has a claim to being protected by the First Amendment.

The DMCA and the posting prohibition are applied to DeCSS solely because of its capacity to instruct a computer to decrypt CSS. That functional capability is not speech within the meaning of the First Amendment. This type of regulation is therefore content-neutral, just as would be a restriction on trafficking in skeleton keys identified because of their capacity to unlock jail cells, even though some of the keys happened to bear a slogan or other legend that qualified as a speech component.

As a content-neutral regulation with an incidental effect on a speech component, the regulation must serve a substantial governmental interest, the interest must be unrelated to the suppression of free expression, and the incidental restriction on speech must not burden substantially more speech than is necessary to further that interest. The Government's interest in preventing unauthorized access to encrypted copyrighted material is unquestionably substantial, and the regulation of DeCSS by the posting prohibition plainly serves that interest. Moreover, that interest is unrelated to the suppression of free expression.

Posting DeCSS on the Appellants' web site makes it instantly available at the click of a mouse to any person in the world with access to the Internet, and such person can then instantly transmit DeCSS to anyone else with Internet access. It is true that the Government has alternative means of prohibiting unauthorized access to copyrighted materials. But a content-neutral regulation need not employ the least restrictive means of accomplishing the governmental objective. It need only avoid burdening "substantially more speech than is necessary to further the government's legitimate interests." The prohibition on the Defendants' posting of DeCSS satisfies that standard.

In considering linking, we need to clarify the sense in which the injunction prohibits such activity. A hyperlink is a cross-reference (in a distinctive font or color) appearing on one web page that, when activated by the point-and-click of a mouse, brings onto the computer screen another web page. The hyperlink can appear on a screen (window) as text, such as the Internet address ("URL") of the web page being called up or a word or phrase that identifies the web page to be called up, for example, "DeCSS web site." Or the hyperlink can appear as an image, for example, an icon depicting a person sitting at a computer watching a DVD movie and text stating "click here to access DeCSS and see DVD movies for free!" The code for the web page containing the hyperlink contains a computer instruction that associates the link with the URL of the web page to be accessed, such that clicking on the hyperlink instructs the computer to enter the URL of the desired web page and thereby access that page. With a hyperlink on a web page, the linked web site is just one click away.

[A] hyperlink has both a speech and a nonspeech component. It conveys information, the Internet address of the linked web page, and has the functional capacity to bring the content of the linked web page to the user's computer screen (to "take one almost instantaneously to the desired destination"). Application of the DMCA to the Defendants' linking to web sites containing DeCSS is content-neutral because it is justified without regard to the speech component of the hyperlink. The linking prohibition applies whether or not the hyperlink contains any information, comprehensible to a human being, as to the Internet address of the web page being accessed. The linking prohibition is justified solely by the functional capability of the hyperlink.

Strict liability for linking to web sites containing DeCSS would risk two impairments of free expression. Web site operators would be inhibited from displaying links to various web pages for fear that a linked page might contain DeCSS, and a prohibition on linking to a web site containing DeCSS would curtail access to whatever other information was contained at the accessed site. To avoid applying the DMCA in a manner that would "burden substantially more speech than is necessary to further the government's legitimate interests," Judge Kaplan required clear and convincing evidence that those responsible for the link (a) know at the relevant time that the offending material is on the linked-to site, (b) know that it is circumvention technology that may not lawfully be offered, and (c) create or maintain the link for the purpose of disseminating that technology.

The Appellants ignore the reality of the functional capacity of decryption computer code and hyperlinks to facilitate instantaneous unauthorized access to copyrighted materials by anyone anywhere in the world. The injunction's linking prohibition validly regulates the Appellants' opportunity instantly to enable anyone anywhere to gain unauthorized access to copyrighted movies on DVDs.

Decision. Decryption software that defeats the standard technical protection measures for the DVD video format violates the DMCA.

Case Questions

1. Which of the three DMCA prohibitions could be violated by DeCSS, its creator, or its users?
2. Discuss the legal impact of the difference between hyperlinking to known infringing or prohibited materials on line and the simple publication of URL web addresses that have prohibited content (infringement, obscenity, defamation, national security matter).

Anticircumvention Exceptions

During Congressional debate on the DMCA, many groups argued that the anticircumvention provisions would adversely affect law enforcement, education, scholarly research, the fair use exception, and the development of encryption (as a form of technical protection measure) and would prevent many traditionally legal methods of reverse engineering. As a result, Congress created several limited exceptions for the six uses listed previously. Exceptions were also created for parents to protect minor children from obscenity or other objectionable material, for accessing or disabling privacy intrusions (e.g., cookies), and for testing the effectiveness of security or encryption technologies.

The DMCA also directed the librarian of Congress to periodically review whether the anticircumvention rules were adversely affecting parties. In 2001, two exemptions were created: (1) decrypting filtering software to evaluate the propriety of website databases that block children's access to inappropriate material and (2) circumvention of malfunctioning software or databases if the copyright owner has not fixed the problem quickly. In the rule making, the Copyright Office rejected many exemptions proposed by various groups. Conflict will probably continue between copyright owners and users on these anticircumvention rules.

COPYRIGHT MANAGEMENT INFORMATION

Accompanying the digital content sought by consumers, there is increasingly additional information used for identification, to make records, to meter fees, or to discover infringement. The additional data are called **copyright management information.** Consider how meta-tags in webpages or in e-mail messages contain routing and subject information. Similarly, copyrighted works may contain the owner's contact information, pricing, links, and licensing terms. This information could be revealed to users as needed, provide record keeping of authorized and unauthorized uses, or be used by electronic agents in automated contract negotiations. The DMCA prohibits intentional tampering with copyright management information that is conveyed with the work.

SAFE HARBOR FOR ISPs

Like the Communications Decency Act, the DMCA provides safe harbors from liability for Internet service providers (ISPs) when they are innocent and acting as mere conduits for their users' infringement. ISPs are not liable for copyright infringement or for contributory infringement as long as they enforce a program to terminate subscribers who repeatedly infringe. Additionally, the ISP may not interfere with standard technical protection measures used by copyright owners. ISPs are not liable for providing a hyperlink to infringing material if they meet several strict requirements, including compliance with the DMCA's **notice and take down** provisions, which require the ISP to remove or block access to infringing materials when the ISP is sufficiently notified by the copyright owner. The DMCA also provides an ISP safe harbor for system caching and ephemeral copies.

MORAL RIGHTS

The author or owner's right to make derivative works may not be enough to prevent negative side effects. In general, Europeans historically feel strongly that only the author has a natural right to prevent desecration of the author's unique, creative works; that is, the author should be able to prevent others from changing the work if the author believes the changes are harmful to the work's artistic integrity. These natural rights are called **moral rights** because they naturally extend from the author's own personality to prevent dishonor or damage to the author's reputation. There are four major components to moral rights: (1) the right of paternity, attribution, or acknowledgment; (2) the right of disclosure; (3) the right of integrity; and (4) the right of withdrawal. Moral rights are most compelling when the author's creative contribution is largely artistic.

The **right of attribution** is essentially a statement that accurately identifies the author as the creator. This right also prevents false claims that someone was the author or creator of a work that she or he did not really create. The **right of disclosure** allows the author control over when, how, and where the work is publicly displayed or performed. Authors can make sure their works are not displayed in galleries, art shows, or public places that they believe might damage their reputation. The **right of integrity** allows authors to prevent physical mutilation, distortion, modifications, or any other changes they believe would injure their reputation. This right can also prevent destruction of the work. Finally, the **right of withdrawal** allows the author alone to change the work and to prevent others from making reproductions. The United States has never adopted this comprehensive, European vision of moral rights. However, aspects of federal and some state laws (e.g., California), as well as federal implementation of the Berne Convention, approximate several aspects of moral rights.

The leading U.S. moral rights case involved an instance when the ABC network cut substantial portions before it rebroadcast the taped shows of a British comedy,

Monty Python's Flying Circus.[10] By shortening the shows, the network violated the express license and created an unauthorized derivative work. This new, shortened work was inaccurately attributed to Monte Python, violating the federal unfair competition law, §43(a) of the Lanham Act. State laws may also provide authors with remedies for moral rights violations. For example, the torts of defamation or privacy might protect some aspects of moral rights. In addition, some states have passed art preservation laws to protect works of fine art, either by prohibiting its destruction or by prohibiting display of altered works. However, these laws may be preempted by the **Visual Artists Rights Act** of 1990 (VARA), which implements U.S. participation in the Berne Convention.

VARA protects only works of visual art that are either in a single copy, such as a famous painting or sculpture, or are part of a limited set of reproductions, such as signed and numbered print editions of 200 or fewer copies. **Visual arts** under VARA include paintings, drawings, prints, sculptures, and photographs. Other visual works are specifically excluded from VARA's moral rights: posters, maps, globes, motion pictures, A/V works, books, periodicals, databases, electronic publications, advertising

International Commentary

"Look What They've Done to My Song, Ma": Contrasting the Hegelian and American Visions of Moral Rights

This early-1970s-era pop song was performed by the New Seekers. It really captures the essential vision of author-composers' attitudes about unauthorized adaptations of their works. In this case, the composer apparently believes the derivative work falls below the composer's minimum standards. Creators are often *very* sensitive in their personal expectations for follow-on versions of their original work. Of course, creators should be realistic and recognize that if their works have enduring quality, other artists will want to reproduce them. Furthermore, audiences may enjoy the renewal of the original's impact. Perhaps the new version could become more popular, maybe even better than the original. Such adaptations can be verbatim, embellish and transform, or reinterpret the original by replacing elements, by softening, or by intensifying stylistic aspects.

Imitation is the sincerest form of flattery, so adaptation to new markets or different media can add recognition to the original work. However, creators can be very tough critics; some are impossible to please. The original creator may become convinced that the adaptation reflects badly on her or him. Indeed, the adaptation may actually diminish the market for the original. A poorly executed adaptation may tarnish the creator's reputation. There is also a fine line separating violation of the moral rights and criticism that uses parody as the vehicle. Consider how Weird Al Yankovic parodies popular songs. The U.S. law does not give authors strong rights to prevent adaptation, as does European law. Indeed, many creative disciplines are ***transformative***; that is, there is an expectation that later creators will have some access to original works so that steady progress can be made in the art. For example, software and music make good progress only when parts of older, original works are adapted and improved to attain new functionality or to create and satisfy new markets.

The differences between the U.S. and the European visions of moral rights help distinguish their underlying philosophical differences. Europeans prefer an individualistic, natural rights vision of ownership of creative accomplishment. By contrast, the United States relies on a more practical vision of personal incentives to enlarge the public domain and contribute to social progress through commercial transactions.

10. *Gilliam v. American Broadcasting Cos.*, 538 F.2d 14 (2d Cir., 1976).

materials, and works for hire. Neither musical works nor sound recordings are included. The moral rights under VARA include (1) attribution to claim authorship and (2) integrity to prevent intentional distortion, mutilation, or modification that prejudices the author's honor. The author has VARA rights even if the work was sold to another person. Unlike in Europe, VARA permits the author to expressly waive these rights in writing. VARA moral rights last for the life of the artist.

COPYRIGHT PROCEDURES

ONLINE

Library of Congress Search Facility
http://www.loc.gov/copyright/search

Copyright protection is much easier to obtain than protection for a patented invention or a trademark. The general requirements under copyright law are only that some unique authorial expression be fixed in a permanent medium of expression. Since the 1976 revision to the U.S. copyright law, it is no longer necessary to register the copyright, deposit a copy with the Library of Congress, publish the work, or attach copyright notice to the work. However, there are still some advantages to using these procedural steps.

COPYRIGHT OFFICE

The **Copyright Office** of the **Library of Congress** is the primary U.S. regulatory agency for copyrights. It serves as the point for registration of works and for deposit of works into the Library of Congress, it advises Congress on copyright policy, and it has some rule-making authority. The chief administrative officer is the **register of copyrights**, who is appointed by the librarian of Congress. The Copyright Office provides records of 50 million catalogue entries showing copyright ownership and ownership transfers. These records help potential users discover if a work is in the public domain, and they assist in locating owners so users can seek permission or license to use copyrighted works. These and other copyright records dating back to 1978 are available for on-line electronic search.

Much of the law of copyright, the Copyright Office's various records, copyright regulations, and links to related sites are available on line. This section discusses the copyrighting procedures of registration, deposit, and notice, as well as the duration or term of copyright protection.

http://
www.loc.gov/copyright/

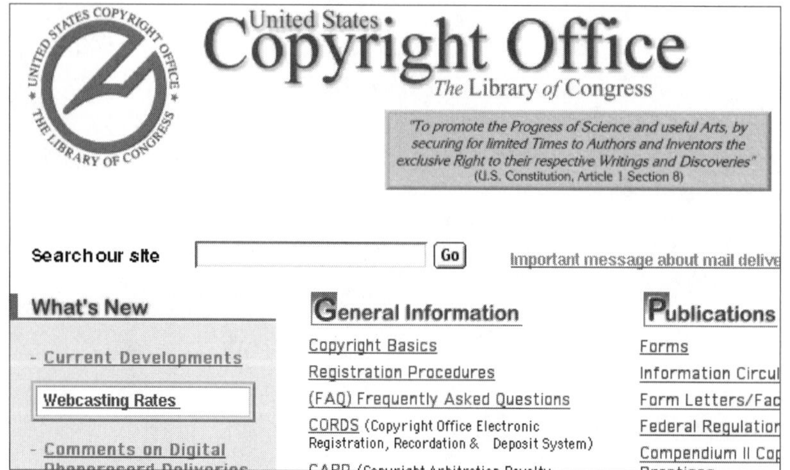

COPYRIGHT REGISTRATION

The United States stands alone in the world by requiring a registration system for copyrighted works. Registration provides initial validity of copyright ownership, it documents the timing of first creation, and it facilitates a market for copyrighted works. The formalities of registration, deposit, and notice are complicated because of changes in the copyright laws that Congress implemented in 1978 and 1989.

Therefore, careful attention is required to determine the creation date for existing works. Registration was important for works created before 1978 because owners could extend their term of copyright protection by filing a renewal with the Copyright Office in the twenty-eighth year, as discussed later. For works created between 1978 and 1989, registration was required if copyright notice was left off a substantial number of copies.

To comply with the Berne Convention, copyright registration was made optional for works created after March 1, 1989. However, even for these newer works, registration is still a useful step because it enables infringement remedies: An infringement suit cannot be brought until after registration if the work was created in the United States or in other nations not part of the Berne Convention. Registration is a prerequisite to seeking statutory damages and attorney's fees, and the owner has few remedies for infringements occurring before registration. The fee for registration is $30 until 2004, when the register of copyrights may make adjustments for inflation.

Most interactions with the U.S. Copyright Office are painless, particularly when compared with interactions with many of the other regulators discussed throughout this book. First, there is no qualification or examination process by the Copyright Office to determine copyrightability, as there is for patents and trademarks by the Patent and Trademark Office (PTO). Fewer interactions with the Copyright Office are adversarial, unlike so many interactions with some agencies (e.g., IRS, Justice Department). Second, copyright registration is relatively easy, inexpensive, and straightforward. The Copyright Office is testing an on-line registration system, the **Copyright Office Registration and Deposit System (CORDS)**, that will permit authors and owners to register and deposit their works via the Internet. The payment of license fees is facilitated by electronic funds transfers using the FedWire system.

ONLINE

Copyright Registration Forms Online
http://www.loc.gov/copyright/forms

Deposit

Copyright law requires the applicant to **deposit**—that is, to submit—two copies of the best edition of the work. This requirement applies to all types of works. Deposit enhances the archival collection of the Library of Congress. Fines are levied for failure to make the deposit within three months after publication. Clearly, deposit would be impractical, if not impossible, for three-dimensional works, such as the sole copy of a sculpture. Works published outside the United States generally need not be deposited. The Copyright Office has issued regulations that permit the owner to block out the trade secrets contained in the source code listing of software that is deposited.

http://
www.loc.gov/

COPYRIGHT NOTICE

Copyright notice is a familiar public signal that the author or owner claims copyright and that the work is not in the public domain. It consists of the copyright owner's name, one of three permissible forms of the copyright symbol (the "c in a circle" ©, copr., or copyright), and the year the work was first published. Notice should be placed in a reasonably visible location on the work. Copyright Office guidelines help owners make good placement choices. Right now, check the title page to this book. You should find something like this: ©2003 by West Legal Studies in Business. The United States is the only major nation that still actively encourages the use of copyright notices. Although notice in the United States is an imperfect method to determine what lies in the public domain, the process is even more uncertain and potentially costly when notice is not widely used.

Notice serves to inform the public of the copyright. It provides the year copyright protection begins and identifies the original author or owner. Critics argue that notice can be misleading if ownership was transferred after the initial printing of copies that are still in circulation. Copyright notice was a mandatory requirement for copyright protection until the 1988 copyright law revision by which the United States complied with the Berne Convention. Works created before 1989 were subject to forfeiture: They fell into the public domain if the copyright notice regulations were not complied with strictly.

Although Berne implementation has made copyright notice optional, nevertheless, notice still has some legal impact. For example, infringers will probably not be successful in arguing their infringement was innocent if the owner has placed a reasonably conspicuous copyright notice on the work. In such cases, the court should impose on the defendant full liability for statutory or actual damages. No reduction should be made for innocent violation. Suitable posting of copyright notice adequately warns potential infringers that the work is protected.

DURATION OF COPYRIGHT PROTECTION

When compared with patents lasting only 20 years, copyrights seem quite lengthy, having a term of protection lasting for the remainder of the author's life plus another 70 years. Recall that the U.S. Constitution in Article I, §8, cl. 8 restricts copyright protection to "limited times." This phrase represents a balance between the incentive given authors and the social costs of an excessive monopoly that would deprive the public domain. Copyright term is another complex procedural matter because it varies as a result of some key factors defined in several revision laws: the date of creation or publication, status of the renewal term, and whether the work was created in the United States. As introduced in Chapter 13, many, if not most, authors of commercially viable works assign their copyrights to a publisher in exchange for production and distribution of the work. Given this complexity, only generalizations about copyright terms are made here.

Unpublished works could be perpetually protected under state common law until passage of the 1976 Copyright Act, which eliminated common law copyright altogether. Unpublished works created before 1978 were previously protected forever under state common law of copyright. The 1976 act now preempts all state copyright laws, substituting the federal scheme. Common law copyrights are now protected under federal copyright law, so the life-plus-70-years duration is generally applicable to them. For works published before 1964, the author had an initial 28-year term and then a chance for a renewal term of another 28 years. This option permitted the author to renegotiate terms with the publisher. For example, assume a record company acquired a famous and commercially successful blues song from an indigent blues artist for a mere pittance. Copyright law gave the artist a chance to renegotiate more favorable royalties before the second copyright term began by requiring that the artist apply for the extension. The second term was extended from 28 years to 67 years by the 1976 Act. Term renewal was made automatic by the Copyright Renewal Act of 1992. Renewals are eliminated altogether for works created after 1977. Works published before 1923 are now in the public domain. (See Exhibit 15.4.)

The **Sonny Bono Copyright Term Extension Act** was passed in 1998 to extend the terms of some existing copyrights by 20 years. This act results in the general duration of life plus 70 years rule. However, there is a different term for anonymous or pseudonymous works and works for hire created primarily by institutional "authors." They all have a term of 120 years after creation or 95 years after publication, whichever term is shorter. At this writing, there is a Supreme Court challenge pending to the Sonny Bono extension law that could either invalidate Congress's lengthening of copyright term or validate it. Opponents of the extension law claim the Constitution limits copyright duration to "reasonable" terms and that the term extension is unreasonably long.[11]

COPYRIGHT INFRINGEMENT

Much of copyright law focuses on the unauthorized intrusion into one of the bundle of exclusive rights held by the author or owner. An infringement occurs when the infringer makes an unauthorized copy, distributes, performs or displays in public, or makes a derivative of the original work. Infringement analysis requires a complex assessment that often focuses on (1) copying, (2) illicit copying, and (3) whether the copying might be excused because copyright law tolerates some infringements that are fair or necessary for the progress of science and the useful arts. This section focuses on the first two of these factors that must be proved by the owner of the original. The third factor, detailed in a later section, must generally be proved by the alleged infringer.

EXHIBIT 15.4 Copyright Duration

Date of Work	Date Protection Starts	Duration of Copyright Protection
Published before 1923	When published with copyright notice attached	Now in public domain
Published between 1923 and 1977	When published with copyright notice attached	Up to 95 years for works published between 1923 & 1977 under "two term" systems: • Works first published before 1964—first term 28 years from publication; second term 28 years from renewal; 1976 law increased second term to 67 years; author required to initiate official renewal process if first term ended before 1964 • Works first published after 1963—first term 28 years from publication; second term 67 years from renewal; renewal automatic
Created after 1977	When fixed in tangible medium of expression	Remaining life of author plus 70 years Exception for works for hire (institutional author): • 95 years after publication, or • 120 years after creation, whichever is shorter

11. See, e.g., *Eldred v. Ashcroft*, U.S. Sup.Ct. No.01-618 (2002).

INFRINGEMENT ANALYSIS

The author or owner's case of infringement first requires proof of a valid copyright (appropriate subject matter, originality, procedural compliance). Registration is a prerequisite to many infringement remedies. Analysis of infringement involves two steps: first consider expert testimony to determine whether copying has occurred, and second consider interpretations by laypeople, usually a jury, about whether the amount taken is qualitatively substantial.[12]

Proof of copying can be difficult. Proving infringement is easy in the case of blatant plagiarism, where the infringer made a substantial, literal, word-for-word copy by "lifting" exact portions from the original work. However, few alleged infringers ever admit to copying, and it is often done secretly, so it must be proved by comparing the two works. This difficulty is made worse because Congress has never successfully defined infringement with precision. Therefore, infringement is an ad hoc determination that varies, depending on the type of work involved: literary, software, musical or visual art. Generally, a comparison is made between the original work that was allegedly infringed and a second work that allegedly infringes on the original work.

Copying

If the second work was independently created, not copied, it cannot infringe the original. Two works could conceivably be protected under copyright, even if they were identical, as long as the second work was created independently. This rule is like the rule in trade secrets but different from the rule under patent law. Independent creation is a complete defense to trade secret misappropriation, but independent creation is no defense to patent infringement. Therefore, the owner of the original copyrighted work must prove that the infringer derived the second work from the first.

In the real world, many copyright infringements are not verbatim takings from the original; that is, many second works are not identical in all respects to the original. Instead, the infringer copies only certain aspects, perhaps paraphrasing prose, changing the meter of poetry or song lyrics, taking only a catchy melody, or modifying some of the instrumental parts or the medium (e.g., oil on canvas to computer graphics, carved stone sculpture to plastic casting).

It is still infringement if the infringement is innocent and the author of the second made no conscious effort to take from the original. Consider the famous example of the 1970s hit song "My Sweet Lord," written and recorded by the late Beatle, George Harrison. The court held he infringed the basic melody of the 1962 hit "He's So Fine," which was written by Ronald Mack and recorded by the Chiffons. Note what the trial judge concluded after inquiring closely into Harrison's inspiration in writing the song:

The composer, in seeking musical materials to clothe his thoughts, was working with various possibilities. A particular combination pleased him . . . this combination of sounds would work. Why? Because his subconscious knew it already had worked in a song his conscious mind did not remember. It is clear that My Sweet Lord is the very same song as He's So Fine with different words, and Harrison had access to He's So Fine.[13]

Typically, the owner of the original may ask the judge or jury to infer copying from circumstantial evidence. If the alleged infringer had **access** to original work and

12. *Arnstein v. Porter*, 154 F.2d 464 (2d Cir., 1946).

13. *Bright Tunes Music Corp. v. Harrisongs Music, Ltd.*, 420 F.Supp. 177 (S.D.N.Y., 1976) *aff'd sub nom ABKCO Music, Inc. v. Harrisongs Music, Ltd.*, 722 F.2d 988 (2d Cir., 1983).

there is **substantial similarity** between the two works, these points may support an inference of copying. The Internet provides considerable and nearly unfettered access to many works, and disproving access to Internet postings may become difficult.

Of course, access should not be conclusive of infringement because copyright does not protect the ideas in the original, only the form of expression. Scientific progress would be difficult unless researchers could have legitimate access to the prior works of previous scholars, but most important, they need access to their ideas. Therefore, the testimony of experts is often helpful to determine whether the similarities result from two independently gifted artists who simply worked from the same public domain reservoir or whether they resulted from copying protected expression. Both unprotected ideas and protected expression are compared, then, to determine whether there was copying and whether the copying was unlawful. Disproving access is a key part of the clean room techniques discussed later.

Access can also be inferred if the two works have **striking similarity**; that is, the similarities are so numerous and so close that it is hard to believe the infringer did not have access to the original and use it. Striking similarity is evident by comparison. For example, try to listen to George Harrison's "My Sweet Lord" after first listening to the Chiffons' "He's So Fine." The court found three musical phrases to be identical in both songs: (1) sol-me-re, (2) sol-la-do-la-do, and (3) sol-la-do-la-re-do.[14] Clearly, listening is the most effective comparison. Many songs have similar melodies or patterns, but infringement analysis is concerned with similarities in the most dominant portions, the creative essence. Once the first step of copying is proved, the judge or jury must then move to the second step: Is the copying illicit?

Illicit Copying

Once expert testimony has helped the judge or jury determine that the original was copied, the testimony of laypersons is used to determine if the copying was an illicit, unlawful appropriation. The substantial similarity standard is again used—this time to determine if the original's expression was taken. The similarities, not the differences, are the critical factor. At this second stage, similarity in the ideas of both works is also irrelevant. Therefore, lay observers who are potentially in the market for that type of work may testify as to whether there is substantial similarity in the expression of the two works. When the case is tried before a jury, they may represent a lay audience and make this determination.

Infringement may take a wide variety of forms, at least as broad as the bundle of rights. First, a common form of infringement occurs when the infringer violates the reproduction right, which generally means the infringer made a verbatim partial or complete copy. For example, software and sound recordings might be infringed by making analog tapes or digital copies saved on disk. Photographs and books might be copied by photographic means such as photocopiers or even with another photograph. Controversy surrounds the temporary ephemeral copies of audio, video, software, or other digital media made in computer RAM or on other intermediary facilities. Ephemeral copies are necessary to transmit, rebroadcast, load, or use the work.

Second, infringement also frequently occurs when the infringer makes a derivative work that uses only parts of the original while adding original expression. For example, George Harrison's "My Sweet Lord" probably constituted a derivative work of the original "He's So Fine"; it was not a verbatim copy. Third, the distribution right is

14. These notations are called *tonic sol-fa*. You may recognize these syllables because they represent the different notes of the musical scale (do-re-me).

also infringed when infringing copies or derivative works are distributed to the public. Similarly, infringing copies publicly performed or displayed are another form of infringement.

COMPUTER APPLICATIONS OF INFRINGEMENT ANALYSIS

Infringement analysis for computer programs is a process that has matured through an evolution of cases in the 1980s and 1990s. A three-step software infringement analysis involves (1) abstraction, (2) filtration, and (3) comparison.[15] The first step, **abstraction**, requires a conceptualization of the original work. The program's sequence, structure, and organization are determined, revealing the original program's functions. Second, the various elements dissected in the abstraction phase must be forced through **filtration**, a process of separating unprotected ideas from protected expression. There can be no infringement of elements already in the public domain or for external elements, such as interfaces and communications protocols; mechanical computer specifications permitting compatibility and widely accepted programming practices are removed from consideration. For example, the "video game" cases have established that the interface connecting game cartridges to the game console are functional elements and generally not protected expression. It would be impossible to build compatible software if a competing manufacturer could not determine how the cartridge communicated with the game console. The third step is **comparison**, in which only protected expression of the second work remains and is compared with the original work. It is similar to the illicit copying step discussed previously.

The design of compatible software and hardware has been a daunting task. A copy of the original work must be acquired legally and then reverse-engineered to discover its functions. Only ideas can be duplicated; the expression cannot be used by the maker of the compatible product. However, many vendors do not want unauthorized competitors to produce compatible products. Recall the discussion of network effects in Chapter 11. The owner of the original has an incentive to block compatible products. The resulting competition would undermine the monopoly profits the original's owner enjoys because consumers become locked in and can use only the original owner's "family" of compatible or licensed products. Owners of the original often license or lease their software and hardware so they can prohibit reverse engineering. Nevertheless, reverse engineering may still be permissible as a fair use, as discussed later.

Clean Room Techniques

A special technique—the **clean room** method—is used to reverse-engineer software and hardware. It typically involves two separate teams: The first team analyzes the original work, and the second team designs the competing product. The first team works in a dirty room, where reverse engineering reveals the unprotected ideas and separates them from the protected expression. The dirty room team clearly has access to the original work and must separate unprotected ideas from the protected expression. The designers in the clean room do not see the protected expression but must develop their own from scratch.

For example, a potential competitor seeking to produce compatible game cartridges would first use a dirty room team to decompile the software and discover

15. *Computer Assoc. Int'l, Inc. v. Altai, Inc.*, 982 F.2d 693 (2d Cir., 1992).

how the programming conventions are used to make the game work. Expression items such as the graphics and the characters in the original must be separated from the unprotected ideas that show how the game functions and operates. The dirty room team prepares a report that contains only unprotected ideas, public domain expression, and, most important, the functional characteristics of the game. The clean room team uses only the report, not the original work. The clean room team works independently to develop the new game so it is different but still functionally compatible. The clean room technique was legitimized in the watershed case *Sega Enterprises v. Accolade, Inc.*[16]

SECONDARY LIABILITY

In another watershed case, *Sony v. Universal City Studios*,[17] the owners of video content attempted to expand secondary liability theories to hold other parties liable for infringement if they assisted infringers. **Contributory infringement** would hold liable someone who provided technology to or otherwise assisted the infringer. Unlike the patent law, the copyright act has no explicit provisions for **vicarious infringement**, but such liability can be implied when someone is responsible for others who actually do the infringement. For example, a publisher, studio, or broadcaster may be held vicariously liable for the actions of its employees. The *Sony* case held that the maker or seller of a device, the VCR, could not be liable for contributory infringement because the VCR has **substantial noninfringing uses.** VCRs can make legal, imperfect analog copies of public domain works, VCRs can make legal copies when the works' owners authorize copying, and VCRs can "time shift" by copying protected works to enable more convenient viewing.

Despite this broad language in *Sony* and similar rulings (such as *RIAA v. Diamond Multimedia*, discussed earlier), copyright owners and the entertainment and software industries continue to press for application of vicarious infringement. The most frequent targets of vicarious infringement are manufacturers, distributors, and resellers of copying technologies (VCRs, CD burners, PCs); the communications intermediaries used to broadcast or download infringing copies (ISPs); and authors of software that facilitates copying.

Liability of ISPs

Printing presses, broadcasting transmitters, distribution contracts with bookstores or local TV affiliates, and the like were the unique facilities needed for effective large-scale infringement in the traditional world. However, in cyberspace, nearly anyone can become a publisher by distributing works through chat rooms, by e-mail spam, or by providing hyperlinks to infringing materials stored elsewhere or stored directly on their own websites. Owners of original works who want to halt infringement must now focus attention on even more entities to remedy infringement.

Internet and on-line service providers are logical targets for secondary liability for various wrongs or offenses: obscenity, defamation, and harassment, as well as infringement. Early cases had conflicting holdings: some held ISPs liable for infringement,[18] and others denied contributory infringement liability if the ISP was unaware of the infringing material.[19] Remember the previous discussion in this chapter about

16. 977 F.2d 1510 (9th Cir., 1992).

17. 464 U.S. 417 (1984).

18. *Playboy Ent., Inc. v. Freena*, 838 F.Supp. 1552 (M.D.Fl. 1993).

19. *Religious Tech. Ctr. v. Netcom On-Line Comm.Servs., Inc.*, 907 F.Supp. 1361 (N.D.Cal. 1995).

the DMCA's safe harbor for ISPs. The DMCA releases ISPs from secondary liability for merely transmitting infringing materials if the material is stored for only short times. However, if the ISP hosts websites for users or otherwise stores allegedly infringing materials for long periods, then more complex notice and take down procedures apply under the DMCA. Generally, the ISP must remove or block access to infringing materials when sufficiently notified by the copyright owner.

INFRINGEMENT REMEDIES

The author or owner's rights under copyright law would be superficial without legal remedies to halt and compensate for the infringement. The Copyright Act provides for equitable remedies (injunctions, seizure, destruction) and legal remedies (statutory damages, actual damages, lost profits, costs and attorney's fees). In addition, criminal penalties deter infringement under the Copyright Act, the DMCA, and the No Electronic Theft Act.

Equitable Remedies

Often the most effective remedy is to simply halt the infringement as soon as possible. The injunction is a classic court order prohibiting the infringer from continuing the infringement. For example, an injunction would stop further infringing performances of a Broadway play or a movie. An injunction would halt further sales of infringing sound recordings or books. A permanent injunction is possible only after a potentially long trial. However, preliminary injunctions are frequently used to halt the infringement before a full trial can be held if the author or owner of the original work can prove three things. First, the owner must have a strong probability of success at the infringement trial on the merits of the case. Second, the owner must show that it will suffer irreparable harm unless the infringement is enjoined immediately. Third, the court hearing the motion for the preliminary injunction must balance the harms of continued infringement to the author against the harm of shutting down the alleged infringer's business. Typically, hearings for preliminary injunctions are held on short notice, they are not lengthy, and the preliminary injunction is effective only temporarily, until a ruling following the full trial.

After infringement is determined at the full trial, another remedy may be available if there are infringing copies in the supply chain or there is special production equipment suitable just to make them. Infringing copies may be impounded, and production facilities unique to the infringing articles may be destroyed. For example, infringing books, phonorecords, or CDs can be seized from warehouses and retailers. The photographic negatives, presses, plates, or molds used to produce the infringing articles may be destroyed. Destruction is a severe remedy that should be reserved for serious cases.

Legal Remedies

The legal remedies most often given in infringement cases are compensatory, the payment of money damages. Infringers may be held liable either for actual damages, including the infringer's profits, *or* for statutory damages. **Actual damages** are computed as the drop in market value of the author or owner's work that results from the infringement. This determination is difficult, so lost profits are a somewhat more reliable measure. For example, the owner's lost sales might be determined by comparing periodic sales volumes over the period before the infringement with the reduced sales volume after infringement. Of course, economic factors can affect sales, and the infringer may be selling at lower prices, so the lost sales measure is often too speculative to be useful. In addition to lost profits, the owner is entitled to the infringer's profits. In both computations, assumptions must be made about the production costs and the allocation of overhead. Infringer profits and the owner's lost profits can be quite contentious issues at trial.

Because actual damages are difficult to determine, Congress provided for an alternative measure, **statutory damages**. Recall that U.S. law requires registration of the original copyright before statutory damages are available. There can be no statutory damages for even proven infringements that occurred before registration. This legal point is an important inducement for copyright registration. Statutory damages are within the trial court's discretion between $500 and $20,000. If the infringement is willful, the court may assess up to $100,000 in statutory damages.

The trial court may also order the losing party to pay the winner's costs for the infringement trial and the winner's attorney's fees. Traditionally, attorney's fees were paid to winning authors or owners routinely but were difficult for winning defendants to receive when they were absolved of infringement. Does that seem fair? In *Fogerty v. Fantasy, Inc.*,[20] the Supreme Court held this disparity was not fair to defendants because it gave authors and owners an advantage in choosing to go to trial. John Fogerty, a songwriter and member of the band Creedence Clearwater Revival (Southern country-blues) was sued by the owner of a song John Fogerty originally wrote, "Run through the Jungle." John Fogerty recorded a similar song on another label with different words that he titled "The Old Man on the Road." John Fogerty won the infringement suit but was denied attorney's fees by the trial court. The Supreme Court found no compelling reason to favor owners over successful defendants, so it reversed the trial court on the attorney's fee issue.

Criminal Penalties

It is a federal felony to willfully infringe copyright in any type of work for commercial advantage or private financial gain. The federal crime is committed when ten or more copies or phonorecords having a retail value of more than $2,500 are reproduced or distributed within a 180-day period if done without the owner's authorization. Fines of up to $250,000 can be levied for individual repeat offenders or $500,000 for organizations. Imprisonment for individuals for up to five years is alternative. Before passage of the **No Electronic Theft Act** (NETA) in 1997, criminal penalties for copyright infringement applied only to willful infringement for personal financial gain. NETA amendments now include a sliding scale of penalties for aggregate retail values down to $1,000 and also increase possible imprisonment to six years. This means that unauthorized Web posting or e-mail distribution of stolen software, audio, or other works on line is illegal under NETA, even if the infringer makes no profit.

Only the Justice Department (DOJ) can prosecute criminal copyright actions. The DOJ has the tougher "beyond a reasonable doubt" burden of proof in criminal copyright infringement cases. Criminal penalties for violation of the DMCA are even more severe, fines up to $500,000 or imprisonment for first-time offenders and fines up to $1,000,000 or imprisonment up to 10 years for repeat offenders. The DMCA's statute of limitations is five years. Not-for-profit organizations are not subject to the DMCA's criminal penalties.

20. *Fogerty v. Fantisy, Inc.*, 114 S.Ct. 1023 (1994).

FAIR USE DEFENSE

Many intellectual property theorists argue that copyrights were never intended to be as strong as patents. Patents are strong rights. They protect ideas but last for a much shorter time, generally only 20 years. The secrets behind a patent are disclosed to the public when the patent is granted. By contrast, copyrights last a long time, so the public should not be made to suffer a strong monopoly over the ideas embedded in copyrighted works. As the preceding sections illustrate, infringement analysis is highly uncertain and carries the threat of severe civil and criminal liability. These factors suggest society is best served by a narrowing of owners' control over copyrighted works. The courts and legislatures have long shown some agreement with these arguments. The English courts originally created an exception to strong copyright protection, called the **abridgment** of the owner's rights. It permits later authors to advance learning by building on existing works.

The abridgment right has evolved into today's most important limitation on an owner's bundle of rights: the fair use exception. Fair use is a defense to copyright infringement that permits reasonable uses of the owner's work without permission. Fair use was developed in English common law cases and then adopted by famous U.S. Justice Story in the 1841 case *Folsom v. Marsh*.[21] Congress codified fair use in §107 of the 1976 Copyright Act so that the threat of infringement litigation does not produce unfair results or weaken the progress of science and the useful arts.

§107 Fair Use Doctrine

Notwithstanding [the author or owner's bundle of rights under §106] the fair use of a copyrighted work, including such use by reproduction in copies or phonorecords or by any other means specified by that section, for purposes such as criticism, news reporting, teaching (including multiple copies for classroom use), scholarship, or research, is not an infringement of copyright.

Fair use is an ambiguous concept. Its uncertainty is further complicated because the case law and statutes do not provide clear guidance and often seem contradictory. Fair use determinations nearly always require ad hoc, case-by-case analysis. Users who forthrightly seek to stay within the lawful bounds of fair use still risk infringement litigation. When they feel uncertain about a particular use, they may decline to use another work because of this risk. Of course, copyright owners prefer narrow fair use, and they may think they benefit when users reluctantly choose not to make a fair use because of their apprehension and the law's ambiguous guidance. The available guidance is too often worthless for most users and probably results in two inferior outcomes: (1) careful users conservatively avoid fair uses they could legally make, and (2) scofflaws ignore the limits of fair use and frequently infringe.

TRANSFORMATIVE USES

One important and developing theory of fair use is that transformative uses are a very important type of fair use. **Transformative uses** are productive uses of the original work that add potentially valuable and creative expression. For example, new works derived from an original may advance the art by adding new information, reinterpreting ideas in light of new conditions, providing more imaginative insights,

21. 9 F.Cas. 342 (C.C.D.Mass. 1841).

using different creative or artistic expressions, reaching different conclusions, or targeting different audiences. Transformative uses are more defensible than reproductive uses. Reproductive uses probably seldom qualify as fair uses because they seek only to mimic the original or compete with the original and do not serve new markets or new purposes.

THE FOUR FACTORS OF FAIR USE

Case law and §107 of the Copyright Act set out a list of the types of situations that may constitute a fair use: "criticism, news reporting, teaching, scholarship, or research." This list is not exclusive because the language in §107 precedes the list with the phrase "for purposes such as . . ." This phrasing clearly indicates that the list is not exhaustive but depends on the circumstances. The determination of fair use is an equitable inquiry about the reasonableness of the use. In the 1841 case of *Folsom v. Marsh*, Justice Story first suggested a set of factors that should be used to identify reasonable uses. These criteria have since grown in judicial decisions until this history was codified by Congress in the 1976 Copyright Act.

These factors balance the hardships on the owner against those of the user by applying a form of the rule of reason. Today, all four factors must be used, they are weighed, and some are given greater weight in particular cases. Also, the courts may consider other factors, such as good faith and usages in the trade. They identify new types of reasonable uses, and they are also used to evaluate whether a claimed use is reasonable. The factors are (1) the purpose and character of the use, (2) the nature of the copyrighted work, (3) the amount and substantiality of the portion used, and (4) the effect of the use on the potential market for the work. These complex criteria are discussed next but are probably familiar to most people who have seen them posted in libraries and on photocopiers.

The Four Factors of Fair Use

1. the ***purpose and character of the use***, including whether such use is of a commercial nature or is for nonprofit educational use;
2. the ***nature of the copyrighted work***;
3. the ***amount and substantiality of the portion used*** in relation to the copyrighted work as a whole; and
4. the ***effect of the use upon the potential market for the work*** or the value of the copyrighted work.

Purpose and Character of the Use

The first factor focuses on the alleged infringer's purpose and type of use of the original work. The factors clearly favor some types of uses over others. (See Exhibit 15.5.) For example, nonprofit educational uses are more likely to be considered fair use, and the user's personal commercial purpose is less likely to be fair use. Other uses more likely to be fair include scholarship, protected forms of speech, and uses that transform the original work. Most publishers are *for-profit* businesses, so the profit motive standing alone does not prohibit a fair use. Instead, the commercial character must be less significant than other meritorious factors. Uses less likely to be judged fair under this factor are those in which the commercial aspects predominate. Commercial use weighs most strongly against the user if the uses are simple reproductions of the original that are in competition with the original or if the user could have easily paid for a license.

Nature of the Copyrighted Work

The second factor focuses on the amount of creative expression in the original work. Highly creative and entertaining works with substantial artistic or fictional content are given maximum protection against unauthorized use. Also, unpublished works are given stronger protection. The unauthorized use of an unpublished work probably involves a breach of confidence or maybe even misappropriation. Theft clearly contradicts any "fairness" in the use.[22] Unpublished works are a recurring and legitimate source for news reporting. By contrast, factual or scientific works contain more public domain information, so users may exploit them more readily than they can exploit creative works. However, there are limits. Fair use of factual works should not undermine the only market for authorized copies of the original, such as for educational consumables like preprinted tests, worksheets, or exercises.

Amount and Substantiality of the Portion Used

Many people crave a mechanical rule of thumb that would enable them to comfortably use just under the threshold amount that would surpass fair use. Indeed, some publishers use a proportional **quantitative** maximum—say, no more than 5% of the original. Others use absolute limits, such as no more than 200 words from a book or no more than 25 words from a magazine before permission must be obtained. These methods have only gross validity because sometimes just a small portion constitutes the **qualitative** "creative essence" of the original work. The proper quantitative comparison is between the original work and the amount taken, not how much the portion taken constitutes in the infringer's work. Fair use is less likely as more is taken quantitatively and/or more important parts are taken qualitatively.

The famous case of *Campbell v. Acuff Rose*[23] dramatically illustrates the distinction between quantitative and qualitative substantiality. Roy Orbison's famous ballad "Oh Pretty Woman" was the subject of a parody by the rap group Two Live Crew. The two versions were very different in style, lyrics, most of the melody, and audience. In finding the parody was a fair use, the Supreme Court insisted that the parodist should take only enough of the original work to conjure up the original in the audience's mind.

Effect of Use on the Potential Market

The fourth factor concerns the negative impact that the use might have on the market for the original work. It often carries the most weight. Indeed, this factor is already considered in the first factor, which disfavors commercial uses, and again in the third factor, because taking large amounts effectively becomes a substitute for the original work. This substitution would occur if the use diminished the potential sale of the original, interfered with the original's potential marketability, or substituted for potential demand for the original work.[24] There is an important exception to this rule. When criticism is effective, it weakens demand for the work. Criticism and parody are not really substitutions for the original work, so they are generally permissible as fair uses.

AUDIOVISUAL ENTERTAINMENT

Fair use continues to plague the entertainment and software industries as new technologies enable consumers to make copies of audio, video, games, and software

---

22. *Harper & Row, Pub. v. Nation Ent.*, 471 U.S. 539 (1985).
23. 510 U.S. 569 (1994).
24. *Hustler Magazine, Inc. v. Moral Majority Inc.*, 796 F.2d 1148 (9th Cir., 1986).

EXHIBIT 15.5 Fair Use Factors

Fair Use Factor	Analysis of Use for "Fairness"
1. Purpose and character of the use	More favored uses: • Nonprofit educational uses • Transformative uses Less favored uses: • Commercial uses; user must prove use is reasonable • Verbatim reproductions or no permission fee paid
2. Nature of the copyrighted work	More favored uses: • Original was factual, scientific work Less favored uses: • Original was creative, fictional, artistic work, was unpublished, or if factual was an educational consumable
3. Amount and substantiality of the portion used	More favored uses: • Small amounts of the original's expression used Less favored uses: • Large amounts of the original's expression used • Significant qualitative amount taken, the "creative essence" of original even if just a small amount
4. Effect of use on potential market	More favored uses: • Does not directly compete with original work • Criticism or parody of the original work Less favored uses: • Directly competes with original work

more easily, cheaply, and perfectly. There have been several expansions of fair use theory in influential cases and also in legislation directly involving entertainment. Consider the watershed *Sony* Betamax case previously discussed. The Supreme Court legitimized **time shifting**—that is, taping a broadcast show for later viewing—largely for two reasons: (1) There are substantial noninfringing uses for the VCR, and (2) the permitted taping is only for personal, noncommercial purposes. The MP3 case interpreted the AHRA so that general-purpose PCs are not digital audio recording devices. This effectively reaffirms that there are substantial noninfringing uses for computers and computer memory. Similar theory underlies the home copying of music authorized by the AHRA because it is for personal use, as well as the making of software backup copies.

Peer-to-peer (P2P) file-sharing technologies like Napster may have finally reached the limits of fair use. Courts are now limiting the growth of entertainment-related fair use and the first sale doctrine. For example, Napster enabled hundreds of thousands of unrelated strangers to make and distribute millions of copies of musical sound recordings. P2P networks are essentially virtual databases of information and copyrighted works that can search, find, download, and save multiple new copies of a single copy of a purchased work. Napster facilitated the unauthorized reproduction and distribution of original works. Was Napster contributing to the wholesale infringement of the musical sound recordings, or should Napster be excused under the fair use doctrine?

A&M Records, Inc. v. Napster

239 F.3d 1004 (9th Cir., 2001)

Facts. Napster designed and operated a P2P file-sharing system that permitted searching for MP3 sound recordings on other users' computers and then transmitting selected files for storage on the searcher's computer by using Napster's MusicShare software. The trial court held that Napster users are engaged in the wholesale reproduction and distribution of copyrighted works, all constituting direct infringement. Up to 87% of the files on the Napster database were copyrighted works. The several plaintiffs represented a significant number of musicians and record companies. Napster appealed the trial court's injunction against its continued operation for unauthorized P2P file sharing of works protected by copyright.

Legal Issue. Are the uses by Napster and by its registered participants excused from infringement of the MP3 music files as fair use?

Opinion. The evidence establishes that a majority of Napster users use the service to download and upload copyrighted music . . . the uses constitute direct infringement of plaintiffs' musical compositions, recordings." The district court also noted that "it is pretty much acknowledged . . . by Napster that this is infringement." We agree that plaintiffs have shown that Napster users infringe at least two of the copyright holders' exclusive rights: the rights of reproduction, and distribution. Napster users who upload file names to the search index for others to copy violate plaintiffs' distribution rights. Napster users who download files containing copyrighted music violate plaintiffs' reproduction rights. Napster contends that its users do not directly infringe plaintiffs' copyrights because the users are engaged in fair use of the material. The district court concluded that Napster users are not fair users. We agree.

1. Purpose and Character of the Use

This factor focuses on whether the new work merely replaces the object of the original creation or instead adds a further purpose or different character. In other words, this factor asks "whether and to what extent the new work is 'transformative.'" The district court first concluded that downloading MP3 files does not transform the copyrighted work. Courts have been reluctant to find fair use when an original work is merely retransmitted in a different medium. A commercial use weighs against a finding of fair use but is not conclusive on the issue. The district court determined that Napster users engage in commercial use of the copyrighted materials largely because (1) "a host user sending a file cannot be said to engage in a personal use when distributing that file to an anonymous requester" and (2) "Napster users get for free something they would ordinarily have to buy." Direct economic benefit is not required to demonstrate a commercial use. Rather, repeated and exploitative copying of copyrighted works, even if the copies are not offered for sale, may constitute a commercial use. In the record before us, commercial use is demonstrated by a showing that repeated and exploitative unauthorized copies of copyrighted works were made to save the expense of purchasing authorized copies.

2. The Nature of the Use

Works that are creative in nature are "closer to the core of intended copyright protection" than are more fact-based works. The district court determined that plaintiffs' "copyrighted musical compositions and sound recordings are creative in nature . . . which cuts against a finding of fair use under the second factor."

3. The Portion Used

"While 'wholesale copying does not preclude fair use per se,' copying an entire work 'militates against a finding of fair use.'" Napster users engage in "wholesale copying" of copyrighted work because file transfer necessarily "involves copying the entirety of the copyrighted work." Under certain circumstances, a use is fair even when the protected work is copied in its entirety.

4. Effect of Use on Market

"Fair use, when properly applied, is limited to copying by others which does not materially impair the marketability of the work which is copied." "[T]he importance of this [fourth] factor will vary, not only with the amount of harm, but also with the relative strength of the showing on the other factors." The proof required to demonstrate present or future market harm varies with the purpose and character of the use:

> *A challenge to a noncommercial use of a copyrighted work requires proof either that the particular use is harmful, or that if it should become widespread, it would adversely affect the potential market for the copyrighted work. . . .* If the intended use is for commercial gain, that likelihood [of market harm] may be presumed. But if it is for a noncommercial purpose, the likelihood must be demonstrated.

The district court concluded that Napster harms the market in "at least" two ways: it reduces audio CD sales among college students and it "raises barriers to plaintiffs' entry into the market for the digital downloading of music." The district court relied on evidence plaintiffs submitted to show that Napster use harms the market for their copyrighted musical compositions and sound recordings. Plaintiffs' expert, Dr. E. Deborah Jay, conducted a survey (the "Jay Report") using a random sample of college and university students to track their reasons for using Napster and the impact Napster had on their music purchases. [Although] the Jay Report focused on just one segment of the Napster user population [it] found "evidence of lost sales attributable to college use to be probative of irreparable harm for purposes of the preliminary injunction motion."

Plaintiffs also offered a study conducted by Michael Fine, Chief Executive Officer of Soundscan (the "Fine Report"), to determine the effect of online sharing of MP3 files in order to show irreparable harm. Fine found that online file sharing had resulted in a loss of "album" sales within college markets.

The district court made sound findings related to Napster's deleterious effect on the present and future digital download market. Moreover, lack of harm to an established market cannot deprive the copyright holder of the right to develop alternative markets for the works. The "record company plaintiffs have already expended considerable funds and effort to commence Internet sales and licensing for digital downloads." Having digital downloads available free on the Napster system necessarily harms the copyright holders' attempts to charge for the same downloads.

5. Identified Uses

Napster maintains that its identified uses of sampling and space-shifting were wrongly excluded as fair uses by the district court.

a. Sampling

Napster contends that its users download MP3 files to "sample" the music in order to decide whether to purchase the recording. The district court determined that sampling remains a commercial use even if some users eventually purchase the music. Plaintiffs have established that they are likely to succeed in proving that even authorized temporary downloading of individual songs for sampling purposes is commercial in nature. The record supports a finding that free promotional downloads are highly regulated by the record company plaintiffs and that the companies collect royalties for song samples available on retail Internet sites. Evidence relied on by the district court demonstrates that the free downloads provided by the record companies consist of thirty- to sixty-second samples or are full songs programmed to "time out," that is, exist only for a short time on the downloader's computer. In comparison, Napster users download a full, free and permanent copy of the recording. The record supports the district court's preliminary determinations that: (1) the more music that sampling users download, the less likely they are to eventually purchase the recordings on audio CD; and (2) even if the audio CD market is not harmed, Napster has adverse effects on the developing digital download market.

b. Space-Shifting

Napster also maintains that space-shifting is a fair use. Space-shifting occurs when a Napster user downloads MP3 music files in order to listen to music he already owns on audio CD. Napster asserts that we have already held that space-shifting of musical compositions and sound recordings is a fair use.

We conclude that the district court did not err when it refused to apply the "shifting" analyses of *Sony* and *Diamond*. Both *Diamond* and *Sony* are inapposite because the methods of shifting in these cases did not also simultaneously involve distribution of the copyrighted material to the general public; the time or space-shifting of copyrighted material exposed the material only to the original user. In *Diamond*, for example, the copyrighted music was transferred from the user's computer hard drive to the user's portable MP3 player. So too *Sony* where "the majority of VCR purchasers . . . did not distribute taped television broadcasts, but merely enjoyed them at home." Conversely, it is obvious that once a user lists a copy of music he already owns on the Napster system in order to access the music from another location, the song becomes "available to millions of other individuals," not just the original CD owner.

Decision. P2P file sharing of compressed music files using a central server and database is not a fair use of the underlying musical works.

Case Questions

1. Other architectures may be developed to make P2P services work differently from Napster despite the injunction affirmed in this case. How is it possible for these other services to "get around" the Napster injunction?
2. If left unchecked by the law of infringement or if permitted by fair use, what other types of copyrighted works might be at risk to P2P file-sharing technologies?
3. What should be the responsibility of Napster's lawyers if they advised the firm that Napster's methods and uses were a fair use?

ONLINE

What services does Napster provide today?
http://www.napster.com

Continuing Saga of P2P File Sharing in *Napster's* Aftermath

Many Internet visionaries see P2P file sharing as one of the most important new technologies of the digital age. By contrast, the entertainment and software industry view unregulated P2P as anathema to their existing business models because P2P can be used for widespread infringement. After the injunction just cited shuttered Napster, the top five record companies finally became more serious and began to create two separate joint ventures to distribute music over the web. However, Judge Marilyn Patel, the trial court judge in *Napster*, is weighing the public interest in the ongoing Napster infringement suit. Judge Patel will permit Napster to defend itself against infringement if it can prove the antitrust defense: copyright misuse. Misuse, mentioned here, is further detailed in Chapter 19.

At this writing, users and the entertainment industry are widely reported to be locked in an arms race over P2P file sharing. Users now find several music-swapping services (e.g., Gnutella, Aimster, Morpheus) available that eliminate the central

Ethical Issue

Why Pay Full Retail for Entertainment?

Copying technologies that have developed over the years tend to undermine the business models traditionally used to exploit copyrighted entertainment works. Books and sheet music can be hand-copied, photocopied, scanned, or even created by computer software as a sound recording is played. Albums recorded on vinyl, cassette tape, or CD can be recorded on tape, computer hard drive, or CD. Software and games can be copied onto new disks. TV programs and movies can be recorded on VCR, DVD, or hard drives. In the 1990s, a huge rogue industry used transient, mass-production facilities to make unauthorized and infringing musical and software CDs in many countries, although most were produced in a few Asian nations. Pirated copies are often illegally shared with friends or sold to strangers. What is the harm in this? Anyway, many selections of recorded entertainment are simply not good enough to be worth their expensive sale prices. Right?

Entertainment is protected by copyright because, as intangible assets, copyrighted works are too easily copied and the owners derive no revenue from pirated copies. Federal law makes infringement unlawful, even criminal in some instances. Nevertheless, many people somehow believe they deserve free entertainment. After all, the music industry gives away music as it is played on the radio. The TV and movie industries give away A/V works when they are broadcast on free TV. Does the adoption of such substantial "free sampling" signal that these owners forfeit *all* their rights to exploit their works? Absolutely not! Audio and video piracy undermines the incentives needed to attract new talent and creativity to entertainment. Most broadcast entertainment is not free; instead, it is paid for by using various business models: advertising, subscription, pay-per-view.

Some observers argue that the cost of music has risen substantially. In the 1970s, albums cost about a quarter of what CDs cost today. Further, many popular albums contained several "good" tunes, and most CDs today contain fewer "good" tunes. Of course, the difference drops in half if current prices are adjusted for inflation. And things could get worse: The recording industry is introducing musical CDs that may not play on computer CD players. The music and software industries are developing business models around pay-per-use and may eventually discover how to charge premium prices to the most enthusiastic or wealthiest fans. It's no wonder that users and the electronic equipment industry continue to develop technical methods (e.g., P2P, MP3, decryption) to weaken the market power of the entertainment industry.

Three factors will probably persist in the future of entertainment and copyright. First, innovative piracy technologies will continue to be developed. Second, the business models and practices used by the entertainment industry will continue to arouse strong consumer reaction. Demand will continue for new technologies that challenge the entertainment industry's control over content, as well as its business models. Third, copyright law will become an even less coherent hodgepodge of special interest protections for the prevailing and most lucrative business models of the entertainment industry.

server and database features found unlawful in the Napster case. The entertainment industry is introducing music CD copy protection that may prevent the use of MP3 and computer CD-R/W drive technologies. However, early versions are reportedly imperfect and may not play on some CD players, so customer resistance may further depress sales—and anger artists. Similar P2P file sharing may soon proliferate (e.g., Morpheus) now that DeCSS, discussed earlier in the *Corley* case, enables decryption of DVD video programming. It should now be clear that the fair use exception does not provide clear guidance for users. However, one thing seems assured: The content industries will try to severely limit fair use, and users will gravitate to each new threatening technology as it becomes available.

OTHER DEFENSES TO INFRINGEMENT

Fair use is the most important defense to infringement. Nevertheless, a few other defenses deserve a brief mention. The alleged infringer may argue **invalidity** of the original work's copyright. For example, the work may not be copyrightable subject matter, or the technical requirements of registration may have been violated. The owner may have waited too long before bringing suit, beyond the statute of limitations period, which is three years after infringement. The owner may be unable to convincingly prove infringement or cannot overcome the user's fair use claims. The first sale doctrine provides a defense to infringement by distribution because the distribution right of the owner of the original ceases when a copy or phonorecord is first sold to a consumer. However, purchasers may not use the first sale defense if they are renting or leasing copies or phonorecords. There is a discussion of the **copyright misuse** defense in Chapter 19.

QUESTIONS

1. Music is a complex form of intellectual property. There are potentially several forms of copyrightable subject matter in music and several exclusive rights held by the author or copyright owner. Explain (a) how musical expression can fit into different forms of the classification of works of authorship and (b) the various exclusive rights owners have for music under copyright law.
2. Copyrighted works, like other intangibles, are vulnerable to misappropriation or infringement. Discuss the four fundamental reasons that copyrights in the digital age are more susceptible to unauthorized use and transfer than were traditional copyrighted works such as books and vinyl record albums.
3. The latest musical CDs now have a form of copy protection that makes them impossible to play on computers to prevent users from duplicating them with CD burners. A computer hacker has posted on the Internet a new software program for public availability that will neutralize the musical CD copy protection scheme. A friend sends you the URL and encourages you to download the program and use it to make a complete duplicate of a new CD he bought. Explain how the DMCA has changed the traditional process of reverse engineering, the exchange of devices or software that override copy protection, and the use of that software to make duplicate copies.
4. Carter was engaged under a work for hire to design and build a huge walk-through sculpture that nearly filled the lobby of a building. The original building owner, which had hired Carter, went into bankruptcy, and Helmsley-Spear took over building management. After a dispute with the building management, Carter was fired and ordered to leave before completion of all the sculpture projects. Carter filed suit under the Visual Artists Rights Act (VARA) when Helmsley-Spear threatened to remove or alter the walk-through sculpture. What rights does Carter have under VARA? See *Carter v. Helmsley-Spear, Inc.*, 71 F.3d 77 (2d Cir., 1995), *cert.denied*, 716 S.Ct. 1824 (1996).

5. Explain the purposes underlying the U.S. traditions of copyright registration, deposit, and notice. What are the continuing effects of these procedures?

6. Sega made a video game console that works with standard TVs. The console has a special use computer inside, but the actual games are contained on cartridges that plug into a proprietary bus on the game console. The game cartridges include software and formatting that create images on the screen and change the sequence of the game, depending on the player's inputs with a joystick. Accolade makes only game cartridges that work on game consoles made by various manufacturers. Several of its games are quite popular; they have somewhat more realistic action for players. Accolade reverse-engineered the Sega Genesis game console to discover how the proprietary bus worked but did not copy any particular Sega game cartridges. Information on how the game console works was passed on from these reverse engineers to game software writers, who wrote compatible but very different games to run on the Sega Genesis console. Describe this process; explain what can be done by the reverse engineers and what must be hidden from the software writers. Is Accolade's reverse engineering a fair use? Explain. See *Sega Enterprises Ltd. v. Accolade, Inc.*, 977 F.2d 1510 (9th Cir., 1992).

7. Identify, define, and give examples of the four fair use factors.

8. What are the criminal penalties under the Copyright Act? What are the criminal penalties under the DMCA? What are the challenges for prosecuting criminal copyright infringement cases?

9. Computer Associates (CA) and Altai, Inc., both write and market computer software. CA sold ADAPTER, a translation program to allow applications programs to run on several operating systems. Thereafter, Altai developed OSCAR, which performed similar functions. Claude Arney had worked for CA on the ADAPTER project and then worked at Altai to design OSCAR. Nearly 30% of OSCAR's code was taken directly from ADAPTER. Explain the infringement analysis for computer software that would likely be used in CA's infringement suit against Altai. See *Computer Assoc. Int'l, Inc. v. Altai*, 982 F.2d 693 (2d Cir., 1992).

Trade Secrets and Database Protection

How does the law fill in the gaps of intellectual property rights? Patents protect ideas but are expensive to prosecute. Patents can be difficult to acquire, they last for only 20 years, and their details are published for the whole world to see. Although copyrights last much longer, they protect only the form of expression and not the underlying ideas or concepts, which are often the primary source of value. Trademarks protect only commercial symbols, goodwill, and brand image. What is the incentive to innovate in data management when it falls outside these federal protection schemes?

Consider the problem of an Internet business called Everything-Anywhere (EA). Assume EA provides mobile-commerce services to thousands of fiercely loyal clients. EA uses its wireless network to provide travel information, instant discounts at nearby merchants, shopping bot searches, transaction payments, instant messaging, and other services by using clients' various Web-enabled, portable devices such as PDAs, wireless Web phones, and laptops. To fulfill these services, EA has invested considerable sums to build and maintain a huge, perpetually updated database of information. EA integrates private information from multiple sources and continually creates valuable customized reports, which are delivered frequently each day to each client. These services are made possible by EA's use of confidential, proprietary software, both on its servers and installed on each customer's device. Other firms could save a great deal of investment by copying confidential portions of the software, by marketing their competing services to existing EA customers, and by mimicking the favorable relationships EA has with vendors who sell the goods and services EA filters and selects for its clients. A few technologies in this system are protected by patents, copyrights, and trademarks. However, EA can best exploit its unique business model, valuable data, and proprietary software only if they are protected as trade secrets.

A **trade secret** is secret business information, protected by various laws against misappropriation via improper means or breach of a confidential relationship. The problems facing EA might be solved by using some protective measures to maintain secrecy. For example, the most vulnerable assets are EA's customer list, the architecture of its software, and the database of its clients' preferences. Trade secret law provides a remedy when such things are misappropriated. This chapter discusses the creation and protection of trade secrets, as well as remedies for trade secret misappropriation under various theories of contract, tort, and criminal law. The chapter concludes with a discussion of database protection. References are made throughout to technology transfer and employment concepts detailed in Chapter 13.

NATURE OF TRADE SECRETS

Trade secret law sets standards for business ethics. These standards are often derived from visceral notions of fairness and morality. They constrain competitive practices used among competing firms as well as between firms and their employees. Trade secret law distinguishes information already in the public domain from the product of unique ingenuity developed at the employer's expense. Employees create most trade secrets, and employers and employees often have adverse interests in information uniquely developed for the employer. It can be difficult to distinguish trade secrets from practices recently adopted and widely used throughout the trade or profession. The pace of change increases the importance of trade secret protection, particularly for products that combine various technologies. Today, the predominant innovative activity of business is the creation of proprietary information and business models that are largely protected as trade secrets.

HISTORY OF TRADE SECRET LAW

Trade secret law dates back at least to Roman times, when *actio servi corrupti* was the wrongful corruption of another citizen's slave. Damages were recoverable against outsiders who maliciously enticed the slave to divulge business secrets.[1] Society eventually balanced these property rights with the employee's rights. Even after involuntary servitude ended, during the guild era, there remained long-term employment restrictions for apprentices. The apprentice's livelihood was seen as unduly restricted by a long-term indenture under the master's direction.

Many influential early English trade secret cases involved recipes for medicine. The English courts of equity upheld agreements promising confidentiality for non-patented secrets. Later, the U.S. courts of equity upheld trade secrets, finding that licenses were not unlawful restraints of trade, such as in a secret process for chocolate making[2] or pump design plans secretly copied by a repairman.[3]

SOURCES OF TRADE SECRET LAW

In a sense, there is no law of trade secrets like there is for other forms of IP. Other forms of IP give more comprehensive protection than does trade secret law. For example, patent and copyright law defines the property interest fairly precisely. They also give the owner exclusive rights for use and possession. By contrast, trade secret law blends various laws that address the challenge of trade secrets' unique vulnerabilities.

1. Schiller, Trade Secrets and the Roman Law: The Actio Servi Corrupti, *Columbia Law Review* 30 (1930), 837.
2. *Vickery v. Welch*, 36 Mass. 523 (1837).
3. *Tabor v. Hoffman*, 23 N.E. 12 (1889).

Modern trade secret law has its roots in confidentiality duties that are implied from fiduciary principles and are often expressed in employment contracts. Modern trade secret practice is traced to the 1939 publication of *Restatement of Torts* by the American Law Institute (ALI). They are syntheses of the common law in several major subject areas. They are produced by judges, academics, and prominent lawyers to provide uniformity and predictability.

A major problem with the *Restatement*'s vision is that it refused to allow trade secrets to be an innovation incentive. Under this view, trade secrets are not a form of IP but instead are simply a form of commercial morality, which the law remedies for victims of breach of faith.[4] Although the *Restatement* helped make trade secret law uniform, only six states still use it.[5] The ALI eventually dropped the trade secrets provisions from later versions of the *Restatement*, so most states are transitioning to the similar Uniform Trade Secrets Act. In 1995, a new *Restatement* covering trade secrets resurfaced when the ALI first published the *Restatement of Unfair Competition*.

American Law Institute
http://www.ali.org

Today, 44 states have adopted the **Uniform Trade Secrets Act** (UTSA). The UTSA was published in 1979 by the National Conference of Commissioners for Uniform State Laws (NCCUSL). Thirty-four of these states have adopted the 1985 UTSA revision. The UTSA is now the predominant trade secret law in the United States. This uniformity encourages the courts to examine decisions from other UTSA states for interpretation guidance. Coverage of trade secrets in this chapter largely follows the UTSA, but some court interpretations of the *Restatement* are still valid, and the *Restatement* clearly inspired the UTSA. Exhibit 16.1 summarizes the major trade secret laws.

ONLINE

NCCUSL
http://www.nccusl.org

Several states reinforce trade secret law with criminal sanctions. The state laws vary from outlawing theft or possession of stolen computer information to criminal sanctions for unlawful use of secret scientific material. However, the most significant criminal law is federal: the **Economic Espionage Act of 1996** (EEA). Two separate EEA offenses are intended to overcome weaknesses in the civil law of trade secrets and increase the deterrence to trade secret theft. First, the EEA defines the

EXHIBIT 16.1 Sources of Trade Secret Law

Trade Secret Laws	Application
Restatement of Torts	Only 6 states now, main source before UTSA, civil tort-style remedy
Uniform Trade Secrets Act (UTSA)	43 states, civil tort-style remedy
Restatement of Unfair Competition	Minimal current impact
State criminal laws: trespass, theft	Local prosecutor or state attorney, general enforcement, varying standards and penalties
Economic Espionage Act (EEA)	Federal criminal statute, DOJ enforcement, severe penalties
Confidentiality duties derived from agreement	Reinforces civil remedies and criminal penalties
Confidentiality duties derived from employment or agency fiduciary duty	Reinforces civil remedies and criminal penalties

4. *Restatement of Torts* §757, comment b.

5. The *Restatement* is the law of trade secrets in North Carolina, New Jersey, New York, Pennsylvania, Texas, and Massachusetts.

crime of **economic espionage.**[6] Second, the EEA outlaws the **theft of trade secrets.**[7] Both crimes require proof that the defendant (1) stole or, without permission, obtained, destroyed, or conveyed trade secret information and (2) knew the information was proprietary. The economic espionage offense also requires the Justice Department (DOJ) to prove that the defendant intended the action to benefit a foreign government or foreign instrumentality or agent. To convict under the theft of trade secrets offense, the DOJ must also prove that the defendant (3) intended to benefit someone other than the trade secret owner (4) and knew the owner would be injured, and (5) the trade secret was related to a product in commerce.

ONLINE

U.S. Justice Department
http://www.us.doj.gov

There are significant penalties for firms under the EEA: maximum fines of $10 million for economic espionage and $5 million for theft of trade secrets. Penalties for individuals include fines up to $500,000 and/or prison terms up to 25 years for economic espionage or 15 years for theft of trade secrets. Substantial forfeiture sanctions may require disgorgement of profits made and forfeiture of any property used during the crime. Congress clearly intended the EEA to apply to crimes involving computer information and theft methods using network communications.

Ethical Issue

Societal Forces Underlying Trade Secret Law

Trade secrets offer advantages over other forms of IP, although they also have some drawbacks. Like other forms of IP, trade secret protection offers an incentive for useful ingenuity that ultimately benefits society with improved products and services. Trade secret protection allows innovators to capture the fruits of their labor. Those who can gain such benefits are more likely to invest resources and ingenuity. The resulting innovation is good for society. Trade secrets function as a safety valve for the shortcomings of other forms of IP. Trade secrets permit some protection where the objective qualifications for patents or copyrights cannot be satisfied. For example, the high fixed costs of patenting are often too burdensome. Compared with the federal registration of patents, trademarks, and copyrights, trade secrets may offer some simple protection. Historically, there were no costly regulatory agencies to administer trade secret protection. There are also societal benefits from propounding commercial morals critical of trade secret theft. Employers have cost savings by using similar form contracts for employment when employees are uniformly required to maintain confidentiality. This helps spread the costs of security and monitoring.

Evaluations of the trade secret system should also consider the costs. Trade secrets are not beneficial when implementation costs outweigh the owner's commercial advantage. First, the security precautions, monitoring, and confidentiality needed to protect trade secrets are costly. Second, trade secrets inherently frustrate the disclosure function of patent law. A successful trade secret is never misappropriated, lost, or discovered with reverse engineering, so the trade secret never enters the public domain or enlightens other inventors. Further, this secrecy fails to signal competitors to avoid costly duplication, so they may needlessly spin their wheels. Competitors suffer opportunity costs because their R&D is diverted away from different but still deserving technologies. Trade secrets may impose societal costs for reinventing the wheel while patent disclosure discourages these social costs.[8]

6. 18 U.S.C. §1831 (2000).

7. 18 U.S.C. §1832 (2000).

8. *See* further discussion in David D. Friedman, William M. Landes, and Richard A. Posner, Some Economics of Trade Secrets, *Journal of Economic Perspectives* 5 (1991), 61.

DOES FEDERAL INTELLECTUAL PROPERTY LAW PREEMPT STATE TRADE SECRET LAW?

State trade secret law and the policies underlying the federal IP laws are sometimes in conflict. For example, trade secret law might frustrate the objectives of patent law, such as when trade secrets persist beyond the defined 20-year duration of a patent or trade secret owners must not disclose their invention, as is required for patents. These potential conflicts raise criticisms that perhaps trade secret protections are inappropriate or that trade secrets are a class of lesser inventions. However, consider the impact of Coca-Cola's trade secret formula. The formula has been of potent commercial value for more than a century. Only in recent years have technologies developed (i.e., spectral analysis) that permit reverse engineering to discover the components and proportions of ingredients in the Coke recipe. As the following landmark case illustrates, state trade secret laws coexist with federal patent law policy.

Kewanee Oil Co. v. Bicron Corp.

416 U.S. 470 (1974)

Facts. Harshaw Chemical Co., a division of Kewanee, is a leading manufacturer of synthetic crystals used to detect ionizing radiation. Between 1949 and 1966, Harshaw spent more than $1 million in R&D to improve crystal-growth techniques, enabling it to increase the size of crystals it grows from just 2 inches to 17-inch crystals, something no one else could do. This R&D refined many processes, procedures, and manufacturing techniques to purify raw materials and encapsulate the growing crystals. Harshaw treats some of these processes as trade secrets. Former Harshaw employees who formed or later joined Bicron were bound to nondisclosure agreements concerning these trade secrets learned while employees at Harshaw. Bicron was formed to compete with Harshaw, and by April 1970 it had grown a 17-inch crystal.

Legal Issue. Is Ohio's law of trade secrets preempted by U.S. patent laws?

Opinion. Mr. Chief Justice Burger. delivered the opinion of the Court. The patent law does not explicitly endorse or forbid the operation of trade secret law. The stated objective of the Constitution in granting the power to Congress to legislate in the area of intellectual property is to "promote the Progress of Science and useful Arts." The patent laws promote this progress by offering a right of exclusion for a limited period as an incentive to inventors to risk the often-enormous costs in terms of time, research, and development. The productive effort thereby fostered will have a positive effect on society through the introduction of new products and processes of manufacture into the economy, and the emanations by way of increased employment and better lives for our citizens.

In return for the right of exclusion—this "reward for inventions"—the patent laws impose upon the inventor a requirement of disclosure. To insure adequate and full disclosure so that upon the expiration of the 17-year period "the knowledge of the invention enures to the people, who are thus enabled without restriction to practice it and profit by its use." The patent laws require that the patent application shall include a full and clear description of the invention and "of the manner and process of making and using it" so that any person skilled in the art may make and use the invention. When a patent is granted and the information contained in it is circulated to the general public and those especially skilled in the trade, such additions to the general store of knowledge are of such importance to the public weal that the Federal Government is willing to pay the high price of 17 years of exclusive use for its disclosure, which disclosure, it is assumed, will stimulate ideas and the eventual development of further significant advances.

The maintenance of standards of commercial ethics and the encouragement of invention are the broadly stated policies behind trade secret law. "The necessity of good faith and honest, fair dealing, is the very life and spirit of the commercial world." [E]ven though a discovery may not be patentable, that does not "destroy the value of the discovery to one who makes it, or advantage the competitor who by unfair means, or as the beneficiary of a broken faith, obtains the desired knowledge without himself paying the price in labor, money, or machines expended by the discoverer."

Since no patent is available for a discovery, however useful, novel, and nonobvious, unless it falls within one of the express categories of patentable subject matter, the holder of such a discovery would have no reason to apply for a patent whether trade secret protection existed or not. Abolition of trade secret protection would, therefore, not result in increased disclosure to the public of discoveries in the area of nonpatentable subject matter. Also, it is hard to see how the public would be benefited by disclosure of customer lists or advertising campaigns; in fact, keeping such items secret encourages business to initiate new and individualized plans of operation, and constructive competition results. This, in turn, leads to a greater variety of business methods than would otherwise be the case if privately developed marketing and other data were passed illicitly among firms involved in the same enterprise.

Certainly the patent policy of encouraging invention is not disturbed by the existence of another form of incentive to invention. In this respect the two systems are not and never would be in conflict. Similarly, the policy that matter once in the public domain must remain in the public domain is not incompatible with the existence of trade secret protection. By definition a trade secret has not been placed in the public domain.

The more difficult objective of the patent law to reconcile with trade secret law is that of disclosure, the quid pro quo of the right to exclude. As to the trade secret known not to meet the standards of patentability, very little in the way of disclosure would be accomplished by abolishing trade secret protection. With trade secrets of nonpatentable subject matter, the patent alternative would not reasonably be available to the inventor. Trade secret law will encourage invention in areas where patent law does not reach, and will prompt the independent innovator to proceed with the discovery and exploitation of his invention. Competition is fostered and the public is not deprived of the use of valuable, if not quite patentable, invention.

Even if trade secret protection against the faithless employee were abolished, inventive and exploitive effort in the area of patentable subject matter that did not meet the standards of patentability would continue, although at a reduced level. Alternatively with the effort that remained, however, would come an increase in the amount of self-help that innovative companies would employ. Knowledge would be widely dispersed among the employees of those still active in research. Security precautions necessarily would be increased, and salaries and fringe benefits of those few officers or employees who had to know the whole of the secret invention would be fixed in an amount thought sufficient to assure their loyalty. Smaller companies would be placed at a distinct economic disadvantage, since the costs of this kind of self-help could be great, and the cost to the public of the use of this invention would be increased. The innovative entrepreneur with limited resources would tend to confine his research efforts to himself and those few he felt he could trust without the ultimate assurance of legal protection against breaches of confidence. As a result, organized scientific and technological research could become fragmented, and society, as a whole, would suffer.

Another problem that would arise if state trade secret protection were precluded is in the area of licensing others to exploit secret processes. The holder of a trade secret would not likely share his secret with a manufacturer who cannot be placed under binding legal obligation to pay a license fee or to protect the secret. The result would be to hoard rather than disseminate knowledge.

Nothing in the patent law requires that States refrain from action to prevent industrial espionage. In addition to the increased costs for protection from burglary, wiretapping, bribery, and other means used to misappropriate trade secrets, there is the inevitable cost to the basic decency of society when one firm steals from another. A most fundamental human right, that of privacy, is threatened when industrial espionage is condoned or is made profitable; the state interest in denying profit to such illegal ventures is unchallengeable.

Where patent law acts as a barrier, trade secret law functions relatively as a sieve. The possibility that an inventor who believes his invention meets the standards of patentability will sit back, rely on trade secret law, and after one year of use forfeit any right to patent protection is remote indeed. Nor does society face much risk that scientific or technological progress will be impeded by the rare inventor with a patentable invention who chooses trade secret protection over patent protection. The ripeness-of-time concept of invention, developed from the study of the many independent multiple discoveries in history, predicts that if a particular individual had not made a particular discovery others would have, and in probably a relatively short period of time. If something is to be discovered at all very likely it will be discovered by more than one person. We conclude that the extension of trade secret protection to clearly patentable inventions does not conflict with the patent policy of disclosure.

Decision. Federal patent and state trade secret law are not incompatible, even though they may cover similar subject matter. Patent law provides strong property rights but requires the inventor to disclose the invention. By contrast, trade secret law requires secrecy to be maintained. Inventors may freely choose between these two schemes.

Case Questions

1. What are the alleged conflicts between state trade secret law and federal patent policy? How can the two bodies of law be interpreted to coexist without conflict?
2. What are the relative advantages of trade secret protection versus patent protection for inventions? Why should society prefer retaining trade secret protection?

Could copyright law preempt state trade secret protection? The 1976 copyright revision eliminated the state common law of copyrights. That law also preempts any other state IP laws if they create rights equivalent to any of the exclusive rights under federal copyright—that is, to reproduce, distribute, make derivative works, display, or perform, as discussed in Chapter 15. Therefore, state trade secret protections that mainly protect the subject matter of copyrights are preempted and invalid. Furthermore, trade secret law is preempted even for the elements not protected by copyright if the trade secret law protects the elements protected by copyright law. All this means that it could be difficult to archive trade secrets because any trade secret embodied in expression that is fixed in a tangible medium is preempted because it is covered exclusively by copyright. Most trade secrets are written or stored in electronic form, so they are clearly covered by federal copyright law. How do trade secret laws survive preemption when most trade secrets are stored in forms protected by copyright?

Fortunately, many courts try to preserve trade secret law when the trade secret is contained in a copyrighted work. The key to the continued validity of trade secret laws is that there must be some "extra element" in the trade secret law beyond the requirements of copyright law. This point is usually satisfied where the misappropriation law involves something more, such as the theft of physical copies (documents, disks, files) or a breach of confidentiality. Trade secret laws are not generally preempted by copyright law because they contain additional wrongful acts that are qualitatively different components from the elements of copyright law.[9] Separately, the Copyright Office permits copyright holders of software programs to blank out printed code showing trade secrets when they submit their source code to the Library of Congress.

SUBJECT MATTER OF TRADE SECRETS

Trade secrets include confidential information that has commercial value. Recall that the *Restatement* originally took a conceptual view of trade secrets, recognizing them only as a tort arising from the breach of a confidential relationship. This view effectively denied that trade secrets were property. However, society expects trade secrets will have property-like characteristics, so the UTSA and many courts hold that "**information is property.**"[10] Status as property gives the trade secret owner some special rights, and the importance of this distinction is evident.

9. *Alcatel USA Inc. v. DGI Technologies, Inc.*, 166 F.3d 772 (5th Cir., 1999).

10. *U.S. v. Carpenter*, 484 U.S. 19 (1987) (material nonpublic information is property in insider trading context) and *Ruckelshaus v. Monsanto Co.*, 467 U.S. 986 (1984) (trade secrets are property interests for government takings purposes).

DEFINITIONS OF TRADE SECRETS

The definitions of trade secrets are very important because they indicate both what subject matter can be protected as trade secrets and the essential steps to create them. Definitions under the *Restatement*, the UTSA, and the EEA are quite similar. Note that over time these laws include specific types of eligible subject matter in progressively greater detail. The *Restatement* definition is worded most generally.

> **_Restatement of Torts_ Trade Secret Definition**
> [A]ny formula, pattern, device or compilation of information which is used in one's business, and which gives him an opportunity to obtain an advantage over competitors who do not know or use it. It may be a formula for a chemical compound, a process of manufacturing, treating or preserving materials, a pattern for a machine or other device, or a list of customers. [It may include] a process or device for continuous use in the operation of the business [but not] information as to a single or ephemeral event.[11]

The *Restatement* requires continuous use of the trade secret; the UTSA does not and so permits protection for one-shot deals, such as takeovers, mergers, business plans, or salaries.[12] The UTSA definition includes most of the same elements yet adds some broad forms of eligible information and clarifies the need for reasonable efforts to maintain secrecy.

> **UTSA Trade Secret Definition**
> Information, including a formula, pattern, compilation, program device, method, technique or process, that:
> (i) derives independent economic value, actual or potential, from not being generally known to, and not being readily ascertainable by proper means by, other persons who can obtain economic value from its disclosure or use, and
> (ii) is the subject of efforts that are reasonable under the circumstances to maintain its secrecy.[13]

The EEA definition is modeled on the *Restatement* and the UTSA. However, the EEA is more recent legislation, which gave Congress an opportunity to include some more specific examples of eligible subject matter. The EEA clearly recognizes that information is processed, stored, and protected on networked computers.

> **EEA Trade Secret Definition**
> [T]he term "trade secret" means all forms and types of financial, business, scientific, technical, economic, or engineering information, including patterns, plans, compilations, program devices, formulas, designs, prototypes, methods, techniques, processes, procedures, programs, or codes, whether tangible or intangible, and whether or how stored, compiled, or memorialized physically, electronically, graphically, photographically, or in writing if
> (A) the owner thereof has taken reasonable measures to keep such information secret; and
> (B) the information derives independent economic value, actual or potential, from not being general known to, and not being readily ascertainable through proper means by the public.[14]

11. *Restatement of Torts*, §757, comment b.
12. New York uses the *Restatement*, so *Lehman v. Dow Jones & Co., Inc.*, 783 F.2d 285 (2d Cir., 1986) held that the attractiveness of a takeover target was ineligible for protection.
13. UTSA §1(4).
14. 18 U.S.C. §1839(3) (2000).

Case law interprets these lists to include many additional specific types of information. For example, the following are eligible subject matter for trade secret protection: engineering data, customer information, lists or preferences, raw material sources, manufacturing processes, design manuals, operating and pricing policies, price codes, bid information, bookkeeping methods, market studies and research, sales data, marketing plans and strategies, new product information, business plans, optimal use of equipment and machinery, software, flow charts, drawings, blueprints, negative results, and know-how. Even a unique selection, compilation, or combination of information taken from the public domain can be protected, an important feature of database protections discussed later in this chapter.

Note that many items on this supplemental list are competitively valuable confidential business information. Some are **know-how,** the experience and intelligence to make processes work most effectively. Know-how is similar to the specifications in a patent that reveal the best mode to practice the patent—that is, the inventor's knowledge of the optimal method to use the patent in a useful way. **Negative results** show what does not work as desired; they come from experiments or testing. Negative results are valuable because competitors might need to repeat the tests, which gives the trade secret owner an economic advantage. The eligible subject matter for trade secrets is much broader than the subjects for patenting: machines, processes, and compositions of matter.

CUSTOMER INFORMATION

Many trade secret cases are litigated over lists of customers, customers' personal preferences, and other related information. Customer lists are more likely to receive protection if effort and expense is used to compile the list and the list includes associated information that creates a database, such as contact agents and sales histories. Lists known generally throughout the industry or that are readily ascertainable from public sources may not be protected. This means that trade secret protection is more likely when the information is difficult to obtain.[15]

An interesting contrast is evident between the law of agency and the emerging interpretation of trade secret law. Agency law provides that customer information retained in a former employee's memory (brain) is exempt from trade secret protection.[16] However, some recent trade secret cases would hold otherwise, such as *Ed Nowogroski Ins. v. Rucker,*[17] in which a former employee recalled, by unaided memory alone, customer lists from a former employer. This was found to be a misappropriation of trade secrets, even though no physical files were copied or stolen.

TRADE SECRETS IN SOFTWARE AND ON THE INTERNET

Trade secrets are increasingly used in software and Internet applications. The major criteria are whether the information, algorithm, links, indexes, methods, or processes would save a competitor time in developing the software or making it more useful. If so, the software information could be a trade secret. Similarly, secret Internet operations, methods, or application programs may qualify as trade secrets. In both cases, the owner must use confidentiality restrictions to retain the secrecy. Users and support

15. *Morlife, Inc. v. Perry,* 56 Cal.App.4th 1514 (Cal.Ct.App. 1997).
16. *Restatement of Agency* §396.
17. 971 P.2d 936 (Wa., 1999).

personnel can be obligated by agreement to maintain confidentiality and not misappropriate the trade secrets. For example, most software licenses prohibit the licensee from decompiling the program. Decompiling is a form of reverse engineering that could reveal trade secrets to a skilled programmer. Reverse engineering is discussed later in this chapter, and confidentiality agreements are discussed in Chapter 13.

ACQUISITION, CONTROL, AND OWNERSHIP OF TRADE SECRETS

Unlike most other forms of IP, trade secrets do not depend on government agencies to create them. Trade secrets are largely created and maintained by the owner's efforts, based on fundamental factors discussed in this section. Trade secret ownership largely depends on contractual controls and confidentiality agreements. These methods cover users as well as the innovators who contribute to devising and assembling the secret information. Confidentiality must be exercised over all people exposed to the secrets. Other types of control—physical, administrative, and contractual—may be needed, depending on the circumstances.

Trade secret rights are not perfected by making applications or filing registrations with regulators. That is not to say that government enforcement is never involved with trade secrets. Increasingly, the criminal aspects of trade secret misappropriation, such as trespass or theft, are addressed by the FBI, state attorneys general, the DOJ, or other law enforcement agencies. Also, many regulatory agencies use procedures to maintain the secrecy about the regulated entities under their control or about investigatory matters.

Traditional trade secret law under the *Restatement* envisioned that the subject matter must have **concreteness**. The trade secret should be more specific and certain than a mere idea or theory, and the trade secret must relate to some useful application. Although the UTSA does not require concreteness, many courts impose this requirement implicitly, such as when they define what is eligible subject matter. Some courts would not require that the trade secret have novelty—some unique newness—but other courts impose a **novelty** requirement. It is not so stringent that it amounts to an invention requirement, as is required by patent law. Novelty is closely related to secrecy, discussed in the next section. Interestingly, court decisions requiring concreteness for trade secrets somewhat parallel patent law's specific requirements for an adequate description and novelty. Exhibit 16.2 lists six factors from the *Restatement* that provide guidance for giving trade secret protection.

Conceptually, trade secret status could be perpetual if the owner keeps the information secret. It is difficult to measure the average value of trade secrets or their longevity because so many are successfully kept secret and firms' own records are incomplete. Recall the long-standing success of the Coke formula. As a practical matter, when the existence of highly valuable trade secrets becomes known, competitors probably expend considerable effort to reverse-engineer, misappropriate, or independently develop similar or alternate methods. This section discusses how these *Restatement* factors inspire the de facto trade secret requirements: secrecy, commercial and economic value, and use causing damage.

REASONABLE EFFORTS TO MAINTAIN SECRECY

Secrecy is the critical element in most trade secret cases for two main reasons: First, the owner must undertake reasonable measures to preserve the secrecy; otherwise,

EXHIBIT 16.2 Trade Secret Factors: *Restatement of Torts*

1. Extent to which the trade secret is known outside the business.
2. Extent to which it is known by employees and others involved in the business.
3. The extent of measures taken to guard the secrecy of the information.
4. The value of the information to [the owner and to] competitors.
5. The amount of effort or money expended in developing the information.
6. The ease or difficulty with which the information could be properly acquired or duplicated by others.[18]

the information will not be protected practically or under trade secret law. Second, there is no reason to sue unless the trade secret has been stolen, misappropriated, or disclosed. Absolute privacy is not needed because the cost burden would too often overwhelm the secret's economic value. Instead, an ad hoc, case-by-case analysis of the circumstances is made to determine whether the owner has "taken all proper and reasonable steps . . . considering the nature of the information sought to be protected as well as the conduct of the parties."[19] Although trade secret laws do not directly define secrecy, many cases discuss it, and the trade secret laws define it negatively; that is, they define when secrecy is lacking. For example, the *Restatement* denies trade secrecy to "matters of public knowledge or of general knowledge in an industry." Secrecy can be lost even if the general public does not know the secret. A potential competitor's knowledge is enough.[20]

Relevant factors in secrecy include the general knowledge of security in the industry and the offensiveness of the misappropriator's conduct. In building a secrecy program, it may be necessary to examine past trade secret practices in the industry, conduct periodic IP audits (including the firm's trade secrets and existing protections), develop scenarios of misappropriation, and design protocols to avoid loss. The audit team needs expertise in several areas, including IP law, technical expertise in the invention field, computer security, and business decisions (strategy, marketing, and/or finance).

These efforts can seem burdensome. However, many management service firms provide consulting to develop new control programs and update existing programs. For example, big accounting firms, law firms specializing in IP, security consultants, and computer security firms regularly help perform IP audits and design trade secrets protections. The major methods are discussed later in this chapter. They are useful beyond trade secrets; much of this regimen is important to develop patents or copyrights.

Will trade secret law still provide remedies if information is inadvertently disclosed outside the "circle of approved employees and third parties"? Secrecy is always most effective when the information is retained by a controlled inner circle. However, there are several recurring situations in which information is released and the courts must determine whether trade secrecy continues as a practical matter. First, information may be determined through **reverse engineering** of products embodying the trade secret that are acquired legally. Second, published information that is **readily ascertainable** from trade journals, reference books, or other published materials is not secret. Third, trade secrets may be revealed to government entities.

18. *Restatement of Torts* §757, comment b.
19. *USM Corp. v. Marson Fastner Corp.*, 393 N.E.2d 895 (Mass. 1979).
20. UTSA §1 comment.

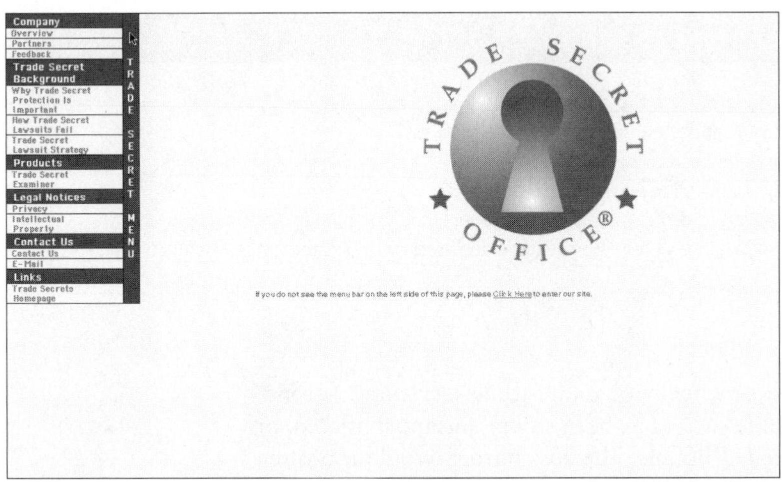

Courtesy, The Trade Secret Office, Inc.

http://
www.thetso.com/

Trade Secrets Revealed to Government

Another regular form of trade secret disclosure is the information contained in patents. Patent law requires the PTO to keep confidential trade secrets divulged in patent applications during examination. If worldwide patent protection is sought, patent applications are published after 18 months, revealing these secrets. Once patents are granted by the PTO, publication of the patent reveals the invention's trade secrets. These trade secrets then enter the public domain. Of course, patent law gives the inventor a limited monopoly to prevent others from directly using the secrets, but their revelation often encourages innovation to work around and even surpass the patent's claims. The patent applicant may withdraw the application at any time before the patent application is rejected or published or the patent is issued. This usually preserves trade secrets contained therein.[21]

Some trade secrets are revealed to government, such as disclosures to regulatory agencies or during litigation. Most agencies have rules requiring that trade secrecy be respected whenever possible. However, agencies sometimes release trade secrets for the public good or during enforcement litigation with the secret's owner. The Freedom of Information Act (FOIA) requires federal agencies to release information whenever a reasonable request is made by any person.[22] FOIA permits most agencies to exercise discretion[23] to withhold disclosing trade secrets in satisfying FOIA requests. Further, an agency can override its promise to maintain secrecy of information submitted by its owner. Nevertheless, a regulator's disclosure of a trade secret may constitute a taking, entitling the owner to compensation under the Fifth Amendment, because "information is property."[24] Similar trade secrecy problems arise with state open records laws; many are patterned after the federal FOIA.

Trade secret information could be revealed during litigation over IP, trade secrets, product liability, or environmental or other issues. Information presented at most trials is placed in the "public record," permitting examination by anyone. However, all is not lost in litigation because many judges place protective orders on information revealed during pretrial discovery. **Protective orders** are court orders to preserve secrecy. Further, testimony likely to reveal trade secret details may be taken **in camera**—that is, privately before the judge and not in open court. Finally, judges often **seal records** from the trial that would reveal trade secrets. Judges also order the opposing parties and witnesses not to disclose trade secret details without court approval.

21. 35 U.S.C. §122 (2000).
22. 5 U.S.C. §552 (2000).
23. *Chrysler v. Brown*, 441 U.S. 281 (1979).
24. *Ruckelshaus v. Monsanto Co.*, 467 U.S. 986 (1984).

WHAT ARE REASONABLE SECURITY PRECAUTIONS?

Firms with substantial or key trade secret assets must develop security protection programs and keep them updated. These programs are even useful to competitors to disprove charges of misappropriation because they provide a complete catalogue of the firm's trade secrets that helps prove rightful development and use. Many components to these programs should be familiar to law enforcement, management accountants, auditors, security professionals, and national security experts because the design of similar systems are so important to these professionals.[25] The firm should first establish sound policies on trade secrecy. From these policies, security measures should be generated that address activities of and interactions among three separate areas: (1) information-centered controls, (2) employee-centered controls, and (3) outsider-centered controls. Of course, there are other ways to classify controls, and many security measures could be usefully applied in two or more classifications. Deliberate evaluation of trade secret protection is necessarily a **risk-benefit analysis**. The cost of each security control measure must be balanced against the financial risk of losing the secret to competitors. Then this analysis is adjusted by the probability that particular combinations of controls can prevent or impede misappropriation, resulting in the net benefits likely to be derived.

Information-Centered Controls

The initial focus should be made on the information itself: Identify sensitive information; list all employees and outsiders who have access; create a "need to know basis" for future access; place warning labels and then log sensitive documents, files, and facilities; use lock-out techniques such as vaults, restricted areas, and computer and network passwords; encrypt or otherwise code data; erase, shred, or destroy stale information; control photocopying; segregate data that has value when integrated; and install alarms, video surveillance, and monitoring devices. With so much proprietary information now created by computer, distributed throughout the firm's locations, and stored for retrieval on networks, the importance of computer security is seldom overstated. Network security techniques such as changing passwords, firewalls, hacker prevention, and Internet policies are becoming very important. Logs should be kept showing when network information was accessed, downloaded, printed, or saved and by whom (IP address).

Reconsider the Coke formula example. The formula is reputedly separated into two major components: one is locked up at one facility, accessible by only one scientist; the other is locked up at a different location and known only to another scientist. The two scientists never meet; their contact is largely prevented. Batches of the two formula components are assembled separately and later combined at a third site. Such information-centered controls significantly reduce misappropriation risk.

Employee-Centered Controls

Few firms can create or use trade secrets without divulging some portion of them to the employees who invent or implement firm activities. Employee-centered controls are directed at delegating strong confidentiality duties and controlling the misuse of trade secrets. The most basic controls are created in employment agreements in which the employee is bound to confidentiality in various nondisclosure agreements

25. M. Epstein and S. Levi, Protecting Trade Secret Information: Plan for Proactive Strategy, *Business Law* (May 1988).

(NDA); a noncompete clause; the nonsolicitation of clients, customers, and co-workers; required sign-in after hours, identification cards while on site, and special access codes to enter sensitive areas; and various work rules generally prohibiting misappropriation and specifically prohibiting personal misuse of employer trade secrets and other assets. Many employers clearly inform their employees that phone records are retained, e-mail using the firm's computers or networks belong to the employer, and workplace surveillance must be expected. Employers generally require employees to assign their IP ownership rights to the employer and agree to assist in obtaining patents or copyrights. Exit interviews and posttermination reminders may encourage compliance. They can also provide a convenient opportunity for the return of the employer's documents, computers, and files. Many of these employment contracting terms are detailed in Chapter 13. Additionally, Chapter 13 discusses the developing inevitable disclosure doctrine, under which a court may impose restrictions that prevent former employees from using trade secrets for a competitor.[26]

Employee-centered controls run some risks. Constant reminders seem advisable so employees are encouraged not to relax their vigilance. However, overextensive security controls may harm morale. They can show a lack of trust, raise employee turnover, and ultimately discourage beneficial risk taking. When controls are well balanced and periodically reviewed during IP audits, employees may better appreciate how their ingenuity contributes to the firm's value.

Outsider-Centered Controls

It is almost inevitable that outsiders will be exposed to at least some trade secrets. Visitors are given plant tours. Employees of service and maintenance firms are often summoned in emergencies. Specifications and new product plans are shared with suppliers who design parts and provide expertise. Consultants are exposed to strategies, product specifications, and production processes to help the firm. Customers are diverted from competitors when shown details of promising, innovative products. As with employee exposure to trade secrets, it is best to reveal only on a need-to-know basis, solicit NDAs, and reveal incomplete information wherever practical. Firms should carefully review product catalogues and specifications, website postings, and press releases to prevent disclosure of important trade secret data. Although licensing trade secrets can be tricky, study the techniques discussed in Chapter 13. For example, most software contains trade secrets, most purchasers of software license its use, and licensors generally impose confidentiality through prohibitions on decompiling or other reverse engineering.

Individuals often submit ideas to firms perceived as capable of effectively developing them into profitable businesses. Idea submissions require delicate progressive revelation and NDAs to create confidentiality and prevent the recipient from appropriating the idea. These techniques are also detailed in Chapter 13. Some of this effort may seem to be unnecessary, excessive secrecy that will only create mistrust and is hardly conducive to good relations. The professional duties of many consultants, accountants, and lawyers prohibit disclosure of client confidences, even without NDAs. Maybe this is so, but it is usually advisable to log and specify confidentiality for all valuable trade secrets shared with outsiders to facilitate their consultation with the owner. Many nations around the Pacific Rim develop long-term,

26. See *PepsiCo, Inc. v. Redmond*, 54 F.3d 1262 (7th Cir., 1995) and *EarthWeb, Inc. v. Schlack*, 71 F.Supp.2d 299 (S.D.N.Y. 1999).

Commentary

When Secrecy Discourages Innovation

Academics and researchers operate in a culture of sharing and disseminating ideas, theories, and other valuable information. Many of the major technologies in medicine, genetics, chemistry, engineering, electronics, materials, and the social sciences were developed in open research settings at major research universities, research institutes, and government laboratories. With the exception of military and weapons development, most researchers subscribe to deeply felt norms that compel them to share information freely and quickly. Researchers take great pride in public recognition that their creativity contributed important ideas.

There are several policy reasons for research openness. First, many of these research projects are publicly financed, so the researcher's societal duties require communication of knowledge quickly into the public domain. Second, academic research depends on building from existing theory, previous discoveries, and known facts. Secrets stall discovery and innovation; they can cause expensive duplication of effort to reinvent the wheel, and this diverts R&D investment from other deserving projects. Third, successful academic researchers *must* publish their research. Publications are the most important evidence of their abilities and performance and demonstrate the significance of their work.

How can academics and research scientists reconcile their fundamental preference for sharing discoveries with trade secret law requirements for secrecy? This puzzling conundrum is becoming more so as universities ramp up their IP programs to capture royalty revenue or start new ventures to fund further research and build prestige. The proper balance remains elusive, but many of the more successful research universities initially insist their researchers publish their discoveries to enhance the public domain. Universities make choices ad hoc to provide confidentiality when research sponsors condition the funding on confidentiality. Researchers and students in university labs are often bound by NDAs covering certain aspects of their research. Researchers on top secret or trade secret projects are sometimes evaluated without placing as much emphasis on publications. Ultimately, students expect to make full use of their educational experiences in their jobs after graduation, so considerable tension is likely to continue.

trusted relationships with suppliers and customers to improve confidentiality expectations resulting from loyalty and trust. Such cultural norms may substitute for some costly controls.

COMMERCIAL VALUE

The *Restatement* implicitly requires the trade secret to have commercial value, derived from the requirement that the secret must give an advantage over competitors. The UTSA and EEA more clearly require trade secrets to give the owner some commercial advantage; these laws require that the owner "derives independent economic value, actual or potential, from [the information] not being generally known." For example, the trade secret could give the owner a cost advantage in raw materials, production, or distribution. Alternatively, the trade secret might make the product superior in quality, features, or performance.

USE CAUSING DAMAGE

The final requirement is that trade secret protection will be available when the owner is damaged by the use of the trade secret. This use arises when a competitor can avoid costs or increase quality or productivity by using the trade secret. Damage from use also arises when the misappropriation occurs because the owner will suffer potential loss from a competitor's future use of the trade secret or from public disclosure.

TRADE SECRET OWNERSHIP

Ownership generally falls to the inventor, discoverer, or developer of the trade secret. Employers may rightfully capture secrets developed at the firm's expense and by its employees by using employment contract provisions such as work for hire, hired to invent, NDAs, noncompetes, and work rules establishing ownership. Ownership is so closely related to secrecy that ownership is lost when the information enters the public domain. Nevertheless, the owner has remedies under trade secret law against employees or outsiders who misappropriate the trade secret or cause it to be publicly disclosed. Misappropriation is discussed next, remedies are discussed later in the chapter, and employment contracting is discussed in Chapter 13.

MISAPPROPRIATION

Although secrecy is the fundamental concept in creating trade secrets, the fundamental concept in trade secret infringement is misappropriation. Misappropriation is the conduct triggering liability and legal action. Suits for wrongful misappropriation are the primary means to protect trade secrets. Misappropriation is both a tort and a violation of contractual confidentiality; many trade secret owners make claims under both theories. A general definition of **misappropriation** covers a range of unethical activities including knowing, wrongful conduct resulting in theft, and wrongful disclosure of secret information using either improper means or in violation of a confidential relationship. The UTSA definition of misappropriation is somewhat complex.

Misappropriation under UTSA

(i) acquisition of a trade secret of another by a person who knows or has reason to know that the trade secret was acquired by improper means; or

(ii) disclosure or use of a trade secret of another without express or implied consent by a person who

(A) used improper means to acquire knowledge of the trade secret; or

(B) at the time of disclosure or use, knew or had reason to know that his knowledge of the trade secret was

(I) derived from or through a person who has utilized improper means to acquire it;

(II) acquired under circumstances giving rise to a duty to maintain its secrecy or limit its use; or

(III) derived from or through a person who owed a duty to the person seeking relief to maintain its secrecy or limit its use; or

(C) before a material change of his or her position, knew or had reason to know that it was a trade secret and that knowledge of it had been acquired by accident or mistake.[27]

Although the *Restatement* definition is substantially similar, there is one major difference. Before an alleged misappropriation violates the *Restatement*, a disclosure or use of the information must be proved. By contrast, the UTSA provides a tougher standard. The UTSA is violated by mere wrongful acquisition—activities that can occur even before a wrongful use or disclosure might occur. The UTSA definition

27. UTSA §1(2).

can be clarified by reclassifying the misappropriation factors into four major forms of misappropriation: (1) improper means, (2) receipt, (3) disclosure, and (4) use. As illustrated in the section on reasonable security precautions, any form of misappropriation could be performed by employees, trusted third parties (e.g., consultants, suppliers, customers), or third-party strangers.

MISAPPROPRIATION: ACQUISITION BY IMPROPER MEANS

Acquisition of trade secrets by using improper means includes actions such as "theft, bribery, misrepresentation, breach or inducement of a breach of duty to maintain secrecy, or espionage through electronic or other means."[28] These are probably the most severe forms of trade secret misappropriation because they involve actions often unlawful under criminal law. For example, employees and entrusted third parties often have access to trade secrets needed to perform their jobs. This type of "information is property"; it belongs to the employer and not to the employee or the entrusted third party. It is misappropriation if one of these parties acquires the information by stealing, bribing others, or using espionage. Similar activities committed by competitors or complete strangers, such as while on a plant tour or by enticing an employee or entrusted third party, are also wrongful.

This form of misappropriation specifically targets unlawful capture of electronic information or unpermitted access into computers, networks, or telecommunication systems. It includes both trespass to land and trespass to chattels. Trespass is an ancient legal concept that is experiencing a revival as hackers probe computers attached to networks and the Internet. All these situations involve intrusion into the zone of expected privacy, a topic developed more fully in Chapter 13. Many physical and computer security controls are regularly used to prevent this problem.

MISAPPROPRIATION BY DISCLOSURE

Trade secret law seeks to prevent disclosure of trade secrets, mostly by employees or entrusted third parties. However, it also prohibits disclosure by strangers who receive the information unlawfully. For example, it is unlawful to disclose trade secrets acquired *directly* from a discloser who used improper means or to *indirectly* acquire information known to come through a chain of tipping. It is also unlawful to disclose trade secrets for a person who knows the information was originally acquired through improper means or in breach of a confidence. Note that disclosure is a separate wrong that is derived from another wrong: acquisition by improper means. Why should there be two separate wrongs in what might often be a single act? Trade secret law reinforces commercial morality by assuring that several forms of the wrong are made illegal and that wrongdoers cannot easily escape liability.

MISAPPROPRIATION BY RECEIPT

Trade secret law also prohibits the receipt of protected information. Misappropriation often involves a "tipping chain" that transmits stolen information from an insider or thief through others to a competitor. Passive and accidental receipt of

---

28. UTSA §1(1).

EXHIBIT 16.3 Chain of Unlawful Forms of Misappropriation

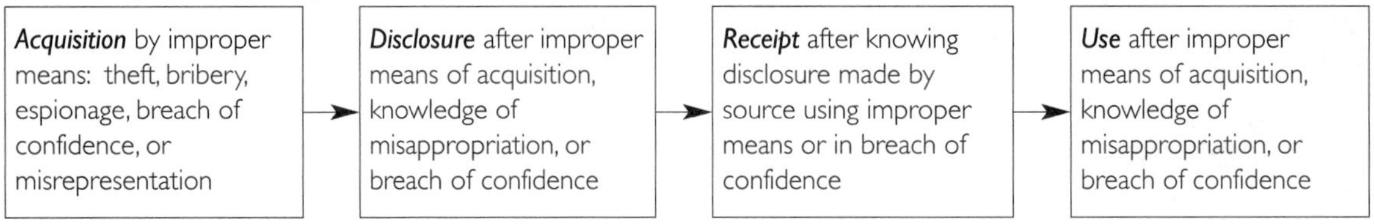

Acquisition by improper means: theft, bribery, espionage, breach of confidence, or misrepresentation	→	*Disclosure* after improper means of acquisition, knowledge of misappropriation, or breach of confidence	→	*Receipt* after knowing disclosure made by source using improper means or in breach of confidence	→	*Use* after improper means of acquisition, knowledge of misappropriation, or breach of confidence

trade secrets is not generally unlawful. Instead, it is wrongful for a recipient to encourage another person, insider or outsider, to communicate the information, when the recipient knows the secret was misappropriated by improper means or a breach of confidentiality. For example, when a competitor receives trade secrets from a former employee of the owner, this constitutes misappropriation by receipt. The recipient could also be another employee of the owner, an entrusted third party, or some other stranger.

MISAPPROPRIATION BY USE

The most direct damage occurs to the owner when the trade secret is used, usually by a competitor, to gain an economic advantage. The owner loses the advantage, and the value of the trade secret is at least partially lost. For example, like with unlawful disclosure, it is unlawful to use trade secrets acquired *directly* from a discloser who used improper means or *indirectly*, if the user knows the information came through a chain of tipping. It is also unlawful to use trade secrets if the user knows the information was originally acquired through improper means or in breach of a confidence. Use is the final but most damaging activity along the chain of misappropriation, as depicted in Exhibit 16.3.

What follows is the classic industrial espionage case involving improper means of discovery. Note how activities ordinarily legal, such as flights in airspace over private property and photography of activities in open view, are transformed into wrongful misappropriation by the court's balancing of the equities. This case distinguishes proper from improper means of discovery. It was cited with approval years later by the Supreme Court in the *Kewanee v. Bicron*, so this precedent is still valid.

E. I. du Pont de Nemours & Co. v. Christopher

431 F.2d 1012 (5th Cir., 1970)

Facts. Rolfe and Gary Christopher were hired by an unknown third party to take aerial photographs of new construction at du Pont's Beaumont, Texas, chemical plant. Du Pont contended the area photographed contained trade secrets on its novel, secret process for the distillation of methanol, a more efficient method than was in current practice in the chemical industry. Du Pont contended these photographs would make it possible for a person skilled in the construction and operation of large-scale distillation operations to detect the trade secrets.

Legal Issue. Is aerial photography an improper means of discovering trade secrets?

Opinion. Circuit Judge Goldberg. This is a case of industrial espionage in which an airplane is the cloak and a camera the dagger [and] a case of first impression, for the Texas courts have not faced this precise factual issue, and sitting as a diversity court we must sensitize our *Erie* antennae to divine what the Texas courts would do if such a situation were presented to them. The Christophers argue that for an appropriation of trade secrets to be wrongful there must be a trespass, other illegal conduct, or breach of a confidential relationship. We disagree.

It is true, as the Christophers assert, that the previous trade secret cases have contained one or more of these elements. However, we do not think that the Texas courts would limit the trade secret protection exclusively to these elements. On the contrary, the Texas Supreme Court specifically adopted the rule found in the *Restatement of Torts*. Thus, although the previous cases have dealt with a breach of a confidential relationship, a trespass, or other illegal conduct, the rule is much broader than the cases heretofore encountered. Not limiting itself to specific wrongs, Texas adopted subsection (a) of the *Restatement* which recognizes a cause of action for the discovery of a trade secret by any "improper" means.

We do not read [the *Furr's* case] as limiting the trade secret protection to a breach of confidential relationship when the facts of the case do raise the issue of some other wrongful conduct on the part of one discovering the trade secrets of another. If breach of confidence were meant to encompass the entire panoply of commercial improprieties, subsection (a) of the *Restatement* would be either surplusage or persiflage, an interpretation abhorrent to the traditional precision of the *Restatement*. We therefore find meaning in subsection (a) and think that the Texas Supreme Court clearly indicated by its adoption that there is a cause of action for the discovery of a trade secret by any improper means.

The question remaining, therefore, is whether aerial photography of plant construction is an improper means of obtaining another's trade secret. We conclude that it is and that the Texas courts would so hold. The Supreme Court of that state has declared that "the undoubted tendency of the law has been to recognize and enforce higher standards of commercial morality in the business world." That court has quoted with approval articles indicating that the proper means of gaining possession of a competitor's secret process is "through inspection and analysis" of the product in order to create a duplicate. Another Texas court explained:

The means by which the discovery is made may be obvious, and the experimentation leading from known factors to presently unknown results may be simple and lying in the public domain. But these facts do not destroy the value of the discovery and will not advantage a competitor who by unfair means obtains the knowledge without paying the price expended by the discoverer.

We think, therefore, that the Texas rule is clear. One may use his competitor's secret process if he discovers the process by reverse engineering applied to the finished product; one may use a competitor's process if he discovers it by his own independent research; but one may not avoid these labors by taking the process from the discoverer without his permission at a time when he is taking reasonable precautions to maintain its secrecy. To obtain knowledge of a process without spending the time and money to discover it independently is *improper* unless the holder voluntarily discloses it or fails to take reasonable precautions to ensure its secrecy.

In the instant case, the Christophers deliberately flew over the du Pont plant to get pictures of a process which du Pont had attempted to keep secret. The Christophers delivered their pictures to a third party who was certainly aware of the means by which they had been acquired and who may be planning to use the information contained therein to manufacture methanol by the du Pont process. The third party has a right to use this process only if he obtains this knowledge through his own research efforts, but thus far all information indicates that the third party has gained this knowledge solely by taking it from du Pont at a time when du Pont was making reasonable efforts to preserve its secrecy. In such a situation du Pont has a valid cause of action to prohibit the Christophers from improperly discovering its trade secret and to prohibit the undisclosed third party from using the improperly obtained information.

We note that this view is in perfect accord with the position taken by the authors of the *Restatement*. In commenting on improper means of discovery the savants of the *Restatement* said:

f. Improper means of discovery. *The discovery of another's trade secret by improper means subjects the actor to liability independently of the harm to the interest in the secret. Thus, if one uses physical force to take a secret formula from another's pocket, or breaks into another's office to steal the formula, his conduct is wrongful and subjects him to liability apart from the rule stated in this Section. Such conduct is also an improper means of procuring the secret under this rule. But means may be improper under this rule even though they do not cause any other harm than that to the interest in the trade secret. Examples of such means are fraudulent misrepresentations to induce disclosure, tapping of telephone wires, eavesdropping or other espionage. A complete catalogue of improper means is not possible. In general they are means which fall below the generally accepted standards of commercial morality and reasonable conduct.*

In taking this position we realize that industrial espionage of this sort here perpetrated has become a popular sport in some segments of our industrial community. However, our devotion to freewheeling industrial competition must not force us into accepting the law of the jungle as the standard of morality expected in our commercial relations. Our tolerance of the espionage game must cease when the protections required to prevent another's spying cost so much that the spirit of inventiveness is dampened. Commercial privacy must be protected from espionage which could not have been reasonably anticipated or prevented. We do not mean to imply, however, that everything not in plain view is within the protected vale, nor that all information obtained through every extra optical extension is forbidden. Indeed, for our industrial competition to remain healthy there must be breathing room for observing a competing industrialist. A competitor can and must shop his competition for pricing and examine his products for quality, components, and methods of manufacture. Perhaps ordinary fences and roofs must be built to shut out incursive eyes, but we need not require the discoverer of a trade secret to guard against the unanticipated, the undetectable, or the unpreventable methods of espionage now available.

In the instant case du Pont was in the midst of constructing a plant. Although after construction the finished plant would have protected much of the process from view during the period of construction the trade secret was exposed to view from the air. To require du Pont to put a roof over the unfinished plant to guard its secret would impose an enormous expense to prevent nothing more that a school boy's trick. We introduce no new or radical ethic since our ethos has never given moral sanction to piracy. The marketplace must not deviate far from our mores. We should not require a person or a corporation to take unreasonable precautions to prevent another from doing that which he ought not do in the first place. Reasonable precautions against predatory eyes we may require but an impenetrable fortress is an unreasonable requirement and we are not disposed to burden industrial inventors with such a duty in order to protect the fruits of their efforts. "Improper" will always be a word of many nuances, determined by time, place and circumstances. We therefore need not proclaim a catalogue of commercial improprieties. Clearly, however, one of its commandments does say "thou shall not appropriate a trade secret through deviousness under circumstances in which countervailing defenses are not reasonably available."

Decision. Aerial photography of a secure plant site is an improper means of discovering trade secrets and a form of unlawful industrial espionage.

Case Questions

1. How can the separately legal activities performed by the Christophers be combined to create the unlawful misappropriation by improper means as concluded by this court? Explain how and why the Christopher's client is liable for receiving the secret.
2. How might the reasoning of this case be used to find such network activities as hacking, sniffing, and interception and decryption of transmissions to be unlawful as improper means? How do the generally accepted standards of commercial morality and reasonable conduct apply to Internet activities? What is the impact of the reasonable precautions discussed here on computer and network security expense?

DEFENSES TO MISAPPROPRIATION

Someone accused of misappropriation may counter the trade secret owner's allegations with evidence disproving the owner's claims or even with an excuse—a defense. Several defenses partially or fully relieve the alleged misappropriator from liability: (1) independent development, (2) proper means of discovery, (3) innocent receipt, (4) reverse engineering, (5) public domain, and (6) various standard equitable and procedural defenses.

INDEPENDENT DEVELOPMENT

Unlike the protection under a patent, a trade secret may be rightfully developed and used by multiple inventors or discoverers. By contrast, it is patent infringement for a second inventor to practice the innovation contained in an existing patent, even if the second inventor was unaware of the patentee's invention. Not so with trade secrets—independent development, either before or after the owner's development, is a complete defense to misappropriation. Of course, the independent development must not have been informed or inspired by confidential information received from the owner. For example, assume one firm has developed an algorithm to evaluate the sale price of derivative securities. After a second firm became known for using a similar technique that it developed previously, the first firm sues for misappropriation. The second firm may use the algorithm because it was developed independently by that second firm.

INNOCENT RECEIPT

There is no duty to refrain from using information received accidentally and innocently. The recipient can defend against a misappropriation suit when no confidentiality breach was known to the recipient or no improper means was used. For example, consider the innocence of a recipient of information overheard in public. If the recipient made no effort to extract the information and there is no indication that the speaker breached a confidence, then there is no liability.

Recipients' innocence reduces to whether they had notice the information was confidential. Notice can take many forms but is answered with this analysis: Did the recipient actually know or, given the circumstances, should they have known that the disclosure was confidential or came from a confidential source? Sometimes notice comes after the recipient has in good faith paid value for the secret or the recipient so changed its position that it would be inequitable to hold it liable. For example, the recipient may have licensed the trade secret from an imposter and then invested heavily in making products using the secret. In these cases, the *Restatement* urges courts to balance the equities by not giving an injunction or damages to the original trade secret owner. In these late-notice situations, the UTSA would require the innocent recipient to pay a reasonable royalty to the original owner.

REVERSE ENGINEERING

Throughout this chapter, reverse engineering is discussed as a legitimate method to discover trade secrets and a complete defense to a misappropriation suit. **Reverse engineering** is the analysis of a product to discover its components and structure. The *Restatement* generally defines it as "inspection or analysis of the commercial product embodying the secret." The UTSA defines it as "starting with the known product and working backward to find the method by which it was developed."

Reverse engineering can often reveal trade secrets in the structure or design of products. The process involves retracing the steps in design and then re-creating the formula or process used in production. For example, when GM embarked on a program to improve the crashworthiness of its sedans, it bought ten Volvos and painstakingly disassembled them to discover how Volvo makes such safe cars. By contrast, trade secrets in the production or administrative process generally cannot be revealed when products are disassembled by experts in the fields of design or manufacturing so they are naturally safer from reverse engineering.

There are limits to reverse engineering. First, software licenses routinely prohibit disassembly—reverse engineering by decompiling object code to become source code. Analysis of source code by experienced programmers would usually reveal trade secrets. Second, the products studied must be acquired legally, according to the UTSA: "The acquisition of the known product must, of course, be by a fair and honest means, such as purchase of the item on the open market for reverse engineering to be lawful." For example, it would not be legitimate to reverse-engineer stolen preproduction products or bribe suppliers to provide components containing the trade secrets.

INFORMATION ALREADY IN THE PUBLIC DOMAIN

Information in the public domain cannot be a trade secret and therefore cannot be misappropriated. Unique combinations, including selection and arrangement of public domain information, could be a trade secret. The public domain defense is directly tied to secrecy. Remember the discussion earlier that information provided to governments or which is readily ascertainable from trade journals, reference books, or other published materials is not secret. But what about secret information wrongfully published? The Internet is a very effective and convenient way to quickly destroy trade secrecy for vindictive or altruistic reasons. Given the breadth of the First Amendment's freedoms of speech and press and absent a confidentiality duty or theft, preventing such postings may be difficult, at least beforehand. Some cases hold that Internet postings destroy secrecy and place the information into the public domain.[29] However, if the owner acts quickly to contain the damage by taking down postings, some courts may be willing to analyze the extent of the publication without mechanically ruling that trade secrets are always destroyed by Internet posting.[30]

OTHER DEFENSES TO MISAPPROPRIATION

Other defenses to misappropriation deserve passing mention. The **statute of limitations** for tort suits is usually applicable. Trade secret owners waiting too long to bring suit may be barred. Equitable defenses are also generally available because the injunction remedy can be so effective. For example, laches is equity's flexible version of a statute of limitations. The **unclean hands** defense could bar an owner who used improper means in acquiring the trade secret. **Laches** would bar an owner's misappropriation suit if there were unexplained delays in bringing suit. If the owner proves its trade secret was misappropriated and no defense applies, the owner is entitled to remedies.

REMEDIES

Trade secret owners suffering misappropriation have two major civil remedies: (1) an injunction against further disclosure or use of the trade secret and (2) money damages resulting from loss of the competitive advantage from the secret information. Separately, the owner may initiate a criminal complaint for state crimes (e.g., theft, trespassing, burglary) or federal crimes, such as the EEA or privacy crimes discussed in Chapter 14, including the Computer Fraud and Abuse Act or the Electronic Communications Privacy Act. Of course, political pressures may influence criminal prosecutors. Their investigatory resources are limited, and they must allocate their constrained resources among a wide variety of crimes and current criminal investigations.

---

29. *Religious Technology Center v. Netcom On-Line Communications Services, Inc.*, 923 F.Supp. 1519 (N.D.Cal. 1995).

30. *DVD Copy Control Association, Inc. v. McLaughlin*, 2000 WL 48512 (Cal.Sup. 2000).

INJUNCTIONS

Injunctions are the most basic and immediately effective remedies. A court order can prohibit the misappropriator from actual or threatened use of the secret. An injunction is also useful to prohibit further disclosures of the secret to others. These may be the most effective remedies when the information is still secret and has not been disclosed widely into the public domain because they effectively prevent economic damages. The injunction may target an entrusted outsider, a competing firm, or a former employee, such as in the inevitable disclosure situation, from disclosing or using the information.

An injunction should be limited to the time the information remains secret. Once the trade secret goes into the public domain, the misappropriator should be able to use the information just as anyone else could. However, a few courts delay this use to prevent any head start in getting products to market made possible by the misappropriation. A temporary restraining order (TRO) or **preliminary injunction** can be appropriate where disclosure is imminent. For example, if the misappropriator is ready to deliver to a client a report containing the secrets, then a preliminary injunction would delay the disclosure until after a trial is held on the secrecy and misappropriation issues.

MONEY DAMAGES

If an injunction to prevent disclosure or use of a trade secret is not possible, then money damages are the next most effective remedy. Damages may result from the owner's loss of sales or market share to competitors' sales that include the infringing trade secret, lower prices for the owner's sales due to competitors' sales, and the misappropriator's profits from products sold using the trade secret. Under the UTSA:

Damages can include both the actual loss caused by misappropriation and the unjust enrichment caused by misappropriation that is not taken into account in computing actual loss.

The owner must prove the compensatory damage amount. The misappropriator has the burden of proving that none of its profits are attributable to the trade secret. If damages are too difficult to prove, a reasonable royalty may be ordered. The UTSA permits punitive damages up to double the amount of the compensatory damages for willful, wanton, and malicious misappropriation. Additionally, attorneys' fees are sometimes ordered in cases of blatant, oppressive, and bad faith conduct. Attorneys' fees could be ordered against the trade secret's owner for a bad faith claim of misappropriation or bad faith opposition to terminate an injunction after the trade secret has gone into the public domain. In extraordinary cases, where the misappropriator has produced products that include the trade secret technology, called embodiments, these products could be seized and destroyed.

PROTECTION OF DATABASES

The information age runs on data, facts, collections of artistic expression, and the like. Consider the business models for such profitable firms as Lexis-Nexis, Westlaw, Moody's, eBay, DoubleClick, Rand-McNally, and proprietary libraries. The one common thread is their need for a reasonable cash flow to fund investment in acquiring data, both digital and analog. Without some legal protection for their databases, only public libraries and universities would be apt to make systematic accumulations of data available for research, learning, and commerce. Databases are as old as manual record-keeping systems, as ubiquitous as telephone books and CD-ROMs, and as new and innovative as Napster was in creating peer-to-peer (P2P) network applications.

Databases are collections of works, data, or other materials arranged in a systematic or methodical way for retrieval or access by manual or electronic means. Data are raw facts that most often become meaningful only when collected and arranged in some logical fashion so that meaning can be given. Then users can access the information and aggregate particular aspects of it in different ways that reveal meaningful relationships. Many useful databases are constantly updated with new information, purged periodically of useless or stale information, and constantly managed to maintain usefulness, data security, confidentiality, and value.

The types of information contained in databases often are such diverse subject matter as literary works, artistic works, texts, sounds, images, numbers, facts, production figures, shipping information, transactions, financial data, geographic information, and personal data. Today, databases are most useful when compiled electronically. Databases are usually stored on computers and electronic media so they can be retrieved according to defined aspects of the data. The function of databases is often to create reports that are communicated to remote locations via telecommunications, such as the public Internet or in closed, proprietary intranets.

Database technology has advanced significantly from ledger paper and spreadsheets. Today a database may stand alone on a PC or mainframe computer or be part of a distributed processing system. Either is well suited to database construction and operation. For example, modern databases may be composed of several separate repositories that are formally linked together by telecommunications. Many firms link their geographically dispersed databases into an enterprise-wide intranet. Increasingly, informal links are arising under the P2P techniques of survey, indexing, and access.

Some databases contain so much information and are so huge that they are comprised of terabytes of information. They are often called **data warehouses**. The dramatic drop in costs for electronic storage and retrieval makes such mass data techniques practical. Large-scale and distributed databases raise both database protection and privacy concerns. (The latter was discussed in Chapter 14.) Relational databases run quickly and efficiently, revealing associations among data and permitting talented people to find new relationships, a practice called **data mining**. New associations are discovered, new sequences are uncovered, and new data classifications or clusters are constructed. All this enables better forecasts, a clear competitive advantage that can also be sold to others.[31]

The Europeans have gone much further than the United States in protecting databases. As discussed later, the EU Directive on the Legal Protection of Databases[32] rewards people or firms who gather data and invest in its organization into a potentially useful database. The EU Directive requires each separate EU nation to enact national laws that create **sui generis** forms of IP. These modern databases are thus new forms of IP, not previously recognized under traditional copyright, patent,

---

31. Jane Kaufman Winn, and James R. Wrathall, Who Owns the Customer? The Emerging Law of Commercial Transactions in Electronic Consumer Data, *Business Lawyer* 56 (2000), 235.
32. OJ 1996 L77/20.

trade secret, or trademark law. However, this "sweat of the brow" theory is not part of current U.S. law. In the United States, databases receive incomplete protection under one or a combination of several theories of law: tort, trade secret, copyright, and contract. This section discusses these incomplete protections that U.S. law offers for databases.

TORT THEORIES

Tort theories of database protection have existed for decades but offer rather limited protection. Several tort theories are available to database owners to protect their databases from unauthorized access, use, or resale by an infringing outsider: misappropriation, trespass, conversion, and trade secrets. Database infringement may include aspects of one or more of these theories, as well as some other legal bases such as breach of contract, database license violations, and breach of employment or confidentiality agreement.

Hot News

The landmark case resolved a 1918 misappropriation dispute in *International News Service v. Associated Press.*[33] International News Service (INS) transmitted news stories about World War I as reports on its wire service. INS originally acquired these stories off the Associated Press (AP) newswire. INS members used these reports as the basis of newspaper stories in direct competition with AP member newspapers that wrote similar stories based on the same timely **"hot news."** The U.S. Supreme Court held that it is wrongful to unfairly misappropriate factual material acquired by another to compete with the data's owner. This decision spawned a form of database protection called the hot news theory, so named because the time value of the information was the property of the original owner.

Later legislation and cases have severely limited this doctrine. Recall from the trade secret preemption discussed before that state law is invalid if it covers copyright subject matter and creates rights similar to those under federal copyright. Hot news is expression covered under copyright, and copying is one of the copyright bundle of rights. However, state misappropriation laws may still protect hot news because they involve "extra element(s)" protected beyond the copying. For example, state misappropriation law generally addresses other elements, such as the time-sensitive nature of the facts, the investment by the owner ("sweat"), the infringer's free riding, the infringer's direct competition with the database originator in using the information, breach of confidence, or passing off. Hot news data may be protected against misappropriation if one or more of these (or other) noncopyright elements are protected by the state law.

Problems with hot news protections were addressed in a series of more recent sports information cases involving real-time play-by-play and score information delivered via wireless or the Internet to various devices, including pagers, PDAs, and PCs. Consider *National Basketball Association* (NBA) *v. Motorola, Inc.*,[34] Motorola marketed a pager promising to deliver real-time NBA scores but failed to license this content from the NBA. This information was acquired through Sports Team Analysis and Tracking Systems, Inc. (STATS), which gathered the data from various

33. *International News Service v. Associated Press*, 248 U.S. 215 (1918).
34. 105 F.3d 841 (2d Cir., 1997).

broadcast sources. STATS then transmitted the data to Motorola via satellite, and Motorola distributed the information to pagers and through the Internet. About the same time, the NBA was attempting to launch its own "Gamestats" service. The New York trial court protected the NBA data and decided in favor of the NBA. It held that STATS and Motorola made no contributions to the data and that they deprived the NBA of its property. However, this trial court decision was reversed on appeal. The Second Circuit found no "extra elements" in this case because the copyrighted broadcasts and noncopyrightable scores should not be separated to permit state claims. This case narrows the hot news protection for databases substantially.

Trespass to Chattels

Trespass to chattels or **cyber trespass** may be a more promising tort theory to protect databases, as well as any data on individual computers or spread among Internet websites. Trespass is an intentional invasion of another person's property interest, the owner's exclusive right to possession. In the electronic database context, trespass could be accomplished locally or remotely by (1) physical acts on site that intrude into another's computer storage or remote intrusion and (2) remote access, probably via Internet or network connections, wired or wireless, by which the trespasser gains access to a computer's memory, storage, or data transmission. Trespass causes harm by reducing the condition, quality, or value of personal property even if there is no physical damage.

Trespass seems to be a robust theory whenever there has been unauthorized access to another's computer, any unauthorized storage onto or destruction of data residing on another's computer, and any unauthorized reading or accessing of data taken from another's computer. Trespass could be a major threat to several computer and networking transaction methods, such as cookies, copying data from a local hard drive during an interactive session to make capacity available for the session, or any other probing of another computer for information. Courts could excuse the trespass and thereby permit remote access if (1) permission is granted in a user agreement, (2) the public gains a widespread understanding and accepts that many Internet methods require access to user data, or (3) users realize their RAM and permanent storage must be invaded by outside programs or probes to accomplish the user's on-line experience. However, there is evidence that few users understand either the fact of outsider probes or the privacy and security significance of such probes. It may take some time before there is widespread user acceptance.

Data Aggregation

Data aggregation requires probing another's website for information. **Data aggregators** are a cottage industry that locates data from widely varying Internet sources to produce reports useful to users. In many of these situations, the firms initially posting the raw data would prefer to shield the data from the "prying eyes" of these new Internet firms. The originators hope to capture for themselves the value of reselling the information, prevent competition, force the aggregators to license the data, or generally prevent the diversion of user attention away from the originator's site. In a simple sense, search engines and Web crawlers are a form of data aggregator because they compare the user search terms with meta-tag and content or text files to produce reports that rank order the information by relevance. The owner of the probed website may claim the probe was an intrusive trespass in an attempt to prevent the aggregator's activity.

Commentary

Content Aggregation

Networks generally and the Internet in particular offer seemingly unlimited opportunities for ingenuity. Content may be posted, access broadened or regulated, and particular content found from among various unaffiliated sites. All this is done in shorter times and by using increasingly sophisticated technologies that cost less. However, all these benefits threaten database owners. It is increasingly easy to assemble databases instantaneously, without much effort and drawn from fragmented content posted almost anywhere. Consider the compelling example of the Napster technology. The MP3 audio format permits "ripping" musical recordings for digital storage on computers. Inexpensive CD burners permit cheap storage. Users can play CDs anywhere or physically exchange CDs with friends. The music can also be played back on computers (RealPlayer), and an unlimited number of perfect copies can be made by using computers. The Internet makes it possible to transfer musical selections freely as computer files in Internet downloads or e-mail attachments. Finally, the P2P indexing of Napster made it possible to find and exchange the music among strangers anywhere in the world. Napster is now a classic example of unleashing the Internet's power to undermine long-established business models that previously relied on physical security systems made obsolete by technology. Napster also illustrates how P2P file sharing creates databases from physically dispersed and independent sources.

Proponents of database protection laws argue that P2P technologies like Napster will undermine the incentive to create databases because the proven piracy of such data could make it impossible to fund further data creation. The loss of incentive in the music world could reduce new recordings. In some other fields, data not directly needed for business operations would not be produced or published, limiting its availability. However, the direct losses from misappropriation of information in many other fields are not as clear-cut.

How can it be that the Internet simultaneously enhances the power to manipulate databases as it impairs the incentive to produce, collect, or publish facts? Is this apparent conundrum best resolved with new sui generis database protection laws? There is no easy or universal answer. Certain industries must produce at least some data to operate. In these industries, incentives are not needed to produce their data. For example, the transportation industry must provide its reservations information to attract new business and run efficiently at capacity. Booking travel would be very inconvenient without the publication of flight or train departure times, destinations, and unsold seat availability. No new incentive is needed to create travel reservation data. However, consider other industries that do not directly depend on publishing certain data. For example, stock-trading data are not directly necessary for a seller to offer or buyer to accept a particular trade. Of course, database incentives or mandatory disclosure of such transaction data improves market efficiency.

Some types of data must be collected and handled very carefully to assure quality. Database protections are important incentives for careful data management that would not otherwise occur. For example, much of the free content on the Internet is not double-blind refereed, nor do experts check it for accuracy. Database protections are best justified to encourage information management that would not otherwise occur or would not be done carefully and completely. It is not necessary to create new IP rights to encourage the creation or publication of many other types of useful data already produced sufficiently, particularly if such rights would diminish the public domain.

Many content aggregators use even more sophisticated methods. For example, on-line bill-paying services probe the bank accounts of bank customers to process automated bill paying. This practice has become known as **screen scraping** because the banking customer grants permission and password access to the aggregator to access the customer's account information, which is "scraped" or taken off the bank's site to facilitate the automated bill payment. Some banks hope to capture fee income from such services when they finally implement their own electronic bill presentment and payment services. The factual data about a bank customer's account are not protected by copyright. Indeed, the data are arguably the customer's property, not the bank's property. A few banks have sued, using trespass and IP theories, to prevent probes by such aggregators. For example, a few banks include copyrighted screen designs or trademarks so that when aggregators probe bank website information with the customer's consent the screen scraping inadvertently infringes the bank's IP rights. If banks are successful with trespass or infringement theories, bill payment services could be forced to license the data or go out of business.[35]

ONLINE
Content aggregator—bill payment service
http://www.paytrust.com

Shopping Bots

Intelligent agent software improves the accuracy and usefulness of information obtained from Internet sites. **Shopping bots** can search for particular models or classes of goods and then return comparative reports showing on-line sellers that satisfy the customer's price and other specifications. Shopping bots may run each search de novo or create databases from which other customers' comparison shopping requests are provided. For example, Bidder's Edge would satisfy customer requests for on-line auction data by searching well-known auction sites such as eBay. However, eBay attempted to block Bidder's Edge and finally sued, claiming the bot trespassed on eBay's website. A preliminary injunction against Bidder's Edge illustrates that trespass may be a viable theory to shield publicly available data from wholesale extraction by using its terms and conditions for website access to stop information scavengers like the shopping bots.[36]

COPYRIGHT PROTECTION OF DATABASES

As discussed in Chapter 15, copyright law protects the form of expression but not the underlying ideas in the expression. This limitation makes copyright law only a weak protection for databases. Copyright may protect a database as a compilation when it includes a unique selection and arrangement of facts. A **compilation** is the product of selecting, coordinating, arranging, or organizing existing material, irrespective of whether these underlying facts were ever protected under copyright. For example, compilations may include personal organizers, standardized tests, a country music show, greeting cards, a collection of logarithms, and a directory of seed suppliers.

It is copyright infringement if another person copies the selection and arrangement of a protected compilation. Others may independently make similar selections and arrangements. A second compiler may use the first compilation to check for errors or omissions. The copyright law recognizes that there can be sufficient originality or creativity for copyright protection in the selection and arrangement of facts into a database. Creativity is the element of making nonobvious choices from among numerous choices.[37] The following landmark case ended some courts' practice of giving copyright protection to compilations of facts without regard to the creative element of selection and arrangement.

35. See discussion of bots, intelligent agents, and similar automated data collection services in Ballon, Ian, *E-Commerce and Internet Law*, Glasser LegalWorks (2000) at Chapter 13.
36. *eBay, Inc. v. Bidder's Edge, Inc.*, 100 F.Supp.2d 1058 (N.D.Cal. 2000).
37. *Matthew Bender & Co. v. Hyperlaw, Inc.*, 168 F.3d 674 (2d Cir., 1990).

Feist Publications, Inc. v. Rural Telephone Service Co., Inc.

499 U.S. 340 (1991)

Facts. The Kansas Corporation Commission required all telephone company franchisees providing telephone service to compile and publish a telephone directory, the well-known "white pages." Rural's white pages were compiled by using information provided by telephone customers when their phone service was started. Rural arranged the listings alphabetically by surname and included addresses and phone numbers. Feist copied portions of Rural's directory to publish a competing directory.

Legal Issue. Is there sufficient originality in a telephone company white pages listing of customers to deserve protection as a compilation under the copyright law?

Opinion. Justice O'Connor. This case concerns the interaction of two well-established propositions. The first is that facts are not copyrightable; the other that compilations of facts generally are. The most fundamental axiom of copyright law is that "no author may copyright his ideas or the facts he narrates." At the same time, however, it is beyond dispute that certain compilations of facts are within the subject matter of copyright. There is an undeniable tension between these two propositions.

The key to resolving the tension lies in understanding why facts are not copyrightable. The sine qua non of copyright is originality. Original, as the term is used in copyright, means only that the work was independently created by the author (as opposed to copied from other works) and that it possesses at least some minimal degree of creativity. To be sure, the requisite level of creativity is extremely low; even a slight amount will suffice. Originality does not signify novelty; a work may be original even though it closely resembles other works so long as the similarity is fortuitous, not the result of copying.

Facts may not be copyrighted because they are not created. Rather, they are discovered. The same is true of all facts—scientific, historical, biographical, or news of the day. "They may to be copyrighted and are part of the public domain available to every person." Factual compilations, on the other hand, may possess the requisite originality. The compilation author typically chooses the facts to include, in what order to place them, and how to arrange the collected data so that they may be used effectively by readers. These choices as to selection and arrangement, so long as they are made independently by the compiler and entail a minimal degree of creativity, are sufficiently original that Congress may protect such compilations through the copyright laws. This protection is subject to an important limitation. The mere fact that a work is copyrighted does not mean that every element of the work may be protected.

[Some] courts have developed a new theory to justify the protection of factual compilations. Known alternatively as "sweat of the brow" or "industrious collection," the underlying notion is that copyright was a reward for the hard work that went into compiling facts. The 1976 Act [clarified this, stating when protection is not available:] "In no case does copyright protection for an original work of authorship extend to any idea, procedure, process, system, method of operation, concept, principle, or discovery, regardless of the form in which it is described, explained, illustrated or embodied in such work."

Not every selection or arrangement will pass muster. Originality requires only that the author make the selection or arrangement independently and that it display some minimal level of creativity. Presumably, the vast majority of compilations will pass the test, but not all will. There is no doubt that Feist took from the white pages of Rural's directory a substantial amount of factual information. The question that remains is whether Rural selected, coordinated or arranged these uncopyrightable facts in an original way. The selection and arrangement in Rural's selection of listings could not be more obvious: It publishes the most basic information—name, town and telephone number.

Because Rural's white pages lack the requisite originality, Feist's use of the listings cannot constitute infringement. This decision should not be construed as demeaning Rural's efforts in compiling its directory, but rather as making clear that copyright rewards originality, not effort; "great praise may be due to the plaintiffs for their industry and enterprise in publishing this paper, yet the law does not contemplate their being rewarded in this way."

Decision. There is insufficient authorial creativity for copyright protection of a telephone book's white pages that simply provide an alphabetical list of phone customers. Compilations must have some originality in selection and arrangement of its contents for copyright protection to arise.

Case Questions

1. How might the outcome in *Feist* have been different if the underlying information in the database had been ideas rather than facts?
2. In computerized databases or in information collected from the Internet, which is more important to the creative element necessary for copyright protection: the selection or the arrangement? Why? How has key word search reinforced this distinction?

TECHNICAL AND CONTRACT PROTECTIONS

In U.S. database protection experience, two common methods are probably the most useful: technical security measures and contract restrictions against infringement. Technical methods include a variety of electronic, security, programming, and physical safeguards that lock up the data. For example, encryption of the data on a CD-ROM would impede infringement. Similarly, it would be very time-consuming to acquire all the data served from a website if the site's search engine responds to queries with only piecemeal answers. Database protection is available to the extent the database owner can use technical security measures to restrict access, meter use, and generally impede comprehensive extraction of large portions of its data. However, technical progress eventually overcomes many of these security controls. Therefore, technical security measures are best reinforced with contractual restrictions.

Contractual terms of use and restrictions on decompiling, reverse engineering, and reselling data are all important means to prevent database infringement. Owners of databases often treat their information as IP and choose to license the content rather than sell it or assign it outright. Licensing is completely appropriate for databases containing IP, such as a collection of copyrighted works, video, music, or images. However, licensing factual databases requires the owner to exert physical and contractual controls that make the database into a trade secret. Contract terms may limit the licensee's use, resale, and manipulation of the database. Assent to these terms of use is likely to be part of a negotiated transaction between businesses. However, on-line access to databases is increasingly accomplished when agreement is made by clicking an "I accept" button in a dialog box. The impact of the *ProCD, Inc. v. Zeidenberg* case on these "click-wrap" agreements is discussed in detail in Chapter 10. Tort and contract theories of database protection merge because the tort theory of misappropriation becomes useful when employees and licensees are bound by contract to preserve secrecy and make only allowable uses under the license.

The Uniform Computer Information Transactions Act (UCITA) is a new law for the licensing of computer information. When adopted, UCITA would make licensing databases much easier and more certain. UCITA would give the database owner very strong control over database licenses and uses. UCITA is controversial because it deviates from the consumer expectations developed over many years in sales contracts for goods. UCITA and its controversies are detailed in Chapters 10, 11, and 12.

http://

www.nap.edu/catalog/9692.html?se_side

SUI GENERIS DATABASE PROTECTION

In recent years, particularly following the 1991 *Feist* decision, pressures from the database management industry, from media giants, and from foreign nations have resulted in international treaty negotiations for new forms of database protection. These new forms are called

38. OJ 1996 L77/20.

sui generis database protections because they are unique, one of a kind, and new to the type of IP interests involved. In 1996, the EU urged the WIPO to add two forms of database protection to the international trade agenda: (1) copyright protections and (2) sui generis database protections. Since that time, the EU adopted (March 1996) the **EU Directive on the Legal Protection of Databases,**[38] which has been implemented with national legislation by about half the EU member nations. Since that time, the U.S. Congress has introduced several controversial database protection bills. As of this writing, the prospects for sui generis database protections in the United States are improving.

EU Database Protection Directive

The EU database directive calls for two independent types of protection for databases. First, the EU directive calls for copyright protection that closely parallels U.S. law: protection for the selection or arrangement of the database contents produced by the author's own intellectual creativity. Much like in the United States, the contents (facts and ideas) may not be protected by national copyright laws. In most respects, the EU's copyright protection of databases must provide all the characteristics of other copyright rights, as discussed further in Chapter 15.

The second form of EU database protection is a sui generis right. The maker of a database who has made a substantial investment in either obtaining, verifying, or presenting the database's contents has a right to prevent others from infringing. Infringement is wrongful and unpermitted extraction or reutilization of the whole or a substantial part of the database's contents. EU database rights can be economically exploited through licensing, transfer, assignment, or other grant. National laws passed under EU directives generally apply only to EU citizens. For EU databases, the law is applicable from the nation of residency of the database owner. For corporations, this means the nation of its incorporation if it has its central administration or principal place of business within the EU or where it has a registered office and genuine ongoing operations. The actual data entry or other investment may be made in another nation. For example, considerable keyboarding is done in India for firms from around the world. An English firm could outsource the actual database construction to India yet be protected under the UK's database protection legislation.

ONLINE

EU Database Directive
http://europa.eu.int/eur-lex/en/lif/dat/1996/en_396L0009.html

http://
www.europa.eu.int/eur-lex/en/lif/dat/1996/en_396L0009.html

EU database rights nominally last 15 years from the date of completion. However, the 15-year period is restarted in two major ways that may extend the duration to more than 30 years in some instances or indefinitely in typical practice. First, a 15-year extension is granted if the database owner makes the database available to the public "in any manner" before the first 15-year term expires. Second, the 15-year term restarts from the time the owner makes a substantial change to the database contents, whether additions, deletions, corrections, or other

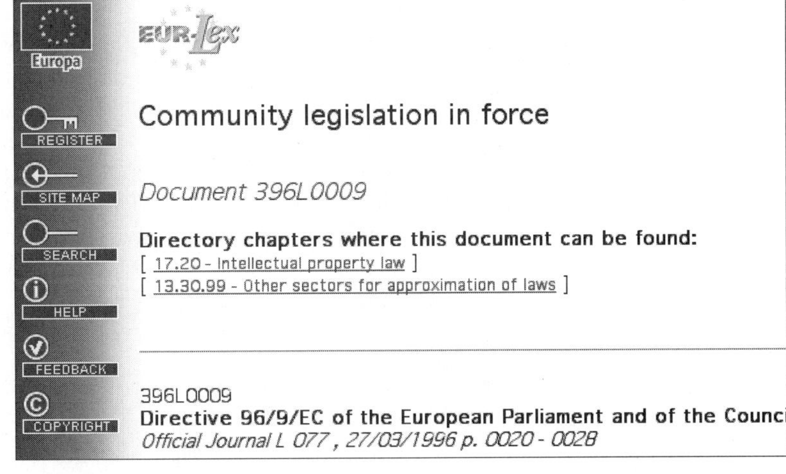

International Commentary

Will Strong Database Rights Help or Harm the Public Interest?

There are mounting pressures in Congress to create new and stronger database rights. The content industry's professed needs and pressures to harmonize U.S. law with the EU's database directive may soon sway Congress to pass sui generis database protections. Even if this effort remains unsuccessful, several states are proposing similar database protection laws, and there is no assurance these laws will be uniform.

What are the arguments against creating new forms of IP to cover databases? Several groups of concerned scientists forcefully argue that strong database rights will hinder scientific research without providing enough offsetting public benefit.[39] Any creation of new property rights and most extensions of existing IP rights withdraw valuable information and works from the public domain. The ultimate question is whether the benefits of new or expanded IP rights will offset their costs. Most of these benefits and costs are highly speculative, and some costs are too often overlooked by advocates of new IP rights. For example, the costs of infringement enforcement and compliance are systematically underestimated.

Congressman Kastenmeier has suggested that the burden of proof that new IP rights are needed should be high.[40] He argues that any new, sui generis IP rights must meet the following requirements before they should be enacted: (1) The new IP right will fit harmoniously with other IP regimes, (2) the new IP rights can be defined in a reasonably clear and satisfactory manner, (3) the proposed new IP rights must be based on an honest cost-benefit analysis, and (4) the new rights must clearly enrich and enhance the public domain. If these criteria are to be met before sui generis database protections are enacted, there is much homework yet to be done.

Going forward, a more thorough understanding of the diverse types of databases seems essential to any deliberate creation of new sui generis database rights. Tracking the EU experience seems fundamental. This analysis will more precisely target any database protection rights to sectors most deserving of property rights incentives. At the same time, it will help to confine the inevitable harmful externalities of an abrupt introduction of a new property rights regime on scientific inquiry, small business, and innovation incentives. At the outset, databases are susceptible to some obvious classifications that may affect the reasons to grant or deny new sui generis database rights. For example, the nature of the data, the source of incentive or funding for its collection, innovation in database architecture and functionality, the most likely uses, compatibility of technical security with the known useful business models, bearing of enforcement costs, and the public interest are all potentially important factors. Without this basic understanding, it is highly likely that European-style new sui generis database rights will not help society as much as their proponents argue.

alterations. Of course, database management is a common practice because maintaining the database keeps it a valuable asset. Protections for many EU databases will last indefinitely.

Both copyright and sui generis database protection rights have exceptions similar to fair use that permit unconsented or unlicensed use. It is permissible to extract or reutilize insubstantial portions, but not repeatedly or systematically. Database contents may be used for noncommercial teaching or scientific research if the source is attributed. EU nations may also add exceptions for public security or administrative and judicial procedures. The EU directive leaves it up to the EU nations to design remedies. Copyright infringement actions are envisioned for the copyright database right. The sui generis right presumes the owner may sue to prevent infringement or use a breach of contract action for users exceeding the rights they actually acquired. (See Exhibit 16.4.)

39. See Committee for a Study Promoting Access to Scientific and Technical Data for the Public Interest, National Research Council, *A Question of Balance: Private Rights and the Public Interest in Scientific and Technical Databases* (Washington, D.C.: National Academy Press, 1999).

40. Robert W. Kastenmeier and Michael J. Remington, The Semiconductor Chip Protection Act of 1984: A Swamp or Firm Ground? *Minnesota Law Review* 70 (1985), 417.

EXHIBIT 16.4 Database Protection Laws

Type of Database Law	Strengths	Weaknesses
Tort: misappropriation	Protects data even if technical security measures or contractual restrictions are not used	Protects only "hot news" or other elements not part of copyright law protections
Tort: trade secrets	Most common in U.S.; requires technical security measures or contractual restrictions	Rights are lost when information is disclosed into the public domain
Tort: trespass to chattels	Protects information stored in owner's personal property, such as computer or network storage	Trespass theory could be expanded so far that interactivity would be severely impeded in network settings
Copyright	Strong prohibition against copying; rewards creativity in selection and arrangement	*Feist* limits protection to compilations made with creativity in selection and arrangement; underlying ideas and facts are not copyrightable
Contract	Common protection in the U.S.; enforceable to prevent misuse, disclosure, copying, or reverse engineering	Requires privity; not applicable unless user assents to restrictions; form and conscious understanding of assent required remains unclear
Sui Generis	Stronger protection than under nearly any other theory; validates the "sweat of the brow" theory	Constitutionality suspect; could impede research and narrow the public domain; offers excessive rewards for some uncreative work

QUESTIONS

1. Explain how traditional laws of patents and copyrights arguably provide insufficient protection for some types of IP. Why should society tolerate special laws to protect trade secrets or databases?
2. What types of law are trade secret protections? Are they more like tort law, are they property rights, do they result from contracts, are they an extension of fiduciary principles from agency law, or are they part of the criminal law?
3. Four Merrill Lynch brokers spent the Labor Day holiday weekend compiling a detailed list of 2,800 clients they serviced, which they then took with them to their new employer, Paine Webber, in violation of their confidentiality and noncompete agreement with Merrill Lynch. Is this client list a proper subject of trade secret protection? Was the brokers' secretive access to their serviced accounts an improper means of acquiring this information? Should the court grant a temporary restraining order barring the former Merrill Lynch brokers from soliciting clients they serviced at Merrill Lynch? Should the dispute be submitted to arbitration as required by the brokers' employment contracts? See *Merrill Lynch, Inc. v. Ran, et al.*, 1999 WL 958464 (E.D. Mich. 1999).
4. Aliotti designed stuffed animals for Favorite Things (FT). FT sought to be taken over by Dakin and displayed several prototype designs that Aliotti developed for stuffed dinosaurs. After FT became insolvent, it assigned all rights in Aliotti's designs to Aliotti. Dakin soon introduced a similar dinosaur line, allegedly copies of Aliotti's prototypes. Is there implied-in-fact liability on Dakin for the designs revealed by Aliotti during the acquisition negotiations with FT or for breach of confidence by Dakin? Must confidentiality be specifically imposed to create trade secrecy? See *Aliotti v. Dankin & Co.*, 831 F.2d 898 (9th Cir., 1987).
5. Newlin and Vafa developed several generic software modules at great time and expense while they were employed at ICM. The software modules worked together and were often used in customized applications. ICM sold the software to banks, which resold the software at retail to the banks' commercial customers. Newlin and Vafa signed nondisclosure-nonuse agreements (NDA) covering the software with ICM. After they quit ICM, the two former employees started a new firm that very quickly developed and marketed similar programs. Should a court enjoin the further use and disclosure of the former employer's trade secrets? Is the NDA sufficient to create trade secrecy over the program modules developed on the jobsite? See *Integrated Cash Management Services, Inc. v. Digital Transactions, Inc.*, 920 F2d 171 (2d Cir., 1990).

6. Chicago Lock manufactured locks, each with a unique serial number. Chicago Lock created a secret database of serial numbers associated with the key code specifications needed to produce an identical new key. Although lock owners could order replacement keys from Chicago Lock, they often used local locksmiths who recorded the serial number and key code after picking the lock for the lock owner. Fanberg published a manual booklet listing these data, and Chicago Lock sued for misappropriation. Was reverse engineering by the locksmiths a defense to misappropriation, or was it an improper means of discovery? Does publishing the list breach a duty the locksmiths owed to their customers? Should this case apply to computer and network security devices such as passwords, private key encryption codes, dongles, or anticircumvention techniques to prevent copying of copyrighted material? Does publication of the list directly infringe Chicago Lock's serial number-key code database? See *Chicago Lock Co. v. Fanberg*, 676 F.2d 400 (9th Cir., 1982).
7. Explain the difference between the remedies of an injunction and money damages. When is an injunction appropriate? When are money damages appropriate? Could there be a situation in which both remedies are appropriate? What other components of remedy are possible in trade secret cases?
8. Lane was a student who published a website called blueovalnews.com, formerly fordworldnews.com. In 1998, Lane posted several Ford-related documents, including (1) an article quoting from confidential Ford documents received from an anonymous source that discussed quality issues about the Ford Mustang Cobra engine; (2) a document entitled "Powertrain Council Strategy & Focus," an internal Ford memo containing its future fuel economy and vehicle emissions strategies; (3) powertrain technology advances; and (4) a Ford engineering blueprint, along with Lane's announcement of an offer of other blueprints for sale. Is Ford entitled to an injunction restraining Lane from selling the blueprints? Does it matter that Lane may have obtained these documents from a Ford employee bound to confidentiality about Ford's trade secrets? See *Ford Motor Co. v. Lane*, 52 U.S.P.Q.2d 1345 (E.D. Mich. 1999).
9. Describe the "sweat of the brow" theory of database protection. Explain how it relates to the following statement: "One should not be permitted to reap where they have not sown." In what situation(s) would the sweat theory be inadequate to support database protection? In what situation(s) is the sweat theory a major reason for database protection or a major factor in protecting a database?
10. Compare and contrast the U.S. and EU protection of databases. What aspects are similar? Which are different? How can a U.S.-based firm be protected under the EU database protection regime?

CHAPTER 17

Patents

Innovation is essential to the increasingly competitive business environment. Innovation is pervasive. For societal progress, these must be innovation in new materials, new products, and more effective and more efficient production processes. In all markets—in the traditional bricks-and-mortar economy, in the "new" e-commerce sector, and in the convergence of these two industrial sectors—innovation is important. Firms in both the goods and service sectors must also enhance their business methods by refining existing processes or creating brand-new methods.

However, business innovation is becoming more difficult, particularly for individual entrepreneurs and small to medium-sized firms. One important reason is that business methods are now clearly patentable. Consider the highly publicized examples of Amazon.com's "one-click" e-commerce ordering system[1] or Priceline.com's "reverse auction" process.[2] Literally thousands of business method patents have been issued since the 1998 watershed case of *State Street Bank vs. Signature Financial Group*.[3] Now business method patents exist in such diverse areas as accounting and bookkeeping, payment systems, electronic commerce transaction processing, pricing and marketing techniques, inventory control, manufacturing, financial instruments, and transactions systems for telecommunications. Business method patenting has been hotly controversial.

This chapter discusses patents—a strong form of IP. Patents are the primary protection for inventions. Patents cover much more than business methods; they are a fundamental source of value for nearly all technology firms. In the future, few firms will be able to rely solely on their IP attorneys to adequately understand the strategies needed to manage IP assets and infringement risks. This chapter first previews the field of patents. Next, the patentability of inventions is discussed, followed by a description of the patenting process. Throughout this chapter, patenting strategies are explored, including the avoidance of infringement litigation and, when necessary, the

1. *Amazon.com, Inc. v. Barnesandnoble.com, Inc.*, 73 F.Supp.2d 1228 (W.D.Wash., 1999). U.S. Pat. No. 5,960,411, Method and System for Placing a Purchase Order via a Communications Network.
2. U.S. Pat. No.5,794,207, Method and Apparatus for Effectuating Buyer-Driven Commerce.
3. 149 F.3d 1368; *cert.denied* 525 U.S. 1093 (1999).

Commentary

The Role of Business Method Patents in Innovation

A major problem with business method patents is that they are written in the technical language of networked computers, the implementation of data processing, and the description of patentable software. Many patent professionals urge that business method patents should be considered simply a subset of software patents. This orientation tends to elevate algorithmic design and network architecture as the main components contributing to the uniqueness of business method patents. It diminishes the significance of the tools developed in applied economics and social science: record keeping, estimation and measurement of economic or behavioral phenomena, identification and shifting of risks, and transaction processing. These latter "arts" are the real and essential building blocks of business processes and innovative business models. Computer programs and network infrastructure are simply the language and mechanized means to implement business methods.

Traditional business disciplines are discovering the patentability of business methods, which is ushering in new and valuable inventions from professionals in industrial engineering, management science, accounting, financial economics, advertising, consumer behavior, media effectiveness, and human behavioral management. Designers of commercial, corporate, and securities transactions are the primary architects of transaction design for supply chain relations, corporate combinations, and new forms of investment. Consider some of the most significant business methods underlying the twentieth-century business progress: (1) discounted cash flow analysis, used in most lending, securities analysis, and portfolio management; (2) double-entry bookkeeping, which is part of all tax accounting and financial control; and (3) inventory models and economic order quantity (EOQ), which made possible the revolution in supply chain efficiency.

Clearly, telecommunication networks offer great promise to business method patents, and many will be implemented most efficiently on computers. Historically, business methods have migrated through various platforms as these techniques are upgraded: from paper calculations, through calculators, on to programmable digital computers, and now to electronic communications networks.

However, there are flaws in the patenting of business methods that could stifle business innovation. The invention of business methods is essentially a highly distributed, individualized process. Much of twentieth-century business methods and recent business method patents originated with dispersed individuals and small groups. Many inventions come from entrepreneurs and small and medium-sized businesses. For most of these small firms, the technicalities and snares of intellectual property (IP) practice seem irrelevant. There are opponents of this view. They argue that large, high-tech companies can more easily adapt; they can develop IP programs to identify, protect, and defend their business method patents much more easily than can small entities.

Like software innovation, business method patents development is incremental. The technical surprises of the IP system raises costs of IP management and transactions. Indeed, influential members of the patent bar (community of practicing patent lawyers) caution that IP infringement and litigation costs are escalating at an alarming rate. Although these costs are no surprise to large firms in high-tech industries, they will be a rude awakening to nearly everybody else. Imagine the surprise to the many low-tech business innovators when they receive threatening letters from a big high-tech firm alleging they have infringed some business method patents and demanding they stop. Smaller business innovators will need to expend unexpectedly huge sums on IP just for the freedom to refine their business processes.

A particularly troubling aspect of this problem is the very nature of innovation in business methods. "Big science" in the biotech and software industries is currently produced largely out of big R&D labs. By stark contrast, the "germ" of business method inspiration is infinitely dispersed. Such innovations originate from the desks of line managers, programmers, and financial managers and from nearly anywhere on the floor of factories, warehouses, and trading rooms. Software innovation was once described as similarly ***ubiquitous***; that is, innovation occurred mostly in garages, basements, and dorm rooms, and nearly anywhere was a potential worksite for writing computer code. This is no longer true, and the most valuable software is written by the big software houses and for big firms. The only real exception these days seems to be in the open source movement, such as Linux. Few small to medium-sized businesses can afford hundreds of thousands in expenses to defend business method patents infringement cases. Even patenting costs, generally estimated from $10,000 to $50,000 can be prohibitive. Smaller businesses can neither afford nor achieve the strategy that big, high-tech firms now use to build their patent portfolios.

realization of remedies. This chapter concludes with a discussion of some special forms of patent-related IP: plant patents, design patents, and semiconductor chip designs.

OVERVIEW OF PATENT LAW

Patent law protects **invention(s)**. Invention is both a process and the thing(s) resulting from the invention process. The invention process involves the production or contrivance of something previously unknown—that is, discovery achieved through study, experimentation, or imagination. The invention thing is a physical object or device or finding that contributes to the creation of a new procedure or practice. A **patent** is a limited monopoly granted by government to the first creator of a useful, novel, and nonobvious invention. Patents are granted on machines, articles of manufacture, compositions of matter, and processes.

Many patentable inventions are difficult to distinguish from trade secrets. The overlap between trade secrets and patents is discussed in Chapter 16. A simple distinction is that trade secrets are information that was not generally known. Patents go further by implementing such unknown information into an **embodiment**—that is, a thing or process that becomes functional by using the basic information in some beneficial way. For example, a trade secret might result from a discovery made by experimentation that shows properties of a new type of metal alloy. A patent might put that raw information into practice in several ways. First, a patent might cover a new process used to produce the new alloy (e.g., smelting, casting, forging, coating). Second, a separate patent might cover a new product made from the alloy that benefits from the alloy's unique characteristics (e.g., strength, lightness, corrosion resistance, flexibility).

What types of things should society recognize as patentable? This old but recurring question has again become important in recent years, as several scientific advances have raised cultural, philosophical, theological, and practical concerns. For example, should life forms or clones be patentable? Should the human genome be patentable? Should patents be granted to hospitals on new medical therapies derived from raw material such as the tissue samples of their patients? Other types of new inventions threaten to weaken the public domain by taking basic laws of nature, formulae, or algorithms away from the public during the patent's near 20-year-long term. For example, the courts worried about protecting the public domain for nearly 22 years before the patentability of software was clarified. Similar reasons kept the patentability of business methods in doubt for more than a century before their patentability was clearly established in 1998.

Patentability is a complex **qualification** procedure—an adversarial process that tests the invention under the stringent standards of patentability. Inventors typically must carefully and confidentially document their diligence in the invention process. A registered patent lawyer or registered patent agent is usually hired to assist in preparing the patent application, which contains highly technical patent claims describing the invention, with drawings and specifications. After the application is filed with the Patent and Trademark Office (PTO), a long and iterative process follows, called **patent prosecution**. It can take 12 to 24 months, or even longer for complex new technologies. During prosecution, an expert PTO **examiner** reviews the application. The inventor must typically negotiate with the PTO to narrow the scope claimed for the patent, which gives the patent applicant a narrower monopoly. If the invention is novel and nonobvious, the PTO issues the patent. The patent application generally remains confidential during prosecution but is eventually published when the patent is issued. However, if the inventor also applies for patents in nearly any foreign nation, the patent application will be published in that country 18 months after filing.

The theory of IP was first introduced as a Constitutional matter in Chapter 4 and then revisited in Chapter 15. Thomas Jefferson was an active inventor and the father of the U.S. patent system. He believed that stringent patentability standards are desirable because government should not suffer the "embarrassment" of a patent monopoly without something substantial and useful given to the public in return. His sentiment here implies the limitations on patents that underlie the **contract theory** of IP. This theory holds that patents are a bargain between society and the inventor. Society provides the inventor with a monopoly to exploit the invention. In return, the inventor's rights are limited: (1) The invention must be "qualified" through stringent patentability standards before the patent is issued, (2) the patent is limited to a fixed term (today 20 years) after the patent application is filed, and (3) when the patent is issued, the inventor must publicly disclose the invention's secrets. All parties should benefit because the patent is an incentive to innovate, disclosure adds new knowledge, useful new information becomes available, and the invention eventually becomes part of the public domain.

Qualification of patentability is *the* major problem in patent law. The inventor must prove the invention is novel, nonobvious and useful. Experts examine the technology claimed in the patent application to determine novelty and nonobviousness. This entails an iterative **examination process** involving several parties: (1) the inventor, who is usually represented by a registered patent lawyer or patent agent, and (2) examiners working for the PTO. The PTO is a federal agency and a branch of the U.S. Department of Commerce. The examination process is designed to assure that the invention is not already in the public domain (part of the prior art) and was not too easily foreseen by persons skilled in the art (nonobvious). Patent litigation sometimes occurs during this patent prosecution process but may occur later if there is infringement.

The inventor may try to personally exploit the invention. However, others may be more effective in using the invention in their existing products or processes or in incorporating the invention as part of existing or new products. Sometimes established firms are better at marketing the new product through existing and successful supply chains. These matters are part of patent strategy, an area that is becoming vitally important to business decisions because managers need an understanding of IP.

The Constitution's framers included details about the purpose and governmental powers over IP in Article I, §8, clause 8. Several patent laws or revisions have been passed by Congress, the first in 1790 and others in 1793, 1836, 1890, and 1909. The 1952 act is still in effect, but amendments were passed in 1982, 1984, 1988, and 1999.

INTERNATIONAL PATENT PROTECTION

International treaties have had a significant influence on U.S. patent law. Usually, the presidential administration authorizes the United States to participate in negotiations in an international organization. Sometimes these negotiations result in multi-lateral agreements among several major industrialized nations, and some treaties also include developing countries. Thereafter, the U.S. Senate considers the treaty; many are officially ratified. International treaties require each signatory nation to pass legislation that implements the treaty. This pattern has been followed in numerous instances by the U.S. Congress and by the European Union (EU).

There are several important IP treaties with impact on patents. First, the **Paris Convention** requires "national treatment"—foreign patents are given all the same rights and status as domestic patents. However, the impact of the Paris Convention is limited because it does not require common patentability or patenting standards among the nearly 80 signatory nations. Second, the **Patent Cooperation Treaty** creates procedural advantages for patent applications made in the nearly 100 signatory nations. Third, the **European Patent Convention** applies to the 19 "member states" of the EU. This treaty simplifies and harmonizes patent application filing requirements and requires EU nations to enact uniform domestic patent legislation. Fourth, the **Patent Law Treaty** was an attempt by the World Intellectual Property Organization (WIPO), a division of the United Nations, to harmonize substantive patent law in member nations. However, its impact has been limited because the United States refused to change certain policies.

Fifth, the World Trade Organization (WTO) concluded various **Trade Related Intellectual Property (TRIPS)** agreements that are probably the most successful of all international IP treaties. TRIPS requires phased compliance deadlines, creates dispute resolution mechanisms in the WTO, has effective national IP enforcement and remedies, and requires criminal sanctions and judicial review of IP matters. The United States has changed several aspects of its patent law to comply with TRIPS, including changing to the 20-year patent term, broadening the subject matter of patents and requiring publication of patent applications before issuance, after 18 months.

Finally, the North American Free Trade Agreement (NAFTA) requires eventual harmonization and effective enforcement of national IP laws in Canada, Mexico, and the United States. The most significant patent treaties are summarized in Exhibit 17.1.

EXHIBIT 17.1 International Patent Policy

International Intellectual Property Agreement or Treaty	Unilateral, Bilateral, or Multilateral	Major Participants	Major Provisions and Impact
Paris Convention	Multilateral	80 signatories	Requires national treatment, but success limited; requires no common standards
Patent Cooperation Treaty	Multilateral	100 signatories	Procedural advantages for patent applications within signatory nations
European Patent Convention	Multilateral, regional	EU's 19 member states	Simplified and harmonized patent application filing requirements; requires signatories to enact uniform domestic patent legislation on certain substantive points
Patent Law Treaty	Multilateral	Several nations but not U.S.	WIPO (UN) attempted harmonization of substantive patent law in member nations; momentum stalled after U.S. refused to change certain policies
World Trade Organization (WTO): TRIPS	Multilateral	Many nations participating	Phased compliance deadlines; WTO dispute resolution mechanisms, effective national enforcement and remedies, criminal sanctions, judicial review; must comply with Paris Convention, 20-year patent terms, broadened subject matter, limited compulsory licensing; probably most successful international IP treaty.
North American Free Trade Agreement (NAFTA)	Multilateral, regional	Canada, Mexico, and U.S.	Calls for harmonization and effective enforcement of national law

PATENTABILITY

Probably the most important and contentious issues in patent law are whether a particular invention should be patentable and the scope of the patent. **Patentability** is determined by the complex analysis of whether the invention has: (1) patentable subject matter (statutory subject matter), (2) novelty, (3) nonobviousness, and (4) utility. Section 101 of the patent law defines the proper subjects for patenting.

> **Patentability under §101**
> Whoever invents or discovers any new and useful process, machine, manufacture or composition of matter, or any new and useful improvement thereof, may obtain a patent therefore, subject to the conditions and requirements of this title.

Initially, the inventor has control over how the invention is classified and defined as it is tested for patentability. The patent application must accurately and fully describe the invention's architecture and function in detailed patent claims and specifications—the heart of the patent application. The four key patentability issues are now explored.

PATENTABLE SUBJECT MATTER

Utility patents are possible on only four types of subject matter: (1) machine, (2) manufacture, (3) composition of matter, and (4) processes. (See Exhibit 17.2.) Special forms of patents and patentlike protections (sui generis) exist for plants, designs, and semiconductors, discussed at the end of this chapter. The four utility patent categories overlap somewhat but are largely identical to the original definition from the 1793 act. Some complex inventions can be classified in more than one category.

The four classes are not well defined in the Patent Act, so the courts have largely used definitions from the dictionary. A **machine** is a mechanism, device, apparatus, or instrument with parts that are organized to cooperate when set in motion to produce predictable results. An article of **manufacture** is produced from raw or processed materials and/or from component parts. Manufacturing with labor or machinery gives new forms and characteristics to these components. This is the catchall category, and it includes goods and "anything under the sun" human made and not clearly within the other categories. A **composition of matter** is any combination of two or more substances. Compositions of matter include composite articles derived from chemical union or mechanical mixture, such as life forms, gases, liquids, powders, and solids.[4]

A **process** is defined in the Patent Act in terms of itself: "process is a process, art or method, and includes a new use of a known process, machine, manufacture, composition of matter, or material." Cases refine this as "a mode of treatment of certain materials to produce a given result . . . an act or series of acts, performed upon the subject matter to be transformed and reduced to a different state or thing."[5] New uses of known materials are also processes. For example, assume a pharmaceutical firm develops an arthritis drug that was only partially successful. If another firm testing the drug accidentally discovers that it can grow hair, this would be a patentable process separate from the original patent on it as a composition of

4. *Diamond v. Chakrabarty*, 447 U.S. 303 (1980).
5. *Cochrane v. Denver*, 94 U.S. 780 (1877).

EXHIBIT 17.2 Patentable Subject Matter: Utility Patents

Subject Matter	Definition	Examples
Machine	Mechanism with parts organized to cooperate in motion to produce predictable results	Engine, appliance, computer, vehicle
Manufacture	Articles produced by labor or machinery in which new form and characteristics are given to raw or processed materials and/or components	Catchall category, includes most goods as well as machines and compositions of matter
Composition of matter	Combinations of two or more substances; composite articles derived from chemical union or mechanical mixture, including gasses, liquids, powders, and solids	Molecules, chemical compounds, life forms
Process	"Process means process," art or method and includes a new use of a known process, machine, manufacture, composition of matter, or material; also treatment of materials, act, or series of acts that transform a subject matter	Chemical production, business methods, software, new uses of known materials

matter. Finally, **improvements** on existing machines, manufactures, compositions of matter, or processes are also patentable. Patent law encourages additional research into new uses and into enhancements to the functioning of existing products. Interesting strategic issues, such as blocking patents, arise when the new use or the improvement is made on an item already protected under an existing patent. These strategies are discussed throughout this chapter.

NONPATENTABLE SUBJECT MATTER

The policies of patent law are much more thorough in protecting the public domain than is copyright law. This is evident in the rigorous qualification process for the patentability of new inventions and in the **nonpatentable subject matter** defined by statute and cases. Exceptions to patentable subject matter are called **nonstatutory subject matter**. First, patent protection is not available for **naturally occurring** things such as life forms. For example, many herbalist remedies come from plant extracts or other living things. Perhaps a cure for cancer might be found in the bark of a yew tree. Although such research is very important, there can be no patent protection for this type of discovery. However, a patent might be appropriate if the naturally occurring substance is changed in a newly invented process or its modified form is new and human-made.

A second major area of nonpatentable subject matter is **abstract ideas, laws of nature,** and **mathematical formulae.** Like naturally occurring things, ideas and natural laws are not invented; they already exist. Their discovery is laudable, but it is not invention. The public domain must be protected so that others can use ideas and formulae (algorithms), which are the fundamental building blocks of science and engineering. For example, Albert Einstein's theory of relativity is generally considered a colossal contribution to theoretical physics. However, Einstein's $E = mc^2$ is a law of nature, which other scientists must be able to use. Similarly, Isaac Newton could not have patented the law of gravity. Of course, the laws of nature, algorithms, and abstract ideas are part of the functioning of nearly all inventions. Practical applications and implementations of ideas and algorithms, are patentable, just not the underlying laws themselves.

These two nonstatutory subject matters lie at the heart of the controversy over the patentability of biotechnology inventions, software, and business methods. All three new areas are now clearly patentable. However, a long period of resistance preceded the patentability of each because many people were concerned that such matters were merely discovered, not invented. Also, many people strongly believe there is a duty to protect the public domain. Biotechnology inventions trigger strong theological opinions. Each of these new technologies has followed a similar three-phase trajectory. First, the courts refused patentability by designating them as nonstatutory subject matter. Second, there was an intermediate, maturing phase when some courts were more careful with their reasoning and contradictory case law resulted; some cases permitted partial patentability. Third, there was final acceptance and recognition of patentability.

BIOTECHNOLOGY

The patentability of biotechnology is a very broad subject. Congress has clearly provided for sui generis protection of new, bioengineered plant species in two laws: the Plant Patent Act of 1930 protecting asexually reproduced plants and the Plant Variety Protection Act of 1970 protecting new plant varieties bred with sexual reproduction techniques. Utility patents are also now possible for new plant species.[6] Plant patent protections are discussed in a later section.

Nearly two-thirds of all prescription and over-the-counter drugs have at least some naturally occurring components. Patents on such drugs cannot cover the natural components but may cover the unique mixture, any novel processes to produce them, or a human-made, purified version of the naturally occurring component. Monopoly profits for critical drugs raise fairness questions and controversy in developing nations (AIDS treatment) and in national crises (Cipro, the anthrax antibiotic).

Medicines are a very important part of biotechnology patenting. The pharmaceutical industry continues to successfully argue that strong patentability is needed to maintain private-sector funding of research into lifesaving or life-enhancing drugs. The Food and Drug Administration (FDA) has authority over the regulation of drugs. The distribution or sale of new drugs is prohibited until after clinical trials prove their **efficacy**—their effectiveness in treating the conditions as intended. FDA qualification of new prescription and over-the-counter drugs often discovers that the drugs have side effects. These drug trials may continue for several years before the FDA releases the drugs for public use, and extended trials can cut short the patentee's 20 years of monopoly protection. Shortened patent terms for drugs, medical devices, and some other inventions makes it more difficult to recoup research expenses from the monopoly profits before generics (work-alike or identical formulations) undercut their monopoly profits. Congress relieved some of this "unfairness" in the **American Inventor's Protection Act (AIPA)**. The AIPA authorizes the PTO to extend patent terms if delays in patent prosecution or FDA trials continue for more than three years.

The protection of genetic engineering, cloning, or other more modern biotechnology methods for reproduction of both plants and animals was an uncertain and controversial issue until 1980. Many cases denied utility patents to bioengineered life forms for two reasons. First, naturally occurring life forms are unpatentable subject matter. Second, many forms of bioengineering evoke strong theological

6. *J.E.M. AG Supply v. Pioneer Hi-Bred Int'l.,* 121 S.Ct. 2566 (2001).

emotions and religious issues. Should some corporation be permitted to patent life forms, animals, or humans? Consider the storm of controversy surrounding the acquisition of stem cells ("harvesting" from human embryos) and their use in disease research.

The watershed 1980 case of *Diamond v. Chakrabarty*[7] shattered much of the resistance to modern biotechnology patents. During the patent prosecution, a PTO examiner rejected Chakrabarty's claims for an oil-eating strain of bacteria that could be used to clean up oil spills. The U.S. Supreme Court permitted patentability, stating that "Chakrabarty's microorganism plainly qualifies as patentable subject matter." Citing congressional intent in the 1952 Patent Act, the court reiterated that patentable subject matter includes "anything under the sun that is made by man." The PTO had argued that broad new types of subject matter should not be permitted patentability until Congress accepts them after considering the competing economic, social, and scientific considerations. However, this argument contradicts the very core of patent law: Patents are issued only for novel and unforeseen inventions.

The Supreme Court also dismissed the PTO's lament that patentability of life forms might trigger a "gruesome parade of horribles" such as "frankenfoods," genetically engineered plants or animals with unknown side effects; resistant forms of fungi, bacteria, or viruses that could devastate whole species; monsters made up of genetic components from different species of plants and animals; and further destruction of biological diversity if genetically engineered species harm natural species. These complex questions are well beyond the purposes of patent law. Any additional incentive offered by patentability is minor, given the well-financed biotechnology industry and the rather considerable health research system.

COMPUTER SOFTWARE

Computer programs met with similar strong resistance to patentability. In early cases, courts fretted that patenting software might result in removing the mathematical formulae contained in the program's code from the public domain; that is, algorithms that cause the software to function could become unavailable to others if the software was patented. These courts prohibited software protection by permitting patentability only if the program was embedded in a machine. In the 1980s, the courts applied the Freeman-Walter-Abele test denying patentability if the software merely solved equations.[8] This test required that physical changes occur in work performed by physical processes before patentability would be permitted. However, after a watershed case in the 1990s,[9] the PTO issued new guidelines for software patentability that now permit patents over software embedded in a machine or on a chip as well as software that can be loaded from disk on a general-use programmable computer. Software patentability does not hinge "on whether there is a mathematical algorithm at work, but on whether the algorithm-containing invention, as a whole, produces a tangible, useful, result."[10]

7. *Diamond v. Chakrabarty,* 447 U.S. 303 (1980).

8. A trilogy of companion cases comprise this test: *In re Freeman,* 573 F.2d 1237 (C.C.P.A., 1978); *In re Walter,* 618 F.2d 758 (C.C.P.A., 1980); *In re Abele,* 684 F.2d 902 (C.C.P.A., 1982).

9. See *In re Alappat,* 33 F.3d 1526 (Fed.Cir., 1994).

10. *ATT Corp. v. Excel Communications, Inc.,* 172 F.3d 1352, 1361 (Fed.Cir.), *cert. denied* 120 S.Ct. 368 (1999).

METHODS OF DOING BUSINESS

Another new area of patentability involves methods of doing business, as introduced at the beginning of this chapter. **Business method patents** are now available for a wide range of business processes. For more than a century, business methods were not generally considered patentable. The **business method exception** was widely believed to make business methods unpatentable, and many business methods are implemented in computer software, a type of invention that was also generally considered unpatentable before 1994. Furthermore, process patents were long disfavored. This point was illustrated in one business method patent case that held a standardized fire-fighting system as merely unpatentable "mental steps."[11]

Cases at the turn of the twentieth century denied protection of bookkeeping systems under both copyright and patent law as "methods of transacting common business."[12] In another case, a 1934 forerunner to computerized trading systems like the NASDAQ was held unpatentable.[13] Also the now well-known drive-in theater was unpatentable.[14] The business method exception became such a significant barrier that few inventors ever attempted to patent their business methods.[15] However, things are different today. The next watershed case opened the floodgates to thousands of business method patent applications after 1998.

State Street Bank v. Signature Financial Group

149 F.3d 1368, *cert.denied* 525 U.S. 1093 (1999)

Facts. U.S. patent # 5,193,056 ('056 patent), *Data Processing System for Hub and Spoke Financial Services Configuration*, was invented by R. Todd Boes, who assigned it to Signature Financial. The system facilitates daily settlement of separate, independent member mutual funds (spokes), which pool their assets into an investment portfolio (hub). The hub is organized as a partnership to obtain tax benefits and economies of scale. State Street's negotiations to license the hub-and-spoke system from Signature broke down, and State Street brought a declaratory judgment action challenging the '056 patent's validity and the owner's claims of infringement.

The system monitors and records the financial information flow and then makes all calculations necessary for maintaining each partner's funds. At the close of each day, the assets in the common hub are allocated to the spokes according to their percentage share maintained in the hub. This allocation reflects daily changes both in the value of the hub's investment securities and in the amount of each spoke's assets, which enables the determination of a true asset value of each spoke. The system also tracks all the relevant daily data to aggregate year-end income, expenses, and capital gain or loss for accounting and tax purposes of the hub, the spokes, and the shareholders and investors in the spokes. The system makes the essential calculations quickly and accurately to adequately service each spoke's shareholders; it calculates the value of the shares to the nearest penny within 90 minutes after the market closes. Given the complexity of the calculations, a computer or equivalent device is a virtual necessity to perform the task.

Legal Issue. Are business methods patentable as processes?

Opinion. Circuit Judge Giles Rich. Whoever invents or discovers any new and useful process, machine, manufacture,

11. *In re Patton*, 127 F.2d 324, 327-38 (C.C.P.A., 1942).
12. *Hotel Security Checking Co. v. Lorraine Co.*, 160 F. 467 (2d Cir., 1908).
13. *In re Wait*, 73 F.2d 982 (C.C.P.A. 1934).
14. *Loew's Drive-In Theatres v. Park-In Theatres*, 174 F.2d 547 (1st Cir., 1949).
15. One notable exception was the Merrill Lynch Cash Management System that hastened the combination of investment and commercial banking; *Paine, Webber, Jackson & Curtis v. Merrill Lynch*, 564 F.Supp. 1358 (D.Del. 1983); U.S. Patent No. 4,346,442 ("Securities brokerage-cash management system" issued Aug. 24, 1982).

or composition of matter, or any new and useful improvement thereof, may obtain a patent therefore, subject to the conditions and requirements of this title. The plain and unambiguous meaning of §101 is that any invention falling within one of the four stated categories of statutory subject matter may be patented, provided it meets the other requirements for patentability. The repetitive use of the expansive term "any" in §101 shows Congress's intent not to place any restrictions on the subject matter for which a patent may be obtained. Indeed, the Supreme Court has acknowledged that Congress intended §101 to extend to "anything under the sun that is made by man."

The "Mathematical Algorithm" Exception

The Supreme Court has identified three categories of subject matter that are unpatentable, namely "laws of nature, natural phenomena, and abstract ideas." Of particular relevance to this case, the Court has held that mathematical algorithms are not patentable subject matter to the extent that they are merely abstract ideas. In *Diehr* the Court explained that certain types of mathematical subject matter, standing alone, represent nothing more than abstract ideas until reduced to some type of practical application, i.e., "a useful, concrete and tangible result." Unpatentable mathematical algorithms are identifiable by showing they are merely abstract ideas constituting disembodied concepts or truths that are not "useful." From a practical standpoint, this means that to be patentable an algorithm must be applied in a "useful" way. In *Alappat* we held that data, transformed by a machine through a series of mathematical calculations to produce a smooth waveform display on a rasterizer monitor, constituted a practical application of an abstract idea (a mathematical algorithm, formula, or calculation), because it produced "a useful, concrete and tangible result"—the smooth waveform. Today, we hold that the transformation of data, representing discrete dollar amounts, by a machine through a series of mathematical calculations into a final share price, constitutes a practical application of a mathematical algorithm, formula, or calculation, because it produces "a useful, concrete and tangible result"—a final share price momentarily fixed for recording and reporting purposes and even accepted and relied upon by regulatory authorities and in subsequent trades.

After *Diehr* and *Chakrabarty*, the Freeman-Walter-Abele test has little, if any, applicability to determining the presence of statutory subject matter. The test could be misleading, because a process, machine, manufacture, or composition of matter employing a law of nature, natural phenomenon, or abstract idea is patentable subject matter even though a law of nature, natural phenomenon, or abstract idea would not, by itself, be entitled to such protection. The mere fact that a claimed invention involves inputting numbers, calculating numbers, outputting numbers, and storing numbers, in and of itself, would not render it nonstatutory subject matter, unless, of course, its operation does not produce a "useful, concrete and tangible result." The dispositive inquiry is whether the claim as a whole is directed to statutory subject matter. It is irrelevant that a claim may contain, as part of the whole, subject matter which would not be patentable by itself. "A claim drawn to subject matter otherwise statutory does not become nonstatutory simply because it uses a mathematical formula, computer program or digital computer." [The Supreme Court's decisions] "stand for no more than these long-established principles" that abstract ideas and natural phenomena are not patentable. [E]very step-by-step process, be it electronic or chemical or mechanical, involves an algorithm in the broad sense of the term. [But the invention is nevertheless patentable] even if the useful result is expressed in numbers, such as price, profit, percentage, cost, or loss.

The Business Method Exception

As an alternative ground for invalidating the '056 patent, the court relied on the judicially-created, so-called "business method" exception to statutory subject matter. We take this opportunity to lay this ill-conceived exception to rest. Since its inception, the "business method" exception has merely represented the application of some general, but no longer applicable legal principle, which was eliminated. Since the 1952 Patent Act, business methods have been, and should have been, subject to the same legal requirements for patentability as applied to any other process or method.

The business method exception has never been invoked by this court to deem an invention unpatentable. Application of this particular exception has always been preceded by a ruling based on some clearer concept. Even the case frequently cited as establishing the business method exception, *Hotel Security Checking,* did not rely on the exception to strike the patent. In that case, the patent was found invalid for lack of novelty and "invention," not because it was improper subject matter for a patent. The court stated "the fundamental principle of the system is as old as the art of bookkeeping, i.e., charging the goods of the employer to the agent who takes them." "If at the time of [the patent] application, there had been no system of bookkeeping of any kind in restaurants, we would be confronted with the question whether a new and useful system of cash registering and account checking is such an art as is patentable under the statute."

This case is no exception. The district court announced the precepts of the business method exception as set forth in several treatises, but noted as its primary reason for finding the patent invalid under the business method exception [was that it was too broad:] "*the '056 Patent is claimed sufficiently broadly to foreclose virtually any computer-implemented accounting method necessary to manage this type of financial structure.*" Whether the patent's claims are too broad to be patentable is not to be judged under §101, but rather under §§102, 103 and 112. Assuming the above statement to be correct, it has nothing to do with whether what is claimed is statutory subject matter.

It comes as no surprise that in the most recent edition of the [PTO's] Manual of Patent Examining Procedures (MPEP) (1996), a paragraph of §706.03(a) was deleted. In past editions it read: "Though seemingly within the category of process or method, a method of doing business can be rejected as not being within the statutory classes." This acknowledgment is buttressed by the U.S. Patent and Trademark 1996 Examination Guidelines for Computer Related Inventions which now read:

Office personnel have had difficulty in properly treating claims directed to methods of doing business. Claims should not be categorized as methods of doing business. Instead such claims should be treated like any other process claims.

We agree that this is precisely the manner in which this type of claim should be treated. Whether the claims are directed to subject matter within §101should not turn on whether the claimed subject matter does "business" instead of something else.

Decision. Everything under the sun human-made is patentable. Business methods are patentable subject matter, as processes. The business method exception was an illusion but is abandoned to the extent it may have existed.

Case Questions

1. Why were business methods not considered patentable? Which type of subject matter are business methods?
2. As a result of this decision, what must business innovators now do to protect themselves from charges of infringement as they develop new business processes?

Following the business method patent revolution ignited by the *State Street* decision, the PTO has issued thousands of business method patents. The quality of these business method patents raises concerns for several key reasons. First, in the early years, most PTO examiners were not trained in business. Expertise in the underlying art has always been a key requirement for the quality of a "qualification" patenting system. Second, PTO examiners initially searched mainly through existing patents to see if the business method was already protected by patent or in the public domain. However, so few business method patents were issued before *State Street* that the PTO was unlikely to find any useful prior art—they were looking in the wrong place. Furthermore, most academic business journals and the business press are not organized or indexed to reveal precisely when business methods were first used or invented or by whom. Therefore, PTO examinations were not informed by any comprehensive or accurate understanding of business processes. Third, business methods are not clearly defined under patent law. Members of the patent bar are trying to characterize business methods as something else—software or other types of processes—to avoid business method patent difficulties. Fourth, the cost of patent practice may make business method patents a luxury for only large, high-tech firms that can afford the expense of patenting and infringement risk management. Fifth, the quality of business method patent has been highly suspect. There is reasonable evidence that many of the dot.com firms that suffered bankruptcy in 2000 were largely based on business method patents that could not sustain profitability. Further, observers allege that many of these business method patents would satisfy neither the novelty nor nonobviousness requirements.

At least two factors may now begin to reduce the problems with business method patents, Internet patents, and e-commerce patents. First, Congress included a **prior user** or **first inventor's defense** with the passage of the AIPA in 1999. Many business methods are developed and used in confidence as trade secrets. If another party receives a patent on that business method, the AIPA permits the first inventor to continue using the business method without risk of infringement liability. A workable definition of business method patents is critical because this first inventor's defense applies only to business methods and not to any other subject matters. Many in the patent community are apprehensive that the first inventor user defense concept might spread to other processes, machines, manufactures, or compositions of matter. Some case law already suggests that there is a prior user defense for other patentable subject matters.[16]

The second reason there is hope for entrepreneurs and small and medium-sized businesses despite these problems is the widespread belief that the many bad business method patents issued in the early years will make infringement litigation inevitable. The courts will likely test the validity of these business method patents at great social cost over the next several years. Many of the early business method patents issued will be invalidated because they were obvious, not novel, or both. As business method patent case law and settlements expand the body of knowledge over business methods, fewer bad business method patents will be written and issued by the PTO in the future.

NOVELTY

Patent law is intended to protect the public domain. No patent monopoly should remove knowledge that is freely available to all from the storehouse of human knowledge. The novelty requirement is designed to prevent patents being granted on known ideas or on inventions already in use. The potentially very lucrative patent monopoly should not be given for inventions already in the public domain.

Section 102 of the Patent Act defines novelty in a complex set of "statutory bars." These bars are significant legal barriers to patentability. They define instances when the invention is not patentable, hence they "bar" or disqualify patentability for an invention that was previously publicly known, used, published, made, or sold.

35 U.S.C. §102 Conditions for Patentability: Novelty

A person shall be entitled to a patent unless—

(a) the invention was known or used by others in this country, or patented or described in a printed publication in this or a foreign country, before the invention thereof by the applicant for patent, or

(b) the invention was patented or described in a printed publication in this or a foreign country or in public use or on sale in this country, more than one year prior to the date of the application for patent in the United States,

(c) he has abandon the invention, or

* * *

(g)(2) before such person's invention thereof, the invention was made in this country by another inventor who had not abandoned, suppressed, or concealed it. In determining priority of invention under this subsection, there shall be considered not only the respective dates of conception and reduction to practice of the invention, but also the reasonable diligence of one who was first to conceive and last to reduce to practice, from a time prior to conception by the other.

16. *Dunlop Holdings Ltd. v. Ram Golf Corp.*, 524 F.2d 33 (7th Cir., 1975); *cert.denied* 424 U.S. 958.

The public domain in patents is known as the **prior art**. It represents the accumulation of specialized knowledge that describes the status of technology, and it informs all inventors. The prior art is important in determining novelty and later in determining nonobviousness. It is also important to analyze the prior art aspects of novelty and nonobviousness from the perspective of **persons of ordinary skill** in the art. They are hypothetical professional specialists in the technologies involved. They can be expected to know the prior art and to have struggled with making improvements.

Publicly Available Knowledge

Section 102(a) focuses on the extent of publicly available knowledge about the invention before the inventor conceives of the invention. It prohibits inventors from patenting knowledge in the previously existing public domain. The scope of this knowledge is defined in §102(a) as whether the invention was publicly known or used in the United States, whether it was patented anywhere in the world, or whether it was disclosed in a printed publication anywhere in the world. No patent may be issued on an invention that is sufficiently described in a single reference or single source found in the prior art. This means that an invention is unpatentable if *other persons* have known or used the invention in the United States. Section 102(a) also bars patentability if the invention was described in a publication or previously patented by *someone else* anywhere in the world. Was the prior art description or patent sufficient to describe the new invention? If so, the prior art reference is said to **anticipate** the later invention. The sufficiency of the description is judged by hypothetical persons of ordinary skill in the art. For example, experienced accountants, finance professionals, or database designers would understand the prior art describing a new record-keeping invention.

Section 102(a) is the most important definition of the prior art. It helps preserve the public domain by prohibiting patenting of information already described in various ways. For example, an invention is unpatentable by anyone in the United States if a foreign scientist presented findings at an academic conference, published the findings in an international research journal, obtained a U.S. or EU patent, demonstrated a prototype at a U.S. trade show or shipped an embodiment into the United States. Sales, uses, or demonstrations of the invention can reveal the invention's secrets or be reverse-engineered to expose the new technologies.

The limitation to printed publications in §102(a) is an anachronism. Prior art is expanding to include electronic information retrieval systems. Scientific journals and patent offices around the world are posting prior art on the Internet and using other modern database techniques to make prior art available electronically.

What is the date of invention or knowledge of prior art? Why are these dates important? **Conception** is the "aha moment" when the inventor conjures up how the invention's components will interact to produce its function. It usually concludes a design phase when a mental or written plan is finally composed that envisions how the invention will work. Conception is complete when it would be possible for a hypothetical person of ordinary skill in the art to use the plans to produce a working model, prototype, or embodiment. After the inventor conceives (largely a mental step), there must be the physical construction of an embodiment, a step known as the reduction to practice. Invention occurs at conception if there is sufficient detail in drawings and plans describing the invention. Reduction to practice is also relevant because it is an important way for prior art to become known or used by others. Both events may become important if multiple inventors claim the invention in competing applications as discussed later.

Inventors, including the firms that employ inventors, must be careful to document the invention process so they can prove the date of conception. The date that an embodiment is made public is important because that is an important way for it to become part of the prior art. Secret uses of a similar invention are not usually sufficient to become part of the prior art. Either the date of conception, the date of reduction to practice, or both may become issues at trial about the patent's validity. Therefore, record keeping, as discussed further in a later section, is an important regimen under the patent law.

One-Year Grace Period

The United States is one of the few nations to give the inventor some development time to perfect the invention before the patent application must be filed. Under §102(b) the inventor may delay filing the application for up to a full year after conception and reduction to practice, during which time the inventor may publicly disclose, sell, publish descriptions in scholarly journals, and otherwise reveal the invention to the public, to venture capitalists, or to other firms that are better able to finance or develop the invention. The one-year rule applies to actions of anyone but overlaps with §102(a), which already covers public use, publication, or patenting by others. Patentability is "barred" by §102(b) if the invention was patented or described in a printed publication by anyone, anywhere in the world, more than a year before application.

Section 102(b) also denies patentability if the invention was on sale or in use in the United States more than a year before the inventor's application. Section 102(b) most clearly affects the inventor because it gives a **grace period** after invention to find financing or test the market's reaction to the invention. It adds another important disqualifier to those found in §102(a) by creating the **on-sale bar**. No patent will be issued for an invention "on sale" more than one year prior to filing the patent application. "On sale" means actual completed sales, held "for sale," demonstrated at trade shows, or described in literature available to potential buyers. There are exceptions for **experimental uses** or experimental sales purposes. Experimental uses or sales do not trigger the §102(b) statutory bar so long as the public cannot discover the invention's secrets. For example, the buyer of a prototype must be using the invention for testing and must be restricted to secrecy in a nondisclosure agreement like those discussed in Chapter 13.

The one-year rule is very important for academic scientists and entrepreneurs and in marketing strategy. The "publish or perish" regimen requires that academics publish their work quickly. Furthermore, many academics have deep convictions that their work should be shared freely with their colleagues and become part of the public domain. Their scholarly reputations are their most important assets. Academics are only mildly interested in patent protection, particularly given the patenting costs and considerable uncertainty over their inventions' value when exploited in the market. Entrepreneurs and marketers often must "sell" their invention to venture capitalists or corporate management and then arouse the interest of potential buyers before they can afford the costly patenting process. They may feel the need to disclose new products to the market quickly to preempt competitors' sales and build their firm's brand image. Although a year may seem like a long time for some simpler technologies, those inventions containing complex technologies require considerable additional work to perfect them. It can be difficult for entrepreneurs and small businesses to fund the $10,000 to $50,000 patenting costs. On balance, §102(b) gives inventors some breathing room but requires that they act diligently to apply for a patent.

First to Invent

Section 102(g) grants patentability to the inventor who first invented. The United States is also the only significant nation to award patents to the **first to invent**.

Nearly all other industrialized nations award patents to the inventor who is **first to file**. The difference may seem technical, but it has enormous consequences. The first-to-invent standard rewards the original inventor with the patent irrespective of the inventor's financial or technological resources. First to invent denies the patent to later inventors who are shrewd or better financed and use these advantages to file earlier than the original inventor. By contrast, first to file rewards the quickest to start the patenting process and probably works to the advantage of firms most experienced in filing patent applications.

The side effects of these two systems are considerable. In the United States, the first-to-invent rule and the one-year grace period encourage entrepreneurs and small inventors, even if they do not have large R&D and IP budgets. By contrast, first-to-file systems reward large, well-financed high-technology firms. These firms can much better afford the considerable expense of developing the invention quickly. Firms with big IP budgets can command IP resources and rush to make patent applications. But a balance must be drawn between two public policies: Fairness dictates rewarding the original inventor, but society is best served by diligent, methodical, and pragmatic inventors who move steadily to refine the invention in a practical way.

Many other nations are pressuring the United States to abandon the first-to-invent system in favor of first to file. Many IP observers expect the United States could give up first to invent in negotiations on some future international IP treaty in return for other concessions. The most persuasive reason to adopt first to file is that the first-to-invent standard is vague and inefficient. Litigation is arguably required more often in the United States to settle inventorship disputes under the first-to-invent standard. By contrast, first to file seems more decisive, and fewer conflicts should arise over which among competing inventors is entitled to the patent. The U.S. defenders of the first-to-invent standard argue that the certainty of first to file unfairly penalizes entrepreneurs and small to medium-sized businesses that can never be as savvy or financially prepared for the considerable IP and patenting expenses to which large technology firms are already accustomed.

The first inventor who conceives of the invention and then diligently reduces it to practice is the first to invent and should be entitled to the patent. Among competing inventors, the patent is awarded to the one with priority. However, there can be difficult questions of priority when one inventor conceives first buts moves slowly to reduce the invention to practice. During this interval, another inventor might conceive of the same invention and move more quickly to reduce it to practice before the first inventor. Although this scenario may seem far-fetched, it actually occurs quite often. For example, in many of the biotechnology and software fields, several scientists or inventors may be working independently to solve similar problems. It is quite possible that two inventors might conceive of the same invention nearly simultaneously. Actual physical reduction to practice is not always required. A **constructive reduction to practice** is possible if the patent application is so detailed that it clearly informs the hypothetical person of ordinary skill how to build a working prototype or use the process.

Inventors must be conscientious in reducing their inventions to practice and in filing their patent applications. This duty of **diligence** is required by at least two provisions of the Patent Act. First, §102(c) bars patentability if the inventor has abandoned the invention, expressly or by implication. For example, an inventor can expressly dedicate the invention to the public, thereby waiving all rights to a patent. Alternatively, the inventor could simply wait too long after reduction to practice before filing the patent application, which can imply an **abandonment**. Second,

§102(g), introduced previously, denies priority to an inventor who abandons, suppresses, or conceals the invention, which can occur if there are unexcused delays in reducing to practice. **Concealment** is precisely the strategy used to protect trade secrets. The original inventor who chooses trade secrecy protection rather than a patent filing could lose rights in the trade secret if a later inventor is diligent and files before the first inventor. These strategies are discussed in this and other chapters. Finally, **suppression** is the deliberate act of hiding the invention. An inventor who suppresses an invention may lose priority to a second, diligent inventor.

Searching the Prior Art

It should be clear by now that "knowing" and understanding all the prior art for the technologies underlying an invention is a difficult but important task. This task is made worse when the invention is complex or includes several different types of technologies. Patent law assumes that inventors know the prior art. However, prior art is highly dispersed, it is often expressed in foreign languages, and it lurks in the files of foreign patent offices, in obscure scientific journals, or in B2B and industrial advertising. An inventor working with his or her patent attorney or agent should usually search the prior art to assure the invention is novel. Prior art is becoming much more accessible today than was possible just a decade ago. The U.S. PTO has posted published patents dating back to 1790 online at uspto.gov. Many of the more recent patents include complete drawings and specifications.

Many publishers of law and technical materials archive, index, and sell access to huge databases of published patents and scientific literature. These were traditionally available only in print publications but are now contained on CD-ROM or through on-line pay-per-use databases such as Lexis and Westlaw. IBM provided much needed stimulus for the on-line versions of patent databases and the vastly superior capabilities of electronic database search. In 2000, IBM's on-line patent database was sold to Delphion Corporation, which operates it as a subscription-fee service. It has some unique search capabilities and offers some of them free at its website.

Delphion's patent search engine
http://www.delphion.com

In the next few years, expect that new, more complete, and better indexed databases or prior art will become available. More foreign patents may be translated into English, and more inexpensive search services may be performed by third parties (technical professionals). Better search engines will use plain language queries and a more complete electronic thesaurus of equivalent technical terms, and these databases will be distributed on high-capacity media (DVD).

http://
patft.uspto.gov/netahtml/search-adv.htm

Many scientific disciplines are supplementing their printed journals with on-line publications. Some are even abandoning print publications altogether because the publication process simply takes too long. For example, in high-energy physics, the most important research papers are largely available on line soon after drafting. This practice enhances distribution to all in the community of relevant scientists who might be

USPTO PATENT FULL-TEXT AND IMAGE DATABASE

Home | Quick | Advanced | Pat Num | Help
View Cart

Data current through 04/09/2002

Query [Help]

Example: ttl/needle or ttl/syringe andnot (sew or thread$)

Select Years [Help]
1996-2002
Search
Reset

Field Code	Field Name	Field Code	Field Name
PN	Patent Number	IN	Inventor Name
ISD	Issue Date	IC	Inventor City
TTL	Title	IS	Inventor State
ABST	Abstract	ICN	Inventor Country
ACLM	Claim(s)	LREP	Attorney or Agent
SPEC	Description/Specification	AN	Assignee Name
CCL	Current US Classification	AC	Assignee City
ICL	International Classification	AS	Assignee State

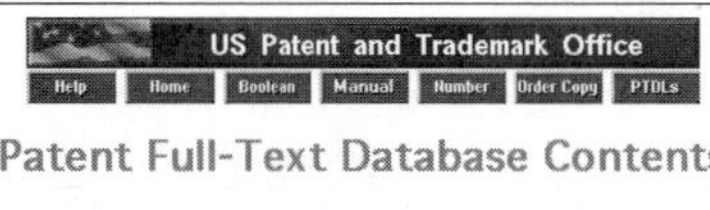

Patent Full-Text Database Contents

Patent numbers in the US Patent Full-Text Database, by type and year, current through 09 April 2002.

Database	Utility***	Design	Plant	Reissue (RD,RE, RX)*	Defensive Pub. **	SIR	AI***
2001-2002	6,167,569- 6,370,689	D435,713- D455,536	PP11,728- PP12,543	RE37,006- RE37,652		H1,930- H2,019	
1996-2000	5,479,658- 6,167,568	D365,671- D435,712	PP9,413- PP11,727	RE35,136- RE37,005		H1,512- H1,929	
1991-1995	4,980,927- 5,479,657	D313,301- D365,670	PP7,408- PP9,412	RE33,510- RE35,135		H863- H1,511	
1986-1990	4,562,596- 4,980,926	D282,020- D313,300	PP5,622- PP7,407	RE32,061- RE33,509	T106,201- T109,201	H7- H862	
1981-1985	4,242,757- 4,562,595	D257,746- D282,019	PP4,612- PP5,621	RE30,469- RE32,060	T100,201- T106,101	H1- H6	
1976-1980	3,930,271- 4,242,756	D242,583- D257,745	PP3,987- PP4,611	RE28,671- RE30,468	T100,001; T942,001-T999,003		
1790-1975	X1- X11,280; 1- 3,930,270	D1- D242,880	PP1- P4,000	RX1-RX125;RE1-RE29,094	T855,019-T941,025		AI2-AI318

* RDs and REs are issued in the same numeric sequence; RXs are issued in a separate numeric sequence.

** T patents were not numbered in a continuous sequence; numbers were issued in batches based on OG volume.

http://

www.uspto.gov/patft/contents.html

interested, and it enables electronic search. Search of printed journals is long, arduous, and limited by the indexing and classification scheme used by authors and editors.

Consider a hypothetical example of patent search problems, which are not that different from Internet search difficulties. Imagine that a finance professor was the first person to invent a new valuation method that used a modified version of the discounted cash flow technique. The new invention was described in an article published in a finance journal six months before the inventor filed a patent application. Before the publication, a financial engineer working at an investment banking firm separately invents a similar evaluation technique but is unaware of the finance professor's prior work. In searching the prior art, the financial engineer fails to use the academic term "discounted cash flow" but instead uses the industry term "present value" in searching for prior art. In a paper-based search system, only patent lawyers or agents who are intimately familiar with both the academic *and* industry perspectives would understand that "discounted cash flow" and "present value" are sufficiently equivalent to represent similar methods of using the "time value of money" for a new valuation method.

As electronic search engines become more sophisticated, they should become capable of translating such technical terms at the conceptual level, much as an expert in the field could. Search engines show great promise for the quality and efficiency of prior art searches, which should improve dramatically over the next few years. This progress will probably parallel similar improvements in Internet search engines and shopping bot technologies that are used by web surfers. Prior art and the hypothetical persons of ordinary skill in the art are also critically important to the second fundamental patentability standard: nonobviousness.

ONLINE

Additional patent search databases
http://www.lexis.com
http://www.westlaw.com

NONOBVIOUSNESS

The third major criteria for patentability, the **nonobviousness** requirement, is stated in §103(a) of the Patent Act. Nonobviousness was added by the 1952 revision that replaced, but closely parallels, a former requirement for **inventiveness**. Today, a patent should not be granted on a novel invention if the advancement is small and represents merely minor improvements over the prior art. Minor improvements make the invention obvious to the hypothetical person of ordinary skill in the art.

35 U.S.C. §103 Conditions for patentability; nonobvious subject matter.

(a) A patent may not be obtained though the invention is not identically disclosed or described as set forth in §102 of this title, if the differences between the subject matter sought to be patented and the prior art are such that the subject matter as a whole would have been obvious at the time the invention was made to a person having ordinary skill in the art to which said subject matter pertains.

The *Graham v. John Deere* Test

The Supreme Court first requires a three-step analysis of nonobviousness, which was expressed in *Graham v. John Deere Co.*[17] First, a court reviewing a patent for obviousness must determine the scope and content of the prior art. This requires a meticulous search and analysis of the prior art that was available at the time the invention was made. Prior art is found in published patents, scientific journals, textbooks, and the like. There is often so much prior art in a particular technology that it must be selected carefully, or this step could quickly become overwhelming. For example, imagine the difficulties of determining obviousness of a novel e-commerce electronic payment method. Is the prior art limited just to the necessary steps for electronic funds transfers, or should the processing of payments by checks and drafts also be explored? Perhaps the search should grow even larger to include all computerized network communication technologies from the telecommunications field, encryption techniques from computer science, and the network effects of currencies from the literature of economics.

Second, there must be a determination of the level of skill held by the hypothetical person of ordinary skill in the pertinent art. This step is necessary because the reviewing court must take only the perspective of experts before evaluating obviousness. The nonobvious test is made only from the perspective of possible inventors, who are assumed to be from among those skilled in the art. These people are the most likely to have the skill and inclination to conceive of such an invention. Obviousness can be judged only after the prior art and persons of ordinary skill in those arts are accurately identified.

The third step is to compare the prior art with the invention to evaluate whether the invention has made any significant advances. If the differences are slight, the invention is obvious and not patentable. However, if the advance is substantial, the invention is nonobvious and may be patentable. Judges make this comparison from the perspective of one skilled in the art and knowledgeable of the prior art. However, experience has shown that nonobviousness tests are difficult to apply because lay judges are seldom skilled in the art. Too often they may try to second-guess the hypothetical person of ordinary skill or substitute their own judgments using hindsight or common knowledge.

That is precisely what happened in *Panduit Corp. v. Dennison Mfg.*[18] The trial court used improper perspectives in holding a patent on the "cable tie" was obvious. Panduit invented the cable tie, a one-piece plastic fastener that holds together a bundle of wires. The cable tie is a strap that wraps around the bundle, and the pointed end is inserted into a looped opening on the other end that locks the strap together. There are teeth all along the cable tie that engage with the one-way locking device in the looped opening. Panduit spent several million dollars on R&D over a nine-year period to develop the locking mechanism so it would be easy to insert but difficult to remove. This effort was needed to make the cable tie convenient but effective in tightly holding the bundle of wires. Dennison's R&D effort had failed, but eventually Dennison became the second largest supplier of cable ties by copying Panduit's patented design. When Panduit sued for infringement, Dennison claimed the locking device was obvious. The trial court erred by improperly using hindsight, ignoring the perspective of persons of ordinary skill, and dissecting the claims in Panduit's patent.

---

17. 381 U.S. 1 (1966).
18. 774 F.2d 1022 (Fed.Cir., 1985), *on remand* 810 F.2d 1561 (Fed.Cir., 1987).

Both obviousness and nonobviousness must be measured at the time the invention was conceived, not later, when a judge has the benefit of hindsight. But obviousness is determined by actuality, while nonobviousness is determined hypothetically, without inventive insight. Hindsight is a later perception that benefits from seeing the significance of events that were much more difficult to see previously. Judges using hindsight later on during suit over validity and/or infringement are unfairly using the very insight of the inventor to conclude that the invention was obvious. Second, the court substituted its judgment for that of persons of ordinary skill. Third, the *Panduit* court erred by dissecting Panduit's claims into the component parts of the cable tie invention. Nearly every invention combines at least some existing technologies. Nonobviousness must be judged by considering the invention as a whole: A unique combination of existing factors constitutes inventiveness.

Secondary Considerations (Objective Factors)

Nonobviousness is the most important patentability criteria. The *Graham* three-part analysis is the conceptually accurate method, but it is too often difficult to apply. Prior art determinations are lengthy and complicated, judges have difficulty accurately mimicking the perspective of persons of ordinary skill that change with every technology, and the temptation is strong to use hindsight, general principles, and common experience. For these reasons, the Supreme Court has acknowledged that sometimes **secondary considerations** may be appropriate. These are additional factors that tend to show that the invention was not obvious at the time it was invented. The Federal Circuit now considers these factors to be very important and much easier to apply than the *Graham* test, so they are now called **objective factors**: (1) long-felt, but unmet need, (2) commercial success, and (3) use or copying by others.

First, **long-felt, but unmet need** occurs when an industry has unsuccessfully tried to solve a problem that the invention finally does resolve. The failure of others' efforts, when combined with the inventor's success, is often convincing evidence that the invention was not obvious; otherwise, others would have invented it. Second, if the **commercial success** of the invention is strong, it can be inferred that it was not obvious; otherwise, other inventors would surely have developed a similar invention sooner. The invention's success must come from its inventive, nonobvious features and not from some other cause, such as promotional expenditures, the seller's market dominance, or other product features not part of the invention. Third, **use of copying by others** can be persuasive. The authorized licensing or outright infringement by competitors is an additional market test of the invention's nonobviousness. Licensing implies competitors accept that the patent is valid; infringing copies imply that competitors were unable to develop adequate substitutes, so the invention must have been nonobvious. For example, in the *Panduit* case, Dennison was not successful in designing a workable cable tie other than by using the method Panduit used to solve these problems in its patent. Both Panduit and Dennison had tremendous commercial success in producing the patented version of the cable tie.

The following case is a recent high-profile illustration of nonobviousness in the business method patent, Internet e-commerce area. What was particularly remarkable about this case is that it received considerable press coverage and provoked many people to publicly participate in the debate over what constitutes nonobviousness. Such technical discussions seldom occur outside the close-knit members of the patent bar or among experts in the technologies involved. Indeed, this case became the cause célèbre on the public policy issues of business method patentability.

Amazon.com v. Barnesandnoble.com, Inc.

73 F.Supp.2d 1228 (W.D.Wash., 1999)

Facts. Sometime before May 1997, Amazon.com CEO Jeffrey Bezos conceived of an idea to enable Amazon.com customers to purchase items with a single click of a computer mouse button. This idea was commercially implemented by Amazon.com in September 1997. On September 21, 1997, a patent application was made on this system, "Method and System for Placing a Purchase Order via a Communications Network." On September 28, 1999, the PTO issued U.S. Patent #5,960,411 ('411 patent) on Bezos's method. The '411 patent describes a method and system in which a consumer can complete a purchase order for an item via the Internet by using only a single action (such as a single click of a computer mouse button) after information about the item is displayed. The retailer must already have purchaser information on file (address, credit card number), and the purchaser's personal computer must have an identifier that enables the retailer's server system to authenticate the purchaser's identity (e.g., cookie). Amazon.com alleged that Barnesandnoble.com's "Express Lane" ordering feature infringes various claims of the '411 patent and sought a preliminary injunction to enjoin infringement by Barnesandnoble.com. Barnesandnoble.com claimed the patent was invalid as obvious.

Legal Issue. Is the Amazon.com "one-click" on-line ordering system obvious, given the prior art and therefore unpatentable?

Opinion. District Judge Pechman. Before granting the patent, the examiner assigned to the patent searched the data base of patents available at the PTO, and obtained a search of private databases through the PTO's Science and Technology Information Center. Additionally, the examiner commissioned a third-party search firm to perform a search for potential non-patent prior art. The evidence indicates that the patent was thoroughly examined by the PTO before issuance. Plaintiff's expert testified that except for single-action ordering and the implementation of single-action ordering without a shopping cart model, everything in the '411 patent is in prior art.

Defendants presented evidence regarding an on-line ordering system called "Web Basket" that requires users to accumulate items into a virtual shopping basket and to check these items out when they are finished shopping. Web Basket requires several confirmation steps for even pre-registered users to complete their purchases. The Court finds that Web Basket requires a multiple-step ordering process from the time that an item to be purchased is displayed. These multiple steps are inconsistent with the single-action requirements of the '411 patent.

A prior art reference an excerpt from a [Netscape] book entitled "Creating the Virtual Store" that was copyrighted in 1996 focused on the following language: "Merchants also can provide shoppers with an instant buy button for some or all items, enabling them to skip check out review. This provides added appeal for customers who already know the single item they want to purchase during their shopping excursion." [However,] apart from the words "instant buy," there is no indication that this Netscape system implements a single-action ordering component [as does the '411 patent].

Pages were presented from a website entitled "Oliver's Market The Ordering System." Although it begins with the sentence: "A single click on its picture is all it takes to order an item," the ordering system described by the reference is a multi-step shopping cart model.

There are key differences between each of the prior art references cited from the '411 patent. None of the prior art references offered anticipate the claims of the '411 patent. The differences between the prior art references and the '411 patent claims are significant. The Court finds particularly telling [that the Barnesandnoble.com's expert witness admitted] that it never occurred to him to modify his Web Basket program to enable single-action ordering, despite his testimony that such a modification would be easy to implement. This admission serves to negate Dr. Lockwood's conclusory statements that prior art references teach to one of ordinary skill in the art the invention of the '411 patent.

Barnesandnoble.com's Express Lane allows customers who have registered for the feature to purchase items by simply clicking on the Express Lane button shown on the detail or product page that describes and identifies the book or other item to be purchased. The text beneath the Express Lane button invites the user to "Buy it now with just 1 click!" The strong similarities between the Amazon.com 1-click feature and the Express Lane feature subsequently adopted by Barnesandnoble.com suggest that Barnesandnoble.com copied Amazon.com's feature.

Anticipation is a question of fact and is a defense only if "all of the same elements are found in exactly the same situation and united in the same way . . . in a single prior art reference." The issue of obviousness is a mixed question of fact and law. The ultimate question is one of law, but it is based on several factual inquiries, including: (1) the scope and content of the prior art; (2) the differences between the prior art and the claims; (3) the level of ordinary skill in the pertinent art; and (4) applicable secondary considerations. Whether it would be, at the present time, an "obvious" or "trivial" modification of the Web Basket system to include the "single action" feature of the '411 patent is legally irrelevant. The law is clear that the time period for any obviousness determination is "at the time the invention was made."

"Secondary considerations [such] as commercial success, long felt but unsolved needs, [and] failures of others" are relevant as evidence of obviousness. Copying of the invention by Barnesandnoble.com and others is additional evidence of nonobviousness. "It gives the tribute of its imitation, as others have done." The adoption of single-action ordering by other e-commerce retailers following Amazon.com's introduction of the feature, coupled with the need to solve the problem of abandoned shopping carts by e-commerce customers, is additional evidence of nonobviousness.

In light of its consideration of the factors and evidence related to the question of obviousness, the Court finds Barnesandnoble.com is unlikely to succeed in showing by clear and convincing evidence that the claims of the '411 patent were obvious. Barnesandnoble.com's reliance on the simplicity of the invention is unavailing. "Defining the problem in terms of its solution reveals improper hindsight in the selection of the prior art relevant to obviousness."

Therefore, the Court hereby ORDERS that Defendants Barnesandnoble.com LLC and Barnesandnoble.com Inc., their offers, agents, servants, employees and attorneys and those in active concert or participation with them or Defendants ARE HEREBY RESTRAINED AND ENJOINED from continuing to infringe the '411 patent including by continuing to make or use within the United States Defendants' Express Lane feature as currently configured or any other single-action ordering system that employs the methods or systems of the '411 patent.

Decision. Amazon.com's '411 patent was nonobvious and therefore valid because the prior art references involved multistep ordering systems and the one-click system was not anticipated by these previously known methods.

Case Questions

1. What was the unique feature of the Amazon.com one-click ordering system?
2. What was the impact of the expert acting as the hypothetical person of ordinary skill in foreseeing the reduction of the ordering process to a single click?

UTILITY

Recall that §101 permits patents to be granted to "whoever invents or discovers any new and *useful* process, machine, manufacture or composition of matter." This creates a requirement that the invention have **utility**, beneficial use for the invention or for products produced by a patented process. This threshold of practical value is low because the invention need not work any better than technologies in the prior art. Indeed, many inventions are refined long after they are patented. Some older cases denied utility if the invention was frivolous, injured public well-being, or was immoral. However, later cases prefer to leave the public policy aspects of the invention's function to other laws, such as regulation of gambling devices or sexual devices. A few cases prohibit patentability of inventions for not being useful if the primary function is illegal or unsafe. For example, patented drugs must prove their efficacy both under FDA drug trials and under the utility standard of patentability.

THE PATENTING PROCESS

Obtaining a patent on an invention is a much more complicated and expensive process than is obtaining a copyright or perfecting a trade secret. Patenting requires qualification, an adversarial process proving the invention is patentable subject matter and that it is novel, nonobvious, and useful. Patenting is seldom successful without careful record keeping during the invention process, the preparation of the patent application advised by a patent attorney or patent agent, and many months of interaction between the inventor and the PTO's patent examiner. Frequently, the inventor is an employee, so employment responsibilities are involved, such as patent assignment and assistance duties often contained in the employment contract. Patenting is so costly ($10,000 to $50,000 in out-of-pocket expenses plus various opportunity costs) that patentability and commercialization sometimes involve third-party experts and venture capitalists. This section discusses the regulatory requirements for patent prosecution.

THE PATENT AND TRADEMARK OFFICE (PTO)

The U.S. PTO is a division of the Department of Commerce. This makes the PTO different from the Copyright Office, which is an agency of Congress and independent of the president. The PTO is a dependent regulatory agency under direct control of the president through the Cabinet. The PTO is the agency Congress created to qualify patents and trademarks, to promulgate interpretive regulations on patent and trademark issues, and to organize the fields of patentable technologies. The PTO's regulations set procedures for various patent-related activities. For example, the procedures that PTO examiners must follow in examining patent applications are assembled into the **Manual of Patent Examination Procedure (MPEP)**. Like most other federal administrative agencies, the PTO must follow the Administrative Procedure Act (APA) in its rule making, hearings, investigations, and responses to requests by the public under the Freedom of Information Act (FOIA) for information held in the PTO's files. The PTO's work burden is enormous. With the number of patent applications approaching a quarter million each year, it is impressive that the PTO manages the workload fairly well. Of course, as with other information businesses, the PTO's computerization efforts have improved productivity.

ONLINE
PTO's MPEP
http://www.uspto.gov/web/offices/pac/dapp/mpepmain.html

THE PATENT APPLICATION

Despite the U.S. first-to-invent standard, it is still sensible to file a patent application as soon as the invention is reduced to practice. This is particularly important for firms engaged in active international trade that expect their patented products to be competitive in international markets. The first-to-file standards in other nations

ONLINE
Trilateral website
http://www.trilateral.org

Patent Regulators around the World

Most industrialized nations have a government agency equivalent to the U.S. PTO. The patent law and patenting procedures used in other nations can vary greatly. For adequate worldwide patent protection, it is still often necessary to file in those other nations where there are meaningful markets for the invention, where infringing production processes might be used, or where infringing products could be manufactured.

The European Patent Office and the Japanese Patent Office are very important patent regulatory agencies. In recent years, these offices have been cooperating with the U.S. PTO as part of the Trilateral organization to eliminate some of the paperwork and uncertainties of differing patent systems. Many hope that someday a single patent office could process patent application(s) that would result in enforceable patents in many or all nations. However, there are still substantial differences in patentable subject matter and patentability criteria among the major industrialized nations. Additionally, barriers such as national pride and economic advantage may delay attainment of a truly one-stop international patent system.

ONLINE

European Patent Office
http://www.european-patent-office.org
Japanese Patent Office
http://www.jpo.go.jp

create risks if filing in foreign nations is delayed. Similarly, many other nations do not have the one-year grace period. Therefore, publication, sales, or use of the invention before filing in many other nations risks patent rights.

An important step before filing is to assure that the inventor keeps detailed records in lab notebooks that are periodically signed and witnessed. Lab notebooks should be bound with no blank or missing pages to represent an accurate chronological journal that logs the invention process in accurate sequence. An initial patentability search of the prior art can be advisable so the benefits of patenting costs are better known and thereby provide an initial assessment of novelty that can encourage continuing with the expense of a patent application.

There are several major parts to a patent application. The inventor must describe the invention in a specification including at least one claim that provides sufficient detail that a person of ordinary skill in the art would be enabled to practice (reproduce or use) the invention. The specification should describe the invention and the manner and process of making and using it. Drawings are required when needed to illustrate the invention's architecture and aid in understanding it. The inventor must make an oath declaring original inventorship. The appropriate filing fee must also be included. After the patent is granted there are periodic **maintenance fees** owed by the patent owner.

Ethical Issue

The Inventor's Risks in Conducting Prior Art Searches

A patent search is not required before an application is filed. The PTO's examination process involves a patent search, so why should the inventor even bother? Many inventors are professional researchers who are generally familiar with the prior art in their fields. Knowing this is precisely how a person of ordinary skill can be in a position to conceive of an important innovation. The inventor has a ***duty of candor***; essentially, the application must disclose any prior art that the inventor knows might be material to patentability. Additionally, the inventor cannot make misrepresentations or misstate test data or other relevant facts in the application or during the examination process. Violation of the duty of candor can make the patent unenforceable.

Some patent lawyers advise their clients not to do a search because it might uncover some prior art that could make the invention obvious or not novel. By remaining unaware of prior art that could risk patentability if disclosed, the inventor does not violate the duty of candor. If the PTO examiner fails to locate the damaging prior art, the patent might be issued, so ignorance is bliss, right? Is this system ethical? Congress never intended that the PTO expend so many resources that the prior art would be thoroughly revealed. Patent prosecution is somewhat adversarial but still must depend on forthright and cooperative revelations by applicants. These problems have worsened in recent years as the PTO's budget has been cut and its fee income diverted to fund other government programs. The salaries paid to examiners are generally lower than for similar services in the private sector. Indeed, the most experienced PTO examiners are regularly lured away from the PTO to IP firms after a few years of excellent training at the PTO.

These business method patent quality-control problems led Congress in 2000 to propose requiring business method patent inventors to search for business method prior art and disclose the extent of their searches. This legislation has not passed, but it nevertheless provoked the PTO to change its rules. Now PTO examiners are clearly given the authority to require that applicants provide additional information relevant to examination, including commercial databases, prior art from nonpatent sources (e.g., scientific journals, technical reports, or advertising) known to the applicant, prior art used in drafting the application, and prior art used in the design process. PTO examiners may also require applicants to certify whether a prior art search was made. These new rules apply to all technologies, business method patents, and other subject matters.

Inventorship

As first introduced in Chapters 13 and 15, inventorship under patent law is a different matter than authorship under copyright law. Although an employer can claim authorship for a work made for hire by one or more employees, this is generally not possible for inventorship. Generally, a patent application is made by the actual human inventor. The inventor must sign the application and declare that he or she is the first inventor. Of course, employers often contract with their employees for an assignment of patent rights and further require confidentiality and assistance in prosecuting the patent application.

A sole inventorship occurs when only one person conceives of the essential elements that are the "germ" of the invention's novel aspects. There is but a sole inventor even if others assist in the effort, pose problems to solve, or make minor suggestions. However, many inventions are made in large R&D laboratories where several human contributors collaborate. It is possible to have co-inventors if each makes a substantial contribution to the conception of the patent's novel aspects. If two or more persons conceive of the essential germ of the novel idea, then they are equal joint inventors. Some joint inventors may contribute different aspects, but all must be contributors to the novel aspects. All **joint inventors** must sign and participate in the application process.

Provisional Patent Applications

Since 1995, it has been much easier to establish the date of invention and obtain priority in international patent filings by using an abbreviated **provisional application.** As discussed next, a patent application must provide a highly accurate and detailed description of the invention. The provisional application can omit most of this. It allows the inventor to file an abbreviated description without taking the time and care necessary to meticulously draft clear and complete patent claims. Provisional applications have advantages: (1) First-to-file standards and shorter grace periods in foreign nations are satisfied by a provisional application, and (2) the inventor may have up to an additional year to test the invention's market appeal before investing in a full patent application. The inventor has one year after filing the provisional application before the full application must be filed.

The PTO's Electronic Filing System (EFS)

As part of the PTO's modernization initiatives, it has established the **Electronic Business Center** (**EBC**), a group of related transaction-processing systems. The EBC processes upgrade interaction with the PTO from the historical use of paper-based, in-person, mail, and telephone interactions to electronic transaction processing. These are similar to the e-government initiatives being implemented throughout other federal agencies and in many states and some municipalities. The EBC includes electronic search for issued patents and trademarks, including full graphic images, the electronic payment of fees and account maintenance, electronic PTO job applications, and PTO subcontractor qualification. The EBC also includes the **Electronic Filing System** (**EFS**) for electronic filing of patent applications and **Patent Application Information Retrieval** (**PAIR**), a faster and less costly method to check the status of a patent application.

Generally, the EBC systems require an initial registration of each individual or corporate user so all communications can be authenticated before transmission of highly confidential information. Registration and the use of bar codes simplifies interaction between the PTO and large, high-technology firms that have numerous applications filed at any one time. Public Key encryption Infrastructure (PKI) helps assure confidentiality. Special software is used for "clients" (inventors or assignees) to interact with the PTO's EBC. All these systems hold promise to improve service, reduce service times, and reduce the costs of the ever burgeoning patent information system.

DISCLOSURE

The major premise of patent law is that a limited monopoly on the invention is given in exchange for the inventor's **disclosure** of the invention's secrets. Disclosure occurs in a **specification** that has two parts. First, claims describe the invention, the "what description" that precisely defines the scope of the patent owner's rights. Second, specifications are the "how description" details of construction and use that must enable a person of ordinary skill in the art to practice (make or use) the invention in the best mode known by the inventor. PTO regulations require a ten-part format, including the inventions title, various cross-references, a summary, a brief as well as a detailed description of the drawings, claims, an abstract, the oath, and the drawings. Although there are no rigid requirements for the format of claims, successful patent claim drafters tend to use esoteric and somewhat standard terminology to describe the particular physical functions of an invention. The language of claims often seems convoluted to the layperson.

Enablement and Best Mode

Adequate description can be a difficult problem. There are natural incentives that create tension between inventors and everyone else (PTO, competitors). Inventors want their claims written broadly to maximize the value of their patent monopoly. Inventors are often reluctant to be as clear and complete as PTO examiners might demand. Ambiguous claims are more difficult to copy or design around, and this also makes the patent potentially stronger than the law permits. Two tests of adequacy are applied to the disclosures: (1) They must provide **enablement** (to a person of ordinary skill in the art), and (2) they must reveal the **best mode** for practicing (using, making) the invention.

The specification need not be a step-by-step production task list or cookbook approach. However, if a person of ordinary skill would be required to perform extensive experimentation before they could construct a working embodiment, then the disclosure is not enabling; that is, it is insufficient and must be revised by the inventor. The best mode requirement is intended to prevent inventors from concealing known examples of the best ways they have discovered to practice the invention. For example, consider the difference between a good cookbook and a bad one. The author of a good cookbook knows the common mistakes that cooks of ordinary skill might make, such as taking steps out of order, inaccurate measurement, improper mixing, inaccurate heating, and insufficient interlude between procedures. The good cookbook warns of these trouble spots and thereby strives to communicate the best mode for cooking the recipe (practicing the invention). By contrast, a bad cookbook fails to warn of possible problems, raising the probability of failure and requiring even cooks of ordinary skill to be persistent and experiment until they get it right.

It takes considerable experience in the technology involved before most people can develop an adequate understanding in the reading, interpretation, and writing of good claims. Technical professionals, patent lawyers, and patent agents usually develop expertise in only a few narrow but related technologies because the technical details are just too numerous in the most valuable arts. Nevertheless, it is useful to see how claims and supporting specifications are written so that the enablement and best mode standards are better understood.

Commentary

Wrestling with Patent Claims

Take some time to read a few patents from the uspto.gov website. Select patents from the main page, then select the search utility. Alternate sources include Lexis.com or Westlaw.com if you have access to these subscription services. Also try delphion.com, various CD-ROM services, or the U.S. PTO's *Official Gazette*, the print publication held in most law libraries and Federal Depository libraries. What patents should you examine? Perhaps you know of a controversial patent from the news or a website. Perhaps you know an inventor. Anyway, consider using one or more of the patents identified in this chapter or the cases; use the by number, or the official title or the inventor's full name in the appropriate search field.[19] The following patent is a particularly interesting example and is easier to read and grasp fairly quickly than are most patents. It involves a business method patent but does not need software for successful implementation. It raised considerable controversy soon after it was granted, as you will immediately see after retrieving it.

"Building Block Training Systems and Training Methods," U.S. Patent No. 5,851,117

Secrecy

Traditionally, patent applications have remained secret during prosecution. Only the inventor, the patent attorney or agent, various employees, the PTO examiner, and a few PTO staff are typically exposed to a patent application until after the patent finally issues. All these parties already are obligated to maintain secrecy until the patent is issued, or they should be. After issuance, the patent is published for anyone to see. Secrecy of patent application contents serves very useful purposes for the inventor. If the patent is rejected, the inventor can try to maintain it as a trade secret. Often during prosecution, the PTO examiner demands that claims be reduced in scope, which diminishes their value. Applicants may become dissatisfied if a narrow patent results. They can still withdraw their application and try to use the invention as a trade secret. Secrecy encourages frank and open prosecution activities between the PTO examiner and the inventor.

The advantages of secrecy largely benefit the inventor. Society also has an interest in patent applications before patents are issued. For example, the public could often contribute to the examination process. Persons of ordinary skill might supply prior art that might narrow the patent's scope or invalidate it. Publication of patent applications reduces the surprise element that surfaces when "submarine" patents undercut industry practices. Most other industrialized nations now require the publication of patent applications at some fixed time after filing irrespective of whether the patent is yet issued.

---

19. The patents described in this chapter include:
    1. Amazon.com: U.S. Pat. No. 5,960,411, Method and System for Placing a Purchase Order via a Communications Network.
    2. State Street: U.S. Patent No. 5,193,056; Data Processing System for Hub and Spoke Financial Services Configuration (issued March 9, 1993, inventor R. Todd Boes).
    3. Priceline.com: U.S. Pat. No.5,794,207, Method and Apparatus for Effectuating Buyer-Driven Commerce.
    4. Merrill Lynch: U.S. Patent No. 4,346,442, Securities Brokerage-Cash Management System (issued Aug. 24, 1982).
    5. Excel: U.S. Patent No. 5,333,184; Call Message Recording for Telephone Systems (issued July 26, 1994).
    6. Panduit: U.S. Patent No. 3,965,538, Integral Cable Tie (issued: June 29, 1976, inventor(s): Caveney, Jack E.; Moody, Roy A.).
    7. Graham: U.S. Patent No. 2,627,798, Clamp for Vibrating Shank Plows.
    8. Pennwalt: U.S. Patent No. 4,106,628, Sorter for Fruit and the Like (inventors: Aaron J. Warkentin and George A. Mills).

The United States finally gave up the absolute secrecy rule for patent applications when the examination process takes more than 18 months. If the application is also filed in foreign patent offices, the AIPA requires publication. The AIPA implemented the WTO and TRIPS treaties by standardizing the secrecy of patent applications to 18 months. Small U.S. inventors won an important exception: Secrecy may continue beyond 18 months if the inventor does not also file in foreign nations. This rule pressures the PTO to speed up the average examination process closer to 18 months. PTO examination can take several years for new and complex technologies like software, business methods, and biotechnology. Applicants uncertain about their application's prospects can still withdraw them before 18 months to avoid publication. This strategy can be used to preserve trade secrecy. Secrecy orders are possible for technologies with national security or defense reasons (secret weapons system), so these are also exempt from publication. Patent applications are now available from the PTO website and from other sources.

ONLINE

USPTO Patent Application Searches
http://www.uspto.gov/patft/

PATENT INFRINGEMENT

Patents are strong IP rights because, unlike copyrights, the patent protects both the idea and the expression (embodiments). The patent owner, often an assignee from the original inventor, has several exclusive rights that are protected by the threat of infringement litigation. These are the rights to exclude others from (1) making embodiments of the patented invention, (2) using the patented invention, and (3) selling (making the first sale) the patented invention. If the patent covers a process, ownership includes the right to exclude others from (1) using the process and (2) selling goods produced by the process. These are the most basic rights from the bundle held by the patent owner. Additional rights permit the patent owner to exclude others from importing into the United States infringing goods or goods produced using infringing processes made outside the United States and provide export restrictions on components of patented combinations and making an application to sell patented drugs.

LITERAL INFRINGEMENT

Infringement analysis is a three-step process: (1) a literal infringement inquiry, (2) a doctrine of equivalents inquiry, and (3) and a reconsideration of the inventor's history of negotiating the claims during patent prosecution. First, the court will look to whether there was **literal infringement**. This is similar to literal infringement under copyright because there is a comparison made between the patent claims and the alleged infringing embodiment. If every element claimed in the patent is also present in the allegedly infringing thing, then there is literal infringement. An exact duplicate infringes under the rule of **exactness**. If one of the claimed elements is missing, there can be no literal infringement under the rule of **omission**. However, there may still be infringement under the doctrine of equivalents discussed next. The rule of **addition** applies when all the claimed elements are reproduced in the infringing embodiment but additional elements are added. Infringement by addition is still a literal infringement even if it is an improvement.

For example, imagine a patent on a machine used to cut grass to an even height between three and six inches; it is called a "lawn mower." The original patent claims describe a nonpower, manual mechanism with the following elements: (1) a long handle, (2) metal frame and housing, (3) cutting blades, (4) the riding wheels drive the blade, and (5) the riding wheels adjust to maintain a variable but uniform cutting height. It would be literal infringement by exactness if a competitor produced a closely resembling machine with all five of these elements. It would be literal infringement by addition if another competitor produced a power mower with the only difference being a gasoline motor to drive the blades. However, it would not be literal infringement by subtraction if an electric motor powered a wheelless power mower that used a propeller-like blade to force airflow downward to hold the mower's cutting blades at a uniform height. Nevertheless, the wheelless mower might still be infringing under the doctrine of equivalents unless the PTO examiner rejected the cutting height claim during the original prosecution under the doctrine of file wrapper estoppel.

DOCTRINE OF EQUIVALENTS

The second step in patent infringement analysis frequently determines whether the allegedly infringing thing is highly similar to the patented invention. The doctrine of equivalents is one aspect of patent law that is stingy with the public domain. The **doctrine of equivalents** defines infringement more broadly by including competing products that closely resemble the patented invention's design, even when they are not literally infringing. For example, the wheelless mower had many of the same elements as the original mower; it added an engine for power, omitted the wheels, and substituted a propeller-like blade to maintain the uniform cutting height. Should patent law recognize the wheelless mower as an infringement?

Since 1853, the Supreme Court has recognized infringement when similar elements are substituted in an effort to avoid infringement.[20] There can still be infringement under the doctrine of equivalents if obvious changes are made by using known substitutes and the resulting product "performs substantially the same function, in the same way, to achieve the same result."[21] This is an ad hoc determination that must compare the prior art, from the perspective of a person of ordinary skill in the art, as to the substituted element(s). It is essentially a nonobviousness test; it is applied to the element substituted for the missing element(s). It is not judged from the perspective of when first invented, as was nonobviousness. Instead, it is judged from a later perspective: at the time of alleged infringement. Would the designers of lawn and garden implements easily think to use blowing air rather than wheels to maintain the mower's cutting height? The doctrine of equivalents is justified as a method to prevent "fraud on the patent" and unscrupulous copiers. Clearly, the doctrine of equivalents tends to expand patent rights but at the cost of making IP infringement determinations much more uncertain and costly. However, there are two limitations that may reduce some of this ambiguity: file wrapper estoppel and the Federal Circuit's 2000 *Festo* decision.

File Wrapper Estoppel

What if the substitute element had been the subject of contention during the inventor's prosecution history with the PTO examiner? Should the inventor be allowed to resurrect a claim rejected by the PTO examiner during prosecution? For example, suppose that the PTO examiner rejected the inventor's claim to use a gasoline motor

20. *Winans v. Denmead*, 56 U.S. 330 (1853).
21. *Graver Tank & Mfg. v. Linde Air Products Co.*, 339 U.S. 605 (1950).

to power the cutting blade but instead allowed the claim for a manual, wheel-driven, push-powered blade finally described by the original patent as issued. Given that the inventor was required to give up the gasoline motor during prosecution, should the inventor be allowed to use the doctrine of equivalents to prevent infringement if a competitor later sells a power mower? The doctrine of **file wrapper estoppel** prevents the original inventor from bringing back a claim as an equivalent in infringement litigation that was surrendered during to a PTO examiner during prosecution.

Prosecution is a process in which the PTO examiner carefully studies the invention claims and looks through prior art cited by the inventor and for other prior art the examiner finds independently by using other sources, databases, and cross-referencing indexes. The PTO examiner might find that some aspect of the invention's claims is already in the prior art. Some claims are written so broadly that they could include things already in the prior art. It is common for the PTO examiner to require the inventor to revise the application by making **amendments**. Only when the examiner is satisfied with these revisions is the patent, as rewritten, **allowed** when the PTO examiner recommends the patent be granted. Patent prosecution takes a long time because newer technologies are complex, the PTO has a substantial workload, and patent prosecution is iterative, requiring amendments to the application. If the PTO examiner finds there are no novel or nonobvious claims, the application can be totally denied in a **final rejection**.

Possible Narrowing of Equivalents under *Festo*

The doctrine of equivalents creates costly uncertainty because of the ambiguity in determining equivalents that arise later in time. It effectively requires mastery over hundreds of different esoteric fields, arts, and technologies. The doctrine of equivalents raises three very serious risks and thereby imposes costs on society and competitors and also confers benefits on patent owners. Many observers argue that these are unnecessary to maintain the fairness balance drawn by patent law. First, competitors using elements that are possible equivalents may be sued for infringement. Second, many competitors are deterred from using equivalents because of uncertainty that these might be infringing. This leads them to forgo innovation that might have been beneficial to society. Third, competitors probably pay license fees to inventors to avoid these two risks, but such payments may be unnecessary. Society suffers dead-weight welfare loss when innovation is prevented or unnecessary payments are made to patent holders.

Some of these problems finally came to light in the 2000 case of *Festo*.[22] If the Federal Circuit's decision withstands the current challenge in the Supreme Court, then file wrapper estoppel may be expanded to further curtail the infringement risks posed by the doctrine of equivalents. *Festo* would give greater power to PTO examiners because any claim narrowed during prosecution, for *any* reason, could not be expanded during infringement litigation under the doctrine of equivalents. *Festo* threatens patent owners of broad and pioneering patents, as well as those who benefit from patent litigation. By contrast, many high-tech firms with large patent portfolios may actually like *Festo* because it reduces infringement uncertainties. The Supreme Court may modify *Festo* by early 2003. The next case illustrates infringement analysis.

22. *Festo v. Shoketsu Kinzoku Kogyo Kabushiki Co.*, 234 F.3d 558 (Fed.Cir., 2000), *cert.granted* (June 18, 2001).

Pennwalt v. Durand

833 F.2d 931 (Fed.Cir., 1987)

Facts. Pennwalt sued Durand-Wayland for infringing U.S. Patent No. 4,106,628 ('628 patent), entitled "Sorter for Fruit and the Like." The '628 patent describes an invention that sorts items, like fruit, by color, weight, or a combination. The sorter moves items along a track that does electronic weighing by producing an electrical signal proportional to the weight of the item. The specification describes the details of a "hard-wired" network consisting of discrete electrical components that perform each step of the claims, for example, by comparing the signals from the weighing device to reference signals and sending an appropriate signal at the proper time to discharge the item into the container corresponding to its weight. An optical scanner sends an electrical signal proportional to the color of the item. The signals from the weighing device and color sensor are combined to send another signal at the proper moment to eject the moving item into the correct container for its color and weight. Durand-Wayland manufactures and sells two different types of sorting machines. The first accused device (alleged infringing product), the "Microsizer," sorts by weight only. The second accused device sorts by both color and weight through the use of the "Microsizer" in conjunction with a color detection apparatus called a "Microsorter."

Legal Issue. Is there infringement by literal means or under the doctrine of equivalents?

Opinion. Circuit Judge Bissell. Under the doctrine of equivalents, infringement *may* be found if an accused device performs substantially the same overall function or work, in substantially the same way, to obtain substantially the same overall result as the claimed invention. That formulation, however, does not mean one can ignore claim limitations. To be a "substantial equivalent," the element substituted in the accused device for the element set forth in the claim must not be such as would substantially change the way in which the function of the claimed invention is performed.

Pennwalt argues that the "accused machines simply do in a computer what the patent *illustrates* doing with hard-wired circuitry," and asserts that "this alone is insufficient to escape infringement." If Pennwalt was correct that the accused devices differ only in substituting a computer for hard-wired circuitry, it might have a stronger position for arguing that the accused devices infringe the claims. The claim limitations, however, require the performance of certain specified functions. Theoretically, a microprocessor could be programmed to perform those functions. However, the district court found that the microprocessor in the accused devices was not so programmed.

Certain functions of the claimed inventions were "missing" from the accused devices and those, which were performed, were "substantially different." The district court observed that "because the 'Microsizer' uses different elements and different operations than the elements and operations disclosed in the patent-in-suit to achieve the desired results, infringement can only be found if the different elements and operations are the legal equivalents of those disclosed in the patent-in- suit." It is clear from this that the district court correctly relied on an element-by-element comparison to conclude that there was no infringement under the doctrine of equivalents, because the accused devices did not perform substantially the same functions as the Pennwalt invention. However, the machine described in the patent-in-suit produces signals that indicate where the fruit is, i.e. track the progression of each cup. The "Microsizer" does not. Here, if the district court was not clearly erroneous in finding that even a single function required by a claim or an equivalent function is not performed by the Durand-Wayland sorters, the court's finding of no infringement must be upheld.

[The court-appointed expert] Dr. Vacroux's statement that the accused devices performed only "some of the same type of operations" supports the court's finding that some were not. It does not conflict with any of his other testimony or with his written report. Thus, on the issue of whether the accused devices performed *each* of the functional limitations of the claim or its equivalent and, thus, operated in substantially the same way, the district court followed its expert precisely. The court cannot be faulted for finding no infringement where the expert's testimony as to facts negates a finding of equivalency under the correct legal standard.

The invention was not a pioneer, but an improvement in a crowded art. The claims are "broad" with respect to what type of product can be sorted, i.e., "items" and, thus, sorters of all types of "items" fall within the relevant prior art. The claims are *narrow*, however, with respect to how the claimed sorter operates. Originally, the claims contained no position indicating means element with its associated functional limitations. The addition of that element was crucial to patentability. A device that does not satisfy this limitation at least equivalently does not function in substantially the same way as the claimed invention.

The testimony of Dr. Alford, Durand-Wayland's expert, was that the accused machine had no component which satisfied either of the above limitations defining position indicating means, and Pennwalt has admitted that the accused machines do not sort by keeping track of the physical location of an item in transit, continuously or otherwise, as required by each of these limitations. Pennwalt argues that there is a way to find out where an item is physically located on the track in the accused machine. Its witness, Dr. Moore, testified "*you could find* the location of a particular fruit as it moves from the scale to the drop by counting the distance from the stored value for that fruit back to the place the pointer is indicating at the start of the queue." Dr. Alford, Durand-Wayland's expert, admitted this was *possible*. Thus, Pennwalt asserts that the accused devices have "position indicating means."

One need not explain the technology to understand the inadequacy of Dr. Moore's testimony. As Dr. Moore himself indicates, the accused machine simply *does not do* what he explains "could" be done. It is admitted that the physical tracking of fruit is not part of the way in which the Durand-Wayland sorter works, in contrast to the claimed sorter which requires some means for "continuously indicating the position of an item to be sorted." While a microprocessor theoretically could be programmed to perform that function, the evidence led the court to a finding that the Durand-Wayland machines performed a *substantially different* function from that which each of the claims requires.

In interpreting the claims, the district court committed fundamental legal error when it analyzed each by a single word description of one part of the claimed tie. In patent law, a word ("teeth";"hinge";"ledge") means nothing outside the claim and the description in the specification. A disregard of claim limitations, as here, would render claim examination in the PTO meaningless. If, without basis in the record, courts may so rewrite claims, the entire statutory-regulatory structure that governs the drafting, submission, examination, allowance, and enforceability of claims would crumble.

Thus, the facts here do not involve later-developed computer technology which should be deemed within the scope of the claims to avoid the pirating of an invention. On the contrary, the inventors could not obtain a patent with claims in which the functions were described more broadly. Having secured claims only by including very specific *functional* limitations, Pennwalt now seeks to avoid those very limitations under the doctrine of equivalents. This it cannot do. Simply put, the memory components of the Durand-Wayland sorter were not programmed to perform the same or an equivalent function of physically tracking the items to be sorted from the scanner to the scale or from the scale to its appropriate discharge point as required by the claims

We affirm the judgment based on the finding of no infringement, the award of costs, and the denial of attorney fees to Durand-Wayland.

Decision. There was no literal infringement of means plus function patent where the accused sorting device differs from the plaintiff's patent by not continuously tracking throughput and uses digital computer logic rather than the plaintiff's claimed hardwire.

Case Questions

1. How is the doctrine of equivalents applied in this case?
2. Explain how the continuous tracking technique differs from the other method to know when to eject the fruit into the appropriate receptacle bin.

DEFENSES TO INFRINGEMENT

Those accused of infringement have only a few recognized excuses. The most important defense is **invalidity**. Those alleged to have infringed commonly attempt to show that the patent is invalid, nonstatutory subject matter, not novel, obvious, or not useful. Indeed, much patent litigation involves both claims of infringement and of invalidity. There is a presumption of validity for patents issued by the PTO, making issued patents very strong rights. The burden of proof is on the infringer or other person challenging validity to prove the invention was not patentable. For example, the incentives to do more thorough prior art searches are much greater during infringement litigation. Challengers often expend considerable resources to **scour the prior art** or enlist other competitors to help "bust the patent" by finding prior art that makes the patent seem obvious or not novel. The inventor's conduct is also closely examined for fraud or other inequitable conduct that might help invalidate the patent. Some upstart companies actively solicit prior art to help invalidate bad patents.

ONLINE

BountyQuest patent information service
http://bountyquest.com

IP is highly regulated because it is clearly a form of monopoly and remains an exception to the general public policy disfavoring monopolies. Indeed, many IP professionals carefully avoid using the term *monopoly* because most people feel that monopolies are exploitive. Owners of all forms of IP, but particularly patents, may be tempted to extend their patent monopoly to other things that are not protected by IP laws. This is called a **misuse** of the patent. Misuse is a defense to patent infringement and may also be a separate, illegal act under antitrust laws. Antitrust law and patent misuse are discussed in detail in Chapter 19.

Two additional infringement defenses deserve brief mention. Infringement suits are not well limited by statutes of limitations. The six-year limitation on damages or injunctive relief restarts as to each new wrongful act of infringement: producing, selling, offering for sale, or using an infringing embodiment or process. Although suit on some very old acts of infringement may be barred, the continuing nature of infringement usually assures that the patent holder will still have a remedy. Nevertheless, the equitable concept of **laches** may be used to bar an infringement suit if it is delayed too long. Recall the **first sale doctrine** in copyright law that permits buyers of a copyrighted work to resell. This doctrine also applies to embodiments containing patented parts or produced using a patented process.

REMEDIES

The right to exclude others from making, using, or selling a patented invention would be hollow without fairly reliable remedies to enforce these rights. Patent remedies closely parallel those for copyrights discussed in detail in Chapter 15: (1) equitable relief by injunctions and (2) legal remedies in the form of lost profits, reasonable royalties, a form of punitive damages, interest on damages, and attorneys' fees. Typically, the patent owner must first prove infringement as discussed in the previous section. Then, a remedies phase is conducted in the infringement litigation that often raises additional complex issues. Both equitable and legal relief are appropriate in many instances. (See Exhibit 17.3.)

EQUITABLE REMEDIES

Court orders to cease the infringement are important because they can be more immediate. First, the patent owner may seek a **preliminary injunction** at an abbreviated hearing. The four equitable elements must be proved: (1) likelihood of success at a full trial held later on the merits of the infringement case, (2) the patent owner will suffer irreparable harm unless the infringer's conduct is stopped immediately, (3) the hardships on the patent owner and the alleged infringer are balanced, and (4) the public interest is considered. At one time, preliminary injunctions were difficult to obtain, but this has changed in recent years. A full trial on the infringement questions must be held before a **permanent injunction** is issued. An injunction is dissolved after the patent expires.

LEGAL REMEDIES

A court evaluating infringement may choose from several measures of monetary damages: (1) lost profits, (2) reasonable royalty, (3) treble damages, and (4) attorneys' fees. Remember the difficulties of determining these measures of compensatory damages for copyright infringement, as discussed in Chapter 15. Lost profits

EXHIBIT 17.3 Remedies for Patent Infringement

Remedy	Definition of Remedy	Impact of Remedy
Preliminary injunction	Temporary court order prohibiting infringement until full trial; must prove: (1) likelihood of success, (2) irreparable harm, (3) balancing of hardships, and (4) public interest	Prevents alleged infringer from continuing acts of alleged infringement until full trial; dissolved after full trial
Permanent injunction	Court order following full trial on merits of case; prohibits further infringement; must prove infringement	Prevents infringer from making, using, or selling infringing products or process; dissolved after patent expires
Lost profits	Projection of profits patent holder would have made if infringer's competition had not diverted sales; may include price erosion—lower profitability on patent holder's sales	Requires reasonable prediction of additional sales patent holder would have made without the infringement; not available if reasonable royalty is awarded
Reasonable royalty	Projection of royalties patent holder might have made if infringer had negotiated license; may base on rates from recent licenses on similar technologies or patent holder's standard royalty rate	May require hypothetical "negotiation" of license fees; not available if lost profits are awarded
Treble damages	Assessed in addition to other damages if infringement is willful	Strong deterrent to infringement
Attorneys' fees	Assessed in addition to other damages if infringement is willful	Most fully compensates patent holder for expense of defending patent

arise when the court can reasonably predict that the patent owner would have made additional sales if competition from the infringer's products had not diverted sales. Another component of these damages is **price erosion**, which involves another forecast of damages in which the higher prices the patent owner "might have received" are projected if the infringing products had not competed. As was discussed in greater detail in Chapter 15, all these profitability measures require estimates of costs and overhead, which can be quite contentious, arbitrary, and speculative. Two alternative measures of royalties are possible: (1) a **reasonable royalty** based on rates used in recent agreements concerning similar technologies and (2) an **established royalty** computed at a rate the patent owner is already charging other licensees. Patent owners may recover either lost profits or royalties but not both. However, treble damages and attorneys' fees may be assessed in addition to compensatory damages if the infringement is willful.

INTERNATIONAL REMEDIES

Since the 1980s, trade relations with other nations have changed significantly by international treaties and by U.S. law. Several laws now improve the U.S. patent owner's remedies for infringement from activities in foreign nations. For example, §337 of the Tariff Act authorizes the U.S. Customs Service to block importation of infringing goods. The special 301 powers of the Omnibus Trade and Competitiveness Act authorize the U.S. Trade Representative (USTR) to monitor foreign nations suspected of repeated infringement. Under §301 of that Act, the USTR can negotiate stronger IP protections in other nations and impose trade sanctions on nations that are the source of repeated infringement. Finally, the **Process Patent Amendments of**

1988 make it an infringement to import goods produced using patented processes if the patent owner has not authorized use of the process. The law is complex and includes due diligence so that resellers are not excessively burdened. International patent remedies are summarized in Exhibit 17.4.

SUI GENERIS PROTECTIONS

Several additional types of IP protections have been added to the law in the United States and other nations to protect unique forms of property. For example, recall from Chapter 16 that a new form of IP is currently proposed for the U.S. to protect databases. These new forms of IP are often called **sui generis** (pronounced "sue-eye generous"), meaning unique, special, or original. Sui generis subject matter does not usually fit neatly into the subject matter acceptable in the existing fields of copyright, trademark, patent, or trade secret. Also, political pressures may prevent the inclusion of sui generis subject matter because the protection might be too great. For example, databases are not well protected under copyright law because they represent public domain ideas and often have little creativity. Similarly, databases do not fit well in patent law because the information they contain is often in the public domain. Furthermore, expanding copyright or patent law to protect databases might not be politically acceptable because the very long term of copyright protection or the strong protection of patent law could stifle research.

Three sui generis forms of IP are discussed here: (1) design patents, (2) plant patents, and (3) semiconductor chip (mask works). Additional sui generis forms are not detailed here but may arise from time to time in other nations, such as in Europe with the European database protection, the German **petty patent**, and the Japanese **utility model.** These rights protect industrial designs that are not well protected in the United States.

DESIGN PATENTS

Congress authorized design patents for ornamental objects to encourage the elimination of unsightly industrial mechanical devices. They created a separate type of patentable subject matter for ornamental design that is fixed in an article of manufacture under §171 of the Patent Law.

EXHIBIT 17.4 Patent Infringement Remedies under International Trade Law

Trade Law	Impact on Patent Infringement Remedies
§337, Tariff Act	Authorizes International Trade Commission (ITC) hearings and findings; may issue exclusion order directing U.S. Customs Service to block imports of infringing products
Special 301, Omnibus Trade and Competitiveness Act	Authorizes the U.S. Trade Representative (USTR) annual review of foreign nations' acts, policies & practices affecting U.S. IP; various watch lists signal dissatisfaction; closely monitor or trigger investigation and possible trade sanctions; successfully raising IP protection in several nations
§301	Authorizes USTR to investigate and negotiate trade agreements to enforce IP rights
§271(g), Process Patent Amendments	Creates new infringement remedy against importer of goods produced using patented processes if unauthorized; due diligence procedures for importers and resellers

Design Patents under §171

Whoever invents any new, original, and ornamental design for an article of manufacture may obtain a patent therefore, subject to the conditions and requirements of this title.

Design patents differ somewhat from utility patents. First, design patents are intended to encourage the decorative arts by protecting ornamental designs on useful articles. Second, the term of protection is 14 years from issuance rather than the 20 years from filing used for utility patents. They do not protect the useful aspects of inventions. Third, the ornamentation must generally be visible during normal use. By contrast, an invention, including a utility patent, may well hide the patented aspect as a component. For example, the novel decoration on a sports shoe achieves its purpose when seen. However, the utility of a patented fuel injection pump is typically hidden inside the engine of a vehicle when it is working as intended. Fourth, infringement analysis requires a perspective more like copyright or trademark—a comparison of similarities in the overall appearance between the patented article and the alleged infringing article. Further, the test is for similarities as perceived by an ordinary observer. Finally, the application procedure to acquire a design patent is much simpler to complete than is a utility patent application. The primary focus is on whether the drawings accurately capture the design rather than on verbal descriptions of functions, as are needed for a utility invention.

There is an important limitation on design patents: Only ornamental designs are protected, so the patented design cannot serve primarily a functional purpose. Patented ornamental designs may have functional aspects but the design cannot be dictated by the functional needs. Designers are often advised that to better assure design patentability of the ornamental design, it should be made severable from its functional aspects. This controversy is similar to the severability discussion about trademarks in Chapter 18.

Conjure up an image of the bicycle rack that is simply a multiple s-shaped metal tube fixed into the ground, usually set in concrete. This item would seem to be the perfect example of the merger of "form into function." However, there is no practical way to separate the ornamental curves from the functional bike slots, so the bike rack is probably not a patentable design. By contrast, the ornamental design of soles on athletic shoes was held patentable despite the function of the sole in the shoe.[23]

Design and utility patents share several aspects. First, the PTO is the regulator that qualifies both types of patents. Second, both must be qualified under similar novelty and nonobviousness standards. However, the relevant scope of prior art for design patents is broader, including anything with similar appearance regardless of its function. Third, similar processes are followed. **Double patenting** is generally prohibited; a single item cannot receive both a utility and design patent. This is not to say that a particular article of manufacture might not have various patents on some of its components. For example, the typical computer is protected under several patents. However, the component protected as a utility patent must be separate from the portions of the article covered by the design patent.

Modern design patent problems include the visual aspects of computers, software, websites, and e-commerce screens. Many observers argue that design patents are an imperfect protection scheme for industrial designs. Designers should explore whether trademark, trade dress, or copyright protection might be an alternative to design patent protection in some instances.

23. *Avia Group Int'l v. L.A. Gear California, Inc.*, 853 F.2d 1557 (Fed.Cir., 1988).

PLANT PATENTS

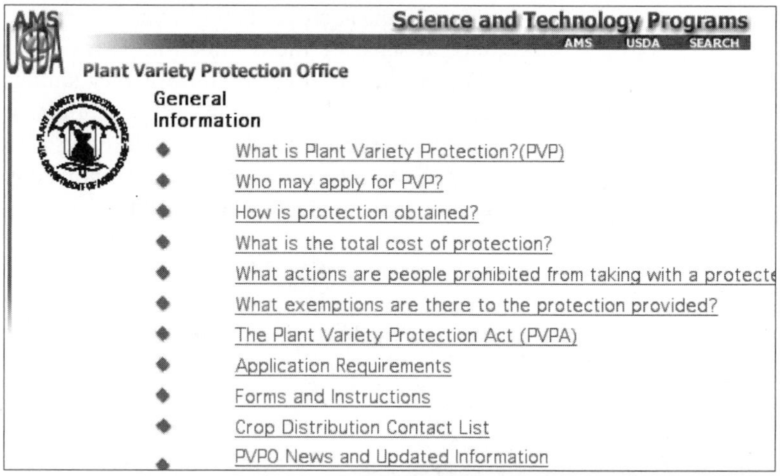

Science and Technology Programs
AMS USDA SEARCH
Plant Variety Protection Office
General Information
- What is Plant Variety Protection?(PVP)
- Who may apply for PVP?
- How is protection obtained?
- What is the total cost of protection?
- What actions are people prohibited from taking with a protect
- What exemptions are there to the protection provided?
- The Plant Variety Protection Act (PVPA)
- Application Requirements
- Forms and Instructions
- Crop Distribution Contact List
- PVPO News and Updated Information

http://
www.ams.usda.gov/science/pvpo/pvp.htm

The United States has two sui generis laws to protect plants. They are different systems administered by two different regulatory agencies. These two sui generis schemes predated the third basis for plant protection, utility patents, which became available under the landmark *Chakrabarty* ruling discussed previously and as clarified in 2001.[24]

The first scheme is administered by the U.S. PTO. Under the **Plant Patent Act** of 1930, plant patents are an extension of utility patent procedures. They provide patent protection to distinct, new, asexually reproduced plant varieties. **Asexual reproduction** includes horticultural techniques such as the rooting of cuttings, layering, budding, and grafting. Reproduction of plants from seeds and reproduction of bacteria are not covered. The patentability standards of novelty and nonobviousness are generally applicable. The term of protection is 20 years after filing, just like utility patents. Successful plant patent applications concentrate more on the adequacy and quality of color drawings than do utility patents. The drawings must reveal all the new variety's distinctive characteristics.

ONLINE
PTO's Plant Patent information
http://www.uspto.gov/web/offices/pac/plant/

The second form of sui generis plant protection was created by the 1970 **Plant Variety Protection Act.** This law protects sexually reproduced plant varieties. This technique involves cross-pollination that creates a hybrid in the next generation. Patentability standards are much reduced; there is no nonobviousness requirement. The act is administered by an agency of the Department of Agriculture's Agricultural Marketing Service. The Plant Variety Protection Office examines applications and issues plant variety protection certificates. Fungi and bacteria are excluded but may receive utility patent protection. Protection lasts for 18 years.

SEMICONDUCTOR CHIP PROTECTIONS

The Semiconductor Chip Protection Act was passed in 1984 to provide sui generis protection for **mask works,** the microscopic electronic circuit schematic diagram containing thousands of transistors as found in integrated circuits. Their development requires considerable time and investment, but they are easy to copy and pirate. Copyright and patent law standards and processes were unsuitable for the short useful lives of semiconductor chips. Chips are useful articles inseparable from their graphical design. While seemingly appropriate for patent protection, they are more like expression covered by copyright. Congress created a sui generis protection administered by the Copyright Office to protect the investment in chip design, essentially a form of programming. The term *mask* is used because chip making is essentially a photographic technique. The mask is a diagram of each layer of the chip's

24. *J.E.M. AG Supply v. Pioneer Hi-Bred Int'l.,* 121 S.Ct. 2566 (2001).

wiring. The mask stops the light used to etch the tiny circuit pathways into a silicon wafer that separate the conducting pathways from the insulating parts.

The act has standards that are very similar to copyright law. For example, the mask work must be fixed in a chip product, it must represent original design that was created independently, the underlying ideas are not protected, a first sale doctrine applies, and a form of fair use permits copying for teaching, analysis, or evaluation. Further, there is no rigorous qualification as is required for patents. The mask work designer, usually a chip manufacturing firm, must register the work with the U.S. Copyright Office. Mask work protection provides a limited bundle of rights to reproduce, sell and license or assign. Protection lasts for ten years after registration or it is first exploited commercially.

QUESTIONS

1. Explain how patent protection differs from copyrights and trade secrets. What are the possible forms of subject matter? How long does protection last? What regulators are involved? Describe their relative strengths and weaknesses. Why choose one form over another? What are the qualifications to get protection under each system?
2. Identify, define, and discuss the four major forms of subject matter that can be patented. What are they? Define them and give examples. How do they overlap?
3. The '184 patent simply adds a data field to the data burst that accompanies long-distance telephone calls. It permits differential billing treatment for subscribers, depending on which among several potential long-distance companies the caller has selected as the primary service provider. It enables various marketing programs, similar to MCI's "Friends and Family" discount program and also permits various billing and record-keeping innovations. Is this system patentable as a method of doing business? Why or why not? See *ATT Corp. v. Excel Communications, Inc.*, 172 F.3d 1352 (Fed.Cir.), *cert.denied* 120 S.Ct. 368 (Oct. 12, 1999).
4. Alex conceives of a new mechanism that shortens the time needed to clean engine parts undergoing renovation. Alex has a day job and cannot afford the time or money needed to develop the idea, build a working prototype, or prosecute an expensive patent application anytime soon. Nevertheless, he continues to tinker with his invention and eventually reduces it to practice two years later by using a pay bonus he received from his employer. However, during this two-year period, the LD Corp.'s R&D Dept. solves the cleaning problem by reducing to practice a nearly identical invention. LD files for a patent before Alex. Who is entitled to the patent and why?
5. Sections 102 and 103 of the Patent Act define the two major patentability criteria. They also effectively define the public domain. Explain how the prior art affects patentability, explain from whose perspective the prior art is judged, and discuss the function of the U.S. PTO in protecting the public domain during patent examination.
6. Arrhythmia Research Technology, Inc., received a patent for a method to analyze electrocardiograph signals to detect when a heart attack patient might soon suffer a dangerous arrhythmia condition. Early detection can help signal the need for treatment that could be lifesaving. The process patent describes the interception of electrical signals and the application of a mathematical formula on the signal, whereupon the result is compared with predetermined values taken from research showing how to evaluate whether the arrhythmia condition is imminent. Should Arrhythmia's patent be invalidated as embracing an algorithm or law of nature? Explain. See *Arrhythmia Research Technology, Inc. v. Corazonix Corp.*, 958 F.2d 1053 (Fed.Cir., 1992).
7. What is the function of secrecy given patent applications during their processing of patent prosecution? What are the arguments for and against such secrecy? How has the United States changed its patent application secrecy laws? Why were these changes made?
8. The East Corp. holds a patent on the process of making industrial conveyor pulley wheels from steel that is highly resistant to wear. Manufacturing systems using East pulleys are much less prone to breakdown;

their assembly lines do not need to be shut down as often, and this translates into considerably higher productivity than for manufacturing plants using pulley wheels from other makers. East Corp.'s sales have not increased as much as expected, so its field sales staff has asked several former customers why they are not switching to East Corp.'s new pulley wheels. One customer showed a foreign-made pulley wheel that appeared to have the same wear resistance characteristics as those made with the East Corp. patented process. What if East Corp. can prove the imported pulley wheels were made in foreign factories by using East Corp.'s patented process but without authority from East Corp.? What are East Corp.'s alternatives to deal with this infringement?

9. Explain how the doctrine of equivalents makes the protection of a patent larger and more effective than when an allegedly infringing product is analyzed under the standards of literal infringement.

10. There are several sui generis protections for various types of IP. Explain the major sui generis laws, describe their subject matter, explain why these subjects are not well protected by other forms of IP (e.g., copyright, patent), compare their duration of protections, and identify the regulatory agencies responsible for administering these programs.

CHAPTER 18

Trademarks

Commercial symbols are powerful tools that build and enhance brand image. Firms spend a lot on their brand images: (1) advertising to stay in the public's consciousness and (2) developing easily recognized logos and other unique identifiers that conjure up favorable memories to trigger repeat transactions. Indeed, much of a firm's goodwill directly results from the brand image sustained by the firm's name, commercial symbols, and reputation. Commercial symbols use imagery and mental pictures to communicate a firm's reputation and thereby distinguish the product's source and qualities from competitors or substitutes. Their vivid verbal descriptions and visual images are enhanced with artistic, literary, or musical expression. Commercial symbols make easy, direct, and influential connections with memories that can reliably direct purchasing decisions.

Trademarks are the most valuable form of modern commercial symbols. Trademarks are a subset of commercial symbols that receive legal protection under the federal laws (e.g., Lanham Act), state common law, and state statutes. Think of a **trademark** as a commercial symbol, word, name, or other device that identifies and distinguishes the products of a particular firm. Trademark law entitles the owner of the trademark, or **mark**, to prevent others, both competitors and those in other industries, from using the trademark to market their products. The principles of trademark infringement illustrate that there are a few exceptions: similar marks for very different products owned by different firms (e.g., Yahoo! chocolate drink vs. Yahoo! Internet portal, Lexis on-line research portal vs. Lexus automobiles). Trademarks are used to help customers find, identify, and distinguish the products of individual firms. Trademarks are the central organizing principle for franchises, detailed in Chapter 13.

This chapter covers trademarks, related intellectual property (IP) rights including trade dress and trademark-related unfair competition, and the trademark implications of the Internet. Trademark law is a complex and challenging area because the standards of analysis and much of the case law are based on artistic and cognitive judgments about human perception and commercial behavior. Increasingly, social science research is needed to prove the impact of trademarks on consumer perceptions and activities. Indeed, market research based on consumer behavior is becoming an important tool in trademark litigation and in administrative determinations by the U.S. Patent and Trademark Office (PTO).

Commentary

Trademarks Meet the Internet

Trademarking seems like a great way to create uniqueness, but how much of a business can be linked to commercial symbols? How many aspects of a firm's products will trademark law protect? Consider an important modern example: the power of websites and their commercial symbols to "connect" with so many people. The most memorable aspects of websites are the domain names users need to visit. These are computerized telecommunications addresses, the "root word" of a universal resource locator (URL). Users can fairly easily remember URLs and type them into a browser to view or download website material. Many URLs are hidden within the hyperlinks of websites. URLs were originally designed to permit convenient access to websites, not to serve as trademarks. However, domain names are clearly commercial symbols, and they have many and sometimes all of the attributes of trademarks. Should trademark owners have the exclusive right to domain names identical or closely similar to their trademarks? The Internet raises the importance of commercial symbols in building brand image, expanding the traditional role for trademarks.

NATURE OF TRADEMARK AS AN INTELLECTUAL PROPERTY RIGHT

Trademarks differ conceptually from other forms of IP such as patents, trade secrets, or copyrights. The constitutional and economic rationales for most other forms of IP are based on two premises: (1) The limited IP monopoly is a powerful incentive to creativity that ultimately benefits society, and (2) IP is really a contract between government and innovators in that a limited monopoly is given in exchange for disclosure of details describing the innovative design. By contrast, trademark policy rewards investment in goodwill only as a byproduct of preventing consumer deception. Indeed, trademark law provides little reward to the visual artist who uses creative imagination and aesthetic skills to design the commercial symbol. Many well-known trademarks were the product of only nominal compensation given to an employee who won a contest to rename the firm; for example, the Standard Oil Co. of New Jersey changed from Humble Oil to Exxon, and Andersen Consulting became Accenture.

GOALS OF TRADEMARK LAW

Trademark law balances four broad goals: (1) the promotion of business ethics, (2) the refinement of distributional efficiency, (3) the development and maintenance of goodwill, and (4) the preservation of competition by expanding the public domain. These broad goals are implemented by three main trademark concepts that pervade this chapter: inherent distinctiveness, likelihood of consumer confusion, and functionality.

First, trademarks promote business ethics. They discourage competitors' promotional activities that weaken the link between a commercial symbol and the firm it represents. Trademark policy evolved from the common law of unfair competition. Competitors may not deceive or confuse consumers about the origin or nature of their products by pretending their products are related to a more reputable firm. Trademarks enable a firm to accurately and exclusively identify itself as the source of particular products. Trademark owners have the right to prevent others from free-riding on the trademark owner's promotional expenses. For example, enforceable trademarks help prevent competitors from palming off their inferior products, such as a competitor that pretends its products were really produced by the trademark owner. These laws may also prevent a counterfeiter from knocking off products protected by a trademark with look-alike imitations. Trademark owners use the infringement remedy to assert these rights.

Second, trademarks enhance distributional efficiency. Buyers and sellers often expend considerable resources to do their business together. Sellers have large advertising, sales, and promotional expense. Many smart buyers spend considerable time and sometimes even money to research product performance before making purchases. Effective use of trademarks helps reduce search costs to connect buyers and sellers. Buyers can more quickly, easily, and cheaply find sellers using well-known trademarks to avoid making purchase mistakes. Commercial symbols more directly associate the seller's products with that seller's reputation. For example, the McDonald's golden arches can be spotted by motorists even when they are driving quickly along a busy Interstate highway. Motorists' search costs to find a fast food restaurant are lower when the golden arches are so reliably and safely located.

Third, trademark law encourages investment in brand image. The incentive to invest in goodwill would diminish without some assurance that firms would capture the benefits of their investments in making their products uniform in quality. Trademark law helps to prevent unfair competition when a competitor passes off its products as produced by another seller. Consumers clearly benefit from investments in quality. Markets function better when the seller's reputation becomes a primary method to communicate accurate marketing information. For example, if all automakers could use the three-pointed star logo on their cars, Mercedes-Benz could have less incentive to produce high-quality cars. Note that the investment in uniform product quality encouraged by trademark law is often different from the investment in innovation encouraged by patent and copyright law. Investments in quality under trademark incentives need not result in new technologies to the same extent that IP investment encourages R&D efforts to develop new technology.

Finally, there are limitations on trademarks to encourage active competition. Some words, descriptions, or symbols are necessary for all competitors to adequately and accurately describe their products. Therefore, no one should acquire a trademark monopoly over the clearest descriptive terms or images for a particular product. Such a trademark would give its owner an unfair advantage over competitors who could not adequately describe their competing products. As a result, trademark law prohibits the registration of generic trademarks, thereby leaving the major descriptive terms for that type of product in the public domain for use by all competitors. For example, if Sony held a trademark to the term TV, other TV makers would be at a significant disadvantage. Finally, protection should not extend to functional aspects of trademarks, elements that affect the purpose, action, or performance of the product. Trademark protection of such functional or useful characteristics would conflict with the balance drawn under patent law by denying competitors the use of key operating elements.

SOURCES OF TRADEMARK LAW

Unlike federal patent and copyright law, the congressional power to enact federal trademark law is not generally based on the IP clause of the U.S. Constitution.[1] Recall that the IP clause, found in Article I, §8, authorizes IP legislation only "To

1. *Trademark cases*, 100 U.S. 82 (1879).

promote the Progress of Science and useful Arts, by securing for limited times to Authors and Inventors the exclusive Right to their respective Writings and Discoveries." The main purpose of trademark law is not directly related to this grant. Instead, trademark law is derived from the state law of unfair competition. Therefore, Congress's legislative power for trademark law is based on the commerce clause to regulate interstate commerce.

The regulation of unfair competition began in state common law and spread to both state and federal statutes on trademarks; it also includes palming off and dilution statutes. Early cases applied equitable principles to prohibit unfair competitive activities that hinder competition through the use of deceptive, improper, or unfair methods of competition. These laws hold that consumers are harmed when one seller pretends its goods are made by a competitor. This is **free riding** on the other firm's reputation, and it harms both consumers and the competitor. Today, trademarks are protected under state common law and state statutes of unfair competition. In addition, many states permit trademark registration.

State trademark law has been significantly supplemented by federal trademark laws enacted in 1870, 1881, and 1905. The **Lanham Act** of 1947 is the primary federal trademark law in force today. It was revised in 1988 and again in 1996. There is stronger protection under the Lanham Act for trademarks used in interstate commerce. Federal trademarks are registered with the PTO. Applications for trademark registration are subject to **qualification**; that is, applicants should conduct a search to assure their proposed trademark is not already used by another. The applicant's trademark counsel gives an opinion of the uniqueness of the proposed trademark, and then PTO examiners also search to confirm the trademark's uniqueness.

Many protections of state and federal trademark law apply even to unregistered marks. However, registration facilitates stronger rights and remedies. Registration is important to strengthen international rights for exclusive use of the trademark in foreign nations. Trademark-related legislation is summarized in Exhibit 18.1. Some aspects of the commercial symbols covered by trademark law may also be protected by copyright or as design patents.

INTERNATIONAL TRADEMARK LAW

International trademark rights are becoming increasingly important as some nations try to recapture their cultural and national symbols or prevent counterfeit branded goods from flooding their markets. Foreign nations' trademark laws differ; protection is often given to the firm that first registered the mark, not the firm that used the trademark first, as in the United States. Firms entering international commerce must assess the desired strength for their trademarks in foreign markets, both in nations where they intend to sell products and in nations where competitive products might be produced.

International organizations are important in international trademark matters. For example, affiliated trading groups such as NAFTA and the EU are trying to harmonize trademark protections. Master international trade treaties negotiated through GATT and the WIPO are working toward uniformity. Three multilateral treaties have direct impact on trademarks. The **Paris Convention** gives reciprocity for each separate nation's treatment of trademarks but grants few substantive rights, lacks a centralized registration or filing system, and lacks effective enforcement mechanisms. The **Madrid Agreement** and the **Madrid Protocol** have yet to have major influence but hold some promise for harmonization. The **Trademark Law Treaty** was a 1994 product of the WIPO, and the U.S. Congress passed legislation in 1998 to conform U.S. procedures to this treaty.

EXHIBIT 18.1 Applicability of Trademark Laws

Trademark Law	Basic Provisions	Applicable in Which Jurisdictions
State unfair competition statutes and common law	Prohibits: unfair competition, palming or passing off, dilution	Limited to activities affecting interests in that state
State trademark statutes	Trademark registration, qualification, infringement, remedies	Limited to activities affecting interests in the state of enactment
Lanham Act of 1943	Trademark registration, qualification, infringement, remedies; enables PTO regulation	U.S. interstate commerce and foreign activities with substantial impact within the U.S.
Federal Trademark Dilution Act of 1996	Extends state antidilution remedies to famous marks throughout the U.S.	U.S. interstate commerce and foreign activities with substantial impact within the U.S.
Anti-Cybersquatting Protection Act of 1999 (ACPA)	Prohibits domain name pirating or ransom	U.S. interstate commerce and foreign activities with substantial impact within the U.S.
Trademark System of the European Union	Trademark Law Harmonization Directive of 1988 requires EU nations to pass uniform legislation on trademark subject matter and grounds to refuse registration and defines trademark rights; Community Trademark System of 1993 permits central registration	All 13 EU member nations
Paris Convention	Requires national treatment to foreigners from signatory nations, protection for marks well known in signatory nation	In all signatory nations that implement the treaty's provision with national legislation (U.S.)
Madrid Agreement and Madrid Protocol of 1996	Permits central filing after registration in home nation	In all signatory nations that implement the treaty's provision with national legislation (U.S.-Protocol)
Trademark Law Treaty	Restructures and simplifies trademark registration procedures in signatory nations	In all signatory nations that implement the treaty's provision with national legislation (U.S.)
ICANN Uniform Domain Name Resolution Process	ADR process to settle rightful trademark preemption of domain name registration	All nations bound by WIPO treaties

TRADEMARK SUBJECT MATTER

Trademarks, also known as marks, may consist of words, names, symbols, devices, or any combination of these elements. Cases have expanded this list to include other elements, including slogans, numbers, colors, smells, sounds, and the overall design of a product's package or the vendor's premises. For example, many of the images used on websites are potential subject matter of trademark or trade dress. There is a trend to include new types of elements if they help to distinguish the vendor's products from competitors. It is often necessary to examine what particular products are sold under the mark in question in the analysis of both the subject matter of marks and their distinctiveness.

WORDS, TITLES, NUMERALS, ABBREVIATIONS, AND SLOGANS

Single words and short groups of words are among the most common forms of marks. Single words, titles, abbreviations, and nicknames are all eligible to become marks if they are distinctive. For example, the abbreviation BMW for Bavarian Motor Works is eligible because consumers readily recognize that the abbreviation relates to the firm as a manufacturer of automobiles. Pepsi is eligible as a nickname for Pepsi-Cola.

Titles of literary or other entertainment works generally cannot become registered marks because they describe the contents of those publications. However, titles that are arbitrary, suggestive, or have secondary meaning can be registered. Titles to literary or other entertainment works might also be registered for use on companion goods such as clothing or toys.[2] The use of names is problematic because the Lanham Act conditionally excludes marks that are "primarily merely a surname." **Conditional exclusion** means that names might be trademarked if they are mixed with other words or have acquired secondary meaning (discussed later).

Letters, numerals, and other typeface characters and symbols may be combined to create marks if they are distinctive and not mainly descriptive of the product. It is common practice to use alphanumeric characters that distinguish models of automobiles or electronics as produced by particular manufacturers. However, they cannot be trademarked if these letters and numerals are used to clearly identify product specifications from among several with differing characteristics. For example, if model numbers are intentionally chosen to refer to a progression of increasing size specifications in the product, they are descriptive and not protectable. Protection can be lost if competitors in the industry use similar numerals to designate their competing products (e.g., Intel's 386 CPU chips).

Slogans and groups of words are also eligible. Slogans could lose their distinctiveness if they are too long to be easily remembered, are buried in text, or mostly convey promotional information. Nevertheless, long slogans may still be copyrightable as advertising copy. A trademarked slogan can validly contain components that are separate marks; the mark "Coke" is part of the slogan "Coke is it," and "Allstate" is used in "You're in good hands with Allstate." To become registered marks, all words, phrases, abbreviations, and slogans must be distinctive.

SENSORY ELEMENTS: DISTINCTIVE SHAPE, COLOR, ODOR, OR SOUND

Trademarks need not be expressed only in text or graphic images. A common and distinctive element in corporate logos is shape. There are also **design marks** that use some nontext elements, such as oval borders, unique fonts, and geometric designs to serve as backgrounds to word marks. These elements contribute to the distinctiveness of many trademarks. Shape may not be merely ornamental. Shapes must create a commercial impression separate from the word mark. Consider the traditional Coke bottle. It uses a vertically ribbed, hourglass shape as its design mark. Even the location of a label might be recognized by consumers as the distinctive element for the producing firm, and therefore it acquired secondary meaning, as discussed later. For example, the red fabric tab on the right rear pocket of Levi's jeans is a trademark separate from the LEVI mark stitched to the tab.[3] However, the Levi's tab did

2. *Lucasfilm, Ltd. v. High Frontier*, 622 F.Supp. 931 (D.D.C. 1985).
3. *Levi Strauss & Co. v. Blue Bell, Inc.*, 632 F.2d 817 (9th Cir., 1980).

not transfer into a different market, for shirts, where the Levi's tab on the front pocket was not protected as a separate mark.[4]

Other sensory elements can also be used as trademarks or as components of trademarks, including distinctive color, odor, or sound. Color patterns or shapes have long qualified as components of design marks. In recent years, color standing alone, even without being part of a fixed pattern, may also be protectable.[5] For example, color was distinctive when applied to replacement fabric covers for ironing presses in commercial laundries.[6] Critics charge that permitting color trademarks, apart from a graphic symbol or design, could eventually deplete the limited number of available colors in the palette. The protection of color marks may depend on consumer ability to differentiate between subtle shades and hues, a difficult task.

Smells can be registered if they are distinctive and not the product's major feature. For example, scented embroidery yarn was held registrable.[7] However, the scents of particular perfumes are not likely to be trademarkable because their smell actually describes the product's main characteristic. Although smell may not seem to be relevant as a trademark in e-commerce, someday computers may have an electronic odor transducer that could transmit an aroma sample. Finally, sounds may now be trademarked. Other motorcycle manufacturers cannot meticulously copy the distinctive rumble of a Harley-Davidson motorcycle in their attempts to duplicate the "hog" experience. Use of distinctive sounds on the Internet may further extend the protectability of sounds as marks. Electronic transducers of aroma are becoming possible so if PCs become equipped with them, trademarked smells might become associated with websites.

CHARACTERS AND CELEBRITIES

The personae of characters and celebrities can be powerful marketing tools. Consider the power of cartoon characters to capture repeat business for related products such as theme park admissions, movie attendance, and video sales and for sales of toys, clothing, music, and food (Disney, Warner Bros.). Similarly, the endorsement of famous artists, musicians, or sports figures enhances advertising and brand image (Britney Spears, Michael Jordan). Characters may appear in works that are literary or entertainment or on the Internet. Trademark protection may extend to a character's name, nickname, or outward appearance, but not to their traits or talents.

Certain elements of a celebrity's persona may be trademarked, including their look, dress, actions, and sound. The line separating trademark or unfair competition aspects of celebrity rights from their privacy rights is fuzzy. Digital technologies to morph or simulate a character or celebrity in video or on-line performances will probably raise both trademark and privacy risks if celebrity images are used without license. The privacy aspects of celebrities are discussed further in Chapter 14, and the licensing aspects are discussed in Chapter 13. Clearly, many video games and websites use characters extensively as part of entertainment and to distinguish themselves from other websites.

---

4. *Levi Strauss & Co. v. Blue Bell, Inc.*, 778 F.2d 1357 (9th Cir., 1985).

5. *In re Owens-Corning Fibreglas*, 774 F.2d 966 (Fed.Cir., 1985) (pink for fiberglass insulation was distinctive, not functional).

6. *Qualitex Co. v. Jacobson Products Co., Inc.*, 514 U.S. 159 (1995).

7. *In re Clarke*, 17 USPQ2d 1238 (TTAB, 1990).

TRADE DRESS

Trademark law can also protect the combination of visual design elements used in the overall appearance of a product, its labels and packaging, the business's premises, or a website's distinctive look and feel. These visual design features are known as **trade dress**. They cover the way the product or service is "dressed up" and creates a total image. To serve as a protectable mark, the trade dress must be distinctive and indicate that the mark owner is the source of the products. For example, trade dress is a major element of many consumer product franchise businesses. Consider how McDonald's restaurants have a uniform look: rectangular red brick building, yellow accents, golden arches (a separate mark) where permitted by local zoning ordinances, uniform service counter, and similar dining room design.

Trade dress is a very broad and vague term because it includes an arrangement of many elements: size, shape, three-dimensional design, ornamentation, color scheme, sounds, and smells. Trade dress for restaurants or taverns includes the emotional, sensory, and aesthetic elements of mood, environment, air, and atmosphere—all part of the "ambience." Trade dress is not merely decoration but must make a commercial impression. It seems likely that trade dress will become even more important as a feature of standardized website design.

Several factors are used in determining whether trade dress is inherently distinctive.[8] First, distinctiveness is more likely if the shapes and designs are uncommon. Second, the trade dress should be unusual in the market for that type of product. Third, simple refinements on traditional ornamentation used in that product's market are less likely to be distinctive. Trade dress cannot be functional when taken as a whole; that is, the whole look and feel should not be essential to the product's use or have a direct impact on the cost of production or the product's quality. Trade dress analysis considers all the trade dress components taken together as a whole.[9] The individual components may have functions if the whole of the trade dress is not functional. For example, the quarry floor tiles used in the Taco Cabana Mexican restaurants discussed later are functional: They seal the floor and provide a finished, decorative surface. However, the tile is only a component of the whole restaurant's ambience, a trade dress that is not functional and not necessary to operate a Mexican restaurant successfully. The analysis of functionality should inquire whether there are commercially feasible alternatives for a competitor's trade dress, whether the trade dress is the simplest and least costly means to manufacture, and whether the trade dress aspects (e.g., color) are inherent and therefore necessary for other competitors.[10] Functionality of website features may become problematic for the protection of website designs. For example, common color bars, clickable button locations, and locations for particular functionality (e.g., search box, terms and conditions, privacy policies) may eventually limit a website's ability to protect these elements as they become standard.

EXCLUDED AS INELIGIBLE SUBJECT MATTER

The Lanham Act prohibits registration of several types of marks. These marks can also be canceled or denied protection under the common law. First, **generic words**

---

8. *Lisa Frank, Inc. v. Impact International, Inc.*, 799 F.Supp. 980 (D.Ariz., 1992).
9. *Fuddruckers, Inc. v. Doc's B.R.Others, Inc.*, 826 F.2d 837 (9th Cir., 1987).
10. *Sega Enterprises Ltd. v. Accolade, Inc.*, 977 F.2d 1510 (9th Cir., 1992).

that are the common description of the product cannot be trademarked. This implements the fourth goal of trademark law: to maintain competition and safeguard the public domain. (Generic terms are discussed later.) Second, scandalous or immoral marks are disqualified. These are marks that are shocking to a sense of propriety and offensive to moral feelings, inspire condemnation by a large portion of the population, or refer inappropriately to religious matters. Unlike copyright, the First Amendment does not give the right to register immoral or scandalous marks, even if they are not obscene. Only a few cases interpret this provision. The following marks were disqualified as immoral or scandalous: "Madonna" as a brand name for wine,[11] a defecating dog as a satirical design mark for clothing,[12] and "Booby Trap" for feminine underwear (bras).[13]

Another class of ineligible subject matter includes fraudulent or deceptive marks. **Deceptive marks** falsely connect the product with persons, institutions, beliefs, or national symbols or cause them contempt or disrepute. They are deceptive if consumers are likely to be influenced by the connection. For example, it would be deceptive if a firm unconnected with the family of a famous army general used the general's name as a mark for rifles. A **deceptively misdescriptive** mark makes a false inference about an influential matter such as an inaccurate geographic origin. Much of the litigation over trademarks on the Internet concern deception in the use or descriptive power of marks (meta-tags).

Additional ineligible subjects include government insignia, flags, coats of arms, names, portraits, or signatures of any living person without their permission or of a deceased U.S. president during the life of the widow(er) without permission. Marks that are primarily geographic are ineligible unless they acquire secondary meaning. Such marks can include the names of states, cities, regions, geographic features, or their nicknames ("Big Apple"). If the products are not associated with the geographic place, then the mark is either deceptive or misdescriptive. Names are discussed later.

TYPES OF TRADEMARKS

Trademark law traditionally focused on marks that identified a single source or producer of goods. Eventually marks also became useful to identify services, uniform product characteristics from various producers and members of industry-wide organizations. In the narrowest sense of the term, *trademark* refers to a mark that distinguishes the source or origin (e.g., producing firm) of goods. As discussed further in Chapter 10, **goods** are tangible personal property (not real estate, employment or services). The Uniform Commercial Code (UCC) defines goods as "all that are movable at the time" of contracting." The Lanham Act's definition for *trademark* addresses only goods:

> **Trademark**
>
> any word, name, symbol, or device or any combination thereof . . . used by the producer or reseller . . . to identify and distinguish [its] goods, from those manufactured or sold by others and to indicate the source of the goods.[14]

11. *In re McGinley*, 660 F.2d 481 (CCPA, 1981).
12. *Greyhound Corp. v. Both Worlds, Inc.*, 6 U.S.P.Q. 863 (TTAB, 1988).
13. *In re Runsdorf*, 171 U.S.P.Q. 443 (PO TTAB, 1971).
14. 15 U.S.C. §1127; Lanham Act §45.

A trademark is generally registered in relation to a particular type of product or a line of related products. Legal questions about a mark are generally considered as they relate to use with particular types of products. For example, trademarks on particular goods include Pepsi® for various versions of soda pop, IBM ThinkPad® for a broad line of laptop PCs, Toyota Tundra® for pickup trucks with various body and drivetrain configurations, and Sony Diskman® for a line of somewhat different portable CD players. Trademarks registered with the PTO may be displayed with the "R in a circle" symbol right after the registered trademark: ®. Trademarks claimed under state common law or trademark statute may be displayed with the small capital letters "TM" right after the trademark: ™. Domain names function like marks but are not yet recognized under the Lanham Act as a separate category of mark. Mark owners must use notices, or they may not be able to sue for damages. Marks and domain names are discussed later.

SERVICE MARKS

Eventually, trademark law began to recognize that services have become a significant part of commerce and that marks should also protect services. The same questions of source identity, consumer confusion, and investment in quality control are important to markets for services, particularly in dispersed business systems like franchises. Indeed, the information age signals a shift from a predominance of goods transactions in the early twentieth century to a predominance of services in the twenty-first century.

What are services? Provisionally, consider **services** to be contracts in which the predominant value is derived from a customized application of human labor, expertise, and/or information. Service businesses perform human activity, manual labor, or professional practice. The sale of goods is at most a minor, incidental part of a service contract, such as the oil in an oil change, meat in a fast-food hamburger, or the shampoo used in hair styling. The Lanham Act does not define services, but the courts have defined the term expansively. For example, as consulting practices flourish, firms purchase customized "solutions" to operate their business systems.

A key factor in hastening the shift to service products is the characterization of information, software, and computer information as services and not as goods or real estate. Therefore, as the ingenuity of humans increases, services will probably be broadly defined and include activities beyond those in most common use today: lodging, restaurant, consulting, advertising, professional practices, entertainment, financial, software, information, transportation, and Web portals, as well as repairs and maintenance. Marks associated with services are registered under the Lanham Act "in the same manner and with the same effect as are trademarks" for goods.

Service Marks

any word, name, symbol, or device or any combination thereof [used to] identify and distinguish the services of one person . . . from the services of others and to indicate the source of the services, even if that source is unknown."[15]

A service mark is registered in relation to a particular type of product or a line of related services. For example, service marks used on particular services include McDonalds℠ for restaurant services, Mr. Goodwrench℠ for automotive maintenance

15. 15 U.S.C. §1053.

and repairs, and eBay℠ for auction and intermediary sales services. Note that many services include an incidental sale of goods: foodstuffs for restaurant services and parts for maintenance and repair services. Some of these goods may be trademarked separately, such as the Delco® or Delphi® parts used in GM's Mr. Goodwrench service or Boar's Head® cold cuts in a deli franchise like Schlotsky's.

Service marks are commonly used with franchise businesses, such as laundry, insurance, restaurants, fast lubes, and product service centers. In the future, product sales and performances may be directly made by computer. Automated performances most closely resemble services unless goods are the predominant output produced by the automated performance. Even if the human labor component declines in these automated performances, they are likely to be classified as services for service mark purposes. A service mark may be displayed with the small capital letters "SM" beside the service mark: ℠. It is a prerequisite to using the damage remedy.

Service Marks Must Be More Than Ancillary

Whether service marks can be registered is also limited by the principle that the public domain must be protected. Service marks must be more than merely ancillary; the service must be sufficiently separate from the sale of goods, and each service must be separately significant. This requirement is intended to prevent mark owners from registering excessive service marks to accompany their trademarked goods, which could result in "a whole raft of service mark registrations covering each and every 'service' that every other competitor also provides as an adjunct to the sale of goods."[16] This **more than ancillary rule** helps discourage trademark owners from creating an excessive number of service marks to cover services that other competitors must also necessarily provide. The problem is that competitors could be blocked from adequately promoting "generic" ancillary services if they are covered by ancillary service marks. For example, most full-service gasoline service stations perform oil changes and chassis lubrications, services provided by many other service stations. Service marks like "OilChanger" or "LubeJobber" are probably ancillary, so they should not be registered to only one oil company.

CERTIFICATION AND COLLECTIVE MARKS

Marks are important to indicate the sole source of products but are also useful to indicate more than just a *single* source. For example, franchises operate under systemwide service marks and trademarks. Franchises, detailed further in Chapter 13, are actually groups of independent businesses operating under a single set of quality control and operational guidance imposed by the franchisor, the mark owner.

Two more distinctive types of marks impose systemwide quality control, require uniform product origin, and/or impose operational guidance on independent entities: collective marks and certification marks. These marks should function in the same manner and with the same effect as trademarks. They are generally owned by independent parties and not by the "industrial or commercial" firm producing the products. Instead, they may be owned by "nations, states, municipalities and the like" if the noncommercial owner exercises "legitimate control over the use of the marks." These marks are not registered if the noncommercial owner misrepresents

16. See J. Thomas McCarthy, *Trademarks and Unfair Competition*, 2d ed. §19.30 (San Francisco: Lawyers Cooperative Publishing Co./Bancroft-Whitney, 1984).

that it is the actual producer. For example, regional government units in agricultural regions do not produce the foodstuffs under these marks. Instead, independent growers in that region produce the products under the auspices of the regional authority, such as California Raisin Growers.

Certification Marks

Certification marks certify that the products of all producers using the mark have the characteristics of the group operating under that certification mark. Mark owners cannot discriminate against or deny use of the mark as long as the producers meet the objective certification standards. Otherwise, the mark could be used to exclude disruptive competitors. Note in the **certification mark** definition that the mark's owner must be independent of the producers who produce their products. Otherwise, there could be conflicts of interest and increase the potential that the mark owner would not be objective in overseeing the matters certified. For example, if the state government of Florida owns the "OJ" certification mark, no state agency can either produce orange juice under the mark or use "OJ" as a service mark in promoting the Florida citrus industry.

> **Certification Mark**
> any word, name symbol, device or combination thereof [used by producers other than the certification mark owner] to certify regional or other origin, material, mode of manufacture, quality, accuracy or other characteristics . . . or that the work or labor on the goods or services was performed by members of a union or other organization.

As with service marks, the certification mark owner must exercise some quality control to assure that its standards are met. Consider how Underwriters Laboratories monitors the use of its "UL" certification mark. Use of the mark by product sellers assures a level of safety in operations of mechanical and electrical goods. UL tests samples from participating product manufacturers and then uses a listing contract to require the covered manufacturers to promise that all other goods using the "UL" mark will also meet the safety criteria. This is about all that UL could practically do to assure compliance. It is impractical for a certification mark owner like UL to test every product or impose absolute control over producers' use of the certification mark. Instead, the certification mark owner must impose a compliance program of reasonable steps under the circumstances to prevent the public from being misled.[17]

ONLINE
Underwriters Laboratories
http://www.ul.com

Several certification programs are becoming important in e-commerce, such as assurance services for encryption security, privacy, and electronic payment security. For example, the Better Business Bureau provides privacy assurance through its BBBonline program. TRUSTe provides similar certification. New standards and other certification authorities are likely to emerge as e-commerce grows. Service and certification and marks on the Internet will become more important as safe shopping, privacy protection certification, and secure payment mechanisms require standardization to attract customer loyalty and trust.

ONLINE
Privacy, e-commerce certification
http://www.bbbonline.org
http://www.truste.org

Collective Marks

Collective marks are similar to certification marks, but collective marks are used by members of an organization to identify their members. They overlap with certification

17. *Midwest Plastic Fabricators, Inc. v. Underwriters Laboratories, Inc.*, 906 F.2d 1568 (Fed.Cir., 1990).

International Commentary

Trademark Protection for Generic Identifications of Origin

The geographic origin of products can be very important to consumers and helps firms succeed in the particular producing region. "Colombian coffee" and "Juan Valdez" are familiar certification marks over the geographic origin of coffee. Europeans use marks to indicate the *source d'origine* of wines, liquor, and other foodstuffs. However, such marks may become so successful that they eventually lose their distinctiveness, and U.S. vintners may describe their sparkling wines as "champagne" even though they are not produced in that region of France. There is a similar result for "Swiss" (-style) cheese produced in other nations. Nevertheless, the EU continues to defend these and many similar marks, particularly in negotiations with other nations by imposing reciprocal protections.

marks if the organization imposes quality control or other standards on its members. For example, the mark "Realtor" refers to members of the National Association of Realtors. They are real estate professionals who pass professional testing and are bound to professional rules of conduct. Membership is the key distinction between certification and collective marks, particularly when the organization requires its members to adhere to codes of conduct or they certify professional conduct or members' moral character.

Collective Mark

Trademark or service mark . . . used by members of a cooperative, an association or other collective group or organization . . . to indicate membership.

SPECTRUM OF DISTINCTIVENESS

Thus far, we have examined several ways to classify trademarks: first, according to the type of subject matter or thing afforded protection, such as words, shapes, and sensory phenomena; second, the source of law affording the protection, either state, federal, or international; and third, the type of commercial activity associated with the mark, either products, services, or groups of producers. This section discusses a fourth and perhaps the most important categorization of marks: the perceived relationship between the mark and its owner. Trademark law provides the strongest protection for identifying marks, the most important function of marks. Identifying marks clearly trigger human memory to associate the mark directly with only one producing firm. A second function of marks is to convey some aspect or attribute of the product. All marks communicate one or both of these two aspects: (1) identification of the producing source and (2) description(s) of the product's attributes. Trademark law makes determinations about distinctiveness and then dictates whether a mark should be registered to one firm or left in the public domain for use by all competing producers.

Firms usually have many choices in selecting the best mark for its products. At one extreme, marks can be chosen that *do not* automatically cause consumers to think about the type of product; that is, the mark does not suggest or describe the characteristics, properties, or features common to all competing products in that category. These marks are the strongest and most distinctive because they uniquely refer to the mark's owner, not to the product category. They are distinctive marks because they are not needed by other competitors to describe their versions of the same product. Marks serve the policies of trademark law best when they promote competition. Trademark law preserves commercial symbols best describing the product for the public domain. No one firm may own the best words, phrases, or symbols that identify the product category.

On the other extreme are marks that do describe each generic category of products. They are the weakest marks because they do not connect directly with a particular producer of the goods. Nevertheless, firms have a natural incentive to use brand names that conjure up images of the product or suggest images of its best features. Suggestive marks may cause consumers to experience multiple hints about the product's suitability or desirability. Some product names strongly imply the product's characteristics as well as identifying the particular producing firm. Trademark law and policy seek to limit this. Only a limited number of best descriptors are available for each product. The best descriptors are generic, so they should remain in the public domain for all producers to describe their products.

The categorization system for marks is known as the **spectrum of distinctiveness.** There are several categories positioned between the two extremes: from arbitrary and fanciful, through suggestive and descriptive, and then finally to generic. The spectrum of distinctiveness discussed in this section is summarized in Exhibit 18.2.

ARBITRARY AND FANCIFUL MARKS

Arbitrary and fanciful marks are inherently distinctive, strong marks that can be protected immediately. The PTO should register arbitrary and fanciful marks without difficulty, and courts should recognize their distinctiveness. The adoption of an arbitrary or fanciful mark easily permits the mark owner to use the mark. **Arbitrary and fanciful** marks in no way describe the whole category of competing products. They are the strongest marks because they identify only a particular producer, or sole source, for the product.

Some arbitrary and fanciful marks have components that are well-recognized words or symbols. For example, Blue Diamond uses a familiar color and shape but this mark has no relationship to the product: nuts (food). Similarly, Carnival[18] is arbitrary and fanciful for a cruise ship line, as is "Just do it"[19] for sportswear and related equipment. Some arbitrary marks are coined or made-up words that did not exist before registration. They have no relationship to the product category: Rolex for watches,[20] Kodak for photographic supplies and services,[21] and Exxon for petroleum products and services.

SUGGESTIVE MARKS

Suggestive marks have at most a vague relationship to the category of goods. **Suggestive marks** are not precisely descriptive; they require some imagination, thought, or perception by consumers to connect the mark to the goods. They indirectly suggest some relevant characteristic, feature, interesting quality, or concept about the goods. For example, an insecticide function is suggested with the Roach Motel brand of insect traps, skin coloration change is suggested by Coppertone suntan

---

18. *Blumfield Development Corp. v. Carnival Cruise Lines, Inc.*, 669 F.Supp. 1297 (E.D.Pa. 1987).
19. *Nike, Inc. v. Just Did It Enterprises*, 799 F.Supp. 894 (N.D.Ill. 1992).
20. *Rolex Watch U.S.A., Inc v. Caner*, 645 F.Supp. 484 (S.D.Fla. 1986).
21. *Eastman Kodak Co. v. Weil*, 243 N.Y.S. 319 (N.Y.Sup. 1930).

EXHIBIT 18.2 Spectrum of Distinctiveness

Descriptiveness Category	Definition	Trademark Protection	Examples of Marks and Associated Products
Arbitrary or fanciful	Inherently distinctive, no connection between mark and product category	Strong protection, immediate protection possible	Blue Diamond (nuts), Exxon (petroleum), Kodak (photographic), Rolex (watches), Carnival (cruises), "Just do it!" (sport equipment), Penguin (books), Arrow (shirts), Beefeater (gin)
Suggestive	Mark indirectly suggests feature(s) of goods, but a connection is required using human imagination	Strong protection, immediate protection possible	Coppertone (suntan lotion), Accenture (consultant), Sportstick (lip balm), Gung-Ho (action figure)
Descriptive	Mark describes major feature(s) of the type of product	Weak protection, secondary meaning is required	Beer Nuts (salted snack), Bufferin (buffered aspirin pain reliever), Chap Stick (lip balm), Fashion Knit (sweaters), Beef and Brew (restaurant), Healthy Choice (diet foods), Super-Soaker (high-powered water gun)
Generic	One of the few terms necessary to adequately describe the type of product	No protection, remains in public domain for use by all competitors	TV, phone, blouse, shoe, watch, computer, tape, and almost any term designating a product category; terms adjudged generic: shuttle (airline), 386 (CPU), Swiss Army (multiblade pocketknife); distinctive terms before genericide: escalator, cellophane, aspirin, thermos

lotion, expertise with an *accent* on a fu*ture* orientation is suggested by the Accenture brand of consulting services, and macho abandon is suggested by the Gung-ho mark for an action figure toy.[22] Suggestive marks are inherently distinctive and deserve immediate protection.

DESCRIPTIVE MARKS

Descriptive marks immediately conjure up some important characteristic about the product. They do so without the need for much imagination. Such marks are weak because they tend to more clearly describe products from all the producers in that category. Because of the scarcity of adequate descriptive terms, trademark policy imposes a conditional exclusion on descriptive marks. Descriptive marks must remain in the public domain and cannot be registered or protected unless they acquire secondary meaning, as discussed later.

Descriptive terms are often adjectives, adverbs, or descriptive nouns because they address aspects of the product, such as the product's nature, quality, characteristics, ingredients, components, or intended use. Marks that are primarily a surname

22. *Hasbro, Inc. v. Lanard Toys, Inc.*, 858 F.2d 70 (2d Cir., 1988).

(last or family name) are conditionally excluded from registration. Marks that are primarily geographic are conditionally excluded. Examples of descriptive marks include Beer Nuts (salted snack), Bufferin (buffered aspirin pain reliever), Chap Stick (lip balm), Fashion Knit (sweaters), Beef and Brew (restaurant), Healthy Choice (prepared foods), and Super-Soaker (high powered water gun toy). Descriptive marks neither are protectable under state unfair competition law nor can they be federally registered until they have acquired secondary meaning.

Secondary Meaning

There is a major exception to the trademark policy that prohibits descriptive terms in marks. Trademark protection can be allowed but only after a descriptive term has acquired secondary meaning. In this context, the mark's **primary meaning** is in its description of the goods. The mark's **secondary meaning** develops only after time passes. Public exposure during this time creates an association between the mark and the mark owner as *the* single producing source. Secondary meaning exists only when consumers immediately link the mark with the mark owner and not with the class of products from all producers. For example, assume the Internet service provider JetWire.com, a suggestive mark, begins using "BroadBand" as the brand name of its Internet access service. BroadBand is probably descriptive because most high-speed Internet access service firms would find the term a useful description for their services. However, secondary meaning develops after the public associates the BroadBand mark with only the JetWire.com firm. Descriptive terms like BroadBand cannot be registered until secondary meaning develops in the public's eyes. When will that happen?

Proving secondary meaning is generally an empirical process that considers the mark's economic impact by examining past events and current conditions. For example, data from validly conducted consumer surveys are direct and fairly persuasive evidence of consumer perception. There is an immediate link of the mark to the particular producer as the only source producing the product under the mark. Consumer survey data can prove the perception of relevant buyers, past purchasers, and prospective consumers for the type of product in question. Circumstantial evidence is also useful to infer secondary meaning. For example, courts may consider long and continuous use of the mark, the amount and nature of advertising using the mark, and the sales volume of products under the mark. These factors help to show the effectiveness of developing a secondary meaning.

Descriptive terms are not immediately permitted registration by the PTO on the **principal register**. This is the more favorable federal registration list because (1) it gives strong notice of the mark's ownership throughout the United States, (2) infringement suits and remedies are enhanced, (3) international registration and protections are enhanced, and (4) a mark becomes incontestable after registration for five years on the principal register.

A secondary list of marks is also maintained by the PTO: the **supplemental register**. It is used when marks do not qualify for the principal register. Generally, the supplemental register is available for descriptive terms but not for generic terms. Supplemental registration permits use of trademark notice symbols ®, as well as reciprocal registration between the United States and some other nations, and it enhances some infringement remedies. However, supplemental registration does not provide the benefits of the principal register. After a descriptive mark is in exclusive and continuous use for five years and is listed on the supplemental register without legal challenge, it may be moved to the more advantageous principal register. The following case illustrates trade dress and secondary meaning.

Two Pesos, Inc. v. Taco Cabana, Inc.

505 U.S. 763 (1992)

Facts. Taco Cabana, Inc., operates a chain of fast-food Mexican restaurants in Texas. The first was opened in San Antonio in September 1978, and five more were opened by 1985. Taco Cabana's trade dress is "Mexican patio café-style" that the firm describes as:

[A] festive eating atmosphere having interior dining and patio areas decorated with artifacts, bright colors, paintings and murals. The patio includes interior and exterior areas with the interior patio capable of being sealed off from the outside patio by overhead garage doors. The stepped exterior of the building is a festive and vivid color scheme using top border paint and neon stripes. Bright awnings and umbrellas continue the theme.

A Two Pesos, Inc., restaurant opened in Houston in 1985 with a motif very similar to Taco Cabana's trade dress. Two Pesos expanded rapidly in Houston and other Texas markets but did not enter San Antonio. In 1986, Taco Cabana entered the Houston and Austin markets and expanded into other Texas cities, including Dallas and El Paso, where Two Pesos was also doing business. Taco Cabana sued Two Pesos for trade dress infringement and for theft of trade secrets.

Legal Issue. May the trade dress of a restaurant be protected under trademark law based on inherent distinctiveness and without proof of secondary meaning?

Opinion. Justice White. Marks, which are merely descriptive of a product, are not inherently distinctive. When used to describe a product, they do not inherently identify a particular source, and hence cannot be protected. However, descriptive marks may acquire the distinctiveness, which will allow them to be protected under the Act. [A] descriptive mark that otherwise could not be registered under the Act may be registered if it "has become distinctive of the applicant's goods in commerce." This acquired distinctiveness is generally called "secondary meaning." The general rule regarding distinctiveness is clear: an identifying mark is distinctive and capable of being protected if it *either* (1) is inherently distinctive *or* (2) has acquired distinctiveness through secondary meaning. There is no persuasive reason to apply to trade dress a general requirement of secondary meaning which is at odds with the principles generally applicable to [ordinary trademark] infringement suits.

Engrafting onto §43(a) a requirement of secondary meaning for inherently distinctive trade dress also would undermine the purposes of the Lanham Act. Protection of trade dress, no less than of trademarks, serves the Act's purpose to "secure to the owner of the mark the goodwill of his business and to protect the ability of consumers to distinguish among competing producers. National protection of trademarks is desirable, Congress concluded, because trademarks foster competition and the maintenance of quality by securing to the producer the benefits of good reputation." By making more difficult the identification of a producer with its product, a secondary meaning requirement for a nondescriptive trade dress would hinder improving or maintaining the producer's competitive position. [It] could have anticompetitive effects, creating particular burdens on the start-up of small companies. It would present special difficulties for a business that seeks to start a new product in a limited area and then expand into new markets. Denying protection for inherently distinctive nonfunctional trade dress until after secondary meaning has been established would allow a competitor, which has not adopted a distinctive trade dress of its own, to appropriate the originator's dress in other markets and to deter the originator from expanding into and competing in these areas. [P]rotecting an inherently distinctive trade dress from its inception may be critical to new entrants to the market and withholding that protection until secondary meaning has been established would be contrary to the goals of the Lanham Act.

Decision. Distinctive restaurant trade dress may be protected under trademark law without a showing of secondary meaning.

Case Questions

1. What is the difference between establishing trade dress that is inherently distinctive and requiring that the trade dress have secondary meaning before it can be protected?
2. Who decides if trade dress is inherently distinctive? How and when is it decided whether trade dress has acquired secondary meaning?
3. Why must a mark owner show that its trade dress has acquired secondary meaning before it can be protected under trademark law? How is this done?

ONLINE

Taco Cabana's trade dress
http://www.tacocabana.com

Until the *Taco Cabana* case, trade dress could be protected only after it had acquired secondary meaning. *Taco Cabana* permits adoption and PTO registration of trade dress even before secondary meaning is established. Unfortunately, a 2000 case obscures this issue again. In *Wal-Mart Stores, Inc. v. Samara Brothers, Inc.*,[23] the Supreme Court openly worried that registering product design before it develops secondary meaning would give existing mark owners too much power to lock up product designs. The justices are concerned that juries may be too easily convinced to make the vague determination that a particular product design is inherently distinctive. Such unpredictable results could discourage new or upstart firms from costly litigation over product designs that another firm already has registered. The issue may now turn on whether trade dress is a form of product design or whether it is simply a form of product packaging. If trade dress is a form of product design, then secondary meaning would be required for protection. However, if trade dress is merely packaging, then *Taco Cabana* would permit trade dress to be protected immediately after PTO registration. This quandary may encourage firms engaged in e-commerce to characterize website trade dress as product packaging to avoid the more onerous requirement of secondary meaning for product designs.

GENERIC MARKS

Trademark law's primary goal is to promote fair competition, without deception. To further this goal, the common law and the Lanham Act deny protection for marks that are **generic**. They are the most common names and descriptions of the class of products in question. No producer should be given a monopoly over the genus name or class descriptors for all competing products. By definition, generic terms cannot identify the producer as source because all competitors' products are identified by the generic term. The legal question in cases interpreting generic terms is whether the term serves as one of the more common names for products in the minds of most relevant consumers.

The particular generic term in question need not be the only name for the product. Consider how the electronic transmission and reception of full-motion video for entertainment purposes is known by various generic terms: television, TV, the tube, or video. Many generic terms are nouns or adjectives because they designate a product category, such as phone, blouse, shoe, watch, computer, or tape. Some terms are adjudged generic, such as shuttle (airline), 386 (CPU; thereafter Intel adopted Pentium rather than 586), and Swiss Army (multiblade pocketknife).

Genericide

Some mark owners are so successful with their advertising and promotional activities that the consuming public eventually associates the mark with the whole product category. Marks that were once suggestive or distinctive may eventually become the primary term describing the class of products. This outcome is **genericide** because the owner loses protection for the mark. The test of genericide is whether the mark's primary significance to the consuming public is to identify the mark owner as the sole producing source or the mark has come to describe the class of products from all sources. As with many other factual questions in trademark law, the proofs used in a genericide case include data from consumer surveys, advertising, use by competitors, and authoritative sources such as dictionaries and expert lexicographers.

23. *Wal-Mart Stores, Inc. v. Samara Brothers, Inc.*, 529 U.S. 205 (2000).

Note that many contemporary mark owners actively seek to avoid genericide of their more valuable marks. For example, the Xerox Corp. frequently advertises that there are no "Xerox copies," and instead there are xerographic copies made on photocopy machines. Similarly, RollerBlade has taken a subtler approach by including the following wording right after its mark, RollerBlade: "brand of in-line skates." In each instance, the mark owner discourages the public from using its mark as the generic descriptor for the product category. Famous genericide examples include aspirin, escalator, thermos, and cellophane. All these marks were distinctive, but after they became widely known as the generic description of the product class, the marks were no longer capable of identifying the mark owner as the sole producing source. The following famous case discusses the spectrum of distinctiveness.

Abercrombie & Fitch v. Hunting World, Inc.

537 F.2d 4 (2d Cir., 1976)

Facts. Abercrombie & Fitch (A&F) registered several trademarks using the word "Safari." Since 1936, it has used the mark on a variety of men's and women's outer garments, hats, shoes, and sporting goods. A&F has spent large sums of money in advertising and promoting products identified with the "Safari" mark and has policed its rights in the mark, including successful trademark infringement suits. Hunting World (HW) sells sporting apparel, hats, and shoes, some identified by use of "Safari" alone or by expressions such as "Minisafari" and "Safariland." HW sought to invalidate A&F's "Safari" marks as an ordinary, common, descriptive, geographic, and generic word that "is commonly used and understood by the public to mean and refer to a journey or expedition, especially for hunting or exploring in East Africa, and to the hunters, guides, men, animals, and equipment forming such an expedition."

Legal Issue. Has A&F created a secondary meaning in its use of the word "Safari" as identifying the source and showing that purchasers are moved to buy it because of its source?

Opinion. Circuit Judge Friendly. The cases, and in some instances the Lanham Act, identify four different categories of terms with respect to trademark protection. Arrayed in an ascending order which roughly reflects their eligibility to trademark status and the degree of protection accorded, these classes are (1) generic, (2) descriptive, (3) suggestive, and (4) arbitrary or fanciful. The lines of demarcation, however, are not always bright. Moreover, the difficulties are compounded because a term that is in one category for a particular product may be in quite a different one for another, because a term may shift from one category to another in light of differences in usage through time, because a term may have one meaning to one group of users and a different one to others, and because the same term may be put to different uses with respect to a single product. In various ways, all of these complications are involved in this case.

A generic term is one that refers to the genus of which the particular product is a species. The [Lanham] Act provides for the cancellation of a registered mark if at any time it "becomes the common descriptive name of an article or substance." This means that even proof of secondary meaning, by virtue of which some "merely descriptive" marks may be registered, cannot transform a generic term into a subject for trademark. The term which is descriptive but not generic stands on a better basis. Any claim to an exclusive right must be denied since this in effect would confer a monopoly not only of the mark but of the product by rendering a competitor unable effectively to name what it was endeavoring to sell. The category of "suggestive" marks was spawned by the felt need to accord protection to marks that were neither exactly descriptive on the one hand nor truly fanciful on the other. Having created the category the courts have had great difficulty in defining it. Judge Learned Hand made the not very helpful statement: "It is quite impossible to get any rule out of the cases beyond this: That the validity of the mark ends where suggestion ends and description begins." Another court has observed, somewhat more usefully, that: "A term is suggestive if it requires imagination, thought and perception to reach a conclusion as to the nature of goods. A term is descriptive if it forthwith conveys an immediate idea of the ingredients, qualities or characteristics."

The English language has a wealth of synonyms and related words with which to describe the qualities, which manufacturers may wish to claim for their products and the ingenuity of the public relations profession supplies new words and slogans, as they are needed. The decision of the Patent Office to register a mark without requiring proof of secondary meaning affords a rebuttable presumption that the mark is suggestive or arbitrary or fanciful rather than merely descriptive. Of course, a common word may be used in a fanciful sense; indeed one might say that only a common word can be so used, since a coined word cannot first be put to a bizarre use. Nevertheless, the term "fanciful," as a classifying concept, is usually applied to words invented solely for their use as trademarks. When the same legal consequences attach to a common word, i.e., when it is applied in an unfamiliar way, the use is called "arbitrary."

Applied to specific types of clothing "safari" has become a generic term; "safari" has not, however, become a generic term for boots or shoes; it is either "suggestive" or "merely descriptive" and is a valid trademark even if "merely descriptive" since it has become incontestable. The word "Safari" has become part of a family of generic terms which have come to be understood not as having to do with hunting in Africa, but as terms within the language referring to contemporary American fashion apparel. These terms name the components of the safari outfit well-known to the clothing industry and its customers: the "Safari hat," a broad flat-brimmed hat with a single, large band; the "Safari jacket," a belted bush jacket with patch pockets and a buttoned shoulder loop; when the jacket is accompanied by pants, the combination is called the "Safari suit." Typically these items are khaki-colored.

This outfit, and its components, were doubtless what Judge Ryan had in mind when he found that "the word 'safari' in connection with wearing apparel is widely used by the general public and people in the trade." Many stores have advertised these items despite A&F's attempts to police its mark. There is no evidence that "Safari" has become a generic term for boots. A&F's registration of "Safari" for use on its shoes has become incontestable.

HW contends that even if "Safari" is a valid trademark for boots, it is entitled to the defense of "fair use" [under] the Lanham Act. [HW's] parent company has been primarily engaged in arranging safaris to Africa since 1959; the president of both companies is the author of a book published in 1959 entitled "Safari Today: The Modern Safari Handbook" and has, since 1961, booked persons on safaris as well as purchased safari clothing in Africa for resale in America. [HW's] use of "Safari" with respect to boots was made in the context of hunting and traveling expeditions and not as an attempt to garner A&F's good will. When a plaintiff has chosen a mark with some descriptive qualities, he cannot altogether exclude some kinds of competing uses even when the mark is properly on the register.

The generic term for A&F's "safari cloth Bermuda shorts," for example, is "Bermuda shorts," not "safari"; indeed one would suppose this garment to be almost ideally unsuited for the forest or the jungle. The same analysis holds for luggage, portable grills, and the rest of the suburban paraphernalia, from swimtrunks and raincoats to belts and scarves, included in these registrations. "Safari" as applied to ice chests, axes, tents and smoking tobacco does not describe such items. Rather it is a way of conveying to affluent patrons of A&F a romantic notion of high style, coupled with an attractive foreign allusion. As such, these uses fit what was said many years ago in upholding "Ideal" as a mark for hair brushes: The word "Ideal" has no application to hair brushes, except as we arbitrarily apply it, and the word is in no sense indicative or descriptive of the qualities or characteristics or merits of the brush except that it meets the very highest ideal, mental conception, of what a hair brush should be.

Decision. The "safari" term has acquired secondary meaning for A&F in relation to some of its products.

Case Questions

1. How can a term be classified as generic for some products from a single source firm like A&F yet be descriptive or suggestive for other products of that same firm?
2. What purposes are served by the spectrum of distinctiveness and its classification of marks into the four different categories?

CLASSIFYING MARKS ON THE SPECTRUM OF DISTINCTIVENESS

It can be difficult to differentiate suggestive marks from descriptive marks[24] or even to distinguish arbitrary or fanciful marks from suggestive marks. The spectrum of distinctiveness is a continuous range of classifications; it is not abruptly defined

24. *Franklin Knitting Mills, Inc. v. Fashionit Sweater Mills, Inc.*, 297 F. 247 (S.D.N.Y. 1923).

or clearly expressed. Determinations of distinctiveness have very important consequences because an owner may be denied the use of a mark if it is not inherently distinctive: arbitrary, fanciful, or suggestive. In judging how to classify a mark, we must look to actual usage and use one or more of several factors, including (1) recognized meanings from the dictionary or thesaurus, (2) judge or jury determination of what constitutes the reasonable cognitive judgment of average or ordinary customers, (3) empirical evidence of consumer attitudes and perceptions, or (4) a factual history of coining terms or local business traditions. Many distinctiveness determinations are based on subjective judgments by PTO examiners, judges, and juries.

It is also challenging to distinguish suggestive marks from descriptive marks. There are two tests to differentiate them. One test examines the degree of imagination needed to connect the mark with the product. If less imagination is needed, then the mark is weaker and more descriptive; if more imagination is needed, then the mark may be suggestive. A second test looks to whether the mark is a term or descriptor needed by competitors to describe their similar products. If so, the mark is more likely to be descriptive, and the mark owner will have difficulty acquiring exclusive rights. The spectrum of distinctiveness is summarized in Exhibit 18.3.

FUNCTIONALITY

The trademark policy goal of promoting competition by preserving the public domain is again addressed by the functionality limitation. **Functionality** is a product's feature that affects its purpose, action, or performance or the facility or economy of processing, handling, or use.[25] Functional aspects of product design cannot be protected by trademark; otherwise, competitors could not compete effectively. For example, trade dress often involves physical aspects of product packaging or the architecture of business premises. Trademark protection extends only to the distinctive visual elements of the design and not to the functional aspects. Consider the purpose of the garage doors in the *Taco Cabana* restaurant case. These doors should be considered functional and not protected as trade dress. They serve an important climate-control function, permitting the enlargement of the dining room onto

EXHIBIT 18.3 Classifying Marks along Spectrum of Distinctiveness

Mark	Product	Classification	Rationale for Classification
Suave	Shampoo	Suggestive	Suave and results of haircare are desirable human characteristics
Accuride	Tires	Suggestive	Accuracy is desirable trait of tire performance
Wearever	Cookware	Suggestive	Durability is desirable
Verbatim	Floppy disks	Suggestive	Exacting recall is desirable
Tylenol	Pain reliever	Arbitrary	Coined, new word name
Amtrak	Transportation	Suggestive	Coined, suggests America and tracked transportation
Hard Rock Café	Restaurant	Arbitrary/fanciful	No relationship to service
Tea Rose Flour	Food	Arbitrary/fanciful	No relationship to type of food

25. *Restatement of the Law, Torts, 1st.*

the adjoining patio areas in good weather while protecting the inside dining space during inclement weather. By contrast, the vertically ribbed hourglass shape of the Coca-Cola bottle is mostly ornamental and unnecessary to strengthen the container.

When is a trademark feature functional? The courts have developed several tests, but unfortunately they do not provide consistent answers. The courts reject the colloquial or de facto definition that the feature simply performs some function. Instead, the courts inquire into whether (1) there are equally appealing alternative ways to accomplish the function, (2) whether the feature was once patented, or (3) whether the mark owner touts the feature as functional in advertising.[26] If these facts are true, the feature will probably not be protected because it is functional. A trademark feature could also be considered functional if it lowers production costs, as was the case with a bicycle rim design used by Schwinn. Some cases even hold that consumer demand may be enhanced with aesthetically pleasing designs. Under this reasoning, an artistic element of a mark or trade dress might not be protected because its function is to increase demand.

Of course, certain aspects of functional designs may be protected under patent law if they satisfy the patentability standards of novelty, nonobviousness, and utility. Recall from Chapter 17 that design patents have similar limitations on functionality. Functional designs enter the public domain more quickly, at the expiration of the limited patent term. Another reason to prohibit functional aspects of trademarks is that the potential duration of a trademark is perpetual. The functionality rule helps preserve the public domain and defers to the rigors and limitations of patent law for functional elements.

ACQUISITION, REGISTRATION, AND MAINTENANCE OF TRADEMARKS

Trademark rights are created or acquired in two major, sometimes overlapping ways: (1) use and (2) registration. The commercial reputation necessary for trademarks cannot be created until the owner makes **actual use** of the mark. Use makes consumers aware so they can rely on the mark to identify the owner as producer. Therefore, to obtain such rights, trademark law traditionally requires the mark owner to be the first to adopt and use the mark. The mark must be affixed to the product. For goods, this means placing the mark directly on the goods, containers, packaging, displays, documentation, or labels. For services, the mark should be displayed along with sales or advertising.

No registration is necessary under state common law. However, stronger rights are available under state or federal trademark registration. To qualify for federal trademark protection and registration, the applicant must be the first to use the mark in interstate commerce or the first to acquire secondary meaning for descriptive marks. Recall the discussion of interstate commerce in Chapter 4. The Supreme Court interprets interstate commerce broadly to include many *intra*state activities that affect *inter*state or foreign commerce.[27] The technology transfer and franchising aspects of trademark licensing are discussed in Chapter 13.

---

26. *In re Morton-Norwich*, 671 F.2D 1332 (CCPA, 1982).
27. *In re Silenus Wines*, 557 F.2d 806 (CCPA, 1977).

FEDERAL REGISTRATION UNDER THE LANHAM ACT

The Lanham Act provides stronger trademark protection than the automatic protections under the state common law of unfair competition. There are several federal registration alternatives under the Lanham Act and its amendments. Registration and other trademark regulatory matters are handled by the Patent and Trademark Office (PTO). The PTO is currently a separate office within the U.S. Department of Commerce, although there have been proposals to privatize the agency.

ONLINE
USPTO's Trademark website
http://www.uspto.gov/main/trademarks.htm

There are two main types of registration on the principal register: §1(a) for marks already in use and §1(b) for intent-to-use applications. Marks may be registered if they are already in use in interstate commerce. The application must identify the owner and the products covered, state the date of the mark's first use, and include a drawing of the mark and specimens of how it is actually used. The applicant must claim that no other rightful user is known. **Disclaimers** can be made, indicating descriptive or generic elements of the mark such as common shapes (circle, oval) and descriptive words (pizza). Disclaimers excluded the matters listed from protection. The PTO may require disclaimers for particular mark elements. Registration on the supplemental register is also available for "would-be marks," typically descriptive terms, geographic names, or surnames. Supplemental registration, discussed previously, is appropriate for marks that are in the process of acquiring secondary meaning. The PTO now encourages electronic filing using the eTEAS: *T*rademark *E*lectronic *A*pplication *S*ystem.

ONLINE
USPTO's eTEAS online registration
http://www.uspto.gov/teas/index.html

Intent-to-Use Application

The 1988 Trademark Revision Act reversed an old prohibition against trademark registration: the **token use doctrine**. Trademark policy did not develop to encourage the needless proliferation of unused commercial symbols or to reward artists and marketing innovators by granting property rights in unused designs. Instead, the trademark goal of preventing consumer confusion is the most important policy. Therefore, mark owners could not lock up a particular mark by making sham transactions—that is, mere token use—to simulate the mark's use in interstate commerce. No trademark protection was permitted for inactive marks: "Ownership of a trademark accrues when goods bearing the mark are placed on the market."[28] Some mark owners actively "warehoused" appealing marks with only vague plans for their future use. These practices frustrate trademark policies of maximizing the public domain because their registration was based on deception. Competitors were denied the use of good but inactive marks.

The token use doctrine was abolished in 1988 when the intent-to-use application process began. When an applicant has a bona fide intention to use the mark in interstate commerce in the future, the applicant may lock in its priority; the application date establishes the date of first use. This "start date" is an important focus when other users try to use the same or a confusingly similar mark. An intent-to-use application is valid for only six months, during which the applicant must begin actual use. A six-month extension is usually granted, and up to three additional six-month extensions may be granted with proof of good cause (e.g., unforeseen production delays). Once the mark is in actual use, a statement should be filed to move the mark to the principal register.

28. *Blue Bell, Inc. v. Farah Mfg. Co.*, 508 F.2d 1260 (5th Cir., 1975).

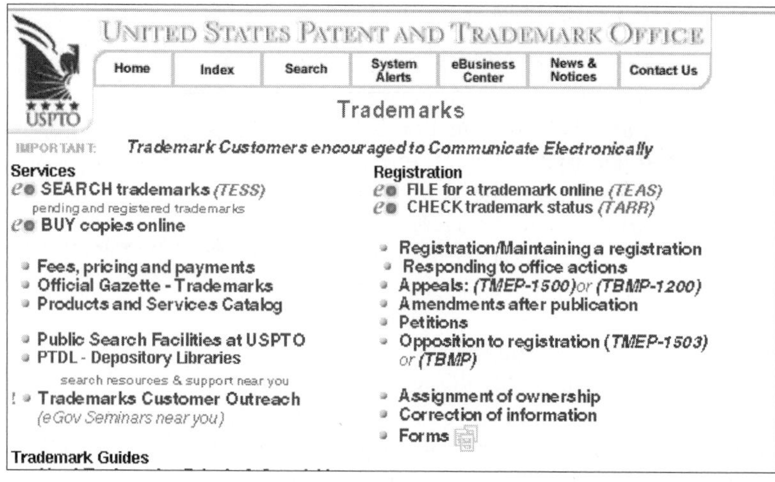

http://

www.uspto.gov/main/trademarks.htm

Trademark Searches

Some research is sensible before investing too much in a trademark. A search of trademark databases is useful to uncover similar marks. Searches can be done by many trademark-savvy individuals, but serious and high-stakes searches are best left to professional trademark search firms and trademark law practitioners. Searches are best made before doing certain things: prosecuting an application, advertising to build brand image, or ramping up production if the mark is permanently affixed. As discussed later, searches should include Internet domain name registrations.

Although trademark searches are optional, they are a good risk-averse strategy because trademark searches often uncover others' claims and other uses of the mark. A search is particularly important for suggestive and descriptive marks because another owner may be a direct competitor selling similar products. Trademark applications must confirm that the applicant in good faith knows of no confusingly similar marks already in use. Searches help to confirm this good faith belief. Trademark infringement suits are costly, as are the wasted costs of advertising or production that used another's mark.

Searches can be made on one or more public domain or proprietary databases, including the *Official Gazette* (the PTO's paper-bound publication), the PTO website, CD-ROM databases such as CASSIS, on-line databases (Lexis, Westlaw, Dialog), and print publications from public libraries. A cursory, surface search looks for existing marks with nearly identical spelling or pronunciation or close visual similarity. A deeper, analytical search examines synonyms, homonyms, alternative and phonetic spellings, and similar overall shapes or visual components. For example, an analytical search for marks similar to "e-commerce" or "cyberlaw" should examine all marks beginning with the lower case *e* or including the prefix *cyber* or the suffix *law*. A deep search covers even more: directories (yellow pages, B2B or trade catalogues), business service firms, and participants in the supply chain. Software using pattern recognition to search digital images is becoming available and should make searches more complete and efficient. In complex searches, professional search assistance may be best to benefit from experienced judgment. Searches range from $100 to several hundred dollars.

ONLINE

Trademark search firm, Thompson & Thompson **http://www.t-tlaw.com**

Prosecution and Examination

After filing, there is an interactive process of **trademark prosecution** between the applicant and the PTO that can take many months. The PTO examines the application to assure compliance with registration procedures and trademark requirements (e.g., proper subject matter, distinctiveness), and a PTO examiner conducts a search to determine the likelihood of confusion. The PTO examiner will issue an office action letter refusing the registration if generic or descriptive terms are used or there is a confusing similarity with an existing mark. The applicant usually responds by negotiating over elements of the proposed mark and with reinterpretation of similar existing marks. If the applicant fails to overcome the examiner's objections, a **final**

refusal is issued; failure to respond within six months results in **abandonment** of the application. A mark is approved when the examiner is satisfied with the applicant's responses and the mark is published in the *Official Gazette*. A **registration certificate** is issued for marks in actual use, or a **notice of allowance** is issued for an intent-to-use application.

RENEWAL AND TERMINATION

Marks are renewable every ten years if they are in continuous use. The first renewal must occur in the fifth year and requires filing an affidavit declaring continuous use. After publication in the *Official Gazette*, another person may challenge the registration in an **opposition** proceeding. This permits outsiders to question the mark's confusing similarity to existing marks or claim that the mark contains descriptive elements or generic terms. If a confusingly similar mark is already in use, the PTO may grant concurrent but restricted use. During the first five years of registration, the mark is vulnerable to **cancellation** for the same reasons used in the opposition process. After the first five years, marks become **incontestable**; they cannot be cancelled, even if they are not inherently distinctive or they lack secondary meaning. However, after five years, marks remain vulnerable to cancellation if they become generic, are abandoned, were obtained by fraud, or are ineligible subject matter. The abandonment of a mark is inferred if there is a substantial period of nonuse, if the owner intends to not resume use, or if the owner fails to control use of the mark (unpoliced licensees).

LIMITATIONS ON THE SCOPE OF USE

Historically, there were two major limitations on a mark's scope of use: (1) geographic or territorial and (2) product field of use. Modern statutes diminish the importance of these limitations. Under the common law, a mark's owner held exclusive rights only in the geographic territory where the mark was actually used. Another person could use the same or a confusingly similar mark in a remote geographic territory, if the first mark owner had no presence in that other region and the second user acted in good faith. The remote territory must not be influenced by advertising or reputation of the first mark. **Good faith** means the second user had no notice or knowledge of the first user's use. For example, imagine that a restaurant chain began operating in the 1940s in New Jersey under the mark "Acme Diner." In the 1960s, a California restaurant chain started operating under the "Acme Diner" mark, but the owner had no knowledge or notice of the New Jersey chain or its use of the mark. The California chain would have a defense to infringement in a suit brought by the New Jersey chain's owner.

Traditional trademark law permitted exclusive rights only in relation to specific products with which the mark was used. For example, assume a blues club, the Bent Note, sold no goods under its mark. Anyone else could use the "Bent Note" mark to sell products other than nightclub services. Today, state and federal antidilution statutes provide some protection to mark owners from noncompeting uses of their marks. Dilution laws are discussed further in the next section.

TRADEMARK INFRINGEMENT

The trademark industry continues to refine its methods of describing and distinguishing marks. Despite this progress, marks will probably continue to be defined

Is Good Faith an Ethical Standard for Trademarks?

Ethical Issue

The good faith rule is severely limited today for federally registered marks. Registration gives national rights. There is no good faith defense for a later adopted mark if the prior user previously registered the mark. For example, if the New Jersey Acme Diner registered the mark before use by the California chain, there would be no good faith defense for the California chain. However, if the registration comes after acquisition and use by the remote user, the later user's rights in the remote territory must be carved out of the registered user's national rights. It is still possible for two common law mark owners to coexist in separate geographic regions. However, eventually this excuse may be eliminated if the Internet is effective in expanding communication and notice.

by very vague criteria. Further, the incentive remains strong to use descriptive terms or to ride free on the brand image of successful competitors. Such acts can be concealed because the law uses so many imprecise standards such as "spectrum of distinctiveness" and "likelihood of consumer confusion." Trademark law permits a mark owner to defend its rights by proving infringement and then seeking remedies. **Infringement** occurs when an outsider uses the same or a similar mark and thus weakens the value of the owner's mark. This section discusses the difficult task of determining when a mark is violated or encroached upon by another mark.

LIKELIHOOD OF CONFUSION STANDARD

The primary test for trademark infringement and unfair competition is the **likelihood of confusion** standard: Would the use of the same or a similar mark by an offending user cause confusion to an appreciable number of consumers about the source of products? This question focuses on whether average, reasonable consumers would be misled into believing the alleged infringer's products were produced by the mark owner or were confused about who produced the products. This concept is fundamental because trademark law primarily remedies consumer misunderstanding about the source of supply for products. The likelihood of confusion standard is also used by the PTO in examining trademark applications. How is the likelihood of confusion determined?

Several key factors are used in determining the likelihood of confusion. Although no one factor alone is decisive, the courts consider a preponderance of factors by weighing and combining them. Unfortunately, the courts do not agree on a single set of factors, but the following summarizes the factors most frequently used. First, the *strength of the mark* is relevant. It measures whether the mark is inherently distinctive—typically more so if the mark is arbitrary or fanciful, but less so if it is descriptive. A mark is also strengthened if the public already associates the mark with its owner, much like the analysis of secondary meaning. Second, a comparison is made to find *similarities between the two marks*. Confusion is more likely if the two marks are closely related in their visual appearances, their phonetic sound (perhaps using a linguistic analysis), and their meanings. Third, the *relationship between the two products* is compared. Products that directly compete or are in related markets would be more likely to confuse people than would products in totally unrelated markets. It is also important to consider how the two products are distributed in the supply chain.

Fourth, empirical *evidence of actual confusion* is very persuasive. This evidence may be drawn from witness testimony. However, consumer behavior data are even more valid if based on scientifically designed and administered surveys or on focus group interrogation. Fifth, *buyer sophistication* is relevant because as purchasers become more discriminating or knowledgeable, they should be more careful about origin. Also, more costly products cause most consumers to do more careful research. Sixth, the *defendant's intent* may show a motive to use a similar mark to ride free on the mark owner's reputation. However, some types of evidence could weigh against an inference of infringement intent. For example, intent might be disproved if the alleged infringer performed an exhaustive search, commissioned a trademark analysis before using the mark, or did considerable advertising. Finally, the courts may examine the *potential for expansion* by either user. If either producer's product lines might move to become in more direct competition, future consumer confusion could result. The likelihood of confusion factors are summarized in Exhibit 18.4.

The likelihood of confusion standard essentially identifies when the goods of the infringer are being passed off as those of the mark owner. An infringer who intends this result is guilty of palming off. State unfair competition law provides remedies for wrongs similar to infringement: misrepresentation and false advertising. **Reverse passing off** occurs when the infringer removes the marks from products made by the mark owner and then sells them as its own. It is a reverse of normal passing off because the infringer pretends the goods of another were produced by the infringer. **Trademark disparagement**, a form of trade libel, protects a mark owner from injurious falsehoods, false statements about another's products. Trademark service firms can help monitor other mark users for potential infringement. Monitoring services scan various media, print and broadcast as well as Internet sites, to find offending uses of an owner's mark. Search bots are also in widening use to find infringers on the Internet.

ONLINE

Infringement monitoring services
http://www.cyveillance.com

DILUTION

Several state and federal laws protect a somewhat different interest than infringement by confusion. **Dilution** is a mark owner's interest in maintaining brand image, the commercial magnetism of its brands. Dilution may occur when another party uses the owner's mark on products and this use diminishes the mark's value. The dilution may occur through **tarnishment** of the mark or by **blurring** the distinctiveness of the mark from the diluting mark. The wrongdoer need not be selling products directly competitive to the mark owner's products. Dilution damage may be

EXHIBIT 18.4 Likelihood of Confusion Factors

Factors Determining Likelihood of Confusion	How Likelihood of Confusion Factors are Evaluated
Strength of the mark	Distinctiveness; secondary meaning
Similarities between marks	Visual appearance, sound, meaning
Relationship between products	Competing products, related vs. separate markets, supply chain considerations
Evidence of actual confusion	Scientifically valid empirical studies, consumer surveys, focus groups
Buyer sophistication	Confusion less likely where buyers research before purchasing
Intent of alleged infringer	Free riding on mark owner's reputation suggests attempt to cause confusion
Potential for expansion	Suggests potential for future confusion if two mark owners eventually become direct competitors

greatest when the wrongdoer has a reputation for poor quality or for offensive products (e.g., pornography). The difficulties of linking, framing, and the use of meta-tags all implicate infringement, particularly dilution and tarnishment. These matters are detailed in Chapter 13.

Damages from trademark dilution are greatest when the mark is famous and has built up considerable goodwill. The **Federal Trademark Dilution Act of 1996** (FTDA) provides a federal remedy for famous trademarks, whether or not registered. Some famous marks include the McDonald's golden arches,[29] Toys "R" Us,[30] and the uniforms of the Dallas Cowboys cheerleaders.[31] FTDA guidelines help to identify **famous trademarks** as listed in Exhibit 18.5.

DEFENSES TO INFRINGEMENT

Someone charged with infringement or another wrong under trademark or unfair competition law often argues that the mark owner has a weak case. Alleged infringers often argue the mark in question is invalid, was improperly registered, includes a generic term, or is descriptive but without secondary meaning, that there is no likelihood of confusion, that the mark is functional, or that the owner abandoned the mark. Sometimes the alleged infringer tries to justify its own actions with a **defense to infringement**. Some defenses are invalid after the five-year incontestability period under the Lanham Act.

There is a **fair use** defense to trademark infringement that is similar to copyright fair use. Descriptive and suggestive words used in a mark must remain available for use by others to describe their own goods. For example, surnames and geographic descriptions may be used by others from that region or who have that surname. When a mark is not used in its trademark sense (to identify the origin of products), then the other party's use should be allowed as a fair use. For example, the website of a Playboy model accurately described her as a "Playmate of the Month" and "Playmate of the Year" in the site's meta-tags and these titles were prominently displayed on her website. This display was a fair use because she was accurately describing herself as well as her past activities and accomplishments.[32] The First

EXHIBIT 18.5 FTDA Guidelines for Famous Trademarks

- Mark's degree of inherent or acquired distinctiveness
- Duration and extent of mark's use with product
- Duration and extent of advertising and publicity with mark
- Geographical extent of trading area in which mark is used
- Channels of trade for products sold under the mark
- Degree of recognition of the mark by the alleged infringer as well as in the relevant market and supply chain
- Nature and extent of usage by third parties of the same or similar marks
- Registration on the PTO's principal register

29. *McDonalds Corp. v. Arche Technologies*, 17 U.S.P.Q.2d (BNA) 1557 (N.D. 1990).
30. *Toys "R" Us v. Akkaoui*, 1996 WL 772709 (N.D.Cal. 1996).
31. *Dallas Cowboys Cheerleaders, Inc. v. Pussycat Cinema, Ltd.*, 604 F.2d 200 (2d Cir., 1979).
32. *Playboy Enterprises Inc. v. Welles*, 7 F.Supp.2d 1098 (S.D.Cal. 1998).

Amendment permits news reporting and parody even when trademarks are viewed or described. Some infringement examples are summarized in Exhibit 18.6.

REMEDIES

Owners of marks have several Lanham Act remedies against others whose infringement or dilution causes damage. The most direct and powerful relief is often an equitable remedy, such as an injunction, because it halts the infringement and prevents further damage. Monetary remedies include compensation for two types of loss: damages to the mark and the infringer's profits. The mark owner must have given notice of use (™) or notice of registration (®) or prove the infringer knew the mark was in use. In exceptional cases, such as where the infringement is deliberate, attorneys' fees and costs may be awarded. There are enhanced civil and even criminal penalties for using counterfeit marks. Remedies under state law generally parallel the Lanham Act. Unlike federal remedies, some states may permit punitive damages. Attorneys' fees are seldom permitted under state law, but this may be changing. The seizure of imported counterfeit goods by U.S. Customs is discussed later.

Injunctions that order the infringement stopped may be cast in several ways. A **preliminary injunction** can be issued quickly if the mark owner is likely to succeed in the later infringement trial, and fairness favors the mark owner for such an immediate and drastic action. **Permanent injunctions** are the most common remedy under the Lanham Act. After an injunction is ordered, the infringer may also be ordered to **recall** the infringing products—that is, pay to have all products in the supply chain returned. In some cases, the injunction may also order the products destroyed if the infringing aspects cannot be separated (e.g., logos not easily removed). In the Internet context, an injunction might be directed to force the infringer to take down and cease further use of the infringing material.

Under the **Trademark Counterfeiting Act** and the **Anticounterfeiting Consumer Protection Act**, even tougher remedies are authorized: seizure, impoundment, treble damages, criminal penalties, and racketeering remedies under Racketeering Influenced and Corrupt Organization (RICO), discussed in Chapter 7. **Counterfeiting** is

EXHIBIT 18.6 Examples of Infringing and Noninfringing Marks

Primary Mark: Product	Secondary Mark: Product	Likelihood of Confusion?
Toys "R" Us: retail toy sales	Guns Are Us: retail gun sales	None; toys is national, guns only local[33]
Post-It: adhesive note pads	Post-it.com	Yes; infringement and intentional consumer confusion likely[34]
Miracle Whip: food	Yogowhip: food	None; *whip* not the most important element of mark
Little Caesar: pizza	Pizza Caesar: pizza	None; toga-clad character sufficiently different from chariot riding character
McDonald's: various fast foods	McPretzel: soft pretzel	Yes; existing family of marks includes similar uses

33. *Toys "R" Us Inc. v. Feinberg*, 26 F.Supp.2d 639 (S.D.N.Y. 1998).

34. *Minnesota Mining & Mfg. v. Taylor*, 21 F.Supp.2d 1003 (D.Minn. 1998).

the use of a spurious mark, identical to or indistinguishable from a registered mark. Counterfeit goods are fake copies made with the intent to defraud consumers into believing they were produced by the mark owner. For example, fake designer jeans, complete with distinctive labels and unique stitching, are a recurring problem. Destruction of fake jeans may be unnecessary if the counterfeit labels are removed.

Injunctions are the preferred remedy because they are immediate and because monetary damages are often difficult to prove. To get monetary relief, there must be actual consumer confusion, a somewhat more rigorous standard than the infringement standard: likelihood (potential) of confusion. Consumer surveys and testimony are relevant. Confusion is presumed for intentional infringement. **Actual damages** include lost sales and injury to reputation and goodwill. For example, lost sales might be based on the mark owner's reasonable marketing estimates projected from past sales. However, damages are difficult to prove, partly because economics and accounting do not yet provide reliable measures of goodwill and because there are no reliable valuation methods for reputational losses.

By contrast, it may be easier to disgorge the infringer's **undeserved profits** if reliable financial data are available. The mark owner must first prove the infringer's gross sales. Next, the infringer has the burden of proving production costs or profits not due to infringement (e.g., noninfringing components). In some cases, the trial court judge may find the damages computed are substantially lower than the overall damage apparently suffered by the mark owner. In such cases, the trial court may order **treble damages**—up to three times the actual damages as computed. These are not punitive damages.

INTERNATIONAL TRADEMARK

As with most forms of IP, a registration in one nation, as well as satisfaction of a particular nation's laws, does not assure protection in other nations. Unfortunately, there are difficulties in assuring IP rights in international commerce. International trademark law has similar challenges. The Internet offers global opportunities for visual communications associated with commercial symbols. As cross-border sales of trademarked information products expands, the potential for international trademark disputes may also expand. Soon the global reach of trademarks will be much greater than the gray market and counterfeit goods problems discussed here.

Gray goods are imported products sold outside the normal supply chain. For example, the price of Mercedes-Benz cars is significantly higher in the United States than in Germany. This huge price discrepancy gives U.S. car dealers an incentive to purchase cheaper new and slightly used Mercedes cars from foreign distributors, dealers, Mercedes employees, and customers for import into the United States. The manufacturer, Daimler-Chrysler, conditions the use of the Mercedes mark, the familiar circled three-point star, on compliance with strict importation rules it imposes on its U.S. subsidiary and local franchised dealers. This system is fairly effective in preventing importation and sale of Mercedes cars outside the official supply chain. A portion of the gross profits from U.S. sales of Mercedes cars made through the official supply chain is used to fund advertising and warranty repair costs. Cars imported through other nations or directly from Germany do not carry their share of these legitimate marketing expenses, and these unlicensed importers ride free on expenses paid in the regular supply chain. Of course, if there was a cheaper, alternate supply channel, Mercedes would be unable to keep prices so much higher in the United States. Also recognize that some goods first sold abroad are illegal or unsuitable for sale in some other nation. Cars sold in the United States must meet stringent safety and emissions standards that are not used in other nations. As a result, many imported gray market products must be heavily modified. Television sets use incompatible broadcast standards, NTSC in the United States and Canada versus PAL in Europe, making such gray goods nearly useless.

Sales of counterfeit goods in the United States are likely to be trademark infringement. By contrast, sales of gray market goods in the United States are not trademark infringement. If the foreign manufacturer is related to the U.S. importer that has registered the mark, there is no right under the U.S. Tariff Act to request the U.S. Customs Service to block imports of gray market goods. However, if the U.S. importer and foreign manufacturer are independent, importation of the gray market goods can be blocked.[35] The Lanham Act §42 has been used to block goods rightfully produced under the mark overseas if they have different characteristics than do the goods sold in U.S. markets (e.g., differences in soap fragrance or sudsing).[36] However, these laws cannot stop importation of personal purchases by domestic tourists traveling abroad.

TRADEMARKS AND THE INTERNET

The Internet magnifies many things: communication, depth and breadth of discovery, and the visibility of commercial symbols. The full implication of the Internet on trademarks is uncertain but already emerging in several key areas. First, websites permit broad communication of commentary and criticism that can adversely affect mark owner reputation through tarnishment. Second, the practices of linking, framing, and meta-tag usage raise the potential for passing off and other false association problems discussed in Chapter 13. Third, this section discusses the connection between trademarks and domain names and how the relationship triggers problems such as cyber squatting.

DOMAIN NAMES AND TRADEMARKS

In the Internet's early years, the assignment of domain names was done largely by Network Solutions Incorporated (NSI), operating under a subcontract form the National Science Foundation (NSF). Domain names were granted on a first-come, first-served basis, and few processes were established to settle ownership or trademark conflict disputes. However, today it is becoming evident that TLDs serve a trademark function much like other components of marks (color, smell, trade dress). Domain names are becoming an integral part of the trademark system because they often satisfy trademark standards.

Some Internet traditionalists are troubled by this development. They insist that URLs are merely technical addresses and were never intended to be marks. However, URLs function like telephone mnemonics (e.g., 1-800-FLOWERS) because they are often accurately guessed. Case law and legislation in the 1990s now recognize that domain names serve trademark functions of source identification, indicate quality, and are repositories of goodwill. URLs are susceptible to trademark problems such as

35. *KMart Corp. v. Cartier, Inc.*, 486 U.S. 281 (1988).
36. *Lever Bros. Co. v. U.S.*, 877 F.2d 101 (D.C.Cir., 1989).

Commentary

Domain Names on the Internet

Each computer has a unique identifier or address so computers can locate each while connected to the Internet. ***IP addresses*** consist of 12 digits separated by periods into four groups of three numerals, (i.e., 131.211.131.111). Domain names, also called uniform resource locators (***URL***), are renamed versions of IP addresses that are more easily recognizable (e.g., Thompson.com). However, URLs often closely resemble commercial symbols and trademarks. Webpages also display trademarks for advertising and other purposes.

URLs are most often structured into four or more distinct subelements: First, the transfer protocol is stated (http:// or ftp://); second, a network sector is given (e.g., www for World Wide Web); third, a particular domain name is used, divided into the unique portion (e.g., thomson for Thomson Inc.) and a generic portion, the top level domain (TLD) name indicating the type of entity owning the domain name—.com for commercial, .edu for educational institution, .org for nonprofit organization, and .gov for government. Creating new TLDs has been a very political process, but several more were introduced in 2001, including .biz, and .info, expanding the potential URLs dramatically. Following the TLD, there can be several other different pieces of address information that more precisely identify or direct access to the content sought. They include country codes for various nations, state codes for the 50 U.S. state governments, and subdirectories or filenames for the particular documents sought. The specific file information often includes a file extension (e.g., .htm, .html, .pdf, .jpg). These filenames may be quite long because they can be located on complex, nested subdirectories and sometimes include database search terms.

consumer confusion and functionality. Nevertheless, there are some important differences between URLs and domain names. Domain names are acquired through registration with a domain name registry, a process separate from trademark acquisition through use or PTO registration.

REGISTRATION OF DOMAIN NAMES

The monopoly NSI held over administering the Internet domain name system expired in June 1999. Since that transitional period, several other domain name registrars have emerged (http://www.register.com) who are accredited by the Internet Corporation for Assigned Names and Numbers (ICANN) (http://www.icann.org). Someone seeking to operate a website must first obtain an IP address from an Internet service provider (ISP) (find ISPs at http://www.thelist.com). Next, provide the IP address to an accredited registrar, and, if the domain name chosen is not already registered, it can be registered for a fee. The Internet makes it easy to search for an available domain name or to actually register and pay the registration fee. Domain name registration does not assure all the Lanham Act protections offered to trademarks. It is still necessary to register the inherently distinctive mark with the

http://
www.icann.org/

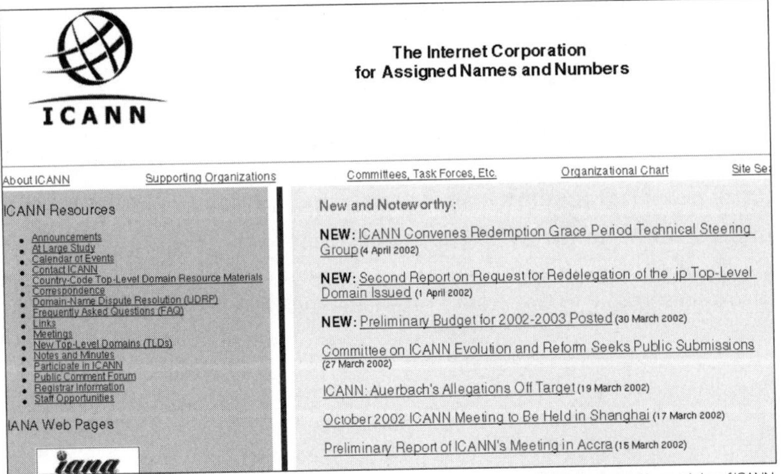

PTO, a step most established firms have already done for their most valuable marks. Domain names can be transferred, an important step in the process of completing a corporate acquisition or merger.

CYBER SQUATTING

Before 1999, many firms still remained unconvinced that the Internet was important in their business models. Indeed, many mark owners could not see why they should register their marks as domain names. Still, there are significant risks that outsiders may register domain names identical to owners' marks. Some outsiders have registered variations of others' marks or combined others' domain names with alternate TLDs (.org rather than the typical .com). Also outsiders sometimes register common misspellings of others' marks as well as their nicknames (bigblue.com for ibm.com). Recall that the domain names are registered on a first-come, first-served basis. There are no qualification standards, such as those to avoid confusing similarity that are required for trademark prosecution and PTO examination. Instead, domain name registrars simply accept applications unless the precise domain name sought is already registered to another owner. These circumstances contributed to **cyber squatting,** the practice of acquiring domain names for ransom and resale to the original owners of similar marks.

Consider the landmark example of Panavision International, which owned two famous marks, Panavision and Panaflex.[37] These marks were used in connection with the firm's photographic imaging business. In 1995, Dennis Toeppen registered panavision.com and later registered panaflex.com before Panavision International fully appreciated the importance of Internet commerce or the risk that others could use these marks as domain names. On simple websites using these domain names, Toeppen displayed only an aerial view of the town Pana, Illinois, and on another site he posted only "hello." Toeppen never did any real business using the domain names. Panavision demanded Toeppen cease using these domain names, and Toeppen demanded a $13,000 ransom. When Panavision sued to enjoin this use, the court held Toeppen had diluted Panavision's marks. Dennis Toeppen registered other famous marks and attempted other acts of what is now called cyber squatting.

Anticybersquatting Consumer Protection Act

Congress passed the **Anticybersquatting Consumer Protection Act (ACPA)** in 1999 to remedy this practice. ACPA makes it unlawful to traffic in or use domain names that are identical or confusingly similar to distinctive marks protected under state trademark law or the federal Lanham Act. APCA creates a civil action authorizing the mark owner to sue if the cyber squatter has bad faith intent to profit from the cyber squatting. Remedies include cancellation of the cyber squatter's registration, transfer to the mark owner, actual money damages, and profits or statutory damages up to $100,000. The suits are ***in rem,*** which means that for jurisdiction purposes, it is irrelevant whether legal process has effectively notified a cyber squatter who provided false contact information, cannot be located with due diligence, or cannot be effectively reached using personal jurisdiction.

ACPA does not address all uses or dilution of a mark by someone other than the mark owner. For example, recall the discussion of First Amendment freedom of speech and the press in Chapter 4. Trademark law and dispute resolution of domain

37. *Panavision Int'l v. Dennis Toeppen*, 945 F.Supp. 1296 (C.D.Cal. 1996), *af'd.* 140 F.3d 1316 (9th Cir., 1998).

EXHIBIT 18.7 ACPA Factors in Determining "Bad Faith" Cybersquatting

1. Trademark ownership rights by mark owner
2. Closeness between domain name and cyber squatter's name
3. Cybersquatter's use of the domain name in commerce for access to a website
4. Cybersquatter's intent to divert Web traffic from the mark owner
5. Cybersquatter's offer to ransom the domain name to the mark owner
6. Whether cybersquatter gave misleading information in domain name registration
7. Cybersquatter's repeated, similar cybersquatting on other owners' marks
8. Whether mark is distinctive and famous

names should not prevent legitimate news reporting, parody, criticism or even griping directed against a mark owner. For example, the legality of the dot.sucks sites or simply adding *–sucks* after a mark to create a domain name is a hotly debated question. Mark owners legitimately seek to protect their marks. However, the use of trademark law to stifle criticism probably violates the First Amendment. On the other extreme are uses of domain names by fans and admirers of the mark owner (fan clubs).

ACPA remedies are triggered when the cyber squatter is guilty of **bad faith** in registering the mark owner's trademark as a domain name. ACPA lists nine factors that courts may consider in determining the cyber squatter's bad faith, as listed in Exhibit 18.7. The following case illustrates an application of the ACPA bad faith standards.

Shields v. Zuccarini

254 F.3d 476 (3d Cir., 2001).

Facts. Shields operated a cartoon business for 15 years and registered the joecartoon.com domain name in June 1997. Shields operates a "shock site," where interactive cartoons are displayed for visitors. For example, "Frog Blender" permits visitors to click on a cartoon blender to watch a cartoon frog spin inside a food blender until the frog explodes into a bloody mess. A similar cartoon microwave oven displays the cooking and explosion of a rodent in "Micro-Gerbil." Shields licenses these and other images for T-shirt and coffee mug sales and can earn 10 to 25 cents per banner ad click-through from the approximately 700,000 visitors each month. Zuccarini registered and operates five close and predictable misspellings: joescartoon.com, joecarton.com, joescartons.com, joescartoons.com, and cartoonjoe.com. Visitors intentionally diverted to Zuccarini's sites cannot exit the mistaken site unless they click on banner ads ("mousetrapping").

Legal Issue. Is the registration and use of intentionally misspelled versions of popular website URLs a violation of the ACPA? Is intentional cyber squatting so egregious as to constitute "exceptional," permitting the award of attorneys' fees?

Opinion. [ACPA] was intended to prevent "cybersquatting," an expression that has come to mean the bad faith, abusive registration and use of the distinctive trademarks of others as Internet domain names, with the intent to profit from the goodwill associated with those trademarks. Under the ACPA, successful plaintiffs may recover statutory damages in an amount to be assessed by the district court in its discretion, from $1,000 to $100,000 per domain name. To succeed on his ACPA claim, Shields was required to prove that (1) "Joe Cartoon" is a distinctive or famous mark entitled to protection; (2) Zuccarini's domain names are "identical or confusingly similar to" Shields' mark; and (3) Zuccarini registered the domain names with the bad faith intent to profit from them.

Shields runs the only "Joe Cartoon" operation in the nation and has done so for the past fifteen years. This suggests both the inherent and acquired distinctiveness of the "Joe Cartoon" name. Shields has used the domain name joecartoon.com as a web site since June 1997 to display his animations and sell products featuring his drawings. The longevity of his use suggests that "Joe Cartoon" has acquired some fame in the marketplace. The *New York Times* ran a page one story that quoted Shields and cited Joe Cartoon. Joe Cartoon T-shirts have been sold across the country since at least the early 1990s, and its products appear on the web site of at least one nationally known retail chain, Spencer Gifts. Shields has advertised in an online humor magazine with a circulation of about 1.4 million. The Joe Cartoon web site receives in excess of 700,000 visits per month, bringing it wide publicity. According to Shields, word-of-mouth also generates considerable interest in the Joe Cartoon site. Shields trades nationwide in both real and virtual markets. The web site gives Joe Cartoon a global reach. Shields's cartoons and merchandise are marketed on the Internet, in gift shops and at tourist venues. The Joe Cartoon mark has won a huge following because of the work of Shields. In light of the above, we conclude that "Joe Cartoon" is distinctive, and, with 700,000 hits a month, the web site "joecartoon.com" qualifies as being famous. Therefore, the trademark and domain name are protected under the ACPA.

The domain names—joescartoon.com, joecarton.com, joescartons.com, joescartoons.com and cartoonjoe.com—closely resemble "joecartoon.com," with a few additional or deleted letters, or, in the last domain name, by rearranging the order of the words. To divert Internet traffic to his sites, Zuccarini admits that he registers domain names, including the five at issue here, because they are likely misspellings of famous marks or personal names. The strong similarity between these domain names and joecartoon.com persuades us that they are "confusingly similar." Shields also produced evidence of Internet users who were actually confused by Zuccarini's sites. A reasonable interpretation of conduct covered by the phrase "confusingly similar" is the intentional registration of domain names that are misspellings of distinctive or famous names, causing an Internet user who makes a slight spelling or typing error to reach an unintended site. The ACPA's legislative history contemplates such situations:

[C]ybersquatters often register well-known marks to prey on consumer confusion by misusing the domain name to divert customers from the mark owner's site to the cybersquatter's own site, many of which are pornography sites that derive advertising revenue based on the number of visits, or "hits," the site receives. For example, the Committee was informed of a parent whose child mistakenly typed in the domain name for "dosney.com," expecting to access the family-oriented content of the Walt Disney home page, only to end up staring at a screen of hardcore pornography because a cybersquatter had registered that domain name in anticipation that consumers would make that exact mistake.

We conclude that Zuccarini's conduct here is a classic example of a specific practice the ACPA was designed to prohibit.

Zuccarini's conduct satisfies a number of [ACPA's bad faith] factors. Zuccarini has never used the infringing domain names as trademarks or service marks; thus, he has no intellectual property rights in these domain names. The domain names do not contain any variation of the legal name of Zuccarini, nor any other name commonly used to identify him. Zuccarini has never used the infringing domain names in connection with the bona fide offering of goods or services. He does not use these domain names for a noncommercial or "fair use" purpose. He deliberately maintains these domain names to divert consumers from Shields's web site. In so doing, he harms the goodwill associated with the mark. He does this either for commercial gain, or with the intent to tarnish or disparage Shields's mark by creating a likelihood of confusion. He has knowingly registered thousands of Internet domain names that are identical to, or confusingly similar to, the distinctive marks of others, without the permission of the mark holders to do so.

Zuccarini argues that his web sites were protected by the First Amendment because he was using them as self-described "protest pages." Therefore, he contends, his use falls under the safe harbor, which states that "[b]ad faith intent . . . shall not be found in any case in which the court determines that the person believed and had reasonable grounds to believe that the use of the domain name was a fair use or otherwise lawful." The district court rejected this argument based on its conclusion that Zuccarini's claim of good faith and fair use was a "spurious explanation cooked up purely for this suit." Zuccarini admitted that he is in the business of profiting from the public's confusion and that he does, in fact, profit from this confusion. The district court properly concluded that this injunction would be in the public interest.

[T]he district court made a proper finding that, under the circumstances, this case qualified as "exceptional" and merited the award of attorneys' fees. The record indicates that Zuccarini's conduct was particularly flagrant and that he showed no remorse for his actions.

Decision. Registration and use of intentionally misspelled version of website URL violates ACPA and merits award of attorney's fees.

Case Questions

1. Compare how confusing similarity expands a trademark beyond its precise spelling and look to similar words and images with the protection offered by APCA beyond precise domain names to include various misspellings.
2. Explain the three main inquiries used under ACPA to find a cyber squatting violation. How do these standards compare with the likelihood of confusion standard for trademark infringement?

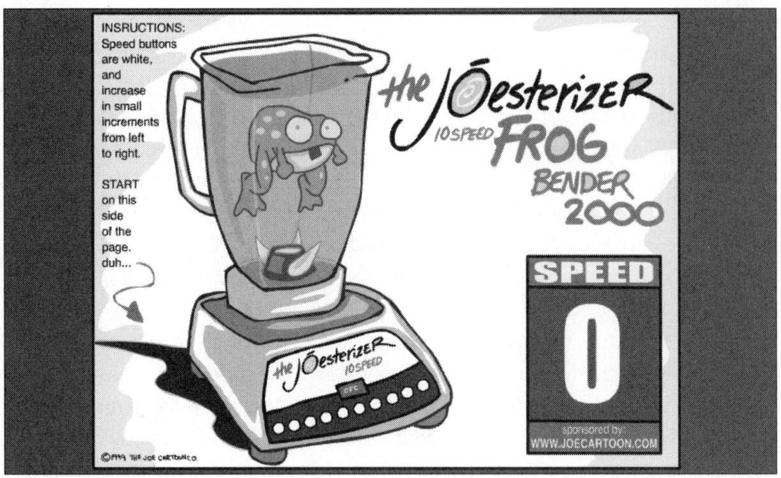

http://
www.joecartoon.com/cartoons/frog.html

ICANN's Uniform Domain Name Dispute Resolution Policy

Before 1999, NSI operated a domain name dispute resolution policy, but it was criticized and there was litigation. A white paper by the National Telecommunications and Information Agency (http://www.ntia.doc.gov) of the Department of Commerce recommended that the World Intellectual Property Organization convene a study to recommend a new dispute resolution procedure. This resulted in the ICANN Uniform Domain Name Dispute Resolution Policy (UDRP), a form of international arbitration that has been in effect since December 1999. In the first year, various ICANN-approved "providers" (arbitrators) used the UDRP to settle more than 2,000 disputes. ICANN claims that nearly 75% of domain name disputes filed under the UDRP have resulted in cancellation of the cyber squatter's domain name registration.

Most of the UDRP standards for cyber squatting are similar to the ACPA standards. However, the UDRP differs from litigation in the United States under ACPA in five major ways. First, the UDRP is arbitration, so it has many cost, timing, and confidentiality differences with litigation. Second, the UDRP ostensibly applies to international domain name disputes. Third, the UDRP hearings are ex parte, and all proceedings are based on documents filed; there are no parties present, no witnesses are examined, and legal counsel is not present. Fourth, UDRP awards are not binding on the courts and, *unlike* most other forms of arbitration, they can be appealed. Fifth, the UDRP may be used before or after litigation. UDRP decisions are listed on the ICANN website (http://www.icann.org/udrp).

QUESTIONS

1. What are the major goals of trademark law? Relate these goals with the major questions and analyses used in resolving the major questions under trademark law: distinctiveness, consumer confusion, and functionality.
2. Why does trademark law protect the public domain? What aspects or elements of trademarks does trademark law closely examine to preserve the public domain? Trademark law encourages investment by mark owners into what type of asset: artistic innovation, goodwill, or quality control? Why?
3. As originally introduced in Exhibit 7.3 and shown again in the first row of the example, complete the following table by (1) classifying each mark in the third column as arbitrary/fanciful, suggestive, descriptive, or generic for its use with the product listed and (2) giving a short phrase in the fourth column to justify your classification.

Mark	Product	Classification	Rationale for classification
Wrangler	Clothing—jeans	Suggestive	Evokes cowboy image
L.A. Gear	Shoes		
Glacier	Ice		
Apple	Fruit		
Apple	Personal computer		
Bed & Breakfast Registry	Lodging reservation service		
"You've got mail"	E-mail service notification		

4. The size, shape, and color combinations used in prescription drugs are often very distinctive. At a glance, an elderly person, emergency room nurse, or an EMS technician can identify such pills, even when the original packaging is missing or repackaged in some other bottle. Many popular and profitable new wonder drugs have patent protection for many years, and these patent terms can be extended to account for premarket efficacy testing before sales are permitted to the public. Drug manufacturers use unique trademarks and trade dress appearance to distinguish their brand of such drugs. However, when these patents expire, highly profitable drugs are often met with competition from generic products. Should trademark law prevent generics from using similar pill designs under the theory that generics are confusing consumers by palming off their products as the original? Is it reasonable to presume consumers are really all that confused, given consumer involvement in choosing generics because they are often so much cheaper? Consider the public policy impact. What trademark limitation would work in the favor of generics in this instance? See *Ives Laboratory, Inc. v. Darby Drug Co.*, 601 F.2d 1379 (2d Cir., 1979).
5. Consider the legal theories applicable to the drug capsule appearance problem discussed in the previous question. A parallel argument can be made about compatibility, both aesthetic and functional. The maker of plastic molded office stacking trays argued that the connecting points that allow its brand of paper trays to lock together are not functional and thus protected under trademark law. Under this argument, another manufacturer would be prevented from using a design that securely interlocks with those of the mark owner. Should trademark or trade dress law prevent a competitor from producing replacement or additional products to work with the mark owner's product? See *W. T. Rogers Co. Inc. v. Keene*, 778 F.2d 334 (7th Cir., 1985).
6. Compare and contrast the principal register and the supplemental register. What types of marks are most appropriate for each? What different protections are offered marks registered on one versus the other? How and why would a mark move from one register to the other?
7. Bensusan operates a famous jazz club in New York City under the federally registered trademark The Blue Note. Richard King operates a small club in Columbia, Missouri, also called The Blue Note and uses a logo similar to Bensusan's logo. Bensusan discovered King's use of the mark when the Missouri club posted its website on a server located in Missouri. Should jurisdiction over King be permitted in an infringement suit brought by Bensusan in federal courts in New York? If jurisdiction issues are resolved, how could the two marks be accommodated? Explain how the standard of infringement will be used in this case? See *Bensusan Restaurant Corp. v. King*, 937 F.Supp. 295 (S.D.N.Y. 1996) *aff'd*, 126 F.3d 25 (2d Cir., 1997).
8. PanaSony of Japan manufactures a line of high-quality portable MP3 personal listening systems about the size of a fountain pen. In the first few years, they were imported by PanaSony of the U.S., a wholly owned subsidiary of PanaSony of Japan. The PanaSony PenMan prices range from $200 for a basic model with wired headphones to $500 for a tiny but powerful "wireless ear bud" model. In Japan and much of the Pacific Rim, "street" retail prices for nearly identical models sell for less than half the U.S. wholesale price. Some enterprising exporters in Hong Kong and importers in San Diego begin to ship large quantities of the PenMan through Tijuana, Mexico, and then through nearby San Diego to other U.S. markets. PanaSony suspects the large wholesale quantities sold to Hong Kong distributors may be part of a gray market supply chain into the United States. Explain the gray goods problem, including the purposes and likely impact of regulating gray goods. What remedies are available to PanaSony under trade law? What are the trademark law remedies?
9. Define the grievance known as cyber squatting. What is the apparent motive in cyber squatting? What remedies are available under the ACPA law? What is a reasonable strategy for trademark owners as they start e-commerce activities using the Internet or as new TLDs emerge?
10. Compare and contrast the standards for infringement under U.S. trademark law with the standards used in the ICANN process for resolving disputes between domain name registrants and trademark owners of identical or similar marks.

Regulation

PART V

In the early days of the Internet, really just a decade ago for most people, law was rarely invoked. The Internet community was self-regulated, supplemented by contractual agreements among owners/operators of the communications and computing infrastructure. The U.S. government and the National Science Foundation provided seed money and nominal oversight to assure that the system functioned. Standardization emerged to "regulate" functionality but the lack of central control was the Internet's primary design objective. This autonomy makes the Internet robust and relatively immune to attack. Many long-time Internet participants are really libertarians at heart. They believe this lack of regulation amounts to utopia. However, this vision is artificial. An unregulated Internet could not be sustained after large sectors of the population discovered the Internet's power and utility.

Through the 1990s, the many risks of the Internet's open architecture became apparent, one by one, and regulatory responses developed. This book chronicles the progressive identification and resolution of these risks. It reviews how some solutions are destined to failure while many traditional legal concepts adapt fairly well to cyberspace. Fences are going up in cyberspace; that is, property rights are protected, dependable commercial relations are emerging, and public order is restored by legal and regulatory institutions, in much the same way the Wild West was made safe for civilization and commerce. Regulation over e-commerce and other Internet activities is spreading rapidly.

The regulation of business has been pervasive, perhaps among the most significant legal and economic developments of the twentieth century. Administrative agencies at the local, state, and federal levels create regulations and enforce laws covering most aspects of business activity. There has been a long-standing trend toward deregulation—the dismantling of regulatory programs and the reform of regulatory processes. Nevertheless, regulation imposes significant constraints and will continue to do so for the foreseeable future. For business to effectively manage its regulatory environment, managers must understand the public policy pressures for re-regulation, the substance of existing and proposed regulations, and the administrative processes agencies use. These matters, including the processes used by particular regulatory programs, are discussed throughout this book.

The regulatory focus of Part V includes six major areas and several sub-areas of regulation with significant impact on businesses in the converging economies. Chapter 19, Antitrust, discusses efforts to discourage monopolies and thereby assure the benefits of full and complete competition. Chapter 20, Labor and Employment, reviews the regulation of unionization and the resulting labor-management relations as focused through collective bargaining. Chapter 21, Equal Employment Opportunities, focuses on legal restrictions against employment discrimination that unlawfully rely on demographic factors rather than actual job performance. Chapter 22, Securities Regulations, discusses special rules for publicly-traded companies when they access capital through the public investment markets. Chapter 23, Environmental Law, covers the local, state, and federal regulation of pollution abatement. Finally, Chapter 24, Internet Regulation, focuses on several matters important to both traditional businesses and e-commerce in consumer protection, telecommunications, and taxation of business and the Internet.

CHAPTER 19

Antitrust

Antitrust law is a complex area of regulation that affects strategic planning, business modeling, marketing strategy, pricing, and the conduct of most supply-chain relations with suppliers, competitors, and customers. Antitrust was originally derived from English law that prohibited restraints of trade. It grew to prominence in the United States as the robber barons of the gilded age built huge monopolies. Antitrust analysis cannot be well understood without some familiarity with the economic theory of industrial organization. Economics strongly suggests that when compared with the ideal of perfect competition, monopolies charge higher prices, innovate more slowly, and reduce their output below what the market needs. Repeated experiences with monopolists prove these predictions. Antitrust regulates a wide range of activities involving horizontal relations with competitors, vertical relations with suppliers and customers, and conglomerate relations in other industries.

Antitrust takes on renewed importance as intellectual property (IP) becomes a major source of most firms' value in the future. For example, IP law grants monopoly-like rights to software companies through software copyrights, trade secrets, patents, and trademarks. Microsoft makes the operating systems (Windows) and applications software (Office, Internet browsers) used on 80% to 90% of all personal computers (PCs). Software companies must be compatible with Microsoft's Windows operating system or with its browser, Internet Explorer. Without compatibility, these competitors are nearly locked out of the PC market.

How does society reconcile the monopolies of IP law with the antitrust laws? Each is intended to encourage innovation and efficiency. On one hand, antitrust prohibits monopolization and promotes vigorous, direct rivalry by numerous competitors. On the other hand, IP law grants limited monopolies and gives the patent or copyright holder the power to control or prohibit direct competition. Accommodating these two major bodies of law poses big challenges for the information age. Former Chairman Robert Pitofsky of the Federal Trade Commission (FTC) argues that these laws must be balanced because IP is "now a principal, if not the principal, barrier to new entry in high-tech markets."

FOUNDATIONS OF THE ANTITRUST LAWS

The encouragement of competition is a primary goal of the antitrust laws. Other goals include maintaining liberty, assuring fairness, and providing economic opportunity. The nineteenth-century populists promoted antitrust law as a way to sustain a system of small, independent businesses and preserve the American dream. They thought that further concentration of political and economic power would encourage the growth of power centers, reminiscent of feudalism, that might eventually rival the power of government. Populists considered the diffusion and decentralization of both political and economic power to be necessary conditions for democracy and liberty.

"The Sherman Act was designed to be a comprehensive charter of economic liberty aimed at preserving free and unfettered competition. It rests on the premise that unrestrained interaction of competitive forces will yield the best allocation of our economic resources, the lowest prices, the highest quality, and the greatest material progress."[1] This statement justifies antitrust laws as an incentive to innovate, maintain productive efficiency, and maximize the range and selection of goods. Monopolies are damaging because they limit production, risk poor quality, and empower monopolists to fix prices and exclude competitors. These outcomes directly conflict with the goals promised by competition. Antitrust laws are intended to maintain a competitive environment.

The Microsoft antitrust litigation has focused attention on two important public policy questions going forward. First, in the future, will the world's economy become so dominated by information products that markets for industrial products will become far less relevant? Second, will the economic theory and laws designed for the twentieth-century industrial economy become unsuitable to the evolving marketplace, making the antitrust laws inappropriate for an information economy? This chapter reviews the antitrust laws and gauges their impact on the traditional economy and on IP and the network economy as a means to resolve the question of whether the antitrust laws and the perfect competition model are becoming obsolete or whether a strong economy can be sustained by balancing strong antitrust values with IP rights.

TRADITIONAL MARKET STRUCTURES

Traditional economic analysis defines five basic market structures: perfect competition, monopoly, oligopoly, monopolistic competition, and monopsony. This analytic model is used to predict the purchasing behaviors of consumers and the pricing, production, and collusive behaviors of sellers. Under **perfect competition**, there are a large number of buyers and sellers. No individual firm or consumer has sufficient market power to influence prices or the quantity of production. Perfect competition presumes there are low barriers to entry, uniform products, and perfect information concerning market conditions that is shared by all. Antitrust enforcement would be unnecessary if all markets were perfectly competitive. These assumptions are unrealistic in the real world, but perfect competition is useful as a model for economic analysis and as an objective. The securities markets and the markets for gasoline or groceries in larger cities often come close to perfect competition.

1. *Northern Pacific Railway Co. v. United States*, 365 U.S. 1 (1958).

Monopoly describes a market dominated by one large seller. Typically, there are no close substitutes for the seller's product. There are usually high **barriers to entry** that make it difficult for other firms to compete. Legal barriers to entry include IP (patents, copyrights, trade secrets), franchises, international trade barriers, and restrictive licenses. Natural barriers to entry include high transportation costs and high capital equipment costs. Some utilities have natural monopolies in their service areas because of the expense to duplicate the power generators or distribution wiring and plumbing. Utilities have been regulated to reduce their monopolistic tendencies. An **oligopoly** is a small number of sellers protected by high barriers to entry. These strong sellers typically have market power to influence prices and quantity. The U.S. domestic steel market was long regarded as an oligopoly: Steel is an interchangeable commodity, and there was little price competition. Prices tend to be higher and output lower in oligopolistic markets than under perfect competition. **Monopolistic competition** involves markets with few sellers offering somewhat substitutable but differentiated products. Examples include automobiles, soft drinks, beer, and PCs. Each producer distinguishes its models in consumers' minds, even though most products are somewhat interchangeable for their basic purposes. Monopolistic competitors possess some market power, are considered slow to innovate, and spend more on marketing than in perfectly competitive markets.

Monopsony exists when a single buyer possesses monopoly buying power. **Oligopsony** exists when a few buyers have market power. For example, the employer in a company town is a monopsonist because, as the predominant buyer of labor, it can affect prices (wages) and set them lower than under perfect competition.

NETWORK EFFECTS AND ANTITRUST

Recall that **network effects** were introduced in Chapter 11 as the main challenge to developing new payment systems. In the antitrust context, network effects are used to criticize traditional **industrial organization economics** as the focus of antitrust law. At the heart of this debate are three key arguments used to oppose antitrust enforcement against firms in the information economy. First, in the future, the information economy will sell ideas and intangibles, and this sector will dominate the whole economy. This argument presumes that the impact of traditional industrial production of physical goods will diminish significantly. Second, it is argued that the information economy is not governed by an industrial age concept, the **law of diminishing returns**, which is based on the scarcity of raw materials. The law of diminishing returns predicts that profitability drops after the production of physical goods expands beyond some point of optimal efficiency. In information businesses, there is an unlimited supply of ideas and intangible assets. They have potentially unlimited **economies of scale** that produce increasing returns as IP or network products are sold to more and more customers.[2] The third argument is that a strong system of IP rights is an adequate substitute as an innovation incentive, so society should abandon antitrust enforcement, particularly in high-technology industries. Such New Age economists believe that society does not long suffer under an IP monopoly because the IP laws provide a strong incentive to develop **substitutes**—new competing technologies that do not directly infringe the monopolist's IP.

2. See W. Brian Arthur, Increasing Returns and the New World of Business. *Harvard Business Review*, July–August , 1996.

These three arguments support a **winner-take-all** system for information products. This results from **positive feedback**, a consumption-side economy of scale produced by the network effects of information products. Information products are most successful if they are allowed a limited-time monopoly to pay back the significant initial R&D expense and technical know-how needed for development. Information products are more valuable to users and producers when they are standardized.

The **first-mover advantage** is also strong for sellers of information products. Sellers have an incentive to enter the market quickly and discount their products. Some even buy their customer base by selling their products below cost to **lock in** a large user base. Thereafter, customers have high **switching costs**, making it difficult to change vendors or adopt new standards. The seller has a loyal customer base that can be exploited with highly profitable sales throughout the product's useful life. Consider the example of a firm-wide computer network, telephone system, or software purchase. These systems often require training and installation. The costs of switching to competing systems can be so prohibitive that switching occurs only after the assets are fully depreciated or become obsolete.

Some opponents of antitrust enforcement against network industries hope to rely exclusively on the innovation incentive of IP to eventually produce potential competitors. Under this theory, they advocate only a diminished role for antitrust enforcement. The natural behavior and benefits of network industries may produce benefits for society. However, it may be necessary to monitor firms achieving dominance so that innovation by potential competitors is not thwarted. As you become more familiar with antitrust law in this chapter, consider how the traditional antitrust theories could apply to firms in the information economy: monopolization, restraints of trade, and mergers that create monopolies. The application of traditional antitrust theory to IP, to network industries, and to the new economy are discussed throughout this chapter.

THE PRIMARY ANTITRUST LAWS

The U.S. antitrust laws broke new ground by directly regulating restraints of trade and monopolies. The early common law had only indirect prohibitions on covenants not to compete in employment contracts and in sales of businesses, introduced in Chapter 13. The rule of reason, discussed later, is a direct descendent from these principles. The contract law concepts of duress and economic duress underlie other antitrust laws, such as the prohibition on tying arrangements and boycotts. As the industrial revolution progressed, these common law principles were unsuitable to encourage competition sufficiently. Contract law failed to protect the competitive structure of the economy because most customers, competitors, and suppliers of monopolists lacked privity, so there was no enforceable legal remedy. The shortcomings of the common law and pressure from populists eventually spawned the federal and state antitrust laws.

SHERMAN ACT

The **Sherman Act** was passed in 1890 as the first major antitrust law. It uses vague and general terms to prohibit anticompetitive devices that restrain trade and erect the barrier of monopoly to any trade or other aspect of interstate commerce. Section 1 of the Sherman Act makes it an unlawful criminal act to enter into a "contract, combination . . . or conspiracy in restraint of trade." Section 2 of the Sherman Act prohibits monopolization by stating that "every person who shall monopolize, or attempt to monopolize, or combine or conspire with any other person or persons, to monopolize any part of the trade of commerce among the several states, or with foreign nations shall be deemed guilty of a felony."

CLAYTON ACT

Initially, the federal courts were quite lenient in their interpretations of the Sherman Act. One early case held that manufacturing was not interstate commerce, so the federal government could not regulate it.[3] Although that view was soon abandoned, it illustrates how the courts' laissez-faire ideology restrained antitrust enforcement. Eventually Congress responded to the mounting criticism in 1914 by passing the **Clayton Act**. It was written in more explicit terms, outlawing specific anticompetitive activities. Whereas the Sherman Act requires proof of completed anticompetitive effects, the Clayton Act can be violated earlier, when anticompetitive tendencies arise from conduct even before competition is damaged. Section 7 of the Clayton Act prohibits interlocking directorates and mergers or stock acquisitions that result in a substantial lessening of competition. Section 3 prohibits tie-in sales, exclusive dealing arrangements, and requirements for contracts that "substantially lessen competition or tend to create a monopoly."

FEDERAL TRADE COMMISSION ACT

The Federal Trade Commission Act was also passed in 1914. It created the FTC and gave the FTC broad powers to enforce the Sherman and Clayton Acts, as well as "unfair methods of competition" and "unfair or deceptive acts or practices." Practices that are not clearly illegal under other antitrust laws may still be unlawful under the FTC Act. The rule-making power of the FTC permits it to fill in the gaps of the antitrust laws through investigation and enforcement of unfair trade practices. FTC proceedings usually involve an internal hearing held before an administrative law judge. The FTC often resolves such complaints with a **consent decree**, settling charges without an admission or denial. Defendants must usually promise to refrain from the practice in the future. The FTC may also issue **cease and desist orders**, which are stronger than injunctions because the defendant must stop the activity that is an unfair trade practice. Also, the defendant bears the stigma of a repeat offender. The FTC's orders are enforced with contempt citations, fines, and imprisonment. Appeals may be taken to the FTC commissioners and ultimately through the U.S. Court of Appeals and on to the U.S. Supreme Court.

http://

www.ftc.gov/bc/compguide/index.htm

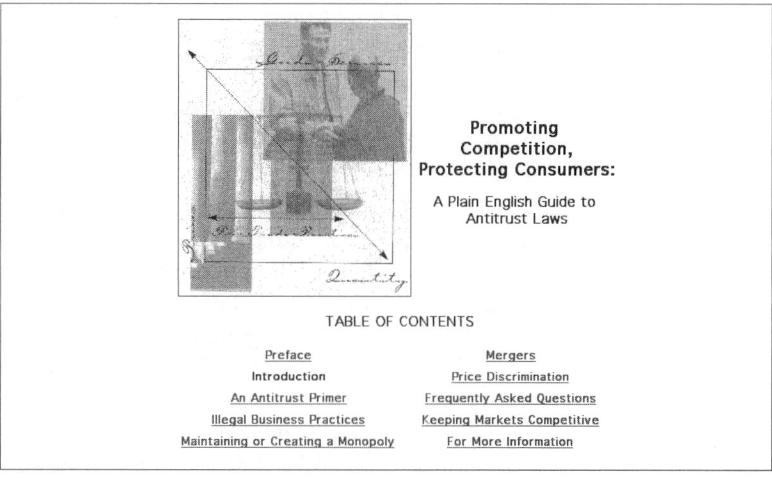

3. *United States v. E.C. Knight Co.*, 156 U.S. 1 (1896).

Like many other agencies, the FTC provides guidance and detailed notice of what the FTC considers unfair trade practices. These guidelines sometimes create **safe harbors** for specific conduct; that is, the FTC promises not to prosecute a business that conforms its transactions to the guidelines. However, FTC advisory opinions and guidelines do not have the force of law and may be reinterpreted by the courts. The FTC may also issue specific trade regulation rules that do have the force of law, for example, the FTC's requirement that gasoline retailers post octane numbers on gas pumps. Private parties may also request the FTC to issue an **advisory opinion** regarding the legality of specific proposed conduct.

ADDITIONAL FEDERAL AND STATE ANTITRUST LAWS

Over the years, Congress has strengthened the antitrust laws. In 1936, price discrimination was specifically outlawed by the **Robinson-Patman Act**. In 1950, the **Celler-Kefauver Amendment** closed a loophole by extending the merger prohibition to include corporate acquisitions in which the assets of another firm are purchased. In 1976, the **Hart-Scott-Rodino Antitrust Improvement Act** expanded the DOJ's investigative powers. Hart-Scott-Rodino requires public notice of mergers prior to their completion, and it permits prosecution of antitrust violations by the attorneys general of the states for damages caused to state citizens. The **Tunney Act** was passed after Congress became concerned that the DOJ might settle antitrust suits by favorably approving mergers and monopolization activities conducted by corporations that were substantial campaign contributors. The Tunney Act requires federal district court review of antitrust settlements negotiated between the DOJ and antitrust defendants because of the potential for political influence on the presidential administration.

Most states have antitrust laws that parallel the federal antitrust laws and the FTC Act. Typically, state antitrust laws outlaw particular anticompetitive acts such as restraints of trade, price-fixing, exclusive dealing, and tying. In recent years, several states' attorneys general have cooperated to enforce both their state and federal antitrust laws. The National Association of Attorneys General (NAAG) has coordinated various suits. Business must not be lulled into complacency over antitrust enforcement, even if federal regulators temporarily relax their enforcement activity. State attorneys general and private parties may use state laws as an alternate basis for antitrust litigation, making enforcement less susceptible to lobbying or ideological shifts in Washington.

ONLINE

National Association of Attorneys General
http://www.naag.org

ANTITRUST ENFORCEMENT

The United States has four basic antitrust law enforcers: the DOJ, the FTC, state attorneys general, and private parties. The DOJ Antitrust Division is the only enforcer with both criminal and civil enforcement powers under the Sherman Act, and the DOJ also has civil enforcement powers under the Clayton Act. The DOJ is directed by the attorney general, a cabinet member who is usually a close ideological confidant of the president. The FTC may bring civil enforcement actions for violations of the Clayton Act and has sole enforcement authority of the FTC Act. The FTC is a quasi-independent regulatory agency headed by five commissioners appointed by the president and confirmed by the Senate. This gives the FTC some political independence from the president and Congress.

Private parties may bring civil damage suits under the Sherman Act or the Clayton Act. A private party may wait to sue until a government agency successfully prosecutes the violator—a good tactic for private plaintiffs because a successful government enforcement action often provides convincing evidence of fault. **Class action** antitrust lawsuits are permissible in certain limited situations, such as when several individuals are harmed in a similar way by the defendant's monopolistic conduct. State attorneys general may sue in their ***parens patrie*** role—that is, on behalf of their state's consumers or competitors. Congress permitted these broad antitrust enforcement alternatives to promote vigorous enforcement of the antitrust laws.

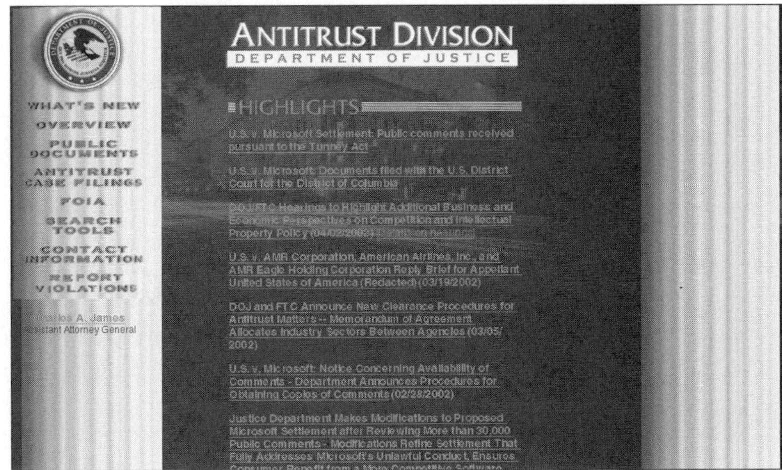

http://
www.usdoj.gov:80/atr/

CRIMINAL PENALTIES

There are substantial penalties to deter anticompetitive conduct. The Sherman Act imposes criminal sanctions on individuals, including fines of up to \$100,000, prison sentences of up to three years, or both. Corporations may be fined up to \$1 million per occurrence. Criminal convictions require proof of criminal intent, which means that the defendant must have had "knowledge of the probable consequences" of the anticompetitive action. The intent and burden of proof requirements make it difficult to obtain criminal convictions, and the predominant enforcement emphasis is on civil suits. No criminal sanctions are authorized by the Clayton or FTC Acts.

PRIVATE RIGHTS OF ACTION

The Clayton Act grants standing to "any person . . . injured in his business or property by reason of anything forbidden in the anti-trust laws," under either the Sherman Act or the Clayton Act. Private plaintiffs may recover **treble damages** (three

Antitrust Jurisdiction

Traditionally, the United States was much more concerned with antitrust enforcement than other nations. Indeed, many nations have only one or two domestic firms in a particular market, and antitrust enforcement would threaten their own firm's dominance. However, since Europe has become a common market, the EU and some other successful industrialized economies have been adopting new antimonopoly laws that resemble U.S. law. The Treaty of Rome that created the EU includes prohibitions against collusion among competitors to fix prices, control production, allocate markets, or limit the development of products or geographic markets. The EU business competition law prohibits tying, monopolization, and discretionary supply contract terms.

In recent years, the EU's Directorate General, who is responsible for enforcing the competition laws, has increased enforcement by imposing large fines for price-fixing and for collusive exchanges of sensitive price information within trade associations. Premerger competitive analysis of the affected markets is now required before regulators approve mergers. Several proposed U.S. mergers have been modified to satisfy EU antitrust concerns. The EU antitrust officials are deeply involved in litigation against Microsoft and may impose more restrictive limitations on Microsoft's marketing activities than has the DOJ.

times the actual damage sustained), plus litigation costs and reasonable attorneys' fees. Treble damages are similar to punitive damages and they are an incentive to sue. Injured competitors, consumers, suppliers, state attorneys general, and even foreign governments may sue for treble damages, but the plaintiff must be a direct purchaser. Indirect purchasers, those who purchase further down the distribution chain, are not directly injured by the anticompetitive conduct, so they may not bring treble damage claims.[4]

CIVIL REGULATORY REMEDIES

Both the FTC and the Justice Department use enforcement devices to obtain innovative remedies. First, **equitable relief** such as an injunction to prohibit future antitrust violations, is possible. This broad power permits the federal courts to restrain a particular anticompetitive conduct, compel divestiture of subsidiaries, dismember monopolies to create more competitive industries, cancel a merger, order licensing of patents with reasonable royalty payments, and cancel existing contracts. Second, consent decrees permit the government and the defendant to avoid trial by agreeing to a settlement. Typically, the defendant is notified that the regulator will file charges and then voluntarily agrees to cease its anticompetitive actions. Usually the defendant neither admits nor denies any violation of the law, and a court approves the settlement but issues a permanent injunction against future violations. **Consent decrees** avoid costly litigation and appeals. Subsequent damage suits by private plaintiffs may not take advantage of the consent decree to prove the violation; their cases must be proven separately, an added incentive for defendants to accept a consent decree. The FTC is limiting the duration of consent decrees to 20 years, and the DOJ's orders average only about 10 years.

Some settlements and consent decrees are controversial. The Tunney Act requires that a federal court must review settlements to avoid politically inspired collusion and assure that settlements are in the public interest. A federal judge found that the 1995 DOJ settlement with Microsoft was not in the public interest. Microsoft's alleged "vaporware" (premature product announcements that deter consumer purchases of competitive products) and other exclusionary practices were not addressed in the settlement, disappointing competing software companies who alleged that Microsoft restrains trade and monopolizes the software and operating system markets.[5]

INTERNATIONAL ANTITRUST ENFORCEMENT

ONLINE

European Union Laws
http://www.europa.org

The Sherman and Clayton acts apply to both domestic and foreign commerce that affects the United States. Some observers argue that U.S. antitrust laws should apply to all foreign firms' anticompetitive practices. The U.S. courts examine several factors before applying U.S. antitrust law to foreign firms' activities. Certain principles of international law restrict antitrust litigation against foreign firms. For example, the **act of state doctrine** and **sovereign immunity** prevent application of U.S. laws if the foreign activity is sponsored by a foreign government. These principles prevented challenges to Japanese firms' collusion because their activities were promoted by MITI, Japan's Ministry of Trade and Industry. **Comity** generally permits a

4. *Illinois Brick Co. v. Illinois*, 431 U.S. 720 (1977).
5. *United States v. Microsoft Corp.* (Civ. No. 94-1564), 1995 W.L. 59580 (D.D.C.).

Commentary

Laissez Faire versus Antitrust Enforcement

Laissez-faire would restrict government intervention in markets. However, observers continue to identify market failures they argue should justify some government regulation. Even Adam Smith observed that the development of monopolies and collusion should be regulated because it is inevitable. However, it is difficult to design a regulatory system that stops short of destructive interference with the beneficial activities of markets.

Theories of ***industrial organization*** attempt to explain how markets perform by examining competitor interaction and their relations with suppliers and customers. The three basic approaches to antitrust enforcement are structuralist, conduct, and performance. The ***structuralist approach*** examines the organization of each industry, identifying particular characteristics that are believed to cause anticompetitive effects. Their analysis includes the number of buyers and sellers, substitute products, industry concentration, barriers to entry, the size and geographic location of the market, and market power. Structuralists believe in strong antitrust enforcement and often advocate structural remedies, such as breaking up monopolies and divestiture.

The middle ground is a ***conduct approach***, focusing inquiry on firms' actual behaviors. Collusive or unfair business practices that are inefficient or monopolistic are condemned. For example, firms' pricing and production policies, advertising, and research and innovation practices are reviewed for anticompetitive impact. Conduct remedies focus on monitoring and preventing future illegal acts.

The actual outcomes of an alleged monopolist's conduct are the focus of ***performance analysis***. These analysts question how well the market performs and how this satisfies antitrust goals and economic efficiency. Attention focuses on technological innovation, reasonable profit performance, and reasonable barriers to entry. Often, complex economic analysis is used to determine these aspects in particular industries: costs, investments, investment return, innovation, and sales. There is very little emphasis on anticompetitive potential or conduct. Big business often supports performance analysis because it permits greater freedom of action.

There are two schools of thought on antitrust enforcement policy: the Harvard (or traditional) school and the Chicago school. The ***Harvard school of antitrust enforcement*** prefers vigorous antitrust enforcement to maintain "atomized" competition among very numerous independent businesses. It argues that concentration of economic power will nearly always lead to monopolistic or collusive behaviors. By contrast, the ***Chicago school of antitrust enforcement*** insists on more restrained enforcement, such as using a separate economic analysis in every antitrust case. It would tolerate some monopolistic behaviors if the anticompetitive effects were short-term, the monopolist competed internationally, or the monopoly profits were used for innovation. The Chicago school has become more influential in recent years. What approach seems best for an economy moving toward greater reliance on high technology, IP, and network industries?

foreign court to refuse enforcement of foreign antitrust laws unless that nation has similar laws. Strong U.S. antitrust enforcement also risks trade retaliation by foreign governments. However, when a foreign firm has assets, affiliates, or operations on U.S. soil, antitrust liability can be enforced.

Some foreign nations have further impeded U.S. antitrust suits against their home industries with **blocking laws** that prohibit compliance with U.S. pretrial discovery requests. Canada, France, and the UK passed these laws in the 1970s after aggressive U.S. antitrust enforcement against the uranium cartel. For example, it is common for antitrust plaintiffs to request from foreign firms numerous documents crucial to prove their case. Blocking laws often require precompliance notification to the foreign government, enabling foreign regulators to bar compliance with a U.S. production of documents request, effectively frustrating the antitrust suit.

During the twentieth century, most nations have had weaker antitrust enforcement than the United States. Many nations promote domestic monopolies so that they can compete more effectively in international commerce. Many educated people in developing nations are torn between the two extremes of nationalist monopoly and the consumer benefits of competition. On one hand, popular nationalism motivates governments to grant monopolies to strengthen domestic industry. On the other hand, many of these supporters also denounce the inevitable decline in their personal standard of living caused by paying high monopoly prices for domestic products and services. This tension has led to anticompetitive and protectionist laws regulating foreign trade: discriminatory taxes, tariffs, quotas, and excessive inspections. There is often hostility toward foreign competition, particularly large foreign firms. Overall, the efforts of GATT negotiations to reduce international trade barriers parallel antitrust enforcement that targets industry restraints of trade. They are remarkably the same problem at different levels.

The U.S. economy no longer acts in isolation. It is increasingly part of an interconnected global marketplace, with implications for the stringent antitrust enforcement of the past. Excessive enforcement could weaken U.S. competitors, particularly if foreign competitors receive government sponsorship or are permitted to monopolize in their home markets. Many nations subsidize their sole producers of various products for nationalistic pride or perceived self-sufficiency purposes. Some industries may need to consolidate and become larger to gain the economies of scale necessary to effectively compete, or to maintain national security.

ONLINE

Antitrust Enforcement Guidelines for International Operations
http://www.usdoj.gov/atr/public/guidelines/internat.htm

ANTITRUST EXEMPTIONS

Antitrust regulation of some industries, such as insurance companies and financial institutions, is the responsibility of other government agencies. To ensure their survival, some industries are permitted to use restraints of trade more freely than would be legal for other industries. For example, IP owners receive government-granted monopoly-like rights. The holders of patents, copyrights, and trademarks are encouraged to innovate by having exclusive rights to exploit the product of their creativity. Congress and the courts have also granted antitrust exemptions to certain industries. These exemptions are narrowly construed under the strict constructionism policy, and there is little flexibility to exempt a new variation of an exempt activity unless it is almost identical to the original.

The Clayton Act specifically exempts nonprofit **agricultural cooperatives** organized to provide mutual assistance to farmers. The **Capper-Volstead Act** extended this exemption to "persons engaged in the production of agricultural products such as farmers, planters, ranchmen, dairymen, or nut and fruit growers." Fishing cooperatives are also exempt. The exemption applies only to "persons engaged in agricultural production" and not to packing houses or to associations involved in both production and distribution. The court's unwillingness to extend this exemption to packing houses illustrates strict constructionism.

The **National Labor Relations Act** is considered a sufficient regulatory program for **labor unions**. The antitrust laws do not apply to most labor union activities that pursue their members' welfare. However, the exemption does not protect conspiracies to restrain trade. Labor union activities that provide aid to nonlabor groups or that tend to create monopolies or control marketing are not exempt. For example, labor agreements that require the employer to avoid dealing with a particular supplier or customer may be anticompetitive. Such agreements are enforceable only if they are designed to protect a legitimate labor union interest.

Restraints of trade or monopolizations that result from valid governmental actions are exempt from the Sherman Act under the **state action** exemption.[6] For example, state licensing of liquor stores or firearm sales often creates oligopolies that restrict the number of sellers, an anticompetitive condition. However, these restraints of trade are not illegal if state licensing is for the public's protection. Adequate supervision provided by the state's regulations is considered to justify the exemption. For the state action exemption to apply, there must be a clearly defined state policy permitting or requiring the particular activity or restraint. The exemption does not apply to nongovernmental functions the state supplies by itself. For example, the state action exemption did not protect (1) alleged conspiracies by municipally owned utilities to exclude the services from utilities outside the municipality and (2) a conspiracy between a city's sports stadium and its airport authority to exclude a particular brand of beer sold at both facilities. The city of Boulder, Colorado, violated the Sherman Act by preventing a cable television company from expanding its service territory.[7] Boulder's action in that case was not taken pursuant to a valid and clearly articulated state policy.

Until 1944, the insurance industry was not considered part of interstate commerce, so antitrust regulation of insurance was prohibited. The **McCarran-Ferguson Act** was passed in 1945 to continue this special exemption in states that regulate the insurance industry, such as by setting premium rates, regulating selling and advertising of policies, and the licensing of insurance agents. The insurance industry's exemption does not exempt other activities, except sharing actuarial data. For example, antitrust law would prohibit an insurance company's boycott, coercion, or intimidation of competitors.

Stock exchanges have a limited form of antitrust exemption because they are considered necessary to support the regulatory framework of the securities laws. Bank and other financial institution mergers are exempt from antitrust laws because they are regulated by federal and state agencies, such as the Federal Reserve Board,

Ethical Issue

Should Collusion Protect Consumers?

For many years, some ***professions*** such as the practice of law or engineering were exempt from antitrust enforcement. They argued that their rules of practice were needed to protect their clients from the professions' inclination toward unethical conduct. For example, local bar associations imposed "minimum fee schedules" for attorneys' services—minimum prices that attorneys could not discount under the threat of discipline by the bar association. Today, such activities are considered illegal as price-fixing.[8] Similarly, the ethical code of engineers once prohibited competitive bidding for engagements. The ethical justification was that competitive bidding would draw prices below what practicing engineers needed to do good work, so competitive bidding was outlawed to avoid unsafe cost-cutting. The engineers' rule effectively created an illegal agreement among competing engineers to refrain from discussing price with customers. There was no overwhelming justification for the antitrust exemption for professions, and their use of it to shield their "ethics" rules is now generally prohibited.

6. *Parker v. Brown*, 317 U.S. 341 (1943).
7. *Community Communications Co. v. City of Boulder, Colorado*, 455 U.S. 40 (1982).
8. *Goldfarb v. Virginia State Bar*, 421 U.S. 773 (1975).

the Comptroller of the Currency, the Federal Deposit Insurance Corporation, and the Office of Thrift Supervision. The exemption for formerly regulated transportation industries is largely removed now, although there is some uncertainty as to which regulator has jurisdiction. As utility and telecommunication deregulation continues, their exemptions may diminish.

Most **professional sports** involve at least some restrictive actions among club owners, players' representatives, and facility owners (e.g., arenas, stadiums). For example, the limits on "free agency" prohibit players from moving between teams at will. Football, boxing, basketball, and hockey are all subject to antitrust enforcement, but the Supreme Court exempted professional baseball in 1922, 1953, and again in 1972. However, the baseball exemption is probably an aberration inconsistent with other laws.

Groups of businesses may join together to take mutually advantageous **political action** without violating the Sherman Act. The Supreme Court has refused to apply the Sherman Act to bona fide political activities of competitors, even if their objective is noncompetitive legislation, regulations, or administrative action. The **Noerr-Pennington doctrine** is based on two First Amendment rights: freedom of speech and the right to petition the government for redress of grievances.[9] However, a **sham exception** to the Noerr-Pennington doctrine does not exempt intentional efforts to harass a competitor. For example, purposeful interference with potential competitors' access to either the courts or regulatory agencies is not protected under *Noerr*. Conspiracy with a foreign government agency to restrain competition is also not protected. Several other laws create some limited exemptions for certain aspects of export goods, R&D, defense activities, oil marketing, and production joint ventures.

MONOPOLIES

Monopolies are the basic evil addressed by the Sherman Act because monopoly power enables price-fixing, reduction of output, and exclusion of competitors. An illegal monopoly arises when monopoly power is intentionally exercised by acts of monopolization.

MONOPOLY POWER

The most fundamental question in most antitrust cases is whether monopoly power exists. The next is whether it is exercised illegally by the defendant. Economists define monopoly power on the basis of the **elasticity of demand**. Perfectly competitive markets are highly elastic: When the price of a product rises, consumers can stretch and substitute purchases of similar products; when the price falls, consumers can quickly shift to purchase that product. The markets for investment securities and certain foodstuffs are highly elastic. There are many substitutes, and most consumers can easily find some alternative.

In an **inelastic market**, consumer demand is relatively unresponsive to small price changes, and consumers cannot easily change their purchases to satisfactory alternatives. Firms in inelastic markets have greater market power that enables them to control prices to a greater extent. An imperfect market is characterized by inelastic

9. *Eastern Railroad Presidents Conference v. Noerr Motor Freight, Inc.*, 365 U.S. 127 (1961).

demand that gives some degree of market power to monopolists, oligopolists, and monopolistic competitors. Such firms can raise their prices without losing all of the customers because substitute products are not suitably equivalent replacements. The market for patented or copyrighted component parts (microprocessor chips) is often inelastic because buyers cannot easily substitute chips made by other manufacturers. Defining the relevant market is the first step in measuring monopoly power.

Relevant Market

Monopoly is not definable unless some boundary is set on the alleged monopoly in a particular market under analysis. A monopolist's illegal use of market power must exist over (1) an identifiable geographic area and (2) a particular product. The **relevant market** must be defined in cases involving monopolies, mergers, and restraints of trade. It includes all the producers of products or services that are functionally interchangeable and reasonably available to the same pool of consumers.

The first relevant inquiry is a determination of the specific geographic area within which competition is affected. Evidence is presented about consumers' buying patterns to construct a region within which consumers can readily obtain the product or service from any available seller, including the alleged monopolist. The **geographic market** may be local (e.g., city, county, metropolitan area), regional (e.g., state, multiple states), national, or even international. Generally, geographic markets are limited or bounded by the costs of transportation and by the ease with which consumers can gain access to other sellers. Within a particular geographic market, there may also be **submarkets** in which a group of local sellers compete more directly. For example, the shops in a neighborhood commercial area could be a submarket within the broader citywide geographic shopping market. It is often argued that the Internet creates massive, borderless markets for buyers and sellers. However, this may be true only for information transferred over networked computerized telecommunications. Language, cultural, and trade barriers still constrain the cross-border flow of goods and services, even if they are marketed over the Internet.

Next, the **product market** is determined. Consumers' preferences and their willingness to substitute physically different products for the same basic purpose or use are the key factors. The issue is usually whether two products are perceived as reasonably interchangeable or substitutable. To make this determination, courts examine the price, use, and quality of all reasonable substitutes, using the cross-elasticity of demand method of analysis to measure relationships between two possible substitutes. **Cross-elasticity of demand** is defined as the percentage change in the quantity demanded of one product divided by the percentage change of the substitute product's price. When these numbers are large and positive, the two products compared are highly substitutable for each other and should be considered part of the same market (e.g., butter versus margarine). Small positive numbers show some, but imperfect substitutability. Negative cross-elasticities often exist between complementary products. They are not substitutable for each other but might be purchased for use together (e.g., automobiles and tires). Cross-elasticity analysis is not a perfect method of determining product markets because consumers may not be willing to substitute dissimilar products priced at vastly different levels. For example, someone may be willing to ride a bus to work only when it becomes significantly cheaper than commuting by personal automobile.

The relevant market is large if there are many positive cross-elasticities between the monopolist's products and other products. However, if cross-elasticities are low, there may be no reasonable substitutes, and the relevant product market is as small as the market for the alleged monopolist's product. A particular firm's market share in a market with many direct competitors and/or many substitutes is usually small. By contrast, a particular firm's market share is likely to be large if there are few competitors or substitutes. Plaintiffs and enforcement agencies have an incentive to allege that few substitutes exist (low cross-elasticities), and defendants have an incentive to allege that there are many substitutes (high cross-elasticities).

Cross-elasticity analysis has narrowed the product market definition in some cases. For example, professional championship boxing matches are considered a market distinct from other boxing matches. Championship matches are the "cream" of the boxing business, appealing to a broader audience than other boxing matches. A similar analysis could be used to separate the major league baseball market from the minor leagues. Gospel music is considered a market distinct from popular music. A submarket for leasing large IBM mainframes was differentiated from the market for purchasing the same computers.

How do we analyze markets in e-commerce? The same principles apply. The costs of consumers gaining access to other sellers helps determine the geographic market. The cross-elasticity between substitutes determines the product market. The market for information and digital products will be very large if they are easily browsed (located), sold (transaction processed), and delivered over the Internet. Such markets could be expected to extend well beyond national borders if language and currency barriers are low and confidence is good that the transactions will be fully and adequately performed. As for the substitutability of products sold in e-commerce, the range of possibilities is very broad. Standardized goods purchased from various Internet vendors would normally all be part of the same product market. Customized products from different vendors might not be satisfactory substitutes. Different forms of similar goods are substitutable if consumers accept their various forms. For example, antivirus or firewall software can be purchased on a disk at computer stores, via mail or phone order, or directly from websites of manufacturers or retailers. Such software can also be downloaded in digital format from the vendor, or a subscription could be renewed. Some vendors, such as bookstores sell in parallel channels, through physical retail outlets as well as over the Internet. All these issues must be carefully measured and considered in determining market boundaries in e-commerce.

Market Share

Once the court has defined the relevant product and geographic markets, it must determine the alleged monopolist's market power within that market. Market power is typically measured as **market share**: the percentage of the relevant market the alleged monopolist controls. Measurement requires computing a fraction or percentage; the fraction's numerator is the defendant's unit sales, and the denominator is the total unit sales of all that product from all vendors. There is no litmus test for determining what market share constitutes a monopoly. Market shares of 90%, 85%, and 75% have been considered monopolies, but shares of 20% or 50% are not usually monopolies. However, in the analysis of mergers, a relatively lower market share for the merged firms could be sufficient to prohibit the merger.

MONOPOLIZATION

The mere existence of monopoly power does not violate the Sherman Act. Indeed, some industries (e.g., utilities) have been more efficient when operated as a monopoly. A monopoly becomes illegal when market power is used illegally. This is a **monopolization**, which represents the intentional use of monopoly power to gain an illegal monopoly. The **abuse theory of monopoly** analyzes both the structure of the market and the conduct of the alleged monopolist. A monopoly is illegal if a firm with monopoly power abuses its market power by undertaking purposeful acts to harm competitors and consumers. Market power is not illegal or abusive if it is acquired by historical accident or is obtained or maintained by selling better products, using business savvy, or applying superior skill, foresight, and industry.

The types of monopolistic acts that constitute monopolization vary. Whenever a monopolist engages in predatory and coercive conduct in direct violation of the antitrust laws, monopolization intent can be inferred. Acts considered legal in many circumstances may be illegal if the monopolist's market power is employed with monopolistic intent. For example, conduct that is intended to prevent the entry of competitors, such as systematically increasing aluminum production capacity in anticipation of new demand, has been held illegal.[10] In another case, IBM's policy of leasing but never selling computers was considered exclusionary and unlawful.

Predatory Pricing

Predatory pricing, pricing below the producer's marginal cost, may also constitute deliberate and purposeful acts of monopolization. Although predatory pricing results in losses on those sales, it often forces competitors out of business. After monopoly is obtained, the monopolist can raise prices to recoup the earlier losses. If a monopolist lowers prices to undercut or restrict the entry of competitors, the intent to monopolize may be inferred. **Marginal cost** is the manufacturer's additional expense to produce one more unit beyond the number produced up to that point. **Average variable cost** is the average of all of the variable expenses for all of the units produced. Some commentators have urged that pricing below average variable cost should be presumed to be predatory pricing. Predatory pricing is monopolistic if it tends to immediately eliminate rivals, thus creating a monopoly. A related tactic is to charge monopoly prices in one geographic or product market and lower prices in the monopolized market to drive out competitors. Discriminatory pricing allows the monopolist to undercut potential competition by taking temporary losses that are made up with profits at other times or in other geographic or product markets.

There may be justifications for predatory pricing. One is to gain a toehold in a market dominated by large rivals. Information products and network industries in e-commerce may justify some acts that look like predatory pricing. For example, many sellers take losses on early product sales in hopes of raising switching costs and locking in consumers so higher prices can be charged later. Losses on the early predatory pricing are recouped later when the customer base must purchase more expensive products going forward.

ATTEMPTS TO MONOPOLIZE

The Sherman Act also outlaws **attempts to monopolize**, even if the alleged monopolist is unsuccessful at monopolizing. To prove liability, it must be shown that the defendant employed methods, means, and practices that would, if successful, accomplish monopolization. Even though the defendant fell short of monopolization, nevertheless it approached closely enough to create a dangerous probability of monopolization. The defendant in such cases must be proved to have had the specific intent of excluding competitors through the exercise of monopoly power. The

10. *United States v. Aluminum Co. of America*, 148 F.2d 416 (2d Cir., 1945).

specific intent standard for attempts to monopolize requires a higher burden of proof than other monopolization crimes. Nevertheless, intent may be inferred from unfair conduct. For example, inducing others to boycott a competitor's product, using discriminatory pricing, or refusing to deal with a particular customer are all evidence of the specific intent to attempt monopolization. When two or more persons combine their efforts in such acts, their agreement may also constitute a separate crime: **conspiracy to monopolize.**

ONLINE

Microsoft antitrust documents
http://www.usdoj.gov/atr/cases/ms_index.htm

The monopolization case against Microsoft was called the antitrust trial of the century. Microsoft appealed the trial court decision that follows here, and the U.S. Court of Appeals reversed only the severe "structural" remedies ordered by the trial judge. It then remanded the case back but to a different trial court judge after concluding that the original judge was biased against Microsoft.[11] Soon thereafter, DOJ settled the case with Microsoft, but several holdouts—nine states, private plaintiffs, and the EU antitrust enforcers—continue to pursue antitrust claims against Microsoft on the issues discussed here. As of this writing, the case remains unresolved and is an ongoing and potent political question.

U.S. v. Microsoft Corp.

84 F.Supp. 2d 9 (D.D.C., 1999) (Findings of Fact)
87 F.Supp. 2d 30 (D.D.C., 2000) (Conclusions of Law)

Facts. The DOJ and 20 states' attorneys general filed a civil antitrust suit against Microsoft in May 1998, alleging monopolization, attempted monopolization, tying, and exclusive dealing. The trial lasted more than two years. Extensive Findings of Fact were issued in November 1999, and the Conclusions of Law were delayed until April 2000 to allow for mediation by Judge Richard A. Posner. Microsoft appealed the order requiring a major "structural" remedy—divestiture of Microsoft into two separate companies, an operating systems business (i.e., Windows) and an applications business (e.g., Office)—as well as the "conduct" remedies—internal control systems for antitrust compliance and periodic inspections by the DOJ for antitrust compliance.

Judge Jackson made several tightly reasoned findings of fact. Windows running on Intel-compatible CPUs are the relevant market. Consumers face significant switching costs to change to competing systems (e.g., Mac OS, Linux, Unix). "Middleware" programs—Netscape Internet browser, Java applets—that work on various operating system, are not yet part of this relevant market. Middleware threatens the Windows dominance if applications can easily run without modification on other operating systems. Microsoft has monopoly power because (1) its market share for Intel-compatible PC operating systems is extremely large and stable; (2) its dominance is protected by the high "applications barriers to entry" posed by the vast libraries of existing Windows-compatible software, not generally available on other systems; and (3) there is no commercially viable alternative to Windows. Microsoft used its monopoly power to displace Netscape as the dominant browser because Microsoft believed that Netscape threatened to render Windows irrelevant, thus undercutting Microsoft's market dominance.

Netscape refused Microsoft's offer to divide the browser market. Microsoft monopolized the operating system market by discouraging Netscape from circumventing the Windows direct control over hardware (monitor, keyboard, mouse, printer, communications, disk drives) at the level of "application programming interfaces" (APIs, computer information flow at deep levels in the operating system that directs various functions of input, output, processing, display, storage, etc.). Microsoft withheld key interoperability specifications or delayed granting licenses to pressure concessions from Netscape, Intel, IBM, Apple, and RealNetworks. Microsoft spent heavily to develop a rival browser, Internet Explorer, and then actively sought market share by distributing Explorer free. Eventually, Explorer was tightly but unnecessarily integrated into each later version of Windows: 95, 98, 2000, ME, and XP.

11. *United States v. Microsoft Corp.*, 253 F.3d 34 (D.C.Cir., 2001).

Microsoft pressured computer manufacturers (OEMs) and Internet service providers (ISPs) with restrictive terms in their supply contracts that essentially required the distribution of Microsoft Explorer to the exclusion of Netscape. OEMs were forbidden from modifying Windows's opening or desktop screens, which prominently featured Explorer. This restriction effectively exiled Netscape from "the crucial OEM distribution channel"; Explorer's market share increased, and Netscape's decreased. Microsoft took similar actions to make Java incompatible across operating systems. These actions sent a clear message to software developers that new applications must be written to run directly on Windows and not on middleware like Netscape or Java. Microsoft feared middleware could make Windows irrelevant.

Legal Issue. Did Microsoft maintain its monopoly power by using anticompetitive means? Did Microsoft attempt to expand its monopoly in the operating system market into the browser market? Did Microsoft tie the purchase of Windows to the purchase of Explorer? Did Microsoft's use of exclusive dealing arrangements foreclose competition by Netscape? Did Microsoft violate 20 states' antitrust laws?

Opinion. Judge Thomas Pennfield Jackson. Section 2 of the Sherman Act declares that it is unlawful for a person or firm to "monopolize . . . any part of the trade or commerce among the several States, or with foreign nations. . . ." Specifically, a firm violates §2 if it attains or preserves monopoly power through anticompetitive acts. [O]nce it is proved that the defendant possesses monopoly power in a relevant market, liability for monopolization depends on a showing that the defendant used anticompetitive methods to achieve or maintain its position. The threshold question in this analysis is whether the defendant's conduct is "exclusionary"—that is, whether it has . . . or threatens to restrict significantly, the ability of other firms to compete in the relevant market on the merits of what they offer customers. As the D.C. Circuit stated:

[P]redation involves aggression against business rivals through the use of business practices that would not be considered profit maximizing except for the expectation that (1) actual rivals will be driven from the market, or the entry of potential rivals blocked or delayed, so that the predator will gain or retain a market share sufficient to command monopoly profits, or (2) rivals will be chastened sufficiently to abandon competitive behavior the predator finds threatening to its realization of monopoly profits.

In this case, Microsoft early on recognized middleware as the Trojan horse. [M]iddleware threatened to demolish Microsoft's coveted monopoly power. Alerted to the threat, Microsoft strove over a period of approximately four years to prevent middleware technologies from fostering the development of enough full-featured, cross-platform applications to erode the applications barrier. In pursuit of this goal, Microsoft sought to convince developers to concentrate on Windows-specific APIs and ignore interfaces exposed by the two incarnations of middleware that posed the greatest threat, namely, Netscape's Navigator Web browser and Sun's implementation of the Java technology. Microsoft's campaign succeeded in preventing—for several years, and perhaps permanently—Navigator and Java from fulfilling their potential to open the market for Intel-compatible PC operating systems to competition on the merits. Because Microsoft achieved this result through exclusionary acts that lacked procompetitive justification, the Court deems Microsoft's conduct the maintenance of monopoly power by anticompetitive means.

Microsoft realized that the extent of developers' reliance on Netscape's browser platform would depend largely on the size and trajectory of Navigator's share of browser usage. Microsoft thus set out to maximize Internet Explorer's share of browser usage at Navigator's expense. Microsoft fails to advance any legitimate business objectives that actually explain the full extent of this significant exclusionary impact. The Court has already found that no quality-related or technical justifications fully explain Microsoft's refusal to license Windows 95 to OEMs without version 1.0 through 4.0 of Internet Explorer, or its refusal to permit them to uninstall [Explorer] versions 3.0 and 4.0. Microsoft's decision to tie Internet Explorer to Windows cannot truly be explained as an attempt to benefit consumers and improve the efficiency of the software market generally, but rather as part of a larger campaign to quash innovation that threatened its monopoly position. [I]f Microsoft was truly inspired by a genuine concern for maximizing consumer satisfaction, as well as preserving its substantial investment in a worthy product, then it would have relied more on the power of the very competitive PC market, and less on its own market power, to prevent OEMs from making modifications that consumers did not want. Considering that Microsoft never intended to derive appreciable revenue from Internet Explorer directly, these sacrifices could only have represented rational business judgments to the extent that they promised to diminish Navigator's share of browser usage and thereby contribute significantly to eliminating a threat to the applications barrier to entry.

In sum, the efforts Microsoft directed at OEMs and [ISPs] successfully ostracized Navigator as a practical matter from the two channels that lead most efficiently to browser usage. While the evidence does not prove that they would have succeeded absent Microsoft's actions, it does reveal that Microsoft placed an oppressive thumb on the scale of competitive fortune, thereby effectively guaranteeing its continued dominance in the relevant market. More broadly, Microsoft's anticompetitive actions trammeled the competitive process through which the computer software industry generally stimulates innovation and conduces to the optimum benefit of consumers.

Viewing Microsoft's conduct as a whole also reinforces the conviction that it was predacious. Microsoft paid vast sums of money, and renounced many millions more in lost revenue every year, in order to induce firms to take actions that would help enhance Internet Explorer's share of browser usage at Navigator's expense. These outlays cannot be explained as subventions to maximize return from Internet Explorer. Microsoft has no intention of ever charging for licenses to use or distribute its browser. Moreover, neither the desire to bolster demand for Windows nor the prospect of ancillary revenues from Internet Explorer can explain the lengths to which Microsoft has gone. In fact, Microsoft has expended wealth and foresworn opportunities to realize more in a manner and to an extent that can only represent a rational investment if its purpose was to perpetuate the applications barrier to entry. Microsoft's campaign must be termed predatory.

Section 1 of the Sherman Act prohibits "every contract, combination ..., or conspiracy, in restraint of trade or commerce ...." Pursuant to this statute, courts have condemned commercial stratagems that constitute unreasonable restraints on competition, among them "tying arrangements" and "exclusive dealing" contracts. Tying arrangements have been found unlawful where sellers exploit their market power over one product to force unwilling buyers into acquiring another. Liability for tying under §1 exists where (1) two separate "products" are involved; (2) the defendant affords its customers no choice but to take the tied product in order to obtain the tying product; (3) the arrangement affects a substantial volume of interstate commerce; and (4) the defendant has "market power" in the tying product market. The plaintiffs allege that Microsoft's combination of Windows and Internet Explorer by contractual and technological artifices constitute unlawful tying to the extent that those actions forced Microsoft's customers and consumers to take Internet Explorer as a condition of obtaining Windows. [T]he Court holds that Microsoft is liable for illegal tying under §1.

[C]onsumers today perceive operating systems and browsers as separate "products," for which there is separate demand. This is true notwithstanding the fact that the software code supplying their discrete functionalities can be commingled in virtually infinite combinations, rendering each indistinguishable from the whole in terms of files of code or any other taxonomy. The "essential characteristic" of an illegal tying arrangement is a seller's decision to exploit its market power over the tying product "to force the buyer into the purchase of a tied product that the buyer either did not want at all, or might have preferred to purchase elsewhere on different terms." Microsoft has conditioned the provision of a license to distribute Windows on the OEMs' purchase of Internet Explorer. The fact that Microsoft ostensibly priced Internet Explorer at zero does not detract from the conclusion that consumers were forced to pay, one way or another, for the browser along with Windows. [L]icensees, including consumers, are forced to take, and pay for, the entire package of software and that any value to be ascribed to Internet Explorer is built into this single price. Microsoft is the only firm to refuse to license its operating system without a browser. Microsoft's decision to offer only the bundled—"integrated"—version of Windows and Internet Explorer derived not from technical necessity or business efficiencies; rather, it was the result of a deliberate and purposeful choice to quell incipient competition before it reached truly minatory proportions.

Decision. Microsoft used its dominance in the Windows operating system to monopolize the browser market and unlawfully tied purchase of its Internet Explorer to Windows.

Case Questions

1. What is the application barrier to entry? What did the court find were Microsoft's actions that were taken to reinforce the application barrier to entry? How would maintaining the application barrier to entry help Microsoft maintain its market power in operating systems and applications software? How would middleware threaten to weaken Microsoft's application barrier to entry?
2. Many consumers who regularly use Microsoft software products oppose structural remedies because they presume they could weaken the advantages of Microsoft's integrated products. Which of the remedies in the Microsoft trial court's judgment and order are structural, and which are conduct remedies? How do these two general forms of remedy differ?

MERGERS

Business combinations involve corporate finance and strategy. They implicate legal areas such as SEC regulations, state corporate law, and antitrust law. Antitrust law poses a difficult question of industrial organization: Will the market structure that results from a merger or an acquisition create an illegal monopoly or otherwise restrain trade?

TYPES OF MERGERS AND BUSINESS COMBINATIONS

Mergers often seem to be the quick and easy expansion method. A **merger** brings together two independent firms, one of which survives, and the other is dissolved. A **consolidation** combines two independent firms; both are terminated and replaced by a newly created combined entity. A **purchase of assets** involves the transfer of an acquired firm's assets to the acquiring firm, neither firm must be dissolved. In an **acquisition**, a firm acquired by another firm may operate as a separate division or subsidiary. For the purposes of antitrust analysis, all of these transactions are considered mergers.

Early interpretations of the Sherman Act held that mergers destroyed the competition that previously existed between the merged firms. However, this overly restrictive theory would prohibit most mergers simply due to the concentration of power that would result. Eventually the courts refused to use the Sherman Act to restrict mergers so Congress passed §7 of the Clayton Act to specifically prohibit mergers, if they tend to lessen competition.

. . . no person engaged in commerce, or in any activity affecting commerce shall acquire, directly or indirectly, the whole or any part of stock or other share capital . . . [or] . . . the whole or any part of the assets of another person engaged also in commerce or in any activity affecting commerce, where in any line of commerce or in any activity affecting commerce in any section of the country, the effect of such acquisition may be substantially to lessen competition, or tend to create a monopoly.

Section 7 was amended in 1950 by the Celler-Kefauver Act to (1) prohibit noncompetitive market structures (e.g., oligopolies, monopolistic competition), (2) encourage internal growth and expansion, and (3) preserve local industrial control and small business viability. Celler-Kefauver also closed a major loophole in the Clayton Act by covering the sale of assets. The amendments apply to all three of the basic merger variations; horizontal mergers between competitors, vertical mergers among suppliers and customers, and conglomerate mergers with firms in other industries.

HORIZONTAL MERGER ANALYSIS

Horizontal mergers are the most basic type and arguably the most harmful to competition. They are combinations of firms that compete at the same level of production in the same industry (see Exhibit 19.1). Merger analysis is very similar to monopoly analysis because the relevant market and market share controlled by the merged firms are determined. Horizontal mergers are challenged when there is increased market dominance after the merger, and a substantial lessening of competition in the relevant market results.

The first step is to determine the **line of commerce**, both the geographic and product markets as introduced previously. Mergers are prohibited when they tend to substantially lessen competition in a particular "section of the country." Markets

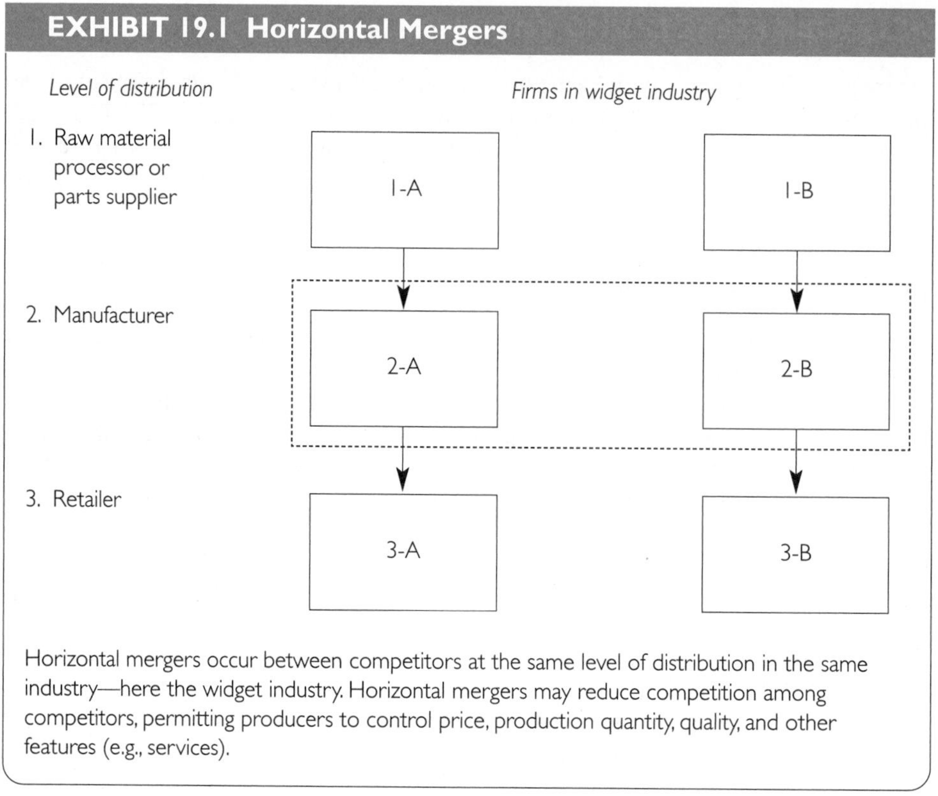
EXHIBIT 19.1 Horizontal Mergers
Level of distribution
Firms in widget industry
1. Raw material processor or parts supplier
2. Manufacturer
3. Retailer
1-A
1-B
2-A
2-B
3-A
3-B
Horizontal mergers occur between competitors at the same level of distribution in the same industry—here the widget industry. Horizontal mergers may reduce competition among competitors, permitting producers to control price, production quantity, quality, and other features (e.g., services).

are defined on a local, regional, or national basis, and submarkets may also exist. The next step examines the relevant product market. Substitute products and their cross-elasticities of demand are identified, and consumers' perceptions of product substitutability are examined. There may also be inquiries into the correlation of price movements between similar products that suggest substitutability. In merger cases, it is necessary to identify all major firms serving a relevant market so that their individual market shares can be computed. Additional firms may be included if they are capable of easily (1) switching to produce the relevant product, (2) reconditioning other products to make them good substitutes for that product, or (3) vertically integrating into the relevant product market. All the merging firms' product lines are considered separately and then aggregated.

ONLINE

FTC-DOJ Horizontal Merger Guidelines **http://www.ftc.gov/bc/docs/horizmer.htm**

The FTC and DOJ have issued merger guidelines that are used to approve or oppose mergers on the basis of **market concentration**, an indication of the potential for exercise of monopoly power. There is greater concentration if there are fewer firms, each with larger market shares. There is less concentration if more firms compete because the market approaches perfect competition.

The **Herfindahl Index** calculates market concentration by *summing the squares of each firm's individual market share*. High Herfindahl numbers result if the market is dominated by monopolists or oligopolists with large market shares. For example, if just one firm in the relevant market had 75% of the market, the Herfindahl Index would be at least $75^2 = 5{,}625$. By contrast, if 10 firms in the relevant market possessed a market share of 10% each, the Herfindahl Index would be $10^2 + 10^2 + 10^2 + 10^2 + 10^2 + 10^2 + 10^2 + 10^2 + 10^2 + 10^2 = 1{,}000$. The Herfindahl Index can range from 10,000 for a pure monopoly (100^2) to less than 1 for a perfectly competitive market with near infinite competitors.

The DOJ is unlikely to challenge mergers if the Herfindahl Index remains below 1,000. If the index lies between 1,000 and 1,800, DOJ will challenge a merger that results in an increase of 100 or more Herfindahl points. For index numbers above 1,800, DOJ will challenge a merger that results in an increase of more than 50 points. Markets with Herfindahl indexes greater than 1,800 are considered highly concentrated. The Herfindahl Index does not have the force of law, but DOJ uses it to indicate when prosecution should be undertaken.

The question to be determined is whether a proposed merger would result in the combined firm's having a market share so high that there would be a substantial lessening of competition. Unlike monopolization cases, there is no necessity to prove attempts at predatory conduct or monopolistic acts. Probabilities, not "ephemeral possibilities," must be demonstrated by the party attacking the merger. DOJ considers the competitive impact of most mergers, and most parties will not pursue a merger if DOJ publicly opposes it. Courts prohibit mergers if the newly created firm "controls an undue percentage share" of the relevant market and produces "a significant increase in concentration." In one case, a prohibited merger would have resulted in a combined firm with a 30% market share. In another case, the absorption of a small, aggressive, and innovative firm by Alcoa was prohibited because the merger adversely affected competition.

In *United States v. Von's Grocery Co.*,[12] the Supreme Court upheld a DOJ challenge to a merger between two grocery store chains in the Los Angeles area: Von's and Shopping Bag. The combined sales of the two chains would have been only 7.5% of the metropolitan Los Angeles grocery market. However, the court noted that these two firms had experienced tremendous growth and that the "mom and pop" grocery stores were in steady decline. Merger analysis of industry trends toward consolidation may be used to prevent a merger with short-term procompetitive effects but longer-range concentration permitting future collusion. Consider this: Mom-and-pop stores resemble atomized perfect competition, but will they produce the lowest consumer prices?

VERTICAL MERGER ANALYSIS

Vertical mergers combine firms that stand in a supplier-customer relationship along the same chain of distribution (see Exhibit 19.2). **Vertical integration** is an expansion into retail and/or supplier levels along the supply chain. Firms naturally desire control over their customers and suppliers. Vertical mergers enable the resulting firm to squeeze out unintegrated competitors, limit future competition, and erect barriers to entry. Vertically integrated firms tend to exclude competitors from sources of supply or from customers, causing a supply squeeze. Vertically merged firms may also refuse to deal with nonintegrated firms and preferentially allocate products to their own affiliates.

Vertical merger analysis is similar to horizontal merger analysis. First, the relevant geographic and product markets are determined. Second, the probable effect of the merger on the foreclosure of competition because of the acquisition of excessive market share is analyzed. Third, the courts analyze historical trends toward concentration, the nature and purpose of the merger, and resulting barriers to entry.

12. 384 U.S. 270 (1966).

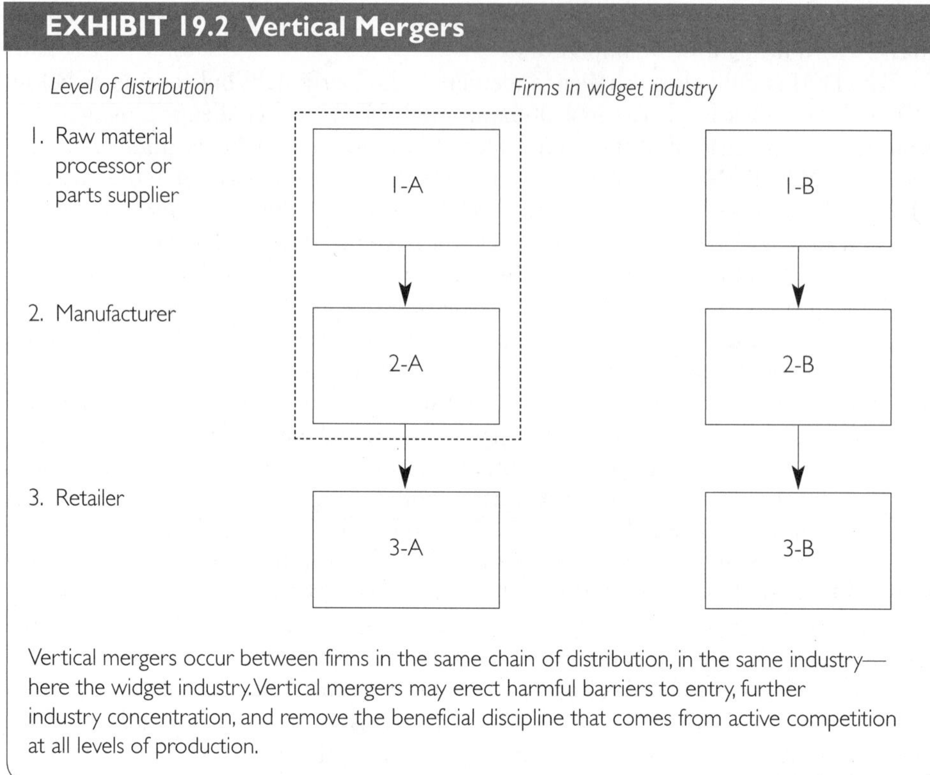

Vertical mergers occur between firms in the same chain of distribution, in the same industry—here the widget industry. Vertical mergers may erect harmful barriers to entry, further industry concentration, and remove the beneficial discipline that comes from active competition at all levels of production.

Because vertical mergers do not immediately result in more concentrated markets, however, this analysis is more difficult.

The potential foreclosure of competition and the resulting barriers to entry by new firms are important factors. A merger is objectionable if potential competitors must thereafter integrate vertically to compete effectively against the merged firm. Challenge of vertical mergers is controversial if the vertical integration makes the industry more efficient, but vertical mergers are challenged when collusion is likely in a highly concentrated **upstream market**—concentration at the supplier level. For example, if suppliers own their retail outlets, then the prices of competing suppliers are apparent when they try to sell to the merged firm's retail outlets. This knowledge can facilitate price-fixing among all suppliers. However, if there are independent and disruptive buyers, then suppliers may be forced to compete for their business.

CONGLOMERATE MERGER ANALYSIS

Conglomerate mergers are all other mergers not classified as horizontal or vertical (Exhibit 19.3). They typically involve acquisition of a firm in another industry or selling other product lines and at any level of production. **Product extension** conglomerate mergers allow a firm to acquire complementary product lines that can be used with existing products. For example, a computer manufacturer's acquisition of a software producer would be a product extension merger because software is used with computers. **Market extension** mergers enable the merging firm to operate in new geographic markets. Totally unrelated mergers are often referred to as

EXHIBIT 19.3 Conglomerate Mergers

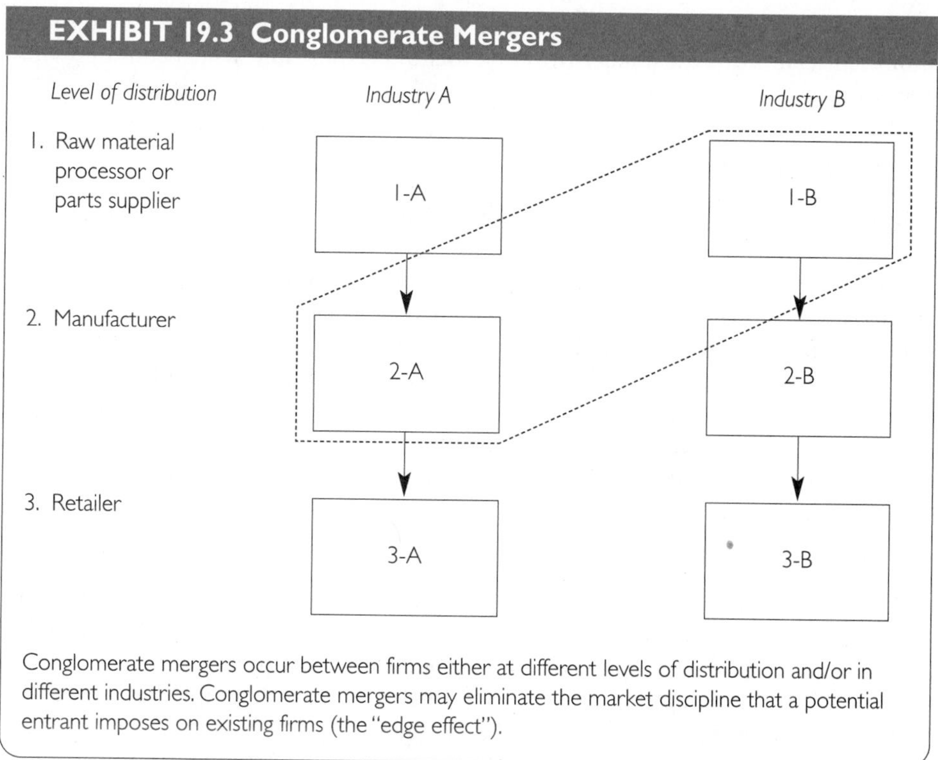

Conglomerate mergers occur between firms either at different levels of distribution and/or in different industries. Conglomerate mergers may eliminate the market discipline that a potential entrant imposes on existing firms (the "edge effect").

diversification mergers. They may allow the firm to smooth out its cash flows and profit in other markets when its main market is in a downturn.

Mergers that result in conglomerates appear to involve little or no anticompetitive effect. However, some structuralists argue that conglomerate mergers may reinforce oligopoly conditions, further weakening independent firms and eventually eliminating competition. Large acquiring firms often have financial resources and goodwill from popular brand names that make it more difficult for independent firms to compete or enter the market. After a conglomerate merger, the larger merged firm may use discriminatory and exclusionary practices to discipline smaller competitors, thereby lessening competition.

Conglomerate mergers can also eliminate the **potential entrant** or potential competitor. As long as competitors perceive that outsiders may come into the market, they are disciplined to remain efficient. They will tend to price below monopoly levels, which discourages new entrants. Potential entrants waiting in the wings create an **edge effect** that pressures existing competitors to remain competitive. However, the edge effect is eliminated when a potential entrant simply merges with an existing firm. If, instead of merging, that firm had entered the market **de novo** on its own, competition would increase.

Challenging a conglomerate merger is difficult. First, there must be proof that existing competitors perceived and were influenced by the potential entrant. Second, the acquiring firm must have had reasonable means to enter the given market without merging. Third, the number of potential entrants cannot be excessive; otherwise, the elimination of only one would not have any significant impact on competitive discipline. It can be argued that a conglomerate merger between an outsider and the largest or leading seller in a concentrated industry is anticompetitive. The outsider should instead acquire a smaller firm in a **toehold acquisition**, which could preserve competition.

MERGER DEFENSES

A legal challenge to merging firms may be turned away with a **merger defense.** For example, merging firms commonly claim greater efficiency. Another merger justification is the **failing firm defense**. The defendant may argue that one of the merger partners would soon be insolvent, making the merger necessary for the failing firm's survival. For this defense to apply, the failing firm must be unable to reorganize successfully under Chapter 11 of the bankruptcy laws. In addition, the failing firm must have made unsuccessful good faith efforts to find other merger partners that might reduce market concentration. Another defense recognizes that purchases of another corporation's stock solely for investment does not substantially lessen competition.

MERGER ENFORCEMENT PROCEDURES

DOJ antitrust enforcement priorities change when presidential administrations change. Because the attorney general is a cabinet-level officer appointed by the president, the DOJ is likely to pursue the president's antitrust philosophy. By contrast, the FTC is a quasi-independent federal agency not directly under the president's control. Its enforcement may reflect the philosophies of the FTC commissioners, some of whom were appointed during the previous president's term. The courts' attitudes may reflect a third set of priorities. Most mergers are reviewed after submission to the FTC, DOJ, or another agency that closely regulates that industry. For example, mergers in telecommunications are overseen by the Federal Communications Commission (FCC). Premerger negotiations are subject to scrutiny by federal agencies and the press, which affect merger activity by indicating approval or threatening a court challenge. Hart-Scott-Rodino premerger notification is required if the acquiring firm has sales or assets exceeding $100 million and the target has sales or assets exceeding $10 million. Notice is required at least 30 days before the merger and

The Politics of Antitrust Enforcement

Ethical Issue

In 2002, the DOJ and FTC updated their allocation of industries for the approval of mergers. The FTC agreed to take primary responsibility for analyzing mergers in airframes, vehicles, chemicals, computer hardware, energy, health care, groceries, retailing, pharmaceuticals, biotech, professional services, and textiles. The DOJ has primary responsibility for analysis of mergers in agriculture, avionics, beer, computer software, cosmetics, financial services, glass, insurance, industrial equipment, media and entertainment, metals, mining, photography, paper, timber telecommunications transportation, and waste. It remains an unsettled question whether these agencies could effectively review mergers in industries that the other agency had jurisdiction over.

This allocation raises controversy because the DOJ is a political agency bound to philosophies of the president's administration and the FTC is quasi-independent of political pressures. For example, DOJ supervision of the media and Internet businesses is likely to result in these industries' lobbying and exercising political influence toward the presidential administration. Some observers believe these industries will more effectively use political processes than related sectors of their industry (computer hardware) could. This unfair mismatch will probably favor some industries in close cases.

must contain basic information to aid in the evaluation of the acquisition. The EU is becoming stricter when mergers anywhere in the world would lessen competition in EU markets requiring EU review of U.S. mergers.

HORIZONTAL COMBINATIONS, RESTRAINTS OF TRADE

Horizontal restraints of trade can arise when competitors collaborate, see Exhibit 19.4). They are the least justifiable restraints. Adam Smith, the famous laissez-faire economist, strongly urged government to actively ensure competition to counteract the natural tendency of competitors to collude:

People in the same trade seldom meet together, even for merriment and diversion, but [that] the conversation ends in a conspiracy against the public, or in some contrivance to raise prices.

Early Supreme Court interpretations of the Sherman Act were so broad that "every contract, combination . . . or conspiracy in restraint of trade" was condemned. Later cases modified this approach by recognizing that some restraints are reasonable. Two legal tests for restraints developed eventually. The **rule of reason** that emerged from nineteenth-century contract law outlawed only unreasonable restraints. However, the **per se rule** requires a strict interpretation of the Sherman Act's "plain meaning" and leaves little wiggle room for any defense or justification.

RULE OF REASON

Section 1 of the Sherman Act literally prohibits "every contract, combination . . . or conspiracy in restraint of trade." However, if this provision was strictly applied, every contract would be illegal because contracts always restrain trade in some small way. For example, goods or services purchased by one person become unavailable to others, and so the buyer does not purchase them from a competitor. Trade is restrained even more by outputs or requirements contracts, by exclusive dealing or supply contracts, and by covenants not to compete. Yet these restraints can be justified in certain circumstances. The Sherman Act is intended to encourage free markets and should not prohibit reasonable restraints of trade.

The rule of reason permits courts to be more flexible by using a less stringent market share analysis than was used in monopolization or merger cases. The rule of

EXHIBIT 19.4 Horizontal Restraints of Trade

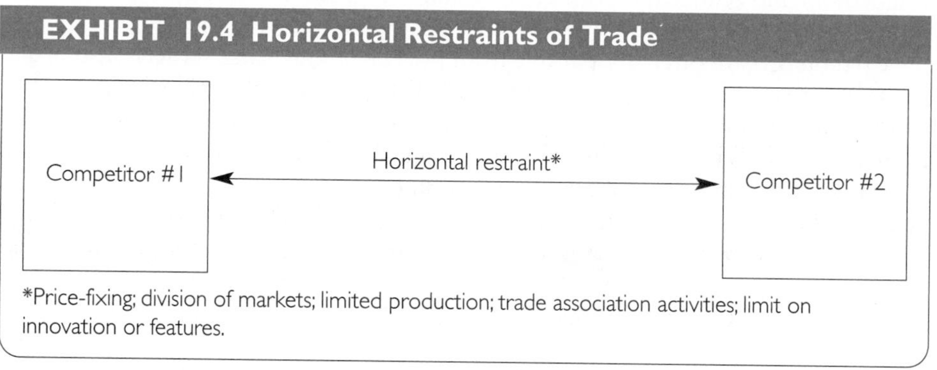

*Price-fixing; division of markets; limited production; trade association activities; limit on innovation or features.

reason developed to prohibit contracts that will reduce competition if they are intended to *unreasonably* restrict competition, if the parties have the power to implement their scheme, and/or if they have a less restrictive alternative to the scheme. In 1918, Justice Brandeis announced the rule of reason analysis in *Chicago Board of Trade v. United States:*[13]

The true test of legality is whether the restraint imposed is such as merely regulates and perhaps thereby promotes competition or whether it is such as may suppress or may even destroy competition. To determine that question, the court must ordinarily consider the facts peculiar to the business to which the restraint is applied; its condition before and after the restraint was imposed; the nature of the restraint and its effect, actual or probable. The history of the restraint, the evil believed to exist, the reason for adopting the particular remedy, the purpose or end sought to be obtained, are all relevant facts.

PER SE VIOLATIONS

Courts have encountered many types of agreements that are almost always unjustifiable. The rule of reason is an inefficient use of judicial and regulatory resources. Some business agreements, such as price-fixing, are designated illegal per se, and so they are never justified. Therefore, the inquiry ends if a per se violation is proven. Trials are shortened and simplified by avoiding unnecessary attempts to justify the restraint. The per se rule also provides business managers with clearer guidance. Per se offenses include price-fixing, division of markets, group boycotts, concerted refusals to deal, and tie-in relationships. The courts first determine whether the conduct in question falls within one of these per se categories. Thereafter, no further analysis is necessary because unlawful anticompetitive effect is presumed.

Price-Fixing

The most direct way for competitors to reduce competition is to agree to set prices artificially. **Price-fixing** is illegal per se because it tends to eliminate competition and passes on the inefficiencies of the oligopoly to consumers. Price-fixing is never justified by good intentions to set "reasonable" prices or to eliminate "ruinous" competition. But what constitutes illegal price-fixing? Agreements to fix minimum prices are illegal. For example, at one time state and local bar associations had minimum fee schedules requiring lawyers to charge a minimum price for particular services such as writing a will or drafting a contract. These fee schedules are illegal per se as price-fixing. It is also illegal to set maximum resale prices, even though fixing "low" prices might not seem harmful. Low prices tend to stabilize prices; they drive out competitors and reduce nonprice competition for optional features, improvements, or additional services.

Credit terms are often inseparable from price, so fixing these terms is also illegal per se. In one case, an agreement among beer distributors to eliminate trade credit to retailers was found to be illegal price-fixing as an equivalent to eliminating discounts. Several plywood producers allegedly agreed to charge a uniform freight rate regardless of the source of supply or the destination. This illegal scheme is known as **phantom freight** because it equalized freight charges without considering the actual distance or transportation charges. Phantom freight eliminates competition based

13. 246 U.S. 231 (1918).

on the purchaser's closeness to the source of supply and may also be a form of price discrimination. An agreement among oil companies to buy excess spot market supplies of crude oil was considered a disguised form of price-fixing.[14]

Some restraints of trade involving incidental price-fixing are judged under the rule of reason. Cooperation is sometimes necessary to advance the market. For example, it is impractical for music copyright owners to separately negotiate licensing fees for every performance of their works on television or radio or in public. The rule of reason applied to the blanket fee arrangement with Broadcast Music, Inc. (BMI) or the American Society of Composers, Authors and Publishers (ASCAP). These performing rights organizations (Chapter 13) provide clearinghouse services essential to effective licensing because they actually encourage the licensing and enforcement of music copyrights.[15]

The rule of reason has been used to judge a price-fixing scheme illegal. The National Collegiate Athletic Association (NCAA) negotiated television contracts for all college football games between 1982 and 1985. However, television fees paid to schools were based neither on the size of the viewing audience nor on the popularity of the teams. The NCAA contracts with ABC and CBS limited the number of televised games and precluded price negotiation between the networks and the schools. The NCAA scheme was invalid price-fixing under rule of reason analysis because both price and output were restrained, thereby effectively raising television fees above competitive levels with a system unresponsive to viewer demand. The per se rule was inapplicable because some horizontal restraint in athletics is needed to make the product available.[16]

Trade Association Activities

The prohibition against collusion and price-fixing is very strong. Competitors must be careful about their collective activities. For example, competitors' exchange of price information generally makes price-fixing easier. An unreasonable restraint may arise if a trade association acts as a clearinghouse for competitors to exchange price information. Critics of this approach charge that to remain competitive in world markets, competitors should be permitted to "network" by joining together for legitimate purposes that promote their collective success and improve product quality. For example, trade associations regularly engage in activities protected by the First Amendment: political lobbying, public affairs, and distributing information about suppliers and new technologies.

Despite the good intentions of trade associations, some have disguised their price-fixing when distributing price information. In the 1920s, for example, 365 hardwood manufacturers exchanged details of individual sales, production, inventories, and current price lists through their trade association. An expert analyst constantly warned members against overproduction. The plan was found illegal after hardwood prices increased sharply. The paper box industry voluntarily exchanged price quotes that identified transactions with particular customers, so the plan was held illegal because it tended to stabilize prices. By contrast, the maple flooring trade association circulated average costs, freight rates, and past transaction information without identifying individual buyers or sellers. This exchange was not illegal because future prices were never discussed. The exchange of information through

14. *U.S. v. Socony-Vacume Oil Co., Inc.*, 310 U.S. 150 (1950).
15. *Broadcast Music Inc. v. CBS*, 441 U.S. 1 (1979).
16. *NCAA v. Board of Regents of the University of Oklahoma*, 468 U.S. 85 (1984).

trade associations is not illegal if it is not intended to lessen competition. For example, a cement manufacturers' association distributed a list of construction contractors that abused the free delivery of cement, a measure that was justifiable to prevent fraud on the cement manufacturers.

Bidding rings are illegal per se as a form of price-fixing. They have arisen among construction contractors and in some auction markets. For example, contractors could preselect a different winner for each of several successive construction projects. The designated "losers" agree to bid high, and the selected winner rigs its bid to appear as the "lowest." The selected winner's price is typically higher than it would have been under genuine competitive bidding. It was once a common practice in Japan for construction contractors to consult each other before bidding on public works projects, a form of bid-rigging.

Industry self-regulation by trade groups is gaining favor as an alternative to government regulation and costly litigation. Care must be taken to prevent "industry codes of conduct" from becoming disguised methods for collusion or price-fixing. Recall the examples of the National Society of Professional Engineers' prohibition against competitive bidding and the bar associations' minimum fee schedules. The quality control arguments for these trade association activities was weak when compared with their anticompetitive impact. Excessive discipline of a highly competitive member suggests that other members are really suppressing competition—an ironic misuse of a professional association's powers, particularly when rationalized as ethical rules.

Some trade associations limit their membership, which may be procompetitive if membership reflects integrity, quality, or reliability. Trade guilds and the apprenticeship system were once justified on this basis. However, excluding members from practice becomes anticompetitive when it limits the number of competitors or limits access to some valuable facility operated by the trade association. Consider that local real estate associations enhance their members' sales of listed properties by operating multiple listing services. Denying membership or limiting nonmember access to these print or Web-based catalogs of real estate offerings reduces competition in commission rates.

Electronic business-to-business (B2B) exchanges (Chapter 10) pose some similar antitrust problems. These on-line auction markets might be tempted to use collusive practices, unfair discipline or outright exclusions of competitive members, and standards-setting activities that risk antitrust enforcement. For example, it could be anticompetitive if some potential members were excluded, a division of markets resulted, the auction operated as a group boycott of particular members, the market's information-reporting system facilitated price signaling or price fixing, or the auction was an attempt to monopolize or a conspiracy to monopolize.

ONLINE

B2B–Antitrust Guidelines for Collaborations among Competitors
http://www.ftc.gov/os/2000/04/ftcdojguidelines.pdf

Division of Markets

Competitors may attempt to divide markets so that only certain producers serve particular regions or specified customers. A **division of markets** is illegal per se because it gives the producer an effective monopoly in an assigned market segment. Even if there are other competitors selling in the affected region, the preferred firm has some market power. In one case, a group of independent local grocers formed a group buying chain. Their joint exercise of buying power was illegal because many members were forced to locate their stores in designated territories. This division of markets was not justified by the grocers' intent to compete more effectively against larger chain stores.

Group Boycotts

Individuals are usually free to deal with whomever they please. But when a group of competitors agree to boycott certain individuals or groups, it may be illegal. **Group boycotts** are generally illegal per se, but some courts use the rule of reason. It may be illegal for competing sellers to agree not to sell to a particular customer, reseller, or class of persons. A group of buyers with market power (monopsony or oligopsony) may also be guilty of an illegal boycott if certain sellers are shunned. In one case, an apparel manufacturers' trade association urged its members to boycott any retailers selling pirated designs (e.g., fake designer jeans). In another case, a National Football League rule required a team to compensate the former team of a free agent if the player changed teams. Both actions were illegal concerted refusals to deal. At one time, the American Medical Association had rules of ethics that prohibited doctors from participating in prepaid medical plans or from receiving a salary for practicing medicine. Those rules were illegal because they tended to destroy competition among professional groups. How might such rules affect evolving health care systems like HMOs?

JOINT VENTURES

A **joint venture** is a form of partnership in which two entities (i.e., persons, partnerships, corporations) enter into a limited business activity together. Joint ventures are subject to rule of reason analysis because they are sometimes justifiable, such as when economic efficiency is the purpose and effect. The test is whether the restraint is really necessary to achieve the lawful purpose. The courts balance the joint venture's potential anticompetitive effects against its alleged efficiency. For example, the Associated Press is a cooperative wire service with thousands of members. Access to this service is often critical to effective competition. At one time, the bylaws of the Associated Press contained a veto clause permitting any member to blackball a competitor seeking membership. This arrangement was held illegal under rule of reason because competitors' exclusion from the joint venture posed a substantial barrier to entry for new firms in the newspaper business. A joint ownership of theaters by moviemaking companies was also held illegal because new releases were not freely available to nonmember theaters, substantially lessening competition.

PROOF OF AN ILLEGAL AGREEMENT OR COMBINATION

Participants in an unlawful collusion or restraint of trade are usually very careful to avoid leaving any clear trail of evidence. Their agreements are hidden and off the record, and clandestine tactics such as secret meetings or secret codes might be used. Because the Sherman Act's criminal provisions require proof beyond a reasonable doubt, it is difficult to prove such hidden guilt with direct evidence. Therefore, illegal concerted activity is usually inferred from circumstantial evidence. Many types of business and supply chain contracts are restricted from disclosure to the press or competitors by nondisclosure agreements (NDAs).

Some firms in monopolistic or oligopolistic industries mimic the pricing decisions of an industry leader. This is **conscious parallelism** so there is no overt agreement. In 1939, the Supreme Court stated: "[i]t is enough that, knowing that concerted action was contemplated and invited, the distributors [of feature films] gave their adherence to the scheme and participated in it." This is the *Interstate* formula, which permits proof of an illegal collusive agreement if there is conscious parallelism.[17] The more modern formulation of conscious parallelism is more limiting. It recognizes that legal conduct may incorrectly appear to be conscious parallelism. Businesses must often respond quickly to changes in market conditions or to new contract terms offered by their competitors. For example, changes in the price of crude oil often quickly lead to similar changes in the gasoline pump prices charged by independent gasoline retailers. "[T]he crucial question is whether the respondents' conduct . . . stems from an independent decision or from an agreement, tacit or expressed. But, this court has never held that proof of parallel business behavior conclusively establishes agreement."[18]

Section 8 of the Clayton Act outlaws certain **interlocking directorates**—that is, the same person sitting on the board of two competitors. It prohibits any person from "at the same time be[ing] a director in two or more corporations . . . if such corporations are or shall have been theretofore, by virtue of their business and location of operation, competitors, so that the elimination of competition by an agreement between them would constitute a violation of any of the provisions of any of the antitrust laws." A common director between competitors could provide a convenient conduit for collusive communication. Although FTC enforcement is lax, the DOJ is more aggressive, extending the prohibition to firms engaged in "related businesses." For example, it could be unlawful for a single individual to sit on the boards of a computer mainframe manufacturer and a manufacturer of mainframe software.

The interlocking directorate prohibition has exceptions. Interlocking directorates may exist between firms that are in a vertical relationship or in different industries. Suppliers and customers commonly solidify their relationship with common directors. Indirect interlocks are also permissible. For example, a bank employee may legally sit on the boards of two competing industrial firms. A nondirector employee of one firm may sit on the board of a competing firm. These interlocks are actively used in Japanese Keiretsu ("feudal families of firms"). Given the post-Enron trend toward increased director liability, attracting competent, experienced directors can be challenging. Vigorous enforcement of §8 could impair the overall quality of corporate management and directorships. It may also be inconsistent with the closer contacts firms may need to assure total quality and technological compatibility from suppliers and to customers.

VERTICAL RESTRAINTS OF TRADE

Vertical restraints of trade are significantly different from horizontal restraints. Vertical relationships are intended to restrict certain activities along the supply chain between manufacturers, wholesalers, and retailers, despite the impact on consumers. Vertical restraints usually include resale price maintenance, restrictions on territorial or customer access, or restrictions on the freedom to sell competing brands. Vertical restraints may also require the purchase of less desirable goods in order to receive desirable ones. Exhibit 19.5 illustrates vertical restraints.

VERTICAL PRICE RESTRAINT: RESALE PRICE MAINTENANCE

The most direct vertical restraint is a manufacturer's **vertical price-fixing.** It requires the retailer to charge consumers a specified retail price, usually a minimum price.

17. *Interstate Circuit, Inc. v. United States*, 306 U.S. 208 (1939).
18. *Theatre Enterprises v. Paramount Film Distributor Corp.*, 346 U.S. 537 (1954).

EXHIBIT 19.5 Vertical Restraints of Trade

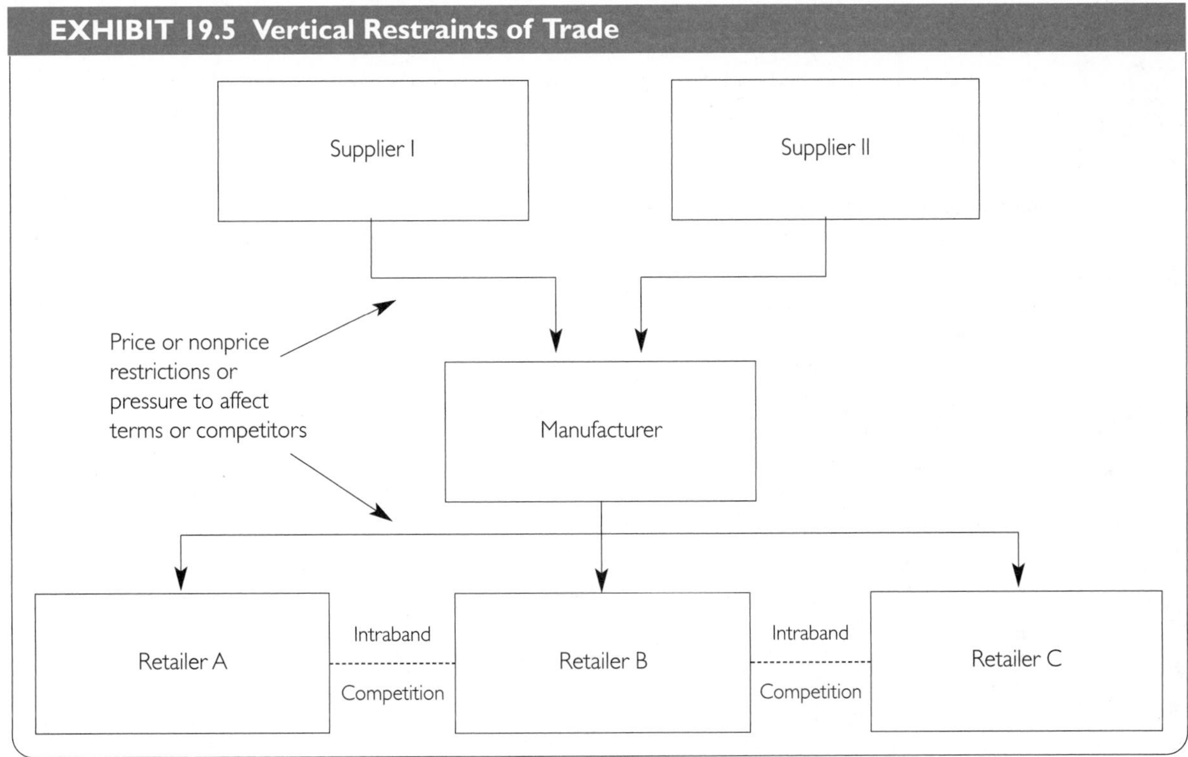

However, even a maximum price is considered **resale price maintenance.** Today, the courts apply the rule of reason, and resale price maintenance is no longer a per se violation. Pressures for resale price maintenance sometimes come from retailers. They may secretly request the manufacturer to set minimum prices as a hidden method to achieve horizontal price-fixing. A specified maximum retail price often becomes an unspoken minimum price, and all retailers sell only at that price.

Political pressure from small retailers urged Congress to abandon per se illegality of resale price maintenance. In 1937, the **Miller-Tydings Act** permitted state statutes to legitimize resale price maintenance if required by a manufacturer's supply contract with retailers. After the Great Depression, chain stores proliferated, forcing many small and inefficient retailers and wholesalers out of business. Small businesses insisted that products should be sold at higher and "fairer" prices that allow them a fair rate of return. By the early 1950s, 45 state statutes permitted resale price maintenance agreements. At one point, more than 1,500 manufacturers enforced the fair-trade laws through agreements with retailers that required them to charge at least the "manufacturer's list price." Congress further reinforced these agreements in 1952 with the **McGuire Act**, extending resale price maintenance to retailers that never agreed under **nonsigner provisions.** Resale price maintenance prevented discounting of many consumer goods, such as name-brand clothes, furniture, cameras, and consumer electronics in the 1950s to 1970s. By the 1960s, however, mail order houses in the few states without fair-trade laws eroded the increasingly unpopular resale price maintenance. Eventually, Congress repealed both the Miller-Tydings and McGuire Acts in 1975, again permitting more widespread intrabrand competition.

The failure of resale price maintenance caused manufacturers to develop alternative methods to discipline retailers who refused to observe minimum prices.

Commentary

Vertical Restraints of Trade

Why should vertical restraints be illegal? Participants in the supply chain use vertical restraints of trade to maximize profits and improve the longevity of their product lines. Retailers with low profit margins advertise less and provide lower quality customer service, and low prices cheapen the product's image. Although overpriced products may deter some customers, higher prices can also create an image of quality. High profit margins encourage retailers to hire trained sales staff and service technicians, provide technical expertise and customer service, and invest in advertising, inventory, parts, broader selection, and better product display.

A ***free rider*** problem arises when the same goods are sold by both high-profit retailers and discount stores. Many customers learn about a technically complex product at a high-priced retailer but then purchase the same model product from low-overhead discounters. These customers and discounters "ride free" on the promotional and technical expenditures of the higher-profit retailers. Widespread free riding forces the higher-profit retailers out of business, leaving little technical expertise available in the market. Free riding plagues the markets for consumer electronics and PCs. Manufacturers or suppliers often impose vertical restraints to prevent free riding and maintain brand image. They may require minimum resale prices, grant exclusive dealerships, or impose territorial restrictions on dealers to reduce cutthroat competition. Higher retail prices can permit adequate customer service. However, critics argue that vertical restraints harm consumers by reducing price competition. The legality of vertical restraints is subject to the rule of reason under provisions of the Sherman or Clayton Acts.

Manufacturers generally prefer interbrand over intrabrand competition. Vertical restraints reduce ***intrabrand competition*** among sellers of the same brand and models, which arguably enhances ***interbrand competition*** between different brands of the same type of product. Interbrand competition helps make various retailer services an important product feature. Consumers can select a different mix of service and price only by buying a competing brand from another dealer specializing in a different brand. Vertical restraints discipline retailers and reduce intrabrand competition because they are an exercise of supplier market power. Vigorous intrabrand competition benefits consumers with price competition, which is more appropriate if customers do not need much retailer service.

Manufacturers often initiated a **refusal to deal** with disruptive retailers. In *United States v. Colgate,*[19] the Supreme Court permitted certain refusals to deal as long as there was no contract agreement requiring sales at specific prices. The Colgate Company announced publicly that it would refuse to deal with distributors that failed to participate in its announced resale price maintenance policy. Later cases severely limit *Colgate* but have not overruled it. Today, resale price maintenance and refusals to deal are judged under the rule of reason. A refusal to deal is illegal and coercive if there is any active harassment or monitoring of the retailer's pricing behaviors or if the manufacturer uses a suspension or reinstatement system to discipline retailers. For example, Parke Davis distributed its pharmaceuticals through wholesalers and drug retailers.[20] Its wholesale catalogue announced a refusal to deal with discounters, and its retail prices often included a 50% markup. Parke Davis's wholesalers ceased filling orders for several retailers who advertised discounted prices on Myadek vitamins. The Supreme Court held that Parke Davis went beyond mere announcement of a refusal to deal by implementing an illegal resale price maintenance combination and conspiracy.

---

19. 250 U.S. 300 (1919).
20. *U.S. v. Parke Davis & Co.*, 362 U.S. 29 (1960).

VERTICAL NONPRICE RESTRAINTS

Manufacturers, unable to rely on vertical price restraints often try to impose nonprice restraints to more directly control the free riding behaviors of retailers. One method prevents retailers from selling to discounters for resale. Another imposes territorial limitations that prohibit retailers from engaging in intrabrand competition. Both devices are vertical nonprice restraints. Although nonprice restraints may have legitimate purposes, they can be used to enforce illegal resale price maintenance.

Exclusive Dealing

The term **exclusive dealership** indicates some sort of restriction in the resale arrangement. **Exclusive** often refers to fashionable or privileged status. However, in antitrust law it has two different meanings. First, the sole right to sell a manufacturer's products within a given region is known as an **exclusive distributorship**. No other dealer in the same region may sell the manufacturer's products. An exclusive distributor might also sell competitors' products. Manufacturers generally have wide freedom to pick their retailers or wholesalers, but an exclusive distributorship may not be justified if there are few substitutes for a manufacturer's products. Exclusive distributorships are judged by the rule of reason, though some recent cases hold that abuses within them are illegal per se. For example, it is illegal for one distributor to pressure the manufacturer to terminate sales to the only competing distributor.

The second use of the term *exclusive* relates to **exclusive dealing**—requiring the buyer to resell only the products of a single manufacturer. Exclusive dealing is illegal under §3 of the Clayton Act if it tends to create a monopoly or substantially lessens competition: "shall be unlawful for any person engaged in commerce to lease or make a sale . . . of . . . commodities . . . on the condition, agreement or understanding that the lessee or purchaser thereof shall not use or deal in . . . commodities of a competitor . . . of the lessor or seller, where the effect of such . . . [agreement] may substantially lessen competition or tend to create a monopoly in any line of commerce."

Manufacturers and suppliers cannot generally insist that a retailer refuse to carry a competitor's products. Exclusive dealing contracts are judged by the **quantitative substantiality** test, which presumes exclusive dealing adversely affects competition when it covers a substantial dollar volume. Thus, a violation of §3 of the Clayton Act may occur with a far lower percentage of market control than would be considered a monopoly or merger violation. Recent cases focus more on unit market share rather than dollar volume.

A subtler way to enforce an exclusive dealing arrangement is to rely on the protection of the *Colgate* doctrine by simply refusing to sell to nonexclusive dealers. Manufacturers seeking this protection have replaced exclusive dealing language in their supply contracts with **adequate representation clauses**, which require retailers to make substantial efforts to market the manufacturer's products. Manufacturers can terminate dealers that do not provide advertising, inventory maintenance, service expertise, or sales effort that is specified in their supply contract.

Customer and Territorial Restrictions

Manufacturers' efforts to restrict retailers from selling to particular customers or in specific territories are probably illegal. Arrangements that restrict retailers' sales to a geographic region or that require retailers to sell only to a particular list of customers deny retailers the right to sell to others, so they are illegal. At first, such arrangements were considered illegal per se under the *Schwinn* rule.[21] In 1977, however, this rule was replaced with the rule of reason, now applicable to nearly all vertical nonprice restrictions. The EU has banned territorial restraints in an effort to lower the barriers imposed by its member nations' national borders. Some vertical nonprice restrictions are valid because they enhance interbrand competition. There are two important questions in the analysis of vertical territorial or customer restrictions: (1) Does the restriction tend to limit competition? (2) Are there legitimate economic and business objectives for the restriction?

Vertical nonprice restrictions may be illegal if there is little interbrand competition, if the manufacturer has considerable market power, or if high barriers to entry exist for new producers. GTE Sylvania limited the number of retail franchises within specified geographic territories to strengthen its retail network.[22] Franchised retailers could sell GTE Sylvania products only at locations specified in their supply contracts. Continental was one of Sylvania's most successful retailers in San Francisco. It complained when Sylvania granted a franchise to another local retailer. Sylvania had refused to give Continental a franchise in Sacramento after Continental canceled a large Sylvania order. The U.S. Supreme Court overruled the *Schwinn* per se rule and justified Sylvania's actions by referring to the free rider controversy.

Dealer Terminations

Manufacturers have the freedom to select new dealers or terminate existing dealers for reasons such as performance, breach of contract on key provisions in the distributorship agreement (e.g., adequate representation), and deviation from announced pricing or from the manufacturer's marketing strategy. However, the power to terminate the dealers is not unlimited. Both federal and state laws protect against some types of arbitrary franchise termination, as noted in Chapter 13. Some state laws require manufacturers to exercise "good faith" or limit terminations to "just cause." Many foreign nations provide similar protection for local dealers of foreign-made goods. Dealer terminations are permitted if no concerted action is taken to maintain resale prices. *Monsanto Co. v. Spray-Rite Service Corp.*[23] subjects vertical nonprice restrictions to the rule of reason.

TYING

The Clayton Act generally prohibits tying arrangements. **Tying,** or a tie-in agreement, requires customers to purchase certain commodities or goods. Typically, the seller refuses to sell a desirable **tying product** unless the customer agrees to purchase a less desirable **tied product.** The tie-in relationship coerces buyers to purchase the less desirable product if they want to obtain the more desirable product. This practice ties their main purchases to other purchases of supplementary goods. A tie-in is effective only when the seller has some market power in the desirable or tying product, perhaps resulting from a patent, a secret process, or a uniquely superior product. The Clayton Act prohibits tying only of goods, not services or land sales. However, tying could be illegal under the Sherman Act for markets in real estate, intangibles, and services. Tying is often called a per se violation, but the cases show

21. *United States v. Arnold Schwinn & Co.*, 388 U.S. 365 (1967).
22. *Continental T.V., Inc. v. GTE Sylvania, Inc.*, 433 U.S. 36 (1977).
23. 465 U.S. 752 (1984).

courts often do thorough rule of reason analysis in tying cases. Recall that the *Microsoft* case discussed the tying offense.

Tying usually arises in one of three types of relationships. First, the tied and tying products are used together in fixed proportions (e.g., nuts and bolts, tires on automobiles). Second, the tied product may be necessary for use with the tying product (e.g., computer cards or peripherals with a computer). Third, the products may be only loosely usable together and may even be used separately (e.g., seed and fertilizer). Three elements must be established before tying is illegal. First, there is an analysis of the relevant market for the tying product and the relevant market for the tied product. It requires evidence of the seller's sale of one product conditioned on the purchase of another. Second, the seller must have sufficient economic or market power to force the tie-in, which may be shown where buyers clearly prefer the seller's tying product. If several buyers agree to a coercive tie-in, the seller may be presumed to have market power. Third, the level of competition restricted in the less desirable tied product must be more than insubstantial. There must be proof of a substantial amount of commerce in the tied product. For example, $500,000 of the salt market and $60,000 of the film market were considered substantial, regardless of the market shares involved.

Justifications for Tying

Tying relationships force buyers to purchase tied products in larger quantities than they would without the tie-in. Otherwise, purchasers could probably obtain the tied product or a substitute more cheaply from other sellers. Tying reduces the buyer's freedom to use the least-cost vendor and permits the tying seller to charge near-monopoly prices for the tied product. Tying unjustifiably expands the seller's near-monopoly in the tying product to the tied product's market and raises entry barriers for potential competitors.

It can be difficult to determine whether there really are two products rather than just one product. For example, both a picture tube and the accompanying television set or an automobile and its built-in radio can be viewed as either separate or single products. The real question here is whether there is a substantial market for the installation of the tied product into the tying product. There is only a replacement and repair market for television picture tubes, but a healthy and competitive installation aftermarket exists for car radios and stereos. Ford has repeatedly tried to tie higher-priced and/or lower-quality car stereos (tied product) to their automobiles (tying product) by making its electrical system technically incompatible with aftermarket stereos. Some automakers permit buyers to delete standard-equipment radios for a credit.

Financing can be seen as an integral part of a product. U.S. Steel (later U.S.X.) insisted on selling high-priced prefabricated homes by providing low-cost loans. Homes and loans are obviously not a single product. Consumers might be willing to pay higher prices for the less desirable prefabricated homes (the tied product) if they receive desirable low-cost loans (the tying product).[24] Today, many automobile and appliance manufacturers use their captive finance companies (e.g., GMAC, FOMOCO Credit, GE Credit) to provide low-cost financing without violating the tying prohibition.

24. *U.S. Steel Corp. v. Fortner Enterprises, Inc.*, 429 U.S. 610 (1977).

Tying relationships can be justified if they result in economic efficiency. During start-up, new businesses may need to assure the proper functioning of their complex products. Once a business has become established, the tying relationship may be no longer justified. For example, a TV antenna manufacturer required the purchase of service contracts with the purchase of its equipment. This tie-in was justified only until the business had become well established. Tying relationships are also justified if the quality of the tied product is higher than that of competitors' similar products. The seller may claim that without the tie-in the goodwill it derives from the tying product will suffer. This argument is not always successful. At one time, IBM required that only the IBM brand of punch cards could be used with its tabulating machines. Although other vendors sold similar punch cards, IBM argued that only the IBM cards could prevent fouling of the machines.[25] Similarly, the Bell System once required its customers to use only Western Electric–brand telephones and switching equipment. In both instances, the alleged low quality of competitors' products was solved by other reasonable means, such as measurable design and performance specifications. Specifications for the thickness and resilience of tabulating cards are sufficient to prevent damage to IBM's machines. Specifications for the electrical characteristics of telephone equipment can be sufficient to prevent damage to the Bell System's equipment. The quality-control argument is weak if the company is well established and specifications can be drawn up to ensure compatibility.

The quality-control justification generally protects the product specifications required in franchise businesses. In *Principe v. McDonald's Corp.*,[26] a form of tying was justified under the quality-control requirements for federal trademark usage under the Lanham Act. McDonald's franchises must pay royalties for the franchise, rent their storefront from a McDonald's affiliate, purchase particular foodstuffs from specified suppliers (e.g., Coke products), and adhere to exacting production quality standards. Tying the storefront lease to the franchise license was found to be a single product rather than two products. Recall that tying Microsoft's browser Explorer to the Windows operating system was a major part of the monopolization case discussed earlier in this chapter. Tying is the major antitrust problem for owners of IP, as discussed next.

ANTITRUST AND INTELLECTUAL PROPERTY RIGHTS

Antitrust and IP use seemingly opposite approaches to achieve consumer welfare. Although both encourage innovation and competition, antitrust disfavors monopolies and market power. By contrast, IP grants monopoly-like property rights to incentivize R&D investment. These two legal regimes must coexist, requiring close scrutiny of IP rights when IP owners go beyond exploitation of their invention or expression to commit anticompetitive acts. The primary antitrust constraint on IP is a corollary of the equitable doctrine **unclean hands** that limits the IP owner's rights when there is an unreasonable extension of the IP right through **misuse**.

INTELLECTUAL PROPERTY MISUSE

Misuse most typically occurs through tying. A patent holder conditions the grant of patent rights (in a license of a patented process or sale of patented products) to the

25. *International Business Machines v. U.S.*, 298 U.S. 131 (1936).
26. 631 F.2d 303 (4th Cir., 1980).

buyer's purchase of unpatented collateral products or services. Applying the tying analysis, the patent holder must have power in the market for the patented, tying product and then use this power to require the purchase of unpatented, tied products, which has an adverse impact on competition in the tied product's market. Misuse can also arise in other situations: (1) **package licensing** if both the tied and tying products are patented, (2) a customer is forbidden from purchasing other vendors' products that could substitute for the tying product, and (3) a patent or copyright is acquired by fraud. A 1988 statute makes it clear that patent holders may simply refuse to license or use their patent rights. Trademark misuse is unlikely because the imperative to preserve the goodwill of a trademark permits tying to maintain quality control. However, the trademark misuse theory is still possible.

In re Independent Service Organizations Antitrust Litigation

203 F. 3d 1322 (Fed. Cir., 2000)

Facts. Xerox manufactures, sells, and services high-volume copiers. It enforced a policy of not selling the patented replacement parts for its copiers to independent service organizations (ISOs), including CSU. Xerox cut off CSU's direct purchase of restricted parts and implemented an "on-site end-user verification" procedure to confirm that the parts ordered by certain ISOs or their customers were actually for their end-user use. To maintain its existing business of servicing Xerox equipment, CSU used parts cannibalized from used Xerox equipment, parts obtained from other ISOs, and parts purchased through a limited number of its customers. For approximately one year, CSU also obtained parts from Rank Xerox, a majority-owned European affiliate of Xerox, until Xerox forced Rank Xerox to stop selling parts to CSU and other ISOs. CSU filed suit, alleging that Xerox violated the Sherman Act by setting the prices on its patented parts much higher for ISOs than for end-users to force ISOs to raise their prices.

Legal Issue. Is it misuse under the Sherman Act for the manufacturer of patented parts or copyrighted manuals to refuse to sell them to independent service firms?

Opinion. Chief Judge Mayer. Intellectual property rights do not confer a privilege to violate the antitrust laws. "But it is also correct that the antitrust laws do not negate the patentee's right to exclude others from patent property." "The commercial advantage gained by new technology and its statutory protection by patent do not convert the possessor thereof into a prohibited monopolist." A patent alone does not demonstrate market power, such "market power does not 'impose on the intellectual property owner an obligation to license the use of that property to others.' A patent owner who brings suit to enforce the statutory right to exclude others from making, using, or selling the claimed invention is exempt from the antitrust laws, even though such a suit may have an anticompetitive effect, unless the infringement defendant proves one of two conditions. First, he may prove that the asserted patent was obtained through knowing and willful fraud. Or he may demonstrate that the infringement suit was a mere sham to cover what is actually no more than an attempt to interfere directly with the business relationships of a competitor.

CSU relies on a footnote in *Eastman Kodak Co. v. Image Technical Services, Inc.*, that "[t]he Court has held many times that power gained through some natural and legal advantage such as a patent, . . . can give rise to liability if 'a seller exploits his dominant position in one market to expand his empire into the next.' " There are no claims in this case of illegally tying the sale of Xerox's patented parts to unpatented products. Properly viewed within the framework of a tying case, the footnote can be interpreted as restating the undisputed premise that the patent holder cannot use his statutory right to refuse to sell patented parts to gain a monopoly in a market beyond the scope of the patent. The cited language from Kodak does nothing to limit the right of the patentee to refuse to sell or license in markets within the scope of the statutory patent grant. In fact, we have expressly held that, absent exceptional circumstances, a patent may confer the right to exclude competition altogether in more than one antitrust market.

We have held that "if a [patent infringement] suit is not objectively baseless, an antitrust defendant's subjective motivation is immaterial." We see no more reason to inquire into the subjective motivation of Xerox in refusing to sell or license its patented works than we found in evaluating the subjective motivation of a patentee in bringing suit to enforce that same right. In the absence of any indication of illegal tying, fraud in the Patent and Trademark Office, or sham litigation, the patent holder may enforce the statutory right to exclude others from making, using, or selling the claimed invention free from liability under the antitrust laws. We therefore will not inquire into his subjective motivation for exerting his statutory rights, even though his refusal to sell or license his patented invention may have an anticompetitive effect, so long as that anticompetitive effect is not illegally extended beyond the statutory patent grant. Xerox was under no obligation to sell or license its patented parts and did not violate the antitrust laws by refusing to do so.

The Copyright Act expressly grants a copyright owner the exclusive right to distribute the protected work by "transfer of ownership, or by rental, lease, or lending." "[T]he owner of the copyright, if [it] pleases, may refrain from vending or licensing and content [itself] with simply exercising the right to exclude others from using [its] property." The Supreme Court has made clear that the property right granted by copyright law cannot be used with impunity to extend power in the marketplace beyond what Congress intended. The Tenth Circuit has not addressed in any published opinion the extent to which the unilateral refusal to sell or license copyrighted expression can form the basis of a violation of the Sherman Act. We are therefore left to determine how that circuit would likely resolve the issue; the precedent of other circuits is instructive in that consideration.

Perhaps the most extensive analysis of the effect of a unilateral refusal to license copyrighted expression was conducted by the First Circuit in *Data General Corp. v. Grumman Systems Support Corp.* There, the court noted that the limited copyright monopoly is based on Congress' empirical assumption that the right to "exclude others from using their works creates a system of incentives that promotes consumer welfare in the long term by encouraging investment in the creation of desirable artistic and functional works of expression. . . . We cannot require antitrust defendants to prove and reprove the merits of this legislative assumption in every case where a refusal to license a copyrighted work comes under attack." The court went on to establish as a legal standard that "while exclusionary conduct can include a monopolist's unilateral refusal to license a copyright, an author's desire to exclude others from use of its copyrighted work is a presumptively valid business justification for any immediate harm to consumers." The burden to overcome this presumption was firmly placed on the antitrust plaintiff. The court gave no weight to evidence showing knowledge that developing a proprietary position would help to maintain a monopoly in the service market in the face of contrary evidence of the defendant's desire to develop state-of-the-art diagnostic software to enhance its service and consumer benefit.

We believe the First Circuit's approach is more consistent with both the antitrust and the copyright laws and is the standard that would most likely be followed by the Tenth Circuit. We therefore reject CSU's invitation to examine Xerox's subjective motivation in asserting its right to exclude under the copyright laws for pretext, in the absence of any evidence that the copyrights were obtained by unlawful means or were used to gain monopoly power beyond the statutory copyright granted by Congress. In the absence of such definitive rebuttal evidence, Xerox's refusal to sell or license its copyrighted works was squarely within the rights granted by Congress to the copyright holder and did not constitute a violation of the antitrust laws. Accordingly, the judgment of the United States District Court for the District of Kansas is affirmed.

Decision. Manufacturers of patented products and copyrighted diagnostic software may refuse to sell replacement parts to independent repair firms without violating antitrust prohibition against patent misuse.

Case Questions

1. What must be proven in a misuse case if courts will not presume anticompetitive motive from a refusal to license or sell? Does this make the proof of misuse any different from proof of other forms of intentional monopolization?
2. What are the three types of conduct that might expose an IP owner to charges of misuse under the antitrust laws?

ESSENTIAL FACILITIES DOCTRINE

Some firms control an **essential facility**: an asset indispensable for competition in the market. The moniker "bottleneck monopoly" aptly describes how competition was substantially lessened in *U.S. v. Terminal Railroad Ass'n.*[27] The famous robber baron

27. 224 U.S. 383 (1912).

Jay Gould controlled the railroad tunnels, bridges, terminals, and switching yards around St. Louis, Missouri. In the 1880s, rail transportation was predominant, and much transcontinental traffic was funneled through St. Louis. There were only a few key bridges over the Mississippi. Gould charged discriminatory surcharges (arbitraries) to pass through his St. Louis chokehold, which was deemed an essential facility. Antitrust law required Gould to open up membership in the cartel to outsiders, and the Interstate Commerce Commission provided regulatory oversight thereafter.

There are four factors used in essential facilities cases: (1) a monopolist controls the essential facility, (2) competitors are unable to duplicate the facility, (3) the competitor is denied use of the essential facility, and (4) a parallel facility is infeasible. Several facilities have been deemed essential under the doctrine, including newswire services, stock exchanges, wholesale produce markets, real estate multiple listing services, airline reservation systems, electricity distribution lines, petroleum pipelines, storage facilities, airport terminals, and shipping piers. Many essential facilities cases involve restrictions on competition in B2B markets that harm downstream customers. For example, MCI gained access to the essential facilities of AT&T's local consumer telephone connections and switching system to offer competition in long-distance telephone service.[28]

In some cases, find there is no essential facility and therefore no antitrust violation, such as when meaningful competition is emerging. For example, the essential facility doctrine is being argued to allow various ISPs access to broadband, high-speed Internet lines. Consumer choice in picking some other ISP than the cable or landline phone provider has been limited to the owner of the essential facility. This situation may change as broadband becomes available through parallel cable TV lines, telephone DSL, wireless telephony, and satellite systems. There was no antitrust violation in the Washington Redskins' exclusive access to RFK Stadium that prevented an American Football League team from entering the Washington sports market.[29]

Standards

High-technology products often have characteristics of an essential facility, generally through their standardized operation. **Standards** are agreed-upon specifications for the production or operation of functionally compatible goods and services. Standards are the method by which network industries gain increasing economies of scale as more users adopt products complying with the standards, such as fax machines, telephones, music or video recording and playback devices (HDTV, MP3), computer operating systems, computer file formats (ASCII, HTML), Internet communications using packet technologies, and even rules for playing sports or the attachment of bottle caps. Government agencies, trade associations, and individual firms influence the standardization of products, services, or service providers to improve quality, safety, and interchangeability. It can clearly benefit consumers unless standardization becomes a hidden way to fix prices, thwart innovation, or exclude vigorous competitors. However, **closed standards** are a barrier to entry when they are owned or controlled by a monopolist or a cartel.

Antitrust law scrutinizes the development process and ownership of standards to avoid monopolization. **Proprietary standards** controlled by a single firm or consortium tend to develop more quickly, gaining wide acceptance as **de facto standards.**

---

28. *MCI Comm. Corp. v. ATT*, 708 F.2d 1081 (7th Cir., 1982).
29. *Hecht v. Pro-Football, Inc.*, 570 F.2d 982 (D.C.Cir., 1977).

By contrast, consensus standards are adopted more slowly and may require a government mandate to achieve network effects. Antitrust risks may arise when, in the standards-setting context, the participants discuss prices, market allocations, discrimination in licensing, or exclusion of participants from the process and use of the standards. Standards can erect barriers to entry when proprietary IP underlies the standard. Antitrust may be violated when the standard is not made generally available or when participants in the standard setting prevent the emergence of new technologies based on revised standards.

ONLINE

Standards Setting Organizations
http://www.ansi.org
http://www.ieee.org

LICENSING AND ANTITRUST

The FTC and DOJ have issued antitrust guidelines for the licensing of intellectual property. They recognize that IP is vulnerable to misappropriation and does not automatically confer market power and that licensing is frequently a procompetitive activity. The guidelines create an **antitrust safety zone** or safe harbor so that the agencies will not challenge a particular IP licensing activity if it satisfies two criteria:

1. The restraint is not facially anticompetitive.
2. The licensor and its licensees collectively account for no more than 20% of each relevant market significantly affected by the restraint.

ONLINE

FTC/DOJ Licensing Guidelines
http://www.usdoj.gov/atr/public/guidelines/ipguide.htm

Licenses often impose potentially anticompetitive restrictions of one or more of the following types: exclusivity, exclusive dealing, resale price maintenance, cross-licensing, patent pooling, or extending royalties beyond the patent's term.

PRICE DISCRIMINATION

Price discrimination is a seller's practice of charging different prices to different buyers for goods of like grade and quality. It is illegal under the Robinson-Patman Act if it substantially lessens competition or tends to create a monopoly. The FTC has enforcement powers under Robinson-Patman, and a private right of action exists for competitors or buyers damaged by price discrimination. Price discrimination would be impossible in a perfectly competitive market. Any buyer faced with a higher price than that offered to others would simply buy from another seller. However, few markets are perfectly competitive, and some buyers or sellers usually have some market power.

Robinson-Patman was passed to protect small businesses competing with big chain stores that had oligopsony (buyer's) market power. Critics claim that Robinson-Patman has outlived its economic usefulness. Price discrimination can occur when buyers have imperfect information or are ignorant of the prices paid by other buyers or when some buyers are given secret discounts.

PROOF OF PRICE DISCRIMINATION

To establish a violation of the Robinson-Patman Act, a plaintiff or the FTC must prove six elements: (1) discrimination in price, (2) between two different purchases, (3) affecting interstate commerce, (4) concerning sales of commodities of like grade and quality, (5) causing a substantial lessening of competition or a tendency to create a monopoly, and (6) injury to competitors of the seller or the buyer or to their customers.

The two discriminatory transactions must occur within a contemporaneous time frame; an excessive interval probably reflects changing market conditions. There must be two different sales prices as stated in the contracts of sale. Nonprice differences may also be discriminatory. For example, preferential credit terms given to one buyer but not others are prohibited. Quantity discounts theoretically open to all purchasers but in practice denied to small buyers are also discriminatory.

Robinson-Patman does not apply to intangibles, services, and certain mixed sales of goods and services. It is lawful to discriminate in the price charged for securities, mutual fund shares, patents, licenses, real estate leases, and consulting services. Airfares, rental car rates, and hotel rates are commonly discriminatory. Price discrimination in intangibles or services could conceivably violate the Sherman Act as a restraint of trade or an attempt to monopolize, or it could be an unfair method of competition under the FTC Act.

The goods sold must be of like grade and quality; that is, their physical and chemical composition must be similar. If buyers willingly substitute two seemingly different products as interchangeable, they may be of like grade and quality. Subtle differences in the brand names or labels of two similar products do not usually justify price discrimination if consumers perceive the two products as functionally similar.

COMPETITIVE INJURIES FROM PRICE DISCRIMINATION

Liability for price discrimination arises when any person discriminates or knowingly benefits from discrimination, thereby causing someone else to suffer lost profits or missed business opportunities. The level in the supply chain of the business suffering the injury must be identified. Injuries may occur at the seller's level, the buyer's level, or the level of the customers of the buyer. Price discriminations tending to injure those in competition with the discriminating seller are **primary-line injuries**. Price discriminations a seller makes are **secondary-line injuries** if between two reselling buyers that are competing for the same customers. If two buyers have different costs for the same goods, the buyer paying higher prices suffers because the buyer paying lower prices can pass the savings on to its customers. If Buyer A and Buyer B were in distinct geographic markets, no secondary-line injury would occur because their two sets of customers could not practically choose one seller over the other. A more controversial theory of price discrimination involves injury to the buyer's customers. Theoretically, injury may occur at any level in the supply chain, no matter where price discrimination occurs. A **tertiary-line injury** may occur if customers of the buyers are injured by price discrimination such as when the cost savings are passed on through wholesalers to retailers.

PRICE DISCRIMINATION DEFENSES

Price discrimination is sometimes justified by affirmative defenses. The seller may attempt to show that the competitive effect of differential pricing is trivial so there is no competitive injury. Export sales are exempted because the Robinson-Patman Act applies only to "commodities . . . sold for use, consumption, or resale within the United States." There are also three statutory defenses: changing conditions, cost differential, and meeting the competition in good faith.

The Robinson-Patman Act provides a defense when the market has changed so that prices previously charged are no longer realistic. The **changing conditions** defense provides that "nothing herein shall prevent price changes from time to time in response to changing conditions affecting the marketability of the goods concerned, such as (but not limited to) actual or imminent deterioration of perishable goods, obsolescence of seasonal goods, distress sales under court process, or sales in good faith in discontinuance of business." This defense is confined strictly to temporary situations in which the physical nature of the commodity requires a distress sale. A classic example is the lowering of retail automobile prices on the leftover inventory of the prior model year.

The second defense is differences in selling costs: The **cost differential** defense provides that "nothing herein contained shall prevent differentials which make only due allowance for differences in the cost of manufacture, sale, or delivery resulting from the differing methods or quantities in which such commodities are sold or delivered." In practice, this defense is difficult for sellers to rely on. One problem is that there is no universal definition of costs. Robinson-Patman was designed to prevent predatory pricing in which one producer subsidizes low-priced sales from profits earned elsewhere and later raises prices above competitive levels after competitors are driven from the market. Computation of average variable costs requires an allocation of indirect costs (e.g., overhead), a complex and controversial process. The amount of overhead allotted to each unit in addition to average variable costs varies under different assumptions. The cost differential defense is most often successful when discriminatory pricing is based on legitimate quantity discounts that are due to actual savings in packaging, handling, and transportation costs.

Robinson-Patman also permits a seller to discriminate in price if the lower price "was made in good faith to meet an equally low price of a competitor." The price discriminator must have a reasonable belief that granting the lower price is necessary to win the sale. The lower price must exactly meet, but not beat, the competitor's price. Antitrust has a problem of conflicting goals, evident in satisfying this defense. Communications with competitors concerning price strongly suggests price-fixing. Good faith is crucial to the competition defense because price discrimination and price-fixing enforcement must be harmonized. Sellers may show good faith if they investigate the truth of a buyer's claim that a competitor charges a lower price. For example, some retailers require buyers to bring the competitor's ad or a written estimate to prove the lower price. When the necessity of meeting the price has ceased and market conditions return to normal, the seller must cease discriminatory pricing. Sellers may discriminate only in meeting their own competition and may not discriminate to assist a customer in meeting its competition.

The Robinson-Patman Act applies to both buyers and sellers. It is unlawful for "any person . . . knowingly to induce or receive a discrimination in price." Thus, if the buyer has knowledge that the price it obtained was discriminatory, either the buyer or the seller may be held liable. A buyer inducing price discrimination may take advantage of any defense the seller has.

INDIRECT CONCESSIONS

The Robinson-Patman Act also prohibits price discriminations effected through indirect price concessions. It is unlawful for "any person to pay, grant, or receive any brokerage or allowance in lieu thereof except for services rendered in connection with the sale or purchase of goods." This provision prohibits kickbacks, which are effectively a secret discount. Robinson-Patman also prohibits the seller from discriminating by providing promotional payments, services, or facilities, such as giving only select customers some special assistance, allowance for advertising, or display materials. The disadvantaged buyer need prove only (1) that the promotional service or allowance was provided only to other purchasers or (2) that a competitor was favored in its "business stature." Such services are permissible if triggered at specified dollar volumes or are equally available to all buyers.

Price discrimination may also occur when shippers charge discriminatory freight rates. If the quoted sale prices for two sales are identical but either customer pays more or less than the actual cost of shipment, then there is an indirect price discrimination. There is no discrimination if the buyer pays legitimate freight and delivery charges. However, some informal "delivered price" quotes include freight charges. If all buyers pay the same freight charges, as part of a uniform delivered price, then buyers geographically closer to the seller's plant pay higher freight charges per mile than do buyers located farther away. Equal freight rates charged for unequal delivery distances may constitute phantom freight, an illegal price discrimination. Recall that it can also be a form of price-fixing. Phantom freight is classified as (1) a single basing point system if the freight is actually shipped from another place, (2) zone pricing if the same freight rates are imposed on all customers within a zone, regardless of the distance, or (3) a multiple basing point system if the nearest of several base points of origin governs the freight charge.

THE FUTURE REGULATION OF PRICE DISCRIMINATION

Robinson-Patman is often regarded as a widely violated law. Critics charge it perpetuates inefficient small retailers, reduces price competition, and raises consumer prices to uniform levels. However, many of the international fair-trade laws, particularly the antidumping rules, are essentially price discrimination regulations. **Dumping** is a foreign firm's practice of selling in another nation's market at prices lower than in that firm's home market. The same policy arguments are made in opposition to both practices: Dumping and price discrimination encourage cross-subsidies that drive out competitors, eventually leaving the discriminator with a monopoly.

Finally, as discussed further in Chapter 14, aggressive marketing strategies in the Internet age may seek to achieve **perfect price discrimination**. As website operators learn and purchase private information about their customers, they develop customer profiles or dossiers. Profiling permits a better understanding of customers' intensity of interest in products, services, and information and of customers' wealth. Target marketers can then raise prices for customers who value the products more highly and lower prices for those who do not. Although the impact of Robinson-Patman may continue to decline, pressures will intensify to practice price discrimination, and public policy may focus on these trends.

QUESTIONS

1. Compare and contrast the three antitrust enforcement approaches. How might these approaches change as there is more widespread recognition that the efficiencies of network industries increase rather than decrease as production rises?
2. For what reasons are foreign nations less likely to vigorously enforce U.S-style antitrust laws against their own nationals and their own firms? How do foreign nations resist enforcement of U.S. antitrust laws?
3. Describe the source and reasoning behind the rule of reason and the per se rule. Compare and contrast the reasoning for each of the per se categories of antitrust violations.
4. Discuss the differences between horizontal and vertical restraints of trade.
5. A computer manufacturer designed a central processing unit that was demonstrably better than any other central processing unit on the market. It then

designed peripherals (units that plug into the central processing unit) and redesigned the central processing unit so that no other peripherals could be used with it. A peripherals manufacturer sued the computer manufacturer for monopolization under §2 of the Sherman Act. Did the computer manufacturer violate the Sherman Antitrust Act? Discuss. See *Telex Corp. v. IBM*, 367 F.Supp. 258 (N.D.Ok., 1973).

6. The publishers of more than 12,000 newspapers are members of the Associated Press (AP), which collects and assembles news and distributes news stories to its members. The bylaws of the AP prohibited its members from selling news to nonmembers and set up a system by which AP members could block nonmember competitors from joining. The United States filed a complaint charging that these provisions violated §1 of the Sherman Act. What was the result and why? See *Associated Press v. U.S.*, 326 U.S. 1 (1945).

7. The Justice Department challenged a merger between two waste disposal companies: Waste Management, Inc., and EMW Ventures, Inc. Both were large and dominant firms in this business. The merged firm would have a nearly 50% market share, with a Herfindahl Index over 2,700. Barriers to entry were rather low. Market entry by "mom and pop" waste disposal firms was easy, requiring only a home office and a waste disposal truck. On what basis could the merger be challenged? What defense might the firms offer to justify the merger? See *United States v. Waste Management, Inc.*, 743 F.2d 976 (2d Cir. 1984).

8. Stacy Corporation produces a unique "add-on" software program that enhances spreadsheet analysis of differing budget alternatives. Usually, budget categories must be painstakingly replicated in most spreadsheets, and the alternative assumptions of sales, expenses, interest rates, and overhead expense must be entered manually. Stacy's product, Budget-Ease, automatically projects different assumptions for these variables, greatly reducing the time spent on projecting budget alternatives. However, Stacy insists that customers must purchase Stacy-Calc, the company's own spreadsheet program, in order to use Budget-Ease. Compare and contrast the legal and ethical analyses of this problem.

9. Licensed physicians belong to a nonprofit corporation, the Maricopa Foundation for Medical Care (Maricopa), which was intended to provide an alternative medical coverage plan to traditional health insurance systems. Maricopa set a maximum fee schedule, which its members agree to follow as a method to control health care costs. Insurers using Maricopa physicians agree to pay up to the limit. What type of restraint of trade do these activities constitute? What is the reasoning behind the court's decision? What constraint does this decision place on national health care design? See *Arizona v. Maricopa County Medical Society*, 457 U.S. 332 (1982).

10. Mutt and Jeff are both sole proprietors of building cleanup services in Atlanta. They have been friends for several years. Recently, they discussed an idea of mutual interest: the possibility of coordinating their pricing so that downtown office building managers do not pit them against each other in bidding for cleanup jobs. What are the antitrust implications? What must a nonparticipating competitor prove to show that it is illegal?

Labor and Employment

INTRODUCTION

HISTORICAL BACKGROUND

The early laws affecting the employment relationship in the United States dealt with wages, hours, and the character of the work force. Several statutes prevented employers from taking advantage of child workers, immigrants, and the poor. An important milestone occurred in the 1930s, when the right of employees to band together in unions to demand better wages and working conditions was recognized, as the National Labor Relations Act became law. The right of employees to affiliate in unions represents the most important exception to the employment-at-will concept that still forms the basis for employer-employee relations.

Today, although unions still constitute an important part of today's employment law environment, the percentage of employees in the U.S. labor force who are union members has declined. In the late 1950s, just under 25% of the labor force were union members. By 2000, union members were less than 14% of the workforce. However, unions are more coordinated. The Internet makes it easier for unions to notify members and sympathizers of plans for pickets, strikes, or demonstrations. Unions now e-mail messages to members around the globe in an instant, and they use webpages with links to search engines and discussion forums to enlist support for their cause.

The recent laws that most affect employer-employee relations deal with safety in the workplace, family and medical leave, drug testing of employees, and privacy issues related to workplace monitoring of employees, particularly regarding their Internet use while at work.

FEDERAL AND STATE LAWS

Labor law is found in both federal and state statutes. The federal laws include three interrelated statutes that establish rights and duties of employers and unions. The Fair Labor Standards Act regulates child labor and sets minimum wages, the standard workweek, and overtime compensation. The federal laws protecting employees from discrimination are covered in the next chapter. In 1970, the Occupational Safety and Health Act (OSHA) established workplace safety standards by requiring most employers in interstate commerce to maintain safe working conditions. Several federal tax and labor laws regulate workers' retirement income from Social Security and private pension plans.

State laws set the eligibility qualifications for unemployment compensation and provide workers' compensation standards. A workers' compensation system provides compensation for employees injured at work through a no-fault, employer-financed insurance program that encourages employers to minimize worksite risks. Most states also have workplace safety laws that are coordinated with OSHA. A number of states have extensive and distinct wage-and-hour and nondiscrimination laws.

EMPLOYMENT AT WILL

Before the twentieth century, all employment contracts in the United States were based on laissez-faire economic theory. Under that theory, broad freedom of contract was given to both employers and employees. Thus, either party could terminate the employment relationship at any time (at will) and without need for any justification.

THE EMPLOYMENT-AT-WILL THEORY

Today, this freedom of contract, known as **employment at will,** continues to be important to many employers and employees. As forcing individuals to work involuntarily for an employer would be slavery, the employee should be free to terminate the employment relationship at his or her will. Thus, employees cannot be required to work, if even they have contracted to do so for a specified period, because that would interfere too much with their personal freedom. If employees have the right to quit at any time, the mutuality of contract law suggests that the employer should also have the right to fire them at will. It would be unfair to require the employer to accept substandard services from an employee or to retain an untrustworthy or even an unwanted employee. Despite the importance of the at-will theory, a number of exceptions now affect the employer-employee relationship.

EROSION OF EMPLOYMENT-AT-WILL DOCTRINE

The Union Environment

In the early twentieth century, the right of employees to form unions and bargain collectively with their employers was recognized. A key feature of most management-union contracts was protection against arbitrary firing of employees by the employer. The collective bargaining agreement, discussed later, constitutes a major exception to the employment-at-will doctrine.

Protection of the Whistle-Blower

Most states have created several exceptions to the employment-at-will doctrine to protect employees from arbitrary dismissal. The **abusive discharge** exception states that an employer who seeks to terminate an employee for refusing to obey a supervisor's order to violate the law or clearly articulated public policies is abusing the employee's rights. Similarly, an employee may not be fired for publicly reporting that the employer is committing crimes. The protection of the employee against the employer's use of this abusive discharge is referred to as the **whistle-blower** exception. A federal law and many state laws offer legal protection to whistle-blowers.

The Policy Statement

In some states, an employee's job is protected if the employer makes an express or implied guarantee of continued employment. Such statements are often found in written policy guidelines or personnel manuals. For example, a personnel manual may state that employees will be discharged only for "good cause" or "just cause." Written or oral statements by an employer who promises continued employment as long as employees "do the job" may be considered to offer job security for employees.

Some courts have held that policies stated in policy guidelines or manuals are regarded as terms of the employment contract. The *Touissant* case, discussed in this chapter, exemplifies such decisions. In such cases, the employer wanting to fire a worker may be required to prove that he or she was insubordinate or negligent or performed poorly on the job. Employers have responded to these cases that limit the "at-will" doctrine by either removing the "just cause" language from personnel manuals or by requiring employees to sign a document stating that they are employed at will or that the personnel manual is not part of their employment contract.

A Good-Faith Requirement

A few states have taken even stronger approaches. Some courts imply the covenant of good faith and fair dealing into employment contracts. In one case, a salesman was terminated just prior to becoming qualified for retirement benefits. Because the employer did not act in good faith, the court found the employer liable to pay the benefits to the employee who was wrongfully terminated.

Discriminatory Firing

Of course, federal civil rights laws also protect employees from being fired on discriminatory grounds. In addition to the classic discrimination cases, sexual harassment cases that lead to firings also fall into this category. This topic is discussed in detail in Chapter 21.

Protection of Statutory Rights

State and federal statutes prohibit employers from firing employees who exercise their statutory rights. All employees are protected from discharge if (1) their wages are garnished, (2) they cooperate in legal proceedings brought against the employer for pollution or work safety violations, (3) they exercise self-organization rights under the labor laws or their rights under laws governing minimum wages or overtime pay, or (4) they refuse a lie detector test. Some of these topics are discussed later in this or the following chapter.

Toussaint v. Blue Cross & Blue Shield of Mich.

292 N.W.2d 880 (Mich. 1980)
Michigan Supreme Court

Facts. Toussaint was a middle manager at Blue Cross for five years before he was unexpectedly discharged. His supervisors had assured him that his employment would continue as long as he was "doing the job." When Toussaint inquired about job security, his supervisor handed him the Blue Cross personnel manual. The manual stated that company policy was to release employees "for just cause only." Toussaint was unexpectedly fired after five years of good performance. He sued Blue Cross, claiming that his discharge had not been for good cause. Blue Cross claimed that despite the provision in its policy manual, it still had the right to terminate an employee at will. The trial court held for Toussaint, but the Court of Appeals reversed and ordered judgment entered for Blue Cross. Toussaint then appealed to the Michigan Supreme Court.

Legal Issue. Where a company's policy manual states a policy that employees will be released only for "just cause" does the policy create an exception to the company's right to terminate an employee "at will"?

Opinion. Justice Levin. Employers are most assuredly free to enter into employment contracts terminable at will without assigning cause. We see no reason why an employment contract which does not have a definite term—the term is "indefinite"—cannot legally provide job security. When a prospective employee inquires about job security and the employer agrees that the employee shall be employed as long as he does the job, a fair construction is that the employer has agreed to give up his right to discharge at will without assigning cause and may discharge only for cause (good or just cause). The result is that the employee, if discharged without good or just cause, may maintain an action for wrongful discharge.

Where the employment is for a definite term—a year, 5 years, 10 years—it is implied, if not expressed, that the employee can be discharged only for good cause and collective bargaining agreements often provide that discharge shall only be for good or just cause. There is, thus, no public policy against providing job security or prohibiting an employer from agreeing not to discharge except for good or just cause.

While an employer need not establish personnel policies or practices, where an employer chooses to establish such policies and practices and makes them known to its employees, the employment relationship is presumably enhanced. The employer secures an orderly, cooperative, and loyal work force, and the employee benefits from the peace of mind associated with job security and the conviction that he will be treated fairly.

No pre-employment negotiations need take place and the parties' minds need not meet on the subject; nor does it matter that the employee knows nothing of the particulars of the employer's policies and practices or that the employer may change them unilaterally. It is enough that the employer chooses, presumably in its own interest, to create an environment in which the employee believes that, whatever the personnel policies and practices, they are established and official at any given time, purport to be fair, and are applied consistently and uniformly to each employee. The employer has then created a situation "instinct with an obligation."

We all agree that where an employer has agreed to discharge an employee for cause only, its declaration that the employee was discharged for unsatisfactory work is subject to judicial review.... A promise to terminate employment for cause only would be illusory if the employer were permitted to be the sole judge and final arbiter of the propriety of the discharge. There must be some review of the employer's decision if the cause contract is to be distinguished from the satisfaction contract. In addition to deciding questions of fact and determining the employer's true motive for discharge, the jury should, where such a promise was made, decide whether the reason for discharge amounts to good cause: Is it the kind of thing that justifies terminating the employment relationship? Does it demonstrate that the employee was no longer doing the job?

An employer who agrees to discharge only for cause need not lower its standard of performance. It has promised employment only so long as the employee does the job required by the employment contract. The employer's standard of job performance can be made part of the contract. Breach of the employer's uniformly applied rules is a breach of the contract and cause for discharge. Where, however, the employer promises the employee that any discharge will be based on cause, the employer has given up its right to discharge at will.

Decision. We hold that an employer's statements of policy such as the Blue Cross Supervisory Manual and Guideline can give contract rights to employees. The question of whether Toussaint's termination was for cause and in compliance with the defendant's procedures is for the jury. Reversed and remanded.

Case Questions

1. Why might an employer want to change its policy from "at will" terminations to "for cause"?
2. What questions does a jury decide in a case involving a discharge for "good cause"?
3. Does this case indicate that a long-term employee is protected from a firing that is not related to job performance if there is no "just cause" policy statement from the employer?

International Commentary

"At-Will" Employment

The "at-will" employment concept is not followed in many other nations. Labor laws in many countries prohibit employee terminations without just cause. Usually, even those terminations can occur only after the employer provides notice of several weeks or months. Consider, for example, the requirements in Bolivia, France, and Japan, countries on three different continents.

In *Bolivia,* there is complete freedom to hire and dismiss employees, but the employer must provide 90 days' notice or payment of an equivalent salary. If an employee is hired for a fixed term, the worker can be dismissed without notice or payment of the 90-day equivalent salary, but such workers are entitled to one month of salary for each year of work. If the worker has worked for 5 years, the equivalent salary has to be paid, even if the worker resigns or is dismissed for cause.

In *France*, if the employment term is fixed, it can be terminated only for a serious breach of contract. If the term of employment is for an indefinite term, a specific procedure must be followed. For example, the employee must usually be notified by registered mail of the reason for the dismissal and, in most cases, must have a meeting with the employer. The employer also must make payments to the employee; the amount of the payments varies, depending on the grounds for dismissal, the status of the employee, and the employee's seniority.

In *Japan,* theoretically, both employers and employees can terminate an employment contract by providing 30 days' notice to the other party. However, employers must also prove that the employee has made a material breach of the labor contract or that another reasonable and unavoidable reason exists. However, courts have found that dismissing an employee whose performance has been found unacceptable is unconstitutional. In practice, only the employee can terminate by providing the notice to the employer. Layoffs are also not recognized by law or by practice. Thus, Japanese employers are hiring more employees on a term basis—for three- or five-year contracts. Those employees need not be rehired at the end of the term.

FEDERAL LABOR STATUTES

The labor laws that govern the employees' right to organize and operate collectively in a union were established less than a hundred years ago. Two early labor laws, the Railway Labor Act and the Norris-LaGuardia Act, established the right of workers to organize into unions and bargain collectively while curtailing court injunctions and employer practices that interfered with those rights. The National Labor Relations Act, the Labor-Management Relations Act, and the Labor-Management Reporting and Disclosure Act are the three federal statutes that establish the basic rights for unions, employers, and union members.

THE EARLY LAWS

In 1926, Congress passed the Railway Labor Act (RLA), the first permanent federal legislation regulating labor-management relations. It gave railroad workers (and later airline employees) the right to organize into labor organizations and required employers to bargain collectively. The RLA provides for noncoercive labor elections to select workers' bargaining representatives. The law also created two regulatory boards to facilitate the settlement of labor disputes: the National Mediation Board (NMB) and the National Railroad Adjustment Board (NRAB).

The Norris-LaGuardia Act of 1932 prohibits federal courts from enjoining labor disputes unless unlawful acts are threatened or committed or a union strikes in violation of a valid no-strike agreement. Labor disputes include strikes, walkouts, labor union meetings, joining a union, and payment of strike or unemployment benefits. Prior to 1932, federal injunctions against these activities demoralized strikers and undermined the impact of strikes. The act also outlaws **yellow-dog contracts**—contracts that require employees to refrain from joining a union or risk losing their jobs.

THE NATIONAL LABOR RELATIONS ACT (WAGNER ACT)

The 1935 National Labor Relations Act (NLRA), known as the Wagner Act, was intended to alter the balance of power between employers and employees that previously had rested almost totally with the employer. The NLRA noted that the unequal bargaining power between employers and employees led to economic instability and that the refusal of employers to bargain collectively led to strikes that burdened the flow of interstate commerce.

The NLRA contains three important provisions that form the basis for modern labor law. First, Section 7 grants employees the right to form, join, or assist labor organizations; the freedom to bargain collectively with the employer; and the right to engage in concerted activity. Second, it defines several employer practices as being unfair labor practices: interference with the employees' right to form, join, or assist labor organizations; discrimination in hiring or awarding tenure to employees because of union affiliation; and refusal to bargain collectively with the employees' representative (union). Third, the National Labor Relations Board (NLRB) was created as the principal regulatory body responsible for administering the act.

THE LABOR-MANAGEMENT RELATIONS ACT (TAFT-HARTLEY ACT)

In the decade following passage of the NLRA, a growing dissatisfaction with the powers exercised by labor unions led to the 1947 enactment of the Labor-Management Relations Act (LMRA). Known as the Taft-Hartley Act, the LMRA defines certain union practices as unfair labor practices. Discrimination in favor of union members, refusal of unions to bargain in good faith, and charging of excessive or discriminatory initiation fees were among the prohibited practices.

The LMRA also made the closed shop illegal. A **closed shop** required a person to be a union member to be eligible for employment. By contrast, a **union shop**, one that requires union membership after a certain time working on a job, was considered legal. However, the LMRA also recognized the right of states to pass **right-to-work laws**, which make it illegal to require union membership for continued employment. In a right-to-work state, a union shop is illegal. Right-to-work laws are found in approximately 20 western and southern states.

THE LABOR-MANAGEMENT REPORTING AND DISCLOSURE ACT (LANDRUM-GRIFFIN ACT)

In 1959, Congress reacted to corruption and misconduct by labor officials by passing the Labor-Management Reporting and Disclosure Act (LMRDA), also known as the Landrum-Griffin Act. The LMRDA requires fair, democratic procedures in the election of union officials. Unions are prohibited from restricting a member's rights of free speech, assembly, or participation in union elections. Unions must notify members of any increase in dues and assessments and give them a right to vote on such proposals by secret ballot. Requiring officials and candidates for union offices to provide extensive financial disclosures about all union transactions is intended to eliminate corruption.

The major federal labor laws administered by the NLRB are listed in Exhibit 20.1.

THE NATIONAL LABOR RELATIONS BOARD

The National Labor Relations Board (NLRB) provides a neutral forum for workers seeking protection from undue pressures by the employer or the union, certifies the selection of a union as the employees' bargaining representative, and investigates unfair labor practices by employers or by unions. (see http://www.nlrb.gov). During contract negotiations, the employer is represented by members of management, labor consultants, and lawyers who sit across the bargaining table from union representatives accompanied by their consultants and attorneys. Collective bargaining results only when both parties willingly negotiate in good faith over contract terms. Several activities must precede collective bargaining, including the grouping of employees into a bargaining unit, the election of a bargaining representative (union), and the employer's recognition of the union as the valid employee representative.

ONLINE

The National Labor Relations Board (NLRB)
http://www.nlrb.gov

ORGANIZATION OF THE NLRB

The NLRB is organized into two major divisions: the board itself and the Division of General Counsel. The board is five members appointed by the president with the "advice and consent" approval of the Senate. Although the board sometimes sits as a full panel, it often delegates its power to review hearings to a three-member panel. Trial-like hearings about labor matters are first heard by one of the administrative law judges (ALJs) sitting in the various regional NLRB offices.

The Division of General Counsel is headed by an independent counsel, who is appointed for a four-year term by the president with Senate confirmation. This office has final authority with respect to the investigation of the charges and

EXHIBIT 20.1 Principal Federal Labor Laws

Date	Name of Law	Purposes and Provisions
1926	Railway Labor Act	Comprehensive coverage of collective bargaining between railroad or airline employers and unions representing their employees
1932	Norris-LaGuardia Act	Prevents federal courts from enjoining collective union activities (e.g., meetings, picketing, strikes) during labor disputes unless unlawful acts occur Outlaws yellow-dog contracts Permits unionization activities
1935	National Labor Relations Act (NLRA or Wagner Act)	Comprehensive coverage of collective bargaining for all employers not covered by Railway Labor Act Gives employees the right to form, join, or assist labor organizations Requires collective bargaining Created National Labor Relations Board (NLRB)
1947	Labor-Management Relations Act (Taft-Hartley Act)	Defines unfair labor practices of unions, such as discrimination and failure to bargain in good faith
1959	Labor-Management Reporting and Disclosure Act (Landrum-Griffin Act)	Requires fair and democratic procedures for elections of union officials Requires disclosure by union officials, unions, and employers to avoid embezzlement and conflicts of interest

issuance of complaints and with respect to the prosecution of complaints before the board. The general counsel is independent of the NLRB.

INVESTIGATION OF UNFAIR LABOR PRACTICES

NLRB procedures begin after the filing of a charge that an employer or a union representative has committed an unfair labor practice. Typically, field examiners investigate the matter, taking affidavits (sworn statements) to discover facts supporting or denying the charge. Even if the person filing the charge withdraws the complaint, the NLRB may continue the investigation and possible prosecution. A charge must be filed within six months after the event in question.

Unfair labor charges may be settled either in an informal proceeding or at an ALJ hearing. The ALJ hearing is similar to a court trial because the parties present their cases and the rules of evidence apply. An appeal from the ALJ hearing may be made to the whole board or its hearing panel. In unfair labor practice cases, appeals from the NLRB are taken to the federal Court of Appeals. In representation and election cases, the NLRB is the final authority in designating bargaining representatives. Exhibits 20.2 and 20.3 list the unfair labor practices of labor employers and unions.

REPRESENTATION ELECTIONS

Representation elections are used to select a particular union as the employees' bargaining representative. After a petition and evaluation by the NLRB that determines that the statutory requirements are met, a hearing is held to determine when the election should take place. After the election, the NLRB rules on its effect. If there is evidence of coercion or threats, the NLRB may order a new election. Employees often file petitions for a representation election and thereby assist an uncertified union in its organizational efforts. A union's petition must show support from at least 30% of the bargaining unit members to appear on an election ballot.

There are several types of representation elections. A consent election is held if the employer and the proposed union agree on which employees would be a part of the union. A contested election arises if the employer and the prospective union disagree on which employees are in the bargaining unit and on the time and place of the election. A globe election is held when a group of employees chooses between merging into a larger bargaining unit and operating separately.

A certification election is held when an employer willingly recognizes and bargains with a union that proves support by showing authorization or membership

EXHIBIT 20.2 Unfair Labor Practices of Employers

1. Interfering with employee efforts to form, join, or assist labor organizations
2. Interfering with employees' concerted activities for mutual aid or protection
3. Dominating a labor organization
4. Supporting a labor organization
5. Discriminating in hiring, firing, benefits, or other conditions of employment due to employee's union affiliation
6. Discriminating due to employee's exercise of rights under the labor law
7. Refusing to bargain collectively and in good faith with a duly certified labor organization
8. Agreeing with a labor organization to conduct a secondary boycott
9. Failing to reinstate unfair labor practice strikers

EXHIBIT 20.3 Unfair Labor Practice of Unions

1. Restraining or coercing employees who are exercising self-organization rights
2. Coercing an employer to discriminate against nonunion employees
3. Refusing to bargain in good faith with an employer if the union is certified as the employees' representative
4. Engaging in illegal strikes, picketing, or secondary boycotts
5. Charging excessive or discriminative dues in a union shop
6. Featherbedding—requiring the employer to pay for work not actually performed
7. Picketing to coerce the employer to recognize a noncertified union
8. Agreeing with an employer to engage in a secondary boycott
9. Failure to represent all members of the appropriate bargaining unit without regard to their union membership status

cards, membership applications, dues receipts or records, or petitions signed by employees. A certification election prevents rival unions from interfering with the certified union for one year following the election. A decertification election is held when employees become dissatisfied with an existing union and seek to remove it.

APPROPRIATE BARGAINING UNIT

The **appropriate bargaining unit** includes all "employees" in a group who have similar interests in employment conditions and should be entitled to vote together as a unit. Bargaining representatives are selected for each appropriate bargaining unit. Employers must bargain with only a single bargaining representative for any group of workers. Of course, a large employer with many separate employee groups may have to bargain with several unions representing different bargaining units. For example, one union may represent production workers, another may represent truck drivers, and a third may represent maintenance workers. The NLRB selects the bargaining unit to ensure that employees in the unit have similar economic interests, job classifications, and bargaining powers.

The NLRA requires that employees within an appropriate bargaining unit have similarities at the level of the employer, the craft unit, or the plant unit or within a recognized subdivision of these levels. For example, professional employees may not be included with nonprofessionals unless a majority of the professionals consent. Similarly, plant guards, who must protect the employer's property, may not be included with other employees because during intense labor disputes there might be a conflict of interest between plant guards and those employees.

CONCERTED ACTIVITIES BY UNIONS

The NLRA grants employees the right to engage in "concerted activities for the purpose of collective bargaining or other mutual aid or protection." When a particular union becomes the certified bargaining representative for a bargaining unit, employees must focus grievance activities through that union. Even unorganized employees with no certified union representative are entitled to engage in concerted activity. In a 2000 case, excerpted here, the NLRB ruled that an employee's right to act collectively includes the right of a nonunionized employee to have a coworker attend an investigatory interview that could lead to discipline for the employee.

Epilepsy Foundation of Northeast Ohio

National Labor Relations Board
8-CA-28169 and 8-CA-28264 (2000)

Facts. Arnis Borgs and coworker Ashradul Hasan together wrote a memorandum to their supervisor, Rick Berger, expressing their view that his supervision was no longer required. A copy of the memo was sent to the Epilepsy Foundation's executive director, Christine Loehrke. Loehrke directed Borgs to meet with her and Berger. Borgs, who had received an earlier reprimand, felt intimidated and asked if he could bring Hasan to the meeting. Loehrke refused the request. After he continued to express concern about meeting with his supervisors alone, he was sent home. The next day he was terminated for failing to meet with Loehrke and Berger.

Borgs filed an unfair labor practice charge with the NLRB. The administrative law judge (ALJ) dismissed the charge, and the NLRB initially sided with the ALJ. Later, the NLRB reconsidered because of the U.S. Supreme Court's ruling in *N.L.R.B. v. Weingarten*,[1] which dealt with an employee's right to engage in concerted activities for the purpose of mutual aid and protection.

Legal Issue. Does a nonunion employee who is asked to attend a meeting with supervisors that could lead to disciplinary action against the employee, have the right to have a coworker attend the meeting?

Opinion. Judge Truesdale. Our examination of this case begins with the Supreme Court's seminal *Weingarten* opinion. There, the Court held that an employer violated Section 8 (a)(1) by denying an employee's request that a union representative be present at an investigatory interview which the employee reasonably believed might result in disciplinary action. The Court explained: "The union representative whose participation he seeks is however safeguarding not only the particular employee's interest, but also the interests of the entire bargaining unit by exercising vigilance to make certain that the employer does not initiate or continue a practice of imposing punishment unjustly.

The Court in *Weingarten* said that an employee seeking the assistance of a union representative at a confrontation with the employer clearly falls within the wording of Section 7 [of the NLRA] granting employees the right to engage in concerted activities for the purpose of mutual aid and protection. The employee in that case clearly sought "aid or protection" against a perceived threat to her employment security. The *Weingarten* decision, however, left unanswered the question of whether such rights applied to nonunion workers.

We recognize that in several subsequent cases, the NLRB concluded that the right to representation during an investigatory hearing does not exist where there is no certified or recognized union. The distinctions made by the Board in the *Sears Roebuck* and *Dupont* cases are not consistent with the Supreme Court's *Weingarten* decision. The proper interpretation of *Weingarten* is that an employee, whether or not a union member, has a right to engage in concerted activities for the purpose of mutual aid and protection. Just as a union representative aids an employee by acting collectively to address the concern that the employer might impose unjust punishment, a co-worker's presence at an investigatory interview can serve the same purpose.

It should be noted, however, that the employer is free to forgo the investigatory review altogether. It can pursue other means of resolving the matter with the employee and it could take disciplinary action against the employee for the conduct in question, even without providing an employee a hearing. If, however, the employer acts without obtaining the employee's side of the story, any disciplinary action could be challenged.

Decision. We hold that the rule enunciated in *Weingarten* applies to employees not represented by a union as well as to those that are. We also shall apply the rule ennuciated today to the facts of this case and find that the Respondent violated Section 8 (a)(1) of the Act by terminating Borgs for insisting on having his coworker, Hasan, present at an investigatory interview.[2]

Dissent. Two of the five members of the NLRB dissented. They argued that the protected representational rights should be reserved only for the unionized setting.

Case Questions

1. Would a nonunion employee have the right to have a coworker attend regular meetings or interviews with supervisors?
2. What would be some of the reasons the dissenting judges might offer to distinguish granting such rights to union employees but not to nonunion employees?
3. If an employee wanted to bring a specific coworker to an investigatory interview and you, as the employee's supervisor, were concerned about that person's ability to keep the investigation and interview confidential, what would you do?

---

1. 420 U.S. 251 (1975).
2. The Court of Appeals decision reviewing this case upheld the NLRB's decision that the *Weingarten* decision applies to nonunion employees. However, it held it was unfair to apply the "newly clarified" ruling retractively to this case. See *Epilepsy Foundation of Northeast Ohio v. NLRB*, 268 F.3d 1095 (D.C., Cir., 2001).

Strikes, picketing, and boycotts exemplify common concerted activities of employees. Concerted activities must be lawful, advanced in good faith, and directed toward a specific objective. In one case, some employees discouraged the public from patronizing their employer. Where employees failed to connect the boycott to a specific grievance or to benefits they sought, their concerted activity was disloyal and unprotected.

REGULATION OF STRIKES

Legality of Strikes

Strikes are concerted activities of employees who stop work simultaneously to pressure their employer. The Constitution protects employees involved in a strike over wages, hours, or conditions of labor; the discipline or discharge of an employee; or the employment of nonunion labor, as well as employees striking in aid of others engaged in such controversies. The NLRA-based right to "engage in concerted activity" also guarantees the right to strike.

Illegal strikes involve violence, discrimination against certain employees, violation of a cooling-off period, or attempts to coerce recognition of a noncertified union when another union has already been certified. In illegal *sit-down strikes*, employees at the job site suddenly refuse to work but occupy the employer's premises by sitting down at their workstations. Sporadic or disruptive shutdowns or partial work stoppages are also illegal. *Wildcat strikes* are illegal because the striking employees do not give the employer advance notice and the strike lacks the approval of other union members.

It is an unfair labor practice for an employer to interfere with legitimate concerted activities such as strikes. Most strikers may not be fired for legal strike activities. Although the employer may hire temporary replacements to continue business operations during any strike, after an unfair labor practices strike, strikers are entitled to reinstatement even if temporary replacements must be fired. Such strikers must be paid "back wages," beginning on the date they were fired for striking.

Legal strikes frequently are economic strikes that concern matters other than the employer's unfair labor practices. Economic strikers have no right to reinstatement if replacements are hired. They are entitled only to a nondiscriminatory review of a reapplication for their old jobs. In addition, the employer may abolish the positions or the whole work unit of strikers if economic or business conditions radically change. For example, if the strike causes the loss of key customers, the employer may shut down the struck plant.

Economic strikes typically are intended to gain increased employee benefits or improved working conditions. Striking employees take the risk of permanent replacement if a strike is considered economic. By contrast, the employer hiring permanent replacements, as can be done in economic strikes, can be liable for breach of contract if the strike is found to be in response to alleged employer unfair labor practices. Following most economic strikes, the union insists that the new contract include a term requiring nondiscriminatory reinstatement of all replaced strikers.

Limitations on Strikes

Unions must notify the employer at least 60 days before engaging in an economic strike and must offer to negotiate a new or modified contract. The 60-day notice is designed to prevent hasty decisions based on emotion or hysteria. Some labor contracts contain **no-strike clauses** that obligate the union to refrain from striking or from causing work stoppages or slowdowns during the life of the contract. Unions often agree to no-strike clauses in return for the employer's agreement to arbitrate grievances. Certain public employees are prohibited by law from striking. Although the Norris-LaGuardia Act prohibits federal court injunctions against strikes, if there is an arbitrable grievance, unions may be enjoined from striking in violation of a valid no-strike clause.

The Taft-Hartley Act includes a cooling-off provision that is intended to prevent severe strikes that might impair the national health or safety. If a threatened strike or lockout is expected to affect an entire industry, then the president of the United States is granted special powers. After an investigation process, the president may seek an injunction prohibiting the threatened activity. The issue at the trial is whether that activity will impair the national health or safety. If an injunction is issued, the 80-day cooling-off period begins. During that period, the parties usually engage in negotiations and, it is hoped, reach an agreement. However, if no agreement is reached, the strike or lockout may resume after 80 days. Congress then has the responsibility for curing the national emergency.

REGULATION OF PICKETING

Protection for Picketing

Picketing, if conducted in a peaceful manner and for a lawful objective, is another concerted activity protected by the Constitution. **Picketing** generally involves a gathering and patrolling of persons who intend to inform or disrupt others. Picketing may be enjoined as unlawful if it (1) violates federal law, (2) represents an unfair labor practice, or (3) violates state law—such as picketing that is not done in a peaceful manner. Picketing may involve confrontations between the picketers and other employees of the picketed employer. Simply posting signs may not be sufficient to constitute confrontation, but confrontation may arise if the picketers remain close to the posted signs, because verbal or threatening exchanges are more likely.

Types of Picketing

The picketing of an employer by its employees is considered **primary picketing** and receives the greatest degree of constitutional protection. **Secondary picketing** takes place at a business site other than the site of the employer with which the picketing employees have a dispute. For example, a restaurant owner who wishes to build a restaurant at a new site might hire a nonunion construction contractor. It is illegal secondary picketing for construction workers to picket at the site of the original restaurant to pressure the restaurant owner into bringing pressure on the contractor to hire union construction laborers. **Informational picketing** is designed to inform the employer's customers about a labor dispute. It may be legal even if it results in a consumer boycott of the employer. Informational picketing becomes illegal only when it disturbs deliveries or physically disrupts customer access to the employer's premises.

BOYCOTTS AND SECONDARY PRESSURE ACTIVITIES

Secondary Pressure Activities

Secondary pressure activities are concerted union activities directed toward a secondary employer, one with which the union has no dispute. For example, a union may seek to pressure the employer with which it has a dispute—the primary employer—by inconveniencing that employer's customers or by pressuring suppliers, who are secondary employers. Secondary pressure exerted through picketing, strikes, or boycotts is generally prohibited.

A **secondary boycott** intends to stop customers or suppliers from entering or purchasing goods from or dealing with a targeted firm. Such activities are illegal if the union strikes or refuses to handle goods or induces nonmembers to strike or refuse to handle goods. Courts have adopted a case-by-case approach to define secondary activities. They are generally prohibited if an innocent secondary employer is forced into a labor dispute.

Consumer Boycotts

A union is entitled to advise the public about the products of the employer with which the union has a dispute. For example, a union's distribution of informational leaflets outside the primary employer's plant is permissible. Moreover, informational distributions, known as *handbilling*, conducted at a shopping mall are legal if the union is not picketing, patrolling, or engaged in other intimidating conduct. Such handbilling activities may advocate a consumer boycott of all the mall's stores even if the union's dispute is only with a contractor building a shop for a single mall tenant.

A union's campaign to provide the public with information may be prohibited in certain more coercive situations. Under the *Tree Fruits*[3] doctrine, such a campaign is illegal if it tends to cause a work stoppage or interfere with deliveries to a secondary employer. For example, a union that has a dispute with a food processor may choose to picket a supermarket that sells the food processor's products. The *Tree Fruits* doctrine permits this secondary picketing only if it causes no interference with suppliers' deliveries or customers' shopping. The secondary picketing permitted under *Tree Fruits* must be noncoercive, peaceful, and designed only to induce customers to refrain from buying the boycotted product.

THE LABOR NEGOTIATION PROCESS

After an appropriate bargaining unit selects a particular union as its bargaining representative, both the employer and the union must bargain in good faith. **Good faith bargaining** is an interactive process in which each side makes offers and counteroffers in an effort to reach an agreement over wages, hours, and other terms and conditions of employment. The labor negotiation process reflects the overall social and economic pressure of the financial, product, and labor markets. Contracts negotiated during this process allow labor markets to reach economic equilibrium.

COLLECTIVE BARGAINING NEGOTIATIONS

Collective bargaining is an interactive process between two parties that often have opposite goals. In many instances, gains made by one party represent losses for the other party, a zero-sum game. There are few opportunities for both parties to "win" on compensation issues. Typically, one party compiles a set of proposals into a first offer. For example, the union may seek to improve or maintain the benefits currently received by employees.

---

3. *N.L.R.B. v. Fruit and Vegetable Packers and Warehousemen, Local 760*, 370 U.S. 58 (1964).

The union's offer usually specifies an amount of compensation for each classification of employees, a designation of the work hours and overtime contingencies, a package of fringe benefits, and a classification of all the employees. Unions often seek to establish systems of seniority, grievance processes, protections against loss of work to outside contractors or the cessation of business, and methods to schedule work and work shifts. Wage-related proposals include base salaries, cost-of-living and productivity increases, a wage scale rewarding seniority and higher levels of skill, and fringe benefits such as pension funds.

In most negotiations, the early offers from either party are more favorable to the offeror and less favorable to the opposing party. As a result, the opposing party may either decline the initial offer or make a counteroffer with terms more favorable to itself. Eventually, most negotiations result in a compromise by reaching some middle ground.

THE BARGAINING PROCESS

Usually, the negotiating teams are well prepared for their first meeting. Elaborate financial statements and cost projections often accompany both the union's demand for higher wages and management's refusal to grant increases. Because negotiations held on either party's home turf may provide a home court advantage, neutral premises are often selected for negotiations. Negotiations are often held behind closed doors because a damaging and inflammatory atmosphere may result from public exposure or adverse publicity.

The parties often negotiate the noneconomic items first because their expectations are often closer on such items. For example, the existing grievance procedures, no-strike clauses, seniority provisions, and work assignments are usually acceptable to both parties. Management may seek greater flexibility through being able to replace restrictive work rules that limit assigning employees to performing multiple or different tasks.

Both the union and the employer are required by the NLRA to meet at reasonable times and confer in good faith with respect to wages, hours, and other terms and conditions of employment. It is an unfair labor practice for either party to refuse to bargain collectively. Neither party may engage in bargaining that has no real intent of reaching agreement. The parties should be willing to meet at reasonable times, put their agreement in writing, negotiate with each other, and bargain on mandatory subjects (discussed later). For example, the offer of totally unreasonable proposals may indicate bad faith. Reasonable requests for management to disclose cost and compensation information to the union must be taken into account.

The teams representing both management and the union must have sufficient authority to bargain. The employer's representatives must have the authority to act as its agents in making offers or accepting union proposals. For union negotiators, the authority requirement is less restrictive because the rank-and-file employees generally must approve the contract in a **ratification vote**.

A certified union has exclusive authority to represent all of the employees in the bargaining unit. Individual employees may not enter into separate bargains with the employer that are inconsistent with the collective bargaining agreement. For example, if the collective bargaining agreement covers all compensation issues, an individual union employee may not cut a separate deal to receive higher pay. Individual employees are considered third-party beneficiaries of the collective bargaining contract. In return for its exclusive bargaining right, the union must bargain fairly on behalf of all bargaining unit employees, both union members and nonmembers.

SUBJECTS OF BARGAINING

Management and unions bargain over subjects that fall into three basic categories. The first category comprises **mandatory collective bargaining subjects**: "wages, hours, and other terms and conditions of employment, or the negotiation of an agreement, or any questions arising thereunder." The parties are required to bargain over these subjects because the employment relationship is directly affected by them. Bargaining on these subjects may continue to the point of impasse.

Mandatory subjects also include merit increases, pension retirement benefits, vacations, rest periods, work assignments, seniority, no-strike provisions, and major grievances concerning working conditions. Safety rules and practices may also be considered mandatory subjects, even though they are regulated under federal law. Ford was required to bargain over the prices it charged employees for food in its lunchrooms.[4] Food prices were a significant part of the employment relationship, and the whole automobile industry bargained over them. More recent mandatory collective bargaining subjects include the use of video surveillance and drug testing, as is noted in the *Colgate-Palmolive* case in this chapter.

The second basic category of bargaining subjects is **permissive subjects**. These subjects are "bargainable," but only if both parties voluntarily agree to negotiate them. Permissive subjects include company or union policies that only indirectly affect the employment relationship, modifications of an existing labor contract before it expires, public policies such as the employer's contributions to charities, the organization or size of the employer's corporation, the types of supervisors, general business practices, and the location of production facilities. Neither party may refuse to bargain on mandatory subjects in an attempt to force bargaining on permissive subjects.

Some employers want to reduce their operations and eliminate union jobs. If, as a result, company supervisors will perform production work, depriving union members of negotiated overtime pay, the employer must bargain. Many employers contract out work once performed by union employees. This practice, known as **outsourcing**, often leads to plant closure or to the sale or transfer of business operations. Employers have an incentive to reduce in-house work that an outsider paying lower wages can do more cheaply.

Managerial business judgments like outsourcing are considered mandatory subjects only if they directly affect the employment relationship. For example, managerial decisions to retrain or transfer employees or to give employees severance pay are usually considered mandatory subjects. However, in *First National Maintenance*,[5] the employer decided to discontinue certain operations. First National had contracted to supply housekeeping and maintenance services to a nursing home, but when it lost the contract, it decided to discontinue those operations altogether. Because the employer did not intend to replace the union employees it discharged, the decision to cease operations was not a mandatory bargaining subject.

The third category of bargaining subjects is **illegal and prohibited subjects**. For example, the employer may not insist that the union bargain away its status as bargaining representative, and the employer must recognize a certified union. Some subjects may never become part of any collective bargaining agreement. For example, no collective bargaining agreement may prohibit employees from distributing union literature on company property or require employees to become union members before being hired.

---

4. *Ford Motor v. NLRB*, 441 U.S. 488 (1979).
5. *First National Maintenance Corp. v. N.L.R.B.*, 452 U.S. 666 (1981).

Confrontation vs. Cooperation Between Unions and Management

Adversarial relations between unions and employers dominate the labor-management environment in many nations, including countries in North America, Western Europe, and Southeast Asia. Under a ***confrontational approach***, the parties bring economic pressure on their adversaries to influence the bargaining process. Proponents argue that confrontation produces an optimal compromise that becomes embodied in their collective bargaining agreement.

Some other nations, such as Japan and Germany, seek cooperation between unions and management. A ***cooperative approach*** involves unions in some management decisions, either formally, as in Germany, or informally, as in Japan. In Germany, union representatives become involved in setting corporate policy under a ***codetermination*** system Although this system does not prevent strikes, it does force management to consider workers' well-being. In Japan, the culture encourages cooperation and the appearance of harmony. Japanese labor relations manifest this tradition by confining unions to the role of craft unions as practiced by the original craft guilds. Japan's culture also reduces adversarial relations between management and labor by encouraging the two groups to share information. ***Quality circles*** are based on Japanese worker groups dedicated to increasing quality and eliminating production problems. Managers wait to implement decisions until a consensus has developed in worker groups.

THE FAIR LABOR STANDARDS ACT

The Fair Labor Standards Act of 1938 (FLSA) is intended to stabilize the economy by (1) placing a floor under wages (the "minimum wage") and (2) encouraging broader-based employment of more workers by imposing a "standard workweek," with maximum regular working hours and higher pay required for overtime. The FLSA applies to all employers engaged in interstate commerce, as well as employees in any "enterprise" with gross annual sales in excess of $250,000. The FLSA does not apply to federal government employees or to government contractors because similar but separate statutes establish labor standards for them.

The FLSA's **white-collar provision** exempts "executive, administrative, and professional" employees. This exemption includes the traditional professions of law and medicine as well as artistic professions and positions that require the exercise of discretion and judgment. Certain workers in agriculture, commercial fishing, household domestic service, retail establishments, and white-collar jobs are exempt if they are paid a salary rather than an hourly wage.

COMPUTATION OF THE MINIMUM WAGE AND OVERTIME PAY

The FLSA sets standards and methods for the computation of minimum wages, overtime pay, and compensable time. The **minimum wage** paid may be reduced by an amount equal to "reasonable costs of food, lodging, and other facilities" furnished to the employee. When employees regularly receive more than $20 per month in tips, the employer may take these into account. Transportation to and from the employer's place of business is not considered "compensable time."

The **overtime pay** provisions require the payment of time and a half of the regular rate of pay for each hour worked in excess of the standard 40-hour workweek. No overtime has to be paid if a 40-hour week contains workdays with more than eight hours. Overtime pay computation becomes more complex if the employee receives nonstandard compensation in addition to the hourly wage. For example, regularly earned bonuses or incentive pay must be included in the base pay rate to which the time-and-a-half premium is applied. Overtime premiums do not apply to bonuses or expense reimbursements.

Although the minimum wage and overtime provisions do not cover executive and administrative personnel, the next case illustrates that it can be difficult to apply this exemption.

Donovan v. Burger King Corp.

675 F. 2d 516 (2d Cir., 1982)
United States Court of Appeals

Facts. Burger King's assistant managers usually performed managerial and supervisory functions. However, they also performed production activities during peak service hours at mealtime. They were not given overtime pay for the hours they worked in excess of 40 hours per week. Burger King argued that these employees were exempt from the overtime record-keeping and pay provisions of the FLSA because they were "executives." The secretary of labor, believing that the assistant managers were "employees" and not "supervisors," sued, alleging violations of the FLSA provisions. After the trial court found for Burger King, Secretary of Labor Donovan appealed.

Legal Issue. Are assistant managers at fast food restaurants, who spend at least half their time doing the same work as hourly employees, while also performing supervisory and managerial functions, entitled to overtime pay as employees?

Opinion. Circuit Judge Ralph K. Winter, Jr. Judge Sifton found as a fact that the Burger King Assistant Managers "spent at least half of their time doing the same work as the hourly employees." This was a direct consequence of a deliberate corporate policy at the regional level which dictated "ideal" ratios of hourly labor to production and thereby required Assistant Managers to serve as an "extra hand" during high volume meal periods. Were the Assistant Managers to abstain from production work, more hourly employees would be needed, "thereby 'blowing payroll'—that is, spending more than the store's budgeted amount for hourly labor."

The regulations provide a different test for employees earning at least $250 per week. Such employees are exempt if their "primary duty consists of management of the enterprise . . . or of a . . . subdivision thereof . . . and includes the customary and regular direction of the work of two or more employees. . . ."

We agree with Judge Sifton that the "short test" determines whether Assistant Managers have, as their "primary duty," managerial responsibilities. Five factors must be weighed in determining an employee's primary duty: (1) time spent in the performance of managerial duties; (2) relative importance of managerial and non-managerial duties; (3) the frequency with which the employee exercises discretionary power; (4) the employee's relative freedom from supervision; and (5) the relationship between the employee's salary and the wages paid employees doing similar non-exempt work.

The record fully supports Judge Sifton's finding that the principal responsibilities of Assistant Managers, in the sense of being most important or critical to the success of the restaurant, are managerial. Many of the employees themselves so testified and it is clear that the restaurants could not operate successfully unless the managerial functions of Assistant Managers, such as determining amounts of food to be prepared, running cash checks, scheduling employees, keeping track of inventory, and assigning employees to particular jobs, were performed.

Such employees also exercise discretionary powers, criterion (3). They schedule work time for employees according to estimates of business based on factors such as weather and local events and assign them to particular work stations. They . . . move employees from task to task and see that they are performing their jobs. They represent management in dealings with employees when they are in charge of the restaurant and, while they do not exercise the power to hire and fire frequently, there are some instances thereof in the record. Given that the ten to twenty-five employees under their direction are teenagers, many on their first job, this supervision is a not insubstantial responsibility. Assistant Managers order supplies in quantities based on their judgments as to future sales and are responsible for dealing with the public. Finally, they must deal with case or inventory irregularities.

We do not understand the Secretary to dispute the existence of these powers and responsibilities so much as to disparage them as wholly dictated by the detailed instructions issued by Burger King. We fully recognize that the economic genius of the Burger King enterprise lies in providing uniform products and service economically in many different locations and that adherence by Assistant Managers to a remarkably detailed routine is critical to commercial success. The exercise of discretion, however, even where circumscribed by prior instruction, is as critical to that success as adherence to "the book." . . . In the competitive, low margin circumstances of this business, the wrong number of employees, too many or too few supplies on hand, delays in service, the preparation of food which must be thrown away, or an under directed or under supervised work force all can make the difference between commercial success and failure.

The record also shows that for the great bulk of their working time, Assistant Managers are solely in charge of their restaurants and are the "boss" in title and in fact. We take that fact to satisfy criterion (4), the relative lack of supervision. That the Restaurant Manager is available by phone does not detract in any substantial way from this conclusion. Being available for advice is in no sense the exercise of supervision. Finally, the evidence is that the employees doing exclusively non-exempt work were paid the minimum wage. Assistant Managers earning $250 or more were paid substantially higher wages even taking their longer hours into account. That fact satisfies criterion (5).

Decision. We affirm the judgment of the trial court.

Case Questions

1. Why do FLSA provisions apply only to hourly employees and not to administrators, professionals, or supervisors?
2. Why did Burger King require assistant managers to perform the same work as hourly production workers?
3. What factors most clearly make these assistant managers exempt as "supervisors"?

CHILD LABOR PROVISIONS

The FLSA includes provisions intended to prevent the abuse of children's labor. During the Industrial Revolution, child laborers worked 12 or more hours a day for pennies an hour, even in mining and other heavy industries. In 1938, child labor provisions added to the FLSA prohibited the shipment of goods in interstate commerce if produced by an employer involved in "oppressive child labor."

Child labor laws are also designed to encourage school attendance. Generally, children under 13 may not be employed, and the employment of children between the ages of 13 and 17 is restricted. For example, children 16 or 17 years old may not be employed in hazardous industries (mining, explosives, roofing, logging, or excavation). Children 14 or 15 years old may work only in approved jobs (retail stores, food service establishments, gasoline service stations). Children may engage in agricultural employment if their parents give consent. Child actors may work with parental consent, but state laws often require an approved school-like tutorial training.

http://
www.ilo.org/public/english/standards/ipec/index.htm

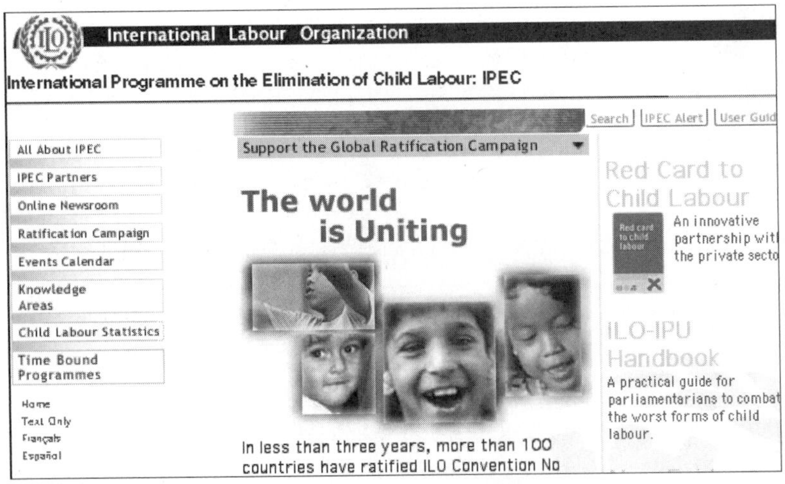

Internationally, many countries are becoming more concerned with child labor abuses. In 1999, many members of the International Labor Organization (ILO) unanimously adopted a new convention to combat the worst forms of child labor. As shown at the organization's website, http://www.ilo.org, as of February 2002, more than 100 nations had ratified the convention.

UNEMPLOYMENT COMPENSATION

During the Great Depression, nearly a third of the workforce was unemployed. Such tremendous hardship was suffered that Congress gave states an incentive to implement unemployment compensation. It devised a tax-offset incentive system that reduces the Social Security withholding tax (FICA) in a state if the state imposes an unemployment compensation tax on employers' payrolls. All of the states have enacted unemployment compensation taxes. Employers support such statutes because they would pay a 3% federal excise tax if a state had no unemployment compensation law.

EMPLOYER QUALIFICATIONS

The **unemployment compensation** system provides benefits to the employees of covered employers. Almost all employers are covered by this system. Employers in the agricultural and domestic household services areas are notable exceptions. Federal, state, and some local governments as well as railroads have other systems for their employees. Employers pay into a fund, and the proceeds from those payments are used to make payments to qualified employees. The employers pay a federal tax on a set amount (such as the first $7,000) of each worker's wages. The employer's tax payment is partially offset by tax credits.

EMPLOYEE QUALIFICATIONS

Most states set a maximum period during which the unemployed may collect benefits, but the length of that period (usually between 26 and 39 weeks) varies with changing economic conditions. The total benefits payable to each unemployed worker are based on a percentage of that worker's average base earnings while employed. Typically, they cover about half the worker's former weekly wage, with set minimums and maximums. The worker must also have met a minimum earnings requirement in the preceding year to qualify. Most unemployment benefits help between a third and half of the unemployed.

To qualify for benefits, an applicant must be actively seeking employment, be available and able to work, and follow the procedure for claims processing. Applicants may be disqualified if they refuse to accept new employment, have quit without just cause, or have been fired either for serious misconduct or as the result of a labor dispute. Unemployment compensation is usually not available to fired striking workers.

The rates paid by employers vary with the number of their employees who are terminated. Employers with low employee turnover generally pay lower premiums because of their favorable **experience rating.**

WORKERS' COMPENSATION

DEVELOPMENT OF THE LAW

Workers' compensation laws are designed to provide compensation for workers who are injured while at work. The system of laws developed because the common law system holding employers liable only for negligent torts imposed difficult burdens on employee suits claiming injury due to the negligence of their employers.

Three common defenses to negligence suits limited the liability of employers for injuries suffered by their workers. First, the **fellow servant doctrine** prevented an injured employee's suit if a fellow employee negligently contributed to the injury. Second, the **assumption of risk** defense prevented suits where the injured employee voluntarily accepted the job's risks. An injured employee who was aware of the job site risks was barred from recovering for the injury. Finally, the **contributory negligence** defense barred an injured employee's suit if the employee in any way contributed to creating the dangerous condition.

Because this negligence "fault system" provided very limited remedies, the states created no-fault, employer-financed workers' compensation systems. Under these systems, workers' compensation benefits are "exclusive remedies." Employees cannot recover in suits against their employers for compensatory, pain and suffering, or punitive damages. Workers' compensation laws create a form of compulsory insurance. Depending on the particular state's law, an employer may self-insure, purchase private insurance, or participate in a state-managed fund. Employers that take effective steps to minimize job risks pay reduced premiums. The risk-adjusted employer premiums of this **merit rating system** provide employers with an incentive to maintain a safe work environment.

WORKERS' COMPENSATION COVERAGE

The first issue in a workers' compensation claim is whether the employee's injury is work related. Employees are covered by workers' compensation only while on the job; off-the-job injuries are covered by traditional tort law. Most workers' compensation benefits are restricted to injuries occurring "in the course of and arising out of employment."

In the Course of Employment

To determine whether the act occurred "in the course of employment," courts frequently look at the time, place, and circumstances of the employment. As the following examples indicate, courts usually tilt in favor of finding coverage for injured workers.

As to time, employees en route to or from the workplace usually are not covered by workers' compensation. This **going and coming rule** restricts workers' compensation coverage to the time that the employee is at the employer's work site if the work site is located at a fixed and limited place. Workers' compensation provides coverage only after the employee arrives at the employer's premises. An employee who parks in the employer's lot and is injured while walking to a locker room to put on safety gear before being shuttled by the employer to a job site would be covered.

As to place, problems may arise if employees must leave the employer's workplace as part of the job. If employees are required to leave the premises to eat lunch, they are covered under workers' compensation. Employees who are required to travel away from the employer's premises are also usually covered.

As to circumstances, if a worker is hurt by a coworker's intentional act, such assaults are not covered. If an injury is the result of a coworker's normal horseplay, however, workers' compensation covers the injured party. For example, in *Murray v. Industrial Commission of Illinois*[6] Murray's coworker hit him behind the knees,

6. 516 NE.2d 1039 (Ill.App.3d, 1987).

causing them to buckle, so that he slipped on oil on the floor. The court ruled that Murray's injuries were a result of horseplay and thus were compensable.

Arising Out of Employment

This test usually requires a close relationship between the injury and the nature of the worker's employment. Although different states use different methods to examine this relationship, some look to see if the nature of the job itself increases the risk of injury. This test is used in the UPS case that follows. The court looks to see if the nature of Fetterman's job was the cause of his injury.

Other states, however, look to see if the person's employment causes the person to be at the place and time where the injury occurred. Here, if an employee is injured while carrying out the business of the employer, such as meeting a client at a public restaurant or at a bar, the injury would be compensable. However, another employee, at that same location, who is not at that time furthering the employer's business, would be unable to recover for injuries some other patron might inflict on the employee.

United Parcel Service v. Fetterman

336 S.E.2d 892 (Va., 1985)
Supreme Court of Virginia

Facts. Randall Fetterman, a UPS driver, was required to load, unload, and deliver packages as part of his job duties for UPS. While unloading packages one day, Mr. Fetterman noticed his shoe was untied so he raised his foot to the back of the truck and bent over to tie the shoe. He immediately noticed an acute back pain; Fetterman had suffered an accidental lumbosacral strain. The deputy commissioner of the Virginia Industrial Commission denied Fetterman's worker's compensation claim, holding that his injury did not arise out of employment because it was not traceable to employment as a proximate cause and was not a natural incident of the work. The full commission reinstated Fetterman's claim, prompting UPS and its insurer to appeal.

Legal Issue. Does a truck driver's back pain injury, which occurred after he bent over to tie his shoe while at work, "arise out of" his employment so as to be covered by worker's compensation?

Opinion. Per Curiam. An accident arises out of employment where there is a causal connection between the claimant's injury and the conditions under which the employer requires the work to be performed. Under this test, an injury arises "out of" the employment when it has followed as a natural incident of the work and has been a result of the exposure occasioned by the nature of the employment. Excluded is an injury that comes from a hazard to which the employee would have been equally exposed apart from the employment. The causative danger must be peculiar to the work, incidental to the character of the business, and not independent of the master-servant relationship. The event must appear to have had its origin in a risk connected with the employment and to have flowed from that source as a rational consequence.

The injury did not arise out of the claimant's employment. Under these circumstances, the act of bending over to tie the shoe was unrelated to any hazard common to the workplace. In other words, nothing in the work environment contributed to the injury. Every person who wears laced shoes must occasionally perform the act of retying the laces. The situation of a loose shoelace confronting the claimant was wholly independent of the master-servant relationship.

Decision. No. the injury did not arise out of Fetterman's employment. The award was reversed, and Fetterman's application dismissed.

Case Questions

1. Should loose shoelaces or other clothing be considered workplace hazards? What if a loose shirttail became caught in a workplace conveyer, dragging an employee into certain injury?
2. Would your answer to the first question be different if the employer supplied special protective gear or clothing and an accident similar to Fetterman's was caused by his reaching to tighten or straighten it?

WORKERS' COMPENSATION BENEFITS

Workers' compensation benefits are paid out of the workers' compensation insurance fund directly to the employee or the employee's family. Typically, these benefits include medical payments and disability or death benefits. Medical payments are made for the services of physicians and nurses, hospitalization, and the use of rehabilitation equipment. Disability benefits indemnify employees for wages lost during their convalescence and usually range between one-half and two-thirds of the employee's normal wages.

Specific **scheduled benefits** are paid for the loss of certain bodily functions. Such benefits are established to reflect the likely extent and duration of the disability. For example, **temporary total disability** prevents the employee from working at all for a while. **Temporary partial disability** prevents the employee from performing certain activities for a while. Such disability might affect only eyesight, hearing, or the use of an arm or leg. **Permanent partial disability** prevents the employee from performing certain activities for the remainder of his or her work life. Finally, **permanent total disability** prevents the employee from ever working again. Permanent disabilities include the loss of both eyes, hands, or legs or total paralysis, as well as less drastic losses where impairment prevents work.

Death benefits are very limited; they are paid to the employee's next of kin to cover only burial expenses (typically about $2,000). A few states pay substantial death benefits to replace the decedent's lost wages for surviving family members. Life insurance is usually still necessary to adequately replace the employee's lost income for survivors.

COMPENSABLE INJURIES

Loss of limb or bodily functions is a clear indication of compensable injury. However, some other conditions and maladies are more controversial, particularly those that involve only mental injuries.

Physical Injuries and Diseases

As for diseases, workers' compensation benefits apply to **occupational diseases**, those caused by a person's occupational environment, but not to the ordinary diseases of life. Ordinary diseases are contracted away from the job site or communicated by coworkers. The precise cause of an employee's disease is difficult to prove unless specific job hazards are positively linked to the disease. For example, it is difficult to prove that cancer is caused by occupational exposure because the disease often takes so long to develop and its cause is difficult to pinpoint. Cancer and allergic reactions are compensable only if the employee proves there was job-related exposure and causation.

Mental Disease or Injuries

Although the causation of mental injuries is quite difficult to prove, courts increasingly provide benefits for diseases caused by the pressures of employment. Before ordering payment, most courts require that a physical impact accompany any alleged mental injury. For example, anxiety depression resulting in numbness of hands and feet, high blood pressure, and vertigo are compensable physical injuries. Mental injuries resulting from a physical blow—and sometimes from the ordinary strain of work without physical injury—are generally also covered.

ADMINISTRATION OF WORKERS' COMPENSATION

Most states have a state industrial commission or state workers' compensation bureau or board administer the workers' compensation statute. The agencies perform legislative, executive, and judicial functions. They make rules regarding claims procedures, manage the receipt and disbursement of funds, and adjudicate workers' compensation claims. Injured workers begin processing their claims by applying for benefits at the state administrative agency. Typically, a claims examiner investigates to verify the extent of the compensable injury. Most legitimate claims are quickly certified, with payment following almost immediately. However, if the agency disallows claims, contested cases are heard by a hearing officer in an informal proceeding. After review in the agency, novel questions and the coverage of new diseases are usually appealed through the state court system.

RETIREMENT INCOME AND PENSIONS

Prior to 1935, very few workers had any form of old-age or retirement benefits except for personal savings. Many workers continued to work until they died or became disabled. In 1935, Congress passed the Social Security Act to prevent such severe economic hardship. Social Security benefit payments are intended to supplement the income of retirees.

Social Security covers nearly all U.S. workers. Unlike most European retirement systems, although it provides some benefits for children or spouses of workers, the U.S. system generally does not apply directly to people who have never worked. The Social Security system is compulsory, requiring employers to withhold Social Security payments from the paychecks of most employees. Each employer must match the amount withheld, which effectively doubles the Social Security tax. The actual name of the Social Security system is Old Age, Survivors, and Disability Insurance (OASDI). In recent years, private pension systems have also developed as an important supplementary source of retirement benefits.

SOCIAL SECURITY

Social Security taxes are paid into the Social Security Trust Fund under provisions of the **Federal Insurance Contributions Act (FICA)**. FICA withholding does not become part of a savings or investment fund that is eventually repaid directly to the retiree. Instead, the system is designed on a pay-as-you-go basis. Contributions from current employees immediately pay benefits to current retirees. Contrary to the common misconception that these contributions are held for employees until they retire, the system remains solvent only while current contributions exceed current benefits payments. As the population ages and the number of retirees increases, and the number of paying employees remains constant or decreases, the solvency of the system has come into question. This problem is magnified by cost-of-living adjustments (COLAs), which increase Social Security payments when the consumer price index increases.

Social Security Taxes

Nearly all employees and their employers must pay the compulsory FICA tax. The tax is determined by multiplying the rate (6.2% in 2001) by the wage base. That base equals the employee's actual pretax earnings up to a statutory maximum ($80,400 in 2001) that has steadily increased in recent years. The FICA tax paid by self-employed people is nearly double that paid by employed people because self-employed people pay both the employee's and the employer's share.

Social Security Benefits

The Social Security system provides retirement income primarily to those who have actively participated in the workforce. A worker's eligibility and amount of benefits are based on the worker's income level and on the work credits given while employed. **Fully insured** employees receive full old-age and survivors benefits. Reduced benefits are available to employees who worked at least 6 calendar quarters in the previous 13 quarters if this time period ends in retirement, disability, or death. Benefits may also be paid to the dependents and surviving spouse of a deceased person who qualified for Social Security benefits. In some cases, the spouse or former spouse of a person eligible for Social Security benefits is also entitled to separate benefits.

Disability benefits may be paid to any former employee with a medically determined physical or mental impairment. The Social Security Administration automatically recognizes several severe impairments, such as loss of limbs or sight. New impairments are determined on a case-by-case basis. Disability payments under Social Security are determined by criteria different from those used in determining disability under workers' compensation. Some disabled people may receive both Social Security and workers' compensation payments.

MEDICARE

Since 1965, health insurance for the aged and disabled has been available for all qualified persons in the system known as Medicare. Hospital insurance pays for many hospital expenses. Those 65 years old may qualify for such insurance even if they are not eligible for Social Security. Optional supplementary and medical insurance coverage is available to beneficiaries who pay additional premiums. As with Social Security, both the employer and the employee contribute a percentage of all wages and salaries to Medicare. Unlike Social Security, there is no cap on the amount of wages subject to the Medicare tax. Because Medicare does not pay enough to defray all medical costs, an active private insurance system provides plans to supplement Medicare coverage.

PRIVATE PENSION PLANS

Although private pension plans have existed for more than a century, their growth as a major source of retirement benefits has occurred mainly in the last 60 years. Historically, pension payments were made largely at the employer's discretion, not as part of a regular and mandatory compensation package. Because so many private pension plans were discriminatory and unpredictable, Congress in 1974 passed the Employee Retirement Income Security Act (ERISA) to standardize retirement plans. ERISA regulates eligibility for pension benefits and the taxation of pension plan earnings and benefit payments. Private pension plans that meet ERISA requirements are entitled to tax-free treatment in the years that employers and employees contribute to the plans.

ONLINE

A good website for examining ERISA and other employee benefit issues is **http://www.benefitslink.com/articles/usingweb.html**

The Plan Administrator's Fiduciary Duties

Qualified pension plans must be administered by a person responsible for handling the pension funds. This fiduciary must carefully invest the funds and act only in the beneficiaries' best interest, using the skill and care of a reasonably prudent person. Pension administrators must diversify their investments to minimize the risk of large losses. They must disclose certain information to the Labor Department and to the plan's beneficiaries: the terms of the plan, annual financial reports, and annual summaries of each beneficiary's interest.

Vesting and Participation

Before ERISA was passed, pension plan beneficiaries could lose all their benefits under certain circumstances. For example, a beneficiary whose employment was terminated prematurely or interrupted by a temporary layoff could have benefits denied or severely limited. As a result, ERISA established the **pension vesting** concept, requiring that the beneficiary's interest becomes irrevocable after employment for a minimum time period. Pension plans must give an irrevocable right to the employer's contributions to beneficiaries once they have worked for the employer for at least five years. Of course, the employee has a right to eventually receive all of his own contributions.

Many ERISA plans are defined benefit plans. Such plans provide beneficiaries with payment amounts based on the employee beneficiary's age and length of service. By contrast, a defined contribution plan requires each employee or employer to make a particular contribution. These plans pay beneficiaries different retirement benefit amounts depending on the return from the investments made during the employee's work life. In recent years, the defined contribution plans, which place more of the financial risk and management responsibilities on the employee rather than on the employer, have become more popular.

OCCUPATIONAL SAFETY AND HEALTH ACT

In the 1950s and 1960s, there was growing public sentiment that workers' compensation and other incentives to reduce workplace risks were ineffective. This pressure accelerated as new manufacturing technologies introduced new and incalculable risks. For example, microwaves, atomic energy, lasers, new chemicals, and high-speed processing machinery significantly reduced the safety of workplaces. The problem was heightened by inadequate workplace safety regulations in most states.

Congress reacted by passing the 1970 **Occupational Safety and Health Act (OSHA)**. The act is intended to "insure so far as possible every working man and woman in the nation safety and healthful working conditions to preserve our human resources." The act applies to any employer with at least one employee engaged in a business affecting interstate commerce. Exemptions exist for industries regulated under other safety laws. Domestic household employees and the religious activities of religious organizations are also exempt.

ADMINISTRATION OF OSHA

OSHA created three new federal agencies: the Occupational Safety and Health Administration (OSHA Administration), the National Institute for Occupational Safety and Health (NIOSH), and the Occupational Safety and Health Review Commission (OSHRC). The OSHA Administration is authorized to implement the act by promulgating regulations and setting safety standards. The agency also inspects employers' premises for compliance with its safety standards. It is a part of the Department of Labor.

ONLINE

The Occupational Safety and Health Administration
http://www.osha.gov

NIOSH conducts research into health and safety hazards and recommends new regulations and standards to the OSHA Administration. It is also responsible for educating and training employers and employees to make the workplace safe. NIOSH is housed in the Department of Health and Human Services. OSHRC is an independent commission that conducts appeals from determinations made by the OSHA Administration. Its independence is designed to reduce bias that might be exerted by employers, employee groups, or the political system. OSHRC members are appointed by the president for staggered six-year terms and must be confirmed by the Senate.

THE EMPLOYER'S DUTY OF SAFETY

OSHA imposes a **general duty** on employers to provide a safe work environment free from recognized hazards that are likely to cause death or serious physical injury. The OSHA Administration also promulgates specific health and safety standards through its regulations. These standards impose a **specific duty** on employers to comply with those regulations affecting particular workplace safety and health conditions.

SAFETY AND HEALTH REGULATIONS

Although early OSHA regulations were concerned with safety conditions in the workplace, a recent trend in its regulations has been away from the primary focus on safety regulations and toward protecting employee health. Unsafe conditions are obvious dangers because they cause sudden and obvious disability. However, delayed-manifestation diseases are becoming linked to low-level workplace exposure to hazardous or toxic substances. OSHA's performance standards now tend to provide increased protection from health hazards, overlapping the environmental regulations discussed in Chapter 23.

COST-BENEFIT ANALYSES

As business is always concerned with the cost of complying with new federal regulations, particularly those coming from OSHA, all new OSHA regulatory proposals must provide societal benefits greater than the expected costs. An executive order now requires a full cost-benefit analysis before new OSHA regulations are imposed. For example, the cost of proposed regulations focusing on ergonomics—designing office furniture and machinery to accommodate frequent use of computers and to reduce repetitive motion syndrome—has been cited by businesses as too high to justify the benefit coming from possible new standards. As a result, Congress has specified that OSHA cannot impose any ergonomic-based regulations.

OSHA ENFORCEMENT PROCEDURES

The OSHA Administration enforces OSHA and the agency's own regulations by collecting information submitted by employees and employers and from on-site inspections. It issues citations for minor violations and assess penalties for more serious violations.

Record-Keeping and Reporting Requirements

OSHA requires employers to report unsafe incidents, accidents, fatalities, lost workdays, job transfers and terminations, medical treatments, and restrictions of work.

These reports must be filed with the secretary of labor. Detailed logs of all recordable incidents must also be maintained. Employers with fewer than 11 employees are exempt from record keeping. OSHA must be notified within 48 hours of an accident if it results in a fatality or in the hospitalization of more than four employees. OSHA requires employers to post information regarding OSHA rights and obligations for all employees to review.

OSHA Inspections

The OSHA Administration also conducts on-site inspections. An employer's work site may be inspected if the OSHA Administration inspector has a search warrant, the violation is in "plain view," or the employer consents. Typically, the employer or one of its representatives accompanies the OSHA inspector during the visit. The OSHA inspector confers directly with employees or the employees' representative (such as a union steward).

OSHA Administration inspectors may conduct four types of investigations. First, accident investigations usually follow reports of fatalities and catastrophes. Second, employee complaints trigger one-third of all investigations. Third, programmed inspections are conducted in industries with a history of dangerous hazards. Inspections are routine in industries with higher-than-average injury reports. Fourth, the OSHA Administration often conducts follow-up inspections where it has previously issued citations for violations of safety standards.

OSHA Violations: Citations and Penalties

The OSHA Administration may issue written citations and impose penalties for violations of safety standards. Citations must be posted near the location of the violation to give employees notice. Penalties usually involve monetary fines and a requirement that the employer remove the violation. Penalties vary according to the size of the business, the employer's good faith and safety record, and the severity of the violation.

A *de minimis violation* has no direct relationship to safety, so the employer is usually notified and no penalty is imposed. For example, the lack of private toilet facilities or waste containers is considered a *de minimis* violation. A *nonserious violation* relates to job safety but is unlikely to cause death or serious physical harm. A monetary penalty for nonserious violations may be levied at the discretion of the director of the OSHA Administration. Examples include a hazard of tripping due to poor housekeeping and failure to provide instructions for the use of machinery.

Violations that pose a substantial probability of death or serious physical harm are *serious violations*. Repeat violations and violations that might lead to imminent danger of likely death or serious physical harm carry penalties of up to $10,000 and/or up to six months in jail. Willful repeated violations carry a $20,000 fine and up to one year's imprisonment.

Protection from Employer Retaliation

Employers are forbidden to discharge or discriminate against employees who report safety violations. The secretary of labor determines whether employer retaliation has occurred. Should an employer be required to reinstate a fired employee and give back pay or other relief to replace benefits of which a wrongfully discharged employee has been deprived? The following case illustrates how OSHA protects employees who report safety or health violations.

Whirlpool Corp. v. Marshall

445 U.S. 1 (1980)
United States Supreme Court

Facts. The secretary of labor adopted a regulation permitting employees to refuse an assigned task if a reasonable apprehension existed that death or serious injury would result from its performance. Two Whirlpool employees refused to perform assigned maintenance work, fearing that a wire mesh used to prevent objects from falling from an overhead conveyer was unsafe. The employees were sent home without pay for insubordination, and their refusal to work was noted on their records. The district court found the regulation was invalid, but the Court of Appeals reversed that finding. Whirlpool appealed to the Supreme Court.

Legal Issue. As OSHA already gives an employee the right to inform OSHA of an imminently dangerous workplace condition that needs inspection, can OSHA also adopt a regulation permitting employees to refuse to perform an assigned task if they reasonably believe that death or serious injury could result from its performance?

Opinion. Justice Stewart. The Act itself creates an express mechanism for protecting workers from employment conditions believed to pose an emergent threat of death or serious injury. Upon receipt of an employee inspection request stating reasonable grounds to believe that an imminent danger is present in a workplace, OSHA must conduct an inspection. In the event this inspection reveals workplace conditions or practices that "could reasonably be expected to cause death or serious physical harm immediately or before the imminence of such danger can be eliminated through the enforcement procedures otherwise provided by" the Act, the OSHA inspector must inform the affected employees and the employer of the danger and notify them that he is recommending to the Secretary that injunctive relief be sought. The court may then require the employer to avoid, correct, or remove the danger or to prohibit employees from working in the area.

To ensure that this process functions effectively, the Act expressly accords to every employee several rights, the exercise of which may not subject him to discharge or discrimination. An employee is given the right to inform OSHA of an imminently dangerous workplace condition or practice and request that OSHA inspect that condition or practice. He is given a limited right to assist the OSHA inspector in inspecting the workplace and the right to aid a court in determining whether or not a risk of imminent danger in fact exists. Finally, an affected employee is given the right to bring an action to compel the Secretary to seek injunctive relief if he believes the Secretary wrongfully declined to do so.

In the light of this detailed statutory scheme, the Secretary is obviously correct when he acknowledges in his regulation that, "as a general matter, there is no right afforded by the Act which would entitle employees to walk off the job because of potential unsafe conditions at the workplace." By providing for prompt notice to the employer of an inspector's intention to seek an injunction against an imminently dangerous condition, the legislation obviously contemplates that the employer will normally respond by voluntarily and speedily eliminating the danger. And in the few instances where this does not occur, the legislative provisions authorizing prompt judicial action are designed to give employees full protection in most situations from the risk of injury or death resulting from an imminently dangerous condition at the worksite.

As this case illustrates, however, circumstances may sometimes exist in which the employee justifiably believes that the express statutory arrangement does not sufficiently protect him from death or serious injury. Such circumstances will probably not often occur, but such a situation may arise when: (1) the employee is ordered by his employer to work under conditions that the employee reasonably believes pose an imminent risk of death or serious bodily injury, and (2) the employee has reason to believe that there is not sufficient time or opportunity either to seek effective redress from his employer or to apprise OSHA of the danger.

Decision. The regulation clearly conforms to the fundamental objective of the act—to prevent occupational deaths and serious injuries. The regulation thus on its face appears to further the overriding purpose of the act and rationally to complement its remedial scheme. In the absence of some contrary indication in the legislative history, the secretary's regulation must be upheld, particularly when it is remembered that safety legislation is to be liberally construed to effectuate the congressional purpose.

Case Questions

1. Would OSHA be effective if employers could threaten employees with discipline or dismissal for seeking its protection?
2. Is an employee's refusal to work under unsafe conditions the best method for discovering workplace hazards?

ADDITIONAL CONCERNS

Two of the more recent concerns affecting the employer-employee relationship deal with the employee's family and his or her right to privacy. The Family Medical Leave Act is the newest federal statute to offer employment rights to employees.

FAMILY AND MEDICAL LEAVE ACT

The 1993 Family and Medical Leave Act (FMLA) requires employers who have 50 or more employees to provide employees with up to 12 weeks of unpaid family or medical leave during any 12-month period. Employees must have worked with their employer for at least one year to be eligible. During the employee's leave, the employer must continue to provide health care coverage and generally must guarantee employment in the same or a comparable position upon return to work. Key employees, those whose pay is in the top 10% of the firm's workforce, are not guaranteed to be reinstated to their same or a similar job.

Employees can take family leave to care for a newborn baby or an adopted child. In *Knussman v. State of Maryland*,[7] a male state trooper requested to use his accumulated sick leave as family leave after his wife gave birth and experienced a difficult recovery. His employer said that only the mother, as the primary caregiver, was eligible for such use of sick leave under state law. A jury found Knussman was discriminated against because of his gender and awarded him $375,000.

Medical leave can be whenever a "serious health condition" of the employee or the employee's spouse, child, or parent needs care. Pending legislation would extend the coverage to employers with 25 or more employees and would provide leave for specified school-related purposes.

EMPLOYEE PRIVACY CONCERNS

Employee privacy is an area of significant concern to most employees at the start of the twenty-first century. The major privacy concerns of employees center around employer testing and monitoring activities. Each has attracted significant attention and some regulation. The Electronic Communications Privacy Act, which requires consent from the employee for an employer to monitor and intercept an employee's e-mail messages, and related privacy laws are discussed in Chapter 14. Drug testing, genetic testing, polygraph testing, video surveillance, and electronic monitoring exemplify the activities that employers may undertake that affect the privacy of the employee.

Many employers require interviewees to take batteries of tests, including psychological, medical, drug, intelligence, and skills tests. Psychological testing may reveal an applicant's work ethic, criminal tendencies, ability to work with others, performance under stress, and aptitude for leadership. Intelligence and skills tests may reveal an applicant's knowledge and capability to perform the tasks necessary for the job. Medical tests may reveal an applicant's predisposition to certain diseases that require expensive treatment. For example, HIV testing is a controversial procedure. As noted in the next chapter, some employers have even considered genetic

7. The district court's decision appears at 65 F. Supp. 2d 353 (1999). On appeal, the appellate court determined the jury award, which was for emotional damages only, was excessive and remanded the case for a redetermination as to damages. See 272 F. 3d 625 (2001).

testing to predict an applicant's honesty, criminal tendencies, or future health care needs. The use of intrusive tests, particularly those without a scientific consensus on reliability, raises profound public policy, legal, and privacy issues.

Drug Testing

Considerable evidence shows that employees' abuse of certain substances can adversely affect their performance, productivity, health, and workplace safety. Nearly all the Fortune 100 companies have drug-testing programs, many for prospective new hires, usually performed through urinalysis or the assay of hair samples. The Drug Free Workplace Act of 1988, which allows drug testing, applies to all federal employees and private employers doing business with the government. Most states also have statutes that permit drug testing.

Employers who have a written drug-testing policy generally prevent exposure to an invasion of privacy claim and also are given greater latitude in testing. Drug and alcohol testing are mandatory subjects of bargaining under NLRB guidelines. Courts consider both the privacy rights of the employee and the employer's right to protect property and the safety of others in cases involving drug surveillance and testing. Although random or investigative testing is less common, it can be permitted if public safety is involved or it is job related.

Polygraph Tests

The Employee Polygraph Protection Act of 1988 prohibits most employers' use of polygraphs (lie detectors) unless there is reasonable suspicion of losses caused by employees. A lie detector test may be conducted if the employer provides a written statement showing a reasonable suspicion that the employee had access to damaged or missing material and was involved in the matter. The questions must relate only to the alleged misconduct and may not be the only basis for an employee's dismissal. Employers may not retaliate against employees who refuse to take a lie detector test. Violators are subject to liability for punitive damages, civil fines, and attorney's fees. There are exemptions from the act for governments, government defense contractors, drug producers, and security protection companies.

http://

www.businessweek.com/2000/00_28/b3689172.htm

Monitoring

When it comes to privacy in the workplace, as the article appearing in a *Business Week* website indicates, most employees don't have any. Nearly 75% of companies surveyed admit they actively monitor their workers' communications—including e-mail and Internet usage. For a variety of reasons, employers now commonly adopt an Internet acceptable use policy (IAUP):

- Loss of productivity from improper use
- Shield of employer from possible sexual harassment suits
- Reduced cost associated with providing computer resources
- Reinforced need for confidential use of company information.

BusinessWeek online

Search
Advanced Search

BW MAGAZINE | DAILY BRIEFING | INVESTING | GLOBAL BUSINESS | TECHNOLOGY | SMALL BUSINESS | B-SCHOOLS | CAREERS

Full Table of Contents
Cover Story -- Can Amazon Make It?
Asian/Latin American Cover -- The Global 1000
European Cover -- Airbus: Birth of a Giant
Frontier -- The Resource for Small Business and Entrepreneurs
Up Front
Readers Report
Corrections & Clarifications
Books
Technology & You
Economic Viewpoint
Economic Trends
Business Outlook
News: Analysis & Commentary
In Business This Week
Washington Outlook

BUSINESSWEEK ONLINE : JULY 10, 2000 ISSUE

Discover the trends in our special **WIRELESS REPORT.**
BusinessWeek online
Click here to see inside

BUSINESSWEEK LIFESTYLE

Someone to Watch Over You

More employers punish those who violate e-mail and Net rules

When it comes to privacy in the workplace, you don't have any. Time and again, courts hav
when it comes to spying on employees. Your boss can monitor the time you spend on the
your voice mail. Employers can review your computer files and copy and read your e-mail
when you're surfing the Internet. They can even put video cameras in washrooms--though

Employee surveillance has mushroomed recently, and you can blame it on the Internet. Ne
companies say they actively monitor their workers' communications and on-the-job activiti
the number four years ago, according to an American Management Assn. poll of its memb
to-large organizations that together employ a quarter of the U.S. workforce. Some 54% trac
Internet connections; 38% admit to storing and reviewing their employees' e-mail. Three ye
monitored e-mail.

Seventy-five percent of the problems with Internet and e-mail use and abuse revolve around two issues: sexual harassment and the disclosure of confidential information.[8] From the employer perspective, the employee is using the company's equipment, and, as it can be held liable for the actions of its employees, the employer has the right to monitor and seek to control the actions of employees in the workplace. The employer's legal obligation to prevent harassment, and its financial obligation to its shareholders or owners to protect confidential information, dictate the necessity for such monitoring policies. More than 40% of surveyed companies have punished employees for violating company policies. Some of these issues are being settled through case decisions. For example, the NLRB has already ruled that video monitoring activities are legitimate employee concerns.

Colgate-Palmolive Company

National Labor Relations Board
323 N.L.R.B. 82 (1997)

Facts. Colgate-Palmolive (C-P) installed hidden cameras throughout the workplace environment, including the restrooms and fitness areas, in order to reduce employee theft and employee misconduct. Many C-P employees were represented by the International Chemical Workers Union (Union). The Union, in a letter to C-P, argued that as employees could be dismissed from their jobs on the basis of misconduct documented by the camera, the use of video surveillance was a mandatory subject of bargaining. C-P refused to bargain, and the Union filed an unfair labor practice complaint with the NLRB. An administrative law judge found for the Union, and C-P appealed to the board.

Legal Issue. Is the use of video surveillance a "term and condition of employment" so as to be a mandatory subject of collective bargaining?

Opinion. The mandatory subjects of collective bargaining described in the NLRA include "wages, hours, and other terms and conditions of employment, or the negotiation of an agreement, or any questions arising thereunder." The parties are required to bargain over these subjects because the employment relationship is directly affected by them. In *Ford Motor Company v. NLRB*,[9] the Supreme Court outlined two factors for determining the mandatory subjects of bargaining. A decision is mandatory if it is both: (1) plainly germane to the work environment, and (2) not among those managerial decisions, which lie at the core of managerial control. Video surveillance is analogous to physical examinations, drug testing, and polygraph testing in that all are investigatory tools an employer may use to discharge an employee. As a result, the subject of video surveillance was "unquestionably germane" to the work environment.

As for the second factor, the cameras are not fundamental to the direction of the enterprise. They did not directly impinge on the security concerns of the employer. Thus, the decision to implement video surveillance is not at the core of managerial control.

Decision. Consequently, Colgate-Palmolive has a duty to bargain with the union regarding the use of video surveillance of employees. As it has not done so, it has violated sections 5 and 8 of the NLRA.

Case Questions

1. The court finds that video surveillance is "germane to the work environment." How would the work environment change with the presence of video surveillance?
2. How do you think the employer and the union could settle this issue through collective bargaining? What result would you expect? What restrictions would the employer agree to, and what activities would the union likely consent to?

8. Michael A. Verespej, Inappropriate Internet Surfing, *Industry Week*, February 7, 2000.
9. 441 U.S. 488 (1979).

QUESTIONS

1. Galvcoat Metals Co. uses numerous toxic chemicals in its metal coatings business. Technicians recently discovered that applications of increased concentrations of sulfuric acid (SO_2) improved the preparation of the sheets of raw steel for the electroplating process applied by Galvcoat. However, management considered the new technique to be a "trade secret process," so it refused to disclose the higher SO_2 concentrations to employees or to provide additional protective gear as required by OSHA regulations. This failure to disclose helped to conceal why Galvcoat metals performed better than competitors' products, which enabled Galvcoat to charge higher prices for its "superior" products. However, Galvcoat paid for none of the additional safety expenses needed to protect workers from the higher concentrations of SO_2. Comment on the ethical and legal problems presented here.
2. Hauck sued his former employer, Sabine Pilot Service, for wrongful discharge, claiming that he was discharged for refusing to pump the bilges of the boat on which he worked. He had been told by an official of the U.S. Coast Guard that pumping bilges into the water was illegal. Sabine Pilot Service claimed that Hauck was discharged for insubordination, for refusing to swab the deck, and for not following through on other duties. Should Hauck recover for wrongful discharge? How does the employment-at-will doctrine apply? See *Sabine Pilot Service, Inc. v. Hauck*, 687 S.W.2d 734 (1985).
3. TWA, a major commercial air carrier, trained all TWA flight attendants at its training academy, located in Kansas. Flight attendant positions were highly desirable, and TWA received thousands of applications for these positions each year. It carefully selected trainees from a large group of applicants. During the four-week training period, most of the trainees resided in dormitory-like accommodations located on the grounds of the training academy. They did not receive any wages from TWA, but it did provide them with meals, lodging, and transportation.

   Trainees were not permitted to work on regular commercial flights or to supplement the work of regular flight attendants until they had completed the training course. Completion of the course qualified them as flight attendants, but TWA did not guarantee that all of the successful trainees would be hired upon graduation. Were the TWA flight attendant trainees "employees" within the meaning of the Fair Labor Standards Act? See *Donovan v. Transworld Airlines, Inc.*, 726 F.2d 415 (1984).
4. What qualifications must an employee meet to receive unemployment compensation?
5. GMAC, which provides financing for buyers of General Motors automobiles, had employees at each of its offices whose job was to collect overdue accounts and repossess cars. These employees put in long and irregular hours, and they usually worked on their own and without direct supervision. The upper management of GMAC regularly encouraged the accurate reporting of hours worked. However, lower-level supervisors set strict limits on the number of hours that could be reported. These supervisors gave the collection employees substantially more work than could be done in a 40-hour week but generally permitted them to report only 40 to 42 hours. On the average, the collection employees actually worked about 53 hours per week. Has GMAC violated the overtime provision of the Fair Labor Standards Act? Why? See *Brennan v. GMAC*, 482 F.2d 825 (1973).
6. A contract between Boeing and its largest labor union, the International Machinists and Aerospace Workers, states that Boeing will give the union 180 days' notice prior to entering into any subcontracts. Boeing said it was considering allowing Japan's Mitsubishi corporation to build major portions of several of its planes, as it could do so at lower cost. Should a court enjoin Boeing from unilaterally farming out work to subcontractors? Why?
7. Communication Workers of America (CWA) recommended a nationwide strike of Bell Telephone in 1971. In New York, the strike continued for seven months. Because the state's unemployment insurance law provided no exemption for striking workers, the 38,000 striking CWA members in New York filed for and received unemployment compensation. The amounts they received were charged back to the employer under the state's system of establishing employer contributions. Bell Telephone claimed that the New York law had been preempted by the National Labor Relations Act. Did the National Labor Relations Act implicitly prohibit New York from paying unemployment compensation to strikers? See *New York Telephone Co. v. New York Department of Labor*, 440 U.S. 519 (1979).
8. Continental Airlines required all of its pilots to learn their schedules and flight assignments by accessing its computerized crew management system. For a fee, airline personnel accessed the system via an Internet service provider and also could use an electronic bulletin board known as Crew Members Forum. Blakey, the first female Continental Airlines pilot to captain

an A300 aircraft, filed a sexual harassment claim with her employer. Later, she filed suit in federal court, and in the midst of that litigation, other pilots posted derogatory and gender-based comments about her on the bulletin board. Could Blakey hold Continental liable for the defamatory statements posted by its pilots? See *Blakey v. Continental Airlines* 751 A.2d 538 (N.J., 2001).

9. What is the relationship between workers' compensation and OSHA safety and health efforts?

10. Read and comment on an article found at one of the employee benefits websites referred to by David Rhett Baker, the publisher of BenefitsLink at http://www.benefitslink.com/articles/usingweb.html.

CHAPTER 21

Equal Employment Opportunities

INTRODUCTION

The United States is a country of great diversity, yet many of its residents were denied numerous opportunities well into the twentieth century. By the middle of the twentieth century, the need for greater legal protection of civil rights became obvious. Most of the equal employment laws grew out of the civil rights movement in the early 1960s. Although the movement was mainly concerned with providing access for minorities to public places like parks, restaurants, motels, and the voting booth, many people also recognized the long-term importance of providing equal access to employment opportunities. The federal legislative protection offered by the civil rights laws that emerged from that period form the basis for today's legal restrictions on discriminatory employment practices.

The **Equal Pay Act of 1963** prohibits sexual discrimination in pay for work that requires "equal skill, effort, and responsibility." The best-known and most comprehensive antidiscrimination law is the **Civil Rights Act of 1964.** It prohibits any employment-based discrimination based on race, color, religion, sex, or national origin. This act effectively extended civil rights protections to a broad spectrum of categories of protected persons. Employment-based discrimination includes decisions related to hiring, promotion, job assignments, eligibility for training programs, layoffs, and firings.

The **Age Discrimination in Employment Act of 1967** prohibits employment discrimination on the basis of age against those 40 years of age or older. Thus, everyone becomes a member of this protected class on attaining age 40. Employers who seek to cut costs by replacing older, higher-paid workers with younger, lower-paid workers can be held liable if the employee can prove that the discharge is motivated, at least in part, by age. The **Vocational Rehabilitation Act of 1973** and the **Americans with Disabilities Act of 1990** extended antidiscrimination protection to people with handicaps.

The Equal Employment Opportunity Commission (EEOC) enforces the federal antidiscrimination laws by rule-making, investigation, and adjudication. Most

EEOC complaints are settled through conciliation. State fair employment practice laws in approximately 45 states supplement federal laws, but their provisions are quite varied. From time to time, the president issues executive orders that are administered by the Office of Federal Contract Compliance Programs. Some of these orders prohibit discrimination by contractors that perform work for the federal government. The unwary employer that does not comply with the antidiscrimination statutes, executive orders, and administrative agency regulations and rulings may be exposed to significant legal liability.

EQUAL PAY ACT

The Equal Pay Act amended the Fair Labor Standards Act (discussed in Chapter 20) by prohibiting unequal pay for equal work by either sex. The act, enforced by the EEOC, is quite narrow in the protection it provides. It does not apply to discrimination in hiring, promotion, or firing on the basis of sex; such discrimination is regulated by the Civil Rights Act of 1964. The Equal Pay Act does apply if an employer has two substantially similar jobs, one held by a male and the other by a female. The act prohibits the employer from paying the two employees at different rates. For this prohibition to apply, the two jobs must require "equal skill, effort, and responsibility . . . [if] performed under similar working conditions." A recurring issue under the Equal Pay Act is the content analysis of jobs. Employers must specify a job description for each job so that if two jobs are substantially similar, then the pay given for performing each of them should be equal.

The Equal Pay Act does not apply to pay differentials resulting from factors other than sex, such as the differentials that result from bona fide seniority or merit systems or from the quantity or quality of output. Exhibit 21.1 depicts the situations the law recognizes as exceptions to the requirement of equal pay for equal work. The "factors other than gender" exception includes pay differences based on education or experience.

http://

www.eeoc.gov/stats/epa.html

If one new employee has a college education and the other does not, or one applicant has had previous work experience related to the potential job and the other does not, then a difference in pay can be justified. Similarly, shift differentials—pay that varies based on the time of day of a work shift—are usually valid. However, such differentials may be illegal if the working conditions are almost identical and one shift is staffed predominantly by males and another by females.

New workers involved in training programs may be rotated through several departments and perform work substantially similar to that done by workers permanently assigned to the departments. Pay differentials between such trainees and permanent workers are not illegal if the training programs are open equally to both sexes.

The U.S. Equal Employment Opportunity Commission

Equal Pay Act Charges
(includes concurrent charges with Title VII, ADEA, and ADA)
FY 1992 - FY 2001

The following chart represents the total number of charge receipts filed and resolved under the EPA.

Receipts include all charges filed under the EPA and those filed concurrently under Title VII, ADA, and ADEA. Therefore, the sum of receipts fo statutes will exceed total charges received.

The data are compiled by the Office of Research, Information, and Planning from EEOC's Charge Data System - quarterly reconciled Data Summa Reports.

	FY 1992	FY 1993	FY 1994	FY 1995	FY 1996	FY 1997	FY 1998	FY 1999	FY 2000	FY 2001
Receipts	1,294	1,328	1,381	1,275	969	1,134	1,071	1,044	1,270	1,251
Resolutions	1,185	1,120	1,171	1,249	1,235	1,172	1,134	1,026	1,235	1,158
Resolutions By Type										
Settlements	105	80	106	94	88	71	71	89	80	96
	8.9%	7.1%	9.1%	7.5%	7.1%	6.1%	6.3%	8.7%	6.5%	8.3%
Withdrawals w/Benefits	87	100	95	81	61	54	49	58	70	62
	7.3%	8.9%	8.1%	6.5%	4.9%	4.6%	4.3%	5.7%	5.7%	5.4%
Administrative Closures	305	272	390	452	339	302	327	226	250	201

EXHIBIT 21.1 Equal Pay Act

Recognized Justifications for Wage Differentials
- Seniority system
- Merit system
- Pay system based on quantity or quality of production
- System based on a factor *other than* gender—such as education, work experience, or participation in a training program

THE CIVIL RIGHTS ACT OF 1964

Of all the antidiscrimination laws, Title VII of the Civil Rights Act of 1964 has had the greatest impact on the employment relationship. It prohibits discrimination by employers with 15 or more employees, by unions that bargain with such employers or operate hiring halls, and by employment agencies. Title VII makes it illegal to discriminate in hiring, firing, compensation, or the terms, conditions, or privileges of employment if the different treatment is based on race, color, religion, national origin, or sex. Any classification of employees based on these protected classes is prohibited if it deprives people in these classes of employment opportunities.

ONLINE

Read Title VII of the Civil Rights Act of 1964 at **http://www.eeoc.gov/laws/vii.html**

INTENTIONAL AND UNINTENTIONAL DISCRIMINATION

Under Title VII, employers can be held liable for either intentional (**disparate treatment**) or unintentional discrimination (**disparate impact**). Of course, employers may legitimately discriminate among job applicants or employees on the basis of their ability to perform work or their prospects for success. It is important to recognize that Title VII outlaws only "discrimination" predicated on race, sex, religion, color, and national origin. Discriminations based on measurable differences in qualifications closely related to job performance are justifiable and legal.

Disparate Treatment

Title VII prohibits employers, unions, and employment agencies from treating one group of employees or job applicants more favorably than a protected class. An illegal disparate treatment occurs when an employer intentionally conducts discriminatory hiring, promotion, or firing policies.

Proof of such discrimination is easy when the employer overtly states, for example, "Blacks need not apply" or "this is a man's job." Today, overt practices are rare. Disparate treatment typically results from subtler conduct, so courts accept inferences based on circumstantial evidence. To prove disparate treatment, the plaintiff must first establish a **prima facie case** (the first impression) that shows that the basic elements of discrimination have occurred. The burden of proof then shifts to the employer. If the employer can show a legal justification, the burden then shifts back to the plaintiff. To establish a prima facie case of disparate treatment, a plaintiff must prove:

1. Membership in a protected class
2. Qualification for the job sought

3. Rejection despite adequate qualifications
4. That the position remained open after the plaintiff was rejected

After the plaintiff establishes the prima facie case, the burden of proof shifts to the defendant, who must prove that there was a legitimate reason for the disparate treatment. In the case that follows, a female accountant who claimed she was discriminated against because of her gender first makes a prima facie case. Then the employer presents a reason, such as her lack of appropriate interpersonal skills, which it argues was the real reason for her dismissal. The final step in the trial requires the plaintiff to show that the reason given by the employer was not the true reason for its actions. Although such proof is often difficult for the plaintiff to provide, if the plaintiff can show that the employer's decision was motivated in part by illegal discrimination, the plaintiff is entitled to a legal remedy. Review the Supreme Court's analysis and discussion of the various stages of a case as it determines whether the employer's conduct constitutes disparate treatment.

Price Waterhouse v. Hopkins

490 U.S. 228 (1989)
United States Supreme Court

Facts. Ann Hopkins, a senior manager at the Washington, D.C., office of the Price Waterhouse accounting firm, was proposed by the partners in her office for a promotion to partner in 1982. However, her candidacy was held over for reconsideration to the following year and thereafter dropped. Only 7 of 662 Price Waterhouse partners nationwide were women, and Hopkins was the only woman among the 88 partner candidates that year. Both her supporters and opponents indicated that Hopkins was "overly aggressive, unduly harsh, difficult to work with, and impatient with staff." She was described as "macho" and "overcompensating for being a woman." She was advised to take a "course at charm school" and to walk, talk, and dress "more femininely, wear make-up, have her hair styled, and wear jewelry."

When Hopkins sued Price Waterhouse for violating Title VII, Price Waterhouse claimed that its decision was based primarily on legitimate interpersonal factors. The trial court held that the firm had unlawfully discriminated against Hopkins on the basis of sex by consciously giving credence to sexually stereotyped comments. Price Waterhouse appealed that decision.

Legal Issue. If a firm making a promotion decision for an applicant considers sexually stereotyped comments, does a decision based in part on the applicant's gender violate Title VII?

Opinion. Justice Brennan. In passing Title VII, Congress made the simple but momentous announcement that sex, race, and national origin are not relevant to the selection, evaluation, or compensation of employees. The statute does not purport to limit the other qualities and characteristics that employers may take into account in making employment decisions. The critical inquiry in this case is whether gender was a factor in the employment decision at the moment it was made. Title VII was meant to condemn even those decisions based on a mixture of legitimate and illegitimate considerations.

To say that an employer may not take gender into account is not the end of the matter. Title VII preserved the employer's remaining freedom of choice. The employer shall not be liable if it can prove that, even if it had not taken gender into account, it would have come to the same decision. In saying that gender played a motivating part in an employment decision, we mean that, if we asked the employer at the moment of the decision what the reasons were and if we received a truthful response, one of those reasons would be that the applicant or employee was a woman. An employer who acts on the basis of the belief that a woman cannot be aggressive has acted on the basis of gender. We are beyond the day when an employer could evaluate employees by assuming or insisting that they match the stereotype associated with their group.

An employer who objects to aggressiveness in women but whose positions require this trait places women in an intolerable and impermissible Catch-22: out of a job if they behave aggressively and out of a job if they do not. Title VII lifts women out of this bind. Price Waterhouse invited partners to submit comments; some of the comments stemmed from sexual stereotypes; the Policy Board's decision on Hopkins was an assessment of the submitted comments; and Price Waterhouse in no way disclaimed reliance on the sex-linked evaluations.

Decision. The decision of the defendant was based in part on the applicant's gender. The defendant may avoid a finding of liability only by proving by a preponderance of the evidence that it would have made the same decision even if it had not taken the plaintiff's gender into account. Thus, we affirm the Court of Appeals' holding, but remand the case to the trial court to determine whether Price Waterhouse's decision would have been the same if it had not considered the gender of the applicant.

[After remand on whether Price Waterhouse would have made the same decision without considering sex stereotyping, the trial court ordered that Hopkins be made a partner.]

Case Questions

1. If an employer's promotion decision is based partly on the person's gender and partly on the basis of other appropriate factors, is the employer discriminating on the basis of gender?
2. If the employer did consider gender in making the promotion decision, under what circumstances could its decision be legal?
3. What are the first things that Hopkins has to prove in this case? What then must the defendant prove to avoid liability?

Disparate Impact

A Title VII violation may also be found if it can be shown that a disparate impact resulted from the employer's hiring policies or evaluation process. Employers often use interview and testing procedures to determine if applicants are suitable for particular jobs. The need to have a high school diploma, several years of college, or a college degree is a common requirement. However, such a requirement may have a disparate impact on a protected class.

Despite vigorous protest from four dissenting justices, the U.S. Supreme Court recently limited the enforcement of disparate impact cases to the government. *Alexander v. Sandoval*[1] determined that Title VII does not allow private parties to challenge discrimination cases based on disparate impact. The ruling means that, despite contrary opinions from numerous federal courts of appeal, the EEOC can bring disparate impact cases, but private parties who are the victims of such discrimination cannot.

If an employer's workforce does not reflect the percentage of nonwhites, women, or other members of a protected group that would be reflected in the appropriate labor market, the plaintiff has presented a prima facie case of disparate impact. Similarly, if an educational requirement excludes members of a protected class from an employer's workforce, regardless of the racial balance in the employer's workforce, a prima facie case of disparate impact discrimination exists. No proof of intentional discrimination is needed. It is then up to the employer to show that the educational requirement is closely related to the qualifications needed to perform the job. Without proof that physical requirements, general intelligence tests, or specified educational achievements are directly related to necessary job qualifications, they may result in a disparate impact.

TITLE VII'S PROTECTED CLASSES

Title VII of the Civil Rights Act of 1964 prohibits discrimination in employment practices on the basis of membership in a protected class. A **protected class** is a

1. 532 U.S. 275 (2001).

demographic variable or classification of persons who have historically been subjected to discrimination in hiring. The protected classes include race, color, religion, national origin, and sex. An employment practice is prohibited if it discriminates against an applicant on the basis of his or her membership in a protected class and if disparate treatment or disparate impact results.

Race or Color

Any policy or practice that has the effect of discriminating against applicants or employees on account of race or color is illegal unless it is protected by one of the recognized exceptions (discussed later in this chapter). The most common of these exceptions, the bona fide occupational qualification, does not apply to discrimination based on race or color.

Although there is little overt racial discrimination today, court cases have unmasked numerous subtler forms of discrimination on the basis of race or color. Both the Civil Rights Act of 1964 and the much earlier act of 1866 were enacted to protect blacks. However, court interpretations have consistently applied them to all other races. Thus, **reverse discrimination**, where preference based on race is given to blacks or other members of this protected class who historically have suffered discrimination, can also be illegal.

National Origin

Discrimination based on the country in which a person was born or from which the person's forebears came is national origin discrimination. It is sometimes legal for employers to indirectly discriminate against aliens or noncitizens. For example, some jobs, particularly those involving communication with customers, suppliers, or fellow employees, may require fluency in English. However, if fluency in English is not a business necessity, then making it a job qualification could be prohibited if it has an adverse impact on certain groups, such as Hispanics.

Unlike discrimination based on race or color, the bona fide occupational qualification defense can apply in cases involving discrimination based on national origin. For example, although English-only laws and workplace rules have been challenged as discriminatory because language can be closely connected to a person's national origin, states like Nebraska, New Hampshire, South Carolina, and South Dakota currently have enforceable English-only language laws for their public employees.

Religion

A fundamental concern addressed in the Constitution is discrimination based on religious practices and beliefs. The separation of church and state and the First Amendment freedoms of religion form the basis for the law's protection of religious beliefs. In addition, the 1964 Civil Rights Act prohibits employment discrimination on the basis of religion. From the standpoint of the law, the term *religion* includes all aspects of religious observations and practices, as well as belief. Thus, in addition to protecting the traditional religions—Christianity, Judaism, Islam, Buddhism, and Hinduism—Title VII also protects atheism and agnosticism. In addition, EEOC guidelines state that protected religious practices include moral or ethical beliefs as to what is right and wrong that are held with the strength of religious views.[2]

Title VII requires employers to "reasonably accommodate" the religious practices of its employees, unless to do so would cause an undue hardship on the employer's

2. 29 C.F.R. sec. 1605.1

business. Where an employee's religious practices tend to interfere with the employer's business, the law tries to find a delicate balance between imposing a hardship on the business and a hardship on the employee's beliefs. Where an employer convincingly demonstrates that accommodating an employee's religious beliefs would impose undue hardship on the business, discrimination on the basis of religion is permitted. In a 2001 case, a court of appeals affirmed a district court opinion that an employer's policy that restricted employees from adding religious greetings, such as "Have a Blessed Day," on their e-mail communications with business customers, while permitting such greetings on internal communications, constituted a reasonable accommodation.[3]

Sex

It is illegal to discriminate on the basis of sex. This prohibition was originally designed to correct the stereotypical societal roles of the sexes, which tended to discriminate against females. During the twentieth century, the role of women in the workforce expanded significantly; today, women are more than 40% of the workforce. The *Price Waterhouse* case exemplifies cases involving illegal discrimination based on sex or gender.

Congress passed the Pregnancy Discrimination Act as an amendment to Title VII in 1978 to assure protection against employment discrimination during pregnancy. More than 70% of all women who become pregnant are working at that time; half return to work after the newborn reaches three months of age, and almost three-fourths return by the child's first birthday. The act prohibits employers from requiring that pregnant employees take leaves of absence if they are still qualified to do their jobs.

Pregnancy leaves may not be treated differently from other temporary disability leaves. Employers may not specify the length of postdelivery leaves of absence. Women may not be denied a promotion or job assignment on the basis of pregnancy. Employee benefits programs must not discriminate against pregnant women. In other words, women who are affected by pregnancy or childbirth must be treated the same as all others with similar ability to work in all employment-related decisions.[4]

Discrimination on the basis of sex occurs when an employee is subject to sexual harassment. As sexual harassment cases may involve both employees and non-employees in a number of different circumstances, this topic is discussed at greater length in the next section.

SEXUAL HARASSMENT

Title VII also protects against **sexual harassment** in employment. EEOC guidelines on sexual harassment apply the general principles of Title VII to employers and supervisors irrespective of whether the sexually harassing acts are authorized. Sexual harassment actions are generally classified as either quid pro quo or hostile environment harassment. Sexual harassment can involve harassment by a person of either gender, and same-sex harassment is prohibited to the same extent as harassment aimed at the opposite sex. In a 1998 case, the U.S. Supreme Court said that nothing in Title VII necessarily bars a sex discrimination claim merely because the

---

3. *Anderson v. U.S.F. Logistics*, 274 F. 3d 470 (7th Cir., 2001).
4. 42 U.S.C. sec. 2000 et. seq.

plaintiff and defendant are of the same sex.[5] The case reversed lower court decisions that said Title VII did not grant a cause of action to a male who was being harassed by male coworkers.

Quid pro Quo Harassment

Quid pro quo means that one person receives something in exchange for something else. Thus, **quid pro quo harassment** occurs when an employment benefit such as a promotion, favorable performance rating, desired job assignment, or bonus payment is given in exchange for sexual favors. An employee experiences harassment when unwelcome sexual advances are encountered, requests for sexual favors are received, or verbal or physical conduct of a sexual nature is received. If the overall circumstances either explicitly or implicitly suggest that submission to the sexual advances is a term or condition of employment, those actions would constitute quid pro quo sexual harassment. A right of action also arises if an employee is denied a promotion or a pay raise because a less qualified person who did grant sexual favors was promoted instead.

In quid pro quo cases, an employer is liable for harassment of an employee by a supervisor or manager even if the employer did not know about the harassment. Thus, lack of knowledge of the harassment is not a defense for the employer.

Hostile Environment Harassment

Hostile environment harassment occurs when the workplace is permeated with intimidation, ridicule, and insult that is sufficiently severe or pervasive to create an abusive working environment. Even less blatant actions may constitute sexual harassment. Most hostile environment cases involve an employer's responsibility for actions of supervisors who harass employees. Employers that know or should know about the sexually harassing acts of supervisors or employees may be held responsible and liable for damages if they fail to take appropriate corrective action.

In the late 1990s, Mitsubishi Motors Manufacturing of America, Inc. was involved in a long-running and notorious case brought by the EEOC. In 1996, the EEOC sued Mitsubishi and claimed that more than 400 men sexually harassed more than 300 female employees by grouping them, calling them "bitches" and "whores," and drawing female body parts on car fenders. The EEOC said the sexual harassment was pervasive, persistent, and defended by the plant manager, who retaliated against complainers. In 1997, 29 female employees received $10 million from Mitsubishi to settle a separate private lawsuit. The next year, its executive vice president apologized and settled with the EEOC. Mitsubishi agreed to pay $34 million, the largest sexual harassment settlement ever obtained.

The Internet, E-Mail, and Sexual Harassment

Courts have made it clear that a pervasive and hostile work environment that is sexually harassing may exist if a supervisor introduces pornography into the workplace via the Internet. In *Coniglio v. City of Berwyn, Illinois*, the plaintiff, and several of her colleagues, complained that her supervisor frequently viewed pictures of topless women on his computer monitor and that she also observed him viewing pictures of completely naked women on Internet websites. She said she saw them when she went into his office and also from outside his office because of the picture window in his office wall. The court noted that a jury would have to evaluate the frequency and duration of the supervisor's conduct, but such conduct could constitute the cre-

5. *Oncale v. Sundown Offshore Services, Inc.*, 523 U.S. 75 (1998).

Commentary

Insurance Premiums Against Harassment and Discrimination Are on the Rise

According to an article in the January 09, 2002, *New York Times*, referred to by the HRnext website, http://www.hrnext.com/news/view.cfm?news_id=1811, insurance premiums for policies against harassment or discrimination suits from employees are doubling and even tripling, with some insurers simply opting to quit the business. The premiums had underestimated both the number of small awards and the growing size of jury verdicts, one-fifth of which are for $1 million or more.

Michael Maloney, an executive with Chubb, one of the largest providers of such insurance, said, "Premiums could double or triple at some large companies that already pay hundred of thousands of dollars a year." Roughly 30% of companies surveyed in 1999 by the Society for Human Resource Management had some sort of employment practices liability coverage. In the beginning, insurers were all too happy to cover companies without paying too much attention to whether the companies were at significant risk for lawsuits. Analysts and consultants told the *Times* that since the insurers accumulated some experience, they are beginning to charge more, which is leading firms to take potential harassment or discrimination seriously.

ation of a hostile work environment in violation of Title VII. As the mayor, the supervisor's boss, had been informed of the problem, the city could be held liable.[6] Although a number of companies have adopted policies and purchased insurance to cover their legal risks, there are signs that both insurers and the companies they cover are more aware of the importance of these problems.

Employer Defenses in Sexual Harassment Cases

When is an employer liable for harassment of an employee by a supervisor or by a coworker? Does the employer need to have knowledge of the harassment to be liable? Does it matter if the employer has established policies for harassed employees to follow? Would an employer still be liable if an employee does not follow those procedures? These questions were answered by the U.S. Supreme Court in the *Faragher* case that follows. That case and a companion case decided the same day provide some guidelines for employers seeking to prevent or defend against sexual harassment claims.

Faragher v. City of Boca Raton

524 U.S. 775 (1998)
U.S. Supreme Court

Facts. Beth Faragher worked for the City of Boca Raton, Florida, as an ocean lifeguard during various periods from September 1985 to June 1990. Faragher alleged that two supervisors, Terry and Silverman, had subjected her to unwanted sexual advances, including touching her on her shoulder and waist, patting her thigh, and slapping her buttocks. She was also subjected to unwanted verbal sexual comments. Another female lifeguard was treated similarly. Neither woman complained to the city's recreation department, but they did speak to one of their supervisors in a personal capacity. That supervisor never passed on the information he received.

In 1992 Faragher sued the city, alleging it was liable under Title VII for her supervisors' sexual harassment. She

6. 2000 U.S.Dist. LEXIS 9841 (D.C., N.D. Il., 2000).

also argued that the harassment was pervasive and that the city had constructive knowledge of her hostile work environment. The city argued that the supervisors were acting in their personal capacity and that it did not know of the harassment. It noted that when another lifeguard wrote a letter to the city to complain of the advances of her supervisors, the city investigated and reprimanded them. The trial court held for Faragher, the court of appeals reversed and held for the city and Faragher brought this appeal.

Legal Issue. Can a city be held liable for sexual harassment of employees by supervisors if the supervisors did not follow city policy (in part because they were not informed of its requirements) and the employees did not complain to the city through established channels for grievances?

Opinion. Justice Souter. We have repeatedly made clear that although the statute [Title VII] mentions specific employment decisions with immediate consequences, the scope of the prohibition includes sexual harassment so "severe or pervasive" as to "alter the condition of the victim's employment and create an abusive work environment."

The proper analysis here calls . . . for an enquiry into the reasons that would support a conclusion that the harassing behavior ought to be held within the scope of a supervisor's employment, and the reasons for the opposite view. In the case before us, a justification for holding the offensive behavior within the scope of Terry's and Silverman's employment was well put in Judge Barker's dissent: A pervasive hostile work environment of sexual harassment is never (one would hope) authorized, but the supervisor is clearly charged with maintaining a productive, safe work environment. The supervisor directs and controls the conduct of the employees, and the manner of doing so may inure to the employer's benefit or detriment, including subjecting the employer to Title VII liability. It is by now well recognized that hostile environment sexual harassment by supervisors (and, for that matter co-employees) is a persistent problem in the workplace. One might justify the burden of the untoward behavior to the employer as one of the costs of doing business, to be charged to the enterprise rather than the victim.

Two things counsel us to draw the contrary conclusion. First, there is no reason to suppose that Congress wished courts to ignore the traditional distinction between acts falling within the scope and acts amounting to what the older law called frolics or detours from the course of employment. The second reason goes to an even broader unanimity of views among the holdings of District Courts and Courts of Appeals thus far. These courts have held not only that the sort of harassment at issue here was outside the scope of supervisors' authority, but by uniformly judging employer liability for co-worker harassment under a negligence standard, they have also implicitly treated such harassment as outside the scope of common employees' duties as well.

Faragher points to several ways in which the agency relationship aided Terry and Silverman in carrying out their harassment. She argues that in general offending supervisors can abuse their authority to keep subordinates in their presence while they make offensive statements. . . . We agree that in implementing Title VII it makes sense to hold an employer vicariously liable for some tortious conduct of a supervisor made possible by abuse of his supervisory authority.

In order to accommodate the principle of vicarious liability for harm caused by misuse of supervisory authority, as well as Title VII's equally basic policies of encouraging forethought by employers and saving actions by objecting employees, we adopt the following holding in this case and in Burlington Industries also decided today. An employer is subject to vicarious liability to a victimized employee for an actionable hostile environment created by a supervisor with immediate authority over the employee. When no tangible employment action [such as firing, denial of promotion] is taken, a defending employer may raise an affirmative defense to liability or damages: that (a) the employer exercised reasonable care to prevent and correct any sexually harassing behavior, and (b) that the plaintiff employee unreasonably failed to take advantage of any preventative or corrective opportunities provided by the employer or to avoid harm otherwise.

Decision. Applying these rules here, we believe the judgment of the Court of Appeals must be reversed. The District Court found that the degree of hostility in the work environment rose to actionable level and was attributable to Terry and Silverman. These supervisors were granted virtually unchecked authority over their subordinates. The District Court found the City had entirely failed to disseminate its policy against sexual harassment among the beach employees and its officials made no attempt to keep track of the conduct of supervisors like Terry and Silverman. The City's policy also did not include any assurance that the harassing supervisor could be bypassed in registering complaints.

Case Questions

1. What two guidelines emerge from this case for employers to follow regarding conduct by supervisors?
2. Why do you think the Court concludes that the acts of the supervisors here are within the scope of their authority?

Employer Liability for Sexual Harassment by Nonemployees

Under some circumstances, an employer can be held liable for sexual harassment of an employee by a person who is not an employee. For example, if a customer or supplier with whom an employee has frequent contact is harassing the employee, the employer, who exerts some control over the harassing party, may be held liable. Of course, if the employer has no control over the actions of the harassing party, it could not be held liable for that person's actions.

Lockard v. Pizza Hut, Inc.

Court of Appeals (10th Cir.)
162 F.3d 1062 (1998)

Facts. Renal Lockard, a waitress at a Colorado Pizza Hut restaurant, brought suit against Pizza Hut, Inc., and A & M Food Services, Inc., asserting claims under Title VII for hostile work environment sexual harassment. On one occasion prior to the incident in question, she had waited on two crude and rowdy male customers who had made sexually offensive remarks to her, such as " I would like to get in your pants." At that time she informed her supervisor, Jack, that she did not want to wait on them, but there is no record that she told him why or what they said.

When these two men came into the restaurant on November 6, the wait staff, including young male waiters, argued over who would seat them because no one on the staff wanted to serve them. Jack instructed Lockard to wait on them. After being seated, one of the customers commented that she smelled good and asked what kind of cologne she was wearing. After she responded that it was none of his business, the customer grabbed her by the hair. She informed Jack that she did not want to continue waiting on them, but he refused, saying, "You were hired to be a waitress. You waitress."

She returned to the table, and when she reached to put beer on the table, the customer pulled her to him by her hair, grabbed her breast, and put his mouth on her breast. At that point, Lockard told Jack she was quitting; she called her husband, who picked her up. The next day, Selby, the manager of that Pizza Hut unit, questioned her. She offered Lockard a job as a production person that would not require her to be in contact with any customers, but Lockard declined. Lockard's resignation form included Selby's note that she was "sexually harassed by a customer and got understandably upset and quit."

Lockard filed a complaint with the EEOC and then sued Pizza Hut. Pizza Hut claimed it was not responsible for the conduct of customers. The trial court found for Lockard, awarding her $200,000 in compensatory damages and $37,000 in attorneys' fees, and Pizza Hut appealed.

Legal Issue. Can an employer, who has notice of actions of customers that could create an abusive environment for an employee, be liable for failure to remedy the creation of a hostile work environment?

Opinion. Chief Judge Seymour. The conduct of these customers on November 6 was more than a mere offensive utterance. Grabbing Ms. Lockard's hair and breast is physically threatening and humiliating behavior which unreasonably interfered with her ability to perform her duties as a waitress. Defendants argue that the physically threatening conduct of these two customers was simply a one-time incident and thus not pervasive enough to create an abusive environment. Conduct is actionable if it is sufficiently severe or pervasive. We therefore disagree with defendants' assertion that a single incident can never be sufficient to create an abusive environment. Looking at all the circumstances, we are persuaded the record contains sufficient evidence to support the jury's conclusion that the harassing conduct created an actionable hostile work environment.

Defendant asserts that even if a hostile environment was created, an employer cannot be held vicariously liable for the harassing conduct of customers. We have not yet ruled on this issue and must therefore decide whether Title VII applies to acts of harassment by customers. If we answer in the affirmative, we must then determine the appropriate standard of employee liability for non-employee harassment and determine whether Ms. Lockard has satisfied this standard.

The regulations specifically provide that an employer may be responsible for the acts of non-employees where the employer or its agents knows or should have known of the conduct and fails to take immediate and corrective action. The focus of the inquiry in a hostile work environment claim is whether the workplace is permeated with discriminatory intimidation, ridicule and insult. An employer who condones or tolerates the creation of such an environment should be held liable regardless of whether the environment was created by an employee or a non-employee, since the employer ultimately controls the conditions of the work environment.

Mr. Jack clearly had authority over Ms. Lockard and her co-workers. [Also] Mr. Jack had control over the working environment and the ability to alter those conditions to a substantial degree. Ms. Lockard had informed Mr. Jack of the hair-pulling incident and had told him on several occasions that she did not wish to serve these customers.

Decision. We hold that this information was sufficient to place Mr. Jack on notice that these customers were likely to sexually harass Ms. Lockard. Instead of following the guidelines set forth in Pizza Hut's policy manual, Mr. Jack ordered Ms. Lockard to continue waiting on the two customers. Because Mr. Jack had notice of the customers' harassing conduct and failed to remedy or prevent the hostile work environment, the defendant is liable for Mr. Jack's failure.

Case Questions

1. What is the primary reason that the court finds Pizza Hut liable for the conduct of its customers?
2. Although the case excerpt omits the court's discussion of the guidelines in Pizza Hut's policy manual, what policies would you want to include in a manual that might guide managers in dealing with a situation like this one?

STATUTORY EXCEPTIONS TO TITLE VII

There are three major statutory exceptions to prohibited discrimination under Title VII. These exceptions permit employers to discriminate against employees on the basis of sex, age, national origin, and religion and sometimes on the basis of race. The exceptions are (1) bona fide occupational qualification, (2) professionally developed aptitude tests, and (3) valid nondiscriminatory seniority systems.

Bona Fide Occupational Qualification

The first major statutory exception to Title VII permits an employer to discriminate where religion, national origin, or sex is a **bona fide occupational qualification** (BFOQ). Discrimination is permitted if an applicant's membership in one of these protected classes is a **business necessity** and employment of people from other groups would undermine the business. The employer must prove that hiring people outside the BFOQ class entails more than mere inconvenience. Race or color discrimination is never justified by a BFOQ.

Religious institutions may validly require that candidates for certain jobs have certain religious characteristics. For example, a Methodist church wanting to hire a Sunday school teacher could require that person to be a Methodist. Kosher slaughterhouses may require their butchers to be Jewish. Female models may be required to display women's fashions. Fluency in a particular language may be necessary for tour guides or for people working with the public or with coworkers.

BFOQs are not granted easily by the courts; the employer must show absolute business necessity to invoke these exceptions. For example, airlines may not insist on female flight attendants, even though females may be superior to males in providing reassurance to anxious passengers, giving courteous personalized service, or making flights more pleasurable. Similarly, the preference of gourmet restaurant customers for male waiters or other restaurants for female waitresses does not justify a BFOQ for males or females only.

A suit against Hooters restaurant by men seeking to be servers was contested by Hooters because it said the restaurant and its female servers provided entertainment as well as food. The case was settled out of court when Hooters paid the plaintiffs and their attorneys $3.75 million and agreed to create more nonserving jobs for men. Similarly, ethnic restaurants may not insist on waiters or waitresses of a particular national origin by arguing that they create a better ambience.

A valid BFOQ can require female locker room attendants in a female exercise club. By contrast, it is discriminatory to exclude female sportswriters from the male locker rooms of professional sports teams. This is probably because sportswriters spend only short times in the locker room, but locker room attendants spend nearly all their work hours there.

Professionally Developed Ability Tests

The second major exception to the prohibitions of Title VII permits employers to discriminate on the basis of an applicant's performance on professionally developed ability tests. The employer may require certain education qualifications or require demonstration of the skills needed on the job. These qualifications must be directly related to the job and constitute a business necessity. The qualifications or tests must be validated as accurate and reliable predictors of job performance. These requirements make it difficult for employers to use tests that are not scientifically designed or have not been proven to offer direct evidence of successful job performance.

The EEOC has issued guidelines to assist employers in designing valid tests. Tests that have an adverse impact on a protected class must be validated by any one of three test validation methods. The first requires that criterion validity be established. Tests with criterion validity demonstrate a strong statistical relationship between test results and observed job performance. Content validity exists when the test contains a representative sample of the job tasks that are part of the job description. Construct validity exists when the test measures the characteristics that are useful on the job. For example, a typing or keyboarding test would exhibit both criterion and content validity for a word processing position. The test would identify those applicants with good keyboard skills when using a keyboard is the primary job activity. Construct validity might exist for a test to establish a police officer's emotional stability or leadership ability, and a psychological test that demonstrates these traits might serve this purpose.

The EEOC guidelines require employers to publish job descriptions that carefully catalogue the tasks required for each job. The employer may use only tests that validly discriminate between applicants who can and cannot accomplish the tasks listed in a job description. This requirement leads to greater precision in specifying job characteristics.

Seniority System

The third major Title VII exception permits job discrimination pursuant to a bona fide seniority system if it is not designed to discriminate. In decisions to lay off, promote, or give merit raises, employers may legitimately discriminate in favor of more senior employees if the union contract includes a seniority provision. Such provisions are intended to eliminate favoritism and permit the employer to retain more experienced employees.

Some seniority systems tend to perpetuate the effects of discrimination because the newest workers were typically hired under conditions of less discrimination than existed when many of the older workers were hired. During times of economic downturn, more recently hired workers are laid off first, even though they represent higher percentages of protected class members. Nevertheless, as the following case illustrates, bona fide seniority systems prevail over anti-discrimination laws.

International Brotherhood of Teamsters v. United States

431 U.S. 324 (1977)
United States Supreme Court

Facts. The United States sued the Teamsters Union and a trucking company employer, alleging a pattern or practice of discrimination against blacks and persons with Spanish surnames who were hired in lower-paying and less desirable driving jobs than the people hired to be long-haul and over-the-road drivers. The collective bargaining agreement between the employer and the Teamsters Union provided for a seniority system that perpetuated and locked in the effects of past discrimination.

The district court ordered the union to take steps to reduce this discrimination. Then the court of appeals reversed the district court's decision but gave retroactive seniority to blacks and Hispanics to secure the better jobs. The union appealed to the Supreme Court.

Legal Issue. Can a union, pursuant to the terms of a collective bargaining agreement, use a bona fide seniority system to assign employee/union members to desirable jobs even if doing so discriminates against "Title VII protected class" employees?

Opinion. Justice Stewart. The primary purpose of Title VII was "to assure equality of employment opportunities and to eliminate those discriminatory practices and devices which have fostered racially stratified job environments to the disadvantage of minority citizens." To achieve this purpose, Congress "proscribe[d] not only overt discrimination but also practices that are fair in form, but discriminatory in operation." Thus, the Court has repeatedly held that a prima facie Title VII violation may be established by policies or practices that are neutral on their face and in intent but that nonetheless discriminate in effect against a particular group.

The heart of the seniority system in this case is its allocation of the choicest jobs, the greatest protection against layoffs, and other advantages to those employees who have been line drivers for the longest time. Where, because of the employer's prior intentional discrimination, the line drivers with the longest tenure are without exception white, the advantages of the seniority system flow disproportionately to them and away from Negro and Spanish-surnamed employees who might by now have enjoyed those advantages had not the employer discriminated before the passage of the Act. This disproportionate distribution of advantages does in a very real sense "operate to 'freeze' the status quo of prior discriminatory employment practices."

Although a seniority system inevitably tends to perpetuate the effects of pre-Act discrimination in such cases, the congressional judgment was that Title VII should not outlaw the use of existing seniority lists and thereby destroy or water down the vested seniority rights of employees simply because their employer had engaged in discrimination prior to the passage of the Act.

The seniority system in this litigation is entirely bona fide. It applies equally to all races and ethnic groups. To the extent that it "locks" employees into non-line-driver jobs, it does so for all. The city drivers and servicemen who are discouraged from transferring to line-driver jobs are not all Negroes or Spanish-surnamed Americans; to the contrary, the overwhelming majority are white.

The placing of line drivers in a separate bargaining unit from other employees is rational, in accord with the industry practice, and consistent with National Labor Relations Board precedent. It is conceded that the seniority system was negotiated and has been maintained free from any illegal purpose. In these circumstances, the single fact that the system extends no retroactive seniority to pre-Act discriminates does not make it unlawful.

Decision. The union's conduct in agreeing to and maintaining the system did not violate Title VII. On remand, the District Court's injunction against the union must be vacated.

Case Questions

1. How could a seniority system have a discriminatory effect?
2. Does the Civil Rights Act permit seniority systems that might arguably have a discriminatory effect?
3. How can a seniority system be designed to avoid a claim of discrimination?

THE AGE DISCRIMINATION IN EMPLOYMENT ACT

APPLICATION OF ACT

Although discrimination on the basis of an employee's age is not a prohibited activity under Title VII, discrimination against people 40 years of age and older is protected under the Age Discrimination in Employment Act of 1967. The act applies to both public and private employees with 20 or more employees. Because the act applies to all people who attain the age of 40 and who then work for a covered employer, most people will be members of this protected group.

Numerous age discrimination claims have been brought by middle-aged professional workers dismissed in favor of equally qualified but lower-paid younger workers. Some employers prefer younger workers to older ones because seniority systems tend to raise wage costs with age. Some employers insist on the perceived strength and appearance of younger workers. However, researchers find that older workers usually have more experience and greater loyalty than do younger workers.

PROOF OF AGE AS A FACTOR

An employee who claims age discrimination must prove that the employer's action was motivated, at least in part, by age bias. If layoff or firing decisions are made on the basis of cost savings achieved by targeting higher-salaried workers, even though salaries are closely correlated with age, there is no violation of the law. However, if the employee can show relevant correspondence or comments that relate to age as a factor in the employer's actions, age discrimination can be proven.

An employer may impose physical fitness standards that are directly related to job activities without violating the law, even though few people in the protected class may meet the standard. For example, if public safety is involved, performance tests may be used even if they result in hiring fewer employees over age 40 (i.e., as bus drivers, pilots, firefighters, or police officers). Although it once seemed justifiable to require all employees to retire at age 65, federal law now prohibits this employer rule for most employees.

AGE DISCRIMINATION AND TWO MEMBERS OF THE PROTECTED CLASS

What if a person over the age of 40 is discriminated against by not being promoted, but the promotion goes to another person who is also over that age and in the protected group? Is the employer still liable for age discrimination? Consider the comment of U.S. Supreme Court in *O'Connor v. Consolidated Coin Caterers Corp.* (517 U.S. 308) 1996:

The discrimination prohibited by the ADEA is discrimination "because of an individual's age," though prohibition is "limited to individuals who are least 40 years of age." This language does not ban discrimination against employees because they are aged 40 or older; it bans discrimination against employees because of their age, but limits the protected class to those who are 40 or older. The fact that one person in the protected class has lost out to another person in the protected class is thus irrelevant, so long as he lost out because of his age. *Because ADEA prohibits discrimination on the basis of age, and not class membership [i.e., 40 or over], the fact that a replacement is substantially younger than the plaintiff is a far more reliable indicator of age discrimination than is the fact the plaintiff was replaced by someone outside [i.e., under age 40] the protected class.*

REMEDIES

The primary remedy for a wronged plaintiff is recovery of lost wages and/or reinstatement in a job. The act does not explicitly provide for compensatory damages to address the damage or injury done to the plaintiff. Nevertheless, most courts award damages to a wronged plaintiff in some situations. Consider the language of the court, and the other court cases it refers to, regarding the ADEA and its relationship to some other labor and employment statutes.

Eggleston v. South Bend Community School Board

858 F.Supp. 841 (1994)
Federal District Court for the Northern District of Indiana

Facts. Eggleston, a high school teacher and football coach employed by the South Bend School Corporation, filed an age discrimination case with the EEOC in 1988, asserting he had been denied a teaching position because of his age. The EEOC supported his claim, and in March 1990, it, the plaintiff, and the School Corporation entered into a conciliation agreement stating that Eggleston would be hired as a permanent teacher for the 1990–91 year and that there would be no discrimination or retaliation of any kind, including consideration for coaching positions. During the next several years, the plaintiff encountered numerous problems and harassment, leading him to file several charges of retaliation with the EEOC and then with the district court. The defendant said that, as the plaintiff's job had not changed, it had not violated the ADEA.

Legal Issue. Is an employer who retaliates against an employee who has filed an ADEA claim liable for creating a hostile environment even if the employee's job and salary have not been adversely affected?

Opinion. Judge Sharp. The plaintiff's prima facie case is based on the ADEA provision that says: "It shall be unlawful for an employer to discriminate against any of his employees . . . because the employee has opposed any practice made unlawful by this section, or because the employee has made a charge in an investigation, proceeding, or hearing under this chapter." The EEOC, as amicus curiae [friend of the court], argues that by retaliating against Eggleston, the defendant has created a "hostile environment" that constitutes discrimination regardless of whether the plaintiff has suffered a change in his job status.

The EEOC argues that the U.S. Supreme Court in *Vinson* found that a hostile work environment violates Title VII's prohibition against "discrimination in the terms, conditions, or privileges of employment." It then notes that the ADEA makes it unlawful for an employer to discriminate against any individual "with respect to his compensation, terms, condition, or privileges of employment," because of such individual's age. This language is identical to Title VII's prohibition against discrimination "on the basis of race, color, religion, sex, or national origin."

This court finds that a claim based on a hostile environment is viable under the ADEA. The Supreme Court [*Lorillard v. Pons,* 434 U.S. 575 (1978)] has noted the similarities between the two statutes and indicated that "the prohibitions of the ADEA were derived . . . from Title VII. Having found that an ADEA claim based on a hostile environment is feasible, this court must ascertain whether the plaintiff's claim is viable. [After referring to several incidents and remarks of other administrators about Eggleston, the court said:] This court finds the plaintiff has presented a viable claim, and this creates a rebuttable presumption of retaliation and the burden shifts to the defendant. If the employer articulates a legitimate nondiscriminatory reason for the retaliation, the burden shifts back to the employee to show that the employer's proffered reasons are pretext. We note that the employee here seeks compensatory damages for his pain and suffering.

In two court of appeals cases, the courts said. "This court notes that 'the ADEA is in some sense a hybrid of Title VII and the Fair Labor Standards Act; the prohibitions in the ADEA generally follow Title VII, but the remedies are those of the FLSA. Neither the original Act nor the 1978 amendments explicitly address the issue of compensatory damages for pain and suffering.' " [The court then noted that most ADEA case interpretations allow the award of compensatory but not punitive damages.]

Decision. Therefore, This Court finds the plaintiff has a viable claim based on the retaliation provisions of the ADEA and can seek compensatory, but not punitive damages. This case is set for jury trial.

Case Questions

1. In what way is the ADEA like Title VII, and in what way is it like the Fair Labor Standards Act?
2. What is the remedy for a plaintiff who has not been paid the minimum wage by an employer pursuant to the Fair Labor Standards Act? What is the remedy for a plaintiff who is discriminated against according to the ADEA? Are they comparable? Why or why not?
3. If Eggleston still has his job, on what basis can you argue that he is being discriminated against in his employment?

DISCRIMINATION AGAINST PERSONS WITH DISABILITIES

Title VII did not originally include handicapped workers as a protected class. In 1973, Congress passed the Vocational Rehabilitation Act, which requires employers that receive federal contracts to consider handicapped job applicants. Employers covered by the act must consider hiring a handicapped applicant if a job can be performed after a **reasonable accommodation** has been made, permitting the minimum level of performance. Note that employers are not required to hire unqualified handicapped workers.

Handicaps are physical or mental impairments that substantially limit one or more person's major life activities. Handicaps that result from diabetes, epilepsy, deafness, disfigurement, heart disease, cancer, retardation, blindness, paraplegia, quadriplegia, alcoholism, or drug abuse are protected by the act. If a handicap does not adversely affect successful job performance, the employer may not take it into consideration in offering employment.

For example, people with communicable diseases may be "handicapped" under the Vocational Rehabilitation Act and receive its protections. In *School Board of Nassau County Florida v. Arline,*[7] Arline was discharged from her position as a teacher after her inactive tuberculosis again became active. The Supreme Court held that because the risk of transmitting the disease was slight, Arline was still qualified as a teacher. Employers must make reasonable accommodation for diseased employees to continue employment.

DISABILITY

The Americans with Disabilities Act of 1990 (ADA) expanded the coverage of the Rehabilitation Act to most private employers. The definition of **disability** was broadened to include additional mental and physical handicaps. It focuses on whether a person has or is regarded as having a physical or mental impairment that substantially limits one or more of that person's major life activities.

ONLINE

Find the text ofthe ADA at **http://www.usdoj.gov/crt/ada/pubs/ada.txt**

In a case decided at the beginning of 2002, the Supreme Court sought to clarify the meaning of the term *disability.*

7. 480 U.S. 273 (1987).

Toyota Motor Mfg., Ky., Inc. v. Williams

534 U.S. 184 (2002)
United States Supreme Court

Facts. Williams worked at Toyota's engine fabrication plant in Georgetown, Kentucky, handling pneumatic tools. The use of tools eventually caused pain in her hands, wrists, and arms that was diagnosed as carpal tunnel syndrome and bilateral tendinitis. She was then assigned to modified jobs for several years before being reassigned to work on a team in quality-control inspection operations. There, she was required to hold her hands and arms up at shoulder height for several hours at a time. After she again experienced pain, she was diagnosed with thoracic outlet compression and soon began missing work on a regular basis. After being placed on a no-work-of-any kind restriction by her physicians, she was terminated for poor attendance. She filed suit with the EEOC and, after receiving a right to sue letter, filed suit against the defendant for failing to reasonably accommodate her disability in violation of the Americans with Disabilities Act. The trial court granted Toyota a motion for summary judgment on the basis that the plaintiff had not been disabled as defined by the ADA. The Court of Appeals reversed, finding she had suffered a disability in performing manual tasks at her work. Toyota appealed to the Supreme Court.

Legal Issue. Is a person "disabled" as defined in the Americans with Disabilities Act if (s)he is unable to perform tasks associated with a specific job even though being able to perform those tasks is central to a person's daily life?

Opinion. Justice O'Connor. The ADA requires covered entities, including private employers, to provide reasonable accommodations to the known physical or mental limitations of an otherwise qualified individual with a disability . . . unless it can demonstrate that the accommodation would impose an undue hardship. The act defines a disability as a physical or mental impairment that substantially limits one or more of the major life activities of such individual . . . To qualify under the ADA's definition of disability, a claimant must initially prove that he or she has a physical or mental impairment.

Merely having an impairment does not make one disabled for purposes of the ADA. A claimant must also demonstrate that the impairment limits a major life activity. The HEW Rehabilitation Act regulations provide a list of "major life activities," that includes "walking, seeing, hearing," and, as relevant here, "performing manual tasks." To qualify as disabled, a claimant must further show that the limitation on the major life activity is "substantial." According to EEOC regulations, "substantially limited" means unable to perform a particular major life activity that the average person in the general population can perform.

The parties do not dispute that respondent's medical conditions, which include carpal tunnel syndrome and thoracic outlet compression, amount to physical impairments. The relevant question is whether the Sixth Circuit correctly analyzed whether these impairments limited respondent in the major life activity of performing manual task. "Substantially" in the phrase "substantially limits" suggests considerable or to a large degree. "Major" in the phrase "major life activities" means important. "Major life activities" thus refers to those activities that are of central importance to daily life. We therefore hold that to be substantially limited in performing manual task, an individual must have an impairment that prevents or severely restricts the individual from doing activities that are of central importance to most people's daily lives.

It is insufficient for individuals attempting to prove disability status under this test to merely submit evidence of a medical diagnosis of an impairment. Instead, the ADA requires "those claiming the Act's protection . . . to prove a disability by offering evidence that the extent of the limitations in terms of their own experience . . . is substantial. An individual assessment of the effect of an impairment is particularly necessary when the impairment is one whose symptoms vary widely from person to person. Carpal tunnel syndrome, one of respondent's impairments, is just such a condition. Studies have shown that, even without surgical treatment, one quarter of carpal tunnel cases resolve in one month, but in 22 percent of cases, symptoms last for eight years or longer.

Even assuming that working is a major life activity, a claimant would be required to show an inability to work "in a broad range of jobs," rather than a specific job. With respect to the major life activity of *working*, the term *substantially limits* means significantly restricted in the ability to perform either a class of jobs or a broad range of jobs in various classes compared to the average person having comparable training, skills and abilities. When addressing the major life activity of performing manual tasks, the central inquiry must be whether the claimant is unable to perform the variety of tasks central to most people's daily lives, not whether the claimant is unable to perform the task associated with her specific job. Even more critically, the manual tasks unique to any particular job are not necessarily important parts of most people's lives. As a result, occupational-specific tasks may have only a limited relevance to the manual task inquiry. Household chores, bathing, and brushing one's teeth are among the tasks of central importance to people's daily lives and should have been part of the assessment of whether respondent was substantially limited in performing manual task.

Decision. As the trial court did not focus on the plaintiff's ability to perform the tasks that are most central to most peoples' daily lives, we reverse the Court of Appeals' judgment granting partial summary judgment to the respondent and remand the case for further proceedings consistent with this opinion.

Case Questions

1. What type of evidence would you offer if you were claiming a disability? Would a doctor's opinioin be important? Why?
2. Will application of this test make it easier or more difficult for the plaintiff to prove a disability? What might be the impact of this decision on other disability cases?
3. What three things must the plaintiff prove to show she is disabled under the ADA's definition?

EMPLOYER INQUIRIES

Employers are limited in their ability to make disability-related inquiries or to require medical examinations at three stages: before an employment offer, after an employment offer, and during employment. For example, an employer cannot require an applicant to undergo a medical examination prior to offering that person a position. However, once an offer is extended, a medical exam can be required, if the requirement is imposed on all employees entering the same job category.

After employment begins, such inquiries and examinations may be made only if they are "job-related and consistent with business necessity." Tests to determine illegal drug usage or physical agility related to job performance are not subject to the ADA policies. Blood, urine, and breath analyses and psychological tests are considered "medical examinations."

REASONABLE ACCOMMODATION AND UNDUE HARDSHIP

Employers are required to make reasonable accommodation to an employee's disability, as long as doing so does not cause the employer undue hardship. The first key concept is that of reasonable accommodation, which requires the employer to accommodate an employee in the performance of his or her job. It does not, however, generally require the employer to assign an employee to another shift or another supervisor. The second key concept is that of undue hardship. If the accommodation requires significant expense or would affect a large number of persons, the employer would probably be considered to suffer undue hardship. A waitress who suffered from stress and anxiety on the job asked to be assigned to less stressful work hours, but almost all times were stressful at the restaurant, and reassigning her would have imposed hardship on a number of other waitresses. The court denied her claim of discrimination because the remedy she wanted would cause undue hardship to her employer.

The ADA makes all Title VII remedies and procedures available to people with disabilities. Thus, basing employment decisions on an applicant or employee's disability is prohibited. Discrimination may occur in job application or hiring procedures, compensation, job training, promotions, or discharge activities. The ADA also imposes a duty on employers and operators of public facilities to provide reasonable accommodation to the disabled; employers must make work stations usable by handicapped employees as long as no undue hardship is imposed. Operators of public facilities such as motels, hotels, restaurants, theaters, passenger trains, buses, and retail stores must ensure that their premises accommodate the disabled with reasonable access.

The EEOC has issued enforcement guidelines on what constitutes reasonable accommodation and undue hardship. The types of reasonable accommodation include (1) modifications of adjustments to a *job application process* so that a qualified applicant with a disability can be considered for a position, (2) modifications to the *work environment* or how the work is normally performed so that a qualified individual with a disability could perform the essential functions of the position, and (3) modifications that enable an employee with a disability *to enjoy equal benefits* and privileges of employment.

Undue hardship should be based on the nature of and cost of the accommodation needed, the financial resources of the facility making the accommodation, and the impact of the accommodation on the operation of the facility. The EEOC guidelines reject using a cost-benefit analysis that compares the cost to the employer and the benefit to the employee. Instead, the undue hardship depends only on the employers resources, not on the status or salary of the employee.

Ethical Issue

Is Genetic Testing of Employees by an Employer Ethical? Does It Violate the ADA?

In April 2001, the U.S. Equal Employment Opportunity Commission settled a court action that represented its first challenge to the use of workplace genetic testing under the ADA.

The EEOC had brought suit against Burlington Northern and Santa Fe Railroad Company. The company admitted it was performing genetic testing on about 25% of the 130 employees who had filed claims against the company claiming a disability because of the repetitive motion injury carpal tunnel syndrome. The company wanted to see if the employees had a predisposition to suffer from the condition.

The EEOC case was based on the section of the ADA that bars employment decisions based not on an individual's actual physical or mental disabilities but on the basis of medical problems that the employer "regards" as a disability. Since 1995, the EEOC has interpreted the ADA to apply if an employer conducts genetic tests to uncover an individual's propensity toward developing what is perceived as a serious illness.

According to EEOC Chairwoman Ida Castro, only a few charges involving genetic testing have been filed to date. She notes that genetic testing of current employees is theoretically possible under the ADA if it is "work-related" and a "business necessity" but that those terms have yet to be analyzed by an appellate court.

In addition to the ADA, 26 states have enacted laws to protect against on-the-job genetic testing. The states are trying to stop problems before they occur. Even though only 2 of more than 1,600 companies queried in a survey published by the American Management Association said they engaged in true genetic testing in the year 2000, more than 15% admitted to using some kind of medical tests to uncover employees' susceptibility to workplace hazards.

A 1998 case, *Bloodsaw v. Lawrence Berkeley Laboratory* (135 F.3d 1260), involved administrative employees at a research facility operated at the University of California. They were secretly tested during a pre-employment examination for their propensity to develop sickle cell anemia. The court of appeals said they could pursue their claim based on invasion of privacy rights but not on violation of the ADA. The case was settled for $2.2 million.

Do you think there are some cases where employers could legally and ethically use genetic testing on some (or all) of its employees? What situations could meet the "work related" or "business necessity" test? How would you feel about this as an employee? As an employer?

ENFORCEMENT OF THE ANTIDISCRIMINATION LAWS

The Equal Employment Opportunity Commission (EEOC) was created by the Civil Rights Act of 1964 and was granted additional powers by the Equal Opportunity Act of 1972 and the ADA in 1990. The EEOC may investigate, conciliate, and litigate grievances filed by existing and prospective employees who claim violation of the various employment discrimination laws. It is also authorized to issue rules implementing the various antidiscrimination laws. Approximately 45 states have similar fair employment practice laws with widely varying provisions. They typically establish a state fair employment practices commission with powers paralleling those of the EEOC.

RECORD-KEEPING REQUIREMENTS

The EEOC requires record keeping and disclosure to provide evidence for pattern or practice and disparate impact suits. Employers, unions, and employment agencies covered by the record-keeping regulations must keep biographical and demographic records for all applicants for new positions and for all employees who receive promotions, demotions, transfers, layoffs, and pay rate changes. These records must be made available whenever an employment discrimination suit arises. Each year, employers must audit their minority populations.

EEOC INVESTIGATIONS

An EEOC right of action arises when an aggrieved employee perceives unlawful discrimination. If the state in which the alleged discrimination occurred has an antidiscrimination statute, the aggrieved employee must initially file charges with the state agency. If the state agency takes no action for 60 days, the employee may file charges with the federal EEOC. EEOC filings must be made within 180 days after the discriminatory act or within 300 days if the state antidiscrimination law requires a local filing first. This statute of limitations is shorter than that for most other legal rights.

The EEOC must notify the employer of the discrimination charges and then investigate the incident by visiting the employer's premises and questioning the employer and employees. It may subpoena any documents relevant to the investigation. If reasonable cause exists for believing that a Title VII violation has occurred, the EEOC notifies the employer of its intent to seek a meditated settlement known as conciliation. Otherwise, the EEOC dismisses the charges and advises the aggrieved employee that it will not pursue them but that the employee may proceed. This "right to sue letter" permits the employee to file suit within 90 days.

CONCILIATION

Most EEOC complaints are settled through **conciliation**. Typically, a confidential proceeding is conducted between the EEOC, representing the aggrieved person, and the employer. If the EEOC presents convincing evidence of a discriminatory practice or a resulting disparate impact, then the employer and the EEOC may voluntarily agree to a remedy. A conciliation agreement is binding on both parties; neither party may turn to the courts except to enforce the agreement. If no agreement is reached, the EEOC regional office may bring suit in a federal district court.

AFFIRMATIVE ACTION

Although the Civil Rights Act of 1964 specifies certain remedies, in some cases the courts have granted additional rights and permitted proactive antidiscrimination remedies. These remedies may require employers to use more positive approaches—such as actively encouraging the employment of minorities and women—to reduce the underlying conditions leading to discrimination.

In its conciliation process, the EEOC has often required employers to take "affirmative action" to achieve equal employment opportunities. **Affirmative action** programs actively recruit minorities and may establish goals and timetables for greater employment participation among certain employers by members of classes that have historically suffered patterns of discrimination. Affirmative action plans can also be adopted voluntarily or result from collective bargaining with unions. Affirmative action plans are required for most federal contractors. Their use in university admission programs and some other employment situations is currently the subject of several lawsuits.[8]

EXECUTIVE ORDER PROGRAMS

Since the passage of the Civil Rights Act of 1964, several presidents have issued executive orders dealing with discrimination by the federal government or by private employers that contract with the federal government. Executive Order 11,246 requires that all contracts between the federal government and federal contractors include a provision prohibiting discrimination on the basis of race, color, creed, or national origin. Other executive orders also prohibit age and sex discrimination. Federal contracts must also include a provision requiring nondiscriminatory hiring practices. If discriminatory practices are proved, federal contracts may be canceled or suspended, and contractors may be declared ineligible for future contracts.

Executive Orders 11,246 and 11,375 created the Office of Federal Contract Compliance Programs. This agency oversees the affirmative action programs required of most federal contractors. The larger federal contractors must develop affirmative action programs to remedy imbalances among protected classes in their workforce. Typically, a federal contractor must compare its minority employee profile with that of the workforce in general or of the population at large. To implement affirmative action programs, federal contractors often establish goals and timetables for hiring from protected classes.

OTHER REMEDIES

State statutes, court decisions, and other federal laws establish enforcement mechanisms to supplement EEOC enforcement, state agency enforcement, affirmative action programs, and the executive order program techniques just discussed. For example, the EEOC has negotiated court-approved **consent decrees** with employers charged with widespread discriminatory practices. The employer typically agrees to adopt new employment practices, often involving affirmative action plans. EEOC and state agency remedies include **reinstatement** for an individual dismissed or constructively discharged by the discrimination. **Back pay** (with interest) is often ordered to compen-

8. See, for example, *Hunter v. The Regents of the University of California*, 190 F.3d 1061 (9th Cir., 1999) and *Grutter v. Bohlinger* 137 F.Supp.2d 821 (E.D., Mi., 2001).

International Commentary

Employment Discrimination Laws— How Is the World Doing?

A few countries in other areas of the world—such as Afghanistan under the Taliban government—promoted discrimination, particularly against women. In Afghanistan, Taliban laws such as the ban on women's work outside the home, the bans on talking with male shopkeepers, going outside the home without a male relative, laughing loudly, and many others (see http://rawasongs.fancymarketing.net/rules.htm) indicate some of the more stringent discriminatory practices. The website for Columbia University's Middle East and Jewish Studies includes a section on women in the Middle East at http://www.cc.columbia.edu/cu/lweb/indiv/mideast/cuvlm/women.html. Included are the above link to the Taliban's restrictions on women, and many others for websites regarding the status of women in several Arab countries.

sate for earnings lost by the individual while he or she was denied the job or promotion. Awards of **retroactive seniority** from the time of discrimination are also made.

The **Civil Rights Act of 1991** authorized recovery of **punitive damages** for intentional, malicious, or reckless indifference to the discrimination laws. In a 1999 U.S. Supreme Court case involving a claim of gender discrimination, *Kolstad v. American Dental Association*,[9] the Court interpreted the intentional discrimination language of the law to require malice or reckless indifference on the part of the employer. However, an employer who made a good faith effort to comply with Title VII cannot be held liable for the malicious or recklessly indifferent acts of one of its managerial agents. The use of formal nondiscrimination policies can demonstrate good faith in meeting Title VII.

QUESTIONS

1. List the defenses that are available to an employer under the Equal Pay Act. Why are certain pay differentials permitted?
2. Ace Airlines required an applicant for flight officer to have a college degree for employment. Joan Jones, a female who did not have a college degree but was otherwise qualified for the position, applied for the position and was denied employment. She filed a complaint with the EEOC. At the hearing, Ace Airlines testified: "All flight officers undergo a rigorous training program on being hired and then are required to attend intensive refresher programs at six-month intervals in order to remain at peak performance ability. Possession of a college degree indicates that the applicant is able to understand and retain the concepts and information imparted in a classroom atmosphere and is more apt to cope with these programs than a person without a college degree." Will Joan win? Discuss the issues that the court should consider.
3. Melody Sherrod worked for AIG Healthcare Management Services first as a clerk typist, later as a billing coordinator, and then as a systems trainer, where she trained people at other sites how to perform data entry for medical billing. She was informed by her supervisor that she could not engage in personal activities at work and could not use office equipment for non-work-related activities. After receiving complaints from coworkers that Sherrod had a picture of a naked man on her computer, an investigator searched her hard drive and found 23 pictures of erect, naked men, two revealing photos of the plain-

9. 525 U.S. 1170 (1999).

tiff, and one of a female coworker. Sherrod said she had downloaded the images from e-mails sent to her by colleagues she trained in her job. She claimed that as the photos had come to her from colleagues, she could not be discharged for violating her employer's policy. The violation, if any, came from the colleagues who sent the material to her. Do you agree? See *Sherrod v. AIG Healthcare Mgmt. Servs.*, 2000 U.S. Dist. LEXIS 1626 (USDC, N.D. Tex., 2000).

4. The Los Angeles Department of Water and Power provided an employee retirement program in which benefits were funded by employer and employee contributions and computed on the basis of monthly salary and years of service. Because standard mortality tables show that the average female would live longer and thus receive more benefits than the average male, female employees were required to make monthly contributions that were almost 15% higher than the contributions of male employees. Manhart, a female employee, filed a class action suit alleging that this differential contribution requirement constituted sex discrimination in violation of Title VII of the 1964 Civil Rights Act. With what result, and why? See *Los Angeles Department of Water and Power v. Manhart,* 435 U.S. 702 (1978).

5. Do the following fact situations present a legal problem? Why or why not?

   a. A company is laying off employees, starting with the employees who have least seniority. The first group to be laid off consists of 25 white women and 15 black men and women.

   b. A company refuses to hire male receptionists, maintaining that business callers, mostly male, want to see a "pretty face" in the reception area.

   c. A company has traditionally hired males to do its assembly line work. The assembly line positions include some jobs that require fitting and some that do not. Males are rotated between these jobs and all male assembly line workers are on the same pay scale. The company has recently started to hire women for the assembly line, but they work only in nonlifting positions. For this reason, they are paid a lower wage scale than the men.

6. Mieritz was employed at Hartford Fire Insurance Company, working without incident for seven years, until 1992. After he suffered a stroke in early 1993, he became a born-again Christian and began attaching Scripture verses to his e-mails and expressing his faith to his coworkers and clients. In 1996, he was transferred from Houston to Dallas, received a poor interim performance review, and then received an adequate annual review. He continued to regularly place Scripture references on e-mails to coworkers. In 1997, the firm implemented a "no solicitation or proselytizing policy" for employees using the company systems—voice mail, faxes, intranet, and electronic mail.

   Because of budget concerns, the firm decided to eliminate one of the Texas auditor positions, and its skills assessment test of all auditors found Mieritz's skills to rank between commendable and does not meet standards. Later, Mieritz's supervisor informed him that some people had taken offense to the Scripture verses he placed on his e-mails; Mieritz did not voice any objection to that statement. Hartford terminated Mieritz several months later, one year before he was eligible for early retirement. Several employees a few years younger than he, all of whom were over 50, were not let go. Is the fact that Mieritz was 55 years of age and one year shy of the retirement age sufficient to make out a prima facie case of age discrimination? Does he have a valid claim of discrimination on account of his religion? See *Mieritz v. Hartford Fire Ins. Co.,* 2000 U.S. Dist. LEXIS 4965 (ND, TEX, 2000).

7. Philbrook's religious beliefs required him to miss six workdays each year. The Ansonia Board of Education allowed him to use three personal leave days and to take the other three days as unauthorized leave, for which he received no pay by was not otherwise disciplined. The school board refused Philbrook's request to allow him to pay for a substitute teacher and not have his pay docked. Did the school fulfill its duty to accommodate Philbrook's religious beliefs? See *Ansonia Board of Education v. Philbrook,* 107 S.Ct. 367 (1986).

8. Rawlinson, a woman, applied for a position as a correctional counselor in a male maximum security prison in Alabama. The Alabama Board of Corrections adopted a rule forbidding women to be employed in "contact" positions requiring close physical proximity to inmates. Rawlinson sued under Title VII. Who should win and why? See *Dothard v. Rawlinson,* 433 U.S. 321 (1977).

9. Sandra Flowers was employed for two years as a medical assistant at Southern Regional Physicians Services in Baton Rouge, Louisiana. After her supervisor found that Flowers was infected with the human immunodeficiency virus, which she had contracted from her husband, he stopped socializing with her, began to intercept her phone calls, and eavesdropped on her conversations. She was forced to undergo four random drug tests in one week. Southern Regional's president refused to shake hands with her and called her a bitch. After she was discharged, she claimed she was harassed and sued under the ADA. Does the ADA cover workplace

harassment of disabled people? Is she disabled? See *Flowers v. Southern Regional Physicians Services,* 247 F.3d 229 (5th Cir., 2001).

10. Kimberly Elleth, a salesperson at Burlington Industries, was subjected to offensive remarks and gestures by her supervisor, Ted Slowick. Although Ellerth refused all of Slowik's advances, he did not retaliate against her, even though he threatened to do so on several occasions. Does Ellerth have a claim against Burlington Industries based on the hostile environment created by sexual harassment? If Burlington had a policy against sexual harassment, which Ellerth did not pursue, and it had no knowledge of the hostile environment, would it still be liable? See *Burlington Industries v. Ellerth,* 524 U.S. 742 (1998).

Securities Regulations

Before the Great Depression, there was little regulation of the securities markets. Laissez-faire allowed the markets to police themselves, supplemented mainly by state common law remedies for breach of contract and fraud. However, this relatively unregulated financial market was abandoned after the 1929 stock market crash and the depression that followed. Governments worldwide now take responsibility for curbing abuses such as securities fraud and manipulation that were rampant during the Roaring Twenties. Today, the U.S. securities markets are the fairest and most efficient and liquid in the world, the Enron crisis notwithstanding. There are usually enough buyers and sellers to satisfy any trader's supply or demand, and most transactions occur at prices close to true value. As the financial markets in other nations' securities grow, they are developing regulations parallel to U.S. law. A global capital market is emerging.

The financial services industry was among the first to "go electronic." Each new wave of technological advancement was fairly quickly adopted by insurance companies and commercial and investment banks. Communication has progressed from the unwritten, through paper mailings, to telegraphy and telephony, and to modern network computerized telecommunications. Technology has reduced service time and transaction costs, increasing the availability of financing at lower cost. Secure uses of technology can greatly enhance **market integrity**—that is, the trust that investors and firms need before lively and reliable capital markets can emerge.

Going forward, finance and banking balance two opposing influences: standardization and customization. Standardized financial products (stocks, bonds, options) produce reliable and liquid markets, yet greater profitability results from new financial product designs. Among the earliest business method patents that addressed the processing of financial transactions were accounting systems, electronic trading facilities, and financial service packages, like those discussed in Chapter 17.

Regulators and the securities exchanges have installed computerized systems to track transactions that identify the parties, participating floor traders, actual trade timing, and prevailing prices. Securities law enforcement is enhanced with new electronic eavesdropping methods (wireless, Internet, e-mail) that deter harmful insider trading, financial fraud, and conflicts of interest. Already the financial markets are evolving so that investors in one nation can quickly, easily, and reliably make trades in other nations' markets. Most nations have bourses (stock markets), and many new markets are emerging in developing nations. Twenty-four-hour trading, much of it electronic, is available in many stocks. Nations with antiquated or guarded markets will have difficulty attracting capital or accessing other nations' capital markets.

THE PRIMARY FEDERAL SECURITIES STATUTES

There are two main securities laws and several related amendments. In addition, several ancillary laws target particular sectors of the securities industry. Most industrialized nations have some form of primary securities law, although these laws differ widely in form and substance. Long and thorough experience with capital markets in the United States has helped to refine its securities laws, which have become a model for other nations. Capital tends to move into markets with balanced, comprehensive, and fair securities laws, as investors worldwide realize that inadequately regulated markets are rigged and unfair.

SECURITIES ACT OF 1933

The **Securities Act of 1933** (1933 Act) is the original federal securities law, passed as part of President Franklin D. Roosevelt's New Deal. The 1933 Act requires disclosure of financial information by firms that issue new securities to the public in "primary markets" for **initial public offerings** (IPOs). Somewhat less rigorous requirements apply for firms that make private placements. New issues of securities must be registered with the Securities and Exchange Commission (SEC). For example, when the Krispy Kreme doughnut firm first went public, its stock was registered with the SEC before the shares were sold to public investors.

SECURITIES EXCHANGE ACT OF 1934

http://

www.sec.gov/

The **Securities Exchange Act of 1934** (1934 Act) created the SEC to administer the securities laws and regulate the **secondary trading markets** (e.g., stock exchanges, options exchanges, bond markets). The 1934 Act outlaws fraud in securities transactions, prohibits insider trading, and regulates corporate democracy under the proxy and tender offer provisions. Brokers, dealers, investment advisers, issuers, securities exchanges, and **self-regulatory organizations (SROs)** must also register with the SEC. The 1934 Act requires continuous disclosure of pertinent corporate financial information.

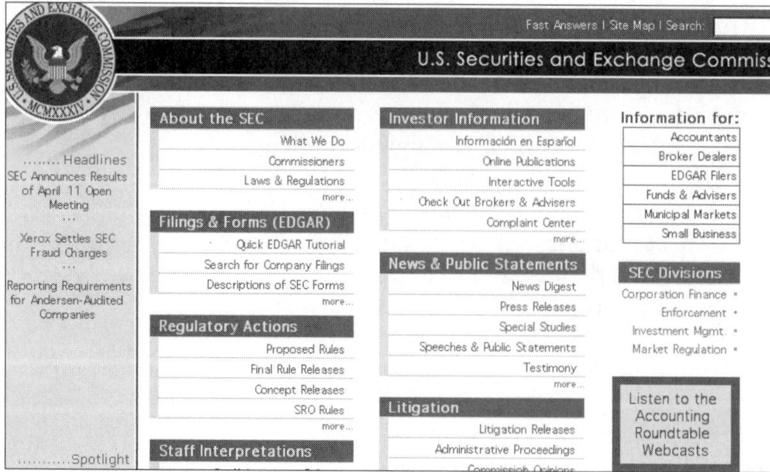

SECURITIES AND EXCHANGE COMMISSION

The SEC is responsible for licensing securities professionals and SROs, it manages the system of financial disclosure, and it enforces the securities laws.

The SEC has considerable power to promulgate regulations, investigate alleged violations, and bring civil enforcement actions. The SEC has various offices and divisions with specialized expertise about the many securities market mechanisms and businesses. For example, the SEC now has an **Office of Internet Enforcement** to better oversee the securities offerings, trading, and fraudulent scams on the Internet. Most nations have a regulator like the SEC, although their powers vary greatly. For example, the Canadian securities markets are regulated largely by Canadian provincial regulators, not by the Canadian federal government.

Other Regulators

The investment markets are also regulated by the states and other federal agencies. All U.S. states regulate securities offerings made to their residents under their own securities laws, called **blue sky laws**. Each state has a securities commission or empowers its corporation commission, attorney general, or department of state to oversee blue sky regulations. Insurance and banking are also regulated. Criminal violations of the securities laws are enforced by the U.S. Justice Department (DOJ).

ONLINE
North American Securities Administrators Association
http://www.nasaa.org

The futures markets are regulated by the **Commodities Futures Trading Commission (CFTC)**, which has jurisdiction over standardized, exchange-traded commitments for the future delivery of commodities. Traditionally, **futures** involved agricultural products such as grains, livestock, timber, and processed commodities, as well as other materials such as petroleum products and metals. The biggest growth is now in financial futures that cover currencies, precious metals, market indexes, and various industry-specific financial assets or liabilities.

Controversy rages over increasing speculation in relatively unregulated **derivatives**, which are investment contracts that fluctuate as the value of some underlying financial asset changes. Traditional derivatives include options and futures, which are most often standardized and traded on exchanges. However, financial engineers continue to develop new forms of derivatives, including swaps between firms of various assets or liabilities and novel commodities such as kilowatt-hour futures. The behavior and risks of many derivatives are not well understood by investors, regulators, or the financial community. This has led to huge derivative losses by large corporations and governments (Orange County, California). Controversy over derivatives may eventually lead to much needed research into their behavior, new regulations, and a modernization of financial disclosure rules for firms with large derivative trading programs. For example, observers believe that the Enron bankruptcy would have been less severe if the financial community better understood energy futures and the accounting profession had developed better methods to measure and disclose derivative risks.

http://
www.cftc.gov/cftc/cftchome.htm

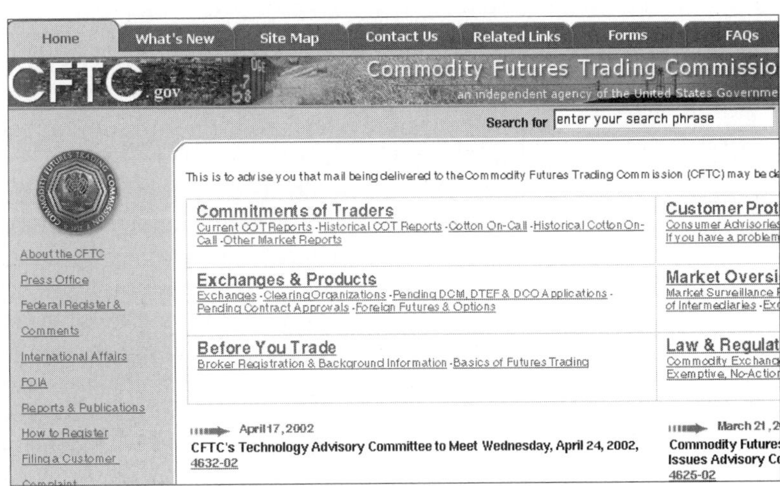

Securities regulation depends heavily on private **self-regulation** by SROs. The SEC oversees all SROs. Most investor complaints against brokers are settled by mandatory binding arbitration conducted by private arbitrators under SEC rules and oversight by the **National Association of Securities Dealers (NASD)**. The

ONLINE

American Institute of Certified Public Accountants
http://www.aicpa.org
Financial Accounting Standards Board
http://www.fasb.org

NASD also licenses securities brokers and dealers, and it operates the huge, electronic over-the-counter (OTC) securities market known as the **NASDAQ**. The New York Stock Exchange (NYSE) and the other physical securities exchanges regulate their members and exchange trading. Accounting rules (generally accepted accounting principles, or GAAP) used in corporate financial disclosure are generally set by the Financial Accounting Standards Board (FASB), and auditing standards (GAAS) are set by the American Institute of Certified Public Accountants (AICPA).

MISCELLANEOUS SECURITIES LAWS

The SEC also administers several specialized laws. In 1935, Congress passed the **Public Utility Holding Company Act** to correct abuses in financing, operations, and the pyramid-type capital structure of natural gas and electric utilities. In 1939, Congress passed the **Trust Indenture Act** to protect bondholders from the conflicts of interest of bond indenture trustees. In 1940, Congress reacted to abuses in two more sectors of the securities industry with passage of the **Investment Advisors Act** to license and regulate advisers and the **Investment Company Act** to regulate mutual funds. After the back office paperwork crisis that brokerage firms experienced in the late 1960s, Congress passed the **Securities Investor Protection Act** of 1970 (SIPA). The SIPA established the Securities Investor Protection Corporation, an insurance fund to protect investors' securities and accounts from broker negligence or bankruptcy. The **Racketeer Influenced Corrupt Organizations (RICO)** provisions of the Organized Crime Control Act and the **Foreign Corrupt Practices Act (FCPA)** are also important; they are discussed in Chapter 7.

Congress passed the **Gramm-Leach-Bliley Act** in 1999 to permit universal banking—the combination of insurance, commercial banking, and investment banking into the same firms. These three financial functions were separated by the Glass-Steagall Act in 1933 after Congress became convinced that concentrations of these financial functions contributed to the market crash and allowed a few big banks to have monopoly control over financing. Universal banking was reintroduced in 1999 at the behest of the financial services industry, which argued that the pre–Depression era conditions no longer exist. Because most other nations permit universal banking, the Glass-Steagall restrictions had put the U.S. financial services industry at a competitive disadvantage. Chapter 14 introduced Gramm-Leach-Bliley because it imposes financial privacy regulations.

REGISTRATION OF SECURITIES

An IPO raises funds from the investing public in the primary securities markets. **Underwriting** is the process investment bankers use to distribute a new issue of securities. Often, a closely held corporation like Krispy Kreme, the **issuer**, negotiates an underwriting contract with an **investment banking syndicate**. Underwriters can make a firm commitment to sell the whole issue, promising the issuer a specified amount of proceeds. In such cases, the syndicate takes the risk that the securities may not sell well. Firms not yet well established may be unable to use firm commitment underwriting. Instead, investment bankers might only serve as sales agents promising their "best efforts" to sell all the securities.

The 1933 Act broadly defines **underwriters** to include (1) any person who purchases from an issuer with a view to distribute the security or (2) any person who offers or sells any security for the issuer's benefit in the distribution. Underwriting occurs whenever an individual or firm receives compensation for selling an issuer's securities for the issuer's benefit. Underwriters must take great care to avoid potential liabilities for violating the 1933 Act. There may be unintentional liability if someone is unexpectedly designated as an underwriter. It is unlawful under §5 of the Securities Act to sell unregistered securities unless there is an exemption. These issues are discussed next.

REGISTRATION STATEMENT AND PROSPECTUS

Issuers must provide investors with sufficient financial information to make an informed investment decision. The 1933 Act requires issuers to provide a prospectus, the primary sales and promotional tool in securities sales. The **prospectus** is broadly defined to include nearly every communication to potential investors: "Any notice, circular, advertisement, letter, or communication, written or by radio or television which offers any security for sale or confirms the sale of any security." Issuers must also file a **registration statement** with the SEC that has content nearly identical to the prospectus. Both documents must include or refer to the issuer's financial statements. The **statutory** or **formal prospectus** is a specific document that contains basic financial information. Well-established issuers may omit certain financial information by referencing it if it is contained in a current annual and quarterly report, disclosure documents that are detailed later.

Information Required in a Prospectus

1. Audited financial statements
2. Five years of comparative financial information
3. Management's discussion and analysis of financial condition (MD & A)
4. Information describing the issuer's management
5. A description of the security offered
6. An explanation of how the proceeds will be used

THE IPO REGISTRATION PROCESS

Firms that are going public use a three-stage process. Before actual registration, there is a **prefiling period**, during which the issuer negotiates with the underwriting syndicate and prepares the prospectus and registration statement. Prefiling ends when the registration statement is filed with the SEC. Sales of securities are not permitted in the United States until the securities are registered with the SEC. **Sales** include contracts of sale or transfers of any interest in a security for value.

"Gun-jumping" during the prefiling period is prohibited. This practice is also known as **preconditioning** because when public statements are made before registration they can arouse investor interest in the imminent offering of new securities. For example, press releases or speeches that predict, project, forecast, or estimate the value of the new security are prohibited as preconditioning. Announcements of forthcoming products, profitability, or the firm's success are also prohibited because they can create demand before investors can adequately evaluate the issuer's prospects. Nevertheless, the issuer may continue to advertise its products and respond truthfully to inquiries by shareholders, securities analysts, or the press. The appearance of business as usual should be maintained during the prefiling period because publicity about the new securities must be avoided.

The second stage is the **waiting period** that begins when the issuer files the registration statement with the SEC. No sales are permitted, and most other forms of sales effort are illegal during the waiting period. However, **statutory offers** are permitted as long as they indicate only an interest to sell or buy. Other permissible communications during the waiting period include (1) **tombstone ads,** which are simple announcements with lined borders resembling tombstones that usually appear in the financial press; (2) the preliminary or **red herring prospectus** that conspicuously disclaims any formal offer; (3) **formal oral offers** that have not yet been accepted; and (4) the **summary prospectus,** containing condensed information. These contacts were traditionally made in print publications, face to face, or by phone between the issuer, dealers, and investors. In some instances, issuers may host **roadshows**—live presentations with sophisticated and institutional investors. Conference calls and video conferencing expanded the scope of roadshows. Now webcasting on the Internet further enhances opportunities to market the forthcoming IPO or private placement to the public.[1]

The effective date of the registration statement starts the third stage, the **posteffective period.** Actual sales may begin. This stage usually begins 20 days after the registration statement is filed unless the SEC accelerates (moves sooner) the effective date or it threatens to halt sales. A fully amended final prospectus must be delivered, along with all confirmations of sale, all deliveries of securities, written offers, and distributions of supplementary sales literature. The issuer, underwriters, dealers, and brokers are responsible for delivering a prospectus to all potential buyers. Electronic deliveries of the prospectus are permissible. The initial sales period lasts for about 40 days or until all of the new issue is sold. The SEC's review of the registration statement does not ensure the accuracy of the issuer's claims, nor does the SEC verify that the securities are good investments. The three stages of SEC registration are illustrated in Exhibit 22.1.

EXHIBIT 22.1 SEC Registration Process

	Prefiling Period	File with SEC	**Waiting Period** 20 days or until SEC accelerates effective date of registration statement	Registration effective	**Posteffective Period** 40 days or until all the securities have been sold to investors
Prohibited actions	No contracts to sell securities No announcements conditioning the market (gun jumping)		No contracts to sell securities		No preliminary or "red herring" prospectuses
Permitted/required actions	Can contact investment bankers for advice Can negotiate with underwriters for possible participation in underwriting syndicate Must prepare registration statement, preliminary prospectus, and supporting documents for SEC filing Must maintain "business as usual" communications with security holders, customers, suppliers, the press, and securities analysts		Can publish or distribute statutory offers to buy or sell securities, including: • Tombstone ads • Preliminary prospectus • Formal oral offers • Summary prospectuses Distribution of preliminary "red herring" prospectus		Must forward formal prospectus before or with all confirmations of sales, deliveries of securities Must attempt to sell all of the newly registered securities unless registered as a shelf offering

1. *NetRoadshow, Inc.*, 1997, SEC NO-Act LEXIS 864 (SEC No-Action Letter, Sept. 8, 1997).

Shelf Registration

Traditionally, the issuer must attempt to sell all the securities immediately after the registration becomes effective. However, **shelf registration** is an alternative process that permits the issuer to comply with the complex registration procedures well in advance of the firm's need for proceeds. These preregistered securities are held in inventory—"on the shelf"—until financing is needed or market conditions become optimal. Issuers often sell shelf securities directly to investors and thereby save some underwriting costs.

On-line Offerings

On-line offerings started cautiously, with private offerings made only to institutional investors. Today, public offerings are made on-line if there are safeguards that disclosures and confirmations of sale are made effectively to all purchasers. The following case is an SEC No Action letter—the SEC's statement that a particular form of transaction would comply with the law if done as promised. No Action letters are not precedents the courts must follow. They only prevent the SEC from bringing an enforcement action against the firm if the transaction is done precisely as disclosed.

Wit Capital

2000 WL 1013585 (S.E.C. No Action Letter, July 20, 2000)

Facts. Wit Capital sought SEC approval in its request for an SEC No Action letter for an Internet auction system using the "Vostock super" auction method. The Vostock auction method is a transparent order book; its workings are visible to those with Internet connections. Each customer, as well as the general public, regulators, and anyone else with Internet access, may view the aggregate demand in the auction, including small and large bids, at each price level. Each auction will have a maximum price and a minimum price that bidders may bid. This Vostock auction preserves anonymity: The issuer and the underwriters will not disclose the identity of bidders to any other bidder.

The Vostock auction will operate "after hours" after exchange trading closes in these securities, and only for registered follow-on, secondary, and combination offerings of stock. The underwriters will conduct the auction after trading closes in the primary market session for the issuer's stock on a trading day. The maximum price will be set at a price lower than the closing price of the security in its primary market. Auctions will be conducted only after the registration statement for an offering has been declared effective. The underwriters and dealers will notify their customers about the auction by phone, fax, e-mail, website posting, in person, or by another means. Notices will specify the number of shares to be auctioned, the URL address for the auction, the minimum bid size, the price increment for bids, and the time the auction begins and ends. A so-called cul-de-sac mechanism will record each bidder's binding transaction for immediate processing.

Legal Issue. Will the Internet Vostock auction proposed by Wit Capital comply with the Securities Laws?

Opinion. [It is the view of the SEC's Division of Corporation Finance] that Wit Capital Corporation may conduct auctions of common equity securities by [publicly traded firms] through the Internet system described in your letter in compliance with the Securities Act of 1933. After the effectiveness of a registration statement for the sales of securities using the auction system, Wit Capital Corporation [must file]:

a final prospectus supplement that provides a fair and accurate description of the information, including price information, as will have been presented electronically in the Internet auction, by presenting

- the final terms of the offering;
- the summary of bidding activity described in your letter; and
- any other interim screen shots that evidence a substantive change in the information already filed with the Commission.

In reaching these positions, we note particularly

- that the Internet auction screens will be a part of the prospectus;
- that the Internet auction screens will be accessible only through that electronic prospectus;
- that a complete presentation of all bidding and other auction activity visible to participants on the Internet auction screens need not be filed because [they will] include all substantive changes from information already filed; and
- that, because the Internet auction screens, as described in your letter, are part of the prospectus, all bidding and other auction activity visible to participants on the Internet auction screens are part of the prospectus.

The positions expressed above are limited to the presentation and manner of conducting the Internet auction, we take no position regarding whether any announcement of the Internet auction would constitute a "prospectus," [under] the Securities Act. These positions are based on the representations made to the Division in your letter. Any different facts or conditions might require another conclusion.

Sincerely, Michael Hyatte, Special Counsel, SEC

Decision. Wit Capital may conduct auctions of securities on the Internet consistent with the design described in its request for this SEC No-Action letter.

Case Questions

1. What aspects of Securities Act disclosure were needed for SEC approval of Wit Capital's Internet auction system?
2. How could the Wit Capital posting system be considered a prospectus?

On-line Trading Systems

Before the Internet, securities traded in the secondary markets, long after the IPO was completed, occurred in three major ways: (1) face-to-face trades between acquainted parties such as friends, colleagues, or employer and employee; (2) over-the-counter through brokers who traded from their own holdings or through a network of brokers representing other individuals or institutions generally known to trade in the particular securities; and (3) in organized stock exchanges with physical trading floors and facilities. The definition of an exchange has expanded to include electronic market mechanisms such as the **National Association of Securities Dealers Automated Quotation** (**NASDAQ**) system. The NASDAQ evolved from a screen-based computerized telecommunications price-posting system into a genuine electronic market, capable of executing, clearing, and settling transactions. Should securities law encourage additional forms of electronic markets to create liquidity and lower transaction costs?

The SEC seems persuaded that it is a good thing for the market to develop novel and carefully designed mechanisms to communicate availability of particular securities for sale, offers to buy or sell, and price quotations and to execution transactions. These mechanisms hold promise to expand the national market system. Several electronic market mechanisms were proposed, and many have been approved since the late 1990s. Some systems are simply **electronic communication networks** (**ECN**), essentially bulletin boards that communicate availability or price. Other forms offer **alternative trading system** (**ATS**) capabilities that match orders and provide clearance and settlement. The Internet is blurring the difference between the primary markets for IPOs or private placements and the secondary markets that trade in previously issued securities. With integration of the disclosure systems of the 1933 and 1934 acts as discussed later, eventually the distinction will be less important for regulatory purposes.

WHAT IS A "SECURITY"?

The securities laws regulate only those investments known as securities. In the abstract, a security may be considered an intangible transaction or contract right requiring one party to make payments or future performances to another party. Although *security* can also mean collateral or reduced risk and danger, the securities laws use the narrower meaning. The term **security** means "any note, stock, treasury stock, bond, debenture, evidence of indebtedness, transferable share, investment contract, voting trust certificate, certificate of deposit for a security, fractional undivided interest in oil, gas, or other mineral rights, any put, call, straddle, stock option, warrant, or in general, any interest or instrument commonly known as a security." The SEC regulates transactions and professional services in securities.

Any instrument on this statutory list is covered by the securities laws, with a few exceptions. Purely commercial, consumption, or consumer transactions, such as short-term commercial paper (corporate IOUs maturing in 9 months or less) and notes that facilitate trade credit and credit sales of consumer assets, are exempt. Notes that bear a "family resemblance" to these commercial transactions are also exempt from securities regulations. *Reves v. Ernst & Young*[2] held that notes are securities depending on the following four factors: (1) the parties' purposes, (2) the seller's distribution plan, (3) the public expectation for securities law protection, and (4) whether another factor reduces the instrument's risk so the protection of the securities laws becomes unnecessary. The securities issued by banks, government agencies, and charities are also exempt from SEC regulation.

The courts can designate new forms of investments as securities. For example, securities include limited partnership interests, equipment trust certificates, some franchises, time shares, variable annuity insurance policies, and pyramid selling schemes. The definition of a security includes a catchall—"investment contract"—that captures new forms. The following classic case illustrates the four elements of **investment contracts:** (1) an investment of money (2) in a common enterprise, (3) from which the investor is led to expect profits (4) derived solely from the promoter's efforts.

S.E.C. v. Howey

328 U.S. 293 (1946)

Facts. Several investors purchased parcels of a common orange grove in Florida as part of the capital-raising efforts of the W. J. Howey Company. Each of the prospective purchasers was offered both a land sale contract and a separate service contract for planting, harvesting, and marketing the crop offered by Howey-in-the-Hills, a subsidiary of W. J. Howey. Such services were provided for 85% of the land purchasers. The 10-year service contracts granted Howey-in-the-Hills full and complete possession of the acreage. The various parcels of land were contiguous, and no fences or markers divided the parcels owned by the various investors. The harvested crops were combined; investors shared profits in proportion to the land owned. Most investors were nonresident professionals with no expertise in citrus growing. They were guests of an adjacent hotel that helped in the sales effort. The SEC challenged the sales as the sale of unregistered securities.

Legal Issue. Does the definition of a security under the Securities Act of 1933 include investments in land that are typically marketed along with cultivation, harvesting, and marketing services?

Opinion. Justice Murphy. Section 2(1) of the Act defines the term "security" to include the commonly known documents traded for speculation or investment. This definition also includes "securities" of a more variable character, designated by such descriptive terms as "certificate of interest or participation in any profit-sharing agreement," "investment

2. 494 U.S. 56 (1990).

contract" and "in general, any interest or instrument commonly known as a 'security.'" The legal issue in this case turns upon a determination of whether, under the circumstances, the land sales contract, the warranty deed and the service contract together constitute an "investment contract" within the meaning of §2(1). An investment contract came to mean a contract or scheme for "the placing of capital or laying out of money in a way intended to secure income or profit from its employment." An investment contract for purposes of the Securities Act means a contract, transaction or scheme whereby a person invests his money in a common enterprise and is led to expect profits solely from the efforts of the promoter or a third party, it being immaterial whether the shares in the enterprise are evidenced by formal certificates or by nominal interests in the physical assets employed in the enterprise. It embodies a flexible rather than a static principle, one that is capable of adaptation to meet the countless and variable schemes devised by those who seek the use of the money of others on the promise of profits.

The transactions in this case clearly involve investment contracts as so defined. The respondent companies are offering something more than fee simple interests in land, something different from a farm or orchard coupled with management services. They are offering an opportunity to contribute money and to share in the profits of a large citrus fruit enterprise managed and partly owned by respondents. They are offering this opportunity to persons who reside in distant localities and who lack the equipment and experience requisite to the cultivation, harvesting and marketing of the citrus products. Such persons have no desire to occupy the land or to develop it themselves; they are attracted solely by the prospects of a return on their investment. Indeed, individual development of the plots of land that are offered and sold would seldom be economically feasible due to their small size. Such tracts gain utility as citrus groves only when cultivated and developed as component parts of a larger area. A common enterprise managed by respondents or third parties with adequate personnel and equipment is therefore essential if the investors are to achieve their paramount aim of a return on their investments. Their respective shares in this enterprise are evidenced by land sales contracts and warranty deeds, which serve as a convenient method of determining the investors' allocable shares of the profits. The resulting transfer of rights in land is purely incidental.

Thus all the elements of a profit-seeking business venture are present here. The investors provide the capital and share in the earnings and profits, the promoters manage, control and operate the enterprise. It follows that the arrangements whereby the investors' interests are made manifest involve investment contracts, regardless of the legal terminology in which such contracts are clothed. The investment contracts in this instance take the form of land sales contracts, warranty deeds and service contracts which respondents offer to prospective investors. And respondents' failure to abide by the statutory and administrative rules in making such offerings, even though the failure result from a bona fide mistake as to the law, cannot be sanctioned under the Act.

Decision. The definition of security includes a catchall item, investment contract, that includes nontraditional investments of money into a common enterprise, where investors are induced with the promise of profitability derived from the efforts of others.

Case Questions

1. What contemporary investment forms have a similar structure of an enterprise operated by a management company, with individual portions owned by investors?
2. What is the importance of investors' need for protection of the securities laws? Would these reasons change if the investors were sophisticated local citrus growers?

Later cases refine *Howey* when applied to novel and innovative instruments. For example, a security was offered when a seller issued warehouse receipts to each purchaser of scotch whiskey while it was aging for years in the cask.[3] The receipts were to be repurchased later and the scotch blended by the seller in bottles. In another case, the sale of all the common stock of a business to a buyer who intended to personally run the business was not considered exempt, rejecting the so-called sale of business doctrine.[4]

3. *S.E.C. v. Haffenden-Rimar Intl., Inc.*, 496 F.2d 1192 (4th Cir., 1974).
4. *Landreth Timber Co. v. Landreth*, 471 U.S. 681 (1985).

New forms of investment have not been designated as a security in other instances. For example, an employee's interest in a noncontributory and compulsory pension plan is not a security. In another case, the so-called stock, which permitted a tenant to lease a publicly subsidized co-op apartment, was not a security. These "stock certificates" lacked the traditional aspects of a security, such as the right to vote, a share in profits, or the potential for capital gains appreciation. During the late 1990s, many websites tried to cash in on the public's exuberance for hot issue stocks and stock options during the dot.com bubble. Various website promotions promised **free stock** in exchange for personal information or URL link referrals. Even though web surfers made no money investment for this free stock, the SEC has generally determined that these are unregistered offerings of securities, made in violation of the 1933 Act.

Questions are again being raised about the largely unregulated derivative markets. Some derivatives are clearly listed as securities or can easily fit in the "investment contract" category defined by *Howey*. For example, options on securities (e.g., puts, calls) are derivatives but are regulated as securities. However, many derivatives are privately negotiated through commercial or investment bankers and are exempt from registration. **Swaps** are becoming a common form of derivative in which two parties exchange cash flows, receivables, or payables. The CFTC and SEC continue to battle about jurisdiction over derivatives, as speculators lobby hard to keep privately negotiated derivatives unregulated. However, the Enron bankruptcy may trigger more disclosure about the sometimes significant but uncertain risks posed by derivatives.

EXEMPTIONS FROM 1933 ACT REGISTRATION

The IPO registration process is extremely costly: There are fees for registration, investment banking services, auditing, legal services, and printing. These tasks traditionally cause months of delay. However, Congress and the SEC believe the securities markets should be available to both small and large businesses. The 1933 Act includes some **transaction exemptions** that reduce the cost for issues of small size and limited scope or distribution. Issuers must be careful to establish their exemption because the sale of nonexempt and unregistered securities is prohibited. Also exempt are "any *security exchanged* by the issuer with its existing security holders exclusively when no commission . . . is paid." This exemption affects three types of corporate reorganizations: (1) voluntary recapitalizations; (2) reorganizations made by the federal courts, bankruptcy courts, or authorized state agencies; and (3) securities issued in a merger, consolidation, or other transfer of assets approved by shareholders.

Intrastate Exemption

The **intrastate exemption** allows a complete relaxation of all registration requirements. Based on the federalism principle, it defers to state blue sky securities laws. The **SEC's Rule 147** exempts intrastate sales that meet strict requirements. First, all purchasers must be residents of the state. Second, the issuer must be domiciled and doing business within the state. Third, the issuer must satisfy three 80% rules: (1) At least 80% of the issuer's gross revenues are derived in the state, (2) 80% of the issuer's assets are located in the state, and (3) 80% of the proceeds will be spent in the state. A restrictive legend must be placed directly on intrastate security certificates warning that resale is restricted in intrastate sales. For example, consider a Pennsylvania corporation, PennCorp, which manufactures asphalt used almost exclusively to resurface Pennsylvania highways. PennCorp may avoid expensive registration if it issues stock only to Pennsylvania residents and the three 80% limitations are satisfied. State blue sky disclosure requirements must be satisfied.

Small Issue Exemption

Because small businesses are generally limited to raising capital through bank loans, partnerships, government loan guarantees, or venture capital, the small issue exemption partially opens the capital markets to small firms. **Regulation A**, the short form, permits the issuance of $5 million of securities each year without a complete registration statement. The only required filing is an **offering statement** that includes unaudited financial statements and a description of the issuer and the securities offered. An **offering circular** containing similar information must be delivered to all potential buyers solicited. Issuers may "test the waters" by soliciting investor interest before registration, a practice that was previously prohibited as preconditioning of the market.

Private Placement Exemption

The market for the private placement of securities is huge, particularly those sold to large institutional investors. Historically, this market was mostly for small or risky firms that issued lower grade securities such as junk bonds. Today, this market is evolving to include healthy blue chip corporations. Private placements permit more efficient capital raising and the avoidance of most SEC regulations. Many leveraged buyout loans and asset-backed securities are privately placed, and they can be kept confidential, which is attractive to issuers suffering from adverse publicity. The most popular form is **Regulation D**, combining aspects of small issues with private placements.

Generally, sales may be made to an unlimited number of **accredited investors**, who are parties with financial sophistication and sufficient net worth, experience, and knowledge of investments to withstand the risk. They include certain institutional investors, employee benefit plans, corporations, the issuer's upper management, and certain "well-to-do" individuals. Issuers must have a reasonable basis for believing investors are accredited before soliciting them for most forms of private placement. They must carefully prequalify sophisticated investors, a task sometimes performed by brokers and dealers. How could the Internet be used to qualify accredited investors? IPONet proposed to permit password access to private placement listings on its Internet site to only accredited investors qualified by W. J. Gallagher & Co. An on-line questionnaire was used to prescreen before providing individuals with passwords. The SEC may permit such new methods if it finds them appropriate.[5]

Rule 504 permits unregistered offerings by nonpublic issuers for amounts up to $1 million within 12 months and defers to registration under state blue sky law. Rule 505 limits offerings to $5 million within 12 months. Rule 506 has no upper dollar limit. Sales under both 504 and 505 may be made to no more than 35 nonaccredited and any number of accredited investors. There is no specific disclosure requirement when sales are made to accredited investors; however, the issuer must provide them with the information they request. Publicly traded issuers must provide their current annual reports when sales are made to nonaccredited investors.

An alternate private placement method exists under §4(2) of the 1933 Act. It has few limitations: no upper dollar limit, no maximum number of offerees, and no

5. *IPONet*, 1996 WL 431821 (SEC No Action Letter, July 26, 2000).

specified form for disclosures. However, all offerees must be sophisticated investors who have access to the type of information contained in a prospectus. There can be no general solicitation of the public and no advertising, and the resale of these securities must be restricted, as discussed later. The SEC has facilitated §4(2) offerings under SEC Rule 146, but this rule limits sales to 35 purchasers.

Integration of Exempt Offerings

The securities a firm sells could be intentionally spread into several separate exempt transactions to avoid SEC registration. Such disintegrations could really be a single plan of financing. To protect investors from such sham transactions, the SEC may **integrate** or combine, several apparently separate exempt offerings if they are made too close together in time and the proceeds are used for the same general purpose. Consider the example of a Michigan firm that issues $4 million of stock to purchase an old factory, exempt under Rule 505. Soon, the firm makes a separate exempt intrastate offering of $2 million in promissory notes to Michigan residents to renovate the factory with new machinery. Even if the firm claims the two offerings are separate, the proceeds are being used for the same plan of financing the new facility. Because the $6 million total exceeded the dollar limit of Rule 505, the two separate sales are integrated and result in the unlawful sale of unregistered securities.

Resale Restrictions

Not all securities can be readily sold whenever the investor desires. Securities law may impose **resale restrictions** on exempt securities. Resale restrictions discourage an issuer from circumventing the registration requirements. For example, the issuer might first sell new securities as exempt but really intend that the initial purchasers function as underwriters and immediately resell the securities to the public. Unsuspecting investors would be deprived of adequate disclosure. An initial buyer who intends to own for only a short time and resell immediately at a profit is considered an underwriter, triggering potential liability. Under **SEC Rule 144**, initial purchasers may resell exempt securities only if they originally had **investment intent**—the desire to hold the securities for longer-term investment purposes. Initial purchasers of exempted securities must hold them for a minimum period, usually a year or two, then sell only small quantities periodically. A boldface warning of resale restrictions is required.

DISCLOSURE

The heart of securities regulations is assuring a continuous flow of high-quality information that investors need to make reasonable choices. The disclosure regime of securities law is intended to equalize the asymmetries of information—when investors are poorly informed by the issuer or its insiders. Economics insists that markets work best when all parties are well informed, which is precisely the aim of securities law. Investors are willing to risk their capital only when they can predict how the issuer will perform in operations and financially. Investors lose confidence in the system when the information they receive is deficient. Disclosure aims to maintain **integrity of the market**—confidence that markets are not rigged, that they represent a "fair game," and that firms compete for capital on a level playing field.

The SEC requires numerous types of disclosures, from issuers going public, issuers making private placements, publicly traded firms whose securities are traded on national securities exchanges, brokers and dealers, investment advisers, mutual

International Commentary

Global Securities Trading

IPOs in some foreign nations do not follow the complex process described here. For example, even though the securities laws of the European Union require IPO registration, the Germans have received an exception for their "universal banking" practices. New IPO securities are generally not registered in Germany. Therefore, issuers disclose far less financial information to potential shareholders than in the United States, particularly about management's compensation and activities.

How do citizens of one nation trade on foreign stock exchanges or invest in the securities of other nations' firms? Traditionally, U.S. citizens have invested in ***American Depository Receipts (ADRs),*** derivative certificates that entitle the U.S. investor to the benefits of particular foreign securities held in trust by a foreign bank. ADRs are securities and must be registered. Increasingly, larger and more successful foreign firms are registering their securities to trade directly on U.S. exchanges. Also, big brokerage firms from most industrialized nations have foreign branch offices to facilitate trading in other nations by their domestic customers. Electronic trading links are used to connect various foreign securities exchanges and permit brokers to receive price quotes and last-sale information on a foreign nation's securities exchange. Outside the United States, the world's major stock exchanges include Canada (Toronto and Montreal), United Kingdom (London), Japan (Tokyo), Hong Kong, Australia (Sydney), Germany (Frankfurt), France (Paris), Switzerland (Zurich), Italy (Milan), Netherlands (Amsterdam), Sweden (Stockholm), Belgium (Brussels), and Spain (Madrid). Other markets are emerging in developing nations, the Pacific Rim, and Eastern Europe. The risks of dealing through a foreign broker include changes in exchange rates, delays in settlement and clearance procedures (payment and delivery of security certificates), higher withholding taxes, and higher transaction costs.

The SEC has liberalized access to U.S. capital markets for foreign issuers. ***Regulation S*** permits registration of new IPOs by foreign issuers with significantly reduced disclosure requirements. ***Rule 144A*** permits nearly unlimited resales of certain privately placed securities among ***qualified institutional buyers (QIB).*** A QIB is a sophisticated institutional investor managing a portfolio of more than $100 million. Under these schemes, foreign issuers need disclose only the same type of information as required in their home nation. They constitute a smaller secondary market for private placements. They are interconnected with electronic screen-based quotation systems.

funds, public utility holding companies, exchanges, and SROs. The disclosure regime also involves other securities market professionals, such as accountants who review financial statements, investment bankers who orchestrate IPOs and other financial transactions (mergers), and lawyers who give opinions about transactions. Adequate disclosure depends on forthright performance by all these participants because their activities are crucial to market integrity. Discussed here are two major disclosure regimes for firms going public and firms with securities already trading. These disclosure regimes are (1) structured, periodic financial statement disclosure and (2) nonfinancial disclosures.

PERIODIC FINANCIAL DISCLOSURE

Financial information is a key component in every IPO, in private placements, and in reports distributed every fiscal quarter and fiscal year for publicly traded firms. These statements include a balance sheet showing major classes of assets and liabilities, an income statement showing major sources of revenue and expenses, and a funds flow statement showing more precise sources and uses of funds. In addition, text explanations clarify the particular accounting treatments used, and management must interpret and give meaning to the firm's liquidity, capital resources, and the results of operations in the **management's discussion and analysis** (MD&A).

SEC Regulation SX defines the format and content of the financial statements. It is supplemented by generally accepted accounting principles (GAAP). The nonfinancial and explanatory disclosures are largely governed by **SEC Regulation SK.** Unaudited quarterly reports are required for the first three quarters of each fiscal year. The annual report to shareholders must be independently audited and then filed with the SEC and delivered to shareholders. All these disclosures are traditionally made in print. The filed documents were traditionally made on paper to the SEC. The registration statement and Form 10K (annual report) or Form 10Q (quarterly reports) and printed copies of the prospectus and annual report are sent to shareholders. However, the SEC was an early adopter of electronic disclosures as discussed later.

Since 1997, the SEC has crusaded for the use of **plain English** in disclosure documents. Disclosures must be in clearer and more concise language, understandable to the likely lay investor audience. Techniques include the use of active rather than passive voice, short sentences, everyday language, avoidance of multiple negatives, and, whenever possible, tables, bulleted lists, and figures to simplify complex information. As firms continually disclose the complexity of their transactions in plain English, there should be fewer disturbing revelations that lead to adverse impact on stock prices and the markets.

ONLINE
SEC's Plain English Handbook
http://www.sec.gov/pdf/handbook.pdf

NONPERIODIC DISCLOSURE

Issuers must also disclose particular information in special circumstances. This disclosure duty is specified in a few instances but implied in others. Regular disclosures and press releases suggest the issuer will not be deceptive and therefore must update previous disclosures with current information as conditions change. The issuer's disclosure duty may arise when false rumors are circulating, there are merger negotiations, the issuer makes forecasts, or there is selective disclosure to favored recipients (analysts).

Issuers can minimize their liability when making projections by including adequate cautionary language make it clear that the statements are not facts—the **bespeaks caution** approach.[6] When projections are clearly labeled as **forward-looking**, made on a reasonable basis and in good faith, they are protected from liability under the Safe Harbor for Projections.[7] Two additional disclosure issues are relevant: the unfairness of selective disclosure to favored analysts and the use of website postings by publicly traded firms to keep investors better informed in real time.

Fair Disclosure

In 2000, the SEC issued Regulation FD, "Fair Disclosure," to prohibit firms from convening small groups of analysts who were the first to hear of important news, such as earnings forecasts, new products, or joint ventures. Such voluntary disclosure is generally a good thing. However, selective disclosure provides analysts and their clients with early inside information before other investors are informed. Analysts who are favored with selective disclosure then have a conflict of interest; they are more apt to publish favorable reviews of the firm, improving the performance of its stock price. Selective disclosure closely resembles tipping that enables analysts' clients to engage in insider trading—a subject detailed later in this chapter.

6. *In re Donald J. Trump Casinos Securities Litigation*, 7 F.3d 357 (3d Cir., 1993).
7. 15 U.S.C. 77z-2, 78u-5(c), based on the SEC Safe Harbor Rule for Projections, 17 C.F.R. §230.175.

Publicly traded firms and third-party consultants and representatives may not make selective disclosures. Disclosures of material nonpublic information made to analysts must be effectively released to the public simultaneously. Suggested methods for public release include press releases, firm website posting, e-mail to existing shareholders, and "furnishing" a copy to the SEC. Sometimes a firm's spokesperson may "inadvertently" disclose a material fact in an interview without making a simultaneous public release. Regulation FD requires the firm to release the information promptly—within 24 hours or by the opening of the NYSE's next trading session.

ELECTRONIC DELIVERY OF INVESTOR COMMUNICATIONS

ONLINE

SEC website
http://www.sec.gov

The SEC was among the first agencies to require electronic communications for the securities transactions and corporate disclosures that fall within its jurisdiction. For example, the SEC's website has an astounding amount of information about its operations, its rules, and public comments that influence rule-making.

The securities laws and SEC rules require written documents. However, pressure for electronic interactions among investors, issuers, brokers, advisers, and exchanges has come from both regulators and market participants. The SEC established guidelines in 1996,[8] which were revised in 2000,[9] to allow electronic communications. Today, considerable trading volume is executed electronically, and many communications with investors are delivered electronically, including prospectuses, annual reports, proxy solicitations, tender offers, going-private transactions, and private placement–offering documents.

The SEC guidelines establish several important principles. First, electronic media can be used to satisfy publicly traded firms' disclosure and communications duties to investors. Second, new media must provide substantially the same information to investors as do paper documents. Third, the issuer must assure that investors have notice that information is available (e.g., downloadable) and that they can retain a permanent copy of all communications received electronically. For example, the pdf document format is becoming so ubiquitous that it can be used if the issuer makes it easy for the investor to successfully download Acrobat Reader, typically with a link to the Adobe website. Fourth, investors must consent to the use of electronic communications, either for particular communications (e.g., one year's proxy) or globally (all future communications). Adequate safeguards are needed if investors give consent by phone, by e-mail, or in writing. Fifth, the firm must take reasonable precautions to assure the security and integrity of all communications with investors. Sixth, investors must have a reasonable opportunity to call and receive paper copies if the electronic delivery is deficient. Seventh, the **envelope theory** permits the firm to use hyperlinks to other required data on its website. However, it is impermissible to link to analysts' reports from within a prospectus. An issuer must take care in linking to content posted by outside firms because the issuer can be liable for misrepresentations the outsider makes.

EDGAR

Since the 1980s, the SEC has ramped up its computerized database of corporate disclosures and many other documents that firms file with the SEC. Probably the SEC's most important electronic effort is the **Electronic Data Gathering Analysis and**

8. Use of Electronic Media for Delivery Purposes, SEC Securities Act Rel. No. 7289 (May 9, 1996).
9. Use of Electronic Media, SEC Securities Act Rel. No. 7856 (April 28, 2000).

Ethical Issue

Management Duties to Disclose Corporate Information

Should management use its control over corporate affairs to hide its performance from shareholders and the public? Corporate information is owned by the firm and is ultimately produced for the benefit of shareholders and to encourage efficient capital markets. Material inside information may not be misappropriated for personal use by anyone, such as a manager's insider trading. The securities markets, exchanges, and securities professionals serve the public by providing places for firms to raise capital and for investors to trade reliably and with confidence that the markets are fair. Actions that compromise these fiduciary duties take unethical advantage of the beneficiaries of the trust. Accurate periodic financial disclosure is needed to prevent subversion of the capital markets. The securities laws legislate corporate morality. Managers have a disclosure duty that limits secrecy, makes them more responsive to shareholders, improves the integrity of the capital markets, and creates a "fair game."

Retrieval (EDGAR) system, which posts SEC filings and corporate disclosures on line. Although EDGAR was somewhat cumbersome in its early years, it is now a model for making the disclosure of important information accessible. Since 1996, all domestic, publicly traded firms are required to submit most of their disclosure filings on EDGAR. Visit EDGAR at the URL listed here. Browse through the disclosures of publicly traded firms cited in the text and cases in this book or from current news reports.

ONLINE

SEC's EDGAR website
http://www.sec.gov/edgar.shtml

EDGAR automatically collects, validates, indexes, accepts, and posts corporate disclosures, such as registration statements, quarterly reports (Form 10Q), annual financial reports (10K), and current reports (Form 8K). EDGAR accelerates the dissemination and analysis of time-sensitive corporate information. Annual reports to shareholders are often available on the firm's own websites. Third-party information resellers may also post similar information, often repackaged to add some value to research and analysis. Currently documents are available as text or html documents, but firms may supplement them with pdf files, including graphics, which are not yet considered "official" filings. Both the SEC and the NASD operate websites for investor complaints and assistance. For example, the litigation history of **rogue brokers** can be viewed on line.

ONLINE

National Association of Securities Dealers
http://www.nasd.com

INSIDER TRADING

The securities laws require publicly traded firms to disclose material information. Fraud is outlawed in connection with purchases or sales of securities. Insider trading is considered a form of securities fraud because the insider knows secret information that is unavailable to most other traders in the markets. Since the 1980s, the SEC and the DOJ have focused considerable enforcement attention on insider trading and other forms of securities fraud that enhance insider trading opportunities. The law of insider trading has many issues that require interpretation and definition: (1) *Why* is insider trading unlawful? (2) *Who* is an insider? (3) *What* is inside information? (4) *When* is insider trading restricted as unlawful? (5) *Where* is the jurisdiction with authority to enforce insider trading law? This section addresses these critical issues.

A provisional definition of insider trading is needed to proceed. Generally, **insider trading** is the practice whereby a person's access to confidential and nonpublic information gives an unfair advantage over others in the trading of a firm's securities. The insider's silence about confidential information while trading with unsuspecting investors is a form of fraud by omission. Why is insider trading illegal?

Confidential inside information is a form of trade secret. Most of the risks of misappropriation and defensive safeguards discussed in Chapter 16 are applicable to insider trading. Technology has significantly increased the opportunities for trade secret theft and for insider trading. First, networked computers and electronic database storage make inside information accessible beyond the limited circle of authorized personnel. They expose the firm's secrets to employees and hackers. Second, Internet communications increase the opportunities for tipping inside information and manipulating the securities markets. For example, e-mail is used to unlawfully disclose inside information, and bulletin boards and chat rooms can spread false rumors that manipulate stock prices. However, just as phone and cell phone records reveal tipping and helped to prove insider trading during the 1980s and 1990s, Internet records are used to prove trade secret theft and tipping. SEC, FBI, and DOJ investigators can subpoena ISP records and brokerage trading records, and they can identify the source of Internet messages. This type of evidence is generally admissible to prove insider trading and tipping.

SHORT-SWING PROFITS: SECTION 16

Congress first attempted to prohibit insider trading with the 1934 Act, which restricts some forms of insider trading by defining insiders fairly precisely, requiring insiders to disclose their trading activities, defining insider trading as short-swing profits, and giving the corporation the remedy for return of the short-swing profits. **Short-swing profits**—insider trading profits made by specified insiders—are prohibited. This law presumes that high-level insiders regularly have access to confidential, market-moving information. Short-swing profits made in trading any class of exchange-listed equity security must be repaid to the corporation. When a statutory insider both purchases and sells the issuer's equity securities (stock) within any six-month period, §16 is violated. Section 16 essentially borrows the corporate opportunity doctrine from state corporation law to make it a federal wrong for a high-level insider to use confidential corporate information for personal profit.

There are two major provisions in §16. First, §16(a) requires statutory insiders to disclose their trading in the firm's stock through filings with the SEC. Second, §16(b) prohibits short-swing profits. Most of the public's knowledge about the trading activity of insiders results from the insider trading reports required by §16(a). Not only are these records available through the SEC but also private news services specialize in tracking insider trades.

ONLINE

Track the Trades of Statutory Insiders
http://www.thomsonfn.com

Statutory Insiders: Officers, Directors, and 10% Shareholders

Section 16(a) requires insiders to report to the SEC all trades they make in their company's equity securities to facilitate enforcement and notify the public. The only insiders who are required to disclose their trades and who are restricted from short-swing profiting are the firm's officers, directors, and 10% shareholders. For years, commentators speculated that §16(a) reports were the most frequently violated provisions of the securities laws. However, in 1991 the SEC imposed strict new reporting rules that required firms to disclose when their officers' or directors' reports are delinquent.

Brokerages and banks often give "officer-like" titles to middle-level managers. However, if these employees do not perform significant corporate executive decision-making functions, they are not restricted as statutory insiders. The title of **officer**

Commentary

The Controversy over Insider Trading

Insider trading enforcement is quite controversial. Proponents of restricting insider trading argue the practice is unfair because insiders have an informational advantage that outsiders cannot overcome, no matter how much they research the firm. As insider trading proliferates, the perception that the capital markets are unfair becomes widespread. If the public loses confidence, as in the Great Depression and after the Enron scandal, firms will have difficulty raising capital and the whole economy will suffer.

On the other side of this controversy are those who oppose restricting insider trading. They claim that it is a victimless crime because the firm's shareholders can simply prohibit the practice. Some even argue that insider trading is part of a corporate manager's implied compensation. Proponents say that insider trading is beneficial by contributing to a more efficient market because insider trading sends a "signal" to the market about the direction the firm's stock price should move. Insiders buy on good news and sell on bad news. Insider trading permits the market to infer that some traders have access to confidential nonpublic information. The market may then presume that insiders' trading activities show the correct direction for stock price movements. Following the Enron scandal, some observers continued to raise this proposition by arguing that Enron insider selling was the "best" method to signal the low quality of Enron's earnings.

The opponents of restricting insider trading apparently ignore the reality of shareholder democracy. Shareholders are probably unable to detect insider trading, and any corporate rule prohibiting it will not be as effective as regulatory enforcement. If given a knowing chance, the victim of insider trading would insist on trading at a price adjusted for the insider's nonpublic information.

Condoning insider trading encourages employees to manipulate the release of corporate information to enhance their profit opportunities by making the firm's price more volatile. For example, knowledgeable insiders could profit from the firm's misfortunes by selling short. But this is market manipulation and totally inconsistent with every employee's fiduciary duty of loyalty. Opponents of insider trading argue that management should be required to disclose information more quickly to the whole public and be generally prohibited from trading on inside information. Information formerly kept secret can be disseminated more rapidly as more investors and analysts rely on the Internet and media for disclosure. Open and timely information reinforces fairness, preserves market efficiency, and restores the public's confidence.

includes the president, any vice president in charge of a principal business function, other officers of the issuer's parent or subsidiaries who perform policy-making functions for the issuer, the principal financial officer, and the principal accounting officer.

The term **director** includes all board members. In addition, some board members are "interlocking directors"; that is, they hold seats on the boards of two or more corporations. In such situations, the director definition may be expanded to include the other corporation because the interlocking director could easily tip the other corporation about inside information. Therefore, the second corporation may be restricted from short swing trading in the first corporation's stock. In such situations, the interlocking director is considered a "deputy" of both corporations because the director may be a convenient conduit to transfer inside information.

There are similar problems in defining 10% shareholders. For example, a shareholder might buy stock in the name of a spouse, minor child, or another close relative. A shareholder who owns less than 10% could actually control more than 10%. To avoid this situation, the 10% shareholder restrictions apply to all stock held in *beneficial ownership*; that is, all the shares owned by a related group are presumed to be owned by one person to test for the minimum 10% threshold. This presumption is rebuttable if the shareholder can prove no actual control was exercised over stock held by a relative. There are exemptions for certain securities market participants who may temporarily hold more that 10%, such as market makers, specialists, dealers and underwriters during an IPO, and arbitrageurs. However, most institutional investors (e.g., pension funds, mutual funds, insurance companies) are not exempt.

Short-Swing Profit Liability

A sliding six-month scale is applied to capture *any* two purchase and sale transactions within *any* six-month period. A purchase or sale occurs when there is an actual transfer or even a contract to purchase or sell an equity security. Options and other derivative securities (e.g., warrants, convertible securities, stock appreciation rights) are considered purchased when they are initially acquired. Exercise or conversion is generally exempt. Such derivatives are considered sold when the *converted* security is sold. A firm's stock option program may be exempted if shareholders approve and other strict SEC guidelines are followed.

Short-Swing Damages

Who brings suit to recover a statutory insider's short-swing trading profit? The plaintiff may be either the corporation or any shareholder acting on the corporation's behalf. Damages are computed as the difference between the purchase and sale prices. These damages belong to the corporation, not to any shareholder personally. This aspect makes §16(b) suits similar to shareholder derivative suits under state corporation law.

In computing short-swing profits, the courts do not apply the FIFO (first-in, first-out) method to match particular stock certificates. The prices of shares purchased first are not always compared with the prices of shares sold first to determine short-swing profit damages. Instead, the lowest purchase price is matched to the highest sale price within any six-month period. This method maximizes the measure of illegal trading profit. For example, assume a statutory insider sells 100 shares at \$10 in January, purchases 100 shares in March at \$5, and then purchases another 100 shares in April at \$4. The profit realized is \$600 (\$10 – \$4 = \$6 per share × 100 shares), even though the sale occurred first. The comparison between the \$5 purchase and the \$10 sale is ignored because the lower purchase price of \$4 occurred within six months of the \$10 sale, as illustrated in Exhibit 22.2.

EXHIBIT 22.2 Short-Swing Liability

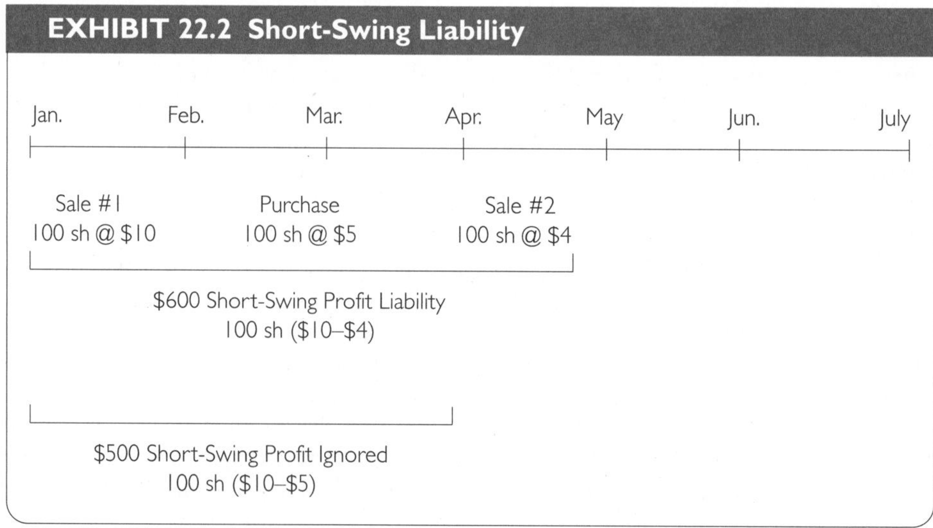

The computation of short-swing profit liability is intentionally maximized to hold statutory insiders to a high standard of conduct and to provide a strong deterrent. The law prohibits sales before purchase because insiders could profit from bad news by "selling short" the issuer's securities. Although §16 was Congress's original and objective method to prohibit insider trading, emphasis has shifted to the subjective approach to insider trading enforcement as a form of securities fraud prohibited by SEC Rule 10b-5.

INSIDER TRADING UNDER SEC RULE 10B-5

The SEC originally promulgated **SEC Rule 10b-5** in response to rumors that "the president of some company in Boston . . . is going around buying up the stock of his company from his own shareholders at $4 a share . . . telling them that the company has been doing very badly, whereas in fact the earnings are going to be quadrupled and will be $2 a share."[10] SEC Rule 10b-5 is the most pervasive antifraud provision in the securities laws. It prohibits (1) insider trading, (2) misleading and fraudulent financial disclosures, and (3) manipulation of the securities markets.

SEC Rule 10b-5

It shall be unlawful for any person, directly or indirectly, by the use of any means or instrumentality of interstate commerce, or of the mails, or of any facility of a national securities exchange,

1. to employ any device, scheme, or artifice to defraud,
2. to make any untrue statement of a material fact or to omit to state a material fact necessary in order to make the statements made, in the light of the circumstances under which they were made, not misleading, or
3. to engage in act, practice or course of business which operates or would operate as a fraud or deceit upon any person, in connection with the purchase or sale of any security.

SEC Rule 10b-5 requires corporate officers, directors, and any other insider to either *disclose* their inside information before trading or *abstain* from trading altogether. This is the so-called **disclose or abstain** rule. This seemingly simple choice actually places the insider in a dilemma. The insider's fiduciary duty of loyalty to the corporation usually prohibits a corporate insider from revealing secret information before trading because disclosure divulges important confidential corporate information.

This problem arose in a leading insider trading case, *SEC v. Texas Gulf Sulphur Company.*[11] The Texas Gulf Sulphur Company (TGS) made a substantial mineral discovery in Canada. To acquire the mineral rights on land surrounding the discovery site at favorable prices, TGS publicly denied rumors of the discovery. At the same time, some TGS employees who knew about the discovery purchased TGS stock. If these employees had disclosed the mineral discovery before purchasing TGS stock, they would have violated their fiduciary duty of confidentiality. These employees were guilty of illegal insider trading, and TGS was guilty of securities fraud in making materially misleading disclosures. Although TGS employees had no duty to inform surrounding landowners of the discovery before acquiring their mineral rights, a stronger duty applies to corporate insiders who are trading in the securities markets.

10. Statement of Milton Freeman in American Bar Association, Section of Corporation, Banking and Business Law, Conference on Codification of the Federal Securities Laws, *Business Lawyer* 22 (1967), 921–923.
11. 401 F.2d 833 (2d Cir., 1968).

SEC Rule 10b-5 makes illegal any insider trading in any security, debt or equity, whether the issuer is publicly traded or closely held. Defrauded sellers or purchasers may sue for civil damages, the SEC may bring enforcement actions and seek civil fines, and the DOJ may prosecute insider traders by seeking fines and prison terms.

Who Is an "Insider"?

Under Rule 10b-5, **insiders** include employees at lower levels than are targeted by §16 restrictions on officers and directors. Rule 10b-5 prohibits insider trading by *any* employee with access to confidential information. It also applies to certain outsiders, nonemployees such as tippees who receive inside information from insiders, consultants and other temporary insiders, and others involved in mergers and acquisitions. The SEC established criteria for the identification of an insider in the leading case *Cady, Roberts & Co.*[12] The trading restriction applies where (1) a relationship gives access to information, (2) information is intended only for corporate purposes, and (3) it is used unfairly for the personal benefit of the insider.

Since the 1960s, a **possession theory** has circulated. At first the SEC promoted the theory to prohibit *any* trading by any person who had mere possession of nonpublic information irrespective of whether the person used the information to make the trading decision. However, the Supreme Court halted expansion of this *parity of information* theory in the famous *Chiarella*[13] case. In *Chiarella*, a financial printer invested in takeover targets, which he identified by misappropriating the information from his employer, the printing firm. The Supreme Court held that without any evidence of wrongfulness, the mere possession of nonpublic information is not sufficient to prohibit trading. The *Chiarella* rule preserves the incentive for securities analysts to do research and investment analysis. Analysts and individual traders can learn or develop nonpublic information for use in their own trading or to advise clients. However, most employees possessing nonpublic information have a duty to maintain confidentiality. If they trade, the mere possession of inside information taints their trading. This shifts to them the burden of proving they did not actually *use* the information in deciding to trade.[14]

Scienter must be proved in cases of securities fraud; that is, regulators or private parties must prove that the insider actually made *use* of the confidential inside information in deciding to trade. It seems obvious that inside information influences the trade if an insider or tippee knew material, secret information. Despite this presumption, an insider or tippee may prove otherwise—that the trading decision was made independently of the inside information. The SEC has tried to clarify this matter with **SEC Rule 10b5-1**, presuming liability if the insider was "aware" of the inside information while trading.

SEC Rule 10b5-1 provides an important exception from the presumption of the trader's awareness. An insider's trade will not be presumed to be "on the basis of" confidential inside information if the insider's trades are done mechanically and not by a direct command. This exception applies if the decision to sell or buy stock is made automatically as part of a preexisting plan, contract, or instruction. So if there is a fixed algorithm or formula that makes the critical trading decisions of timing, price, and volume, the insider may prove that inside information had no influence on these regular purchases or sales. The exception applies only to trades made under

12. *In re Cady, Roberts & Co.*, 40 SEC 907 (1961).

13. *Chiarella v. United States*, 445 U.S. 222 (1980).

14. *United States v. Teicher*, 987 F.2d 112 (2d Cir., 1993).

the plan, and there is no defense to insider trading charges if the insider's trading deviates or the insider also makes hedging trades or holds offsetting positions in the employer's stock.

For example, many employees automatically buy their employer's stock in various employee stock ownership plans (ESOPs), for their 401K pension investment accounts, and in executive stock option plans. Sales can also be made regularly and automatically. Many executives regularly exercise their stock options and then immediately sell the stock to realize incentive compensation. The Enron bankruptcy in 2001 emphasized how some of these programs work and that these programs are generally less flexible and advantageous for ordinary employees. The Enron story also suggests that there are more lucrative insider trading opportunities for top executives.

Insider trading enforcement can be brought under a variety of theories by regulators and in private damage suits by victims of insider trading. Five major types of insider trading are explored here: (1) traditional or classical theory, (2) tipping theory, (3) temporary insider trading, (4) misappropriation theory, and (5) tender offer insider trading. In addition to these major theories, several other theories are also noted.

Traditional or Classical Insider Trading

Traditional theory insider trading has its roots in common law fraud and the fiduciary duty of loyalty. In *Strong v. Repide*[15] a controlling stockholder who purchased shares from minority stockholders failed to disclose that he knew about the firm's impending asset sale, which would boost share value. This constituted **special circumstances**, giving the insider a type of trusteeship status. This status required him to disclose what he knew before purchasing others' shares because the price was artificially depressed by their ignorance of the inside information. Traditional theory also is rooted in the SEC's original purpose in promulgating Rule 10b-5 and progressed into the disclose or abstain rule.

Traditional theory is probably the most widely understood and accepted method to prohibit insider trading. The corporate insider is an employee with ready access to material, nonpublic information who uses this advantage to trade in the firm's securities. This trading is a deceptive device prohibited by SEC Rule 10b-5 because "a relationship of trust and confidence [exists] between the shareholders of a corporation and those insiders who have obtained confidential information by reason of their position with that corporation. That relationship, we recognized, gives rise to a duty to disclose [or to abstain from trading] because of the necessity of preventing a corporate insider from . . . tak[ing] unfair advantage of . . . uninformed . . . stockholders."

Examples of traditional theory insiders are rather predictable and straightforward: statutory insiders under §16(a) (officers, directors), upper-level managers with access to trade secrets or other market-moving confidential information, lower-echelon employees who from time to time help create or are briefed on confidential information to perform their work, and even otherwise naive employees if they seek out secret information to enhance their trading advantages. The graphic in Exhibit 22.3 illustrates the insider's fiduciary link to the issuing firm and the shareholder's justifiable expectation of fair dealings with the issuing firm. It illustrates insider selling, typical if the inside information is bad news. Insiders with knowledge of nonpublic information indicating good news are tempted to buy stock from a naive trading partner.

15. 213 U.S. 419 (1909).

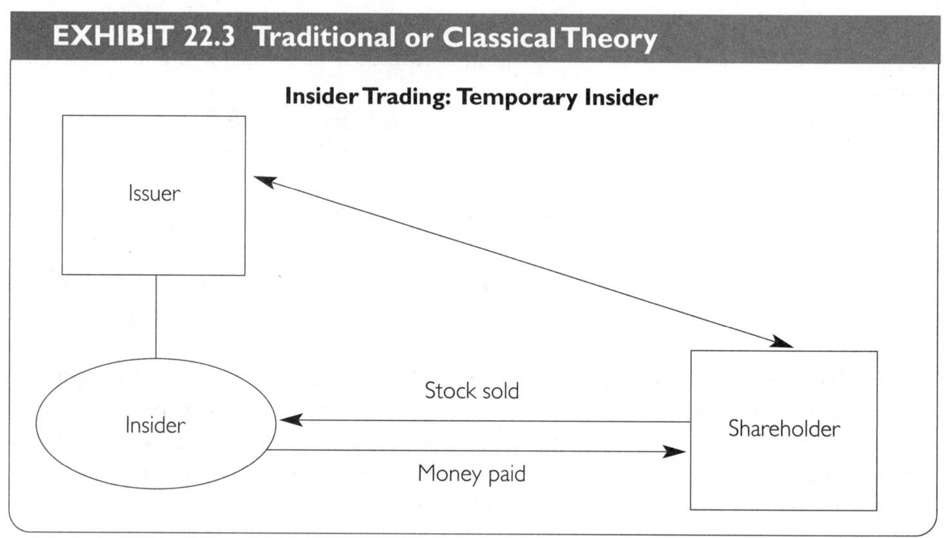

Tipping Liability

Insider trading prohibitions also apply to certain outsiders. Tippees were probably the first group of noninsiders to have their trading prohibited. Often tippees are nonemployees who receive inside information from a tip originating from an insider. What circumstances taint inside information so that outsider tippees may not trade on the information? The famous case *Dirks v. SEC*[16] clearly prohibits tipping by insiders and trading by tippees—the recipients of a tip. Dirks was a securities analyst who received information from a former officer of Equity Funding of America that its assets were vastly overstated because of fraudulent corporate practices. Dirks's investigation with Equity Funding employees confirmed the fraud. Dirks openly discussed his findings with clients and fellow brokers at his firm before he notified the SEC. These clients quickly sold off nearly $16 million in Equity Funding stock before the news became public and Equity Funding's stock price plummeted from $26 to $15. The SEC censured Dirks for transmitting the inside information. Dirks was not guilty as a tippee because the insiders breached no fiduciary duty in revealing the Equity Funding fraud. A tippee is restricted from trading only if the insider conveyed the inside information *improperly*, such as when the insider expects a personal benefit from the tippee.

The *Dirks* case defines tipping liability for both the tipper and tippee. Tipping liability depends on connecting the tipper's fiduciary duty, through the tip, and to expectations about the tippee. Tipping liability exists where (1) the tip involves confidential nonpublic information, (2) the tippee knew or had reason to know the tip breached the tipper's fiduciary duty, and (3) the tip was made for an improper purpose, such as a personal benefit expected by the tipper.

The improper purpose required is broadly construed to include many tipper-tippee relationships: intrafamily, among business colleagues, and between friends. Also, the types of improper purposes are broadly defined to include the tippee's payment for the information, quid pro quo expectation for future return tips from the

16. 463 U.S. 646 (1983).

tippee, and even the intangible personal benefit of the tipper's increased reputational stature in the tippee's eyes. *Dirks* reinforces that analysts need incentives to do securities research. Analysts perform critical functions for market efficiency; their work informs the market.

A tippee inherits the insider tipper's duty to disclose or abstain if the tippee knows or has reason to know of the insider's fiduciary breach in tipping the information. There can be tipping liability for the tipper making the tip and for the tippee in trading on the tip. Some remote tippees down the chain of tipping may also be liable. A tipping relationship is depicted in Exhibit 22.4. Note that the insider's fiduciary relationship is inherited by the tippee. This provides a pathway for the imposition of the disclose or abstain duty running from the tippee to shareholders in the issuing firm.

Wireless and networked computerized communications tempt insiders to make tips and tippees to request them. However, records of wireless telephone and e-mail communications are increasingly available to SEC and DOJ enforcement investigators. Sophisticated computer analysis of trading patterns by the exchanges can help identify potential violators. Phone and Internet records help find possible tipping links.

Temporary Insiders

The *Dirks* case included a now famous footnote #14 that established another category of outsider liability. **Temporary insiders** include underwriters, accountants, lawyers, and consultants working for the firm whose shares are traded. Temporary insiders owe a fiduciary duty to their employer and ultimately to the issuer. Client firms have the right to expect their consultants and the consultants' employees will keep confidential any information discovered in the consulting engagement. Such confidentiality is usually implied, but engagement agreements should also expressly require confidentiality.

EXHIBIT 22.4 Tipping Theory

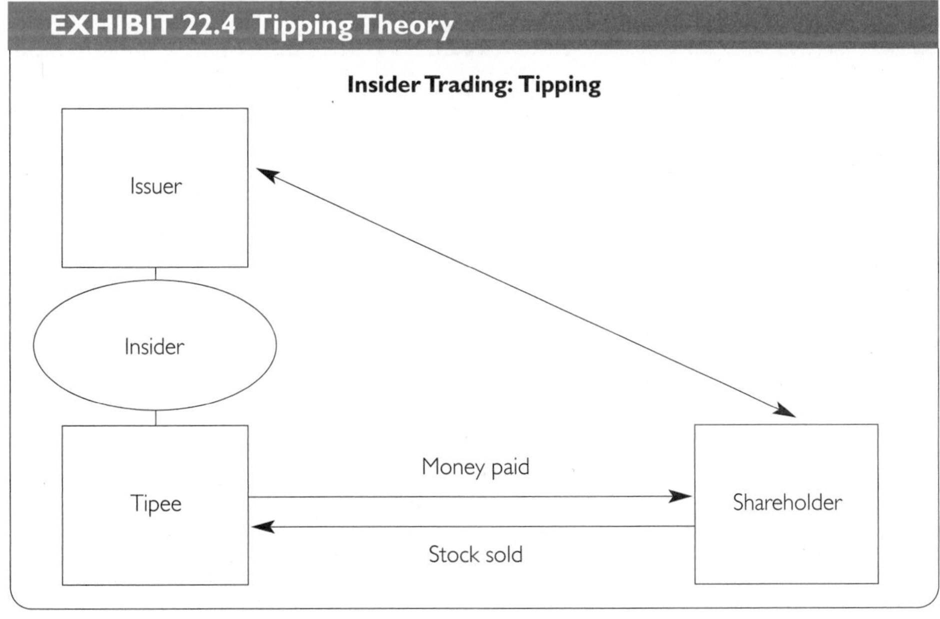

Temporary Insiders under Definition in *Dirks* footnote #14

Under certain circumstances, such as where corporate information is revealed legitimately to an underwriter, accountant, lawyer, or a consultant working for the corporation, these outsiders may become fiduciaries of the shareholders. The basis for recognizing this fiduciary duty is . . . that they have entered into a special confidential relationship . . . and are given access to information solely for corporate purposes. When such a person breaches his fiduciary relationship, he may be treated more properly as a tipper than a tippee.

The graphic in Exhibit 22.5 shows that a consulting firm has a contractual duty of confidentiality. The consultant's employees become temporary insiders owing a fiduciary duty through their employer, the consultant, to the issuing corporation. Ultimately, the temporary insider's disclose or abstain duty extends to shareholders of the client firm.

The Misappropriation Theory

Under the **misappropriation theory,** it is irrelevant whether nonpublic, confidential information originates from inside or from outside the issuer whose shares are traded. There are two common misconceptions about insider trading that the misappropriation theory now discredits. The first is that only employees of the issuer whose shares are traded are restricted by insider trading rules. This is wrong. Trading by various outsiders is restricted (e.g., tipping, temporary insiders, tender offers). The second major misconception is that the confidential, nonpublic information can come *only* from sources within the firm whose shares are traded. This is also wrong. Secret information about a takeover, major corporate transaction, corporate combination, or tender offer is generally known only by outsiders (takeover bidder, employees, bidder's consultants, consultants' employees).

The misappropriation theory presumes that information is property. Any firm's confidential information or trade secrets can qualify as property rights. The owners of information suffer if their agents misappropriate it for personal trading purposes.

EXHIBIT 22.5 Temporary Insider Theory

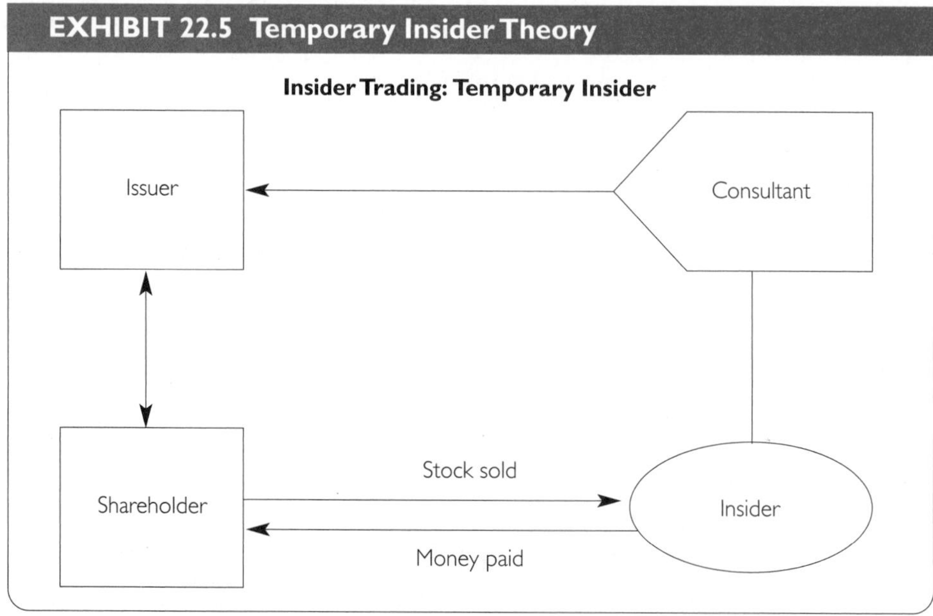

For example, there can be extensive insider trading just before a takeover that raises the price that the bidder must pay for the target firm. Therefore, even though the source of information was outside the firm whose shares are traded, this outside source suffers financial damage when its insiders trade in the stock of a target firm.

Any person, whether an insider or an outsider, who breaches fiduciary duty by misappropriating confidential information may be liable for insider trading. For example, an employee of a financial printing firm who trades on information stolen from the firm is guilty of insider trading. Similarly, employees of law firms or investment banks that represent takeover participants may not trade on confidential information learned in their employment. Other common examples include financial analysts, financial journalists, takeover bidders, courts, regulators, even physicians and psychiatrists. Misappropriation is illustrated in Exhibit 22.6.

The damage caused to outside firms by misappropriation was well stated in *United States v. Newman*:

In a tender offer situation, the effect of increased activity in purchases of the target company's shares is to drive up the price of the target company's shares; but this effect is damaging to the offering company because the tender offer will appear commensurately less attractive and the activity may cause it to abort. The deceitful misappropriation of confidential information by a fiduciary, whether described as theft, conversion, or breach of trust, has consistently been held to be unlawful."[17]

Many people believe that inside information is received through some privileged channel. Just like under the corporate opportunity doctrine, employees may not misuse their employer's contacts and resources for personal profit. Misuse entitles the corporation to recompense because the assets were placed at employees' disposal

EXHIBIT 22.6 Misappropriation Theory of Insider Trading

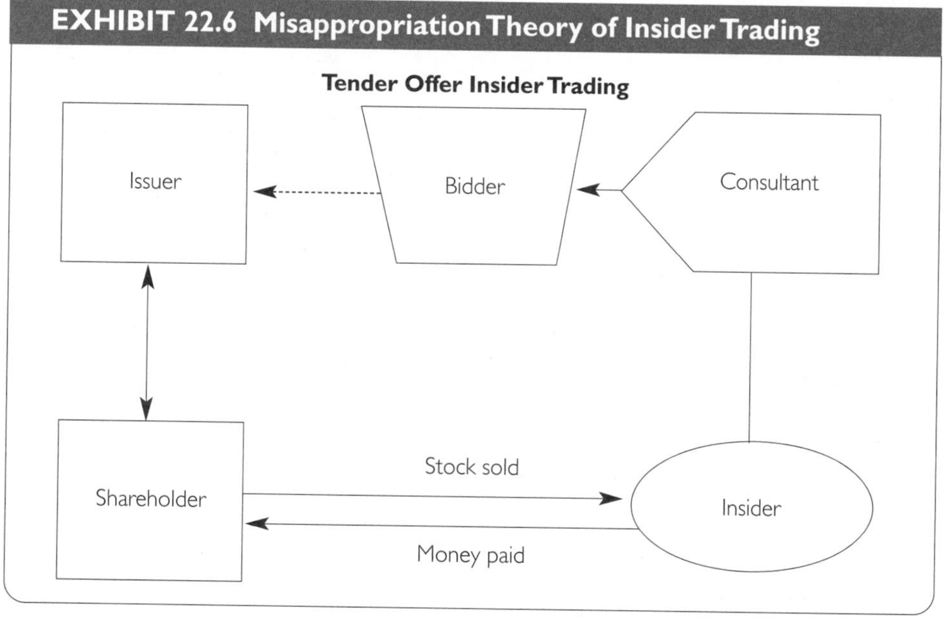

17. 664 F.2d 12 (2d Cir. 1981). Employees at several investment banking firms traded on confidential takeover information they secretly exchanged before the information became public.

only for corporate purposes. Although traditional theory prohibits insider trading based on a "fraud on the naive trading partner" theory, misappropriation theory broadens the trading prohibition to include "fraud on the informational source." In the famous *Wall Street Journal* "Heard on the Street" case, the Supreme Court first approved criminal insider trading prosecution but only under the federal mail and wire fraud statutes.[18] Should misappropriation suits also be based on §10(b) of the 1934 Act and SEC Rule 10b-5? That remained unclear until the following case.

United States v. O'Hagan

521 U.S. 642 (1997)

Facts. O'Hagan was a partner in the law firm representing Grand Met during early stages of its takeover attempt for Pillsbury. Although O'Hagan did not participate in representing Grand Met, he nevertheless learned of the takeover plans. O'Hagan purchased options and stock in Pillsbury before the public announcement of the takeover. O'Hagan was convicted on numerous counts of insider trading under SEC Rule 10b-5, mail fraud, tender offer insider trading under SEC Rule 14e-3, and money laundering.

Legal Issue. Is the misappropriation theory a valid theory under §10b and SEC Rule 10b5? Is the possession theory under SEC Rule 14e-3 a valid exercise of the SEC's rule-making powers under the Williams Act?

Opinion. Justice Ginsburg. Criminal liability under §10(b) may be predicated on the misappropriation theory. The "misappropriation theory" holds that a person commits fraud "in connection with" a securities transaction when he misappropriates confidential information for securities trading purposes, in breach of a duty owed to the source of the information. Under this theory, a fiduciary's undisclosed, self serving use of a principal's information to purchase or sell securities, in breach of a duty of loyalty and confidentiality, defrauds the principal of the exclusive use of that information. The misappropriation theory is designed to "protec[t] the integrity of the securities markets against abuses by 'outsiders' to a corporation who have access to confidential information that will affect th[e] corporation's security price when revealed, but who owe no fiduciary or other duty to that corporation's shareholders."

In this case, the indictment alleged that O'Hagan, in breach of a duty of trust and confidence he owed to his law firm and to its client traded on the basis of nonpublic information regarding Grand Met's planned tender offer for Pillsbury common stock. [M]isappropriators deal in deception. A fiduciary who "[pretends] loyalty to the principal while secretly converting the principal's information for personal gain," "dupes" or defrauds the principal. Deception through nondisclosure is central to the [misappropriation] theory of liability. Similarly, full disclosure forecloses liability under the misappropriation theory: Because the deception essential to the misappropriation theory involves feigning fidelity to the source of information, if the fiduciary discloses to the source that he plans to trade on the nonpublic information, there is no "deceptive device" and thus no §10(b) violation—although the fiduciary turned trader may remain liable under state law for breach of a duty of loyalty.

We turn next to the §10(b) requirement that the misappropriator's deceptive use of information be "in connection with the purchase or sale of [a] security." This element is satisfied because the fiduciary's fraud is consummated, not when the fiduciary gains the confidential information, but when, without disclosure to his principal, he uses the information to purchase or sell securities. The securities transaction and the breach of duty thus coincide. This is so even though the person or entity defrauded is not the other party to the trade, but is, instead, the source of the nonpublic information. A misappropriator who trades on the basis of material, nonpublic information, in short, gains his advantageous market position through deception; he deceives the source of the information and simultaneously harms members of the investing public.

Although informational disparity is inevitable in the securities markets, investors likely would hesitate to venture their capital in a market where trading based on misappropriated nonpublic information is unchecked by law. An

18. *United States v. Carpenter*, 484 U.S. 19 (1987).

investor's informational disadvantage vis-à-vis a misappropriator with material, nonpublic information stems from contrivance, not luck; it is a disadvantage that cannot be overcome with research or skill. It makes scant sense to hold a lawyer like O'Hagan a §10(b) violator if he works for a law firm representing the target of a tender offer, but not if he works for a law firm representing the bidder.

The governing statutory provision, §14(e) of the Exchange Act prohibits fraudulent, deceptive, or manipulative acts or practices, in connection with any tender offer [and gives the SEC rulemaking powers to define such acts]. Rule 14e-3(a) qualifies under §14(e) as a "means reasonably designed to prevent" fraudulent trading on material, nonpublic information in the tender offer context. A prophylactic measure, because its mission is to prevent, typically encompasses more than the core activity prohibited. Section 14(e)'s rulemaking authorization gives the Commission "latitude," even in the context of a term of art like "manipulative," "to regulate nondeceptive activities as a 'reasonably designed' means of preventing manipulative acts, without suggesting any change in the meaning of the term 'manipulative' itself." The Commission may prohibit acts, not themselves fraudulent under the common law or §10(b), if the prohibition is "reasonably designed to prevent . . . [fraudulent] acts and practices."

Decision. The misappropriation theory validly applies the insider trading prohibition of SEC Rule 10b5 to outsiders. SEC Rule 14e-3 validly invokes the possession theory of tender offer insider trading under the Williams Act.

Case Questions

1. Explain how this case reconciles the extension of insider trading prohibitions to outsiders under a common understanding of insider trading.
2. How does *O'Hagan* affect insider trading rules for firms' employees?

A concise formulation of the misappropriation theory aids in analysis of either traditional insider or outsider trading cases. The four elements to misappropriation apply to outsider trading when the nonpublic information is (1) misappropriated from a *confidential source*, (2) the source has *rights* to keep the information confidential, (3) the source has *intent* to retain the confidentiality, and (4) the source has undertaken *efforts* to maintain secrecy of the information.

What kinds of relationships strongly suggest confidential inside information will be misappropriated or tipped? Experience shows that professional colleagues, close acquaintances, and members of families too often disclose inside information among themselves. Should misappropriation and use of the inside information be presumed with these close relationships if the insider had inside information and the recipient trades in the firm's stock? This was the issue in *U.S. v. Chestman*[19] in which a corporate employee entrusted nonpublic information to her husband. The court refused to impose a duty of trust and confidence needed to trigger misappropriation liability, even though the husband traded the firm's stock because the wife had not imposed confidentiality on her husband.

In 2000, the SEC promulgated **SEC Rule 10b5-2** to close the *Chestman* loophole. The misappropriation theory applies to trades following a tip that occurs through a relationship of trust and confidence. The outsider will be liable (1) if the recipient promises confidentiality; (2) there is a reasonable expectation of mutual confidentiality from history, practice, or pattern of sharing confidences; or (3) the information source is a spouse, child, parent, or sibling of the recipient. Each case is evaluated ad hoc, so proving the relationship creates only a rebuttable presumption of misappropriation.

19. 947 F.2d 551 (2d Cir., 1991).

Tender Offer Insider Trading

Tender offer insider trading (TOIT) theory under SEC Rule 14e-3 is somewhat different than under the other insider trading theories that treat insider trading as a form of deception or fraud. The SEC's TOIT rule resurrects the old possession theory and parity of information rule rejected by the Supreme Court in *Chiarella* and *Dirks*. *O'Hagan* validated the possession theory because of the SEC's broader authority to regulate tender offers. In that section 14(e) of the Williams Act empowers the SEC to design means to prevent fraudulent, deceptive, or manipulative practices, the SEC can regulate beyond traditional common law fraud. The TOIT rule includes the disclose or abstain duty for anyone in mere possession of material information that the person knows or has reason to know is nonpublic and that has been acquired from a confidential source. For example, employees of the target or bidder, consultants of the target or bidder, and employees of these consultants are constrained by 14e3. When combined with the tipping rule, the TOIT rule also restricts the trading of tippees who receive tender offer tips.

TOIT liability under SEC Rule 14e-3 is illustrated in Exhibit 22.7. Note that the insider is really an outsider with a fiduciary duty to the bidder, which is often the source of the confidential information. However, there is no confidential relationship, based on fiduciary principles or contract, between the bidder and issuer. Traditional insider trading theory is often ineffective in prohibiting TOIT because the duty path between insider and naive trading partner (shareholder) cannot be drawn.

OTHER INSIDER TRADING LAWS

Between 1984 and 1990, Congress enacted three laws strengthening insider trading enforcement. The **Insider Trading Sanctions Act** of 1984 (ITSA) imposes a civil penalty of up to three times the insider's trading profit in enforcement actions brought by the SEC. The SEC may sue for the full treble penalty or for a lesser

EXHIBIT 22.7 Tender Offer Insider Trading Theory

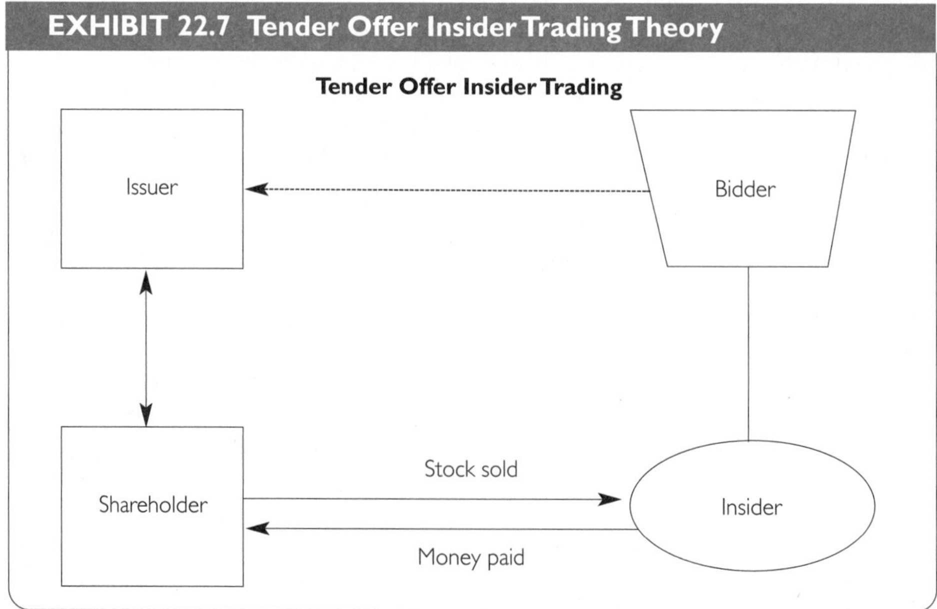

International Commentary

Insider Trading Abroad

The insider trading laws in the United States are the most stringent in the world. Many nations have traditionally permitted insider trading as an innocent executive perk. Some nations have simply ignored it. Insider trading enforcement in most other nations has been lax until recent years. Insiders may try to hide their trading by conducting their trades through anonymous accounts they hold in foreign banks or foreign brokers. To make matters worse, many foreign nations fail to cooperate with the SEC's enforcement efforts. For example, in a 1983 case involving Santa Fe International Corp., the Swiss Supreme Court refused to adopt the misappropriation theory. The Swiss found no direct fiduciary relationship between two strangers trading anonymously through brokers on the impersonal stock exchange.[20]

Some commentators argue that the U.S. insider trading laws are excessively stringent and that U.S. markets will therefore lose trading volume to other nations' securities markets. However, several other nations are finally abandoning their protection of insider traders since scandals in the early 1990s damaged the reputations of securities markets in the United Kingdom, Ireland, France, Germany, and Japan. Most nations are beginning to enforce insider trading rules, and their regulators now cooperate more fully with the SEC in insider trading enforcement.

amount, which is payable into the federal treasury. ITSA actions are tried by only a judge, not a jury. It does not eliminate existing remedies under §16(b), Rule 10b-5, or Rule 14e-3. ITSA damages are the "profit gained or loss avoided" through illegal insider trading. This is the difference between the insider's purchase price and the trading price right after the inside information is disclosed publicly. The ITSA penalties are cumulative with other insider trading liabilities. Investors who trade contemporaneously with the insider are entitled to sue for such damages. ITSA cases must be brought within one year after the wrongful act is discovered. The SEC usually sets aside a fund for payment of disgorged profits (insider's repayment of unlawful insider trading profits) to private insider trading victims.

Congress further toughened the insider trading penalties and the SEC's enforcement powers in the **Insider Trading and Securities Fraud Enforcement Act** of 1988 (ITSFEA). This law (1) increases criminal penalties, (2) provides for payment of a bounty to informants, (3) requires brokers and dealers to supervise their employees to prevent tipping or insider trading, (4) establishes a statutory right for injured investors to sue for damages, and (5) gives the SEC authority to assist foreign investigations of international securities fraud.

The **Enforcement Remedies and Penny Stock Reform Act** of 1990 further expands the SEC's civil enforcement powers applicable to insider trading and other securities law violations. The SEC may seek money penalties and disgorgement in SEC administrative proceedings without prosecuting the defendants in federal court. Officers and directors may be debarred from practice before the SEC, effectively preventing their employment in high offices for publicly traded companies. The SEC may issue cease and desist orders against repeat offenders. This act also significantly restructured the penny stock industry and gives the SEC powers over program trading and emergency enforcement powers over securities firms.

There is often substantial overlap among the various insider trading theories. When takeover bidders use a tender offer to acquire the target's shares, insider trading by employees of the bidder is prohibited by both the misappropriation rule and

20. The *Santa Fe* Case, *Intl. Leg. Mat.* 22 (1983), 785.

by SEC Rule 14e-3. Employees of the bidder's consultants are also restricted as temporary insiders. This proliferation of theories demonstrates three important points: (1) Insider trading is so widely viewed as offensive that common law, statutory law, and administrative regulations may all prohibit it; (2) insider trading is broadly unlawful as a crime, a regulatory offense, and a private right to damages; and (3) the numerous insider trading theories provide regulators with a full array of enforcement tools.

PROXY SOLICITATIONS AND TENDER OFFERS

There is a market for corporate control in which individual financiers, takeover specialists, firms, and dissident shareholders (in opposition to management) struggle for control. State corporation law and federal securities law are both involved. The federal proxy rules regulate how management and outsiders communicate with shareholders and advocate their action in proxy contests and votes taken at shareholder meetings. The tender offer rules regulate how takeovers are achieved through tender offers.

PROXY SOLICITATIONS

The 1934 Act regulates proxy solicitations of shareholders in publicly traded corporations, and the proxy process for closely held corporations is regulated primarily under state law. The term **proxy** has several different meanings: (1) the intangible agency or power of attorney a shareholder gives to another to vote their shares, (2) the written or electronic absentee ballot, and (3) the agent who actually casts the vote. The 1934 Act confines the term *proxy* to "any proxy, consent, or authorization to vote shares." Proxies are used to assure sufficient shareholder votes are present (or represented by proxy) at shareholder meetings to satisfy quorum requirements so that valid business is conducted.

Proxy solicitations involve electioneering to convince shareholders to vote for particular proposals or director candidates. Solicitations include any verbal, audio, printed, video, or electronic request to give or revoke a proxy or furnish a shareholder a proxy form. It also includes advertising in print or electronic media and solicitations by direct mail or over the Internet. The proxy rules are intended to maintain fairness by promoting full disclosure, prohibiting fraud, and facilitating shareholder participation. Proxy solicitations are made by both management and dissident shareholders. All their communications must comply with the SEC's proxy rules. Most are filed in print or electronically with the SEC. The SEC rules on electronic delivery of documents, discussed previously, apply to all communications in the proxy context.

Proxy Statements

Any person soliciting proxies must file a **proxy statement** containing certain information to inform shareholders of the issues and of the solicitor's motives. This information includes the identity of the solicitor, the proxy's legal terms, and details about board elections or extraordinary corporate transactions (merger, issuer's financial statements). Management annually solicits proxies in board elections, so the SEC requires the issuer to distribute its latest annual report as part of the disclosure package. To make it easier for shareholders to assess management's performance, the compensation of the top five senior executives is juxtaposed against shareholder return for recent years. Management can be held liable for inaccuracies or misstatements in the annual report. Even if management decides not to solicit proxies for director elections, it must nevertheless distribute an **information statement** containing similar information.

The proxy itself must be formatted much like a standard ballot, with a blank date line and boxes for each proposition to permit the shareholder to vote for approval or disapproval or to abstain. If the proxy is solicited by the board or its legal terms permit the board to vote incomplete proxies, these facts must be conspicuously stated. Electronic proxy solicitation and voting is becoming commonplace. Internet proxy sites are usually operated by third-party proxy solicitation firms. As with electronic deliveries of other documents to investors, the SEC requires investors to consent to receiving electronic delivery of proxy documents. Further, the disclosures must include information equivalent to the printed versions, and the investor must be capable of retaining a permanent record (saved, printed). These must be reasonably secure from interference or tampering.

Many shareholders' stock is held in **street name**; that is, the shares are not registered in stockholders' names but instead are in the name of their broker. Street name shares actually belong to the investor but are held in street name to facilitate quick settlement of trades or as collateral for margin loans made to the investor to purchase securities. When shares are held in street name, the issuer and broker must forward all proxy solicitation materials to the beneficial or actual owner.

ONLINE

Automated Data Processing's Proxy Processing
http://www.proxyvote.com

PROXY CONTESTS

Proxy contests are the major tool of shareholder democracy in corporate governance. Some contests are so divisive they are covered extensively in the press, and the opponents take out full-page ads in the national press and on detailed websites. Shareholders are best served by receiving accurate information from all proxy solicitors. Preliminary drafts of proxy solicitation materials are filed with the SEC. The firm's management has the most effective ability to electioneer in that management's proxy solicitation expenses are paid from the corporate treasury.

Management alone possesses the complete and accurate list of eligible shareholder voters. Dissident shareholders have a more difficult time soliciting proxies. The SEC regulates shareholder proxy solicitations in two ways. First, dissidents can pay for their own solicitation—often an expensive campaign that may not generate sufficient benefits from winning the vote. SEC rules give management the choice to either provide the dissident solicitor with a shareholder list or mail the solicitation for the dissident. Direct mailing makes it difficult for dissidents to match management's advantage in follow-up electioneering by contacting big shareholders directly, a point made clear in the 2002 proxy approval of the merger between Compaq and Hewlett-Packard. Second, small shareholder proposals are financed by the firm.

Mandatory Shareholder Proxy Proposals

Corporations must pay solicitation expenses and include certain shareholder proposals in management's own proxy mailing. This procedure is intended to give small shareholders at least some minimal voice in corporate governance. Some shareholders abused this process in the 1960s by airing their personal political and social views that were arguably unconnected to the issuer's operations. For example, one shareholder who opposed the Vietnam War proposed a charter amendment prohibiting a defense contractor from producing napalm. The proxy process is not designed for political grandstanding, so the SEC tightened these requirements. Dissident shareholders must have a serious financial interest in the corporation: The shareholder has held the shares for at least one year, owns at least 1% or $1,000 in market value, and is limited to only one proposal each year. Management can choose to limit the dissident's proposal to no more than 500 words and may omit shareholder proposals that violate the guidelines in SEC Rule 14a-8(c).

Management Exclusion of Shareholder Proposals: Rule 14a-8(c)

1. Proposal is illegal.
2. Proposal violates SEC proxy rules.
3. Proposal furthers a personal grievance.
4. Proposal is unrelated to the issuer's business.
5. Proposal concerns issuer's ordinary business operations.
6. Proposal duplicates another pending proposal.
7. Proposal is moot.
8. Proposal attempts to censure a particular director.
9. Proposal requires declaration of a dividend.

In recent years, shareholders have put forth various types of questions for shareholder votes. For example, many proposals have sought changes in management compensation systems, shareholder voting (cumulative voting, confidential voting), takeover defenses (staggered boards, poison pills, golden parachutes), and social issues (discontinuing business with oppressive foreign governments, controlling corporate political action committees, animal rights). In the future, shareholders are likely to seek more control over the choice of auditors and consulting firms, redefine the metrics used in executive bonus and stock option plans, narrow the choice of particular accounting treatments, and curtail the use of special purpose entities such as the limited partnerships used by Enron.

TENDER OFFERS

After the wave of conglomerate mergers in the 1960s, American financiers began to adopt a British takeover tactic, the takeover bid or tender offer. A **tender offer** typically involves a public offering of cash and/or securities in exchange for a controlling interest in a target corporation. After a successful tender offer, the bidder can restructure the target firm or merge it into an affiliated firm. For example, Chevron Oil Co. used a tender offer to take over Gulf Oil Co. Tender offers occurred very quickly, with little time for shareholders to evaluate the transaction. Before 1968, many individual shareholders had little notice of tender offers and were often panicked into selling their shares. In other cases, large institutional investors, large-block shareholders, and Wall Street insiders crowded out small shareholders, who learned of the tender offer too late to participate. In 1968, Congress passed the Williams Act, which requires tender offer disclosures and slows the process so all shareholders are treated equally.

Williams Act Notification Requirements

Under the Williams Act, a **Schedule 13D** is filed to give early warning to potential takeover targets and their shareholders. The 13D identifies the potential takeover bidder when it accumulates a large block of the target's stock. Shareholders of more than 5% of any equity security must file a 13D when they acquire 2% or more of any registered equity security and the purchase results in their ownership of 5% or more. The 13D must also disclose the purchaser's background, the source and amounts of funds used, any present or likely future plans to control the target, the number of shares owned, and any contracts the purchasers has concerning the issuer's securities (e.g., options).

A tender offeror must file a **Schedule 14D-1** tender offer statement when the tender offer begins. The 14D-1 includes all the 13D information, plus negotiations with the issuer, the bidder's purpose and plans for the target, the bidder's financial statements, the precise terms of the tender offer, and communications sent to shareholders or press releases used during the tender offer. The tender offer target must immediately advise its shareholders in a **Schedule 14D-9** that gives management's opinion of the tender offer.

WHAT IS A TENDER OFFER?

Tender offer is defined only in cases and SEC interpretations. Tender offers usually involve a widespread public announcement and solicitation of shareholders and are not privately negotiated stock purchases. Tender offer bidders usually attempt to acquire a large block of shares by paying a premium above the prevailing market price. Tender offers remain open for only a short time, and their terms are usually nonnegotiable. All this creates pressure to sell. A tender offer is usually made contingent on receiving a minimum percentage of shares the bidder seeks. Tender offers are not always made for 100% of the outstanding stock because firms can be controlled with less. Sometimes the bidder offers a higher price in the first step of a two-tiered tender offer. Shareholders realize they could receive less in the second tier or "back end," and they feel pressured to tender early.

Tender offer bidders can refuse to purchase any tendered shares unless the minimum is tendered. Undersubscribed tender offers may be terminated, and the bidder may refuse to purchase any of the shares tendered. What if the bidder then immediately makes several substantial block purchases of the target's shares in large, privately negotiated transactions? The SEC calls this a **street sweep** and believes it is covered by the tender offer rules. Alternatively, the bidder could raise the offer to attract enough shares.

Mechanics of the Tender Offer

Even though tender offers are made public by the press, they must be separately and personally communicated to all shareholders. Tender offer communications are based on the proxy solicitation model. The target corporation's management usually distributes the tender offer documents. The target's management may either provide a shareholder list to the offeror or directly mail the tender offer at the bidder's expense.

The SEC clearly encourages the electronic delivery of communications to investors (e-mail, website links, and documents). However, the tender offer rules may still require that the offeror to distribute some of the tender offers by mail and through the financial press. Two rules create a conflict. First, the SEC's electronic disclosure rules require that the investor be given notice and then consent to electronic delivery. Second, the tender offer rules require equal treatment of all investors. Should investors unwilling or unable to receive electronic delivery be excluded from a tender offer? Clearly not, so these difficulties must be resolved before electronic tender offers fully deliver on their promise of transactional efficiency.

Tender offers must remain open for at least 20 days. If more shares are tendered than the bidder requests, all shares must be accepted pro rata. Thus, if a limited tender offer is oversubscribed, all tendering shareholders may still own some of their original shares after acceptance. Tendering shareholders may withdraw their shares

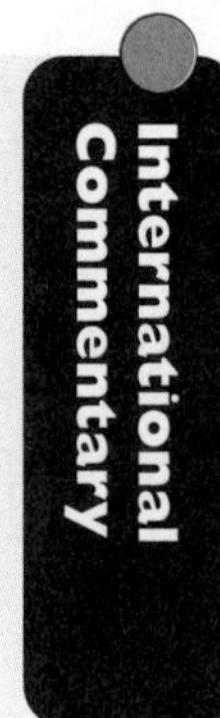

International Takeovers

Hostile takeovers are a phenomenon known largely in the nations of the former British Empire: the United Kingdom, United States, Canada, and Australia. The laws and cultures of most other industrialized nations erect significant barriers to hostile takeovers and to interference from foreigners. For example, most European and Japanese laws prevent foreigners from gaining controlling interests in their domestic corporations. When mergers occur in these nations, they are usually negotiated amicably with another domestic merger partner. This helps guard against layoffs and avoids abrupt changes in the merging firms' business practices. Since the 1980s, even the United States has restricted some hostile takeovers. For example, the United States impedes foreigners from controlling much of the defense contracting industry, and state anti-takeover statutes are generally valid.

within 15 business days after they tender. During a tender offer, it is illegal for the bidder to manipulate the target's shares. Tender offer insider trading is also illegal, and shareholders may not **short tender** by tendering borrowed shares.

STATE TENDER OFFER REGULATIONS

Most states have passed some type of takeover legislation. Some observers believe these statutes have similar objectives to foreign restrictions of takeovers; that is, they are really intended to retain the target corporation's employment and tax base within these states. State takeover regulations arguably attract businesses that seek protection from hostile takeovers. However, some state antitakeover laws interfere with the Williams Act. An Illinois antitakeover statute was invalidated in *Edgar v. MITE Corp.*[21] because it created delays inconsistent with the Williams Act. Later cases validate state antitakeover statutes that regulate only corporate shareholder democracy. States have a traditional role in structuring corporations and shareholder rights. The Indiana Control Share Acquisition Act was validated in *CTS Corp. v. Dynamics Corp. of America*[22] and quickly became a model for other states. Control share acquisition provisions permit other shareholders to take a vote that can remove the voting powers of a takeover bidder that acquires a large, "control" block of stock.

Some state laws have other takeover defenses. For example, target management may need to consider the interests of corporate constituencies other than shareholders (e.g., employees, customers, suppliers, surrounding communities). Some takeovers are permitted only at "fair prices." Some laws prohibit the bidder from merging with the target until after a long time elapses. These laws impede hostile takeovers, force the bidder to negotiate with the target's management, and clearly shift power to the target firm's management.

LIABILITIES UNDER THE SECURITIES LAWS

The two major components of the securities laws—the 1933 Act and the 1934 Act—have significant remedial provisions. These are the enforcement "teeth" used to deter negligent or intentional wrongdoing that endangers investors' interests and

21. 457 U.S. 624 (1982).
22. 481 U.S. 69 (1987).

the integrity of the capital markets. If the deterrence fails, the liability provisions give investors rights to remedies, such as damages and recision (cancellation). Regulators like the SEC, DOJ, the SROs, and state attorneys general also have enforcement powers. The major remedies are discussed next. Insider trading enforcement and remedies were discussed previously.

SECURITIES ACT LIABILITIES

The 1933 Act includes remedies that encourage compliance with the registration procedures. Investors may return nonexempt unregistered securities to the issuer and demand return of their investment. Investors may also bring private damage suits against those responsible for material omissions or misstatements. Those subject to this liability include the issuer, its underwriters, control persons, and any individual who signs the registration statement, such as an officer, director, or auditor. If found guilty of intentional fraud in a securities offering, they are liable for both civil damages and, in severe cases, criminal penalties. Under Section 12 of the 1933 Act, it is illegal to offer or sell an unregistered security, to fail to deliver a prospectus, or to use an illegal prospectus in making illegal offers or sales during the prefiling or waiting periods. These provisions are quite successful because most issuers carefully follow the registration and prospectus delivery requirements. The 1933 Act liabilities apply only to IPOs.

Most securities market participants can minimize their liability risk exposure by acting reasonably and professionally under the circumstances. Defendants accused of participating in misstatements can use the **due diligence** defense by proving they reasonably believed the registration statement disclosures were true. Must the various parties investigate separately to be protected by the due diligence defense? Each party must devote attention and expertise consistent with their experience and their position. For example, due diligence duties depend on the sophistication of the investor, reasonable expectations of trust created by fiduciary duties, access to superior information, active concealment of material information, the opportunity to detect fraud, the initiator of transaction, and the specificity of information that is misstated.

The watershed case of *Escott v. BarChris* is frequently cited for its extensive list of negligence and deception by various parties, each of which had key responsibilities for the integrity of the financial statements.[23] BarChris financed and built bowling alleys during that industry's 1960s expansion. BarChris needed a public offering of debentures for cash flow after bowling alleys became overbuilt and many customers defaulted in their payments to BarChris. BarChris's financial statements had significant errors and omissions about its cash flow, sales, income, earnings per share, assets, and liabilities. Each participant who was expected to assure accuracy in financial statements failed to stop the fraud, including the firm's founders, president and CEO, the CFO, directors, in-house counsel, the underwriter, and the auditors. The BarChris failure is much like the Enron bankruptcy in 2001 as an example of catastrophic failure of numerous major control systems expected to assure integrity of the capital markets and corporate governance.

LIABILITY FOR PROXY AND TENDER OFFER VIOLATIONS

Electioneering in corporate governance contests is a sensitive matter. Solicitations from management or dissident shareholders risk liability for proxy rule violations.

23. 283 F.Supp. 643 (S.D.N.Y., 1968).

SEC Rule 14a-9 is a proxy antifraud provision that prohibits false or misleading solicitation statements. Proxy fraud is judged by the "total mix" of communications made to shareholders from all sources. Proxy solicitors are also liable for negligent misstatements or omissions, a great potential liability.[24] The proxy rules exempt proxy solicitations by foreign issuers, issuers in insolvency proceedings (bankruptcy, reorganization), and public utility holding companies. Most proxy rules do not apply to tombstone ads, to small solicitations of 10 or fewer persons, or to presolicitation discussions such as those among institutional investors. Misstatements or omissions must be material to be actionable as proxy fraud. Proxy settlements are increasingly used when shareholder votes are predicted to favor the dissident(s), often implementing much of the dissident's objective(s).

Violators of the tender offer rules may be liable for fraud, failure to file the required schedules, or commission of any manipulative acts. Although the Williams Act was originally passed to protect tendering shareholders, other parties such as the SEC, target corporations, or competing bidders may also enforce the rules.

MATERIALITY

Throughout this chapter, there is a primary focus on the accuracy and timeliness of disclosure. The securities laws are concerned primarily with accurate information that is important to evaluate the risks and appropriateness of particular transactions. The measure of this importance is called **materiality**—a focus on the importance and relevance of a misstatement or omission. There is no liability for inadvertent or immaterial errors or omissions about insignificant matters. Materiality is a limiting principle in securities law, accounting practice, the due diligence defense, and many other aspects of contract performance.

Each profession may have a slightly different perspective on evaluating materiality. For example, accounting traditionally uses a rule of thumb quantitative method to measure the importance of inaccuracies in accounts. Errors are insignificant if they are less than 5% of an account; errors become material if they rise above 5%. However, such "mechanical" measures of materiality do not apply in securities law. This difference can be confusing for accountants because auditors of financial statements must follow the securities law definition of materiality.

Materiality under securities law is defined in *TSC Industries v. Northway*, an influential proxy case in which the materiality of misstatements in proxy disclosures was evaluated in relation to the vote that shareholders were asked to make.[25] A misrepresented or omitted fact is material if there is a substantial likelihood that a reasonable investor would consider it important in making an investment decision. Put another way, had the fact been truthfully disclosed, the investor would consider it to have significantly altered the mix of available information.

SECURITIES LITIGATION REFORM

Securities litigation tends to wax and wane, depending on the market. When the market is up, investors show less dissatisfaction. When the market falls, however, investors are quick to allege their losses are due to fraud by management, auditors, brokers, or investment advisers rather than to the business cycle or their own bad

24. *Arron v. SEC*, 446 U.S. 680 (1980).
25. 426 U.S. 438 (1976).

investment decisions. The securities laws are not investment insurance, nor should their liability provisions be misused to recoup losses not caused by securities fraud. However, there are recurring eras when numerous securities fraud suits are brought by shareholders citing violations of the federal securities laws or state corporation law. Many are brought as class actions because numerous shareholders can be joined in a single suit. As discussed in Chapter 3, class action suits are sometimes efficient but can also be harassing. Some innocent firms have settled shareholder class action suits because the opportunity costs and reputational losses of defending them are too high. There have been many regulatory, tort, and liability reforms at both state and federal levels. Similar reforms were discussed in Chapters 7 and 8. Two securities laws passed in the 1990s that addressed the excesses of the securities liability system are discussed next.

Private Securities Litigation Reform Act of 1995

The first major reform was the **Private Securities Litigation Reform Act of 1995 (PSLRA)**. PSLRA significantly limits the previously common abuses of shareholder class actions. Class actions must have a lead plaintiff, who is the named party in the suit. PSLRA presumes the largest shareholder should be the lead plaintiff unless it clear that another is more appropriate. For example, if the CEO is the largest shareholder but is alleged to be responsible for the fraud, another large shareholder plaintiff should be chosen. Selection of plaintiff's counsel is also regulated. The plaintiff must plead the fraud with particularity, which means more evidence must be shown to connect disclosure misstatements or omissions with shareholder losses. Management and auditors are less vulnerable to liability when stocks in a whole sector of the market (e.g., high tech) all lose value at one time. The pretrial discovery stage of litigation is very costly, and threat of prolonged discovery pressures defendants to settle frivolous suits. PSLRA now allows a **stay**—a court order halting discovery until the defendants argue a motion to dismiss frivolous suits. The law also codified the bespeaks caution and safe harbor for forward-looking statements discussed previously. PSLRA reformed the racketeering law, making it very difficult to allege securities fraud as a predicated offense under RICO, discussed in Chapter 7. PSLRA imposes proportionate liability rather than joint and several liability, and any one defendant is not held liable for the whole damage amount, only the proportionate part a defendant caused.

The accounting industry made a historic compromise in return for these very favorable securities litigation reforms, as well as an additional exemption from private securities fraud liability. PSLRA requires auditors to detect and report fraud more than was previously required under the auditing standards that the accounting industry set for itself. Auditors of publicly traded firms perform different societal functions than do attorneys and consultants. The latter are fiduciaries owing their ultimate loyalty to the firms that engage them. By stark contrast, auditors are public watchdogs who must maintain their independence from conflicts and the selfish, personal influences of the firm's management.[26]

PSLRA has whistle-blower provisions that require auditors to detect illegal acts, identify transactions with parties related to the firm, and evaluate the firm's ability to continue as a going concern. When illegal acts are discovered or suspected, the auditor must determine the likelihood of reoccurrence and their potential impact on financial statements. Next, the auditor must inform the firm's management. If the impact is material and management fails to take timely remedial action, then the

26. *U.S. v. Arthur Young & Co.*, 465 U.S. 805 (1984).

auditor must inform the board, which must immediately inform the SEC. Auditors must immediately resign if they do not soon hear back that the SEC was notified. Auditors are exempt from private plaintiffs' fraud suits by security holders if the SEC is informed in a timely manner. PSLRA changes so reduced shareholder suits in the federal courts that they flooded state courts, and Congress narrowed this loophole with a second reform law in 1998.

Securities Litigation Uniform Standards Act of 1998

The second major reform was the **Securities Litigation Uniform Standards Act of 1998**, which severely limits plaintiffs who try to bring shareholder class action suits in state courts against firms traded on national exchanges. There are exceptions for violations of state corporation law, enforcement actions brought by state regulators, and corporate governance matters such as going private, tender offers, mergers, and dissenters' appraisal rights. This law also reinforces the safe harbor for forward-looking statements discussed previously. Despite these securities litigation reforms, the number of suits is again rising. Of course, the bursting of the dot.com bubble in 2000 and 2001 probably explains some increase in securities litigation. However, modern cases seem to be much stronger in pleading, process, and proof. The elimination of frivolous suits is precisely the objective of securities litigation reform.

ONLINE

Impact of securities litigation reform
http://securities.stanford.edu

Additional Reforms of Auditor Liability and Audit Professionalism

In addition to the litigation reforms that accountants enjoy under PSLRA and the Uniform Standards Act, several other sources of litigation reform directly benefit auditors. The accounting industry is routinely sued when publicly traded firms allegedly have "cooked books." There is no aiding and abetting liability in private securities fraud suits against auditors or underwriters following *Central Bank of Denver v. First Interstate Bank*,[27] and this exemption is codified in PSLRA. Since 1991, most states have enacted new laws permitting general partnerships to re-form as **limited liability partnerships (LLPs)**. LLPs are particularly popular with accounting firms because the LLP form limits the joint and several liability. Malpractice liability is limited for those partners who are not directly involved in the audit engagement of the firm found liable for securities fraud. Most LLP laws require the LLP to maintain adequate malpractice insurance. The aftermath of the Enron bankruptcy may raise malpractice insurance rates significantly for auditors and lawyers.

The Enron bankruptcy has caused more serious calls for reform of the accounting profession, particularly its client relations and professional standards. Litigation reform has immunized the accounting industry from many suits, so future reform efforts will focus on prevention of fraud. These issues include the process and participation of financial statement user groups in setting accounting and auditing standards. Auditor independence and conflicts of interest in large accounting firms attempting to maintain **multidisciplinary practices (MDPs)** are under much closer scrutiny. The existing regulatory systems—state, federal, and self-regulatory—that discipline the accounting industry are likely to more closely control how the accounting industry performs, consistent with society's expectations. For example, quality control reviews may not be perfunctorily performed by competing accounting firms. Public oversight will shift to a more publicly selected group that is more independent of the accounting profession, and the standards-setting process for accounting and audit methods will be examined for excessive influence by the firms audited.

---

27. 511 U.S. 164 (1994).

QUESTIONS

1. Under the Securities Act of 1933, three important periods affect the offering of securities for sale. Name and describe these three periods, and give reasons for their apparent importance in the public policy on regulating the securities markets.
2. What factors are presumed to be part of every "security"? Give three examples of transactions other than the sale of stock or bonds that have been interpreted as involving the sale of a security, and explain why they are considered securities.
3. Claiming the intrastate exemption of the Securities Act of 1933, Jones Investment Company did not register its offering of shares with the SEC. Jones Investment is a Georgia corporation whose only offices are in that state. It sold shares only to Georgia residents. However, the funds were raised to finance the company's real estate developments in Florida. Why or why not is the intrastate exemption available for Jones Investment? See *Busch v. Carpenter,* 827 F.2d 653 (10th Cir., 1987).
4. Consider the following example and calculate the short swing profits liability under Section 16(b):
   - On January 1, Insider purchased 100 shares of Atlantic stock at $30 a share.
   - On February 28, Insider sold 100 shares of Atlantic stock at $20 a share.
   - On April 15, Insider purchased 100 shares of Atlantic stock at $40 a share.
   - On May 20, Insider sold 100 shares of Atlantic stock at $50 a share.
5. John Smith is a junior executive of the Widget Company. In the course of his employment, he has accumulated $25,000 of its common stock (at its current market value of $12.50 per share), having first received a stock bonus eight years ago and having last made a purchase of 200 shares at $10 per share four months ago. During the last four months, since a new president was brought in from the outside, he has felt that the company was drifting downhill. Some rather weak executives have been hired, apparently because they were friends or relatives of the new president. A disappointment is in the offing because a new device that was rumored to be a breakthrough (and was prominently mentioned in the trade journals) is having production difficulties that will probably prevent it from being offered in the market for a long time to come.

   Smith thinks that when the facts about the new device are announced, Widget stock will go down several points. It is unlikely, however, to descend to its level a year ago for some time, perhaps not until its annual financial report is released in about seven months. Smith would like to sell his stock as soon as possible and would also like to advise some friends who have followed his lead and invested heavily in it to do so too. Discuss his potential liability and the statutes that might apply. See *Shapiro v. Merrill Lynch, Pierce, Fenner & Smith*, 495 F.2d 228 (2d Cir., 1974).
6. How would you apply the misappropriation theory to the fact pattern in the previous question? For example, suppose that John Smith passed on the information to his friends and that the friends tipped off other outsiders. Discuss how this would this violate Rule 10b-5? See *U.S. v. Chestman*, 947 F.2d 551 (2d Cir., 1991).
7. James Jones has access to information on Atlantic Company that is not available to the general investor. He wants to buy stock in the company, and he is also preparing a proxy statement that is to be distributed to all of its shareholders. What standard should he apply to determine whether the information in his possession is "material," so that he cannot invest in his company prior to its public release? What standard should he apply to determine whether the information should be included in the proxy statement?
8. Compare and contrast the analytical steps taken to evaluate the legal and ethical problems of the following securities markets activities:
   a. Stock parking, the practice of acquiring and holding large blocks of the stock of potential takeover targets through friends, family, and business associates in order to conceal the identity of the acquirer.
   b. Trading on inside information acquired from corporate employees of another firm by promising to return the favor with a tip of inside information on the trader's company.
   c. Disclosure of false information about your companies' lower expected earnings for the next quarter in order to sell your holdings in the stock before the market price plunges.
   d. Falsifying the accounting records of your company to show a false profit so that the company can float a new issue of bonds to secure financing that may help turn around the company's ill fortunes.
   e. Failing to disclose in management's proxy solicitation that urges approval of a merger that the officers of the company currently own large amounts

of corporate stock and have lucrative golden parachutes (huge severance pay bonuses). Approval of the merger will trigger the officers' rights to these stock profits and severance bonuses. However, the officers have not secured any advice on a fair merger price from an independent investment banker, and the merger price is far below the company's value.

9. A top executive of a publicly traded company and graduate of the University of Oklahoma was seated at a track meet near the football coach, Barry Switzer. The executive made a nonintimate revelation, supposedly to his wife, which was very optimistic financial news about his firm. The statement was so loud that it was easily overheard by the coach and others seated nearby in this crowded public place. Soon thereafter, Coach Switzer purchased the stock and made significant profits before the information was disclosed to the public. Was the executive's tip made for the improper purpose of giving cost-free compensation to a cherished football coach? Is the coach liable as a tippee for insider trading? See *SEC v. Switzer*, 590 F.Supp. 756 (W.D.Ok., 1984).

10. How can Internet securities market mechanisms such as bulletin boards, on-line trading systems, EDGAR, and on-line IPO auctions improve the securities markets? Include various factors such as transaction costs, underwriting fees, widespread notice of offerings, updated disclosures, and the quickness and accuracy of transaction processing.

Environmental Law

INTRODUCTION

The environment is all of the surrounding physical conditions and influences that affect the development of living things. Environmental law regulates our interaction with the surrounding air, water, and land through limitations imposed by law. Worldwide public concern over the deteriorating environment is increasing, and environmental laws are growing in importance for business managers. Although motor vehicle manufacturers and chemical, petroleum, and mining firms have for years faced extensive regulation of the environmental effects of their activities, today financial services firms, insurers, and real estate developers are also deeply affected by environmental regulation. The cost of compliance with numerous regulations seems to constantly increase, and managers may even face criminal charges for intentional violations of environmental laws.

Serious environmental threats to human health have become too common and too dangerous to ignore. In the past, the dumping of solid, liquid, and gaseous products into streams and harbors, on land, and into the air was largely unregulated. Medical science was unaware of the health effects of waste, pollution, and decaying products. Centuries ago, the London smog came into being when soft coal became a common fuel. Venice has encountered serious water and air pollution problems for centuries. For decades, the water from lakes and rivers near many cities throughout the world has been virtually undrinkable because of the wastes residents and business firms have dumped into them. The poor in some major cities live at garbage dumps that create and spread disease and other health hazards. The laissez-faire attitude toward the environment that prevailed throughout the first half of the twentieth century led to the dumping of wastes in waterways, the burning of low-grade coal, and lead emissions from millions of cars.

Today, environmental law in the United States is based on pervasive federal regulation. The Clean Water Act, Clean Air Act, Resource Conservation and Recovery Act, Superfund legislation, Solid Waste Disposal Act, and Toxic Substances Control Act exemplify the statutory laws intended to address environmental problems. In addition to federal laws, state and local legislation also regulate many business activities that

http://

www.greenpeace.org/

affect the environment. Some comparisons of U.S. law with those in other countries provide several different approaches to protecting the environment while promoting economic development. Although recent attempts to reach a global accord have been unsuccessful, international agreements will be needed to deal with a host of problems affecting the worldwide environment.

Environmental activists for decades have urged greater social accountability for corporate actions that degrade the environment. By using the Internet, the activists can better coordinate their activities and campaigns to target governmental and business leaders. The Greenpeace site depicted here includes its views on a number of the topics considered in this chapter.

This chapter examines recent laws regulating the use and abuse of the environment in the United States. Unlike many other fields of law, environmental law is primarily statutory and federal in scope; the common law plays only a minor role in American environmental regulation. The major federal environmental statutes are depicted in Exhibit 23.1.

ONLINE

Among the more prominent sites maintained by environmental activists are
http://www.greenpeace.org
http://www.earth-link.com
http://www.corpwatch.org

MAJOR FEDERAL ENVIRONMENTAL STATUTORY LAWS

Although pollution differs from region to region, its effects do not stop at state or national borders. This chapter focuses first on the most important federal environmental statute: the National Environmental Policy Act. Next, it takes up other important federal statutory laws dealing with air, water, and land pollution. Then, it considers more specific environmental concerns—nuclear power and wildlife protection. Finally, it discusses the role of the states and local communities in enforcing environmental laws.

THE NATIONAL ENVIRONMENTAL POLICY ACT

The 1970 National Environmental Policy Act (NEPA) makes it federal policy to consider the environmental impact of various activities. It also establishes the Council of Environmental Quality, which gathers information on the environment, reviews and recommends changes in federal policies, and makes annual reports on environmental conditions.

Purpose

NEPA lists several general purposes:

to declare a national policy that will encourage productive and enjoyable harmony between man and his environment;

to promote efforts that will prevent or eliminate damage to the environment and the biosphere and stimulate the health and welfare of man; and

EXHIBIT 23.1 Major Federal Environmental Laws

Act	Coverage
Clean Air Act (CAA)	Protects ambient (outdoor) air quality through national ambient air quality standards, state implementation plans, and controls on both stationary (point source) and movable (automotive) sources.
Clean Water Act (CWA) and Federal Water Pollution Control Act (FWPCA)	Protects quality of surface water by setting water quality standards and limiting industrial and municipal discharges into those waters by a permit system. Prohibits filling or dredging of wetlands without a permit.
Hazardous and Solid Waste Amendments (HSWA)	These amendments to the Solid Waste Disposal Act and to RCPA seek to eliminate hazardous waste from landfills and to protect groundwater.
Marine Protection, Research and Sanctuaries Act (MPRSA)	Regulates dumping of all materials into ocean water.
Nuclear Waste Policy Act (NWPA)	Establishes a national plan for nuclear waste disposal.
Oil Pollution Act (OPA)	Imposes liability for damages and cleanup cost on anyone discharging oil into navigable waters or an adjoining shore.
Resource Conservation and Recovery Act (RCRA)	Amends the Solid Waste Disposal Act and establishes a regulatory system for the generation, transportation, and disposal of hazardous waste.
Safe Drinking Water Act (SDWA)	Protects and enhances quality of drinking water. Requires municipal systems to disclose compliance information to the user.
Solid Waste Disposal Act (SWDA)	Assists states and municipalities in addressing waste disposal problems.
Toxic Substance Control Act (TSCA)	Requires testing of toxic chemicals and regulates chemicals that pose an unreasonable risk to health or the environment.

to enrich our understanding of the ecological systems and national resources important to the nation.

The Environmental Protection Agency (EPA) was created in 1970 to coordinate the federal government's environmental policies. Congress recognized that the problems of air pollution, water pollution, and solid waste disposal were interrelated. Subsequent laws addressed control of pesticides, ocean dumping, and hazardous waste problems. The EPA is headquartered in Washington, D.C., and has 10 regional offices throughout the country.

ONLINE

The EPA website, lists a number of different topics as well as recent news items.
http://www.epa.gov

Although the EPA is the nation's primary federal agency for the environment, the Nuclear Regulatory Commission and the Department of Interior also have specific environmental responsibilities.

Environmental Impact Statements

An NEPA provision requires preparation of an environmental impact statement before authorization of certain proposed federally financed or approved projects that are likely to have a significant effect on the quality of the human environment. When the federal government plans to build a dam or power plant, the appropriate federal agency must prepare an environmental impact statement. State roads or prisons built with federal funds also require such a statement. Private companies that

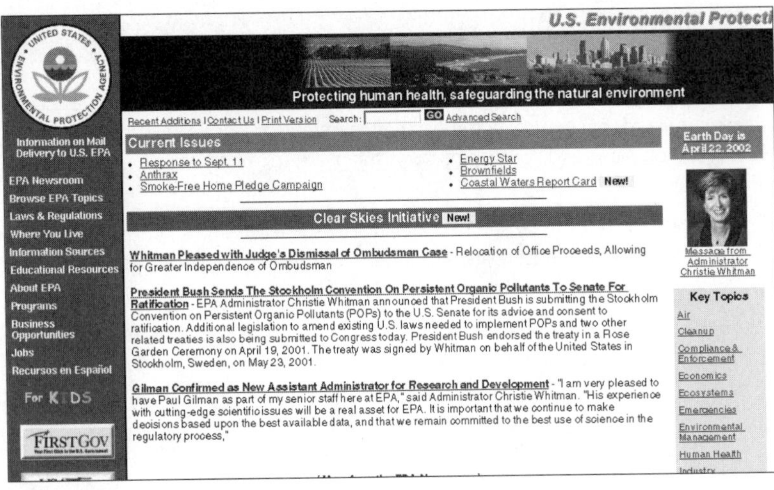

http://
www.epa.gov

receive federal contracts or that are granted permits to cut timber or drill for oil on federal property may be required to assist in preparing environmental impact statements.

The law requires an analysis of the impact the action will have on the environment, its adverse impact, and a consideration of alternative actions. Environmental impact statements are submitted to the president and the Council on Environmental Quality and disclosed to the public. Several other laws, including the Fish and Wildlife Coordination Act and the Endangered Species Act, also require federal agencies to consider the environment in their decision making.

An environmental impact statement (EIS) must contain the following information:

1. The environmental impact of the proposed action
2. Any adverse environmental effect that can be avoided, should the proposed action be implemented
3. Alternatives to the proposed action
4. The relationship between local short-term use of the environment and the maintenance and enhancement of long-term productivity
5. Any irreversible and irretrievable commitments of resources that would be involved, should the proposed action be implemented

AIR POLLUTION

The first federal statute dealing with air pollution was passed in 1955. Then the Clean Air Act was passed in 1963 and amended in 1970, 1977, and most recently in 1990. That act requires the EPA to set national ambient air (atmospheric air as opposed to air inside buildings) quality standards (NAAQS) for such pollutants as carbon monoxide, hydrocarbons, lead, nitrogen oxide, ozone, and sulfur dioxide. Originally, each state was required to develop a state implementation plan (SIP) to achieve a level of air pollution below the maximum level specified by EPA standards. States also were required to inform the EPA about the methods used to achieve the standards for each industrial plant and meet the attainment dates.

The EPA controls both mobile and stationary sources of pollution. Mobile sources of pollution account for more than 50% of the air pollution in the United States. Motor vehicles are subject to emission and fuel standards established by the EPA. The use of unleaded gasoline has diminished the amount of lead in the air. Manufacturers' installation of pollution-control devices has lessened the emission of carbon monoxide and hydrocarbons (a source of smog) from cars, trucks, and buses. Stationary sources of pollution, such as industrial plants, are more difficult to control. A number of the nation's heavily industrialized areas have been unable to attain the EPA's air quality standards.

ONLINE

Additional webpages that provide numerous environmental links include EnviroLink, **http://www.envirolink.netforchange.com** Indiana University's virtual law library, **http://www.law.indiana.edu** and the Essential Organization webpage, **http://www.essential.org**

Commentary

Wireless Communication Devices Versus Environmental Static

Any cell phone user knows that dropped calls, fast busy signals, and dead zones where service is unavailable continue to plague the wireless industry. Carriers are spending big bucks to increase the number of cell sites—antennas, computers, and software—to improve service. In 2000, the 104,288 cell sites were almost five times the 22,663 sites that existed only five years earlier.

A key part of providing the cellular service that customers are demanding requires building more cellular towers. Although hundreds of towers are built each year, the demand for service suggests that many additional towers must continue to be built for the next few years. The Federal Communications Commission (FCC) already requires wireless companies to file environmental impact statements with each tower application. The studies must examine the impact of electromagnetic emissions on surrounding wildlife and vegetation.

Recently, environmental groups have started to complain about the ecological impact of the towers, particularly in sensitive areas. They argue that vegetation and animal habitat in wetland and flood plain areas can be damaged as companies fell trees, string power and communication lines, and build access roads to support the towers. The Friends of the Earth and the Forest Conservation Council asked the FCC to delay approving the construction of 40 towers until further environmental studies are completed. The studies could take a year to complete, and the industry, which claims $300,000 in lost revenue for each month the FCC deliberates, says delays threaten the industry's ability to expand its network to meet current and future demand.

Do you want to remove the static in your phone and the dead zones, or do you want a more careful review of the environmental impact of the thousands of cellular towers across the country?

See the *Wall Street Journal*, July 23, 2001, B1.

MOBILE SOURCES OF AIR POLLUTION

Motor vehicle manufacturers must follow the Clean Air Act's regulations regarding exhaust emissions. The 2004 model cars are required to be able to cut nitrogen oxide from tailpipe emissions. By 2007, the emissions are to be 10% less than the 1998 vehicles. Trucks, sport utility vehicles, and automobiles are all required to meet the same standard. In addition to emission standards, motor vehicles are subject to corporate automotive fuel economy (cafe) standards. A legislative proposal that would have required all cars and light trucks to average 35 miles per gallon by 2013, as compared with the existing requirement of 24 mpg, was defeated in March 2002.

STATIONARY SOURCES OF AIR POLLUTION

The law seeks to limit emissions from stationary sources by imposing standards to be met for existing sources of pollution and for new construction that will emit pollution at either an existing source or a new one. In areas that meet the NAAQ standards, plants that are major sources of toxic emissions must use equipment that meets the maximum available control technology (MACT) standard. In areas that have not attained the NAAQ standards, new construction must use the lowest achievable emission rate (LAER) equipment. By enforcing these controls, the law seeks to reduce the ozone pollution in almost all major cities to healthful levels by 2005.

Acid Rain

The 1990 amendments also addressed the acid rain problems for the first time. The emission of sulfur dioxide from more than 100 power plants in 21 states had to be reduced by 2000. Most electricity-generating facilities had to install control devices, scrubbers, or some form of clean-coal technology. A bonus system allowed companies whose emissions are clearer than that allowed by law to sell their rights to emit more sulfur dioxide to other companies that do not meet the standards.

Toxic Emissions

Toxic air pollution is also significantly affected. Whereas the pre-1990 law had identified and regulated only 7 chemicals, now firms that emit 189 chemicals must use the best technology to reduce emissions. The EPA issued guidelines as to what equipment meets the standards. These cancer-causing pollutants include asbestos, benzene, mercury, and vinyl chloride.

Alternative Fuels

The most striking legacy of the 1990 Clean Air Amendments will probably be the use of alternative fuels. The law required that by 1998 fleets of 10 or more cars must run 80% cleaner than 1990 autos; trucks must be 50% cleaner. In addition, since 1995, all gasoline in the nation's nine smoggiest cities has had to be cleaner-burning, with less emission of hydrocarbons and toxic pollutants.

More cars and trucks will run on methanol, electricity, or other alternative fuels. Several models coming on the market in the next few years will incorporate alternate fuels. The major automobile manufacturers have each decided to develop hydrogen fuel-cell technology, either on their own or in alliance with firms focusing on the technology. If they succeed in making the fuel cells cost-competitive and reliable across a broad range of temperatures and operating conditions, the auto makers will begin selling the first fuel cell–powered vehicles by 2010.[1]

A provision inserted into the Clean Air Act made it unlawful to tamper with existing devices on automobile exhaust systems that were installed to reduce the emission of carbon monoxide and hydrocarbons. In the following case, a muffler center that was sued by the EPA presented several arguments. Note that the law provides for a fine of up to $2,500 per violation. Do you think such a fine is too stiff?

United States of America v. Economy Muffler & Tire Center, Inc.

762 F.Supp. 1242
U.S. District Court (Virginia, 1991)

Facts. Economy Muffler operates an automobile repair shop in Richmond, Virginia, that routinely services motor vehicle exhaust systems. On 32 occasions during the past five years, Economy Muffler service personnel replaced three-way catalytic converters with two-way catalytic converters on a total of 51 motor vehicles.

Two-way catalytic converters contain platinum and palladium, chemical substances that reduce the emissions of carbon monoxide and hydrocarbons. Three-way catalytic converters also contain rhodium, a chemical substance that reduces the emissions of nitrogen oxides. Since the early 1980s, most passenger cars sold in the United States have been equipped with three-way converters, in accordance with EPA emission control standards.

Economy Muffler representatives regularly received and signed certificates, also known as statement forms, labeled "Notice to Professional Installers." The statement forms contained the following excerpt from the Section 203(a)(3)(B)

1. See J. Lynn Lunsford, UTC Fuel Cells Signs Pact with Nissan To Develop Technology for Automobiles, *Wall Street Journal,* February 19, 2002, p. A4.

enforcement policy published by the EPA at 51 *Fed. Reg.* 28118 on August 5, 1986: "In order not to be considered a violation of Section 203(a)(3) of the Clean Air Act, the converter must be the same type of converter as the original (i.e., oxidation, three-way, or three-way plus oxidation), and be the proper converter for the vehicle application as determined and specified by the Catalog."

On December 3, 1990, the United States sued Economy Muffler, charging violations of Section 203(a)(3)(B) of the Clean Air Act of 1990 and seeking penalties of up to $2,500 for each violation.

Legal Issue. Does replacing a three-way catalytic converter with a two-way converter on automobiles violate the Clean Air Act and subject the firm doing the replacement to civil penalties under the Clean Air Act?

Opinion. District Judge Richard L. Williams. Section 203(a)(3)(B) of the Clean Air Act of 1990, known as "the tampering provision," prohibits "any person engaged in the business of repairing or servicing . . . motor vehicles" from "knowingly . . . removing or rendering inoperative any device or element of design installed on or in a motor vehicle . . . in compliance with regulations under this title." In *United States v. Haney Chevrolet, Inc.* (1974), a Florida District Court held that a service manager violated Section 203(a)(3)(B) by removing an automobile's original carburetor and accompanying idle speed solenoid and installing a new carburetor without the idle speed solenoid. The Court reasoned that the transmission control spark system and the idle speed solenoid are emission control devices or elements of design within the meaning of the statute. The replacing of the original carburetor with a different carburetor that lacked the idle speed solenoid rendered the solenoid inoperative. The same reasoning is applicable here. Three-way catalytic converters contain rhodium, a "device" or "element of design" without which a motor vehicle's exhaust system cannot reduce emissions of nitrogen oxide. Replacing a three-way converter with a two-way converter effectively removes rhodium or renders it inoperative and is therefore subject to civil penalties under the Clean Air Act.

The legislative history of the Act suggests that Congress intended the statute to be interpreted in this manner. The Senate Report explains that the provision does not prohibit the use of after market parts "except where the use of such parts or the service performed would adversely affect the emission control system of the vehicle." Installing a two-way converter in place of a three-way converter adversely affects a vehicle's emission control system by destroying its capacity to prevent the harmful emission of nitrogen oxides.

The EPA has consistently interpreted the statute to bar the replacement of three-way catalytic converters with two-way catalytic converters. The tampering enforcement policy published by the EPA on August 6, 1986, and reproduced on statement forms distributed to repair shops, specifically requires that a replacement converter "be the same type of converter as the original."

Defendant argues that the tampering policy imposes a new set of legal obligations not contained in the statute and, for this reason, should have been enacted or promulgated as regulations in accordance with the Administrative Procedure Act's (APA's) notice and comment rulemaking requirements. The defendant's characterization of the EPA enforcement policy is inaccurate. The tampering enforcement policy falls under Administrative Procedure Act Section 553(b)(3)(A), which exempts interpretive rules, general statements of policy, and rules of agency organization, procedure, and practice from the APA's rulemaking requirements.

Economy Muffler also claims that its employees did not knowingly violate the Clean Air Act because they were not aware of the Act's requirements with respect to converters. In adopting the 1977 amendments to the Clean Air Act, the House Committee on Interstate and Foreign Commerce endorsed the construction of the term "knowingly," given by the Federal District Court in *United States v. Haney Chevrolet, Inc.*, that "an act is done knowingly when it is done voluntarily or intentionally, and not by mistake."

Finally, Economy Muffler challenges the statute as void for vagueness. In reviewing a business regulation for vagueness, "the principal inquiry is whether the law affords fair warning of what is proscribed." Fair warning is interpreted more loosely in the context of economic regulation because businesses, which face economic demands to plan behavior carefully, can be expected to consult relevant legislation in advance of action. The company president's claim that he and other employees were unaware of the legal requirements even though they had received and signed dozens of statement forms bearing the text of the enforcement policy strains credibility.

Decision. For these reasons, the defendant's motion for summary judgment is denied and the government's motion for partial summary judgment is granted.

Case Questions

1. Why does replacing a three-way converter with a two-way converter violate the Clean Air Act?
2. How did the EPA notify firms like Economy Muffler that replacing converters would violate the Clean Air Act?
3. Do you agree with the court that the employees did "knowingly" violate the Act?

International Commentary

Kyoto Protocol and Global Warming

Representatives from 178 nations have agreed to continue the process of ratifying the agreement they reached in Kyoto, Japan, to cut greenhouse gas emissions, such as carbon dioxide, which are blamed for warming the earth's atmosphere. Fifty-five nations, responsible for more than half of the global greenhouse gas emissions, have agreed to a 5% average cut in their total emissions of greenhouse gases, including carbon monoxide.

The United States did not sign the treaty because President Bush said reducing emissions to meet the treaty's requirements could reduce the country's gross domestic product by more than 4% annually. He also questions whether global warming is in fact occurring. President Bush also seeks assurance that developing countries like China and India will commit to reduce rather than increase their emissions.

Despite Bush's complaints, scientists claim that the burning of the rainforest in the Amazon Basin is destroying the planet. The loss of trees and foliage reduces the area's photosynthesis capacity to take in carbon dioxide, and the Amazon region is now said to spew 7% of the carbon dioxide that is responsible for global warming. Among the programs trying to deal with the problem is a British government offer of approximately $300 million in a competitive auction to companies that agree to cut their emissions the most over the next five years. The Dutch government is offering more than $25 million to clean up outmoded plants in the developing world and in Eastern Europe, and the reductions in those areas will count for cutbacks the Netherlands has agreed to make. Despite the U.S. stance on the Kyoto Agreement, some U.S. firms are lobbying as the Business Environmental Leaders Council for adoption of a U.S. to adopt a greenhouse gas policy.[2] International agreements are the only way to address some of these worldwide environmental problems.

WATER POLLUTION

Federal regulations governing water pollution began more than a century ago with the 1899 Rivers and Harbors Appropriation Act. Although the early focus of regulation was on **navigable waters,** that term today includes both coastal and freshwater wetlands. In 1948, Congress passed the Federal Water Pollution Control Act (FWPCA), which was amended in 1972 with what is now known as the Clean Water Act. The **Clean Water Act** requires a permit before pollutants can be discharged into navigable waters from any point source, private or public, regardless of whether the discharge existed prior to the legislation. Criminal sanctions may be imposed if pollutants are discharged without a permit. A firm with a discharge permit must monitor its own performance regarding the discharge of pollutants and report the results to the state and the EPA. The states have the option of administering the permit program or allowing the EPA to do so.

THE CLEAN WATER ACT STANDARDS

For both private and public organizations that discharge pollutants into the nation's waters, the Clean Water Act establishes two standards: the best practicable technology (BPT) and the best available technology economically achievable (BAT). All

2. See. Geoff Winestock, Efforts to Cut Greenhouse Gases Percolate on Back Burner, *Wall Street Journal,* February 1, 2002, p. A 14.

plants were required to install water pollution control devices representing the best practicable pollution control technology by 1977. Such factors as the cost of equipment, the amount of time required to install it, and the severity of the pollution were considered in determining whether a firm had complied with the **best practicable technology** (BPT). The Clean Water Act provided that a more stringent standard of **best available technology** (**BAT**) economically achievable had to be met by 1987. With this standard, less effective alternatives were not acceptable even if they were significantly less expensive. After 1987, firms had to install the most effective water pollution control equipment available.

Federal and State Laws

The federal law establishes minimum water quality standards, but it also allows the states to adopt more stringent standards. Once the EPA has approved such state standards, they must be met by everyone in the state who seeks a permit. Are the states free to consider any factors they choose in establishing more stringent state water quality standards? Consider following the excerpt from *the Homestake Mining case,* which examined water quality standards established in South Dakota:

The FWPCA states that "standards shall be established taking into consideration" the various factors listed. The applicable federal regulation states that "the State should take into consideration" the various factors. It must, therefore, be determined what the phrase "taking into consideration" requires. Nothing in the statute seems to indicate that the states must give equal weight to all the factors listed. The Weyerhaeuser *case indicates that the amount of weight to give each individual factor is within the State's discretion.*

In United States Steel Corporation v. Train, *the Court dealt with the issue of more stringent state standards. The Court held that the FWPCA was not designed to inhibit the states from adopting more stringent standards and in forcing industry to create more effective pollution control technology. Furthermore, the Court held that EPA has no authority to set aside or modify state standards which are more stringent than those mandated by the Act.*

The FWPCA clearly indicates that the states are to play a significant role in the reduction of water pollution. The statute itself and the case law make it clear that the states can adopt more stringent standards and can force technology. South Dakota was not required to consider economic and social factors, and thus its failure to do so does not invalidate its water quality standards. EPA's approval of those standards was not arbitrary and capricious or violative of the Act.[3]

Wetlands

In addition to regulating pollution in navigable waters as defined by the act, the Clean Water Act prohibits filling or dredging wetlands unless a permit is obtained from the Corps of Engineers. Wetlands are the areas between land and open waters. The regulation of wetlands can affect property located in many areas of the United States, and the need for a permit before any filling or dredging can occur sometimes significantly limits the landowner's use of his or her property, as is illustrated in the following case.

---

3. *Homestake Mining Co. v. U.S. Environmental Protection Agency*, 477 F.Supp. 1279 (S.D., 1979).

Joseph F. Gazza v. New York Department of Environmental Conservation

New York Court of Appeals
679 N.E.2d 1035 (1997)

Facts. Gazza purchased property in a residential zone in the village of Quogue in the town of Southampton for $100,000. Approximately 65% of the 43,500-square-foot parcel had previously been classified as tidal wetlands by the defendant, New York Department of Environmental Conservation (DEC). Gazza sought a variance from two setback requirements so that he could build a home on the property. One requirement prohibited building within 75 feet of the tidal wetland boundary, and the second required a 100-foot setback between the wetland boundary and the planned septic tank. Gazza estimated that, if the variance was granted, the property would be worth almost $400,000.

An administrative law judge recommended denying the application for a variance, and the DEC agreed with that decision. Their decision was based on the plaintiff's failure to prove that the variance would not have an undue adverse impact on the present or potential value of the tidal wetland. In fact, the proposed project would eliminate or diminish several tidal wetland benefits in one of the few functioning wetlands in an otherwise developed area.

Plaintiff then filed a case with the Supreme Court (the trial court in the New York system), which found that he had not proven that his property had lost all but a bare residue of its value. It noted the testimony that the property with the wetlands restriction was worth between $50,000 and $80,000. The Appellate Division, citing *Lucas,* a U.S. Supreme Court case, said that Gazza knew the wetlands restriction was in place when he bought the property and that there was no taking when his request for a variance was denied. The decision of the Court of Appeals, New York's highest court, follows.

Legal Issue. Is the denial of a building variance pursuant to environmental regulations designed to preserve wetlands an unconstitutional taking of property if the property has lost some, but not all, of its value?

Opinion. Justice Smith. In 1973, the Legislature concluded that "tidal wetlands constitute one of the most vital and productive areas of the natural world, and their protection and preservation are essential." It then enacted the Tidal Wetlands Act and directed DEC to inventory all wetlands in the state of New York and empowered it to regulate the wetlands and the areas adjacent thereto. The legislature also enacted strict guidelines for the application and granting of permits to landowners desiring to conduct regulated activities in and around the wetlands.

Judicial review is a two-step process. If the court finds the permit denial is supported by substantial evidence, a second determination is made to determine whether the restriction constitutes an unconstitutional taking requiring compensation. Turning to the first step, the DEC's denial of the setback variances in *Gazza* is supported by substantial evidence. It must next be determined whether the wetlands act, coupled with the denial of the permit, has placed such an onerous burden on the property that a taking must be deemed to occur. In *Lucas v. South Carolina Coastal Council* (505 U.S. 1003), the Supreme Court stated: Where the State seeks to sustain regulation that deprives land of all economically beneficial use, we think it may resist compensation only if the logically antecedent inquiry into the nature of the owner's estate shows that the proscribed use interests were not a part of his title to begin with. . . .

In this case, the petitioner's claim is based upon the denial of the setback variances. Petitioner had a reasonable expectation that the DEC would consider his request in accordance with the standards and purposes of the wetlands regulations generally and as applied to other landowners. Petitioner does not dispute that the DEC's determination is supported by substantial evidence. Although petitioner's permit application was entitled to due consideration, petitioner's claim that the denial of his variance was a "taking" must fail because he never owned an absolute right to build on his land without a variance. Since the enactment of the wetlands regulations, the only permissible uses for the subject property were dependent upon those regulations which were a legitimate exercise of the police power.

Courts have enunciated several tests to resolve the fact-intensive question of the impact of regulation upon a landowner. Whether a taking has occurred may be determined by an examination of various factors such as those set forth in *Penn Central*: the economic impact of the regulation, the extent to which the regulation has interfered with reasonable investment-backed expectations, and the character of the governmental action. A taking may be found only if an onerous burden forces property owners "alone to bear public burdens, which in all fairness and justice should be borne by the public as a whole" (*Armstrong v. U.S.*).

Decision. Here, no per se taking occurred. Even if petitioner's "bundle of rights" includes the "stick" he claims was taken, any burden resulting from the denial of the setback variances would not rise to the level of a taking. The order of the Appellate Division should be affirmed.

Case Questions

1. What was the standard Gazza had to meet to have the DEC grant a variance? Explain why that standard was not met.
2. Evaluate the three factors as they apply to this case that are examined to see if a regulation about a landowner's use of wetlands constitutes a taking.
3. The court notes that the state regulation here is part of its "police powers." Based on your recollection from Chapter 4, which part of the state's police power justifies this regulation?

Enforcement

The Clean Water Act provides for both civil and criminal penalties. The civil penalties include fines of up to $10,000 per day for each violation, in addition to cleanup costs. Criminal penalties, levied only for intentional violations, include fines of up to $1 million and 15 years' imprisonment.

Other Legislation

Several other laws aim to protect our water. The Safe Drinking Water Act, the Marine Protection Research and Sanctuaries Act, and the Oil Pollution Act have all been enacted or modified during the last several decades.

Safe Drinking Water The Safe Drinking Water Act, passed in 1974 and amended in 1986 and 1996, is designed to protect the quality of drinking water. According to the World Health Organization, approximately 1.2 billion people, one-sixth of the globe, currently have no access to clean water.[4] The 1996 amendment gives the EPA significant authority to control contaminants from pesticides or landfill waste leaks that make their way into underground wells. Although the states have primary responsibility for complying with the regulations, all water suppliers are subject to the act. The EPA requires that community water systems must provide annual reports to consumers concerning the source water, regulated contaminants in the waters, and information on how the communities are meeting the Safe Drinking Water Act's requirements.

Ocean Dumping The Marine Protection Research and Sanctuaries Act, known as the Ocean Dumping Act, is a 1972 U.S. law that establishes a permit system to regulate dumping of materials into the ocean. The act banned dumping specific types of industrial waste after 1995, while establishing a permit system for the transportation and dumping of other materials. Internationally, the 1972 London Convention on the Prevention of Marine Pollution by the Dumping of Waste and Other Materials has been replaced and updated by a 1996 protocol. Approximately two dozen countries have agreed to abide by its requirements.

Oil Spills The Oil Pollution Act of 1990 provides that any oil facility, oil shipper, vessel owner, or vessel operator that discharges oil into navigable waters or onto an adjoining shore may be liable for cleanup costs as well as damages. The legislation, inspired by the Exxon Valdez oil spill in Alaska, creates a $1 billion cleanup fund and establishes civil penalties of up to $1,000 per barrel spilled for each violation.

---

4. See Jim Carleton, Report Aims to Ease Water Privatization in Developing World, *Wall Street Journal,* February 5, 2002, p. B12.

By 2011, all oil tankers using U.S. ports must be double-hulled to limit the severity of accidental spills. Some shipping lines have already purchased doubled-hulled vessels to guard against such spills.

LAND POLLUTION

Pollution of the earth is caused by disposal of toxic and nontoxic solid wastes. Millions of tons of solid wastes are generated each year and disposed of in open dumps or landfills. Trash from residences and small businesses is usually taken by disposal companies to county or municipal landfills. However, some solid wastes are burned by the individuals or firms generating them. Agricultural operations produce the largest portion of solid wastes; mining operations also generate significant solid waste land pollution.

Solid waste disposal is not just a land pollution problem. Burning solid wastes contributes to air pollution, and dumping solid wastes in or near sources of water may contaminate waterways, lakes, and streams. Many sources of pollution fit into more than one pollution category.

Until very recently, the federal government paid less attention to solid waste disposal than to air and water pollution. Today, however, three federal statutes are concerned with land pollution: the Solid Waste Disposal Act, the Toxic Substance Control Act, and the Comprehensive Environmental Response, Compensation, and Liability Act (Superfund).

SOLID WASTE DISPOSAL ACT

The **Solid Waste Disposal Act** was enacted in 1965 and amended in1970. Its purpose is to assist states and municipalities in addressing waste disposal problems. Grants from the federal government are made for waste disposal studies and for the construction of facilities that turn solid waste into energy. Several events in the 1970s—for example, the land and water contamination caused by the improper disposal of chemical wastes in New York state's Love Canal and by the improper disposal of an insecticide in Virginia—focused the attention of Congress on the need for more specific regulation of the disposal of certain types of wastes. The 1976 amendments to the act, known as the **Resource Conservation and Recovery Act,** and the 1984 amendments, known as the **Hazardous and Solid Waste Management Act,** are each briefly reviewed.

Resource Conservation and Recovery Act

In 1976, the Resource Conservation and Recovery Act (RCRA) created a federal permit system. All businesses that use, transport, or store hazardous wastes—those that contribute significantly to a serious, irreversible illness or pose a hazard to human health when improperly managed—are required to comply with its standards.

Firms that generate such wastes have cradle-to-grave responsibility for it. Each generator obtains an EPA identification number that follows the waste when it is stored, transported, or disposed of. If it is transported off-site for disposal, a manifest must identify the nature and quantity of the wastes and the names of both the transporter and the receiving firm. The transporter must make entries on the manifest and is responsible for intentional or accidental waste discharges during transportation. Firms generating hazardous waste must make annual reports to the EPA.

Facilities for the disposal of hazardous wastes must have a permit. Such permits are issued only if certain performance standards are met. A disposal facility of this kind must sign the manifest it receives from the transporter of hazardous wastes and return the manifest to the generator of the wastes. Each disposal facility has an EPA identification number. Representative samples of the hazardous wastes must be analyzed before the wastes are stored or treated. EPA inspectors are authorized to enter the disposal facilities at reasonable times to conduct inspections or review records.

Currently, only 15 states have commercial dumps for hazardous waste. Although several of these states have attempted to limit out-of-state waste from being dumped at their facilities, federal courts have consistently found such laws to interfere with interstate commerce. Restrictions in Alabama, Michigan, Ohio, and South Carolina have been struck down by courts in the last decade or so. Usually, the opinions suggest that if every state was allowed to determine the amount and type of out-of-state waste it would accept, the results would be catastrophic for the national economy. The Michigan case, excerpted next, is typical of those decisions.

Fort Gratiot Sanitary Landfill, Inc. v. Michigan Department of Natural Resources

504 U.S. 353 (1992)
United States Supreme Court

Facts. In 1978, Michigan enacted its Solid Waste Management Act (SWMA), which required every Michigan county to establish the amount of solid waste that would be generated in that county in the next 20 years and to adopt a plan for its disposal that complied with state health standards. After the St. Clair County Board of Commissioners adopted a solid waste plan for St. Clair County, the Michigan Department of Natural Resources issued a permit to Ft. Gratiot Sanitary Landfill to operate a sanitary landfill as a solid waste disposal in that county.

In December 1988, the state legislature amended its SWMA to prohibit acceptance of out-of-county waste unless such waste was authorized by the approved county plan. In 1989, Fort Gratiot applied to St. Clair county for authority to dispose of up to 1,750 tons per day of out-of-state waste at its landfill. The county refused and Fort Gratiot then sued, claiming the restriction on the import of waste violated the commerce clause of the U.S. Constitution. The trial court and appellate court found the regulation constitutional because the restriction affected waste from other Michigan counties as well as from out-of-state sources and because it was necessary to protect the public health and environment. Fort Gratiot appealed to the U.S. Supreme Court.

Legal Issue. Does a county's restriction on the import of waste that applies to waste from in-state as well as out-of-state sources violate the commerce clause of the U.S. Constitution?

Opinion. Justice Stevens. In *Philadelphia v. New Jersey* (1978) we held that a New Jersey law prohibiting the importation of most "solid or liquid waste that originated or was collected outside the territorial limits of the State" violated the commerce clause of the U.S. Constitution. In this case, petitioner challenges a Michigan law that prohibits private landfill operators from accepting solid waste that originates outside the county in which their facilities are located. Adhering to our holding in the New Jersey case, we conclude that this Michigan statute is also unconstitutional.

Philadelphia v. New Jersey provides the framework for our analysis of this case. Solid waste, even if it has no value, is an article of commerce. As we have recognized, the "negative" or "dormant" aspect of the commerce clause prohibits States from advancing their own commercial interests by curtailing the movement of articles of commerce, either into or out of the state. A state statute that clearly discriminates against interstate commerce is therefore unconstitutional unless the discrimination is demonstrably justified by a valid factor unrelated to economic protectionism.

The Waste Import Restriction enacted by Michigan authorizes each of its 83 counties to isolate itself from the national economy. In view of the fact that Michigan has not identified any reason, apart from origin, why solid waste coming from outside the county should be treated any differently than solid waste from within the county, the foregoing reasoning would appear to control the disposition of this case. Michigan and St. Clair County assert that the Waste Import Restrictions are necessary because they enable individual counties to make adequate plans for the safe disposal of future waste. Michigan could attain that objective without discriminating between in- and out-of-state waste. Michigan could, for example, limit the amount of waste that landfill operators could accept each year.

Decision. The Waste Import Restrictions unambiguously discriminate against interstate commerce and are appropriately characterized as protectionist measures that cannot withstand scrutiny under the commerce clause. We reverse the lower court decision.

Case Questions

1. Under what conditions might it be constitutional for a state to limit certain waste originating from other states?
2. In dissent, Justice Rehnquist argued that because the Michigan law was a part of a comprehensive plan to control and plan for waste disposal, it should be held valid. Would adopting that reasoning encourage states to make plans for their own solid waste disposal?
3. Would your state want to prevent waste coming from other states, or would it be in favor of allowing states, like your state, to ship waste to other locales? Why?

Hazardous and Solid Waste Amendments

In 1984, the Hazardous and Solid Waste Amendments amended RCRA to increase the EPA's regulatory powers. Many small waste generators that were exempt from RCRA were required to use the manifest system for tracking the use, transport, and disposal of hazardous wastes. The 1984 amendments also established a timetable for the gradual elimination of landfills as sites for the disposal of many hazardous substances. Existing landfills were required to use specific equipment to limit the harmful effects of leakage, and regulatory programs for underground storage tanks and the protection of groundwater were established.

THE TOXIC SUBSTANCES CONTROL ACT

Congress enacted the **Toxic Substances Control Act** in 1976 to identify, test, and control chemicals that were believed to pose an unreasonable risk of injury to human health or the environment. Many chemicals that are manufactured for useful purposes, such as dioxins, PCBs, and Agent Orange, pose grave dangers to human health and to the environment for years after they have been discarded. Initially, the EPA was charged with developing a comprehensive list of all manufactured chemicals, including thousands of chemicals used in industry and agriculture.

The Toxic Substances Control Act requires manufacturers to test toxic chemicals. The EPA can halt the manufacture of high-risk substances and issue regulations concerning the manufacture, distribution, commercial use, and disposal of toxic chemical substances. The Toxic Substances Control Act does not cover pesticides, which are regulated under the Pesticide Control Act. It provides that pesticides that are classified for restricted use may be applied only by certified persons.

More than a hundred nations have signed an international agreement on toxic waste exports. The international accord requires the government of any country exporting toxic waste to obtain written permission from the government of any country to which the waste is to be shipped. Toxic waste from industrial countries has often found its way to developing countries that have accepted it in exchange for much-needed hard currency. Although developing countries may not have the technical know-how to safely dispose of the waste they accept, they realize it is dangerous. The treaty provides them with greater assurance that there will not be secret dumping of foreign waste in their territory.

THE COMPREHENSIVE ENVIRONMENTAL RESPONSE, COMPENSATION, AND LIABILITY ACT OF 1980 (SUPERFUND)

Until 1980, most of the environmental laws enacted by Congress were aimed at preventing future environmental problems. However, the Superfund legislation was intended to create a fund for the identification and cleanup of hazardous waste disposal sites. The money for the fund has been raised primarily through taxes levied on manufacturers of certain dangerous chemicals. Since its beginning, more than $15 billion in tax funds has been spent to clean up such Superfund sites.

However, since 1995, corporate polluters have paid less as Congress has let the tax on corporations expire. In 1994, taxpayers paid about 21% of the $1.2 billion paid for Superfund cleanups. In 2003, taxpayers will pay more than 50% of the $1.3 billion fund. By 2004, under current conditions, all the money will come from the taxpayers.[5] It is estimated that over the next 50 years more than $100 billion will be required to clean up additional waste sites. A national priority list notes the sites that, pursuant to a hazard ranking score, present the highest degree of risk to the environment and public health.

The Right to Know Act

Congress amended the Superfund law in 1986 with the Emergency Planning and Community Right-to-Know Act. The act was passed in response to the chemical plant disaster in Bhopal, India, that resulted in more than 3,000 deaths. The act requires companies to notify the government if they release any extremely hazardous chemicals into the environment. Inventories of hazardous substances must be submitted to the government, and state and local planning to deal with emergencies is required.

Compensation and Liability Provisions

An important aspect of the Superfund legislation is its compensation and liability provisions. Owners and operators of polluting facilities or vessels, as well as those who generate, treat, and dispose of hazardous waste, are held strictly liable for all cleanup costs. Each responsible party is held jointly and severally liable for all cleanup costs. Thus, the government can seek total recovery from one party and put the burden of collecting from other responsible parties on that defendant. These costs include the government's response costs and the damage to natural resources.

The EPA may perform the cleanup itself or require the responsible persons to do so. The Act defines a responsible person to include:

1. The present owner or operator of the facility
2. The owner or operator of the facility at the time of disposal of the hazardous substance
3. Any person who arranged for the treatment or disposal of hazardous substances at the facility
4. Any person who transported hazardous substances to and selected the facility

Owners who cooperate in cleanup and whose acts are not willfully negligent have limited liability. A due diligence defense exists if commercial developers run tests and examine EPA records and title documents to discover previous toxic dumping.

5. Katherine Q. Seelye of the *New York Times,* quoted in Polluters to Pay Far Less for Superfund Cleanups in *Kalamazoo Gazette,* February 24, 2002, p. A3.

In 1998, the EPA promulgated a policy that provided specific mathematical formulae that could be used to determine the financial responsibility of municipalities and other parties who entered into settlements with the EPA to resolve their Superfund liability. The formulae could be used for any party who generated or transported municipal solid waste and for municipal owners, but not private owners, of co-disposal sites on the Superfund national priorities list. Co-disposal sites contain both hazardous and nonhazardous waste. The potentially responsible parties who settle with the EPA obtain statutory protection from actions by private third parties seeking contributions.

Representatives of private parties challenged the EPA's ruling, saying that they were allowed not to settle for the formula amount and thus would bear a disproportionate share of the site response costs. A federal trial court ruled in favor of the EPA's policy but noted that its ruling left open the opportunity to challenge specific settlements.[6] Such challenges by private parties are likely in the coming years.

The imposition of liability on the "owner and operator" of polluted sites caused banks to severely limit their commercial real estate lending. After complaints from businesses that were affected by the credit crunch brought about by the Superfund liability provisions, the EPA made some modifications to the liability portions of the law. The Superfund legislation does not make polluters liable for injuries to private persons, although such persons may bring private suits in state courts under common law rules. In addition, those injured by hazardous waste may make a limited claim for compensation from the Superfund if the owner of the hazardous waste site is unknown.

ENVIRONMENTAL COMPLIANCE

Because business firms face significant penalties and possible criminal punishment for not complying with environmental laws and regulations, many firms are using environmental audits to better understand the risks these laws present to their operations. The EPA defines an environmental audit as a systematic, documented, periodic, and objective review of regulated entities or facility operations and practices related to meeting environmental regulations.

Such audits are usually performed by attorneys, consultants, and company personnel. Attorneys are involved so that, where possible, the attorney-client privilege may be used to protect documents created in the auditing process. Audits can be beneficial in a number of ways:

- Audits can provide data to managers charged with prioritizing investments among environmental projects.
- Early discovery of problems can minimize the cost of responding.
- Voluntary correction can minimize or eliminate some enforcement actions.
- Compliance audits are used to meet insurance and government requirements.

Exhibit 23.2 depicts the elements usually found in an effective environmental audit.

OTHER FEDERAL ENVIRONMENTAL CONCERNS

Two other environmental concerns that have been addressed by significant federal legislation are nuclear energy and wildlife preservation. In the early days of nuclear energy, the federal government had a monopoly on its use and did not allow its use

6. *Chemical Manufacturers Ass'n. v. EPA*, No. 98-1255 (D.D.C, 1998) .

EXHIBIT 23.2 Elements of an Effective Environmental Compliance Audit

Element	Comment
1. Top management support	A written policy articulating support for the audit and compliance with all regulations is vital. Follow-up comments should also be distributed to key people in the firm.
2. Independence of audit	There should be no conflict of interest, and auditors should be free from interference or possible retribution.
3. Adequately trained auditors	Audits should have appropriate knowledge and skill and demonstrate currency in technical and analytical components.
4. Clear objectives and adequate resources	Compliance with all regulations and evaluation of company policies, practices, and training should be clear objectives.
5. Process for collection, analysis, and interpretation of data	Information should be sufficient, reliable, relevant, and useful to provide a basis for audit findings and recommendations.
6. Process to report on findings and correct problems	Reports should be sent internally to those responsible for follow-up activities and externally to appropriate regulators.

for civilian purposes. More recently, the federal government's concerns with nuclear energy have focused on nuclear accidents and nuclear waste. Because wildlife is regarded as subject to federal regulation under the commerce clause, the state laws affecting wildlife are subject to preemption by federal laws.

NUCLEAR POWER AND NUCLEAR WASTE

Nuclear power is a controversial source of energy in the United States and, to a lesser extent, throughout the rest of the world. Although it has the potential for supplementing fossil sources of energy such as coal and oil, it poses significant dangers in the form of nuclear radiation, nuclear accidents, and terrorist acts against nuclear power plants. Nuclear power currently provides approximately 10% of the energy used in the United States, more than 30% of the energy used in Japan and Great Britain, and close to 65% of the energy used in France.

The Regulation of Nuclear Power Plants

Nuclear power has been heavily regulated by the federal government since the beginning of the atomic age during World War II (1941–1945). The Atomic Energy Act was amended in 1954 to authorize the Atomic Energy Commission (now the Nuclear Regulatory Commission) to license a variety of private, commercial uses for nuclear energy. In 1959, Congress permitted the states to establish restrictions regarding the location of nuclear power plants and the disposal of nuclear wastes. Under the Clean Air Act, the states may also establish limits for the emission of radioactive particles by nuclear power plants. Some states have such restrictive standards with regard to the use of nuclear power that nuclear power plants cannot be constructed in them. Since the 1986 disaster at the Chernobyl nuclear power facility in the former Soviet Union, it has been clear that a nuclear accident can cause substantial damage and injury to thousands of people. Although the most disastrous consequences are felt by those close to the accident site, radiation in the atmosphere and in the food supply adversely affects the lives of millions of people in distant locations.

Ethical Issue

Nuclear Waste: Where in the World Should We Put It?

On February 15, 2002, President Bush authorized the construction of a huge, centralized site, located in the Yucca Mountains 90 miles northwest of Las Vegas, for the storage of U.S. nuclear waste. Currently, 131 above-ground facilities store more than 40,000 tons of spent nuclear material. In Nevada, the waste is to be stored in metal cannisters several hundred feet underground. Because the waste would have to be transported there from sites across the nation, opponents of the plan worry about accidents in transit. They also question whether the scientific and technical problems associated with the decision have been carefully analyzed. Of course, the people in Nevada oppose dumping the nation's waste in their back yard. Their argument is that the communities that generate the waste should be responsible for it. (See Eric Pianin, Nuclear Waste Site Picked amid State's Protests, *Washington Post,* February 17, 2002, p. A30.)

The problem is not only a U.S. problem. What about other countries that have or will soon have nuclear waste? An article in England's *Guardian* newspaper said it will cost Britain one billion pounds annually for the next 10 to 25 years to safely store its nuclear waste. New plants are needed to pack and compact the waste into concrete to be stored. Britain is organizing a new agency that will take over the decommissioning of old plants and make plans to deal with the waste problem. The storage would need to last for 100 years. (See Paul Brown, Safe N-Waste Will Cost Pounds 1bn a Year, *Guardian,* February 20, 2002, p. 7.)

Is it safer to store the nuclear waste where it is produced or at national sites in more remote locations and with better geological characteristics? Is this a problem for each country to solve on its own?

Regulation of Nuclear Waste

The accumulation of nuclear wastes is a second concern associated with nuclear energy. Radioactive wastes are created as the fissions of uranium release energy in nuclear reactors. Because those wastes may take centuries to become harmless, safe storage or disposal sites are critical. Nevertheless, more than two decades have passed since Congress passed the Nuclear Waste Policy Act to establish a national plan for the disposal of highly radioactive nuclear wastes. Although construction of several appropriate storage facilities was to begin in the 1990s, at least another decade will pass before any nuclear waste is moved from the present locations. The United States currently plans to move all its nuclear waste to the Yucca Mountains in Nevada. We won't know for a long time whether that in fact happens and, if so, whether that is a good plan.

WILDLIFE PROTECTION

Numerous federal laws seek to protect wildlife. The most comprehensive of these laws is the **Endangered Species Act**. This act, enforced by the Environmental Protection Agency and the Department of Commerce, protects endangered and threatened animal species. It prohibits the taking of any animal on the endangered species list, with taking defined as harassing, harming, pursuing, hunting, shooting, trapping, collecting, or capturing. Federal projects must not adversely affect endangered species or their habitats. It is a federal offense to buy, sell, or possess any species listed as endangered or threatened or any product made from such a species. For example, the Endangered Species Act prohibits the sale or purchase of products made from some furs or reptile skins.

The Migratory Bird Treaty Act, the Fishery Conservation and Management Act, and the Marine Mammal Protection Act are among other federal laws designed to protect wildlife. States also enact laws to protect wildlife within their borders. Granting state hunting and fishing permits is often dependent on the need to protect state fishing and gaming resources.

STATE AND LOCAL CONCERNS

Most states have detailed legislation requiring environmental impact statements for actions by state or local governments that will affect environmental quality. This legislation generally also requires private industrial and commercial firms to prepare such statements for their actions of this kind. Some states are addressing environmental concerns that are more appropriately handled on a state level, such as solid waste bans for yard waste, mandatory use of recyclable materials, and more stringent limits for automobile emissions. Cities, counties, and other local governments also enact legislation designed to protect their environment.

PRESERVING NATURAL RESOURCES

The Michigan case that follows exemplifies a common concern: the conflict between preserving natural resources and opening land to development, particularly for oil and other energy resources. This case may shed light on the recent debate over drilling for oil in Alaska on government-owned land, with numerous precious natural resources.

West Michigan Environmental Action Council, Inc. v. Natural Resources Commission of the State of Michigan

Supreme Court of Michigan
275 N.W.2d 538 (1979)

Facts. The Michigan Department of Natural Resources (DNR)* sold oil and gas leases covering 500,000 acres of state land, including part of a state forest. After filing an environmental impact statement, the DNR permitted Shell Oil Company and several other oil companies to drill exploratory wells in a portion of the state forest. The plaintiffs filed a complaint under the Michigan Environmental Protection Act, claiming DNR's agreement with the oil companies did not properly consider the environmental impact of the drilling on wildlife, particularly elk. The trial court upheld the agreement, and the plaintiffs appealed to the Supreme Court of Michigan.

*[*For purposes of this case, the Department of Natural Resources is considered to be the same party as the Natural Resources Commission of Michigan.]*

Legal Issue. If drilling exploratory wells could cause serious and lasting damage to the area's elk herd, does that constitute an impairment or destruction of a natural resource so as to be a "significant adverse impact" as defined under the state's environmental protection act?

Opinion. Justice Moody. Perhaps the single most revealing piece of evidence is the Environmental Impact Statement for Potential Hydrocarbon Development in the Pigeon River County State Forest (EIS) prepared by the DNR. Many of the EIS's conclusions directly apply to the effects of exploratory drilling. Testimony before the trial court indicated that six of the ten proposed sites were not adjacent to any road, requiring that roads be built to such sites. The EIS cites studies in Montana which concluded that "[e]lk avoid roads even when there is no traffic." The EIS also observed that "[w]hether the elk will return to their former range following completion of the last seismic survey work is unknown."

Some quantification of the adverse impact of exploratory drilling on the elk can be gained from comparing the EIS's Matrix for Proposed Hydrocarbon Development in the Southern Portion of the Forest with Dr. Inman's testimony. Dr.

Inman, who participated in the development of the EIS, testified that a slow recovery time is considered to be 40 to 50 years or more, a short recovery time less than 20 years, and a great recovery time is 100 years or more.

The Environmental Impact Matrix defines a significant adverse impact as "a change in the element that is impacted from its present status to a status that may take a long time for recovery, at least during the duration of the project." Applying Dr. Inman's definitions of what constitutes a slow recovery time to the matrix predictions, it would appear that elk would avoid the impacted areas for 40 to 50 years.

We recognize that virtually all human activities can be found to adversely impact natural resources in some way or other. The real question before us is, when does such impact rise to the level of impairment or destruction? The DNR's environmental impact statement recognizes that "[e]lk are unique to this area of Michigan" and that the herd is "the only sizable wild herd east of the Mississippi River. Several attempts to introduce elk elsewhere in Michigan have been unsuccessful." It is estimated that the herd's population, which numbered in excess of 1,500 in 1963, now probably lies between 170 and 180. Expert testimony has established that the Pigeon River County State Forest, particularly unit 1 in which the exploratory drilling is to take place, provides excellent habitat for elk and that the elk frequent this area. Furthermore, it is clear from the record that available habitat is shrinking.

Decision. In light of the limited number of the elk, the unique nature and location of this herd, and the apparently serious and lasting, though unquantifiable, damage that will result to the herd from the drilling of the ten exploratory wells, we conclude that defendants' conduct constitutes an impairment or destruction of a natural resource. Accordingly, we reverse the remand to the trial court for entry of a permanent injunction prohibiting the drilling of the wells.

Case Questions

1. Why would the exploratory drilling damage the elk?
2. If it is impossible to drill without adversely affecting some animals, would drilling ever be permitted?

ANTILITTER LAWS

A few states have enacted laws aimed at reducing the litter along state highways, which is frequently in the form of disposable beverage bottles or cans. Some states have passed **bottle laws** that require buyers to pay a cash deposit on all beverage containers. The purchaser receives the deposit back for empty containers returned to any authorized center. Usually, stores selling beverages must also handle returns and refund the deposit. The states with bottle laws have significantly decreased roadway litter.

NUISANCE, TRESPASS, AND LAND USE LAWS

Nuisance Laws

Common law nuisance statutes have long been used by state and local governments to deal with environmental problems. A **nuisance** is a substantial and unreasonable interference with the use and enjoyment of a person's interest in property. A public nuisance causes damage to the property of many people or to public facilities, whereas a private nuisance deprives other property owners of their right to use and enjoy their property

Trespass

Trespass is an unlawful interference with the property of another. The person who sets foot on the property of another is a trespasser, but so is the firm that causes soot, dust, or other particles to intrude onto the land of another. The hacker who invades a computer network or hard drive also is a trespasser. Recall the case Intel brought against one of its ex-employees for slamming—invading its e-mail system and sending thousands of derogatory messages about the firm to current employees.

Trespass invades the property owner's exclusive right of possession, whereas a nuisance interferes with the property owner's use and enjoyment of the property. If the cement dust from a nearby factory is deposited on another's land, a trespass has occurred because something else is now on that land. Because trespass and nuisance often overlap, it is generally less important to determine which exists than to determine whether either has occurred.

Land Use Laws

Zoning ordinances and land use regulations have recently begun to play a larger role in addressing environmental problems. As the *Gazza* case notes, in addition to state laws such as those designed to protect wetlands, municipalities enact zoning ordinances to control the use of land. These laws usually require detailed development plans to be submitted before permits are issued to build or alter existing buildings. State laws frequently require municipalities to prepare land use plans that accommodate differing uses of land within its area.

QUESTIONS

1. Discuss the purpose of the National Environmental Policy Act. Why is government regulation of the environment important to the business community?
2. Your firm has been hired to build a new federal post office near a large in-town neighborhood. A group of residents oppose the building of the new government facility. What factors must you consider in an environmental impact statement (EIS)?
3. What are hazardous wastes? How does the EPA regulate hazardous wastes?
4. The Commission of the European Union in 2002 proposed a law that would hold polluters liable for damages to the environment in member countries. The law could help prevent water, soil, and air pollution and hold polluters liable for the loss of biodiversity. It is somewhat akin to the Superfund law of the United States but would apply only to environmental damage that occurs after the law takes effect. The law changes the current law that does not make a polluter liable for cleanup costs. Should polluters, rather than taxpayers, pay for environmental damages they cause? Won't such a law make companies in countries that impose such liability (the EU or the United States) less competitive than the firms in countries where no such liability is imposed (India or China)?
5. In 2001, Japan enacted the Law on Promoting Green Purchasing. The law is aimed only at products purchased by the government or by institutions that work closely with the government. It seeks to ensure that goods they purchase are environmentally friendly. Surveys taken in that country indicate that more than 80% of people try to buy environmentally friendly products. Japan's law does not require products to meet appropriate standards, but it encourages producers to consider scientific knowledge and provide appropriate information to consumers. In contrast to Japan's approach, U.S. laws generally impose certain requirements on those who generate or dispose of waste related to the production of goods. As far as environmental practices regarding materials and packaging are concerned, do you think it is better for the law to allow producers and consumers to establish standards, or is it better to impose legal mandates and financial consequences on producers? Why?
6. The city of Chicago enacted an ordinance banning the use of detergents containing phosphates. Procter & Gamble lost $4.8 million in sales in the Chicago area during the first five months following the enactment of this ordinance because a number of Chicago-area wholesalers that sold in Midwestern states other than Illinois refused to carry phosphate-based detergents. Procter & Gamble sued, alleging that the ordinance resulted in an impermissible interference with interstate commerce. Do you think that state and local governments should have the power to regulate such products as phosphates? See *Procter & Gamble v. City of Chicago*, 501 F.2d. 69 (1975).
7. Why has the federal government enacted extensive legislation in the environmental area? Do you favor international regulation or national regulation? Federal regulation or state regulation? Why?

8. The World Resources Institute has developed an international standard for reporting six greenhouse gases that are key contributors to global warming. It envisions that corporations will need to account for their greenhouse gases in the same way as they do for other assets and liabilities. Review the policy and indicate whether you think the standard, called the Greenhouse Gas Protocol Initiative or GHG Protocol, makes sense. See http://www.wri.org/press/ghg_protocol.html.

9. Water pollution caused by oil spills has occurred in the waters of Alaska, California, Delaware, Florida, Louisiana, and Texas. Beaches have been inundated with medical debris that apparently had been discarded from hospitals or medical clinics. In some cases, the polluter responsible for an oil spill is a corporation that has little insurance and few assets and is thus unable to pay the cleanup costs. In a few cases, the waste disposal firm is responsible for the pollution. In other cases, it is impossible to trace the debris dumped into an open sea to one or more polluters. In these cases, what should be the government policy? Should the government absorb the cost of cleanup? Should the cost be spread among all manufacturers of certain products or to all waste disposal firms, even if many are not polluters? What if the cost of cleanup to private industry or to a particular polluting firm will cause that firm to go bankrupt or to reduce employment? Is the benefit derived from having the firm pay for its pollution worth the cost to society of having the firm go out of business? Will enforcing pollution laws make U.S. firms less competitive with foreign firms that may not have to bear such costs?

10. The Comprehensive Environmental Response Compensation Liability Act (CERCLA) imposes liability on individuals and companies who own, once owned, operate, or formerly operated a facility that contained hazardous substances. Farmland Industries was going to be held liable for cleanup costs at several different sites by the EPA. Farmland then sought to recover from its insurer, Republic Insurance Co., for the amount of cleanup costs it had agreed to pay in a settlement agreement with EPA. Republic Insurance said the cleanup costs are not "damages arising from property damage and personal injury as that term is used in its policy." It also argued that it should not be liable for paying the firm's cleanup costs at its own property when the policy was to cover the costs of damages suffered by others at the firm's property. Should an insurer that is liable for damages on a policyholder's property be required to cover CERCLA cleanup costs imposed by EPA? See *Farmland Industries v. Republic Insurance Co.*, 941 S.W. 2d 505 (Mo. Banc, 1997).

Internet Regulation

Before the Internet, individual and mass communications were made individually and in mass using face-to-face methods, print, and electronic means (mostly phone and broadcast). Freedom to communicate is an essential right given in the Bill of Rights; the First Amendment assures freedom of speech, press, and assembly. As discussed in Chapter 4, these freedoms are not limited to political expression but are also important for the proper functioning of commerce and the self-expression needed for true liberty.

Internet growth continues to suffer, at least in part, because of opposing visions of regulation. Early Internet adopters embraced a laissez-faire attitude. In their view, the Internet was a borderless new cyberspace that could not be tamed by traditional government means. The history of government political processes shows they are usually limited to influencing physical, geographic space. This Internet libertarianism truly reawakened the eighteenth- and nineteenth-century laissez-faire spirit on which much of America's public policies were originally built.

The Internet eventually encountered difficulties much like the nineteenth-century westward expansion that temporarily produced the Wild West. The prevailing conception of the role of law and order in this new space is changing. Now governments all over the world are trying to rein in abuses (hacking, fraud, stalking, theft, espionage, vandalism) that have become widespread. Nevertheless, cyberspace libertarians continued to argue that Internet regulation is impossible and largely ineffective.

Eventually, the defense of Internet laissez-faire shifted to another perspective: cost-benefit analysis. Cyberspace libertarians now argue that regulation will mute the efficiency and freedoms seemingly possible in unfettered cyberspace. They claim that governments will never understand cyberspace and too readily impose restrictions that dampen innovation and prevent e-commerce from achieving its efficiency and productivity promises. They perceive government to be largely incompetent and ignorant of the issues and capabilities of the Internet. Further, government enforcement will probably remain underfunded and unable to regulate as effectively as it has in traditional areas. Government regulators are unlikely to remain current in the technical capabilities necessary for effective and efficient regulation. From this standpoint, industry should embrace self-regulation as a means to achieve society's goals and avoid the draconian overregulation that too often follows scandal or catastrophe.

Many aspects of Internet regulation are covered elsewhere in this book. For example, criminal and tort liability, gambling and obscenity, the creation and defense of intellectual property rights, commercial law processes and safeguards, privacy, and monopolies were discussed in preceding chapters. This chapter discusses several remaining areas of Internet regulation: consumer protection, taxes, and telecommunications. First, the conceptual basis for regulation is presented. This theoretical framework developed during the industrialization of the nineteenth and twentieth centuries. Now, many aspects are adapting to cyberspace and e-commerce. Second, consumer protection, largely administered by the Federal Trade Commission (FTC) and the states, is discussed. Third, the highly controversial problem of Internet taxation is covered. Finally, the regulation of e-commerce infrastructure—telecommunications—is discussed.

CONCEPTUAL BASIS FOR BUSINESS REGULATION

Traditional business and e-commerce are both regulated by local, state, federal, and international governmental authorities. In addition, there is a trend toward private regulation by professional associations and self-regulatory organizations (SROs). This was not always so. Before the New Deal era, U.S. Supreme Court interpretations reinforced the historical U.S. preference for public policy decision making largely by the free market. This philosophy was founded on the colonists' contempt for the British crown's authoritarian rule and the economic restraint imposed by British mercantilism. Indeed, the Constitutional framers designed the Bill of Rights with broad social, political, and economic freedoms to encourage free markets and other libertarian fundamentals. These laissez-faire principles have limited the role of government in the economy and thereby minimized governmental intrusion on business. Even today, U.S. economic freedom stands in stark contrast to the pervasive intrusion of other governments into their national economies. Government decision making has historically prevailed throughout the world's developed and developing economies at most times in history. Provisions of the U.S. Constitution illustrate this preference. The contracts clause prohibited states from legislating to impair the obligations of contracts. Regulation can diminish the value of private property, so regulation is generally limited by the economic due process concept.

Adam Smith probably makes the best-known statement of this laissez-faire preference in his 1776 publication *The Wealth of Nations*. The "invisible hand" of capitalism is implemented through self-interest that "naturally" drives the market to optimize social welfare. Private property incentivizes risk and innovation as long as actors can retain the fruits of their effort (profits). Competition disciplines the participants to become efficient. New competitors are attracted when any endeavor makes abnormally high profits. The primary economic questions are answered with allocative efficiency: what is produced, how is it produced, who receives that production, and how production changes or maintains flexibility. Adam Smith was a career British bureaucrat.

Adam Smith's model makes some assumptions similar to those in the perfect competition model: (1) There are numerous rational buyers and sellers in all markets, (2) all have perfect information, (3) no barriers restrict the entry of new firms into markets, (4) only standardized products are sold, and (5) no participant has market power (e.g., no monopoly power). The market "clears" for quantities and at prices that form an equilibrium. Adam Smith believed that government intrusion into such free markets was "unnatural." Therefore, there is only limited justification for government intervention. Smith saw only three legitimate governmental roles: (1) national defense, (2) administration of justice to preserve property rights and facilitate enforcement of transactions, and (3) establish public works or other public goods that are valuable throughout society but that private enterprise might neglect (e.g., roads, dams, parks). This section discusses some of the traditional market failure arguments and the regulatory programs that grew up to cure them.

MARKET FAILURES

Considerable real-world experience illustrates that Adam Smith had a simplistic view of markets. His assumptions seldom hold true in the real world, and markets often do not behave as predicted. Sometimes market inefficiencies or market failures occur. Market failures harm society's welfare because there is an injurious side to self-interest. For example, the side effects of pollution are often hidden, eventually harming society. Critics often justify government intervention to correct market failures through the tool of regulation. Some free market critics argue that competitive market systems cannot adequately address social problems. Therefore, the public's policy preferences are also focused through pluralistic democracy. Public consensus brings pressure through government to distribute income more equitably, conserve natural resources, eliminate discrimination, pursue nationalistic goals, and stabilize economic volatility.

Monopoly Power

The perfect competition model can allocate scarce resources efficiently only when no seller possesses monopoly power and no buyer possesses monopsony power. Monopolies are the antithesis of perfect competition. A monopolist has power to set high prices, reduce the quantity produced, and be slow to innovate. The result is an artificial equilibrium that gives the monopolist high monopoly profits and society a lower level of products. There is a dead-weight loss that transfers wealth from society to the monopolist. Monopolists can reinforce their monopoly power by thwarting competition—for example, by raising barriers to entry with patents, high fixed costs, or trade barriers.

Opponents of monopoly argue that regulatory policies should limit monopoly power and force the market back toward the benefits of competition. For example, antitrust laws are designed to correct for the market failure of monopolies. The "free trade" movement among nations serves a similar purpose. Trade barriers erect monopolistic barriers to entering foreign markets. They tend to preserve market power for each nation's domestic producers at the expense of more perfect competition.

In another form of monopolization, one or a few sellers supply less of scarce commodities than the market demands. The seller(s) can earn windfall profits that trigger political pressures to regulate or tax them if no particular skill or ingenuity was involved and the windfall profits are very large. For example, regulation may impose windfall profit taxes to transfer the windfall back to society from producers. After the Arab oil embargo raised energy prices nearly 20-fold during the 1970s, Congress regulated oil and gas pricing and taxed the oil industry's windfall profits. A similar theory leads to rationing scarce commodities during wartime and to price controls to control inflation. President Nixon imposed such a price control program in the early 1970s. Cornering a market in commodities by buying or tying up all the available supply is illegal under the commodities laws.

Monopsony is buyers' market power that creates unequal bargaining power. This problem is significant in the labor markets. Most employees have a weak bargaining position because they are dispersed and unconnected as individuals. Large employers thus have a monopsony—more accurately, oligopsony—power, to buy services. Employers' inherent bargaining advantage was particularly evident during the early industrial revolution. The inevitable reaction was the unionization movement, and it also inspired the more severe backlash of socialism and communism.

Natural Monopolies and Destructive Competition

An area of particular importance to e-commerce is natural monopolies. **Natural monopolies** are believed inevitable in some industries because monopoly is occasionally more efficient than competition. The theory is that industries with declining long-run average costs provide cheaper products with a monopoly than is possible with direct competition. For example, recall the discussion of network economics in Chapter 11. It seems foolish to have numerous competing utilities serving the same customers, each with duplicate physical distribution systems, such as electric wires or pipes for water, natural gas, or sewers. Utilities have high fixed costs to establish their generation capacity; to pay for the expenses of generation, pumping, and transport; and to create and maintain their distribution networks of miles of wires or pipe. These are natural monopolies like the winner-take-all philosophy underlying network industries today.

At the turn of the twentieth century, the fledgling electric power industry became a natural monopoly after experience with another market failure, **destructive competition**. Rampant price-cutting between competing electric utilities led to selling below cost. Eventually, most went bankrupt, leaving the lone survivor as an unregulated monopoly. Every state and most foreign nations adopted public utility rate regulation to permit the economies of scale that utilities need, along with avoiding costly duplication of their network capacities. Another example of destructive competition periodically plagues the U.S. airline industry. After deregulation in 1980, the airlines had more capacity than demand, so they began a period of destructive competition. Several U.S. airlines eventually went bankrupt.

Destructive competition causes an inefficient waste of societal resources. Competition in a natural monopoly requires competitors to duplicate their networks. None can offer prices as low as could a single monopolist. Therefore, the regulatory response is for government to grant an exclusive franchise creating the legal monopoly for each utility. State public utility commissions regulate prices and profits to avert the natural monopolist's tendency to raise price and cut output.

Natural monopolies are not perpetual. Over time, technology can eliminate the cost advantages of a natural monopoly. For example, deregulation of long-distance telephone service, local cellular phone service, and cable television occurred after competition became a more efficient way to discipline these markets than regulation. Also, the railroad's natural monopoly eventually disappeared as pipelines, motor transport, and airlines became more acceptable, reliable, and cost-effective.

Externalities

The pursuit of self-interest through competitive markets often produces side effects that affect others—negatively and positively. **Externalities** are by-products of an individual's economic activities that can impose costs and/or bestow benefits on others. Externalities are a form of market failure that economists define as any cost or benefit transfer of the activity that is not bargained for in the contractual exchange.

Pollution is a classic negative externality. Consider the manufacturing process that produces wastewater dumped into rivers and particulate and toxic gases released into the air. What are the manufacturer's natural incentives to control pollution? Abatement equipment is costly, and outsiders may be unable to discover or prove the pollution's source. If the polluter externalizes these costs on the environment, pollution harms the public. Polluters are **free riders** because others actually bear the costs of pollution in cleanup, disease, and lost productivity. Free markets encourage pollution when it is difficult to detect or the damage manifests slowly, such as a latent disease. Free riders take advantage by shifting the cleanup costs component of their production costs to society.

As the pollution example suggests, many externalities are eventually discovered, triggering political pressure for regulation. Regulation and tax policies can address the market's failure to discipline the producers of negative externalities. Public policy sometimes encourages **positive externalities**, which are beneficial effects of economic activity. For example, many states and local governments use tax and industrial incentives to attract new industry that benefits local merchants, employment, the surrounding community, and the tax base for local governments.

There are critics of using externalities to justify regulation. Ronald Coase has suggested that bystanders may already be compensated for externalities through cheaper land purchases or higher wages for employees in dangerous industries. The costs of controlling externalities should be weighed against the benefits expected before society implements any costly regulatory policy.

Public Goods

Markets sometimes fail to provide certain types of goods or services. **Public goods** are the prime example, and often government provides them. Public goods are nonrival and typically underproduced by competitive forces. The additional or marginal cost of providing more public goods to an additional person is usually small. Also, it is difficult to exclude people from consuming them. For example, private enterprise is unlikely to provide the sea navigational assistance of a lighthouse. Ship owners, consumers, and suppliers share the benefit of safe and reliable trade, so government supplies lighthouse safety services. In general, government provides tax-financed public goods or regulation to cure the market's failure to supply them.

Garrett Hardin's famous narrative on the **Tragedy of the Commons** illustrates the public goods problem. Consider the capacity problem of the U.S. open range in the late 1800s. Each cattle rancher expanded his herd in order to raise his income. The public open range appeared to be in limitless supply, and feeding cattle there seemed costless. However, the range could not feed all the cattle as the number of ranchers and their herds grew. Eventually the forage grass was stripped away and did not regenerate, ranchers' herds were malnourished, and many cattle died off, bankrupting ranchers. Hardin commented, "Ruin is the destination toward which all men rush, each pursuing his own best interest in a society that believes in the freedom of the commons. Freedom in a commons brings ruin to all." Advocates of laissez-faire economics and libertarianism cite this "Tragedy" to justify converting public lands into private property and hold that individual ranchers are not likely to overgraze if they must personally bear the negative "wealth effects" of overusing land they own.

Can this same analysis be applied beyond land to other common things? How could air and water resources be cordoned off? Are they "commons" subject to a similar tragic destruction? Critics of pollution argue they are public goods that must be regulated to avoid the "Tragedy." The debate between free-marketers and regulators reinforces the significance of distinguishing between private and public goods. Society has experimented with privatizing several previously public goods: (1) police and fire protection, (2) roads and turnpikes, (3) mail service, and (4) utilities. Many

EXHIBIT 24.1 Potential Public Goods

Grain elevators	Airports	National defense	Waterworks
Docks and wharves	Train stations	Justice system	Utilities
Parks, public lands	Bus terminals	Public education	Public sanitation
Public markets	Roads and streets	Basic research	Fireworks displays
Locks and dams	Harbors	Public universities	Emergency service
Scenic views	Public broadcasting	Law enforcement	Mail services
Communications	Industrial policy	Civil defense	Public airwaves
Internet			

nations still own their telephone service. There are few "pure" public goods because most goods and services have some aspect of rivalry or excludability. The "goods" listed in Exhibit 24.1 are often cited as public goods. Each has been "underproduced" by private enterprise at some time in history, so they became the subject of regulation or public financing.

Asymmetric Information

Free market economists predict the market will operate efficiently when buyers and sellers are well informed. Transactions entered without key information about the value of the products or the reliability of the obligor may lead to **adverse selection.** Information is costly in the real world. Many market participants have limited ability to effectively process the information they acquire. Further, parties have an incentive to hide critical information. For example, employees often have incomplete information about workplace hazards or pollution. With better information, employees might demand higher wages, bargain for safety and health protections, or pressure politicians for enhanced safety protection. Imperfect information is the reality of most markets. Political pressures for disclosure regulations result, such as the food and drug labeling laws and the securities and franchising laws. These regulations seek to improve information and avoid adverse selection.

EVALUATING REGULATORY JUSTIFICATIONS

Regulatory programs usually result from social and political pressures to cure market failure. Such regulatory programs are always evaluated by value judgments about the **fairness** or the redistribution of income, but regulation can also be evaluated by economic analysis. **Economic efficiency** is cited to justify regulations that arguably reduce the waste of societal resources for a given level of economic activity. **Pareto optimality** is another measure of regulatory success. Under this model, a regulation or any other action produces optimal efficiency when it causes society, as a whole, to become better off, while no one is made worse off. Pareto efficiency is used to protect some faction of the economy from carrying the whole burden of the change.

Few regulatory programs are based on a single justification. Sometimes the market failure explanation is weak, but the political pressures are strong and persistent. In other instances, a regulatory program may be rationalized as correcting multiple market failures. For example, product liability laws attempt to correct the market's failure to supply consumers with more perfect information about products. Product liability laws can be explained as a method to prevent manufacturers from externalizing their costs of defective design or negligent production techniques.

Commentary

What Should Government's Role Be in E-Commerce?

The role of government and the private sector in regulating e-commerce is hotly debated. On one side are libertarians and the original Internet community. They find little helpful from government. On the other side are many sectors of society that find too many aspects of the Internet dangerous and culturally destabilizing. Internet regulation becomes a political question because these opposing forces are unlikely to find much comfortable compromise. Governments around the world are experimenting with vigorous controls over the Internet and e-commerce. As discussed throughout this book, many of these regulations ignore many cherished American liberties such as freedom of speech and privacy. Therefore, it is sensible to be pragmatic in Internet regulation.

As the dot.com revolution was taking hold in the mid-1990s, the U.S. presidential administration created a conceptual framework for e-commerce in *Framework for Global Electronic Commerce*. The *Framework* acknowledges that there are tough choices ahead, so it tries to establish libertarian policies where feasible. The *Framework* acknowledges that the Internet has become an "appliance of everyday life, accessible from almost every point on the planet" and that "many businesses and consumers are still wary of conducting extensive business over the Internet because of the lack of a predictable legal environment governing transactions." The *Framework* foresaw the range of pressures for regulation in areas such as "taxes and duties, restrictions on the type of information transmitted, control over standards development, licensing requirements and rate regulation of service providers."

Several key principles were established that still resonate clearly. First, the *Framework* recognizes that the private sector should lead. Innovation largely starts in private enterprise, and government action risks being perpetually behind in discovering and resolving societal problems. Second, governments should avoid undue restrictions on e-commerce. Overregulation will distort the development of the electronic marketplace by decreasing the supply and raising the cost of products and services. Business models must evolve rapidly to keep pace with the speed of technological change, making government regulations likely to be outmoded when finally enacted.

The third major e-commerce regulatory policy is that when government is needed, it should support and enforce a predictable, minimalist, consistent, and simple legal environment for e-commerce. The fourth principle is that government policies must accommodate the unique qualities of the Internet. For example, the Internet is decentralized and has a successful tradition of bottom-up governance. Regulation should be imposed only as a necessary means to achieve important goals when there is broad consensus. While some existing regulations work, they may be appropriate only for existing technologies and business models. Laws can hinder e-commerce, so they should be reviewed and revised or eliminated as needed for the new electronic age. Finally, the *Framework* recognizes the Internet's reach, making global e-commerce possible. Policies that are harmonized among the world's governments will lead to predictable results, regardless of where buyers or sellers reside.

The *Framework* concludes with an important role for government in facilitating standardization. Recall the antitrust aspects of standards that were discussed in Chapter 19. Standards allow products and services from different vendors to work together. Standards encourage competition and reduce uncertainty. Standards assure reliability, interoperability, ease of use, and scalability in areas such as: electronic payments, security (confidentiality, authentication, data integrity, access control, nonrepudiation), security services infrastructure (e.g., public key certificate authorities), electronic copyright management systems, video and data conferencing, high-speed network technologies (e.g., asynchronous transfer mode, synchronous digital hierarchy), and digital object and data interchange.

Nonstandard technical methods raise costs and introduce errors. Premature standardization, however, can lock in outdated technology or become nontariff trade barriers that lock out businesses from foreign markets. The *Framework* suggests that the marketplace, not governments, should determine technical standards. Numerous private sector bodies have contributed to developing voluntary standards that promote interoperability. The United States encourages the development of voluntary standards through private standards organizations, consortia, test beds, and R&D activities.

The regulatory programs discussed throughout this book should be evaluated with market failure criteria. Pressures to regulate e-commerce and the Internet should also be subjected to these analyses. Consider the major regulatory issues of cyberspace mentioned in this and previous chapters: obscenity, privacy, monopolization, law enforcement, Internet communications infrastructure, and the expansion of intellectual property rights. Each area should be examined under this law and by economics analysis to aid public policy making and guide regulators to make effective and least costly regulations.

CONSUMER PROTECTION

Before the 1930s, there was little comprehensive consumer protection regulation. Only the common law contract and tort principles of misrepresentation, warranty, and interference with economic relations provided any legal protection. However, they were insufficient, and Congress expanded the regulatory powers of the **Federal Trade Commission** (FTC) in 1938. The FTC directs much of its energy toward product marketing, where evidence has mounted that some sellers take advantage of unsophisticated buyers and fail to admit their products' shortcomings. As some industries became known for their abusive practices, pressures to legislate eventually addressed these abuses. This section examines the FTC's consumer protection regulatory powers over deceptive advertising and unfair and deceptive trade practices.

THE FEDERAL TRADE COMMISSION

The FTC is an independent regulatory agency with five commissioners appointed by the president and confirmed by the Senate. There must be political balance on the FTC, with no more than three members from any one political party. The FTC is entrusted by Congress to promote a competitive business environment. Originally created to enforce the antitrust laws in 1914 under the FTC Act (discussed in Chapter 19), the FTC has had consumer protection authority since the Wheeler-Lea Act of 1938. The FTC's powers in consumer finance under the Fair Credit Reporting Act were discussed in Chapter 14.

There is considerable overlap between the FTC's consumer protection function and its powers to promote competition. The FTC fosters competition by monitoring business practices and setting policies for consumer protection such as prohibiting practices found to be deceptive that might divert sales from honest competitors. Deceptive advertisements distort consumers' information, making their purchasing decisions inferior. Therefore, deceptive advertising undermines the goals of perfect competition. The FTC's interpretation of this mission undergoes change as the political makeup of the commissioners changes. For example, the FTC's vigorous industrywide enforcement of the 1960s and 1970s gave way to a restrained case-by-case approach in the 1980s, and then stricter enforcement returned in the mid-1990s.

The FTC also has the power to prosecute violations of §5 of the FTC Act, which prohibits unfair methods of competition and unfair or deceptive trade practices. The courts have interpreted trade practices to be *unfair* if they offend established public policy and are immoral, unethical, oppressive, unscrupulous, or apt to substantially injure consumers. FTC interpretations may be different from those of the courts, reflecting the prevailing ideology of the FTC and the judiciary. Trade practices are usually found "deceptive" if they *tend to deceive* the consumer, even if no actual deception is proved.

FTC Powers

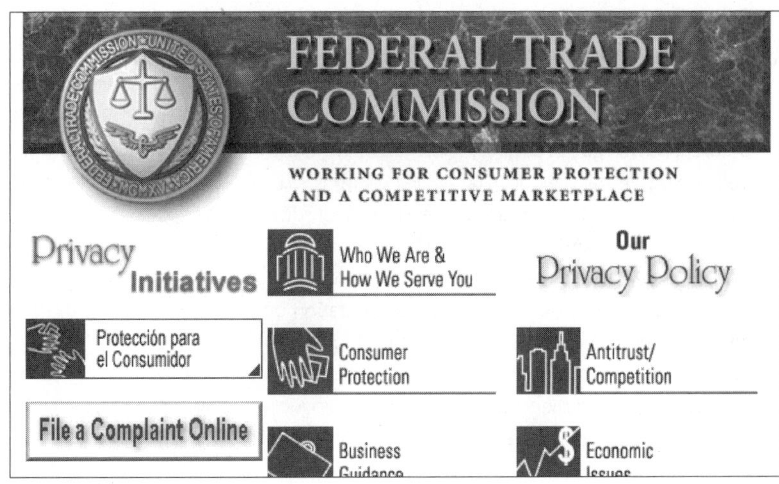

http://
www.ftc.gov

The FTC exercises several powers that facilitate enforcement of the consumer protection laws. The FTC defines unfair and deceptive trade practices by issuing **trade regulation rules**, which have the force of law. These rules prohibit deceptive activity in one or more industries. For example, there are trade regulation rules that address abuses in door-to-door sales, bait-and-switch sales tactics, direct marketing schemes, and used car sales. The FTC also may issue **advisory opinions** to individual firms seeking to avoid charges of unfair or deceptive trade practices in their proposed activities. More comprehensive advice is sometimes available through **industry guides** that address the trade practices of an entire industry. FTC advisory opinions and industry guides do not bind the courts, but there is often deference to the FTC's expertise. Of course, these policy statements may be amended later by the FTC itself. Influential members of President George W. Bush's administration have actively sought to stop federal agencies from issuing such guidelines as part of a deregulation effort originally started in the 1980s by his father, George H. W. Bush, then vice president under Ronald Reagan.

Some industries are exempt from FTC regulation if they are regulated by another federal, state, or local agency (e.g., public utilities, securities). A few industries, such as food and consumer credit, are regulated by both the FTC and another agency. For example, the FTC and the Food and Drug Administration (FDA) have overlapping jurisdiction over food labeling and food ads. The two agencies are beginning to cooperate to avoid costly and conflicting regulations. The FTC can share its investigatory files with other agencies such as the Justice Department to trigger a criminal prosecution.

FTC Consumer Protection Remedies

FTC investigations and enforcement actions are initiated after consumers, business competitors, administrative agencies, or Congress complains. The FTC also initiates its own investigations. The FTC's Bureau of Consumer Protection monitors consumer sales practices to obtain evidence of potential violations. The FTC may then conduct an investigation and gather sufficient evidence to bring an enforcement action. The FTC may issue **cease and desist orders** or settle charges with a **consent decree**, without going to trial, in which the defendants agree to eliminate the deception.

The FTC may also issue an **affirmative disclosure order** requiring an offender to provide information in future ads. A **corrective advertising order** may be issued to require new ads to correct past misleading ads. A **multiple product order** prohibits future deceptive advertising by a firm with a history of false advertising in selling any of its products. The FTC has also successfully sought rescission of contracts, returns of property, refunds of the purchase price, and damage payments to consumers. In one case, the FTC settled charges of false ad claims by requiring a health product retailer to fund health research.

If the business under investigation disputes the charges, an administrative hearing may be held before an administrative law judge (ALJ). Appeals from the ALJ's

Ethical Issue

Dilemmas in Consumer Protection

Consumer activist groups view product marketing as involving excessive sales pressure and some unfair practices. When goods are oversold, there may be evidence of unethical conduct. The ethical dilemma presented is whether the selling organization, individual salesperson, or advertising consultant has made a conscious decision to mislead prospective purchasers. Unethical conduct arises when a sales presentation or an advertisement makes untrue, fraudulent, or exaggerated claims. Misrepresentations or intentional fraud may appear in documents, sales literature, catalogues, price lists, allegedly "certified" test results, testimonials, advertising, websites, chat rooms, e-mail messages, or verbal sales talk provided by the seller or made in response to the buyer's inquiry.

Even where there is no misrepresentation during contracting, a transaction may be viewed as unethical during its performance. The knowing delivery of poor-quality goods or goods unsuitable for the buyer is unethical unless the seller notifies the buyer that the substandard delivery is an accommodation. Unfair advantage taken of uneducated consumers is also unethical. Telemarketing and on-line fraud are practiced increasingly on the unsophisticated and the elderly, who are often considered vulnerable to exaggerated claims. Too few people consciously follow the old adage "if it's too good to be true, it probably is."

decision go to the FTC commissioners. Appeals then go to the U.S. Circuit Courts of Appeals for judicial review. Violators of FTC regulations or cease and desist orders may be fined up to $10,000 per violation per day. Although the FTC's powers are generally intended to be preventive, the power to fine can add up. For example, Reader's Digest was fined $7.75 million for violating an FTC order.[1] However, a 1994 report indicated that since 1980 the FTC had collected only about one-third of the nearly $363,000,000 in fines for advertising or marketing fraud it has levied on 187 companies.

ADVERTISING REGULATION

The advertising of consumer products has contributed to the tremendous industrial expansion of the twentieth century. A legitimate function of advertising is to inform consumers and eliminate information asymmetries. However, advertising and promotional activities are less legitimate when the advertising is deceptive, false, or misleading. The U.S. Constitution protects free speech against government censorship unless the censorship is very closely related to a compelling governmental purpose, such as the prevention of fraud, defamation, riots, or subversive activities. Although political speech is given the greatest protection, **commercial speech** such as advertising is well protected. Information is essential to the efficient operation of markets. Advertising can be regulated under the common law and by the FTC for consumer protection purposes.

Regulation addresses advertising in all its traditional forms as well as many new forms. Consumer protections discussed in this chapter apply to print, electronic media, billboard, TV, and radio forms, as well as to newer forms such as ads on commercial websites, banner ads, bulletin boards, chat sites, e-mail, and spam ads. Some aspects of advertising regulation are adapted to the special circumstances of the Internet.

1. *United States v. Reader' Digest Ass'n, Inc.*, 662 F.2d 995 (3d Cir.1981).

Common Law Remedies

The common law remedies for victims of deceptive advertising are generally ineffective. For example, a seller's advertisement is seldom treated as an offer. If the product's actual specifications, its price at the store, or its characteristics as delivered differ from the advertised specifications, there is no breach of contract because no enforceable contract had been made. Warranty liability discussed in Chapter 8 may arise from advertising and other language in the sales materials or contract. Warranties may also become the basis for a consumer's complaint about deception.

The tort of deceit or fraud may exist if an advertiser knowingly makes material misrepresentations of fact on which an injured purchaser justifiably relies. Protection of trademarks and trade names exists under both common law and federal statutes. If an advertiser makes untrue statements in comparing its goods with the goods of a competitor, the defamed competitor may sue for trade libel, slander, or disparagement, as discussed in Chapter 18.

Deceptive Advertising

Congress found the common law remedies were ineffective to protect consumers so it passed the Wheeler-Lea Act in 1938 to deal with **deceptive advertising.** The FTC is authorized to prosecute unfair or deceptive trade practices in advertising. To measure deception, the FTC uses a deception policy that requires assessment of ads by the total impression created in the consumer's mind. To be deceptive, an ad must make a *misrepresentation or omission* in its communication to consumers. The misleading statement need have only a capacity to mislead consumers about some *material* aspect of the product. This test is interpreted by using a hypothetical "typical ordinary consumer . . . who is acting reasonably under the circumstances." It is not necessary to prove either that the advertiser intended to deceive or that actual deception occurred. However, the deceptiveness must be so strong that a reasonable person, not just a gullible one, would be deceived. Courts have admitted survey evidence to show how a reasonable consumer might interpret an ad.

False or Unsubstantiated Claims

Ads are deceptive if patently false or if the claims are not supported by a reasonable basis in scientific evidence. Demonstrations must accurately depict the performance of the product advertised and illustrate some relevant or meaningful product attribute. Test results that create an impression of the product's superiority must be based on studies or surveys conducted scientifically. This means that clinical tests must be well controlled and use reasonable statistical inference. This is the **prior substantiation** rule: It requires that the evidence used in an ad must be gathered *before* the ads are run. FTC enforcement can require advertisers to submit substantiation.

Product performance claims about composition, durability, capacity, or endurance under adverse conditions must be true. For example, a dishwasher retailer was ordered to cease and desist from claiming that no prewashing was necessary.[2] Numerous sellers of nutritional and health products have been ordered to stop advertising false or unsubstantiated health improvement claims. Kraft was ordered to discontinue ads falsely suggesting its cheese slices had the same calcium content as five ounces of milk. Haagen-Dazs agreed to refrain from advertising that its frozen yogurt bars were 98% fat free because several flavors allegedly contained more than 2% fat,

2. *Sears, Roebuck & Co., v. FTC*, 676 F.2d 385 (9th Cir., 1982).

Ethical Issue

Dilemmas in Advertising

If advertising creates demand and additional use of some dangerous products or exposure to them increases accidents, then is it safer to restrict advertising? This type of ethical dilemma has been the foundation for advertising controls or bans in dangerous products such as firearms, cigarettes, and alcohol. Some groups believe that promoting dangerous products—such as ads for three-wheel all-terrain motorcycles or ads targeting children that glamorize of smoking and drinking—is unethical.

Children are a particularly vulnerable audience for certain types of advertising. The use of hero advertising and the merging of children's programming into advertising also pose ethical dilemmas. Advertisers and the media have used self-regulation in these areas. For example, the television code encourages clear transitions between children's shows and the accompanying ads to weaken the influence of heroes in the ads. Advertisers should carefully consider how the audience receives their claims as well as the lifestyle and activities presented. An ethical dilemma is presented by advertisements that overreach the consumer's ability to appreciate the risks, costs, or utility of a product.

some averaging 8 to 12 grams of fat per serving.[3] The FTC prohibited Stouffer Foods from falsely advertising that Lean Cuisine was low in sodium.[4] The FTC order required Stouffer to compare its sodium content to established public guidelines for "low-sodium" and FDA "recommended daily allowances (RDA)." Now these are called "daily values."

Green Ads and Eco-Labeling

The so-called green ads targeting environmentally conscious consumers are susceptible to abuse. Ad claims such as "recyclable" or "biodegradable" are not well defined and subject to abuse because many consumers are swayed by the desire to satisfy their environmental responsibilities. The FTC worked with the EPA to issue voluntary environmental advertising guidelines in 1992, which were revised in 1998 and are now published in *Complying with the Environmental Marketing Guides*. For example, products labeled "recycled" must be made from 100% recycled materials; otherwise, it should state an accurate proportion of recycled material.

The green guidelines urge that claims be true and not meaningless. They discourage exaggerated environmental benefits of advertised products, and claims must be specific and substantiated like any other ad claim. In one FTC case, the manufacturer of a spray product was ordered to stop claiming it was environmentally safe because it contained an ozone depleting propellant. The manufacturer of a gasoline additive was ordered to stop claiming fuel economy improvements of "up to 15%" without significant evidence that actual consumers could regularly achieve such performance. There have been various experiments with **eco-labeling,** voluntary and mandatory. For example, some firms eco-label, touting environmental benefits of their products. In some other instances, governments have mandated eco-labeling requirements that would require products sold to follow particular environmental processes. They can erect trade barriers if the products are from nations that do not follow the eco-standards.

ONLINE

FTC Environmental Marketing Compliance
http://www.ftc.gov/bcp/conline/pubs/buspubs/greenguides.htm

Consumers in many nations have nationalistic pride that encourages them to purchase domestic products. For example, the South Koreans are actively discouraged

3. *In re Haagen-Dazs Co. Inc.*, FTC File 942-3028 (Nov. 7, 1994).
4. *Stouffer Foods Corp.*, FTC Docket 9250 (Aug. 6, 1993).

from buying "luxury goods" produced abroad. Many U.S. manufacturers and retailers encourage consumers to "Buy American" or claim their goods are made in the USA. This has raised questions about the "domestic content" of goods. Wal-Mart's "Made in the USA" advertising program was subjected to national TV criticism after discovery that much of its apparel was foreign-made. Other products, such as sneakers and computers, touted as made in America are often just assembled in the United States from foreign-made components.

Most automobiles made by the Big Three U.S. manufacturers have at least some foreign content, and many are assembled in Canada or Mexico. The U.S. law requires window stickers on all new cars citing the precise "North American Content." There are similar domestic content labeling laws for apparel. The increasing globalization of the market may eventually curtail such claims unless more laws are passed that arbitrarily set some minimum measure for the "domestic value added" of goods with foreign content that would then permit ads claiming "Made in the USA." Other nations have similar domestic content laws.

ONLINE

FTC's domestic content guidelines
http://www.ftc.gov/os/statutes/usajump.htm

Puffing

Puffing is the seller's opinion or generalized commendation of value. Puffing is not a misrepresentation under contract law, nor does it form the basis for an express warranty. Puffing in ads is *not* generally considered deceptive by the FTC unless accompanied by more concrete but false statements about the product's characteristics or performance. Obviously false and exaggerated ad claims may not be illegal as puffing if reasonable consumers could easily see that a statement such as "faster than lightning" is an exaggeration.

Mockups

A **mockup** is a false demonstration to improve the appearance or effect of an ad. The mockup is deceptive if the viewer believes it represents the real thing. A mockup that fails to disclose important facts or clearly acknowledge that the demonstration is not genuine is an unfair or deceptive practice. For example, Volvo has an enviable and deserved reputation for safety. Its ad agency chose to tout the structural integrity and crashworthiness of Volvo cars in a staged mockup of a car-crushing event. The ad showed a Volvo surviving uncrushed as it was driven over by "big-wheel" four-wheel-drive vehicles in an arena while other brands were quickly and easily crushed. Volvo's ad agency could have cited extensive valid scientific evidence of Volvo's safety. However, the agency decided the repeated trials necessary to adequately catch the event on film would eventually crush even the Volvo. Later Volvo fired the ad agency when it was discovered the Volvo in the film was extensively reinforced to survive the many film "takes" necessary to shoot a successful commercial. This ad was a mockup because viewers were led to believe the Volvo in the ad was standard.

Colgate-Palmolive used a series of one-minute commercials allegedly showing that the use of Rapid Shave would enable a razor to "cut right through this tough, dry sandpaper." Actually, a mockup of loose sand applied to Plexiglas was used. Real sandpaper would require 80 minutes of soaking with shaving cream to soften enough to be shaved as shown. The U.S. Supreme Court acknowledged the FTC's expertise in determining the deceptiveness of ads and held: "We think it inconceivable that the ingenious advertising world would be unable to conform to the FTC's insistence that the public be not misinformed."[5]

5. *FTC v. Colgate-Palmolive Co.*, 380 U.S. 374 (1965).

Omissions and Half-Truths

Advertisers must also refrain from deception by disguising it with some truth that omits facts necessary for clarification. An **omission** or **half-truth** is deceptive if more information is necessary to keep the ad from being misleading. For example, the selective use of data, comments, or conclusions from scientific studies may be deceptive half-truths. The FTC ordered P. Lorillard to stop advertising that Old Gold cigarettes were lower in tar and nicotine than the six leading brands because the differences were statistically negligible. The ads cited selective data from a *Reader's Digest* article concluding Old Gold's lower tar and nicotine content was not meaningful for smokers' health. Only the article's most favorable portion was extracted. The more negative conclusion was omitted, creating an "entirely false and misleading impression" in the ad about the article's content and Old Gold's health impact.[6]

In some ads, a false impression is created about the seller's credentials, which is also a misleading omission.[7] For example, persons falsely appearing to be scientists or medical doctors are misleading half-truths. Misleading health claims can emerge from literal truths that withhold other important information. For example, the ad for a water purification device claimed to remove several contaminants but failed to mention it added another potentially hazardous chemical. Food ads claiming health benefits such as reduced heart disease from a product's low-fat or low-cholesterol content are misleading if they contain high sodium content, which is directly connected to heart disease.

Endorsements

The FTC has issued several guidelines for endorsements. Endorsements by sports figures, celebrities, or experts, such as those found in shaving, beer, and medical insurance commercials, should reflect the actual opinions of these people. An advertiser may use such an endorsement only while the celebrity actually uses the product. Ads appearing to be the endorsements of consumers must use actual consumers and not actors. By contrast, fictional dramatizations without endorsements may use unknown actors. When fictional, the actor need not have a heartfelt positive opinion of the product or actually use the product. Many responsible advertisers use disclaimers indicating the commercial is a fictional dramatization, although some such disclaimers are in small type or run across the TV or computer screen too fast for careful detection. False endorsements may trigger liability for fraud for the advertiser and for the celebrity.

Corrective Advertisements

When an advertiser makes misstatements in advertisements, the FTC assumes that the misconception may be durable, remaining in the consumer's mind for some time. Only further advertising of a similar magnitude, duration, and creativity can correct such "resilient" false impressions. In some cases, a court-approved consent decree requires the advertiser to conduct corrective advertising or **counteradvertising** to rebut the misleading claims of prior ads. The FTC has used corrective advertising orders since the well-known Listerine case, in which Warner-Lambert was ordered to conduct $10 million of new ads correcting its former claims that Listerine killed millions of "germs." The germs Listerine eliminated did not cause colds, even though reasonable consumers might interpret this from the ads. The FTC's power to

---

6. *P. Lorillard v. FTC*, 186 F.2d 52 (4th Cir., 1950).
7. *Erickson v. FTC*, 272 F.2d 385 (7th Cir., 1959).

International Commentary

Ad Regulation

Comparison advertising was long condemned by most U.S. businesses as ultimately harmful to their whole industries. However, comparative ads are appearing with greater frequency, particularly as surveys proliferate from independent research firms. Japanese businesses still avoid active comparison ads because they are believed to disturb the traditional appearance of industrial harmony important in Japanese culture.

The regulation of advertising varies considerably in other nations. The United States is generally among the strictest. The huge size of the U.S. market, the broad diversity of products available, and the much larger U.S. marketing budgets bring about generally more marketing experimentation there than in most other nations. Many deceptive marketing practices are devised in the United States long before the same products, marketing channels, or promotional devices are known in most other nations. However, several northern European nations also have strict ad regulations. The standard in the UK is somewhat less stringent, holding ads illegal if a product is misrepresented. Government nonintervention in many developing nations may actually indulge misleading advertisers. As advertising becomes even more important in other nations, their ad regulations can be expected to follow the U.S. lead, at least to some extent.

order a corrective ad was upheld on appeal; the required ads stated: "Contrary to our prior advertising, Listerine will not help prevent colds or sore throats or lessen their severity."[8] Another manufacturer was ordered to run corrective ads for a year, admitting its products were not superior insulation to regular glass storm windows. In another case, Novartis claimed its product Doan's Pills were particularly effective against back pain and contained an ingredient not found in other over-the-counter analgesics. While literally true, the FTC found that consumers would mistakenly believe the product was superior to its competitors. Corrective ads were ordered and affirmed by the Court of Appeals.[9] The FTC's corrective ad standard appears in Exhibit 24.2.

Comparative Ads and the Lanham Act

The FTC favors the recent trend toward scientifically verifiable comparative advertising because it encourages competition. The "Pepsi Challenge" blind taste tests were conducted over decades, using large random samples and performed nationwide by independent testing agents. Therefore, there is strong scientific validity to such consumer preference comparisons. However, not all comparative ads are as rigorous. Invalid comparisons may be false and deceptive, exposing the advertiser to damages under the common law tort of trade disparagement and for lost profits under §43(a) of the Lanham Act (federal trademark law). The disparaged competitor may sue if the comparison makes false or misleading statements of fact or misrepresentations about the nature, characteristics, geographic origin, or quality of a competitor's products, services, or commercial activities. The false statement must have a tendency to deceive a substantial segment of the intended audience, it must influence purchasing decisions, and it must be likely to injure the disparaged trademarked product.

Comparative ad cases under the Lanham Act illustrate that a false advertiser is subject to suit even if the competitor's precise product is not directly identified in the ad. It

8. *Warner-Lambert Co. v. FTC*, 562 F.2d 749 (D.C. Cir. 1977).
9. *Novartis Corp. v. FTC*, 223 F.3d 783 (D.C.Cir. 2000).

EXHIBIT 24.2 Corrective Advertising Standard

[I]f a deceptive advertisement has played a substantial role in creating or reinforcing in the public's mind a false and material belief that lives on after the false advertising ceases, there is clear and continuing injury to competition and to the consuming public as consumers continue to make purchasing decisions based on the false belief. Since this belief cannot be averted by merely requiring respondent to cease disseminating the advertisement, we may appropriately order respondent to take affirmative action designed to terminate the otherwise ill effects of the advertisement.

is enough if the advertiser misleads consumers about important features, such as a false statement about a computer monitor's compatibility with a new video standard.[10]

Packaging and Labeling

Congress has passed numerous consumer protection laws directly regulating product packaging and labeling. Generally, the law requires accuracy in labels. The **Fair Packaging and Labeling Act of 1966** provides for general labeling requirements. As increased packaging obscures the consumer's actual view of the product, accurate label descriptions become important for product evaluation. Labels must (1) identify the product; (2) identify the name and address of the manufacturer, packer, or distributor; and (3) list the quantity and serving size in a specific manner.

FTC rules require particular labeling of numerous diverse products. For example, accurate octane numbers must appear on gasoline pumps. There are numerous additional federal and state labeling laws regulating wool products, cigarettes, flammable fabrics, textiles, poisons, food, drugs, and cosmetics. Many of these laws empower various agencies to regulate labeling or deceptive practices.

Internet and On-line Ad Regulation

The FTC issued guidelines in 2000 reaffirming that its advertising regulations apply to deceptive marketing on line. These guidelines largely emphasize the principles discussed previously, applying them to on-line marketing. The FTC's ad rules apply to all advertising media, including the Internet. Key terms must be disclosed in a clear and conspicuous manner, and on-line customers often do not see everything on a full webpage. They may not click through or find disclaimer language that generally benefits the marketer. Therefore, forthright disclosure is even more critical on line. Disclosures must be placed close to the Web page areas where most consumers will view them, not in tiny type on another page. The type size must be large enough to be readily seen, moving features in the ad must not distract from the disclosure message, and disclosures unlikely to be readily seen may need to be repeated or made in multimedia (audio, video, text) to assure communication.

ONLINE

FTC Dot Com Disclosure Guidance
http://www.ftc.gov/bcp/conline/pubs/buspubs/dotcom/index.html

Website designers may be held liable for unfair and deceptive ads. Since on-line ads have proliferated, the FTC has brought hundreds of enforcement actions against websites for violation of the ad rules. Examples include pyramid sales schemes, credit and investment scams, unfair auctions, health care swindles, website hijacking, and unauthorized credit card transactions.

10. *Princeton Graphics v. NEC Home Electronics*, 732 F.Supp. 1258 (S.D.N.Y. 1990).

Ethical Issue

Food Labeling

Recent trends toward better nutrition have generated a flurry of new and repackaged foods and nutritional products. Unfortunately, some food producers pander to the public's obsession with healthy eating by taking advantage of consumers' limited nutrition knowledge. Many make exaggerated claims of product performance that confuse consumers. There are ethical dilemmas when such ads prey on consumers' fears of ill health and their prejudices about body image. The FDA monitors unfair and deceptive trade practices in marketing food, drugs, and nutritional products. The FDA closely scrutinizes product claims about food contents, fad diets, and product descriptors such as "diet," "light," "fresh," "natural," and "low-fat."

The promotion of some products as "no-cholesterol" or "low-cholesterol" falsely suggests that similar products from other manufacturers do contain cholesterol. For example, no major national brand of peanut butter contains cholesterol. There is no cholesterol in peanuts, and no domestic producers add cholesterol-laden lard to peanut butter as in the past. Even when factual, a producer's claim of low cholesterol may be an unethical half-truth. High blood cholesterol levels are more closely linked to eating foods high in saturated fat than to foods simply high in cholesterol.

Health claims that products contain lower amounts of suspected unhealthy substances can also be misleading because the comparative descriptors "diet," "lower," and "light" have no meaning except when compared with similar foods that regularly contain more of that substance. For example, the term "light" beer is meaningless unless it contains significantly fewer calories than some average beer. "Light" can also be understood as suggesting lighter flavor, smell, or color.

TRADE REGULATION RULES AND DECEPTIVE TRADE PRACTICES

The FTC may use the notice and comment rule-making procedure to issue consumer protection regulations. The FTC's proposed regulations are first published in the *Federal Register*, which permits affected parties to comment. Comments can influence the FTC to change the final rule. The following sections discuss some of the more significant FTC trade regulation rules issued under §18 of the FTC Act and as deceptive practices challenged under §5. One such rule was discussed in Chapter 11, the FTC's **holder in due course disclosure rule**, issued in 1976, which suspends the HDC rule from the UCC for individual consumer purchases or leases of goods and services. This rule requires that any consumer credit contract must contain a boldface clause permitting the consumer to stop paying on debts if the seller committed fraud or breached the contract or if the goods are defective.

Bait and Switch

Some sellers stock a limited supply of inexpensive "loss leader" merchandise as "bait" to lure potential buyers into the store, hoping that sales personnel can "switch" them into purchasing products with higher profit margins. This **bait-and-switch** tactic violates FTC guidelines if a salesperson refuses to show the cheaper merchandise, represents that the bait will be out of stock for a long time, holds an inadequate supply of the bait, or is following instructions to actively switch customers to alternative goods. For example, it is illegal to hold insufficient inventory of an inexpensive color TV advertised and then instruct salespeople to encourage buyers to switch to more expensive models. Ads for cheap eyeglass frames often result in purchases of more expensive "designer" frames.

Direct Marketing and Mail Order

The FTC promulgated a 30-day rule in 1975 for telephone and mail order. The rule prohibits sellers from soliciting orders unless the goods can be shipped within 30 days after receiving a prepaid order. Sellers cannot sit on orders, must clearly state expected shipping dates, and must ship promptly. If there are unanticipated delays, the seller may (1) cancel orders and refund payments or (2) notify consumers of the delay and provide an option of shipment or cancellation. High-quality mail order retailers wait until after shipment to charge customers' credit cards, notify customers of their order's status, and remind customers of their alternatives. Many states impose similar mail order rules. In 1993, the rule was extended to include orders transmitted by computer, fax, or other means using telephone lines. A U.S. Postal Service rule makes unsolicited merchandise sent by mail a gift to the recipient and a penalty to the sender.

Door-to-Door Sales

The FTC imposes a **cooling-off period** for door-to-door sales that gives consumers an opportunity to reassess purchases for three days following sales over $25. The rule counteracts the high-pressure tactics often used to sell such merchandise as vacuum cleaners and encyclopedias. Door-to-door sales contracts must warn the buyer that the cancellation right exists and provide a cancellation form. Several types of sales are exempt: real estate, insurance, securities or commodities from a registered broker, and most sales solicited by the buyer. Some state laws also apply to door-to-door sales, including those exempt under the FTC rule.

Telemarketing

The "boiler room" technique used in high-pressure securities marketing moved into the consumer market as telemarketing expenses dropped and database mining for private information made target marketing feasible (see Chapter 14). **Telemarketing** consists of several marketing techniques: unsolicited sales calls, fax contacts, and even toll-free inquiries or orders initiated by consumers. Telemarketing can impose costs on consumers because the calls divert consumer time (during the dinner hour), tie up the recipient's line, and consume the consumer's fax capacity and consumables (paper, ink). Spam e-mail was discussed in Chapter 14.

Congress passed two laws to address consumer dissatisfaction with the annoyance of telemarketing. First, the **Telephone Consumer Protection Act of 1991**, discussed later, authorizes the Federal Communications Commission (FCC) to regulate telemarketing. The TCPA prohibits automatic dialing systems and prerecorded messages. The call recipient must be able to effectively disconnect by hanging up. Senders must get permission before sending fax ads. The TCPA gives consumers a private right of action in state court against telemarketers for the greater of their actual damages or $500 for each violation. Marketers have been generally unsuccessful at challenging the TCPA on First Amendment grounds, as discussed later. Second, the **Telemarketing and Consumer Fraud and Abuse Act of 1994** empowers the FTC to regulate the content of telemarketing calls. The FTC has rulemaking authority and may enforce this law against telemarketers. In 1995, the FTC promulgated its telemarketing sales rule that requires several disclosures by telemarketers: The caller must identify himself or herself and the product offered, the recipient must be informed the call is for sales purposes, misrepresentation is prohibited, the total cost of the product and special contractual terms must be disclosed, and calls may be made only after 8 A.M. and before 9 P.M. Many state telemarketing laws are even more stringent. This rule is inapplicable to transactions made entirely using the Internet. Several key industries are exempt: financial institutions, telecommunications carriers, airlines, and nonprofits. The FTC may seek injunctions and civil penalties up to $10,000 per violation.

Other Trade Regulations

There are several other FTC trade regulation rules. A used car rule requires a window sticker or buyer's guide on used cars clearly stating the warranties, whether the car is sold "as is," estimated repair costs after the sale, suggesting an independent mechanical inspection, and reminding consumers that the dealer's oral promises are difficult to prove. The insulation rule requires standardized testing and disclosure of home insulation "R-value" to facilitate comparison-shopping. The funeral rule recognizes consumers are seldom careful comparison shoppers at the time of a loved one's death. It requires itemized price lists and provides consumer information about various funeral services in the FTC Funeral Guide. Other rules have addressed unfair and deceptive trade practices in the following industries: correspondence schools, hearing aid sales, automobile repairs and estimates, entertainment clubs, health spas, dance studios, insurance, and home improvement. Medical services are under investigation at this writing. For example, there is evidence that excessive and often unnecessary hysterectomies are performed.

Pay-per-call services, such as 900 numbers, charge the caller's phone bill largely for "information services" provided by the call recipient. Some considerable abuses, particularly dial-a-porn targeting youth, caused the FTC to impose a **900-Number Rule.** The call recipient must identify herself or himself and the cost of the call early in the call to give the caller an opportunity to hang up without incurring a charge. Further, 900 services may not target children under 12 unless for bona fide educational services, and contests or sweepstakes must disclose additional information.

The FTC's early cases focused mostly on "deceptive" trade practices. Increasingly, it also focuses on unfairness, originally defined as immoral, unethical, oppressive, or unscrupulous activity that violates fairness and causes substantial consumer injury. Later refinements to *unfairness* include conduct causing substantial and unavoidable consumer injury not outweighed by consumer benefits or the competition. Is it unfair to raise a fixed fee originally agreed in a consumer contract? Unfairness is illustrated in the following case.

Orkin Exterminating Co. v. F.T.C.

849 F.2d 1354 (11th Cir., 1988)

Fact. Orkin offered lifetime continuous protection guarantees on termite extermination services it provided to more than 200,000 customers. For a fixed annual fee, these customers could have their homes retreated if the home was ever reinfested. Orkin discovered it was losing money on retreatments, so it raised the fees by approximately 40%. Orkin's sales personnel pretended there was a billing error if surprised customers insisted the price was fixed in their contracts. The FTC issued a cease and desist order to Orkin, and Orkin appealed.

Legal Issue. Did the FTC exceed its §5 authority by applying precedents from the deception standard and not the unfairness standard it now applied to Orkin?

Opinion. Judge Clark. We must decide whether the FTC exceeded its authority in deciding that one company's unilateral breach of over 207,000 consumer contracts could meet the Commission's definition of unfairness. The policy statement's consumer injury standard was the focus of its analysis. The unfairness standard requires a finding of substantial injury to consumers. "The harm resulting from Orkin's conduct consists of increased costs for services previously bargained for and includes the intangible loss of the certainty of the fixed price term in the contract." The Commission's finding of "substantial" injury is supported by undisputed fact that Orkin's breach generated more than $7,000,000 in revenues from renewal fees to which the Company was not entitled. Although the actual injury to individual customers may be small on an annual basis, this does not mean such injury is not "substantial." Because the "increase in the fee was not accompanied by an increase in the level of service provided or enhancement of its quality," no consumer benefit had resulted from Orkin's conduct. Customers could not have reasonably avoided the harm caused by Orkin's conduct. The Commission generally relies on free and informed consumer choice as the best regulator of the market.

Nothing indicates that the Commission did anything other than that which it purported to do: apply the unfairness standard contained in its Policy Statement. The Commission's conclusion was simply that it was an "unfair" practice to breach over 200,000 contracts. We think that this was a reasonable application of the Commission's unfairness standard. Section 5 by its very terms makes deceptive and unfair practices distinct lines of inquiry. While a practice may be both deceptive and unfair, it may be unfair without being deceptive. The Commission's policy statement assumes the unfairness doctrine differs from, and supplements, the prohibition against deception. For the foregoing reasons, we affirm the Commission's cease and desist order.

Decision. The FTC did not exceed its authority in issuing a cease and desist order based on its conclusion of unfairness and not only on established elements of deception.

Case Questions

1. What is the issue in "unfairness" in FTC enforcement actions under §5?
2. What is the future impact of an agency's prior enforcement interpretations?

STATE LAWS PROHIBITING UNFAIR COMPETITION

States have legislation paralleling the FTC Act, the so-called **Mini-FTC Acts.** These laws typically empower the state attorney general or a special administrative agency to enforce prohibitions against unfair and deceptive trade practices and unfair methods of competition. Several states permit private rights of action by damaged consumers for damages, treble damages, punitive damages, attorney's fees, injunctions, rescission of contracts, and class action suits. State attorneys general may seek injunctions, restitution, civil penalties, criminal punishment, and other remedies. One of the most notable developments in the 1980s was the coordination of enforcement efforts by various states' attorneys general through their National Association of Attorneys General organization. Various other state statutes regulate particular aspects of consumer fraud, such as lemon laws, door-to-door sales, and use of plain English in insurance contracts. Business must remain aware of this expanding area of federal and state consumer protection.

INTERNET TAXATION

"The power to tax is the power to destroy."[11] This famous quote illustrates the pervasiveness of power held by the federal, state, and local government. Most U.S. taxes are levied on retail transactions, property, and income. Many other nations have huge social benefit programs funded by high-level consumption and income taxes. By contrast, a major impetus for U.S. independence from England was strong feelings about the fairness and scope of the tax system (e.g., Boston Tea Party).

There is widespread concern that the states and local taxing authorities may specifically target new taxes to e-commerce and Internet access. Opponents are concerned that such new taxes create uncertainties, and inconsistencies among them could stifle e-commerce development. This tax controversy is really part of the

11. *McCulloch v. Maryland*, 17 U.S. 316 (1819) (Chief Justice Marshall's oft quoted passage).

Constitutional question over the connection between a governmental unit and a particular regulated activity. It is the classic issue of jurisdiction constrained by Constitutional principles, as introduced in Chapters 3 and 4, and e-commerce increases the opportunities for tax avoidance, making e-commerce taxation hotly controversial. This section explores the Constitutional and definitional difficulties in applying traditional taxes to e-commerce. Particular emphasis is given to the multijurisdictional aspects of taxation and potential new forms of taxation.

COMPLEXITY OF TAXATION OF E-COMMERCE

Tax compliance is a highly complex matter consuming the full-time attention of legions of accountants and lawyers. Individuals and businesses must be constantly aware of their tax liability, and this is much more than the annual income tax ritual. Internet activity poses some tax definitional questions and reopens some strong controversies over taxation. Taxation of traditional commerce and e-commerce can occur in numerous ways, and the various levels and units of government should be expected to use existing taxes aggressively, as well as search for new forms of tax on nearly any identifiable aspect of Internet use. In the United States, much more than in most other nations, the forms of tax and its scope are constrained by two major institutions: the U.S. Constitution and the political legitimacy of particular taxes and the government programs they fund.

Types of Taxes

There are three basic forms of taxation. First, income taxes are levied on individuals, corporations, and other business entities by municipalities, states, and the federal government. Taxable income is generally defined as gross receipts net of allowable expense deductions. There is considerable complexity, particularly in the federal income tax, over the treatment of different types of income, such as salary, business profits, capital gains, royalties, and rents. Also important are choices among accounting treatments used to determine deductions, such as amortization, depreciation, ordinary and necessary expenses, and capitalization.

Property taxes are levied on the owners or lessees of property, usually levied on one day each year—tax day. Real estate taxes levied by school districts, counties, municipalities, and states are the primary method of financing public education. Personal property taxes on vehicles and intangibles taxes on investment securities are additional examples. Some states levy severance taxes on mining and petroleum extraction.

Taxes on transactions are also quite common. States and municipalities levy sales and use taxes, mostly on consumer purchases. State and federal taxes are levied on the sale of fuels to fund road building and maintenance. There are state and federal taxes on sales of alcohol, tobacco, and firearms, as well as excise taxes on certain luxury goods. Transfer taxes are levied on real estate and securities transactions. Most forms of taxes that yield significant revenue can be classified as income, property, or transaction. There are also a few additional types of tax that combine some aspects of these three main types of tax, such as the estate, gift, and inheritance taxes and tariffs on international trade.

Several existing forms of tax either already apply or could be made to apply to Internet activity. Most centrally, e-commerce produces income that can be taxed by the federal government. However, the imposition of state or local income taxes could be more problematic for particular Internet businesses that have uncertain "tax domiciles." Property taxes may be less significant for e-commerce than for traditional bricks-and-mortar industries. For example, virtual businesses with few major facilities and just-in-time inventories may have few assets to tax. However, such pure-play dot.coms are probably less significant today than are the hybrid businesses with both traditional and e-commerce presence. These converging firms have property tax liabilities that are already well established.

The most controversial e-commerce taxes are sales and use taxes on purchases made over the Internet. Sales taxes are transaction taxes applicable generally to consumer sales of most goods. Several major classifications of exemptions vary widely by state. For example, groceries and clothing are exempt in Pennsylvania and New Jersey, and most states exempt newspapers and some services. As discussed later, states have been generally unsuccessful in requiring out-of-state vendors to collect and remit their sales or use taxes. This traditionally left a major loophole for phone and mail order businesses that now appears similarly significant for out-of-state e-commerce firms. Businesses that sell at a distance or directly to consumers from out of state do not generally collect or remit sales and use taxes. However, distance sellers generally must charge separately for shipping and handling. This difference creates a distinct "advantage" for distance sellers when the goods are small, light, and high value. The advantage diminishes when the goods are bulky, heavy, and low value. For example, local retailers generally do not charge shipping and handling but must collect and remit sales tax. Mail, phone, and Internet businesses generally charge shipping and handling but do not collect and remit sales and use taxes. Mail, phone, and Internet sellers have an advantage for certain products such as small and expensive electronics and jewelry.

ONLINE

Internet tax challenges
http://www.nasbo.org/pubs/newslett/9604/nettax.htm
http://www.nga.org/internet/equality.asp

Several other taxes affect e-commerce. The federal telecommunications tax is a form of excise tax that was traditionally levied only on "luxury" items. Increasingly, excise taxes cover items generally considered "quasi-necessities." State and local sales tax may also apply to telecommunication services. Sometimes local property taxes are levied at higher rates on some types of business, such as service industries or utilities. Perhaps the utility's natural monopoly gives it the market power to pass its taxes through to customers. In some states, there are fees paid to government to acquire and maintain rights of way for utility connections (phone, CATV). Much of the controversy leading to the Internet Tax Freedom Act (ITFA) discussed later is based in concerns over new forms of tax primarily targeting Internet use. For example, before passage of the ITFA, a few states and local governments imposed Internet access taxes, which are essentially sales or excise taxes. Another tax proposal is the bit tax—a tax levied for each bit of data transferred. The bit tax causes great anxiety because it varies with the amount of use and taxes large files most heavily (streaming video, audio, images). The value-added tax (VAT), a common form of consumption tax in most other nations, is discussed later.

STATE TAXATION OF INTERSTATE BUSINESS

States may impose burdens on interstate commerce by taxing out-of-state businesses. Taxation is justifiable if the out-of-state business has some connection, local operations, or **nexus** with the taxing state. The nexus is a valid basis for taxation because all residents and nonresidents should pay for their use of governmental benefits, including the protection of the state's laws, police, fire department, and courts, as well as use of its public facilities, such as the direct use of roads or the indirect use of parks or schools by employees. **Use taxes**, as a substitute for sales tax, can be legitimately levied on out-of-state mail order sales if the purchaser resides within the taxing state and the retailer actively solicits orders by mail or phone order.

Commentary

Controversy over Strengthening State Enforcement of Sales and Use Taxes

Internet taxation is a highly controversial topic that has assumed the political spotlight as states try to attract e-commerce business. Views on Internet taxation range from the libertarian cyberspace community who fear taxes will stifle e-commerce to the small businesses disadvantaged by the Internet's illusion of tax freedom. Many states and local governments worry that the Internet's growth will seriously erode their tax base.

Many well-meaning citizens fail to realize that although purchases made from out-of-state vendors are seldom taxed in the seller's state, the purchaser nevertheless owes a substitute tax, called the "use" tax, which is a replacement for sales tax in the consumer's home state. As a result, there is seldom sales or use tax paid on the vast majority of mail order, catalogue, phone order, and now Internet sales from out-of-state vendors. Wholesale purchases among businesses are largely exempt from sales or use taxes.

It is argued that enforcement of sales and use taxes on catalogue, mail order, phone order, and Internet retail is too complex and costly. This criticism lies at the heart of the continuing gridlock blocking federal legislation to harmonize state sales and use tax systems. Mail, phone, and Internet order business significantly lags bricks-and-mortar businesses in local markets in collecting and remitting such taxes. Growing on-line sales will pose ever-greater problems for the states because most states rely heavily on their sales taxes for substantial portions of their budgets. States legitimately fear major budget crunches if taxes on Internet sales remain uncollected. Until this collection and remittance problem equalizes, local small businesses will remain at a significant disadvantage in competing with the growing volume of remote sales by phone, mail, or the Internet.

The collection and remittance of taxes typically occur at points that are most efficient and effective for compliance. For example, income and sales taxes are largely collected and remitted to the state by employers and sellers, respectively. However, the states have been unsuccessful in overcoming due process and commerce clause barriers to imposing collection and remittance duties on out-of-state vendors that have no nexus with the taxing state. This means that some taxes must be collected from individuals, a more costly and less effective process. Use tax collections are much like the difficulty of withholding income taxes on income from nonsalary sources. Both use taxes on self-employment income require a self-reporting honor system. A series of cases on state taxation of interstate commerce has left the states with few good options for collection and remittance of use taxes.

In *National Bellas Hess v. Illinois Dept. of Revenue*,[12] the U.S. Supreme Court held that Illinois could not force a Missouri mail order seller to collect Illinois use tax. Bellas Hess had no facilities within Illinois. Constitutional principles for imposing tax collection and remittance duties on out-of-state businesses were established in *Complete Auto Transit v. Brady*.[13] A sufficient nexus exists to impose these duties when (1) the activity taxed has substantial nexus to the taxing state, (2) the tax is apportioned fairly, (3) the tax does not discriminate against interstate commerce, and (4) the tax fairly relates to services provided by the taxing state. The following is the leading case that still exempts many out-of-state businesses from the tax collection and remittance duty.

12. 386 U.S. 753 (1967).
13. 430 U.S. 274 (1977).

Quill Corp. v. North Dakota

504 U.S. 298 (1992)

Facts. Quill is a Delaware corporation with offices and warehouses in Illinois, California, and Georgia selling office equipment and supplies. Quill's presence in North Dakota is insignificant. Quill solicits business through catalogues and flyers, advertisements in national periodicals, and telephone calls. Quill has annual national sales of more than $200,000,000; almost $1,000,000 in sales are made to about 3,000 North Dakota customers. Quill's deliveries to North Dakota are made by mail or common carrier from out-of-state locations. North Dakota imposes a use tax on property purchased for storage, use, or consumption within the state and requires every "retailer maintaining a place of business in" the state to collect the tax from the consumer and remit it to the state. "Retailer" includes every person who engages in regular or systematic solicitation of a consumer market in the state. Since 1987, mail order companies that solicit customers are required to collect and remit the tax, even if they have no property or personnel in North Dakota.

Legal Issue. Does the due process clause prohibit North Dakota from requiring out-of-state "retailers" to collect and remit a use tax? Does the commerce clause prohibit North Dakota from requiring out-of-state "retailers" to collect and remit a use tax?

Opinion. Justice Stevens. The Due Process Clause and the Commerce Clause reflect different constitutional concerns . . . they are not always sharply separable . . . we consider each constitutional limit in turn.

Building on the seminal case of *International Shoe Co. v. Washington*, we have framed the relevant inquiry as whether a defendant had minimum contacts with the jurisdiction "such that the maintenance of the suit does not offend 'traditional notions of fair play and substantial justice.'" We have abandoned more formalistic tests that focused on a defendant's "presence" within a State in favor of a more flexible inquiry into whether a defendant's contacts with the forum made it reasonable, in the context of our federal system of government, to require it to defend the suit in that State. Applying these principles, we have held that if a foreign corporation purposefully avails itself of the benefits of an economic market in the forum State, it may subject itself to the State's *in personam* jurisdiction even if it has no physical presence in the State. It is an inescapable fact of modern commercial life that a substantial amount of business is transacted solely by mail and wire communications across state lines, thus obviating the need for physical presence within a State in which business is conducted. Thus, to the extent that our decisions have indicated that the Due Process Clause requires physical presence in a State for the imposition of duty to collect a use tax, we overrule those holdings as superseded by developments in the law of due process. In this case, there is no question that Quill has purposefully directed its activities at North Dakota residents, that the magnitude of those contacts are more than sufficient for due process purposes, and that the use tax is related to the benefits Quill receives from access to the State.

Article I, §8, cl. 3 of the Constitution expressly authorizes Congress to "regulate Commerce with foreign Nations, and among the several States." The clause "by its own force" prohibits certain state actions that interfere with interstate commerce. Under *Complete Auto*'s four part test, we will sustain a tax against a Commerce Clause challenge so long as the "tax [1] is applied to an activity with a substantial nexus with the taxing State, [2] is fairly apportioned, [3] does not discriminate against interstate commerce, and [4] is fairly related to the services provided by the State."

The Commerce Clause, and its nexus requirement, is informed not so much by concerns about fairness for the individual defendant [the concern in due process] as by structural concerns about the effects of state regulation on the national economy. Under the Articles of Confederation, State taxes and duties hindered and suppressed interstate commerce; the Framers intended the Commerce Clause as a cure for these structural ills. The *Complete Auto* analysis reflects these concerns about the national economy. The second and third parts of that analysis, which require fair apportionment and non-discrimination, prohibit taxes that pass an unfair share of the tax burden onto interstate commerce. The first and fourth prongs, which require a substantial nexus and a relationship between the tax and State provided services, limit the reach of State taxing authority so as to ensure that State taxation does not unduly burden interstate commerce. Thus, the "substantial nexus" requirement is not, like due process' "minimum contacts" requirement, a proxy for notice, but rather a means for limiting state burdens on interstate commerce. Accordingly, a corporation may have the "minimum contacts" with a taxing State as required by the Due Process Clause, and yet lack the "substantial nexus" with that State as required by the Commerce Clause. It is not unlikely that the mail order industry's dramatic growth over the last quarter century is due in part to the bright line exemption from state taxation created in *Bellas Hess*.

This aspect of our decision is made easier by the fact that the underlying issue is not only one that Congress may be better qualified to resolve, but also one that Congress has the ultimate power to resolve. No matter how we evaluate the burdens that use taxes impose on interstate commerce, Congress remains free to disagree with our conclusions. Indeed, in recent years Congress has considered legislation that would "overrule" the *Bellas Hess* rule. Congress is now free to decide whether, when, and to what extent the States may burden interstate mail order concerns with a duty to collect use taxes.

Decision. North Dakota's use tax is not unconstitutional under the due process clause, but is invalid under the commerce clause because it fails the nexus requirement.

Case Questions

1. Why should it be a legislative question for Congress to resolve the interstate sales and use tax question?
2. How do due process and commerce clause analysis differ?

Sufficient nexus with the taxing state is the key issue in use tax collection cases. Nexus is the same issue discussed in Chapter 3 for jurisdiction purposes and again in Chapter 9 to identify when foreign corporations must be domesticated because they are "doing business" within the state. A preponderance of the following factors is used to identify when a firm has sufficient nexus with a taxing state for the state to impose duties to collect and remit without unduly burdening interstate commerce. Most important, a nexus exists when the firm has a substantial physical presence in the state. Physical presence can arise when it has offices, warehouses, and physical inventories within the taxing state. These may be owned or rented spaces. Presence may arise if the firm has sales staff calling on clients in the state, the firm attends trade shows there, uses a Web server in the taxing state, licenses software in the state, or hires agents in the state. For example, out-of-state mail order businesses are generally immune from collecting sales and use taxes in a state where they have neither agents nor physical facilities and contact customers only via phone, mail, delivery carrier, and/or the Internet. However, if the retailer has a single mall or outlet store in the state, a sufficient nexus exists, and the taxing state can require collection and remittance of sales and use taxes. All states have taxing authorities, usually their departments of revenue. These agencies supply use tax forms to customers who purchase taxable goods out-of-state. It is the purchaser's responsibility to pay use taxes.

INTERNET TAX FREEDOM ACT

Throughout the late 1990s, political forces supported continued freedom of e-commerce from new taxes and new compliance burdens. The *Framework* asserted that no new taxes should be imposed on Internet commerce but any Internet taxes should be consistent with the established principles, should avoid inconsistent tax jurisdictions and double taxation, and should be simple to administer and easy to understand. Several important principles were established. First, Internet taxes should neither distort nor hinder commerce. No tax system should discriminate among types of commerce, nor should it create incentives that will change the nature or location of transactions. Second, the tax system should be simple and transparent, capable of capturing most appropriate revenues, and with burdens of record keeping minimized. Third, the system should accommodate various tax systems in use. Fourth, adaptation of existing taxation concepts and principles is desirable. The *Framework* urges states and local governments to cooperate and develop a uniform approach to e-commerce taxation.

Congress acted on the *Framework* with passage in 1998 of the **Internet Tax Freedom Act (ITFA)**. The ITFA places a temporary moratorium on new application of existing taxes or on the imposition of any new taxes on the Internet. The ITFA did not disturb sales and use and Internet access taxes existing when the act was passed. ITFA appointed a multidisciplinary commission to study and recommend revisions to the labyrinth of different taxes imposed at nearly every level of government. The **Advisory Commission on Electronic Commerce (ACEC)** was chaired by former Virginia Governor James Gilmore. There was no broad consensus in its findings to Congress due in May 2000, so Congress extended the moratorium for another three years.

ONLINE

Commission on Electronic Commerce (ACEC)
http://www.ecommercecommission.org/about.htm

Partisans in the Internet taxation controversy propose solutions that fall into three major groupings. First, there are still Internet advocates who argue that all taxes should be eliminated because they stifle growth in Internet commerce. This position seems unlikely to prevail in the long run. Second, a group advocating tax simplification hopes to achieve a permanent reduction of tax categories applicable to all aspects of Internet use. This proposal holds great promise for efficiency, but many interests can be expected to oppose it. For example, states are likely to resist eliminating their unique tax subjects or methods, and tax preparation professionals probably prefer the status quo. A third group seeks to simplify and standardize taxation mechanisms: forms, exemptions, rates, remittance responsibility, and audit procedures. This view also holds great promise but seems unlikely to prevail without some strong incentive from Congress.

The Internet and computerization reduce the burden of multijurisdictional complexity. Spreadsheets or other computer programs can much more easily accommodate the various rates and exemptions of all U.S. jurisdictions and any revisions. Complexity is no longer a good excuse for tax simplification or elimination, given that technology now exists to manage the calculation, collection, and remittance of varying taxes. Many of the arguments against state taxation of interstate or international transactions simply are no longer valid. However, reconciling the parochial and historical interests to achieve harmonization of Internet taxation may be a monumental political achievement.

INTERNATIONAL TAXATION

Just like the U.S. municipalities and states, many nations are looking to the Internet for new sources of revenue, particularly for the rather considerable social welfare programs in Europe and Canada. Some are trying to levy taxes and/or tariffs on global e-commerce. The United States is working through the World Trade Organization (WTO) to declare the Internet a tariff-free environment when used to deliver products or services. However, the prospects for success are limited. Already the EU is seeking to force U.S. phone, mail, and Internet sellers to collect and remit their VAT taxes.

Value-Added Taxes (VAT)

The **value-added tax** (VAT) is an enormously successful tax in most industrialized nations. VAT is a hidden tax that is seldom enumerated on sales invoices. VAT is most often a huge tax applied to the value added at each point along the supply chain. VAT ranges from 15% in Luxembourg to 25% in Sweden and Denmark. VAT is owed by a manufacturer on the difference between the cost of raw materials or component parts and the sale price of finished goods. Similarly, VAT is owed by the wholesaler and retailer on their markup. Therefore, large VAT amounts are collected and remitted all along the supply chain. VAT is a major source of funding for social programs in most other industrialized nations. Of course, VAT makes the cost of comparable goods much higher in those nations than in the United States. By contrast, sales and use taxes are consumption taxes that are highly visible, and taxpayers are always cognizant of their tax burden.

The EU has a complex system to account for and remit VAT for goods sold within EU nations and in cross-border transactions. Usually, the nation with VAT taxing authority is the nation of origin of the product. VAT becomes more problematic when the products sold are intangible, such as software, information, or other digital or "virtual goods." When the products are digital, EU nations suffer a problem similar to the interstate use tax collection discussed previously. Non-EU nations cannot be compelled to collect VAT on deliveries into the EU from outside the EU. The EU proposes to require all non-EU sellers to "domesticate" by registering to do business with at least one EU nation that would give tax nexus and require VAT collection and remittance duties. The EU may try to impose VAT collection and remittance duties on U.S. sellers of digital products.

TELECOMMUNICATIONS REGULATION

E-commerce must use communications networks to carry the electronic messages that negotiate, conclude, and perform contracts. This communications infrastructure includes several evolving technologies and sectors of the telecommunications industry. Historically, two major regulatory programs address communications: (1) federal regulation of broadcast and telephone service and (2) state or local regulation of utilities. Much of telecommunications regulation has changed because of the **Telecommunications Act of 1996**. This law partially deregulates the industry, and it encourages competition in various services. This section discusses these regulatory methods as traditionally used for communications infrastructure, the impact of their deregulation, and the prospects for this type of regulation on new services in the converging telecommunications technologies.

REGULATORY FRAMEWORK FOR TELECOMMUNICATIONS

The states have regulated public utilities since the turn-of-the-twentieth-century experience with destructive competition. Under this theory of regulation, utilities are seen as natural monopolies because competition would be inefficient and create duplicate networks. As introduced earlier, the states responded to destructive competition and the resulting natural monopolies by regulating public utilities. The states qualify competent utility firms, grant monopoly-like franchises to provide service in a defined geographic region, require service to all customers, and fix each utility firm's prices by using rate-of-return regulation on their invested capital. Franchise regulation covers various utilities: water, electricity, sewers, natural gas, phone, and cable television (CATV). Utilities are generally viewed as necessities of life (heat in winter), so much of utility regulation concerns assuring all customers access at fair prices (rates).

Although the federal government has also regulated utilities (energy, power), the most enduring federal regulation concerns telecommunications. Regulation of the radio spectrum began in 1910, when radio was expected to have only military and emergency applications. The **radio spectrum** is a limited and scarce public resource. All the available frequencies must be shared by broadcast and communication by radio, TV, wireless, and two-way radio. Only so many users can use the radio spectrum before interference degrades quality. By 1927, Congress created the Federal Radio Commission, assuming that the airwaves are a form of public good. Use of the public airwaves by firms is a privilege that carries public duties.

Although technology continues to expand the capacity of the existing radio spectrum, the increase in users strains this scarce public resource. For example, consider that a decade ago few people used cellular service. Today, many people have landlines at home and work as well as cellular service. This increased usage strains the available phone numbers and the public airwave capacity, as calls and Internet usage shift to wireless. The Communications Act of 1934 created the **Federal Communications Commission** (**FCC**) to maximize effective use of this scarce telecommunications capacity. The radio spectrum is a scarce resource used for radio and TV broadcasts, wireless telecommunications (portables, cellular, PCS), two-way radio (CB, ham, walkie-talkie, emergency, military), radar, weapons guidance systems, and many promising future uses.

ONLINE

The radio spectrum can be viewed at **http://www.jsc.mil/images/speccht.jpg** or **http://www.ntia.doc.gov/osmhome/allochrt.pdf**

During the twentieth century, regulation by local municipalities, the states, and the FCC has varied as technology has broadened the range of available services and firms have developed new business models. Congress borrowed heavily from the Interstate Commerce Commission's regulation of transportation as it designated telephone firms as common carriers. **Common carriers** offer communication services (telephony, telegraphy) for hire to the public; common carriers have special duties in the public interest.

Telecommunications regulatory programs address five basic objectives. First, regulators limit the firms that may provide telecommunications services. Firms are licensed or allotted franchise territories when these firms qualify as responsible telecommunications providers. Second, the structure of ownership and corporate affiliation among media and telecommunications firms is regulated to capture the benefits of competition when possible and to avert the disadvantages of monopolies and complex corporate affiliations. Third, the prices charged customers by telecommunications firms with natural monopolies are controlled under rate regulation. Fourth, the technologies and technical methods used by telecommunications firms are regulated to achieve standardization and reduce interference. Finally, regulators occasionally exert some control over content. **Content** is the objectives, substance, meaning, and style of the communication's subject matter. Content regulation is sometimes influenced directly but is also influenced indirectly by telecommunications regulation of entry, structure, and rates. The First Amendment constrains content regulation by the states and the FCC.

FEDERAL COMMUNICATIONS COMMISSION

The FCC is a quasi-independent federal agency charged with regulating interstate and international communications by radio, TV, wire, satellite, and cable. The FCC is directed by five commissioners appointed by the president with Senate confirmation for five-year terms. One of the commissioners is designated by the president to serve as chairperson. The FCC must have political balance; no more than three commissioners may be from the same political party. The FCC's jurisdiction over **communications** includes "transmissions of writings, signs, signals, pictures and sounds of all kinds." This includes analog and digital data and all the infrastructure and apparatus used in such transmissions.

The FCC has six operating bureaus and ten staff offices. Among the most important here is the **International Bureau**, with responsibility for satellite and international matters. The **Media Bureau** regulates AM and FM radio and television broadcast stations, as well as multipoint distribution (i.e., cable and satellite) and instructional television fixed services. The **Wireless Telecommunications Bureau** oversees cellular and PCS phones, pagers, and two-way radios and regulates use of the radio spectrum. The **Wireline Competition Bureau** oversees regulation of telephone companies that provide interstate telecommunications services over wire-based transmission facilities (corded and cordless phones). The **Office of Engineering and Technology** allocates spectrum for nongovernment use in cooperation with the Departments of Commerce and Defense and provides the FCC with expert advice on many technical issues (electrical engineering, computer science).

FCC Rule-Making and Enforcement Powers

The FCC's rule-making powers span its regulatory programs in broadcast and telecommunications. The FCC has had some difficulties when new technologies create new businesses outside the FCC's traditional regulatory spheres. For example, CATV was not clearly broadcast TV, nor was it common carriage. Although the FCC could assert some jurisdiction over CATV, the FCC's powers were limited until Congress expressly broadened the FCC's authority over CATV. The Internet and other new technologies are raising similar difficulties for the FCC. For example, Internet telephony, broadband carried over wireless, CATV, or DSL phone lines, and other **enhanced telecommunications services** continue to raise questions of the FCC's power to regulate entry, rates, competition, technical standards, and content. Should the FCC have rule-making authority to regulate how new technologies are used in advertising? The following case addresses Constitutional issues triggered by most new technologies.

Moser v. F.C.C.

46 F.3d 970 (9th Cir., 1995)

Facts. The Telephone Consumer Protection Act (TCPA) banned prerecorded telemarketing phone calls and gave the FCC rule-making authority to create exemptions. Congressional hearings revealed that automated dialing devices could call up to 1,000 phone numbers per hour to play prerecorded sales pitches. Customers who wanted to be removed from calling lists had to wait until the tape ended, prerecorded messages cluttered answering machines, and automated dialers did not disconnect immediately after the recipient hung up. Forty-one states and the District of Columbia restricted or banned intrastate automated commercial calls but could not regulate interstate calls. The telemarketing trade association (NATO) estimated that only 3% of telemarketing calls were automated, but the FCC estimated the number as between 17% and 30%.

Legal Issue. Does the TCPA ban on automated dialing and prerecorded telemarketing calls violate advertisers' First and Fifth Amendment rights?

Opinion. Circuit Judge Fletcher. Congress concluded that telemarketing calls to homes constituted an unwarranted intrusion upon privacy and such calls were "more of a nuisance and a greater invasion of privacy than calls placed by 'live' persons" because such calls "cannot interact with the customer except in preprogrammed ways" and "do not allow the caller to feel the frustration of the called party...." The Telephone Consumer Protection Act (TCPA), amending the Communications Act of 1934, provides in part:

It shall be unlawful for any person within the United States

... (B) to initiate any telephone call to any residential line using an artificial or prerecorded voice to deliver a message without the prior express consent of the called party, unless the call is initiated for emergency purposes or is exempted by [FCC]rule or order.

Under the statute, prerecorded messages may be used only if a live operator introduces the message or if the consumer consents. All live solicitation calls, as well as automated calls to most businesses, are permitted.

The statute does not require that the FCC distinguish between commercial and noncommercial calls, [therefore] the appropriate inquiry is whether a ban on automated telemarketing calls is narrowly tailored to the residential privacy interest, and whether ample alternative channels of communication remain open. There was significant evidence before Congress of consumer concerns about telephone solicitation in general and about automated calls in particular. "When Congress makes findings on essentially factual issues . . . those findings are of course entitled to a great deal of deference, inasmuch as Congress is an institution better equipped to amass and evaluate the vast amounts of data bearing on such an issue." We conclude that Congress accurately identified automated telemarketing calls as a threat to privacy. The ban on automated, prerecorded calls is not an attempt to favor a particular viewpoint. Congress may reduce the volume of intrusive telemarketing calls without completely eliminating the calls.

The restrictions in the Act leave open many alternative channels of communication, including the use of taped messages introduced by live speakers or taped messages to which consumers have consented, as well as all live solicitation calls. That some companies prefer the cost and efficiency of automated telemarketing does not prevent Congress from restricting the practice.

Decision. Congress adequately demonstrated that automated, prerecorded calls to residences pose a threat to residential privacy. The TCPA ban does not violate the First Amendment because it is content-neutral, narrowly tailored and leaves open ample alternative channels of communication.

Case Questions

1. To what extent does the TCPA give the FCC rulemaking power over content?
2. How much evidence must Congress have before regulating speech?

STATE AND LOCAL REGULATORS

State and local regulation of telecommunications has generally followed the public utility regulation model. Various regulatory agencies seek to qualify entry by licensing only one or a few firms to become natural monopolies that will exclusively serve a geographic area. Both phone service and CATV rates have been regulated by state and local regulators. However, two forces are reducing the regulatory powers of state and local governments over telecommunications. First, the deregulation movement in the 1980s significantly reduced the power of states and municipalities to regulate monthly cable fees except for basic cable. There is continuing controversy over inflation in CATV rates. CATV rate rises outpace inflation, yet the CATV industry argues that video sales and rentals, video game consoles, movie theaters, and broadcast TV provide sufficient competition so that rates should be completely deregulated. Second, programming and phone service can be delivered using new technologies, and these are introducing some competition (e.g., Internet or CATV telephony, video downloads). The deregulation movement, FCC preemption, and competition from other technologies all suggest that state and local telecommunication regulation will continue to decline.

LICENSING AND ENTRY

A basic function of telecommunications regulation in broadcast and telephony is to create legal barriers to entry. Only firms qualified to do business are given a license or granted operating authority under a franchise. Qualification scrutinizes various factors believed to lead to successful service: which firms are financially sound and which firms are most likely to serve the **public interest**. Over the years, many factors have been used to define public interest, many of which overlap with content regulation; these factors include avoiding indecency, maintaining political balance, maintaining a balanced range of programming (talk, music, news, public affairs), and avoiding excessive commercialization, among others. All these factors are constrained by the First Amendment's freedom of expression. Licensees are qualified by examination of their technical capability to provide the services (transmitters, wiring, trained operators); they must be of good character, free of criminal convictions, have no substantial foreign ownership, and not be guilty of misrepresentations made to regulators.

Access

An important part of telecommunications regulation is **access**, also known as universal service. Telecommunications firms may become common carriers, many with natural monopoly franchises or broadcast over the public airwaves. In exchange for this privilege, telecommunications firms must provide their services to everyone at reasonable rates. The access principle is at the heart of several well-recognized telecommunications issues: public access CATV channels, equal time in political campaign advertising, and scheduling of neighborhood CATV wiring and rollout. Access is the main issue in the **digital divide**—the difficulty some people experience in accessing the Internet because of their income, lack of broadband in their neighborhood, inappropriate website design for people with disabilities, and similar issues.

Access is a two-way street. Website owners also argue they should not be denied access to post and maintain websites to conduct e-commerce or to speak freely over the Internet. In the Internet world, access by suppliers or telecommunications firms is less the traditional issue of radio spectrum scarcity than it is of financial resources and quality performance of these firms. As licensing and other legal barriers to entry decline in importance for telecommunications, access may emerge as a bigger social issue.

STRUCTURAL REGULATION

Structural regulation is an issue related to entry qualification for the firms providing telecommunications services. Structural regulation seeks to prevent monopolies from controlling the major sources of media and communications. Monopolies in telecommunications are undesirable because monopolists who own the infrastructure could slant programming, particularly the news, and influence political questions or provide favoritism to affiliated businesses. The famous antitrust case that resulted in the breakup of the Bell System in 1980 is a dramatic example of antitrust theory applied to the structure of the telecommunications industry.

In recent years, the FCC has relaxed some of its structural regulations. Most of these prevented firms from owning all the major media outlets (radio, TV, newspaper) in metropolitan areas and prohibited affiliated firms from owning more than five TV stations. Structural regulation is an indirect form of content regulation. Competition is used to assure diverse programming and reasonable access by and to various societal factions. Structural regulation was the major issue in the simplification of ownership and control in the electric utility industry after implementation of the Public Utility Holding Company Act of 1935, discussed in Chapter 22. Such matters are still problematic. For example, the complex affiliation structure of Enron was a major problem leading to its bankruptcy. Enron was an energy company that operated a large pipeline network, traded in energy futures and derivatives, and "dabbled" in broadband telecommunications.

REGULATION OF RATES

Rate regulation is the mechanism intended to balance the public interest with the natural monopoly aspects of network industries. It is too inefficient for several utilities to serve the same customers with duplicate service networks and generation capacities. Public utility commissions and the FCC conduct rate regulation because natural monopolies are more efficient but monopolists are not trusted to treat customers fairly. In the twentieth century, a very extensive experience by the FCC and state utility regulators developed. These adversarial proceedings examined financial measures to set the maximum rates that a utility can charge. Even the deregulation and competition movement in electricity does not convince that rate regulation is passé. Indeed, California's electricity deregulation experience in 2001 and allegations that energy trading firms manipulated wholesale and retail electricity prices suggest that rate regulation is not a dead letter. Periodically, phone and CATV rates have been subject to rate regulation.

TECHNOLOGY AND STANDARDS

Recall the discussion of network industries in Chapters 11 and 19. Telecommunications is the classic network industry because it becomes more valuable as more users participate and there are many technical specifications needed to permit interoperability by all participants. Another major function of telecommunications regulation has been to identify technical specifications needed for interoperability and then establish them as standards. The FCC both sets and recognizes standards so the networks can operate. For example, precise electronic signaling methods must be used in broadcast and telephony so that equipment will work and can be efficiently produced (e.g., phones, ringer equivalency, NTSC, TVs, radios, switches, transmitters, cabling, modems). Technical specifications are also needed so that licensees are confined to use only their limited portion of the radio spectrum. For example, the location and power of broadcast transmitters is important for TV, radio, and cellular services. These limitations help assure adequate signal delivery within the coverage area without creating interference for other rightful users of the radio spectrum.

TELECOMMUNICATIONS REGULATION AND E-COMMERCE

Going forward, telecommunications will continue to be the crucial infrastructure for effective e-commerce. Whether firms implementing EDI use dedicated systems or consumers connect to the Internet via landline or wireless common carriers, this infrastructure is the key component. Telecommunications is historically a closely regulated industry, treated largely like a utility. New technologies replacing old methods and deregulation are two strong forces that may limit the growth of telecommunication regulation. However, the **convergence** of technologies continually raises new questions of consumer protection, competition, and content regulation. For example, the emerging use of the Internet to bypass long-distance telephone carriers illustrates that traditional classification of these infrastructure systems or the business models of telecommunications firms is subject to abrupt change. Many of these issues have been covered in this chapter and elsewhere in this book.

QUESTIONS

1. The Pantron Corp. sold its hair restoration product, claiming that it "works some of the time for a lot of people," that it reduced hair loss, and that it promoted hair growth. The trial court accepted that there was a "placebo effect" in that there were a few instances of the product's efficacy when the users believed it would. There is no cure for male pattern baldness; even transplants have no lasting effect. On what basis might the FTC charge the advertisements were unlawful? See *FTC v. Pantron I Corp.*, 33 F.3d 1088 (1994).
2. USDrives Corp. assembled CD-ROM drives from foreign made components at its manufacturing facility in California. After 1998, USDrives moved all its assembly operations to Asia. USDrives packages touted "Made in the U.S.A." and were colored red, white, and blue, and some packages included the American flag and American eagle. A disclaimer in small type on packages indicated "Made in China." How should the FTC proceed, and what remedies would be appropriate? See *In re USDrives Corp.*, 1999 F.T.C. LEXIS 78 (April 6, 1999).
3. Whirlpool Financial National Bank and Gulf Coast Electronics sold satellite dishes to the elderly and illiterate for $1,100 each, but the price increased to nearly $1,800, including four-year financing. Similar dishes were available locally for $200. Does the sales technique violate FTC rules as unfair and deceptive sales practices?
4. Explain the concept of market failure. How are alleged market failures used by advocates of regulation to lobby legislatures and regulators into regulating markets? Which of the market failure arguments and economic justifications are most compelling in the regulation of cyberspace and e-commerce?
5. What can government do to reduce the negative effects of regulation of the Internet? Identify and discuss five major principles of government's role in facilitating e-commerce.
6. Compare and contrast the principles of jurisdiction introduced in Chapter 3 with the power of states or nations to tax multijurisdiction transactions. Identify and describe the factors that establish nexus. Identify and explain the two constitutional provisions that are implicated in this analysis.
7. The Illinois telecommunications excise tax of 5% applied to all intrastate long-distance calls and to interstate long-distance calls made from within Illinois. The tax applied even if the call was billed in another state (collect). Is the Illinois tax unconstitutional under the due process or commerce clauses? See *Goldberg v. Sweet*, 488 U.S. 252 (1989).
8. What is the justification for the regulation of rates charged by telecommunications, CATV, or broadcast firms. Why should these services be deregulated? Explain how technological changes provide substitutes that make deregulation attractive.
9. Discuss how consumer access to the Internet and various telecommunications services creates a "digital divide" between consumers with plentiful access to the Internet and those without such access.

Appendix: The United States Constitution

We the People of the United States, in Order to form a more perfect Union, establish Justice, insure domestic Tranquility, provide for the common defence, promote the general Welfare, and secure the Blessings of Liberty to ourselves and our Posterity, do ordain and establish this Constitution for the United States of America.

ARTICLE I

Section I

All legislative Powers herein granted shall be vested in a Congress of the United States, which shall consist of a Senate and House of Representatives.

Section 2

The House of Representatives shall be composed of Members chosen every second Year by the People of the several States, and the Electors in each State shall have the Qualifications requisite for Electors of the most numerous Branch of the State Legislature.

No Person shall be a Representative who shall not have attained to the Age of twenty five Years, and been seven Years a Citizen of the United States, and who shall not, when elected, be an Inhabitant of that State in which he shall be chosen.

Representatives and direct Taxes shall be apportioned among the several States which may be included within this Union, according to their respective Numbers, which shall be determined by adding to the whole Number of free Persons, including those bound to Service for a Term of Years, and excluding Indians not taxed, three fifths of all other Persons. The actual Enumeration shall be made within three Years after the first Meeting of the Congress of the United States, and within every subsequent Term of ten Years, in which Manner as they shall by Law direct. The Number of Representatives shall not exceed one for every thirty Thousand, but each State shall have at Least one Representative; and until such enumeration shall be made, the State of New Hampshire shall be entitled to choose three, Massachusetts eight, Rhode Island and Providence Plantations one, Connecticut five, New York six, New Jersey four, Pennsylvania eight, Delaware one, Maryland six, Virginia ten, North Carolina five, South Carolina five, and Georgia three.

When vacancies happen in the Representation from any State, the Executive Authority thereof shall issue Writs of Election to fill such Vacancies.

The House of Representatives shall choose their Speaker and other Officers; and shall have the sole Power of Impeachment.

Section 3

The Senate of the United States shall be composed of two Senators from each State, chosen by the Legislature thereof, for six Years; and each Senator shall have one Vote.

Immediately after they shall be assembled in Consequence of the first Election, they shall be divided as equally as may be into three Classes. The Seats of the Senators of the first Class shall be vacated at the Expiration of the second Year, of the second Class at the Expiration of the fourth Year, and of the third Class at the Expiration of the sixth Year, so that one third may be chosen every second Year; and if Vacancies happen by Resignation, or otherwise, during the Recess of the Legislature of any State, the Executive thereof may make temporary Appointments until the next Meeting of the Legislature, which shall then fill such Vacancies.

No Person shall be a Senator who shall not have attained to the Age of thirty Years, and been nine Years a Citizen of the United States, and who shall not, when elected, be an Inhabitant of that State for which he shall be chosen.

The Vice President of the United States shall be President of the Senate, but shall have no Vote, unless they be equally divided.

The Senate shall chuse their other Officers, and also a President pro tempore, in the Absence of the Vice President, or when he shall exercise the Office of President of the United States.

The Senate shall have the sole Power to try all Impeachments. When sitting for that Purpose, they shall be on Oath or Affirmation. When the President of the United States is tried the Chief Justice shall preside: And no Person shall be convicted without the Concurrence of two thirds of the Members present.

Judgment in Cases of Impeachment shall not extend further than to removal from Office, and disqualification to hold and enjoy any Office of honor, Trust or Profit under the United States: but the Party convicted shall nevertheless be liable and subject to Indictment, Trial, Judgment and Punishment, according to Law.

Section 4

The Times, Places and Manner of holding Elections for Senators and Representatives, shall be prescribed in each State by the Legislature thereof; but the Congress may at any time by Law make or alter such Regulations, except as to the Places of chusing Senators.

The Congress shall assemble at Least once in every Year, and such Meeting shall be on the first Monday in December, unless they shall by Law appoint a different Day.

Section 5

Each House shall be the Judge of the Elections, Returns and Qualifications of its own Members, and a Majority of each shall constitute a Quorum to do Business; but a smaller Number may adjourn from day to day, and may be authorized to compel the Attendance of absent Members, in such Manner, and under such Penalties as each House may provide.

Each House may determine the Rules in its Proceedings, punish its Members for disorderly Behaviour, and, with the Concurrence of two thirds, expel a Member.

Each House shall keep a Journal of its Proceedings, and from time to time publish the same, excepting such Parts as may in their Judgment require Secrecy; and the Yeas and Nays of the Members of either House on any question shall, at the Desire of one fifth of those Present, be entered on the Journal.

Neither House, during the Session of Congress, shall, without the Consent of the other, adjourn for more than three days, nor to any other Place than that in which the two Houses shall be sitting.

Section 6

The Senators and Representatives shall receive a Compensation for their Services, to be ascertained by Law, and paid out of the Treasury of the United States. They shall in all Cases, except Treason, Felony and Breach of the Peace, be privileged from Arrest during their Attendance at the Session of their respective Houses, and in going to and returning from the same; and for any Speech or Debate in either House, they shall not be questioned in any other Place.

No Senator or Representative shall, during the Time for which he was elected, be appointed to any civil Office under the Authority of the United States, which shall have been created, or the Emoluments whereof shall have been encreased during such time; and no Person holding any Office under the United States, shall be a Member of either House during his Continuance in Office.

Section 7

All Bills for raising Revenue shall originate in the House of Representatives; but the Senate may propose or concur with amendments as on other Bills.

Every Bill which shall have passed the House of Representatives and the Senate, shall, before it become a Law, be presented to the President of the United States; If he approve he shall sign it, but if not he shall return it, with his Objections to that House in which it shall have originated, who shall enter the Objections at large on their Journal, and proceed to reconsider it. If after such Reconsideration two thirds of that House shall agree to pass the Bill, it shall be sent, together with the Objections, to the other House, by which it shall like wise be reconsidered, and if approved by two thirds of that House, it shall become a Law. But in all such Cases the Votes of both Houses shall be determined by Yeas and Nays, and the names of the Persons voting for and against the Bill shall be entered on the Journal of each House respectively. If any Bill shall not be returned by the President within ten Days (Sundays excepted) after it shall have been presented to him, the Same shall be a Law, in like Manner as if he had signed it, unless the Congress by their Adjournment prevent its Return, in which Case it shall not be a Law.

Every Order, Resolution, or Vote to which the Concurrence of the Senate and House of Representatives may be necessary (except on a question of Adjournment) shall be presented to the President of the United States; and before the Same shall take Effect, shall be approved by him, or being disapproved by him, shall be repassed by two thirds of the Senate and House of Representatives, according to the Rules and Limitations prescribed in the Case of a Bill.

Section 8

The Congress shall have Power To lay and collect Taxes, Duties, Imposts and Excises, to pay the Debts and provide for the common Defense and general Welfare of the United States; but all Duties, Imposts and Excises shall be uniform throughout the United States;

To borrow Money on the credit of the United States;

To regulate Commerce with foreign Nations, and among the several States, and with the Indian Tribes;

To establish an uniform Rule of Naturalization, and uniform Laws on the subject of Bankruptcies throughout the United States;

To coin Money, regulate the Value thereof, and of foreign Coin, and fix the Standard of Weights and Measures;

To provide for the Punishment of counterfeiting the Securities and current Coin of the United States;

To establish Post Offices and post Roads;

To promote the Progress of Science and useful Arts, by securing for limited Times to Authors and Inventors the exclusive Right to their respective Writings and Discoveries;

To constitute Tribunals inferior to the supreme Court;

To define and punish Piracies and Felonies committed on the high Seas, and Offenses against the Law of Nations;

To declare War, grant Letters of Marque and Reprisal, and make Rules concerning Captures on Land and Water;

To raise and support Armies, but no Appropriation of Money to that Use shall be for a longer Term than two Years;

To provide and maintain a Navy;

To make Rules for the Government and Regulation of the land and naval Forces;

To provide for calling forth the Militia to execute the Laws of the Union, suppress Insurrections and repel Invasions;

To provide for organizing, arming, and disciplining, the Militia, and for governing such Part of them as may be employed in the Service of the United States, reserving to the States respectively, the Appointment of the Officers, and the Authority of training the Militia according to the discipline prescribed by Congress;

To exercise exclusive Legislation in all Cases whatsoever, over such District (not exceeding ten Miles square) as may, by Cession of particular States, and the Acceptance of Congress, become the Seat of the Government of the United States, and to exercise like Authority over all Places purchased by the Consent of the Legislature of the State in which the Same shall be, for the Erection of Forts, Magazines, Arsenals, dock-Yards, and other needful Buildings;—And

To make all Laws which shall be necessary and proper for carrying into Execution the foregoing Powers, and all other Powers vested by this Constitution in the Government of the United States, or in any Department or Officer thereof.

Section 9

The Migration or Importation of such Persons as any of the States now existing shall think proper to admit, shall not be prohibited by the Congress prior to the Year one thousand eight hundred and eight, but a Tax or duty may be imposed on such Importation, not exceeding ten dollars for each Person.

The Privilege of the Writ of Habeas Corpus shall not be suspended, unless when in Cases of Rebellion or Invasion the public Safety may require it.

No Bill of Attainder or ex post facto Law shall be passed.

No Capitation, or other direct, Tax shall be laid, unless in Proportion to the Census or Enumeration herein before directed to be taken.

No Tax or Duty shall be laid on Articles exported from any State.

No Preference shall be given to any Regulation of Commerce or Revenue to the Ports of one State over those of another; nor shall Vessels bound to, or from, one State, be obliged to enter, clear or pay Duties in another.

No Money shall be drawn from the Treasury, but in Consequence of Appropriations made by Law; and a regular Statement and Account of the Receipts and Expenditures of all public Money shall be published from time to time.

No Title of Nobility shall be granted by the United States: And no Person holding any Office of Profit or Trust under them, shall, without the Consent of the Congress, accept of any present, Emolument, Office, or Title, of any kind whatever, from any King, Prince or foreign State.

Section 10

No State shall enter into any Treaty, Alliance, or Confederation; grant Letters of Marque and Reprisal; coin Money; emit Bills of Credit; make any Thing but gold and silver Coin a Tender in Payment of Debts; pass any Bill of Attainder, ex post facto Law or law impairing the Obligation of Contracts, or grant any Title of Nobility.

No State shall, without the Consent of the Congress, lay any Imposts or Duties on Imports or Exports, except what may be absolutely necessary for executing its inspection Laws: and the net Produce of all Duties and Imposts, laid by any State on Imports or Exports, shall be for the Use of the Treasury of the United States; and all such Laws shall be subject to the Revision and Control of the Congress.

No State shall, without the Consent of Congress, lay any Duty on Tonnage, keep Troops, or Ships of War in time of Peace, enter into any Agreement or Compact with another State, or with a foreign Power, or engage in War, unless actually invaded, or in such imminent Danger as will not admit of delay.

ARTICLE II

Section 1

The executive Power shall be vested in a President of the United States of America. He shall hold his Office during the Term of four Years, and, together with the Vice President, chosen for the same Term, be elected, as follows:

Each State shall appoint, in such Manner as the Legislature thereof may direct, a Number of Electors, equal to the whole Number of Senators and Representatives to which the State may be entitled in the Congress: but no Senator or Representative, or Person holding an Office of Trust or Profit under the United States, shall be appointed an Elector.

The Electors shall meet in their respective States, and vote by Ballot for two Persons, of whom one at least shall not be an Inhabitant of the same State with themselves. And they shall make a List of all the Persons voted for, and of the Number of Votes for each; which List they shall sign and certify, and transmit sealed to the Seat of the Government of the United States, directed to the President of the Senate. The President of the Senate shall, in the Presence of the Senate and House of Representatives, open all the Certificates, and the Votes shall then be counted. The Person having the greatest Number of Votes shall be the President, if such Number be a Majority of the whole Number of Electors appointed; and if there be more than one who have such Majority, and have an equal Number of Votes, then the House of Representatives shall immediately chuse by Ballot one of them for President; and if no Person have a Majority, then from the five highest on the List the said House shall in like Manner chuse the President. But in chusing the President, the Votes shall be taken by States, the Representation from each State having one Vote; a quorum for this Purpose shall consist of a Member or Members from two thirds of the States, and a Majority of all the States shall be necessary to a Choice. In every Case, after the Choice of the President, the Person having the greatest Number of Votes of the Electors shall be the Vice President. But if there should remain two or more who have equal Votes, the Senate shall chuse from them by Ballot the Vice President.

The Congress may determine the Time of chusing the Electors, and the Day on which they shall give their Votes; which Day shall be the same throughout the United States.

No Person except a natural born Citizen, or a Citizen of the United States, at the time of the Adoption of this Constitution, shall be eligible to the Office of President; neither shall any Person be eligible to that Office who shall not have attained to the Age of thirty five Years, and been fourteen years a Resident within the United States.

In Case of the Removal of the President from Office, or of his Death, Resignation, or Inability to discharge the Powers and Duties of the said Office, the Same shall devolve on the Vice President, and the Congress may by Law provide for the Case of Removal, Death, Resignation, or Inability, both of the President and Vice President, declaring what Officer shall then act as President, and such Officer shall act accordingly, until the Disability be removed, or a President shall be elected.

The President shall, at stated Times, receive for his Services, a Compensation, which shall neither be encreased nor diminished during the Period for which he shall have been elected, and he shall not receive within that Period any other Emolument from the United States, or any of them.

Before he enter on the Execution of his Office, he shall take the following Oath or Affirmation:—"I do solemnly swear (or affirm) that I will faithfully execute the Office of President of the United States, and will to the best of my Ability, preserve, protect, and defend the Constitution of the United States."

Section 2

The President shall be Commander in Chief of the Army and Navy of the United States, and of the Militia of the several States, when called into the actual Service of the United States; he may require the Opinion, in writing, of the principal Officer in each of the executive Departments, upon any Subject relating to the Duties of their respective Offices, and he shall have Power to grant Reprieves and Pardons for Offenses against the United States, except in Cases of Impeachment.

He shall have Power, by and with the Advice and Consent of the Senate, to make Treaties, provided two thirds of the Senators present concur; and he shall nominate, and by and with the Advice and Consent of the Senate, shall appoint Ambassadors, other public Ministers and Consuls, Judges of the supreme Court, and all other Officers of the United States, whose Appointments are not herein otherwise provided for, and which shall be established by Law: but the Congress may by Law vest the Appointment of such inferior Officers, as they think proper, in the President alone, in the Courts of Law, or in the Heads of Departments.

The President shall have Power to fill up all Vacancies that may happen during the Recess of the Senate, by granting Commissions which shall expire at the End of their next Session.

Section 3

He shall from time to time give to the Congress Information of the State of the Union, and recommend to their Consideration such Measures as he shall judge necessary and expedient; he may, on extraordinary Occasions, convene both Houses, or either of them, and in Case of Disagreement between them, with Respect to the Time of Adjournment, he may adjourn them to such Time as he shall think proper; he shall receive Ambassadors and other public Ministers; he shall take Care that the Laws be faithfully executed, and shall Commission all the Officers of the United States.

Section 4

The President, Vice President and all Civil Officers of the United States, shall be removed from Office on Impeachment for, and Conviction of, Treason, Bribery, or other high Crimes and Misdemeanors.

ARTICLE III

Section 1

The judicial Power of the United States, shall be vested in one supreme Court, and in such inferior Courts as the Congress may from time to time ordain and establish. The Judges, both of the supreme and inferior Courts, shall hold their Offices during good Behaviour, and shall, at stated

Times, receive for their Services, a Compensation, which shall not be diminished during their Continuance in Office.

Section 2

The judicial Power shall extend to all Cases, in Law and Equity, arising under this Constitution, the Laws of the United States, and Treaties made, or which shall be made, under their Authority;—to all Cases affecting Ambassadors, other public Ministers and Consuls;—to all Cases of admiralty and maritime Jurisdiction;—to Controversies to which the United States shall be a Party;—to Controversies between two or more States;—between a State and Citizens of another State;—between Citizens of different States,—between Citizens of the same State claiming Lands under Grants of different States, and between a State, or the Citizens thereof, and foreign States, Citizens or Subjects.

In all Cases affecting Ambassadors, other public Ministers and Consuls, and those in which a State shall be Party, the Supreme Court shall have original Jurisdiction. In all the other Cases before mentioned, the supreme Court shall have appellate Jurisdiction, both as to Law and Fact, with such Exceptions, and under such Regulations as the Congress shall make.

The Trial of all Crimes, except in Cases of Impeachment, shall be by Jury; and such Trial shall be held in the State where the said Crimes shall have been committed; but when not committed within any State, the Trial shall be at such Place or Places as the Congress may by Law have directed.

Section 3

Treason against the United States, shall consist only in levying War against them, or in adhering to their Enemies, giving them Aid and Comfort. No Person shall be convicted of Treason unless on the Testimony of two Witnesses to the same overt Act, or on Confession in open Court.

The Congress shall have Power to declare the Punishment of Treason, but no Attainder of Treason shall work Corruption of Blood, or Forfeiture except during the Life of the Person attainted.

ARTICLE IV

Section 1

Full Faith and Credit shall be given in each State to the public Arts, Records, and judicial Proceedings of every other State. And the Congress may by general Laws prescribe the Manner in which such Acts, Records and Proceedings shall be proved, and the Effect thereof.

Section 2

The Citizens of each State shall be entitled to all Privileges and Immunities of Citizens in the several States.

A Person charged in any State with Treason, Felony, or other Crime, who shall flee from Justice, and be found in another State, shall on Demand of the executive Authority of the State from which he fled, be delivered up, to be removed to the State having Jurisdiction of the Crime.

No Person held to Service or Labour in one State, under the Laws thereof, escaping into another, shall, in Consequence of any Law or Regulation therein, be discharged from such Service or Labour, but shall be delivered up on Claim of the Party to whom such Service or Labour may be due.

Section 3

New States may be admitted by the Congress into this Union; but no new State shall be formed or erected within the Jurisdiction of any other State; nor any State be formed by the Junction of two or more States, or Parts of States, without the Consent of the Legislatures of the States concerned as well as of the Congress.

The Congress shall have Power to dispose of and make all needful Rules and Regulations respecting the Territory or other Property belonging to the United States; and nothing in this Constitution shall be so construed as to Prejudice any Claims of the United States, or of any particular State.

Section 4

The United States shall guarantee to every State in this Union a Republican Form of Government, and shall protect each of them against Invasion; and on Application of the Legislature, or of the Executive (when the Legislature cannot be convened) against domestic Violence.

ARTICLE V

The Congress, whenever two thirds of both Houses shall deem it necessary, shall propose Amendments to this Constitution, or, on the

Application of the Legislatures of two thirds of the several States, shall call a Convention for proposing Amendments, which, in either Case, shall be valid to all Intents and Purposes, as Part of this Constitution, when ratified by the Legislatures of three fourths of the several States, or by Conventions in three fourths thereof, as the one or the other Mode of Ratification may be proposed by the Congress; Provided that no Amendment which may be made prior to the Year One thousand eight hundred and eight shall in any Manner affect the first and fourth Clauses in the Ninth Section of the first Article; and that no State, without its Consent, shall be deprived of its equal Suffrage in the Senate.

ARTICLE VI

All Debts contracted and Engagements entered into, before the Adoption of this Constitution, shall be as valid against the United States under this Constitution, as under the Confederation.

This Constitution, and the Laws of the United States which shall be made in Pursuance thereof; and all Treaties made, or which shall be made, under the Authority of the United States, shall be the supreme Law of the Land; and the judges in every State shall be bound thereby, any Thing in the Constitution or Laws of any State to the Contrary notwithstanding.

The Senators and Representatives before mentioned, and the Members of the several State Legislatures, and all executive and judicial Officers, both of the United States and of the several States, shall be bound by Oath or Affirmation, to support this Constitution; but no religious Test shall ever be required as a Qualification to any Office or public Trust under the United States.

ARTICLE VII

The Ratification of the Conventions of nine States, shall be sufficient for the Establishment of this Constitution between the States so ratifying the Same.

AMENDMENT I (1791)

Congress shall make no law respecting an establishment of religion, or prohibiting the free exercise thereof; or abridging the freedom of speech, or of the press; or the right of the people peaceably to assemble, and to petition the Government for a redress of grievances.

AMENDMENT II (1791)

A well regulated Militia, being necessary to the security of a free State, the right of the people to keep and bear Arms, shall not be infringed.

AMENDMENT III (1791)

No Soldier shall, in time of peace be quartered in any house, without the consent of the Owner, nor in time of war, but in a manner to be prescribed by law.

AMENDMENT IV (1791)

The right of the people to be secure in their persons, houses, papers, and effects, against unreasonable searches and seizures, shall not be violated, and no Warrants shall issue, but upon probable cause, supported by Oath or affirmation, and particularly describing the place to be searched, and the persons or things to be seized.

AMENDMENT V (1791)

No person shall be held to answer for a capital or otherwise infamous crime, unless on a presentment or indictment of a Grand Jury, except in cases arising in the land or naval forces, or in the Militia, when in actual service in time of War or public danger; nor shall any person be subject for the same offense to be twice put in jeopardy of life or limb; nor shall be compelled in any criminal case to be a witness against himself, nor be deprived of life, liberty, or property, without due process of law; nor shall private property be taken for public use, with out just compensation.

AMENDMENT VI (1791)

In all criminal prosecutions, the accused shall enjoy the right to a speedy and public trial, by an impartial jury of the State and district wherein the crime shall have been committed, which district shall have been previously ascertained by law, and to be informed of the nature and cause of the accusation; to be confronted with the witnesses against him; to have compulsory process for obtaining Witnesses in his favor, and to have the Assistance of Counsel for his defense.

AMENDMENT VII (1791)

In Suits at common law, where the value in controversy shall exceed twenty dollars, the right of trial by jury shall be preserved, and no fact tried by a jury, shall be otherwise reexamined in any Court of the United States, than according to the rules of the common law.

AMENDMENT VIII (1791)

Excessive bail shall not be required nor excessive fines imposed, nor cruel and unusual punishments inflicted.

AMENDMENT IX (1791)

The enumeration in the Constitution, of certain rights, shall not be construed to deny or disparage others retained by the people.

AMENDMENT X (1791)

The powers not delegated to the United States by the Constitution, nor prohibited by it to the States, are reserved to the States respectively, or to the people.

AMENDMENT XI (1798)

The Judicial power of the United States shall not be construed to extend to any suit in law or equity, commenced or prosecuted against one of the United States by Citizens of another State, or by Citizens or Subjects of any Foreign State.

AMENDMENT XII (1804)

The Electors shall meet in their respective states and vote by ballot for President and Vice President, one of whom, at least, shall not be an inhabitant of the same state with themselves; they shall name in their ballots the person voted for as President, and in distinct ballots the person voted for as Vice-President, and they shall make distinct lists of all persons voted for as President, and of all persons voted for as Vice-President, and of the number of votes for each, which lists they shall sign and certify, and transmit sealed to the seat of the government of the United States, directed to the President of the Senate;—The President of the Senate shall, in the presence of the Senate and House of Representatives, open all the certificates and the votes shall then be counted;—The person having the greatest number of votes for President, shall be the President, if such number be a majority of the whole number of Electors appointed; and if no person have such majority, then from the persons having the highest numbers not exceeding three on the list of those voted for as President, the House of Representatives shall choose immediately, by ballot, the President. But in choosing the President, the votes shall be taken by states, the representation from each state having one vote; a quorum for this purpose shall consist of a member or members from two-thirds of the states, and a majority of all the states shall be necessary to a choice. And if the House of Representatives shall not choose a President whenever the right of choice shall devolve upon them, before the fourth day of March next following, then the Vice-President shall act as President, as in the case of the death or other constitutional disability of the President—The person having the greatest number of votes as Vice-President, shall be the Vice-President, if such number be a majority of the whole number of Electors appointed, and if no person have a majority, then from the two highest numbers on the list, the Senate shall choose the Vice-President; a quorum for the purpose shall consist of two-thirds of the whole numbers of Senators, and a majority of the whole number shall be necessary to a choice. But no person constitutionally ineligible to the office of President shall be eligible to that of Vice President of the United States.

AMENDMENT XIII (1865)

Section 1

Neither slavery nor involuntary servitude, except as a punishment for crime whereof the party shall have been duly convicted, shall exist within the United States, or any place subject to their jurisdiction.

Section 2

Congress shall have power to enforce this article by appropriate legislation.

AMENDMENT XIV (1868)

Section 1

All persons born or naturalized in the United States and subject to the jurisdiction thereof, are citizens of the United States and of the State wherein they reside. No State shall make or enforce any law which shall abridge the privileges or immunities of citizens of the United States; nor shall any State deprive any person of life, liberty, or property, without due process of law; nor deny to any person within its jurisdiction the equal protection of the laws.

Section 2

Representatives shall be apportioned among the several States according to their respective numbers, counting the whole number of persons in each State, excluding Indians not taxed. But when the right to vote at any election for the choice of electors for President and Vice President of the United States, Representatives in Congress, the Executive and Judicial officers of a State, or the members of the Legislature thereof, is denied to any of the male inhabitants of such State, being twenty-one years of age, and citizens of the United States, or in any way abridged, except for participation in rebellion, or other crime, the basis of representation therein shall be reduced in the proportion which the number of such male citizens shall bear to the whole number of male citizens twenty-one years of age in such State.

Section 3

No person shall be a Senator or Representative in Congress, or elector of President and Vice President, or hold any office, civil or military, under the United States, or under any State, who, having previously taken an oath, as a member of Congress, or as an officer of the United States, or as a member of any State legislature, or as an executive or judicial officer of any State, to support the Constitution of the United States, shall have engaged in insurrection or rebellion against the same, or given aid or comfort to the enemies thereof. But Congress may by a vote of two-thirds of each House, remove such disability.

Section 4

The validity of the public debt of the United States, authorized by law, including debts incurred for payment of pensions and bounties for services in suppressing insurrection or rebellion, shall not be questioned. But neither the United States nor any State shall assume or pay any debt or obligation incurred in aid of insurrection or rebellion against the United States, or any claim for the loss or emancipation of any slave; but all such debts, obligations and claims shall be held illegal and void.

Section 5

The Congress shall have power to enforce, by appropriate legislation, the provisions of this article.

AMENDMENT XV (1870)

Section 1

The right of citizens of the United States to vote shall not be denied or abridged by the United States or by any State on account of race, color, or previous condition of servitude.

Section 2

The Congress shall have power to enforce this article by appropriate legislation.

AMENDMENT XVI (1913)

The Congress shall have power to lay and collect taxes on incomes, from whatever source derived, without apportionment among the several States, and without regard to any census or enumeration.

AMENDMENT XVII (1913)

The Senate of the United States shall be composed of two Senators from each State, elected by the people thereof, for six years; and each Senator shall have one vote. The electors in each State shall have the qualifications requisite for electors of the most numerous branch of the State legislatures.

When vacancies happen in the representation of any State in the Senate, the executive authority of such State shall issue writs of election to fill such vacancies: Provided, That the legislature of any State may empower the executive thereof to make temporary appointments until the people fill the vacancies by election as the legislature may direct.

This amendment shall not be so construed as to affect the election or term of any Senator chosen before it becomes valid as part of the Constitution.

AMENDMENT XVIII (1919)

Section 1
After one year from the ratification of this article the manufacture, sale, or transportation of intoxicating liquors within, the importation thereof into, or the exportation thereof from the United States and all territory subject to the jurisdiction thereof for beverage purposes is hereby prohibited.

Section 2
The Congress and the several States shall have concurrent power to enforce this article by appropriate legislation.

Section 3
This article shall be inoperative unless it shall have been ratified as an amendment to the Constitution by the legislatures of the several States, as provided in the Constitution, within seven years from the date of the submission hereof to the States by the Congress.

AMENDMENT XIX (1920)

Section 1
The right of citizens of the United States to vote shall not be denied or abridged by the United States or by any State on account of sex.

Section 2
Congress shall have power to enforce this article by appropriate legislation.

AMENDMENT XX (1933)

Section 1
The terms of the President and Vice President shall end at noon on the 20th day of January, and the terms of Senators and Representatives at noon on the 3d day of January, of the years in which such terms would have ended if this article had not been ratified; and the terms of their successors shall then begin.

Section 2
The Congress shall assemble at least once in every year, and such meeting shall begin at noon on the 3d day of January, unless they shall by law appoint a different day.

Section 3
If, at the time fixed for the beginning of the term of the President, the President elect shall have died, the Vice President elect shall be come President. If a President shall not have been chosen before the time fixed for the beginning of his term, or if the President elect shall have failed to qualify, then the Vice President elect shall act as President until a President shall have qualified; and the Congress may by law provide for the case wherein neither a President elect nor a Vice President elect shall have qualified, declaring who shall then act as President, or the manner in which one who is to act shall be selected, and such person shall act accordingly until a President or Vice President shall have qualified.

Section 4
The Congress may by law provide for the case of the death of any of the persons from whom the House of Representatives may choose a President whenever the right of choice shall have devolved upon them, and for the case of the death of any of the persons from whom the Senate may choose a Vice President whenever the right of choice shall have devolved upon them.

Section 5
Sections 1 and 2 shall take effect on the 15th day of October following the ratification of this article.

Section 6
This article shall be inoperative unless it shall have been ratified as an amendment to the Constitution by the legislatures of three fourths of the several States within seven years from the date of its submission.

AMENDMENT XXI (1933)

Section 1
The eighteenth article of amendment to the Constitution of the United States is hereby repealed.

Section 2
The transportation or importation into any State, Territory, or possession of the United States for delivery or use therein of intoxicating liquors, in violation of the laws thereof, is hereby prohibited.

Section 3
This article shall be inoperative unless it shall have been ratified as an amendment to the Constitution by conventions in the several States, as provided in the Constitution, within seven years from the date of the submission hereof to the States by the Congress.

AMENDMENT XXII (1951)

Section 1
No person shall be elected to the office of the President more than twice, and no person, who has held the office of President, or acted as President, for more than two years of a term to which some other person was elected President shall be elected to the Office of the President more than once. But this Article shall not apply to any person holding the office of President when this Article was proposed by the Congress, and shall not prevent any person who may be holding the office of President, or acting as President, during the term within which this Article becomes operative from holding the Office of President or acting as President during the remainder of such term.

Section 2
This article shall be inoperative unless it shall have been ratified as an amendment to the Constitution by the legislatures of three fourths of the several States within seven years from the date of its submission to the States by the Congress.

AMENDMENT XXIII (1961)

Section 1
The District constituting the seat of Government of the United States shall appoint in such manner as the Congress may direct:

A number of electors of President and Vice President equal to the whole number of Senators and Representatives in Congress to which the District would be entitled if it were a State, but in no event more than the least populous State; they shall be in addition to those appointed by the States, but they shall be considered, for the purposes of the election of President and Vice President, to be electors appointed by a State; and they shall meet in the District and perform such duties as provided by the twelfth article of amendment.

Section 2
The Congress shall have power to enforce this article by appropriate legislation.

AMENDMENT XXIV (1964)

Section 1
The right of citizens of the United States to vote in any primary or other election for President or Vice President, for electors for President or Vice President, or for Senator or Representative in Congress, shall not be denied or abridged by the United States or any State by reason of failure to pay any poll tax or other tax.

Section 2
The Congress shall have power to enforce this article by appropriate legislation.

AMENDMENT XXV (1967)

Section 1
In case of the removal of the President from office or of his death or resignation, the Vice President shall become President.

Section 2
Whenever there is a vacancy in the office of the Vice President, the President shall nominate a Vice President who shall take office upon confirmation by a majority vote of both Houses of Congress.

Section 3
Whenever the President transmits to the President pro tempore of the Senate and the Speaker of the House of Representatives his written declaration that he is unable to discharge the powers and duties of his office, and until he transmits to them a written declaration to the contrary, such powers and duties shall be discharged by the Vice President as Acting President.

Section 4
Whenever the Vice President and a majority of either the principal officers of the executive departments or of such other body as Congress may by law provide, transmit to the President pro tempore of the Senate and the Speaker of the House of Representatives their written declaration

that the President is unable to discharge the powers and duties of his office, the Vice President shall immediately assume the powers and duties of the office as Acting President.

Thereafter, when the President transmits to the President pro tempore of the Senate and the Speaker of the House of Representatives his written declaration that no inability exists, he shall resume the powers and duties of his Office unless the Vice President and a majority of either the principal officers of the executive department or of such other body as Congress may by law provide, transmit within four days to the President pro tempore of the Senate and the Speaker of the House of Representatives their written declaration that the President is unable to discharge the powers and duties of his office. Thereupon Congress shall decide the issue, assembling within forty-eight hours for that purpose if not in session. If the Congress, within twenty-one days after receipt of the latter written declaration, or, if Congress is not in session, within twenty-one days after Congress is required to assemble, determines by two-thirds vote of both Houses that the President is unable to discharge the powers and duties of his office, the Vice President shall continue to discharge the same as Acting President; otherwise, the President shall resume the powers and duties of his office.

AMENDMENT XXVI (1971)

Section 1

The right of citizens of the United States, who are eighteen years of age or older, to vote shall not be denied or abridged by the United States or by any State on account of age.

Section 2

The Congress shall have power to enforce this article by appropriate legislation.

AMENDMENT XXVII (1992)

No law varying the compensation for services of the Senators and Representatives shall take effect until an election of representatives shall have intervened.

Glossary

A

A/V Audiovisual; a work involving both hearing and sight.

abandonment (1) Failure to file for a patent within the required time or waiver of rights in the invention to the public. (2) Failure to protest a final refusal of trademark registration within six months.

abridgment The principle that later authors may advance learning by building on existing works.

abrogation of state sovereign immunity Nullification of *sovereign immunity*, a government's immunity from suit.

absolute privilege Immunity from charges of defamation for statements made during court or legislative proceedings.

absorption Doctrine under which rights such as those in the Fifth Amendment are applied to the states under the Fourteenth Amendment.

abstract ideas Ideas that are not related to any practical application.

abstraction An analysis of a software program's sequence, structure, and organization to reveal its functions.

abuse theory of monopoly Analysis of both the structure of the market and the conduct of a firm to determine whether it is a monopoly.

abusive discharge Terminating an employee for refusing to obey an order to violate the law or clear public policy.

acceleration clause A holder's right to demand early payment on a negotiable instrument for some stated reason.

accept or return The user's choice with regard to a *shrink-wrap agreement*; either accept all terms of the license or return the product to the seller.

acceptance The response to an offer to contract which indicates agreement with the offer's terms.

access (1) The opportunity of an alleged copyright infringer to copy from the protected work. (2) The opportunity to use telecommunications services at reasonable rates and for public purposes such as public access channels and equal time for political advertising. (3) The right to timely, accurate, and inexpensive review of the file of personal information collected about one's self.

access contracts Contracts for electronic access to information, such as with Internet service providers, remote data processing, and e-mail systems.

access device Elements of control procedures required by Federal Reserve Board Regulation E for ATM point-of-sale and other electronic payment devices, such as PIN numbers, magnetic strips on debit cards, and photographs.

accessory A person who aids the perpetrator of a crime but is not present at its commission.

accessory after the fact An accessory who provides assistance after the commission of a crime.

accessory before the fact An accessory who provides assistance before the commission of illegal acts.

accord and satisfaction An agreement to substitute a different performance than what a contract calls for, and the performance of that agreement.

accredited investors Financially sophisticated investors such as corporations, employee benefit plans, and certain wealthy individuals.

acquisition One firm's purchase of another firm that may operate as a separate division or subsidiary.

act of state doctrine Restriction of lawsuits against activity sponsored by a foreign government.

actual authority The authority granted to an agent by a principal either based on express statements or implied from those statements or from actions of the principal.

actual damages Compensation for the actual harm suffered by the plaintiff, such as lost profits and injury to reputation.

actual use Affixing a trademark to a product or container, or displaying a service mark with services or advertising.

actus reus A criminal act.

ad valorem tariff A tax based on a percentage of the value or price of an imported item.

addition The rule that an item that reproduces all the claimed elements of a patented invention and adds other elements is still an infringement.

adequate representation clauses Contract provisions that require retailers to make substantial efforts to market a manufacturer's products.

adhesion contract A take-it-or-leave-it contract that favors the seller and is unconscionable or violates public policy.

adjudication Agency determination of existing facts, application of rules or laws to the facts, and decision of the matter being heard.

adjudicatory hearings Hearings in which agencies determine whether an individual or business has violated a legislative statute or an administrative regulation.

administrative agency A governmental body that is not included in the constitution as part of the legislative, executive, or judicial branches.

administrative law Law that concerns the organization and operation of administrative agencies.

administrative probable cause The probable cause that an agency must show to obtain a warrant.

administrative procedures The procedures used by administrative agencies for rule-making, adjudication, and ministerial actions.

Administrative Procedures Act (APA) Act of Congress that establishes the procedures a federal agency must follow in *rule-making* and *adjudication.*

admission An exception to the UCC statute of frauds on the sale of goods, where the party who denies the contract has also admitted it in judicial proceedings or pleadings.

adversarial process The procedure by which parties to a dispute, usually through their attorneys, are responsible for presenting evidence and proving their claims.

adverse selection Bad decisions by creditors based on lack of relevant information that is withheld because of consumers' privacy concerns. (2) Less-than-optimal business choices that are made because market participants do not have enough information.

advising bank In a letter of credit transaction, the seller's bank which receives the letter from the buyer's issuing bank and advises the seller regarding payment.

Advisory Commission on Electronic Commerce (ACEC) Commission appointed to study and make recommendations on taxation for the Internet.

advisory opinion An agency opinion to a private party regarding the legality of specific proposed conduct.

affectation doctrine The doctrine that Congress may regulate a commercial activity only if there is a link between the activity and interstate commerce.

affirm The appellate court's action when it agrees with the decision of the lower court.

affirmative action Employer efforts to actively recruit minorities and women in order to attain equal employment opportunities for those groups.

affirmative defense A statement of legal justification for the defendant's conduct that may be made part of the defendant's answer.

affirmative disclosure order FTC order requiring an offender to provide information in future advertisements.

after-acquired property clauses Property of the debtor that is acquired after the execution of a security agreement.

Age Discrimination in Employment Act of 1973 Federal law that prohibits employment discrimination on the basis of age against those 40 years of age or older.

agency See *principal-agent relationship.*

agency coupled with an interest The situation where an agent has a property interest in the agency relationship, such as an agreement for a percentage of the principal's earnings.

agent One who acts on behalf of or represents another person or firm.

aggregate To combine personal information about individuals from multiple sources.

aggregator A database manager who combines personal information about identified individuals from several sources.

agricultural cooperatives Nonprofit organizations that provide mutual assistance to farmers; exempt from the *Clayton Act.*

all-or-nothing rule Another name for the *contributory negligence* rule.

allowed (1) The status of a patent application that is recommended for approval; (2) The authority to hear a case involving particular parties or subject matter.

alternative trading system (ATS) An electronic market mechanism that can match orders and settle sales of securities.

amendments Revisions of an inventor's claims on a patent application.

American Depository Receipts (ADRs) Derivative certificates that entitle U.S. investors to the benefits of foreign securities held in trust by foreign banks.

American Inventor's Protection Act (AIPA) Federal law that authorizes the Patent and Trademark Office to extend the term of a drug patent if delays in FDA trials continue for more than three years.

Americans with Disabilities Act of 1990 Federal law that gives certain employment and other rights to persons with disabilities as defined by the act.

ancillary Necessary to protect the interests transferred in a contract, for example as a covenant not to compete protects trade secrets divulged to an employee.

answer The defendant's response to the allegations in the plaintiff's complaint.

anticipate A description in the *prior art* that sufficiently describes a later invention is said to anticipate it.

anticipatory breach An action or indication by a contract party prior to the time of its performance that it will not perform the acts or promises it agreed to undertake.

Anticounterfeiting Consumer Protection Act U.S. law prohibiting sale of counterfeit goods using a spurious mark, identical to or indistinguishable from a registered mark. Counterfeit goods are fake copies made with the intent to defraud consumers.

Anticybersquatting Consumer Protection Act (ACPA) Federal law that makes it unlawful to traffic in domain names that are identical or confusingly similar to distinctive marks protected under state trademark law or the Lanham Act.

antidumping duties A tax imposed on imported goods that are dumped, or sold in the importing country at a price lower than the price in the home market.

Anti-Federalists Early American party that supported stronger states' rights relative to the central government.

antitrafficking provisions Prohibition of the manufacture or sale of software or devices that circumvent access or use controls over copyrighted materials.

antitrust safety zone Guidelines for licensing of intellectual property; actions that follow them will not be challenged as anticompetitive.

anything of value Description of the bribery payments outlawed by the *Foreign Corrupt Practices Act.*

apparent authority The authority created when a principal does something that leads a third party to believe that the agent is authorized to act for the principal.

appellant The party that brings an appeal from the decision of a lower court.

appellate brief A written submission to an appellate court that argues the party's position on the case and refers to prior cases that support the position.

appellee The party against whom an appeal is brought.

apprehension Expectation of an immediate, harmful touching, based on the victim's state of mind as judged by a reasonable person standard.

appropriate bargaining unit All the employees in a group who have similar interests in employment conditions and should be entitled to vote together as a unit.

appropriation right The right to control the commercial value of one's endorsements and public reputation.

arbitrary and fanciful Marks that in no way describe the product they identify; some are made-up words.

arbitration A form of alternative dispute resolution in which an arbitrator hears evidence and makes a binding decision.

Architectural Works Protection Act Federal law extending copyright protection to architectural plans.

arraignment A defendant's formal appearance before a judge in order to enter a *plea* to the charges.

arrangement An adaptation or modification of a musical composition.

Articles of Confederation The fundamental law that governed the original confederation of American colonies.

articles of incorporation Document submitted to the designated state agency by incorporators who intend to form a corporation.

as is A phrase that is understood to effectively exclude an implied warranty of *merchantability.*

asexual reproduction Plant propagation techniques including rooting, layering, and grafting; not by seeds.

assault A crime and an intentional tort resulting from intentionally putting another person in *apprehension* of immediate, offensive, harmful touching.

assignment The outright transfer of a right.

assignment of rights Transfer to another party of the right to enforce duties under a contract.

assistance feature A franchisor's significant assistance to the franchisee on managerial or operational matters.

assumption of risk (1) A defense alleging that the plaintiff knew or should have known that a situation was dangerous and voluntarily assumed the consequences. (2) The doctrine prior to workers' compensation that barred recovery for an injured employee who was aware of the dangers on the job site.

attachment A court order allowing the plaintiff to sell the defendant's personal property and use the proceeds to pay off a judgment.

attempt All the activities of the perpetrators to plan and carry out a criminal act, such that, if successful, would result in the criminal act.

attempts to monopolize Methods and practices that would, if successful, accomplish monopolization.

auction with reserve An auction in which the bids are considered offers and the seller reserves the right to withdraw the goods before final sale.

auction without reserve An auction in which the bids are considered acceptances and the seller does not reserve the right to withdraw the goods before final sale.

Audio Home Recording Act Federal law that requires digital audio recording devices to prevent making copies from copies.

authenticated record A signed or electronically executed piece of information in writing or stored in retrievable format.

authentication Signing or otherwise executing by means of a symbol with the intent to establish a document as genuine.

automated clearing house (ACH) Electronic networks for processing electronic payments and payment orders.

automated transactions Machines acting as electronic agents to form contracts without human intervention between electronic agent and individual or between two electronic agents.

Automobile Dealer Day in Court Act Federal law that protects automobile dealers from bad-faith termination of their franchises.

average variable cost The average of all of the variable expenses for all of the units produced.

B

B2B electronic marketplaces Software systems that enable buyers and sellers to form contracts for goods and services using industry-wide computer systems.

back pay Compensation, with interest, to an employee for wages lost because of being denied a job or being unjustly fired.

bad faith The standard used to find a violation of the *Anticybersquatting Consumer Protection Act,* including the cyber squatter's intent to divert Web traffic from the mark owner, offer to ransom the name to the mark owner, and whether the mark is distinctive and famous.

bail Money deposited with the court to ensure that

a defendant released before trial will be present when required.

bailees Temporary custodians of goods who usually act for the true owner's benefit.

bait and switch Stocking a limited supply of inexpensive merchandise in order to lure customers into a store where they may be switched to higher-priced items.

balancing the equities Consideration of whether unfairness would best be avoided by enforcing or not enforcing a promise.

bankruptcy stay A court order that temporarily stops creditors from taking legal action against a debtor who has filed for bankruptcy.

barriers to entry Circumstances that make it difficult for new firms to enter a market.

barter A method of payment involving the direct exchange of goods for goods.

battery The intentional offensive touching of another person without justification or consent, including the use of an instrumentality, such as a bullet, put in motion by the aggressor.

battle of the forms The situation in which parties to a contract use forms containing language that differs.

bearer paper Commercial paper that is negotiable by anyone who rightfully possesses it.

beneficiary A person who benefits from a contract; a person who is to receive property, such as an insurance policy, owned by another party.

Berne Convention A copyright treaty subscribed to by many nations.

bespeaks caution A firm's approach when it uses cautionary language in making projections of future performance.

best available technology (BAT) The best technology without consideration of factors such as cost.

best mode Disclosure that includes the best way to make or use an invention.

best practicable technology The best technology under circumstances such as cost of equipment, time required to install it, and severity of pollution to be controlled.

beyond a reasonable doubt The standard of proof necessary in a criminal case, higher than in a civil case.

bifurcated trial A trial separated into a guilt phase and a sentencing phase, where judge or jury may hear evidence of the defendant's background or insanity as part of sentencing.

bilateral contract Contract that requires a promise of performance from each party.

bilateral mistake A mistake in contracting made by both parties.

bill of lading A document of title used by carriers and freight forwarders that can also serve as the contract of carriage.

Bill of Rights The first ten amendments of the U.S. Constitution, guaranteeing many fundamental rights.

biometrics Identification technology such as fingerprinting, retinal scanning, and DNA analysis.

blank endorsement The signature of the payee without further restriction, converting the instrument to *bearer paper.*

blanket licenses Standardized performance licenses at standardized rates.

blocking laws Laws that prevent compliance with pretrial discovery requests from foreign courts.

blue pencil test Legal theory that permits a judge to limit unreasonable aspects of a covenant not to compete.

blue sky laws State laws regulating securities offerings within the state.

blurring Lessening the distinctiveness of an owner's mark, thereby causing *dilution.*

board of directors A group elected by the *shareholders* of a corporation to provide management oversight and establish policies for operating the corporation's business.

boilerplate Language in a form contract that sets "take-it-or-leave-it" terms.

bona fide occupational qualification A characteristic required of employees as a matter of business necessity; it may justify an exemption from laws prohibiting discrimination based on religion, national origin, or sex.

bona fide purchasers for value Intermediaries in the negotiation process who have greater rights than ordinary assignees of contracts.

bottle laws State laws that require payment of a refundable deposit on beverage containers, designed to decrease litter.

branches Parts of a parent firm that are not independent entities.

breach (1) Failure to perform duties under a contract. (2) Failure to use reasonable care in a negligence situation.

brief A summary of a case, including the facts, issues, holding, and reasoning behind the court's decision.

bundle of exclusive rights See *statutory rights.*

burden of proof Legal standards that indicate which party to a lawsuit has the obligation to submit proof to the court and the quantity and quality of the evidence that is needed to prevail.

business ethics The application of traditional ethical analysis to business decisions.

business method exception The former principle that business methods were not eligible for patents.

business method patents Patents covering systems and methods used in business, such as financial recordkeeping software.

business necessity A valid reason for employers to require employees with certain characteristics, such as restricting clergy positions to members of the religion.

business-opportunity franchise A franchise in which the franchisor supplies goods to the franchisee, secures retail outlets, and receives a fee.

bylaws The rules by which a corporation is to be governed, including the number of directors, their powers, and how they are to be elected.

C

Cable Communications Policy Act of 1984 (CCPA) Federal law that protects information about viewing habits of cable television subscribers.

cancellation The act of withdrawing approval of a trademark because of similarity to existing marks or for containing descriptive elements or generic terms.

capital offense A felony potentially punishable by death.

Capper-Volstead Act Federal law that exempts agricultural producers from the *Clayton Act.*

capture Interception and storage of data during its creation and transmission.

Carnivore Internet monitoring software used by the FBI.

case or controversy An actual dispute that a court may adjudicate, in contrast with rendering an advisory opinion in a hypothetical case.

caveat emptor The doctrine that a buyer has the responsibility to investigate products before making a purchase; Latin for "let the buyer beware."

cease and desist orders Court orders that a party must stop an activity such as unfair trade practices.

Celler-Kefauver Amendment Federal law that prohibited noncompetitive market structures and extended a merger prohibition to corporate acquisitions in which the assets of another firm are purchased.

certificate of deposit A note in which a bank acknowledges the receipt (deposit) of customer funds and promises to repay them at a future time with interest.

certification mark A mark owned by an independent party and used to certify that producers allowed to use the mark have the characteristics of the group that the mark identifies.

chain of title The history of transfers of a negotiable instrument.

challenge for cause A party's right to have a prospective juror excluded because of bias that might influence the juror's decision in the case.

changing conditions Reasons for temporary instances of price discrimination, such as disposing of perishable or seasonal goods.

charitable subscriptions The situation where a charitable organization relies on a donor's promise to contribute and the promise will therefore be enforceable.

check The most common form of *draft,* ordering the *drawee* bank to pay a specific sum to the *payee* or whoever has endorsed the check.

Chicago school of antitrust enforcement Restrained antitrust enforcement, believing that monopolistic behavior may be permissible in some cases.

chief privacy officers Those in charge of coordinating firms' privacy policies and ensuring compliance.

Children's Online Privacy Protection Act (COPPA) Federal law that prohibits collecting personal information from children on-line without parental consent.

Chinese wall Physical and administrative procedures intended to isolate functions to avoid misappropriation or transfer of information such as to protect trade secrets or prevent insider trading.

choice The right to intentionally consent or not consent to data collection, including secondary uses of the information.

choice of law Designation in a contract of the jurisdiction whose law will govern interpretation of the contract.

choreographic works Dance movements and patterns.

circumstantial authority Authority of agent inferred from circumstances such as for ostensible authority or ratification.

citation A reference stating the page and volume where the report of a case may be found.

civil law Law concerned with the rights of individuals and corporations or the duties owed to people in society.

civil law legal system Legal system organized around a comprehensive legal code.

Civil Rights Act of 1964 Federal law that prohibits discrimination based on race, color, religion, sex, or national origin; Title VII covers employment.

Civil Rights Act of 1991 Federal law that authorizes punitive damages for intentional, malicious, or reckless indifference to discrimination laws.

class action A lawsuit brought by named plaintiffs on behalf of themselves and all others who have the same interest in the case.

Clayton Act Federal law barring specific anticompetitive activities.

clean room A method of reverse engineering in which one team discovers the unprotected ideas of the target product and provides only that information to a second team that develops a competing product.

Clean Water Act Federal law that deals with prevention of water pollution.

click-wrap agreement An agreement under which access to a website or installation of software is prevented unless the user clicks to accept the terms of the agreement; analogous to a *shrink-wrap agreement.*

closed shop The requirement that a person must be a union member to be eligible for employment.

closed standards Standardization that is owned or controlled by a monopolist or a cartel.

closing statement A party's summary of the evidence that it has presented in the trial.

codetermination Involving union representatives in setting corporate policy.

collateral estoppel Doctrine that prevents litigating facts or issues that were previously resolved in another suit.

collective bargaining Negotiation between an employer and a labor union, usually concerning conditions of employment.

comity A court's refusal to enforce laws of another nation unless that nation's laws are similar to those of the forum nation.

commercial impracticality Circumstances where a party to a contract is relieved of its obligation because its performance, through no fault of its own, has become impracticable.

commercial paper Negotiable instruments that include checks, notes, drafts, certificates of deposit, and bankers' acceptances.

commercial speech Advertising, a protected form of free speech.

commercial success Success of an invention in the marketplace that is caused by its inventive, nonobvious features.

Commodities Futures Trading Commission (CFTC) Agency with jurisdiction over commodities *futures* markets.

commoditization of private information Transformation of private information into a commodity that is easily shared and sold.

common carriers Firms that offer communication or transportation services for hire to the public and have special duties in the public interest.

common law Law derived from the decisions of courts and used as precedent in later cases.

common law legal system Legal system in which both court decisions and legislative acts are important sources of law.

common market An economic community that goes further than a *customs union* by making uniform standards and laws among member nations.

communications Transmissions of writings, signs, signals, pictures, and sounds of all kinds, as defined for the FCC.

comparative negligence Rule under which damages in a negligence case are apportioned based on the percentage of negligence of both plaintiff and defendant.

comparison Comparison of a software program's protected expression with the allegedly infringing software to detect similarities.

compensatory damages Payments to reimburse damages such as medical expenses, lost income, and pain and suffering.

compilation The result of selecting, coordinating, arranging, or organizing existing material in a unique way.

compliance programs A corporate plan designed and implemented to prevent and detect criminal conduct.

composition (1) A written piece of music. (2) An agreement among creditors that each will accept a lesser sum from the debtor to satisfy their debts.

composition of matter Any combination of two or more substances.

compulsory licensing Government-mandated permission to use intellectual property at a fee set by the government rather than market forces.

computer crime Offenses that at least partially involve computers.

Computer Fraud and Abuse Act (CFAA) Federal law that provides civil and criminal penalties for unauthorized access or molestation of protected computer systems.

Computer Software Copyright Act Federal law protecting software, both source code and object code, as a literary work under copyright.

concealment Keeping an invention secret from the public, as is done with trade secrets.

conception The moment when an inventor envisions how the invention will work.

conciliation A process of voluntary agreement between an employer and the EEOC on behalf of an employee to settle discrimination complaints.

conclude an agreement To reach mutual agreement on the terms of a contract.

concreteness A trade secret's quality of specificity and certainty.

concurrent conditions Each party's performance conditioned on the other party's nearly simultaneous tender of counterperformance.

concurrent powers Powers that both federal and state governments possess, such as taxation.

condition precedent An uncertain future event that must happen before a duty is owed.

condition subsequent An event that occurs after a duty is being performed that relieves one party of any further duty to perform.

conditional acceptance A counteroffer in which the offeree appears to accept but adds additional or different conditions.

conditional exclusion

conditions Events that must happen before a party's rights under a contract become enforceable.

conduct approach Examination of firms' actual behaviors, focusing on preventing future inefficient or monopolistic practices.

conduit theory The theory that an entity that must report its income, such as a partnership, is not itself responsible to pay taxes, but is a means for the income to be transferred to and taxed on its owners.

confederation A form of government in which states unite to achieve limited common goals; the central government is relatively weak.

confidentiality agreements See *nondisclosure agreements.*

confirmatory records Records that provide the exclusive source of terms of a contract.

confirming bank In a letter of credit transaction, the bank in the seller's country that confirms the issuing bank's obligation to pay to the seller, and itself becomes obligated to pay , under the terms specified in the letter of credit.

conflicts of law Law that involves which state's law to apply in cases where the parties have contacts with more than one state.

conforming goods Goods that conform to contract specifications.

confrontational approach An approach to labor-management relations that is largely adversarial.

congestion pricing Charging higher prices during times of greater demand.

conglomerate mergers Mergers that are not horizontal or vertical, such as acquisition of a firm in another industry or another product line.

conscious parallelism Mimicking the pricing decisions of an industry leader without overt agreement.

consent A defense based on the victim's consent to the defendant's action.

consent decree A court order agreed to by a defendant, without admitting the charges, that defines how the defendant will improve its future conduct, for example by adopting new employment practices.

consequential damages Compensation to replace lost profits or earnings of a user injured by a defective product.

consideration The giving of value or making of obligations by each party that is necessary to make a contract enforceable.

consignee The recipient of goods as designated in the document of title.

consolidation The combination of two firms, terminating both and replacing them with a new firm.

conspiracy An agreement between two or more persons who plan the commission of a crime.

conspiracy to monopolize The agreement by two or more parties to attempt to monopolize.

constructive reduction to practice An exception to the need for *reduction to practice* if the patent application is so detailed that it clearly informs the hypothetical person of ordinary skill how to build a working prototype or use the process.

consumer leases Leases made from merchants to consumers for personal or household goods.

consumer reports Credit histories about individuals provided by credit reporting agencies.

content The substance and style of a communication's subject matter.

contract An enforceable set of mutual obligations for which the law recognizes a duty and provides for enforcement of remedies.

contract clause Constitutional provision that prohibits states from impairing private contracts.

contract theory The theory that patents represent a contract between the inventor and society, providing a monopoly for a limited time in return for public disclosure of the invention's secrets as an incentive to further innovation.

contributory infringement The liability of one who provided technology that assisted another to infringe copyrighted material.

contributory negligence (1) Rule that prohibits any recovery for the plaintiff in a negligence suit if the plaintiff was in any way negligent. (2) The former doctrine that barred recovery for an injured employee who in any way contributed to creating the dangerous circumstances.

control feature A franchisor's significant control over the franchisee's business operations.

convergence Movement of elements closer together.

conversion Appropriation of personal property that is rightfully in another person's possession.

cookies Small files placed on a Web user's hard drive when a website is visited; they may persist for years or disappear when the browser is closed.

cooling-off period FTC rule that gives consumers three days to cancel a purchase made in their home.

cooperative approach An approach to labor-management relations that involves the union in some management decisions.

copyright A creator's rights in an original work, including reproducing, distributing, and adapting the work and assigning rights to it.

Copyright Arbitration Royalty Panels (CARP) Dispute resolution panels that settle royalties for cable television, digital audio recording technologies, and so forth.

copyright management information Data included with copyrighted work that is used for identification, making records, metering fees, or discovering infringement.

copyright misuse Defense to copyright infringement by which copyright owner violates antitrust laws by tying a transaction in copyrighted work to another transaction.

copyright notice A claim of copyright placed in a reasonably visible location on a work, consisting of the owner's name, a copyright symbol, and the year of first publication.

Copyright Office The primary regulatory agency for copyrights in the United States, a part of the Library of Congress.

Copyright Office Registration and Deposit System (CORDS) An on-line system for registering works and *depositing* copies.

copyright term The length of a holder's copyright.

corporate crime Illegal behavior intended to benefit a firm.

corporate stakeholders Groups or entities affected by a firm's activities, such as shareholders, customers, suppliers, and employees.

corporation Form of business organization created by state law that is regarded as an entity distinct from its owners.

corrective advertising order FTC order requiring new advertising to correct past misleading ads.

cost differential A reason for price discrimination based on difference in selling costs, such as a legitimate quantity discount.

counteradvertising New advertising to correct misleading information in prior ads.

counterclaim A related or unrelated claim by the defendant against the plaintiff that may be made part of the defendant's answer.

counterfeiting The use of a spurious mark, identical to or indistinguishable from a registered mark, on fake copies made with the intent to defraud consumers.

counterterrorism Antiterrorism preparedness.

countertrade A barter type arrangement often found in international business where in exchange for a sale of a product or service, the seller agrees to also make a purchase from the original buyer.

countervailing duties A tax assessed to counteract foreign subsidies of imported products that materially injure competing domestic products.

course of dealing A common practice followed by contracting partners in their previous dealings.

course of performance Expectations of the parties based on repeated performances in the course of a contract; for example, setting a precedent of allowing late deliveries.

covenant not to compete A contract term prohibiting an employee from competing with the employer after termination of employment.

cover A remedy for the buyer under the UCC that allows the buyer, after a breach by the seller, to purchase goods from another seller and substitute them for the goods due from the seller.

covered A composition recorded in its original form.

covered entities Health care providers, insurance plans, and other organizations regulated under the *Health Insurance Portability and Accountability Act* with regard to disclosing individuals' private medical information.

credit history Data about a debtor's timely payments or payment defaults.

creditor third-party beneficiary A *third-party beneficiary* who receives a benefit from the promisor that discharges a duty previously owed by the promisee to the third party.

criminal intent The intent to commit an act that is a crime.

criminal law Law whose purpose is to protect society as a whole rather than a single member.

cross-elasticity of demand The percentage change in the quantity demanded of one product divided by the percentage change of a substitute product's price.

cross-examination Questioning of a witness called by the opposing party.

cross-licensing Exchange of licensing rights between a licensor and a licensee that develops an improvement to the originally licensed technology.

culpability multiplier Part of the *U.S. Sentencing Guidelines* that provides leniency to convicted firms that can show various kinds of *compliance programs,* cooperation, and acceptance of responsibility.

cure Under the UCC, the right of a party who tenders nonconforming goods to correct his performance within the contract period.

custom anthologies Collections of copyrighted articles and book chapters created by college faculty for student readings.

customer proprietary network information (CPNI) Information that must be kept private by a telephone carrier, including the quantity, technical configuration, type, destination, location, and amount of use of a telecommunications service.

customs union An area in which member nations agree to eliminate tariffs among themselves and to create a common external tariff.

cyber crime *Computer crime* committed over telecommunications networks.

cyber notaries Third-party certification authorities that attest to the identity of a signatory.

cyber squatting The practice of acquiring domain names that suggest established firms and reselling them to those firms as a form of ransom.

cyber stalking A form of *stalking* that involves telecommunications, such as intercepting the target's e-mail or interacting in chat rooms.

cyber terrorism Criminal activities committed against computer systems, such as theft of information, malicious destruction, spying, or fraud.

cyber trespass Invasion of another's property interest in an electronic database by physical acts on site or by remote access.

D

data acquisition Observation of an activity followed by collecting and coding information into data storage.

data aggregators Firms that gather data from various Internet sources to produce reports for users.

data controller identification Notice of the data collector's identity, purpose for data processing, and other information required by the European Union.

data controllers Data managers and their clients.

data creep The use of data for purposes other than the original purpose for which it was collected.

data mining Analysis of database information to find relationships and associations among the data.

data warehousing A mechanized method of data collection and organization.

databases Collections of works, data, or other materials arranged in a systematic or methodical way for retrieval or access by manual or electronic means.

de facto standards Standards that informally become widely accepted.

de novo New or as if new.

debtor relief laws Legislation that modifies debt contracts for the benefit of the debtor.

deceptive advertising Advertising that makes a misrepresentation or omission to consumers.

deceptive marks Marks that falsely connect a product with persons, institutions, or national symbols.

deceptively misdescriptive A mark that makes a false inference about an important matter, such as the product's geographic origin.

decompile To convert machine-readable *object code* into *source code.*

deductive reasoning The process of examining general principles derived from induction or legislation and applying them to specific situations.

deep linking Linking that bypasses the home page of an Internet site and accesses internal pages.

deep pocket theory The theory that an employer generally has greater financial resources and insurance coverage with which to pay a claim than an individual employee who directly commits a tort.

defamatory per se Certain statements that are automatically considered defamatory without specific proof of damage to reputation.

default judgment A judgment in the plaintiff's favor that is entered if the defendant fails to respond within the prescribed period.

defendant The party being sued or prosecuted.

defense An excuse or justification that partially or completely relieves a defendant of criminal liability.

defense to infringement Legal reasons against finding trademark infringement, such as *fair use* or lack of distinctiveness.

definite time Required condition of a note or draft, making clear the time for payment.

delayed manifestation Principle that limits injured plaintiffs from suing after a period that begins with the onset of symptoms or the last use of the product, whichever comes first.

delegation The transfer of power from one governmental body such as the legislature to another such as an administrative agency.

delegation of duties Transfer to another party of the obligation to perform duties under a contract.

demand for arbitration A notice by the party initiating arbitration that is served on the other party under a prior agreement to arbitrate.

demand instrument A negotiable instrument payable on demand (when presented).

deposit Submission of two copies of a work to the Copyright Office as part of the copyright process.

deposition The taking of testimony from a witness outside of court under examination by attorneys; used to discover the witness's testimony and preserve a transcript for possible use at trial.

deprivation of liberty Deprivation of a right guaranteed under the Fifth Amendment; usually denotes incarceration.

deprivation of life Deprivation of a right guaranteed under the Fifth Amendment; usually denotes capital punishment.

deprivation of property Deprivation of a right guaranteed under the Fifth Amendment; usually denotes payment of fines or damages or loss of property by government confiscation.

derivative works Adaptations of a work.

derivatives Investment contracts that fluctuate as the value of some underlying financial asset changes.

descriptive marks Marks that describe major features of the products they identify and can be registered only if they have acquired a *secondary meaning.*

deservedly discrediting information Unfavorable but true information about an individual.

design marks Trademarks that use nontext elements such as borders, unique fonts, and geometric designs.

destructive competition Wasteful competition in a natural monopoly that causes duplication of capacity.

detrimental reliance Reliance on a promise and acting in some definite and substantial way because of it.

digital audio recording devices Machines that produce digital recordings.

digital audio recording technology (DART) Technology such as digital audio tape.

digital divide The difficulty some people experience in accessing the Internet because of low income, disability, or lack of broadband.

Digital Millennium Copyright Act (DMCA) Federal law that creates civil and criminal prohibitions against tampering with copy protection technology.

Digital Performance Right in Sound Recordings

Act Federal law that manages rights and uses of digital sound recording transmission.

digital phonorecord deliveries Music streamed or downloaded via the Internet.

digital privacy rights management A form of *digital rights management* that can enforce restrictions on collection and use of personal information.

digital rights management Systems that attach hidden data to the primary data in order to identify and track sources and enforce restrictions.

digital signatures Encrypted data used to authenticate electronic records.

digital transmissions Communications accomplished by means of digital technology.

digital watermarks A form of hidden data used in *digital rights management.*

diligence The duty of an inventor to reduce the invention to practice and file a patent application in a timely manner.

dilution Use of an owner's mark by an outsider in such a way as to diminish the mark's value and diminishes the owner's interest in maintaining brand image.

direct examination Questioning of a witness by the party who called the witness.

direct liability One's liability for one's own tortious acts.

direct perception The act of reading a book or viewing a photo, painting, or sculpture.

direct use Use of information by the party that collected it.

directed verdict The defendant's motion that a judge may grant if the plaintiff has not proved its case at the end of the testimony on plaintiff's behalf; the verdict is directed in favor of the defendant.

director A member of the board of directors of a corporation.

disability A physical or mental impairment that substantially limits one or more of the major life activities of an individual.

disaffirm To avoid or set aside a contract obligation.

discharged In contract law, when a party fulfills its legal obligations, it no longer has the obligation to perform. In bankruptcy law, a discharge releases the debtor from all debts that by law can be excused.

disclaimers Statements with a trademark application that indicate the generic elements of the mark that are excluded from protection.

disclose or abstain SEC rule that requires corporate officers, directors, and any other insiders to either disclose their inside information before trading or abstain from trading.

disclosed A principal is disclosed if a third party knows the principal's identity when contracting with the principal's agent.

disclosure Opening an invention's secrets to public access.

discovery The process of obtaining information from opposing parties before trial in a lawsuit.

discovery procedures Methods that the parties to a lawsuit use to obtain facts, documents, and other things from the opposing party; examples are depositions, examinations, inspections, and interrogatories.

discretionary activities Actions that an agency may decline to take as a matter of discretion, such as filing a complaint.

dishonor To refuse to pay as in dishonoring a promissory note.

disintermediation Elimination of intermediaries such as wholesalers and resellers from a commercial transaction.

disparagement False, disparaging statements about a business that result in specific business losses; also called *trade libel.*

disparate impact Discrimination caused by employment policies unrelated to job qualifications, but without the intent to discriminate.

disparate treatment Intentional discrimination by employers.

display Showing a work directly or by mechanical means.

distance contracts Contracts concerning goods or services that are concluded by means of technology.

distribute To sell copies of a work.

distribution Transfer of a product to another by sale, rental, lease, or other means.

distributor A person or firm that purchases products from a seller and assumes the economic and legal risk involved with reselling them.

diversification mergers Combination of totally unrelated firms.

division of markets Assignment of certain segments of a market to different sellers.

doctrine of equivalents The rule that infringement may be found if a device makes obvious changes using known substitutes and the resulting product performs substantially the same function, in the same way, to achieve the same result.

documents of title Written instruments entitling the holder to possess, receive, or dispose of specified goods.

domestic concerns Firms in the United States.

donee third-party beneficiary A *third-party beneficiary* who is intended to receive a gift.

double jeopardy Being tried twice for the same crime arising out of the same incident.

double patenting The rule that an invention cannot receive both a utility patent and a design patent.

draft A three-party instrument in which a *drawer* issues a draft that orders a *drawee* to pay money to the third-party payee.

dramatic works Directions guiding the portrayal of a story in a performance by use of dialogue or acting.

drawee The party to be paid when a *drawer* issues a *draft.*

drawer The party who issues a *draft.*

dual auction A method by which buyers post their bids and sellers post their asking prices to an electronic marketplace.

dual federalism Another term for *federalism.*

due care Reasonable consideration of the possible effect of an action on others.

due diligence The defense that one used reasonable efforts to assure that disclosures in a registration statement were true.

dumping The practice of selling in another country at prices lower than in the firm's home market.

duress A defense based on a credible threat of serious bodily harm to the defendant unless he or she commits the crime to avoid the threatened harm.

duty of candor The duty of a patent applicant to disclose any material prior art that the inventor is aware of and to make truthful statements in the application.

duty of good faith The duty to act in a reasonable and honorable way in commercial transactions.

duty to exercise due care The duty to use reasonable care in one's actions; the failure to use due care may result in negligence.

duty to mitigate damages The duty imposed on the plaintiff to lessen or minimize the damages caused by the defendant.

duty to use reasonable care One of the elements that must be proved in a negligence case.

E

eco-labeling Advertising that cites the environmental benefits of the product.

economic due process An early doctrine used to invalidate economic regulation on the basis of unjustified restriction of business.

economic efficiency Characterized by reducing the waste of societal resources.

economic espionage Theft of trade secret information with knowledge that it was proprietary and with intent to benefit a foreign government or instrumentality.

Economic Espionage Act of 1996 Federal criminal law that prohibits economic espionage and theft of trade secrets.

economic union An economic community that requires member nations to adopt a common currency and to integrate their economic policies.

economies of scale The reduction of unit costs brought about by increased productive capacity.

edge effect The effect of a potential entrant that pressures current firms in the market to remain efficient and keep prices competitive.

efficacy The effectiveness of drugs in treating medical conditions as intended.

Eighth Amendment Prohibition of excessive fines or bail, and of cruel and unusual punishment.

elasticity of demand A demand for a product that depends to a large extent on the price, because consumers can substitute alternate goods when prices are high.

electronic agent Computer program, or electronic or other automated means, used by a person to initiate an action or to respond to electronic messages or performances, on the person's behalf, without review or action by another individual.

electronic bill payment and presentment (EBPP) Analog or digital electronic means—telephone, fax, e-mail, third-party electronic bill payment service, and the like—to transmit billing and payment information.

Electronic Business Center (EBC) A group of electronic transaction-processing systems in the Patent and Trademark Office, including patent searches.

electronic check presentment (ECP) Federal Reserve Board proposal for a system of automated clearinghouse debits in which the depository bank would make and transmit an electronic image of the check, an image replacement document for collection from the drawee bank.

electronic communication networks (ECN) Electronic bulletin boards that communicate availability and price of securities.

electronic communications Transfer of signs, signals, writing, images, sounds, data, or intelligence of any nature transmitted in whole or part by wire, radio, electromagnetic, photoelectric, or photooptical system.

Electronic Communications Privacy Act (ECPA) Federal law that expanded the provisions of wiretapping law to cellular phones, voice mail, Internet downloads, and e-mail.

Electronic Data Gathering Analysis and Retrieval (EDGAR) SEC system for posting corporate filings and disclosures on line.

electronic data interchange (EDI) Transactions using a system of interconnected computers that exchange data among merchant buyers, sellers, banks, carriers, warehouses, and other parties on a regular basis.

electronic error Under UCITA, occurs in an electronic message if the information processing system provides no reasonable method to detect and correct or avoid errors.

Electronic Filing System (EFS) A feature of the Patent and Trademark Office for filing applications electronically.

Electronic Freedom of Information Act (eFOIA) Federal act extending the provisions of the *Freedom of Information Act* to electronic files.

electronic record A record created, generated, sent, communicated, received, or stored by electronic means.

electronic self-help Under UCITA, right of licensor to disable software or information availability on the licensee's system, such as when the licensee's access to programs or databases is refused by the licensor's server or software use is not reauthorized.

electronic signature An electronic symbol or process attached to or logically associated with a record, used with the intent to sign the record.

Electronic Signatures in Global and National Commerce Act Federal legislation on electronic signatures.

electronic records Record that is created, generated, sent, communicated, or received by electronic means; UETA and federal E-SIGN make equivalent to written documents for most purposes under law.

electronic transferable record An *electronic record* that has only one holder at a time and is protected from alterations; used in electronic data exchange and can be used as a negotiable instrument if the parties so agree.

embargo A government order prohibiting trade with another country.

embezzlement The wrongful appropriation of property entrusted to an individual.

embodiment A thing or process that becomes functional by using basic information in some beneficial way.

eminent domain The power of government to take private property for public purposes, such as highway construction.

Employee Polygraph Protection Act Federal law prohibiting use of polygraphs by employers unless they have reasonable suspicion that an employee has caused a loss.

employer–independent contractor relationship A relationship in which a person or firm hires a contractor to perform specific tasks but does not have the right to control how the contractor performs the work.

employment at will An employment contract in which either employee or employer can terminate the relationship at any time and without justification.

enablement Disclosure of details about an invention that would allow a person of ordinary skill in the art to construct it.

enabling legislation Laws that grant some lawmaking authority to an agency and specify the activities that the agency may perform, such as to subpoena witnesses; also called enabling acts.

encryption Conversion of recognizable text to a coded format readable only with a decryption key.

Endangered Species Act Federal law designed to protect wildlife on the endangered species list.

endorsement (1) The signature of the payee on a negotiable instrument. (2) The principle that data collection and management must have mechanisms to enforce privacy practices.

Enforcement Remedies and Penny Stock Reform Act Federal law that governs the SEC's civil enforcement powers, including administrative actions.

enhanced telecommunications services New communications technology such as Internet telephony and DSL phone lines.

entrapment A defense based on acts of law enforcement personnel who stage circumstances and suggest criminal acts to a defendant who is not predisposed to commit a crime.

entrepreneur One who organizes, manages, and assumes financial responsibility for a business or other enterprise.

enumerated powers Powers expressly delegated to the federal government by the states.

envelope theory The principle that electronically delivered communications to investors can include hyperlinks to other information on the firm's website.

ephemeral copies Audio, video, or software copies in computer RAM, which disappear when the computer is turned off.

equal dignities rule In most states, a rule that where a contract is to be in writing, an agent's express authority to act on behalf of the principal must also be in writing.

Equal Employment Opportunity Commission Federal agency that enforces antidiscrimination laws by rule-making, investigation, and adjudication.

Equal Pay Act of 1963 Federal law that prohibits sexual discrimination in pay for work that requires "equal skill, effort, and responsibility."

equitable relief Broad powers based on the discretion of the court, such as injunctions.

E-SIGN See *Electronic Signatures in Global and National Commerce Act.*

essential facility An asset that is indispensable for competition in a market, such as electricity distribution lines or real estate multiple listing service.

established royalty The royalty rate a patent holder charges licensees.

ethics A field of philosophy that examines motives and actions from the perspective of moral principles

EU Directive on the Legal Protection of Databases European Union policy calling for copyright protection of the selection and arrangement of database information and *sui generis database protections.*

EU Personal Data Protection Directive The requirement that European Union member nations enact strong personal information privacy laws.

European Patent Convention Treaty that simplifies patent application filing requirements for European Union nations and requires members to enact uniform domestic patent legislation.

ex parte Court proceedings held without the presence of the person who is the subject of the proceedings.

ex parte warrant A warrant granted without notice or hearing to the party to be searched.

exactness The rule that an exact duplicate of an invention is an infringement.

examination A physical or mental examination of a litigant or examination of personal or real property.

examination process Determination of whether an invention is novel (not already known) and nonobvious (not easily foreseen by persons skilled in the field).

examiner An expert employee of the Patent and Trademark Office who determines whether an invention qualifies for a patent.

exclusion order An order to the U.S. Customs Service to block imports of products that infringe patents.

exclusionary rule Principle that evidence obtained illegally cannot be introduced at trial.

exclusive (1) Limited to a single individual or group. (2) Rights under a license that may be used only by the *licensee* but not by the licensor or other parties.

exclusive dealership A restriction in resale arrangements.

exclusive dealing Requiring a buyer to resell only the products of a single manufacturer.

exclusive distributorship The sole right to sell a manufacturer's products within a given region.

exclusive powers Powers that only the federal government has, such as regulation of interstate commerce and conduct of foreign affairs.

exculpatory clauses A clause that releases a party from liability for injury to another, regardless of who is at fault.

executed contract Contract for which all the duties have been fully performed.

executive agencies Administrative agencies that assist the executive in carrying out the functions of the executive branch.

executive privilege A privilege invoked by presidents to withhold information from public disclosure.

executory contract Contract for which at least some duties of either or both parties have not yet been fully performed.

exhaustible A quality of tangible property; the rightful owner loses all value in the property if it is transferred or wrongfully misappropriated.

experience information Personal financial information based on direct transaction history with a creditor.

experience rating The relative turnover among an employer's workforce, which affects the size of the employer's unemployment compensation premiums.

experimental uses Exceptions to the *on-sale bar* for testing or experimental sales.

exports Good sold outside the country where they are produced.

express authority Authority given directly by a principal to an agent orally or in writing.

express contracts Contracts that arise from the parties' outward expressions of mutual assent, such as oral or written statements.

expropriation Government takeover of the ownership and management of a private firm without payment of compensation.

externalities (1) By-products of economic activities that create costs or benefits for others. (2) The coincidental benefits of a contract enjoyed by *incidental beneficiaries*.

F

failing firm defense The argument that a merger target would have become insolvent and could not find other merger partners that might reduce market concentration.

Fair Credit Reporting Act (FCRA) Federal law regulating the credit reporting system, requiring the removal of obsolete information and allowing individuals to examine and submit corrections of mistakes in their own files.

fair information practices Elements of information privacy identified by an advisory committee to the Department of Health, Education and Welfare, including notice, choice, access, security, and enforcement.

Fair Packaging and Labeling Act of 1966 Federal law that requires accuracy in labeling.

fair use (1) An exemption from copyright infringement that permits reasonable use in research, teaching, news reporting, criticism, or parody. (2) The right of others to use the descriptive and suggestive words in a trademark, such as geographical terms or surnames, or to use the trademark in news reporting or parody.

fairness Characterized by justness and equity.

Fairness in Music Licensing Act Federal law that regulates the licensing of music for use in businesses, restaurants, and so forth.

false imprisonment Intentional confinement of a nonconsenting individual within a bounded area for an appreciable time.

false light The tort of making a false connection between a person and illegal, immoral, or embarrassing activity.

famous trademarks Trademarks identified as famous under the *Federal Trademark Dilution Act* based on degree of distinctiveness, duration of use, extent of publicity, geographical extent, and other factors.

Federal Communications Commission (FCC) Agency that regulates use of radio, TV, wire, satellite, and cable.

Federal Insurance Contributions Act (FICA) Federal law that requires employers and employees to contribute to the Social Security trust fund.

Federal Register Official publication for federal agency rules and regulations.

Federal Trade Commission (FTC) Independent agency that enforces antitrust, consumer protection, and consumer finance laws.

Federal Trademark Dilution Act of 1996 Federal law that provides a remedy for dilution of famous trademarks.

federalism A general theory of government that recognizes power at both the central level and the state and local level.

Federalists Early American party that desired a strong central government.

fellow servant doctrine The rule that prevented an injured employee from suing the employer if a fellow employee negligently contributed to the injury.

felonies More serious crimes that are punishable by larger fines and longer prison sentences than *misdemeanors*.

fiduciary One who has the obligation to be faithful to the principal who places trust and confidence in the fiduciary.

fiduciary duty The duty of loyalty that requires confidentiality and prohibits conflict of interest.

fiduciary duty of loyalty The duty of trust and confidence that the agent or employee owes the employer.

Fifth Amendment Guarantee of fair judicial process, including protection against self-incrimination, right to grand jury indictment, protection against double jeopardy, and right to due process.

file wrapper estoppel The rule that the original inventor cannot allege infringement based on a claim that was surrendered during the examination process.

filing system A storage and retrieval system for data.

filtration Separation of a software program's unprotected ideas from protected expression.

final refusal The Patent and Trademark Office's administrative refusal to register a trademark.

final rejection The status of a patent application that is found to have no novel or nonobvious claims.

finance leases A three-party lease involving a lessee, a lessor who finances the lease, and an original supplier of goods.

financial institutions Businesses regulated under the *Gramm-Leach-Bliley Act,* such as banks, securities brokers, credit card issuers, and trust services.

financing statement A document prepared by a secured creditor that is filed with a local or state office to give notice to the public that the creditor claims an interest in the collateral belonging to the named defendant.

finder or middleman One who brings parties together in a business deal, but neither party relies on the finder for advice and assistance.

firm offer An offer made in writing in which a merchant promises that the offer is irrevocable.

First Amendment Guarantee of rights to freedom of speech, freedom of the press, freedom of assembly, and freedom of religion.

first inventor's defense The right to use business methods developed as trade secrets if the methods are subsequently patented by another.

first sale doctrine (1) Principle that prohibits a licensor from exercising control after the product embodying the IP is sold the first time. (2) Principle that the individual purchaser of a copyrighted work such as a book may sell it without committing infringement; applies also to items containing patented parts or produced using a patented process.

first to file Policy that awards a patent to the quickest filer, who may be best financed and most experienced in filing patent applications.

first to invent Policy that awards a patent to the actual inventor, regardless of the inventor's financial resources.

first-degree felony A crime punishable by up to life imprisonment.

first-mover advantage The advantage of the first firm to attract customers to a product that will be hard to switch away from.

fixed in a tangible medium of expression A stable, permanent, and physical rendering of a creative work.

fixed sum of money Required condition of a note or draft, making the extent of the obligation clear.

flat rate tariff A tax levied on each unit of an imported product.

for cause The type of challenge that dismisses a juror who, for example, is related to one of the parties or has formed an opinion about guilt or innocence.

forbearance A promise not to do something or actually refraining from doing it; can constitute sufficient consideration for a contract.

force majeure A contract provision that stipulates the unforeseen events—wars, Acts of God, certain strikes—that will excuse a party from its duty to perform the contract.

foreclosure A proceeding in which a mortgagee either takes title to or forces the sale of a debtor's property to satisfy a debt.

Foreign Corrupt Practices Act (FCPA) Federal law that prohibits corporations from bribing foreign officials and establishes accounting practices to prevent bribery.

foreign direct investment Investment by a foreign firm that gives it at least a 10% ownership in the local firm.

foreign officials Description of those who may not be bribed under the *Foreign Corrupt Practices Act,* including government officials, political officials, candidates, and officials of international organizations.

foreign portfolio investment Investment by a foreign firm that gives it less than a 10% ownership in the local firm.

foreign sales corporation (FSC) A subsidiary firm incorporated under one of several specified foreign laws.

foreign subsidiary An affiliated firm organized in a foreign country under the corporation laws of that country.

forgery The fraudulent making or altering of an instrument that apparently creates or alters a legal liability of another.

form contracting Transactions based on prepared forms, in which there is little or no bargaining between the parties.

form contracts Documents designed to impose appropriate restrictions on a firm's relations with others.

formal oral offers Oral offers to buy securities.

formal prospectus A specific document that contains basic financial information about a security and its issuer.

forum non conveniens The principle that a case should be heard in a court of the place where parties, witnesses, and evidence are primarily located.

forum selection Designation in a contract of the jurisdiction where any trial concerning the contract will take place.

forum selection clause Part of the terms and conditions imposed on users by a firm; it requires that any claims may be heard only in a specified court.

forum shopping The practice of looking for a state whose law is more favorable to a party's case.

forum state The state in which a lawsuit is brought.

forward-looking The way projections should be characterized for fair disclosure to investors.

Fourth Amendment Guarantee of right to be secure from warrantless searches and seizures.

framing Displaying parts of two websites simultaneously.

franchise A license to conduct business under a registered trademark in which all participants share a community of interest in selling goods or services under specified conditions.

franchisee Independent operator of a business who buys a franchise and operates under control of the franchisor.

franchising A form of *license* by which the franchisor of trademarks and copyrights grants a license to the franchisee to use the trademarks and copyrights in selling goods or services under specified conditions; examples are McDonald's and Holiday Inn.

franchisor The party that develops a product or service and licenses it to franchisees.

fraud A misrepresentation of fact , knowingly made, with the intention of deceiving another, on which a reasonable person can and does rely to his or her detriment.

free rider (1) A discounter that benefits from the advertising paid by a high-profit retailer for the goods that both sell. (2) A seller that pretends its goods are made by a competitor, thus "riding" on the other firm's reputation. (3) A polluter whose damages to the environment are paid for by others.

free stock Stock given without charge by website promoters in exchange for personal information or referrals.

free trade area Geographic area in which member nations agree to eliminate or phase out tariffs and other trade barriers among themselves.

freedom of contract Principle that parties are generally free to contract for any legal objective.

Freedom of Information Act (FOIA) Federal law that requires disclosure of most federal records upon request.

freedom of religion Constitutional prohibition against government establishment of religion and protection of free exercise of religion.

fruit of the poisonous tree doctrine The legal principle that evidence is not admissible in a criminal trial if it was discovered because of leads obtained from illegally seized evidence.

frustration of purpose Court doctrine that relieves a party of its obligation to perform a contract obligation if the purpose for such performance no longer exists for reasons not due to that party's conduct.

FTC Act §5 Federal law that prohibits unfair and deceptive trade practices.

full faith and credit clause Constitutional provision that requires each state to recognize the laws and legal proceedings of all other states.

full performance Fulfillment of the duties of both parties under a contract.

full warranty A warranty, under the Magnuson-Moss Warranty Act, that must provide the consumer with reasonable replacement or repair rights without other charges or conditions.

fully insured The level at which workers whose income level and work credits entitle them to full retirement benefits from Social Security.

functionality A feature of a product that affects its purpose, action, or performance or the facility or economy of processing, handing, or use.

fundamental right A constitutional right that is given more careful protection than other rights; voting rights, interstate travel, immunity from mandatory sterilization, and criminal procedural protections, as applied in equal protection analysis.

futures Commitments for the future delivery of agricultural products, petroleum, metals, currencies, and other assets.

G

gambling Risk taking for the purpose of gain or loss, based on games of chance, sports outcomes, or games of skill and chance.

gap-filling terms Terms that supplement vague sales contracts.

garnishment A court order used to help a party enforce a money judgment; for example, ordering a bank to pay the amount from the defendant's bank account, or ordering an employer to turn over some of the defendant's wages.

general creditors In bankruptcy, those creditors who have no specific security or collateral for debts owed to them; they are also known as unsecured creditors.

general duty The employer's duty under OSHA to provide a safe work environment free from recognized hazards that are likely to cause death or serious physical injury.

generally accepted practices Customs and practices that over time have been accepted by most nations.

generic A mark that is a common name or description and applies to all instances of a product; it does not qualify for trademark protection.

generic words Common descriptive words that cannot be trademarked.

genericide Loss of trademark protection because the public has come to perceive the mark as identifying the entire product class made by all manufacturers.

geographic market A region within which consumers can readily obtain a product or service.

going and coming rule The rule that workers' compensation covers injuries sustained after an employee arrives at the employer's premises.

good faith (1) Honest dealing in commercial transactions. (2) The standard, acting without knowledge or notice, required to use a mark that is used by another as a trademark in a different geographical area.

good faith bargaining An interactive process in which each side makes offers and counteroffers in an effort to reach an agreement.

goods Tangible items of personal property that are movable at the time of contracting.

governmental privilege Licensing of the privilege to practice a profession, operate a business, or carry on an activity such as driving.

grace period The one-year period permitted by the Patent Act between invention and filing of a patent application.

Gramm-Leach-Bliley Act (GLB) Federal law permitting the consolidation of financial service firms (insurance, commercial banking, and investment banking) and regulating privacy aspects of personal financial information.

grand jury A panel of citizens that reviews the evidence for probable cause and may issue an *indictment* against the accused.

grant The clause in a license that describes the right to be transferred, creates the right, and transfers it to the licensee.

gray goods Imported products sold outside the normal supply chain.

grease Facilitating payments to lower-echelon foreign government agents for *routine governmental actions;* not considered bribes under the *Foreign Corrupt Practices Act.*

group boycotts Agreement among competitors to boycott individuals or groups.

guarantee A collateral contract by which a third party promises to pay a debtor's debt; one of the situations requiring a written contract under the statute of frauds.

H

hackers People skilled in computer programming; usually derogatory.

half-truth Factual information that fails to give other damaging facts.

handicaps Physical or mental impairments that substantially limit one or more of a person's major life activities.

Hart-Scott-Rodino Antitrust Improvement Act Federal law that requires public notice of mergers prior to completion and allows state attorneys general to prosecute antitrust cases.

Harvard school of antitrust enforcement Vigorous antitrust enforcement, believing that concentration of economic power nearly always leads to collusive behavior.

Hazardous and Solid Waste Management Act Federal law that strengthened regulation of hazardous waste in landfills.

Health Insurance Portability and Accountability Act (HIPAA) Federal law designed to permit freer movement of employees among different employer-sponsored health plans and to protect the privacy of medical information.

Herfindahl Index A statistical calculation of *market concentration.*

highly material terms Essential contract terms such as the parties' identity, the price, and significant descriptions of the quantity or subject matter.

highly sensitive data European Union classification of data that receives greater protection, including ethnic or racial demographics, political or religious opinions, health or sexual information, and union membership.

hindsight A later perception that benefits from seeing the significance of events that were much more difficult to see previously.

hired to invent A relationship between employer and employee that vests ownership of an employee's innovation in the employer with regard to specific technologies.

historical facts The allegations in the plaintiff's complaint that recite the circumstances of the case and the defendant's wrongful acts.

holder One who rightfully possesses (has actual physical control) of an instrument and has good title to it.

holder in due course The special status granted to intermediaries in the processing of negotiable instruments, making them immune to many defenses the original maker might assert against a normal contract assignee.

holder in due course disclosure rule FTC rule that consumer credit contracts must notify the consumer of rights to stop paying on a debt where the seller committed fraud or breached the contract or if the goods are defective.

horizontal mergers Combination of firms that compete at the same level of production in the same industry.

horizontal restraints of trade Collaboration between competitors to restrain trade by fixing prices, dividing markets, and the like.

hot news Information with a time value that is the property of its original owner.

I

idea-expression dichotomy The principle that ideas cannot be copyrighted; only the expression of ideas can be copyrighted.

identified Goods designated as being for the buyer.

illegal and prohibited subjects Matters that may not become part of a collective bargaining agreement, such as disregarding employee rights.

illegal strikes Strikes that involve violence, discrimination against certain employees, violations of a cooling-off period, or attempts to coerce recognition of a noncertified union.

illusory Term for a promise that is entirely within the control of the promissor and therefore not sufficient consideration for a contract.

image replacement document (IRD) Electronic facsimile of an original paper check or draft that is considered equivalent to the original check for all legal and evidentiary purposes.

immunity A bar to prosecution in exchange for the defendant's cooperation and information leading to prosecution of other criminals.

implied authority Authority that is implied from the responsibilities granted to an agent by the principal.

implied in fact contracts Contracts inferred from the parties' actions.

implied warranties Warranties, such as the warranty of merchantability, that are imposed by law; they do not arise from expressions or actions of the principal.

implied warranty of fitness for a particular purpose An implied warranty that arises whenever the buyer relies on the seller's expertise to select goods to suit the buyer's intended use.

imports Foreign goods or services that enter the economy of a country.

impossibility of performance In contract law, a party is excused from its obligation to perform if it is impossible for anyone, not just the contract party, to perform the required action.

improvements Enhancements to existing machines, manufactures, compositions of matter, or processes.

in camera Conducted privately before a judge rather than in open court.

in money Required condition of a note or draft, making money the only acceptable means of payment.

in pari delicto Equally at fault in tort or crime.

in rem Lawsuits brought against property as compared with those against a person; the court's jurisdiction does not depend on notice to the property owner.

incidental beneficiaries Outsiders who receive benefits by coincidence from the side effects produced by others' contracts.

incidental use The doctrine that the press can report on celebrities without liability for misappropriation.

incontestable A trademark's status of being immune to cancellation for lack of distinctiveness or secondary meaning.

incorporate by reference To make an independent document part of a contract, as an employee manual becomes a binding part of an employment contract.

incorporation Doctrine under which rights such as those in the Fifth Amendment are applied to the states under the Fourteenth Amendment.

INCOTERMS *Mercantile terms* as recognized by the International Chamber of Commerce.

indecent An incompletely defined term used in the Communications Decency Act.

indemnification The right of a party ordered to pay a judgment to receive reimbursement from the ultimately responsible party.

indemnify To make good any losses the agent suffers on account of doing the principal's business.

independent contractor A contractor who works as specified in the contract but not under the control of the other party as to how the job is to be done.

indictment The grand jury's finding of probable cause to recommend prosecution.

indirect perception The use of a machine or device such as a CD player to experience a creative work.

inductive reasoning The process of examining specific situations to determine whether they have some common attributes.

industrial organization economics A theory of economics organized around traditional industrial production of goods.

industry guides FTC policy statements that address the trade practices of an entire industry.

industry self-regulation Codes of conduct and policies adopted by the members of an industry.

inelastic market A market in which consumers cannot easily change to alternative goods.

inevitability injunction A court order that prevents an employee from taking a new job with a competing employer for a specified time.

inevitable disclosure doctrine The principle that a former employee cannot work for a competitor without disclosing confidential information.

infancy A defense for those under the legal age of majority.

informal actions Ordinary administrative acts such as granting permits, determining eligibility, or gathering information.

information A document that brings formal criminal charges.

information is property The principle that trade secrets have commercial value and should be treated like property.

information statement A statement distributed to shareholders by management that provides specified information.

informational picketing Picketing designed to inform the employer's customers about a labor dispute.

infringement (1) An outsider's use of the same or similar mark that weakens the value of an owner's mark. (2) Use of a copyright holder's work without permission.

initial public offerings The first offering of a stock for investment by the public.

injury Harm caused to the plaintiff, such as physical injury, property damage, lost profits, or pain and suffering.

inquiry regarding terms A response by an offeree that requests the offeror to send additional information or consider changing the terms; not considered a *rejection*.

inquisitorial The system of criminal justice in most civil law nations, where judges serve as prosecutors and have broad powers of discovery.

inquisitorial process The procedure by which the judge takes an active part in determining the facts of a case.

insanity A defense based on a lack of *criminal intent*.

insider Any employee with access to confidential information and certain outsiders who receive inside information.

insider trading The practice whereby a person's access to confidential and nonpublished information gives an unfair advantage over others in the trading of a firm's securities.

Insider Trading and Securities Fraud Enforcement Act Federal law that governs enforcement of insider trading laws, including bounties to informants, supervision of brokers' employees, and investors' right to sue for damages.

Insider Trading Sanctions Act Federal law that imposes a civil penalty of up to three times an insider's trading profit.

insolvency Inability to pay one's obligations as they come due.

instructions The judge's statements to the jury that summarize the law to be applied to the evidence presented during the trial.

insurable interest The right to insure goods; the buyer has an insurable interest when the goods have been *identified*, and the seller for as long as it has title or a security interest.

intangibles Classification of a nontangible property that has no physical substance, such as contract rights and intellectual property rights such as patents, copyrights, trademarks, trade secrets, and information.

integrate SEC action to combine apparently separate exempt offerings if they are made too close together and the proceeds are used for the same general purpose.

integration Written contract which the parties intended to be their complete agreement.

integrity of the market See *market integrity.*

intellectual property Classification of intangible property rights based on ideas, expression, and inventions.

intellectual property audit Analysis of a firm's intellectual property assets and the enforceability of those rights.

intentional infliction of emotional distress Outrageous acts that cause detectable emotional injury; some physical injury may also be required for recovery of damages.

interbrand competition Competition among different brands of the same type of product.

interest in land Ownership of a right to real property such as full ownership, easement, or mineral rights; one of the situations requiring a written contract under the statute of frauds.

interference with contract relations Intentional tampering with the contract of a person or business, inducing a party to breach the contract.

interlocking directorates The case where one person sits on the boards of directors of two firms that compete or engage in related businesses.

intermediary banks Banks that pass documents such as letters of credit to and from the buyer's Issuing Bank and the seller's Advising or Confirming Bank.

International Bureau FCC bureau responsible for satellite and international matters.

international business law The international, regional, and national laws affecting international business transactions.

international investment Purchasing a significant interest in a foreign firm or starting business operations in a foreign country.

international law Legal principles in the international sphere, derived from national laws, treaties, generally accepted practices, and regional and international organizations.

international organizations Organizations of nations on a global basis, such as the World Trade Organization.

international trade The purchase of goods or services produced in one country by firms or individuals located outside the country of origin.

Internet Tax Freedom Act (ITFA) Federal law that placed a temporary moratorium on new taxes or new application of existing taxes on Internet transactions.

interrogatories Written questions submitted to the opposing party in a lawsuit that must be answered under oath.

intoxication A defense based on a lack of *criminal intent* associated with intoxication, especially if it is involuntary.

intrabrand competition Competition among sellers of the same brands and models.

intranet An in-house electronic communication system.

intrastate commerce Aspects of commerce that pertain within the boundaries of one state.

intrastate exemption Securities transactions between issuers and purchasers located within a single state; they are exempt from registration requirements.

intruder The finder of information, contrasted with the individual about whom the information is collected.

intrusion A tort involving violation of the right to be let alone.

invalidity (1) A defense asserting that a copyright is invalid because of failure to follow technical requirements or because the work's subject matter may not be copyrighted. (2) A defense to infringement that claims the original invention was unpatentable.

invention The process of producing or contriving something previously unknown; also the physical object, device, or finding created.

inventiveness Former requirement for patentability, replaced by *nonobviousness.*

Investment Advisors Act Federal law to license and regulate investment advisors.

investment banking syndicate A firm in the business of underwriting securities.

Investment Company Act Federal law to regulate mutual funds.

investment contracts New forms of securities that are investments of money in a common enterprise from which the investor is led to expect profits derived solely from the promoter's efforts.

investment intent A purchaser's desire to hold securities for longer-term investment purposes.

involuntary petition A petition filed by creditors that forces a debtor into bankruptcy.

IP addresses Unique 12-digit numbers that identify every computer connected to the Internet.

irresistible impulse The principle that one is criminally insane if the crime was committed under the influence of an irresistible impulse.

irrevocable offer An offer with which the offeror makes a binding promise not to withdraw the offer.

Islamic law legal system A legal system based on principles revealed in the Koran.

issue The original making of a negotiable instrument and first delivery to another person.

issuer The firm that issues securities in order to raise funds from the public.

issuing bank In a letter of credit transaction, the buyer's bank that issues a letter of credit payable to the seller.

J

joint inventors Co-inventors who each make a substantial contribution to the invention's novel aspects.

joint venture (1) A partnership between a foreign firm and a firm located in the country where the investment is being made. (2) A form of partnership in which two entities enter into a limited business activity together.

judgment The court's decision that ends trial proceedings.

judgment notwithstanding the verdict (JNOV) The judge's alteration of a jury's verdict upon a finding that the verdict is not based on the evidence or does not follow the instructions on the law.

judgment-proof Uninsured, insolvent, or otherwise unable to pay a judgment.

judicial review A court's power to hold statutes invalid because of conflict with the U.S. Constitution.

jurisdiction The power of a court to hear and decide cases; for example, original jurisdiction at the trial level and appellate jurisdiction in courts that hear appeals.

jurisdictional facts Statements in the plaintiff's complaint that show why the court has jurisdiction over the case.

juvenile court system A separate court system for children under a specific age.

K

know-how The experience and intelligence to make processes work most effectively.

L

labor unions Organizations of workers for the purpose of bargaining with employers and arranging benefits for the membership.

laches A defense that bars a lawsuit started so long after the injury that the rights of other parties would be affected or evidence would be unavailable.

lacking serious literary, artistic, political, or scientific value Part of the test for determining obscenity.

landlines Physical elements of communications systems, such as telephone wires and cables.

Lanham Act The primary federal trademark law, covering registration, qualification, infringement, remedies, and regulation of the Patent and Trademark Office.

law Established, binding standards or guidelines for action or behavior in a society.

law merchant Laws and customs used for centuries that govern the sale and movement of goods.

law of diminishing returns An economic theory that profitability drops after production reaches a point of optimal efficiency.

laws of nature Relationships and processes found in the natural world, such as the law of gravity.

L/C beneficiary Party to a letter of credit transaction for whom the assurance of funds is directed.

leading object See *main purpose*.

lease A contract granting possession and use of property in exchange for payment of rent.

lease agreement Contract that defines the transfer of rights and possession of property.

least cost provider The party that has the lowest cost of performing a service.

legal analysis The study of general legal principles and analysis of how those principles are applied to specific situations.

legal benefit The promise of a contracting party to be obligated to provide some benefit to the other party that was not previously an obligation.

legal detriment The promise of a contracting party to be obligated to some condition that was not previously an obligation.

legal environment of business The laws, legal institutions, and processes that affect business.

legal injury An injury that is recognized by law, whether physical injury, monetary injury or loss of a legal right.

legal strikes Strikes that involve wages, hours, or conditions of labor, discipline or discharge of a employee, employment of nonunion labor, or aid to other unions on strike.

legal system A nation's legal, regulatory, and political institutions and legal processes.

legitimacy of data processing European Union requirement of consent or other specified reasons for data collection.

lessee The party acquiring temporary possession of property under a lease.

lessor The owner of property who grants rights to use the property.

letter of credit (L/C) An instrument containing a promise, if specific documents are submitted, to pay to a named person (such as a seller) or to the bearer money or something of value and to look to the drawer of the document (such as the buyer's bank) for payment.

libel Written dissemination of an untrue statement about another person that injures the person's reputation or character.

Library of Congress The national library of the United States, including the Copyright Office.

license Permission for the licensee to produce or distribute the licensor's product under the licensor's name.

license fee An initial or fixed payment made to purchase the license right or to acquire a franchise that includes license rights.

licensee The firm or person who receives a right to property conferred under contract.

licensing in The *licensee's* receipt of rights such as IP.

licensing out The *licensor's* transfer of rights such as IP.

licensor The owner of property or producer of a service who confers a right to use the property or service under contract.

lien An interest in another's real property that permits the lienholder to receive money when the property is sold.

life, liberty, or property Under the Fifth Amendment, the three elements that the government may not take from a person without due process of law.

likelihood of confusion The primary test for trademark infringement and unfair competition, whether an appreciable number of consumers would be confused about the source of a product.

limited liability company Form of business organization that combines limited liability with taxation only to the individual members.

limited liability partnerships (LLPs) Partnership form that limits malpractice liability for partners who are not directly involved in an incident.

limited partnership A partnership in which some partners are allowed to limit their liability to the amount of their original investment, while general partners have unlimited liability.

line of commerce A firm's geographic and product markets.

linked site The website to which another website provides a hypertext link.

linking Providing a hypertext link from one website to another.

linking site The website that provides a link to another website.

liquidated damages The damages that are agreed upon in a contract to be paid to a party should the other party breach the contract.

literal infringement The case where every element claimed in a patent is also present in the allegedly infringing item.

literary works Expressions using words or numbers, such as books, magazines, or databases.

litigation A dispute resolution process that involves parties presenting evidence to the judge or jury that decides the case.

location referencing Technology that can track location, time, and activities, such as electronic toll systems, wireless phones, global positioning, and traffic video.

lock in To obtain a large base of long-term customers.

long-felt but unmet need The case when an industry has unsuccessfully tried to solve a problem.

look-alike Advertising that uses a model resembling a celebrity.

M

M'Naghten test The principle that one is criminally insane if incapable of distinguishing right from wrong.

machine A mechanism, device, apparatus, or instrument with parts that are organized to cooperate when set in motion to produce predictable results.

Madrid Agreement A treaty that permits a central filing of trademarks after registration in the owner's home country.

Madrid Protocol See *Madrid Agreement.*

magic words of negotiability The words "payable to order or bearer," which must appear on commercial paper to make it negotiable.

mail covers Transactional information on the outside of a mailing envelope or in headers of an e-mail message.

mailbox rule Rule covering acceptances that makes the acceptance effective when the communication is dispatched.

main purpose An exception to the *statute of frauds* requirement of a written memorandum for a guarantee, where the primary purpose of the guarantee is to protect the guarantor's own interests.

maintenance fees Additional fees to be paid after a patent is granted.

maker The party who makes a note promising to pay the *payee* a specified sum in the future.

malice Intentional performance of a wrongful act without just cause or excuse.

malpractice Negligence or other unreasonably poor practice by a professional.

management's discussion and analysis (MD&A) The part of a financial statement in which management interprets and gives meaning to the firm's liquidity, capital resources, and operations.

mandatory collective bargaining subjects Matters directly affecting the employment relationship that union and management must bargain over: wages, hours, and other terms and conditions of employment like pensions, vacations, and seniority.

Manual of Patent Examination Procedure (MPEP) The procedures followed by patent examiners.

manufacture Production from raw or processed materials or from component parts to give new forms and characteristics to the components.

marginal cost A manufacturer's additional expense to produce each extra unit.

mark A trademark.

market concentration The potential for exercise of monopoly power, based on number of firms in the market.

market extension Acquisition of a firm in a new geographic market.

market integrity Confidence that the securities markets are not rigged and that firms can compete for capital on a level playing field..

market share The percentage of the relevant market that a firm controls.

market share liability Principle that allows plaintiffs to recover in product liability cases from all makers of a dangerous type of product when it is impossible to prove which maker produced the product that was used; damages depend on each maker's market share.

mask works The microscopic electronic circuit schematic diagrams found in integrated circuits.

mass customization Mass production of products customized to customer order, promising the quality control and efficiency advantages of mass production but with made-to-order customization; it would reduce inventory costs and shorten production delays; e.g., manufacturing to order in on-line ordering and configuration of personal computers.

mass market Licenses involving routine transactions directed to consumers.

mass market transactions Sales of software to consumers in retail markets.

master Legal term for the principal in a master/servant relationship, often a business firm.

material alteration A significant alteration made on a negotiable instrument by a person other than the maker.

material breach A breach of performance that is so severe that it excuses the other party from its duties under the contract.

material change A substantial change in duties or rights of a party if the other party transfers performance of the contract to another; a material change can make such a transfer unenforceable.

material terms Contract terms that would cause surprise to either party, such as changes in standard warranty terms or credit terms.

materiality The importance and relevance of information under the circumstances of a case.

mathematical formulae Mathematical expressions in the abstract.

McCarran Ferguson Act Federal law that exempts

the insurance industry from antitrust regulation in states that regulate it.

McGuire Act Federal law that extended *resale price maintenance* to retailers that had never made such agreements; now repealed.

mechanical license A license to make an independent recording of a composition already recorded by another group.

mechanical right A compulsory licensing right pertaining to nondramatic phonograph records.

Media Bureau FCC bureau that regulates radio and television stations, cable and satellite TV, and instructional services.

mediation A form of alternative dispute resolution in which a third party, usually professionally trained, helps the parties to resolve their differences.

meeting of the minds Exact agreement by both parties on the terms of a contract.

member states European nations that belong to the European Union.

memorandum A written document or documents that set forth a particular transaction.

mens rea The mental state that makes an act criminal.

mercantile terms Recognized terms such as FOB that designate terms of delivery and passage of title and risk.

mercantilists Medieval European businessmen who developed payment systems based on transfer of the right to receive payment.

merchant A seller or buyer who deals in goods of the kind involved in the contract or who professes to be an expert in the particular trade.

merchantability A warranty that is implied whenever goods are sold by a *merchant,* one who deals in the goods in question.

merger The bringing together of two independent firms, one of which survives and the other dissolves.

merger clause Provision in a contract that states the parties' intention that the writing is an *integration* of their agreement.

merger defense A defense that negates a claim of antitrust violation.

merit rating system A system that reduces workers' compensation premiums for employers who take steps to minimize job risks.

metatags Hidden html codes in Web pages that describe the website's content to search engines.

micropayment Small electronic payments made automatically at low transaction costs.

milk import cases Cases illustrating the proposition that states may not regulate in the area of health and safety beyond what is necessary to achieve their limited purpose.

Miller-Tydings Act Federal law that permitted state statutes to legitimize *resale price maintenance;* now repealed.

Mini-FTC Acts State laws that parallel the Federal Trade Commission Act.

minimum wage The lower limit for wages that can be paid to employees covered by the Fair Labor Standards Act.

Miranda warnings Constitutional rights that police officers must recite to suspects before custodial interrogation; derived from the *Miranda v. Arizona* case.

mirror image The principle that the offered terms and accepted terms must be exactly alike or no contract is formed.

misappropriation (1) Wrongful appropriation of another's tangible property or intangible property, such as intellectual property rights. (2) Wrongful, knowing conduct resulting in theft of trade secrets, and wrongful disclosure of secret information using either improper means or in violation of a confidential relationship.

misappropriation theory The theory that a misappropriation of a firm's confidential information by insiders or outsiders is a breach of a fiduciary duty and constitutes insider trading.

misdemeanors Less serious crimes traditionally punishable by smaller fines and incarceration for a year or less.

misrepresentation A false representation of material facts about a product that leads to injury to a purchaser who justifiably relies on the representation.

mistake A defense based on a genuine mistaken belief in the objective of the defendant's act.

misuse (1) A form of *assumption of risk* based on improper use of a product. (2) Extension of a patent monopoly to things that are not protected by intellectual property law. (3) Unreasonable use of a right.

mockup A false demonstration designed to improve the appearance or effect of an ad.

Model EDI Trading Partner Agreement Standard terms for use in electronic data interchange transactions.

Model Penal Code A codification of criminal laws in a form recommended by legal scholars.
money laundering Transactions designed to disguise the origin and movement of criminal proceeds.
monopolistic competition A market with few sellers offering somewhat substitutable but differentiated products.
monopolization The intentional use of market power to gain an illegal monopoly.
monopoly A market dominated by one large seller.
monopsony A market in which a single buyer possesses monopoly buying power.
moral reasoning The process of moving from premises to conclusions in determining the right course of action.
moral rights The natural rights of an author to prevent changes to the work that would be harmful to the work's artistic integrity, including attribution, disclosure, integrity, and withdrawal.
morality Human behavior that is good and just.
morals clause Provision in an endorsement contract to terminate the agreement if the celebrity's image is tarnished.
more than ancillary rule The principle that service marks cannot be registered for generic services that competitors must also provide.
morphing Digitally changing an image gradually into a different image.
most-favored nation Status that requires signatories to a treaty to treat goods from all member countries on an equal basis; also known as *normal trade relations*.
motion A request to the court for some type of order, which is granted or denied usually after arguments by the parties.
motion picture A series of related images shown by machine and accompanied by sounds.
multidisciplinary practices (MDPs) Accounting firms that also offer services other than accounting.
multimedia Combinations of various types of content, which can include text, audio, graphics, and video.
multiple product order FTC order prohibiting future deceptive advertising in selling any of a firm's products.
musical works Words and tune as fixed in sheet music, sound recordings, and arrangements, but not the sound track of a motion picture.
mutual assent Agreement by both parties on the terms of a contract.
mutual mistake In contract law, a mistake made by both parties to a contract such that there is no real or genuine agreement by them to contract.

N

900-Number Rule FTC rule regulating abuses of pay-per-call services.
National Association of Securities Dealers (NASD) Organization that regulates its stock broker members, settles complaints, and operates the *NASDAQ*.
National Association of Security Dealers Automated Quotation (NASDAQ) A national over-the-counter electronic market for the sale of securities.
national ID cards Identification devices that would use digitized records to verify the holder's identity.
National Labor Relations Act Federal law regulating labor-management relations and collective bargaining.
national laws Legislation passed by a sovereign state and binding on firms that do business there.
national treatment standard The provision that treaty signatories may not discriminate between their own nationals and those of other member nations.
nationalization Government takeover of the ownership and management of a private firm with payment of compensation.
natural monopolies Businesses in which monopoly is more efficient than competition, such as utilities.
naturally occurring Things found in nature, such as life forms.
navigable waters Bodies of water in which boats can be sailed, including wetlands.
necessaries Those items such as shelter and clothing that are essential for living and for which infants (minors) can be held liable despite their lack of contractual capacity.
necessary and proper Constitutional phrase that authorizes Congress to legislate in order to implement enumerated powers.
necessity A defense based on a serious emergency that justifies the criminal act to avert more serious harm.
negative results Knowledge that shows what does not work as desired.
negligence The breach of a legal duty that is the proximate cause of some legal injury.
negligence per se The presumption of negligence when the behavior violates a criminal law.

negotiability The concept that payments can be transferred by the negotiation process for eventual payment.

negotiable instruments Commercial documents, such as checks, that transfer legal rights when negotiated by endorsement.

negotiation A transfer to a *holder* who rightfully possesses an instrument and has good title to it.

netiquette Self-regulated courtesy in the use of the Internet.

network effects Economies of scale derived from standardization and universal acceptance, e.g., facsimile operation standards.

nexus A connection with a state that justifies regulation or taxation by the state.

No Electronic Theft Act Federal law prohibiting willful infringement of copyrighted material online, even if no profit is made.

Noerr-Pennington doctrine Supreme Court decision that the *Sherman Act* does not apply to bona fide political activities of business competitors, based on freedom of speech and right to petition the government.

nolo contendere A *plea* that does not admit guilt but submits to the court's decision.

noncompetes See *covenant not to compete.*

noncompetition clauses See *covenant not to compete.*

nonconforming goods Goods that do not conform to contractual requirements.

nondisclosure agreements (**NDA**) Agreements that require confidentiality and prohibit disclosure of secrets revealed during business presentations or contract performance.

noneconomic damages Damages such as pain and suffering, loss of consortium, emotional distress, embarrassment, and punitive damages.

nonexclusive Rights under a license that may be used by the *licensor* or licensed to additional parties.

nonexclusive agent An agent who acts for more than one principal, if all principals consent to the arrangement.

nonexperience information Personal financial information obtained from sources other than creditors.

nonobviousness The requirement that an invention must not be a minor improvement over prior technology that would be obvious to a hypothetical person of ordinary skill in the art.

nonpatentable subject matter Subjects that cannot be patented, including naturally occurring things, abstract ideas, laws of nature, and mathematical formulae.

nonsigner provisions See *McGuire Act.*

nonstatutory subject matter See *nonpatentable subject matter.*

nontariff barrier Any governmental regulation that discriminates against imports or in favor of exports.

normal trade relations The requirement that treaty signatories treat the goods of all member countries on an equal basis; also known as *most-favored nation status.*

normative principles Ethical principles and religious precepts that suggest ideal goals for conduct.

no-strike clauses Provisions in labor contracts that obligate the union not to strike or cause work stoppage during the life of the contract.

note A two-party instrument in which the *maker* promises to pay the *payee* a specified amount in the future.

notice Notification that data capture activities may affect an individual.

notice and takedown Provisions of the *Digital Millennium Copyright Act* that require an Internet service provider to remove or block access to materials that infringe on copyrights.

notice of allowance The approval document for an intent-to-use trademark application.

novation The discharge of a contract between two parties because a third party contracts to perform the duty required under the first contract.

novelty A unique quality of newness that may be required for a trade secret.

nuisance A substantial and unreasonable interference with the use and enjoyment of a person's interest in property.

O

object code Software in machine-readable form.

objection rights European Union rights to prevent one's personal data from being used in direct marketing.

objective factors *Secondary considerations* concerning whether an invention was nonobvious, including a long-felt but unmet need, commercial success, and use or copying by others.

obligee The beneficiary who is designated to receive the performance on a contract; also called *third-party beneficiary.*

obligor The party who must make the performance on a contract.

occupational diseases Illnesses caused by a person's occupational environment.

Occupational Safety and Health Act (OSHA) Federal law designed to improve workplace safety and health by promulgating regulations and setting safety standards.

offer A proposal to contract that contains all of the necessary contract terms.

offering circular Information given to potential investors about a small issue of securities.

offering statement The registration documentation for small issues that includes unaudited financial statements and a description of the issuer and the securities offered.

Office of Engineering and Technology FCC office that allocates radio spectrum for nongovernmental use and provides expert advice.

Office of Internet Enforcement Division of the SEC that oversees securities offerings, trading, and fraudulent scams on the Internet.

officer The president, vice president in charge of a business function, or other officer of a firm who is required to report personal trades of the firm's stock under insider trading rules.

officers A group hired by the *board of directors* of a corporation to oversee day-to-day operations of the business.

oligopoly A market with a small number of firms protected by high barriers to entry.

oligopsony A market in which a few buyers have buying power.

omission (1) Failure to provide some information that would clarify the truth of a matter. (2) The rule that an item that is missing one element of a patented invention is not an infringement.

omnibus An approach to enacting privacy laws in a comprehensive and uniform way.

Omnibus Crime Control and Safe Streets Act A wide-ranging federal law on aspects of criminal justice, including prohibitions on wiretapping except under a warrant or in cases of national security or permissible employee monitoring.

on-sale bar The Patent Act's bar of patentability for inventions sold, demonstrated, or described in literature more than one year before application for a patent.

open account Payment system that allows a buyer to make payment during future time periods.

open terms Terms in a contract that may be left for future determination or inferred from circumstances.

opening statement A party's overview of the case to be presented.

operating agreement An agreement among the members of a *limited liability company* that covers the firm's methods of making decisions, allocating profits, and dealing with transfer of membership.

opposition An outsider's challenge to the renewal of a trademark.

opt-in A form of consent that requires a clear and affirmative act to permit data collection.

option contract A contractual commitment in which the offeree pays the offeror to give up the right to revoke the offer.

opt-out A form of consent that requires a clear and affirmative act to prevent data collection.

order A direction to some agent to make payment.

order paper Commercial paper that is negotiable only by the person stated as payee or with that person's endorsement.

ordinances The laws and regulations of municipal bodies.

ordinary, reasonable person The hypothetical person whose actions are the standard used to judge the actions of a person accused of a crime or a tort.

organized crime Criminal activity operated by a centrally controlled, formal structure.

original Created independently by an author and not copied from another source.

outputs The amount of goods that a seller actually produces.

outsourcing Contracting out work that was formerly done by union members.

overtime pay Payment of one and one-half times the regular rate of pay for hours worked beyond the standard 40-hour workweek.

P

package franchise A franchise in which the franchisee must use a uniform business format specified by the franchisor and identified by the trademark.

package licensing A tying arrangement that requires purchase of both desirable and less desirable patented items.

pantomimes Performances that tell a story by

means of bodily movements and facial expressions.

paparazzi Freelance photographers who pursue celebrities in the attempt to obtain candid photos

parens patriae A state's role as guardian of the welfare of its citizens.

parental refusal rights The continuing right of parents to refuse collection of personal information about their children online.

Pareto optimality The case when an action causes society as a whole to be better off while no one is made worse off.

Paris Convention Treaty that requires signatories to grant foreign patents the same status as domestic patents.

parol evidence rule Rule of evidence that applies when a written contract is intended to be the complete agreement between the parties; if so, oral promises cannot be enforced.

part payment An exception to the UCC statute of frauds on the sale of goods, where the buyer has made part of the payment or accepted partial delivery.

part performance An exception to the *statute of frauds* requirement of a written land contract, applied when the buyer has paid part or all of the purchase price and has either taken possession or made valuable improvements.

partial delivery An exception to the UCC statute of frauds on the sale of goods, where the buyer has accepted partial delivery.

partial taking Government action that deprives the owner of some but not all rights in property, such as by zoning restrictions; the owner may be entitled to partial compensation.

partially disclosed A principal is partially disclosed if a third party knows there is a principal-agent relationship but does not know the identity of the principal.

partially inexhaustible A quality of intangible property; the rightful owner retains some value in the original property when copies are transferred or stolen.

parties to a communication The sender and recipient of an electronic message.

partnership Form of business organization in which two or more people carry on a business for profit and share the rights and responsibilities of the business.

patent A limited monopoly granted by government to the first creator of a useful, novel, and nonobvious invention.

Patent Application Information Retrieval (PAIR) A feature of the Patent and Trademark Office for checking the status of patent applications electronically.

Patent Cooperation Treaty Treaty that creates procedural advantages for patent applications made in signatory nations.

Patent Law Treaty Treaty that attempted to harmonize patent law in member nations.

patent prosecution Review of a patent application by an expert examiner and negotiation between examiner and inventor over the scope of the patent.

patentability The right to receive a patent if the invention has patentable subject matter, novelty, nonobviousness, and utility.

patently offensive Part of the test for determining obscenity; a description of hard core depiction of sexual conduct.

payee The party to be paid by the *maker* of a *note*.

payment order Order to a financial institution to make a payment from a customer's account.

pension vesting The point at which an employee's interest in a private pension becomes irrevocable after five years of employment.

per se rule A strict interpretation of the Sherman Act that prohibits certain specified acts whenever they are proved.

peremptory challenge Discretionary challenge that a party can use to remove a prospective juror without citing a cause.

perfect competition An economy with a large number of buyers and sellers; no individual firm or consumer has sufficient market power to influence prices or the quantity of production.

perfect price discrimination Pricing goods according to each individual's ability and desire to pay.

perfect tender rule Rule of contract law requiring exact performance as promised, relaxed in many commercial contexts but still used in letter of credit practice as the strict compliance rule.

perfection When a security interest is made valid as against other creditors of a debtor.

performance Presenting a work to the public by reciting, playing, dancing, or acting.

performance analysis Examination of how well a market actually performs, focusing on economic efficiency.

performing rights associations Clearinghouse

organizations that administer permissions, licensing, and collection and distribution of royalties.

permanent injunction A court order prohibiting some action on a permanent basis.

permanent partial disability A disability that prevents an employee from performing certain activities for the rest of his or her working life.

permanent total disability A disability that prevents an employee from ever working again.

permissive subjects Matters that indirectly affect the employment relationship that union and management may bargain over voluntarily, such as general business practices.

personal data The term used in the European Union for *personally identifiable information.*

personal defenses Source of the special status of a holder in due course when the original contracting party could assert the contract defenses of breach of contract, fraud in the inducement (intentional misrepresentation), misrepresentation, mistake, failure of consideration, failure of a condition precedent, or impossibility.

personally identifiable information (PII) Information that can be connected with an individual.

persons of ordinary skill Hypothetical professional specialists in a technology who can be expected to know the *prior art* concerning their field.

Petroleum Marketing Products Act Federal law that gives gas station operators an opportunity to purchase the premises when the franchisor refuses to renew the lease.

petty patent Sui generis intellectual property right in some other nations (Germany), providing shorter and weaker protection than utility patents and requiring a less rigorous qualification process.

phantom freight Equal freight charges without regard to actual distance or transportation charges.

phone rule An FCC rule that prohibits recording a phone call for broadcast without first notifying the caller of the recording.

phonorecord A recorded rendering of a work, including most recordings of sound, video, or software in various media.

picketing A gathering of people who intend to inform or disrupt others.

pictorial, graphic, and sculptural works Two- and three-dimensional works of fine, graphic, or applied art.

plain English Understandable language and format designed for a lay audience.

plaintiff The party that brings a lawsuit.

Plant Patent Act Federal law extending patents to distinct, new, asexually reproduced plant varieties.

Plant Variety Protection Act Federal law extending patents to sexually reproduced plant varieties created by cross-pollination.

plea The defendant's answer to the prosecution's allegations in a criminal case.

plea bargain agreement The written outcome of *plea bargaining.*

plea bargaining Negotiation between prosecution and defense in a criminal case that usually ends with a plea of guilty to a lesser charge.

pledge A security interest whereby the creditor or secured party takes possession of the collateral owned by the debtor.

police power The power of a state to protect its citizens' health, safety, welfare, and morals.

political action Activity designed to bring about legislative or electoral objectives.

positive externalities Beneficial effects of economic activity that spill over to other parts of the community.

positive feedback A consumption-side economy of scale produced by the *network effects* of information products.

possession theory The theory that mere possession of inside information is enough to prohibit trading, whether or not the information was used in the trading decision.

posteffective period The period following the effective date of a registration statement and until all securities have been sold.

potential entrant A potential new competitor in a market.

power of attorney A document that authorizes an agent to act for the principal.

prayer or request for relief Statement in the plaintiff's complaint that sets forth what remedy the court should impose.

preconditioning Public statements about a forthcoming security issue before the filing of the registration statement.

predatory pricing Setting prices below the producer's marginal cost in order to force competitors out of business.

predicate offenses Illegal activities prohibited by *RICO,* such as securities fraud, extortion, drug dealing, mail and wire fraud, and murder.

preemption Congressional legislation that replaces differing state laws.

preexisting legal duty Term for an obligation that cannot be used as consideration for a contract if the promise is merely for something that is already an obligation.

prefiling period The period before the filing of a *registration statement* during which a prospectus is written and underwriting is negotiated.

preliminary hearing Pretrial hearing in which the prosecution must demonstrate the existence of *probable cause* that the evidence connects the defendant to the crime.

preliminary injunction A court order prohibiting a party from carrying out some action until a trial can determine the rights of the parties.

preponderance of the evidence The standard of proof necessary in a civil case; more likely than not.

prescriptive Laws that require minimal levels of conduct.

presentment A demand for acceptance or payment of a negotiable document made upon the maker, drawee or other payor by or on behalf of the holder of the document.

pretrial conference A meeting held by the judge and attorneys before trial in which they seek to narrow the issues in dispute and move the controversy toward either settlement or trial.

price discrimination Charging different prices to different buyers for goods of like grade and quality.

price erosion Lower profits than an inventor might have received in the absence of infringement.

price-fixing Agreements to set minimum prices or maximum resale prices.

prima facie case A case that on first impression shows the basic elements needed to prove a claim.

primary liability The liability to make a payment on a negotiable instrument of makers and drawers as well as for drawees after an instrument is accepted.

primary meaning A mark's direct description of the product it identifies.

primary picketing The picketing of an employer by its employees.

primary-line injuries Price discrimination that tends to injure competitors of the discriminating seller.

principal The firm or person who is represented by an agent.

principal register The registration list of the Patent and Trademark Office that gives strong notice of a mark's ownership and confers advantages with regard to infringement suits, international registration, and final incontestability after five years.

principal-agent relationship A relationship in which the principal authorizes the agent to carry out activities on the principal's behalf and each has duties to the other.

prior art The accumulated specialized knowledge about the status of technology.

prior restraint Prohibition of speech or publication before the fact.

prior substantiation Evidence cited in ads that is gathered before the ad is run.

prior user See *first inventor's defense.*

privacy The ability to prevent disclosure of one's personal information.

Privacy Act of 1974 Federal legislation concerning privacy rights.

privacy fundamentalists People who value privacy highly and seek strong protection of privacy rights.

privacy pragmatists People who balance personal privacy with societal needs for information and support privacy regulation only when industry self-regulation fails.

privacy unconcerned People who are unconcerned with disclosing personal information and are unlikely to support strong privacy regulation.

private facts Information about an individual that is highly embarrassing and not of legitimate interest to the public.

private franchises Grants of the privilege to conduct business defined in a franchise agreement.

private law Law that concerns the relationships among individuals and firms within a society, including contracts, torts, and business organization.

private license A special privilege that is defined and conferred by contract on a firm or person, called the *licensee,* by the owner, called the *licensor.*

private sector Activities controlled by individuals or businesses.

Private Securities Litigation Reform Act of 1995 (PSLRA) Federal law that regulates shareholder class action suits.

privately held Ownership of a firm by a few shareholders, with shares not traded on a national securities exchange.

privileges and immunities clause Constitutional provision that requires states not to discriminate against citizens of other states except in certain permissible ways.

probable cause The legal standard for issuance of a search warrant, requiring that relevant evidence is likely to be found at the place to be searched.

procedural due process The form of due process concerned with fair investigation, arrest, detention, trial, and appeal.

procedural laws Laws that detail the means by which substantive rights or duties will be enforced.

process A process, art, or method, including a new use of a known process, machine, manufacture, composition of matter, or material.

Process Patent Amendments of 1988 Federal law that declared it to be infringement to import goods produced using patented processes without authorization.

processing Operations performed on personal data by either automated or manual means.

product extension Acquisition of a complementary product line that can be used with existing products.

product franchise A franchise in which the franchisee distributes goods bearing the franchisor's trademark and produced by the franchisor or under the franchisor's control.

product market Products that consumers perceive as reasonably interchangeable for the same basic purpose.

product misuse A defense alleging that the plaintiff used the product in a way for which it was not designed.

production and inspection of records and documents Giving a party access to records, notes, and other documents in the possession of the opposing party as required by court rules.

production of documents A request to examine documents in the possession of the opposing party as part of *discovery.*

professional sports Athletic organizations operated for profit.

professions Vocations that require specialized knowledge and long preparation, such as law or medicine.

profiling Description of a Web user's interests based on analysis of browsing patterns.

prohibited powers Powers that may not be exercised by government, such as establishment of religion.

prohibition (1) The policy that made it illegal to manufacture or sell liquor in the United States, imposed by the Eighteenth Amendment and repealed by the Twenty-First. (2) The total restriction on import of a product.

promise A commitment; for example, a commitment to pay.

promissory estoppel The principle that a promise will be enforced, even without consideration, if the promise could induce action or forbearance by the promisee and enforcement would avoid injustice.

property crimes Offenses that cause destruction or deprive owners of their property.

proportionate liability A system that limits the liability of each defendant to the percentage of its fault for the injury.

proprietary standards Standards developed by a single firm or consortium.

proscriptive Laws that forbid certain actions that society views as unacceptable.

prosecutor The person who represents society as the plaintiff in a criminal case; also called district attorney.

prospectus Any communication to investors that offers any security for sale.

protected classes Groups that have historically been subject to discrimination (on the basis of race, color, religion, national origin, or sex) and are protected by the Civil Rights Act of 1964.

protected health information (PHI) Health care personal information as defined by the *Health Insurance Portability and Accountability Act.*

protective orders Court orders to preserve secrecy, for example of information that must be revealed during litigation.

protest Notarized certificate of dishonor refusing payment, as used in international banking.

provisional application An abbreviated preliminary application filed up to a year before the full patent application.

proximate cause The standard used in negligence cases that establishes a reasonable causal relationship between the defendant's behavior and the plaintiff's injury; reasonable foreseeability between action and injury.

proxy (1) The power of attorney that shareholders give another to vote their shares. (2) A written or electronic absentee ballot. (3) The agent who actually casts a shareholder's proxy vote.

proxy contests Disputes between groups that solicit

shareholders' proxies for differing points of view.

proxy solicitations Campaigns to convince shareholders to vote for particular proposals or director candidates.

proxy statement A statement containing certain information filed by any person soliciting proxies.

prurient interest Part of the test for determining obscenity; defined as a tendency to excite lustful thoughts.

public at large The populace as a whole.

public domain The public's freedom to use creative work that is not protected by copyright.

public firms See *publicly traded.*

public goods Advantages to the public that are usually underproduced by competitive forces, so that government provides them; for example, parks.

public interest Factors required for obtaining a broadcast license, including political balance, avoiding indecency, balanced programming, and avoiding excessive commercialization.

public law Law that concerns the relationships between people and their government.

public order crimes Acts that violate society's mores or threaten order, such as sale of drugs, gambling, hate crimes, bribery, counterfeiting, and terrorism.

public performance Presenting a work in public places, where there are a substantial number of persons outside a normal circle of friends or family.

public performance licenses Licenses for broadcasting a sound recording via radio, TV, or Internet, or for performing a composition in public.

public records Records collected for the public's benefit, such as vital records and land transfer records.

public sector Activities controlled by the public equally through governmental entities.

Public Utility Holding Company Act Federal law to regulate natural gas and electric utilities.

publicly traded Ownership of a firm by numerous shareholders, with securities traded on national exchanges.

puffing Generalized statements of value about a product that are too vague to be warranty promises.

punitive damages Damages awarded in cases such as product liability, medical malpractice, and negligence that go beyond the amount needed to compensate the plaintiff for losses suffered; they are intended to punish the wrongdoer and to deter similar acts.

purchase money security interest (PMSI) A security interest when a seller lends the buyer the money to buy the seller'' goods or property.

purchase of assets The transfer of an acquired firm's assets to the acquiring firm, neither firm being dissolved.

Q

qualification (1) The process of confirming that a proposed trademark is not already in use. (2) The process of testing an invention for patentability.

qualified endorsement An endorsement that limits the endorser's liability if the instrument is not paid by the drawee, made by writing "without recourse" on the endorsement.

qualified institutional buyer (QIB) A sophisticated institutional investor as defined under SEC *Rule 144A.*

qualified privilege Immunity from charges of defamation for certain kinds of statements made without *malice* by one who has a duty to make a statement and communicates only with those who have an immediate interest.

qualitative A rule for determining how much of a work may be used under the fair use doctrine based on the creative essence of the work.

quality circles Worker groups dedicated to reaching a consensus about increasing quality and eliminating production problems.

quantitative A rule for determining how much of a work may be used under the fair use doctrine based on an absolute or percentage amount.

quantitative substantiality The presumption that *exclusive dealing* adversely affects competition when it covers a substantial dollar volume.

quasi-strict scrutiny A standard in equal protection analysis midway between *rational basis* and *strict scrutiny.* It applies to classifications that are only partly suspect, such as gender or legitimacy, and to rights that are considered important but not fundamental.

quid pro quo harassment Conditioning employment benefits on submission to sexual advances.

quota A limit on the quantity of a product that may be imported.

R

radio spectrum The range of available radio frequencies, which is considered a scarce public resource.

ratification The act of accepting and giving legal effect to an unauthorized act.

ratification vote An election in which employees accept or reject a contract agreed to by their union negotiators.

rational basis The ordinary standard by which a court will judge the connection between a state classification scheme and a permissible government purpose in deciding whether it is constitutional under the equal protection clause. See also *strict scrutiny.*

readily ascertainable Obtainable published information that is not considered a trade secret.

real defenses Limitation on the special status of a holder in due course when the original contracting party could assert the contract defenses of incapacity (incompetence, infancy), fraud in the execution (tricked into signing the wrong instrument such as a note rather than an autograph as pretended), instrument discharged in bankruptcy, forgery, material alteration, and illegality.

reasonable accommodation Reasonable changes in a job or workplace that an employer can make without undue hardship to help a handicapped person perform the job.

reasonable expectation of privacy A situation in which society recognizes that an expectation of privacy is reasonable.

reasonable justification A test of whether a battery is wrongful under tort law or a reasonable use of force in self-defense.

reasonable person See *ordinary, reasonable person.*

reasonable royalty A projection of royalties a patent holder might have received if an infringer had negotiated a license.

recall To order the return of all products in the supply chain.

receiver bound An exception to the UCC statute of frauds on the sale of goods, where a written confirmation of an oral agreement is not objected to within 10 days.

recidivism The likelihood that the defendant will commit further crimes.

record Information inscribed on a tangible medium or stored in a retrievable format.

records Documents in either paper or electronic form.

red herring prospectus A preliminary prospectus that disclaims any formal offer.

redlining Refusal to approve mortgages in neighborhoods with particular demographic characteristics.

reduction to practice The physical construction of a model of an invention.

refusal to deal Manufacturers' refusal to deal with retailers who fail to charge minimum prices for their products.

regional organizations Organizations of nations in a certain geographical region, such as the European Union.

register of copyrights The chief administrative officer of the Copyright Office.

registration certificate The approval document for a trademark in actual use.

registration statement A statement filed with the SEC by issuers of securities.

Regulation A The SEC regulation governing small issues that do not require a complete registration statement.

Regulation D The SEC regulation governing private placement of securities.

Regulation E Federal Reserve Board regulation promulgated under the Electronic Funds Transfer Act governing the use of debit services.

Regulation S SEC regulation governing the registration of initial public offerings by foreign issuers.

Regulation Z Regulations issued by the Federal Reserve Board to interpret the Federal Truth-in-Lending Act.

regulatory licensing statutes Licensing regulations that are intended to regulate conduct as well as raise revenue.

reinstatement Taking an employee back into the same position.

rejection The offeree's refusal of an offer.

relevant market All the producers of products or services that are functionally interchangeable and reasonably available to the same pool of consumers.

remand The appellate court's action when it returns a case to the lower court for further action.

remittitur The determination of an appellate court to reverse the judgment being appealed.

rent-a-judge or private trial method A form of alternative dispute resolution in which the parties hire a retired judge or a lawyer to hear the case and make a decision; the result is usually not legally binding.

reorganization A bankruptcy process by which a firm's assets are not liquidated but are allowed to continue to be used to continue the business usually in a more limited manner.

replevin A common law action by which the owner recovers the possession of goods.

reply The plaintiff's response to new facts raised in the defendant's answer.

representation elections Elections held to select a particular union as the bargaining representative of a group of employees.

reproduce To make copies of a work.

republishers Intermediaries, such as a phone company, bookstore, or Internet service provider, that transmit the communications of others.

request for proposals A document that defines products and services required and invites concrete proposals from independent suppliers.

requirements The amount of goods that a buyer actually needs.

res ipsa loquitur A rule of evidence that allows negligence to be inferred from the circumstances surrounding the injury; Latin for "the thing speaks for itself."

res judicata The principle that a final judgment of a court with jurisdiction of a case is binding on all parties and bars further legal action on the same claim.

resale price maintenance Requiring retailers to charge consumers a specified retail price, usually a minimum price but sometimes a maximum price.

resale restrictions SEC restrictions on the ability of investors to immediately resell securities.

reserved powers Powers retained by the states with regard to health, safety, welfare, and morals.

residuals *Royalties* paid in the entertainment industry.

Resource Conservation and Recovery Act Federal law that creates a system for tracking and disposing of hazardous waste and licensing disposal facilities.

respect for others' rights Taking steps to avoid infringing the rights of others.

respondeat superior The rule that a principal is liable for the agent's torts committed within the scope of the agent's authority, even though the principal is not at fault; Latin for "let the superior respond."

Restatement (Second) of Contracts A compilation of the common law of contracts by legal scholars.

restrictive covenants See *covenant not to compete.*

restrictive endorsement The signature of the payee that adds some condition, such as "for deposit only," to the negotiability of the instrument.

retroactive seniority Setting seniority at the level it would have been if discrimination had not occurred.

revenue raising A statute that is primarily intended to raise revenue rather than regulate conduct.

reverse The appellate court's action when it disagrees with the decision of the lower court.

reverse auction A method by which buyers post their needs to an electronic marketplace.

reverse discrimination Preference given to members of a class that has historically experienced discrimination.

reverse engineering Analyzing a product to determine how it works and how it was made.

reverse passing off The case when a trademark infringer removes marks from products made by a mark owner and then sells them as its own.

revocation A communication from a person who has made an offer to contract that cancels and rescinds the offer.

RICO Part of the Organized Crime Control Act of 1970 that prohibits racketeer-influenced and corrupt organizations; it has both criminal and civil provisions.

right of attribution The right to be accurately identified as the author of a work and to prevent false claims by another.

right of disclosure The right of control over when, how, and where a work is publicly displayed or performed.

right of integrity The right to prevent physical mutilation, distortion, modification, or any other changes to works that authors believe would injure their reputations.

right of publicity A right not to have one's name or likeness used to advertise another's business without consent.

right of way The right to pass over the property of another, such as in constructing utilities and communications networks.

right of withdrawal The right to alter a work and to prevent others from making reproductions.

right to learn The right to observe, record, and remember information from direct experience.

rights to receive payment Rights to receive obligated payments under a contract that may be transferred to another.

right-to-work laws State laws that make a *union shop* illegal.
risk-benefit analysis Measuring the cost against the benefit to be gained by a certain course of action.
roadshows Live presentations by securities issuers to potential investors.
Robinson-Patman Act Federal law barring price discrimination.
rogue brokers Securities brokers who have been the subject of complaints.
routine governmental actions Ordinary acts for which some foreign officials expect a gratuity.
roving wiretaps Electronic surveillance aimed at any phone used by a suspect, all included in a single warrant.
royalty Consideration paid for licensed use of a patent, copyright, or trademark, or for mineral rights.
royalty base Quantity used to measure the *licensee's* production of goods under a license agreement.
rule An agency statement of general or particular applicability and future effect designed to implement, interpret, or prescribe law or policy.
Rule 144A SEC rule permitting nearly unlimited resale of certain privately placed foreign securities.
rule of reason A flexible standard by which a court may decide whether agreements unreasonably restrain trade.
rule-making The process of making the *rules* of an administrative agency.
rules of evidence Rules adopted to assure that information presented during a trial is relevant to the case, unbiased, and reliable.
running royalties Set annual fees paid under a license, generally not variable by units or dollar volume.

S

safe harbors Guidelines for conduct which, if followed, mean that one will not be prosecuted.
sale on approval Sale that is complete when the buyer has tested the goods and accepted them.
sale or return Sale in which the buyer has the right to return the goods and restore title to the seller.
sales Contracts of sale or transfers of any interest in a security.
sales draft A commercial *draft* used to pay for goods; also known as *trade acceptance*.
Schedule 13D A notice of a potential takeover offer.
Schedule 14D-1 A statement filed by the offeror when a *tender offer* begins.
Schedule 14D-9 A notice to shareholders of a takeover target that gives management's opinion on the offer.
scheduled benefits Specific benefits paid for the loss of certain bodily functions.
scienter Knowledge of a fact, such as an insider's knowledge of confidential information.
scope of employment The limits of the duties an employee is hired to perform, including acts done for the employer's benefit and foreseeable by the employer.
scour the prior art To make a very thorough examination of prior art in order to show a patent was issued invalidly.
screen scraping The practice of a *data aggregator* that accesses a firm's website to obtain information from a customer's account, with permission from the customer; for example, obtaining customer account information to facilitate automated bill payment.
scrivener The author of the language of a contract.
seal program Verification by an independent third party of a firm's compliance with established business standards.
sealed bids An auction method in which the identities of the bidders and the bids are kept confidential.
sealed container doctrine A defense to product liability for the retailer, who has no duty to discover concealed or latent defects.
sealed records Court records that are made unavailable to the public by court order.
SEC Regulation SK SEC regulation that governs nonfinancial and explanatory disclosures.
SEC Regulation SX SEC regulation that defines the format and content of financial statements.
SEC Rule 10b-5 SEC rule that prohibits insider trading, misleading or fraudulent financial disclosures, and manipulation of the securities markets.
SEC Rule 10b5-1 SEC rule that presumes liability if an insider is aware of inside information while trading, unless the trade is done mechanically
SEC Rule 10b5-2 SEC rule that creates insider trading liability for trades following a tip from a trusted source or a family member.
SEC Rule 144 The SEC rule that initial purchasers may resell exempt securities only if they originally had *investment intent*.

SEC's Rule 147 The SEC rule governing eligibility for *intrastate exemption.*

secondary boycott Pressure intended to stop customers or suppliers from entering or purchasing goods from or dealing with a targeted firm.

secondary considerations Additional factors that tend to show an invention was not obvious at the time it was invented.

secondary liability Liability of endorsers on negotiable instruments, typically conditioned on certain events or rights.

secondary meaning An association in the mind of the public between a mark and the mark owner as the only source of the product.

secondary picketing Picketing at a business site other than the site of the employer with which the picketers have a dispute.

secondary trading markets Securities markets such as stock markets, options exchanges, and bond markets.

secondary transmissions The transmission by cable and satellite television companies of the works of other broadcasters.

secondary use Use of information by a party that has obtained it by sale, sharing, or barter.

secondary-line injuries Price discrimination between two reselling buyers that are competing for the same customers.

second-degree felony A crime punishable by imprisonment up to 10 years.

Section 101 Section of the Patent Act that requires a patentable invention to have utility.

Section 102(a) Section of the Patent Act that bars patentability if an invention was publicly known or used in the United States or described in any source.

Section 102(b) Section of the Patent Act that allows patent application within one year of creating an invention, publishing descriptions, or selling the item.

Section 102(g) Section of the Patent Act that grants patentability to the inventor who first invented the item.

Section 103(a) Section of the Patent Act that requires a patentable invention to be nonobvious.

sectoral approach Enacting privacy laws narrowly drawn with reference to particular industries.

secured creditors A person who has a security interest in specific property of a debtor.

secured party Party in a credit transaction with rights to foreclose or otherwise convert collateral into satisfaction of the amount owed.

Securities Act of 1933 Federal law that requires disclosure of financial information by firms that issue new securities to the public and to a lesser extent for private offerings.

Securities Exchange Act of 1934 Federal law that created the Securities Exchange Commission to regulate stock exchanges and bond markets, prohibits securities fraud and insider trading, and requires continuing disclosure of corporate financial information.

Securities Investor Protection Act Federal law to protect investors' securities and accounts from broker negligence or bankruptcy.

Securities Litigation Uniform Standards Act of 1998 Federal law that limits the ability of shareholders to bring class action suits against nationally traded firms in state courts.

security (1) A contract right requiring one party to make payments or future performances to another party, such as a stock share or bond. (2) The principle that operators of databases must take reasonable steps to assure the accuracy of information and its safety from unauthorized access, destruction, misuse, or unauthorized disclosure.

security agreement An agreement that creates or provides for a security interest.

security interests An interest in personal property or fixtures that is used as collateral to secure payment or the performance of an obligation.

self-defense The justifiable use of force to repel a physical attack or in defense of one's home or family, using only as much force as is needed to repel the attack.

self-regulation Methods of setting standards, licensing, and settling disputes with regard to an organization's own operations.

self-regulatory organizations (SROs) Organizations such as the National Association of Securities Dealers and the American Institute of Certified Public Accountants that regulate their own activities under the supervision of the Securities Exchange Commission.

sentencing The process by which the judge or jury decides on the punishment to be given the convicted defendant.

separation of powers The division of governmental powers between legislative, executive, and judicial branches.

serial copy management systems (SCMS) Copy protection technology that prevents making copies of copies with a digital audio recording device.

servant Legal term for the employee or agent who acts for the master or principal in a master/servant relationship.

service of summons Notice delivered to the defendant that a lawsuit has been filed against him or her, assuring the opportunity to offer a defense.

services Activities in which the predominant value is derived from a customized application of human labor, expertise, or information.

Seventh Amendment Guarantee of the right to jury trial in civil suits.

severability rule The principle that the functional aspects of a work, as contrasted with its artistic aspects, are in the public domain.

sexual harassment Creation of a hostile work environment because of sexual intimidation or ridicule, or because of unwelcome sexual advances.

sham exception Activities that are not within the spirit of the *Noerr-Pennington doctrine.*

shareholders The owners of a corporation, who usually are not personally liable for the debts of the corporation.

shelf registration Registered securities that an issuer holds in reserve until it needs to sell them.

shelter rule Special status of holder in due course inherited by later transferees if they take the instrument in good faith.

Sherman Act The major federal law that prohibits anticompetitive devices in restraint of trade.

shop right doctrine An employer's nonexclusive right to use an innovation without paying royalties to the employee who developed it.

shopping bots Software that can search the sites of on-line sellers and return comparative reports on items that satisfy the customer's specifications.

short tender A shareholder's offer to sell borrowed shares in a tender offer.

short-swing profits Insider trading profits made by specified insiders.

shrink-wrap agreement A standardized license agreement enclosed with a piece of software and visible through the plastic wrapping; acceptance of the license terms is inferred from opening the package.

sight draft A *draft* that is payable on sight, immediately upon presentation and demand for payment.

signature The name of the maker of a note or drawer of a draft, written on the instrument in any manner.

site license A license negotiated with a large purchaser of software, such as a corporation, that includes many users.

Sixth Amendment Guarantee of speedy trial, impartial jury, right to confront witnesses, subpoena power, and right to counsel.

slander Oral dissemination of an untrue statement about another person that injures the person's reputation or character.

SLAPP suit Litigation against individuals and interest groups that criticize firms; the acronym stands for strategic litigation against public participation.

Social Security A compulsory system that provides retirement benefits to workers, disability benefits to some workers, and some benefits to the worker's spouse and children.

sole proprietor The owner of a *sole proprietorship.*

sole proprietorship Form of business organization that has a single owner who is personally liable for the debts of the business.

Solid Waste Disposal Act Federal law designed to help states and municipalities cope with problems in disposing of waste.

Sonny Bono Copyright Term Extension Act Federal law that extends the term of some existing copyrights.

sound recording An aural representation of a musical composition.

Sound Recording Act Federal law governing the copyright of sound recordings.

sound recordings The performance of a musical, literary, or dramatic work fixed as a series of musical, spoken, or other sounds on any medium.

sound-alike Use of an impersonation of a celebrity's voice.

source code Software in the form written by programmers.

source code escrow Protection of trade secrets in software through an independent third party, allowing the licensee to decompile or customize when necessary.

sovereign immunity The principle that a sovereign nation cannot be sued.

spam Mass distribution of direct marketing solicitations by means of e-mail.

special circumstances Factors that give a person

with inside information the status of a trustee with regard to other shareholders.

special endorsement The signature of the payee that restricts further negotiation to a person named in the special endorsement.

specially commissioned works Specific creations of independent contractors that are considered *works made for hire*.

specially manufactured goods An exception to the UCC statute of frauds on the sale of goods, where the goods are unsuitable for sale in the seller's ordinary course of business.

specific duty The employer's duty under OSHA to comply with agency regulations affecting particular workplace safety and health conditions.

specific intent The desire to cause a specified result, which may be inferred from conduct

specific performance Performance of the terms of a contract rather than paying damages for nonperformance.

specification The claims that describe an invention and detail the construction and use of it.

spectrum of distinctiveness A range that categorizes how specifically a trademark describes its product.

SSN Abbreviation of Social Security number.

stalking Pursuing another person by tracking in a stealthy manner, usually involving harassment.

standard technical protection measures The technology designed to prevent access to or copying of copyrighted material.

standards (1) Agreed-upon specifications for the production or operation of functionally compatible goods. (2) The activities that specify the concerns to be addressed by an agency.

standby L/Cs Letters of credit used to guarantee the payment in the event that the primary obligor does not pay. They are often used in construction contracts to ensure that contractors are paid by the owner.

stare decisis The doctrine that a court's decision creates precedent for future cases involving similar facts.

state action (1) Involvement of government in an action, necessary to bring the matter under the constitutional guarantees of due process, which do not apply to private action. (2) Valid state governmental acts such as licensing and regulation.

state open records laws State laws that require disclosure of government records upon request.

Statute of Anne The first legislation of the British Parliament dealing with copyright.

statute of frauds Requirement that a valid contract in one of several classes must be written and signed by the party to be charged.

statute of limitations Legal limitation that bars a lawsuit started more than a specified period of time after the injury occurred.

statutory damages Compensation for copyright infringement within a statutorily fixed range according to the trial court's discretion.

statutory law Law enacted by the U.S. Congress, state legislatures, and city councils, along with administrative rules and regulations of governmental agencies.

statutory offers Indications of an interest in buying or selling securities.

statutory preclusion Determination by Congress that an agency decision is not to be reviewed by the courts.

statutory prospectus See *formal prospectus*.

statutory rights The rights of a copyright holder, including the right to reproduce, make derivative works, distribute, perform or display, license and/or assign, and digitally transmit.

stay A court order halting action.

stock photo A photo held in reserve for future use or sale.

storehouse of value Former characteristic of money; intrinsic value derived from the precious metal content of gold or silver coins.

straight bankruptcy A bankruptcy in which a trustee liquidates the debtor's estate and distributes the proceeds to the creditors according to their priority.

street name The status of shares that are registered in the name of the shareholder's broker.

street sweep A takeover bidder's privately negotiated purchase of large blocks of a target's shares.

strict compliance rule The rule that all the terms of a letter of credit must be met or the issuer is not obligated to make payment to the beneficiary.

strict constructionism A judicial philosophy holding that the legislative branch is the more proper body to solve social and economic problems, contrasting with judicial activism, which gives judges more latitude to implement certain policies.

strict liability Liability for damages without proof of either intentional wrongdoing or fault.

strict scrutiny The standard by which a court will judge a state law under the equal protection clause when it affects *fundamental rights* or discriminates against *suspect classes*; a more rigorous standard than *rational basis*.

strikes Concerted activities of employees who stop work simultaneously to pressure their employer.

striking similarity Similarities so numerous and so close as to prove an alleged infringement of a copyrighted work.

structuralist approach Examination of the organization of each industry, identifying particular characteristics that are believed to cause anticompetitive effects and advocating strong antitrust enforcement.

subagencies Administrative agencies that are part of a cabinet-level department.

subchapter S corporation A corporation organized according to regulations of the Internal Revenue Code, under which the income of the corporation is taxed only to the individual shareholders.

subject individual The person described in collected information.

sublease The lease of property from a *lessee* to another person called a sublessee.

sublicensing A *licensee's* right to further license rights to others.

submarkets Groups of sellers within a broader market who compete more directly.

submission to arbitration A contractual agreement to submit a particular dispute to arbitration.

subpoena duces tecum A subpoena that requires a witness to bring documents to a judicial proceeding.

subpoenas Judicial writs that require witnesses to give testimony.

subrogation The right of a party that has paid a claim to sue the ultimately responsible party for reimbursement.

substantial noninfringing uses Ways that a device can be used other than to infringe on copyrighted material; for example, the acceptable uses of a VCR.

substantial performance Performance under a contract that does not fully comply with what is required, but which is close enough so that the other party still must perform its obligation while receiving damages for what is not performed.

substantial similarity A similarity between a protected work and an allegedly infringing work that may support an inference of copying.

substantive due process The form of due process concerned with the fairness of legislation in the way it defines rights and duties.

substantive laws Laws that define rights and impose on members of society the duty to respect those rights.

substituted service A valid alternative method of notifying a defendant of a lawsuit when the defendant cannot be located.

substitutes Products that directly compete or can be reasonably used to replace each other for similar functions.

successor liability The possible responsibility of a purchasing firm for the product liability of a firm it acquires.

suggestive marks Marks that indirectly suggest the qualities of the products they identify.

sui generis Unique; concerning something that is the only example of its kind.

sui generis database protections Rights against infringement for those who make a substantial investment in obtaining, verifying, or presenting a database.

summary prospectus A prospectus for securities that contains condensed information.

summons A court order that gives the defendant notice of a lawsuit and requires the defendant to respond with a prescribed period, such as 30 days.

sunset laws State laws that provide an automatic periodic review of agency performance and determination of whether to reauthorize the agency.

supplemental register The registration list of the Patent and Trademark Office that is used for *descriptive marks* that do not qualify for the principal register; it confers some advantages.

suppletory law Law that provides common terms for agreements when the parties have left them undefined.

supply feature The franchisee's sale of goods or services supplied by the franchisor.

suppression Deliberately hiding an invention.

supremacy clause A provision of the U.S. Constitution that makes federal law supreme and permits the Supreme Court to declare any conflicting state law unconstitutional.

suspect classes Classifications of persons based on factors such as race, national origin, and alien status.

swap A form of *derivative* in which two parties exchange cash flows, receivables, or payables.

switching costs The costs of changing from one product to another.

T

taking The government's confiscation of private property under *eminent domain,* for which it must pay reasonable compensation.

tariff A tax on an imported product, used to protect domestic producers of the product, who are not taxed.

tarnishment Detraction from the value of an owner's mark that causes *dilution.*

technical fraud Fraud committed by means of technological systems.

Telecommunications Act of 1996 Federal law that partially deregulated the telecommunications industry.

telemarketing Marketing technique that uses telephone contact with prospective customers.

Telemarketing and Consumer Fraud and Abuse Act of 1994 Federal law that allows the FTC to regulate the content of telemarketing calls.

Telephone Consumer Protection Act (TCPA) Federal law that regulates telemarketing activities including automatic dialing, unsolicited faxes, and telemarketing lists.

temporary insiders Underwriters, accountants, lawyers, and consultants working for a firm whose shares are traded.

temporary partial disability A disability that prevents an employee from performing certain activities for a certain time.

temporary total disability A disability that completely prevents an employee from working for a certain time.

tender An unconditional offer of payment that produces the money due.

tender offer A public announcement offering cash and/or securities in exchange for controlling interest in a target corporation.

terrorism The threatened use of violence reinforced by actual violent, criminal acts, usually for political or religious purposes.

terrorist organizations Groups that engage in terrorism.

tertiary-line injury Passed-along injury to customers of buyers who are injured by price discrimination.

theft of trade secrets Theft of trade secret information related to a product in commerce, with knowledge that it was proprietary, intending to benefit someone other than the trade secret owner, and knowing that the owner would be injured.

third-degree felony A crime punishable by imprisonment up to five years.

third-party beneficiary Someone other than parties to a contract who is designated to receive the benefit of the performance.

three strikes you're out A sentencing policy that mandates a life sentence for a third felony conviction.

tied product A less desirable product that must be purchased in order to be able to purchase a more desirable tying product.

time draft A *draft* that is payable on a specified date in the future.

time of the essence A contract that states that timely performance by one of the parties is an essential part of the contract.

time shifting Taping a broadcast program for more convenient viewing.

title Ownership of property.

toehold acquisition The acquisition of a small firm in a market by an outsider firm.

token use doctrine The former rule that trademarks could not be registered for possible future use.

tombstone ads Simple advertisements of securities, usually appearing in the financial press.

tortfeasor One who commits a tortious act.

Toxic Substances Control Act Federal law designed to identify, test, and control toxic chemicals.

trade acceptance A commercial *draft* used to pay for goods; also known as *sales draft.*

trade dress The combination of visual design elements used in the overall appearance of a product to create its total image.

trade libel See *disparagement.*

trade regulation rules FTC rules that define unfair and deceptive trade practices.

Trade Related Intellectual Property (TRIPS) Treaties creating dispute resolution mechanisms, enforcement and remedies, criminal sanctions, and judicial review of intellectual property matters.

trade secret Secret business information protected by law against misappropriation by improper means or breach of a confidential relationship.

trademark A commercial symbol, word, name, or other device that identifies and distinguishes the products of a particular firm.

Trademark Counterfeiting Act U.S. law prohibiting

the sale of counterfeit goods, which are fake copies made with the intent to defraud consumers.

trademark disparagement Injurious false statements about a mark owner's product.

Trademark Law Treaty A treaty that restructures and simplifies trademark registration procedures in signatory nations.

trademark prosecution The process of examining a trademark application and searching to determine the likelihood of confusion with another mark, sometimes including negotiation with the applicant.

trading partner agreement An agreement to govern future orders between international customers and suppliers in ongoing business relationships.

Tragedy of the Commons The problem of overconsumption that occurs when no one has a personal interest in conserving a public resource.

transaction exemptions Securities transactions exempt from registration requirements, including small issues and securities exchanged with existing holders.

transfer contracts Contracts that transfer rights and duties owed under a separate contract.

transferee One who receives the transfer of an instrument in the course of negotiation.

transferor One who transfers an instrument in the course of negotiation.

transfers Changes in ownership of a negotiable instrument along the way to final payment.

transformative uses Productive uses of an original work that add potentially valuable and creative expression.

treaties Agreements among different countries, whether between two countries (bilateral) or global.

treble damages Three times the actual damages as computed by a trial court.

trespass Unlawful interference with a property owner's right of possession.

trespass to chattels Intentional and wrongful interference with the possession and use of personal property.

trial court record A transcript of trial testimony, briefs, evidence, and other items that record what happened during a case.

TRIPS The trade-related intellectual property rights agreement among WTO members, designed to establish minimum standards, enforce rights, and settle disputes in a broad range of intellectual property areas.

Trust Indenture Act Federal law to protect bondholders from conflicts of interest of bond indenture trustees.

trusted and reliable third-party intermediaries Intermediaries such as banks, carriers, or warehouses that perform nearly concurrent conditions in transferring payment to the seller and transferring title to the buyer.

truth is a complete defense The principle that libel or slander cannot be found if the statements made are true.

Tunney Act Federal law that requires federal district court review of antitrust settlements.

tying An agreement that requires a buyer to purchase certain goods.

tying product A desirable product that buyers can purchase only if they also purchase a tied product.

U

U.S. Sentencing Guidelines Guidelines adopted by the U.S. Sentencing Commission to standardize sentencing in the federal courts.

Ubiquitous Being everywhere at the same time.

UCP 500 Currently effective law governing letters of credit procedures when UCP is specified by the parties.

ultrahazardous activity Certain inherently dangerous forms of activity, such as using explosives and keeping wild animals.

uncertificated Goods that are not accompanied by paper documents but rather are handled by electronic records.

unclean hands An equitable principle that bars recovery if the plaintiff itself has acted improperly.

unconditional promise or order to pay Required condition of a note or draft, setting the terms of payment.

unconscionability The principle relating to contracts with unfair provisions.

underwriter One who purchases from an issuer with a view to distribute the security or offers or sells any security for the issuer's benefit.

underwriting A commitment to sell an issue of securities for the issuer at specified terms.

undeserved profits A trademark infringer's profits from wrongful use of a registered trademark.

undisclosed A principal is undisclosed if a third party does not know the principal's existence or identity when contracting with the principal's agent.

undisclosed principal A principal is undisclosed if a third party does not know the principal's existence or identity when contracting with the principal's agent.

undue influence Influence and power over another person that makes genuine assent from that person impossible.

unemployment compensation Payments to unemployed workers from a fund to which employers contribute.

unenforceable contract Contract for which the Statute of Frauds requires a written document, but none was signed.

Uniform Commercial Code (UCC) Uniform commercial laws adopted by statute throughout the United States to govern sales of goods, payment mechanisms, title documents, and collateralization.

Uniform Customs and Practices of Documentary Credits (UCP) Private regulations of the International Trade Commission governing International trade practices such as letters of credit.

Uniform Trade Secrets Act A uniform law covering trade secrets, adopted by the majority of states.

unilateral contract Contract that involves a promise from one party and actual performance from the other party.

unilateral mistake A mistake regarding a contract made by only one of the parties; such mistakes do not justify excusing that party's obligation to perform.

union shop The requirement that workers must join the union within a certain period after being hired.

United Nations Convention on the Contracts for the International Sale of Goods (CISG) A common body of law on contracts for the international sale of goods.

universal banking Consolidation of commercial banking, investment banking, and insurance.

universal theory An ethical theory that holds that a commitment to universal principles should guide people.

unlawful access to stored communications Access to data stored in computers on RAM or disk drives, prohibited by the *Electronic Communications Privacy Act.*

unliquidated debt A disputed debt.

unprotected speech Communication that is not protected under the First Amendment, including incitement, sedition, fraud, defamation, and obscenity.

unqualified endorsement The endorser's promise to pay on the instrument if it is not paid by the drawee; presumed for all endorsements unless they are *qualified.*

unsecured creditors A creditor in bankruptcy who has no interest in any specific property of the debtor.

unsolicited commercial e-mail (UCE) See *spam.*

upstream market Concentration of a market at the supplier level.

URL The domain name (universal resource locator) of an Internet site, which restates the *IP address* in letters.

USA Patriot Act Legislation enacted by Congress in 2001 that substantially diminishes the rights of suspected terrorists and others.

usages of trade Methods or expectations in the commercial dealings common to a whole trade or business.

use or copying by others Behavior of competitors that acknowledges the nonobvious nature of an invention.

use taxes A substitute for sales taxes that are levied on out-of-state mail order purchases.

uses and disclosures for treatment, payment, and operations Health care information needed for rendering health care services.

uses and disclosures other than for treatment, payment, and operations Health care information for nonmedical uses, such as hiring decisions.

utilitarian theory An ethical theory that examines the consequences of a given action and defines an action as morally right and ethical if it produces the greatest amount of good for the greatest number of people.

utility A beneficial use for an invention or the products produced by a patented process.

utility model Sui generis intellectual property right in some nations (Australia, Japan), providing shorter and weaker protection than utility patents and requiring a less rigorous qualification process.

V

valid contract Contract that is completely enforceable by either party if it meets all of the necessary legal requirements.

value Cash, property, or compensation for past services.

value-added tax A tax applied to the value added at each point along the supply chain.

values Alphanumeric expressions contained in *cookies.*

verdict The jury's finding in the case, based on the application of the law to the facts it has determined.

verifiable parental consent Reasonable efforts to ensure that parents receive notice and consent to collection of information about their children online, under the *Children's Online Privacy Protection Act.*

vertical integration An expansion into retail or supplier levels along the supply chain.

vertical mergers Combination of firms that stand in a supplier-customer relationship along the same chain of distribution.

vertical price-fixing See *resale price maintenance.*

vicarious infringement Form of infringement liability for a third party not actually involved in infringement due to close relationship or responsibility for actions of the infringer.

vicarious liability A principal's liability for the torts of its agent or employee while acting on behalf of the principal.

Video Privacy Protection Act of 1988 (VPPA) Federal law that protects information about rental and purchase of videos.

violent crimes Offenses against persons, such as homicide, assault, rape, robbery, and kidnapping.

Visual Artists Rights Act Federal law that protects certain *moral rights* for creators of single or limited editions of paintings, drawings, prints, sculptures, and photographs.

visual arts Paintings, drawings, prints, sculptures, and photographs, as defined under the *Visual Artists Rights Act.*

Vocational Rehabilitation Act of 1973 Federal law that requires employees holding federal contracts to consider handicapped job applicants.

void contract Contract that is invalid and unenforceable because it has an illegal objective or because one party was insane or incompetent during negotiations.

voidable contract Contract that allows one or both of the parties to rescind or cancel if there is a problem with incapacity, fraud, misrepresentation, duress, undue influence, or mistake.

voir dire Questioning of prospective jurors to discover biases that would disqualify them from service.

voluntary petition A petition in bankruptcy voluntarily filed by the debtor.

waiting period The period following the filing of a registration statement with the SEC, usually lasting 20 days.

waiver The release of a right; a contract that releases the recipient from liability for misappropriating an idea or breaching confidentiality.

W

warehouse receipt A title document issued by a warehouse that can also serve as the storage contract.

warranty A seller's contractual promise about the condition or performance of a product.

warranty of title The condition implied in every sale that the seller has the right to sell the goods, there are no outstanding liens on the goods, and the seller can pass good title to the buyer.

watch list A list of foreign nations that are suspected of allowing violation of intellectual property rights, for example by importing patent-infringing products.

Web bugs Technology designed to track Web users' browsing habits and product interests.

Web hosting Administration of a client's website.

Webcast Broadcasting from a website by means of streaming audio or video.

whistle-blower An employee who publicly reports an employer who commits crimes.

white lists Lists of non-European nations considered by the EU to provide adequate levels of privacy protection.

white-collar crime Illegal, nonviolent behavior of employees of businesses.

white-collar provision The exemption of executive, administrative, and professional employees from coverage by the Fair Labor Standards Act.

wholly owned foreign enterprise A firm totally owned and controlled by a foreign investor.

winner take all A system, suggested for the information industry, in which the most successful firm is allowed to have a limited-time monopoly.

Wireless Communications and Public Safety Act of 1999 (WCPSA) Federal law on wireless communication, including the requirement that cell phone carriers capture the location of 911 calls made from cell phones.

Wireless Telecommunications Bureau FCC bureau

in charge of cellular phones, pagers, two-way radios, and the radio spectrum.

Wireline Competition Bureau Division of the Federal Communications Commission responsible to oversee regulation of telephone companies that provide interstate telecommunications services over wire-based transmission facilities (corded and cordless phones).

wiretapping Interception and recording of telephone calls during transmission.

with all faults A phrase that is understood to effectively exclude an implied warranty of *merchantability.*

within the scope of their employment The position of employees who create works as part of their employment.

without notice Key factor necessary to establish holder in due course status, showing lack of financial intermediaries' knowledge of problems in transferring negotiable instruments.

work A creative expression written, recorded, or otherwise made into permanent physical form.

work made for hire An exception to the author's usual rights in a work when the work is created for a firm by an employee or independent contractor.

workers' compensation Payments to workers who are injured at work or contract a work-related illness.

works of authorship Creative expressions protected by copyright law.

World Intellectual Property Organization (WIPO) International organization devoted to intellectual property matters.

writ of mandamus A court order to a public official to perform a specified action.

X

XML Extensible markup language, used to prepare commercial documents for *electronic data interchange.*

Y

yellow-dog contracts Contracts that require employees to refrain from joining unions or risk losing their jobs.

Z

zone of privacy Right of privacy inferred under the Ninth Amendment.

Index

A

B

C

F

G

J

N

Q

R

T

W

Z